SINGAPORE
MANAGEMENT
UNIVERSITY

BASIC PRINCIPLES OF SINGAPORE BUSINESS LAW

Andrew Phang
General Editor

THOMSON™

Australia • Canada • Mexico • Singapore • Spain • United Kingdom • United States

THOMSON

Basic Principles of Singapore Business Law

For more information, please contact:
Thomson Learning
(a division of Thomson Asia Pte Ltd)
5 Shenton Way
#01-01 UIC Building
Singapore 068808

Or visit our internet website at *http://www.thomsonlearningasia.com*

Thomson Learning offices in Asia: Bangkok, Beijing, Hong Kong, Kuala Lumpur, Manila, Mumbai, Seoul, Singapore, Taipei, Tokyo.

Printed in Singapore
2 3 4 5 SLP 07 06 05

ISBN 981-243-435-6

To Our Students

Contents

	Foreword	page vii
	Preface	page ix
	List of Authors	page xi
	Table of Cases	page xiii
	Table of Singapore Legislation	page xxxi
	Table of Subsidiary Legislation (Singapore)	page xliii
	Table of Foreign Legislation	page xlv
	Table of Treaties and Conventions	page xlix
PART I	**INTRODUCTORY**	
Chapter 1	Introduction to the Singapore Legal System *Gary Chan & Eugene Tan*	page 3
PART II	**THE LAW OF CONTRACT**	
	Formation of Contract	
Chapter 2	Offer and Acceptance *Andrew Phang*	page 55
Chapter 3	Consideration *Lee Pey Woan*	page 89
Chapter 4	Intention to Create Legal Relations *Lee Pey Woan*	page 115
	Terms of the Contract	
Chapter 5	Terms of the Contract *Austin Pullé*	page 121
Chapter 6	Exception Clauses *Mary Wong*	page 143
	Capacity to Contract	
Chapter 7	Capacity to Contract *Chiu Hse Yu*	page 171
	Privity of Contract	
Chapter 8	Privity of Contract *Andrew Phang*	page 179
	Discharge of the Contract	
Chapter 9	Discharge by Performance, Breach and Agreement *Tham Chee Ho*	page 197

Chapter 10 Discharge by Frustration page 231
Low Kee Yang

Vitiating Factors

Chapter 11 Mistake page 247
Andrew Phang

Chapter 12 Misrepresentation page 279
Low Kee Yang

Chapter 13 Economic Duress, Undue Influence and Unconscionability page 295
Andrew Phang

Chapter 14 Illegality and Public Policy page 325
Andrew Phang

Remedies

Chapter 15 Remedies for Breach of Contract I: Damages page 363
Tham Chee Ho

Chapter 16 Remedies for Breach of Contract II : Specific Performance and Injunctions page 411
Tham Chee Ho

PART III THE LAW OF AGENCY

Chapter 17 Agency page 457
Pearlie Koh

PART IV BUSINESS ORGANISATIONS

Chapter 18 Business Organisations page 477
Pearlie Koh

PART V THE LAW OF TORT

Chapter 19 Negligence page 501
Andrew Phang

Chapter 20 Economic Torts page 555
Lee Pey Woan

PART VI LAW OF INTELLECTUAL PROPERTY

Chapter 21 Law of Intellectual Property page 593
Saw Cheng Lim

PART VII LAW AND INTERNATIONAL BUSINESS

Chapter 22 Law and International Business page 649
Austin Pullé

Index page 679

Foreword

Business is the lifeblood of Singapore. Faith in the law and in the learning and incorruptibility of the personnel of the law explains and maintains its status as the regional capital for business and finance. Against that background the appearance of this new book on the basic principles of business law must be seen as an important event. It is certainly an occasion for congratulation. Appropriately enough it comes from the lawyers of the Business School of the Singapore Management University. Every member of the Law Department in that School has had a hand in the authorship.

Professor Andrew Phang is the general editor. He is a scholar of international reputation. He has moulded his Department into an effective team to produce an up-to-date and economical account which ought to have a market beyond the students who must study to maintain the Singaporean lead in this sector. Teamwork is highly valued in business. The congratulations are shared by every member.

Legal learning can be packaged in many different ways. Some categories, such as property and obligations, are based on unitary concepts which are essential to the currently dominant taxonomy of the whole law. Others are contextual in the sense that they take as their focus some aspect of life, as it might be art or building or cricket, and seek to expound all the law about that particular subject. 'Business' is a contextual category and one with wide boundaries.

All the law about business would run to many volumes. The first task of the SMU team was therefore to select what really mattered so as to make available a compact account on which to build. In that kind of exercise one person always knows better than another. But nobody will disagree that contract must form the core of the core. Secure in that choice, this book adds, by way of necessary introduction, an account of the structure and operation of the legal system and, so to say at the other end, a lively discussion of that part of the law of civil wrongs most likely to be encountered in the course of business activities. Moving out from core the choice becomes more open and more difficult. In deference to its great importance in the modern world this book chooses to present the law of intellectual property and, finally, the international aspects of trade. The latter certainly reflects Singapore's position as a hub in a huge network of overseas activity.

This volume gives the reader the basics which its title promises. At the same time it prepares the way for the distinguished SMU team to follow the success of this work with a second, building out from the foundation now secured. Some great houses never admit to being finished. We have to hope that this team will stay together, for this, it would seem, is only the end of the beginning.

Peter Birks QC, DCL, FBA
Regius Professor of Civil Law in the University of Oxford
and
Fellow of All Souls College Oxford
1 August 2003

Preface

The present book is literally the cooperative effort of the entire Law Department of the Business School of the Singapore Management University. Originally conceived as a textbook for our own students, it is simultaneously an attempt at conveying the basic principles of Singapore business law to the general public as well. We also hope that both lawyers as well as students would find this work useful and stimulating.

Although written in an accessible style, this book does not avoid controversial issues but, rather, sets them out in a systematic fashion in order that the reader might bring his or her analysis to bear on them. This is wholly consistent with the spirit undergirding the university's basic approach towards education: to encourage creative thinking as well as analysis. Much of the work, however, also comprises a clear and systematic restatement of the many principles of Singapore business law. Wherever relevant, it has also incorporated elements of the new economy, in particular, those pertaining to cyberspace.

The book itself is divided into several parts. The first chapter gives the reader a succinct, yet substantive, introduction to the Singapore legal system as viewed in its historical and socio-economic context. The next fifteen chapters take the reader through the various principles of the law of contract, which is not only vitally important in its own right but is also the foundation of many other areas of commercial law as well. The reader is then introduced to two areas in the law of tort that are of particular relevance to the business context: negligence and economic torts, respectively. There follow accounts of the various forms of business organisations as well as the important area of agency law. The final two chapters deal with areas that are of vital relevance in the sphere of business: intellectual property law and law and international business, respectively.

One of the privileges of the general editor of any work is being able to acknowledge the assistance as well as kindness of the very many persons involved, which constitute the true source and strength of the work itself. I must commence by thanking the various authors themselves. This book is the cooperative effort of eleven faculty members (including myself). Any editor will know how difficult it is to coordinate the efforts of so very many persons. In over two decades in academia, however, I have never encountered a more cooperative and committed team of scholars, who delivered manuscripts of the highest quality on time and with relative cheerfulness! The team would also like to express its gratitude to Professor Peter Birks, Regius Professor of Civil Law in the University of Oxford and Fellow of All Souls College Oxford for kindly consenting to write the *Foreword* as well as to the then Dean of the Business School, Associate Professor Tsui Kai Chong, for his encouragement and support. We would also like to thank Professor George Wei and Associate Professor Tan Keng Feng of the National University of Singapore for their comments and suggestions with regard to the intellectual property law and negligence chapters, respectively. Mr Aedit Abdullah of the Attorney-General's Chambers also provided valuable comments on the negligence chapter. Our thanks, also, to Ms Carol Yap, who not only cheerfully and efficiently helps in the Department's administration but also assisted throughout in this project. Last, but by no means least, we would like to to express our gratitude to the team from Thomson Learning, who contributed immensely to the fruition of this work. We would like to thank Mr Paul Tan, Mr Tony Ng, Ms Pauline Lim, Ms Juliana Lim and Ms Gillian Chee. Juliana and Gillian, in particular, were closely involved in the production of the book as it entered its final stages.

Andrew Phang
August 2003

List of Authors

Gary Chan *LLM (London), MA (NUS), LLB (NUS), BA (London)*
Advocate & Solicitor (Singapore)
Assistant Professor of Law, Singapore Management University

Chiu Hse Yu *LLM (Cantab), LLB (NUS)*
Formerly, Lecturer in Law, Singapore Management University

Pearlie Koh *LLM (Melbourne), LLB (NUS)*
Advocate & Solicitor (Singapore)
Associate Professor of Law, Singapore Management University

Lee Pey Woan *BCL (Oxford), LLB (King's College, London)*
Advocate & Solicitor (Singapore)
Assistant Professor of Law, Singapore Management University

Low Kee Yang *PhD, LLM (King's College, London), LLB (NUS)*
Advocate & Solicitor (Singapore)
Associate Professor of Law, Singapore Management University

Andrew Phang *SJD, LLM (Harvard), LLB (NUS)*
Advocate & Solicitor (Singapore)
Professor of Law, Singapore Management University

Austin Pullé *SJD, LLM (Harvard), LLB (Sri Lanka)*
Attorney (Columbia and Massachusetts), Solicitor (New South Wales)
Associate Professor of Law, Singapore Management University

Saw Cheng Lim *LLM (Cantab), LLB (NUS)*
Advocate & Solicitor (Singapore)
Assistant Professor of Law, Singapore Management University

Eugene Tan Kheng Boon *MSc (London School of Economics & Political Science), LLB (NUS)*
Advocate & Solicitor (Singapore)
Lecturer in Law, Singapore Management University

Tham Chee Ho *BCL (Oxford), LLB (NUS)*
Advocate & Solicitor (Singapore), Solicitor (England and Wales),
Attorney and Counsellor-at-law (New York)
Assistant Professor of Law, Singapore Management University

Mary W S Wong *LLM (Cantab), LLB (NUS)*
Advocate & Solicitor (Singapore)
Associate Professor of Law, Singapore Management University

Table of Cases

A

A Schroeder Music Publishing Co Ltd v Macaulay [1974] 1 WLR 1308...**14.90**
Abdul Rahman bin Yusof v PP [1996] 3 SLR 15...**1.136**
Adam v Ward [1917] AC 309...**20.88**
Adams v Cape Industries plc [1990] 2 WLR 657...**18.23**
Addis v Gramophone Company, Ltd [1909] AC 488...**15.15, 15.60, 15.61, 15.64, 15.64**
AG Schuler v Wickman Machine Tools Ltd [1974] AC 235...**5.19, 5.20**
Ailion v Spikermann [1976] 1 All ER 497...**14.95**
Ailsa Craig Fishing Co Ltd v Malvern Fishing Co Ltd & Securicor (Scotland) [1983] 1 WLR 964....**6.5, 6.23, 12.52**
Airbus Industrie GIE v Patel [1999] 1 AC 119...**22.7**
Aircharter World Pte Ltd v Kontena Nasional Bhd [1999] 3 SLR 1...**2.8**
Akerhielm v De Mare [1959] AC 789...12.18
Alcock v Chief constable of South Yorkshire Police [1992] 1 AC 310...**19.17, 19.21, 19.23**
Alec Lobb (Garages) Ltd v Total Oil (Great Britain) Ltd [1983] 1 WLR 87; affirmed [1985] 1 All ER 303...**13.46, 14.87, 14.88**
Alev, The [1989] 1 Lloyd's Rep 138...**13.13, 13.22**
Alexander v Rayson [1936] 1 KB 169...**14.33**
Alfred McAlpine Construction Ltd v Panatown Ltd [2000] 3 WLR 946, [2001] 1 AC 518...**8.23, 15.45**
Allcard v Skinner (1887) 36 Ch D 145...**13.26**
Allen v Flood [1898] AC 1...**20.42**
Allen v Gold Reefs of West Africa Ltd [1900] 1 Ch 671...**18.48**
Alsagoff v Robin [1965] MLJ 56...**11.20, 11.21**
Anderson, Ltd v Daniel [1924] 1 KB 138...**14.16**
Andrews v Parker [1973] Qd R 93...**14.48**
Anglia Television Ltd v Reed [1972] 1 QB 60...**15.49, 16.60**
Anns v Merton London Borough Council [1978] AC 728...**19.15, 19.16, 19.17, 19.18, 19.19, 19.20, 19.21, 19.27, 19.28, 19.29, 19.31, 19.33, 19.34**
Archbolds (Freightage) Ltd v S Spanglett Ltd [1961] 1 QB 374...**14.16, 14.18**
Arcos, Ltd v EA Ronaasen and Son [1933] AC 470...**9.4**
Arctic Shipping Co Ltd v Mobilia AB, The Tatra [1990] 2 Lloyd's Rep 51...**17.17**
Armstrong v Jackson [1917] 2 KB 822...**17.38**
Armstrong v Strain [1952] 1 KB 232...**12.19**
Arthur JS Hall & Co (a firm) v Simons [2002] 1 AC 615...**19.33**
Arul Chandran v Chew Chin Aik (Suit 1896 of 1998, judgment dated 19-06 2000) ...**20.73**
Arul Chandran v Gartshore [2000] 2 SLR 446...**15.60**
Ashford Shire Council v Dependable Motors Pty Ltd [1961] AC 336...**17.8**
Ashmore, Benson, Pease & Co Ltd v AV Dawson Ltd [1973] 1 WLR 828...**14.27**
Asia Polyurethane Mfg Pte Ltd v Woon Sow Liong [1990] 2 MLJ 463...**14.76**
Associated British Ports v Transport and General Workers' Union [1989] 1 WLR 939...**20.49**
Associated Electric & Gas Insurance Services Ltd v European Reinsurance Company of Zurich [2003] 1 WLR 1041...**5.27**
Associated Japanese Bank (International) Ltd v Crédit du Nord SA [1989] 1 WLR 255...**11.10, 11.11, 11.13, 11.14, 11.15, 11.17, 11.18, 11.20, 11.21, 11.22**

Asylum (Colombia v Peru) 1950 ICJ 266...**22.3**
Atlas Express Ltd v Kafco (Importers and Distributors) Ltd [1989] 1 All ER 641...**13.13**
Attorney-General v Blake [2001] 1 AC 268...**15.16, 15.45, 16.92, 16.93**
Attwood v Lamont [1920] 3 KB 571...**14.98**
Attwood v Small (1838) 6 Cl & F 232...**12.21**
Avon Insurance v Swire Fraser [2000] 1 All ER 573...**12.5**

B
Bailey v Bullock [1950] 2 All ER 1167...**15.62**
Baird Textiles Holdings Ltd v Marks & Spencer plc [2002] 1 All ER 737...**3.66**
Balfour v Balfour [1919] 2 KB 571...**4.4, 4.5, 4.8**
Ballet v Mingay [1943] KB 281...**7.20**
Banco de Portugal v Waterlow and Sons, Ltd [1932] AC 452...**15.77**
Bandar Raya Developments Berhad v Ang Yoke Lian Construction Sdn Bhd [1993] 1 AMR 285...**2.36**
Bank Line v Arthur Capel [1919] AC 435...**10.26**
Bank of Credit and Commerce International SA v Aboody [1989] 2 WLR 759...**13.31, 13.34**
Bank of India v Rai Bahadur Singh & Anor [1994] 1 SLR 328...**7.5, 7.6**
Bank of Montreal v Jane Jacques Stuart [1911] AC 120...**13.30**
Bannerman v White (1861) 10 CBNS 844...**5.14, 12.36**
Banque Brussels Lambert SA v Australian National Industries Ltd (1989) 21 NSWLR 502...**4.13**
Barcelona Traction, Light and Power Company, Limited (Belgium v Spain) 1970 ICJ 3...**22.6**
Barclays Bank Plc v Boulter [1999] 1 WLR 1919...**13.39**
Barclays Bank Plc v Coleman [2001] QB 20...**13.33**
Barclays Bank Plc v O'Brien [1994] 1 AC 180...**13.37, 13.38, 13.40, 14.48**
Baretts & Baird (Wholesale) Ltd v Institute of Professional Civil Servants [1987] IRLR 3...**20.41**
Barrett v Enfield London Borough Council [1999] 3 WLR 79...**19.33**
Barton v Armstrong [1976] AC 104...**13.16**
Beattie v E & F Beattie Ltd [1938] Ch 708...**18.46**
Beca (Malaysia) Sdn Bhd v Tan Choong Kuang [1986] 1 MLJ 390...**14.57**
Beecham Group Limited's (Amoxycillin) Application [1980] RPC 261...**21.55**
Bell v Lever Brothers, Ltd [1932] AC 161...**11.10, 11.12, 11.13, 11.14, 11.19, 18.41**
Bennett v Bennett [1952] 1 KB 249...**14.95**
Bennett, Ex parte (1805) 32 ER 893...**17.39**
Bentsen v Taylor, Sons & Co [1893] 2 QB 274...**5.19**
Berenger v Rozario (mw) [1953] MLJ 239...**14.47**
Beswick v Beswick [1968] AC 58...**8.21, 16.21**
Bettini v Gye (1876) 1 QBD 183...**5.21**
Bigos v Boustead [1951] 1 All ER 92...**14.66**
Biogen v Medeva [1997] RPC 1...**21.49**
Birmingham & District Land Co v London & North Western Railway Co (1888) 40 ChD 268...**3.62**
Blackpool and Fylde Aero Club Ltd v Blackpool Borough Council [1990] 1 WLR 1195...**2.8, 2.14**
Blythe v Birmingham Waterworks Co (1856) 11 Exch 781...**19.42**
Bolam v Friern Hospital Management Committee [1957] 1 WLR 582...**19.42, 19.43, 19.73**
Bolitho v City and Hackney Health Authority [1997] 4 All ER 771...**19.43**
Bolton Partners v Lambert (1889) 41 Ch D 295...**17.26, 17.27**
Bolton v Mahadeva [1972] 1 WLR 1009...**16.98, 16.99, 16.100, 16.101**
Bonnard v Perryman [1891] 2 Ch 269...**20.93**

Boomer v Muir 24 P (2d) 570 (Cal App 1933)...**16.80, 16.83, 16.87**
Boone v Eyre (1779) 1 Hy Bl 273n...**9.11**
Boulton v Jones (1857) 2 H & N 564...**11.49**
Boustany v Pigott (1993) 63 P & CR 298...**13.47**
Boustead Trading (1985) Sdn Bhd v Arab-Malaysian Merchant Bank Bhd [1995] 3 MLJ 33...**13.58**
Bowmakers, Ltd v Barnet Instruments, Ltd [1945] KB 65...**14.60, 14.62**
BP Refinery (Westernport) Pty Ltd v Shire of Hastings (1977) 16 ALR 363...**5.25**
Brimelow v Casson [1924] 1 Ch 302...**20.22**
Brinkerhoff Maritime Drilling Corp v PT Airfast Services Indonesia [1992] 2 SLR 776...**22.7**
Brinkibon Ltd v Stahag Stahl und Stahlwaren Handelsgessellschaft GmbH [1983] 2 AC 34...**2.23, 2.24**
Bristow v Eastman (1974) 1 Esp 172...**7.23**
British Crane Hire Corporation Ltd v Ipswich Plant Hire Ltd [1975] QB 303, [1974] 1 All ER 1059...**6.18**
British Motor Trade Association v Salvadori [1949] Ch 556...**20.15**
British Northrop v Texteam [1974] RPC 57...**21.9**
British Russian Gazette and Trade Outlook, Ltd v Associated Newspapers, Ltd [1933] 2 KB 616...**9.86**
British Steel Corporation v Cleveland Bridge and Engineering Co Ltd [1984] 1 All ER 504...**2.14**
British Telecommunications Plc v One In A Million Ltd [1998] 4 All ER 476...**21.96**
British Westinghouse Electric and Manufacturing Company, Ltd v Underground Electric Railways Company of London, Ltd [1912] AC 673...**15.76, 15.84, 15.87**
Brodie v Brodie [1917] P 271...**14.45**
Brogden v Metropolitan Railway (1877) 2 App Cas 666...**2.22**
Brown v Gould [1972] Ch 53...**2.36**
Brown v Harper (1893) 68 LT 488...**7.15**
Brown v KMR Services Ltd [1995] 2 Lloyd's Rep 513...**15.74**
Browning v Provincial Insurance Co of Canada (1873) LR 5 PC 263...**17.35**
Bryan v Maloney (1995) 182 CLR 609...**19.27, 19.28, 19.36**
Buckman Laboratories (Asia) Pte Ltd v Lee Wei Hoong [1999] 3 SLR 333...**14.85**
Bunge Corporation, New York v Tradax Export SA Panama [1981] 1 WLR 711...**5.19, 5.22**
Burnard v Haggis (1863) 14 CB (NS) 45...**7.21**
Butler Machine Tool Co v Ex-Cell-O Corporation (England) Ltd [1979] 1 WLR 401...**2.44, 2.45, 2.46**
Butwick v Grant [1924] 2 KB 483...**17.32**

C
C & P Haulage v Middleton [1983] 1 WLR 1461...**15.51**
C C C Films (London) Ltd v Impact Quadrant Films Ltd [1985] 1 QB 16...**15.51**
Calebar Properties v Stitcher [1984] 1 WLR 287...**15.62**
Calico Printers' Association Ltd v Barclays Bank (1930) 38 Ll L Rep 105...**17.42**
Callisher v Bischoffsheim (1870) LR 5 QB 449...**3.29**
Canada Steamship Lines Ltd v R [1952] 1 All ER 305...**6.26**
Caparo Industries Plc v Dickman [1990] 2 AC 605...**19.7, 19.17, 19.20, 19.21, 19.22, 19.23, 19.27, 19.30, 19.34, 19.36, 19.63**
Carlill v Carbolic Smoke Ball Company [1893] 1 QB 256...**2.5, 3.11, 4.10**
Carnduff v Rock [2001] 1 WLR 1786...**14.32**
Cassell v Broome [1972] AC 1027...**20.92**
Cassidy v Daily Mirror Newspapers Ltd [1929] 2 KB 331...**20.63**
Catnic Components Ltd v Hill & Smith Ltd [1982] RPC 183...**21.59**

CBS Songs Ltd v Amstrad [1988] AC 1013...**20.32, 21.19**
CDL Hotels International Ltd v Pontiac Marina Pte Ltd [1998] 2 SLR 550...**21.91**
Cehave NV v Bremer Handelsgesellschaft mbH (The Hansa Nord) [1976] QB 44...**5.21, 5.22**
Central London Property Trust Ltd v High Trees House Ltd [1947] KB 130...**3.47, 3.61**
Chan Cheng Kum v Wah Tat Bank Ltd [1971] 1 SLR 22...**5.30**
Chapelton v Barry Urban District Council [1940] 1 KB 532...**2.39, 2.41, 6.9**
Chaplin v Hicks [1911] 2 KB 786...**15.47**
Chaplin v Leslie Frewin (Publishers) Ltd [1966] Ch 67...**7.10, 7.16**
Chappell & Co Ltd v Nestlé Co Ltd [1960] AC 87...**3.7, 3.20**
Chapple v Cooper (1844) 13 M & W 252...**7.10**
Charles Rickards, Ld v Oppenhaim [1950] 1 KB 616...**9.83, 9.84**
Che Som Bte Yip v Maha Pte Ltd [1989] 3 MLJ 468...**7.27**
Cheese v Thomas [1994] 1 All ER 35...**13.35**
Chew Kong Huat v Ricwil (Singapore) Pte Ltd [2000] 1 SLR 385...**20.36**
Chiam See Tong v Ling How Doong [1997] 1 SLR 648...**20.64**
China National Foreign Trade Transportation Corporation v Evlogia Shipping Co SA of Panama, The Mihalios Xilas [1979] 1 WLR 1018...**9.59**
China Resources v Magenta Resources [1997] 1 SLR 707...**10.24**
Chong Yeo & Partners v Guan Ming Hardware & Engineering Pte Ltd [1997] 2 SLR 729...**19.33**
Choo Tiong Hin v Choo Hock Swee [1959] 1 MLJ 67...**4.8**
Chop Ngoh Seng v Esmail and Ahmad Bros [1948] 2 MLJ 93...**11.16**
Chromalloy Aeroservices v Arab Republic of Egypt 939 F Supp 907 (DDC 1996)...**22.34**
Chuan Hong Auto (Pte) Ltd v Shell Eastern Petroleum (Pte) Ltd [1996] 1 SLR 415...**14.87**
CIBC Mortgages Plc v Pitt [1994] 1 AC 200...**13.31, 13.32, 13.33**
Clarion Ltd v National Provident Institution [2000] 2 All ER 265...**11.32**
Clarke v The Earl of Dunraven [1897] AC 59...**2.40**
Climax Manufacturing Co Ltd v Colles Paragon Converters (S) Pte Ltd [2000] 1 SLR 245...**2.38**
Coal Cliff Collieries Pty Ltd v Sijehama Pty Ltd (1991) 24 NSWLR 1...**2.38**
Coco v Clark [1969] RPC 41...**21.66**
Collen v Wright (1857) 8 E&B 647...**17.48**
Collins v Godfrey (1831) 1 B & Ad 950...**3.30**
Combe v Combe [1951] 2 KB 215...**3.6, 3.56**
Commercial Bank of Australia Ltd v Amadio (1983) 46 ALR 402...**13.47, 13.49**
Compagnie General Maritime v Diakan Spirit SA (The 'Ymnos') [1982] 2 Lloyd's Rep 574...**5.22**
Consmat Singapore (Pte) Ltd v Bank of America National Trust & Savings Association [1992] 2 SLR 828...**6.55**
Constitutional Reference No. 1 of 1995 [1995] 2 SLR 201...**1.51**
Cooper v Hobart (2001) 206 DLR (4th) 193...**19.24, 19.31, 19.33**
Cooper v Phibbs (1867) LR 2 HL 149...**11.20**
Co-operative Insurance Society Ltd v Argyll Stores (Holdings) Ltd [1998] AC 1...**16.23, 16.29**
Corfu Channel Case (United Kingdom v Albania) 1949 ICJ 4...**22.3**
Costello v Chief Constable of Derbyshire Constabulary [2001] 1 WLR 1437...**14.62**
Coulls v Bagot's Executor and Trustee Co Ltd (1967) 119 CLR 460...**3.18, 8.36**
Courtney and Fairbairn Ltd v Tolaini Bros (Hotels) Ltd [1975] 1 WLR 716...**2.38**
Couturier v Hastie (1856) 5 HLC 673...**11.10, 11.16**
Credit Development Pte Ltd v IMO Pte Ltd [1993] 2 SLR 370...**18.23**
Credit Lyonnais Bank Nederland NV v Burch [1997] 4 All ER 144...**13.47**

Cremdean Properties Ltd v Nash (1977) 244 EG 547…**12.53**
Crescendo Management Pty Ltd v Westpac Banking Corp (1988) 19 NSWLR 40…**13.8**
Cresswell v Potter [1978] 1 WLR 255…**13.45, 13.49**
Crofter Hand Woven Harris Tweed Co Ltd v Veitch [1942] AC 435…**20.33**
CTN Cash and Carry Ltd v Gallaher Ltd [1994] 4 All ER 714…**13.14, 13.20**
Currie v Misa (1875) LR 10 Exch 153…**3.3**
Curtis v Chemical Cleaning and Dyeing Co [1951] 1 KB 805, [1951] 1 All ER 631…**6.11**
Cutter v Powell (1795) 6 Term Reports 320…**9.7, 9.8, 9.10, 9.11**

D
D & F Estates Ltd v Church Commissioners for England [1989] AC 177…**19.19**
D&C Builders v Rees [1966] 2 QB 617…**3.45, 3.55**
Datuk Ong Kee Hui v Sinyium Anak Mutit [1983] 1 MLJ 36…**14.49**
Daulia Ltd v Four Millbank Nominees Ltd [1978] Ch 231…**2.14**
Davies v Beynon-Harris (1931) 47 TLR 424…**7.12**
Davis Contractors v Fareham UDC [1956] AC 696…**10.4, 10.5, 10.18**
DC Thomson & Co Ltd v Deakin [1952] Ch 646…**20.12, 20.14**
De Bussche v Alt (1878) 8 ChD 286…**17.41**
De Francesco v Barnum (1890) 45 ChD 430…**7.11, 16.27**
Deacons v Bridge [1984] 2 All ER 19…**14.91**
Dean v Ainley [1987] 1 WLR 1729…**15.59**
Denny v Denny [1919] 1 KB 583…**14.51**
Derry v Peek (1889) LR App Cas 337…**12.27**
DHKW Marketing v Nature's Farm Pte Ltd [1999] 2 SLR 400…**20.69**
Diamond Peak Sdn Bhd v Tweedle [1980] 2 MLJ 31…**2.45**
Dick Bentley Productions Ltd v Harold Smith [1965] 1 WLR 623…**5.17**
Dickinson v Dodds (1876) 2 Ch D 463…**2.13**
Dickson Trading (S) Pte Ltd v Transmarco Ltd [1989] 2 MLJ 408…**2.14, 2.17**
Dies v British and International Mining and Finance Corporation, Ltd [1939] 1 KB 724…**15.97, 16.95, 16.96, 16.97**
Diesen v Samson 1971 SLT (Sh Ct) 49…**15.62**
Dimpex Gems (Singapore) Pte Ltd v Yusoof Diamonds Pte Ltd [1988] 1 MLJ 87…**14.27**
Dimskal Shipping Co SA v International Transport Workers Federation (The Evia Luck) [1992] 2 AC 152…**13.8**
Djoni Widjaja v Bank of America [1993] 2 SLR 816…**22.7**
Donoghue v Stevenson [1932] AC 562…**19.6, 19.7, 19.8, 19.21, 19.24, 19.73**
Donohue v Armco Inc [2002] 1 Lloyd's Rep 425…**9.43**
Douglas v Hello! Ltd [2001] 2 All ER 289…**21.70**
Dow Jones & Company v Gutnick [2002] HCA 56…**20.98**
Doyle v White City Stadium Ltd [1935] 1 KB 110…**7.10**
Dr Khoo James & Anor v Gunapathy d/o Muniandy [2002] 2 SLR 414…**19.43**
Dunlop Pneumatic Tyre Co Ltd v Selfridge & Co Ltd [1915] AC 847…**8.3, 8.9, 8.35**
Dunlop Pneumatic Tyre Company, Ltd v New Garage and Motor Company, Ltd [1915] AC 79…**15.94**

E
Earl of Oxford's case (1615) 1 Rep Ch 1; 21 ER 485…**1.75**
East v Maurer [1991] 1 WLR 461…**15.20**
Eastwood v Kenyon (1840) 11 Ad & El 438 …**3.24, 3.25**
Ecay v Godfrey (1947) 80 Ll L Rep 286…**5.13, 12.36**
Edgington v Fitzmaurice (1885) LR 29 Ch D 459…**12.7, 12.20**
Edler v Auerbach [1950] 1 KB 359…**14.100**
Edwards v Carter [1893] AC 360…**7.12, 7.13**

Edwin Hill & Partners v First National Finance Corpn [1989] 1 WLR 225...**20.23**
Eldred v Ashcroft (2003) No 01-618 (US Supreme Court)...**21.6**
Enderby Town FC Ltd v The Football Association Ltd [1971] Ch 591...**14.2**
Entores Ltd v Miles Far East Corporation [1955] 2 QB 32...**2.23**
Eshelby v Federated European Bank [1932] 1 KB 423...**15.104**
Esso Petroleum Co Ltd v Harper's Garage (Stourport) Ltd [1968] AC 269...**14.75, 14.87, 14.88, 14.89**
Eugenia, The [1964] 2 QB 226...**10.28**
Eurymedon, The (*see* New Zealand Shipping Co Ltd v AM Sattherwaite & Co Ltd)
Evia, The (No 2) [1983] 1 AC 736...**10.7**
Ex p Island Records Ltd [1978] Ch 122 ...**20.49**
Exxon Corporation v Exxon Insurance Consultants International Ltd [1982] RPC 69...**21.7**

F
FG Minter v Welsh Health Technical Services Organisation (1980) 13 BLR 1...**16.7**
Faccenda Chicken Ltd v Fowler [1986] 1 All ER 617...**14.81, 21.69**
Fairchild v Glenhaven Funeral Services Ltd [2002] 3 WLR 89...**19.46**
Fairclough Building Ltd v Borough Council of Port Talbot (1992) 62 BLR 82...**2.8**
Farley v Skinner [2002] 2 AC 732...**15.45, 15.62, 15.63, 15.64, 15.67**
Fawcett v Smethurst (1914) 84 LJ Ch 473...**7.9**
Federal Lands Commissioner v Benfort Enterprises & Anor [1998] 1 SLR 855...**18.5**
Fender v St John Mildmay [1938] AC 1...**14.44**
Fibrosa Spolka Akcyjna v Fairbairn Lawson Combe Barbour, Limited [1943] AC 32...**10.29, 16.56, 16.72, 16.95, 16.107**
Financings Ltd v Stimson [1962] 1 WLR 1184...**2.18**
Fitch v Dewes [1921] 2 AC 158...**14.74, 14.84**
Foakes v Beer (1884) 9 App Cas 605...**3.44, 3.46, 3.62, 9.81**
Fong Maun Yee v Yoong Weng Ho Robert (practising under the name and style of Yoong & Co) [1997] 2 SLR 297...**15.90**
Fong Whye Koon v Chan Ah Thong [1996] 2 SLR 706...**13.49**
Forsikringsaktieselskapet Vesta v Butcher [1986] 2 All ER 488...**15.90**
Forsikringsaktieselskapet Vesta v Butcher [1988] 3 WLR 566...**15.90**
Foster v Redgrave (1867) LR 4 Ex 32...**7.9**
Freeman & Lockyer v Buckhurst Park Properties (Mangal) Ltd [1964] 2 QB 480...**17.15, 18.30**
Freeth v Burr (1874) LR 9 CP 208...**9.33**
FROOT LOOPS Trade Mark [1998] RPC 240...**21.74**
Fry v Lane (1888) 40 Ch D 312...**13.45**
Fu Loong Lithographer Pte Ltd v Mun Hean Realty Pte Ltd [1989] SLR 300...**3.53, 9.84**

G
Galoo Ltd v Bright Grahame Murray (a firm) [1994] 1 WLR 1360...**15.88**
Garcia v National Australian Bank Ltd (1998) 155 ALR 614...**13.40**
Garnac Grain Co Inc v HMF Faure & Fairclough Ltd [1968] AC 1130...**17.6**
Gaussen v Morton (1830) 10 B&C 731...**17.52**
Gee Hoe Chan Trading Co Pte Ltd, Re [1991] SLR 837...**18.49**
Genelabs Diagnostics v Institut Pasteur [2001] 1 SLR 121...**21.52**
General Tire v Firestone Tyre [1972] RPC 457...**21.52**
George Mitchell (Chesterhall) Ltd v Finney Lock Seeds Ltd [1983] 2 AC 803, [1983] 2 All ER 737...**6.54**
Gibson v Manchester City Council [1979] 1 WLR 294...**2.45**
Gilbert-Ash (Northern) Ltd v Modern Engineering (Bristol) Ltd [1974] AC 689...**15.103**
Glahe International Expo v ACS Computer [1999] 1 SLR 166, on appeal [1999] 2 SLR 620...**10.28**

Glamorgan Coal Co v South Wales Miners' Federation [1903] 2 KB 545…**20.21**
Glasbrook Bros v Glamorgan County Council [1925] AC 270…**3.31**
Godfrey v Demon Internet Ltd [2000] 3 WLR 1020…**20.96**
Gold Coin Limited v Tay Kim Wee [1987] 2 MLJ 271…**2.36**
Goldsoll v Goldman [1915] 1 Ch 292…**14.98**
Goodinson v Goodinson [1954] 2 All ER 255…**14.95**
Gore v Gibson (1843) 13 M & W 623…**7.30**
Gore v Van der Lann [1967] 2 QB 31…**8.17**
Gouriet v Union of Post Office Workers [1978] AC 435…**20.48**
Government of Zanzibar v British Aerospace (Lancaster House) [2000] 1 WLR 2333…**12.47, 12.53**
Governors of the Peabody Donation Fund v Sir Lindsay Parkinson & Co Ltd [1985] AC 210…**19.19, 19.21**
Great Peace Shipping Limited v Tsavliris (International) Limited [2002] 3 WLR 1617…**11.19, 11.21**
Gregory v Rangitikei District Council [1995] 2 NZLR 208…**2.8**
Grist v Bailey [1967] 1 Ch 532…**11.18**
Gross v Lewis Hillman [1970] Ch 445…**12.24**
GWK Ltd v Dunlop Rubber Co Ltd (1926) 42 TLR 593…**20.11**

H

H Dakin & Co, Ltd v Lee [1916] 1 KB 566…**9.11**
H Parsons (Livestock) Ltd v Uttley Ingham & Co Ltd [1978] QB 791…**15.71, 15.72, 15.74**
Hadley v Baxendale (1854) 9 Ex 341…**15.68, 15.74, 16.8**
Hain Steamship Company Ltd v Tate & Lyle Ltd [1936] 2 All ER 597…**16.101**
Halifax Mortgage Services Ltd v Stepsky [1995] 3 WLR 701…**13.38**
Halifax Mortgage Services Ltd v Stepsky [1996] 2 WLR 230…**13.38**
Hamer v Sidway (1891) 27 NE 256…**3.26, 3.27**
Harrington v Kent [1980] IRLR 353…**10.20**
Harris v Nickerson (1873) LR 8 QB 286…**2.9**
Harrison v Harrison [1910] 1 KB 35…**14.45**
Hartley v Ponsonby (1857) 7 El & Bl 872…**3.35**
Hartog v Colin & Shields [1939] 3 All ER 566…**11.37**
Harvela Investments Ltd v Royal Trust Company of Canada (CI) Ltd [1986] 1 AC 207…**2.8**
Hector v Lyons (1988) 58 P & CR 156…**11.41, 11.43**
Hedley Byrne & Co Ltd v Heller & Partners Ltd [1964] AC 465…**6.35, 12.2, 12.30, 19.7, 19.21, 19.35, 19.36, 19.37, 19.39, 19.40**
Heglibiston Establishment v Heyman (1978) 246 EG 567…**14.48**
Heilbut, Symons & Co v Buckleton [1913] AC 30…**5.9**
Heller Factoring (Singapore) Ltd v Ng Tong Yang [1998] 3 SLR 299…**14.74**
Hely-Hutchinson v Brayhead Ltd [1968] 1 QB 549…**17.9, 17.15**
Henderson v Merrett Syndicates Ltd [1995] 2 AC 145…**12.3, 19.2, 19.36**
Herbert Morris Ltd v Saxelby [1916] AC 688…**14.80, 14.83**
Hermann v Charlesworth [1905] 2 KB 123…**14.42, 14.43**
Heron II, The (*see* Koufos v C Czarnikow Ltd, The Heron II)
Heydon's case (1584) 3 Co Rep 73…**1.138**
Heywood v Wellers [1976] QB 446…**15.62**
HIH Casualty & General Insurance Ltd v Chase Manhattan Bank [2001] Lloyd's Rep IR 191…**5.11**
Hill v Chief Constable of West Yorkshire [1989] AC 53…**19.33**
Ho Kian Siang v Ong Cheng Hoo [2000] 4 SLR 376…**16.46**
Ho Seng Lee Construction Pte Ltd v Nian Chuan Construction Pte Ltd [2001] 4 SLR 407…**11.21, 11.37**

Hobbs v The London & South Western Railway Company (1875) LR 10 QB 111...**15.62**
Hollier v Rambler Motors (AMC) Ltd [1972] 2 QB 71, [1972] 1 All ER 399...**6.24**
Home Office v Dorset Yacht Co Ltd [1970] AC 1004...**19.26, 19.33**
Hong Fok Realty Pte Ltd v Bima Investment Pte Ltd [1993] 1 SLR 73...**9.52**
Hongkong and Shanghai Bank Corporation Ltd v Jurong Engineering Ltd [2000] 2 SLR 54...**4.14**
Hong Kong Fir Shipping Co Ltd v Kawasaki Kisen Kaisha Ltd [1962] 2 QB 26...**5.21, 5.22, 6.27**
Hong Leong Leasing Sdn Bhd v Tan Kim Cheong [1994] 1 MLJ 177...**11.20**
Horwood v Millar's Timber and Trading Co [1917] 1 KB 305...**14.51**
Houghton v Trafalgar Insurance Co Ltd [1954] 1 QB 247...**6.22**
Household Fire and Carriage Accident Insurance Co v Grant (1879) 4 Ex D 216...**2.24, 2.25, 2.26**
Howard Marine & Dredging v Ogden & Sons (Excavations) [1978] QB 574...**5.18, 12.34**
Howard v Pickford Tool Co Ltd [1951] 1 KB 417...**9.47**
Hubbard v Vosper [1972] 2 QB 84...**21.26**
Huggins v Wiseman (1690) Carth 110...**7.10**
Hughes Aircraft Systems International v Airservice Australia (1997) 146 ALR 1...**2.8**
Hughes v Metropolitan Railway Company (1877) 2 App Cas 439...**3.49, 3.51**
Hulton v Jones [1910] AC 20...**20.68**
Hutton v Warren (1836) 1 M & W 466...**5.30**
Huyton SA v Peter Cremer GmbH & Co [1999] 1 Lloyd's Rep 620...**13.16**
Hyde Park Residence Ltd v Yelland [2000] RPC 604...**21.26**
Hyde v Wrench (1840) 3 Beav 334...**2.15**
Hyman v Hyman [1929] AC 601...**14.37**

I

Ikumene Singapore Pte Ltd v Leong Chee Leng [1993] 3 SLR 24...**19.30, 19.36**
Imperial Loan Co v Stone [1892] 1 QB 599...**7.27**
Improver Corp v Remington [1990] FSR 181...**21.59**
Inche Noriah v Shaik Allie bin Omar [1929] AC 127...**13.30**
Industries and General Mortgage Co Ltd v Lewis [1949] 2 All ER 573...**17.40**
Info-communications Development Authority of Singapore v Singapore Telecommunications Ltd (No 2) [2002] 3 SLR 488...**16.51, 16.73, 16.115, 16.118**
Ingram v Little [1961] 1 QB 31...**11.43, 11.44, 11.45, 11.46**
Initial Services Ltd v Putterill [1968] 1 QB 396...**21.68**
Interfoto Picture Library v Stiletto Visual Programmes [1989] QB 433, [1988] 1 All ER 348...**6.13, 6.20**
Invercargill City Council v Hamlin [1996] AC 624...**19.27, 19.28**
Irvine & Co v Watson & Sons (1880) 5 QBD 414...**17.32**

J

J Evans & Son (Portsmouth) Ltd v Andrea Merzario Ltd [1976] 1 WLR 1078...**5.9, 5.16, 6.29**
J T Stratford & Sons Ltd v Lindley [1965] AC 269...**20.13, 20.14, 20.39**
James Cundy & T Bevington v Thomas Lindsay (1878) 3 App Cas 459...**11.50, 11.51**
James McNaughton Paper Group Ltd v Hicks Anderson & Co [1991] 2 QB 113...**19.25, 19.32, 19.38**
Jarvis v Swans Tours Ltd [1973] QB 233...**15.62**
Jimat bin Awang v Lai Wee Ngen [1995] 3 SLR 769...**18.25**
John Shaw & Sons (Salford) Ltd v Shaw [1935] 2 KB 113...**18.27**
Johns-Manville Corporation's Patent [1967] FSR 327...**21.55**
Johnson Matthey & Co v Constantine Terminals Ltd and International Express Co Ltd [1976] 1 Lloyd's Rep 215...**8.20**

Johnson v Agnew [1980] AC 367…**9.52, 15.24, 16.47**
Johnson v Gore Wood & Co (a firm) [2001] 2 WLR 72…**15.64**
Johnson v Moreton [1980] AC 37…**14.38**
Johnson v Unisys Ltd [2001] 2 WLR 1076…**15.65**
Jones v Padavatton [1969] 1 WLR 328…**4.4**
Jones Bros (Hunstanton) Ltd v Stevens [1955] 1 QB 275…**20.18**
Joscelyne v Nissen [1970] 2 QB 86…**5.7, 11.27**
Joseph Constantine v Imperial Smelting [1942] AC 154…**10.21**
Joyce v DPP [1946] AC 347…**22.5**
Junior Books Ltd v Veitchi Co Ltd [1983] 1 AC 520…**19.18**

K

Kearley v Thomson (1890) 24 QBD 742…**14.58, 14.65**
Keighley, Maxted & Co v Durant [1901] AC 240…**17.23, 17.34**
Keir v Leeman (1844) 9 QB 371…**14.30**
Kelly v Partington (1833) 4 B & Ad 700…**20.86**
Kendall v Hamilton (1879) 4 App Cas 504…**17.35**
Kennedy v De Trafford [1897] AC 180…**17.2**
Kenrick v Lawrence (1890) 25 QBD 99…**21.9**
Kenwell & Co. Pte Ltd. v Southern Ocean Shipbuilding Co Pte Ltd [1999] 1 SLR 214…**6.55**
King's Norton Metal Co (Ltd) v Edridge, Merrett, and Co (Ltd) (1897) 14 TLR 98…**11.52**
Kiriri Cotton Co Ltd v Ranchhoddas Keshavji Dewani [1960] AC 192…**14.57**
Kleinwort Benson Ltd v Lincoln City Council [1998] 4 All ER 513…**11.3**
Kleinwort Benson Ltd v Glasgow City Council [1997] 4 All ER 641…**12.10**
Kleinwort Benson Ltd v Malaysia Mining Corp Bhd [1989] 1 WLR 379…**4.13**
Koenigsblatt v Sweet [1923] 2 Ch 314…**17.20**
Kong Thai Sawmill (Miri) Sdn Bhd, Re [1978] 2 MLJ 227…**18.49**
Koufos v C Czarnikow Ltd, The Heron II [1969] 1 AC 350…**15.71**
Krell v Henry [1903] 2 KB 740…**10.16**
Kushvinder Singh Chopra v Mooka Pillai Rajagopal [1996] 2 SLR 379…**13.42**

L

L'Estrange v Graucob [1934] 2 KB 394…**6.10, 6.20**
Ladbroke v William Hill [1964] 1 WLR 273…**21.16**
Las Vegas Hilton Corp v Khoo Teng Hock Sunny [1997] 1 SLR 341…**14.13**
Latham v Credit Suisse First Boston [2000] 2 SLR 693…**5.8**
Laurence v Lexcourt Holdings Ltd [1978] 1 WLR 1128…**11.18**
Lavarack v Woods of Colchester Ltd [1967] 1 QB 278…**15.85, 15.86**
Lawrence v Fox 20 NY 268 (1859)…**8.4**
LB (Plastics) Ltd v Swish Products Ltd [1979] FSR 145…**21.16**
Le Lievre v Gould [1893] 1 QB 491…**12.27**
Leaf v International Galleries [1950] 2 KB 86…**12.43**
Lee Christina v Lee Eunice & Anor (executors of the estate of Lee Teck Soon) [1993] 3 SLR 8…**9.53**
Lee Kuan Yew v Davies [1989] SLR 1063…**20.62, 20.75, 20.78**
Lee Seng Heng v Guardian Assurance Co Ltd [1932] MLJ 17…**2.24**
Lee Siong Kee v Beng Tiong Trading, Import and Export (1988) Pte Ltd [2000] 4 SLR 559…**9.14, 9.18, 9.19, 16.101, 16.105, 16.106**
Leigh and Sillavan Ltd v Aliakmon Shipping Co Ltd [1986] AC 785…**19.19**
Leigh v National Union of Railwaymen [1970] Ch 326…**14.36**
Lewis v Averay [1972] 1 QB 198…**11.45, 11.46**
Lifestyle 1.99 Pte Ltd v S$1.99 Pte Ltd (t/a ONE.99 SHOP) [2000] 2 SLR 766…**21.91, 21.92**

Lim Feng Chieh (formerly trading as Intra-Smit Agencies) v GS Auto Supply Pte Ltd [1993] 2 SLR 489…**18.6**
Lim Geok Hian v Lim Guan Chin [1994] 1 SLR 203…**13.49**
Lim Kim Som v Sheriffa Taibah bte Abdul Rahman [1994] 1 SLR 393…**10.19**
Lim Tjoen Kong v A-B Chew Investments Pte Ltd [1991] SLR 188…**9.84**
Linden Gardens Trust Ltd v Lenesta Sludge Disposals Ltd [1994] 1 AC 85…**8.23**
Lion Laboratories Ltd v Evans [1984] 2 All ER 417…**21.68**
Lipkin Gorman v Karpnale Ltd [1991] 2 AC 548…**16.114, 16.117**
Lister v Romford Ice & Cold Storage Ltd [1957] AC 555…**5.27**
Littlewoods Organisation Ltd v Harris [1977] 1 WLR 1472…**14.99**
Liverpool City Council v Irwin [1977] AC 239…**5.27**
Livingstone v The Rawyards Coal Company (1880) 5 App Cas 25…**15.18**
Lloyds Bank v Bundy [1975] QB 326…**13.31**
Lodder v Slowey [1904] AC 442…**16.81**
Loh Siok Wah v American International Assurance Co Ltd [1999] 1 SLR 281…**5.25**
London & Mashonaland Explorations Co Ltd v New Mashonaland Exploration Co Ltd [1891] WN 165…**18.41**
London Artists Ltd v Littler Grade Organisation Ltd [1969] 2 QB 375…**20.79**
London Association for Protection of Trade v Greenlands Ltd [1916] 2 AC 15…**20.86**
London Drugs Ltd v Kuehne & Nagel International Ltd [1993] 1 WWR 1…**8.18**
London, Chatham and Dover Railway Company v The South Eastern Railway Company [1893] AC 429…**16.5**
Lonrho Ltd v Shell Petroleum Co Ltd (No 2) [1982] AC 173…**20.31, 20.37, 20.48, 20.49**
Lonrho v Fayed [1990] 2 QB 479…**20.41, 20.42, 20.44**
Lonrho v Fayed [1992] 1 AC 448…**20.36, 20.37**
Lonrho v Fayed (No 5) [1993] 1 WLR 1489…**20.34**
Lotus (France v Turkey) 1927 PCIJ (Ser A) No 10…**22.3, 22.5**
Louth v Diprose (1992) 175 CLR 621…**13.47**
Lovell & Christmas v Beauchamp [1894] AC 607…**7.12**
Lovelock v Franklyn (1846) 8 Queen's Bench 371…**9.45**
Low Peng Boon v Low Janie [1999] 1 SLR 761…**18.49**
Lubbe v Cape Plc [2000] 1 WLR 1545…**22.7**
Lumley v Gye [1853] E&B 216…**20.6, 20.24**
Lumley v Wagner (1852) 1 De Gex McNaghten and Gordon 604…**16.38, 16.41**

M

Macmillan & Co Ltd v K & J Cooper (1923) 40 TLR 186…**21.9**
Magee v Pennine Insurance Co Ltd [1969] 2 QB 507…**11.18**
Malcomson Nicholas Hugh Bertram & Anor v Naresh Kumar Mehta [2001] 4 SLR 454…**21.70**
Malik v Bank of Credit & Commerce International SA [1998] AC 20…**5.23, 5.26, 5.27, 15.62**
Management Corp Strata Title No 586 v Menezes [1992] 1 SLR 807…**20.48**
Management Corporation Strata Title No 473 v De Beers Jewellery Pte Ltd [2001] 4 SLR 90…**11.3**
Management Corporation Strata Title No 473 v De Beers Jewellery Pte Ltd [2002] 2 SLR 1…**11.3, 15.11, 16.113**
Marc Rich & Co AG v Bishop Rock Marine Co Ltd [1996] AC 211…**19.8**
Maredelanto Compania Naviera SA v Bergbau-Handel GmbH, The Mihalis Angelos [1971] 1 QB 164…**5.19, 9.46**
Maritime National Fish v Ocean Trawlers [1935] AC 524…**10.22**
Market Investigations Ltd v Minister of Social Security [1969] 2 QB 173…**19.3**

Marshall, Re [1920] 1 Ch 284...**7.28**
Mason v Provident Clothing and Supply Co Ltd [1913] AC 724...**14.82**
Mastrobuono v Shearson Lehman Hutton 514 US 52 (1995)...**22.34**
McCutcheon v David MacBrayne Ltd [1964] 1 All ER 430, [1964] 1 WLR 125...**6.17**
McEllistrim v Ballymacelligott Co-operative Agricultural and Dairy Society [1919] AC 548...**14.75**
McElroy Milne v Commercial Electronics Ltd [1993] 1 NZLR 39...**15.81**
McFarlane v Tayside Health Board [2000] 2 AC 59...**19.13**
McLoughlin v O'Brian [1983] 1 AC 410...**19.12, 19.17, 19.21**
McRae v Commonwealth Disposals Commission (1951) 84 CLR 377...**11.2, 11.10, 11.14, 15.21**
Medivac International Management Pte Ltd v John Walter Moore [1988] 1 MLJ 5...**14.81**
Meng Leong Development Pte Ltd v Jip Hong Trading Co Pte Ltd [1984-1985] SLR 27...**9.84**
Merck v Pharmaforte [2000] 3 SLR 717...**21.52**
Meridian Global Funds Management Asia Ltd v Securities Commission [1995] 2 AC 500...**18.18, 18.25**
Merkur Island Corporation v Laughton [1983] 2 AC 570...**20.17, 20.50**
Merritt v Merritt [1970] 1 WLR 1211...**4.5, 4.7**
Millar v Bassey [1994] EMLR 44...**20.9**
Millar's Machinery Co Ltd v David Way & Son (1935) 40 Com Cas 204...**16.69**
Min Hong Auto Supply Pte Ltd v Loh Chun Seng & Anor [1993] 3 SLR 498...**15.24**
Mogul Steamship Co Ltd v McGregor Gow & Co [1892] AC 25...**20.3**
Mohd bin Sapri v Soil-Build (Pte) Ltd [1996] 2 SLR 505...**19.30**
Mooka Pillai Rajagopal v Kushvinder Singh Chopra [1996] 3 SLR 457...**13.42**
Moorcock, The (1889) 14 PD 64...**5.24**
Moorhouse v University of New South Wales [1976] RPC 151...**21.19**
Morris v Baron and Company [1918] 1 AC 1...**9.78, 9.87**
Morris v CW Martin & Sons Ltd [1966] 1 QB 716...**8.20**
Moschi v Lep Air Services Ltd [1973] AC 331...**9.41**
MP-Bilt Pte Ltd v Oey Widarto [1999] 3 SLR 592...**9.64, 16.4, 16.5**
Murphy v Brentwood District Council [1991] 1 AC 398...**19.7, 19.19, 19.21, 19.27**
Mutual Life and Citizens' Assurance Co Ltd v Evatt [1971] AC 793...**19.37**

N

Nash v Inman [1908] 2 KB 1...**7.9**
National Aerated Water Co Pte Ltd v Monarch Co, Inc [2000] 2 SLR 24...**14.89, 14.98**
National Westminster Bank Plc v Morgan [1985] AC 686...**13.31, 13.32, 13.33, 13.42**
Nelson v Dahl (1879) 12 Ch D 568...**5.30**
Nelson v Nelson (1995) 70 ALJR 47...**14.60**
Nelson v Stocker (1859) 4 De G & J 458...**7.23**
Nema, The [1982] AC 724...**10.17**
New York Star, The (*see* Port Jackson Stevedoring Pty Ltd v Salmond and Spraggon (Australia) Pty Ltd)
New Zealand Shipping Co Ltd v AM Sattherwaite & Co Ltd, The Eurymedon [1975] AC 154...**2.41, 3.33, 8.16**
Ng Buay Hock v Tan Keng Huat [1997] 2 SLR 788...**5.11, 12.34**
Nichols Advanced Vehicle Systems Inc v De Angelis (unreported, 21 December 1997)...**16.40**
Nippon Paint (Singapore) Co Pte Ltd v ICI Paint (Singapore) Pte Ltd [2001] 1 SLR 1...**21.91**
Nippon Yusen Kaisha v International Import and Export Co Ltd, The Elbe Maru [1978] 1 Lloyd's Rep 206...**8.17**
Nordenfelt v Maxim Nordenfelt Guns and Ammunition Co [1894] AC 535...**14.72, 14.75, 14.76**

Norfolk County Council v Secretary of State for the Environment [1973] 1 WLR 1400...**17.17**
North Ocean Shipping Co Ltd v Hyundai Construction Co Ltd, The Atlantic Baron [1979] QB 705...**13.12**
North Sea Continental Shelf Case 1969 ICJ 3...**22.3**
North Western Rly v M'Michael (1850) 5 Ex 114...**7.12, 7.13**
Nottebohm (Liechtenstein v Guatemala) 1955 ICJ 4...**22.6**
Nutting v Baldwin [1995] 1 WLR 201...**15.106**

O

Occidental Worldwide Investment Corp v Skibs A/S Avainti, Skibs A/S Glarona, Skibs A/S Navalis (The 'Siboen' and the 'Sibotre') [1976] 1 Lloyd's Rep 293...**13.5**
Office Cleaning Services Ltd v Westminster Window & General Cleaners Ltd (1946) 63 RPC 39...**21.92**
Olley v Marlborough Court Ltd [1949] 1 KB 532, [1949] 1 All ER 127...**6.14**
Ong Seow Pheng v Lotus Development [1997] 3 SLR 137...**21.19**
Ooi Han Sun v Bee Hua Meng [1991] SLR 824...**19.53, 19.56**
Oscar Chess Ltd v Williams [1957] 1 WLR 370...**5.17, 12.36**
Overbrooke Estate v Glencombe Properties [1974] 1 WLR 1335...**12.53**
Overseas Tankship (UK) Ltd v Morts Dock & Engineering Co, The Wagon Mound (No 1) [1961] AC 388...**15.71, 19.49**
Overseas Union Insurance Ltd v Turegum Insurance Co [2001] 3 SLR 330...**2.3, 2.16, 2.46**
Overstone Ltd v Shipway [1962] 1 WLR 117...**16.10**

P

PP v Manogaran s/o R Ramu [1997] 1 SLR 22...**1.136**
PP v Teo Ai Nee [1995] 2 SLR 69...**21.20**
P.R.E.P.A.R.E. Trade Mark [1997] RPC 884...**21.74**
Pacific Rim Investments Pte Ltd v Lam Seng Tiong [1995] 3 SLR 1...**15.98**
Page One Records Ltd v Britton [1968] 1 WLR 157...**16.35, 16.41**
Page v Smith [1996] AC 155...**19.17**
Panatron v Lee Cheow Lee [2001] 3 SLR 405...**12.20, 12.21**
Panayiotou v Sony Music Entertainment (UK) Limited [1994] EMLR 229...**14.90**
Pang Koi Fa v Lim Djoe Phing [1993] 3 SLR 317...**19.17, 19.26**
Pao On v Lau Yiu Long [1980] AC 614...**3.13, 3.15, 3.16, 3.33, 13.9, 13.10, 13.12, 13.17, 13.19**
Paradine v Jane (1647) Aleyn 26...**10.1**
Parker v South Eastern Railway Co (1877) 2 CPD 416...**6.12**
Parmiter v Coupland (1840) 6 M & W 105...**20.59**
Paul Felthouse v Bindley (1862) 11 CB (NS) 869...**2.29, 2.31, 2.32, 2.34**
Payzu, Limited v Saunders [1919] KB 581...**15.79, 15.80**
Pearce v Brooks (1866) LR 1 Ex 213...**14.46, 14.47**
Peh Teck Quee v Bayerische Landesbank Girozentrale [2000] 1 SLR 148...**14.5**
Pek Nam Kee v Peh Lam Kong [1996] 1 SLR 75...**13.49**
Percival v Wright [1902] 2 Ch 421...**18.43**
Perrett v Collins [1998] 2 Lloyd's Rep 255...**19.8**
Perry v Sydney Phillips & Son [1982] 1 WLR 1297...**15.62**
Peter's American Delicacy Co Ltd v Heath (1939) 61 CLR 457...**18.47, 18.48**
Pharmaceutical Society of Great Britain v Boots Cash Chemists [1953] 1 QB 401...**2.7**
Phelps v Hillingdon London Borough Council [2000] 3 WLR 776...**19.33**
Phillip William Carney v John Edward Herbert [1985] AC 301...**14.95**
Phillips Products Ltd v Hyland [1987] 1 WLR 659n, [1987] 2 All ER 620...**6.35**

Phillips v Brooks, Ltd [1919] 2 KB 243…**11.42, 11.43, 11.44, 11.45, 11.46**
Phoenix General Insurance Co of Greece SA v Administratia Asiguralor de Stat [1988] QB 216…**14.18**
Photo Production Ltd. v Securicor Transport Ltd [1980] AC 827, [1980] 1 All ER 556…**6.28**
Pianotist Co's Application (1906) 23 RPC 774…**21.75, 21.79**
Pilba Trading & Agency v South East Asia Insurance Bhd [1998] 2 MLJ 53…**19.26**
Pilmore v Hood (1838) 5 Bing NC 97…**12.15**
Pinnel's Case (1602) 5 Co Rep 117a…**3.44, 3.45, 3.46, 9.81, 9.88**
Pioneer Container, The [1994] 2 AC 324…**8.20**
Pitt v PHH Asset Management Ltd [1993] 4 All ER 961…**2.38**
Pitts v Hunt [1991] 1 QB 24…**19.55, 19.56**
Plus Group Ltd and Others v Pyke [2002] EWCA Civ 370 …**18.41**
Poosathurai v Kannappa Chettiar (1911) LR 47 IA 1…**13.31, 13.33**
Port Jackson Stevedoring Pty Ltd v Salmond and Spraggon (Australia) Pty Ltd, The New York Star [1981] 1 WLR 138…**8.16**
Porter v Freudenberg [1915] 1 KB 857…**14.40**
Portuguese Consolidated Copper Mines Limited, Re (1890) 45 Ch D 16…**17.28**
Poussard v Spiers (1876) 1 QBD 410…**5.21**
President of India v La Pintada Compania Navigacion SA [1985] AC 104…**16.5, 16.8**
Press Automation Technology Pte Ltd v Trans-link Exhibition Forwarding Pte Ltd [2003] 1 SLR 712…**6.20, 6.55**
Preston Corpn Sdn Bhd v Edward Leong [1982] 2 MLJ 22…**2.4**
Price v Strange [1978] Ch 338…**16.23**
Printing and Numerical Registering Co v Sampson (1875) LR 19 Eq 462…**6.2**
Pro Sieben Media AG v Carlton UK Television Ltd [1999] FSR 610…**21.26**
Projection Pte Ltd v The Tai Ping Insurance Co Ltd [2001] 2 SLR 399…**2.3, 2.46, 11.18**
Pub 1997 Pte Ltd v Scorpion [1994] 2 SLR 180…**16.42**
Public Works Commissioner v Hills [1906] AC 368…**15.93**
Pym v Campbell (1856) 6 E & B 370…**5.7**

Q
Quah Kay Tee v Ong & Co Pte Ltd [1997] 1 SLR 390…**20.36**
Quinn v Burch Bros (Builders) Ltd [1966] 2 QB 370…**15.88**

R
R & B Customs Brokers Co Ltd v United Dominions Trust Ltd [1988] 1 All ER 847, [1988] 1 WLR 321…**6.50**
R Leslie Ltd v Sheill [1914] 3 KB 607…**7.20, 7.23**
R v Bow Street Metropolitan Stipendiary Magistrate, Ex Parte Pinochet Ugarte (No 2) [2000] 1 AC 119…**22.5**
R v Clarke (1927) 40 CLR 227…**2.33, 2.34**
'R' v Her Majesty's Attorney-General for England and Wales (2003; Privy Council Appeal No 61 of 2002)…**13.8, 13.32, 13.57**
R v Willans (1858) 3 Kyshe's Reports 16…**1.19**
RSP Architects Planners & Engineers (Raglan Squire & Partners FE) v Management Corporation Strata Title Plan No 1075 [1999] 2 SLR 449…**19.28**
RSP Architects Planners and Engineers v Ocean Front Pte Ltd [1996] 1 SLR 113…**19.27, 19.28, 19.29, 19.41**
Radcliffe v Evans [1892] 2 QB 524…**20.52**
Radford v De Froberville [1977] 1 WLR 1262…**15.58, 15.59, 15.83**
Raffles v Wichelhaus (1864) 2 H & C 906…**11.29, 11.30**
Rajabali Jumabhoy v Ameerali R Jumabhoy [1997] 3 SLR 802; affirmed [1998] 2 SLR 439…**13.49**

Rajeswari Thedshanamurthy v Kin Nam Realty Development Sdn Bhd [1983] 1 MLJ 88...**2.36**
Rama Corporation v Proved Tin and General Investments Ltd (1952) 2 QB 147...**17.14**
Ramsgate Victoria Hotel Co Ltd v Montefiore (1866) LR 1 Ex 109...**2.17**
Re AUVI Trademark [1992] 1 SLR 639...**21.9**
Re Mahmoud and Ispahani [1921] 2 KB 716...**14.18, 14.19**
Reckitt & Colman Products Ltd v Borden Inc [1990] 1 All ER 873...**21.90**
Redgrave v Hurd (1881) 20 Ch D 1...**12.21**
Reed v Madon [1989] Ch 408...**15.62**
Regal (Hastings) Ltd v Gulliver [1942] 1 All ER 378...**18.41**
Regazzoni v KC Sethia (1944) Ltd [1958] AC 301...**14.41**
Renault v Zhang (2002) 187 ALR 1...**22.7**
Rengamah a/p Rengasamy v Tai Yoke Lai [1998] 5 MLJ 260...**14.9**
Richardson v Mellish (1824) 2 Bing 229...**14.2**
Robin v Goh Boon Choo [1965] MLJ 215...**11.20**
Robinson v Harman (1848) 1 Ex 850...**15.17**
Rondel v Worsley [1967] 3 All ER 993 ...**19.33**
Rookes v Barnard [1964] AC 1129...**20.25, 20.27, 20.29, 20.30, 20.45, 20.46**
Rose & Frank Co v JR Crompton & Bros Ltd [1923] 2 KB 261; affirmed [1925] AC 445...**4.11**
Routledge v McKay [1954] 1 WLR 615...**5.15**
Rover International Ltd v Cannon Film Sales Ltd [1989] 1 WLR 912...**16.73, 16.96, 16.97, 16.100**
Rowland v Divall [1923] 2 KB 500...**16.71**
Roxborough v Rothmans of Pall Mall Australia [2001] HCA 68...**16.73**
Royal Bank of Scotland v Etridge (No 2) [1998] 4 All ER 705...**13.32**
Royal Bank of Scotland v Etridge (No 2) [2001] 3 WLR 1021...**12.25, 13.32, 13.38, 13.42, 13.47, 13.52**
Royal British Bank v Turquand (1856) 6 E&B 327...**18.32**
Royscot Trust Ltd v Rogerson [1991] 3 All ER 294...**5.11**
Ruxley Electronics and Construction Ltd v Forsyth [1996] AC 344...**15.45, 15.59**
Ryan v Mutual Tontine Westminster Chambers Association [1893] 1 Ch 116...**16.28**
Rylands v Fletcher (1868) LR 3 HL 330; affirming (1866) LR 1 Exch 265...**19.62**

S

Sadler v Whiteman [1910] 1 KB 868...**18.52**
Sainsbury v Street [1972] 1 WLR 834 ...**10.23**
Sajan Singh v Sardara Ali [1960] AC 167...**14.60**
Saloman v Saloman & Co Ltd [1897] AC 22...**18.19**
San International Pte Ltd v Keppel Engineering Pte Ltd [1998] 3 SLR 871...**9.34, 9.35, 9.36**
Satef-Huttenes Albertus SpA v Paloma Tercera Shipping Co SA (The Pegase) [1981] 1 Lloyd's Rep 175...**15.70**
Saunders v Anglia Building Society [1971] AC 1004...**11.54**
Scally v Southern Health and Social Services Board [1992] 1 AC 294...**5.27**
Scancarriers A/S v Aeteraroa International Ltd, (The 'Barranduna' and 'Tarago') [1985] 2 Lloyd's Rep 419...**2.10**
Schawel v Reade [1913] 2 IR 64...**5.13**
Scotson v Pegg (1861) 6 H & N 295...**3.33**
Scott v Avery (1856) 5 HL Cas 811...**14.34**
Scott v Davis (2000) 74 ALJR 1410...**17.3**
Scott v London and St Katherine Docks Co (1865) 3 H & C 596...**19.53**
Scruttons Ltd v Midland Silicones Ltd [1962] AC 446...**8.16**
Seagate Technology Pte Ltd v Goh Han Kim [1995] 1 SLR 17...**16.114**

Sea-Land Service Inc v Cheong Fook Chee Vincent [1994] 3 SLR 631...**3.40, 3.41**
Selectmove Ltd, Re [1995] 1 WLR 474...**2.31, 3.46, 9.81**
Shaikh Faisal t/a Gibca v Swan Hunter Singapore Pte Ltd [1995] 1 SLR 394...**14.8**
Shanklin Pier Ltd v Detel Products Ltd [1951] 2 KB 854...**2.40, 5.9**
Sharon Global Solutions Pte Ltd v LG International (Singapore) Pte Ltd [2001] 3 SLR 368...**3.41, 13.20**
Shell Eastern Petroleum (Pte) Ltd v Chuan Hong Auto (Pte) Ltd [1995] 3 SLR 281...**14.87**
Shelley v Paddock [1980] 1 All ER 1009...**14.58, 14.60**
Shirlaw v Southern Foundries (1926) Ltd [1939] 2 KB 206...**5.24**
Shogun Finance Ltd v Hudson [2002] 2 WLR 867...**11.46, 11.47**
Sim Tony v Lim Ah Ghee (t/a Phil Real Estate & Building Services) [1994] 3 SLR 224...**14.8**
Sim Tony v Lim Ah Ghee (t/a Phil Real Estate & Building Services) [1995] 2 SLR 466...**3.15, 14.8**
Sim v Stretch [1936] 2 All ER 1237...**20.59**
Singapore Woodcraft Manufacturing v Mok Ah Sai [1979] 2 MLJ 166...**10.19**
Siu Yin Kwan v Eastern Insurance Co Ltd [1994] 2 AC 199...**17.34, 17.35**
Smith New Court Securities v Scrimgeor Vickers (Asset Management) [1997] AC 254...**12.27**
Smith v Eric S Bush [1990] 1 AC 831, [1989] 2 All ER 514...**6.35, 19.36, 19.39**
Smith v Hughes (1871) LR 6 QB 597...**11.31, 11.34, 11.35, 11.37**
Smith v Leech Brain & Co Ltd [1962] 2 QB 405...**19.54**
Smith v Wilson (1832) 3 B & A 728...**5.7**
Société Italo-Belge pour le Commerce et l'Industrie SA v Palm and Vegetable Oils (Malaysia) Sdn Bhd, The Post Chaser [1982] 1 All ER 19...**3.52. 3.54**
Societe Nationale Industrielle Aerospatiale v Lee Kui Jak [1987] AC 871...**22.7**
Solle v Butcher [1950] 1 KB 671...**11.17, 11.18, 11.19, 11.20, 11.21, 11.51**
Sotiros Shipping Inc and Aeco Maritime SA v Sameiet Solholt (The Solholt) [1983] 1 Lloyd's Rep 605...**15.81**
South Australia Asset Management Corporation v York Montague Ltd [1997] AC 191...**15.26, 15.81, 15.88**
South Western General Property v Marton (1982) 263 EG 1090...**12.54**
Southern Foundries (1926) Ltd v Shirlaw [1940] AC 701...**18.34**
Southern Ocean Shipbuilding Co Pte Ltd v Deutsche Bank AG [1993] 3 SLR 686...**2.31**
Southern Water Authority v Carey [1985] 2 All ER 1077...**8.16**
Sovracht (V/O) v Van Udens Scheepvart en Agentuur Maatschappij (NV Gebr) [1943] AC 203...**14.40**
Spartan Steel & Alloys Ltd v Martin & Co (Contractors) Ltd [1973] QB 27...**19.9, 19.11, 19.13**
Spence v Katz Bros (1892) SLR (NS) 61...**2.2**
Spencer v Harding (1870) LR 5 CP 561...**2.8**
Spice Girls v Aprilia World Service [2002] EWCA Civ 15, CA...**12.14, 12.16**
Spiliada Maritime Corp v Cansulex Ltd [1987] AC 460...**22.7**
Spring v Guardian Assurance Plc [1995] 2 AC 296...**19.36**
Spurling v Bradshaw [1956] 2 All ER 121, [1956] 1 WLR 461...**6.13, 6.20**
St John Shipping Corporation v Joseph Rank Ltd [1957] 1 QB 267...**14.15, 14.19, 14.22, 14.25**
Standard Chartered Bank v Coopers & Lybrand [1993] 3 SLR 712...**19.30, 19.36**
Standard Chartered Bank v Pakistan National Shipping (No 2) [2000] 1 Lloyd's Rep 218...**12.27, 12.28**
Stansbie v Troman [1948] 2 KB 48...**15.88**
Star City Pty Ltd v Tan Hong Woon [2002] 2 SLR 22...**14.13**
Steinberg v Scala (Leeds) Ltd [1923] 2 Ch 452...**7.14**

Stevenson, Jacques & Co v McLean (1880) 5 QBD 346...**2.16**
Stickney v Keeble [1915] AC 386...**16.22**
Stilk v Myrick (1809) 2 Camp 317...**3.34, 3.36, 3.38, 3.39, 3.41, 3.42, 3.44, 9.80**
Stocks v Wilson [1913] 2 KB 235...**7.23**
Stovin v Wise [1996] AC 923...**19.21, 19.23, 19.25, 19.33, 19.34**
Strongman (1945) Ltd v Sincock [1955] 3 All ER 90...**14.63**
Strutt v Whitnell [1975] 1 WLR 870...**15.82**
Sudbrook Trading Estate v Eggleton [1983] 1 AC 444...**2.36**
Suisse Atlantique Societe d'Armement Maritime SA v NV Rotterdamsche Kolen Centrale [1967] 1 AC 361, [1966] 2 All ER 61...**6.27, 6.28**
Sumpter v Hedges [1898] 1 QB 673...**9.19, 16.98, 16.100, 16.101**
Super Servant Two, The [1990] 1 Lloyd's Rep 1...**10.22**
Surrey County Council v Bredero Homes Ltd [1993] 1 WLR 1361...**16.89**
Sutherland Shire Council v Heyman (1985) 157 CLR 424...**19.19, 19.20, 19.21, 19.23**
Sutton v Sutton [1984] Ch 184...**14.37**
Svanasio v McNamara (1956) 96 CLR 186...**11.20, 11.21**
Swiss Singapore Overseas Enterprise Pte Ltd v Horng Chang Enterprise Pte Ltd [1993] 2 SLR 478...**19.7, 19.30, 19.36**
Symbian Ltd v Christensen [2001] IRLR 77...**16.36**

T

T Lucas & Co Ltd v Mitchell [1974] 1 Ch 129...**14.98**
Tamplin Steamship v Anglo-Mexican Petroleum Products [1916] 2 AC 397...**10.3**
Tan Sim Lay v Lim Kiat Seng [1996] 2 SLR 769...**13.19**
Tan Soo Leng David v Lim Thian Chai Charles [1998] 2 SLR 923...**15.78**
Tan Yeow Khoon v Tan Yeow Tat (No 1) [2000] 3 SLR 341...**2.36**
Tang Siew Choy v Certact Pte Ltd [1993] 3 SLR 44...**14.81, 21.69**
Tay Ah Poon v Chionh Hai Guan [1997] 2 SLR 363...**16.22, 16.25**
Tay Joo Sing v Ku Yu Sang [1994] 3 SLR 719...**15.24**
Taylor v Caldwell (1863) 3 B & S 826...**10.1**
Taylor v Johnson (1983) 151 CLR 422...**11.21, 11.32, 11.37**
Temple of Preah Vihear (Cambodia v Thailand) 1962 ICJ 6...**22.3**
Tengku Abdullah ibni Sultan Abu Bakar v Mohd Latiff bin Shah [1996] 2 MLJ 265...**13.40, 14.48**
Third World Development v Atang Latief [1990] 1 MLJ 385...**13.9, 13.19**
Thomas Cowan & Co Ltd v Orme [1961] MLJ 41...**14.76**
Thomas v Bradbury, Agnew & Co Ltd [1906] 2 KB 627...**20.80**
Thomas v Thomas (1842) 2 QB 851...**3.23**
Thompson (WL) Ld v Robinson (Gunmakers) Ld [1955] Ch 177...**15.87**
Thomson Plaza (Pte) Ltd v Liquidators of Yaohan Department Store Singapore Pte Ltd [2001] 3 SLR 437...**2.37**
Thornton v Shoe Lane Parking Ltd [1971] 2 QB 163...**2.39, 6.15, 6.42**
Tilden Rent-A-Car Co v Clendenning (1978) 83 DLR 3d 400...**6.20**
Tinn v Hoffmann & Co (1873) 29 LT 271...**2.35**
Tinsley v Milligan [1994] 1 AC 340...**14.55, 14.60**
Tito v Waddell (No 2) [1977] Ch 106...**15.59, 16.88**
Tool Metal Manufacturing Co Ltd v Tungsten Electric Co Ltd [1955] 1 WLR 761...**3.60, 3.61**
Torquay Hotel Co Ltd v Cousins [1969] 2 Ch 106...**20.16, 20.17**
Trade Facilities Pte Ltd v Public Prosecutor [1995] 2 SLR 475...**18.22**
Transniko Pte Ltd v Communication Technology Sdn Bhd [1996] 1 SLR 580...**2.23**
Trendtex Trading Corpn v Central Bank of Nigeria [1977] 1 QB 529...**22.4**
Tribe v Tribe [1995] 3 WLR 913...**14.66**

Tribune Investment Trust Inc v Soosan Trading Co Ltd [2000] 3 SLR 405...**2.3, 11.51, 20.8, 20.9**

Trident General Insurance Co Limited v McNiece Bros Proprietary Ltd (1988) 165 CLR 107...**8.19**

Tsakiroglou v Noblee Thorl [1960] 2 QB 318...**10.14, 10.18**

Turner v Grovit [2002] 1 WLR 107...**22.7**

Turquand, Young & Co v Yat Yuen Hong Co Ltd [1967] 1 MLJ 291...**14.12**

Tweddle v Atkinson (1861) 1 B & S 393...**3.17, 3.18**

U

UCB Corporate Services Ltd v Williams [2002] EWCA Civ 555...**13.34**

Ultramares Corporation v Touche (1931) 174 NE 441...**19.7**

Union Carbide Corp, Re 634 F Supp 842 (SDNY 1986)...**22.7**

Union Discount Co Ltd v Zoller [2001] 1 WLR 1517...**9.43**

Uniphone Sdn Bhd v Chin Boon Lit [1998] 6 MLJ 441...**19.21, 19.26**

United Bank of Kuwait v Hammond [1988] 1 WLR 1051...**17.15**

United Malayan Banking Corp Bhd v Masagoes [1994] 1 SLR 766...**13.49**

United States v Aluminum Co of America 148 F2d 416 (2d Cir 1945)...**22.5**

United States v Yousef (2000) WL 714103 (SDNY 1999)...**22.5**

Universal Cargo Carriers Corporation v Citati [1957] 2 QB 401...**9.39**

Universe Tankships Inc of Monrovia v International Transport Workers Federation [1983] 1 AC 366...**13.8**

V

Vancouver Malt and Sake Brewing Co Ltd v Vancouver Breweries Ltd [1934] AC 181...**14.77**

Viacom International Inc v Elitist Technologies Co Ltd (Singapore Domain Name Dispute Resolution Service Case No. SDRP-2002/0001(F))...**21.95**

Victoria Laundry (Windsor) Ld v Newman Industries Ld [1949] 2 KB 528...**15.69, 15.71, 15.73, 15.74**

Visvasam v Sathasivam [1980] 1 MLJ 266...**13.15**

Vita Food Products Inc v Unus Shipping Co Ltd [1939] AC 277...**22.7**

Vitol SA v Norelf Ltd [1996] AC 800...**9.50, 9.51**

Vizetelly v Mudie's Select Library Ltd [1900] 2 QB 170...**20.90**

W

W J Alan & Co Ltd v El Nasr Export and Import Co [1972] 2 QB 189...**3.52, 9.84**

Wade v Simeon (1846) 135 ER 1061...**3.29**

Wadsworth v Lydall [1981] 1 WLR 598...**16.8**

Wakley v Cooke (1849) 4 Exch 511...**20.73**

Walford v Miles [1992] 2 WLR 174...**2.38**

Walker, Re [1905] 1 Ch 160...**7.28**

Walters v Morgan (1861) 3 GF & J 718...**12.12**

Waltons Stores (Interstate) Ltd v Maher (1988) 164 CLR 387...**3.63, 3.64, 3.65, 3.66**

Ward v Byham [1956] 1 WLR 496...**3.32, 3.68**

Warlow v Harrison (1859) 1 E & E 309...**2.9**

Warner Brothers Pictures, Incorporated v Nelson [1937] 1 KB 209...**16.36, 16.39, 16.41**

Warren v Mendy [1989] 1 WLR 853...**16.33, 16.36, 16.40, 16.41**

Watson v Davies [1931] 1 Ch 455...**17.29**

Watson v Park Royal (Caterers) Ltd [1961] 1 WLR 727...**18.5**

Watt v Longsdon [1930] 1 KB 130...**20.87**

Watts v Morrow [1991] 1 WLR 1421...**15.60**

Webb v Chief Constable of Merseyside Police [2000] QB 427...**14.62**

Wee Richard v Wong Meng Meng & Partners [1995] 3 SLR 68...**20.86**

Weller v Denton [1921] 3 KB 103...**18.5**
West Sussex Properties Ltd v Chichester District Council (unreported judgment dated 28 June 2000)...**11.51**
Westacre Investments Inc v Jugoimport-SPDR Ltd [1998] 3 WLR 770...**14.35**
Westacre Investments Inc v Jugoimport-SPDR Ltd [2000] 1 QB 288...**14.35**
White and Carter (Councils) Ltd v McGregor [1962] AC 413...**9.63, 9.64, 9.65, 16.11**
White v Bluett (1853) 23 LJ Ex 36...**3.25, 3.26, 3.27, 3.32**
White v Chief Constable of South Yorkshire Police [1998] 1 All ER 1...**19.17**
White v Jones [1995] 2 AC 207...**19.36**
Whitehouse v Jordan [1981] 1 WLR 246...**19.42, 19.43**
Whiten v Pilot Insurance Co [2002] 1 SCR 595...**15.16**
Whittingham v Murdy (1889) 60 LT 956...**7.12**
Whittington v Seal-Hayne (1900) 82 LT 49...**12.35**
William Lacey (Hounslow) Ltd v Davis [1957] 1 WLR 932...**2.14**
William Sindall Plc v Cambridgeshire County Council [1994] 1 WLR 1016...**11.13, 11.25**
Williams v Cawardine (1833) 4 B & Ad 621...**2.33**
Williams v Natural Life Health Foods Ltd [1998] 1 WLR 830...**19.36**
Williams v Roffey Bros & Nicholls (Contractors) Ltd [1991] 1 QB 1...**3.27, 3.37, 3.39, 3.40, 3.41, 3.42, 3.46, 3.57, 3.70, 4.15, 9.80, 9.81**
Wilson v Northampton and Banbury Junction Rly Co (1874) 9 Ch App 279...**16.20**
Wilson v Wilson (1848) 1 HL Cas 538...**14.45**
Win Line (UK) Ltd v Masterpart (Singapore) Pte Ltd [2000] 2 SLR 98...**17.6**
Win Supreme Investment v Joharah bte Abdul Wahab [1997] 1 SLR 679...**10.28**
Windsurfing International v Tabur Marine [1985] RPC 59...**21.55**
Winnipeg Condominium Corp No 36 v Bird Construction Co (1995) 121 DLR (4th) 193...**19.27, 19.28**
With v O'Flanagan [1936] Ch 575...**12.16**
Woodhouse AC Israel Cocoa Ltd SA v Nigerian Produce Marketing Co Ltd [1972] AC 741...**3.48**
Wright v British Railways Board [1983] 2 AC 773...**15.60**
Wrotham Park Estate Co Ltd v Parkside Homes Ltd [1974] 1 WLR 798...**16.91**
WT Lamb & Sons v Goring Brick Co [1932] 1 KB 710...**17.4**
Wyatt v Kreglinger and Fernau [1933] 1 KB 793...**14.75**

X

X (Minors) v Bedfordshire County Council [1995] 2 AC 633...**19.33**

Y

Yasuda Fire and Marine Insurance Co of Europe Ltd v Orion Marine Insurance Underwriting Agency Ltd [1995] 2 WLR 49...**17.6**
Yuen Kun Yeu v Attorney-General of Hong Kong [1988] AC 175...**19.19, 19.21, 19.23, 19.31, 19.36**
Yukong Line Ltd of Korea v Rendsburg Investments Corporation of Liberia [1996] 2 Lloyd's Rep 604...**9.48, 9.60, 9.65**
Yuson Bien v Bankers Trust Co Ltd [1980] 1 MLJ 32...**11.27**

Table of Singapore Legislation

A

Administration of Muslim Law Act (Cap 3, 1999 Rev Ed)...**1.113, 1.127**
Application of English Law Act (Cap 7A, 1994 Rev Ed)...**1.22, 1.49, 2.9, 5.11, 5.22, 5.29, 6.6, 6.48, 7.6, 7.22, 11.16, 12.2**
section 3...**1.23**
section 4...**1.23**
section 7...**1.23**
First Schedule...**1.23, 6.31**
Apportionment Act (Cap 8, 1988 Rev Ed)...**9.11**
section 3...**9.10**
Arbitration (Foreign Awards) Act (Cap 10A, 1985 Rev Ed) [repealed]...**1.158**
Arbitration (International Investment Disputes) Act (Cap 11, 1985 Rev Ed)...**22.27**
Arbitration Act (Cap 10, 2002 Rev Ed)...**1.170**

B

Bankruptcy Act (Cap 20, 2000 Rev Ed)...**1.151**
Bills of Exchange Act (Cap 23, 1985 Rev Ed)
section 26...**17.47**
section 27...**8.13**
section 29...**8.13**
Business Registration Act (Cap 32, 2001 Rev Ed)...**18.50**
section 4...**18.4**
section 4(2)...**18.4**
section 5...**18.4**
section 12...**18.4**
section 17...**18.5**
section 17(2)...**18.5**
section 23...**18.6**
First Schedule...**18.4**

C

Children and Young Persons Act (Cap 38, 2001 Rev Ed)...**1.112**
Civil Aviation Authority of Singapore Act (Cap 41, 1985 Rev Ed)...**18.7**
Civil Law Act (Cap 43, 1988 Rev Ed)
section 5 [repealed]...**1.21, 1.22, 1.23**
Civil Law Act (Cap 43, 1999 Rev Ed)
section 3...**1.75**
section 3(f)...**8.17**
section 5...**14.13**
section 10...**19.59**
section 12...**15.7**
section 20...**19.59**
section 21...**19.59**
Community Mediation Centres Act (Cap 49A, 1998 Rev Ed)...**1.162**

Companies Act (Cap 50, 1994 Rev Ed)...**1.152**
section 4...**18.7, 18.13**
section 17(3)...**18.3**
section 18(1)...**18.13**
section 19...**18.14**
section 19(5)...**18.7, 18.14**
section 19(6)...**18.11**
section 22...**18.15**
section 25...**7.37**
section 25(3)...**18.15**
section 39...**18.45**
section 41...**7.34, 17.23, 17.47**
section 145...**18.33**
section 156...**18.41**
section 159...**18.40**
section 184...**18.25**
section 186...**18.31**
section 216...**18.47, 18.49**
section 216A...**18.44**
Fourth Schedule, table A...**18.16, 18.25**
Fourth Schedule, table A, article 66...**18.33**
Fourth Schedule, table A, article 69...**18.33**
Fourth Schedule, table A, article 70...**18.33**
Fourth Schedule, table A, article 79...**18.25**
Fourth Schedule, table A, article 81...**18.41**
Computer Misuse Act (Cap 50A, 1998 Rev Ed)...**19.62**
section 3...**21.70**
section 5...**21.70**
Constitution (Amendment) Act 1965 (No 8 of 1965)...**1.38**
Constitution (Amendment) Act 1969 (No 19 of 1969)...**1.45**
Constitution of the Republic of Singapore, The
article 5A...**1.109**
article 20...**1.101**
article 21...**1.101**
article 22...**1.101**
article 22H...**1.51**
article 23...**1.100**
article 25...**1.102**
article 31...**1.102**
article 35(1)...**1.103**
article 35(7)...**1.103**
article 35(8)...**1.103**
article 39(1)(b)...**1.53**
article 39(1)(c)...**1.55**
article 39A...**1.54**
article 68...**1.97**
article 69...**1.97**
article 78...**1.97**
article 78(7)(c)...**1.97**
article 93...**1.106**
article 94(5)...**1.47**
article 100...**1.51**
article 153A...**1.39**

Consumer Protection (Fair Trading) Act (draft Bill)...**6.61, 6.62**
Contracts (Rights of Third Parties) Act (Cap 53B, 2002 Rev Ed)...**1.96, 8.7, 8.18, 8.25**
section 2...**8.26, 8.27**
section 2(1)(a)...**8.26**
section 2(1)(b)...**8.26**
section 2(2)...**8.26**
section 2(3)...**8.26**
section 2(5)...**8.24, 8.37**
section 3...**8.27**
section 4...**8.28**
section 5...**8.29**
section 6...**8.30**
section 7...**8.31**
section 7(1)...**8.31**
section 7(2)...**8.31**
section 7(3)...**8.31**
section 7(4)...**8.31**
section 7(5)...**8.16**
section 8(1)...**8.16, 8.32**
section 8(2)...**8.32**
section 9...**8.33**
Contributory Negligence and Personal Injuries Act (Cap 54, 2002 Rev Ed)...**1.80, 19.56**
section 2...**15.89, 19.59**
section 3...**15.89, 19.59**
section 3(1)...**15.89**
Copyright Act (Cap 63, 1999 Rev Ed)...**21.3, 21.5, 21.7, 21.14, 21.22, 21.23, 21.24, 21.27, 21.29, 21.30, 21.92**
section 7(1)...**21.7, 21.12, 21.14, 21.26**
section 7(2)...**21.25**
section 7(2A)...**21.25**
section 7A...**21.7**
section 10(1)...**21.16**
section 15...**21.14**
section 15(3)...**21.17**
section 16...**21.10**
section 17...**21.10**
section 24...**21.8**
section 25(3)...**21.20**
section 25(4)...**21.20**
section 25A...**21.14**
section 26...**21.14**
section 26(1)(c)...**21.14**
section 27...**21.9**
section 27(1)...**21.8**
section 27(2)...**21.8**
section 27(4)...**21.8**
section 28(2)...**21.11**
section 28(3)...**21.11**
section 28(6)...**21.11**
section 30(2)...**21.12**
section 30(3)...**21.12**
section 30(4)...**21.12**

section 30(5)...**21.12**
section 30(6)...**21.12**
section 31...**21.15**
section 31(1)...**21.18**
section 32...**21.20**
section 33...**21.20**
section 35–37...**21.25**
section 35(2)...**21.25, 21.26**
section 35(3)...**21.25**
section 35(4)...**21.25**
section 38...**21.3**
section 69...**21.17**
section 70...**21.17**
section 70(1)...**21.40**
section 73...**21.17**
section 73(2)(b)...**21.46**
section 74...**21.17**
section 74(1)...**21.46**
section 74(2)...**21.46**
section 74(3)...**21.46**
section 74(4)...**21.46**
section 82(1)(b)...**21.14**
sections 82-86...**21.14**
section 87...**21.8**
section 88...**21.8**
sections 89–91...**21.8**
sections 92–95...**21.11**
section 96...**21.11**
section 97(2)...**21.12**
section 97(3)...**21.12**
section 98(2)...**21.12**
section 98(3)...**21.12**
sections 103–105...**21.15**
section 103(1)...**21.18**
section 104...**21.20**
section 105...**21.20**
section 106...**21.3**
sections 109–111...**21.25**
section 114...**21.3**
section 119...**21.22**
section 119(2)...**21.22**
section 119(3)...**21.22**
section 119(4)...**21.22**
section 120...**21.22**
section 120A...**21.22**
section 136...**21.20**
section 140B(1)...**21.23**
section 140B(7)...**21.23**
section 140M(1)...**21.23**
section 184...**21.8**
section 188...**21.29**
section 193B...**21.32**

section 193C(1)...**21.32, 21.33**
section 193C(2)...**21.33**
section 193D...**21.34**
section 193E...**21.35**
section 194(3)...**21.13**
section 200(1)...**21.21**
section 246...**21.27**
section 256...**21.27**
section 260(1)...**21.30**
section 260(2)...**21.30**
section 260(3)...**21.30**
section 260(4)...**21.30**
section 261...**21.30**
Part V...**21.22, 21.23**
Part IX...**21.29**
Part XII...**21.27**
Part XIII...**21.30**
Corruption, Drug Trafficking and Other Serious Crimes (Confiscation of Benefits) Act (Cap 65A, 2000 Rev Ed)...**17.40**
Countervailing and Anti-Dumping Duties Act (Cap 65B, 1997 Rev Ed)...**22.8**
section 2...**22.9**
section 3...**22.10**
Part III...**22.9**
Criminal Procedure Code (Cap 68, 1985 Rev Ed)...**1.112**
section 11...**1.124**
section 336(1)...**1.103**
section 336(2)...**1.105**
section 400...**1.84**

D

Defamation Act (Cap 75, 1985 Rev Ed)...**20.58**
section 4...**20.58**
section 5...**20.58**
section 6...**20.54**
section 7...**20.91**
section 8...**20.73**
section 9...**20.77**
section 10...**20.92**
section 11...**20.83**
section 12...**20.89**

E

Economic Development Board Act (Cap 85, 2001 Rev Ed)...**1.42**
Electronic Transactions Act (Cap 88, 1999 Rev Ed)...**2.2, 2.28, 2.48, 6.16, 6.57, 11.57**
section 2...**2.49, 2.52**
section 4(1)...**2.50**
sections 6–9...**2.50**
section 10...**19.64, 20.95, 20.96, 20.97, 21.32**
section 10(1)(a)...**20.95**
sections 11–15...**2.50**
section 11...**2.49**
section 12...**2.49**
section 13...**2.51**

section 14...**2.51**
section 15...**2.51**
Evidence Act (Cap 97, 1997 Rev Ed)...**5.6**
section 2(2)...**5.8**
section 93...**5.8**
section 94...**5.8**
section 94(b)...**5.9**
section 94(c)...**5.7**

F
Frustrated Contracts Act (Cap 115, 1985 Rev Ed)...**10.29, 10.37, 16.108**
section 2(2)...**10.31–10.33**
section 2(3)...**10.33**
section 3(3)...**10.34**
section 3(5)...**10.35, 16.109**

G
Geographical Indications Act (Cap 117B, 1999 Rev Ed)...**21.97**
section 2...**21.97**
section 3(1)...**21.98**
section 3(2)...**21.98**
section 3(2)(c)...**21.98**
section 3(2)(d)...**21.98**
section 4...**21.99**
section 6–9...**21.99**
Government Proceedings Act (Cap 121, 1985 Rev Ed)
section 5...**19.3**

H
Hijacking of Aircraft and Protection of Aircraft and International Airports Act (Cap 124, 1997 Rev Ed)...**1.130**
Hire-Purchase Act (Cap 125, 1999 Rev Ed)
section 1(3)...**6.36**

I
Independence of Singapore Agreement 1965 (9 August 1965)...**1.36**
Industrial Relations Act (Cap 136, 2002 Rev Ed)
Part IV...**1.157**
Intellectual Property Office of Singapore Act (Cap 140, 2002 Rev Ed)...**21.47**
International Arbitration Act (Cap 143A, 2002 Rev Ed)...**1.158, 1.170, 1.188, 22.29**
First Schedule (incorporating UNCITRAL Model Law on International Commercial Arbitration 1985)...**22.29**
article 1(1)...**22.30**
article 1(3)...**22.30**
article 5...**22.31**
article 8...**22.31**
article 9...**22.31**
article 18...**22.32**
article 22...**22.32**
article 28...**22.33**
article 28(3)...**22.33**
article 30...**22.33**
Second Schedule...**22.34**

Interpretation Act (Cap 1, 2002 Rev Ed)
section 2...**1.77**
section 9A...**1.139**
section 10...**1.97**
section 19...**1.98**
section 23...**1.99**

J

Judicial Committee (Repeal) Act 1994 (No 2 of 1994)...**1.110**
Jurong Town Corporation Act (Cap 150, 1998 Rev Ed)...**1.42**

L

Layout-Designs of Integrated Circuits Act (Cap 159A, 2000 Rev Ed)...**21.43**
Legal Profession Act (Cap 161, 2001 Rev Ed)...**1.147, 1.150, 1.152**
section 2...**1.148**
section 3...**1.148**
section 7(1)...**1.148**
section 12...**1.148**
section 14...**1.148**
section 37...**1.153**
section 38...**1.153**
section 81B...**1.152**
section 82...**1.151**
section 82A(12)...**1.151**
section 83(2)...**1.150**
Limitation Act (Cap 163, 1996 Rev Ed)...**15.10, 19.27, 19.59**

M

Maintenance of Parents Act (Cap 167B, 1996 Rev Ed)...**1.96, 1.159**
Minors' Contracts Act (Cap 389, 1994 Rev Ed) (see the references under the Minors' Contracts Act 1987 (UK))
Misrepresentation Act (Cap 390, 1994 Rev Ed) (see the references under the Misrepresentation Act 1967 (UK))
Misuse of Drugs Act (Cap 185, 2001 Rev Ed)
section 8A...**22.5**
Monetary Authority of Singapore Act (Cap 186, 1999 Rev Ed)...**1.42**

P

Parliament (Privileges, Immunities and Powers) Act (Cap 217, 2000 Rev Ed)...**20.82**
section 7...**20.82**
section 8...**20.82**
Parliamentary Elections Act (Cap 218, 2001 Rev Ed)
section 52...**1.53**
Partnership Act (Cap 391, 1985 Rev Ed) (see the references under the Partnership Act 1890 (UK))
Patents (Amendment) Act 1995...**21.47, 21.50**
Patents (Amendment) Act 2001...**21.47**
Part XIX...**21.47**
Patents Act (Cap 221, 2002 Rev Ed)...**21.47, 21.49, 21.65**
section 2(1)...**21.53**
section 13(1)...**21.48**
section 13(2) [repealed]...**21.50**
section 13(3)...**21.48**
section 14(1)...**21.51**

section 14(2)...**21.51**
section 14(4)...**21.53**
section 14(5)...**21.53**
section 15...**21.53**
section 16(1)...**21.56**
section 16(2)...**21.56**
section 16(3)...**21.56**
section 17...**21.51**
section 25(4)...**21.47**
section 30(1)...**21.62**
section 33...**21.57**
section 34...**21.57**
section 36...**21.57**
section 41...**21.64**
section 41(7)...**21.64**
section 43(1)...**21.64**
section 66(1)...**21.49, 21.60**
section 66(1)(a)...**21.60**
section 66(1)(b)...**21.60**
section 66(1)(c)...**21.60**
section 66(2)...**21.61**
section 66(2)(a)...**21.61**
section 66(2)(b)...**21.61**
section 66(2)(g)...**21.61**
section 67(1)...**21.62**
section 67(2)...**21.62**
section 69(1)...**21.62**
section 71(1)...**21.61**
section 71(2)...**21.61**
section 71(3)...**21.61**
section 75...**21.64**
section 76(1)...**21.62**
section 76(3)...**21.62**
section 77...**21.63**
section 80(1)(a)...**21.48, 21.57**
section 82(1)(a)...**21.61**
section 113(1)...**21.58**

Penal Code (Cap 224, 1985 Rev Ed)...**1.130**
section 120A...**20.31**
section 499...**20.58**
section 499 (1)...**20.58**

Prevention of Corruption Act (Cap 241, 1993 Rev Ed)...**17.40**

Professional Engineers Act (Cap 253, 1992 Rev Ed)
section 11...**14.13**
section 12...**14.13**

R

Registered Designs Act (Act 25 of 2000)
section 76(1)(a)...**21.40**

Registered Designs Act (Cap 266, 2001 Rev Ed)...**21.46**
section 2(1)...**21.42, 21.45**
section 5...**21.44**
section 6...**21.43**

section 7...**21.43**
section 19...**21.44**
section 21(1)...**21.41**
section 21(2)...**21.41**
section 30...**21.45**
section 30(5)...**21.45**
section 30(6)...**21.45**
Republic of Singapore Independence Act (No 9 of 1965)
section 7...**1.39**
Reciprocal Enforcement of Commonwealth Judgments Act (Cap 264, Rev Ed 1997)...**22.7, 22.34**
Reciprocal Enforcement of Foreign Judgments Act (Cap 264, Rev Ed 1997)...**22.7, 22.34**
Residential Property Act (Cap 274, 1985 Rev Ed)...**14.13**

S

Sale of Commercial Properties Act (Cap 281, 1985 Rev Ed)...**14.13**
Sale of Goods (United Nations Convention) Act (Cap 283A, 1996 Rev Ed)...**5.29, 22.11**
Schedule, article 1(1)(a)...**22.11**
Schedule, article 2...**22.11**
Schedule, article 3...**22.11**
Schedule, article 5...**22.11**
Schedule, article 16(1)...**22.11**
Schedule, article 16(2)...**22.11**
Schedule, article 18(2)...**22.11**
Schedule, article 19(2)...**22.11**
Schedule, article 19(3)...**22.11**
Schedule, article 25...**22.11**
Schedule, article 30...**22.11**
Schedule, articles 31–44...**22.11**
Schedule, article 35...**22.11**
Schedule, article 41...**22.11**
Schedule, article 53...**22.11**
Schedule, article 54...**22.11**
Schedule, article 57...**22.11**
Schedule, article 58...**22.11**
Schedule, articles 66–70...**22.11**
Schedule, article 71...**22.11**
Schedule, article 72...**22.11**
Schedule, article 74...**22.11**
Schedule, article 82...**22.11**
Sale of Goods Act (Cap 393, 1999 Rev Ed) (see the references under the Sale of Goods Act 1979 (UK))
Securities and Futures Act (Cap 289, 2002 Rev Ed)...**18.13**
Singapore Academy of Law Act (Cap 294A, 1997 Rev Ed)...**1.154**
Singapore Tourism Board Act (Cap 305B, 1997 Rev Ed)...**1.42**
Small Claims Tribunals Act (Cap 308, 1998 Rev Ed)...**1.112**
section 5(1)...**1.115**
section 5(2)...**1.115**
section 5(3)(b)...**1.116**
section 5(4)...**1.115**
section 12(4)...**1.114**
section 15(6)...**1.114**
section 16...**1.114**

section 22(1)...**1.114**
section 23(3)...**1.114**
section 31...**1.116**
section 32...**1.116**
section 38...**1.117**
Subordinate Courts Act (Cap 321, 1999 Rev Ed)...**1.112**
section 2...**1.119, 1.122**
section 9...**1.121**
section 9(3)...**1.121**
section 10(1)...**1.118**
section 10(2)...**1.118**
section 23 ...**1.122**
section 26...**1.123**
section 26(a)...**1.122**
section 27...**1.122**
section 30...**1.122**
section 31(1)...**1.123, 15.8, 16.17, 16.46**
section 31(2)...**1.123, 16.17**
section 50(2)...**1.124**
section 51(2)...**1.120**
section 52...**1.119, 15.8, 16.17, 16.46**
Supply of Goods Act (Cap 394, 1994 Rev Ed) (see the references under the Supply of Goods and Services Act 1982 (UK))
Supreme Court of Judicature Act (No 24 of 1969)...**1.45**
Supreme Court of Judicature Act (Cap 322, 1999 Rev Ed)...**1.126**
section 15...**1.130**
section 16...**1.126**
section 17...**1.126**
section 17A(1)...**1.127**
section 17A(2)...**1.127**
section 17A(3)...**1.127**
section 18(2)...**15.8, 16.17, 16.46**
section 19...**1.130**
section 22...**1.129**
section 29A(1)...**1.132**
section 29A(2)...**1.133**
section 37...**1.132**
section 39(2)...**1.132**
section 54...**1.133**
First Schedule...**1.128**
First Schedule, paragraph 6...**15.8**
First Schedule, paragraph 14...**16.17, 16.46**

T
Trade Marks Act (Cap 332, 1999 Rev Ed)...**21.71, 21.98**
section 2(1)...**21.72, 21.73, 21.74, 21.75**
section 2(2)...**21.72**
section 2(4)...**21.78**
section 2(7)...**21.73**
section 4(2)...**21.89**
section 5(2)...**21.76**
section 6...**21.76**
section 7...**21.74**

section 7(1)...**21.74**
section 7(2)...**21.74**
section 7(3)...**21.74**
section 7(4)...**21.74**
section 7(5)...**21.74**
section 7(6)...**21.74**
sections 7(7)–7(10)...**21.98**
section 8...**21.73, 21.74, 21.75, 21.79**
section 8(1)...**21.73, 21.75**
section 8(2)...**21.73, 21.75**
section 8(3)...**21.73, 21.75**
section 8(6)...**21.75**
section 9(1)...**21.75**
section 10(1)...**21.76**
section 15(2)...**21.77**
section 15(3)...**21.77**
section 18...**21.77**
section 19...**21.77**
section 22...**21.77**
section 22(1)(a)...**21.77**
section 23...**21.77**
section 23(4)...**21.77**
section 26(1)...**21.78**
section 27...**21.79**
section 27(1)...**21.79**
section 27(2)...**21.79**
section 27(3)...**21.79**
section 27(4)...**21.78**
section 27(4)(d)...**21.79**
section 27(5)...**21.79**
section 27(6)...**21.80**
section 28(1)...**21.81**
section 28(2)...**21.82**
section 29(1)...**21.83**
section 29(2)...**21.83**
section 31(2)(a)...**21.84**
section 31(2)(b)...**21.84**
section 32(1)...**21.84**
section 33(1)...**21.84**
section 34(1)...**21.84**
section 35...**21.86**
section 36...**21.87**
section 38(1)...**21.87**
section 38(2)...**21.87**
section 38(3)...**21.87**
section 39(1)...**21.87**
section 39(2)...**21.87**
section 39(3)(a)...**21.87**
section 39(3)(b)...**21.87**
section 39(4)...**21.87**
section 42(1)...**21.87**
section 42(3)...**21.87**

section 44...**21.87**
section 45...**21.87**
section 46(1)...**21.84**
section 46(2)...**21.84**
section 47...**21.84**
section 55...**21.73**
section 55(1)...**21.73**
section 61...**21.97**
section 81...**21.85**
section 82...**21.85**
section 82(1) ...**21.85**
section 82(4)...**21.85**
section 94(1)...**21.85**
Part VI...**21.84**
Part X...**21.85**
Second Schedule...**21.97**

U

Unfair Contract Terms Act (Cap 396, 1994 Rev Ed) (see the references under the Unfair Contract Terms Act 1977 (UK))
United Kingdom Designs (Protection) Act (Cap 339, 1985 Rev Ed) [repealed]...**21.41**

W

Workmen's Compensation Act (Cap 354, 1998 Rev Ed)...**19.56**

Table of Subsidiary Legislation (Singapore)

C

Copyright (Border Enforcement Measures) Regulations 1998 (GN No S 224/98)...**21.23**
Copyright (International Protection) Regulations 1987 (GN No S 110/87)...**21.8**
  Regulation 3(8)...**21.27**

L

Legal Profession (Professional Conduct) Rules (GN No S 156/98)...**1.147**
Legal Profession (Qualified Person) Rules (GN No S 357/2001)...**1.148**

P

Patents Rules 1995 (GN No S 1/95)
  rule 47(1)...**21.62**
Practice Statement on Judicial Precedent (issued on 11 July 1994) [1994] 2 SLR 689...**1.50, 1.136**

R

Rules of Court (GN No S 71/96)...**1.156**
  order 11, rule 1(f)(i)...**20.98**
  order 11, rule 1(f)(ii)...**20.98, 20.99**

T

Trade Marks Rules 1998 (GN No S 635/98)
  rule 54...**21.87**
  Third Schedule...**21.76**
Trade Marks (Border Enforcement Measures) Rules 1999 (GN No S 5/99)...**21.85**

Table of Foreign Legislation

A

Anticybersquatting Consumer Protection Act 1999 (S1255) (US)...**21.94**

B

British Columbia Contract Law Reform Act (draft) (Canada)...**14.102**

C

Companies Act 1985 (UK)
    section 711A...**18.31**
Constitution and Malaysia (Singapore Amendment) Act (Malaysian Act No 53 of 1965) (Malaysia)
    section 2...**1.37**
    section 14...**1.37**
Constitution of the United States of America
    article II, section 2...**22.4**
    First Amendment...**20.99**
    Fourteenth Amendment...**22.6**
Contract Act (India)
    section 16...**13.33**
Contracts (Rights of Third Parties) Act 1999 (UK)...**1.96, 8.24, 8.34**
Corporations Act 2001 (Australia)
    section 130...**18.31**

D

Data Protection Act 1998 (UK)...**21.70**
Defamation Act 1996 (UK)
    section 1...**20.96**
Delaware Revised Uniform Partnership Act (US)...**18.59**

E

Electronic Signatures in Global and National Commerce Act 2000 (US)...**6.57**

F

Family Law Reform Act 1969 (UK)...**7.4, 7.6**
Federal Racketeer Influenced and Corrupt Organizations Act, 18 USC (US)
    §1962(c)...**9.43**

H

Human Rights Act 1998 (UK)...**21.70**

I

Illegal Contracts Act 1970 (New Zealand)...**14.101, 14.102**
Illinois Electronic Commerce Security Act 1999 (US)...**2.48**
Infants Relief Act 1874 (UK)...**7.17, 7.18, 7.19**

J

Judicature Acts 1873–1875 (UK)...**1.75**

L

Law Reform (Contributory Negligence) Act 1945 (UK)...**15.90, 19.59**
section 1...**15.90**
Law Reform (Frustrated Contracts) Act 1943 (UK)...**10.29, 16.72, 16.107, 16.108**
Limited Liability Partnerships Act 2000 (UK)...**18.59**
Limited Partnerships Act 1907 (UK)...**18.57**

M

Matrimonial Causes Act 1973 (UK)
section 34...**14.37**
Ministry of Trade and Industry of Indonesia Decree No 295 (Indonesia)...**22.14**
Minors' Contracts Act 1987 (UK)...**7.17, 7.19, 7.22**
section 3(1)...**7.24, 7.25**
section 3(2)...**7.24**
Misrepresentation Act 1967 (UK)...**5.11, 5.18, 12.2, 12.30, 12.56**
section 1...**12.4**
section 2(1)...**5.11, 12.31, 12.33, 12.39, 12.46, 12.49**
section 2(2)...**12.39, 12.45–12.49**
section 2(3)...**12.49**
section 3...**6.11, 12.51**

P

Partnership Act 1890 (UK)
section 1...**18.51**
section 5...**18.53**
section 8...**18.53**
section 9...**18.54**

R

Registered Designs Act 1949 (UK)...**21.41**
Republic of the Philippines: Build-Operate-Transfer Law [Republic Act No. 7718] (Philippines)...**22.18**
Rules of the London Court of International Arbitration (UK)...**1.186**

S

Sale of Goods Act 1979 (UK)...**5.22, 5.23, 5.29, 6.36, 6.48, 9.18, 11.16, 22.11**
section 3(2)...**7.9, 7.29, 7.32**
section 6...**11.16**
section 6(1)...**11.16**
section 12(1)...**5.29**
section 12(2)...**5.29**
section 13(1)...**5.29**
section 14(1)...**5.29**
section 15(1)...**5.29**
section 30...**9.55**
section 30(1)...**9.17**
section 57(2)...**2.9**
Sonny Bono Copyright Term Extension Act 1998 (US)...**21.6**
State of Singapore Act 1958 (UK)...**1.29**
Statute of Frauds (1677) (UK)...**1.20**
Supply of Goods and Services Act 1982 (UK)
section 2...**6.48**

U

Unfair Contract Terms Act 1977 (UK)...**6.5, 6.6, 6.11, 6.23, 6.25, 6.31, 6.32, 6.55, 12.51, 12.52, 12.54, 15.99, 19.39**
section 1(1)...**6.41**
section 1(1)(c)...**6.31**
section 1(3)...**6.40**
section 1(3)(b)...**6.31**
section 2...**6.33, 6.34, 6.37, 6.39, 6.40, 6.41**
section 2(1)...**6.38, 6.42, 8.32**
section 2(2)...**6.38, 6.43, 6.53, 8.32**
section 3...**6.37, 6.38, 6.40, 6.44, 6.46, 6.53**
section 3(1)...**6.44**
section 3(2)...**6.44**
section 4...**6.37, 6.38, 6.40**
section 5...**6.34, 6.40**
section 6...**6.34, 6.40, 6.53**
section 6(1)...**6.47**
section 6(2)...**6.47**
section 6(3)...**6.47**
section 7...**6.34, 6.38, 6.40, 6.48, 6.53**
section 7(3A)...**6.48**
section 7(4)...**6.48**
section 8...**6.11, 12.51**
section 11...**6.43, 6.53**
section 11(1)...**6.51**
section 11(2)...**6.53**
section 11(3)...**6.52**
section 11(4)...**6.54**
section 12...**6.38, 6.49**
section 13...**6.34, 6.35**
section 14...**6.40, 6.42**
sections 15–25...**6.31**
section 26...**6.39**
First Schedule...**6.37, 6.38, 6.39**
Second Schedule...**6.53, 6.54, 12.54**

Uniform Commercial Code (US)...**1.80, 6.60**

Uniform Computer Information Transactions Act (US)...**6.58, 6.60, 6.62**
section 102(14)...**6.59**
section 114...**6.60**
section 117...**6.60**
section 803(1)...**6.58**

Utah Digital Signature Act (US)...**2.48**

Table of Treaties and Conventions

A

Agreement on Trade Related Aspects of Intellectual Property Rights...**21.3, 21.73, 21.75, 21.97, 21.98, 21.100**
  article 9(1)...**21.28**
  article 13...**21.3, 21.24**
Anglo-Dutch Treaty 1824...**1.11**

B

Berne Convention for the Protection of Literary and Artistic Works...**21.6, 21.8**
  article 6*bis*...**21.28, 21.29**
Budapest Treaty on the International Recognition of the Deposit of Micro-organisms for the Purposes of Patent Procedure...**21.47**

C

Charter of the International Court of Justice
  article 38(1)...**22.3**
Convention of the International Centre for the Settlement of Investment Disputes...**22.27**

G

General Agreement on Tariffs and Trade...**21.3, 22.8, 22.9**

I

Independence of Singapore Agreement 1965...**1.36**
International Institute for the Unification of Private Law
  article 6...**22.20**

M

Madrid Protocol...**21.88**

N

New York Convention on the Recognition and Enforcement of Foreign Arbitral Awards 1958...**1.158, 1.188, 22.29, 22.34**
  article V...**22.9, 22.34**
  article V(1)...**22.34**
  article V(2)...**22.34**
North American Free Trade Agreement...**22.8**

P

Paris Convention for the Protection of Industrial Property...**21.47, 21.51, 21.73, 21.75, 21.76, 21.97**
  article 10*bis*...**21.98**
Patent Co-operation Treaty...**21.47**

S

Second Charter of Justice 1826...**1.12, 1.19, 1.20**

T

Third Charter of Justice 1855...**1.15**
Treaty of Cession 1824...**1.11**

U

UNCITRAL Arbitration Rules 1976...**1.186**
UNCITRAL Model Law on Electronic Commerce...**2.48**
United Nations Convention on the International Sale of Goods...**5.29, 22.11**
US-Singapore Free Trade Agreement...**21.6, 21.72, 22.3, 22.6, 22.8, 22.25**
  chapter XV...**22.25**
  article 15.4.1...**22.25**

V

Vienna Convention on the Law of Treaties (1969)...**22.3**

W

World Trade Organization: Anti-Dumping Agreement...**22.9**
World Trade Organization: Agreement on Subsidies and Countervailing Measures...**22.10**
World Trade Organization: Agreement on Trade Related Aspects of Intellectual Property Rights...**22.8**
World Trade Organization: Agreement on Trade Related Investment Measures...**22.26**
World Trade Organization: General Agreement on Trade in Services...**22.26**

PART I

Introductory

CHAPTER 1

Introduction to the Singapore Legal System

PARAGRAPHS

1.1–1.3 **Introduction**

Legal and Constitutional Development

1.4–1.6 Introduction
1.7–1.11 Arrival of the British: Singapore in the British Realm (1819)
1.12–1.18 Fledgling Legal System: A Fitful and Chaotic Start (1826–1867)
1.19–1.23 Reception of English Law
1.24–1.25 From the British to the Japanese to the British (1942–1945)
1.26–1.31 Path to Self-Government (1948–1959) and Self-Government (1959–1963)
1.32–1.35 Singapore in Malaysia (1963–1965)
1.36–1.40 Disengagement from Malaysia and Independence (1965)
1.41–1.45 Initial Tasks of Nation-Building (1965–1969)
1.46–1.51 Development of an Autochthonous Legal System (1970–Present)
1.52–1.56 Constitutional Remaking in the 1980s and 1990s

The Common Law Tradition

1.57–1.58 Introduction
1.59–1.61 Do Judges Make Law?
1.62–1.73 Doctrine of Judicial Precedent or *Stare Decisis*
1.74–1.76 Common Law Versus Equity
1.77 Common Law Versus Written Law
1.78–1.82 Civil Law Tradition Versus Common Law Tradition
1.83–1.87 Civil Law Versus Criminal Law

The Three Governing Arms

1.88–1.89 Introduction
1.90–1.95 The Legislature
1.96–1.99 (1) The Law-Making Process
1.100–1.105 The Executive
1.106–1.107 The Judiciary
1.108 (1) Various Meanings of 'Jurisdiction'

PARAGRAPHS

The Three Governing Arms (continued)

1.109–1.111 (2) Court Structure and Hierarchy in Singapore
1.112–1.113 (3) Subordinate Courts
1.114–1.117 (a) Small Claims Tribunals
1.118–1.120 (b) Magistrates' Courts
1.121–1.124 (c) District Courts
1.125 (4) Supreme Court
1.126–1.130 (a) High Court
1.131–1.133 (b) Court of Appeal
1.134–1.137 (5) Vertical and Horizontal *Stare Decisis*
1.138–1.140 (6) Interpretation of Written Law
1.141–1.146 (7) Courts and Information Technology

1.147–1.154 **The Legal Profession**

Alternative Dispute Resolution: No More in the Alternative

1.155–1.156 Introduction
1.157–1.164 Overview of ADR in Singapore

Modes of ADR

1.165–1.167 Negotiation
1.168–1.169 Mediation
1.170 Arbitration
1.171 Hybrid Processes
1.172–1.173 Mini-Trial
1.174–1.176 Mediation–Arbitration
1.177–1.180 ADR: Its Popularity and Advantages
1.181–1.184 Key Institutions for Arbitration and Mediation
1.185–1.189 (1) Singapore International Arbitration Centre
1.190–1.196 (2) Singapore Mediation Centre

1.197–1.199 **Conclusion**

Introduction

1.1 Law consists of a set of rules and principles governing the conduct and behaviour of individuals, various entities and bodies as well as the society at large. It is distinct from purely moral rules or principles in that law can be enforced within the parameters of the legal system. The law is therefore concerned with the legal rights and obligations of such individuals, entities and the society *vis-à-vis* each other and the extent to which such rights and obligations may be protected or enforced by the legal system.

1.2 In order to properly understand business law and its interaction with the conduct of business activities in Singapore, one needs to possess at least a basic understanding of the Singapore legal system. The impact of the legal system on the development of business activities can be significant. An intelligent and judicious development of the legal system can facilitate and enhance businesses by providing a predictable and stable environment for the operation of business activities; at the same time, it needs to administer a sufficient dose of flexibility to encourage innovation and creativity, vital ingredients for successful businesses. On the other hand, overly stringent laws and a 'hard-nosed' approach to the implementation of such laws may unnecessarily stifle the development of business activities as well as the economy.

1.3 This chapter aims to provide an overview of the legal and constitutional history, the major legal institutions and traditions as well as to elaborate on some recent developments and innovations of the Singapore legal system. In a nutshell, it hopes to capture the *past* and *present* of the Singapore legal system as the current developments and innovations (whether of a legal nature or otherwise) continue to impinge upon its future direction. To cover the vast array of material within the space constraints of this chapter, the various sections discussed herein will inevitably have to be as concise and succinct as possible. The interested reader is therefore encouraged to refer to the more detailed references provided.

Legal and Constitutional Development

1.4 From its founding by Sir Thomas Stamford Raffles in 1819 to independence in 1965, Singapore's legal development was intricately linked with its British colonial master. In many respects, English legal traditions, practices, case law and legislation were adopted without much consideration as to whether they suited the local circumstances. Indeed, there was a 'slavish adherence to English law' resulting in the 'impoverishment of the common law in Singapore' (see, generally, A Phang, *The Development of Singapore Law: Historical and Socio-Legal Perspectives* (1990) at pp 84, 351–356)).

1.5 With independence, there has been a gradual—and increasing—movement towards developing an autochthonous legal system. The guiding principle is that the adoption of any legal practice or norm must be compatible with Singapore's cultural, social and economic requirements. In this regard, the economic success of Singapore can be attributed, amongst others, to the wisdom of its political leadership, its use of laws and the legal system to build a new society and entrench its economic survival while ensuring that the legal system is attuned to the needs and demands of the international business community.

1.6 The following paragraphs sketch the milestones in Singapore's legal and constitutional development. It is important to note that the brief nature of the overview necessarily means that much detail has been omitted. The interested reader is requested to consult the following titles for more detailed discussion and analysis: CM Turnbull, *A History of Singapore, 1819–1988* (2nd ed, 1989) for a general historical account, and KYL Tan, 'A Short Legal and Constitutional History of Singapore', in KYL Tan (ed), *The Singapore Legal System* (2nd ed, 1999) for an overview of Singapore's legal and constitutional history.

Arrival of the British: Singapore in the British Realm (1819)

1.7 Prior to the arrival of the Portuguese, Dutch and British imperialists from the 17th century in search of spices and trade, Singapore was insignificant in the struggles between Siam (now Thailand) and the Java-based Majapahit Empire for control over the Malay Peninsula. By the early 19th century, Singapore was under the rule of the Sultan of Johor, who was based in the Riau-Lingga archipelago. Little is known of Singapore's legal history prior to the founding of Singapore by Sir Stamford Raffles on 29 January 1819; what is often assumed is that a mixture of Malay customary and *adat* laws (localised traditional law and custom in Indonesia and Malaysia) formed the basis of a rudimentary legal system for a community of fishermen numbering no more than 200.

1.8 Given the Anglo-Dutch economic rivalry in maritime Southeast Asia, the British, through the British East India Company, was seeking to further establish and enhance its sphere of influence. Although the conventional wisdom was that Singapore was a 'sleepy fishing village', Raffles presciently determined that Singapore was a suitable port given its strategic geopolitical location. It would enable the British to ensure a good measure of control over the entrance to the Straits of Malacca as well as the main shipping route between South Asia and Northeast Asia.

1.9 Raffles acted without delay and, on 30 January 1819, concluded a preliminary treaty with Temenggong Abdu'r Rahman, the Johor Sultan's representative in Johor and Singapore, to set up a trading factory in Singapore. On 6 February 1819, a formal treaty was concluded with Sultan Hussein of Johor and the Temenggong, the *de jure* and *de facto* rulers of Singapore respectively, to formalize the earlier agreement. Raffles, who was then Bencoolen's Lieutenant-Governor, placed Singapore under Bencoolen's jurisdiction, which in turn was administered by the Governor-General in Calcutta, India.

1.10 For the proper administration of the island, Raffles sought to put in place a basic but functional legal system with a uniform law that was applicable to all inhabitants. He proceeded to promulgate a code of law known as the 'Singapore Regulations'. These Regulations were *ultra vires* as he had no legal authority to do so—Singapore had yet to be ceded to the British by the Johor Sultan and the Temenggong and the power to legislate resided in Calcutta. Regardless of the *de jure lex loci* (the law of the place; local law) of Singapore, *de facto* English law prevailed between 1819 and 1826 (see further, W Woon, 'The Applicability of English Law in Singapore', in W Woon (ed), *The Singapore Legal System* (1989)).

1.11 Raffles' prescience proved correct and Singapore rapidly evolved into a key trading port. In 1824, Singapore's status as a British possession was confirmed by the Anglo-Dutch Treaty and the Treaty of Cession of March 1824. This treaty provided for the Dutch withdrawing all objections to the British occupation of Singapore and the ceding of Malacca in exchange for the British relinquishing control of the factories in Bencoolen and Sumatra to the Dutch. Later that year, a second treaty was entered into with Sultan Hussein and Temenggong Abdu'r Rahman, by which the Johor Sultanate ceded Singapore to the British in return for increased cash payments and pensions.

Fledgling Legal System: A Fitful and Chaotic Start (1826–1867)

1.12 Up to this stage, Raffles and his successor Residents had no legal authority to promulgate the necessary legal instruments to establish a system for the administration of justice. Whatever regulations and system of justice established by Raffles and Resident John Crawfurd were *ultra vires*. This unsatisfactory state of affairs was resolved with the Second Charter of Justice, granted by the British Parliament on 27 November 1826, on the petition of the East India Company.

1.13 The Charter did not explicitly state that English law was to be applied in Singapore but it had been assumed to provide the legal basis for the general reception of English law in Singapore. It provided for the establishment of the Court of Judicature of Prince of Wales' Island (Penang), Singapore and Malacca with civil and criminal jurisdiction on par with similar courts in England.

1.14 Originally, Singapore, together with Malacca and Penang, the two other British settlements in the Malay Peninsula, collectively became the Straits Settlements in 1826, under the control of British India. With the reorganization of the East India Company's possessions by the British Parliament in 1833, the Governor-General of India was empowered to legislate for the Straits Settlements. During this period, there was much dissatisfaction with the legal system, which was characterized by 'legal chaos of epic proportions' (KYL Tan, 'A Short Legal and Constitutional History of Singapore', in KYL Tan (ed), *The Singapore Legal System* (2nd ed, 1999) at p 33).

1.15 The local business community was unhappy with the inadequate judicial framework which meted out justice infrequently and poorly. Again, on the petition of the East India Company, the Third Charter of Justice was granted in 1855 to help ease the increasing legal workload. However, the Third Charter did not improve the state of affairs. With the abolition of the East India Company in 1858, the Straits Settlements was transferred to the Indian Government. However, there were pockets of unhappiness with the Straits Settlements being administered out of India as it tended to result in their interests being relegated, if not neglected. On 1 April 1867, the Straits Settlements became a Crown Colony under the direct jurisdiction of the Colonial Office in London (see further discussion in (KYL Tan, 'A Short Legal and Constitutional History of Singapore', in KYL Tan (ed), *The Singapore Legal System* (2nd ed, 1999) at pp 34–35).

1.16 In 1868, the Supreme Court of the Straits Settlements was established following the abolition of the Court of Judicature. In 1873, there was further reorganisation with the Supreme Court given the jurisdiction to sit as a Court of Appeal. Prior to this, appeals were to the King-in-Council. In 1878, as a result of the changes to the judicial system in England, the local courts were restructured accordingly to mirror those of the English High Court (see generally, KYL Tan, 'A Short Legal and Constitutional History of Singapore', in KYL Tan (ed), *The Singapore Legal System* (2nd ed, 1999) at pp 36–39).

1.17 The increased use of the steamship in the mid-1860s coupled with the opening of the Suez Canal in 1869 resulted in Singapore's promotion from being a port of call for regional trade to one for international trade and, with it, the movement of people, ideas and finance. Singapore became a major port of call for ships plying between Europe and East Asia. With the growth of the rubber industry and Malaya being a major rubber exporter, Singapore developed rapidly after the 1870s as it became the main sorting and export centre in the world for rubber. Between 1873 and 1913, Singapore experienced unprecedented prosperity and trade expanded eightfold. This in turn attracted more immigrants from Southeast Asia, China and India and farther away.

1.18 AM Atkin was the first member of the Singapore Bar when he was admitted on 4 August 1852. In 1894, Song Ong Siang became the first Chinese barrister to be admitted to the Singapore Bar. The Court of Criminal Appeal was added in 1934 to the Supreme Court structure. In August 1939, after three and a half years of work, Governor Sir Shenton Thomas opened the present Supreme Court building on St Andrew's Road (for more historical anecdotes, see YS Thian, CC Chong and S Lim (eds), *In Session: Supreme Court Singapore–The Building, Her Heritage and Her People* (2002)).

Reception of English Law

1.19 Local case law since the 19th century, following the landmark case of *R v Willans* (1858) in Penang, has adopted the legal position that

English law (both common law and equity as it stood in 1826 as well as pre-1826 English legislation) was introduced to Singapore via the Second Charter of Justice. The assumed intention of the Charter was for English law to apply in Singapore as well as in Penang and in Malacca and this was generally accepted (for a quick overview and listing of academic articles on the reception of English law, see A Phang, 'The Singapore Legal System: History, Theory and Practice' (2000-1) 21 *Singapore Law Review* 23, pp 27–31).

1.20 Thus, the position can be summarised as follows: Subject to suitability and modification to local conditions, the Second Charter of Justice provided the legal basis for the general reception of the principles and rules of English common law and equity and pre-1826 English statutes (only those of general application) into Singapore. Of course, this meant that old English statutes, such as the Statute of Frauds (1677), were law in Singapore. However, the specific difficulty flowing from this was that no one knew for certain the complete list of English statutes (even those that have been repealed in England) that applied here.

1.21 This problem presented itself manifestly with the specific reception of English law via a local statute which provides for the application of English law. Until its repeal in 1993, section 5 of the Civil Law Act (Cap 43, 1988 Rev Ed) was the most significant reception provision in our statute books. Given Singapore's heavy reliance on trade and investment, it was an important legislative provision as it dealt with the introduction of English commercial law. This section provided that if a question or issue on specific categories of law or in general mercantile law arose in Singapore, the law to be administered shall be the same as that administered in England at the corresponding period, unless other provisions are made by any law having force in Singapore.

1.22 Section 5 of the Civil Law Act has since been repealed by the enactment of the Application of English Law Act (Cap 7A, 1994 Rev Ed). This belated amendment has removed much of the uncertainty and unsatisfactory state of affairs that had prevailed over the applicability of English legislation and common law in post-colonial Singapore which was, until recently, heavily dependent on the laws of the former colonial master.

1.23 The Act states that the common law of England (including the principles and rules of equity), so far as it was part of the law of Singapore before 12 November 1993, shall continue to be part of the law of Singapore. Section 3 of the Act provides that the common law, however, shall continue to be in force in Singapore as long as it is applicable to the circumstances of Singapore and subject to such modifications as those circumstances may require. Section 4, read with the First Schedule, specifies the English enactments (in *toto* or in parts), with the necessary modifications, that apply or continue to apply in Singapore. Section 7 effects miscellaneous amendments to local Acts, incorporating relevant English statutory law into local legislation. (There is a voluminous amount of academic discussion on the former section 5 of the Civil Law Act and the reader is advised to consult A Phang, 'Cementing the

Foundations: The Singapore Application of the English Law Act 1993' (1994) 28 *University of British Columbia Law Review* 205 for the references, as well as an overview of the 1993 Act itself).

From the British to the Japanese to the British (1942–1945)

1.24 During the Japanese Occupation of Singapore between February 1942 and September 1945, Singapore was renamed Syonan (Light of the South) by the Japanese and operated under the dictates of the Japanese military administration. The end of the Second World War resulted in the temporary administration of Singapore by the British Military Administration (BMA). By this time, the imperial powers encouraged and promoted self-determination and decolonization.

1.25 With the disbanding of the Straits Settlements in 1946, Penang and Malacca became part of the Malayan Union, and later the Federation of Malaya in 1948. However, given Singapore's strategic and economic importance, Singapore was not destined on the path of independence at the same pace as Malaya. Instead, it was made a Crown Colony with its own constitution. Like many other British colonies, the real power to govern and legislate were vested in the hands of the Governor and the colonial officials with a modicum of local participation and representation through limited elected seats on the Legislative Council. The first such elections were conducted in 1948.

Path to Self-Government (1948–1959) and Self-Government (1959–1963)

1.26 With the declared goal of taking over Malaya and Singapore through violence, the upsurge in communist united front activity led by the Communist Party of Malaya resulted in the Malayan colonial authorities clamping down during a period now known as the Emergency (1948–1960). Draconian laws were enacted (including detention without trial) in an attempt to control the scourge of communism. Singapore was not spared of communist activity and influence either. Indeed, the popular history of the mid-1950s to 1960s is of the ruling People's Action Party riding the communist tiger (D Bloodworth, *The Tiger and the Trojan Horse* (1986), J Drysdale, *Singapore, Struggle for Success* (1984)).

1.27 By this time, the Progressive Party was the leading political party in Singapore having won the Legislative Council elections in 1948 and 1951. Interest in Singapore's political life was nascent and tended to be drawn along the partisan lines of non-communist against pro-communist. In order to catalyse the democratic development in Singapore, a Constitutional Commission, headed by Sir George Rendel (the 'Rendel Commission'), was formed in 1953 with the goal of reviewing the Colony's constitution and enlarging public participation in self-governance. The government accepted most of the Rendel Commission's recommendations including the transformation of the Legislative Council into a chamber comprising mainly of directly elected members.

However, real power continued to be vested in the Governor and the Official Members of the Council of Ministers rather than the elected Assembly members (see further KYL Tan, 'A Short Legal and Constitutional History of Singapore' in KYL Tan (ed), *The Singapore Legal System* (2nd ed, 1999) at pp 42–44).

1.28 In the first Legislative Assembly elections in 1955, which marked the start of mass politics in Singapore, the Labour Front—led by David Saul Marshall—displaced the Progressive Party as the leading party, winning ten of the available 25 seats. The People's Action Party (hereafter the 'PAP'), founded in the same year, won 3 seats. Marshall was made Chief Minister and was adamant about accelerating the movement towards self-government. Constitutional talks on self-government began in 1956 in London with a non-partisan mission comprising of representatives from all the parties in the Assembly.

1.29 However, Marshall's Chief Ministership was short-lived. He resigned on 6 June 1956, after the breakdown of constitutional talks over whether the British High Commissioner in Singapore should have the casting vote on the proposed Defence Council. Lim Yew Hock, Marshall's deputy and Minister for Labour, became the Chief Minister. Lim led the March 1957 constitutional mission, which was successful in negotiating the main terms of a new Singapore Constitution. On 28 May 1958, the Constitutional Agreement was signed in London. The British Parliament passed the State of Singapore Act on 1 August 1958 marking Singapore's transition from a colony to a self-governing state in 1959.

1.30 In May 1959, Singapore's first general election was held to choose 51 representatives to the first fully elected Legislative Assembly. The PAP won 43 seats, garnering 53.4% of the total votes. On 3 June 1959, the new state Constitution was brought into force by the proclamation of the Governor, Sir William Goode, who became the first Yang di-Pertuan Negara (Head of State). The swearing-in of the first government of the State of Singapore on 5 June, with Lee Kuan Yew as Singapore's first Prime Minister, marked the culmination of the road to self-government and the beginning of the arduous path to independence via merger with Malaysia.

1.31 As part of the process towards self-government, the colonial authorities gradually divested the reins of government to the local people. Wee Chong Jin became the first local member of the Singapore Bar to be made a Puisne Judge (equivalent of a High Court Judge) in 1957 and subsequently became Chief Justice of Singapore in 1963, the first Asian to be appointed to the post. He retired as Chief Justice in 1990. Ahmad bin Mohd Ibrahim was appointed the first State Advocate-General of Singapore in June 1959 and became the first Attorney-General on Singapore's independence until January 1967.

Singapore in Malaysia (1963–1965)

1.32 By this time, the PAP was deeply mired in intra-party intrigues which split the party between the Chinese-educated pro-communists and the English-educated anti-communists. The inevitable open split arose in July 1961 with the issue of merger with Malaya being the tipping point. The pro-communists, led by Lim Chin Siong, broke away and formed the Barisan Socialis (Socialist Front). This defection and the Barisan Socialis' subsequent boycott of the 1968 general elections paved the way for the PAP to be the only party in Parliament until 1981.

1.33 On 27 May 1961, the Malayan Prime Minister, Tunku Abdul Rahman, proposed closer political and economic co-operation between the Federation of Malaya, Singapore, Sarawak, North Borneo and Brunei through merger. The PAP favoured merger with the Federation of Malaya for reasons of economic survival and as a means of achieving political independence from the British. The pro-communists took the merger proposal as an imperialist plot.

1.34 The main terms of the merger provided for the federal government in Kuala Lumpur to have responsibility for defence, foreign affairs and internal security. However, it provided for local autonomy in matters pertaining to finance, education and labour. Singapore was also to have her own executive state government. A referendum on the terms of the merger held in Singapore on 1 September 1962 gave the go-ahead for the PAP's plan of merger.

1.35 Brunei having opted out, Malaysia—consisting of the Federation of Malaya, Singapore, Sarawak and North Borneo (now Sabah)—was formed on 16 September 1963. Indonesia and the Philippines opposed the merger. Indonesia's President Sukarno subsequently launched the violent *Konfrontasi* campaign (Confrontation) against Malaysia. With merger, Singapore's court system became part of Malaysia's. Singapore's Supreme Court was replaced by the High Court of Malaysia in Singapore. The final court of appeal was the Federal Court in Kuala Lumpur.

Disengagement from Malaysia and Independence (1965)

1.36 Within two years, the merger was failing for a variety of reasons ranging from the internal politics of Malaysia to personality clashes to the ethnic politics of Malay-Malaysia. All of these, coupled with the threat and eruption of racial violence, as well as the receding threat of communism, prompted a negotiated departure of Singapore from Malaysia on 9 August 1965 (for an account of this tumultuous period in Singapore's history, interested readers can consult the memoirs of Senior Minister Lee Kuan Yew: *The Singapore Story: The Memoirs of Lee Kuan Yew* (1998); *From Third World to First—The Singapore Story: 1965–2000, Memoirs of Lee Kuan Yew* (2000), and Albert Lau, *A Moment Of Anguish: Singapore in Malaysia and the Politics of Disengagement* (1998)). The Independence of Singapore Agreement of 9 August 1965 declared that '…Singapore shall be forever a sovereign democratic and independent nation, founded upon the principles of liberty and justice and ever seeking the welfare and happiness of her people in a more just and equal society'.

1.37 The Malaysian Parliament had also enacted the Constitution and Malaysia (Singapore Amendment) Act (Malaysian Act No 53 of 1965) to 'allow Singapore to leave Malaysia and become an independent and sovereign state and nation separate from and independent of Malaysia' (section 2). Section 14 of this 'Separation Agreement' also provided for the guarantee of the 1961 and 1962 water agreements, which have now become a source of contention between Singapore and Malaysia in recent years (see the Singapore's Government's stand on the sanctity of the agreements in Ministry of Information, Communications and the Arts, *Water Talks?: If Only It Could* (2003) at p 4).

1.38 The Singapore Parliament, surprisingly, took several months to complete the constitutional formalities and legal procedures required for them to be in accord with Singapore's independent status. On 22 December 1965, the Singapore Parliament passed the Constitution (Amendment) Act (No 8 of 1965), with retrospective effect to 9 August 1965, which provided, *inter alia*, for a simple majority requirement (rather than the typical two-third majority) to effect an amendment to the Constitution. It was a pragmatic response to the rapid socio-economic and political re-engineering that was needed in the fledgling nation. The super-majority requirement was only reinstated in 1979.

1.39 Parliament also passed the Republic of Singapore Independence Act 1965 (No 9 of 1965), again retrospectively, for the reception of executive and legislative powers which had previously been vested in the Malaysian Federal government. Section 7 of the Act provided for Malay, Mandarin, Tamil and English to be the four official languages in Singapore and Malay to be the national language (also found in article 153A of the Constitution of the Republic of Singapore (1999 Rev Ed), the Singapore Constitution).

1.40 Singapore was admitted to the United Nations on 21 September 1965 and became a member of the Commonwealth of Nations on 15 October 1965. Yusof bin Ishak was appointed as the Republic's first President on 22 December 1965.

Initial Tasks of Nation-Building (1965–1969)

1.41 The task of building a nation with no natural resources or domestic market and a multi-racial and multi-religious society occupied the Government's attention. In the economic realm, Singapore pursued a labour-intensive, import-substitution industrialization programme, which graduated to an increasing emphasis on foreign direct investment, capital intensive, export-oriented industralisation and the development of a services sector. Various investment incentives, to facilitate job creation and the transfer of technology, were put in place. The laws on employment were also amended to reduce the powers of the trade unions and to make strikes illegal. The goal was to make Singapore an investor-friendly destination through the promotion of industrial peace and discipline among the workforce (see further WG Huff, *The Economic Growth of Singapore: Trade and Development in the Twentieth Century* (1994); C Carter, *Eyes on the Prize: Law and Economic Development in Singapore* (2002)).

1.42 To catalyse the pace of economic development, the Government also created several statutory boards such as the Economic Development Board (see Economic Development Board Act (Cap 85, 2001 Rev Ed)), the Jurong Town Corporation (Jurong Town Corporation Act (Cap 150, 1998 Rev Ed)) and the Singapore Tourism Board (Singapore Tourism Board Act (Cap 305B, 1997 Rev Ed)). In 1970, the Monetary Authority of Singapore (Monetary Authority of Singapore Act (Cap 186, 1999 Rev Ed)), the *de facto* central bank, was established to formulate and implement Singapore's monetary policies.

1.43 The Government also established in December 1965 Singapore's second constitutional commission, headed by Chief Justice Wee Chong Jin, to examine how the rights of the minorities (racial, linguistic and religious) could be constitutionally safeguarded. In its 1966 report, the Commission recommended that the constitutional provisions on fundamental liberties, the judiciary, the legislature, the general elections, minority rights, the special position of the Malays and the amendment procedures be entrenched (that is, amending these provisions require a two-step process: a two-thirds majority in Parliament followed by a two-thirds majority at a national referendum). It also recommended the creation of the office of an Ombudsman as an independent check on the actions and decisions of civil servants (for a more detailed discussion, see KYL Tan, 'A Short Legal and Constitutional History of Singapore' in KYL Tan (ed), *The Singapore Legal System* (2nd ed, 1999) at pp 49–51).

1.44 One recommendation that was accepted and which has a tangible outcome was the creation of an advisory body to offer advice to Parliament on proposed legislation and their impact on the minorities. This body is now known as the Presidential Council for Minority Rights. This is further discussed in paragraph 1.97 below.

1.45 With the passing of the Constitution (Amendment) Act (No 19 of 1969) and the Supreme Court Judicature Act (No 24 of 1969) in December 1969, the anomaly of the Singapore High Court being part of the Malaysian judiciary was finally resolved. These amendments also provided for the Judicial Committee of Her Britannic Majesty's Privy Council as the highest court of the land. Jury trials were also abolished in 1969.

Development of an Autochthonous Legal System (1970–Present)

1.46 The creation of an autochthonous legal system was tentative in the 1970s and 1980s. There was a casual comfort with the inherited traditions, practices and laws of England. The constant shortage of suitable candidates to serve on the Bench mandated two major changes in the 1970s. The first was the constitutional amendment in 1971 to allow for the appointment of supernumerary judges, which has since enabled High

Court judges who have reached the mandatory retirement age of 65 years to remain on the Bench for further periods on a contract basis.

1.47 In 1979, constitutional provisions were made for the creation of Judicial Commissioners to facilitate the disposal of business in the Supreme Court for limited renewable periods between six months and three years. Article 94(5) of the Singapore Constitution also allows for the appointment of a Judicial Commissioner to hear and determine a specified case only. Except for the fact that there is no security of tenure, Judicial Commissioners exercise the same powers and perform the functions of a Judge of the High Court and enjoy the same immunities as a High Court judge.

1.48 The drive to create an autochthonous legal system gained increased momentum in the late 1980s and accelerated with the appointment of Chief Justice Yong Pung How in September 1990. By 1989, appeals to the Privy Council had already been restricted. This was the precursor to the abolition of all appeals to the Privy Council in 1993. A permanent Court of Appeal, presided by the Chief Justice and two Justices of Appeal ('JAs'), was designated Singapore's highest court.

1.49 In November 1993, the Application of English Law Act (Cap 7A, 1994 Rev Ed) came into force and specified the extent to which English law is applicable in Singapore (and see, generally, paragraphs 1.19–1.23, above).

1.50 The impetus for these changes can be explained by the increasing confidence in the growing maturity and international standing of Singapore's legal system as well as the concern that Britain's increasing links with the European Union would render English law incompatible with local developments and aspirations. Further, political, social and economic circumstances have changed enormously since Singapore's independence. Indeed, the landmark Practice Statement on Judicial Precedent, issued on 11 July 1994, declared that the Privy Council, Singapore's predecessor courts as well as the Court of Appeal's prior decisions no longer bound the permanent Court of Appeal. The Practice Statement reasoned that '[t]he development of our law should reflect these changes and the fundamental values of Singapore society'.

1.51 In 1994, a new constitutional provision (article 100) was passed to establish a Constitutional Tribunal, consisting of at least three Supreme Court Judges, to which the President may refer for its binding opinion any question on the effect of any constitutional provision which has arisen or which is likely to arise. Thus far, the tribunal has provided a ruling on article 22H pertaining to the President's veto powers (see Constitutional Reference No 1 of 1995 (1995)).

Constitutional Remaking in the 1980s and 1990s

1.52 The late 1980s and early 1990s was a period of intensive constitutional remaking to develop an autochthonous government and parliamentary system of Singapore. The departure from the Westminster-inspired parliamentary system was evident through the innovations which attempted to handle the unique political circumstances here (for a critique, see LA Thio, 'The Right to Political Participation in Singapore: Tailor-Making a Westminster-modelled Constitution to Fit the Imperatives of "Asian" Democracy', (2002) 6 *Singapore Journal of International and Comparative Law* 181).

1.53 Between 1968 and 1981, the PAP was the only party in Parliament. The clamour for an alternative voice in Parliament resulted in the constitutional innovations to the electoral system. The first was the creation of Non-Constituency Members of Parliament ('NCMPs') in 1984 (see article 39(1)(b) of the Singapore Constitution). Here, up to six best losers in the general election (in terms of the highest percentage of votes polled) securing at least 15 per cent of the vote in the constituency contested may be invited to be NCMPs (see section 52 of the Parliamentary Elections Act (Cap 218, 2001 Rev Ed)).

1.54 In 1988, to ensure that Singapore politics continued to keep faith with the ideal of multiracialism, Parliament amended the Constitution to provide for the creation of the Group Representation Constituency ('GRC') (see article 39A of the Singapore Constitution). Here, several candidates—one of whom must be of a minority race—from a party compete as a team for an enlarged super-constituency (which in essence was an amalgamation of several single-member constituencies). The GRC scheme has evolved and expanded. For example, in the 2001 general election, GRC seats took up 75 of the 84 available seats, with each GRC having between four to six Members. When the GRC was first introduced in 1988, each GRC had only three Members; this was enlarged to four in 1991 and to six under the present structure.

1.55 In 1990, another category of Members of Parliament was created—the Nominated MP ('NMP')—to provide a wider range of non-partisan views from non-politicians. Over the years, the number of NMPs has increased from two and, since 1997, now stands at nine (article 39(1)(c) of the Singapore Constitution).

1.56 The final significant constitutional amendment relating to government was the conversion of the President's office from a mere ceremonial head of state appointed by Parliament to one in which the President was popularly elected. The Elected President scheme had a long gestation period and was driven by the concern that a freak general election could result in the PAP being thrown out of power and replaced by a populist government which may lead Singapore to political and economic ruin. The ostensible objective of the Elected President was to institutionally safeguard Singapore's foreign reserves and the integrity of the civil service. The Elected President serves as a second 'key' to the reserves and is vested with the power of veto on key civil service appointments (for a fuller discussion, see PE Lam and KYL Tan (eds), *Managing Political Change in Singapore: The Elected Presidency* (1997)). President Wee Kim

Wee first exercised the powers of the Elected President when the Constitution was amended in 1991; Ong Teng Cheong won the first ever Presidential elections in August 1993.

The Common Law Tradition

1.57 There are a number of major legal traditions in the world today (instead of the term 'traditions', it is sometimes referred to as legal 'families'; see K Zweigert and H Kotz, *An Introduction to Comparative Law* (3rd ed, 1998) at pp 63-73). These legal traditions include the Common Law, Civil Law, Socialist and other religious legal traditions (there are other ways of classifying the various legal systems in this world, which are based on one or more factors such as legal ideology, the areas of law in question, attitudes towards and expectations of the role of the law and various legal styles; see K Zweigert and H Kotz, ibid. See also A Harding, 'Comparative Public Law: Some Lessons From Southeast Asia' in A Harding and E Orucu (eds), *Comparative Law in the 21st Century* (2001) at p 264 on problems of classification for Southeast Asia laws in terms of legal families). Singapore belongs to the Common Law tradition. More specifically, it has its roots in the English Common Law tradition. However, Singapore is also influenced in part by other legal traditions, such as Islamic law traditions in the area of personal laws (see A Harding, 'Global Doctrine & Local Knowledge: Law in Southeast Asia' (2002) 51 *International and Comparative Law Quarterly* 35 at p 42). The other countries in the Asian region which are part of the English Common law tradition include India, Malaysia, Myanmar and Brunei.

1.58 The English Common Law tradition began to develop from the 11th century in England. It arose out of a need for England to develop laws which were applied equally to litigants in similar disputes. As a result, *assize*, and later, circuit judges were sent to various parts of England to adjudicate disputes. The idea was that these judges would apply the same laws to the resolution of the disputes before them. Further, these laws would be the same (or at least similar) irrespective of the provinces or geographical areas in which the disputes took place. As a result, a 'common' law developed throughout the whole of England (see D Keenan, *Smith & Keenan's English Law* (13th ed, 2001) at pp 6–7).

Do Judges Make Law?

1.59 Modern-day legal scholarship accepts that the English Common Law tradition is premised on the idea that judges make law. In the past, this idea was resisted on the basis that judges are unelected and can only 'declare' the law. The opposing view is that judges should defer to the laws made by the Legislature whenever they are called upon to adjudicate disputes, instead of making new laws.

1.60 However, such resistance to judges making law is not practicable. It is well and good if the Legislature has stipulated clear laws to regulate or govern a particular dispute which is before the judge. If this is the case, judges would then have an easy task of applying the law made by the Legislature to the dispute before him. However, it is quite conceivable that the Legislature may not have foreseen such a dispute occurring and hence has not stipulated at all how the dispute should be resolved. Indeed, it would be apposite to add that it is impossible for the Legislature to predict the infinite variety of fact situations (and for that matter, disputes) which this world presents us. In such a situation, the judge would have to try to fill the *lacunae* (or gaps) in the law in order to reach a proper decision on the dispute based on the facts of the case.

1.61 In order to fill the *lacunae* left by the Legislature, judges relied upon principles of justice, their sense of fairness or made reference to public policy. In time to come, these principles of fairness or justice and public policy considerations as applied in the court decisions developed into legal rules and principles which are utilised as precedents for subsequent court decisions. Alternatively, the *lacunae* have been filled by judges via the drawing of analogies from prior decisions to the present facts of the dispute. In this regard, it is inevitable that judges gradually 'create' a body of law.

Doctrine of Judicial Precedent or Stare Decisis

1.62 It is expected that judges, when adjudicating a dispute, would rely on rational and non-arbitrary principles as far as possible, instead of, for instance, tossing a coin to decide the outcome (see, generally, MDA Freeman, 'Theories of Adjudication' in *Lloyd's Introduction to Jurisprudence* (7th ed, 2001), Chapter 17).

1.63 The English Common Law tradition is characterised by the doctrine of judicial precedent, also known as *stare decisis*. *Stare decisis* is a Latin phrase which means 'standing decision'. According to this doctrine, judges have, when adjudicating disputes between litigants before them, to abide by the previous decisions made by superior judges within the court hierarchy. The previous decisions are also called 'judicial precedents'.

1.64 There are a few reasons for this doctrine of *stare decisis*. Firstly, it promotes *uniformity* and *consistency* of decisions within the court hierarchy as judges are not permitted to adjudicate a dispute and reach a decision based merely on his or her whim and fancy, but on past decisions. Secondly, by virtue of this uniformity and consistency, it also lends a measure of *certainty* to the law. Greater *certainty* in the law confers on the disputing parties the opportunity to decide whether to settle the case outside of the courts. Thirdly, the doctrine is consistent with the respect accorded to the hierarchy within the court system, which is usually based on the experience and seniority of the judges (see, generally, W Woon, 'The Doctrine of Judicial Precedent', in K Tan (ed), *The Singapore Legal System* (2nd ed, 1999) at pp 298–299).

1.65 How is the decision of a judge reached? A decision of the judge is simply a *conclusion* which seeks to resolve the dispute and such a conclusion is invariably based on a *legal principle* applied to the particular *facts* of the dispute. For instance, the legal principle may be that 'a man who commits a criminal act cannot profit from the criminal act'. The facts of the dispute are that X has committed a criminal act and seeks to recover the 'rewards' obtained from the commission of the criminal act. Hence, the judge may, applying the legal principle to the facts of the case, conclude that X shall not be entitled to recover the 'rewards'.

1.66 Where it is apparent from the conclusion of the judge as to the legal principle(s) upon which the conclusion of the case is based, we refer to such a legal principle as the *ratio decidendi* of the case. '*Ratio decidendi*' is a Latin phrase which simply means 'the reason for the decision'. Hence, in the above example, the legal principle that 'a man who commits a criminal act cannot profit from the criminal act' is the *ratio decidendi* for the decision of the judge to disallow recovery by X.

1.67 *Obiter dictum* means a statement 'made by the way' (or, if you like, a 'peripheral' or an 'incidental' statement). *Obiter dictum* refers to a legal principle or statement (made by a judge in the case) which is not directly applied to the decision of the case. *Obiter dicta* is the plural of *obiter dictum*.

1.68 In the context of the doctrine of *stare decisis*, the determination of the *ratio decidendi* and the *obiter dicta* in a decision can be significant. If the particular legal principle or statement in a previous decision is regarded as *ratio decidendi*, then the judge in the present case has to abide by the *ratio decidendi* of the prior decision (that is, the *ratio decidendi* has to be applied in the present case), assuming that it is a previous decision made by a higher court within the hierarchy. In legal parlance, we say that the *ratio decidendi* in the previous decision by a higher ranking court is 'binding' on the judge. If, however, the legal principle in a previous decision is merely regarded as *obiter dicta*, then strictly speaking, the judge in the present case does not need to apply the *obiter dicta* in the case before him, notwithstanding that the previous decision is made by a higher court within the hierarchy. In legal parlance, we say that the *obiter dicta* is merely 'persuasive', and is therefore not binding on the judge in the present case.

1.69 A situation may arise where the facts in the previous decision upon which the *ratio decidendi* is based may be materially different from those in the present case. Hence, the judge adjudicating the present case may regard the facts in the prior decision as being so materially different that the *ratio decidendi* of that previous decision should not be followed or applied in the present case. In legal parlance, we say that the judge has 'distinguished' the prior decision from the present case.

1.70 Clearly, the previous decision of a higher court within the hierarchy is an important factor to determine whether the judge in the present dispute is 'bound' by that previous court's decision ('vertical *stare decisis*'). A judge is not bound by previous decisions made by a lower court. What about previous decisions made by courts at the *same level*? This is known as 'horizontal *stare decisis*'. In Singapore, for example, the High Court is not bound by previous decisions of the High Court. The distinction between 'vertical' *stare decisis* and 'horizontal' *stare decisis* will be dealt with in greater detail in paragraphs 1.134–1.136.

1.71 The need for the judge to follow judicial precedents of a higher court within the hierarchy does not, however, raise any issue if the judge in fact agrees with the judicial precedent. In such a situation, he or she would readily follow the previous decision of the higher court. One could not say, in this sense, that he or she was obliged to follow or was 'bound' to follow the precedent. The doctrine of *stare decisis* becomes significant, however, when the judge disagrees with the judicial precedent or is of the opinion that the judicial precedent should not be applied to the present dispute.

1.72 In summary, the doctrine of *stare decisis* stipulates that the previous decision by a higher court would bind the judge in his or her adjudication of the present dispute, unless the judge can show one or more of the following :

(1) the facts of the present dispute can be materially 'distinguished' from the facts in the previous decision of the higher court so as to render that previous decision inapplicable; or
(2) the previous decision was decided *per incuriam*, ie that it was wrongly decided on the basis that the previous court did not follow the rules of *stare decisis* in reaching that previous decision; or
(3) that the legal principle embodied in the previous decision of the higher court and sought to be applied to the dispute at hand was merely *obiter dicta*, and hence not binding on the judge in the present dispute.

1.73 As an aside (but nonetheless an important one), the proper functioning of the doctrine of *stare decisis* depends on the publication of judicial precedents in a form accessible to the courts as well as the lawyers. Hence, law reports containing prior court judgments are vital for the development of the common law in Singapore. Currently, the *Singapore Law Reports* is the main law reporter for Singapore. This was first published in 1992; prior to that, reports of local cases were published in the *Malayan Law Journal* since 1932 (see A Phang, *A Bibliographical Survey of Singaporean Legal Materials* (1999) at p 17).

Common Law Versus Equity

1.74 To understand the difference between Common Law and Equity, we need to look briefly at the historical development of Equity in England. As indicated above, the Common Law in England began to develop since the 11th century. However, certain defects in the Common Law began to surface. In order for a claimant to bring a claim under the Common Law in England, he or she had to file a form (called a 'writ') in the English courts according to rigid prescriptions. A case which could not fit into the inflexible categories under the writ would be thrown out.

This meant that no action can be brought on that claim. The remedies available under the common law writs were also limited. Further, the high costs of the writ sometimes deterred a party from taking out a claim in the common law courts (see, generally, D Keenan, *Smith & Keenan's English Law* (13th ed, 2001) at pp 8–12).

1.75 Hence, the Lord Chancellor was tasked (by the King then) to handle such cases. New writs were provided to cover complaints which could not fit into the categories under the existing common law writs. Initially, there were complaints about the perceived abuses of discretionary power conferred on the Lord Chancellor. Subsequently, the rules and practices became more formalised and institutionalised and the Chancery courts were set up to deal with the cases formerly handled by the Lord Chancellor. In the Chancery Courts, the judges used principles of fairness and justice (also called Equity) to decide on the disputes. Where there was a conflict between the principles of Equity and the Common Law, Equity would prevail (*Earl of Oxford's* case (1615)). In England, due to the subsequent amalgamation of the equity and common law courts via the Judicature Acts 1873-5, a claimant could seek both common law and equitable remedies in the same action from the same court (see D Keenan, *Smith & Keenan's English Law* (13th ed, 2001) at pp 8–12). Common Law and Equity have also been administered concurrently in Singapore courts (see section 3 of the Civil Law Act (Cap 43, 1999 Rev Ed)).

1.76 Equitable principles are significant in some areas of the law and those areas will be covered in this book. Under Contract Law, for instance, the courts can, in specific circumstances, grant discretionary or *equitable remedies* where there has been a breach of a contract by a contracting party. These equitable remedies consist of *specific performance* and *injunctions* (see Chapter 16). Amongst others, equitable principles such as undue influence (see Chapter 13) and promissory estoppel (see Chapter 3) will be examined in this book.

Common Law Versus Written Law

1.77 The words 'Common Law' can also be contrasted with the notion of 'Written Law'. In Singapore, 'Written Law' refers to both the Constitution and the legislation (section 2 of the Interpretation Act (Cap 1, 2002 Rev Ed)). In this context, 'Common Law' refers to judge-made law or case law whilst 'Written Law' refers to the laws made by the Legislature. The making of laws by the Legislature is discussed in detail in paragraphs 1.96–1.97.

Civil Law Tradition Versus Common Law Tradition

1.78 Before we leave this section on the Common Law tradition, we need to say a few words about the Civil Law tradition, which is the other major legal tradition in the world today. The term 'Civil Law' refers to a particular legal tradition, and in this regard, is contrasted with the notion of the Common Law tradition. The Civil Law tradition refers to the tradition practised in several European countries such as France and Germany as well as in some Asian countries such as Indonesia, Vietnam and China.

1.79 The differences between the Civil Law tradition and the Common Law tradition and its impact on a legal system (such as Singapore) can only be described in general terms. This is due to the fact that each legal system, whether it belongs to the Common Law or the Civil Law tradition, is unique in the way it has been conditioned by historical factors, its distinctive legal institutions, ideology as well as modes of thought or approaches to law.

1.80 The Common Law tradition places a premium on the 'experience' of the law in its incremental development of legal principles, as reflected in the doctrine of judicial precedent described in paragraphs 1.62–1.73. On the other hand, the Civil Law tradition has tended to rely on general, comprehensive and 'rational' legal principles of law found in the *Codes* (essentially a set of comprehensive legislation which seeks to cover a wide area of human and societal interaction), rather than the incremental development of legal principles (for a brief discussion on the impact of the Common Law and Civil Law approaches on economic development, see MDA Freeman, *Lloyd's Introduction to Jurisprudence* (7th ed, 2001) at pp 662–666). Within the Civil Law tradition, the purposes of the Codes are generally to replace prior law and normally seek to present a complete and coherent set of laws which avoids the need for 'gap-filling' by the judges. Whilst codes (eg the Uniform Commercial Code in the US which belongs to the Common Law tradition) and statutes (eg Contributory Negligence and Personal Injuries Act) do exist within the Common Law tradition, the purposes are *generally* to supplement the existing Common Law rather than to replace prior laws. It is not inconceivable for Common Law judges to find, in appropriate situations, the legal bases for resolving disputes outside of such codes or statutes, unlike the situation under the Civil Law tradition (see JH Merryman, *The Civil Law Tradition* (2nd ed, 1985) at pp 26–38).

1.81 The Civil Law tradition is generally characterised by judicial passivism in judicial law-making as compared to the more active law-making role of judges within the Common Law tradition. There is no doctrine of 'judicial precedent' within the Civil Law tradition. Although the Civil Law tradition relies on court cases, less weight is placed on the prior court decisions as a source of law, as compared to court decisions within the Common Law tradition. In general, the judges within the Civil Law tradition have limited discretionary power to exercise Equity, unlike judges within the Common Law tradition.

1.82 Further, the judge operating within the Civil Law tradition tends to take on a more inquisitorial role with respect to the court proceedings. That is, the judge tends to adopt an activist attitude in terms of collecting evidence in a court case. Within the Common Law tradition, the judges will generally leave the arguments as well as the collection and proof of evidence to the disputing parties who adopt 'adversarial' positions *vis-a-vis* each other.

Civil Law Versus Criminal Law

1.83 Within the Common Law tradition, there is a distinction between civil and criminal law. In this context, 'civil law' does not refer to a particular legal tradition; it is used in contrast to the notion of criminal law. One distinction is that a criminal case is prosecuted by the State against the offender, whereas a civil law suit is initiated by one disputing party against the other disputing party.

1.84 The second distinction relates to the contrasting purposes of civil law and criminal law. The general purpose of civil law is to compensate the victim or the innocent party for the damages or losses which he or she has suffered or incurred. However, in criminal law, the primary general purpose is to 'punish' or deter would-be criminals from committing offences. Under civil law, we speak in terms of 'remedies' to compensate the victim or the innocent party. However, in criminal law, the offender may suffer the consequences of a jail term or a fine by the state or both; there is generally no direct compensation under criminal law from the wrongdoer to the victim for the crime committed (as an exception, see section 400 of the Criminal Procedure Code (Cap 68, 1985 Rev Ed) on the discretion of the court (before which a person is convicted of any crime or offence) to order the criminal to compensate any person injured in respect of his person, character or property by that crime or offence).

1.85 Of course, an act committed by a person can give rise to issues under both civil and criminal law. A good example would be an action arising from a motor accident. A negligent driver might (in appropriate circumstances) be prosecuted by the state under the relevant criminal statutes in a criminal case and if convicted, may be imprisoned for a term. At the same time, the injured party can sue the negligent party in a civil suit and if successful, would be compensated by the negligent party.

1.86 The burden of proof in a criminal prosecution is that the prosecution has to prove *beyond reasonable doubt* that the accused has committed the offence as charged. In a civil suit, however, the party making a claim (plaintiff) against the defendant has to prove his or her case merely on a *balance of probabilities*.

1.87 The main focus of the book is civil law. Examples of areas of law under the category of civil law are contract law and tort law. With regard to intellectual property law (see, generally, Chapter 21), for instance, certain infringements of intellectual property rights may attract criminal penalties whilst other infringing acts may only attract a civil suit to compensate the victim.

The Three Governing Arms

1.88 Under the Singapore Constitution, the three main arms of the State are the Legislature (or Parliament), the Executive (or the Government) and the Judiciary. The main role of the Legislature is to enact written laws, the Executive, to implement and enforce the enacted laws and the Judiciary, to adjudicate disputes between disputing parties based on its interpretation of the written law (both the Constitution and the legislation), previous court decisions and a sense of justice and fairness.

1.89 There is a concept known as 'separation of powers' (see Montesqieu, *The Spirit of the Laws* (T Nugent trans, 1949)), that is, the three governing arms of the State are separate and independent of each other. The idea of perfect and complete 'separation' and 'independence' is not possible in practice. However, there are varying degrees of 'separation of powers' in various legal systems in the world. In the case of Singapore, there is little separation between the Legislature and the Executive in the *formal* sense. Members of the Executive are appointed from the Legislature and in most cases, Bills for the making of law in Parliament are initiated by the Executive (though it is also possible for a private Member to initiate Bills). The Executive also has an influential role in the promulgation of subsidiary legislation (see paragraph 1.98). The Judiciary is in a *formal* sense separate and independent from the Legislature and the Executive, in terms of its security of tenure and remuneration (with respect to the judges of the High Court and the Court of Appeal).

The Legislature

1.90 In Singapore, we have only one law-making body, the Parliament. We have a unicameral system, unlike the bicameral system in the United Kingdom consisting of the House of Commons and the House of Lords. The Parliament continues to be dominated by one political party, the People's Action Party (in the most recent 2001 general elections, the PAP garnered an overwhelming 75.3% of the vote; see '75.3%–Resounding Win for PAP', *The Straits Times*, 4 November 2001). At present, the PAP occupies 82 of the 84 elected seats in Parliament.

The Parliament consists of elected Members of Parliament (MPs) as well as non-elected members. As regards elected membership, we have already referred to the creation of the Group Representation Constituency (GRC) in paragraph 1.54, above. In practice, this GRC scheme is somewhat tied to the establishment of Town Councils, whose role is to manage the HDB housing estates at a local level. A Town Council is usually formed from a grouping of constituencies under the GRC scheme. For example, candidates who were victorious in the general elections via the GRC ticket have often banded together to form a Town Council in order to achieve greater economies of scale.

1.91 The non-elected MPs include the Non-Constituency Members of Parliament ('NCMPs') and the Nominated Members of Parliament ('NMPs'). The purposes of the NCMP and NMP schemes have been mentioned in paragraphs 1.53 and 1.55, above.

1.92 Non-elected MPs, unlike elected MPs, are not entitled to vote on certain matters in Parliament: amendments to the Constitution, money bills and votes of no-confidence in the Government.

1.93 There are various parliamentary committees formed for the purposes of providing a more in-depth discussion of specific public issues or Bills. The more commonly publicised parliamentary committees in Singapore are the Select Committees and the Government Parliamentary Committees ('GPCs').

1.94 A Select Committee is usually formed for the purpose of examining a particular piece of legislation. The members of a Select Committee are nominated by the MPs. Each Select Committee is responsible to the whole House of Parliament and is obliged to submit a report on its findings to the House with respect to the legislation under scrutiny. The Select Committee may invite views from members of the public on the particular legislation. One fairly recent example of a Select Committee hearing concerned the constitutional amendments in relation to the Elected President.

1.95 The Government Parliamentary Committee ('GPC') Scheme, which was introduced in 1987, allows individual PAP MPs to be part of a committee focusing on a specific or specialised topic (such as education or transport) so as to engender greater debate in Parliament on these more specialised issues (see also the recent proposal by PM Goh to form an alternative policies group or the 'People's Action Forum' as an alternative to more opposition MPs and the lifting of the party's whip for PAP MPs in 'Party Whip to be Lifted Partially for 20 PAP MPs', *The Straits Times*, 7 November 2001). The GPCs are formed at the initiative of the PAP Government and GPC Members are exclusively drawn from the PAP.

(1) *The Law-Making Process*

1.96 The life of an Act of Parliament begins with a Bill, usually initiated by the Government, though there are, albeit exceptionally, private Members bills which have 'blossomed' into law (for example, NMP Walter Woon initiated a private member's Bill in 1994 which resulted in the Maintenance of Parents Act (Cap 167B, 1996 Rev Ed)). The bulk of the Bills which originate from the Government are usually drafted by the legal officers in the Attorney-General's Chambers (see paragraphs 1.104, below) and approved by the Cabinet and the Ministry concerned before they are tabled in Parliament. Sometimes, the Bill may be based substantially on a statute from a foreign jurisdiction (for example, the Bill which eventually resulted in the Contract (Rights of Third Parties) Act 2001 (Cap 53B, 2002 Rev Ed) was substantially based on the UK Contract (Rights of Third Parties) Act 1999; this Act is discussed in detail in Chapter 8).

1.97 Whether the Bill is initiated by a private Member or the Government, it goes through the following procedures before it is enacted as law:
(1) First Reading—the title of the Bill is read for the first time in

Parliament as a form of introduction to the Bill whereupon a date will be fixed for the Second Reading and the Bill is published in the *Government Gazette*.

(2) Second Reading—at this stage, the Minister usually makes a speech to outline the main objectives of the Bill and the Bill is debated by Parliament. The Members of Parliament then vote on the Bill, except for the non-elected MPs who cannot vote on certain Bills as referred to in paragraph 1.92, above.

(3) Committee Stage—The Bill may be referred to either the Committee of the Whole House or a Select Committee. The Committee of the Whole House (which consists of all the MPs) will deliberate on the Bill in detail with respect to the individual clauses of the Bill. If it is referred to a Select Committee (which consists of a smaller group of selected MPs), the Select Committee will deliberate on the Bill and submit its report to Parliament. The Select Committee report may recommend amendments to the Bill which may be rejected or accepted by Parliament.

(4) Third Reading—If the amended Bill is accepted by Parliament, a motion will be made that the Bill be read for the third time. At this stage, the Bill (including amendments) is usually passed by Parliament.

(5) Presidential Council for Minority Rights—the Speaker of Parliament is then obliged to refer the Bill to the Presidential Council for Minority Rights ('PCMR') which is a body established under the Singapore Constitution (article 69 of the Singapore Constitution). The members of the PCMR are appointed by the President on the advice of the Cabinet. The role of the PCMR is to draw attention to any Bill if in its opinion that Bill is a 'differentiating measure'. A 'differentiating measure' is defined as a measure 'which is, or is likely in its practical application to be, disadvantageous to persons of any racial or religious community and not equally disadvantageous to persons of other such communities, either directly by prejudicing persons of that community or indirectly by giving advantage to persons of another community' (article 68 of the Singapore Constitution). Certain Bills are exempted from the PCMR's scrutiny: Money Bills, Bills on a Certificate of Urgency (where the Prime Minister certifies that the Bill is so urgent that it is not in the public interest to delay its enactment; see article 78(7)(c) of the Singapore Constitution) and Bills which affect the defence, security, public safety, peace or good order of Singapore (article 78 of the Singapore Constitution).

If the PCMR gives a favourable report of the Bill without any amendments, Parliament will submit the Bill to the President for his assent. However, if the PCMR gives an unfavourable report, Parliament can either amend the Bill and refer it back to the PCMR or choose to present the Bill for Presidential assent, notwithstanding the PCMR's adverse report. In the latter case, it will need to garner the support of at least two-thirds of the Members of Parliament in order to reject the amendments proposed by the PCMR.

(6) Assent by the President—upon the assent of the President, the Bill

becomes an Act of Parliament. In legal parlance, we say that the legislation has been 'enacted'. However, the legislation does not come into force until the date of its publication in the *Government Gazette* or upon the commencement date as specified by the legislation or a notification thereof (section 10 of the Interpretation Act (Cap 1, 2002 Rev Ed)).

1.98 An Act of Parliament is known as primary or parent legislation. Due to constraints of Parliamentary time as well as the view that particular Ministries or agencies tasked with implementing the legislation may be better placed to tackle the details of such legislative implementation, an Act of Parliament usually contains provisions stipulating that a particular Ministry or agency has powers to promulgate *subsidiary legislation* to implement the laws provided such subsidiary legislation are not inconsistent with the Act of Parliament (section 19 of Interpretation Act (Cap 1, 2002 Rev Ed)).

1.99 Subsidiary legislation shall be published in the *Government Gazette* (unless otherwise expressly provided in an Act) and shall be in force as of such date of publication (unless otherwise stated in the subsidiary legislation itself) (section 23 of Interpretation Act).

The Executive

1.100 The Executive consists of the President and the Cabinet in whom executive powers are vested. Executive functions may be conferred on other persons by legislation (article 23 of the Singapore Constitution).

1.101 The President shall exercise his or her functions generally in accordance with the advice of the Cabinet. The Elected President has powers in respect of spending national financial reserves and the appointment of senior public officials (articles 21 and 22 of the Singapore Constitution) and is elected for a six-year term (article 20 of the Singapore Constitution). He or she is also obliged to consult the Council of Presidential Advisers with regard to specific constitutional functions (see article 21 of the Singapore Constitution).

1.102 The Cabinet is collectively accountable to the Parliament under the so-called Westminster system. The members of the Cabinet are drawn from the Members of Parliament. The Cabinet comprises the Prime Minister and the other Ministers. The Prime Minister is appointed by the President on the basis that he or she, in the President's judgment, is 'likely to command the confidence of the majority of the Members of Parliament' (article 25 of the Singapore Constitution). The respective Ministers are usually responsible for all governmental matters pertaining to one or more portfolios (such as Education or Trade and Industry). In Parliament, the responsible Minister will have to justify the policies implemented by his/her Ministry, and is thus accountable to Parliament. The President may, acting upon the advice of the Prime Minister, appoint Parliamentary Secretaries from amongst the Members of Parliament to assist the Ministers in their duties (article 31 of the Singapore Constitution).

1.103 The Attorney-General ('AG') is the legal adviser to the Executive (article 35(7) of the Singapore Constitution). The AG is appointed by the President if the latter, acting in his or her discretion, concurs with the advice of the Prime Minister (article 35(1) of the Singapore Constitution). The AG is empowered to commence, conduct and discontinue proceedings for any offence (article 35(8) of the Singapore Constitution). He is the Public Prosecutor who has control and direction of criminal prosecutions and proceedings (section 336(1) of the Criminal Procedure Code (Cap 68, 1985 Rev Ed)).

1.104 The Attorney-General's Chambers is staffed by State Counsel and Deputy Public Prosecutors. There are various divisions and departments within the Attorney-General's Chambers such as the Civil, Criminal Justice, Legislation, International Affairs and Law Reform and Revision divisions.

1.105 The Solicitor-General ('SG') provides legal advice to the Executive. The SG also possesses prosecutorial powers and may act as the Public Prosecutor in the event of the Attorney-General's absence or inability to act (section 336(2) of the Criminal Procedure Code (Cap 68, 1985 Rev Ed)).

The Judiciary

1.106 The primary role of the courts in Singapore is to resolve and adjudicate disputes brought before them. Judicial power is vested in the Supreme Court and such Subordinate Courts as may be provided by written law (article 93 of the Singapore Constitution). The judge is tasked with hearing the dispute between the litigants and decides on the outcome of the dispute based on the law, whether written law (that is, the Constitution and legislation), previous court decisions or a sense of justice and fairness (common law and/or equity). In Singapore, the judge hearing the dispute will apply the relevant legal principles to the facts in order to reach a conclusion on the case.

1.107 In Singapore, the judge is the sole arbiter of both facts and the law. There is no jury system in Singapore, unlike in some other countries where the jury would usually have some decision-making powers relating to the determination of the facts and the outcome of the case (see, generally, A Phang, 'Jury Trial in Singapore and Malaysia: The Unmaking of Legal Institution' (1983) 25 *Malaya Law Review* 50). In determining the law, the judge will need to interpret the Constitution and the legislation to distill the applicable law to be applied to the facts of the case. Sometimes, previous court decisions which have interpreted the particular article of the Constitution or the section of the legislation may be relevant to the judge deciding the case at hand. The judge needs to consider the relevance of previous court decisions (if any) to decide the outcome of the case in accordance with the doctrine of judicial precedent.

(1) *Various Meanings of 'Jurisdiction'*

1.108 The concept 'jurisdiction' can be variously defined, depending on the context in which the word is used. In general, it can refer to the authority or power of a court to do something (for instance, whether a court has the power to hear and decide on a particular dispute). On a more specific level, the word 'jurisdiction' can also refer to the idea of territory or location over which the court exercises judicial powers. For instance, the High Court in Singapore will have territorial jurisdiction over a criminal offence committed within the shores of Singapore, but not over a crime committed in Indonesia involving two Indonesians. The word 'jurisdiction' can be specifically defined with reference to the type of case (criminal, civil or family law, etc) being considered. Hence, in this regard, the Small Claims Tribunal will not have jurisdiction over a divorce matter. It is also possible to distinguish between the civil jurisdiction of a court from its criminal jurisdiction. Lastly, the term 'jurisdiction' can also refer to the monetary limit of the claim beyond which a particular court will not have jurisdiction over the matter. For instance, the Magistrate's Court has jurisdiction to hear and decide civil disputes where the claim does not exceed $60,000.

(2) *Court Structure and Hierarchy in Singapore*

1.109 The Supreme Court consists of the High Court and the Court of Appeal. Within the Supreme Court, a Constitutional Tribunal has also been set up to hear questions referred to by the Elected President on the effect of provisions of the Constitution (articles 5A(2) and 100 of the Singapore Constitution).

1.110 Prior to 1994, appeals from the Court of Appeal were brought before the Judicial Committee of the Privy Council in England. However, appeals to the Privy Council have been abolished pursuant to the Judicial Committee (Repeal) Act 1994 (No 2 of 1994). Hence, after the abolition of appeals to the Privy Council, the Singapore Court of Appeal is the highest court in the land.

1.111 Specialist courts within the Supreme Court such as the Admiralty Court (established on 4 February 2002) and the Intellectual Property Court (see Singapore Supreme Court media release, 19 September 2002) have been established. They are presided over by Judges and Judicial Commissioners who have particular expertise in the abovementioned areas of law.

(3) *Subordinate Courts*

1.112 The Subordinate Courts consist of the following courts:

(1) District Courts (which are constituted by the Subordinate Courts Act (Cap 321, 1999 Rev Ed));
(2) Magistrates' Courts (which are constituted by the Subordinate Courts Act (Cap 321, 1999 Rev Ed));
(3) Juvenile Courts (which administer justice under the Children and Young Persons Act (Cap 38, 2001 Rev Ed));
(4) Coroners Courts (which are responsible for determining the causes of death of natural persons pursuant to its duties conferred by the Criminal Procedure Code (Cap 68, 1985 Rev Ed));

(5) Small Claims Tribunals (which are set up under the Small Claims Tribunals Act (Cap 308, 1998 Rev Ed))(the 'SCT Act');

(Details and updates on the Subordinate Courts can be accessed at http://www.subcourts.gov.sg.)

1.113 There are two other courts, namely the Family Court (which hears matters such as divorce, maintenance, custody, adoptions and granting of protection orders), and the Syariah Court (which hears matters such as divorce, maintenance, child custody and property inheritance amongst Muslims, set up under the Administration of Muslim Law Act (Cap 3, 1999 Rev Ed). Due to constraints of space, we will only focus on the above-mentioned District Courts, Magistrates' Courts and Small Claims Tribunals as well as the Supreme Court.

(a) Small Claims Tribunals

1.114 The Small Claims Tribunals are established under the SCT Act. The purpose of the Small Claims Tribunal is to allow a more expeditious and less costly method of resolving small claims without representation by an Advocate and Solicitor (section 23(3) of the SCT Act). There is no requirement for the Small Claims Tribunal to adhere to strict legal forms or technicalities (see section 12(4) of the SCT Act), unlike in the Magistrates' and District Courts. The proceedings before a Small Claims Tribunal shall be conducted in an informal manner (section 22(1) of the SCT Act). In order to commence proceedings before a Small Claims Tribunal, the claimant simply needs to lodge a claim stating his name and address, name and address of the respondent(s), sum of money claimed and other particulars of the claim as are 'reasonably sufficient' to inform the respondent of the ground for the claim and the manner in which the amount claimed has been calculated (section 16 of the SCT Act). The claim may even be lodged by electronic facsimile or other prescribed electronic means (section 15(6) of the SCT Act).

1.115 The types of disputes covered under the SCT Act are claims in respect of contracts for the sale of goods and the provision of services and any claim in tort in respect of property damage (though claims for property damage arising out of or in connection with the use of a motor vehicle are excluded under the SCT Act) (section 5(1) and (2) of the SCT Act). In terms of monetary limits, the Small Claims Tribunal can hear disputes where the claim does not exceed $20,000 and the disputing parties consent in writing; if there is no consent by the disputing parties, the monetary limit is $10,000 (section 5(4) of the SCT Act).

1.116 Claims must be brought within one year from the date the cause of action accrued (section 5(3)(b) of the SCT Act). Hence, in a case of a contract for sale of goods, the claimant must lodge the claim at the Small Claims Tribunal within one year from the date of the breach of the contract. Costs (other than disbursements) shall not be awarded to or against any party in such proceedings, except in the case of a frivolous or vexatious claim (sections 31 and 32 of the SCT Act).

1.117 There is a right of appeal from the decision of the Small Claims Tribunal to the High Court involving a question of law or on the basis that the claim was outside the jurisdiction of the Small Claims Tribunal (section 38 of the SCT Act).

(b) Magistrates' Courts

1.118 The Magistrates' Courts have both civil and criminal jurisdiction. Magistrates are appointed by the President upon the recommendation of the Chief Justice (section 10(1) of the Subordinate Courts Act). The criteria for eligibility to be appointed as a Magistrate is at least one year's standing as a 'qualified person' (section 10(2) of the Subordinate Courts Act); for a definition of 'qualified person', please refer to paragraph 1.148, below).

1.119 In terms of civil jurisdiction, the monetary limit for the claims brought before the Magistrates' Courts is $60,000 ('Magistrate's Court limit') (section 2 of the Subordinate Courts Act). The Magistrates' Courts have jurisdiction to hear and try any action founded on contract or tort subject to the Magistrate's Court limit. The President may, after consulting the Chief Justice, by order vary the Magistrate's Court limit. The Magistrates' Courts have the same jurisdiction and powers as conferred on the District Courts in respect of certain actions or matters only (such as an action founded on contract or tort claiming a debt, demand or damage and an action for recovery of moneys under any written law) and where the amount claimed or the value of the subject-matter in dispute does not exceed the Magistrate's Court limit (see section 52). For further details, please refer to Chapter 16 of this book.

1.120 In terms of criminal jurisdiction, the Magistrate's Court has jurisdiction over offences committed
(a) within Singapore;
(b) on board any ship or aircraft registered in Singapore;
(c) by any person who is a citizen of Singapore on the high seas or on any aircraft; and
(d) in any place or by any person if it is provided in any written law that the offence is triable in Singapore.
(See section 51(2) of the Subordinate Courts Act.)

(c) District Courts

1.121 The District Courts possess both civil and criminal jurisdiction, like the Magistrates' Courts. District Judges are appointed by the President on the recommendation of the Chief Justice (section 9 of the Subordinate Courts Act). The criteria for eligibility to be appointed as a District Judge is at least 5 years' standing as a 'qualified person' (section 9(3) of the Subordinate Courts Act).

1.122 In terms of civil jurisdiction, the monetary limit of the disputes brought before the District Court is $250,000 (the 'District Court limit') (section 2 of the Subordinate Courts Act). For probate and administration matters, the monetary limit is $3 million with respect to the value of the estate within Singapore (see sections 2, 26(a) and 27 of the Subordinate Courts Act). However, where the claim is founded on contract or tort, and the disputing parties agree in writing, the District Court shall have the jurisdiction to hear and try the matter notwithstanding that the debt, demand or damage claimed exceeds the District Court limit (section 23 of the Subordinate Courts Act). The President may, after consulting the Chief Justice, vary the District Court limit (section 30 of the Subordinate Courts Act).

1.123 The Subordinate Courts Act also specifically confers jurisdiction on the District Court over certain matters such as the execution or declaration of trusts, foreclosure and redemption of mortgages, specific performance, dissolution and winding up of partnership, subject to the District Court limit (section 26 of the Subordinate Courts Act).

The District Court has the power to grant reliefs and remedies as ought to be granted or given in a similar action by the High Court (section 31(1) of the Subordinate Courts Act). Specifically, the District Court is empowered to grant injunctions and make binding declarations of rights in relation to the disputing parties (section 31(2) of the Subordinate Courts Act).

1.124 With regard to criminal jurisdiction, the District Court has the same jurisdiction as the Magistrate's Court, as indicated above in paragraph 1.120 (see section 50(2) of the Subordinate Courts Act). However, it should be noted that the District Court and Magistrate's Court possess different sentencing powers. In general, the District Court has, for example, the power to impose a jail term not exceeding seven years while the Magistrate's Court is only empowered to impose a jail term not exceeding two years (see section 11 of the Criminal Procedure Code (Cap 68, 1985 Rev Ed)).

(4) *Supreme Court*

1.125 The Supreme Court consists of both the High Court and the Court of Appeal. The Judges of the Supreme Court consist of the Chief Justice, the Judges of Appeal who sit on the Court of Appeal and the Judges of the High Court. Judicial Commissioners are appointed on a short-term contract basis (which is subject to renewal) to perform the role of and possess the same powers as a High Court Judge. A Registrar, Deputy Registrar and several Assistant Registrars are also appointed to assist in the administration of justice within the Supreme Court.

(a) High Court

1.126 The High Court has both original and appellate jurisdiction over criminal and civil matters. In terms of civil matters, the Supreme Court of Judicature Act (Cap 322, 1999 Rev Ed) prescribes that the High Court exercises civil jurisdiction *in personam* (that is, jurisdiction in respect of obligations owed by one person to another) based on the service of writ or originating process or where the defendant submits to the jurisdiction of the High Court or where jurisdiction is vested by other written law (section 16 of the Supreme Court of Judicature Act). It also exercises jurisdiction over specific matters such as divorce and matrimonial causes, admiralty, bankruptcy and companies (section 17 of the Supreme Court of Judicature Act).

1.127 The Singapore High Court does not have any jurisdiction over certain matters (ie marriage, divorces known in the Muslim law as *fasakh, cerai taklik, khuluk* and *talak*, and betrothal, nullity of marriage or judicial separation) under the jurisdiction of the Administration of Muslim Law Act (Cap 3, 1999 Rev Ed) in which the parties concerned are Muslims or where the parties were married under Muslim law (section 17A(1) of the Supreme Court of Judicature Act). However, the High Court has concurrent jurisdiction with the Syariah Court over civil proceedings involving matters relating to maintenance for any wife and child, custody of a child, and the disposition or division of property on divorce (section 17A(2) of the Supreme Court of Judicature Act), though the High Court civil proceedings may be stayed in specific circumstances (see section 17A(3) of the Supreme Court of Judicature Act).

1.128 The High Court also has powers which are vested in it by written law as well as the powers set out in the First Schedule of the Supreme Court of Judicature Act (including powers to grant remedies at law and equity, power to enforce a judgment of the court and provide for interim preservation of the subject-matter of the proceedings).

1.129 *Appellate* civil jurisdiction of the High Court consists of the hearing of appeals from District Courts and Magistrates' Courts and from other tribunals prescribed by written law. All appeals to the High Court shall be by way of rehearing (section 22 of the Supreme Court of Judicature Act).

1.130 In terms of criminal jurisdiction, the Singapore High Court enjoys *original* jurisdiction over offences committed

(a) within Singapore;
(b) on board any ship or aircraft registered in Singapore;
(c) by any person who is a citizen of Singapore on the high seas or on any aircraft;
(d) by any person on the high seas where the offence is piracy by the law of nations;
(e) by any person within or outside Singapore where the offence is punishable under and by virtue of the provisions of the Hijacking of Aircraft and Protection of Aircraft and International Airports Act (Cap 124, 1997 Rev Ed); and
(f) in any place or by any person if it is provided in any written law that the offence is triable in Singapore (see, generally, section 15 of the Supreme Court of Judicature Act).

There is no limit to its sentencing powers when it exercises *original* criminal jurisdiction provided the sentence meted out is pursuant to the relevant legislation (eg Penal Code).

The High Court also has *appellate* criminal jurisdiction to hear (1) appeals from the District Courts or Magistrates' Courts; and (2) points of law reserved by special cases submitted by a District Court or Magistrate's Court (see section 19 of the Supreme Court of Judicature Act).

(b) Court of Appeal

1.131 The Singapore Court of Appeal, as the highest court of the land, enjoys both appellate civil *and* criminal jurisdiction.

1.132 The Court of Appeal has appellate *civil* jurisdiction over any appeal from the High Court decision in a civil matter, whether made by the High Court in its original or appellate jurisdiction (section 29A(1) of the Supreme Court of Judicature Act). Appeals to the Court of Appeal shall be by way of rehearing (section 37 of the Supreme Court of Judicature Act). The Court of Appeal may order a new trial where it is of the opinion that some substantial wrong or miscarriage of justice has occurred (section 39(2) of the Supreme Court of Judicature Act).

1.133 Its appellate *criminal* jurisdiction consists of appeals against a decision of the High Court in the latter's exercise of its original criminal jurisdiction (section 29A(2) of the Supreme Court of Judicature Act). On appeal, the Court of Appeal may either confirm, reverse or vary the decision of the trial court, or order a retrial or may remit the matter to the trial court (section 54 of the Supreme Court of Judicature Act).

(5) *Vertical and Horizontal* Stare Decisis

1.134 With the court structure and hierarchy in mind, we can now return to a more fruitful discussion of vertical and horizontal *stare decisis* as referred to in paragraph 1.70, above. Vertical *stare decisis* refers to a situation where a court is bound to follow the previous decisions of a court *higher* in the court hierarchy. For instance, the Singapore High Court is faced with a previous decision of the Singapore Court of Appeal under vertical *stare decisis*. In such a situation, the Singapore High Court is 'bound' by the decision of the Singapore Court of Appeal, unless the High Court judge is able to show that one or more exceptions stated in paragraph 1.72 apply.

1.135 Horizontal *stare decisis* refers to a situation where a particular court is faced with a previous court decision of a court occupying the same level in the court hierarchy. For instance, the Singapore High Court judge is faced with a previous decision of another Singapore High Court judge. In such an instance, the judge is not 'bound' by the previous decision.

1.136 While still on the topic of horizontal *stare decisis*, what about prior decisions of the Privy Council on appeal from Singapore (delivered before such appeals were abolished in 1994)? Is the Singapore Court of Appeal bound by such prior Privy Council decisions? Is the Singapore Court of Appeal bound by its own decisions?

These issues were dealt with in the Practice Statement on Judicial Precedent issued by the Supreme Court on 11 July 1994 following the abolition of appeals to the Privy Council. The Practice Statement stated that the Court of Appeal should not be bound by its own previous decisions and those of the Privy Council which, prior to 8 April 1994, were binding on it, 'where adherence to such prior decisions would cause injustice in a particular case or constrain the development of law in conformity with the circumstances of Singapore'. The Singapore Court of Appeal will continue to treat such prior decisions as normally binding but will, whenever it appears right to do so, depart from such prior decisions (see the decision of *PP v Manogaran s/o R Ramu* (1997), where the Court of Appeal departed from the previous Court of Appeal decision of *Abdul Rahman bin Yusof v PP* (1996)). Bearing in mind the danger of retrospectively disturbing contractual, proprietary and other legal rights, this power to depart from prior Privy Council decisions will be exercised sparingly.

The upshot of the Practice Statement is as follows :

(i) the Singapore Court of Appeal is not bound by its own previous decisions;
(ii) the Singapore Court of Appeal is not bound by prior Privy Council decisions,

though the Singapore Court of Appeal would normally, in practice, follow and apply its own prior decisions or such prior Privy Council decisions (as the case may be).

1.137 Decisions by courts in foreign jurisdictions (such as England, Australia, Malaysia, India, Brunei and Canada), are not binding on Singapore courts, notwithstanding the fact that they belong to the Common Law tradition. These decisions from foreign jurisdictions do not belong to the same hierarchy as our Singapore courts. In practice, however, Singapore courts do treat relevant decisions by such Commonwealth courts as 'persuasive', though not 'binding' (see W Woon, 'The Doctrine of Judicial Precedent', in KYL Tan (ed), *The Singapore Legal System* (2nd ed, 1999) at pp 297–324). For instance, relevant Court of Appeal and House of Lords decisions from England and the High Court of Australia are 'persuasive' precedents for Singapore judges adjudicating a similar dispute.

(6) *Interpretation of Written Law*

1.138 The judge may need to interpret the written law where applicable to reach a decision in a particular case. A few general approaches have been used by judges, namely the following:

(1) Literal rule—the words in the statutory provisions should be construed according to their literal meaning.
(2) Golden rule—the literal rule should be followed unless it leads to an absurd result.
(3) Mischief rule (also known as the rule in *Heydon's* case (1584))—the words should be considered in the light of the mischief which the enactment of the legislation was attempting to remedy.
(4) Purposive rule—the legislative intent of the statute should be examined to ascertain the meaning of the words.

1.139 Some of these approaches have been encapsulated in the Interpretation Act. According to section 9A of the Interpretation Act (Cap 1, 2002 Rev Ed), the judge can refer to, *inter alia*, the explanatory statement to the Bill, the speech made by the Minister in Parliament as well as the Parliamentary debates for the following purposes:

(a) to confirm the ordinary meaning of the provision of the written law taking into account its context in the written law and the purpose or object underlying the written law (ie a combination of the literal rule and purposive rule);

(b) to ascertain the meaning of the provision of the written law if:

  (i) the provision is ambiguous or obscure; or

  (ii) the ordinary meaning of the provision would lead to a result that is manifestly absurd or unreasonable (ie the golden rule).

1.140 There are also various specific technical rules which judges have used to interpret the wording of the Constitutional provisions, the sections of an Act of Parliament or subsidiary legislation. They consist of the following:

(1) *ejusdem generis* rule—where general words follow specific words, the meaning of the general words will be confined to the class given by the specific words;

(2) *noscitur a sociis*—this involves gathering the meaning of words from its context, that is, via association with its neighbouring words;

(3) *expressio unius est exclusio alterius*—that is, words which are expressly indicated excludes those which are not indicated.

(On statutory interpretation generally, see H Chan, *The Legal System of Singapore* (1995) at pp 107–112), and G Williams, *Learning the Law* (12th ed, 2002) and R Cross, *Statutory Interpretation* (3rd ed, 1995).)

(7) *Courts and Information Technology*

1.141 Advances in the use of information technology within the Judiciary started with the creation of a bankruptcy system which allowed faster and more accurate searches of data on bankruptcy matters via the computer, which is subsequently enlarged with the development of the Civil System in the early 1990s.

1.142 LawNet, the nationwide computer network which provides a one-stop shop for numerous information repositories including the local law reports, was launched in 1990. The Supreme Court provides the contents for the Litigation Module under LawNet, which include information on writs of summons, originating summons, company winding up and admiralty matters. This facilitates the lawyers' search for data relating to litigation in Singapore in a fast and efficient way.

1.143 The efforts to integrate information technology in the judiciary continue unabated with the launch of the first Technology Court in the Supreme Court in 1995. Within the Technology Court, a computer network (which links all the computers in the courtroom) permits lawyers and judges access to information as well as to share information online. In addition, features such as multimedia, imaging, graphics, audio recording and data enable the lawyers to prepare and present their cases. Technology Court 2 was subsequently opened in 2000 in the Supreme Court. The Technology Courts allow witnesses to give evidence without having to face the accused person in the court via a standalone video conferencing set and the witness is able to view the court proceedings through a plasma display panel installed in the witness room.

1.144 The Electronic Filing System ('EFS'), a joint project of the Judiciary, the Singapore Network Services Pte Ltd and the Singapore Academy of Law, covers all civil litigation in the Supreme Court as well as the Subordinate Courts. The EFS provides four main services:

(1) an electronic filing system which allows documents to be filed;
(2) an electronic extract service which allows extracts of court documents by lawyers;
(3) an electronic service of documents facility, which allows law firms to serve court documents on the other party; and
(4) an electronic information service which permits law firms to search case information.

1.145 The EFS is moving towards a fully integrated, multi-faceted and comprehensive system to cover all criminal and civil matters. A more recent innovation by the judiciary is to allow lawyers to obtain hearing dates and status of e-filing via Short Message Service ('SMS') on their handphones. Another example of IT advancement is Casewatch which allows users to monitor legal actions involving a company or an individual which the user has included as part of his monitoring list. The users include the media, stock exchange, finance companies and so on. Such users are alerted of legal actions or updates via email or SMS (for more details, see http://www.casewatch.com.sg).

1.146 Some other significant innovations since the 1990s include: (1) the Tickets and Summons System 2000 ('TICKS 2000') launched in 1999 which allows the traffic police to send the charges electronically to the courts whilst the adjudication results are sent electronically to the police as updates; (2) Singapore Case Recording and Information Management System ('SCRIMS') launched in 1999 which allows the automated processing of a criminal case from the registration of the case to the final outcome; (3) Automated Traffic Offence Management System ('ATOMS') which is basically the interactive multimedia kiosk application for members of the public to pay fines for minor traffic offences; and (4) the web-based system at the Small Claims Tribunals for entry and electronic transmission of the details of a claim lodged at the SCTs.

For more details of the Court IT innovations, see BH Tan, 'E-Litigation: The Singapore Experience', *InterSe*, May/June 2002 at pp 25–26 and July/August 2002 at pp 22–23 (a publication of the Singapore Academy of Law). See also BH Tan, 'E-Litigation: The Singapore Experience', *The Law Gazette*, November 2001 (a publication of the Law Society of Singapore) and JJ Koh, 'Singapore Subordinate Courts, Technology for Courts in the Asian Region—The Singapore Experience' at http://www.ejustice.org.sg/archives/whitepapers.html.

The Legal Profession

1.147 In Singapore, legal profession matters are governed by the Legal Profession Act (Cap 161, 2002 Rev Ed) ('LPA'). The LPA governs issues such as the qualifications and disqualifications of Advocates and Solicitors, the rights and duties of practising and non-practising Advocates and Solicitors, professional practice, as well as the conduct and discipline of Advocates and Solicitors. Apart from the LPA, the Legal Profession (Professional Conduct) Rules issued on 1 June 1998 (GN No S 156/98) regulate the discipline of Advocates and Solicitors (on the legal profession, see generally YL Tan, *The Law of Advocates and Solicitors in Singapore and West Malaysia* (2nd ed, 1998)). In Singapore, the legal profession is a 'fused profession' meaning that the lawyer can both represent clients in litigation work in court (advocate's work) as well as conduct solicitor's work (as in drafting of contracts, negotiations as well as preparation of court documents).

1.148 The steps for admission to be an Advocate and Solicitor in Singapore are as follows:

(1) Attain 'qualified person' status—one may attain such status under the LPA by obtaining a law degree either from the National University of Singapore or certain approved overseas universities in the United Kingdom, Australia, New Zealand and Canada, with the required level of academic performance. Such overseas law graduates will also be required to complete and obtain the Diploma in Singapore Law conferred by the National University of Singapore in order to be a 'qualified person' (see Legal Profession (Qualified Person) Rules (GN No S 357/2001)).

As a fairly recent move via a legislative amendment in 2001, the Board of Legal Education ('BLE') may, *in its discretion*, approve a person as a 'qualified person' (notwithstanding that an applicant is not otherwise entitled to become a qualified person under section 2 of the LPA), if he or she, in the opinion of the BLE, possesses such '*qualification or expertise as would contribute to, promote or enhance the quality of legal services in Singapore or the economic or technological development of Singapore*' (section 7(1) of the LPA).

(2) Training requirements—one must serve the prescribed period of pupillage, courses of instruction as prescribed as well as fulfill prescribed dining terms. The current prescribed period of pupillage with an Advocate and Solicitor in private practice is 6 months (section 14 of the LPA).

(3) Postgraduate exam requirements—one must obtain a certificate from the BLE (constituted under section 3 of the LPA) by passing the Postgraduate Law Course exams or such exams prescribed by the BLE.

(4) Other criteria – the petitioner must be at least 21 years old and of good character. (See section 12 of the LPA.)

Upon the fulfilment of the criteria above, a person may be admitted to the Roll of the Advocates and Solicitors of the Supreme Court of

Singapore (or in ordinary parlance, he or she is called to the Bar). For the purposes of legal practice in a Singapore law firm, however, the Advocate and Solicitor would need to apply to the Supreme Court for a practising certificate which has to be renewed on a yearly basis. With the practising certificate, the Advocate and Solicitor can advise clients in various transactions governed by Singapore law and represent clients in the Singapore courts. It is a criminal offence for an unauthorised person to act as an Advocate and Solicitor or wilfully or falsely to pretend to be an Advocate or Solicitor without a practising certificate.

1.149 An Advocate and Solicitor may not wish to obtain a practising certificate for the purpose of legal practice in a local law firm. Firstly, he or she may wish to join the Legal Service as a legal officer. Secondly, the Advocate and Solicitor may join a private company as an in-house legal counsel to advise the company on legal matters; in this regard, the in-house counsel is normally an employee of the company, just like the finance or the human resource manager of a company. Thirdly, he or she may join one of the international law firms (currently dominated by law firms originating from the United States and the United Kingdom) based in Singapore as a legal associate or partner. In the above cases, he or she is not required (and also not entitled) to obtain a practising certificate.

1.150 The practising Advocate and Solicitor is also an officer of the Supreme Court and hence attracts attendant duties and responsibilities as well as discipline by the Supreme Court. The Supreme Court has the power to take disciplinary action against the errant practising Advocate and Solicitor such as by striking the lawyer off the Roll, suspending the lawyer from practice not exceeding five years or censuring the lawyer, upon proof of specified grounds stated in the LPA. Examples of such grounds are the conviction of a criminal offence implying defect of character, indicating that the Advocate and Solicitor is unfit for the profession; or where the Advocate and Solicitor is guilty of fraudulent or grossly improper conduct in the discharge of his or her professional duty (see, generally, section 83(2) of the LPA).

1.151 Non-practising Advocates and Solicitors and legal officers may also be disciplined under the LPA (section 82). Upon due cause being shown (eg where the advocate and solicitor or legal officer was guilty in Singapore or elsewhere of misconduct unbefitting a legal officer or an Advocate and Solicitor as an officer of the Supreme Court or as a member of a honourable profession; or has been adjudicated bankrupt and has been guilty of certain acts or omissions specified in the Bankruptcy Act (Cap 20, 2000 Rev Ed)), the Advocate and Solicitor may be struck off the Roll, prohibited from applying for a practising certificate for a period not exceeding 5 years, censured or otherwise punished (section 82A(12) of the LPA).

1.152 There are three vehicles for setting up a legal practice in Singapore. The practising Advocate and Solicitor can establish (1) a sole-proprietorship; (2) a partnership with other partner(s); or (3) a law corporation. The idea of a 'law corporation' is a recent innovation in the Singapore legal landscape, the relevant provisions having been passed as an amendment to the LPA in 2000. Prior to this innovation, a legal practice in Singapore has to be formed either as a sole-proprietorship or partnership, for which the liability of the sole proprietor and the partner(s) is unlimited. Hence, the setting up of a legal practice as a 'law corporation' avoids such risks involved in setting up sole-proprietorships and partnerships. A 'law corporation' is a limited liability company established under the Companies Act (Cap 50, 1994 Rev Ed) whose primary object is to supply legal services (section 81B of the LPA). There are however restrictions, *inter alia,* with respect to the shares and the rights of the shareholders, directors and employees in a 'law corporation' (which are beyond those normally associated with a limited company which is not a 'law corporation').

1.153 The Law Society of Singapore is a statutory body established under the LPA (section 37). The purposes of the Law Society are, *inter alia,* to maintain and improve standards of conduct and learning of the legal profession in Singapore, facilitate the acquisition of knowledge by members of the legal profession, to protect and assist the public in Singapore on all matters touching or ancillary to the law, and grant pecuniary or other assistance to any association, institute, board or society in Singapore in the interests of the profession of law or for students of that profession (section 38 of the LPA). Updates and details of the Law Society and its work can be accessed at http://www.lawsoc.org.sg.

1.154 The Singapore Academy of Law ('SAL') is a body set up in 1989 pursuant to the Singapore Academy of Law Act (Cap 294A, 1997 Rev Ed). The functions of the SAL are, *inter alia,* to promote and maintain high standards of conduct and learning amongst members of the legal profession, provide continuing legal education for members, promote good relations and social interaction amongst its members, as well as to promote advancement and dissemination of knowledge of the laws and the legal system. Other functions include the appointment of Commissioners for Oaths as well as Notaries Public. Updates and details of the Singapore Academy of Law can be assessed at http://www.sal.org.sg.

Alternative Dispute Resolution: No More in the Alternative

1.155 In commercial matters, litigation has been the dominant form of dispute resolution in Singapore and in many other common law jurisdictions. However, alternative dispute resolution ('ADR') is growing rapidly in importance in Singapore and internationally as a means of dispute resolution for matters ranging from domestic and social conflicts to large-scale, cross-border legal disputes. Indeed, with time, ADR in Singapore may not be as 'alternative' as the term suggests. ADR has gained impetus as an effective, efficient and economical means of resolving a spectrum of disputes in a variety of settings (interested readers can consult J Lee, 'The ADR Movement in Singapore', in KYL Tan (ed), *The Singapore Legal System* (2nd ed, 1999)).

1.156 In tandem with Singapore's quest to be a total business centre, great efforts have been expended towards making Singapore a major centre for dispute resolution (similar to London, New York and Paris). This development is not surprising as the Singapore Government is a strong proponent of ADR and has put in place the institutional and infrastructural framework to support this. The Judiciary is also firmly behind the ADR initiatives in settling disputes and its Rules of Court (Cap 322, Rule 5, GN S 71/96, 1997 Rev Ed) provide ample opportunity for ADR even within a litigation setting.

Overview of ADR in Singapore

1.157 ADR got off to a tentative start in the 1980s when the Government envisaged Singapore as a major dispute resolution centre, capitalizing on its geographic position as well as its goal of developing Singapore into a total and one-stop business centre. Prior to this, ADR was virtually an alien concept to the legal fraternity and was practised in limited circumstances in specific industries. For instance, arbitration was customarily practised in the shipping, building and construction industries. In industrial relations, there is statute-prescribed arbitration for industrial disputes under Part IV of the Industrial Relations Act (Cap 136, 2002 Rev Ed).

1.158 In 1986, the Economic Review Committee recommended the establishment of an arbitration centre in Singapore. In that year, Singapore acceded to the 1958 New York Convention on the Recognition and Enforcement of Foreign Arbitral Awards. Under this Convention, each contracting State is required to recognise and enforce arbitral awards made in another contracting State. As there are more than 120 Convention signatories, arbitral awards rendered in Singapore are potentially enforceable in more than 120 jurisdictions. The Arbitration (Foreign Awards) Act (Cap 10A, 1985 Rev Ed) was enacted in 1986 to give effect to the Convention. This Act was repealed in 1994 and replaced by the International Arbitration Act (Cap 143A, 2002 Rev Ed), which incorporated the United Nations Commission on International Trade Law ('UNCITRAL') Model Law on International Commercial Arbitration.

1.159 In 1991, the Singapore International Arbitration Centre ('SIAC') was established; this was followed in 1997 with the establishment of the Singapore Mediation Centre ('SMC'). In 1994, mediation of civil disputes was first introduced in the Subordinate Courts through the Court Mediation Centre. Since then, it is also routinely conducted in the Small Claims Tribunals, the Family Court, the Juvenile Courts, the Consumer Association of Singapore ('CASE') and the Ministry of Community Development, Youth and Sports and Maintenance of Parents Tribunal. In line with the governmental emphasis on harnessing electronic technology, the Subordinate Courts have also introduced 'e@dr' for parties in e-commerce transactions to resolve their disputes through the Internet (see http://www.e-adr.gov.sg).

1.160 In May 1996, the government created the multi-agency Committee on Alternative Dispute Resolution with the aim of examining how ADR processes and, in particular, mediation, could be promoted in Singapore. The Committee's Report in July 1997 recommended that non-adversarial modes of dispute resolution be introduced and encouraged for all forms of commercial, social and community disputes. The explicit goal was to help prevent Singaporeans from becoming too litigious. Mediation was singled out as being in accord with Singapore's Asian traditions and cultures.

1.161 Since then, constant reference has been made to mediation's similarities with traditional Asian philosophy and practice. The emphasis now is to develop an Asian model of mediation drawing on the customary and influential role of the traditional leaders of the various races such as the *penghulu* (Malay kampong headman), the *panchayat* (the Indian community council) and the senior clansmen of the Chinese clan associations in mediating conflicts within those communities.

1.162 Since 1998, this abiding faith in ADR, especially mediation, is now manifested in the establishment of three Community Mediation Centres ('CMCs') in Marine Parade (1998), Ang Mo Kio (1999) and Woodlands (2001). As part of the national effort to foster a mediation culture, the Community Mediation Centres Act (Cap 49A, 1998 Rev Ed) was enacted in 1997 to spearhead this endeavour.

1.163 Community mediation is envisaged as an effective means of settling relational disputes on the ground, especially in multi-racial, multi-religious Singapore. In this connection, the CMCs will work closely with the Community Development Councils ('CDCs'), the People's Association and schools to create a corp of volunteer 'master mediators' (see Senior Minister of State for Law and Home Affairs, Ho Peng Kee's speech at the First National Mediation Conference, 17 August 2002; NT Tan, 'Community Mediation in Singapore: Principles for Community Conflict Resolution' (2002) 19(3) *Conflict Resolution Quarterly* 289).

1.164 Within Singapore's legal fraternity, efforts, led by the Judiciary, are being made to encourage lawyers' and their clients' reception of ADR as a more satisfactory, faster and cheaper way of settling disputes (see 'Staying out of Court: The Rise of ADR in Singapore', *Inter Se*, July-August 2002). For a long time, arbitral awards were seen as being inferior to judgments and that ADR would affect the livelihood of lawyers. This perspective is rapidly changing as a result of continual education by the proponents of ADR.

Modes of ADR

Negotiation

1.165 Negotiation is the most widely used form of dispute resolution which is featured even within the litigation process. Negotiation, simply put, is the process of parties coming together and agreeing to the issues in a dispute that require resolution.

1.166 The process is private, party-driven and seeks to formulate a range of compromise options for the disputing parties to consider. The parties themselves often attempt negotiation, without or with legal representation. The process is relatively informal in that the parties agree on the rules and procedures governing the negotiations and third parties are seldom involved. This also means that the process can be risky as there are no external rules and little protection for the parties.

1.167 An increasingly popular approach in negotiation is to derive an optimal position that provides the disputants with as much benefits as possible, rather than a situation where one party 'wins' and the other 'loses'. An agreement reached through negotiation is enforceable as a contract.

Mediation

1.168 Mediation is closely associated with negotiation. It is a process of facilitated negotiation using a specially trained, neutral third party (with limited or no decision-making power as well as adjudication power) to assist disputants in presenting their positions, formulate and evaluate options to resolve the dispute. The mediator's role is not to decide which party is right or wrong, but rather, to help the parties understand the whole situation in order to reach a solution that both parties are happy with. When parties reach a settlement, the mediator will, with the assistance of the disputants' lawyers (if present), draw up the terms of settlement.

1.169 Compared with negotiation, mediation is a relatively more formal process as a third party is involved and parties often conduct themselves pursuant to a set of agreed rules and procedures. Like negotiation, the parties could conduct mediation themselves or through their legal representatives.

Arbitration

1.170 More adversarial than mediation is arbitration. Arbitration refers to the resolution of a dispute between parties by a neutral third party (known as the arbitrator) with specialist knowledge of the subject matter of the case and who is selected by mutual agreement. Often described as a private trial, the arbitration process is fairly similar to litigation. There is the presentation of evidence, through witnesses and on the record, as opposed to an agreed or negotiated understanding of the facts. The procedure can either be governed by the applicable statutes viz the International Arbitration Act (Cap 143A, 2002 Rev Ed) and the Arbitration Act (Cap 10, 2002 Rev Ed), or decided by the parties prior to the commencement of the arbitration proceedings. The process is entirely voluntary.

Hybrid Processes

1.171 Two modes of ADR involving hybrid processes worth mentioning are mini trials and mediation-arbitration. They are not as popular as the modes discussed above but could be potentially useful to disputants whose needs may not be met by the more conventional modes of ADR.

Mini-Trial

1.172 A mini-trial enables disputants to structure a dispute resolution process integrating negotiation, mediation and litigation. This mode is popular for commercial disputes as it seeks a resolution, which consciously factors in commercial needs and reality and is not based solely on legal rights and principles. Each party, either through their legal representatives or self-representation, makes a presentation of the case to the senior management representatives of the disputing parties according to a pre-determined format. This is to enable a fair, balanced and meaningful presentation of the case.

1.173 The senior management representatives have the authority to settle the dispute and are regarded as being able to arrive at a negotiated settlement since they are expected to have a better understanding of company policy, commercial needs and practice. There may also be a mediator selected by the parties who plays a variety of roles from the presentation of information stage to the decision-making stage, especially when the senior management representatives are unable to arrive at a settlement.

Mediation-Arbitration

1.174 Mediation-arbitration, as the name implies, is a mixture of mediation and arbitration. This mode was developed originally in the resolution of industrial disputes. Through a mediator, the parties seek to reach an agreement. If they are unable to do so, the case is immediately referred to arbitration for a binding decision by the arbitrator, who could be the mediator as well. Mediation-arbitration affords the informal party-driven process offered by mediation and arbitration while providing for certainty in the eventual resolution of the dispute. It also promotes dispute resolution in the first instance through mediation, the failure of which would trigger the arbitration process with the same third party deciding on a binding award, having witnessed the parties' failure to agree. The disadvantages pertain to the disclosure of information at the mediation stage which may be used against the disclosing party should the arbitration procedure kick in.

1.175 The diagram below is a simple representation of the various modes of dispute resolution in ascending order (from left to right) of adversarial stance:

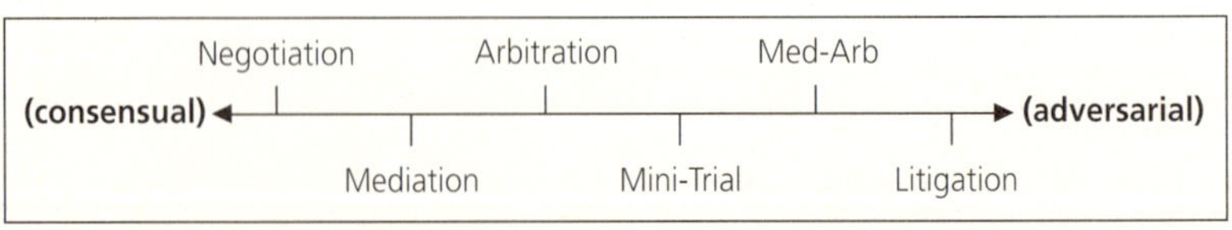

1.176 The table below summarises the **characteristics of the various modes of dispute resolution**.

	Legal Representation Allowed	Rules and Procedure for Conduct of Process	Neutral Third Party Involved?	Formality of Process	Resolution to the Problem(s)?	Agreement Enforceable?
Negotiation	Yes but seldom used	Seldom pre-determined	No	Relatively informal	No guarantee	Yes, as a contract
Mediation	Yes	By mutual agreement of parties	Yes, mediator—with limited or no decision-making and adjudication powers—is selected by the parties or appointed by an independent party	Relatively informal	No guarantee	Yes, as a contract. Where court proceedings have begun, the parties can agree to record the terms of settlement before a judge
Arbitration	Yes	By mutual agreement of parties or applicable statutes	Yes, arbitrator is the decision-maker and is selected by the parties	Relatively formal	Yes, arbitrator makes an award	Yes. Appeal in limited circumstances
Mini-Trial	Yes	By mutual agreement of parties	Possible (eg mediator)	Formal	Yes (assuming representative(s) have full authority to reach settlement)	Yes
Mediation-Arbitration	Yes	By mutual agreement of parties	Yes, mediator and arbitrator (may be the same person)	Relatively formal	No guarantee at the mediation stage. However, resolution is likely especially when the matter proceeds to arbitration	Yes
Litigation	Yes	Yes, statute-prescribed rules and procedures viz the Rules of Court	Yes, a judge and, occasionally, for complicated cases, the solicited views of a amicus curiae (friend of the court), a person who is not party to the suit and often an expert in his field is heard	Formal	Yes, but with a winner-loser outcome. The business relationship can be subjected to potential damage by the adversarial nature of litigation	Yes. Parties can appeal against the court's decision

ADR: Its Popularity and Advantages

1.177 Having looked at some of the more popular modes of ADR, it is useful to briefly mention the features of litigation. A complicated court process and lawyers with a 'winner takes all' outcome characterise litigation. It is also an adversarial mode to conflict resolution with adjudication by a judge according to the facts evidenced in the proceedings and the applicable legal principles. Either party can begin proceedings and compel the defendant to attend court. The process is subjected to a detailed set of statutory rules. In Singapore, these are known as 'Rules of Court'.

1.178 In a business relationship, litigation—which often results in a 'winner' and a 'loser'—can undermine the bonds of trust and detrimentally affect the viability of a long-term business relationship. As such, ADR is advantageous in preventing parties from falling out with each other.

1.179 It should be noted that the various modes of ADR could still be relied upon even if litigation proceedings have begun. For instance, litigants or their legal representatives may either apply to the court for the matter to be referred to mediation or directly to the Singapore Mediation Centre itself. Some of the other benefits of ADR include:

(1) *Confidentiality*: As can be seen from the various modes of ADR, parties have control over the private and confidential nature of their dispute resolution process. As the processes are private, the attempted resolution of such disputes does not arouse public interest nor necessitate a public record as would be the case should the matter be litigated in the courts. Disputants may desire confidentiality for various reasons. Some are concerned that a publicly litigated dispute will affect stakeholders' (actual and prospective) interest and confidence. Others are concerned that litigation may require parties to disclose trade secrets or proprietary information at the hearings. There are also parties who are concerned that the creation of a legal precedent may be harmful to their interests.

(2) *Control*: ADR allows parties to exercise greater control over the dispute resolution process. Most of the procedures for the various modes of ADR are mutually agreed to by the parties themselves to cater to the peculiarities of the dispute and in alignment with the parties' mutual interests. Although the disputants' lawyers increasingly manage more and more disputes under ADR, the flexibility of the ADR process allows for, and actually encourages, more latitude by the disputants to actively manage the settlement process.

(3) *Cost*: ADR is also characterised by cost-efficiency when compared to litigation. Substantive savings can be made even for arbitration. Reductions in costs arise as lawyers' billable charges are lower as the case takes less time to prepare and argue; the various charges such as court fees, document fees, etc in a litigation are dispensed with. The need for expert witnesses is less likely as well.

(4) *Demands of the globalisation of business*: With more cross-border

business transactions, business disputes are made more complicated by conflict of law issues (arising from a difference in the laws of different countries applicable in a case in which a vital connecting factor is linked with two or more jurisdictions). This, in turn, contributes to the legal costs as parties seek to have the dispute adjudicated in a jurisdiction which is likely to be favourable for them. ADR provides a non-threatening mode of dispute resolution, particularly for parties from different jurisdictions and legal traditions, which is likely to gain more receptivity from the disputants than litigation would.

(5) *Flexibility*: Litigation provides a high level of certainty in terms of the procedures and possible outcomes. ADR, without being encumbered by statute-prescribed rules and regulations, allows for more flexibility in the structuring of the conflict resolution process. This means that disputants can customise the process to suit their mutual needs and interests without being confined to the straitjacket that the litigation process requires.

(6) *Non-confrontational approach*: ADR is a non-confrontational form of dispute resolution. Parties attempt to work together towards finding a resolution that they are comfortable with. Parties are encouraged to look forward by resolving the dispute in a manner that does not harm the business relationship. Indeed, the various modes of ADR are characterised by an informal process that is less adversarial and which emphasises working together. Parties are also spared the stress of going through a trial and the potential negative publicity that often follows.

(7) *Ability to have specifically tailored outcomes*: ADR promotes a purposive approach towards dispute resolution. Notwithstanding the dispute that the disputants are locked in, such parties agreeing to ADR are more likely to be interested in preserving a viable business relationship. As such, the outcome is likely to be driven by such motivations with negotiated outcomes quite different from the 'winner takes all' outcome that characterises litigation. The negotiated resolutions in an ADR process are more likely to be in accord with the parties' individual and mutual needs and interests.

(8) *Speed*: Parties in a dispute seek to resolve their differences as quickly as possible so that the business relationship would not be undermined. ADR tends to meet the need for closure more expeditiously than litigation. This is so even in Singapore where the courts have been successful in dramatically reducing the time it takes to resolve a legal suit. Take, for instance, mediation conducted under the auspices of the SMC. Mediations are usually conducted between one to two weeks from the date of the request for mediation. The date for mediation depends on when the disputants, their representatives and a suitable mediator are available to attend the mediation session. In urgent cases, mediations may be arranged within two to three days from the date of request for mediation.

1.180 Further, as ADR is a relatively informal and flexible process, it takes less time as it is not encumbered by the rules governing litigation timelines. In ADR, parties are also discouraged from burdening the process with too many documents.

Key Institutions for Arbitration and Mediation

1.181 In Singapore, the trend has been in the direction of institutionalizing ADR as a private, non-court-based means of dispute resolution. Indeed, even in litigation (the primary and predominant court-based form of dispute resolution), elements of ADR are consciously woven into the litigation process through pre-trial conferences, court-directed mediation and the court's encouragement to settle before judgement is handed down.

1.182 Mediation appears to be the most encouraged form of ADR in Singapore. It is routinely conducted in the Small Claims Tribunals, the Family Court and the Maintenance of Parents Tribunal (see also LY Lim and TL Liew, *Court Mediation in Singapore* (1997)).

1.183 As indicated earlier, the Government is a keen believer of ADR. The Judiciary is also a strong supporter. In April 2003, the Chief Justice appointed Justice Judith Prakash to preside over all arbitration matters brought before the High Court. This is part of the Judiciary's goal of ensuring that Judges with the requisite expertise and experience preside over cases involving specialised areas of law and commercial practice (see Singapore Supreme Court media release, 7 April 2003).

1.184 Two other key players in the ADR movement in Singapore are the Singapore International Arbitration Centre ('SIAC') and the Singapore Mediation Centre ('SMC'). Much of the information below on the SIAC and SMC are taken from their websites at http://www.siac.org.sg/ and http://www.mediation.com.sg respectively.

(1) *Singapore International Arbitration Centre*

1.185 The Singapore International Arbitration Centre ('SIAC') is a non-profit organisation incorporated as a public company limited by guarantee in March 1990. It commenced operations in July 1991. The SIAC aims to:

- provide facilities for international and domestic commercial arbitration;
- promote arbitration as an alternative to litigation for the settlement of commercial disputes;
- develop a pool of arbitrators in the law and practice of international arbitration.

1.186 Parties may mutually agree on the procedure for arbitrations at the SIAC or use the SIAC Rules for Arbitration. These rules are based largely on the UNCITRAL Arbitration Rules and the Rules of the London Court of International Arbitration with some modifications. The modifications are made principally with the intention of shortening the written stage of the arbitration and to stipulate a time limit within which the tribunal must render its award.

1.187 Under the SIAC Rules for Arbitration, parties are required to submit to the tribunal all written pleadings/statements within 60 days. The tribunal is obliged to determine the issues expeditiously and render reasons with its award within 45 days from close of hearing. A normal dispute could be resolved within six months of the commencement of arbitration.

1.188 The SIAC is also the statutory appointing authority under the International Arbitration Act (Cap 143A, 2002 Rev Ed). In support of its objective of making Singapore a centre for arbitration, the SIAC has a panel of international and regional arbitrators. SIAC also prides itself as a cost-effective centre for arbitration when compared with other major international cities. Parties are also free to choose laws they are familiar and most comfortable with. Singapore law is not imposed on the party's rights and obligations without their agreement. As Singapore has acceded to the New York Convention on the Recognition and Enforcement of Foreign Arbitral Awards 1958, a Singapore arbitral award is, in theory, easily enforceable internationally across over 120 countries, including the United Kingdom and the United States of America.

1.189 The SIAC provide support and administrative services which include settling fees of the arbitrators, providing accommodation for hearings, arranging dates for meetings between the tribunal and parties' representatives, and acting as the registry for the depository of pleadings, documents and correspondence. It is likely that the scope of arbitration will expand if Singapore succeeds in being an important financial centre where disputes involving consumer insurance and financial instruments can be beneficially managed through ADR.

(2) *Singapore Mediation Centre*

1.190 Incorporated on 8 August 1997, the Singapore Mediation Centre ('SMC') is the flagship mediation centre of Singapore. The SMC is a non-profit and non-partisan entity funded by the Singapore Government through the Ministry of Law, and guaranteed by the Singapore Academy of Law. It is linked institutionally with many professional and trade associations and has the support of both the Supreme Court of Singapore and the Subordinate Courts of Singapore.

The SMC's functions include:

- the provision of mediation and other alternative dispute resolution services;
- the provision of facilities for negotiation, mediation and other forms of ADR;
- the provision of training in negotiation and mediation skills;
- the accreditation and maintenance of a panel of mediators;
- the provision of consultancy services for dispute avoidance, dispute management and ADR mechanisms; and
- the promotion of mediation and other ADR services.

As of 31 December 2002, 918 of the 1,045 matters referred for mediation at the SMC were mediated. The settlement rate for completed mediations was about 77%. The SMC provides full logistics, administrative and secretarial support for all matters referred for mediation. Disputes may be referred at any stage, whether before or after the commencement of legal proceedings. Mediations can be conducted in any language or dialect, and have been conducted in Malay, Tamil, Mandarin and other Chinese dialects.

1.191 The types of cases handled by SMC are varied and wide-ranging. They include the sale and purchase of goods or property, service contracts, construction and renovation contracts, employment contracts, defamation, shipping matters, contested probate, insurance claims, intellectual property and information technology cases, and matrimonial matters.

1.192 To enhance the services it provides, the SMC maintains a panel of trained and experienced mediators. These SMC mediators are professionals and leaders from different disciplines. All SMC mediators are specially trained by the SMC in a methodology endorsed by it. They are also committed to conducting a minimum number of mediations each year to maintain their skills. They are then matched to cases in which they can best offer their special experience, expertise and language proficiency.

1.193 In 2002, the SMC unveiled DisputeManager.com, a portal for online ADR services. This portal is part of the national infrastructure for e-commerce and as such seeks to be a forum for resolving e-commerce disputes. In 'e-Settlement' of disputes involving simple monetary claims between two parties, parties make an offer and demand using an automated system. If the offer and demand are within a certain range, the system will indicate that there is a settlement at the mid-point between the offer and demand.

1.194 In the same year, the SMC was urged to make a gradual movement away from the facilitative model of mediation to an Asian model of mediation. In the facilitative model of mediation, the mediator merely facilitated negotiations between the parties and refrained from expressing his views on the dispute. In this new paradigm, the mediator played a more interventionist role. Here, mediation sought to imbibe the Asian perspectives and concepts of 'face', the high regard placed on community interests and the concomitant collective good as well as the parties' expectations of a mediator as going beyond that of a mere facilitator (see Chief Justice Yong Pung How's speech at the launch of 'DisputeManager.com', 30 July 2002, on file with author).

1.195 SMC's community outreach continues with the objective of gaining cross-sectoral and corporate acceptance of mediation. SMC has entered into memoranda of understanding with more than 20 trade and professional bodies to promote mediation as the primary mode of resolving disputes. Regular training sessions are also conducted to educate relevant parties on the effectiveness of mediation.

1.196 The SMC and the SIAC jointly operate the Secretariat of the Singapore Domain Name Dispute Resolution Policy ('SDRP'), which provides the Singapore Domain Name Dispute Resolution Service for resolving '.sg' domain name disputes. Besides being the registration authority for '.sg' domain names, the SDRP also offers a quicker and cheaper way of resolving '.sg' domain name disputes compared to litigation in the courts (see further http://www.disputemanager.com.sg/sdrp/what.asp).

Conclusion

1.197 It is evident that the Singapore legal system has gradually become less a copy of the English legal system. The drive towards legal autochthony continues and legal innovations will continue and be guided by, first, the need for relevance to and compatibility with Singapore's needs and local conditions and secondly, with trade and investments being Singapore's lifeblood, the legal system must provide adequate protection to all and inspire confidence in the international business community that the legal system is both effective and efficient while according justice on the basis of fairness, equity and impartiality.

1.198 The Government recognises the importance of law in maintaining political and social order as well as engendering conducive conditions for economic activity. Indeed, law is regarded as a fundamental economic value, which must be carefully nurtured and harnessed to enhance Singapore's aspirations to be a total global business centre. International bodies such as the World Economic Forum ('WEF'), the Political and Economic Risk Consultancy ('PERC') and the International Institute for Management Development ('IIMD') have consistently ranked Singapore's economic competitiveness highly—the success of which owes much to the laws and the legal system.

1.199 Although Singapore's critics argue that the human rights regime and legal protection for individuals is not on par with the legal regime for economic activity, the Government's success in generating economic wealth have legitimated and lent credence to the state's preference for tough laws, social discipline and low incidence of corruption as an integral part of good governance. As Senior Minister Lee Kuan Yew notes in his memoirs, 'Law and order provide the framework for stability and development' (*From Third World to First—The Singapore Story: 1965–2000* (2000) at p 241).

PART II

The Law of Contract

CHAPTER 2

Offer and Acceptance

PARAGRAPHS

2.1–2.3 **Introduction**

Offer

2.4–2.5 Definition and Nature of an Offer
2.6–2.10 Offer Must be Distinguished from Invitation to Treat
Termination of the Offer
2.11 (1) Introduction
2.12–2.14 (2) Revocation
2.15–2.16 (3) Rejection
2.17 (4) Lapse of Time
2.18 (5) Failure of a Condition Subject to Which Offer was Made
2.19 (6) Death

Acceptance

2.20 Definition and Nature of Acceptance
General Principles
2.21 (1) Acceptance Must be Final and Unqualified
2.22 (2) Acceptance Must be Communicated to Offeror
2.22–2.23 (a) General Rule
2.24–2.28 (b) Exception: The 'Postal Acceptance Rule'
2.29–2.31 (c) Can There be Acceptance by Silence?
2.32–2.34 (d) There can be No Acceptance by Offeree Ignorant of Offer

Other Principles

2.35 Cross-Offers
2.36–2.38 Certainty and Completeness
2.39–2.42 Artificiality of the Offer and Acceptance Rules
2.43–2.47 Battle of the Forms
2.48–2.53 Impact of the Electronic Transactions Act

Introduction

2.1 The concepts of offer and acceptance constitute the traditional starting-points for a contract to be validly formed. There are other prerequisites before a contract can be validly formed; these include the requirements of consideration (to be considered in Chapter 3) and intention to create legal relations (to be considered in Chapter 4). However, offer and acceptance are the very first elements in the entire process.

2.2 Simply put, the offer 'starts the ball rolling'. However, at that particular point in time, there is only one potential party (ie the person who *makes* the offer and who is known as the 'offeror'). Common sense and reason tell us that there can be no concluded contract at this point simply because, for there to be a contract, there must be at least two parties who enter into an agreement with each other. In the words of Goldney J in the very early Singapore decision of *Spence v Kutz Bros* (1892) (at p 63): 'No contract is raised by a mere *ex parte* affirmation in discourse or by mere overture or offer to enter into an agreement not definitively and expressly assented to by both parties. A proposal does not produce what can properly be called an obligation and the person bound by the proposal may retract his consent at any time before it is definitely accepted.'

In order, therefore, for there to be a concluded contract, the offer must be accepted by another party (who is known as the 'offeree', ie the one *to whom* the offer is made).

Although the basic concept or idea is simple (and it is), there are many other specific principles which we will need to look at—for example, when is an attempted offer considered an offer in a legal sense? The same applies with regard to an attempted acceptance. Indeed, we will proceed by considering the definition as well as nature of an offer before proceeding to consider the definition and nature of an acceptance. We will then proceed to consider certain other general principles governing both offer and acceptance before touching on the nature of these concepts in the context of (principally) the Electronic Transactions Act.

2.3 As a final general point, it should be noted that that whether or not there is an offer and acceptance depends on an *objective* interpretation of the facts of the case concerned. From this perspective, the concepts of offer and acceptance constitute the objective manifestations of an intention to contract: hence, in addition to reasons of logic and commonsense, the utilisation of them as the starting-points in the ascertainment whether a contract has been validly formed in law.

In this regard, the following observations by Yong Pung How CJ in the Singapore Court of Appeal decision of *Tribune Investment Trust Inc v Soosan Trading Co Ltd* (2000) are instructive (see pp 422–423):

> 'The principles of law relating to the formation of contracts are clear. Indeed the task of inferring an assent and of extracting the precise moment, if at all there was one, at which a meeting of the minds between the parties may be said to have been reached

> is one of obvious difficulty, particularly in a case where there has been protracted negotiations and a considerable exchange of written correspondence between the parties. Nevertheless, the function of the court is to try as far as practical experience allows, to ensure that the reasonable expectations of honest men are not disappointed. To this end, it is also trite law that the test of agreement or of inferring consensus *ad idem* is objective. Thus, the language used by one party, whatever his real intention may be, is to be construed in the sense in which it would be reasonably understood by the other.'

This approach was reaffirmed yet again by LP Thean JA, delivering the judgment of the Singapore Court of Appeal in *Projection Pte Ltd v The Tai Ping Insurance Co Ltd* (2001) (at p 405), and by Judith Prakash J in the Singapore High Court decision of *Overseas Union Insurance Ltd v Turegum Insurance Co* (2001) (at p 340).

Offer

Definition and Nature of an Offer

2.4 A leading contract textbook defines an offer succinctly, as follows: 'An offer, capable of being converted into an agreement by acceptance, must consist of a definite promise to be bound provided that certain specified terms are accepted' (see MP Furmston, *Cheshire, Fifoot and Furmston's Law of Contract* (14th ed, 2001), p 34).

A definition from a local (Malaysian) decision echoes the above definition: 'An offer is an intimation of willingness by an offeror to enter into a legally binding contract. Its terms either expressly or impliedly must indicate that it is to become binding on the offeror as soon as it has been accepted by the offeree' (per Salleh Abas FJ in the *Preston Corp Sdn Bhd v Edward Leong* (1982) at p 23, Malaysian Federal Court).

In summary, an offer, once accepted (without any qualification, a point to which we return below), results in a valid contract (subject to other requirements, such as those relating to consideration and intention to create legal relations, being satisfied (see Chapters 3 and 4, respectively)). The key element of an offer is that of *intention*. This, as we have seen, has to be ascertained objectively (see paragraph 2.3, above). In other words, the offeror *must intend* to be bound if the offeree accepts *all* the terms in the offer *without any qualification*. Logically, of course, all the terms of the offer must have been clearly communicated to the offeree in the first instance for it would otherwise have been impossible for the offeree to have accepted terms which he or she was not even clear about to begin with.

2.5 An important proposition relating to an offer is that an offer can be made to *the whole world*. This was established in perhaps what is one of the most famous decisions in the English common law of contract, the Court of Appeal decision in *Carlill v Carbolic Smoke Ball Company* (1893), which has also been cited in the local context. In that case, the salient facts were as follows.

The defendants (*Carbolic Smoke Ball Company*) were the proprietors and vendors of a medical preparation, not surprisingly called 'The Carbolic Smoke Ball'. They advertised, in the newspapers, offering to pay £100 to any person who contracted influenza after having used the said smoke ball three times daily for two weeks and in accordance with the printed directions supplied with each ball. The plaintiff (Mrs Carlill) utilised the defendants' product for the specified period and in the manner specified but nevertheless contracted influenza. The key issue that arose was whether or not she could claim the £100. Several significant issues arose, which we will briefly consider here. On a more general level, we note at the outset that the court held that the plaintiff could succeed in her claim against the defendants.

First, the court had to consider whether or not the promise by the defendants to pay the £100 was a mere puff, ie that there was no intention to create legal relations inasmuch as the ostensible promise was not intended to have any legal effects whatsoever. We will be considering the topic of 'Intention to Create Legal Relations' in Chapter 4. It will suffice for our present purposes to note that the court rejected this argument. The main reason was that the advertisement itself contained the sentence that '£1,000 is deposited with the Alliance Bank, shewing our sincerity in the matter'. This, the court held, was evidence that the defendants were serious about their promise.

Secondly, the issue arose as to whether the defendants' apparent promise was an offer in the first instance. It was unlike the conventional offer which is addressed to a specific person or specific group of persons. Here, the advertisement was, in effect, to the whole world. The court held that an offer could indeed be made to the whole world and so the defendants failed on this particular issue as well.

Thirdly, there was the closely related issue as to whether the plaintiff should nevertheless fail in her claim because she had not notified her acceptance to the defendants. The court also rejected this argument by the defendants. This was a *unilateral* contract, the nature of which we will briefly consider further at the end of the present paragraph. All that was required was the plaintiff's complete act of performance in accordance with the defendants' instructions and this was effected here. Various explanations were proffered with regard to the fulfillment of the requirement of notice. Lindley LJ was of the view that the defendant offerors would receive the requisite notice *contemporaneously* with the notice of the performance of the condition stipulated (here, to use the smoke ball for the specified period and in the manner specified, but yet still contracting influenza). Both Lindley and Bowen LJJ were of the view that the defendants had *waived* (or dispensed with) the requirement of notice prior to performance: in other words, the defendants had impliedly indicated that they did not require notification of the acceptance of the offer as such. In Bowen LJ's view, this was based on 'common sense' (see p 270); in his words (see ibid), 'If I advertise to the world that my dog is lost, and that anybody who brings the dog to a particular place will be paid some money, are all the police and other persons whose business it is to find lost dogs to be expected to sit down and write me a note saying that they have accepted my proposal?'

Fourthly, there was the issue as to how long such an offer would last. There were differing views amongst the various judges although none thought that the timeframe was so vague or uncertain as to defeat the plaintiff's claim. Indeed, it was held that, whichever view was held, there was a sufficient and reasonable time limit in any event.

Finally, the court held that there was sufficient consideration furnished by the plaintiff for the defendants' promise (to pay the £100). The doctrine of consideration will in fact be discussed in much greater detail in Chapter 3.

Before leaving our discussion of the *Carlill* case, it is important to note that while an offer can indeed be made to the whole world, the offeror *cannot contract with* the whole world. That is an obvious physical impossibility and would be ludicrous in any event. The same, however, is not true when one makes an offer to the whole world; in the words of Lindley LJ in the *Carlill* case itself, 'although the offer is made to the world, the contract is made with that limited portion of the public who come forward and perform the condition on the faith of the advertisement' (see p 268).

It should also be mentioned that the facts and holding of the *Carlill* case very neatly illustrate the nature of a *unilateral contract*. For a unilateral contract, the offeror makes a promise in return for an *act* which is to be performed by the offeree. The act of acceptance is the complete performance of this act (see, further, paragraph 2.14 on possible problems that may arise). It might also be noted that the complete performance of the said act also constitutes the requisite consideration for the offeror's promise, provided that it is recognized in law (on the doctrine of consideration, see generally Chapter 3). A unilateral contract is to be *contrasted* with a *bilateral* contract, where the offeror makes a promise in return for the offeree's *promise*. For a bilateral contract, therefore, the contract is concluded at the point when the offeree makes his or her *promise*.

Offer Must be Distinguished from Invitation to Treat

2.6 As we have seen, an offer 'must consist of a definite promise to be bound provided that certain specified terms are accepted' (see paragraph 2.4, above).

On the other hand, what may look like an offer might turn out to be something else altogether—in legal terms, it is called an *invitation to treat*. In other words, it is an attempt to induce or invite offers, rather than being an offer itself. There is *no* intention to be bound; the person making the invitation to treat is inviting others to make offers instead. Hence, when a response to the invitation to treat is forthcoming, it is merely an offer, which the person who made the invitation to treat can (as an *offeree*) decide to either accept or reject. *No* contract is therefore formed at that particular point in time.

In contrast, the nature of an offer is such that an unqualified response constitutes an acceptance and a binding contract is formed immediately.

How, then, is one to distinguish an offer from an invitation to treat?

As we shall see below, there are certain established results for certain general fact situations. However, where no prior case governs, it is necessary to have recourse to first principles. And the first principle in this regard is simple to state but extremely difficult to apply to the facts at hand—the issue, in the final analysis, is one of the *intention* of the person in question: in other words, is the intention of the person concerned to make 'a definite promise to be bound provided that certain specified terms are accepted' (in which case he or she would be making an *offer*) *or* is the intention of the person concerned simply to attempt to induce offers and initiate negotiations (in which case he or she would be making an *invitation to treat*)? As already mentioned, the general principle is easy to state but difficult to apply in practice. Much depends on the court's objective interpretation of the facts from which it will infer either an intention to make an offer or an intention to merely make an invitation to treat.

The practical impact of a finding either way cannot be overemphasized: to reiterate, if an offer has been made, an unqualified response will result in an immediately binding contract. Any attempt thereafter to escape from the contract will constitute a *breach* of contract (as to which see generally Chapter 9). In contrast, if only an invitation to treat has been made, any response will not result in an immediately binding contract. Indeed, any response will only constitute an offer at best, which might or might not be accepted by the person who had originally made the invitation to treat.

2.7 As mentioned in the preceding paragraph, however, there are established situations where the courts have already decided whether there is an offer or an invitation to treat. The paradigm model is that pertaining to *priced goods on display*. In a practical context, if priced goods on display are offers, then the mere picking up of such goods might result in a binding contract. If, on the other hand, priced goods on display are merely invitations to treat, then in order for a binding contract to be concluded, the person who picks up the good concerned makes an offer to the owner of the good who accepts the offer, whereupon a binding contract is formed.

The leading case in this regard is that of the English Court of Appeal in *Pharmaceutical Society of Great Britain v Boots Cash Chemists* (1953). This case was not a 'pure' contract case as such although the particular contractual issue now discussed was crucial to the outcome of the case itself. Briefly stated, the facts of the case were as follows.

The defendants owned a branch shop which was operated under a self-service scheme. The shop offered products which included some that were regulated under the then Pharmaceutical and Poisons Act. The customer would select the articles he or she wished to purchase and bring it to the cashier's desk for payment. For products which required regulation under the Act just mentioned, the requisite check was made by a registered pharmacist who was stationed at the cashier's desk itself. The plaintiff brought an action against the defendants for alleged infringement of the Act. The key issue which hence arose for decision was whether or not the specific sales of products were properly effected under the supervision of a registered pharmacist in accordance with the provisions of the Act itself. This raised the further issue as to *when precisely* the contract of sale concerned was concluded. If the priced goods on display were merely invitations to treat, then the customer would be offering to purchase them when he or she brings them to the cashier's desk. Since the contract would be concluded at that particular point in time, it would have been effected under the supervision of a registered pharmacist who was in fact stationed at the cashier's desk. If, however, the priced goods on display were offers, then the contract of sale of the goods concerned would have been concluded between the defendants and the customer when the latter picked the items off the shelf—in which case it clearly would *not* have been concluded under the supervision of a registered pharmacist as required under the said Act.

The court unanimously held that the goods in question were mere invitations to treat and not offers and that, therefore, the defendants were entitled to succeed. The specific reasons given by the various judges, however, are interesting and merit the briefest of descriptions. First, Somervell LJ was of the view that if the priced good or article on display were an offer, then the customer concerned would be unfairly bound once the article was placed in the basket and would have no right (without first paying for the said article) to substitute that article with one he saw later of a similar kind and which he perhaps preferred. In other words, the customer would not be able to change his mind once the article concerned had been picked up—a point which was also emphasised by Romer LJ. Birkett LJ was of the view that if the priced good or article on display were an offer, then the store owner or shopkeeper would be in deep legal trouble if he or she ran out of stock.

The general rule, therefore, with regard to priced goods on display appears to be clear: such goods are mere *invitations to treat*, and it is therefore the customer who makes the offer by bringing it to the payment or checkout counter to effect payment.

Notwithstanding the clear proposition as set out above, there have nevertheless been numerous criticisms of this proposition and, in particular, the reasoning of the court in the *Boots* case briefly described above. The best discussion is, perhaps, to be found in Professor Treitel's treatise, *The Law of Contract* (10th ed, 1999) at pp 12–13. To briefly summarise the learned author's various critiques, the first is that the modern shop or supermarket is not, as some argue, a place for bargaining. Secondly, the customer would *not* be *automatically* bound if the priced good on display were an offer because the mere picking up of the good concerned would be, in and of itself, too equivocal an act to constitute an act of acceptance as such. Finally, the argument that there is a danger that the shopkeeper (or owner of the good concerned) would be unfairly bound if he or she ran out of stock could be avoided because (in Professor Treitel's words), 'the offer could be construed as one which automatically expired when the shopkeeper's stock was exhausted: this would probably be in keeping with the common expectation of both shopkeeper and customer' (see p 12). The shopkeeper could, of course, pre-empt these potential difficulties altogether by stating that his or her 'offer' was open 'only while stocks last'. In addition, insofar as the *digital environment* is concerned, it might be argued that software, for example, is always available although availability is obviously subject to the relevant copyright restrictions (see D Rowland and E Macdonald, *Information Technology Law* (2nd ed, 2000), p 297).

Despite these very cogent criticisms, however, the law still remains as stated above. However, the reader is encouraged to consider seriously whether or not the law ought to be changed in the light of the powerful criticisms just considered.

There is also the issue as to what the law would be in the context of *material posted on internet websites*. It is suggested that the basic principle set out above (in paragraph 2.6) to the effect that it all depends on the *intention* of the person or persons responsible for the material on the website concerned is all-important. In other words, it is important to ascertain whether, in constructing the material as well as its context, the intention was to make an invitation to treat or (on the contrary) to make an offer. Although it appears attractive, at first blush, to argue that the material on the website is in the nature of an advertisement and only amounts to an invitation to treat, one cannot endorse such a sweeping proposition. Where, for instance, a website leads the user through a whole battery of terms and then invites the user to click an 'I accept' button, would the entire process constitute an offer instead of an invitation to treat? Would it make any difference if the user had to send an e-mail to conclude the transaction instead? What if the system on the website itself were programmed to reject orders requiring goods stated therein to be delivered to particular jurisdictions (cf D Rowland and E Macdonald, *Information Technology Law* (2nd ed, 2000), p 298)? It is suggested, once again, that what is crucial is the *intention* to be gathered from the particular facts of the situation itself (see also GJH Smith, *Internet Law and Regulation* (3rd ed, 2002), p 451). Reference may also be made to S Christensen, 'Formation of Contracts by Email—Is it Just the Same as the Post?' (2001) *Queensland University of Technology Law & Justice Journal* 22 (this article is available online at the Australian Legal Information Institute website at http://www.austlii.edu.au). The author of this article helpfully distinguishes between non-interactive and interactive websites, arguing (insofar as the latter is concerned) that '[w]here a person is able to log into a website, chose [*sic*] an item for sale, enter payment details and conclude the agreement the display on the site may go beyond a mere invitation to treat' (see p 28). However, no one proposition is conclusive, for '[i]f by analogy the website is considered to be the same as a display of goods in a store window or on a shelf, a court may be reluctant, depending on the terms placed on the website, to find the existence of an offer' (see ibid).

2.8 Another situation where there have been decided cases is that pertaining to *tenders*. The general rule is that invitations to tender are just that: ie invitations to treat and not offers (see, eg the leading English decision of *Spencer v Harding* (1870)). This is perhaps not surprising because there are many other circumstances that the invitor would like to take into account before awarding the contract to a particular tenderer. For example, it does not inexorably follow that the invitor would want to conclude a contract without more with the person who comes in with the lowest tender in the situation where the invitor is inviting tenders to supply goods and/or services to him or her. Other factors that would weigh very heavily with the invitor might include the quantity and/or quality of the product and/or service offered. Naturally, a low tender might be low precisely because the quantity and/or quality of the produce and/or service offered might be lower than what is generally offered on the open market. This might be wholly unacceptable to the invitor and it would be patently unfair to bind the invitor in such circumstances. On the other hand, where tenders are invited and the invitor is offering a product and/or service (for, say, distribution), it also does not follow that the invitor would inexorably want to conclude a contract with the person coming in with the highest tender. For example, the invitor might dislike that particular tenderer on a personal level and hence not want to conclude any business whatsoever with him or her.

Hence, it makes for eminent logic and commonsense for the courts generally not to construe the invitor as having made an offer which would be turned into a binding contract on acceptance by the first person responding or by the person responding with the lowest or highest tender, as the case may be. Indeed, without any clear terms as to what would constitute the first binding acceptance, one could argue that there is sufficient uncertainty in any event and that any invitation must therefore necessarily be an invitation to treat. However, like all general rules, exceptions are possible—depending on the specific facts and circumstances of the particular case. For example, given certain exceptional facts and circumstances, the courts could find that the invitor may have *expressly undertaken* to sell to the *highest bidder* (see, eg *Spencer v Harding* at pp 563–564, the House of Lords decision of *Harvela Investments Ltd v Royal Trust Company of Canada (CI) Ltd* (1986) and the Singapore Court of Appeal decision of *Aircharter World Pte Ltd v Kontena Nasional Bhd* (1999) at p 14). However, where such an undertaking exists, the facts have to be closely examined in order to ascertain whether a fixed bidding sale is intended—in which case referential bids are precluded (see the *Harvela* case, ibid).

On the other hand, the invitor may *expressly state* that he or she is free to accept any, all or even none of the tenders concerned. However, even in situations similar to the one just mentioned, the law may not be altogether clear. In order to do justice in a particular case, the court concerned may actually generate more uncertainty in future cases. A particularly striking example may be found in the English Court of Appeal decision of *Blackpool and Fylde Aero Club Ltd v Blackpool Borough*

Council (1990). In the *Blackpool* case, the defendant authority owned and managed Blackpool Airport. It granted a concession to an air operator to operate pleasure flights. The plaintiff had, for an unbroken period since 1875, been able to secure that concession. The most recent concession was due to expire in 1983 and the defendant therefore sent invitations to tender to seven parties (including the plaintiff). The terms of the invitation were as follows:

> 'The *council* do *not bind* themselves to *accept* all or any part of any tender. No tender which is received after the last date and time specified shall be admitted *for consideration.*
>
> The concession will be for a period of three years commencing on 1 April 1983. Tenderers should note that the concession is NOT to be a sole concession and the council may accept *all or any* tenders submitted in respect of each class of aircraft.
>
> ...
>
> Form of Tender
>
> I/We the undersigned hereby make the following *offers* for the privilege of operating pleasure flights from Blackpool Airport for a period of three years from 1 April 1983' (emphasis added).

Only three of the seven selected tenderers responded (of whom the plaintiff was one). However, although the plaintiff did in fact submit a bid within the stipulated time frame, the defendant thought that the plaintiff's tender was late owing to a mistake on the part of the defendant's staff. As a result, the defendant excluded (in accordance with its standing orders) the plaintiff's tender from consideration. Unfortunately, it was clear that had the plaintiff's tender been considered, it would probably have been accepted by the defendant. The plaintiff was understandably unhappy as another tender was duly accepted. The defendant in fact admitted, through its airport director, that a mistake had been made, and another invitation for tenders was rescheduled. However, the defendant subsequently called off this rescheduled invitation. As a result, the plaintiff brought an action against the defendant for damages for breach of contract and for tortuous negligence. The court held in favour of the plaintiff on the contractual claim and therefore avoided having to rule on the issue of tort (with the exception of Bingham LJ, who made some *obiter* comments on the tort issue).

The court held that the defendant was under a *contractual* obligation to the plaintiff to *consider* the plaintiff's tender when attempting to arrive at a decision as to whom to grant the concession. While the decision appears fair, the court has, unfortunately, 'destabilised' the general rules with regard to offer and acceptance in the context of tenders, as briefly stated above. The result is, it is submitted, an unnecessarily large amount of uncertainty for the business community generally. Indeed, had the court adhered to the established principles, it would have arrived at an *opposite* conclusion. The reader is referred to the material terms of the invitation set out above, in particular, the italicised portions. In other words, the plaintiff's tender (based on the established principles) would have been no more than an offer, hence resulting in no contractual obligation on the part of both the plaintiff and the defendant in the absence of an acceptance by the latter. Indeed, a focus on (in particular) the italicised words in the invitation clearly demonstrates that there was clearly no acceptance by the defendant in the present case. Nor was there an express undertaking on the part of the defendant invitor to award the tender in favour of any designated person.

However, the court chose *another* route in order to do justice in the case at hand: it relied on a *separate collateral contract* to establish a contractual obligation on the defendant's part to *consider* the plaintiff's tender. However, the reader is invited to consider whether or not this alternative route, whilst apparently achieving justice on the *specific* facts of the present case, nevertheless generates *excessive uncertainty* on a more *general* level insofar as *future* cases are unconcerned—an uncertainty that would in fact be detrimental to the expectations of the business community where reasonable commercial parties would accept the risk of a tender being rejected as an everyday fact of commercial life. For a view that adopts this approach, see A Phang, 'Tenders and Uncertainty' (1991) 4 *Journal of Contract Law* 46. Note also, however, that the principle in the *Blackpool* decision has (notwithstanding this critique) been endorsed in subsequent decisions (see, eg *Fairclough Building Ltd v Borough Council of Port Talbot* (1992) (which is an English decision); reference may also be made to the New Zealand decision of *Gregory v Rangitikei District Council* (1995) and the Australian decision of *Hughes Aircraft Systems International v Airservice Australia* (1997); see, further, particularly with regard to the last-mentioned decision, A Phang, 'Tenders, Implied Terms and Fairness in the Law of Contract' (1998) 13 *Journal of Contract Law* 126). Which approach is preferable? Ought the principle in the *Blackpool* case be confined to its special facts, or ought it be extended as a general principle?

2.9 Insofar as *auction sales* are concerned, the general rule is that the bid itself is considered to be the offer, with acceptance occurring at the fall of the hammer (and see section 57(2) of the UK Sale of Goods Act 1979, which is part of Singapore law by virtue of the Application of English Law Act (Cap 7A, 1994 Rev Ed)).

An advertisement of an auction sale does not, in and of itself, constitute a promise to potential bidders that the sale will in fact be held (see the leading English decision of *Harris v Nickerson* (1873)). *However*, if an advertisement states that the auction sale will be 'without reserve', the *auctioneer* may be liable for breach of a *collateral contract* if the auction sale does not in fact take place (see the English decision of *Warlow v Harrison* (1859)).

2.10 A mere *quotation* that is not intended to give rise to any binding legal obligation will not constitute an offer in law. However, the final result is dependent primarily on the construction of the language of the quotation concerned (reference may be made, in this regard, to the Privy Council decision of *Scancarriers A/S v Aeteraroa International Ltd (The 'Barranduna' and 'Tarago')* (1985)).

Termination of the Offer

(1) *Introduction*

2.11 Even after an offer has been made, it can be terminated *provided that* it has not already been accepted. If, of course, it has been accepted, then (in accordance with the general principles set out above), a binding contract has come into being; thereafter, any attempt to disclaim the obligations therein will amount to a *breach of contract* (as to which, see generally, Chapter 9).

(2) *Revocation*

2.12 An offer can be *revoked* at any time prior to acceptance. In order to be effective, however, it must be communicated to the offeree; once communicated, the original offer cannot thereafter be accepted by the offeree.

2.13 Can an offer be *impliedly* revoked? This issue arose in the leading English decision of *Dickinson v Dodds* (1876). The decision appears to suggest that implied revocation is possible, so that if the offeree hears of the revocation of the offer by the offeror through a third party, that would be sufficient to terminate the offer.

However, there are the inevitable difficulties of application of the principle of implied revocation of an offer via a third party to the facts of any given case. In this regard, *Dickinson v Dodds* was an easy case. The third party concerned was the plaintiff offeree's very own agent and, therefore, there was no problem with regard to the reliability of the information relating to the revocation of the offer in that case. Most fact situations are not, however, as clear-cut. How are we to ascertain whether or not the information is reliable? In this regard, a leading textbook has suggested that an *objective test* be applied in order to ascertain whether or not the information in question is reliable (see MP Furmston, *Cheshire, Fifoot and Furmston's Law of Contract* (14th ed, 2001), p 64). This is, of course, but the roughest of guidelines and much will depend on the court's interpretation of the facts of the case at hand.

2.14 Difficulties may also arise in the context of the revocation of an offer insofar as *unilateral contracts* are concerned. In particular, what is the legal position where an offer of a unilateral contract is revoked *before full* performance (and, hence, acceptance of the offer) has taken place? The fact that *partial* performance has taken place makes it appear rather unfair to the offeree that the offeror could revoke the offer at any time before full performance and still retain any benefit that might have accrued to him or her (the offeror) in the meantime. However, the strict legal position is that the offeror can revoke his or her offer at *any* time *prior to* acceptance by the offeree. There, therefore, arises a tension between considerations of fairness (here, to the offeree) on the one hand and that of giving effect to the strict legal position on the other. The arguments for each do appear to be finely balanced. The focus on achieving fairness in the particular case at hand may set an undesirable precedent for the future (hence, the oft-cited saying that 'Hard cases make bad law'; see also the discussion of the *Blackpool* case at paragraph 2.8, above). On the other hand, the desire to maintain the uniformity of the law as manifested in the general (and established) rules (here, that the offer may be revoked at any time before acceptance) may result in unfairness in the particular case at hand. However, this last-mentioned argument of unfairness to the offeree may be somewhat overstated because the parties have entered into the agreement voluntarily and the *offeror* also thus takes the risk that the offeree might default without exposing himself or herself (ie the *offeree*) to any legal liability (see also MP Furmston, *Cheshire, Fifoot and Furmston's Law of Contract* (14th ed, 2001), p 65).

There have been suggested solutions, the chief of which is the so-called 'two-offer approach'. Under such an approach, there is, first, the express (and main) offer which (as we have seen) can be revoked at any time before acceptance; secondly, there is an *implied* offer not to revoke the first (and main) offer once the offeree has begun his or her performance within a reasonable time (in other words, this (second) offer is accepted (and therefore binding on the offeror) when the offeree commences performance). It is suggested, however, that such a solution is artificial as well as question-begging. Professor Treitel has in fact adopted a more realistic and straightforward approach by suggesting that it might be preferable simply to state that the first (and main) offer is *itself* accepted by the commencement of performance by the offeree (see GH Treitel, *The Law of Contract* (10th ed, 1999), p 37). Notwithstanding the learned author's view, however, the 'two-offer approach' was adopted (albeit by way of *obiter dicta*) by Goff LJ in the English Court of Appeal decision of *Daulia Ltd v Four Millbank Nominees Ltd* (1978), where the learned judge observed thus (at p 239):

> 'Whilst I think the true view of a unilateral contract must in general be that the offeror is entitled to require full performance of the condition which he has imposed and short of that he is not bound, that must be subject to one important qualification, which stems from the fact that there must be an implied obligation on the part of the offeror not to prevent the condition becoming satisfied, which obligation it seems to me must arise as soon as the offeree starts to perform. Until then the offeror can revoke the whole thing, but once the offeree has embarked on performance it is too late for the offeror to revoke his offer.'

It might also be noted that, in the Singapore context, Chan Sek Keong JC (as he then was) approved of Goff LJ's *dictum* above in *Dickson Trading (S) Pte Ltd v Transmarco Ltd* (1989) (at p 414).

However, apart from the 'two offer approach', there is *another possible alternative*—to compensate the offeree for his or her trouble by way of a reasonable sum in *quantum meruit* (reference may be made to the English decisions of *William Lacey (Hounslow) Ltd v Davis* (1957) and *British Steel Corporation v Cleveland Bridge and Engineering Co Ltd* (1984)) *or* by way of a bold application of the doctrine of promissory estoppel (this is not very likely under present Singapore law which is premised, in the main, on English law; though compare with the Australian position which is much more radical. And on the doctrine of promissory estoppel generally, see paragraphs 3.47 ff, below).

(3) *Rejection*

2.15 Another way in which an offer may be terminated occurs when there is any variation in the terms of the offer by the offeree. When this happens, the offer is said to have been *rejected*. This legal effect is consistent with the general principle (already briefly referred to in paragraphs 2.4 and 2.6, above) that in order for there to be a valid and binding contract, each and every term of the offer *must* be accepted *without any qualification whatsoever*.

Any qualification renders the offeree's response a *counter-offer*. The effect of a counter-offer is to *destroy* the *original* offer; it simultaneously constitutes a *new offer* which can either be accepted or rejected by the original offeror (who now becomes the (new) counter-offeree, with the original offeree becoming the counter-offeror). There are many cases illustrating these general principles pertaining to the concept and effect of the counter-offer (see, eg the oft-cited English decision of *Hyde v Wrench* (1840) as well as the various local decisions cited in A Phang, *Cheshire, Fifoot and Furmston's Law of Contract—Second Singapore and Malaysian Edition* (1998), p 96, n 71).

2.16 A counter-offer should, however, be distinguished from a request for information (see the (also) oft-cited English decision of *Stevenson, Jacques & Co v McLean* (1880)). But it should be noted that this distinction, whilst easy to draw in theory, may be difficult to apply in practice and really depends, in the final analysis, on the particular facts of the case concerned. For a relevant (and recent) local case, see the Singapore High Court decision of *Overseas Union Insurance Ltd v Turegum Insurance Co* (2001), especially at p 341.

(4) *Lapse of Time*

2.17 An offer can also be terminated by *lapse of time*. There are at least two basic situations.

The first is very straightforward and relates to a situation where the offer itself contains an express term as to when the offer will lapse (see, eg the Singapore decision of *Dickson Trading (S) Pte Ltd v Transmarco Ltd* (1989)).

The second is one where there is no such express stipulation. Here, the courts, not surprisingly, have held that the offer will lapse after *a reasonable period of time* has elapsed. This is, of course, premised on logic and commonsense since an offer cannot be expected to last indefinitely. More importantly, the entire issue in such a situation is one that is obviously very heavily dependent on the particular facts of the case concerned (and see generally the oft-cited English decision of *Ramsgate Victoria Hotel Co Ltd v Montefiore* (1866)).

(5) *Failure of a Condition Subject to Which Offer was Made*

2.18 If such a condition fails, then the offer itself (which was premised on this particular condition) must also terminate. If, for example, the offer made is conditional on the subject-matter of the proposed contract remaining in substantially the same condition until acceptance takes place, *and* the said subject-matter in fact deteriorates, the offer is incapable of being accepted and will in fact terminate (see the oft-cited House of Lords decision of *Financings Ltd v Stimson* (1962)).

(6) *Death*

2.19 This would appear to be another obvious category under which the offer terminates. However, the relevant rules may not be altogether clear, although it does appear that knowledge is a key element. If the offeree knows of the offeror's death, he or she will not be allowed to effect a valid acceptance, but if the offeree is ignorant of the offeror's death, the legal position would appear to be unclear, with the relevant authorities going both ways. The better view in this last-mentioned situation would appear to be that a valid acceptance is possible, save in those situations where some element of personal service or the like is required on the offeror's part. If the *offeree* passes away, it would appear that his or her personal representatives cannot accept the offer on behalf of the decased offeree's estate. For a good general discussion, see MP Furmston, *Cheshire, Fifoot and Furmston's Law of Contract* (14th ed, 2001), pp 68–69.

Acceptance

Definition and Nature of Acceptance

2.20 An excellent and succinct definition of an acceptance is given by Professor Treitel, as follows: 'An acceptance is a *final and unqualified* expression of assent *to the terms of an offer*' (emphasis added) (see GH Treitel, *The Law of Contract* (10th ed, 1999), p 16).

As already explained above, the requirement of acceptance differs according to whether a unilateral or bilateral contract is involved (see paragraph 2.5, above). For a unilateral contract, the complete performance of the act is the requisite acceptance of the offer. On the other hand, for a bilateral contract, the offeree's promise (as opposed to complete performance of the contractual subject-matter) constitutes the requisite acceptance.

General Principles

(1) *Acceptance Must be Final and Unqualified*

2.21 This is an essential principle. As we have already noted above, any qualification of the terms of the original offer renders the offeree's response a *counter-offer*, which destroys the original offer and simultaneously constitutes a *new offer* which can be either accepted or rejected by the original offeror (see paragraph 2.15, above).

(2) *Acceptance Must Be Communicated to Offeror*

(a) General Rule

2.22 The general rule is that the acceptance must be communicated to the offeror in order for it to be effective and a binding contract to come into being. Whether or not the requisite communication has taken place is dependent upon an objective interpretation of the facts (see also paragraph 2.3, above). In this regard, a mere mental assent without more is therefore insufficient but, rather, must be objectively manifested. Such objective manifestation need not, however, be confined to a direct communication through written or spoken words but, rather, could take the form of *conduct* (see, eg the oft-cited English decision of *Brogden v Metropolitan Railway* (1877)).

2.23 It is clear that the general rule as enunciated in the preceding paragraph applies to *instantaneous communications*; these include communications via telex, fax and (possibly) electronic mail. However, the general rule applies on condition that there has been *no fault* on the part of the *offeror.* If, for example, the offeror does not receive the acceptance because he or she has been negligent in, say, maintaining the necessary equipment, then it would be inequitable for the offeror to argue that there is no concluded contract because he or she did not receive the offeree's acceptance.

It should also be noted that the application of the traditional rules of offer and acceptance to *electronic mail* has generated some controversy. At first blush, one would have thought that it must, *a fortiori*, constitute a form (possibly even a paradigm form) of instantaneous communications. However, it has also been argued that electronic mail can be likened to the normal post or mail which may (as we shall see, in the next paragraph) be subject to quite different rules of communication insofar as acceptance is concerned. It is true that electronic mail is not, strictly speaking, instantaneous and is conveyed in 'packets' and might not even arrive at its destination (bouncing back to its original sender). There appears, unfortunately, to be no definitive ruling one way or the other at the present time.

Returning to the relevant precedents which were, given their vintage, decided in the context of telex communications, the English Court of Appeal decision of *Entores Ltd v Miles Far East Corporation* (1955) established that the general rule applied, ie that communication had to be actually communicated to the offeror. This decision was endorsed much later by the House of Lords in *Brinkibon Ltd v Stahag Stahl und Stahlwaren Handelsgesellschaft GmbH* (1983). However, in an interesting observation which emphasises the open-endedness that is inherent in the very enterprise of law itself, Lord Wilberforce canvassed possible exceptions to the general rule, even in the context of instantaneous communications. He observed as follows (at p 42):

> 'I think it [ie the general rule with respect to instantaneous communications] *a sound rule, but not necessarily a universal rule.*
>
> Since 1955 the use of telex communication has been greatly

expanded, and there are many variants on it. The senders and recipients may not be the principals to the contemplated contract. They may be servants or agents with limited authority. The message may not reach, or be intended to reach, the designated recipient immediately: messages may be sent out of office hours, or at night, with the intention, or on the assumption, that they will be read at a later time. There may be some error or default at the recipient's end which prevents receipt at the time contemplated and believed in by the sender. The message may have been sent and/or received through machines operated by third persons. *And many other variations may occur. No universal rule can cover all such cases; they must be resolved by reference to the intentions of the parties, by sound business practice and in some cases by a judgment where the risks should lie ...'* (emphasis added).

It might be useful to note that the position in Singapore is basically the same: see *Transniko Pte Ltd v Communication Technology Sdn Bhd* (1996).

(b) Exception: The 'Postal Acceptance Rule'

2.24 A more *clearly defined* exception (compared to the broader approach utilised by Lord Wilberforce in the *Brinkibon* case as quoted in paragraph 2.23, above) is popularly referred to as the 'postal acceptance rule'. This rule is an *exception* to the general rule: in other words, acceptance does not need to be communicated to the offeror in order for there to be a binding contract. *Instead*, acceptance takes place *at the point of posting of the letter of acceptance itself*. This exception applies equally to telegrams itself although this mode of communication has recently become moribund.

However, an important point should be noted: the 'postal acceptance rule' is effective *even if* the letter of acceptance is *lost* in the post (see, eg the English Court of Appeal decision of *Household Fire and Carriage Accident Insurance Co v Grant* (1879)).

The 'postal acceptance rule' has in fact been endorsed in the Singapore context: see *Lee Seng Heng v Guardian Assurance Co Ltd* (1932) (this case is discussed in more detail in A Phang, *Cheshire, Fifoot and Furmston's Law of Contract—Second Singapore and Malaysian Edition* (1998), p 120).

As to whether or not the 'postal acceptance rule' applies to *electronic mail*, we have already seen above that the arguments are rather finely balanced (see paragraph 2.23, above).

2.25 It is important, however, to note that before the 'postal acceptance rule' can be invoked, certain rather straightforward and commonsensical conditions have to be satisfied.

First, the rule only applies to situations where postal acceptance is either expressly *or* impliedly authorised, for instance, by reason of the terms in which the offer is made *or* by reason of the specific relations between the parties themselves *or* because of general usage (and see per Beggallay LJ in *Household Fire and Carriage Accident Insurance Co v Grant* (1879) at pp 227–228).

Secondly, and this is even more commonsensical, the letter of acceptance must have been *properly stamped and addressed* (reference may also be made to GH Treitel, *The Law of Contract* (10th ed, 1999), pp 26–27).

2.26 Notwithstanding the fact that the 'postal acceptance rule' is in fact well-established, the question arises as to whether or not it ought to be retained. We will briefly proffer some possible critiques of the possible reasons supporting the rule itself for the reader's consideration.

One reason given for the 'postal acceptance rule' is that the post office is the agent for both parties (see, eg per Thesiger LJ in *Household Fire and Carriage Accident Insurance Co v Grant* (1879) at p 221). However, Professor Treitel has argued that this is a highly artificial argument and that, in any event, the post office is (at most) an agent to transmit, not to receive (see GH Treitel, *The Law of Contract* (10th ed, 1999), p 24).

Another reason proffered in support of the 'postal acceptance rule' is that the offeror could always require actual communication of acceptance (see, again, per Thesiger LJ in the *Household Fire and Carriage Accident Insurance* case, p 223). However, one possible critique of this reason is that it begs the question since the issue is whether or not the offeror should be relieved of having to make the above stipulation in the first instance.

Thirdly, Thesiger LJ, yet again, observed that there would otherwise be 'considerable delay in commercial transactions ... for the acceptor would never be entirely safe in acting upon his acceptance until he had received notice that his letter of acceptance had reached its destination' (see p 224). However, Bramwell LJ (who *dissented* in the present case) adopted a quite contrary view: it would be *equally hard* on the *offeror* who might have made *his or her own* arrangements on the footing that his or her offer had somehow *not* been accepted, particularly given the delay in the offeree's response (which might even be permanent if the letter of acceptance had in fact been lost in the post) (see at p 235).

Finally, Professor Treitel considers the argument to the effect that the offeror ought to be the one 'prejudiced' because he or she had initiated the negotiations by post. However, the learned author is of the view that the negotiations may have in fact been initiated by the *offeree* instead and that the offer may have been made on a form provided by the *offeree* who would have control over the transaction generally (see GH Treitel, *The Law of Contract* (10th ed, 1999), p 25).

In the specifically *local* context, it might be further asked whether or not the arguments against the 'postal acceptance rule' are *supported further* by the *small size* of Singapore itself as well as the related point that there is unlikely to be delay or theft in the context of the efficiency of the postal service. Such conditions were not present in England at the time when the rule was formulated, where the post was a slow and ponderous service that was also given (on occasion at least) to the bane of coach or mail robberies. However, such arguments, whilst not unpersuasive, may need to be confirmed by *more empirical research* on the nature of the postal service in the Singapore context.

2.27 Another thorny issue relates to the question as to whether or not a postal acceptance may be *recalled* by the offeree *prior to* such acceptance reaching the offeror. The arguments are, unfortunately, rather finely balanced.

On the one hand, it may be argued that if the 'postal acceptance rule' applies, then the contract is concluded at the point of posting. Hence, it would be too late for the offeree to unravel the contract already made by purporting to recall his or her acceptance. Indeed, the contract having *already* been formed, there is no longer any 'acceptance' to revoke in the first place. *In addition*, if the offeree were accorded the liberty to revoke his or her acceptance, then that would be tantamount to giving the offeree the best of both worlds: he or she could take advantage of the 'postal acceptance rule' if the circumstances suited him or her and yet be able to revoke his or her offer if the circumstances did not.

On the other hand, however, it may be argued that if the letter of acceptance can be intercepted by faster means and the offeror is unaware that this has in fact taken place, then the offeror has really suffered no prejudice whatsoever. It may be further argued that since the offeror had chosen the post as the medium for negotiations, he or she should accept the risks associated with that particular choice.

For a general discussion of the various pros and cons, see, further, MP Furmston, *Cheshire, Fifoot and Furmston's Law of Contract* (14th ed, 2001), p 59.

2.28 An important issue (particularly in the context of the advent of the new economy) is whether or not the 'postal acceptance rule' applies to communications via *electronic mail (or e-mail)*. This is not an issue to which there is an immediately clear answer. It could, for example, be argued that e-mail is not really a form of instantaneous communications since the information contained therein literally travels in packets across the vast expanse of the Internet. On the other hand, many users do treat e-mail as being, in effect, instantaneous, although this particular argument would appear to be somewhat weak, as it is based on mere perception and nothing more. A stronger argument along similar lines, however, would be that since faxes and telexes are considered to be forms of instantaneous communications, then e-mail ought to fall into the same category (on balance) as well. Further, it could be argued that e-mail is akin to a paper letter, albeit in electronic form. However, this argument does not take into account the criticisms of the 'postal acceptance rule' in the first instance (as to which see paragraph 2.26, above).

If, of course, e-mail is considered a mode of instantaneous communications, then the general rule (as opposed to the 'postal acceptance rule') would apply instead (for the general rule, see paragraphs 2.22–2.23, above). Unfortunately, the fairly recently enacted Electronic Transactions Act (discussed at paragraphs 2.48–2.53, below) does not furnish a definitive answer, although the Act does (as we shall see) provide for the mechanics of ascertainment, as it were.

An excellent article that canvasses the various views in an even-handed manner is S Christensen, 'Formation of Contracts by Email—Is it Just the Same as the Post?' (2001) *Queensland University of Technology*

Law & Justice Journal 22 (this article is available online at the Australian Legal Information Institute website at http://www.austlii.edu.au). The learned author does in fact suggest (at p 38) that 'the general principle of acceptance upon communication should be applied in the first instance and only where the parties have provided otherwise should another time of acceptance be adopted'. Another author has also expressed a similar approach as follows (see J Poole, *Textbook on Contract* (6th ed, 2001), p 53):

> '[G]iven the complexities of individual e-mail systems, it would seem preferable to apply an actual communication (or "receipt" rule), especially because the sender will know if the message has not been sent and can resend it. [T]hat ought to mean that responsibility for getting the message through to its destination should lie with the sender.'

The learned author does, however, point to possible difficulties with such an approach as well. For example, 'if the customer makes the offer, the contract will be formed in the customer's jurisdiction, which may suit the customer but will be too risky for suppliers' (see Poole, ibid, p 53).

(c) Can There be Acceptance by Silence?

2.29 The general proposition appears to be that there *cannot* be acceptance by silence. When viewed from the perspective of an objective approach, this makes good sense for, although there may be the necessary mental assent on the part of the offeree, it has to be communicated tangibly to the offeror. We do not have the power to 'read minds', as it were, hence, the need for objective manifestation of acceptance itself. Looked at in this light, the (English) decision of *Paul Felthouse v Bindley* (1862), which is often cited for this proposition, is not unpersuasive. The case itself was not a 'pure' contract case as such, although the contractual issue was of pivotal importance to the decision of the court itself. In order to make this clearer, a brief rendition of the facts and decision might be in order.

In *Felthouse v Bindley*, the plaintiff uncle had wanted to purchase his nephew's horse and had, at the end of his offer to his nephew, stated, 'If I hear no more about him, I consider the horse mine at thirty pounds, fifteen shillings.' The nephew did not reply to his uncle; more importantly, perhaps, he actually desired to sell the said horse to his uncle because he told the defendant auctioneer (who was selling some of his (the nephew's) property, including the horse concerned) *not* to sell the horse. The defendant auctioneer, however, made a mistake and sold the horse to a third party. The plaintiff uncle then brought an action against the defendant auctioneer in tort for conversion of the horse. The action had to be mounted in tort because there was no contractual nexus as such between the plaintiff and the defendant. However, whether or not the plaintiff had a contractual nexus with his nephew was crucial to the outcome of the case. This was because, in order to be able to sue in the tort of conversion, the plaintiff had first to demonstrate that he or she had either possession or the right to possession of the object alleged to have been the subject of conversion by the defendant. In the latter instance, the title to the object or good would have to be proven. Since the plaintiff did not have actual possession of the horse, it was incumbent on him to prove that he had title to the horse by way of a concluded contract between him and his nephew. Hence, the issue arose as to whether or not there was a concluded contract in view of the fact that the plaintiff's nephew had not actually replied to his (the plaintiff uncle's) offer. Could there, in other words, be an acceptance of the (here, plaintiff's) offer by *silence*?

The court held that the plaintiff had *no* title to sue in conversion as there had been no concluded contract for the sale of the horse as such between him and his nephew. The nephew was not contractually bound as he had not communicated his acceptance to his uncle. Silence was, apparently, insufficient. Hence, the general proposition stated at the outset of the present paragraph. It is interesting to note that although there was in fact *mental assent* by the nephew and a consequent intention on his part to conclude a contract with his uncle (as demonstrated by his instructions to the defendant auctioneer not to sell the horse), this was apparently insufficient as it was not accompanied by the *tangible* (and *objective*) *communication* of such assent (the nephew's mere silence, apparently, not being sufficient in this regard). This, as we have already seen, is wholly consistent with the objective approach to contract law utilised by the courts generally today. It is also consistent with the more general rationale of fairness that offerees should not be *forced or coerced into* entering into a contract merely because they have not gone to the trouble to signal their *non*-acceptance. On the facts of *Felthouse v Bindley*, however, this was not the case (where the nephew was neither forced nor coerced). But this point still does not get around the earlier point made in this paragraph to the effect that some objective manifestation of assent or acceptance is required.

However, Professor Treitel, with his characteristic perceptiveness, has pointed to a number of weaknesses in the reasoning of the court in *Felthouse v Bindley* (see GH Treitel, *The Law of Contract* (10th ed, 1999), pp 30–34). First, he points to the fact that the nephew *did* in fact intend to sell the horse to his uncle, a point we have already referred to above. However, this fact alone is insufficient to get around the problem of silence as there was still a need for the nephew to signal, in an *objective and tangible way*, this intention to sell which would otherwise be 'embedded' in his mind—and his mind only. However, a more persuasive criticism is that the offeror (here, the plaintiff uncle) could (and did) *waive* communication of acceptance of his offer (as embodied in his parting words to his nephew quoted above). An equally persuasive criticism, it is submitted, is the author's argument that it is difficult to draw the line between silence on the one hand and conduct on the other. Indeed, purported 'silence' could, for example, be *implied conduct* and, as we have already seen, conduct can in fact constitute acceptance (see paragraph 2.22, above). Could, for instance, the nephew's instructions to the auctioneer have been construed as a form of acceptance by conduct? But would it have had to have been communicated to his uncle? A clearer case would have involved a course of dealing between the parties concerned. There are also possible issues of *estoppel*, which we will be covering in the next chapter (on 'Consideration'; see Chapter 3).

2.30 It would appear that one *cannot* lay down an inflexible or blanket rule to the effect that silence can *never* constitute acceptance. Everything will depend very much on the specific facts of the case at hand. However, it would seem to be reasonable to state that, as a general starting-point, it is reasonable to presume that silence does not constitute acceptance, unless special circumstances exist to demonstrate otherwise (however, the proof of such special circumstances will not, in the nature of things, be easy). This starting-point is reasonable, not least because in most instances, silence is *ambiguous*. Where ambiguity exists, there can be no valid acceptance, taking into account the very nature and requirements of the concept of acceptance itself (see paragraph 2.20, above). However, having just mentioned that there may be exceptional instances where silence may constitute a valid acceptance in law, what might at least some of these instances look like?

2.31 In the Singapore High Court decision of *Southern Ocean Shipbuilding Co Pte Ltd v Deutsche Bank AG* (1993), Punch Coomaraswamy J construed the decision in *Felthouse v Bindley* as one where the *offeror* had stipulated that silence would constitute acceptance. This is obviously less than attractive for, as already pointed out above, the coercion of the offeree militates against all considerations of fairness (see paragraph 2.29, above). In the present case, although the learned judge was of the view that it could therefore still be possible (under certain circumstances) to have a situation where the *offeree* would be under a duty to communicate his rejection of the offer, this was not the case here (involving, as it did, letters of credit). In his words (at p 697), 'nothing short of an unequivocal reply would suffice'.

In the English Court of Appeal decision of *Re Selectmove Ltd* (1995), the court accepted the general proposition to the effect that acceptance cannot be inferred from mere silence, save in exceptional circumstances. On the facts, the court found that it was in fact the *offeree* who had undertaken that he would communicate with the offeror if he did not desire to conclude the contract. In other words, the *offeree* had *initiated* the possibility of acceptance by *his (the offeree's) silence*—quite unlike the fact situation in *Felthouse v Bindley* itself where it was the *offeror* who was attempting to *impose* on the offeree (there, the nephew) the term of acceptance by silence. Unfortunately, in the present case, the court did not wish to express a 'concluded view' as it held that, in any event, it was the offeree's *representative* (as opposed to the offeree himself) who had so initiated the possibility of acceptance by silence *and* that this particular representative had *no authority* from the offeree to conclude such a contract with the offeror in the first place (see p 478, per Peter Gibson LJ).

(d) There can be No Acceptance by Offeree Ignorant of Offer

2.32 The particular situation in issue here is the *exact converse* of the one just considered (viz whether there can be acceptance by silence). There is, here, a tangible manifestation of acceptance insofar as the *physical act* constituting acceptance is concerned. *Unlike* the situation in *Felthouse v Bindley*, however, there is *not* the requisite *mental assent* inasmuch as the purported 'acceptor' is in fact *ignorant* of the offer itself at the point of acceptance.

2.33 The leading case is the Australian High Court decision of *R v Clarke* (1927). In this case, there was a proclamation stating that a reward was offered 'for such information as shall lead to the arrest and conviction of the person or persons who committed the murders' of two police officers. This was, in effect, an offer of a unilateral contract, with the giving of the requisite information constituting acceptance and the consequent entitlement to the said reward (on the nature of unilateral contracts generally, see paragraphs 2.5 and 2.14, above).

The plaintiff gave the required information and claimed the reward. However, at the time he gave this information, *he was acting to secure his own safety without any thought whatsoever of the reward*. The court held that, as the plaintiff had been ignorant of the reward at the crucial moment (when he gave the information and hence completed the act required for acceptance), he could *not* claim the reward: he had not acted 'on the faith of, in reliance upon' the proclamation (see p 242).

However, it appears (from an English case that was distinguished, *Williams v Cawardine* (1833)) that the *mere knowledge of the offer will suffice even though* the offeree was, at the time of the giving of the requisite information, *also motivated by some other consideration* (eg a guilty conscience). What, therefore, will prevent recovery by the plaintiff is a *total ignorance* (by the offeree) of the offer altogether, at least at the point of acceptance. This *was* the case in *R v Clarke* as, on the facts of the case, the offeree *admitted* that, at the point in time when he furnished the requisite information, he was *not advertent at all* to the offer of the reward. This was therefore a *highly unusual* fact situation which is very unlikely to repeat itself. Indeed, on an evidential level, even if the plaintiff offeree were actually totally ignorant of the offer at the point of acceptance, it is a moot point at best whether there would be the very forthcoming admissions that were present in *R v Clarke* itself.

2.34 A general summary of the general approach embodied in both the present as well as the preceding section would appear to be as follows: there must be, it seems, not only mental assent or an intention to accept the offer (which was not the case in *R v Clarke*) but there must also (and simultaneously) be a tangible manifestation of such mental assent by way of physical acts constituting acceptance and, in this regard, silence will not usually constitute such tangible demonstration, especially having regard to the general fact that silence is usually ambiguous (cf *Felthouse v Bindley*).

Other Principles

Cross-Offers

2.35 This is the rather unusual (albeit not impossible) situation where both parties send offers in identical terms at approximately the same time, so that they actually cross each other in, say, the post. For example, A offers to purchase B's car for $20,000 and B offers to sell his car to A for $20,000 and both offers are put into the post at the same time. Is there a concluded contract? The authority most often cited is the English decision of *Tinn v Hoffmann & Co* (1873), where some judges held that no contract could be concluded in the situation of cross-offers. A leading textbook, however, argues that there is no reason why a concluded contract ought not to be the result as there have been both a coincidence of acts *as well as* an unanimity of mind (see MP Furmston, *Cheshire, Fifoot and Furmston's Law of Contract* (14th ed, 2001), p 61). This particular argument is, it is submitted, persuasive and tends to look at the substance as opposed to mere form.

Certainty and Completeness

2.36 It is axiomatic and commonsensical that before there can be a concluded contract in law, the terms of that agreement must be both certain and complete.

Any gaps can possibly be remedied by either a previous course of dealing between the parties or by trade practice. Gaps may also be filled where a definite formula exists (see, eg the oft-cited English decision of *Brown v Gould* (1972)). However, the law appeared to take a rather curious turn in the House of Lords decision of *Sudbrook Trading Estate v Eggleton* (1983), where it was held that even if one of the parties refused to appoint a valuer as provided for under the terms of the contract, the court could nevertheless treat the agreement as if it were one to pay a reasonable price (the court being, of course, able to ascertain what a reasonable price would be). Nevertheless, in the recent Singapore High Court decision of *Tan Yeow Khoon v Tan Yeow Tat (No 1)* (2000), Rubin J applied the decision in *Sudbrook Trading Estate* and helpfully summarised the law in question, as follows (see p 354):

> 'In my view, the true rule ... ought to be that where there is a contract for sale at a valuation, the court ought to decree specific performance and direct an inquiry to ascertain the price, not only where the parties fail to provide the machinery, but also where the machinery provided had broken down: Provided of course that on the true construction of the contract the agreed machinery was subsidiary to the ascertainment of the proper price and was not of the essence of the agreement. The question whether the prescribed machinery was of the essence of the contract is a matter of construction.'

Gap-filling might also occur by way of *statutory provision* (see, eg the Malaysian decision of *Rajeswari Thedshanamurthy v Kin Nam Realty Development Sdn Bhd* (1983)).

It should also be noted there might, on occasion, be at least partial recovery even where there is no binding agreement as such (see, eg the Singapore decision of *Gold Coin Limited v Tay Kim Wee* (1987), where recovery was recovered by way of *quantum meruit*).

The court may also *imply terms* in order to give effect to the contract concerned; the topic of implied terms will in fact be considered in a later chapter (see, generally, paragraph 5.23 ff). Indeed, it has been observed that 'the fact that a term has to be implied into a contract does not make the contract itself uncertain' (see per Ee Ching Seng JC in the Malaysian decision of *Bandar Raya Developments Berhad v Ang Yoke Lian Construction Sdn Bhd* (1993) at p 298).

2.37 There is another significant area which covers agreements that are signed *'subject to contract'*. The general view would be that no binding contract has been concluded, although the particular facts as well as the language utilised are crucial. If, in other words, the actual facts and/or language merit it, the court will hold that a valid and binding contract has been concluded. There are many relevant cases and the reader is referred to the various textbooks for a fuller discussion (see, eg A Phang, *Cheshire, Fifoot and Furmston's Law of Contract—Second Singapore and Malaysian Edition* (1998), pp 97–100; reference may also be made to the recent Singapore High Court decision of *Thomson Plaza (Pte) Ltd v Liquidators of Yaohan Department Store Singapore Pte Ltd* (2001) at p 445).

2.38 Another relevant (and by no means unimportant) issue is *whether or not there is a duty to negotiate in good faith*. The leading House of Lords decision (which reflects, of course, the existing English position) is *Walford v Miles* (1992). In this case, the plaintiffs wished to purchase the defendants' company as well as premises. To this end, they entered into negotiations (subject to contract) to acquire the said interest. As there was no concluded contract (and see paragraph 2.36, above), the plaintiffs relied, instead, on a *collateral contract*, which they claimed had been formed in the following fashion. As the plaintiffs were aware of a rival who also desired to purchase the defendants' interest, they (the plaintiffs) therefore secured an oral undertaking from one of the defendants that the defendants would, in consideration of a letter of comfort relating to the provision of finance by the plaintiffs and of an undertaking by the plaintiffs to continue negotiations and not to withdraw, terminate and not enter into negotiations with any third party. However, for personal reasons, the defendants ultimately decided to sell their interest to the rival third party. The plaintiffs then brought the present action and the House ruled in favour of the defendants.

Turning to the specific reasoning in the case itself, the plaintiffs' arguments were based on two alternative grounds. First, the plaintiffs relied on the 'lock-out' agreement whereby the defendants agreed not to enter into negotiations with any third party. Secondly, they relied on the 'lock-in' agreement to the effect that it was an implied term of the agreement that the defendants would, 'so long as they continued to desire to sell the said property and shares', 'continue to *negotiate in good faith* with the plaintiff' (emphasis added) (see p 178).

Lord Ackner, who delivered a judgment with which all the other Law Lords agreed, held that the 'lock-out' agreement failed for uncertainty, observing (*inter alia*, at p 183) that '[i]t does not specify for how long it is to last'. He further held that a 'reasonable time' could not be implied so as to save the contract as it would *indirectly impose* a duty to negotiate in good faith upon the defendants. As we shall see in a moment, the House had to consider whether or not there was, in law, a duty to negotiate in good faith, but this time with respect to the 'lock-in' agreement. Indeed, it held that there was *not* a duty to negotiate in good faith. However, before we consider the House's ruling on the validity of the 'lock-in' agreement, we should note that it did not totally disapprove of 'lock-out' agreements; however, sufficient certainty had to exist (this was not the case here). An instance where a 'lock-out' agreement might exist, for instance, is where a specific 'try-out' time for negotiations is agreed upon. The subsequent English Court of Appeal decision of *Pitt v PHH Asset Management Ltd* (1993) in fact held that the 'lock-out' agreement in that particular case was valid.

Lord Ackner was of the view that the 'lock-in' agreement was unenforceable as it lacked the requisite certainty (and see the leading English Court of Appeal decision of *Courtney and Fairbairn Ltd v Tolaini Bros (Hotels) Ltd* (1975)). In particular, there was no term with respect to the duration of the alleged collateral agreement and, secondly, no workable criterion or criteria by which it could be ascertained whether or not there was justification for the termination of the alleged contract to negotiate (especially since any such justification had to be based on the ability to ascertain whether a breakdown in good faith had occurred). There were certainly potential problems of subjectivity in this regard; more specifically, Lord Ackner was of the view that the very nature of the negotiations themselves implied an *adversarial* scenario which itself militated against any concept of good faith and which entitled 'either party ... to withdraw from [the] negotiations, at any time and for any reason' (see p 181).

It is significant that the majority of the New South Wales Court of Appeal in *Coal Cliff Collieries Pty Ltd v Sijehama Pty Ltd* (1991) adopted a different approach. More importantly, perhaps, in addition to the existing academic critique of *Walford v Miles* itself (see, eg P Neill, 'A Key to Lock-Out Agreements?' (1992) 108 *Law Quarterly Review* 405), there are in fact indications that it will be reversed should an opportunity arise: see the extrajudicial views of Lord Steyn in 'Does Legal Formalism Hold Sway in England?' (1996) 49 *Current Legal Problems* 43, p 52 and, by the same author, 'Contract Law: Fulfilling the Reasonable Expectations of Honest Men' (1997) 113 *Law Quarterly Review* 433, pp 438–439. It should be noted that Lord Steyn is (at the time of writing) a member of the House of Lords. Indeed, in the former article just referred to, the learned Law Lord observed (at p 52) as follows:

> 'While I do not argue for the introduction of a general duty of good faith in contract law, it is difficult to see why an express agreement to negotiate in good faith should be invalid. A best endeavours undertaking is apparently valid. That is a most

technical distinction. What the difficulty is I do not know. After all, there is no reason to think that English judges are not capable of trying the issue whether a party has acted in bad faith by pretending to negotiate, thereby causing the other party wasted expenditure.'

In the Singapore High Court decision of *Climax Manufacturing Co Ltd v Colles Paragon Converters (S) Pte Ltd* (2000), Judith Prakash J observed that she had 'no quarrel with the holding in *Walford v Miles*' (see p 256). It should, however, be noted that Prakash J did not expressly endorse the decision in *Walford v Miles* as such although this somewhat controversial decision of the House continues to be good law in England (and, presumably, Singapore) in the meantime.

Artificiality of Offer and Acceptance Rules

2.39 The situation can, understandably, become too involved when the rules pertaining to offer and acceptance are being applied. In particular, fine distinctions as well as artificiality may result.

To take but one illustration in some minimal detail, in the English decision of *Chapelton v Barry Urban District Council* (1940), the plaintiff wished to hire a deck chair at a beach. There was in fact a stack of deck chairs together with a notice which set out, *inter alia*, the rates of hire. However, there was nothing within the notice itself which sought to exclude the liability of the defendants (Barry UDC). The plaintiff duly helped himself to a deckchair. An attendant, who came round later, collected the money from the plaintiff and issued the plaintiff a ticket which contained an exception clause. Unfortunately the canvas in the deckchair gave way and the plaintiff was injured. The issue that arose was whether or not the ticket containing the exception clause was part of the contract in the first instance (for exception clauses generally, see Chapter 6). The court held that it was *not* part of the contract: it had come *after* the contract had been concluded and, hence, the exclusion clause contained therein was ineffective. The contract concerned was made in the following manner. The stack of deckchairs together with the notice constituted the offer which was accepted when the plaintiff picked one deckchair (unfortunately, a defective one) from that pile. Some questions may be posed. Was this process of reasoning rather artificial? If so, was it prompted by the desire to achieve some conception of fairness which the court might have felt was owed to the plaintiff? How does the reasoning in this case compare to that in the *Boots* case (see paragraph 2.7, above) and is there a plausible distinction between these cases?

Another case that is of some interest is that of the English Court of Appeal in *Thornton v Shoe Lane Parking Ltd* (1971), yet another case involving an exception clause. Of particular interest is Lord Denning MR's utilisation of the principles of offer and acceptance (which was not utilised, incidentally, by the other two judges).

2.40 Indeed, sometimes courts have even 'invented' entire contracts in order to do justice in the cases concerned. In this regard, reference may be made to the oft-cited English decisions of *Clarke v The Earl of Dunraven* (1897) and *Shanklin Pier Ltd v Detel Products* (1951), both of which are discussed in MP Furmston, *Cheshire, Fifoot and Furmston's Law of Contract* (14th ed, 2001), pp 69–70 and 70–71, respectively.

2.41 Such artificiality notwithstanding, the utilisation of the concepts of offer and acceptance do, on occasion at least, aid in achieving a just result (see, eg the discussion of the *Chapelton* case in paragraph 2.39, above). Indeed, such a just result may be both just and realistic in a commercial sense: see, eg the Privy Council decision of *The Eurymedon* (1975), which is discussed briefly in paragraph 8.16, below. In delivering the judgment of the majority of the Board in this particular case, Lord Wilberforce in fact observed (at p 167) that 'English law, having committed itself to a rather technical and schematic doctrine of contract, in application takes a practical approach, often at the cost of forcing the facts to fit uneasily into the marked slots of offer, acceptance and consideration'.

Another interesting area where pragmatism appears also to be a major consideration is that pertaining to 'shrink wrap' or (in the case of purchases online) 'clickwrap' licences of software. Indeed, the major issues turn on the concept of incorporation of terms, although suggested solutions do include the 'creation' of a contractual nexus as well, particularly between the copyright holder and the acquirer/intended user (and see generally, eg D Rowland and E Macdonald, *Information Technology Law* (2nd ed, 2000), pp 123–130).

2.42 Indeed, although achieving the balance between the attainment of justice in the individual case on the one hand and not generating excessive artificiality on the other is not easy, this is of course the ideal and certainly is one that should be constantly sought to be achieved by the courts.

Battle of the Forms

2.43 As we have seen, if counter-offers are constantly being made in a particular transaction, no concluded contract can ensue as each counter-offer destroys the original offer and itself constitutes a new offer (and see generally paragraph 2.15, above). This could, unfortunately (and theoretically at least), continue indefinitely with no binding agreement arrived at if neither side relents. It would be, in a sense, a 'perpetual tennis match', except for the fact that both 'players' neither tire nor make a mistake. Such conduct is not without a commercial rationale as each party must be assumed, generally, to desire to obtain a concluded agreement on his or her terms (which would, in the ordinary course of things, be more favourable). Such a battle, utilising the respective parties' own standard forms, is popolary known as the 'battle of the forms'.

2.44 The leading decision is that of the English Court of Appeal in *Butler Machine Tool Co v Ex-Cell-O Corporation (England) Ltd* (1979), where, briefly stated, on 23 May, the plaintiffs/sellers/offerors sent an offer to the defendants/buyers/offerees, which terms included a price variation clause. The defendants then replied (on 27 May), but excluding the said price variation clause. The plaintiffs thereafter sent (on 5 June) the defendants' acknowledgment form, accepting the defendant's order 'on the terms and conditions thereon'. *However*, the plaintiffs' *covering letter* stated that delivery was to be made 'in accordance with our revised quotation of May 23 ...'; *this* quotation by the plaintiffs *did*, of course, contain the price variation clause. There was, in fact, a subsequent rise in costs, and the plaintiffs invoked the price variation clause; not surprisingly, the defendants resisted such a claim.

The court held in favour of the defendants. It held that the defendants'/buyers' order of 27 May was a counter-offer which had been accepted by the plaintiffs/sellers on 5 June on the *defendant's terms* (which, of course, *excluded* the price variation clause). However, the potential difficulty lay in the *covering letter*, the terms of which were in fact *contrary* to the purported acceptance, referring (as it did) to the offer of 23 May which *did* contain the price variation clause. The court explained away this potential difficulty by holding that the covering letter was only intended to *identify* the price and the identity of the machine. If the court had held otherwise, there would then have been (in place of an acceptance) a counter-offer instead—and, hence, no binding contract. In the event, because it indeed held that the covering letter was for the purpose of identification as just mentioned, the court held that there was in fact a binding contract on (as we have seen) the defendants' terms. However, it is suggested that it is not entirely clear that such an explanation by the court is wholly persuasive and there is at least some scope for a contrary argument to be made on the facts of the *Butler* case itself.

2.45 Of even more interest are the *approaches* adopted by the judges in the *Butler Machine Tool* case itself. The traditional approach, as briefly described in the preceding paragraph, deals with the situation when a particular party finally concedes by way of an unqualified acceptance (as opposed to a mere counter-offer). This particular approach was in fact adopted by the *majority* of the court in the case (Lawton and Bridge LJJ). Lord Denning MR, however, whilst endorsing the traditional approach, also advocated a relatively more radical alternative approach as follows (at p 404):

> 'The better way is to look at all the documents passing between the parties—and glean from them, or from the conduct of the parties, whether they have reached agreement on all material points—even though there may be differences between the forms and conditions printed on the back of them.'

The learned Master of the Rolls would here have arrived at the *same* result utilising this alternative approach; he would have found that the document of 5 June was the decisive document, thus making it clear that the contract was concluded and on the defendants' terms (which did *not* include the price variation clause).

However, Lord Denning MR's alternative approach has not really found favour with the courts, probably because it is too vague and productive of unnecessary uncertainty. Whilst it might furnish the court concerned with the necessary flexibility to achieve fairness and justice, this has to be weighed against the possible negative effects insofar as the concepts of rules and predictability are concerned. Indeed, it should be noted that this particular approach was all but rejected in the House of Lords decision of *Gibson v Manchester City Council* (1979). The *Gibson* case was in fact cited with approval by Abdoolcader J in the Malaysian decision of *Diamond Peak Sdn Bhd v Tweedle* (1980). It is significant that the learned judge also cited from Lord Denning MR's judgment in the *Butler Machine Tool* case *but omitted* to mention the learned Master of the Roll's alternative (and more radical) approach.

2.46 However, it should be mentioned that the Singapore Court of Appeal in *Projection Pte Ltd v The Tai Ping Insurance Co Ltd* (2001) did, interestingly enough, endorse the approach adopted by Lord Denning MR in the *Butler Machine Tool* case. It also cited *Chitty on Contracts* (27th ed, 1994), Vol I, paragraph 2-017 in support of this approach. It is reiterated, with respect, however, that Lord Denning's approach is subject to the various difficulties briefly mentioned above, although the Singapore High Court decision of *Overseas Union Insurance Ltd v Turegum Insurance Co* (2001) did in fact cite the *Projection* case with approval on this specific issue (see p 340). But it should be noted that the *Projection* case, being a decision of the Court of Appeal, was in fact binding on the High Court in any event. It should also be noted that the *Overseas Union Insurance* case did refer to the basic principles pertaining to the termination of an offer by rejection and the consequent making of a counter-offer and that this focus on both offers as well as counter-offers does (to some extent at least) suggest the endorsement of the more traditional approach compared to the more radical approach suggested by Lord Denning.

2.47 On a practical level, one general lesson seems to be clear: that one must be very careful about how one responds, particularly if there is a desire to conclude the contract on terms which one desires. That having been said, each situation would depend very much upon the particular circumstances and would include whether or not one might want nevertheless to concede to the other party for the sake of long-term business and goodwill.

Impact of the Electronic Transactions Act

2.48 In 1998, the Singapore Parliament enacted the Electronic Transactions Act (hereafter the 'ETA') (Act No 25 of 1998; now Cap 88, 1999 Rev Ed). This Act is based, in the main, upon the UNCITRAL Model Law on Electronic Commerce as well as the Illinois Electronic Commerce Security and Utah Digital Signature Acts.

2.49 The ETA is particularly apposite to the present chapter because, insofar as the substantive law of contract is concerned, the Act itself touches (if at all) upon issues of *formation*; other contractual issues appear to remain governed by the existing common law of contract. However, even with regard to issue of formation of contract, the ETA touches on these in a very broad (and, arguably, even ambiguous) fashion. Take, for example, section 11 of the ETA, which reads as follows:

> '(1) For the avoidance of doubt, it is declared that in the context of the formation of contracts, unless otherwise agreed by the parties, an offer and the acceptance of an offer may be expressed by means of electronic records.
> (2) Where an electronic record is used in the formation of a contract, that contract shall not be denied validity or enforceability on the sole ground that an electronic record was used for that purpose.'

A close perusal of section 11 above suggests that it is merely clarificatory and does not appear to impact on the substantive Singapore common law of contract as such (note that the term 'electronic record' is defined in section 2 of the ETA itself).

A similar view may be taken of section 12 which states that 'a declaration of intent or other statement' between the contracting parties 'shall not be denied legal effect, validity or enforceability solely on the ground that it is used in the form of an electronic record'.

Further, the rest of that Part of the ETA (Part IV, entitled 'Electronic Contracts') in which the above provisions are found do not appear (save with 'pockets' of possible exceptions) to deal with the substantive law of contract as such. The reason for this is perhaps not too difficult to ascertain. As already mentioned (in paragraph 2.48, above), the ETA was based, in the main, on the UNCITRAL Model Law on Electronic Commerce. This Model Law was not, however, intended or envisaged to be a codification of the substantive laws governing electronic transactions. The goals of the Model Law were much more modest, and as the Guide to Enactment of the UNCITRAL Model Law on Electronic Commerce explains (see paragraph 13 thereof):

> 'The Model Law is intended to provide essential procedures and principles for facilitating the use of modern techniques for recording and communicating information in various types of circumstances. However, it is a "framework" law that does not itself set forth all the rules and regulations that may be necessary to implement those techniques in an enacting State. Moreover, the Model Law is not intended to cover every aspect of the use of electronic commerce. Accordingly, an enacting State may wish to issue regulations to fill in the procedural details for procedures authorized by the Model Law and to take account of the specific, possibly changing, circumstances at play in the enacting State, without compromising the objectives of the Model Law. It is recommended that, should it decide to issue such regulation, an enacting State should give particular attention to the need to maintain the beneficial flexibility of the provisions in the Model Law.'

Such a compromise approach is understandable, given the need to encourage the various countries to adopt the Model Law. However, although a '"framework" law' need not necessarily exclude substantive effects altogether, it is apt to generate at least some measure of vagueness and ambiguity. It then becomes (as we shall see) a rather nice question as to whether or not (in the context of Singapore at least) certain provisions of the ETA impact on the substantive Singapore common law of contract insofar as electronic transactions are concerned.

2.50 However, before proceeding to consider briefly some other salient provisions of the ETA, it is important to note the precise *scope of application* of the ETA, which is embodied in section 4(1), as follows:

> '(1) Parts II [comprising sections 6–9 and entitled 'Electronic Records and Signatures Generally'] and IV [comprising sections 11–15 and entitled 'Electronic Contracts'] shall not apply to any rule of law requiring writing or signatures in any of the following matters:
>
> (a) the creation or execution of a will;
> (b) negotiable instruments;
> (c) the creation, performance or enforcement of an indenture, declaration of trust or power of attorney with the exception of constructive and resulting trusts;
> (d) any contract for the sale or other disposition of immovable property, or any interest in such property;
> (e) the conveyance of immovable property or the transfer of any interest in immovable property;
> (f) documents of title.'

2.51 Turning, now, to certain specific provisions of the ETA that might impact on the substantive law of contract in Singapore, it might be noted that section 13 deals with the issue of attribution whilst section 14 deals with the acknowledgment of receipt by the addressee of the electronic record.

More importantly, perhaps, one should note section 15, which is concerned with the time and place of despatch and receipt of an electronic record. An important issue that arises is whether or not section 15 impacts on the substantive law relating to offer and acceptance. The position is certainly not as clear as it should be. If electronic communications are equated with instantaneous communications (as to which see generally paragraph 2.23, above), the contract will only be concluded when the offeror actually receives the acceptance from the offeree (the 'actual receipt' or general rule). However, as already alluded to above (see paragraph 2.23, above), not all forms of electronic communications may in fact be instantaneous: electronic records may be collated and transmitted in batches, may be saved in computer systems for re-transmission, or may even be forwarded from computer system to computer system only when the recipient requests his or her electronic messages. Looked at in this light, it may well be the case that the 'postal acceptance rule' might be appropriate instead (for this rule, see generally paragraph 2.24 ff, above; see also A Phang and D Seng, 'The Singapore Electronic Transactions Act 1998 and the Proposed Article 2B of the Uniform Commercial Code' (1999) 7 *International Journal of Law and Information Technology* 103 at pp 111–112).

Looking at section 15 closely, a literal reading does not indicate why the provision should not impact on the substantive law of offer and acceptance in the context of electronic transactions. It is suggested that section 15 supplements the existing rules relating to offer and acceptance. The Guide to Enactment of the UNCITRAL Model Law on Electronic Commerce states that section 15 is intended to prescribe legal rules to allow parties to ascertain 'the time and place of receipt of information', which would otherwise be difficult to ascertain if rules that were designed for *non*-electronic communications were applied to electronic communication techniques. However, as just mentioned, such an impact is by way of *supplementary* effect only. As we have seen above, it must first be determined whether or not the general rule or the 'postal acceptance rule' applies; then, and only then, can the guidance in section 15 be utilised.

2.52 The ETA also deals with the concept of a 'signature'. There are extensive provisions relating to electronic records and signatures, digital signatures (and the accompanying encryption process utilising an 'asymmetric cryptosystem' (which is, incidentally, defined in section 2)). For a summary of the different provisions as well as processes, see generally A Phang and D Seng, 'The Singapore Electronic Transactions Act 1998 and the Proposed Article 2B of the Uniform Commercial Code' (1999) 7 *International Journal of Law and Information Technology* 103.

2.53 On the ETA generally, see A Phang and D Seng, 'The Singapore Electronic Transactions Act 1998 and the Proposed Article 2B of the Uniform Commercial Code' (1999) 7 *International Journal of Law and Information Technology* 103 and KH Tan, 'Breaking New Ground: The Electronic Transactions Act 1998' (1999) *Asia Business Law Review* (January 1999) 64.

CHAPTER 3 Consideration

PARAGRAPHS

3.1–3.2 **Introduction**

3.3–3.8 **Definition and Nature**

3.9–3.16 **Consideration Must Not Be Past**

3.17–3.19 **Consideration Must Move From the Promisee**

Consideration Must Be Sufficient

3.20–3.22 The Concept of 'Sufficiency'
3.23–3.27 Intangibles and Moral Obligations
3.28–3.29 Forbearance and Compromise
3.30–3.32 Existing Public or Legal Duty
Existing Contractual Duty
3.33 (1) Existing Contractual Duty Owed to a Third Party
3.34–3.35 (2) Existing Contractual Duty Owed to the Promisor
3.36–3.41 (a) Legal or Factual Benefit (or Detriment)?
3.42–3.43 (b) Consideration and Economic Duress
3.44–3.46 (c) Part Payment of Debts

Promissory Estoppel

3.47 Meaning and Origin
Elements of Promissory Estoppel
3.48–3.49 (1) Clear and Unequivocal Promise
3.50–3.53 (2) Reliance
3.54–3.55 (3) Inequitable to Go Back on Promise
3.56–3.59 (4) Shield, Not Sword
3.60–3.62 Effect of Promissory Estoppel—Suspensory or Extinctive?
3.63–3.66 Promissory Estoppel and Consideration

3.67–3.71 **Reappraising Consideration**

Introduction

3.1 Another element (in addition to the presence of an agreement discussed in Chapter 2) required for the formation of a contract is that of consideration. The main function of this requirement is to place some legal limits on the enforceability of agreements, as it is clearly not possible to enforce *all* agreements. Simply put, consideration is *something that has value in the eyes of the law*. A promise is only enforceable if it is supported by consideration, ie where it is given *in exchange for something of value*.

3.2 It should, however, be noted that there is a class of contracts, viz deeds (which are signed, sealed and delivered) which may be enforced even if the promisee has not provided any consideration for the promises therein. The reasons for this are historical, but the rule is well-established.

Definition and Nature

3.3 Traditionally, consideration is defined in the form of a 'benefit-detriment analysis' as follows (*Currie v Misa* (1875) at p 162):

> 'A valuable consideration, in the sense of the law, may consist either in some right, interest, profit, or benefit accruing to the one party, or some forbearance, detriment, loss, or responsibility given, suffered, or undertaken by the other.'

3.4 For instance, if A bought B's car at the price of $50,000, the consideration for A's purchase is the *benefit* of taking ownership and possession of the car, *or* the *detriment* suffered by B in parting with the car. From B's perspective, the consideration for his delivery of the car is the *benefit* of receiving the purchase price from A, or the *detriment* suffered by A in making the payment. Thus it can be seen that both the concepts of benefit and detriment often (though not always) describe the same thing, depending only on the perspective that is adopted. It should be noted, however, that although benefit and detriment will often coincide, the only valid legal requirement is that either benefit *or* detriment is present. Further, there are some limits to the usefulness of the benefit-detriment analysis in explicating the concept of consideration. If A makes a promise to B in consideration for B's *counter-promise* (ie an executory consideration, see paragraph 3.11, below), such a counter-promise is neither a benefit to A nor a detriment to B insofar as it has not yet been performed. If one argues that A has received the benefit of B's counter-promise, then such an argument is in fact circular in nature as it presumes that B's promise is a benefit, ie it assumes the very conclusion which it has set out to establish.

3.5 An alternative way of defining consideration is to regard it as the *price* for *purchasing* a promise. Applying this definition to the example above, A is said to have *bought* B's act of delivery at the *price* or consideration of $50,000, and conversely, B can be said to have *bought* A's act of payment at a *price* or consideration equivalent to the value of the car.

3.6 It is important to note that a benefit or detriment will only constitute a valid consideration if such benefit or detriment has been *requested* by the promisor. This necessarily follows from the definition that consideration is a value given *in exchange for* a promise. In *Combe v Combe* (1951), the plaintiff sued her ex-husband for breach of a promise to pay her an annual maintenance of £100 after their divorce and argued that she had provided consideration for the promise as she had, in reliance on the promise, refrained from applying to the court for maintenance. The court rejected this argument and held that the promise was not supported by any consideration as the defendant ex-husband had not requested her to so refrain.

3.7 Consideration must be distinguished from a *condition* to which a promise is subject. If A says to B 'I will buy you a car when you attain the age of 21', there is clearly no contract but only a gratuitous promise subject to the fulfilment of a condition. However, the distinction between the two concepts is not always obvious, particularly if the fulfilment of the condition involves the performance of some act by the promisee. This difficulty can be illustrated by the case of *Chappell & Co Ltd v Nestlé Co Ltd* (1960). In that case, the defendant company, Nestlé, offered to sell records of the tune 'Rockin' Shoes' at 1*s*/6*d* each but required each intending purchaser to produce three wrappers of their chocolate bars. The majority of the House of Lords held that the chocolate wrappers formed part of the consideration for the purchase of the records as Nestlé had (indirectly) *benefited* from the receipt of the chocolate wrappers since its chocolate sales might have increased in connection with the promotion. Alternatively, the purchaser had suffered a *detriment* on account of being put to the trouble of purchasing the chocolate bars in order to purchase the record. However, as Viscount Simonds (who disagreed with the majority judges) pointed out, the purchase of the chocolate bars and the purchase of the records were clearly two separate and independent transactions and hence the benefit and/or detriment arising from the former (chocolate) transaction was really irrelevant for purposes of the latter (record) transaction. On this view, it would be artificial to say that the valueless wrappers formed part of the consideration for the sale of the records. Instead, the dissenting judges thought that the correct view was that the requirement for the wrappers was merely a condition which a purchaser had to fulfil before he could purchase the records.

3.8 While the notion of consideration as a value of exchange may appear fairly straight-forward at first blush, it will become obvious, on a closer examination, that it is in fact a complex and difficult subject. The main reason for such difficulty lies in the fact that the concept of consideration, and the related concepts of benefit, detriment and value, are all *legal* (rather than *factual*) in nature. For instance, a promisor may consider that he has in *fact* benefited from the other party's act or promise, but such benefit may still not amount to consideration at *law* if there exists a legal rule or principle that does not recognise such benefit as consideration. In the following sections, we will examine these legal principles and ponder over some of the difficulties arising from their application.

Consideration Must Not Be Past

3.9 If an act is done *prior to* and *independently* of a promise, it cannot be regarded as valid consideration for the promise since it is *not* done *in exchange for* the promise. Hence if A voluntarily washes B's car and thereafter, B, impressed by A's kindness, promises to pay $50 to A, the promise is not enforceable as the 'consideration' provided by A is clearly past. Such past acts are conveniently referred to as 'past consideration' though it should be noted that it is somewhat of a misnomer since such acts do not even amount to consideration in a strictly legal sense.

3.10 Past consideration must be distinguished from *executed* consideration. To understand this distinction, it is necessary to briefly explain the concepts of *executory* and *executed* consideration.

3.11 If A promises to deliver goods to B in a month's time in return for B's promise to make payment on delivery, B's *promise* is a valid consideration for A's promise, even though it is *executory* in nature as it has yet to be performed. Where, however, the consideration is present or has been performed at the time of the contract, such consideration is *executed*. This usually occurs where the executed consideration is also the acceptance of the offer. In *Carlill v Carbolic Smoke Ball Co* (1893) (discussed in paragraph 2.5, above), it was held that the plaintiff had accepted the defendant's unilateral offer by acting in accordance with the defendants' instructions, that is, by taking the smoke ball thrice daily for two weeks. At the same time, this act of acceptance also constituted the necessary consideration for the defendants' promise as the defendants benefited from the sale of the smoke ball while the plaintiff suffered a detriment by using the smoke ball as instructed. Thus the consideration provided by the plaintiff was executed at the time the contract was formed.

3.12 Executed consideration is therefore an act or forbearance undertaken *in return for* the promisor's offer and is distinguishable from a past consideration, which involves an act or forbearance undertaken *without* any reference to the promisor's offer.

3.13 As past consideration is usually undertaken *before* a promise is given, it is tempting to conclude that *all* acts or forbearance occurring *before* the promise are not good consideration for the promise. But this is not always so. In *Pao On* v *Lau Yiu Long* (1980), the plaintiffs had agreed, at the defendants' request, not to sell the shares of a company for a period of one year. Subsequently, the defendants agreed to indemnify the plaintiffs for any loss which the latter might suffer as a result of their earlier promise not to sell the shares. Eventually, the plaintiffs did in fact sustain losses and sued the defendants on the indemnity. In defence, the defendants argued that their promise to indemnify the plaintiffs was not enforceable as it was not supported by consideration; the plaintiffs' promise not to sell the shares was given *before* the indemnity and was therefore past consideration.

3.14 The Privy Council rejected the defendants' argument and held that the indemnity was enforceable. Even though the plaintiffs' promise to hold the shares was given before the defendants' promise to indemnify, it was nonetheless good consideration as it satisfied the following conditions:

(1) the act was done at the promisor's request;
(2) there was an understanding between the parties that the act would be paid for; and
(3) such payment would be enforceable if it had been promised in advance.

3.15 The decision in *Pao On* has been endorsed in Singapore in the case of *Sim Tony v Lim Ah Ghee* (1995). In that case, the plaintiff (Sim) had introduced a friend, Goei, to the defendant for the purposes of some property transactions. The plaintiff argued that he was entitled to a share of the commission arising from the property transaction as consideration for the introduction made by him. However, the court found that the 'consideration' provided by the plaintiff was past consideration since the introduction was made before any promise of payment. Even though the court accepted the exception in *Pao On* (see paragraph 3.14, above), this principle could not be applied to the present case as the evidence showed that the plaintiff had not expected any remuneration for his service at the time of the introduction and hence, the second condition laid down by the Privy Council in *Pao On* was not satisfied.

3.16 While the decision in *Pao On* is often regarded as an exception to the general rule that past consideration is no consideration, it is doubtful if it is indeed a true exception. If payment were contemplated by both parties at the time the act was performed, is it not more accurate to say that the act was executed for a payment to be fixed in the future? If that is correct, then the act performed by the promisee is in fact *executed* (and *not* past) consideration for the promised payment. This case thus demonstrates that it is not necessary to take a strictly chronological view of the events in deciding whether an act is in fact past consideration. Rather, the more important question is to ask whether the preceding act and the subsequent promise are in substance part and parcel of *one and the same transaction*.

Consideration Must Move From the Promisee

3.17 Under this rule, a person can only enforce a promise if the consideration for the promise is furnished by him. Hence, in *Tweddle v Atkinson* (1861), A and B, the respective fathers of a married couple, entered into a contract whereby each undertook to pay a sum of money to C (the husband). Subsequently, C sought to enforce the contract against the estate of B but it was held that he could not, as the consideration for the promise was furnished by A and not by him.

3.18 The decision in *Tweddle v Atkinson* can, however, be explained on a different ground: that C was unable to enforce the contract because he was not a party to the contract (for Privity of Contract, see generally, Chapter 8, below). This raises the interesting question of: what relation do the two rules (that consideration must move from the promisee and that a person who is not a party to a contract cannot sue on the contract) bear to each other? Are they in effect one and the same principle? Or are they separate and distinct principles? One situation in which this issue has arisen is that involving *joint promisees*. For instance, if A makes a promise to B and C collectively but such a promise is only supported by consideration moving from B, will C be allowed to enforce A's promise? The Australian decision of *Coulls v Bagot's Executor and Trustee Co Ltd* (1967) suggests that the answer is yes. In effect, this creates an exception to the general rule that consideration must move from the promisee. More importantly, however, this approach suggests that the doctrines of privity of contract and consideration are really separate and distinct —the former is concerned with *who* is entitled to enforce a contract (ie those privy to the contract), whilst the latter is concerned with what *type* of promises may be enforced (ie that which is supported by consideration but not necessarily furnished by the claimant-promisee). We shall return to consider this issue in paragraphs 8.35–8.37 below.

3.19 One other point to note is that while consideration must move from the promisee, there is *no* requirement for such consideration to move *to the promisor*. Hence, if A promises to pay B $50 if B washes C's car, the consideration provided by B is valid even though it does not confer a direct benefit on A, the promisor.

Consideration Must Be Sufficient

The Concept of 'Sufficiency'

3.20 Consideration must be sufficient but need not be adequate. At first sight, this rule may appear nonsensical as the terms 'sufficient' and 'adequate' are commonly used interchangeably. However, in this context, the term 'sufficient' is in fact synonymous with '*legal* validity'. Hence, the phrase 'consideration must be sufficient' is often explained as requiring that consideration be of some value *in the eyes of the law*. However, once an act or forbearance is deemed sufficient or valid consideration at law, it is *not* necessary to show that such consideration is also *adequate*, ie that it has a value that is comparable to the value of the promise. The rationale for this rule lies in the belief that contracting parties are perfectly able to assess the merits of their own bargains; the role of the court is to ascertain whether a bargain has been made but not whether it is a good bargain. Hence, if A agrees to sell his car to B for $20,000 when it in fact has a market value of $50,000, B's payment of $20,000 is undoubtedly good or sufficient consideration even if it may not be a fair price for A's car. A more extreme example can be found in *Chappell & Co Ltd v Nestlé Co Ltd* (1906) (see paragraph 3.7, above), where it was held that even used chocolates wrappers which were discarded on receipt could constitute sufficient consideration for the sale of records.

3.21 Sometimes, however, a grossly inadequate consideration may indicate that the promisor did not willingly consent to a bargain but was in fact coerced or improperly influenced into such agreement. In such situations, the contract may be set aside on the ground of the duress or undue influence. The relevant legal principles will be considered in Chapter 13, below.

3.22 Since it is essential for consideration to have some value in the eyes of the law, the next question to ask is, how do we identify such 'value'? Clearly, where the consideration in question is given in monetary terms or which by its nature may readily be expressed or measured in economic terms, such consideration is sufficient in the eyes of the law. Hence, in the vast majority of commercial contracts, under which parties furnish consideration in the form of monetary payments, or the provision of goods or services the value of which can readily be measured by reference to market prices, the sufficiency of such consideration is not in doubt. Where such 'price-tags' cannot be readily affixed to the consideration in question, the task of identifying such 'value' becomes much more difficult.

Intangibles and Moral Obligations

3.23 If A makes a promise to B in return for B's love and devotion, the promise is not binding. Natural love and affection, as well as other motives of a purely sentimental nature, are generally not sufficient consideration. Hence, where A promised to transfer a property to B so as to fulfil C's dying wish, it was held that C's desire or motive was not sufficient consideration for A's promise (*Thomas v Thomas* (1842)).

3.24 In the later part of the eighteenth century, there was a school of thought that suggested that where a person had a moral obligation to perform an act, and subsequently promised to perform such act, then such promise would be legally binding as the pre-existing moral obligation was sufficient consideration for the promise. This proposition was firmly rejected by the court in *Eastwood v Kenyon* (1840). In that case, the plaintiff, who was the guardian of the defendant's wife, Sarah (when she was an infant), had voluntarily incurred expenses for her benefit. Subsequently, upon the defendant's marriage to Sarah, he promised to reimburse the plaintiff for these expenses. The plaintiff sued the defendant on his promise. The action failed as there was insufficient consideration for the defendant's promise. The expenses were incurred by the plaintiff prior to and independently of the defendant's promise and was thus clearly past consideration. The plaintiff's argument that the defendant's moral obligation to reimburse him was in itself good consideration for his promise also failed. The reason is obvious: if the mere existence of a moral obligation were sufficient consideration, then every promise would, without more, be enforceable as the mere creation of the promise places the promisor under a moral obligation to fulfil such promise. Indeed, if this were correct, such a proposition would abrogate the entire doctrine of consideration.

3.25 *Eastwood v Kenyon* demonstrated that the *promisor's* moral obligation to do something was not in itself sufficient consideration for his subsequent promise to perform that act. What would the position be if a promise were supported by the *promisee's* promise to do an act which he would in any event be morally obliged to do? In *White v Bluett* (1853), a father, who was wearied by his son's frequent complaints that he had distributed his assets unfairly among his children, agreed to release his son from the latter's obligation under a promissory note (which contains the son's promise to pay a specific sum to his father) if he would cease complaining. It was held that the father was not bound by his promise; it was his right to distribute the property as he wished and hence the son had no right to complain. In ceasing his complaints, the son was only doing what he was morally obliged to do and that was no consideration for his father's promise.

3.26 *White v Bluett* may be contrasted with *Hamer v Sidway* (1891), an American decision in which an uncle promised his nephew US$5,000 if he would refrain from drinking, smoking, gambling and swearing until he attained majority at age 21. This promise was held to be enforceable because the court found that the nephew had suffered a detriment in giving up his lawful freedom to drink, smoke, swear and gamble and such detriment constituted good consideration for the uncle's promise. If this reasoning were accepted, could it not equally be argued that the son in *White v Bluett* had furnished consideration by giving up his lawful freedom to complain?

3.27 While the above two cases appear to be irreconciliable, some observations are worth noting. Firstly, *White v Bluett* may be defended on the ground of *policy*—that one should not be encouraged to extort favourable bargains by misbehaving (or threatening to misbehave). In *Hamer v Sidway*, however, there was no evidence that the nephew was taking advantage of his own bad habits to extract any advantage from his uncle. On the contrary, the agreement appeared to have been initiated by the uncle with a view to encourage him to quit these habits. Secondly, however, the correctness of *White v Bluett* must now be doubted in the light of the Court of Appeal's decision in *Williams v Roffey Bros & Nicholls (Contractors) Ltd* (1991). As we shall see in paragraphs 3.37–3.38 below, this case suggests that a *practical* or *factual* benefit enjoyed by the promisor is sufficient to constitute consideration. Following this view, can it not be said that the father in *White v Bluett* had in fact *benefited* from a more harmonious relationship with his son after the latter ceased to complain and hence received valuable consideration for his promise? (See E McKendrick, *Contract Law* (4th ed, 2000), pp 85–86.) Such reasoning would be consistent with the approach taken in *Hamer v Sidway*, where the nephew had in fact suffered a detriment by giving up his preferred lifestyle. Indeed, it is no surprise that *Williams v Roffey Bros* should cast doubt on the correctness of *White v Bluett* as the very reasoning employed in *Williams v Roffey Bros* threatens to dismantle the entire doctrine of consideration. A more detailed consideration of the difficulties generated by the decision in *Williams v Roffey Bros* is contained in paragraphs 3.39–3.41 below.

Forbearance and Compromise

3.28 Where a party has a claim against another, he may agree to *refrain* from enforcing the claim in exchange for a promise given by the latter and such an agreement is described as a *forbearance*. Similarly, the parties to a dispute may consider it more beneficial to enter into a *compromise* whereby one party agrees to *surrender* his claim in consideration for the other's payment or other promises. The clear advantage of such agreements is the avoidance of expending precious resources on costly and time-consuming litigation to enforce the claims. In both instances, the promisor's agreement not to pursue a claim is good consideration for the promises given in exchange.

3.29 Where a person promised not to enforce an *invalid* claim and it is shown that he *knew* such claim to be invalid at the time of his promise, such forbearance is no consideration. This occurred in *Wade v Simeon* (1846), where the court found that there was no consideration because the surrender of a groundless claim is neither a benefit to the promisee nor a detriment to the promisor. However, it is not necessary for a promisor relying on his act of forebearance or surrender to show that he has given up a valid claim. It is sufficient if he could establish, firstly, that he has reasonable grounds for his claim; and secondly, that he honestly believes that he has a fair chance of success and finally, that he has not concealed from the other party any fact which he knew may affect the validity of the claim (see *Callisher v Bischoffsheim* (1870)). This makes practical sense as the vast majority of compromises and settlements relate to *doubtful* claims the validity of which could not be ascertained without a complete trial. To insist that only the forbearance to sue on a valid claim would constitute good consideration would defeat the very object of a compromise: avoiding litigation. In effect, this means that the consideration furnished by the promisor who forbears to sue lies *not* in giving up a valid claim, but rather, in giving up a *right to claim* against the promisee.

Existing Public or Legal Duty

3.30 In general, where A makes a promise to B in consideration for B's promise to do something which B is in any event legally obliged to do, B's promise is not good consideration. Again, the rationale for this rule appears to be that an act which is obliged by law is neither a benefit to the promisee nor a detriment to the promisor. Alternatively, it has been said that such a rule is necessary to prevent public officers from extorting money for services which they were legally bound to render. In *Collins v Godfrey*

(1831), the plaintiff was subpoenaed to testify at a trial in which the defendant was a litigant and he alleged that the defendant had promised to pay him for testifying on the defendant's behalf. The court held that the plaintiff had provided no consideration for the defendant's promise since a subpoenaed witness was in any event under a legal duty to give evidence in court.

3.31 Where the act or conduct in question *exceeds* the requirements of the legal duty, such act or conduct may constitute good consideration. In *Glasbrook Bros v Glamorgan County Council* (1925), the appellant mining company agreed to pay the respondent police authority for garrisoning a troop of police at its mine to protect workers returning to work during a strike. Subsequently, the appellant refused to make the promised payment and argued that the police authority had provided no consideration for the promise as they were merely discharging their legal duty to protect life and property. This argument was rejected by the House of Lords (but by a close decision of 3-2). While the police were legally bound to provide protection, in this case they had done more than what was legally required of them by providing a stationary force instead of a mobile force, which in their view would have been sufficient for the purposes of the appellants.

3.32 A similar reasoning was adopted in *Ward v Byham* (1956). In this case, the father of an illegitimate child agreed to pay her mother a weekly allowance of £1 for looking after the child on the condition that she would be 'well looked after and happy'. The mother sought to enforce the promise when the father stopped making payments. It was argued in defence that no consideration had been provided for the father's promise since the mother was in any event bound to maintain the child under section 42 of the National Assistance Act 1948 (UK). The English Court of Appeal rejected this argument. A majority of the appeal judges found that the care given by the mother in ensuring that the child is 'well looked after and happy' had exceeded the statutory requirements and had therefore furnished consideration for the father's promise. The majority's reasoning in this regard is, however, open to criticism. In substance, the mother's promise to look after her child in this case was not significantly different from the son's promise not to complain in *White v Bluett* (see paragraph 3.25, above), yet, one promise constituted consideration but the other did not. Indeed, the majority's approach in *Ward v Byham* is evidence of how at times judges are willing to artificially invent consideration just so that the promise can, on occasion, be upheld. Sometimes, such cases have led commentators to question the usefulness of, and even the necessity for, consideration as an element of contract formation (see, eg A Phang, 'Consideration at Crossroads' (1991) 107 *Law Quarterly Review* 21). We shall return to briefly consider this issue at the end of this chapter (see paragraphs 3.67–3.71, below).

Existing Contractual Duty

(1) *Existing Contractual Duty Owed to a Third Party*

3.33 The performance of, or the promise to perform, an existing contractual duty owed to a *third party* is sufficient consideration for a promise given in exchange. In *Scotson v Pegg* (1861), A contracted to deliver goods to X or his nominee, and X nominated B to accept the goods. Subsequently, B agreed with A that if A would deliver the same goods to B, B would unload them from the ship at a fixed rate. B did not honour his promise and A sued for breach of contract. B contended that A had provided no consideration because in delivering the goods, it was merely performing its existing contractual duty to X. The court disagreed and held that A provided real consideration for B's promise when it performed its existing contractual duty to X. When A promised B to perform an existing contractual duty which A owed to X, such a promise benefits B by conferring on B the personal right to enforce that promise. This principle has since been affirmed by the Privy Council in *New Zealand Shipping Co Ltd v A Satterwaite, The Eurymedon* (1975) (see below, paragraph 8.16). In *Pao On v Lau Yiu Long* (1980) (see paragraph 3.13, above), the Privy Council extended the principle to *promises to perform* existing contractual duties to third parties (as opposed to the actual performance of such duties).

(2) *Existing Contractual Duty Owed to the Promisor*

3.34 A different analysis is called for in the case where the alleged consideration lies in the performance of, or a promise to perform, an existing contractual duty owed to the *promisor*. The traditional view is that such a promise is generally not regarded as sufficient consideration as the promisor derives no benefit from a performance to which he was already entitled and likewise, the promisee suffers no detriment for doing that which he was already bound to do. *Stilk v Myrick* (1809) is often cited as the leading authority for this proposition. In this case, the captain of a ship, unable to replace two crewmen who had deserted in the course of a voyage, promised to divide the wages of the deserters equally among the rest of the crew if they would work the ship safely back to London. One of the remaining seamen brought an action to enforce this promise after the completion of the voyage. The claim was rejected by the court on the ground that the seamen were already bound, under the terms of their existing contracts, to complete the voyage and hence a subsequent promise to do the same was no consideration for the captain's promise.

3.35 It is clear, however, that any performance which is *over and above* the promisee's existing contractual duty is sufficient consideration for a promise given in exchange. In *Hartley v Ponsonby* (1857), the remaining crewmen were also promised additional wages to continue on a voyage which had become too hazardous after the desertion of 17 (out of a total of 36) sailors. The promise was held to be binding because in such circumstances, the remaining crew were no longer bound to complete the voyage and hence, in agreeing to do so, they had done more than what was required under their original contractual undertakings.

(a) Legal or Factual Benefit (or Detriment)?

3.36 It will only take a moment of reflection to see that in a case such as *Stilk v Myrick*, even though the sailors were discharging an existing contractual obligation, their agreement to sail the ship back did in *fact* benefit the defendant. If the sailors had decided to breach their contractual undertaking and discontinue the voyage, the captain of the ship could in theory sue the sailors for breach but in practice, the value of such action would be minimal compared to the loss which could result from a delayed or abandoned voyage. The avoidance of the expense and inconvenience of hiring another crew and (if such crew were not readily available) the losses resulting from a delayed or abandoned voyage was undoubtedly a *factual* benefit which the captain had enjoyed as a result of the crew's promise to bring the ship back to the destined port. Why should not such factual benefits suffice as consideration?

3.37 This issue arose in the controversial case of *Williams v Roffey Bros & Nicholls (Contractors) Ltd* (1991). The defendants (Roffey Bros) were building contractors who were awarded a contract to refurbish 27 flats. For that purpose, they engaged the plaintiff (Williams) as sub-contractor to carry out the carpentry work for a total price of £20,000. Shortly after commencing work, the plaintiff got into financial difficulty because the agreed price of £20,000 was too low to enable him to carry out the work satisfactorily and this was aggravated by the slow progress of the work due to his own inadequate supervision. The defendants were aware of the plaintiff's problems and were concerned that if the plaintiff did not complete the carpentry work on time, that could in turn render the defendants liable for delay damages under the main contract. After some negotiation, the defendants agreed to pay the plaintiff an *additional* sum of £10,300 at the rate of £575 for each flat completed. Thereafter, the plaintiff resumed work and substantially completed the work on eight more units but received only one further payment of £1,500 from the defendants. The plaintiff then ceased work and brought an action to enforce the defendants' promise of additional payment.

3.38 Relying on *Stilk v Myrick*, the defendants resisted the plaintiff's claim on the ground that he had not furnished any consideration for the defendants' promise of additional payments—his promise to complete the carpentry work was no consideration as he was already bound to do so under the original sub-contract. However, all three judges of the English Court of Appeal rejected this argument. Clearly, the defendants had agreed to the additional payment because they considered it advantageous to do so. The defendants stood to enjoy *practical* or *factual* benefit from the plaintiff's promise to complete the work on time such as avoiding the need to engage another sub-contractor and, more importantly, the avoidance of liability for delay damages under the main contract. Such practical or factual benefits constituted sufficient consideration for the defendants' promise. The result of this decision is that the promise to perform an existing contractual duty owed to the promisor may constitute sufficient consideration if the promisor derived 'practical benefits' from the performance. This position was summarised by Glidewell LJ (at pp 15– 16):

> '(i) if A has entered into a contract with B to do work for, or to supply goods or services to, B in return for payment by B; and
>
> (ii) at some stage before A has completely performed his obligations under the contract B has reason to doubt whether A will, or will be able to, complete his side of the bargain; and
>
> (iii) B thereupon promises A an additional payment in return for A's promise to perform his contractual obligations on time; and
>
> (iv) as a result of giving his promise, B obtains in practice a benefit, or obviates a disbenefit; and
>
> (v) B's promise is not given as a result of economic duress or fraud on the part of A; then
>
> (vi) the benefit to B is capable of being consideration for B's promise, so that the promise will be legally binding.'

3.39 By accepting that 'practical' benefits could constitute consideration, *Williams v Roffey* marks a significant departure from the traditional position represented by *Stilk v Myrick*. As mentioned above, the defendant in *Stilk v Myrick* had also benefited from the crew's promise to sail the vessel back to the destined port, yet such benefit was not held to be sufficient consideration. It is therefore clear that these two decisions are (despite the adamant denials of the appeal judges in *Williams v Roffey* in fact inconsistent with each other. The appeal of the decision in *Williams v Roffey* lies mainly in the fact that it permits a broader and more flexible understanding of the concept of consideration; this appears to accord with the commercial reality that parties do often agree to pay more for the same goods or services (or conversely, render more services for the same price) where they consider it beneficial to do so. If such contractual variations are entered into *voluntarily*, why should not the law uphold such bargains? Ironically, the flexibility afforded by this broad approach is also its weakness. If the slightest benefit could constitute consideration, then it would become virtually impossible to impeach the validity of a modification of a contract for lack of consideration, since the promisor would *almost always* benefit more from the promisee's continued performance than from the breach of his contractual duty. In that case, the requirement for consideration ceases to have a meaningful role in defining the kinds of agreements which are enforceable at law. At present, the inconsistency between *Stilk v Myrick* and *Williams v Roffey* has yet to be satisfactorily resolved and hence substantial uncertainty still surrounds the law in this regard.

3.40 Unfortunately, the position in Singapore is equally unsettled. In *Sea-Land Service Inc v Cheong Fook Chee Vincent* (1994), the defendant employer issued a 30-day termination notice to the plaintiff employee and advised the latter that his severance benefit included an enhanced severance payment of $14,340. However, upon completing the last month of his service, the plaintiff was told by the defendants that he was not in fact entitled to the enhanced severance payment but was offered an *ex gratia* allowance of $4,780 instead. The plaintiff brought an action to enforce the payment of the enhanced severance payment. At trial, the main issue was whether the plaintiff's performance of his existing contractual duty —by continuing in his employment until the expiry of the termination notice—was good consideration for the defendants' promise. Relying on *Williams v Roffey*, the plaintiff argued that the defendants had in fact benefited from his services during the last month of his employment and that constituted real consideration for the promised payment. The Court of Appeal disagreed. In its view, *Williams v Roffey* was a 'limited exception' (at p 634) which would only apply if the defendants obtained a factual or a practical benefit from the plaintiff's performance. In this case, the defendants derived no benefit from the plaintiff's work in the last month because a company would only retrench employees who were no longer essential to its operations and hence the value of such employee's work in the final month was at best minimal. The Court of Appeal's approach in this case suggests that the local courts may prefer a *narrower* understanding of the concept of 'practical benefits', such that only a *real* and *significant* benefit (and not just *any* benefit) would constitute sufficient consideration under the principle established in *Williams v Roffey*. (See, generally, J Carter, A Phang and J Poole, 'Reactions to Williams v Roffey' (1995) 8 *Journal of Contract Law* 248.)

3.41 However, *Williams v Roffey* was applied in the more recent local case of *Sharon Global Solutions Pte Ltd v LG International (Singapore) Pte Ltd* (2001) (see paragraph 13.20, below). In this case, the defendant agreed to make additional payments to the plaintiff in exchange for the latter's promise to deliver goods, which it was already bound to do under its existing contract with the defendant. The Singapore High Court enforced the defendant's promise as it found that the defendant had benefited from the timely delivery of the goods and avoided 'negative commercial consequences' such as the damage to its reputation arising from its failure to meet its customers' orders. In applying the principles in *Williams v Roffey*, the court neither referred to the Court of Appeal's observations in *Sea-Land Service Inc v Cheong Fook Chee Vincent* (see paragraph 3.40, above) nor attempted to reconcile this approach with that in *Stilk v Myrick*. As discussed in paragraph 3.39 above, if the principles in *Williams v Roffey* applied whenever the promisor could be said to have factually benefited from the promisee's performance of his existing contractual obligation, then *Williams v Roffey* comes perilously close to displacing the entire doctrine of consideration by shifting the focus of the enquiry from 'has the promisee provided something that has value *in the eyes of the law?*' to 'did the promisor *in fact* benefit from the promisee's promise?'

(b) Consideration and Economic Duress

3.42 In cases such as *Stilk v Myrick* and *Williams v Roffey*, the central question is whether the modification of an existing contract should be enforced.

However, there is no simple answer to this question because of the tension between two legitimate concerns. On the one hand, one might reasonably take the view that a modification which has been freely agreed to by contracting parties should be upheld even in the absence of consideration. If one party should encounter problems in the performance of his contractual obligations, there is no reason why he should not attempt to resolve his problems by negotiating with the counter-party for a modification or relaxation of the contract terms. In fact, the law should encourage the use of such self-help methods which are generally more time and cost effective than formal dispute resolution processes such as litigation. On the other hand, however, there is the concern that such modification might have been the result of one party's exploitation of the other party's weaker bargaining position. Thus it has been suggested that the correct explanation for the decision in *Stilk v Myrick* was that the bargain for additional pay was not upheld so as to discourage seamen from holding their employer to ransom by threatening to breach their contracts and aggravating the perils of seafaring. According to this view, *Stilk v Myrick* is thus a case in which the court guarded against such risks by insisting on the presence of consideration, the assumption being that where fresh consideration for the variation of contract has been furnished, the agreement is less likely the result of duress or coercion.

3.43 Some commentators have, however, argued that it is no longer necessary to employ the concept of consideration to curb such risks, as this function is now more aptly performed by the doctrine of economic duress (see Chapter 13 and, in particular, paragraphs 13.21–13.22, below; see R Halson, 'Sailors, Sub-Contractors and Consideration' (1990) 106 *Law Quarterly Review* 183 and A Phang, 'Whither Economic Duress? Reflections on Two Recent Cases' (1990) 53 *Modern Law Review* 107 and A Phang, 'Consideration at the Crossroads' (1991) 107 *Law Quarterly Review* 21). Applying this line of reasoning, the validity of a contract modification does not depend on the presence or absence of consideration. Instead, such modification is valid even in the absence of fresh consideration as long as it can be shown that both parties *intended* to be bound by the modification and that no improper pressure has been applied on the promisor in the bargaining process. It is submitted that there is considerable force in this line of reasoning which, if accepted, will bring the law closer to commercial reality (see, further, paragraphs 13.21–13.22, below).

(c) Part Payments of Debts

3.44 A owes B $1,000. A pays $700 to B which B accepts as a complete discharge of A's debt. Can B subsequently sue A for the unpaid balance of $300? In this situation, A does not rely on B's promise to seek additional remuneration (as was the case in *Stilk v Myrick*) but to avoid part of his liability. The general rule, commonly known as the rule in *Pinnel's* case (1602), is that the payment of a lesser sum is not a complete satisfaction of the debt. The rationale appears to be that a promisor is not bound by his promise to forego the unpaid portion of the debt as the promisee has not furnished any consideration for the promise; in making part payment, the promisee has done no more than what he is contractually bound to do. It follows that in the illustration above, B may insist on the full repayment of A's debt notwithstanding his promise to the contrary. The rule in *Pinnel's* case was subsequently affirmed by the House of Lords in *Foakes v Beer* (1884). In that case, F owed B a sum of £2,090 and it was agreed that B would not enforce the debt if F paid £500 upfront and the balance in instalments. F eventually repaid the principal sum in full but B then claimed for the interest which had accrued on the debt. The House of Lords held, applying the rule in *Pinnel's* case, that B was entitled to the interest.

3.45 However, the rule in *Pinnel's* case does not apply where the debtor has provided *something different* to the creditor. Thus, if A owed B $1,000 and B agreed to treat the debt as discharged in full if A washed B's car, the rule in *Pinnel's* case would have no application since A would have furnished consideration for B's promise to forgive the debt. Similarly, B's promise would be binding if A agreed to make a partial repayment of $500 *and* wash B's car, but not if A merely promised to repay the sum of $500. It has also been held that a partial repayment of a debt at a different place or on an earlier date would suffice as fresh consideration for the creditor's promise. In these cases, even a very slight change to the debtor's obligation constitutes sufficient consideration because the court generally respects the parties' freedom to contract and does not inquire into their motives. There is some uncertainty as to whether a partial payment by way of *cheque* should be differentiated from that made in cash. In England, the Court of Appeal had declined to draw a distinction between cheque and cash payments such that if a debtor furnished a smaller payment by way of a cheque, the rule in *Pinnel's* case would similarly apply (*D&C Builders Ltd v Rees* (1966), see paragraph 3.55, below). In Singapore, the position is unclear as some cases decided *before D&C Builders Ltd v Rees* have held that smaller payments by cheques are sufficient to discharge the original debts. However, as cheques are generally of less security than cash in that they are merely conditional payments until they are honoured, it would seem more logical to treat a partial payment by way of cheque no differently from that made in cash (and see, generally, A Phang, *Cheshire, Fifoot and Furmston's Law of Contract—Second Singapore and Malaysia Edition* (1998) at p 189).

3.46 The rule in *Pinnel's* case has been criticised principally on the ground that it runs counter to the ordinary expectations of the business community. As Lord Blackburn observed in *Foakes v Beer*: 'all men of business, whether merchants or tradesmen, do every day recognise and act on the ground that prompt payment of a part of their demand may be more beneficial to them than to insist on their rights and enforce payment of the whole. Even where the debtor is perfectly solvent, and sure to pay at last, this often is so. Where the credit of the debtor is doubtful it must be more so' (at p 622). Indeed, if *Williams v Roffey* were correct in recognising practical or factual benefits as sufficient consideration, then should not the *practical benefit* of receiving a partial payment be accepted as good consideration for the promise to forgive the whole debt? In *Re Selectmove Ltd* (1995), Peter Gibson LJ (in the English Court of Appeal) acknowledged the force of this argument but nonetheless concluded that the principle in *Williams v Roffey* could not be extended to situations involving partial payment of debts as that would in effect be overruling the House of Lords' decision in *Foakes v Beer*, which the Court of Appeal had no power to do. But while the decision correctly adhered to the doctrine of precedent, the unfortunate result is that the inconsistency between *Williams v Roffey* and *Foakes v Beer* remains unresolved. In principle, it is difficult to see why the law should differentiate between these two situations as the practical benefits which a promisor may derive from the receipt of part payment are no less real than the benefits of receiving promised performance (see J Carter, A Phang and J Poole, 'Reactions to Williams v Roffey' (1995) 8 *Journal of Contract Law* 248).

Yet another significant exception to the rule in *Pinnel's* case is often found in the application of the doctrine of *promissory estoppel*, to which we will now turn.

Promissory Estoppel

Meaning and Origin

3.47 In essence, the doctrine of promissory estoppel prevents a person from going back on his word when it would be inequitable to do so. Where the doctrine applies, the result is that the promise is enforced even where such promise is *not* supported by consideration. This doctrine is often said to have originated from Denning J's (as he then was) *obiter dicta* in *Central London Property Trust Ltd v High Trees House Ltd* (1947). That case concerned a 99-year lease granted by the plaintiffs to the defendants in 1937 for a block of flats at a rent of £2,500 per year. In January 1940, the plaintiffs agreed to reduce the rent to £1,250 as the defendants were encountering difficulty securing sub-tenants for the flats owing to the war conditions then prevailing and the defendants thereafter paid the reduced rent. However, the flats were again fully let by early 1945 and the plaintiffs sought to restore the rent to £2,500 from mid-1945. Denning J held that the plaintiffs were entitled to do so as the reduced rent was intended to apply only while the adverse conditions persisted. More importantly, however, Denning J observed that if the plaintiffs had claimed for the full rent for the period *prior to* 1945, they would have been *estopped* from doing so as they could not go back on a promise that was intended to be binding and which was in fact relied upon by the defendants. The result, as stated by Denning J in the *High Trees* case (at p 135), is that 'a promise to accept a smaller sum in discharge of a larger sum, if acted upon, is binding notwithstanding the absence of consideration'.

Elements of Promissory Estoppel

Although significant uncertainty still surrounds the scope and effect of the doctrine of promissory estoppel, there is now sufficient judicial recognition of this doctrine as well as its key constituent elements.

(1) *Clear and Unequivocal Promise*

3.48 First, the promisor must have made a *clear and unequivocal promise* which is intended to affect the future conduct of the parties' relationship. Obviously, the clearer the promise, the more likely it is that the promisee will act in reliance on it and render it inequitable for the promisor to retract his promise. Another reason given for this requirement is that, since the application of promissory estoppel very often creates the same *effect* as that of a *variation* of a contractual obligation, then it must necessarily be in terms no less certain than that which is required for contractual variation (which in turn requires the same degree of certainty as that required for contract formation; see paragraph 2.36, above). For the same reason, whether a promise is sufficiently certain so as to have induced the promisee to rely on it is judged *objectively*, that is, it is sufficient if a promisee could *reasonably* have been so induced in the circumstances. Thus, if A contractually undertook to pay B in Nigerian pounds and B subsequently agreed that 'payment can be made in sterling', that was construed merely as an agreement to accept payment in a *different currency*, but did *not* amount to an unequivocal promise to accept a *lower price*. Thus, when the sterling was devalued by up to 15% as against the Nigerian pound, B was not estopped from claiming the full value of the purchase price as measured in Nigerian pounds (see *Woodhouse Ltd v Nigerian Produce Ltd* (1972)).

3.49 Given the requirement for certainty, it is not surprising that silence or mere inaction would not generally constitute a clear promise for the purposes of promissory estoppel. Thus, a mere failure to enforce a contractual obligation does not amount to a promise to abandon such right of enforcement. However, that does not mean that the promise must always be express, as such promise could be *implied* by words or conduct. In the leading House of Lords decision in *Hughes v Metropolitan Railway Company* (1877), a landlord gave his tenant six months' notice to repair the premises but thereafter, the parties commenced negotiations for the sale of the lease to the landlords. The tenant had indicated that he would not effect the repairs whilst negotiations continued. Soon after, the negotiations broke down and the landlord sought to forfeit the lease on account of the tenant's failure to repair on the expiry of six months from the date of the original notice. It was held that he could not do so as it could reasonably be inferred from his conduct in entering into negotiations with the tenant that the notice period would not run while the negotiations continued and would only continue to run after the negotiations ended.

(2) *Reliance*

3.50 The second requirement that needs to be satisfied is that the promisee must have acted in reliance on the promise. Generally, such reliance is evidenced by the promisee's *change of position* on the faith of the promise, that is, by doing or omitting to do something which he would otherwise not have done or omitted to do.

3.51 A number of cases suggest that it is not sufficient that the promisee merely alters his course of action in reliance on the promise made, but that he must also have suffered some *detriment* or *disadvantage* as a result. The rationale for this suggestion is that only where the promisee has suffered such detriment would it be inequitable for the promisor to go back on his word (see paragraphs 3.54–3.55, below). This was the case in *Hughes v Metropolitan Railway Company* (1877), where the tenant had lost time to effect repairs as a consequence of relying on the landlord's implied promise.

3.52 However, the prevailing view in English law appears to be that there is no such requirement for detrimental reliance. In *W J Alan & Co Ltd v El Nasr Export and Import Co* (1972), Lord Denning rejected the suggestion that a promisee must adduce evidence of detriment in order to invoke promissory estoppel; all he needed to demonstrate was that he had, in reliance on the promise, acted differently from what he otherwise would have done. In the same vein, Goff J (as he then was) made the following observations in the English High Court decision of *Société Italo-Belge pour le Commerce et l'Industrie SA v Palm and Vegetable Oils (Malaysia) Sdn Bhd, The Post Chaser* (1982) (at p 27):

> 'To establish such inequity, it is not necessary to show detriment; indeed, the representee may have benefited from the representation, and yet it may be inequitable, at least without reasonable notice, for the representor to enforce his legal rights. Take the facts of [the *High Trees* case] … The representation was by a lessor to the effect that he would be content to accept a reduced rent. In such a case, although the lessee has benefited from the reduction in rent, it may well be inequitable for the lessor to insist on his legal right to the unpaid rent, because the lessee has conducted his affairs on the basis that he would only have to pay rent at the lower rate.'

3.53 Notwithstanding the English position discussed above, it would seem that detrimental reliance is an essential element of promissory estoppel in Singapore. In *Fu Loong Lithographer Pte Ltd v Mun Hean Realty Pte Ltd* (1989), the defendant seller contracted to sell a part of a factory to the plaintiff buyer. Although the sale agreement specified 31 December 1983 as the completion date, the transaction was only completed at the end of 1985. There was, however, evidence to show that neither party had seriously intended to complete on 31 December 1983 as that date was only arbitrarily selected for the purpose of fulfilling the relevant statutory requirement. In fact, the plaintiffs had, by their words and conduct, assured the defendants that they did not consider the stated date binding and such assurance induced the defendant to embark on some development works on the property which they would not otherwise have done if they had been required to meet the 31 December 1983 deadline. Subsequently, the plaintiff sued the defendant for liquidated damages arising from the delay in completion and the defendants pleaded promissory estoppel in defence. The court held that a plea of promissory estoppel could be made out on these facts as the defendant had suffered detriment in undertaking the developmental works in the belief that such work would not be impeded by the need to meet the stated deadline. In arriving at this conclusion, the court (citing G Spencer Bower and A Turner, *The Law Relating to Estoppel By Representation* (3rd ed, 1977)) defined detriment as the '*injustice* to the promisee which would result if the promisor were allowed to recede from his promise' (emphasis added) (at p 309). So defined, it would seem that it is the very presence of such detriment that gives rise to the inequity of allowing the promisor to retract his promise. As we shall see (paragraph 3.55, below), however, the concept of inequity encompasses detriment but is broader than mere detriment.

(3) *Inequitable to Go Back on Promise*

3.54 A third requirement is that it must be *inequitable* for the promisor to go back on his word. It is virtually impossible to define with any precision a broad concept such as inequity or injustice but this requirement can be understood by looking at how it is applied in a given context. As pointed out in the preceding paragraph, there is clearly a substantial overlap between the concepts of detrimental reliance and inequity. Where a promisor makes a promise upon which the promisee relies and suffers detriment as a result, it seems irrefutable that the inequity of allowing the promisor to recede on his word lies in the fact of the latter's reliance and detriment. In *The Post Chaser* (see paragraph 3.52, above), although the court took the view that detriment was not a necessary element of promissory estoppel, it nonetheless held that it was *not* inequitable for the promisor to recede on his promise because the lapse of two days between the time of the promisee's reliance and the time at which the promisor retracted his promise was too short to have caused any *prejudice* to the promisee. It is thus clear that even if one accepts as correct the English position that excludes detriment as an element of promissory estoppel, the concept of detriment remains a factor of great weight in the general assessment of whether it is just and equitable to permit the promisor to go back on his word.

3.55 Ultimately, the issue of inequity must be determined by taking into account *all the relevant circumstances*. Thus any factor that could tip the balance one way or another must be considered. For instance, if it is shown that a promisor has *dishonestly* induced the promisee to act on his promise, such evidence would undoubtedly weigh in favour of the promisee rendering it inequitable for the promisor to renege. Conversely, if the promisee were guilty of improper behaviour, the balance will be tipped in favour of the promisor. *D&C Builders v Rees* (1966) serves as a useful illustration of the latter situation. The defendant owed the plaintiffs £482 but offered, through his wife, to pay £300 in full settlement of the account, stating in effect that the plaintiffs would get nothing if they did not accept the lesser sum. The plaintiffs were then on the verge of bankruptcy and the defendant's wife was well aware of that fact. For lack of a real option, the plaintiffs accepted the payment but subsequently brought an action to recover the balance of the debt. Lord Denning held that it was not inequitable for the plaintiffs to resile from their promise as the defendant had improperly procured the plaintiffs' agreement by taking advantage of their weak financial position.

(4) *Shield, Not Sword*

3.56 The principle of promissory estoppel is often metaphorically described as one which acts only *as a shield but not as a sword*. This means that the principle may only be invoked to *defend* or *resist* a claim, but it cannot be used to create a new cause of action where none existed before. This is borne out by the decision in *Combe v Combe* (1951), where (as discussed in paragraph 3.6, above) the plaintiff could not enforce her ex-husband's promise as she had not furnished consideration for the promise. The court also rejected her further argument that the defendant was estopped from breaking his promise since to do otherwise would amount to creating a contractual relation between them when none existed before. As Lord Denning explained (at p 219):

> 'That principle [of promissory estoppel] does not create new causes of action where none existed before. It only prevents a party from insisting upon his strict legal rights, when it would be unjust to allow him to enforce them, having regard to the dealings which have taken place between the parties.'

3.57 Similarly, in a case such as *Williams v Roffey* (see paragraph 3.37, above), the doctrine of promissory estoppel would not have aided the plaintiffs who were attempting to *enforce* the defendants' promise of additional payment, an obligation which did not exist in the parties' original agreement. Note, however, that in that case, Russell LJ did (at pp 17–18) observe that the plaintiffs could possibly have relied on promissory estoppel to protect their interests. If such a view were accepted, that would be tantamount to utilising promissory estoppel as a sword (see J Carter, A Phang and J Poole, 'Reactions to Williams v Roffey' (1995) 8 *Journal of Contract Law* 248; see also paragraphs 3.63–3.66, below).

3.58 The restrictive role of promissory estoppel as a shield must not, however, be mistaken as limiting the availability of this armoury to the defendant alone. A plaintiff may also rely on this principle as long as it does not result in the creation of a new cause of action. If, for instance, a plaintiff brings an action against a defendant for breach of contract, he may plead that the defendant is estopped from raising a particular defence which the defendant has in fact promised to forego. This occurred in the Malaysian case *Boustead Trading (1985) Sdn Bhd v Arab-Malaysian Merchant Bank Bhd* (1995). BT bought goods on credit from C, and C assigned the resultant book debts in favour of AMMB (a bank) under a factoring agreement. (A valid assignment confers on the assignee, ie AMMB, a direct contractual right to enforce the assigned debts.) AMMB notified BT of the assignment and stamped all invoices (for goods delivered by C to BT) with an indorsement that any objection to the invoice must be reported to AMMB within 14 days of receipt of the invoice. BT did not at anytime challenge the time constraint of 14 days, nor object to any of the invoices within that time frame. In fact, BT paid AMMB on several invoices but subsequently refused to make payments on the remaining invoices, claiming that it was entitled to offset such payments against liabilities owed to it by C. The Federal Court of Malaysia held that BT was estopped from challenging the time constraint and the invoices as a defence to AMMB's claims on the remaining invoices. Its earlier inaction coupled with its payment on the first few invoices had amounted to the representations that all was in order, and in reliance thereof AMMB had altered its position by making payments to C under the factoring agreement. AMMB, the plaintiff, could invoke the principle of promissory estoppel because it was not using the principle to establish a new right or cause of action (since it already had a right to sue BT by virtue of the valid assignment), but only to prevent BT from denying the fact that it has accepted the invoices as valid for payment.

3.59 It is, however, entirely legitimate to question why the principle of promissory estoppel should be limited to operating only as a shield but not as a sword. If the rationale underlying the principle is concerned with the protection of the reasonable reliance placed on a promise, it is not immediately apparent why such an interest should only be protected for the purposes of a defence but not as a cause of action. In fact, some other jurisdictions such as Australia have not imposed a similar constraint on the operation of promissory estoppel. We shall examine these developments in paragraphs 3.63–3.66 below.

Effect of Promissory Estoppel—Suspensory or Extinctive?

3.60 A number of cases suggest that promissory estoppel merely suspends the enforcement of an obligation but does not extinguish it, such that it may be revived by the promisor upon giving due notice to the promisee. In *Tool Metal Manufacturing Co Ltd v Tungsten Electric Co Ltd* (1955), Tool Metal (TTMC) licensed Tungsten Electric (TECO) to manufacture, use and sell certain hard metal alloys. Under the licence agreement, TECO was required to pay 'compensation' to TTMC whenever the quantity of material used or sold by TECO exceeded a certain monthly quota. On the outbreak of war in 1939, TTMC agreed to suspend its right to compensation and TECO accordingly ceased to make payments. In 1945, TECO brought an action against TTMC alleging fraud, in response to which TTMC counterclaimed (in March 1946) for compensation payable under the agreement. TTMC's counterclaim failed as it was found that they had not given TECO adequate notice of their intention to revive the payment obligation under the agreement. Subsequently, TTMC brought a separate action against TECO seeking the restoration of the compensation from January 1947. The House of Lords held that TTMC was entitled to its claim as their counterclaim in 1946 constituted sufficient notice of their intention to enforce their strict legal rights. For this purpose, it is not necessary that there be an express notice, nor does it have to specify a precise time for it to take effect. What constitutes sufficient notice in each case would depend on its particular facts. Generally, it would suffice if the promisor has by his conduct made clear his intention to withdraw his concession and the promisee is given a reasonable amount of time to make the necessary adjustments thereafter.

3.61 It should, however, be noted that *Tool Metal Manufacturing v Tungsten Electric* was a case which concerned the revival of an obligation involving *periodic payments* and the plaintiff therein only sought the resumption of its rights in respect of *future* instalments. Would TTMC have succeeded if it had attempted to claim for the compensation that was unpaid between 1939 and 1946? It appears unlikely. Similarly, in the *High Tress* case (see paragraph 3.47, above), Lord Denning was of the view that the landlords in that case would not have been able to recover the full rent for the war years. The results of these two cases suggest that it is not possible to recover the payments which accrued before the issue of notice and thus the right to these payments are therefore extinguished; but the general right to payment, insofar as they relate to future payments, is merely suspended and may be revived upon reasonable notice. It remains controversial whether this result as regards former payments is correct as it would necessitate the reversal of the rule laid down by the House of Lords in *Foakes v Beer* (1884) (see paragraph 3.44, above). The suspensory effect as regards future payments is justifiable by the fact that the promises were given in response to acute and temporal circumstances and thus it is likely that the said promises were only intended to be binding while the extenuating circumstances lasted.

3.62 A better view, it is submitted, is to determine the effects of the doctrine by reference to the nature, intent and circumstances of the promise made. In exceptional circumstances, an obligation may be extinguished because the reliance placed on the promisor's assurance makes it impossible for the promisee to perform his original obligation. For instance, in *Birmingham & District Land Co v London & North Western Railway Co* (1888), the plaintiff company was obliged, under several building agreements, to build a certain number of houses on a plot of land owned by one B by 1885. It was further agreed that the plaintiff would be granted separate leases for the houses as they were completed. After the completion of a number of houses, the plaintiff was informed of the defendant railway company's intention to statutorily acquire a part of the land for the construction of a railway line and consequently, B agreed with the plaintiff that the building operations on the houses should be suspended pending the confirmation of the railway scheme. In 1886, the defendant company completed the compulsory acquisition of the land but declined to pay statutory compensation to the plaintiff on the ground that the building agreements had then expired. The court found that the defendant company was estopped from alleging the expiry of the building agreements as they were bound by B's earlier assurance to the plaintiff as regards the suspension of their obligations under the agreements and were therefore liable to compensate the plaintiff. In effect, the application of estoppel in this case was to extinguish the plaintiff's obligation to build under the agreements since it was no longer possible to build on the affected land. In the paradigm case where a creditor accepts a lesser sum in satisfaction of a larger debt, the effect of promissory estoppel should ultimately depend on whether the creditor's intention (objectively determined) is to forgive the entire debt or merely to allow the debtor more time to pay.

Promissory Estoppel and Consideration

3.63 Although the doctrine of promissory estoppel has the effect of binding a party to his promise even when it is not supported by consideration, it does not yet, because of its limited role as a shield, displace the necessity for consideration in contract formation. Such a restrictive approach to the doctrine of promissory estoppel has, however, been challenged in other jurisdictions. Significantly, the Australian courts have refused to so confine the operation of the principle in the landmark case of *Waltons Stores (Interstate) Ltd v Maher* (1988).

3.64 In *Waltons Stores v Maher*, W and M were engaged in an advanced stage of negotiations for the lease of M's property by W, which envisaged that M would demolish the existing building on the property, and build in its place a new building suitable for W's purposes. On 11 November 1983, M executed the lease agreement and forwarded it to W for execution and exchange. M then proceeded to demolish the building on the assumption that W had agreed to the final amendments made to the agreement and that the exchange of document would be a mere formality. Soon after, however, W decided not to proceed with the lease as a result of a change in its retailing policy. Even though W knew that M had commenced works on the demolition, it did not inform M of its change of mind until 19 January 1984, by which time works on the new building had begun. The High Court of Australia held that M was entitled to specifically enforce W's promises. Even though no contract was concluded between the parties due to W's failure to execute and exchange the lease agreement, W was estopped from denying that it had impliedly promised to conclude the contract. It was *unconscionable* on the part of W to stand by in silence when it knew that M had embarked on a detrimental course of action under a mistaken assumption induced by W.

3.65 *Waltons Stores v Maher* is significant because it enables a claimant to wield promissory estoppel as a sword and not merely as a shield. In arriving at this conclusion, the High Court of Australia was careful to point out that such a development did not undermine the doctrine of consideration, as the principle of estoppel was concerned with protecting a party's *reliance* induced by another's *unconscionable conduct*, whilst the doctrine of consideration was concerned with protecting *expectations* engendered by promises made (since a promise supported by consideration is enforceable even where the promisee has not placed any reliance on it).

3.66 The bold approach in *Waltons Stores v Maher* has not (yet) been adopted in England and Singapore. The more restrictive approach (limiting the use of estoppel as a shield) was recently affirmed by the English Court of Appeal in *Baird Textiles Holdings Ltd v Marks & Spencer plc* (2002). It should, however, be noted that two of the judges in that case did in fact acknowledge that the law relating to estoppel has not been fully developed and there is thus a possibility that the House of Lords may, if an appropriate opportunity should arise, reform the law in this regard. A significant deterrence of such development may lie in the broad and amorphous nature of the notion of 'unconscionability', which, if accepted, would result in a measure of uncertainty in the law. Indeed, in a commercial context where self-interest is generally accepted as the primary and legitimate motivation of transacting parties, it is a daunting task to attempt to draw a clear line beyond which such self-serving conduct is considered illegitimate and unconscionable. Notwithstanding such difficulties, however, the more critical question is *whether, as a matter of principle, a person whose interests have been prejudiced by another's unconscionable conduct should be allowed to seek relief against the wrongdoer.* If one takes the view that the right to pursue one's self-interest is not absolute even in a commercial setting, then the line between acceptable and unconscionable conduct must necessarily be drawn. As regards the resultant risk of uncertainty, it might be asked if it could not be minimised as more concrete principles are fashioned through the development of the case law.

Reappraising Consideration

3.67 It must now be apparent to the reader that while the doctrine of consideration is firmly rooted in the law of contract, there has been no lack of attempt at assailing its importance as an essential element of contract formation. Several considerations account for this phenomenon.

3.68 First, one of the traditional justifications for consideration is that it serves as good evidence of the contracting parties' intention to create legal relations. While the exchange of value is undoubtedly an excellent indicator of the parties' intention, it is by no means the only indicator. Where other circumstantial evidence makes it abundantly clear that the parties do intend to be bound by their agreement, there seems to be no compelling reason why such agreements should be denied legal validity simply on account of the lack of consideration. Indeed, it is often the recognition of the need to give effect to the parties' intention in such situations that prompted judges to 'invent' consideration; we have already seen an instance of such contrivance in *Ward v Byham* (see paragraph 3.32, above).

3.69 Yet another justification given for the necessity of consideration lies in the notion that the law should only enforce agreements which amount to 'bargains', and the consideration exchanged between two contracting parties is the very feature that distinguishes a bargain from a mere agreement (see C Hamson, 'The Reform of Consideration' (1938) 54 *Law Quarterly Review* 233). However, such argument does not explain why the law only enforces bargains and not other agreements. In fact, as the development of promissory estoppel has shown, there may indeed be very forceful reasons (such as the need to protect reasonable reliance placed on a promise) for enforcing promises not supported by consideration.

3.70 Finally, the expansion of consideration to include 'practical benefits' in *Williams v Roffey* is yet another development which could severely impair the usefulness of consideration in defining enforceable agreements. If a trifling factual benefit could suffice as consideration, it would be extremely rare to find a promise that is not supported by consideration.

3.71 The above discussion attempts to help the reader understand the uncertainty which still surrounds the very concept of consideration and more importantly, the necessity (or otherwise) for such a concept in our law. While there is at present no sign that we are ready to abandon the notion of consideration altogether, it is hoped that the reader would, at the very least, appreciate that the place of consideration in contract formation is not as immutable as it might have appeared at first sight.

CHAPTER 4

Intention to Create Legal Relations

PARAGRAPHS

4.1–4.3 **Introduction**

4.4–4.8 **Social and Domestic Agreements**

4.9–4.14 **Business and Commercial Agreements**

4.15 **Contractual Intention and Consideration**

Introduction

4.1 Even where it is clear that two parties have reached an agreement which is supported by consideration, such agreement is not necessarily enforceable as a contract in law unless it is also established that the parties have intended the agreement to be legally binding. For instance, if A agrees with B to take a stroll by the Esplanade, the agreement is not enforceable as there is no intention to create legal relations.

4.2 Whether the parties to an agreement did intend to create legally binding relations is a *question of fact*; in other words, whether such intention exists in a particular case is determined largely by the facts of that case. The ascertainment of such intention is also *objective* in nature—the parties to an agreement are said to have the intention to create legal relations if an objective view of the relevant facts suggests that such an intention exists, even if one of the parties should assert the contrary.

4.3 Generally, the cases in which the issue of contractual intention arises are analysed under two broad categories. The first category relates to agreements made in social and domestic contexts and the second relates to agreements arising in business and commercial contexts.

Social and Domestic Agreements

4.4 Where an agreement is in the nature of a social or domestic arrangement, there is a presumption that the parties do *not* intend the agreement to be legally binding. The leading case of *Balfour v Balfour* (1919) is often cited as the authority for this proposition. In that case, the defendant husband who was leaving for an overseas assignment promised to pay his wife, the plaintiff, a monthly sum of £30 until such time when she joined him. The defendant subsequently failed to honour his promise and the plaintiff sued for breach of contract. The English Court of Appeal rejected the plaintiff's claim on the ground that the agreement was motivated mainly by the parties' natural love and affection for each other and not the intention to create legal obligations. Similarly, in *Jones v Padavatton* (1969), a mother's agreement to maintain her adult daughter on the condition that the latter studied to become an advocate was held not to be enforceable as it was merely an informal family arrangement whereby each party depended on the other's good faith for the performance of the promises and was therefore not intended to create any binding arrangement.

4.5 However, the presumption against contractual intent can be rebutted by clear evidence of the parties' intention to create legal obligations. In *Merritt v Merritt* (1970), a husband who had deserted his wife agreed to pay the latter a monthly maintenance of £40 and to transfer the house to her when the mortgage loan had been repaid in full provided that she paid off the outstanding mortgage loan as well as other related expenses. At the wife's insistence, the husband wrote the agreement on a piece of paper and signed against it. The court held that in these circumstances, the presumption against creating legal relations did not apply and the agreement was binding. Unlike the facts of *Balfour v Balfour*, where the couple were living in amity at the time of the agreement, the couple in *Merritt v Merritt* were estranged when the agreement was made. As such, they were clearly making a serious bargain and not merely relying on the other's affection and good faith for the fulfilment of the promises.

4.6 As mentioned earlier, the issue of contractual intent is really a question of fact and hence *all the surrounding facts* of a case are relevant in considering whether the presumption against contractual intent has been displaced. It is therefore not possible to list all the factors that may operate to displace the presumption. However, the cases have shown that two factors are of particular significance in this respect.

4.7 The first is the *certainty* of the terms of the agreement. The more certain the terms, the more likely it is that the parties have given careful consideration to the content and effects of the agreement. Conversely, where the terms are vague and imprecise, the court will be more inclined to construe them as evidence of the parties' lack of contractual intent. The second factor is the *actual reliance* which a party placed on the agreement; evidence of such reliance will tend to suggest that the parties intended the agreement to be binding. Both these factors appeared to have influenced the decision in *Merritt v Merritt* (see paragraph 4.5, above), as the court found that the agreement was written with sufficient certainty and that the wife had acted in reliance on the husband's promises when she paid off the mortgage loan and other related expenses.

4.8 The principles in *Balfour v Balfour* were applied in the local case of *Choo Tiong Hin v Choo Hock Swee* (1959), where agreements between a father and five adopted sons to distribute the wealth jointly acquired by them equally among the sons upon the death of the father were found to 'possess all the characteristics of a private family arrangement depending for its efficacy upon a sense of filial duty and paternal responsibility on the part of the adopted sons and their adoptive father' (at pp 68–69) and therefore lacked the requisite intention to create binding obligations. This decision has, however, been criticised by a commentator as an instance of a 'slavish adherence to English law' without sufficient regard to the different mores of our society leading to unsatisfactory results (see KL Koh, 'Current Legal Research in Singapore' (1979) 21 *Malaya Law Review* 69 at p 71). The commentator was of the view that the arrangements, which were made for mutual benefits and between persons of mature years, should in fact be likened to enforceable contracts of service. Indeed, in the current context where the formation of business or other binding arrangements in the familial context is no longer uncommon, our law should be slow to presume that a presumption fashioned nearly a century ago would have the same relevance today (see A Phang, *Cheshire, Fifoot & Furmston's Law of Contract—Second Singapore and Malaysian Edition* (1998) at p 225). The critical step, in each case, is to carefully consider the entire context and circumstances of the transaction to ascertain the parties' intention.

Business and Commercial Agreements

4.9 Where business and commercial agreements are concerned, the presumption is that the parties intend to create legally enforceable obligations. The burden of rebutting the presumption lies on the party who asserts the absence of contractual intent and it is a heavy one.

4.10 In a commercial setting, the issue of contractual intention can arise in two types of factual situations. First, it can arise in a situation where the very *existence* of a contract is in doubt and has to be determined by reference to the parties' intention. The case of *Carlill v Carbolic Smoke Ball Co* (1893) is an instance of such factual scenario. In that case, the defendant argued that it had not entered into any contract with the plaintiff because the promise made in the advertisement was a mere puff which was not intended to create a binding contract. The court rejected this argument as the defendant's claim that they had deposited £1,000 in its bank account was good evidence of its intention to honour its promise. In the second and more common situation, there is no question that the contract exists but it is uncertain whether a particular statement in the contract was intended to have contractual force. The application of the test of intention in this scenario has been discussed in more detail in a preceding part of this book (see paragraph 2.5, above).

4.11 It is not uncommon for parties to expressly state in their agreement that they have no intention to create legal relations. Where this is done in clear terms, such a statement effectively displaces the presumption of contractual intention. A good illustration is provided by the facts of *Rose & Frank Co v J R Crompton & Bros Ltd* (1923), where the parties included the following clause (commonly known as an 'honour clause') in their agreement:

> 'this arrangement is not entered into as a legal or formal agreement, and shall not be subject to legal jurisdiction in the Law Courts but is only a definite expression of and record of the purpose and intention of the parties concerned to which they each honourably pledge themselves.'

The court held that the arrangement was not enforceable as a contract as the honour clause had clearly stated that they did not intend the agreement to have any legal consequence. In principle, if the parties to a commercial agreement should choose to rely on each other's good faith and honour instead of the formal protection of the law, there is no reason why such preference should not be respected.

4.12 The issue of contractual intention frequently arises in relation to a type of commercial document known as a *letter of comfort*. Typically, such letters are issued by a parent company or a substantial shareholder to encourage a financial institution to extend a loan facility to its subsidiary or investee company. The precise legal effect of a comfort letter turns on the intention of the parties as evidenced by the surrounding circumstances and the text of the letter.

4.13 In *Kleinwort Benson Ltd v Malaysia Mining Corp Bhd* (1989), the defendant parent company issued a comfort letter which contained the statement: 'It is our policy to ensure that the business of [our subsidiary] is at all times in a position to meet its liabilities to you under the above arrangements.' Based on a minute inspection of the wording of the letter, the English Court of Appeal held that this statement was merely a statement of the defendant's intention which did not amount to a contractual promise. In contrast, the Australian Supreme Court upheld a letter of comfort containing a similarly worded statement as having contractual force in *Banque Brussels Lambert SA v Australian National Industries Ltd* (1989). In the latter case, Rogers CJ disapproved of the English court's approach in attempting to resolve a commercial dispute with excessive emphasis on the text of a document. Rogers CJ also took the view that, in general, commercial agreements resulting from hard bargaining should be given significant weight and not be lightly reduced to a 'merely honourable engagement' except in the clearest of circumstances.

4.14 Significantly, in Singapore, the High Court has recently declined to give legal effect to a letter of comfort in the case of *Hongkong and Shanghai Bank Corporation Ltd v Jurong Engineering Ltd* (2000). Though the court acknowledged that the letter of comfort should, as a commercial document, be presumed to have legal effect, it nonetheless held that the presumption was displaced by two important considerations: first, the evidence showed the parties did not seriously place any *reliance* on the comfort letter, and secondly, the text of the letter was *not* sufficiently *certain* to support the creation of binding obligations. This decision suggests that our courts may be more inclined towards a restrictive approach in interpreting letters of comfort, such that documents of this nature are unlikely to be given contractual force except where there is irrefutable evidence of such intention. In reality, however, while the obligations under a comfort letter would generally fall short of those under a guarantee, one may legitimately question whether it is right not to accord any legal significance to such a document at all when they often do perform the critical role of *inducing* the lender to extend the loan to the borrower (see PW Lee, 'Letters of Comfort Revisited' [2002] *Lloyd's Maritime and Commercial Law Quarterly* 169).

Contractual Intention and Consideration

4.15 Finally, it should be noted that the requirement for contractual intention as a necessary element of contract formation has been questioned. In particular, it has been argued that an agreement which is supported by consideration should be enforceable without the need to establish contractual intention (see A Lord (ed), *Williston on Contracts* (4th ed, 1990) at section 3.5; on the topic of 'Consideration', see generally above, Chapter 3). It is true that, generally, the provision of consideration by a party would serve as good evidence of his intention to be bound by the agreement. However, this would not be true of all agreements. For instance, in a domestic context, if A agrees with his brother B that the former would pay for the household utilities while the latter pays for the groceries, it would seem clear that the arrangement would not amount to a binding contract notwithstanding the fact that consideration has been furnished by the parties. Further, if the English Court of Appeal were right to extend, in *Williams v Roffey Bros & Nicholls (Contractors) Ltd* (1991), the concept of consideration to include factual or practical benefits (see paragraphs 3.37–3.39, above), then the usefulness of the doctrine of consideration in identifying legally enforceable agreements would be significantly undermined. In that case, the requirement for intention to create legal relations, far from being displaced by the doctrine of consideration, would more likely assume an even more critical role as a test for enforceability.

CHAPTER 5

Terms of the Contract

PARAGRAPHS

5.1–5.5 **Introduction**

5.6–5.9 **The Parol Evidence Rule**

Terms and Representations

5.10–5.12 Introduction
5.13 Request to Verify
5.14 Importance of the Statement
5.15 Timing of the Statement
5.16 Oral Statements and Written Contracts
5.17 Special Skill and Knowledge
5.18 Impact of the Misrepresentation Act

Relative Importance of Terms

5.19–5.20 Warranties, Conditions and Innominate Terms
5.21 Differentiating Between Conditions and Warranties
5.22 The '*Hong Kong Fir* Approach' and A Suggested Synthesis Between the 'Condition-Warranty' and '*Hong Kong Fir*' Approaches

5.23 **Implied Terms**
5.24–5.25 Terms Implied in Fact
5.26–5.28 Terms Implied in Law
5.29 Terms Implied by Statute
5.30 Terms Implied by Custom

Introduction

5.1 The law relating to contractual terms provides rules on how the precise obligations of the parties to a contract are to be ascertained, and once these have been ascertained, the manner in which such obligations should be categorised to determine the consequences for the breach of such obligations. Judges have developed some of these rules and Acts of Parliament have enacted other rules that in turn have been further clarified by judicial interpretation. The law on contractual terms attempts to achieve several objectives designed to promote contractual efficacy but without violating the principles, first, that courts do not make contracts for the parties and, secondly, that the various technical rules are designed to find out and give effect to the intention of the parties on an objective basis.

In terms of contractual efficacy, the first objective is to promote certainty and to fill gaps relating to matters in the contract that were not addressed by the parties. Rules designed to separate contractual obligations from statements that are not part of the contract, rules for protecting written contracts from being undermined by extrinsic evidence, and rules for implying terms in circumstances not envisaged by the parties are all designed to foster predictability.

The second objective is to integrate social and public interest policy in certain types of contracts so that these contracts will be performed in conformity with such policies. The next chapter will discuss the circumstances under which the law intervenes to limit the scope of terms that attempt to relieve one party for loss or damage caused to the other party. Finally, the law acknowledges the truism that some terms of a contract are so important that if they are breached, the innocent party will be deprived of a substantial benefit under the contract and that he or she should therefore be allowed to terminate the contract, whereas other terms are not so important and if they are breached the contract must still be performed by the innocent party who can be compensated with damages for that breach. Accordingly, the law promotes contractual efficacy by creating a hierarchy of obligations within the contract itself so that breaches of a minor obligation and/or nature will not permit the destruction of the transaction by authorising the party aggrieved by the breach to terminate the contract.

5.2 People may agree that they have a contract but may disagree about what precisely was agreed upon. In the thousands of contracts made every day, the parties explicitly agree only on a few main terms. A buyer-consumer and a supermarket-seller of a product may engage in a sales transaction without actually considering critical issues such as the quality of the product and the seller's title to the product. Likewise, a householder-buyer and a home-repair services contractor may agree on the scope of the repair, the payment to be made and the completion date but leave out other important features in this type of contract. This is often the way it should be. If the parties to a contract try to anticipate and iron out every possible situation over which a dispute may arise, they will squander their precious time and probably not agree on a contract. Moreover, the vast numbers of people who make contracts have not studied contract law and should not be expected to know everything that could go wrong in a particular transaction. Accordingly, the law allows people to contract freely, and what they explicitly agree on, the law refers to as 'express terms'. After this, the law steps in and fills in the blanks, if and when necessary, by terms referred to as 'implied terms' and the process of such gap-filling will be different depending on whether the terms to be implied are those which the courts would regard as terms implied in fact or implied in law.

5.3 Quite often, the parties enter into a contract after lengthy negotiations involving not only themselves but also their advisors such as lawyers and accountants. During these negotiations, each side will try to persuade the other of its point of view and will make various claims for their products or services. Consequently, these negotiations could give rise to two sets of problems. First, when the parties enter into a written contract, one party may later allege that the written contract does not faithfully and comprehensively contain the entire agreement and may demand the right to introduce evidence of terms, whether they be statement of fact or promises, not contained in the written document. To deal with objections of this kind, the law has a rule, the parol evidence rule, which excludes extraneous evidence meant to contradict or vary the language of a written contract except in limited circumstances. Second, one party may allege that the other party induced her to enter into the contract by making a statement of fact that became a part of the contract. After the contract was concluded, she finds that the statement was untrue and wishes to sue for breach of contract. The law would examine her claim by finding out if the statement was a representation or a term and will allow her to sue for a breach of contract only if it was the intention of the parties to make the statement a term of the contract. If, of course, there is representation that is false, the plaintiff might have a possible action for misrepresentation (see, generally, Chapter 12, below).

5.4 Finally, even where the terms of a contract have been ascertained and precisely defined, the law does not treat all the terms as being of equal weight. For instance, in a computer sales contract, a small scratch on the casing of the CPU is not as serious as a defective hard disk. In recognition of the fact of the relative importance of contractual terms, the law regards some terms, known as 'conditions', as so important that when they are breached the innocent party may, if she wishes to, terminate the contract and sue for breach. Other terms, known as 'warranties', do not share the same status as 'conditions'. When a party breaches a warranty, the innocent party may not terminate the contract, which is a radical remedy, but instead must continue to perform the contract and recover compensation for the loss caused by the breach of the warranty by way of damages.

Yet, other terms, known as 'innominate terms' or 'intermediate terms' may attract the legal consequences of a breach of either a warranty or a condition depending on how serious the breach of the innominate term is. If the breach of the innominate term is a grave breach depriving the innocent party of substantially the whole benefit of the contract it was intended that he or she should have had, the courts would treat such breach as a breach of a condition and allow the innocent party the remedies that would have been accorded for a breach of condition. On the other hand, if the breach of the innominate term is less serious because of the less serious consequences ensuing, the courts would require the innocent party to continue with the contract and permit monetary damages to compensate for the loss caused by such breach. Whether a term is an 'innominate term' or something else will not be decided by examining the nature of the breach but rather by the nature of the term itself, viz whether it is capable of sometimes being breached in a serious way as to justify termination and being breached in yet other circumstances in a minor way that would justify only the remedy of damages. However, as we shall see, the actual focus in the situation of an 'innominate term' is, in the final analysis, not so much upon the nature of the term itself which, as we have just seen, is rather amorphous, but is instead on the actual *consequences* of the breach insofar as a finding of whether or not the innocent party is justified in terminating the contract is concerned.

5.5 The discussion that follows addresses four groups of circumstances, broadly illustrated below, that give rise to disputes over contract terms:

(1) The parties (A and B), who engaged in negotiations before the contract was signed, have reduced the contract to writing. Party A discovers that what she thought had been orally agreed with Party B is missing from the written contract or some other clause contradicts what she thought was a verbal understanding. May Party A prove the oral agreement to contradict, vary or add to the written contract?

(2) During the negotiations that preceded the contract, one party made certain claims in respect of the product or service to be sold. After the contact was concluded, the other party finds that the claim with regard to the product or service that she regarded as important proves to be false. May this other party allege that such statement was a part of the contract and sue the party who made the statement for breach of contract?

(3) The terms of the contract do not carry equal weight. Breach of terms, known as 'conditions' gives rise to extensive remedies unlike the breach of those terms known as 'warranties'. How does a court determine which terms are 'conditions' and which terms are 'warranties'? When would a court classify a term as an 'innominate term' taking into account the nature and consequences of the breach of that term?

(4) Where the contract does not provide for a particular eventuality, how do the courts 'fill in the blanks' and what principles do they use?

The Parol Evidence Rule

5.6 The Singapore Evidence Act (Cap 97, 1997 Rev Ed) has codified the parol evidence rule as well as some of, though not all, the exceptions to the rule found at common law.

According to the parol evidence rule, when the parties have reduced their contract to writing, either party may not attempt to show by extrinsic evidence that the terms in the written contract must be changed, added to, or contradicted. Contract law attempts to reduce uncertainty wherever possible. The parol evidence supports this outcome by adopting the position that where the parties have taken the step of reducing their contract to writing, none of these parties should be allowed the opportunity to displace the contents of the written contract by showing that the document is incorrect because there are other oral terms that change or vary the terms found in the contractual document. A little reflection shows what the rule achieves. Absent the rule, the written document may not be worth the paper it is written on. Moreover, third parties, such as banks, that were induced to lend money to one party in reliance on the document may find that the cash flow anticipated under the written contract will be disrupted by terms not found in the written contract.

5.7 Applied rigidly, however, the parol evidence rule can produce great injustice that could outweigh the benefits of certainty. Accordingly, judges have devised certain exceptions to reduce injustices that may flow from an unwavering application of the parol evidence rule. The need for some of these exceptions is, on reflection, quite obvious as they are based on avoiding injustice while other exceptions are based on technical contract rules. The main exceptions at common law are as follows:

(1) A party may dispute the validity of the written contract by showing, through extrinsic evidence, that the contract was the result of mistake, a lack of consideration, or of misrepresentation (see, for example, GH Treitel, *The Law of Contract* (10th ed, 1999) at p 178).

(2) A party may show by extrinsic evidence a mistake in the written contract and prove what the contract should have read instead of its disputed term. For example, a written agreement to sell a recent model of a luxury car may refer to a selling price of $500. The seller will be allowed to introduce evidence to show that the real price agreed upon was $500,000. Reference may also be made to *Joscelyne v Nissen* (1970), where a daughter's undertaking to pay utility bills, although not included in the written contract between father and daughter, was held enforceable.

(3) A party may also adduce extrinsic evidence to show that the written contract has not yet come into existence or that it is no longer in operation. Sometimes, parties agree that their contract would come into existence only upon the occurrence or non-occurrence of a certain event by a certain date, or that if something has not occurred by a certain date the contract would cease to exist. For example, in a contract of employment, the parties may have verbally agreed that

the contract would come into existence only if the employee obtains her professional qualification by a certain date, or the contract would end if the employee did not obtain the qualification by a certain date. Reference may also be made to *Pym v Campbell* (1856) where extrinsic evidence was allowed to the effect that the obligation to buy shares in an invention contained in a written agreement was conditional upon a third party approving the invention, of which the approval had not been received (and see now also section 94 (c) of the Singapore Evidence Act).

(4) A party may be allowed to offer extrinsic evidence to demonstrate that a particular custom of the trade must be implied into, and therefore become part of, the written agreement. See, for example, *Smith v Wilson* (1832), where evidence of local custom to show that '1,000 rabbits' in the written contract really meant '1,200 rabbits' was allowed.

5.8 In Singapore, the policies supporting the parol evidence rule are reflected in sections 93 and 94 of the Singapore Evidence Act that codify the parol evidence rule and its major common law exceptions. Section 93 states that where the parties have reduced their contract to writing, 'no evidence shall be given in proof of the terms of such contract ... except the document itself, or secondary evidence ... in which secondary evidence is admissible under the provisions of this Act'. Section 94 states that where a written contract is shown to exist, no oral evidence shall be admitted 'for the purpose of contradicting, varying, adding to, or subtracting from its terms' subject to certain exceptions. Section 94 enumerates six sets of circumstances in which extraneous evidence could be used to vary the terms of the written contract. The common law on the other hand recognises more exceptions and one issue that has been raised but which has not been settled in Singapore is whether it is possible to invoke exceptions from the common law that are not reflected in the proviso to section 94. Professor Phang has considered the impact of section 2(2) of the Singapore Evidence Act which states that all 'rules of evidence *not* contained in any *written* law, so far as such rules are inconsistent with any of the provisions of *this* Act, are hereby repealed' (emphasis added). Noting that some common law exceptions to the parol evidence rule actually enshrine principles that are inconsistent with the provisions of the Evidence Act, Professor Phang is of the opinion that those common law exceptions to the parol evidence rule insofar as they are consistent with the Evidence Act continue to be applicable: see A Phang, *Cheshire, Fifoot and Furmston's Law of Contract—Second Singapore and Malaysian Edition* (1998) at p 224. However, in *Latham v Credit Suisse First Boston* (2000), Yong Pung How CJ appeared to indicate that the section 94 exceptions are exhaustive when he observed (at p 699) that the section 93 'encapsulation of the common law contractual parol evidence rule applies unless the secondary evidence falls under one of the exceptions found in s 94 of the Evidence Act'. The learned Chief Justice appeared to have had in mind the maxim of statutory interpretation, *expressio unius exclusio alterius* (the expression of one excludes others), in order to view section 94 as preemptively exhaustive with the result that the common law exceptions not found in section 94 are by definition inconsistent with section 94 and are thus inadmissible pursuant to section 2(2) of the Evidence Act.

5.9 Relevant to issues raised by the parol evidence rule as well as to the topic of distinguishing terms and representations is a type of contract known as a 'collateral contract'. The essence of a collateral contract is that one party, in consideration of the other party making a separate and distinct contract, makes a contract with that other party by giving that other party a collateral warranty. For example, in *Shanklin Pier LD v Detel Products LD* (1951), a representative of the defendant manufacturer made certain claims about the paint that it manufactured. As a result, the plaintiff asked its contractor to use the paint on the pier and it turned out that the paint did not have the qualities claimed for it by the representative. The court held that the plaintiff had a collateral contract with the defendant manufacturer of the paint and could recover the damages caused by the use of the unsuitable paint. Before a collateral contract can be said to exist, it must be shown that one party made a representation intending to persuade the other to conclude the contract and that in fact that person concluded the contract with the result that the representation is in the form of a warranty collateral to the main contract and existing side by side with the main contract. In *Heilbut, Symons & Co v Buckleton* (1913), the House of Lords was of the opinion that the courts should be slow to hold that there was a collateral contract. This view has been criticized: see *J Evans & Son (Portsmouth) Ltd v Andrea Merzario Ltd* (1976).

It would appear, however, that under the Evidence Act, the terms of any collateral contract must *not be inconsistent* with those contained in the main agreement; see section 94(b), which reads as follows:

> '[T]he existence of any separate oral agreement, as to any matter on which a document is silent and which is not inconsistent with its terms, may be proved; in considering whether or not this proviso applies, the court shall have regard to the degree of formality of the document.'

There appears, nevertheless, to be some controversy in the case law: see A Phang, *Cheshire, Fifoot and Furmston's Law of Contract—Second Singapore and Malaysian Edition* (1998) at pp 245–246.

Terms and Representations

Introduction

5.10 In many transactions, the parties first discuss aspects of the transaction before they conclude a contract. One party may think that something said by the other during these discussions forms part of the contract while that other party may consider the statement as not involving any promise on her part. Where the parties have reduced their contract to writing, the parol evidence rule could be used to exclude extraneous material but most contracts are made verbally without being put into writing. In the latter category of contracts, it becomes necessary to determine what is part of the contract and what is not. Contract law makes this determination by drawing a distinction between terms and representations. The courts will examine the pre-contractual negotiations and sift what was said into three categories. The first category consists of the puff, the normal exaggeration and grandstanding that is a part of contract negotiation, that the law regards as legally insignificant because it is not meant to be taken seriously. Often, though not always, these statements will be on the borderline of opinion and a statement of fact. The second category consists of representations. When one party makes a statement of fact to another party with the intention of inducing the other party to enter into a contract and that factual statement does in fact induce the other party to enter into the contract but it cannot be said that the statement was intended by the parties to form part of the contract, a representation has been made. The critical feature of the representation is that it induces the contract but if it turns out to be false, the person who relied on it cannot sue for breach of contract. For example, if A tells B that she would sell a necklace to B for $1,000, the price may induce B to buy the necklace but the price is also a part of the contract. But, if in addition, A tells B that the necklace is a precious family heirloom, this statement may induce B to buy the necklace but it is uncertain whether it becomes a part of the contract such that B can sue A for breach of contract if she discovers, after making the purchase, that the necklace was a new piece acquired during the previous Christmas season.

5.11 By virtue of the Application of English Law Act (Cap 7A, 1994 Rev Ed), the UK Misrepresentation Act of 1967 (reprinted locally as Cap 390, 1994 Rev Ed), applies in Singapore and a literal reading of section 2(1) of this Act would expose a maker of a misrepresentation, who cannot prove that he had objectively reasonable grounds for making that misrepresentation, to the same liability as the maker of a fraudulent representation; see the English Court of Appeal decision of *Royscot Trust Ltd v Rogerson* (1991) which, 'although subject to criticism, holds sway' according to the UK Court of Appeal in *HIH Casualty & General Insurance Ltd v Chase Manhattan Bank* (2001). In *Ng Buay Hock v Tan Keng Huat* (1997) Warren LH Khoo J referred to the decision in *Royscot* but held (at p 795) that the plaintiff's claim relieved him of making 'a choice in regard to the measure of damages such as was made in the *Royscot* case'. His comments about *Royscot* must therefore be regarded as *obiter dicta*. As it is possible that *Royscot* might be accepted as good law in Singapore, the proper characterisation of a pre-contractual statement as a term or a representation will be of critical importance in terms of the types of remedies available under contract law or the Misrepresentation Act to both the maker of the statement and the other party who relied on the statement (see further, the discussion of misrepresentation in Chapter 12).

5.12 Whether something said by one party to another during a pre-contractual negotiation is a representation or a term depends on the intention of the parties and thus is a question of fact. This means that if the parties disagree about the status of the statement and go to court, the judge will examine the specific facts of the particular case to determine whether the parties intended the statement in question to be a representation or a term. In making this determination as to the intention of the parties, however, the judge will apply to the specific facts certain guidelines, discussed in the following sections, that the courts have developed over a hundred years.

Request to Verify

5.13 During a negotiation prior to the contract, when one party tells the other party something and then qualifies that statement by telling that party in effect, 'don't take my word for it, get an independent verification and satisfy yourself', the court will probably hold that the party made a representation.

In *Ecay v Godfrey* (1947), the seller told the buyer of a boat that the boat did not have any flaws but then went on to invite the buyer to have the boat inspected. The buyer did not have the boat inspected and after the sale, the buyer found flaws in the boat. He sued for breach of contract. The court rejected this claim holding that the seller's statement about the lack of flaws was a representation and not a term. On the other hand, the court in *Schawel v Reade* (1913) held that the seller's statement was a term. Here, the seller told the buyer, who wished to buy the seller's horse for stud purposes, that the horse was perfectly sound and that the buyer need not look for anything that could be the matter with the horse. The buyer successfully sued the seller for breach of contact upon discovering that the horse was totally unfit for stud purposes.

Importance of the Statement

5.14 If it appears to the court that the statement in question was so important to one party that she would not have entered into the contract but for such statement having been made, the court will likely hold that statement was intended to be a term and not a representation. In *Bannerman v White* (1861), the buyer asked the seller whether the hops that the seller offered had been treated with sulphur. The buyer emphasised that he would not even bother to ask the price if the hops had been treated with sulphur. This exchange clearly showed that the buyer would only buy sulphur-free hops. The seller assured the buyer that no sulphur had been used on the hops. When, after the purchase, the buyer found that sulphur had been used, he sued the seller for breach of contract. The court held that the assurance about the hops being free of sulphur was a term of the contract and not a representation.

Timing of the Statement

5.15 If one party makes a statement about the subject matter of the contract to the other party shortly before they enter into the contract, the courts would probably hold that this statement was a term and not a representation. The relevant time frame would depend on the type of contract. For example, in a contract of employment which the parties had negotiated over for several months, a statement made during the start of the negotiations would probably be a representation and not a term. On the other hand, in a routine buy and sell transaction, there might be so much haggling that it would justify a court finding that a statement made just a week before the contract was a representation and not a term. Thus, in *Routledge v McKay* (1954), the seller had consulted the registration book of the motorcycle to be sold and told the buyer that the vehicle was a 1942 model. One week later, the parties signed the contract. The buyer found that the motorcycle, far from being a 1942 model, was a 1930 model. The court rejected the buyer's claim for a breach of warranty holding that the statement about the year of the model was not a term of the contract. This case illustrates the point made earlier that whether a term or a representation is eventually a question of the intention of the parties, a fact to be determined by looking at the surrounding circumstances. In a country like Singapore, where vehicles are expensive and the parties are choosy and sensitive to Certificate of Entitlement ('COE') issues such as the scrap value of the vehicle, the courts may decide a similar case differently. The court might consider any statement about the model year to be so important that it would qualify as a term because it would be reasonable to hold that, in the context of automobile purchases in Singapore, the parties intend the year of manufacture to be a term and not a mere representation.

Oral Statements and Written Contracts

5.16 Where the parties, after negotiations, put their agreement in writing, the courts would probably hold that what they said during the pre-contractual negotiations was a representation and not a term. Normally, the parol evidence rule would shut out such statements. However, in special circumstances, the court might hold that the parties entered into a contract that was partly written and partly oral; see, for example *J Evans & Son (Portsmouth) Ltd v Andrea Merzario Ltd* (1976), where an oral undertaking to the plaintiffs by the defendants who were forwarding agents that the plaintiff's machines shipped by containers would be stored below deck was held to override the printed exemption from liability.

Special Skill and Knowledge

5.17 If a statement is made by or to a party on a matter about which that party has special knowledge or skill, that special knowledge or skill will be relevant in determining whether the statement is a representation or a term. This is because it is reasonable to assume that it was not the intention of a person making the statement who has little or no expertise in the area to someone who has expertise in the area to expose herself to a breach of contract action in case the representation proves false. Two contrasting English cases that deal with a statement on the model of the car that was the subject of the contract illustrate this approach.

In *Oscar Chess v Williams* (1957), the plaintiff, a hire-purchase firm, agreed with the defendant that he could trade in his car as a part of the hire purchase transaction. The defendant, who was not in the car business, consulted his registration book and told the plaintiff that the car was a 1948 model whereas in fact the car was a 1939 model. The defendant made this false statement in good faith and it was later found that some unknown person had fraudulently altered the particulars in the registration book. Because the plaintiff believed the defendant's statement that the car was a 1948 model, the defendant received more credit that he would got if the plaintiff knew that the car was a 1939 model. The remedy of rescission was available if the false statement was an innocent misrepresentation. The plaintiff could not set aside the contract by the remedy of rescission since this relief must be sought in a timely manner and the plaintiff had delayed in bringing the action. Not being able to bring an action to rescind the contract because of the delay, the plaintiff sued for breach of contract on the ground that the false statement was a term of the contract. The court disallowed the plaintiff's action for a breach of warranty. It reasoned that the defendant who was not a car dealer was not in a position to give a warranty on the year of the model whereas the plaintiffs, a hire-purchase firm that dealt in automobiles, had the technical knowledge to protect themselves.

The roles were reversed in *Dick Bentley Productions Ltd v Harold Smith* (1965). Here, it was the seller who dealt in cars. The odometer of the car showed that it had done only 30,000 miles after a replacement engine had been fitted. In fact, the car had done 100,000 miles. The buyer successfully sued the seller-dealer for breach of warranty.

These two cases demonstrate that where the knowledge of the person who receives the statement is about the same or superior to that of the party making the statement, the courts would likely hold that such statement was intended as a representation and not a term of the contract.

Impact of the Misrepresentation Act

5.18 The Misrepresentation Act (Cap 390, 1994 Rev Ed) has supplemented the common law relating to pre-contractual misrepresentation (see Chapter 12) and the continued relevance of old case law providing guidelines to determine whether a statement is a term or a representation must be assessed in the context of a growing body of consumer protection law, the pervasive influence of hyper-advertising in a media saturated culture on a skeptical consumer public and the possibility that a party who makes a misrepresentation whether innocent or negligent could be liable to the same extent as a person making a fraudulent misrepresentation unless the party making the representation had objectively reasonable grounds to believe and did believe up to the time the contract was made that the facts represented were true. In other words, this Act imposes legal liability on the party making the representation not to state facts during the course of contractual negotiations that he or she cannot prove that he or she had reasonable grounds to believe that the representation was true; see *Howard Marine v Ogden & Sons* (1978). Advertisers and their clients who are averse to exposure to liability under the Act might opt to influence buyers with meaningless sounds and images that cannot be characterised as representations instead of providing information that are of a representational nature and thus attract potential liability under the Act. It should also be borne in mind that jurisdiction over most consumer disputes is now vested in the Small Claims Tribunals that use as a part of their procedure a mandatory mediation process. Insisting on the niceties of legal distinctions between representations and terms and invoking remedies under the Misrepresentation Act may not be an easy exercise in the specific context of effective consumer dispute resolution.

Relative Importance of Terms

Warranties, Conditions and Innominate Terms

5.19 Once a court finds that the contents of a contract include a statement, ie the statement is a term and not a representation, the court might find it necessary to classify the term as a 'condition', 'warranty' or an 'innominate term' because important consequences flow from the accurate classification of such term. Where one party fails to perform a condition, the other party is entitled to treat the contract as at an end. If the breach is in respect of a warranty, the innocent party may seek damages but the breach does not entitle the innocent party to terminate the contract. Thus if the innocent party mistakes a breach of warranty for a breach of condition, purports to terminate the contract because of this mistaken characterisation, and enters into another contract for the performance of the same obligation with a third party, that innocent party will be liable in damages as a result of the wrong assessment of the nature of the term. An innominate term is a term that the parties have expressly or, more usually, impliedly agreed that the effect of non-performance would depend upon the nature and consequences of the breach.

Accordingly, the court's first task is to assess the objective language of the contract to determine whether the parties intended the term in question to be a condition, an innominate term or a warranty. The parties are free to agree expressly that a particular term in a contract will be regarded as a condition with the result that if there is a breach of this term, the innocent party can terminate the contract regardless of how minor the consequence of the breach was. Sometimes, however, the court may conclude that, when the parties characterised a term as a 'condition', they did not intend that technical meaning; see *AG Schuler v Wickman Machine Tools Ltd* (1974). Where there is no express characterisation of a term, the courts will look 'at the contract in the light of the surrounding circumstances, and then [make up its mind] whether the intention of the parties, as gathered from the instrument itself, will best be carried out by treating the promise as a warranty sounding only in damages or as a condition precedent by the failure to perform which the other party is relieved of his liability' (per Bowen LJ in *Bentsen v Taylor, Sons & Co* (1893) at p 281). Sometimes, previous cases examining a standard term in a generic contract would conclude that the term was a condition, and confronted with such a term in the same type of contract, a court may conclude that the term was a condition; see *Maredelanto Compania Naviera SA v Bergbau-Handel GmbH, The Mihalis Angelos* (1971). Sometimes, a statute will classify a particular term as a condition and it will not usually be open to the parties to designate it as a warranty.

However if, after examining the term in question, the court decides that it is not a condition but also concludes at the same time that the breach of the term 'may be attended by trivial, minor or very grave consequences', it will characterise the term as an innominate term and not as a warranty; see per Lord Scarman in *Bunge Corporation, New York v Tradax Export SA Panama* (1981) (at p 717).

5.20 The words 'conditions' and 'warranties' as they appear in contracts also have *secondary* meanings that are quite different from the meanings given above. Thus the word 'condition' as used above, also known as a 'promissory condition', differs from a 'contingent condition'. As its name implies, a contingent condition is a term in the contract that specifies an event or events that must occur if the contract is to come into force or remain in force. These 'conditions precedent' and 'conditions subsequent' are terms but are not 'conditions' in the specialised sense used above. Rather, they are 'conditions' in the layperson sense of the word as in 'conditional'. Thus a sub-contract to build a garage in a house between the sub-contractor and the main contractor may contain a condition precedent to the effect that the contract will come into force only when the owner awards the building contract to the main contractor. Likewise, there might be a 'condition subsequent' to the effect that the sub-contract to build the garage will remain in force only insofar as the main building contract remains in force. In *AG Schuler v Wickman Machine Tool Sales Ltd* (1974), the majority of judges in the House of Lords concluded that the characterisation of a term as a 'condition' was not meant in the technical sense but in the layperson sense.

The word 'warranty' is frequently used in consumer contracts for the sale of goods or of services. The meaning here is different from the technical term 'warranty' when used to differentiate a term that is not a condition or an innominate term. In the consumer context, for example, a seller of a handphone may give a warranty for a certain period. This usually just means that the seller or dealer of the handphone will replace any faulty components and provide repairs free of charge during this warranty period.

Differentiating Between Conditions and Warranties

5.21 Because termination of the contract is an option for the innocent party where a condition in a contract has been breached and this could have serious consequences for both parties, it has been observed that courts should not be too ready to characterise terms as conditions; see *Cehave NV v Bremer Handelsgesellschaft mbH (The Hansa Nord)* (1976). However, parties to commercial contracts place a high value on certainty and certain terms in mercantile contracts, for example, those relating to time, have been regarded as conditions in the absence of evidence to the contrary. A number of possible guidelines as to when a term might be classified as a 'condition' have already been examined in paragraph 5.19, above. Under the traditional approach, if the term is not a 'condition', it would be a 'warranty'. This does not of course take into account the concept of the 'innominate term' under the '*Hong Kong Fir* approach' (as to which, see paragraph 5.22 ff, below). Bearing these observations in mind, just two of the classic cases, because of the similarity of their respective 'factual matrixes', may be considered.

In these two leading cases, opera singers on contract failed to honor the terms of their contracts but one failure was regarded as a breach of condition while the other was held to be a breach of warranty.

In *Poussard v Spiers* (1876), Madame Poussard had contracted to sing in an opera, the first performance of which was due to take place on 28 November 1874. The singer fell ill on 23 November 1874, and the illness prevented her from being able to sing until 4 December 1874. The defendant company had engaged a substitute who had insisted upon being offered the role for the complete engagement. The defendant agreed to this requirement and hired the substitute for the complete engagement. Madame Poussard presented herself for the role on 4 December 1874, and the defendant refused to engage her. She sued the defendant for breach of contract. The court rejected her suit holding that her failure to appear on opening night was a breach of a condition entitling the defendant to repudiate the contract and treat it as discharged.

Bettini v Gye (1876) provides a useful contrast to the *Poussard* case. Here, too, the plaintiff, an opera singer, had agreed to sing for a specified period. She had agreed to sing in England for a period commencing 30 March 1875, and to be in London for rehearsals for six days before the engagement. The plaintiff singer fell ill and arrived in England only on 28 March 1875, late for the rehearsals but in time for opening night. The defendant company rejected the singer's services and treated the contract as terminated. The court upheld the plaintiff's action for breach of contract despite the fact that it was she who did not appear for the rehearsals on time. It held that the obligation to participate in rehearsals was not a condition because participating in rehearsals was merely ancillary to the main purpose of the contract. The principal purpose of the contract was for the singer to engage in the actual performance, a task that she was able to perform.

These cases show that where the term goes to the root of the contract and deals with an obligation or statement of fact, the absence of which would have persuaded the innocent party not to enter into the contract in the first place, the term in question will be treated as a condition. On the other hand, if the term relates to a matter, the non-performance of which will not impair the substance of the bargain expected by the innocent party, the term will be regarded as a warranty.

The 'Hong Kong Fir *Approach' and A Suggested Synthesis Between the 'Condition-Warranty' and* 'Hong Kong Fir' *Approaches*

5.22 Although the distinction between conditions and warranties (the 'Condition-Warranty approach') has existed for more than a century, the characterisation of a new class of terms, *the innominate term*, took place relatively recently in the case of *Hong Kong Fir Shipping Co Ltd v Kawasaki Kisen Kaisha Ltd* (1962), particularly in the judgment of Diplock LJ (as he then was). However, in a later case, *Bunge Corporation, New York v Tradax Export SA Panama* (1981) (at p 717), Lord Scarman observed that *Hong Kong Fir* case represented merely a rediscovery and reaffirmation of a type of term that was neither a condition nor a warranty. Professor Phang has argued that the phrase '*Hong Kong Fir* approach' to this type of term is more appropriate since the term is of a type radically different from the normal 'condition' and 'warranty' because of its focus on *the nature and consequences of the breach of the term rather than on the intention of the parties*: see A Phang, *International Encyclopedia of Laws—Contracts (Singapore)* (2000) at paragraph 465.

Innominate terms are those terms, not explicitly characterised by the parties as 'conditions', that cannot be immediately categorised as conditions or warranties simply by looking at their content because it is possible to envisage both serious as well as extremely trivial breaches of the term. An innominate term could *operate* either as a condition or a warranty depending on the nature and consequences of the breach. If the breach is serious, given the context of the contract, the courts will regard the beach as if it were a breach of condition with all the consequences that such a breach entails. In other words, in the event of a dispute, the task of the court will be to decide whether the parties, if they had been asked what would happen if the breach in question would occur, would have replied, 'it goes without saying that, if that happens, the contract is at an end': see *Bunge Corporation, New York v Tradax Export SA Panama* (1981) (at p 717). On the other hand, if the breach were not serious applying the foregoing criterion, then the court would hold that the breach was as if it were a breach of warranty with the consequence that the innocent party must continue performing the contract and seek only damages. To illustrate, contracts to rent ships, known as charterparty contracts, frequently contain a term that the ship must be seaworthy. If the owner delivers the ship with a nail missing, she would be in breach of the term of seaworthiness, and she would also breach the term if she delivered a ship, the engines of which did not work. Obviously, the two types of breaches, whilst both breaches as to the term as to seaworthiness, are not the same. The absence of a nail would not lead to serious consequences while the defective engines would certainly lead to serious consequences.

In *Bunge Corporation, New York v Tradax Export SA Panama* (1981), the court held that applying the '*Hong Kong Fir* approach' involves a two-step process. First, the court must determine whether the language of the term requires it to be classified as a condition according to the traditional 'condition-warranty' approach. Second, it is only after determining that the term is not a condition but is, rather, an innominate term, must the court consider whether in the circumstances of the case, the breach has deprived the innocent party of substantially the entirety of the benefit of the contract it was intended that the innocent party should have, in which case the consequences of a breach of a condition would follow. The difficulty with such an approach is that when a term is held not to be a condition, it is not automatically treated as a warranty. The scope of the concept of the warranty may well become very drastically reduced as a result (and cf per Robert Goff LJ (as he then was) in *Compagnie General Maritime v Diakan Spirit SA (The 'Ymnos')* (1982) at p 583; see also the discussion at the end of this paragraph).

This alternative approach leads to useful commercial results since it avoids the rigid dualistic classification and allows a court to achieve a pragmatic outcome with regard to terms that are worded in such general and wide language so as to admit minor and major breaches. It would work hardship on the parties if a minor infraction of such terms were to entitle the innocent party to treat the contract as discharged, and conversely, if a serious infraction had occurred instead, prevent discharge by the innocent parties. Some critics argue that adopting such an approach could cause problems where an innocent party mistakenly terminates the contract because she thought that the breach of the innominate term was sufficiently serious. As she made this mistake, she could be liable for wrongfully repudiating the contract. While this possibility exists, the '*Hong Kong Fir* approach' may help to promote justice as illustrated by the case of *The Hansa Nord* (1974). Here, the buyers of citrus pulp rejected the shipment on the ground that it was not in good condition, but thereafter bought the shipment through one of their agents at more than a 60% discount, and used the pulp for the purpose for which the buyers originally purchased the pulp. The court categorised the term relating to quality as an innominate term and found that the slight consequences of the breach did not justify termination. Instead, the buyers had to be content with damages. The recognition of this new category of terms has broken the rigid classification of terms into conditions and warranties. Even though the UK Sale of Goods Act, made applicable in Singapore under the Application of English Law Act (and see Cap 393, 1994 Rev Ed), categorises terms as 'warranties' and 'conditions' without any mention of a third category, 'innominate terms', the English courts have held that the Sale of Goods Act accommodates this third category; see *Cehave NV v Bremer Handelsgesellschaft mbH* (1976). Recognition of this approach now promotes fairer dealings among contracting parties and allows commercial contracts to address flexibly the events that take place during the performance of such contracts. In effect, the courts tell parties to a contract that they are free to designate terms as 'conditions', which designation will be honoured if the courts ascertain that the parties meant what they said in the legal sense. In the absence of such an explicit characterisation of the term by the parties or by statute, the courts would attempt to discover from the objective language of the contract whether the parties intended the term to be a condition. Previous cases characterising the term as a condition, practices of the trade and sector specific terms such as shipping terms will guide the courts in making such a determination (see also paragraph 5.19, above). If this exercise precludes the court from finding that the term in question is a condition, it will look at the range of possible consequences of breaching that term, and if these include both serious and trivial consequences, then the courts will treat the term as an innominate term and attach the consequences of a breach of condition where the breach leads to serious consequences. Quite often, there could be serious as well as trivial consequences flowing from different breaches of the same term. The result is that the scope of coverage of conditions, warranties and innominate terms is immense with warranties being restricted to only those terms where no breach can ever give rise to the discharge of contract: see *Compagnie General Maritime v Diakan Spirit SA (The 'Ymnos')* (1982). As already mentioned, this very drastically reduces both the role and scope of warranties generally.

Implied Terms

5.23 The express terms of a contract, ie those terms that the parties explicitly incorporate in their contract, can hardly envisage and provide for all eventualities, especially in complex transactions. Sometimes, the parties envisage eventualities but prefer not to address them to save time or to avoid a disagreement from preventing the formation of the contract. The law supplements the express terms of a contract by a category of terms known as implied terms. This category of implied terms can itself be divided into sub-categories depending on how the term is implied.

First, there is the category of terms implied in fact. When confronted with a gap in the contract, the court asks itself what the parties would have unequivocally agreed upon had they addressed their minds to the problem or alternatively tries to supply a term that would give business efficacy to the contract.

Second, there is the category of terms implied by law or to use computer terminology favoured by Lord Steyn in *Malik v Bank of Credit and Commerce International SA* (1997) (at pp 108–109) 'default terms'. This category concerns specific types of contracts, usually defining relationships between the parties such as landlord and tenant or employer and employee, where the courts imply a term not because of the presumed intention of the parties but because the implied term gives effect to policies intended to make the relationship work in that particular category of contract. Thus, for example, in employment contracts, the courts will presume that certain terms apply unless the parties negate those implied terms by other terms.

Third, there is a category of terms that a law passed by parliament states must be implied in some types of contract. The Sale of Goods Act (Cap 393, 1994 Rev Ed) furnishes the best example of this category.

Finally, there is a category of terms that relate to contracts relating to specialist subjects like the sale of commodities. These contracts take place in the context of trade associations and practices that have developed rules on how the contract is to be performed and expands on the obligations of the parties.

Terms Implied in Fact

5.24 While the courts have frequently declared that they are unwilling to make contracts on behalf of the parties, they are willing to imply a term into a contract either when the term to be implied is obvious or where the implication is necessary in order to give business efficacy to the contract. Frequently, there is an overlap of these standards.

A court would imply a term in a contract if it is satisfied that the parties, if they had been asked by an officious bystander whether they would have included the term to be implied as an express term, would both testily answer 'Oh, of course!' (per Mackinnon LJ in *Shirlaw v Southern Foundries (1926) Ltd* (1939) at p 124). Because the term to be implied must be so obvious as to not admit of possible disagreement, if there are different possible answers or answers with qualifications, the implication may not take place.

Some terms may not be obvious but the contract will not work if they are not implied. Thus, the courts are willing to imply such terms where the implied term would inject business efficacy to the contract. In *The Moorcock* (1889), the defendants were the owners of a jetty in the Thames River. They contracted with the plaintiff to have the plaintiff's boat, *The Moorcock*, docked at the jetty. Both parties knew that when the tide was low, the vessel would lie on the riverbed. During the low tide, the vessel settled on a ridge of hard ground beneath the mud and was damaged. The defendants had not given a warranty to the effect that the place was safe and that the ship could rest on it without damage. Despite this omission, the court held that there was an implied warranty by the defendants to this effect and therefore were liable for damages caused by the breach of warranty. The court observed that the warranty was implied from the presumed intention of the parties. The purpose of the implication was to give business efficacy to the transaction that both parties must have intended. The alternative, that was unacceptable, was to impose on one party all the risks of the transaction or to free the other side from all chances of failure.

5.25 There have been scores of cases that have expanded on the criteria for implying terms in fact. In *BP Refinery (Westernport) Pty Ltd v Shire of Hastings* (1977), the Privy Council, a court that hears appeals from some Commonwealth countries, enumerated the following conditions that must be present in order for a term to be implied:

(1) the term to be implied must be reasonable and equitable;

(2) the term implied must be necessary to give business efficacy to the contract. Thus, no term will be implied if the contract is effective without it;
(3) the term implied must be so obvious that 'it goes without saying';
(4) it must be capable of clear expression; and
(5) it must not contradict any express term of the contract.

In *Loh Siok Wah v American International Assurance Co Ltd* (1999) (at p 289), Chan Seng Onn JC observed that while there is a considerable overlap between the 'business efficacy' and the 'officious bystander' tests, they should not be regarded as cumulative and may be alternative criteria. Professor Phang argues that the 'business efficacy' and 'officious bystander' criteria both connote a requirement of necessity and, to that extent, the tests are complementary rather than alternative tests, with the 'business efficacy' test serving as the basic theoretical guideline and the 'officious bystander' test providing the practical mode for effecting the general principle (see A Phang, 'Implied Terms Revisited' [1990] *Journal of Business Law* 394 at p 397). The criterion of 'reasonable and equitable' implication (in the above quotation), while vague, merely provides a ground for refusing implication where the term sought to be implied is manifestly unfair or unreasonable. However, unlike 'terms implied in law' (considered in the following paragraph), the criterion of reasonableness alone is insufficient; what is required, rather, is the stricter criterion of necessity, which (as we have seen) is embodied within both the 'business efficacy' and 'officious bystander' tests.

Terms Implied in Law

5.26 The courts imply terms in certain types of contracts, usually contracts that provide for a relationship between the parties such as an employer and an employee. The advantages of having such standardised terms are that certainty is promoted, risk can properly be estimated and important social policies can be given effect. For instance, a human resources manager in a company can find out what terms the law will imply in the employment relationship and can provide for risks by taking insurance. Likewise, a lessor will know what duties will be implied in a lease and can adjust the rent to be charged in order to pay for the costs associated with discharging those duties. Adopting a usage derived from computer use—default printer—the House of Lords has recently referred to these terms as 'default terms' because they will apply unless overridden by the parties to the particular transaction; see, for example, *Malik v Bank of Credit & Commerce International SA* (1998).

5.27 In the leading case of *Liverpool City Council v Irwin* (1977), a landlord of a block of apartments was held to be under an implied obligation to take reasonable care of the common areas and keep them in a reasonable state of repair, and in *Scally v Southern Health and Social Services Board* (1992), employees who had been represented by a union that had negotiated certain pension rights for them were able to obtain damages from the employer who had failed to notify them of these rights because the court implied a term requiring the employers to bring this to the notice of the employees. The House of Lords reasoned that since these rights were derived from a collective bargain, the employees could not be expected to become aware of them on their own.

In *Lister v Romford Ice & Cold Storage Ltd* (1957), the court implied a term of faithful service by the employee in the contract of employment. The implied term also required the employee to indemnify his employer where the employee caused losses to the employer in the course of employment.

In *Malik v Bank of Credit & Commerce International SA* (1998), the court held that there was an implied term in employment contracts that the relationship between employer and employee was one of trust and confidence and that neither party would do anything, without good cause, that would damage this relationship.

The courts are also willing to imply a term in order to facilitate global commerce and the smooth functioning of arbitral agreements. Thus, it is an implied term of an arbitration agreement that the parties will perform the award issued by the arbitral tribunal: see *Associated Electric & Gas Insurance Services Ltd v European Reinsurance Company of Zurich* (2003).

5.28 The list of default terms or terms implied by law is not closed. The New Economy has generated a form of contracts made in cyberspace that have yet to evolve implied terms on a range of issues such as the type of security that a credit card payment may receive and the privacy that would be accorded to the customer who provides personal details about herself. But it is by no means clear that there are a coherent set of criteria that must be satisfied before a court would imply a new term in law or new default term in this or other areas. Some scholars have argued that while the courts state that they are using criteria such as 'necessity', the courts in fact are using a standard of 'reasonableness' and that, by insisting on the use of the concept of 'necessity' instead, the courts are confusingly conflating 'terms implied in fact' with 'terms implied in law': see, for example, A Phang, 'Implied Terms Revisited' [1990] *Journal of Business Law* 394.

Terms Implied by Statute

5.29 A statute may imply terms in a particular type of contract. When a statute implies terms in a contract, it is not trying to anticipate and provide for the intentions of the parties. Instead, the implication is on grounds of public policy with Parliament believing that such contracts must contain these implied terms unless explicitly dislodged by the parties. Perhaps, the most well-known instance of terms implied by statute is the sales of goods legislation contained in the UK Sale of Goods Act ('SOGA'), applicable in Singapore pursuant to the Application of English Law Act (and see Cap 393, 1994 Rev Ed), and the United Nations Convention on the International Sale of Goods which has been made a part of Singapore law (see the Sale of Goods (United Nations Convention) Act (Cap 283A,

1996 Rev Ed)). The terms implied by sale of goods legislation attempt to provide coherence and a framework to a type of contract that is entered into thousands of times a day. These implied terms allow the seller to price goods by reference to the risk exposure created by the implied terms and allows the buyer and seller to routinely engage in sales without wasting time in hammering out details. The following illustrations of terms implied by SOGA show that the content of what is implied is necessary for the smooth functioning of a sale of goods system in a country. For example, section 12(1) of SOGA implies a condition that the seller has a right to sell the goods. Section 12(2) implies a warranty that the goods are free from charges or encumbrances in favour of third parties. Section 13(1) implies a condition that goods sold by description will correspond with their description and Section 15(1) that goods sold by sample will correspond with their sample. Section 14(1) implies a warranty that where a seller sells goods in the course of his business, there is an implied warranty that the goods supplied under the contract are of a satisfactory quality.

By incorporating this 'shorthand' in sales of goods transactions, the SOGA allows the seller and the buyer to focus on the main elements of the transaction and not be distracted by the need to cross the 't's and dot the 'i's. This in turn, reduces transaction costs and frees up time for the parties to engage in more productive economic transactions. Thus, a grocery store manager may work on managing the store without having to meet customers and assure them on these matters while they stand in line at the checkout queue.

Terms Implied by Custom

5.30 Contracts are rarely divorced from their surroundings and context. A particular trade practice, the features of the market and even the customs of the locality may be relevant to the operation of the contract. Accordingly, where a party engages in contracting within a particular trade, for example, the coffee trade, that party will be bound by the usage in that trade if the usage is well-known, certain, reasonable and legal: see *Nelson v Dahl* (1879). In *Hutton v Warren* (1836), the dispute centered on a tenant farmer's claim to a fair share for seeds and allowance. The plaintiff farmer gave the landlord notice of his intention to quit farming the land. However, the lease required the farmer to continue to plant during the notice period. He would no longer be in a contractual relationship when harvest time came around. The issue was whether the farmer was entitled to a fair allowance even though the crop had not been harvested. The court reasoned (at p 475) that this was a type of contract where 'the parties did not express in writing the whole of the contract by which they intended to be bound but to contract with reference to known usages'. If it can be shown that those doing business in a particular community had a generally accepted custom and that anyone inquiring would have been told about that custom, then this custom would bind the parties even if both of them were ignorant of its existence: see *Chan Cheng Kum v Wah Tat Bank Ltd* (1971).

To be implied in a contract, a custom must be a usage that is sufficiently uniform and accepted by the relevant community as controlling in the absence of express agreements. Pointing to the impact of rapid globalisation and industrialisation in Singapore, Professor Phang argues that the emergence of significant local custom that could be implied in Singapore contracts is remote: see A Phang, *International Encyclopedia of Laws—Contracts (Singapore)* (2000) at paragraph 358.

CHAPTER 6 Exception Clauses

PARAGRAPHS

6.1–6.7 **Introduction**

6.8 **Incorporation**
6.9 Methods of Incorporation
6.10–6.11 (1) Incorporation by Signature
6.12–6.16 (2) Incorporation by Notice
6.17–6.18 (3) Incorporation by Prior Course of Dealing Between the Parties
6.19–6.20 Standard Form Contracts

6.21 **Construction**
6.22–6.23 The *Contra Proferentum* Rule
6.24–6.26 The Rule in Cases of Negligence Liability
6.27–6.28 The Doctrine of Fundamental Breach
6.29–6.30 Other Devices Relating to Construction

6.31–6.36 **Statutory Limitations on the Use of Exception Clauses**
6.37–6.39 Contracts to Which the UCTA Does Not Apply
6.40 The Applicability of the UCTA to 'Business Liability' for Contractual and Tortious Claims
6.41–6.43 The Applicability of the UCTA to Negligence Liability
6.44–6.46 The Applicability of the UCTA to Cases of Breach of Contract and Other General Contractual Claims Relating to Performance
6.47–6.48 The Applicability of the UCTA to Liability Arising from the Sale or Supply of Goods
6.49–6.50 The UCTA and Consumer Contracts
6.51–6.56 The Test of Reasonableness

6.57–6.60 **Exception Clauses and Electronic Contracts**

6.61–6.62 **Exception Clauses and Consumer Protection Legislation in Singapore**

Introduction

6.1 A type of express term that is increasingly common in many written contracts is the 'exception clause'. An exception clause is not a specific legal term of art, and although various academic and judicial attempts have been made to define it, it is best illustrated by reference both to its functions as well as its treatment under common and statutory law. Where its functions are concerned, an exception clause seeks essentially to do one of three things: (1) it may attempt to exclude a contracting party's liability completely; (2) it may attempt to limit that liability (eg to a certain money amount); or (3) it may attempt to pass the liability (or the risk thereof) to a third party. These three types of exception clauses may be further described, respectively, as (1) exclusion (or exemption) clauses; (2) limitation of liability clauses; and (3) indemnity clauses. In this chapter, the term 'exception clause' is used to delineate all of these types of clauses.

6.2 Any discussion of exception clauses would be incomplete without noting two developments that serve to place the legal treatment of exception clauses in context. One such development may be classified as theoretical/historical, and the other as a more recent phenomenon in the evolution of contract law. Where the theoretical/historical aspect is concerned, the use and legal treatment of exception clauses hark back to the idea of freedom of contract, while the latter aspect takes into account the growing awareness of consumer protection as a valid interest to be considered and balanced against other commercial considerations in contractual matters, and the reality of modern contractual negotiations and bargaining.

The idea of freedom of contract is inextricably bound up with the emergence of *laissez-faire* economic theory in the 19th century. Under this theory, the free market (through private enterprise) and not the state should determine the pricing, movement and growth of commerce; at the same time, ideas of individual welfare and choice developed such that, where individuals were concerned, they should have the autonomy to make their own rational choices. In terms of contracts, this meant that an individual should have the freedom to determine what he/she is willing to agree to (or not), and the state should not intervene to change what such individuals have agreed on in their contracts with each other. A contract therefore represents a freely-negotiated, voluntary set of rights and obligations that individual parties have rationally agreed to take upon themselves; and neither the courts nor the legislature should interfere with that freedom of choice; rather, they ought to respect the sanctity of the contract that such parties have freely entered into. The courts' role was thus to give effect to the parties' intention, as evident from their contractual promises to each other. This policy is exemplified by the remarks of Sir George Jessel MR in *Printing and Numerical Registering Co v Sampson* (1875) (at p 465):

> 'If there is one thing which more than any other public policy requires it is that men of full age and competent understanding

> shall have the utmost liberty in contracting, and that their contracts when entered into freely and voluntarily shall be held sacred and shall be enforced by the courts of justice. Therefore you have this paramount public policy to consider—that you are not lightly to interfere with freedom of contract.'

Adopting this view, it would follow that an exception clause, however favourably it operated to the benefit of one contracting party (and however unfair its application might therefore be to the other party), should be upheld. To do otherwise would be to intrude on the sanctity of contract and interfere with the parties' freedom of contract.

6.3 As against this view, however, as the 20th century progressed, it became evident that the reality of the contracting process bore less and less resemblance to the idea of individual autonomy in negotiating agreement. Commercial transactions did not necessarily take place between businesses but included business-consumer transactions; they also did not necessarily take place between parties with identical (or even substantially similar) bargaining powers. To underscore the growing divergence between reality and theory, standard form contracts became more commonly used and the variety and complexity of contracts also increased. The reality of 20th century contractual negotiation and agreement was thus, increasingly, one where a standard form contract containing terms (including exception clauses) drafted by one party was agreed to by the other party who, in a growing number of situations, was also a consumer. While it could be argued that this kind of situation would not preclude the consumer (or other parties faced with a standard form contract) from evaluating the risks and potential disadvantages of agreeing to such forms and exception clauses, it was also clear that this was not necessarily the kind of autonomous bargaining situation in which freedom of contract could be completely realised. Similarly, while an exception clause could be viewed also as a means of allocating risks between the parties to a transaction, in cases where the party asked to agree to such a clause was of lesser bargaining power compared to the party attempting to impose the clause, any risk allocation exercise could be an unbalanced one, favouring one party over the other due not to a fully-negotiated bargaining process, but rather to stronger bargaining power on the part of that party.

6.4 Faced with these developments, the English courts began, in the latter half of the 20th century, to adopt a number of devices to mitigate the excessive unfairness that could result from the unrestricted application of exception clauses. These devices were centered on rules of construction that allowed the courts to construe exception clauses narrowly or to restrict the scope of application thereof, in order to prevent unwarranted abuse of exception clauses by those seeking to escape liability.

6.5 One interesting development in this context was the distinction that some courts began to make between exclusion/exception clauses and limitation of liability clauses. The former were thought to be more oppressive (and hence more rigidly construed) while the latter could be considered more reasonably appropriate in commercial contracts, being by their nature more directly related to calculations of risk and monetary losses. For example, in *Ailsa Craig Fishing Co Ltd v Malvern Fishing Co Ltd & Securicor (Scotland)* (1983), Lord Wilberforce stated (at p 966) that:

> 'Clauses of limitation are not regarded by the courts with the same hostility as clauses of exclusion; this is because they must be related to other terms, in particular to the risks to which the defending party may be exposed, the remuneration which he received, and possibly also the opportunity of the other party to insure.'

Lord Fraser thought similarly, stating (at p 971) that 'there is no reason why [limitation clauses] should be judged by the specially exacting standards which are applied to exclusion clauses'. While the passage of the Unfair Contract Terms Act in the UK in 1977 resulted in less need for judicial activism in restraining the more excessive exception clauses that were the subject of dispute, the distinction between exclusion/exception clauses and limitation of liability clauses may still be relevant to the application of the test of reasonableness prescribed by the Act (discussed below).

6.6 Another significant development that led to the courts' readiness to regard exception clauses as abusive and unreasonable was the growing recognition that consumer protection was a necessary consideration in developing and applying contractual rules. With the introduction of consumer protection legislation and fair trading regulations, the common law as regards contracts was also inevitably influenced by the principles and interests behind such laws. In the context of exception clauses, the fact that such laws have been developed and enacted, hence creating valid legal channels for the protection of consumers and disadvantaged parties, may also lessen any judicially perceived need for exception clauses to be construed in such a manner so as to protect these same interests.

In 1977, the Unfair Contract Terms Act became law in the UK, thus finally signalling the legislature's involvement in regulating the application of exception clauses. The Unfair Contract Terms Act ('UCTA') is also law in Singapore (as Cap 396, 1994 Rev Ed), by virtue of the Application of English Law Act (Cap 7A, 1994 Rev Ed), and thus remains significant for determining the scope and applicability of exception clauses in Singapore.

6.7 In order, however, for an exception clause to have its intended effect (as drafted), it has to satisfy the following requirements:

- it has to be properly incorporated into the contract;
- it has to, upon its proper construction, apply to the situation at hand; and
- its operation is not excluded or restricted by statute, viz UCTA.

Incorporation

6.8 As with other express terms in a contract, an exception clause is legally operative only if it forms an integral part of the contract in question. Where incorporation of exception clauses is concerned, there are two related issues that can arise. First, there may be an issue as to whether or not the *method* of incorporation is sufficient to make the clause part of the contract; and secondly, whether or not the clause was incorporated *in time* (ie before or at the time the contract was made). Where the method of incorporation is in issue, a related question that can arise concerns the *form or document* in which the clause appears (ie whether such form or document is by its nature a contractual document or not).

Methods of Incorporation

6.9 There are generally three methods by which an exception clause may be incorporated into a contract:

- by signature;
- by notice; or
- by a prior course of dealing between the parties.

However, the contractual (or non-contractual and hence non-binding) nature of the document containing the exception clause may be relevant even in cases where one of the methods of incorporation may have been used validly. As such, a preliminary issue is often whether or not the document within which the exception clause is found can properly be considered an integral and binding part of the contract. If the document is not one that can be considered a contractual document, the exception clause will then not be effective, as it would be unfair to hold a party bound to a term in a document that she did not reasonably consider to be binding and would not reasonably expect to find contractual terms in. While this question is one of fact in every case, it is clear that a document that a reasonable person would expect to be nothing more than a mere receipt for the payment of money, or an acknowledgment that payment has been made, would not constitute a contractual document. Thus, in *Chapelton v Barry Urban District Council* (1940), deck-chairs were stacked on the beach near a notice that instructed hirers to obtain tickets from the attendant, and to retain the tickets for purposes of inspection. An exception clause was printed on the ticket but no mention of it was found on the notice. The English Court of Appeal held that the defendant council could not rely on the exception clause, as a reasonable person would assume that the ticket was no more than a receipt issued for the money paid over to hire the deck-chairs.

(1) *Incorporation by Signature*

6.10 If a person has signed the contract, which document contains the exception clause, then in the absence of fraud or misrepresentation, that person is bound to all the terms of that contract, including the exception clause. This rule applies regardless of whether or not she read or was aware of the existence of the clause. The strictness of the rule seems to reflect the principle of certainty of contract, possibly over considerations of fairness in individual cases, as a person is essentially deemed to have agreed to whatever she has signed, and to have read and understood the terms thereof, whether or not she actually did so. For example, in *L'Estrange v Graucob* (1934), the purchaser of a cigarette vending machine that turned out to be unfit for the purpose for which it was purchased was held bound by the exclusion clause in the standard form sale contract that she signed, even though the clause was in very small print and she did not read the terms.

6.11 There may, however, be a possible exception to the rule on incorporation by signature. Where the effect of an exception clause was misrepresented to the party against whom the clause is sought to be imposed, before or at the time of the contract, the party seeking to rely on that exception clause may be prevented from doing so by the court. This was the case in *Curtis v Chemical Cleaning and Dyeing Co* (1951), where the plaintiff had been told (by the defendant's employee) that the receipt she had to sign contained clauses that exempted the defendant from the risk of damage to the beads and sequins on the plaintiff's dress. In fact, the clause exempted the defendant from 'any damage, however caused'. The English Court of Appeal held that the defendant could not rely on the exception clause because of the innocent misrepresentation that had been made to the plaintiff by the employee. It should be noted, however, that the applicability of this case may now be affected by section 8 of the Unfair Contract Terms Act ('UCTA'), which amends section 3 of the Misrepresentation Act (Cap 390, 1994 Rev Ed) to the effect that where a contract contains a term that excludes or restricts a person's liability for 'any misrepresentation made by him before the contract was made' or in relation to 'any remedy [available to the other contracting party] by reason of such misrepresentation', the term in question will be effective only if it satisfies the test of reasonableness (which test is discussed below) under the UCTA. There has been some case law on the effect of an operative misrepresentation on the applicability of exception clauses and section 8 of the UCTA. These cases are discussed in Chapter 12 (at paragraphs 12.50 ff).

The validity of exception clauses that are incorporated by signature (even where the signatory does not know or has not read the terms) is a question that takes on even greater significance in the context of standard form contracts. This issue is discussed further below.

(2) *Incorporation by Notice*

6.12 Where the contract containing the exception clause is not signed, or where there is no written contract, it may be possible to incorporate an exception clause into the contract if the person seeking to rely on it (the 'relying party') has given the other party reasonably sufficient notice of the existence of the clause. Thus, in *Parker v South Eastern Railway Co* (1877), the appellate court held that the issue to be decided, in determining whether or not the defendant railway could rely on a clause on a cloakroom ticket limiting its liability, was whether or not the defendant had taken reasonably sufficient steps to notify the plaintiff of the existence of the term in question. The plaintiff had deposited a bag in the cloakroom and received a ticket which had printed conditions on its back. He admitted he knew there was printing on the ticket, but claimed he did not know the printing contained conditions and he had not read them. At the re-trial, three principles emerged, as follows:

- a person who did not know that there was printing on the ticket is not bound by the conditions;
- a person who knows there was printing on the ticket, and who knows or believes that the printing contained or referred to conditions, is bound by those conditions; and
- a person who knows there was printing on the ticket, but does not know or believe that the printing contained or referred to conditions, will, however, nevertheless be bound by those conditions where the party seeking to rely on the conditions has provided reasonable notice that the printing contained conditions.

6.13 What constitutes reasonably sufficient notice in any one case is necessarily a question of fact, although some guidance can be drawn from the leading cases in this area. The general guideline appears to be that the more onerous or unusual the clause, the more the relying party may have to do to bring the clause to the attention to the other party.

Thus, in *Interfoto Picture Library v Stiletto Visual Programmes* (1988), the defendants had hired photographic transparencies from the plaintiffs. The transparencies were delivered to the defendants with a delivery note setting out various printed conditions, including a term that provided for a daily charge to be imposed for late return of the transparencies (the sum was £5 per day, plus value-added tax, for each day after 14 days from the due date, which was 19 March). The defendants never used the transparencies and returned them to the plaintiffs only on 2 April. The late charge that the plaintiffs sought to impose for the period of 19 March to 2 April amounted to £3,783.50. The Court of Appeal held that, as the daily charge was much higher than what would usually be charged, the term was a particularly onerous one that required a greater degree of notice than was given in the instant case, where it was merely printed on the plaintiff's standard terms. The Court also quoted, with approval, Lord Denning's statement in *Spurling v Bradshaw* (1956) (at p 466) to the effect that:

> 'Some clauses are so onerous they would need to be printed in red ink on the face of the document with a red hand pointing to it before notice could be held to be sufficient ... Onerous or oppressive clauses must be drawn clearly to the other party's notice, otherwise they will not be incorporated.'

6.14 Besides the question of adequacy of notice, however, a related issue is that of *when* such notice is given. The principle is that notice has to be given either before, or at the time of, contracting. Any notice of terms that is given after the contract has been concluded, however adequate by the test described above, will not be effective to incorporate those terms into the contract. This is illustrated by the case of *Olley v Marlborough Court Ltd* (1949), where a husband and wife arrived at the Marlborough Court Hotel and paid in advance for a week's lodging. They then went up to their room, where there was a notice stating that '[t]he proprietors will not hold themselves responsible for articles lost or stolen unless handed to the manageress for safe custody'. During their stay at the hotel, a thief entered their room and stole some furs. The majority of the Court of Appeal found that the contract had been concluded before the guests went to their room and as such, the terms of the notice had not been incorporated into the contract.

6.15 The case of *Thornton v Shoe Lane Parking* (1971) is significant for its decision on the same point of law, as well as Lord Denning MR's thorough analysis of the role of automatic booking or ticket machines in determining when a contract is formed, such machines being the latest in the long line of 'ticket cases' that has arisen in English contract law. In this case, where the plaintiff was injured in the defendants' car park, the Court of Appeal held that the defendants could not rely on the exception clause as notice thereof had been given only after the contract had been concluded. Although the actual facts of the case rendered the following statement of Lord Denning MR (at p 689) *obiter dicta*, it is still very instructive:

> 'The customer pays his money and gets a ticket. He cannot refuse it. He cannot get his money back. He may protest to the machine, even swear at it; but it will remain unmoved. He is committed beyond recall. He was committed at the very moment when he put his money into the machine. The contract was concluded at that time. It can be translated into offer and acceptance in this way. The offer is made when the proprietor of the machine holds it out as being ready to receive the money. The acceptance takes place when the customer puts his money into the slot. The terms of the offer are contained in the notice placed on or near the machine stating what is offered for the money. The customer is bound by those terms as long as they are sufficiently brought to his notice beforehand, but not otherwise. He is not bound by the terms printed on the ticket if they differ from the notice, because the ticket comes too late. The contract has already been made.'

6.16 Similar issues of incorporation can arise in the context of cyberspace. Insofar as incorporation by signature is concerned, what, for instance, constitutes a valid signature might be usefully considered. Under Singapore law, the provisions of the Electronic Transactions Act (Cap 88, 1999 Rev Ed) would govern this question. The issue of reasonable notice, in the context of an electronic contract, can also arise; for example, would including an exception clause in such a contract in bold type, but buried more than midway through a long electronic document reproduced onscreen in small fonts such that a computer user has to scroll down through several screens of 'legalese' and text, suffice? It is likely, however, that the basic principles enunciated above would be very similar, notwithstanding the fact that the exception clauses concerned will be found within the context of a computer screen or an electronic record.

(3) *Incorporation by Prior Course of Dealing Between the Parties*

6.17 Where there has been a consistent and sufficiently regular previous course of dealing between the parties to the contract in question, a term from that course of dealing may be found to have been incorporated into the parties' contract even though neither party made reference to such a term at that time. In *McCutcheon v David MacBrayne Ltd* (1964), a farmer who had previously used MacBrayne's services arranged with MacBrayne for a car to be shipped. The car was lost as a result of the ship sinking. The shippers could not rely on an exception clause in the freight invoice as that had been delivered to the farmer only after he had concluded the oral contract with MacBrayne. The same exception clause was contained in a risk note that MacBrayne often used and that the farmer had sometimes signed in the past, although MacBrayne had omitted the note on this occasion. It was held that the exception clause was not incorporated in this case as there had not been a sufficiently consistent course of dealing between the parties. However, whether or not an exception clause is incorporated through a previous course of dealing between contracting parties would depend, in the final analysis, very much upon the actual facts of the particular case itself.

6.18 A variation that, admittedly, does not fall neatly within the present heading is what Professor Treitel describes as 'trade custom or usage' (see GH Treitel, *The Law of Contract* (10th ed, 1999) at p 201). Where this is the case, the court might hold the exception clause concerned as incorporated into the contract even though there may have been no prior dealings as such between the parties. This was the situation in *British Crane Hire Corporation Ltd v Ipswich Plant Hire Ltd* (1975), where the parties were plant hirers who were therefore in the trade of hiring out plant and who were of equal bargaining power. Lord Denning MR observed (at p 311) thus:

> 'I would not put it so much on the course of dealing, but rather on the common understanding which is to be derived from the conduct of the parties, namely, that the hiring was to be on the terms of the plaintiffs' usual conditions.'

Standard Form Contracts

6.19 The issue of incorporation can be particularly important where a standard form contract is used, especially where it is a business-consumer transaction, when it is often the case that the business in question will wish to contract only on the basis of its standard terms (encapsulated in a standard form contract) and the consumer may have little or no choice but to accept those terms without negotiation. Standard form contracts are also commonly used in business-to-business transactions where, although the question of inequality of bargaining power as between a business and an individual consumer may not arise, there may still be a question as to whether the terms contained in such standard form contracts have been validly incorporated.

6.20 A distinction may be drawn between standard form contracts that have been signed by the party who has to accept the terms thereof (including the exception clause in question), which terms were drafted or are being relied upon by the other party, and standard form contracts where the exception clause is contained in a document that is unsigned and that may in fact be a document separate from the standard form contract itself. For example, a contracting party may have signed a standard form (such as a delivery order or sales quotation), which refers to terms contained in a different document (possibly another standard form, such as a set of industry rules, containing an exception clause not found in the signed contract) that she does not sign and may not have seen or read. This type of situation has become fairly common business practice, particularly in regard to the use of standard forms, and combines the issues presented by two methods of incorporation that previously and generally were treated separately, viz incorporation by signature and incorporation by notice.

If the rule in *L'Estrange v Graucob* is applied to this example wholesale, it would not matter that the exception clause is contained in a different, unsigned document, but always provided that there is sufficient evidence to show that the terms contained in this other document form part of the signed contract. The question therefore is not whether the signing party also signed the second document containing the relevant terms, nor whether the second document contained onerous or unusual clauses that required them to be reasonably brought to the signing party's attention. Rather, the question is whether or not the signed document clearly refers to the terms contained in the second, unsigned, document such that these terms can be said to have been successfully incorporated into the contract. Thus, if the signed document makes a specific and express reference to terms found elsewhere, this would be sufficient to bind the signatory even if she has never seen or signed those terms. This is the position under Singapore law, as shown by the case of *Press Automation Technology Pte Ltd v Trans-link Exhibition Forwarding Pte Ltd* (2003), where certain conditions restricting a carrier's liability in relation to a freight transportation contract were not stated in the signed standard acceptance order form, but the form stated expressly that the conditions in question were the standard rules of the industry association, and copies of these were available on application to the carrier. Prakash J held that this statement was sufficient to incorporate the standard conditions into the contract, notwithstanding that the plaintiff customer did not have a copy of the conditions and had not read them. The plaintiff had sought to rely on a line of authorities requiring that the party against whom 'onerous and unusual conditions' were being imposed had to have her attention specifically drawn to them, but Prakash J distinguished the situation before her from that in those cases, including the *Interfoto* case and *Spurling v Bradshaw*, on the basis that they concerned unsigned documents handed over at the time of contracting, without the additional fact of a signed document that referred to conditions found in another unsigned document. Prakash J also declined to follow the Canadian case of *Tilden Rent-A-Car Co v Clendenning* (1978) on the basis that the case did not represent the common law of England or of Singapore (see p 726):

> 'Where a party has signed a contract after having been given notice, by way of a clear incorporating clause ... of what would be included among the contractual terms, that party cannot afterwards assert that it is not bound by some of the terms on the ground that the same are onerous and unusual and had not been drawn specifically to its attention. Contracting parties must have a care for their own legal positions by ascertaining what terms are to be part of a contract before signing it. If they do not do so, they will be bound by those terms except to the extent that the UCTA offers them relief.'

Given that this case is a very recent decision, it can be said also to signify a pragmatic and modern approach by the Singapore courts, in dealing with standard form contracts and commercial practice, at least amongst contracting parties who are business entities. The question of consumer protection interests in Singapore, in the context of exception clauses and standard form contracts, is further discussed below.

Construction

6.21 Even if an exception clause is successfully incorporated into a contract, it will not automatically apply to exempt the relying party from liability. As with all other terms in a contract, the clause has to be interpreted to divine its meaning, ie the exception clause must be construed in order to determine its scope and whether or not it in fact applies to the situation at hand such that the party relying on it may use it to exempt herself from liability in the instant case. As such, it follows that the broader the interpretation given to an exception clause, the greater the protection it will afford to the relying party.

As mentioned previously, the English courts have used a number of devices, centred in the main on construction of contractual terms, to limit the scope and applicability of exception clauses. Essentially, these devices can be classified as follows:

- the *contra proferentum* rule;
- the rule in cases of negligence liability;
- the doctrine of fundamental breach; and
- other devices relating to construction.

The Contra Proferentum *Rule*

6.22 The *contra proferentum* rule dictates that, where there is ambiguity in construing the words of a contractual term, the term will be construed against the person seeking to rely on it, ie in cases where there is doubt as to the meaning of a term, the interpretation taken will be that least favourable to the maker of, or the person relying on, the term. The operation of this rule therefore depends on the court's finding that there is ambiguity in the language used in the exception clause in question. The results in some cases suggest that the courts have been fairly ready to find ambiguity and so apply the rule. In *Houghton v Trafalgar Insurance Co Ltd* (1954), an insurance policy excluded claims in cases where the car was carrying 'any load in excess of that for which the car was constructed'. In finding that the insurance company could not rely on the exception clause where the accident occurred while there were six persons in the car, when it was meant to carry only five persons, the court held that the word 'load' could refer to weight as well as the number of passengers and hence was ambiguous.

6.23 Since the passage of the UCTA, however, which attempts to alleviate some of the harsher results of certain types of exception clauses (discussed below), it would seem that the courts have been somewhat more restrained in applying rules of construction, such as the *contra proferentum* rule, to rein in the use of exception clauses. For instance, in *Ailsa Craig Fishing Co Ltd v Malvern Fishing Co Ltd* (1983), which was decided a few years after the enactment of the UCTA, Lord Wilberforce cautioned that 'one must not strive to create ambiguities by strained construction' and urged that contractual terms be given, as far as possible, their 'natural plain meaning'.

The Rule in Cases of Negligence Liability

6.24 The rule that has been adopted by the courts in cases where a party seeks to exempt her liability, where her negligence was the cause of the other party's damage, is fairly similar to the *contra proferentum* rule. In general, in order to escape liability for negligence, the relying party must point to clear words in the exception clause that unequivocally cover the facts that occurred. As with the *contra proferentum* rule, the courts have sometimes shown themselves ready to find that the exception clause is inapplicable in the circumstances, in that the clause does not clearly cover cases of negligence. For example, in *Hollier v Rambler Motors (AMC) Ltd* (1972), the defendant garage had sought to rely on an exception clause that stated '[t]he company is not responsible for damage caused by fire to customers' cars ...'. The plaintiff's car was damaged by fire caused by the defendants' negligence, and the defendants argued that this fell within the scope of the exception clause. The Court of Appeal disagreed, and held that a reasonable customer could read the clause as attempting to exclude liability for fire damage caused both by and in the absence of negligence, and as such the wording in the clause was not sufficiently clear and unambiguous to cover the instant case.

6.25 If the reason for such strict interpretation against a party seeking to exempt negligence liability is either that it is unreasonable and unrealistic to assume that the other party would readily agree to a clause with such an effect, or that it would be unfair to permit the negligent party to escape the consequences of her own actions so readily, or both, it is arguable that, given the UCTA (which deals specifically with attempts to exclude or limit liability for negligence), the perceived need for the courts to apply such strict rules of construction against a relying party is greatly reduced. In any case, it may not be all that difficult to fulfil the courts' 'clear words' rule in attempting to avoid liability due to negligence. For example, using phrases such as 'the company is not liable for any kind of damage howsoever caused' may be sufficient, particularly if the view that the UCTA removes the need for judicial activism in this area is taken.

6.26 The case of *Canada Steamship Lines Ltd v R* (1952) sets out the following guidelines for determining when an exception clause may be construed so as to cover negligence liability:

'(1) If the clause contains language which expressly exempts the person in whose favour it is made [hereafter called the proferens] … effect must be given to that provision …

(2) If there is no express reference to negligence, the court must consider whether the words used are wide enough, in their ordinary meaning, to cover negligence … If a doubt arises at this point, it must be resolved against the proferens …

(3) If the words used are wide enough for the above purposes, the court must then consider whether the head of damage may be based on some ground other than that of negligence … [which, however,] must not be so fanciful or remote that the proferens cannot be supposed to have desired protection against it; but subject to this qualification, … the existence of a possible head of damage other than negligence is fatal to the proferens even if the words used are prima facie wide enough to cover negligence …'

Despite the 'three-stage' approach seemingly taken in the *Canada Steamship* case, however, these statements by the Privy Council have since been applied as guidelines for construction, rather than strict rules of law classifying cases of negligence liability. This approach is consistent with the fact that contractual terms should be interpreted to discover the parties' intentions and in light of the facts and circumstances of their particular case.

The Doctrine of Fundamental Breach

6.27 The phrase 'fundamental breach' and what constitutes such a breach is not necessarily easily defined, and it remains an interesting academic question whether or not there is (or ought to be) a difference between 'breaching a fundamental term' of the contract, and 'committing a fundamental breach' of the contract. For the purpose, however, of determining the applicability of exception clauses to a case where the breach is of so serious a nature as to be deemed a 'fundamental breach' (eg whether this be to defeat the purpose of the contract, cause a *Hong Kong Fir* type of benefit deprivation to the innocent party, or constitutes some other sufficiently serious event 'going to the root' of the contract (as to which see paragraph 5.22, above)), there is an additional issue. This concerns the *effect* of a fundamental breach (once extant) on the operation of an exception clause.

Up to 1967, the courts were faced with two possible rules to apply to exception clauses in cases of fundamental breach: (1) that as *a rule of law*, a fundamental breach cannot be excluded or limited by an exception clause, regardless of its language; or (2) that as a *rule of construction*, whether or not a fundamental breach could be so excluded or limited depended entirely on the proper interpretation of the exception clause. Thus, under the first possible rule, no fundamental breach could be excluded or limited, whereas under the second possible rule, some fundamental breaches could be so excluded or limited. Whether or not the second rule was possible depended on the scope of the exception clause itself, as reflecting the parties' intention in the event of such a breach. Until the House of Lords case of *Suisse Atlantique Societe d'Armement Maritime SA v NV Rotterdamsche Kolen Centrale* (1967), many decisions emanating from the English courts seemed to favour the first rule, ie that as a rule of law a person could not ever exempt herself from liability for a fundamental breach. However, in the *Suisse Atlantique* case, the House unanimously favoured the second rule, ie that it was a matter of construction whether or not an exception clause could operate in cases of fundamental breach.

6.28 Due, however, to the fact that the House of Lords was not actually required to rule on the matter (since the facts of the *Suisse Atlantique* case did not concern that of a fundamental breach), and the lack of complete agreement in the opinions of the five judges, it was not until 1980, in the case of *Photo Production Ltd v Securicor Transport Ltd* (1980), that the House of Lords clearly affirmed its position in the *Suisse Atlantique* case. In the words of Lord Wilberforce, 'the question whether, and to what extent, an exclusion clause is to be applied to a fundamental breach, or a breach of a fundamental term, or indeed to any breach of contract, is a matter of construction of the contract' (see pp 842–843).

One welcome effect of this rule is that it removes the need to distinguish between a 'fundamental breach' and a 'breach of a fundamental term', at least in the context of construing an exception clause, as the effect of classifying a breach as a 'fundamental breach' is now less drastic, depending as it does on interpretation of the clause rather than an automatic application of a rule of law. This is not to say that being able to determine that a 'fundamental breach' has occurred will be completely irrelevant to the question of construction. For example, to the extent that the parties have not acted otherwise, it may be possible to limit the construction of a particular exception clause (especially an exclusion clause) by arguing that the breach in question is so serious that, unless the clause is crystal-clear in its scope and intent, the parties could not have intended it to apply to such a situation, as the effect would be to allow the breaching party to escape liability totally.

Although there might have been a possible controversy as to what the position in Singapore might have been in the past, this is no longer the case and the better position would appear to be that the doctrine of fundamental breach should be viewed as a rule of construction, rather than as a rule of law (see, generally, A Phang, *Cheshire, Fifoot and*

Furmston's Law of Contract—Second Singapore and Malaysian Edition (1998) at pp 318–312).

Other Devices Relating to Construction

6.29 Where the exception clause is inconsistent with another term of the contract, the question for the court is whether or not the exception clause was intended to override that other term or be subject to it. In *J Evans & Son (Portsmouth) v Andrea Merzario Ltd* (1976), the parties had orally agreed that the plaintiff's goods would continue to be shipped below deck, as had been the case previously, though the defendant now wished to use containers for shipping goods. The written contract contained a clause permitting the defendant to have discretion as to 'means, route and procedure to be followed in the handling and transportation of goods', subject only to a customer's express written instructions. The plaintiff's goods were not shipped below deck, and the English Court of Appeal refused to allow the defendant to rely on the clause, holding that the oral assurance overrode the written clause, on the basis either that a collateral contract had been formed between the parties by reason of the oral assurance, or that the oral agreement formed part of the whole contract, which therefore was not entirely written but, rather, partly written and partly oral.

6.30 The above case should, however, be applied with some degree of caution. In the case of inconsistent terms, given that the basis for overriding a written exception clause in the case of an inconsistent oral promise is either through the device of the collateral contract or the application of an exception to the parol evidence rule, courts may be reluctant to hold that an oral assurance is sufficient to override a written contractual term unless that assurance related to a matter that both parties could be said to have known was fundamental to the contract or its performance. It may also be that it will be more difficult to argue that an oral agreement trumps a written contractual term in cases of negotiated contracts, rather than standard form or other non-negotiated contracts.

Statutory Limitations on the Use of Exception Clauses

6.31 The 1977 Unfair Contract Terms Act ('UCTA') of the UK is also part of the law of Singapore by virtue of the First Schedule to the Application of English Law Act of 1993 (Cap 7A, 1994 Rev Ed, and published locally as Cap 396, 1994 Rev Ed), although there are sections of the UCTA that are excluded from Singapore law, viz sections 1(1)(c) and 1(3)(b) (and the amendments thereto made by the UK legislature) and the whole of Part II (sections 15 through 25). Contracts that are governed by Singapore law and that contain exception clauses, therefore, may be subject to the limitations imposed by the UCTA.

6.32 In order to determine if the UCTA applies to restrict the application of an exception clause, it will be necessary to determine at the outset if the *contract* and, separately, the *clause* in question fall within the scope of the UCTA. As a preliminary matter, however, it must be noted that, despite its name, the UCTA does not limit or affect all contractual terms that could be described as 'unfair'. Its scope is therefore more limited than its name might imply. Further, it does not declare all exception clauses that fall within its scope to be unfair or invalid; rather, depending on the clause in question and which section of the Act applies, the clause could either be deemed invalid and totally inapplicable, or it could be subjected to a statutory test of 'reasonableness' that, if satisfied, would allow the clause to operate. Where an exception clause falls within the scope of the UCTA, therefore, one out of only two possible outcomes will ensue. Either the clause is rendered totally inoperative, or it is subject to the test of reasonableness in order to determine if it is to apply to the situation at hand. Where, however, a clause is subjected to the test of 'reasonableness' and is not found to be reasonable in accordance therewith, the result is that the clause is inoperative (which is the first outcome).

6.33 There are, however, limited situations where the UCTA could apply more widely than its name suggests, namely, to restrict the operation of exception clauses in non-contractual situations involving negligence (as in section 2). More significantly, perhaps, the UCTA does not purport to change the common law as regards the use of exception clauses and limitations that have been developed and applied thereof. This means that, even with the UCTA as part of the law of Singapore, it is necessary in each case to first consider the common law requirements for the applicability of an exception clause (as discussed above) and, to the extent that the clause in question is thereby found to be applicable to the case, to then examine the effect of the UCTA (if any) on that clause.

6.34 Another preliminary point worth noting about the UCTA is that it does not apply only to exception clauses of the 'classic' type (eg those that exclude or limit a person's liability or indemnity for such liability). The UCTA provides (in section 13) that Part I of the Act (which contains the primary provisions dealing with exception clauses in the context of contract and tort) applies also to attempts to '[prevent] making the liability or its enforcement subject to restrictive or onerous conditions; ... excluding or restricting any right or remedy in respect of the liability, or subjecting a person to any prejudice in consequence of his pursuing any such right or remedy; [as well as] excluding or restricting rules of evidence or procedure'. Section 13 also provides that sections 2 and 5 through 7 of the UCTA apply to 'prevent excluding or restricting liability by reference to terms and notices which exclude or restrict the relevant obligation or duty'.

6.35 While the broader view of exception clauses (and their treatment under the UCTA) as described in section 13 does not cover written agreements to submit disputes to arbitration, it is one instance where the UCTA may be considered to live up to its title. However, some difficulty has been caused by the wording that terms and notices, 'which exclude or restrict the relevant obligation or duty', are also covered by the UCTA's provisions. For example, in *Smith v Eric S Bush* (1989) and *Phillips Products Ltd v Hyland* (1987), a fairly liberal interpretation was taken of these words such that it would seem that almost any contractual term or notice (whether contractual or otherwise) could be construed to be one that 'exclude[s] or restrict[s] the relevant obligation or duty'. If this is the case, the scope of the UCTA, at least in respect of the kinds of clauses to which it applies, would be extremely wide indeed. While this point may not be of much practical significance in most commercial contracts (the drafting of which tends to utilise the more common, clear and obvious types of exception clauses), it raises difficult definitional issues, as such a broad approach clearly blurs the distinction between a term (or notice) that merely *defines* a party's contractual or legal obligations and duties, and a term (or notice) that purports to 'exclude or restrict' those obligations and duties, defined elsewhere in the contract or by law. However, what seems clear is that the courts will not allow a party to undermine the policy of the UCTA by attempting to draft itself out of the Act itself. So, for example, in *Smith v Eric S Bush*, which has been mentioned above, the argument by the defendant, that the exception clause disclaiming liability was outside the purview of the UCTA because—applying the principle in *Hedley Byrne & Co Ltd v Heller & Partners Ltd* (1964)—the clause went towards negating the duty of care rather than restricting or excluding liability, was rejected. In other words, the clause was still subject to the statutory test of 'reasonableness' under the UCTA.

6.36 The UCTA will be triggered to apply to exception clauses in cases of contractual claims or negligence if the following two requirements are satisfied:

- First, if the contract in question is a contract within the scope of the Act; and
- Secondly, for all but those cases involving a breach of either the Sale of Goods Act or the Hire Purchase Act, if the case at hand involves 'business liability' (as defined in section 1(3)) for the party seeking to rely on the clause.

In the event the Act applies to the case at hand, it then becomes necessary to determine if liability is based on a general cause of action (ie negligence or breach of contract) as opposed to it arising from a specific type of contract or transaction (ie a contract for the sale or supply of goods). This issue determines which section(s) of the Act applies to the exception clause in question, and thus whether or not the clause will be totally ineffective or subject to the test of reasonableness.

Contracts to Which the UCTA Does Not Apply

6.37 Where most contractual claims and negligence liability arising under a contract are concerned, the First Schedule to the UCTA will be relevant, as it lists the contracts for which sections 2 to 4 (which are the primary sections applicable to exception clauses that attempt to exclude or restrict liability for such claims) will not apply. These are:

- contracts of insurance;

  And in so far as certain contracts deal with the following stated matters, sections 2 to 4 are also inapplicable:
- contracts relating to the creation, transfer or termination of rights or interests in land or intellectual property;
- contracts relating to the formation or dissolution of a company, or to its constitution or the rights or obligations of the corporators or members; and
- contracts relating to the creation or transfer of securities or any rights or interests therein.

6.38 Where marine salvage or towage contracts, ship or hovercraft charterparties, or contracts for the carriage of goods by ship or hovercraft are concerned, the First Schedule provides (in paragraph 2) that sections 2(2) to 4 of the UCTA and section 7 (which covers contracts under or pursuant to which possession or ownership of goods passes, other than sale of goods or hire purchase contracts) will not apply except in favour of a person 'dealing as consumer' (which phrase is defined in section 12, discussed below). Further, in relation to contracts involving the carriage of goods by ship or hovercraft, where the means of carriage are concerned, paragraph 3 of the First Schedule excludes the applicability of sections 2(2), 3 and 4 as well, again except in favour of a person 'dealing as consumer'. It is important to note that, in these contracts described in paragraphs 2 and 3 of the First Schedule, section 2(1) is not excluded from applicability. As will be seen in the discussion on negligence liability (below), this means that contractual terms or notices purporting to exclude or restrict such liability where death or personal injury has resulted will be totally ineffective.

6.39 The First Schedule also provides, in paragraph 4, that section 2 will not apply to exclude or restrict negligence liability in contracts of employment, except in favour of the employee. Paragraph (4) thus does not distinguish between the various kinds of damage that may result from negligence. Finally, section 26 of the UCTA provides that the limits to exception clauses prescribed by the UCTA do not apply to liability arising under sale of goods contracts or contracts under or pursuant to which possession or ownership of goods passes, where the contract in question is an international contract in the sense that the contracting parties have their places of business or habitual residences in different States and where certain relevant acts (such as the carriage or delivery of the goods, or the offer and acceptance of the contract) take place in those different States.

The Applicability of the UCTA to 'Business Liability' for Contractual and Tortious Claims

6.40 Section 1(3) of the UCTA provides that sections 2 through 7 apply to contracts and torts only in cases of 'business liability', meaning 'liability for breach of obligations and duties arising from things done or to be done by a person in the course of a business (whether his own business or another's)'. 'Business' is defined in section 14 as 'includ[ing] a profession and the activities of any Government department or local or public authority.' Sections 2 through 7 of the UCTA will thus be ineffective in cases where the claim for which a party relies on an exception clause arises from liability other than that incurred in the course of running or doing business.

The Applicability of the UCTA to Negligence Liability

6.41 Section 1(1) of the UCTA defines 'negligence' as either the breach of 'any obligation, arising from the express or implied terms of a contract, to take reasonable care or exercise reasonable skill in the performance' of that contract, or the breach of 'any common law duty to take reasonable care or exercise reasonable skill (but not any stricter duty).' This definition implies that the UCTA, despite its name, can apply also to cases of negligence where the liability therefor arises other than in relation to a contract or the performance of a contract. This is confirmed by section 2 of the UCTA, which deals with attempts to exclude or restrict liability for such negligence.

6.42 Section 2(1) is concerned with attempts to exclude or restrict negligence liability that causes death or personal injury. It states unequivocally that a person may not exclude or restrict such liability 'by reference to any contract term or notice given to persons generally or to particular persons'. The inclusion of the word 'notice' thus would include within the scope of section 2(1) not only cases such as *Thornton v Shoe Lane Parking* (discussed above at paragraph 6.15), but implies that this provision of the UCTA would operate also in non-contractual cases of negligence. Thus, for example, if a home owner were to place a notice containing an exception clause outside his house, and that clause purported to exclude or restrict her liability if her negligence causes a visitor death or personal injury, section 2(1) would apply such that she would not be able to rely on the notice to so exclude or restrict her liability. Section 14 further confirms this view, as it provides, *inter alia*, that the word 'notice' 'includes an announcement, whether or not in writing, and any other communication or pretended communication.'

6.43 For damage other than death or personal injury (eg property damage), section 2(2) provides that a person may (whether through a contractual term or notice given) exclude or restrict her liability for negligence only 'in so far as the term or notice satisfies the requirement of reasonableness'. The requirement of reasonableness under the UCTA is dealt with by section 11 and is discussed below (at paragraph 6.51 ff).

The Applicability of the UCTA to Cases of Breach of Contract and Other General Contractual Claims Relating to Performance

6.44 Section 3 of the UCTA deals with cases of breach of contract, including claims of non-performance or 'substantially different' performance in relation to a contract. At the outset, however, it must be noted that section 3, despite (or perhaps because of) its applicability to such claims, will not apply to all such claims. Instead, section 3(1) provides that section 3 applies only where the contracting party against whom the exception clause is being relied upon either 'deals [with the relying party] as consumer or on the other's written standard terms of business'. Section 3 thus covers attempts to exclude or restrict liability for common failures in contractual performance or contractual breaches, where there is a consumer interest or where a standard form is used. The issue as to when a party 'deals as consumer' is discussed further at paragraph 6.49, below.

6.45 Where either a consumer contract or a standard form contract is in issue, section 3(2) prescribes when an exception clause may be relied upon. First, the claim should be either based on the relying party's breach of a contract with the claiming party, or on the relying party's claim to be entitled 'to render a contractual performance substantially different from that which was reasonably expected of him; or … in respect of the whole or any part of his contractual obligation, to render no performance at all'. In such instances, the party relying on the exception clause in the contract will only be permitted to do so 'in so far as … the contract term satisfies the requirement of reasonableness.'

6.46 The fact that section 3 draws a distinction between a breach of contract, 'substantially different' contractual performance and 'no performance at all' raises an interesting if subtle point about the scope of the UCTA. While most obligations of contractual performance would be specified or otherwise clarified such that a 'substantially different' or non-performance would constitute a breach of the contract, section 3 indicates that it will also cover situations where such kinds of contractual performance do not constitute a breach. Thus, it will apply in situations where the performance was different from that which the other party 'reasonably expected' of the performing party (even if these reasonable expectations have not been captured in legally binding form such that their going unmet would not constitute a breach). The right to render 'no performance at all', however, causes more difficulties as that statement seems to go against the basis of any and all contracts. It may perhaps only be reconciled with the idea of a contract requiring performance of some sort if it is construed to mean cases where the party who is to perform claims that, due to the operation of a legal principle or other contractual term triggered by an act or event not related to her lack of performance, she no longer has to perform her part of the contract.

The Applicability of the UCTA to Liability Arising from the Sale or Supply of Goods

6.47 In contracts of sale or hire purchase of goods, section 6(1) of the UCTA prevents the exclusion or restriction of liability relating to a seller's implied undertakings of title. Where such contracts are consumer contracts (in that the buyer is 'dealing as consumer'), the seller also cannot exclude or restrict liability for non-conformity of the goods with their description or sample or their quality or fitness for a particular purpose (section 6(2)). Where the contracts are non-consumer contracts, exception clauses dealing with any non-conformity, quality or fitness of purpose of the goods will be subject to the test of reasonableness (section 6(3)).

6.48 Section 7 states that the same principles, and distinction between a totally ineffective exception clause and one that is subject to the test of reasonableness, apply to contracts that are not governed by the law of sale of goods or hire purchase but that nonetheless deal with the passing of ownership or possession of the goods thereunder or in pursuance thereof. Further, liability for breach of obligations arising under section 2 of the Supply of Goods Act (an English Act applicable in Singapore by virtue of the Application of English Law Act (Cap 7A, 1994 Rev Ed), and published locally as Cap 394, 1994 Rev Ed) cannot be excluded or restricted at all (section 7(3A)), though liability in respect of the right to transfer ownership or give possession, or the assurance of quiet possession of the goods, may be excluded or restricted if the clause in question satisfies the test of reasonableness (section 7(4)).

The UCTA and Consumer Contracts

6.49 Certain sections of the UCTA refer to contracts where one party 'deals as consumer' vis-à-vis the other party. According to section 12, a party 'deals as consumer' if 'he neither makes the contract in the course of a business nor holds himself out as doing so; [and] the other party does make the contract in the course of a business'. In contracts of sale of goods or hire purchase, or of the supply of goods where ownership or possession passes, the buyer 'deals as consumer' if the goods are 'of a type ordinarily supplied for private use or consumption'. However, the buyer in a sale by auction or competitive tender will not be regarded as dealing as consumer. The burden of proof in relation to the question whether a person 'deals as consumer' lies on the other party, ie the person who is claiming that the other party is not dealing as consumer.

6.50 In *R & B Customs Brokers Co Ltd v United Dominions Trust Ltd* (1988), Dillon LJ made the following helpful observations as to what would *not* constitute 'dealing as consumer' (at pp 330–331):

> '... there are some transactions which are clearly integral parts of the businesses concerned, and these should be held to have been carried out in the course of those businesses; this would

> cover, apart from much else, the instance of a one-off adventure in the nature of trade, where the transaction itself would constitute a trade or business. There are other transactions, however, ... which are at highest only incidental to the carrying on of the relevant business; here a degree of regularity is required before it can be said that they are an integral part of the business carried on, and so entered into in the course of that business.'

The Test of Reasonableness

6.51 Section 11(1) provides that, for contractual terms, the test of reasonableness requires that 'the term shall have been a fair and reasonable one to be included having regard to the circumstances which were, or ought reasonably to have been, known to or in the contemplation of the parties when the contract was made'. By its language, this subsection clearly shows that the legislature intended to draw a distinction between exception clauses that would not be legally operative at all (eg those that attempt to exclude liability for negligence causing death) and exception clauses that might in some cases be valid, provided that, in the latter case, an objective standard that strives for fairness as between the parties is met. An important point to note about the reasonableness test under the UCTA is that the time for considering whether the contractual term is a 'fair and reasonable' one is at the time of the contract, ie before the breach, act of negligence or other event resulting in the parties' dispute has happened. It therefore does not matter that the term in question may have been a 'fair and reasonable' one for the party to whom liability falls to rely on, at or after the time that liability arose; rather, what is relevant is whether at the time of contracting, and in light of what was known or should have been known to the contracting parties, it was 'fair and reasonable' for the parties to have included the exception clause in their contract. A subtle point in relation to this may also be made: not only does section 11(1) require that the court have regard to circumstances that the parties knew or should have known, the court should also consider circumstances which were, or should have been, 'in the contemplation of the parties' at the time of contracting.

6.52 Where a non-contractual term, ie a notice with no contractual effect, is subject to the test of reasonableness, section 11(3) provides that the test is whether 'it should be fair and reasonable to allow reliance on [the notice], having regard to all the circumstances obtaining when the liability arose or (but for the notice) would have arisen'. The time for considering reasonableness in cases of non-contractual notices serving as exception clauses is thus different from that in cases of contractual exception clauses, and with good reason. Where in a contract the parties would have had an opportunity to consider and weigh circumstances and facts, and thus negotiate the terms of their contract accordingly, this is not the case where there is no contract or other pre-existing relationship between the parties in dispute.

6.53 Section 11 does not go on to provide any specific factors or guidance as to the operation of the reasonableness test. In cases of the sale, hire purchase or supply of goods, however (as described in sections 6 and 7), section 11(2) states that 'regard shall be had in particular to the matters specified in the Second Schedule'. Several important points and observations may be made about this subsection. First, the use of the mandatory term 'shall' means that a court is given no discretion as to whether or not to refer to the guidelines in the Second Schedule; however, a review of those guidelines will show that they reflect a pragmatic and commonsensical approach to the issue and as such would likely be factors a court would consider in applying the reasonableness test in any case. This is so particularly in view of the second important point, viz that the matters specified in the Second Schedule are to be considered 'in particular', thus implying that the court is free to examine and take into account other factors and circumstances that it believes appropriate or necessary. Thirdly, although section 11(2) mandates that the guidelines in the Second Schedule are to be considered only in cases under section 6 or 7, it is unlikely that a court faced with a different case (eg under section 2(2) or section 3) would not also review and rely on at least some of those guidelines. This has been the approach taken by both the English and Singapore courts.

6.54 The Second Schedule lists the following as matters to which regard is to be had in particular by the court, to the extent that any of these matters 'appear to be relevant':

- the parties' relative strength in bargaining positions vis-à-vis each other, taking into account alternative methods for meeting the customer's requirements;
- whether the customer 'received an inducement' to agree to the exception clause or could have entered into a similar contract with another person without the need for such a term;
- whether the customer knew or should have known of the existence of the term, taking into account matters such as trade custom or previous course of dealing;
- in cases where the term in question excludes or restricts 'any relevant liability if some condition is not complied with', whether it was reasonable at the time the contract was made to expect that complying with such a condition would be 'practicable'; and
- whether the goods in question were manufactured, processed or adapted according to the customer's special order.

Other factors that have emerged through case law as being relevant to a court's determination of the reasonableness requirement include whether it would have been reasonably practicable to obtain advice from an alternative source considering the time and costs involved, whether the liability in question was for a difficult task or obligation that may impose an additional burden on the performing party in order to discharge the task or obligation, and the practical consequences of determining that the clause in question in fact is or is not reasonable (eg if it would have been open to either party to protect themselves against risk by taking out insurance). These factors were highlighted in the case of *Smith v Eric S Bush* (1989). The question of insurance was also relevant in the case of *George Mitchell (Chesterhall) Ltd v Finney Lock Seeds Ltd* (1983). It is also specified as a relevant factor (together with the resources available to the party seeking to rely on an exception clause) in cases where the exception clause is a limitation of liability clause in section 11(4) of the UCTA.

6.55 Several Singapore cases have considered the UCTA test of reasonableness. In *Consmat Singapore (Pte) Ltd v Bank of America National Trust & Savings Association* (1992), although the UCTA was held inapplicable on the facts, the court found that, were it to be applicable, the clause in question would have been reasonable. Factors highlighted by the court in its judgment included the fact that both parties were commercial entities who entered into the contract freely and who had a choice of banks. In the more recent case of *Kenwell & Co Pte Ltd v Southern Ocean Shipbuilding Co Pte Ltd* (1999), the court held that a party who entered willingly into a contract could still raise the issue of reasonableness subsequently, and that a term that was commonly used in the relevant industry could be a reasonable term by reason thereof but that would not necessarily mean it would be considered reasonable as between the actual contracting parties. The *Kenwell* case was accepted as clear authority and applied in *Press Automation Technology Pte Ltd v Trans-Link Exhibition Forwarding Pte Ltd* (2003), a case which also illustrates the court's view that reasonableness as between the parties is a question of fact.

6.56 With the advent of the Internet and the increasing use of online and electronic contracts, other factors may also be relevant, for example, whether it is generally reasonable to expect users to read online contractual terms (a point also alluded to earlier under the topic of 'incorporation') as well as whether or not the Internet itself furnishes users a reasonable source of alternative information and, if so, whether or not this ought also to be a factor to be taken into account insofar as transactions on the Internet are concerned.

Exception Clauses and Electronic Contracts

6.57 In Singapore, the Electronic Transactions Act (legally effective from July 1998) makes it clear that electronic contracts are functionally equivalent to, and legally as valid and enforceable as, written contracts. In the US, the federal Electronic Signatures in Global and National Commerce Act ('E-SIGN') was enacted in June 2000, to similar effect. To the extent that exception clauses are utilised in written (offline) contracts, it must follow that they will also be inserted into contracts in the electronic (online) environment. While the legal rules, tests and issues are likely to remain virtually identical, at least one specific legislative attempt to deal with this issue should be noted.

6.58 In the context of software licenses and other agreements involving the creation, modification, transfer or licensing of 'computer information' (defined as 'information in electronic form which is obtained from or through the use of a computer or which is in a form capable of being processed by a computer', including a copy of such information and any documents or packaging associated therewith), the National Conference of Commissioners for Uniform State Laws ('NCCUSL') in the US has proposed a model state law titled the Uniform Computer Information Transactions Act ('UCITA'). Since its ratification by NCCUSL in July 2000, UCITA has encountered strong opposition from consumer groups and legislators who view its provisions, particularly in relation to the use of contractual warranties and electronic self-help measures, as disproportionately favouring the software industry and merchant licensors and against consumer protection interests. UCITA has to date been enacted into law in only two states (Maryland and Virginia), and several other states have in fact enacted 'anti-UCITA' laws.

In relation to exception clauses, UCITA reflects both commercial practice and general contract law principles in that it provides (in § 803(1)) that a merchant licensor 'may limit or alter the measure of damages recoverable under this [Act] or a party's other remedies under this [Act], such as by precluding a party's right to cancel for breach of contract, limiting remedies to returning or delivering copies and repayment of the contract fee, or limiting remedies to repair or replacement of the nonconforming copies'. The language, scope and effect of this section follow that of the Uniform Commercial Code, which, as enacted into state law, governs most commercial transactions in the US.

6.59 UCITA is also noteworthy in the context of exception clauses as it provides (in § 102(14)) that:

> '"Conspicuous", with reference to a term, means so written, displayed, or presented that a reasonable person against which it is to operate ought to have noticed it ... Conspicuous terms include the following:
> (A) with respect to a person:
> (i) a heading in capitals in a size equal to or greater than, or in contrasting type, font, or color to, the surrounding text;
> (ii) language in the body of a record or display in larger or other contrasting type, font, or color or set off from the surrounding text by symbols or other marks that draw attention to the language; and
> (iii) a term prominently referenced in an electronic record or display which is readily accessible or reviewable from the record or display; and
> (B) with respect to a person or an electronic agent, a term or reference to a term that is so placed in a record or display that the person or electronic agent cannot proceed without taking action with respect to the particular term or reference.'

6.60 As with many other provisions of UCITA, this subsection was modeled after the language and scope of the Uniform Commercial Code, except only that its wording and the illustrations of what constitutes a 'conspicuous' term were crafted deliberately to take into account electronic contracts and the computing environment. The test is stated to be whether the 'reasonable person against which [the term in question] is to operate ought to have noticed it', thereby highlighting a possible difference between the standard adopted and the 'reasonable notice' test for incorporation of an exception clause into a contract under English and Singapore law, which requires only that the person seeking to rely on the exception clause takes reasonable steps to draw the term to the attention of the other party. This distinction, however, is likely to be of little practical significance, since in most cases, taking what the court considers to be reasonable steps to bring a clause to the other party's attention would also consequentially mean that a reasonable person in the shoes of the other party 'ought to have' noticed the clause (whether or not she in fact did so). Further, the Uniform Commercial Code and UCITA standard of conspicuousness seems to assume (eg through the wording 'so written, displayed or presented') that the first enquiry is whether or not the merchant licensor did, in fact, 'so' write, display or present the term such that the other person 'ought to have' noticed it. It is for the court to determine whether or not a term is 'conspicuous' (§ 114, proposed to be revised as § 117).

What is of greater interest, therefore, in this definition in UCITA are the examples given of 'conspicuous' notice. Since the 'reasonable notice' test will apply to exception clauses in electronic and online contracts under Singapore law, Singapore courts tasked with applying the test to such contracts to determine whether or not a particular exception clause has been incorporated may find these illustrations extremely helpful.

Exception Clauses and Consumer Protection Legislation in Singapore

6.61 In March 2001, a task force co-led by the Consumers' Association of Singapore and the Ministry of Trade and Industry was formed to study the feasibility of enacting fair trading legislation in Singapore. The draft Consumer Protection (Fair Trading) Act that was ultimately prepared by the Ministry covered consumer transactions involving goods and services (except for some that were specifically excluded, such as transfers of ownership in immovable property and leases with an annual rent or consumer transactions over $20,000) and provided for civil remedies by consumers against suppliers in such transactions who engaged in unfair practices. 'Unfair practices' meant either an act or omission that may result in a consumer reasonably being deceived or misled, making a false claim, knowingly taking advantage of a consumer or doing certain other specified acts (such as misrepresenting the price of a product, the sponsorship, benefits, standard or quality thereof). In the context of exception clauses, the draft bill also provided that 'taking advantage of a consumer by including in a consumer agreement terms or conditions that are harsh, oppressive or excessively one-sided' or 'using small print to conceal a material fact from the consumer' constituted specific unfair practices as well. However, a person who in the ordinary course of her business 'prints, publishes, distributes, broadcasts or telecasts an advertisement in good faith' on behalf of a supplier is exempted from liability. The provisions of the Act cannot be contracted out of.

In January 2003, the Monetary Authority of Singapore issued an industry consultation paper proposing amendments to the draft Act that would include financial investments and services within the purview of the Act, thereby broadening its scope.

6.62 The enactment of this proposed legislation regulating fair trading in Singapore would provide a hitherto-unknown avenue for legal redress for consumers. Where exception clauses are concerned, should the provisions of the draft Act as described above be accepted by the authorities and enacted into law, the practice of using restrictive or one-sided exception clauses may be curtailed in Singapore, at least with respect to consumer transactions. Although the Act, unlike the UCTA, does not specifically provide that certain exception clauses are invalid, it does permit an aggrieved consumer to sue a supplier and be awarded restitution of the money she has paid or damages for loss she has suffered as a result of the supplier's unfair trading practices. Interestingly, the Act also gives the court the power to 'make an order varying the contract' in question. It remains an intriguing question whether or not a Singapore court will, if the Act becomes law and the basis for a consumer claim, apply this provision to declare an exception clause that it considers 'harsh, oppressive or excessively one-sided' to be void, thereby achieving a result wider than that obtained under the UCTA.

CHAPTER 7 Capacity to Contract

PARAGRAPHS

7.1–7.2 **Introduction**

Minors

7.3–7.7 Definition of Minor
7.8 Effects of Minor's Contract
7.9–7.11 (1) Valid Contracts
7.12–7.16 (2) Voidable Contracts
7.17–7.19 (3) Void Contracts
7.20–7.21 Minor's Liability in Tort
7.22–7.25 Minor's Liability in Restitution

7.26–7.29 **Mental Patients**

7.30–7.32 **Drunkards**

7.33–7.38 **Corporations**

Introduction

7.1 A person's capacity to contract affects the enforceability of the contract against that person. Where a person is found to have lacked capacity to contract, the contract may in some cases be void, and others voidable. It is in the interest of any person, before entering into a contract, to determine if the other party has the capacity to do so.

7.2 There are four situations in which a party's capacity to contract may be questionable: where a party is a minor, a mental patient, under the influence of drink, or a corporation, respectively.

Minors

Definition of Minor

7.3 Minors may be absolved from most contracts as the law must protect minors from contracting with adults who may take unfair advantage of a minor's inexperience. However, the law must also strike a balance in not causing unnecessary hardship to adults who have dealt fairly and in good faith with minors.

7.4 The definition of a minor in Singapore is not found in any statute and the age of majority is therefore governed by the common law. Under the common law, the age of majority is 21 years of age. In contrast, in England, the Family Law Reform Act 1969 has stipulated that the age of majority is 18.

7.5 The issue of whether the English Family Law Reform Act 1969 was applicable to Singapore was tested in court in a local case of *Bank of India v Rai Bahadur Singh & Anor* (1994). In that case, two brothers who were above the age of 18 but below the age of 21 were shareholders of a company which had been extended credit facilities by the Bank of India. The two brothers issued a letter of set-off in favour of the bank, allowing the bank to set off the company's debts against their accounts with the bank. Five years later, the bank executed the set-off and appropriated moneys in the brothers' accounts. The brothers argued that the letter of set-off was void as they were minors at the time of execution and they lacked capacity.

7.6 In that case, a possibility that the English position was applicable to Singapore was raised, as Singapore then had a provision in section 5 of the Civil Law Act which imported English mercantile law generally. As the scope of mercantile law fell to be determined by case law, there was room for argument whether the English Act was in fact imported into Singapore. It should be noted that with the passing of the Application of English Law Act 1993 (now Cap 7A, 1994 Rev Ed) by the Singapore Parliament, the English statutes that are applicable in Singapore are explicitly set out in the Act and section 5 of the Civil Law Act has been repealed. Therefore, there is now no doubt that the English Family Law Reform Act does not apply in Singapore. However, even in *Rai Bahadur*

Singh, it was held that the English Act was not imported into Singapore via section 5 of the Civil Law Act.

7.7 The only English statute that deals with minors that applies in Singapore is the Minors' Contracts Act, as it is expressly imported via the Application of English Law Act. However, the Minors' Contracts Act contains no definition of a minor. Thus, the default position in Singapore is still that a minor is a person under 21 years of age, as under common law.

Effects of Minor's Contract

7.8 A minor's contract may be held as valid against him in some circumstances. In other cases, the contract may be completely void, or voidable, in the sense that the contract binds the minor unless he repudiates the contract.

(1) *Valid Contracts*

7.9 Contracts for necessary goods concluded by minors are valid contracts, if they are made for his benefit and do not contain harsh and onerous terms (*Fawcett v Smethurst* (1914)). This position is also enshrined in section 3(2) of the UK Sale of Goods Act 1969, now imported into Singapore by the Application of English Law Act (and reprinted locally as Cap 393, 1994 Rev Ed). However, it is not so clear what 'necessary goods' mean. Necessaries for a rich man's son may not be held as necessaries with regard to a poor man's son. The onus is upon the supplier of the alleged 'necessary goods' to show that the goods are not just capable of being necessary goods but actually are necessary (*Nash v Inman* (1908)).The courts have even held that if a minor has an adequate supply of the goods already, even if the supplier did not know this, the excess goods would not be held as 'necessary goods' (*Foster v Redgrave* (1867)).

7.10 Certain contracts for services concluded by minors and are for the benefit of the minor may also be held as necessaries and therefore valid. Examples include education (*Chapple v Cooper* (1844)) and medical and legal advice (*Huggins v Wiseman* (1690)), as well as contracts a minor enters into in order to make a living as an athlete, author or entertainer (*Doyle v White City Stadium Ltd* (1935), *Chaplin v Leslie Frewin (Publishers) Ltd* (1966)).

7.11 Service contracts which contain harsh or onerous terms upon the minor are however invalid (*De Francesco v Barnum* (1890)).

(2) *Voidable Contracts*

7.12 A minor is in some cases bound by certain contracts unless he repudiates the contract. These voidable contracts would be contracts to buy or sell land (*Whittingham v Murdy* (1889)), take or grant a lease (*Davies v Beynon-Harris* (1931)), where he or she incurs liability for calls on shares in a company (*North Western Rly v M'Michael* (1850)), contracts of partnership (*Lovell & Christmas v Beauchamp* (1894)), and contracts of marriage settlement (*Edwards v Carter* (1893)).

7.13 A voidable contract may be repudiated by a minor during minority, or within a reasonable time after reaching majority (*Edwards v Carter* (1893)). A repudiation during minority may be withdrawn by the minor before or within a reasonable time of majority (*North Western Rly v M'Michael*, (1850)).

7.14 Where a minor repudiates a voidable contract, he is relieved from future liabilities but he may not recover money paid or property transferred under the contract earlier (*Steinberg v Scala (Leeds) Ltd* (1923)), unless the effect of the repudiation results in 'total failure of consideration'. Total failure of consideration is a situation where the party who has given consideration for the promise does not get any part in return for what he has bargained. However, where some benefit has been obtained for the consideration or some performance of the promise has been carried out, it would not be considered as a 'total failure of consideration'.

7.15 A minor may also ratify the contract upon reaching majority, and he would become liable on the contract. Ratification may be express or implied from conduct such as if the minor continues to act on the contract and regards it as binding on himself (*Brown v Harper* (1893)).

7.16 In a sale of goods situation, property in goods can pass to a minor even if the contract does not bind him (*Chaplin v Leslie Frewin (Publishers) Ltd* (1966)). However, this proposition is limited to situations where property in goods passes by delivery to the minor. This position is sound as it protects third party purchasers of those goods from the minor.

(3) *Void Contracts*

7.17 The UK Infants Relief Act 1874, which was the predecessor of the UK Minors' Contracts Act 1987 (which shall be discussed in greater detail under 'Minors' liability in restitution', paragraphs 7.22–7.25, below) was part of Singapore law by virtue of the Second Charter of Justice which imported English law into Singapore, then a colony of the British empire. The Act provided instances where a contract with a minor would be utterly void.

7.18 Under the UK Infants Relief Act 1874, loans to minors, contracts for goods supplied or to be supplied (other than contracts for necessaries) and all accounts stated with minors were totally void. This would entail the consequence that minors would be absolved from all liability on amounts owed and could take goods supplied to them without having to make restitution as the contract was void.

7.19 In 1984 when the UK Law Commission recommended reforms to the Infants Relief Act 1874, it stated expressly that the courts had been uncomfortable rendering a minor's contract totally void as it would result in injustice for those who have dealt with the minors. Thus, it was a sound move for the UK to repeal the Infants Relief Act and replace it with the Minors' Contracts Act 1987 which provided for some restitutionary relief in equitable cases. This will be discussed under 'Minors' liability in restitution' at paragraphs 7.22–7.25, below. Thus, even under contracts with minors which would have been determined as void, the Minors' Contracts Act has provided an inroad to assuage the harshness of the consequences of rendering a contract as void.

Minor's Liability in Tort

7.20 The general rule is that minors are liable in tort in the same way as adults, except for very young children. However, a minor may not be sued in tort for what may not be sued for under the law of contract due to his incapacity. This is to avoid the circumvention of the protection intended by the law of contract upon minors, and to prevent adults from recovering from minors what they cannot recover under the law of contract. Thus, where he commits a tort in breaching an invalid contract or procuring such a breach, he is not liable in tort (*R Leslie Ltd v Sheill* (1914)). He is liable in tort only for something wholly outside the scope of the acts envisaged by the parties when they entered into the contract (*Ballet v Mingay* (1943)).

7.21 However, the law strikes a balance in protecting minors as well as protecting aggrieved persons who may have no recourse as the minor is shielded by his incapacity. Thus, under some circumstances, a minor is liable in tort—for example, by doing something expressly forbidden in the invalid contract. In the case of *Burnard v Haggis* (1863), a minor hired a horse and the contract expressly forbade jumping on the horse. The minor jumped on the horse and the horse was killed. In a suit for tort, the owner of the horse claimed successfully against the minor.

Minor's Liability in Restitution

7.22 The UK Minors' Contracts Act 1987, received in Singapore via the Application of English Law Act, deals chiefly with a minor's liability in restitution. This Act has in fact been reprinted in the local context (see Cap 389, 1994 Rev Ed).

7.23 Before the UK Act, a minor could only be held liable to restore certain benefits received by him under a void or voidable minor's contract if the minor was guilty of fraud or had to so restore by virtue of the principles in quasi-contract (*Nelson v Stocker* (1859)). The action for restitution in quasi-contract also allowed an adult to sue a minor for certain benefits the minor obtained at the expense of the adult, viz where a minor apprenticed to a master embezzled his master's property (*Bristow v Eastman* (1974)). However, this doctrine of restitution is somewhat limited as it only applies if restitution of the subject matter fraudulently obtained under contract is possible. It does not extend to situations where the minor has ceased to hold on to the goods fraudulently obtained (*R Leslie Ltd v Sheill* (1914)) or where the fraudulent contract is one of a loan. This is because to order restitution in either case would result in the enforcement of a contract that is void. However, in an odd case, where a minor had obtained goods under a contract induced by fraud, he was held liable to account to the original seller the proceeds of those goods (*Stocks v* Wilson (1913)).

7.24 The abovementioned actions for relief are still available under the Minors Contracts Act, as section 3(2) preserves such remedies. However, section 3(1) of the Act goes further than the abovementioned remedies in giving restitutionary relief to an adult who has entered into an unenforceable contract with a minor.

7.25 Section 3(1) of the Minors' Contracts Act allows the contract to order restitution against the minor 'if it is just and equitable to do so' and 'require the defendant to transfer to the plaintiff any property acquired by the defendant under the contract, or any property representing it'. Thus, section 3(1) may allow an adult restitutionary relief even where there is no fraud or no action in quasi-contract if the court is of the view that it is just and equitable to do so. The availability of section 3(1) largely renders resort to the common law action in quasi-contract or equitable action in fraud unnecessary (see Chapter 13 on 'Capacity' in GH Treitel, *Law of Contract* (10th ed, 1999)).

Mental Patients

7.26 Contracts made with persons with mental disorders are generally valid and enforceable except in two situations.

7.27 Where a mental patient is incapable of understanding what he was doing and the other party knows or ought reasonably to know of the patient's disability, the contract would be voidable at the option of the patient (*Che Som bte Yip v Maha Pte Ltd* (1989), *Imperial Loan Co v Stone* (1892)).

7.28 The second situation where contracts made by mental patients would be unenforceable is where a contract is made with a mental patient to dispose of property belonging to him, that is also under the control of the court. The contract is unenforceable as it would interfere with the court's control over the property (*Re Walker* (1905), *Re Marshall* (1920)). It is not however certain, as suggested by Professor GH Treitel in *Law of Contract* (10th ed, 1999) at p 517, as to whether *any* contract made with a mental patient who happens to have property subject to the court's control would be invalidated by this rule.

7.29 The Sale of Goods Act also contains a provision, section 3(2), that states expressly that a mental patient who enters into a contract for necessaries must pay a reasonable price for them. This section applies to a contract for necessaries entered into by a minor, as discussed above, as well as by a drunkard, as will be discussed later.

Drunkards

7.30 The position at law regarding drunkards at the time the contract is entered into is identical to the position at law regarding mental patients. Where a drunkard is incapable of understanding what he (or she) was doing and the other party knows this, the contract would be voidable at the option of the drunkard (*Gore v Gibson* (1843)).

7.31 A drunkard can however ratify a voidable contract when he (or she) is sober and the contract would be enforceable against him or her.

7.32 A drunkard is also liable for necessaries he (or she) contracted for and must pay a reasonable price for them (section 3(2) of the Sale of Goods Act).

Corporations

7.33 A company incorporated under the Companies Act may enter into contracts like any individual. A company's capacity to contract is not affected by issues of minority or infirmity that may affect an individual. However, there are two instances where the capacity to contract by a corporation may be put into doubt.

7.34 The first is where a contract is made in the company's name before its actual incorporation. Would the contract be enforceable if the incorporation does not take place? Section 41 of the Companies Act (Cap 50, 1994 Rev Ed) now governs this issue and states that where the company ratifies the contract after its incorporation, the contract shall be enforceable against the company. Prior to ratification by the company, such persons who purported to act in the name or on behalf of the company shall, in the absence of express agreement to the contrary, be personally bound by the contract. However, a question remains as to what recourse a person may have if he contracts with a pre-incorporated company whose representatives have expressly agreed amongst themselves that they would not be personally bound by the contract. In such a situation, the other contracting party ought to be on alert and assess the risk of unenforceability carefully before he enters into such a contract.

7.35 The other issue relates to the capacity of a company to contract outside its objects clause. Every company is incorporated with its documents of incorporation, ie the memorandum and articles of association. In the memorandum, there would be an objects clause which specifies what the company would be authorised to pursue. The rationale for the objects clause is to protect shareholders by giving them some assurance that the assets of the company would not be used in some wholly unexpected way. Thus, a company that makes a contract that is *ultra vires* its objects clause cannot be bound by the contract.

7.36 However, the limitations of the objects clause can be circumvented by drafting a very wide objects clause, or by amending the objects clause to make it wide or to include the activity that is the subject of an intended contract, previously not within the objects clause.

7.37 Section 25 of the Companies Act also expressly provides that a contract made *ultra vires* shall not by reason of that only be made invalid. Thus, where the enforceability of the contract is concerned, a person who has contracted with a company which acted *ultra vires* would still be able to enforce the contract.

7.38 However, in certain proceedings, the fact that a company has acted *ultra vires* may be asserted or relied upon. These are proceedings by a shareholder or a debenture holder against the company, or proceedings by the company against any present or former officer or member, or any proceedings instituted by the Minister for Finance to wind up a company (see section 25(2) of the Companies Act).

CHAPTER 8 Privity of Contract

PARAGRAPHS

8.1–8.4 **Statement and Illustration of the General Rule**

Exceptions to the General Rule

8.5–8.7 Introduction

8.8–8.11 Exception (1)—Agency

8.12 Exception (2)—Collateral and Multilateral Contracts

8.13 Exception (3)—Statute or Acts of Parliament

8.14 Exception (4)—Law of Trusts

8.15 Exception (5)—Land Law

8.16–8.20 Exception (6)—Special Rules Relating to Exception Clauses and Other Special Situations

8.21–8.23 Exception (7)—Indirect Means: An Action for Damages

8.24–8.34 Exception (8)—The Contracts (Rights of Third Parties) Act 2001

8.35–8.37 **Relationship Between Doctrine of Privity of Contract and Doctrine of Consideration**

Statement and Illustration of the General Rule

8.1 We begin with the general rule or proposition that a person who is not a party to a contract (who is not, in other words, *privy* to that contract) cannot enforce any rights or obligations that arise under that particular contract. Neither can he or she be burdened by any obligations under the same contract.

8.2 A person who is not thus a party to the contract is often referred to as a '*third party*'.

8.3 The House of Lords decision of *Dunlop Pneumatic Tyre Co Ltd v Selfridge & Co Ltd* (1915) is probably the most often cited. In this case, the plaintiffs, who were tyre manufacturers, obtained an undertaking from Dew & Co (who were trade purchasers) *not* to sell the plaintiffs' products below the stipulated list prices. Dew & Co also entered into an additional undertaking to obtain a similar undertaking (with regard to sale of the plaintiffs' products) from their (Dew & Co's) own trade customers. Dew & Co in fact obtained such an undertaking from its trade customer, who were the defendants (Selfridge & Co). However, the defendants sold the plaintiffs' products below the latter's list prices.

The issue arose as to whether or not the plaintiffs could enforce the undertaking entered into between Dew & Co and Selfridge & Co. The plaintiffs were of course not privy to the contract between Dew & Co and Selfridge & Co. For this very reason, the court held that the plaintiffs' action failed. This is a classic illustration of the general rule stated (in paragraph 8.1, above) in action.

8.4 The doctrine of privity of contract is in fact unknown in American law (at least since the New York Court of Appeals decision in *Lawrence v Fox* in 1859). However, the doctrine is still very much embedded in the Singaporean contractual landscape. This is not surprising in view of the fact that Singapore contract law is based, in the main, on the corresponding English law (and see generally Chapter 1). However, as we shall see in the next part, the doctrine of privity is by no means written in stone. There are exceptions and, in the Singapore context, there has in fact been major *legislative* reform as well (see paragraphs 8.24–8.34, below).

It should be added that an understanding of the doctrine of privity and its main exceptions is important simply because the doctrine concerns, in essence, rules and principles with regard to the *standing* to either enforce contractual terms and/or (much more rarely, though) to have contractual terms enforced against oneself.

Exceptions to the General Rule

Introduction

8.5 The general rule pertaining to privity of contract does ensure a measure of order inasmuch as it ensures that not any third party can enforce the terms of the contract; the rights of the actual parties to the contract are also safeguarded as a result.

In a related vein, the general rule also safeguards the rights and liberty of third parties inasmuch as the parties to the contract cannot foist upon third parties obligations under that contract.

8.6 However, while it is understandable that the courts are vigilant that third parties are not *burdened* with obligations under a contract, there appears to be no reason in principle why if the contracting parties intend to confer the *benefit* of terms under their contract on a third party, this should be automatically precluded in law by the general rule. Indeed, it is highly unlikely that a third party would refuse such benefits, although he or she obviously could. The key issue, however, is whether or not such a third party could avail himself or herself of such benefits if he or she is minded to do so. It should be added that such benefits are often sought to be conferred in an attempt to ensure commercial efficiency and convenience (for example, where goods are transhipped across the globe or where, as we shall see below, third parties (such as stevedores) would not be able to practically carry out their work without adequate safeguards against liability).

8.7 It is not surprising, therefore, that the courts have allowed a number of *exceptions* to the general rule, particularly in the context of the attempts by contracting parties to confer the *benefit* of contractual terms on third parties. The exceptions with regard to the imposition of the *burden* of contractual terms on third parties are, understandably, extremely limited in number and highly specialised in nature. Hence, only a very brief description will be attempted, with more space devoted to exceptions where it is sought to confer the benefit of contractual terms on third parties.

It should be noted that the *most important* exception is *legislative* in nature and was recently embodied within the *Contracts (Rights of Third Parties) Act 2001*, which will be discussed as *Exception (8)* below.

Exception (1)—Agency

8.8 In a sense, this is not a true exception. In such a situation, one 'contracting party' deals with the other contracting party. However, the former is not contracting on his own behalf but, rather, as an *agent* for the apparent third party. In the circumstances, therefore, the real contract is in fact concluded between the apparent third party and the other contracting party, with the first-mentioned 'contracting party' acting merely as agent for the former (ie the third party).

8.9 An illustration might be in order. In the *Dunlop* case above (see paragraph 8.3, above), for example, had Dew & Co contracted as *agents* for the plaintiffs, the plaintiffs would have succeeded in their action simply because there would then have been created a direct contractual nexus or link between the plaintiffs and the defendants (with Dew & Co as agents). However, the House of Lords held that Dew & Co had contracted with the defendants not as agents but, rather, as principals in their (Dew & Co's) own right.

It might also be interesting to note that the House also held that *even if* Dew & Co had contracted as agents for the plaintiffs, the plaintiffs' action would nevertheless still have failed because they had furnished *no consideration* for the defendants' undertaking (see generally Chapter 3 for an account of the doctrine of consideration).

8.10 This neatly brings us to an interesting issue—what is the relationship, if any, between the doctrine of privity on the one hand and the doctrine of consideration on the other? We will discuss this in the next part of this chapter (at paragraphs 8.35–8.37).

8.11 It should also be noted that the law of agency is discussed in more detail in Chapter 17.

Exception (2)—Collateral and Multilateral Contracts

8.12 This again (like the exception of agency) is not so much a true exception to the general rule as a situation where the alleged third party turns out *not* to be a third party after all. Here, the alleged third party is in fact claiming as *a party*, albeit under some *other collateral or multilateral contract arrangement*. This is, in a sense, a complete circumvention of the various difficulties by way of a claim under a *separate and independent* contract.

It should be mentioned, however, that on occasion at least, the courts do tend to engage in possible artificiality as they locate, for example, a collateral contract in order to do justice in the case at hand.

Exception (3)—Statute or Acts of Parliament

8.13 This is an obvious exception since under the common law system, statutes or Acts of Parliament take precedence (in situations of conflict) over the common law. Exceptions to privity are sometimes expressly embodied within statutory or legislative provisions (such as sections 27 and 29 of the Singapore Bills of Exchange Act (Cap 23, 1985 Rev Ed)). It should be observed, however, that such exceptions do not (understandably) occur in a generally consistent fashion, although they obviously have significant impact in the area of law concerned as and when they are enacted by Parliament.

Exception (4)—Law of Trusts

8.14 This particular device is equitable in origin. Here, the alleged third party is, in law, a *beneficiary*, who is entitled to the beneficial ownership of the contractual subject-matter. However, such an entitlement is not based on contract law as such but arises, rather, under the law of *trusts*. In other words, the beneficiary can establish and enforce his or her claim by proving a trust arrangement, notwithstanding the lack or absence of privity of contract.

Exception (5)—Land Law

8.15 This exception is similar to the preceding one inasmuch as its origin is not to be located in the law of contract as such. The leading example here pertains to the running of covenants in leaseholds where the absence of privity of contract between the original landlord and the current tenant is overcome by another concept of privity altogether, viz privity of *estate* and one which is, as the concept itself suggests, unique to land or real property law.

Exception (6)—Special Rules Relating to Exception Clauses and Other Special Situations

8.16 Consistent with the general rule relating to privity of contract (see paragraph 8.1, above), third parties cannot, *prima facie*, take advantage of exception clauses to which they are not parties (and on the law relating to exception clauses generally, see Chapter 6). However, owing primarily to commercial circumstances and convenience, an exception at common law has emerged in the *shipping* context. To fully understand this particular exception, it is necessary to begin with the House of Lords decision of *Scruttons Ltd v Midland Silicones Ltd* (1962), where Lord Reid laid down (at p 474) the following *five cumulative conditions* which (if satisfied) might allow a third party to take the benefit of an exception clause in a contract to which it is not a party. The five conditions were as follows:

> 'I can see a possibility of success of the agency argument if (first) the bill of lading makes it clear that the stevedore [the third party in this case] is intended to be protected by the provisions in it which limit liability, (secondly) the bill of lading makes it clear that the carrier, in addition to contracting for these provisions on his own behalf, is also contracting as agent for the stevedore that these provisions should apply to the stevedore, (thirdly) the carrier has authority from the stevedore to do that, or perhaps later ratification by the stevedore would suffice, and (fourthly) that any difficulties about consideration moving from the stevedore were overcome. And then to affect the consignee it would be necessary to show [fifthly] that the provisions of the [English] Bills of Lading Act, 1855, apply.'

Only a very elaborately drafted clause could have possibly satisfied all the five conditions above. And such a clause was in fact successfully pleaded by a third party many years later in the New Zealand Privy Council decision of *New Zealand Shipping Co Ltd v AM Sattherwaite & Co Ltd, The Eurymedon* (1975). The clause itself (now popularly termed a 'Himalaya Clause') read as follows:

> 'It is hereby expressly agreed that no servant or agent of the carrier (including every independent contractor from time to time employed by the carrier) shall in any circumstances whatsoever be under any liability whatsoever to the shipper, consignee or owner of the goods or to any holder of this bill of lading for any

loss or damage or delay or whatsoever kind arising or resulting directly or indirectly from any act neglect or default on his part while acting in the course of or in connection with his employment and, without prejudice to the generality of the foregoing provisions in this clause, every exemption, limitation, condition and liberty herein contained and every right, exemption from liability, defence and immunity of whatsoever nature applicable to the carrier or to which the carrier is entitled hereunder shall also be available and shall extend to protect every such servant or agent of the carrier acting as aforesaid and for the purpose of all the foregoing provisions of this clause the carrier is or shall be deemed to be acting as agent or trustee on behalf of and for the benefit of all persons who are or might be his servants or agents from time to time (including independent contractors as aforesaid) and all such persons shall to this extent be or be deemed to be parties to the contract in or evidenced by this bill of lading.'

The actual facts of *The Eurymedon* were not simple and perhaps a diagram followed by a short elaboration might be in order.

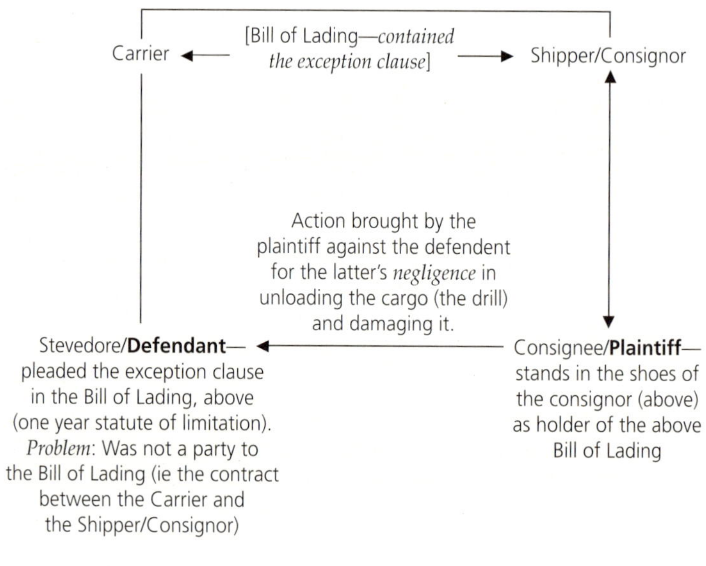

Note: (1) The *Carrier* was a *wholly owned subsidiary* of the Defendant.
(2) The *Carrier had* the *authority* to enter into contracts on behalf of the *Defendant*.

The contract in question was evidenced by the Bill of Lading between the contracting parties, the Carrier and the Shipper/Consignor, respectively. And it was this Bill of Lading contract that contained the exception clause sought to be relied upon by the defendant third parties. The Consignee was the Plaintiff who had purchased the cargo concerned (a drill) from the Shipper/Consignor. It will suffice for our present purposes to note that under the then existing (shipping) law, the Plaintiff/Consignee *stood in the shoes of the Shipper/Consignor as holder of the Bill of Lading, and was therefore a party to the Bill of Lading contract briefly mentioned above.*

The Stevedores were the Defendants. They negligently unloaded the drill and damaged it. The Plaintiff was naturally upset and brought a *tortious* action in *negligence* against the Defendant Stevedores. The Defendant Stevedores sought to rely upon the exception clause in the Bill of Lading contract. However, as we have seen, the Defendant Stevedores were *not privy to* (ie were *not parties to*) the Bill of Lading contract; they were, in other words, *third parties*. One key issue which arose was whether or not they could nevertheless take the *benefit* of the exception clause.

The Judicial Committee of the Privy Council held that the Defendant Stevedores could indeed take the benefit of the exception clause concerned. The court located a *nexus* between the Plaintiff Consignee and the Defendant Stevedores by way of a rather *artificial unilateral contract*. This unilateral contract did not, obviously, exist on the face of the facts themselves but was, rather, '*constructed*' by the court. In the words of Lord Wilberforce, the 'bill of lading brought into existence a bargain initially unilateral but capable of becoming mutual, between the shipper [note, here, that the Plaintiff Consignee was affected because, as already mentioned above, it stood in the shoes of the Shipper/Consignor as holder of the Bill of Lading] and the appellant [ie the Defendant Stevedores], made *through the carrier as agent*' (emphasis added) (see pp 167–168). In other words, the court found an offer of a unilateral contract by the Shipper/Consignor to the Defendant Stevedores *through the Carrier as agent* and that, in return for the Defendant Stevedores unloading the cargo (the drill), the Defendant Stevedores would obtain the benefit of the exception clause in the Bill of Lading contract. It has been noted in an earlier chapter that the act of the Defendant Stevedores in unloading the cargo itself constituted sufficient consideration for the Shipper/Consignor's promise to allow them to receive the benefit of the exception clause (see paragraph 3.33). Again, as an important (albeit technical) point, it should be reiterated that the Plaintiff Consignee was impacted by this contractual arrangement because they stood in the shoes of the Shipper/Consignor as holder of the Bill of Lading.

It can be seen that the unilateral contract situation enunciated by the Privy Council was rather artificial. However, it should also be noted that all five of the conditions laid down by Lord Reid in the much earlier House of Lords decision in *Scruttons Ltd v Midland Silicones Ltd* (above) were satisfied. Indeed, a close perusal of the exception clause above will bear this out. It should be further noted that although the device utilised was rather artificial, on the actual facts of *The Eurymedon* itself, the Carrier could quite reasonably be construed as being the *agent* which established the necessary contractual nexus since it was a *wholly owned subsidiary* of the Defendant Stevedores *and had* the requisite *authority* to enter into contracts (such as the one located by the court here) on behalf of the Defendant Stevedores.

More importantly, although the *means* utilised (an artificially constructed unilateral contract) might strain one's imagination at least slightly, the *ends* sought to be achieved were eminently understandable and reasonable—the facilitation of commerce in a very real and practical context. Indeed, the Privy Council reaffirmed *The Eurymedon* in a subsequent decision (but this time on appeal from Australia) in *Port Jackson Stevedoring Pty Ltd v Salmond and Spraggon (Australia) Pty Ltd, The New York Star* (1981) (which was, perhaps not surprisingly, another shipping law case). It is also important to note that the Privy Council in both these cases was by no means emphasising the proposition that good ends justified bad means. The means may have been a little artificial but they were not wholly beyond the bounds of reasonableness.

An interesting issue which arises is whether or not the legal device utilised to get around the problem of privity of contract in *The Eurymedon* and *The New York Star* could be utilised successfully in a more *general, non*-shipping, context. The stringent conditions as well as the unique (shipping) context in which the device was formulated would seem to suggest a negative answer (as would the case law thus far; see, eg the English decision of *Southern Water Authority v Carey* (1985)).

Finally, it should be noted that this particular exception is in fact expressly preserved by both sections 8(1) and 7(4) of the local Contracts (Rights of Third Parties) Act 2001, with the latter provision making it clear that the proscription against third party benefits with respect to carriage of goods by sea does *not* extend to the contractual exclusion or limitation of liability as such (see also generally paragraphs 8.31 and 8.32, below).

8.17 Another legal device to get around the problem of privity of contract in the context of exception clauses centres around the technique of *drafting*. More specifically, this particular technique involves the inclusion in the contract wherein the exception clause is located *a promise that the plaintiff (contracting party) will not sue the third party*. If the plaintiff does in fact commence an action against the third party, then the *other contracting party* may (*if, and only if, that other* contracting party *so wishes*) *apply to the court* (under *section 3(f) of the Civil Law Act* (Cap 43, 1999 Rev Ed)) for a *stay* of the plaintiff's proceedings against the third party on the grounds (first) that to allow the action to proceed would be tantamount to an abuse of the process of court *and* (secondly) that there would otherwise be a fraud committed upon the applicant (see, eg the English decisions of *Gore v Van der Lann* (1967) and *Nippon Yusen Kaisha v International Import and Export Co Ltd, The Elbe Maru* (1978)). However, there is an important condition that must also be present if this particular legal device is to succeed and a stay of action granted—the applicant for the stay of proceedings (the other contracting party) *must* be under *a legal obligation to indemnify the third party* for any loss suffered as a result of the successful prosecution of the plaintiff's action against the third party.

The rationale of abuse of the process of court as well as a fraud committed on the applicant results as follows. If the plaintiff's action against the third party is not stayed by the court, the third party would then have to pay the plaintiff damages. As the applicant is under a legal obligation to indemnify the third party, the third party would then seek redress from the applicant for the amount of damages which the third party had to pay to the plaintiff. The applicant would then be out-of-pocket and would bring an action against the plaintiff for breach of contract (viz breach of the promise by the plaintiff not to sue the third party, it being recalled that the applicant is the other contracting party). The reader would have discerned by now that there has been a *circularity of actions*, with no real change in the original situation. It is no wonder, therefore, that the court would 'short-circuit' the possible circularity of actions by granting a stay of the plaintiff's action against the third party which would otherwise initiate a process that would not only involve a fraud being committed on the applicant but also (and more importantly) a total waste of the court's time and resources.

8.18 The Canadian Supreme Court decision of *London Drugs Ltd v Kuehne & Nagel International Ltd* (1993) represents yet another departure (at common law) from the doctrine of privity of contract. In that case, the majority of the court held that third party employees could avail themselves of a contractual *limitation clause* (in a contract between their employer and the plaintiff) if:

(1) The benefit of the clause was either expressly or impliedly extended to the employees seeking to rely on it; *and*

(2) The employees concerned must have been acting in the course of their employment and must have been performing the very services provided for in the contract between their employer and the claimant when the loss or damage occurred.

Whether or not the particular fact situation in the *London Drugs* case would have fallen within the ambit of the local Contracts (Rights of Third Parties) Act 2001 (as to which see paragraphs 8.24–8.34, below) may be somewhat controversial (see the discussion by A Phang, 'On Justification and Method in Law Reform—The Contracts (Rights of Third Parties) Act 1999' (2002) 18 *Journal of Contract Law* 32). For a perceptive analysis of this particular case, see J Adams and R Brownsword, 'Privity of Contract—That Pestilential Nuisance' (1993) 56 *Modern Law Review* 722.

8.19 The Australian High Court decision of *Trident General Insurance Co Limited v McNiece Bros Proprietary Ltd* (1988) may also be noted briefly. This particular case concerned the issue as to whether or not a third party was entitled to bring an action on a contract of insurance which was purportedly entered into for his or her benefit. Although a majority of the court found in favour of the third party, there was such a broad variety of reasons as well as qualifications that it cannot be said that, overall, the decision itself represents a clear (and, more importantly, general) exception to the doctrine of privity of contract. Interestingly, this specific situation had since been resolved legislatively so that third parties can now sue on insurance contracts. An excellent analysis of the *Trident* case may be found in FMB Reynolds, 'Privity of Contract, the

Boundaries of Categories and the Limits of the Judicial Function' (1989) 105 *Law Quarterly Review* 1.

8.20 There are also very limited situations under which the *burden* of an exception clause could be imposed on a third party. As we have already noted, the courts are especially concerned that the *burden* of contractual obligations generally are not foisted upon a third party (see paragraph 8.5, above). It would therefore entail a very clear situation before the courts would allow a third party to be burdened with a term or terms of a contract to which he or she was not, of course, a party. It comes as no surprise that these very rare situations are themselves rather specialised in nature. For this reason, we will not deal with them in any detail.

It will suffice for our present purposes to note that the principal exceptions occur in the *bailment* context. A bailment itself involves possession. In particular, in a typical bailment situation, the owner (the bailor) of the goods concerned parts (temporarily) with possession of the goods for a certain stipulated purpose or purposes to the bailee. Indeed, there could even be a *sub*-bailment inasmuch as the latter person could grant possession of the same goods to yet another person (the *sub*-bailee).

Turning to the main exceptions in the bailment context and (in particular) to the judgment of Lord Denning MR in the English Court of Appeal decision of *Morris v CW Martin & Sons Ltd* (1966), it has now been clearly established that if the plaintiff (as bailor) either expressly *or* impliedly *consented* to the bailee making a sub-bailment containing, *inter alia*, the relevant exception clause, with the defendant third parties being the sub-bailees, the plaintiff-bailor would be *bound* by the exception clause. In this particular situation, there is no objection in principle to the third party (sub-bailees) having the burden of the exception clause in a contract to which they are not a party (the exception clause being contained in the contract between the plaintiff-bailor and the bailee) simply because of the presence of *consent* (either express or implied) on the part of the plaintiff.

A second situation (also in the bailment context) is somewhat more complex and controversial. Indeed, even if the exception is viable, it is even more specialised and (at least arguably) involves a step further removed. This particular situation involves a cause of action for *negligence* in the *bailment context*, and *not generally*. Further, the possible effect of the exception clause is to negate the duty of care based on the following reasoning: assuming only a cause of action for negligence in a *bailment context*, the court should hold that the bailor is bound by the terms of the sub-bailment (containing the exception clause) *regardless* of consent because the bailor cannot prove the bailment (upon which the duty and consequent breach and action in negligence are premised) without reference to the very terms of the sub-bailment itself. This approach used to derive some support from the English High Court decision of *Johnson Matthey & Co v Constantine Terminals Ltd and International Express Co Ltd* (1976). However, such an approach was rejected by the Privy Council more recently in *The Pioneer Container* (1994). It has, however, been argued that the approach in the *Johnson Matthey* case was nevertheless based on sound principle and therefore ought to be followed (see A Phang, 'Sub-Bailments and Consent' (1995) 58 *Modern Law Review* 422).

Exception (7)—Indirect Means: An Action for Damages

8.21 This particular category has even less of a claim to the status of an exception. However, it can furnish a possibly effective means around the doctrine of privity of contract and allow the third party to recover benefits under the contract to which he or she is not a party. The route, however, is an *indirect* one and briefly operates as follows: although the third party has no standing to sue (owing to the doctrine of privity of contract), there is nothing precluding the *party* to the contract (who had intended to benefit the third party) from suing the party in breach of contract for *damages*. The plaintiff could then transfer the damages obtained from the party in breach to the third party.

Alternatively (but much more rarely), if the plaintiff sues for (and is granted) a decree of *specific performance*, the third party would likewise be able (in effect) to benefit, the absence of privity of contract notwithstanding. An illustrative case (which also emphasises the likelihood of rarity) is the leading House of Lords decision of *Beswick v Beswick* (1968).

However, the reader would have noticed by now that this particular device (whether in the context of damages or specific performance) will only work if the contracting party concerned is *willing* to sue the party in breach in the first instance.

8.22 It should be noted that significant difficulties do surround the efficacy of the present device.

In the first instance (and as already noted in the preceding paragraph), the grant of *specific performance* is likely to be very rare and would be decreed only in very exceptional circumstances.

8.23 Secondly, and insofar as the remedy of *damages* is concerned, the court might in fact hold that the plaintiff has suffered no real loss—although the third party certainly would have, since the term(s) of the contract were intended to benefit him or her. If so, the court would have no alternative but to award only *nominal* damages. One possible way around this particular difficulty is to *characterise* the plaintiff's loss in such a fashion as to encompass the third party's loss as well. However, this is a rather artificial approach.

Alternatively, there is no reason in logic or principle why the plaintiff ought not to be awarded a substantial sum of damages if he or she can actually prove real loss to him or her. In this regard, the recent House of Lords decision of *Alfred McAlpine Construction Ltd v Panatown Ltd* (2000) may be noted. In this case, the plaintiff (Panatown) sued the defendant contractors (McAlpine). Panatown alleged defects in the completed building. Difficulties arose because Panaltown had never owned the construction site which (at all times) belonged to their associated company (Unex Investment Properties Ltd ('UIPL')), who were the actual developers. It is important to note that on the day the construction contract between the contracting parties was signed, McAlpine (the defendants) had entered into a *separate* Duty of Care Deed ('DCD') with UIPL under which limited liability for negligence was accepted. Put in simple diagrammatic form, the situation was as follows:

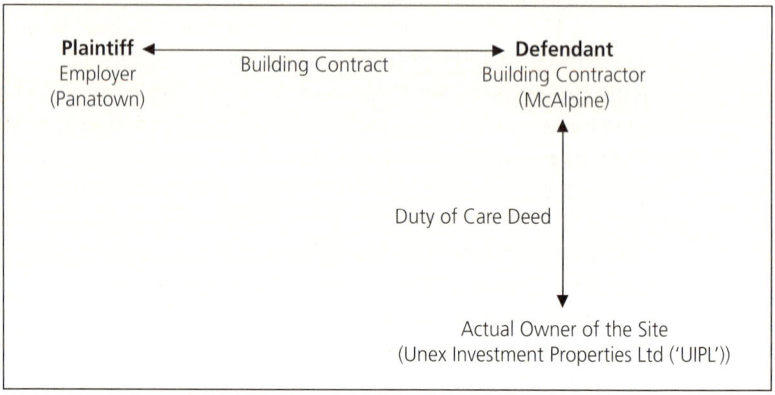

The majority of the House held that the plaintiff could not recover substantial damages from the defendant because of the rights of action conferred on UIPL (here, the third party) under the DCD. However, the minority (comprising Lords Goff and Millett) held for the plaintiff. They were in favour of a broader approach which was (in turn) based upon Lord Griffiths's principle enunciated in an earlier decision of the House in *Linden Gardens Trust Ltd v Lenesta Sludge Disposals Ltd* (1994), which (because of its importance) is set out here in full as follows (see pp 96–97):

> 'I cannot accept that in a contract of this nature, namely for work, labour and the supply of materials, the recovery of more than nominal damages for breach of contract is dependent upon the plaintiff having a proprietary interest in the subject matter of the contract at the date of breach. In everyday life contracts for work and labour are constantly being placed by those who have no proprietary interest in the subject matter of the contract. To take a common example, the matrimonial home is owned by the wife and the couple's remaining assets are owned by the husband and he is the sole earner. The house requires a new roof and the husband places a contract with a builder to carry out the work. The husband is not acting as agent for his wife, he makes the contract as principal because only he can pay for it. The builder fails to replace the roof properly and the husband has to call in and pay another builder to complete the work. Is it to be said that the husband has suffered no damage because he does not own the property? Such a result would in my view be absurd and the answer is that the husband has suffered loss because he did not receive the bargain for which he had contracted with the first builder and the measure of damages is the cost of securing the performance of that bargain by

completing the roof repairs properly by the second builder. To put this simple example closer to the facts of this appeal—at the time the husband employs the builder he owns the house but just after the builder starts work the couple are advised to divide their assets so the husband transfers the house to his wife. This is no concern of the builder whose bargain is with the husband. If the roof turns out to be defective the husband can recover from the builder the cost of putting it right and thus obtain the benefit of the bargain that the builder had promised to deliver. It was suggested in argument that the answer to the example I have given is that the husband could assign the benefit of the contract to the wife. But what if, as in this case, the builder has a clause in the contract forbidding assignment without his consent and refuses to give consent [as was the case here] ... It is then said that neither husband nor wife can recover damages; this seems to me to be so unjust a result that the law cannot tolerate it.'

The minority approach in the *Panatown* case would in fact support the proposition made here to the effect that the plaintiff would be perceived as seeking to recover *his or her own* loss. The issue, in Lord Goff's view, is (in other words) not one of privity but, rather, of *damages*. Interestingly, there also appears to be at least some qualified support for such an approach in the judgments of Lords Clyde, Jauncey and Browne–Wilkinson. However, it should be noted that these judgments embodied a rather more restrictive view of Lord Griffiths's approach. For example, Lords Clyde and Jauncey would confine recovery of substantive damages to situations where the promisee had personally paid in order to obtain alternative performance (see pp 958–959 and 998, respectively), whilst Lord Clyde would also confine such recovery to situations where the promisee was accountable to the third party for any damages awarded (see pp 959–960). Lord Browne–Wilkinson was prepared to assume that Lord Griffiths's broader approach was 'sound in law' but found that there could be no recovery, in any event, on the facts 'because UIPL (the owner of the land) has a direct cause of action under the DCD' (see p 1002). Given the varied views, one cannot dismiss Lord Griffiths's broad approach in the *Linden Gardens* case (which was endorsed by Lords Goff and Millett in the *Panatown* case) out of hand. The way is clearly open for a more definitive view in the future.

For a perceptive analysis and critique of the *Panatown* case, see B Coote, 'The Performance Interest, *Panatown*, and the Problem of Loss' (2001) 117 *Law Quarterly Review* 81.

Exception (8)—The Contracts (Rights of Third Parties) Act 2001

8.24 By far, however, arguably the most important exception is the most recent and is *legislative* in nature. The Singapore Parliament enacted the Contracts (Rights of Third Parties) Act in 2001 (Act No 39 of 2001; now Cap 53B, 2002 Rev Ed). This Singapore Act is in fact closely modelled on the English Contracts (Rights of Third Parties) Act 1999.

However, one significant difference between the Singapore and English Acts is the presence of additional wording in section 2(5) of the Singapore Act which seeks to prevent any argument whatsoever being raised to the effect that the doctrine of consideration could still operate so as to prevent the third party from obtaining the benefit of the terms of the contract under the Act because consideration has not moved from the promisee (here, the third party). The provision itself reads as follows (the emphasis added signifying the principal difference between the Singapore and English provisions):

> 'For the purpose of exercising his right to enforce a term of the contract, there shall be available to the third party any remedy that would have been available to him in action for breach of contract if he had been a party to the contract (and the rules relating to damages, injunctions, specific performance and other *remedy* shall apply accordingly) *and such remedy shall not be refused on the ground that, as against the promisor, the third party is a volunteer.*'

It may well be the case, in fact, that such express additional language is unnecessary. In any event, the Singapore Legislature has gone out of its way to prevent any possible misunderstanding in this particular regard.

8.25 Simply put, the Act seeks to allow, under certain circumstances, third parties to receive the *benefit* of terms of contracts to which they are not (of course) parties.

Consistently with the general nature of this book, only a brief summary can be provided.

8.26 The key provision in this regard is *section 2*; this provision allows the third party to enforce a term of the contract if either 'the contract expressly provides that he may' (see section 2(1)(a)) *or* 'subject to subsection (2), the term purports to confer a benefit on him' (see section 2(1)(b)).

However, section 2(2), as we have just seen, *qualifies* section 2(1)*(b)*; it provides that section 2(1)(b) 'shall not apply if, on a proper construction of the contract, it appears that the parties did not intend the term to be enforceable by the third party'.

Section 2*(3)* is also important and provides that '[t]he third party shall be expressly identified in the contract by name, as a member of a class or as answering a particular description but need not be in existence when the contract is entered into'.

8.27 *Section 3* deals with the circumstances under which the contracting parties may *vary or rescind* the contract in a situation where the third party has the right to enforce a term of the contract under section 2 (some material parts of which were described briefly in the preceding paragraph).

8.28 *Section 4* deals with the availability of any defences or set-offs to the promisor in an action by the third party.

8.29 *Section 5* provides that '[s]ection 2 shall not affect any right of the promisee to enforce any term of the contract'.

8.30 *Section 6* provides the promisor with protection from double liability.

8.31 *Section 7* contains *specific exceptions* which prevent the third party from taking advantage of the provisions of the Act. Section 7*(1)* provides that '[s]ection 2 shall not confer any right on a third party in the case of *a contract on a bill of exchange, promissory note or other negotiable instrument*', whilst section 7*(2)* provides the same with regard to 'the case of *any contract binding on a company and its members under section 39 of the Companies Act*' and section 7*(3)* also provides the same with regard to any attempt by the third party 'to enforce any term of a *contract of employment against an employee*'. Finally, section 7*(4)* provides that '[s]ection 2 shall not confer any right on a third party in the case of—(a) a contract for the *carriage of goods by sea; or* (b) a contract for the *carriage of goods by rail or road, or* for the *carriage of cargo by air, which is subject to the rules of the appropriate international transport convention, except that* a third party may in reliance on that section avail himself of *an exclusion or limitation of liability* in such a contract'.

It should be noted that these exceptions (as the very categories they pertain to suggest) are premised on various public policy and/or commercial grounds.

8.32 *Section 8* contains supplementary provisions. Two of the more significant provisions include the following.

First, Section 8*(1)* provides that '[s]ection 2 shall not affect any right or remedy of a third party that exists or is available apart from this Act'. This provision is important: it not only preserves the existing exceptions at common law but also contemplates new exceptions being created. The issue which arises is whether or not it is desirable for the various common law exceptions to exist side-by-side with the Act (for an analysis of this particular issue, see A Phang, 'On Justification and Method in Law Reform—The Contracts (Rights of Third Parties) Act 1999' (2002) 18 *Journal of Contract Law* 32).

Secondly, Section 8*(2)* provides that '[s]*ection 2(2) of the Unfair Contract Terms Act (Cap 396) (exclusion of or restriction on liability for negligence) shall not* apply where the negligence consists of the breach of an obligation arising from a term of a contract *and* the person seeking to enforce it is *a third party acting in reliance on section 2*'. This particular provision poses the very thorny issue as to whether or not the exclusion of section 2(2) of the Unfair Contract Terms Act from the ambit of this particular Act is justifiable. The English Law Commission itself conceded that the arguments were finely balanced (see its report entitled *Privity of Contract: Contracts for the Benefit of Third Parties* (1996) at paragraphs 13.12 and 13.13).

A very powerful critique of this decision to exclude section 2(2) of the Unfair Contract Terms Act may be found in J Adams, D Beyleveld and R Brownsword, 'Privity of Contract—The Benefits and Burdens of Law Reform' (1997) 60 *Modern Law Review* 238 at pp 258–263. Section 2(2) of the Unfair Contract Terms Act itself pertains to the restriction or exclusion of liability for negligence for damages other than death or personal injury and has been dealt with above at paragraph 6.43 (in the chapter on 'Exception Clauses'). The corresponding provision with regard to the restriction or exclusion of liability for negligence causing death and negligence is to be found in section 2(1). It is understandable, therefore, that the Legislature did not think it appropriate to exclude section 2(1) of the Unfair Contract Terms Act from the scope of the present Act. What, then, about the exclusion of section 2*(2)* of the Unfair Contract Terms Act?

Adams, Beyleveld and Brownsword, in the article referred to above, make the following basic arguments *against* such exclusion: first, to prevent the third party from relying on section 2(2) of the Unfair Contract Terms Act against a defendant who seeks to rely on an exception clause would lead to unevenness in the law; for instance, if the third party were *also* to have an action in *tort*, he could possibly avail himself or herself of section 2(2) of the Unfair Contract Terms Act, *whereas* he or she could *not* if the action were mounted only under the auspices of the Contract (Rights of Third Parties) Act.

Secondly, allowing the third party the benefit of section 2(2) of the Unfair Contract Terms Act would not diminish the power of the contracting parties to regulate their relationship with the third party not only because the concept of respect under the Contract (Rights of Third Parties) Act is in fact for the *joint* intentions of the parties only and not (as in this instance) for the intentions of only one party but also because the defendant ought not to be able to invoke what is in effect a *bad defence* against the third party.

8.33 Finally, *section 9* contains provisions relating to *arbitration*.

8.34 Very useful accounts as well as analyses of the English Contracts (Rights of Third Parties) Act exist in the legal literature. As mentioned in paragraph 8.24 above, the Singapore Act is closely based upon the English Act. To this end, very valuable insights may be gleaned from such literature, particularly since both the English and Singapore Acts are of extremely recent vintage. Two useful collections include R Merkin (ed), *Privity of Contract—The Impact of the Contracts (Rights of Third Parties) Act 1999* (2000) and P Kincaid (ed), *Privity—Private Justice or Public Regulation* (2001). Interesting and comprehensive essays include the following: TM Yeo, 'When Do Third Party Rights Arise Under the Contracts (Rights of Third Parties) Act 1999 (UK)?' (2001) 13 *Singapore Academy of Law Journal* 34; N Andrews, 'Strangers to Justice No Longer: The Reversal of the Privity Rule Under the Contracts (Rights of Third Parties) Act 1999' [2001] *Cambridge Law Journal* 353; M Bridge, 'The Contracts (Rights of Third Parties) Act 1999' (2001) 5 *Edinburgh Law Review* 85; C MacMillan, 'A Birthday Present for Lord Denning: The Contracts (Rights of Third Parties) Act 1999' (2000) 63 *Modern Law Review* 721; and A Burrows, 'The Contracts (Rights of Third Parties) Act 1999 and Its Implications for Commercial Contracts' [2000] *Lloyd's Maritime and Commercial Law Quarterly* 540.

Relationship Between Doctrine of Privity of Contract and Doctrine of Consideration

8.35 The very holding of the House of Lords in the *Dunlop Pneumatic Tyre Co* case (as briefly set out in paragraph 8.3) suggests that the doctrines of privity of contract and of consideration are *separate* concepts as well as requirements (insofar as the doctrine of consideration is concerned, see generally, Chapter 3). However, a leading textbook (see MP Furmston, *Cheshire, Fifoot and Furmston's Law of Contract* (14th ed, 2001)) makes the argument that both doctrines are but two sides of the same coin (see pp 86–88; see also the vigorous arguments made along the same lines in B Coote, 'Consideration and the Joint Promisee' [1978] *Cambridge Law Journal* 301 and Kincaid's essays and notes in P Kincaid (ed), *Privity—Private Justice or Public Regulation* (2001)). In other words, one cannot possibly be privy, be a party, to the contract unless one has *also* furnished sufficient consideration.

8.36 It is suggested, however, that there is no reason in principle why a person cannot be a party to the contract even though he or she has not furnished sufficient consideration. Indeed, the so-called *'joint promisee doctrine'* (first made famous in the Australian High Court decision of *Coulls v Bagot's Executor and Trustee Co Ltd* (1967) and endorsed, fairly recently, by the English Law Commission in its Report entitled *Privity of Contract: Contracts for the Benefit of Third Parties* (1996) at paragraphs 6.10–6.11) supports the view just proffered. Under the 'joint promisee doctrine', so long as a person is one of two or more parties (joint promisees) to the contract, he or she need *not* have *personally* furnished consideration in order to be able to enforce the said contract; it is sufficient that consideration has been furnished by *one* of the said joint promises, which would then be deemed (in law) to have been given on behalf of the other party or parties as well. The 'joint promisee doctrine', in other words, *presupposes* the doctrine of privity and the very term itself imports as well as implies the concept of privity of contract.

There are *other* reasons supporting the argument (made above) to the effect that the doctrines of privity of contract and consideration are separate and distinct. It has, for example, been argued that the doctrines of privity and consideration perform *different* functions: the former relates to *who* can sue under the contract whereas the latter relates to the *enforcement* of the contract (ie what types of promises can be enforced) (see, eg D Beyleveld and R Brownsword, 'Privity, Transitivity and Rationality' (1991) 54 *Modern Law Review* 48 at p 61). Although it is of course an ideal situation where the person entitled to sue under the contract would *also* have furnished the requisite consideration, this need *not necessarily* be the case; to put it another way, there is *no necessary* connection as such between the doctrine of privity of contract on the one hand and the doctrine of consideration on the other (for a more detailed discussion and analysis, see generally A Phang, 'On Justification and Method in Law Reform—The Contracts (Rights of Third Parties) Act 1999' (2002) 18 *Journal of Contract Law* 32).

8.37 An important point should, however, be noted insofar as the third party's rights under the *Contracts (Rights of Third Parties) Act 2001* are concerned: as we have seen, the fact that the third party did not personally furnish consideration is not a bar as such (see above, paragraph 8.24 in general and section 2(5) of the Act in particular).

CHAPTER 9

Discharge by Performance, Breach and Agreement

PARAGRAPHS

9.1 **Introduction**

Discharge by Performance

Precise Performance

9.2 (1) No Breach at All

9.3–9.4 (2) *'De Minimis'* Breach Only

9.5–9.8 (3) Effect of Breach Which is not *'De Minimis'*

Partial Performance

9.9–9.10 (1) Apportionment Act

9.11–9.12 (2) Substantial Performance

9.13–9.15 (3) Quantum Meruit

9.16–9.19 (a) Quantum Meruit on a Contractual Basis

9.20 (b) Quantum Meruit on a Restitutionary Basis

9.21–9.24 Divisible Covenants and Obligations

Discharge by Breach of Contract

9.25–9.27 Manner of Breach

9.28–9.32 (1) Breaching a Contract Term

(2) Repudiation of Contract

9.33–9.34 (a) By Oral or Written Communications

9.35–9.36 (b) By Conduct

9.37 (c) By Omission

9.38–9.40 (3) Making Performance Impossible

Timing of Breach: Actual and Anticipatory Breaches

9.41–9.43 (1) Actual Breach of Contract

9.44–9.48 (2) Anticipatory Breach of Contract

Effect of Breach: Discharge of Contract

9.49 (1) Option to Discharge or Affirm

9.50–9.51 (2) Communicating Decision to Discharge or Affirm

9.52–9.53 (3) Effects of Electing to Discharge for Breach

9.54 Losing Right to Discharge for Breach

9.55–9.56 (1) Contract Itself Excludes Such Right

(2) Affirmation of Contract

9.57–9.58 (a) Terminology

PARAGRAPHS

Discharge by Breach of the Contract (continued)

9.59–9.60 (b) When is Affirmation Effective?

9.61–9.62 (c) Affirmation of Actual Versus Anticipatory Breach

9.63–9.65 (d) Limits on Freedom of Choice to Affirm or Discharge Contract

9.66 (3) Estoppel and Waiver

9.67 Lawful Excuse

9.68–9.69 **Discharge by Agreement**

9.70–9.71 Original Contract Provides for Discharge

Subsequent Agreement to Discharge Original Contract

9.72 (1) Unilateral Release Under Seal

9.73–9.77 (2) Discharge Via Mutual Release

9.78–9.82 (a) Mutual Release Distinguished from Variation

9.83–9.85 (b) Mutual Release Distinguished from Waiver

9.86–9.88 (3) Accord and Satisfaction

Introduction

9.1 A contract may be brought to an end or 'discharged' due to:

- complete or 'precise' performance by all parties to a contract of their mutual rights and obligations ('discharge by performance');
- breach of a term of the contract by one party (the 'party-in-breach') which gives the other party not in breach (the 'innocent party') the power to end the contract ('discharge by breach');
- mutual agreement between the parties ('discharge by agreement'); or
- an unforeseeable event beyond the control of any party to the contract—where no party is at fault—which renders further performance of the contract impossible, or at the very least, essentially different from that originally envisaged by parties to the contract ('discharge by frustration'). This type of discharge arises independently of the actions of the parties to the contract and raises distinct and complicated issues of its own (which will be discussed in Chapter 10).

Discharge by Performance

Precise Performance

(1) *No Breach at All*

9.2 A contract is discharged by performance once all parties have precisely performed their obligations under the contract. In such a case, the contract comes to an end since no obligations remain outstanding. Obviously, there will be no issues relating to damages or discharge by breach (discussed below) since precise performance by all parties to the contract presupposes that there are no breaches of any of the terms of the contract.

(2) *'De Minimis' Breach Only*

9.3 In the real world, truly precise performance will be rare. The strictness of the rule that performance must be precise is therefore eased slightly using various techniques. There is, first, the *de minimis* rule: if the defect in performance is minute and inconsequential, then such defects will be ignored and the contract will be treated as if it was performed precisely.

9.4 When, then, are defects *de minimis*? There is no hard and fast rule. Each case will turn on its own facts as well as the terms of the contract. However, the case of *Arcos Ltd v E A Ronaasen & Son* (1933) provides some useful guidelines (per Lord Atkin at p 479–480):

> '... If the written contract specifies conditions of weight, measurement and the like, those conditions must be complied with. A ton does not mean *about* a ton, or a yard *about* a yard. Still less when you descend to minute measurements does $\frac{1}{2}$ inch mean *about* $\frac{1}{2}$ inch .... No doubt there may be microscopic deviations which business men and therefore lawyers will

ignore ... But apart from this consideration, the right view is that the conditions of the contact must be strictly performed' (emphasis added).

(3) *Effect of Breach Which is not 'De Minimis'*

9.5 Failure by one party to perform precisely resulting in a defect or shortfall in his performance which is *not de minimis* will expose the party-in-breach to liability to pay contractual damages to the innocent party if it suffers any loss as a result.

9.6 As discussed previously in Chapter 5 at paragraphs 5.19 to 5.20, where the failure to provide precise performance only results in a breach of a warranty or an innominate term which is not so serious that it deprives the innocent party of substantially the whole of the benefit of the contract (that is, a breach which does *not* 'go to the root of the contract'), the contract cannot be discharged (although *damages* may be recoverable). Instead, the contract must be allowed to continue. Practically, this may mean giving the party-in-breach more time to try and fulfil the terms of his obligation precisely (assuming time of performance is not of the essence and is therefore not a condition of the contract).

9.7 On the other hand, as discussed at paragraphs 5.19–5.20 of Chapter 5, where the failure in performance *does* result in a breach of a condition or of an innominate term which 'goes to the root of the contract' (and which is therefore treated as if there has been a breach of a condition), the breach may excuse the other parties from further performance of their obligations which are meant to 'follow on' or are due only after precise performance by the first party *if* they opt to accept the breach and discharge the contract. In such a situation, we will have moved away from the realm of discharge by precise performance, into the realm of discharge by breach. Exercise of the option to terminate the contract for breach is discussed at paragraphs 9.49–9.65 below.

This type of outcome is most striking where the only obligation still due from the innocent party is payment of the contract price, but where the innocent party refuses to pay on the ground that there has been a prior failure by the party-in-breach to provide precise performance. If this failure amounts to a breach of a condition of the contract, or constitutes a breach of an innominate term which goes to the root of the contract, the party-in-breach who has yet to complete precise performance cannot make a claim for the contract price. This can be seen in the case of *Cutter v Powell* (1795), the facts of which were as follows:

Cutter was employed as second mate in a vessel sailing from Jamaica to Liverpool. It was agreed that he would be paid 30 guineas upon the completion of the entire voyage. However, Cutter passed away 19 days before the vessel reached Liverpool. Cutter's widow attempted to recover a proportion of the agreed fee of 30 guineas in her capacity as administratix of his estate. Unfortunately, her claim was dismissed on the basis that Cutter had not completed his part of the bargain, and as a result, was not entitled to claim for any part of the fee for his services in the law of contract. Cutter's completion of the journey was a condition precedent before payment of the 30 guineas.

9.8 It should be noted, however, that a failure to perform precisely *in itself* does not necessarily mean that all payment for such performance is completely excused. It may be possible to seek payment on a *quantum meruit* basis within the law of unjust of enrichment if the partial performance can be said to amount to a benefit that would unjustly enrich the other party (this type of recovery is discussed in greater detail in Chapter 16. In *Cutter v Powell* (1795), though, Cutter's obligation was held to be an entire one; as such, there was no benefit to Powell until Cutter had completely performed his obligation. As a result, *quantum meruit* on the basis of unjust enrichment was not available).

Partial Performance

(1) *Apportionment Act*

9.9 The strict position due to the requirement for precise performance creates a situation where one party can potentially gain a benefit from the partial and incomplete performance of the other without having to pay anything for it. Legislation was passed in England in the form of the Apportionment Act in 1870 to address this problem.

9.10 This English Act was incorporated into the statutes of Singapore and takes its latest form in the similarly named Apportionment Act (Cap 8, 1998 Rev Ed). This Act provides in section 3 that 'rents, annuities, dividends and other periodical payments in the nature of income' (which would include most forms of salary paid to an employee), 'shall … be considered as accruing from day to day, and shall be apportionable in respect of time accordingly'. In consequence, if the facts of *Cutter v Powell* (1795) were to be decided in Singapore today, arguably, Cutter's estate could make submissions under the Apportionment Act for a pro-rated proportion (based on the number of days worked) of the total amount that would have been paid had Cutter not passed away prematurely.

(2) *Substantial Performance*

9.11 Outside of contracts caught by the Apportionment Act, the courts have developed other principles which alleviate the potential unfairness of the strict 'precise performance' rule. One of these is the doctrine of 'substantial performance'.

This doctrine originates from the decision of Lord Mansfield in *Boone v Eyre* (1779): if there is a slight deviation from exact and precise performance, but the actual performance approaches quite closely to the contracted-for performance (especially where the cost of rectifying the defects in performance is not too great in comparison with the contract price), then the *full* contract price may still have to be paid, subject to a counter-claim or set-off for the cost of rectifying such defects. For example, in the case of *H Dakin & Co Ltd v Lee* (1916), the plaintiffs agreed to carry out repairs to the defendant's premises for an agreed contract price of £1,500. All necessary repairs were carried out, except in respect of three unimportant respects (which would have cost £80 to rectify). Pickford LJ observed that even if it could be said that the work was badly done, it did not mean that there had been no performance at all. The defendant was accordingly ordered to pay the contract price of £1,500 to the plaintiff, less a reduction for the breach.

This doctrine, however, is not available if, as a matter of construction of the contract, the obligation which has been breached is an *entire* obligation (as in the case of *Cutter v Powell* (1795) discussed at paragraph 9.7, above). If the obligation is an entire obligation, then payment of the price only arises if the condition precedent of entire and precise performance by the counter party to the contract has been satisfied. Fortunately, in the absence of a clear intention by the parties that the obligations owed are entire, most obligations to pay the price will not usually be construed as pre-supposing complete and precise performance. In other words, the scenario described by Pickford LJ in *Dakin* is often more typical.

9.12 Assuming that the contract is *not* construed to impose any entire obligations, the next issue is whether the partial performance tendered is actually 'substantial'. This is also an issue of construction. To wit, we need to reconsider the issues canvassed in Chapter 5 at paragraphs 5.19–5.20 in relation to whether a term of the contract is really a condition, a warranty, or an innominate term which goes to the root of the contract. It may be noted that it will generally be difficult to see how partial performance resulting in a breach of a condition or an innominate term going to the root of the contract can ever be said to be 'substantial performance'.

(3) *Quantum Meruit*

9.13 There may be situations where the tendered performance falls so far short of the contract that the doctrine of substantial performance may not be applicable, that is (generally speaking), where there has been a failure to perform a condition or an innominate term which goes to the root of the contract. If so, the party who has tendered partial performance will not be able to recover the full price that would have been payable by the other party to the contract (minus damages to compensate for the defects in performance) as discussed in the preceding section. However, it may be that he can still recover a proportion of the contract price by using the doctrine of *quantum meruit*.

9.14 As discussed and identified by the Singapore Court of Appeal in the case of *Lee Siong Kee v Beng Tiong Trading, Import and Export (1988) Pte Ltd* (2000), there are two varieties of *quantum meruit*:

- *Quantum meruit* on a contractual basis; and
- *Quantum meruit* on a restitutionary basis.

9.15 These possibilities, however, do not excuse any potential liability in damages for the partial performance, although any damages payable as a result may be reduced to take into account any reduction in the *reliance loss* suffered by the innocent party in relation to the price they would have had to pay had the contract been performed perfectly. (For further discussion as to the various types of losses which may be recovered in damages, please refer to Chapter 15.)

(a) *Quantum Meruit* on a Contractual Basis

9.16 Sometimes, a contract may expressly provide that payment in return for performance will be made in proportion to the amount of work done. In the appropriate circumstances, such a term may even be implied. If so, payment of the price will simply be made in accordance with the manner of apportionment as described in such a term.

9.17 The implication of a term to apportion payment on a *quantum meruit* basis is particularly common in the area of sale of goods where section 30(1) of the Sale of Goods Act (Cap 393, 1999 Rev Ed) provides that:

> 'Where the seller delivers to the buyer a quantity of goods less than he contracted to sell, the buyer may reject them, but if the buyer accepts the goods so delivered, he must pay for them at the contract rate.'

Therefore, in all situations of sales of goods where section 30(1) applies, it will be a term of the contract that partial deliveries will be met with proportional payment at the 'contract rate' (or, in other words, the price per unit measure of the goods in question).

9.18 Of course, in addition to terms implied by statutes like the Sale of Goods Act, a term providing for *quantum meruit* payment can be implied at common law if it was necessary for business efficacy, or if it passed the test of the 'officious bystander' (as discussed at paragraphs 5.24–5.25 in Chapter 5). In certain cases though, implication of such a term may be impossible since it would be inconsistent with the express terms of the contract. For example, in the case of *Lee Siong Kee v Beng Tiong Trading, Import and Export (1988) Pte Ltd* (2000), the Singapore Court of Appeal rejected the appellant's argument that a term to allow for remuneration on a *quantum meruit* basis should be implied into his agency contract with the respondents. The Singapore Court of Appeal agreed with the trial judge (at p 570) that there was:

> '... no ground for implying such a term. The agency agreement is not unworkable without it. There is nothing in the agency agreement pointing to any obligation to pay Mr Lee [the appellant] anything other than the agreed fee ... .'

Since the agency agreement contained specific provisions for remuneration to be paid to Lee, when such payments (if made) should be refunded by Lee, as well as when no such payments should be made at all, there was no room to imply a term to permit *quantum meruit*.

9.19 In some cases and textbooks, it has also been suggested that it may even be possible to imply the existence of an entirely new contract with such terms. Thus, where the innocent party 'accepts' the partial performance by the party-in-breach, it may be possible to infer or imply a *fresh* *agreement* between the two parties, wherein they agree that payment will be made for the work already done (albeit incomplete) or for the goods already delivered (although short or otherwise defective). This type of analysis also requires that the defendant must have had the option to take or not to take the benefit of the work done, following the English decision of *Sumpter v Hedges* (1898). However, in the light of the analysis taken by the Singapore Court of Appeal in *Lee Siong Kee v Beng Tiong Trading, Import and Export (1988) Pte Ltd* (2000), the better position today may be to view this as having been subsumed and superseded by the language and analysis of restitutionary *quantum meruit* (which is discussed in the next section).

(b) *Quantum Meruit* on a Restitutionary Basis

9.20 Strictly speaking, this doctrine lies outside the law of contract. Instead, it lies within the complex and developing realm of the law of unjust enrichment (or law of restitution). In some texts or in very old judgments, it is sometimes described as being part of the law of *quasi-contract*.

Even in the complete absence of any contractual clauses to make payment in proportion to the amount of work done, where partial performance by one party has conferred a benefit upon another, retention of such benefit without a corresponding payment to reflect the value of that benefit, coupled with termination or vitiation of the contract, may be 'unjust'. To use the language of the Roman civil law (as explained and applied by Professor Birks in his seminal work, *An Introduction to the Law of Restitution* (Rev ed, 1989) at p 23):

> 'It is fair by the law of nature that nobody should be made richer through loss and wrong to another (*cum alterius detrimento et injuria*).'

Therefore, in certain cases, a claim may be made for a reasonable sum in relation to the partial provision of work or services, *if* the party who has received the alleged benefit of this partial performance had the option of *freely accepting or rejecting* the benefit of this partial performance. This remedy is more fully discussed in Chapter 16.

Divisible Covenants and Obligations

9.21 A lengthy or complex agreement may consist of a number of *divisible* or *severable* parts. For example, in such an agreement, there may be provision that various payments from one party will become due upon the performance of specified parts of the contract by the other.

9.22 A common example can be found in construction contracts, where the main contractor will usually agree to make staggered payments to its sub-contractors, depending on the stage of completion of the overall project achieved by the sub-contractor. If so, once the sub-contractor completes, say, the pouring of the foundations for the building, and the main contractor has contractually agreed that he will pay, say, 15% of the entire contract price upon the completion of this stage, such staggered payments will become due and payable once the pre-determined portion of the contractual performance is completed. Employment contracts where the salary of the employee is payable periodically (for example, monthly) are yet another common example.

Therefore, where it is possible to divide the contract into a number of individually distinct parts, so far as each part is concerned, the mutual rights and obligations of the parties will come to an end once there is precise performance of each of these parts.

9.23 The arguments and considerations as to what should happen where there is only partial performance of one of these distinct parts will simply be a replication of the discussion above. It is therefore possible to argue that there may have been a *de minimis* breach in relation to a specific severable part of the contract, or that it has been substantially performed, and so forth.

9.24 As to *when* a contract may be said to be divisible, this is an issue of interpretation of the contract and the court will usually take into account issues such as the terms of the contract, customary business practices and any common understanding between the parties due to their past dealings with one another.

Discharge by Breach of Contract

Manner of Breach

9.25 A contract may be discharged by breach in a number of ways. Broadly speaking, the contract may be breached if a party to the contract, *without lawful excuse*:

- completely fails to perform, or defectively performs his own obligations under the contract, thereby breaching a condition, or breaching an innominate term which goes to the root of the contract ('I couldn't do it');
- 'renounces' his liabilities or obligations under the contract ('I won't do it'); or
- makes further performance of the contract impossible ('I won't let you do it').

9.26 Obviously, all three types of discharge by breach may occur at the actual point in time where the party-in-breach ought to have performed his obligations under the contract (in which case, it may be said that there has been an 'actual breach' of the contract).

9.27 The latter two types of discharge, however, may occur while the contract is in an 'executory' stage, that is, before the actual point in time when the obligation was supposed to have been performed. In such a situation, the breach is said to be an 'anticipatory' breach. These two concepts are further expanded below from paragraph 9.41 onwards.

(1) *Breaching a Contract Term*

9.28 In Chapter 5, we made a distinction between 'promissory conditions' and 'contingent conditions'. In the rest of this chapter, however, we will only be considering breaches of promissory conditions and any reference to 'conditions' will be to promissory conditions.

9.29 The innocent party will have no power to discharge the contract if the term which has been breached is:

- a warranty; or
- an innominate term, the breach of which does *not* deprive the innocent party of substantially the whole of the benefit of the contract (and therefore does not go to the root of the contract).

On the other hand, the innocent party may be given this power to discharge the contract when the term which has been breached is:

- a condition; or
- an innominate term, the breach of which deprives the innocent party of substantially the whole of the benefit of the contract (and therefore goes to the root of the contract).

9.30 Such termination presupposes that the obligations owed by the parties to the contract are *interdependent*. In other words, we have a scenario where the innocent party has to perform his obligations only if the party-in-breach has already performed his obligations, or is at least 'ready, willing and able' to perform. This is a question of construction of the contract, and most of the time, the courts will take the view that any obligations owed by the parties to the contract, are intended to be interdependent.

9.31 Nonetheless, it is possible for the contract to be framed in such a way that any, some, or even all of the obligations, may be independent of one another. To give an example, the obligation of a tenant to pay rent to his landlord is *independent* of the landlord's obligation to keep the rented premises in good repair. As a result, even if the tenant is in arrears of rental, the landlord generally cannot refuse to make necessary repairs to his premises (in the hope that it will become so uninhabitable that the tenant will move out).

Such independent obligations are the exception rather than the rule, and the court will not construe the contract in such a manner unless the parties' intentions are very clear. This is because an innocent party will not be able to lawfully withhold performance of his own part of the bargain in response to a breach by the other party where the contractual obligations are independent—as such, there is less 'protection' for such an innocent party. Consequently, in most contracts for goods, work or services, performance of the obligation to pay the price is *dependent* on performance of the obligation to provide such goods, work or service.

9.32 Having determined that the obligations are in fact interdependent, the question naturally then arises, 'How do we differentiate between these different types of terms?' To answer this, we should reconsider the discussion in Chapter 5 from paragraphs 5.19–5.20 on the different types of terms.

(2) *Repudiation of Contract*

(a) By Oral or Written Communications

9.33 Where one party to a contract clearly and unequivocally informs the other party that he no longer intends (or will be unable) to perform any of his material obligations under that contract, he is 'renouncing the contract'. This may be done in words, orally or in writing, or in fact, may even be done by way of conduct. So long as it can be said that he has clearly demonstrated his intention not to be bound by the terms of the contract, he will be said to have 'renounced' the contract, and the contract may come to an end. In the case of *Freeth v Burr* (1874), Keating J stated (at p 214) that:

> '[i]t is not a mere refusal or omission of one of the contracting parties to do something which he ought to do, that will justify the other in repudiating the contract; but there must be an absolute refusal to perform his part of the contract.'

9.34 It should be kept in mind, however, that:

> '[n]ot every intimation of an intention not to perform or of an inability to perform some part of a contract will amount to a renunciation. In the case of an entire and indivisible contract, a refusal to perform any part of the agreement will normally entitle the innocent party to treat the contract as discharged. Otherwise, *a renunciation of some but not all the obligations under a contract will not entitle the innocent party to rescind* [ie discharge] *the contract unless the renunciation amounts to a breach of a condition of the contract or deprive* [sic] *him of substantially the whole benefit which it was the intention of the parties that he should obtain from the obligations of the parties under the contract then remaining unperformed*' (emphasis added) (per Karthigesu JA delivering the decision of the Singapore Court of Appeal in *San International Pte Ltd v Keppel Engineering Pte Ltd* (1998) at p 882).

(b) By Conduct

9.35 The matter is less straightforward in the case of repudiation by way of conduct. The Singapore Court of Appeal has quoted the following passage from Vol 1, paragraph 24-016 of *Chitty on Contracts* (28th ed, 1999), with approval in the case of *San International Pte Ltd v Keppel Engineering Pte Ltd* (1998):

> '... Short of an express refusal or declaration the test is to ascertain whether the action or actions of the party in default are such as to lead a reasonable person to conclude that he [the party in default] no longer intends to be bound by its provisions. The party in default may intend in fact to fulfil the contract but may be determined to do so only in a manner substantially inconsistent with his obligations, or may refuse to perform the contract unless the other party complies with certain conditions not required by its terms' (per Karthigesu JA at p 880).

9.36 In *San International Pte Ltd v Keppel Engineering Ltd* (1998), the Singapore Court of Appeal was faced with a dispute between Keppel Engineering, the main contractors in the construction of a warehouse, and San International, to whom part of the construction works were sub-contracted. The dispute centred around whether San International's cessation of certain works relating to the main office areas of the warehouse amounted to a repudiation of the contract which entitled Keppel Engineering to discharge the contract. In order to determine whether Keppel Engineering had the right to discharge the contract, the Singapore Court of Appeal noted (at pp 882–883) that:

> '[i]n our view the crucial question is what consequences San International's failure to resume work on the main office works had on the project as a whole and not just on the sub-contract works. ... What is needed is direct evidence showing what repercussions the main office works had on the rest of the project, and in particular the main warehouse.'

The Singapore Court of Appeal was willing to assume that San International's refusal to carry on with the construction of the main office was, at best, a breach of an innominate term. As such, applying the observation set out at paragraph 9.35 above, Keppel Engineering could only discharge the contract if it could show that San International's cessation of work had deprived it of substantially the whole of the benefit of the contract. In these circumstances, this required an examination of the repercussions of this delay on the progress of the rest of the project, since the 'benefit' of the sub-contract was to enable Keppel Engineering to complete the entire project—a discussion alone as to the percentage of completion on the sub-contracts was not enough. However, as there was insufficient evidence on these matters, the dispute was sent back for further hearing by the trial court.

(c) By Omission

9.37 As a further complication, the possibility of repudiation by way of omission, inaction, or indeed, by way of silence by the party-in-breach cannot be completely discounted. Admittedly, it will not be a straightforward task to demonstrate that there was in fact, the requisite intention to no longer be bound by the contract, but in appropriate circumstances, the court may have sufficient evidence to make such a finding.

(3) *Making Performance Impossible*

9.38 A contract may also be discharged by breach where the actions of one contracting party make it impossible for the other contracting party or parties to perform their obligations. This is distinct from the scenario where a supervening event *which is beyond the control*—and *not due to the fault*—of any of the parties to the contract, renders further performance impossible, or at the very least, 'essentially different' from that which was originally contemplated: that results in a discharge of contract by frustration (which is dealt with in Chapter 10).

9.39 Where the contract is said to be discharged due to the acts or default of a contracting party which renders performance of the contract *impossible*, the innocent party who wants to discharge the contract must show that further performance is *in fact* impossible—he must demonstrate that the contract is actually impossible of performance. It is not enough to show that a *reasonable person* would conclude that further performance is impossible. This distinction can be illustrated by considering the decision of Devlin J in the English case of *Universal Cargo Carriers Corporation v Citati* (1957):

Universal Cargo Carriers ('UCC') hired a ship to Citati. Citati agreed that he was to nominate by a certain date: (1) a location for the ship to be berthed, (2) someone who would provide cargo for shipment on the vessel and (3) the cargo. Three days before that deadline, Citati had not performed any of these obligations, although he indicated that he would be willing to perform the contract if he could. UCC attempted to discharge the contract and found another party to hire the vessel from them, instead of Citati.

Devlin J held that Citati *had not renounced* the contract (and hence there was no discharge by breach pursuant to the principles discussed in paragraphs 9.33–9.37, above). However, UCC was still entitled to discharge the contract because it managed to show that it was in fact impossible for Citati to actually perform his obligations without incurring a delay which would be so long as to negate the commercial purpose of the hire-contract.

9.40 Although they are distinct, facts amounting to discharge by repudiation may also amount to discharge by the impossibility of further performance through the default of one of the contracting parties: surely the argument exists that the actions or default of one party which have made further performance of the contract by the other impossible, also amounts to an *implied* statement of repudiation of the contract (or in other words, such action or default objectively demonstrates an intention not to be bound by the terms of the contract any more). Indeed, where the fact of *impossibility* of further performance is equivocal, great difficulty in continued performance may well be enough in certain circumstances as to amount to an implied repudiation.

Timing of Breach: Actual and Anticipatory Breaches

(1) *Actual Breach of Contract*

9.41 All three types of breach of contract mentioned earlier may occur at the point in time when actual performance is due: an *actual breach*.

For example, where A has contractually bound himself to deliver goods to B on 1 January 2002, time being of the essence, and payment by B of the contract price for the goods to be upon delivery, A commits an actual breach of the contract (in this case, via breach of a condition) if he fails to deliver anything on 1 January 2002. As such, if B exercises his option to accept the breach and discharge the contract, both A and B will be freed from their *primary* obligations under the contract.

This means that B does not need to fulfil his obligations which would have become due over the course of time had there been no breach. In this case, B does not need to perform his *primary* obligation to pay A the contract price. A's *primary* obligation to deliver the goods is in turn replaced by his *secondary* obligation now to compensate B in damages in respect of any pecuniary (and sometimes, non-pecuniary) losses resulting from A's breach of contract. As observed by Lord Reid in the case of *Moschi v Lep Air Services Ltd* (1973) (at pp 345–346):

> '… [W]hen a contract is brought to an end by repudiation accepted by the other party all the obligations in the contract come to an end and they are replaced by operation of law by an obligation to pay money damages. The damages are assessed by reference to the old obligations but the old obligations no longer exist as obligations. Were it otherwise there would be in existence simultaneously two obligations, one to perform the contract and the other to pay damages. But that could not be right. The only legal nexus remaining is the obligation to pay the damages …'

For more on damages for breach of contract, please refer to Chapter 15.

9.42 If B chooses, however, to reject the repudiation, *waives* the breach and allows A further opportunity to perform (for example, by giving A an extension of time), then B loses his right to discharge the contract that arose from A's breach. Unlike the case of affirmation of an anticipatory breach, though, B may still have the opportunity to recover damages from A arising from any losses he may incur as a result of A's actual breach (for example, for losses due to the delay).

9.43 Apart from the primary and secondary obligations, there is also another category of obligations within many contracts which do not directly relate to performance of the contract. Instead, these are focussed on matters *ancillary* to performance of the contract and are thus often referred to as ancillary obligations. Examples of such obligations include those imposed by contractual terms like exception clauses, choice of forum clauses, jurisdiction clauses, choice of law clauses, and so forth.

These clauses are often aimed at governing actions of parties following a breach and perhaps discharge of the contract. Unlike the primary obligations which are extinguished, they survive the end of the contract, subject to certain limitations (for example, the rules on the enforceability of exception clauses which are discussed in Chapter 6). In fact, breach of these ancillary obligations following an earlier repudiatory breach could well give rise to separate and distinct liabilities in damages. A possible example of this can be seen in the House of Lords case of *Donohue v Armco Inc* (2002):

In this case, Donohue had applied for an injunction against Armco, to restrain them from bringing legal proceedings against him in New York, on the basis that this infringed his contractual right to have all 'legal disputes' between the two of them heard in London. Donohue argued that if the injunction was not granted, he might potentially face liability for exceptionally punitive damages available under the United

States Federal Racketeer Influenced and Corrupt Organizations Act, which would enable a successful plaintiff to be awarded triple, punitive and exemplary damages (none of which would be recoverable in an English court). In addition, Donohue would have to incur potentially irrecoverable additional legal costs in defending himself against such a suit in New York. Armco conceded that if it were the case that bringing an action against Donohue could amount to a breach of the exclusive jurisdiction clause, Donohue would be entitled to sue and recover damages. It thus gave an undertaking that it would not enforce any multiple or punitive damages that might be awarded in the New York proceedings. Interestingly, the concession and undertaking were *accepted* by the House of Lords as the basis for their decision to refuse Donohue's application for an injunction.

Given their acceptance without comment of Armco's concession and undertaking, it appears that the House of Lords is willing to accept that damages may be available for breaches of this type of clause. Damages were also awarded by the English Court of Appeal in *Union Discount Co Ltd v Zoller* (2001) for losses incurred as a result of a breach of an exclusive jurisdiction clause. Despite this, care should be taken since there is as yet, no authoritative approval of such damages from the House of Lords (and, more importantly, the Singapore courts).

(2) *Anticipatory Breach of Contract*

9.44 A breach of contract by repudiation or impossibility can also occur even before any performance is expected of any party to the contract: an *anticipatory breach*. Indeed, breaches by repudiation or impossibility are more likely to occur at an executory stage of the contract, prior to the time of actual performance, than otherwise. For example, following the exchange of promises resulting in the formation of the contract, but before the time of performance of those promises, if the party-in–breach demonstrates an intention not to be bound by his obligations under the contract and repudiates it, such a repudiation will be effective and will be said to be an anticipatory breach. Similar outcomes will apply in cases where repudiation occurs because further performance has been made impossible through the default of one of the parties.

9.45 Generally speaking, in all cases of anticipatory breach, the innocent party can elect to discharge the contract for breach and choose to sue for contractual damages to compensate him for any losses caused by the party-in-breach's actions. As in the case with acceptance of an actual breach (discussed above), all outstanding primary obligations of both parties under the contract are extinguished, and instead, all that remains are the secondary obligations of the party-in-breach to compensate the innocent party in damages for any loss suffered, as well as the ancillary obligations (if any) mentioned above. What is important, however, is that the innocent party does not have to wait until the time of actual performance to discharge the contract and sue for damages. A good example of this can be seen in the case of *Lovelock v Franklyn* (1846), where the defendant had an interest in a lease. He promised to assign this to the plaintiff within seven years from the date of their mutual exchange of promises. In return, the plaintiff promised to pay the defendant £140 upon such assignment. However, before the end of the seven years, the defendant assigned his interest to someone other than the plaintiff, making performance of the contract impossible. This amounted to an anticipatory breach, and the plaintiff successfully sued without having to wait until the seven years had lapsed. Lord Denman CJ observed at (p 378) that the plaintiff in *Lovelock* had the right to tell the defendant:

> 'You have placed yourself in a situation which you cannot perform what you have promised: you promised to be ready during the period of seven years; and, during that period, I may at any time tender you the money and call for an assignment, and expect that you should keep yourself ready; but if I now were to tender you the money, you would not be ready.'

Clearly, the defendant's assignment amounted to a breach of the contract.

9.46 Although the innocent party can immediately claim for damages following acceptance of the anticipatory breach, the damages awarded must still reflect the value of the contractual performance by the party-in-breach which has been lost. Therefore, as observed by Megaw LJ in the English Court of Appeal case of *Maredelanto Compania Naviera SA v Bergbau-Handel GmbH, The Mihalis Angelos* (1971) (at p 210), if such contractual performance could 'by the terms of the contract of being rendered less valuable or valueless in certain events, and if it can be shown that those events were, at the date of acceptance of repudiation, predestined to happen', then the damages that can be recovered should be reduced to reflect such potential diminution in value.

The Mihalis Angelos (1971) involved a dispute over the amount of damages which should be awarded to the owners of a vessel due to the anticipatory breach of the charterparty (the lease agreement for the vessel). The pertinent facts were as follows:

The owners of the Mihalis Angelos hired the vessel to the charterers under a charterparty which contained a clause stating that the ship was 'expected ready to load at Haiphong under this charter about July 1st, 1965'. This clause also provided that the ship was to be ready for loading apatite ore on or before 20 July 1965, and that the charterers would have the option of cancelling the contract if it was not ready by that date. On or about 12 July 1965, the charterers found that they were unable to have their cargo of apatite ore ready for loading at Haiphong in time due to difficulties in land transport which were apparently beyond their control. Meanwhile, by 17 July, it had become obvious that the Mihalis Angelos could not arrive at Haiphong to be ready for loading by 20 July. Instead of waiting until 20 July to exercise their contractual right to cancel the contract, the charterers attempted (wrongfully, as it turned out) to discharge the contract on 17 July on the basis that it had been frustrated by the difficulties in transporting their cargo to the port by land. On the other hand, the owners took the view (rightfully) that this was in reality an anticipatory breach.

Ultimately, however, the owners' claim for substantial damages as a result of this breach failed. Even though the contractual right to cancel the contract on 20 July was lost, as a result of the termination of the contract on 17 July following the owners' acceptance of the charterers' anticipatory breach, the English Court of Appeal accepted that the contractual right to cancel survived for the purpose of determining the quantum of damages that should be awarded for the breach. Since the charterers would definitely have exercised their contractual right to cancel on 20 July, given the delayed arrival of the vessel, the owners suffered no substantial loss from the charterers' anticipatory breach on 17 July.

9.47 Unless and until an anticipatory breach is *accepted* by the innocent party, the contract will stay on foot and the anticipatory breach will be ignored as if it had never occurred. In the colourful (and oft-quoted) words of Asquith LJ in the English Court of Appeal case of *Howard v Pickford Tool Co Ltd* (1951) (at p 421):

> '... An unaccepted repudiation is a thing writ in water and of no value to anybody: it confers no legal rights of any sort or kind....'

9.48 In summary:

> '(1) A [repudiation] of the contract by one party prior to the time for performance is not itself a breach but it gives the other party, the injured party, the right to treat it as a breach in anticipation and thus to treat the contract as discharged immediately. In other words, if a person says he will not perform, the law allows the other to take him at his word and act accordingly.
>
> (2) In such a case the injured party is not ordinarily bound to treat the contract as discharged; the law gives him a choice. He may treat the contract as discharged or he may disregard the repudiation and treat the contract as continuing in full effect, notwithstanding what has occurred. He can, in other words, elect to affirm it.
>
> (3) If the injured party elects to affirm the contract, both parties' rights and obligations under it remain completely unaffected; the renunciation is "writ in water", ...
>
> (4) The choice placed before the injured party is between inconsistent rights, and once the choice has been made and communicated to the other party to the contract, it is irrevocable. Unlike estoppel, election does not depend upon any change in position by the party to whom it is communicated.
>
> (5) Although the injured party is bound by his election once it has been made, the fact that he has affirmed the contract does not of course preclude him from treating it as discharged on a subsequent occasion if the other party again repudiates it. ...'
>
> (per Moore-Bick J in the English case of *Yukong Line Ltd of Korea v Rendsburg Investments Corporation of Liberia* (1996) at p 607).

These observations apply equally to a case of breach where performance has been made impossible due to one of the parties' actions or default.

Effect of Breach: Discharge of Contract

(1) *Option to Discharge or Affirm*

9.49 It must be emphasised that discharge of the contract (following breach of a condition or an innominate term that goes to the root if the contract) does not occur automatically. Regardless of whether it is an actual or an anticipatory breach, the breach will only discharge the contract if the breach is *accepted* by the innocent party. In other words, the innocent party must not *reject the breach.*

(2) *Communicating Decision to Discharge or Affirm*

9.50 To be effective, the decision to discharge the contract must be communicated to the party-in-breach. This is often done via oral or written communication to the party-in-breach, whether personally, or sometimes via an agent. However, this is not mandatory—any mode of communication which unequivocally evidences the intention of the innocent party to discharge the contract is sufficient. Hence, in the House of Lords case of *Vitol SA v Norelf Ltd* (1996), Lord Steyn accepted (at pp 810–811) the following propositions of law:

> '(1) Where a party has repudiated a contract the aggrieved party has an election to accept the repudiation or to affirm the contract ... (2) An act of acceptance of a repudiation requires no particular form: a communication does not have to be couched in the language of acceptance. It is sufficient that the communication or conduct clearly and unequivocally conveys to the repudiating party that that aggrieved party is treating the contract as at an end. (3) It is rightly conceded by counsel for the buyers that the aggrieved party need not personally, or by an agent, notify the repudiating party of his election to treat the contract as at an end. It is sufficient that the fact of the election comes to the repudiating party's attention, *eg* notification by an unauthorised broker or other intermediary may be sufficient ...'

On the other hand, if the contract prescribes a mandatory mode of communication of such decision, it must be complied with. Otherwise, the election will be ineffective.

9.51 What is still unclear is whether *inactivity* by the innocent party in response to a breach may be sufficient, for example, where the innocent party fails to take certain steps which he would have been expected to, if he were of the mindset that the contract was still in force. The case of *Vitol SA v Norelf Ltd* (1996) provides authority that, in the right circumstances, inactivity *could* be sufficient. This case involved a dispute between buyers and sellers of certain goods to be loaded onto a vessel due to arrive, berth and leave port on specified dates. The buyers informed the sellers that they were rejecting the cargo and repudiating the contract while the vessel was loading because the vessel was unlikely to complete loading within the contractual time frame. The House of Lords had to consider whether the seller's subsequent failure to present a bill of lading to the buyer constituted an acceptance of the buyer's repudiatory breach.

Lord Steyn (with whom the rest of the Lords agreed) set out the following analysis (at pp 811–812):

> '... I am satisfied that a failure to perform may *sometimes* signify to a repudiating party an election by the aggrieved party to treat the contract as at an end. Postulate the case where an employer at the end of a day tells a contractor that he, the employer, is repudiating the contract and that the contractor need not return the next day. The contractor does not return the next day or at all. It seems to me that the contractor's failure to return may, in the absence of any other explanation, convey a decision to treat the contract as at an end. Another example may be an overseas sale providing for shipment on a named ship in a given month. The seller is obliged to obtain an export licence. The buyer repudiates the contract before loading starts. To the knowledge of the buyer the seller does not apply for an export licence with the result that the transaction cannot proceed. In such circumstances it may well be that an ordinary businessman, circumstanced as the parties were, would conclude that the seller was treating the contract as at an end. Taking the present case as illustrative, it is important to bear in mind that the tender of a bill of lading is the pre-condition to payment of the price. Why should an arbitrator not be able to infer that when, in the days and weeks following loading and the sailing of the vessel, the seller failed to tender a bill of lading to the buyer he clearly conveyed to a trader that he was treating the contract as at an end? ... *Sometimes in the practical world of businessmen an omission to act may be as pregnant with meaning as a positive declaration. ... [I]n the ... field of repudiation, a failure to perform may sometimes be given a colour by special circumstances and may only be explicable to a reasonable person in the position of the repudiating party as an election to accept the repudiation*' (emphasis added).

(3) *Effects of Electing to Discharge for Breach*

9.52 Having decided to discharge the contract, does the discharge affect any obligations which were due, or which had been performed prior to the decision to exercise one's power to discharge the contract due to breach? The answer is that this type of termination has *no retrospective effect*. This means that all obligations which were performed *prior* to the exercise of the right to discharge are *unaffected*. Any prior obligations which were due to be performed, but which were not performed, are similarly unaffected and still have to be performed. However, in relation to all obligations which were due to be performed at the time when the right to discharge the contract was exercised, as well as all obligations which were due to be performed after such time, all such obligations are discharged. As a result, both the innocent party and the party-in-breach are released from having to perform any of their outstanding primary obligations. The party-in-breach, however, will now have to perform his secondary obligation to compensate the innocent party in damages.

This distinction has been authoritatively summarised by Lord Wilberforce in the House of Lords case of *Johnson v Agnew* (1980) (at pp 392–393):

> '…[I]t is important to dissipate a fertile source of confusion and to make clear that although sometimes the vendor is referred to … as "rescinding" the contract, this so-called "rescission" is quite different from rescission *ab initio*, such as may arise for example in cases of mistake, fraud or lack of consent. In those cases the contract is treated in law as never having come into existence … In the case of an accepted repudiatory breach the contract has come into existence but has been put an end to or discharged. Whatever contrary indications may be disinterred from old authorities, it is now quite clear, under the general law of contract, that acceptance of a repudiatory breach does not bring about "rescission *ab initio*".'

Locally, the Singapore Court of Appeal in *Hong Fok Realty Pte Ltd v Bima Investment Pte Ltd* (1993) has also highlighted the same point (at p 79).

9.53 The decision to accept the breach and discharge the contract is also irrevocable: once made, it cannot be retracted or withdrawn (see, for example, *Lee Christina v Lee Eunice & Anor (executors of the estate of Lee Teck Soon)* (1993)).

Losing Right to Discharge for Breach

9.54 The discussion in the previous sections has listed various situations where a contract may be brought to an end due to breach following an election to discharge the contract by the innocent party. However, this right may be lost in a number of ways.

(1) *Contract Itself Excludes Such Right*

9.55 In certain contracts, the right to discharge the contract for breach may be excluded by the contract itself. For example, in some contracts for the sale of goods, the vendor may include a clause which provides that the purchaser will not be able to reject the goods delivered, even if there is a shortfall in quantity, thereby excluding the operation of section 30 of the Sale of Goods Act (Cap 393, 1999 Rev Ed).

9.56 One might then wonder if such a non-rejection clause might fall foul of the rules relating to exception clauses (discussed in Chapter 6). Although this may be possible, it should be kept in mind that notwithstanding the loss of the right to reject the goods (and hence discharge the contract), the purchaser may still sue the vendor for breach and recover damages for any loss he may have suffered (unless the clause *also* provides for the exclusion of remedies such as damages). In light of this, it is arguable that a non-rejection clause *per se* will not contravene the rules relating to exception clauses.

(2) *Affirmation of Contract*

(a) Terminology

9.57 As mentioned previously, even where there is a breach of the contract which would entitle the innocent party to discharge it, the contract continues to be in force unless he exercises that right. Once the innocent party chooses, instead, to reject the breach and affirm the contract, he will thereafter lose the right to discharge the contract. In doing so, he has decided that he will continue to perform his contractual obligations, and will also expect the party-in-breach to continue to perform his outstanding contractual obligations if any.

9.58 Sometimes, this process of rejection of the breach and affirmation of the contract is referred to as a *waiver* of the breach. This terminology should be used with care to avoid confusion with the concept of what is sometimes described as a *total waiver*. In a situation of total waiver, the innocent party not only waives his right to discharge the contract, he also waives his right to recover any damages for the contractual breach. In other words, the innocent party is abandoning *all* of his rights under the contract. To avoid this confusion, we will only use the language of affirmation of the contract and/or rejection of the breach to refer to the situation where the innocent party is leaving open the possibility that he may still seek damages from the party-in-breach to recover any losses incurred because of the breach of the contract, even though the innocent party has elected to continue with the contract.

(b) When is Affirmation Effective?

9.59 An affirmation is only effective if there is an unequivocal act or statement from the innocent party to the party-in-breach to clearly show this intention to affirm the contract, instead of discharging it. In the House of Lords case of *China National Foreign Trade Transportation Corporation v Eulogia Shipping Co SA of Panama, The Mihalios Xilas* (1979), Lord Scarman observed (at pp 1034–1035) that:

> '[w]hen a man, faced with two alternative and mutually exclusive courses of action, chooses one and has communicated his choice to the person concerned in such a way as to lead him to believe that he has made his choice, he has completed his election.'

9.60 Moore-Bick J summarised these issues neatly in the English case of *Yukong Line Ltd of Korea v Rendsburg Investments Corporation of Liberia* (1996) (at p 607):

> '... (6) The injured party will not be treated as having elected to affirm the contract in the face of the [repudiation] unless it can be shown that he knew of the facts giving rise to his right to treat the contract as discharged and of his right to choose between affirming the contract and treating it as discharged.
>
> (7) A binding election requires the injured party to communicate his choice to the other party in clear and unequivocal terms. In particular, he will not be held bound by a qualified or conditional decision.

(8) Election can be express or implied and will be implied where the injured party acts in a way which is consistent only with a decision to keep the contract alive or where he exercises rights which would only be available to him if the contract had been affirmed.'

(c) Affirmation of Actual Versus Anticipatory Breach

9.61 Affirmation of an actual—as opposed to an anticipatory—breach results in slightly different outcomes. When an actual breach is rejected and the contract affirmed, the innocent party loses his right to discharge the contract, but he retains the right to sue for damages to compensate him for any losses he may suffer because of the breach by the party-in-breach.

9.62 When an anticipatory breach is rejected and the contract affirmed, as mentioned before, the anticipatory breach is treated as if it never occurred and the contract continues in force. Not only is the right to discharge the contract lost, there is also no right to make any claim in damages since there is, in effect, *no breach* at all. Of course, it is conceivable that at the point of actual performance of the contract, the 'party-in-breach' may maintain his earlier position and actually fails to perform, despite the affirmation of the contract earlier. If so, there will be an actual breach of the contract and of course, damages may be available to compensate the innocent party for his losses at that particular point in time. The prior rejection of a prior anticipatory breach does not preclude the innocent party from accepting a subsequent breach, whether actual or anticipatory, and terminating the contract as a result thereof.

(d) Limits on Freedom of Choice to Affirm or Discharge Contract

9.63 Generally speaking, following a breach of contract, the innocent party is free to choose whether to affirm the contract or to accept the breach and discharge the contract. This freedom of choice, however, is potentially subject to a limitation set out in the case of *White and Carter (Councils) Ltd v McGregor* (1962) ('*White & Carter* (1962)'). The facts of the case were as follows:

White and Carter (Councils) Ltd ('White & Carter') supplied litter bins to various local authorities in Scotland in exchange for remuneration by way of paid advertisements placed on these litter bins. McGregor was the sales manager of a company operating a garage who had placed such advertisements with White & Carter. Upon the termination of one such contract, McGregor entered into another contract with White & Carter to continue advertising for another three years. This was within his ostensible authority, although he did not have any actual authority to do so. Consequently, McGregor's employers informed White & Carter about the mistake and attempted to repudiate the contract the very next day. Instead of accepting the repudiatory breach and discharging the contract, White & Carter's management decided to continue with performance of their obligations under the contract: they prepared the necessary plates for attachment to the bins and exhibited them on the bins from 2 November 1957. The contract provided that the first annual payment would become due seven days after the first display. If unpaid for four weeks, then the entire amount due for the three years (being £196 4s) would become payable. When the garage company failed to make the first year's payment on time, the full price for the three years' worth of advertising became payable and White & Carter sued for the entire amount due, instead of suing for the loss of profit from the breach of contract by the garage company.

On appeal to the House of Lords, a bare majority of their Lordships accepted that White & Carter were entitled to act as they did and allowed their claim. Their Lordships were faced with a dilemma because the facts of this case brought up two conflicting principles, namely:

- that an anticipatory breach does not discharge the contract unless the innocent party exercises his option to do so; and
- that the innocent party has to mitigate his losses as a result of the breach of contract.

Three out of five of the Lordships held that White & Carter did not need to mitigate and had the right to choose to perform the contract in full, which therefore entitled them to claim for the price. Consequently, Lord Reid, Lord Tucker and Lord Hodson decided that White & Carter's claim should succeed. Indeed, Lord Hodson (with whom Lord Tucker agreed) took the robust view (at p 445) that:

> '[i]t may be unfortunate that the [garage company] have saddled themselves with an unwanted contract causing an apparent waste of time and money. ... [T]here is no equity which can assist the [garage company]. It is trite that equity will not rewrite an improvident contract where there is no disability on either side. There is no duty laid upon a party to a subsisting contract to vary it at the behest of the other party so as to deprive himself of the benefit given to him by the contract. To hold otherwise would be to introduce a novel equitable doctrine that a party was not to be held to his contract unless the court in a given instance thought it reasonable so to do.'

In other words, there is no duty to 'mitigate' or to act reasonably insofar as the innocent party has a free choice whether to affirm or discharge the contract (mitigation of damages is further discussed at paragraphs 15.76–15.83 in Chapter 15).

Alone of the three judges in the majority, Lord Reid suggested (at pp 430–431) that the right to affirm the contract could (possibly) be curtailed on the basis of some 'general equitable principle or element of public policy'. Lord Reid observed (at p 431) that:

> '*... if it can be shown that a person has no legitimate interest, financial or otherwise, in performing the contract rather than claiming damages, he ought not to be allowed to saddle the other party with an additional burden with no benefit to himself.* If a party has no interest to enforce a stipulation, he cannot in general enforce it: so it might be said that, if a party has no interest to insist on a particular remedy, he ought not to be allowed to insist on it. And, just as a party is not allowed to enforce a penalty, so he ought not to be allowed to

penalise the other party by taking one course when another is equally advantageous to him' (emphasis added).

The difficulty with this limitation is that it is unclear when and where such an interest may be found. In the passage above, Lord Reid suggests that the legitimate interest could include the financial interests of the parties. However, in the very same paragraph, he appears to contradict himself by observing (at p 431) that:

> 'If I may revert to the example which I gave of a company engaging an expert to prepare an elaborate report and then repudiating before anything was done, *it might be that the company could show that the expert had no substantial or legitimate interest in carrying out the work rather than accepting damages*: I would think that the *de minimis* principle would apply in determining whether his interest was substantial, and that he might have a legitimate interest *other than an immediate financial interest*. But if the expert had no such interest then that might be regarded as a proper case for the exercise of the general equitable jurisdiction of the court' (emphasis added).

On the facts of *White & Carter* (1962) itself, no such legitimate interest was *proved*, although it must have been assumed that it was in the advertising company's financial interest to act in the way they did since Lord Reid was with the majority in allowing their claim. Interestingly, Lord Reid also observed (at p 431) that the respondents (that is, the garage company):

> '... did not set out to prove that the appellants [White & Carter] had no legitimate interest in completing the contract and claiming the contract price rather than claiming damages; there is nothing in the findings of fact to support such a case, and *it seems improbable that any such case could have been proved*' (emphasis added).

Therefore, assuming that such a limitation exists, it is of limited assistance to the repudiating party since they seem to have the burden of proving the absence of a legitimate interest on the part of the innocent party in the performance of the contract. If it is difficult to prove the presence of a concept as ill-defined as 'legitimate interest', the difficulty to prove its *absence* must surely be even greater.

9.64 Locally, the scope of Lord Reid's requirement of 'legitimate interest' has been the subject of further discussion by Selvam J in the Singapore High Court case of *MP-Bilt Pte Ltd v Oey Widarto* (1999). This case involved a dispute over the payment of a second instalment of $486,039.80 by Oey for the purchase of a condominium unit being developed by MP-Bilt. One of the issues raised was whether MP-Bilt was under a duty to mitigate or to act reasonably in exercising its option to discharge the contract or to affirm it. Applying *White & Carter* (1962), Selvam J had no hesitation in holding that there was no such duty. Of greater interest, however, are his observations on the doctrine of 'legitimate interest' raised by Lord Reid in *White & Carter* (1962). Accepting that there was in fact such a doctrine, Selvam J observed (at p 607) that it was subject to the following restrictions:

> 'First, it [the requirement of 'legitimate interest'] cannot apply retrospectively to accrued debts. Accrued debts can be sued for even after acceptance of repudiation.
>
> Next, it does not apply where the innocent party can reasonably perform his obligation without the co-operation of the contract-breaker. …
>
> Thirdly and more importantly, the doctrine was conceived in the context of the innocent party rejecting the repudiation by the other party and exercising his right to complete performance when the former has a legitimate interest to protect. *A fortiori*, the doctrine cannot apply when the innocent party is under a legal obligation or practical compulsion to complete performance of the contract in question and other contracts he has entered into on the basis of the contract in question.'

Selvam J's third restriction is particularly interesting: it will be rare indeed to find a contracting party pondering whether or not to reject a repudiatory breach who is *not* under any 'legal obligation or practical compulsion to complete performance of the contract', especially since such legal obligation or practical compulsion includes consideration of *other contracts* which have been entered into on the basis of the contract which has been repudiatorily breached. In addition, it should be remembered that an anticipatory repudiatory breach, once rejected, is treated as if it never existed such that parties continue to be bound to perform their mutual obligations thereunder. As such, it is difficult to see how the innocent party who has rejected the anticipatory repudiatory breach can be said *not* to be under a legal obligation of practical compulsion to complete performance 'of the contract in question'. If Selvam J's qualification to the requirement of 'legitimate interest' correctly represents the view of the courts in Singapore, it may well be that Lord Reid's attempt to ameliorate the apparent harshness of the rule in *White & Carter* (1962) can only be applied locally in the most unusual of cases. Further discussion of the problems relating to *White & Carter* (1962) may also be found in JW Carter, A Phang and SY Phang, 'Performance Following Repudiation: Legal and Economic Interests' (1999) 15 *Journal of Contract Law* 97.

9.65 Following from the extensive discussion on *White & Carter* (1962) above, it is clear that mitigation also does not have any role to play *after* the innocent party has decided to reject an anticipatory breach by the other party and affirms the contract. However, there may be cases where it is unclear whether an anticipatory breach has been rejected and the contract affirmed, or whether it has been accepted and the contract discharged. Faced with such uncertainty, the innocent party may well embark on steps seeking to minimise his own losses (that is, to mitigate them) which may then be inconsistent with affirmation and continuation of the contract.

For example, where a purchaser of certain specific goods commits an anticipatory repudiatory breach of the contract by informing the vendor that he no longer intends to honour his obligation to pay for and take delivery of the goods, if the vendor then enters into another contract with another purchaser for those goods, thereby cutting his losses short, the pressure to mitigate will have caused the innocent party, the vendor, to make it impossible for himself to perform the original contract. In such a situation, he will have lost his right to choose whether to accept or to reject the initial breach by the first purchaser. Using the language of Moore-Bick J in the *Yukong Line* case (discussed at paragraph 9.60, above), it may well be said that this would amount to an 'implied' election by the innocent party to discharge the contract.

(3) *Estoppel and Waiver*

9.66 The right to discharge a contract may be lost if there are circumstances which would estop the innocent part from being able to exercise such a right. The circumstances where promissory estoppel might operate have been discussed extensively in Chapter 3. In appropriate circumstances, an innocent party may be found to have waived his right to discharge the contract and may be unable to exercise such rights if it would be inequitable to do so. This is discussed below from paragaphs 9.83 onwards.

Lawful Excuse

9.67 All of the discussion thus far presupposes that a breach of contract has occurred. However, a contract is only breached if there is no 'lawful excuse' for the failure of performance. Examples of a lawful excuse for a breach of the contract could include the following:

- Where the reason for the non-performance is the prior non-performance by the other party to the contract of his own contractual obligations, where such non-performance constitutes an event of discharge of contract by breach.
- Where after the contract has been formed, external unforeseeable events occur, rendering further performance of the contract by the parties impossible, or at least, rendering continued performance to be fundamentally and essentially different from what was originally envisaged, that is, where a *frustrating event* has occurred, causing the contract to be discharged by frustration. This is discussed in Chapter 10.
- Where there are express (or sometimes implied) terms within the contract itself which provide 'excuses' for the actions in question, which would otherwise constitute an event of discharge of contract by breach. For example, a '*force majeure*' clause excusing non- or delayed performance due to an Act of God, adverse weather, strikes, etc. These are discussed in Chapter 10.
- Where a 'vitiating factor' is present and causes the contact to be either void *ab initio* or enables one of the parties to avoid the contract, thereby rendering the contract as if it never came into existence. This is discussed in detail in Chapters 11 to 14.

Discharge by Agreement

9.68 Just as a contract creates binding obligations on the parties to the contract because of their mutual agreement to be so bound, the parties to a contract can also agree to release themselves from such obligations, that is to say, to discharge the contract by agreement.

9.69 Keeping in mind the potential difficulty with consideration (see paragraph 9.74, below), discharge by agreement may be said to arise in a number of different contexts:

- Where the original contract specifically provides for its own discharge; or
- Where the parties to a contract subsequently agree that they will not take any legal proceedings to enforce the obligations owed under the original contract against one another, and thereby enter into:
  (1) a release under seal (where the seal dispenses with the need for consideration for the release to be legally enforceable)—this is sometimes referred to as a 'unilateral release'; or
  (2) a second agreement supported by consideration which creates a legally enforceable contract. This can take the form of:
    (a) a mutual exchange of promises not to enforce the obligations under the original contract, where the contract is wholly executory—this is sometimes referred to as a 'mutual release'; or
    (b) 'accord and satisfaction', where the contract is either wholly executory or where part of it has been completely executed.

Original Contract Provides for Discharge

9.70 A contract may be drafted in such a way as to give one or more parties to the contract the contractual right to discharge the contract. Usually, a pre-condition will be drafted such that these powers can only be exercised if certain events occur first. For example, most employment contracts incorporate a clause entitling the employer (or the employee) to discharge the contract upon giving a specific period of notice.

9.71 In some contracts, there may be a term that provides for the *automatic* termination of the contract upon the occurrence of a certain event. A good example is a lease of property for a fixed term—once the agreed period of the lease runs out, the entire contract automatically comes to an end. Such terms may, of course, be express. But even in contracts which do not have such express provision, the possibility remains open for them to be implied where the appropriate tests are satisfied.

Subsequent Agreement to Discharge Original Contract

(1) *Unilateral Release Under Seal*

9.72 In any contract, any party can choose to release the other party to the contract from further performance by executing a unilateral release under seal. This possibility is available regardless of whether the contract is wholly executory or otherwise. As noted earlier in Chapter 3 (at paragraph 3.2), the formal process of executing a contract under seal replaces the need for consideration. Accordingly, where the promise not to require the other party (the promisee) to perform is executed under seal, there is no need for the promisee to provide any consideration in exchange, and the release will, nonetheless, be effective.

(2) *Discharge Via Mutual Release*

9.73 Where neither party to a contract has completed performance of its obligations under that contract, a new agreement between them whereby they mutually promise not to enforce against each other any of the obligations under the original agreement is effective in discharging the original agreement. Such a new agreement is effective as the promise of each party to abandon its rights under the original contract is consideration for the other party's promise to likewise abandon its rights.

9.74 Discharge via mutual release, however, is not available if either party has completed all of its obligations under the original contract. For example, if A originally contracted to deliver certain goods to B in exchange for B's counter-promise to pay the contractual price, and A has actually delivered those goods to B, a subsequent agreement between A and B not to enforce the original agreement against one another would be ineffective. In such a situation, A's promise that he would not enforce B's original promise of payment would be ineffective, as B (the promisee) would have provided no consideration for it. B's counter-promise 'not to enforce A's original obligations to deliver' does not render a benefit to A, nor is it a detriment to B (since A has already delivered the goods). In such a case, the subsequent mutual promise not to enforce the original contract would not be legally binding. However, the possibility for an argument based on *promissory estoppel* (discussed at length in Chapter 3) or *waiver* (discussed below from paragraph 9.83 onwards) remains open. In both these cases, detrimental reliance by a party on the promise not to enforce the original contract may be enough to surmount the lack of consideration, and allow the promise of release at least some limited binding force.

9.75 Although such agreements of mutual release may be express, it is possible for a court to conclude that parties have *impliedly* come to an agreement of mutual release through their conduct, for example, through extended periods of delay or inactivity after the original agreement was entered into. This is most likely to occur when one party has acted in a manner whereby the other party can reasonably assume that there is a new agreement for the original contract to be abandoned.

9.76 In addition to a mutual release where the original agreement is simply brought to an end, sometimes the mutual release takes the form of a second agreement which is aimed at replacing or superseding the original one, thereby introducing new terms which were not present in the original contract. Yet a further possibility is a mutual release which takes the form of a subsequent agreement to replace the parties to the contract.

Again, if the terms of the new contract are so inconsistent with the terms of the original contract such that both parties must be taken to have intended the original contract to no longer bind them, the court may be prepared to imply a release from the obligations under the original contract into the terms of the new contract.

9.77 Mutual release via the creation of a new contract with new terms or with new parties in substitution of those under the original contract, may, however, sometimes be confused with mere *variation* of the contract, as well as with waivers. The distinction between mutual releases and these types of situations is discussed below.

(a) Mutual Release Distinguished from Variation

9.78 The distinguishing factor in a mutual release, is that parties intend to bring an earlier contract to an end. It may then be substituted with a second contract with different rights and obligations if so desired by the parties. So, as observed by Viscount Haldane in the House of Lords case of *Morris v Baron and Company* (1918) (at p 19), the changes imposed by the parties must have:

> '... made manifest the intention in any event of a complete extinction of the first and formal contract, and not merely the desire of an alteration, however sweeping, in terms which leave it still subsisting.'

In some situations, parties may not want the original contract to be brought to an end. Instead, what they seek to achieve is to add to the obligations imposed by the original contract, or change some of those obligations, leaving others intact. This is often termed as a 'variation'. So, in some sales contracts, there may be provision for unilateral variation of the price by one party on the occurrence of certain contractually pre-determined events. Alternatively, it is entirely possible for a 'new' agreement to merely add on to the rights and obligations set out in the original agreement, in which case there is no release from those rights. Such an 'add on' variation, then, is really in the nature of a second contract, adding new obligations to or modifying the obligations to be performed under the original contract. As such, the variation contract must be supported by consideration (or a substitute thereof, for example, by execution under seal).

9.79 In the absence of an appropriate substitute, consideration for this type of variation may be found by way of:

- mutually abandoning some, though not all, existing rights in the original contract;
- mutually granting each party new benefits, in addition to the existing rights in the original contract; and/or
- mutually incurring additional obligations thereby incurring an increased detriment.

9.80 What if *only one party* to the contract promises to undertake new and varied obligations and thereby adds to its own detriment or adds to the benefit enjoyed by the other party? Such a promise may be ineffective as being unsupported by consideration. The promisee in such a situation is merely going to perform all that he was already expected to under the original agreement. As such, the promisor gets nothing more than what he was already due from the original agreement, and the promisee suffers no further detriment than what he already expects under the original agreement. The principle of *Stilk v Myrick* (1809) (see paragraph 3.34) would therefore appear to preclude the effectiveness of most 'variations' of this type.

Exceptionally, however, where the counter-promise under the original contract by the promisee entails any kind of performance other than the payment of money, the court may be prepared to find consideration in the form of a 'factual' or 'practical' benefit enjoyed by the promisor resulting from the promisee continuing to perform his obligations under the original contract. Such factual benefit was famously found by the English Court of Appeal in the case of *Williams v Roffey Bros & Nicholls (Contractors) Ltd* (1991) (which we have already encountered in Chapter 3 at paragraphs 3.37–3.39).

9.81 The case where the counter-promise under the original contract by the promisee requires only the payment of money, however, is treated differently. As will be recalled from Chapter 3 at paragraph 3.46, the case of *Re Selectmove Ltd* (1995) rejected the extension of the factual benefit recognised in *Williams v Roffey Bros & Nicholls (Contractors) Ltd* (1991) to include an obligation to make payment. As explained by the English Court of Appeal in *Re Selectmove Ltd* (1995), it is well-settled since the case of *Foakes v Beer* (1884), which applied the rule in *Pinnel's Case* (1602), that payment of a lesser sum than originally contracted for the same performance is not good consideration. By analogy, payment of the same sum under the original contract, but where the promisor promises to perform additional obligations over and above those originally due, is similarly not good consideration.

9.82 A subsequent agreement to impose additional duties may then be contrasted with a subsequent agreement to excuse performance of some of the duties under the original contract. This latter process is sometimes referred to as a 'waiver' which will be discussed below.

(b) Mutual Release Distinguished from Waiver

9.83 The term 'waiver', unfortunately, is used in many different contexts. It is most commonly used to refer to a situation where one party to a contract decides of its own volition to excuse the other party from precise performance of its obligations under that contract. Often, this may involve issues such as the time or place of performance, the precise quantity or quality of goods delivered under the contract, and so forth.

Unlike the case of mutual release or variation, however, where the doctrine of waiver is invoked, it does not appear to matter that the promise to forego strict performance of the contractual obligations is unsupported by consideration. Such a promise does confer a benefit on the promisee who is released from having to fulfil his original contractual obligations strictly. However, the promisee confers no additional benefits upon the promisor in return, nor does he suffer from any additional detriment. Nonetheless, many judicial decisions have upheld the principle that a promisor who grants a waiver cannot go back on his word and immediately reinstate precise performance of the original contract. Unlike mutual release or variation, most judicial decisions also appear to tolerate revocation of a waiver thereby requiring the promisee to revert back to compliance with the original contract, so long as reasonable notice is given. This may be seen in the case of *Charles Rickards Ltd v Oppenhaim* (1950). The facts of the case were as follows:

Oppenhaim ('O') ordered a Rolls Royce car chassis from Charles Rickards Ltd ('CR'). This was delivered to O. O then contracted with CR for CR to build the body of the car on this chassis. The contract provided for completion of the work by 20 March 1948. There was a delay and the completion date went by. O allowed CR to continue work on the body, but on 29 June 1948, O wrote to CR stating that he would not take delivery of the car if it was not completed by 25 July 1948. Despite this extension, CR still failed to complete by 25 July, and O decided to treat the contract as repudiated.

In relation to the initial deadline, the English Court of Appeal agreed that O's conduct in permitting CR to continue with the work on the vehicle past the initial deadline amounted to an implied waiver. This waiver, however, could be brought to an end with reasonable notice and such notice was given in the form of O's 29 June 1948 letter. Consequently, the contract was validly discharged when the new time limit expired without completion of performance by CR.

9.84 As a matter of legal history, the doctrine of waiver was developed as a common law doctrine. However, it should be apparent that the doctrine of waiver is very similar to the doctrine of *promissory estoppel* (which we have already encountered in Chapter 3 at paragraphs 3.47–3.66). Indeed, Denning LJ noted in the case of *Charles Rickards Ltd v Oppenhaim* (1950) (at p 623) that:

> '...[w]hether it be called waiver or forbearance on his part, or an agreed variation or substituted performance, does not matter. It is a kind of estoppel. ... It is a particular application of the principle [of promissory estoppel] which I endeavoured to state in *Central London Property Trust Ltd v High Trees House Ltd* ...'

At first glance, however, the two doctrines might not be completely identical in that promissory estoppel (at least within Singapore) appears to require *detrimental* reliance on the promise by the promisee, following the opinion of the Privy Council delivered by Lord Templeman in an appeal from the Singapore Court of Appeal (see *Meng Leong Development Pte Ltd v Jip Hong Trading Co Pte Ltd* (1984)). In delivering the opinion of the Privy Council, Lord Templeman quoted G Spencer Bower and A Turner, *The Law Relating to Estoppel by Representation* (3rd ed, 1977), paragraph 310 with approval:

> 'Where A, dealing with B, is confronted with two alternative

and mutually exclusive courses of action in relation to such dealing, between which he may make his election, and A so conducts himself as reasonably to induce B to believe that he is intending definitely to adopt the one course, and definitely to reject or relinquish the other, *and B in such belief alters his position to his detriment*, A is precluded, as against B, from afterwards resorting to the course which he has thus deliberately declared his intention of rejecting. It is of the essence of election that the party electing shall be "confronted" with two mutually exclusive courses of action between which he must, in fairness to the other party, make his choice' (emphasis added) (per Lord Templeman at p 34).

This position was reiterated in the Singapore High Court case of *Fu Loong Lithographer Pte Ltd v Mun Hean Realty Pte Ltd* (1989).

On the other hand, detriment (at least in England), does not appear to be strictly necessary in a situation where waiver is being relied upon. Instead, it appears that so long as it would be *unreasonable* or *inequitable* for the promisor to be allowed to go back on his promise not to insist on his strict legal rights, he will not be allowed to do so as he will be said to have *waived* his rights. Hence, there have been cases where a waiver has been found to be effective even though reliance by the promisee did not result in any detriment. An example of this can be seen in the English Court of Appeal case of *W J Alan & Co Ltd v El Nasr Export and Import Co* (1972) where Lord Denning MR pronounced (at p 213) that:

'[t]he principle of waiver is simply this: If one party, by his conduct, leads another to believe that the strict rights arising under the contract will not be insisted upon, intending that the other should act on that belief, and he does act on it, then the first party will not afterwards be allowed to insist on the strict legal rights when it would be inequitable for him to do so ... There may be no consideration moving from him who benefits by the waiver. *There may be no detriment to him by acting on it.* ... Nevertheless, the one who waives his strict rights cannot afterwards insist on them ....'

Admittedly, this may be because Lord Denning was of the opinion that *waiver* and *promissory estoppel* were really one and the same (maintaining consistency with the views he had taken some two decades earlier in *Charles Rickards*), and that in his view (and perhaps for the *English* courts in general, nowadays), promissory estoppel does not require detrimental reliance but merely *inequity* (although as mentioned in Chapter 3, such inequity clearly overlaps with detriment).

There does seem to be some extremely slight authority, however, that although Lord Denning's view that detriment is unnecessary in promissory estoppel is *not* accepted in Singapore, his view that waiver is a form of promissory estoppel *is*. In passing, the Singapore Court of Appeal in *Lim Tjoen Kong v A-B Chew Investments Pte Ltd* (1991) seems to have accepted without comment that waiver is a 'form of promissory estoppel' in *obiter dicta* (at pp 194–195). Admittedly, this authority is extremely weak, and this area of the law remains obscure. It remains to be seen whether the proposition that waiver and promissory estoppel are really one and the same (espoused in English cases such as *W J Alan*) is good authority in Singapore. If so, then *waiver* can only be established if the promisee demonstrates that he has both *detrimentally relied* upon it, *and* that it would be *inequitable* to allow the promisor to withdraw the waiver. This conclusion, however, can only be highly tentative, given the lack of any conclusive local authority.

9.85 Finally, the term 'waiver' is sometimes also used in the context of an *election* between two or more alternative and inconsistent rights. An example of such a 'waiver', or more properly, an election, can be seen in the affirmation of a contract following a repudiatory breach by a party to the contract. The innocent party in affirming the contract is sometimes said to 'waive the breach'. This type of 'waiver' or election to treat the contract as being on foot is discussed above in the section starting from paragraph 9.57.

Such elections are permanent and cannot be revoked, even with reasonable notice. There is also no requirement for reliance or detriment by the other party who receives notice of such an election. Conversely, such an election can only occur if the party said to have made the election, actually knew he had such a right. This is not necessary in relation to waiver as discussed in paragraphs 9.83–9.84 above.

(3) *Accord and Satisfaction*

9.86 As defined by Scrutton LJ in the English Court of Appeal case of *British Russian Gazette and Trade Outlook Ltd v Associated Newspapers Ltd* (1933) (at pp 643–644):

> '... Accord and satisfaction is the purchase of a release from an obligation whether arising under contract or tort by means of any valuable consideration, not being the actual performance of the obligation itself. The accord is the agreement by which the obligation is discharged. The satisfaction is the [fresh] consideration which makes the agreement operative.'

9.87 Accord and satisfaction can discharge any contract, whether executory or executed. The real question is *when* such discharge occurs. It is obvious that once the *satisfaction* (the consideration for the accord) has been performed and executed, discharge must have occurred. However, what if the satisfaction is still executory? Is the promise to provide satisfaction at some point in the future effective to discharge the contract *as at the time the promise is made*? The answer appears to lie in interpretation of the agreement between the parties. As stated by the Lord Atkinson in the House of Lords case of *Morris v Baron & Co* (1918) (at p 35):

> 'There is no doubt that the general principle is that an accord without satisfaction has no legal effect, and that the original cause of action is not discharged as long as the satisfaction agreed upon remains executory. That was decided so long ago as 1611 in *Peytoe's Case*. If, however, it can be shown that what a creditor

> accepts in satisfaction is merely his debtor's promise and not the performance of that promise, the original cause of action is discharged from the date when the promise is made ...'

9.88 Where the satisfaction in the purported discharge of the original contract involves the payment of a smaller sum than that originally due and payable, the rule in *Pinnel's Case* discussed previously in Chapter 3 (see above at paragraph 3.44) will render the accord and satisfaction a nullity, as the payment of such a smaller sum cannot be viewed as sufficient consideration. The accord cannot effectively discharge the earlier contract in such a situation.

CHAPTER 10

Discharge by Frustration

PARAGRAPHS

Introduction

10.1 Scenario
10.2 Legal Development
10.3 Juristic Basis

Concept of Frustration

10.4 Elements of Frustration
10.5 (1) Radically Different Performance
10.6 (2) Neither Party at Fault
10.7 (3) Time of Frustration
10.8 (4) Foresight and Foreseeability

Classification

10.9 General
Impossibility
10.10 (1) Destruction of Subject Matter of Contract
10.11 (2) Death or Incapacity
10.12 (3) Unavailability
10.13 (4) Failure of Source of Supply
10.14 (5) Method of Performance Impossible
10.15 Illegality
Radical Change
10.16 (1) Frustration of Purpose
10.17 (2) Delay, Unavailability
10.18 (3) Impracticability, Increased Costs
10.19 Frustration of a Lease/Sale of Land

Self-Induced Frustration

10.20 General
10.21 Negligence
10.22 Choosing Between Several Contracts

10.23 **Partial Frustration**

Express Provision

10.24–10.25 General
10.26 Construction

PARAGRAPHS

Foresight and Foreseeability

10.27 Foreseen Events
10.28 Foreseeable Events

Effects of Frustration

10.29 Introduction
Frustrated Contracts Act
10.30 (1) General
10.31–10.33 (2) Payments, Expenses, Benefits
10.34 (3) Severability
10.35 (4) Ambit of Act

10.36–10.38 **Conclusion**

Introduction

Scenario

10.1 As with life in general, businesses and business transactions are subject to uncertainties and unexpected events. If, after a contract has been entered into, an event takes place which severely affects the performance of the contract, issues arise as to the rights and liabilities of the parties in the light of the new development. Does the contract continue or does it come to an end? In either case, what are the respective parties' rights and remedies? These and other questions are dealt with by the law of frustration.

It may be observed that frustration is in some measure quite similar to common mistake (see paragraph 11.7, below) in that both doctrines are concerned with unexpected states or events which make the performance of the contract difficult or impossible. However, whilst mistake relates to matters occurring before or at the time of the contract, frustration deals with matters which arise subsequently; and the two doctrines have developed separately and differently.

Legal Development

10.2 At one time, the law held on to a strict theory of contractual performance —that contractual duties are absolute and have to be carried out, supervening events notwithstanding (see, eg *Paradine v Jane* (1647)). Over time, it was felt that such a position was too harsh and was not a satisfactory way of allocating losses between the parties. Eventually, in 1863, in *Taylor v Caldwell*, which involved the accidental destruction of a music hall which was the subject of a hire contract, the doctrine of frustration was introduced into the common law. Through a period of development, the doctrine was applied to other scenarios of unexpected events, such as cases of supervening illegality and those involving the frustration of the commercial purpose.

The extension of the doctrine, however, was one which proceeded cautiously. There are several reasons for narrowing its application. First, the doctrine should not be used by a contracting party to escape what has turned out to be a bad bargain. Secondly, parties are free to make contractual provision with respect to eventualities.

In any case, until the position was rectified by legislation, the common law effect of frustration—that losses lie where they fall (see paragraph 10.29, below)—in many instances, could hardly be considered a fair allocation of losses as between the two parties.

Juristic Basis

10.3 Whilst the doctrine of frustration is now well-established, its legal basis is still uncertain. Three theories, amongst others, have been put forward. The first is the implied term theory, that the parties had contracted 'on the footing that a particular thing or state of things would continue to exist' (Lord Loreburn in *Tamplin Steamship v Anglo-Mexican Petroleum*

Products (1916)). The second is that where the 'foundation' of the contract disappears, the contract itself also vanishes (Lord Haldane in the *Tamplin* case). The third justification is that a court may exercise its discretion and hold that a contract is frustrated when justice demands it. Some commentators have observed that there does not appear to be any practical implication as to which is the true basis of the doctrine.

Concept of Frustration

Elements of Frustration

10.4 The classical definition of frustration was provided by Lord Radcliffe in the leading House of Lords decision of *Davis Contractors v Fareham UDC* (1956):

> '... without default of either party, a contractual obligation has become *incapable of being performed* because the circumstances in which performance is called for would render it a thing *radically different* from that which was undertaken by the contract' (emphasis added).

This definition covers the physical impossibility scenarios, such as the destruction of the subject matter, the cancellation of an event and the death or illness of a performer; but it goes further. It encompasses supervening illegality and, more importantly, cases where the commercial objective or purpose is defeated or has disappeared. The test, simply stated, is: Does the event make the performance of the contract now radically different from what was originally contemplated by the parties?

(1) *Radically Different Performance*

10.5 As mentioned above, the question is whether performance of the contract in the changed circumstances would be something radically different from that which was originally undertaken. Essentially, the court looks first at the contractual promise and the circumstances that existed at the time of the contract. It then looks at the supervening event and what performance would be like if the promise were to be enforced in the new circumstances. Finally, it would compare the performance in the two scenarios and ask whether the latter is radically or significantly different from the former.

In *Davis Contractors v Fareham UDC*, the contractors agreed to build for the Fareham local authority 78 houses within eight months for £92,425. Without the fault of either party, inadequate labour supply delayed the completion by 14 months and increased the contractors' expenses by some £17,000. The contractors argued that the contract had been frustrated and that they could therefore claim, on a *quantum meruit* basis (payment of a reasonable sum for work done), a sum higher than the contract price. The court held that the fact that increased labour costs made the contract more onerous did not make the contractual performance radically different from the performance contemplated at the time of the contract.

(2) *Neither Party at Fault*

10.6 Frustration is premised upon neither party being at fault. Indeed, if a contract is discharged by frustration, this takes place by operation of law, as opposed to any action on the part of a contracting party. In general, if one party was at fault, it is likely that he had breached an express or implied term of the contract. Even in the absence of such a term, the law would not excuse a contracting party whose conduct caused or led to the event. This policy finds expression in the principle that a contracting party cannot rely on 'self-induced' frustration (see paragraph 10.20, below).

(3) *Time of Frustration*

10.7 When a frustrating event occurs, the contract is discharged automatically. The frustrating event may discharge a contract prospectively, in that the time of performance has yet to arrive. The effect of a supervening event is determined at the time the event occurs, or a reasonable time thereafter; one need not, indeed should not, wait till the day of the scheduled performance in order to see how the event would affect the performance of the contract. The rationale for taking a reasonable view of the probable effect of a supervening event upon or shortly after its occurrence is that the parties' rights should not be left indefinitely in suspense. Whether the situation be the outbreak of war affecting a charter of ships or the onset of illness affecting an employee, the contract is frustrated as soon as 'a sensible prognosis of the commercial probabilities' can be made (*The Evia (No 2)* (1983)).

(4) *Foresight and Foreseeability*

10.8 The notion of frustration is somehow naturally associated with the idea of unexpected events. It would seem that a frustrating event is one which was not expected, foreseen or even foreseeable. But the matter is far from simple and is a matter of some debate. The complexities are dealt with in paragraphs 10.27–10.28 below.

Classification

General

10.9 The issue of frustration has arisen in many different settings and different types of contracts. Perhaps the most useful means of classification, from the point of analysis and understanding, is to categorise them into three major categories: impossibility, illegality and radical change. These categories may be divided, in turn, into sub-categories, and may raise particular problems and issues of their own.

Impossibility

(1) *Destruction of Subject Matter of Contract*

10.10 The destruction of the subject matter of the contract is a clear and obvious application of the doctrine of frustration. Case law examples include the destruction of premises, the failure of a crop and the sinking of cargo. However, total destruction may not be necessary; it suffices if the thing is so seriously damaged that, for commercial purposes, it has become something else; or that destruction of a part of the subject matter defeats the main purpose of the contract. The destruction of something which is not the subject matter of the contract but is nevertheless necessary for its performance, such as the building in which the machinery is to be installed, will also frustrate the contract.

In certain contracts, different rules of discharge apply. A prime example is a contract for the sale of goods, where rules as to the passing of risk in the goods are provided for by legislation. For instance, where goods sold are destroyed after the risk has passed to the buyer, the buyer is not discharged from his duty to pay the seller. There is no frustration in such a case. Another example concerns building contracts, where generally the risk of damage or destruction lies with the builder until the work is completed.

(2) *Death or Incapacity*

10.11 Contracts of a personal nature—those where the promisor has to perform the obligation(s) personally—are frustrated by the promisor's death or incapacity. Such contracts include contracts of apprenticeship, employment and agency. The critical factor is the personal nature or character of the contract. If the personal element is absent, the contract may still have to be performed, albeit by another on behalf of the promisor.

In the case of incapacity, such as illness, imprisonment or conscription, whether the contract has been frustrated depends on the likely duration of the incapacity or unavailability, and whether the disruption would make a radical change to the contractual performance. The sudden illness of a performer for a one-night-only concert is certainly quite different from the illness of an employee for a term of years. In the latter situation, the relevant factors for determining whether the contract is frustrated include the nature and duration of the employment, the length of past employment, and the prospects of recovery.

(3) *Unavailability*

10.12 The above situation of the illness of an employee may also fall within the sub-category of unavailability of the subject matter or of the person or thing essential to the performance of the contract. The types of situations and contracts in which this may occur are varied. A charterparty (contract for chartering a ship) may be frustrated by the seizure or detention of the ship; a contract for the sale of goods may be frustrated by the government requisitioning the goods; the sale and purchase of a piece of property may be frustrated by compulsory acquisition by the authorities; and so on.

Whether temporary unavailability results in frustration would again depend on various factors such as the length of the anticipated unavailability, the period of the contract and the commercial purpose of the contract.

(4) *Failure of Source of Supply*

10.13 Where it is expressly provided that goods are to be supplied by a particular source, the contract may be frustrated by the failure of that source. The position is similar where, though there is no express provision, both parties contemplated supply by the particular source; but where only one party intends to use that source, failure of that source does not amount to frustration.

(5) *Method of Performance Impossible*

10.14 A contract may provide for, or the parties may have contemplated, a particular method of performance. In such a case, if that method becomes impossible, the contract is frustrated. But the method stipulated must have been intended to be exclusive; otherwise, alternative methods may have to be resorted to, so long as they are not fundamentally different from the prescribed method. The classic illustration is the House of Lords decision of *Tsakiroglou & Co Ltd v Noblee Thorl GmbH* (1960), involving the shipment of goods from Port Sudan to Hamburg. Though there was no express stipulation to that effect, the parties had expected shipment to be via the Suez Canal. With the sudden closure of the Suez Canal, the alternative route was via the Cape of Good Hope, a journey twice the distance and incurring much greater expense. The House of Lords held that shipment via the alternative route was not a substantially different performance, and that the contract had therefore not been frustrated.

Illegality

10.15 Where at the time of contract the performance is one which is already prohibited by law, the contract is void *ab initio* (from the start) for illegality. On the topic of 'Illegality', see generally below, Chapter 14. The contract is not enforceable because, as a matter of public policy, the law will not give assistance to parties to an illegal transaction. Similar policy considerations apply where there is supervening illegality. Common instances of frustration brought about by supervening illegality include wartime prohibition against trading with the enemy, and subsequent changes in the law, such as a prohibition against exporting a particular product, or a restriction on the movement of capital.

Where the contract is to be performed abroad and its performance has become illegal by the law of the place of performance, the contract is generally frustrated (for further complexities in this area, see the discussion in *Chitty on Contracts*, Vol 1 (28th ed, 1999) at paragraph 24-026).

Whereas in general the doctrine of frustration can be excluded by express agreement, frustration through supervening illegality cannot be so excluded. The reason for this is the strong public interest of not upholding such contracts and transactions. In similar vein, a contract may be frustrated by supervening illegality which was foreseeable or even foreseen but for which no express provision has been made.

Radical Change

(1) *Frustration of Purpose*

10.16 Sometimes, after a turn of events, the literal performance of a contractual obligation remains possible but performance under the changed circumstances would not fulfil the original commercial purpose of the parties. Instinctively, the cancellation of event cases, as in the leading English decision of *Krell v Henry* (1903), which involved the hire of premises to view the coronation procession of King Edward VII (who, unfortunately, fell ill) come to mind. The key question is whether the enjoyment of the event, such as a procession, a fireworks display or the eclipse of the sun, was the common purpose of *both* parties. If it was, then the cancellation of the event frustrates the contract even though the continuation of the contract—such as the hire of premises—is physically possible. The failure of the purpose of one party alone does not bring about frustration.

(2) *Delay, Unavailability*

10.17 The subject of temporary unavailability was discussed in paragraph 10.12 above. Contracts may be delayed by various causes, such as the stranding of a ship, wartime requisitions, bad weather, labour shortages and so forth. In order for a delay to render performance a thing 'radically different', the delay must be so abnormal in its effect or expected duration as to fall outside what was the reasonable contemplation of the parties at the time of contract. Consonant with the approach as to the time of frustration (see paragraph 10.7), at the onset of the supervening event, or soon thereafter, based on the evidence of what has occurred and is likely thereafter to occur, a judgment has to be made as to whether the delay has frustrated the contract (per Lord Roskill in the House of Lords decision of *The Nema* (1982)).

(3) *Impracticability, Increased Costs*

10.18 In the US, many states recognise the doctrine of commercial impracticability as a ground for discharge by supervening events, and this concept of impracticability includes extreme and unreasonable difficulty, expense or loss. The UK (and Singapore) position, however, is that impracticability in itself is insufficient to frustrate a contract.

Tsakiroglou v Noblee Thorl mentioned above (in paragraph 10.14) and the *Davis Contractors* decision are clear testimony of the strict approach taken by English courts. Men of business are taken to be cognizant of the risks and vicissitudes in the business environment, such as rises and falls in prices, interruptions in supply, currency fluctuations, inflation and so on. Impracticability or increased costs, in general, does not frustrate a contract. But where the supervening impracticability is so abnormal as to be outside the ordinary range of commercial risk (such as an astronomical rise in price), performance in the changed circumstances may be considered radically different performance (see per Lord Reid and Lord Hodson in *Tsakiroglou v Noblee Thorl).*

Frustration of a Lease/Sale of Land

10.19 For a time, there was uncertainty as to whether the doctrine of frustration could apply to leases and other contracts pertaining to land. It was thought that the doctrine did not apply for the reason that a lease creates not merely a contract but also an estate. It is now quite settled that, under Singapore law, the doctrine applies to a lease of land (see *Singapore Woodcraft Manufacturing v Mok Ah Sai* (1979)).

Similarly, the Singapore Court of Appeal, in *Lim Kim Som v Sheriffa Taibah bte Abdul Rahman* (1994), has held that the doctrine of frustration can apply to a contract for the sale of land. In the case itself, it was held that the sale and purchase agreement was frustrated by the supervening compulsory acquisition of the property by the government.

For further discussion on the topic, see A Phang, *Cheshire, Fifoot and Furmston's Law of Contract* (2nd ed, 1998) at pp 968–972 and the references there cited.

Self-Induced Frustration

General

10.20 A critical element of frustration is that neither party is at fault. More specifically, frustration should not be due to the act or election of the party seeking to rely on it. A party to a contract cannot rely on self-induced frustration, that is, on frustration due to his own conduct or the conduct of those for whom he is responsible. The act may be a breach of contract, but it need not be so.

Although a contracting party cannot rely on frustration induced by his own conduct, the other contracting party is entitled to do so. So, for example, where an employee committed an offence (not related to his employment and therefore not amounting to a breach of contract) and was imprisoned, the employer was entitled to rely on the circumstances as frustrating the contract of employment (*Harrington v Kent* (1980)).

The onus of proving that the frustration was self-induced lies with the party who asserts that it is so.

Negligence

10.21 A difficult point is whether a contracting party can rely on an event brought about by his own negligence as a ground of frustration. In principle, it seems correct that a party who has been negligent should not escape liability since he is at fault. The problem is that negligence encompasses a wide spectrum of conduct ranging from mere carelessness to gross negligence. In *Joseph Constantine v Imperial Smelting* (1942), Lord Simon seemed to incline to the view that a prima donna who loses her voice through carelessly catching a cold could plead frustration so long as her incapacity 'was not deliberately induced in order to get out of her engagement'.

At first blush, Lord Simon's statement of law sounds simple and correct. Upon closer analysis, there are difficulties. The central problem is the relationship between negligence and deliberateness. The conventional delineation is that a person's action is either intentional (deliberate) or negligent. Lord Simon's dictum, however, seems to suggest that a person can be deliberately careless. In this writer's view, there is sense in what his lordship had said.

Take the example of a singer who is considering a night walk on the eve of her performance. She knows the air is rather cold and there is a slight chance of her catching a chill. However, she thinks and hopes that she will not catch a cold. In this situation, she may be careless but she is does not deliberately want to catch a cold; in fact, she does not want to catch a cold. Suppose we change the scenario a little. She knows that there's a small risk but hopes to catch the cold as, for some reason, she does not want to perform the next day. In this scenario, her action is careless (but not grossly negligent since the chance of catching the cold is slight) but, in a sense, deliberate. If she does catch a cold and is therefore unable to perform, there is frustration in the first scenario but not in the second.

Choosing Between Several Contracts

10.22 A situation can arise whereby as a result of a supervening event, a contracting party is in a position where he is not able to perform all of several contracts but can perform some of them. For example, the supervening event may have substantially reduced his supply of goods or materials. Judicial authority (see *Maritime National Fish v Ocean Trawlers* (1935) and *The Super Servant Two* (1990)) suggests that if the contracting party chooses to perform some of the contracts, he cannot rely on frustration to discharge him from the other contracts; with regard to these other contracts, the frustration would be considered self-induced. The fairness of such a position is questionable as it seems harsh to fault the contracting party for making the best of an unexpected situation. On the other hand, it may be argued that he took the commercial risk of ending up in such an invidious situation.

An alternative is to hold that all the contracts affected by the supervening event are partially frustrated and that the contracting party is permitted to pro-rate the delivery to all the parties. But this solution is problematic from both the practical and theoretical perspectives (see paragraph 10.23, below). A satisfactory solution has yet to be found.

Partial Frustration

10.23 In the preceding paragraph, we have seen that if supervening events put a contracting party into a position where, being unable to perform all of several contracts, he has to choose which to perform, he is not discharged as regards the contracts which he chose not to perform. The reasoning is that the frustration would have been self-induced. Suppose then that the contracting party entered into one contract only and, because of a supervening event, the contract can only be partially performed, as in *Sainsbury v Street* (1972) where, as a result of crop failure, the harvest yielded only 140 tons of barley whereas the contract quantity was 275 tons. It was there held that the seller remained bound to deliver the 140 tons though he was excused with regard to the remaining 135 tons. It would seem, then, that the case is authority for a doctrine of partial frustration. Unfortunately, the term frustration was not used in the judgment at all and the decision proceeded on the basis of construction of the terms of the contract.

The issue is a difficult one. The traditional thinking on frustration takes an all-or-nothing approach; the contract (assuming it is not a divisible contract: see paragraphs 9.21–9.24) as a whole ends if there is frustration or continues if there is no frustration. If partial frustration is accepted as a doctrine, one difficulty is whether and where a line should be drawn as to the proportion of the contract performable before it can be said that the contract is partially frustrated and thus keeping intact the rest of the contract. This writer suggests that, consistent with the law's approach to discharge by performance (see paragraph 9.2 onwards), a reasonable threshold would be whether the contract is still 'substantially performable' in the changed circumstances. Meanwhile, the current legal position remains unclear.

Express Provision

General

10.24 Frustration, it should be recalled, deals with allocation of risks. If the parties have made their own allocation of risks with regard to possible supervening events, generally the law would uphold their contractual allocation. One exception, which has been mentioned earlier, is supervening illegality.

In exceptional circumstances, a court may imply a provision excluding frustration, for example, where the nature of the contract makes it clear that it was intended that one party assumes the risk of the supervening event.

10.25 Express contractual provisions regarding supervening events are often called *force majeure* (act of God) clauses. A *force majeure* clause may deal with supervening events in a variety of ways. For example, it could put the risks of the supervening events on one party alone, in effect making his performance obligation an absolute one. Or, it could provide that upon the occurrence of any of the supervening events, the contract is at an end and the clause could provide in further detail for the legal consequences. Alternatively, it could provide that upon the occurrence of a supervening event, the parties will meet and negotiate as to the continuation of the contract (see, for example, the Singapore case *China Resources v Magenta Resources* (1997) where the clause provided that '[s]hould the effect of the *force majeure* continue for more than 120 consecutive days, the buyer and the seller shall discuss through friendly negotiation... their obligation to continue to perform...').

Construction

10.26 While an express provision can exclude frustration, the courts have tended to construe such a provision narrowly. A *force majeure* clause, it is said, must be 'full and complete' (*Bank Line v Arthur Capel* (1919)) and intended to cover the supervening event in question. The more devastating or catastrophic the event, the more the courts would require particularly clear words to be used.

The supervening events which a *force majeure* clause purports to cover are not restricted to what the law would consider frustrating events. Events which would not have frustrated a contract may also be dealt with, and where pursuant to such a clause a contract is discharged following such an event, the contract is discharged not by frustration but rather by a contractual term either automatically or upon one party exercising his right to cancel, as the clause so provides.

Foresight and Foreseeability

Foreseen Events

10.27 As pointed out in paragraph 10.8 above, despite the fact that frustration is implicitly about unexpected events, the authoritative judicial definitions of frustration omit reference to this aspect. There is much doubt and uncertainty about whether frustration applies to foreseen or foreseeable events.

As for foreseen events, the view generally adopted by commentators is that the occurrence of such events does not frustrate a contract. The reasoning is that since the parties had already envisaged the possibility of such an event and yet chose not to make any express provision regarding it, they must have contracted with reference to the risk of such occurrence. Insofar as Singapore law is concerned, given the position taken on foreseeable events (see paragraph 10.28, below), it may be assumed that an event foreseen by both contracting parties does not frustrate a contract.

Foreseeable Events

10.28 Events not foreseen but nevertheless were foreseeable give rise to greater difficulty. A foreseen event is high on the scale of likelihood of occurrence and, logically, should not be a frustrating event. Conversely, a very remote contingency should qualify as a frustrating event. A foreseeable event, however, covers a wider spectrum of likelihood. The preponderance of academic opinion is that a foreseeable event would not lead to frustration if the degree of foreseeability is high and is one which any person of ordinary intelligence would regard as likely to occur (see GH Treitel, *The Law of Contract* (10th ed, 1999) pp 840–843 for a good discussion of the subject).

The current English position with regard to foreseen and foreseeable events is still unclear, and one is still faced with judicial *dicta* (see, for example, Lord Denning MR in *The Eugenia* (1964)) to the effect that the essential thing is that the event was not provided for in the contract.

Insofar as Singapore is concerned, it is quite established that an event which is highly foreseeable cannot frustrate a contract. In *Win Supreme Investment v Joharah bte Abdul Wahab* (1997), Chao J held that frustration is inapplicable if the event was 'clearly… foreseeable'. In similar vein, in *Glahe International Expo v ACS Computer* (1999), Khoo J decided that an event which is 'reasonably foreseeable' (at p 177) does not bring about frustration. In fact, Thean JA, in the Court of Appeal in *Glahe Internationl Expo* (at p 629), went so far as to say that '… the doctrine of frustration concerns the treatment of contractual obligations upon the onset of an *unforeseeable* event' (emphasis added), which may suggest that even a very low level of foreseeability would displace the notion of frustration. If a very low level of foreseeability suffices to negate frustration, then the application of the doctrine will be very limited. Time will tell whether Singapore courts indeed take such a strict approach towards frustration.

Effects of Frustration

Introduction

10.29 The effect of frustration on a contract is that it brings the contract to an end from the time of the frustrating event. Frustration operates automatically, without the need for any election by either party.

At common law, the effect of frustration on the parties' remedies is summarised by the phrase 'the losses lie where they fall'. While the parties are released from future obligations, accrued obligations remain. Sums paid prior to the event are not recoverable while sums payable at the time of frustration remain payable.

Originally, it was also said that in the case of a frustrated contract, there could be no recovery of moneys for a failure of consideration. Later, following a House of Lords decision (*Fibrosa Spolka Akcyjna v Fairbain Lawson Combe Barbour* (1943)), such a claim was permitted. There was, however, no such recourse where the failure of consideration was only partial. These and other inadequacies were eventually dealt with by legislation. The Singapore Frustrated Contracts Act (Cap 115, 1985 Rev Ed) is identical in substance to the UK Law Reform (Frustrated Contracts) Act 1943.

Frustrated Contracts Act

(1) *General*

10.30 The Frustrated Contracts Act alters and adds to the common law position. The common law effect that all future obligations cease is untouched by the Act, but the Act does alter the remedies in three respects: payments, expenses and benefits.

(2) *Payments, Expenses, Benefits*

10.31 Section 2(2) of the Act provides that all sums paid before the time of discharge are recoverable while all sums payable at that time cease to be so payable. This is a reversal of the common law position.

10.32 The sub-section goes on to provide that if the party to whom the sums are paid or payable had incurred expenses prior to the time of discharge in or for the performance of the contract, the court may, if it considers it just to do so, allow him to retain or recover (as the case may be) part of the sum so paid or payable. Of course, he cannot recover more than his actual expenses.

10.33 The third key aspect of the Act is that it recognises and compensates for benefits enjoyed, supervening event notwithstanding. Section 2(3) provides that if a contracting party has, by reason of any act done by the other party in performance of the contract, obtained a valuable benefit before the time of discharge, the court may, if it considers it just to do so, allow that other party to recover a sum (not exceeding the value of the benefit) which is appropriate in the circumstances.

In arriving at such just sum, the court is to have regard to the expenses that the benefited party had incurred in the performance of the contract as well as the payments retained or recoverable by the first party under section 2(2) (see paragraph 10.32, above). The court also has to consider the effect, if any, that the frustrating event had on the benefit. For example, the event may have damaged the work performed so far and thereby reduced the benefit obtained by the partial performance, whereas if the event brought about the complete destruction of the subject matter, the benefit may be nil (for the intricacies on the subject, see GH Treitel, *The Law of Contract* (10th ed, 1999) at pp 852–853).

(3) *Severability*

10.34 Section 3(3) provides for severable parts of a contract to be treated separately, so that parts of a contract may be frustrated while other parts continue unaffected.

(4) *Ambit of Act*

10.35 The Act has general application but does not apply to contracts for the carriage of goods by sea, insurance contracts and contracts for the sale of specific goods where the cause of frustration is the perishing of the goods (see section 3(5)).

Conclusion

10.36 The concept of frustration is an important one and has serious implications on the performance of contracts. The key elements are reasonably clear: absence of fault on the part of both parties, a supervening event and radical change in performance. Further, under Singapore law, foreseen and reasonably foreseeable events would not frustrate a contract.

10.37 Where frustration applies, the contract comes to an end. Under the Frustrated Contracts Act, existing payment obligations cease and sums paid are recoverable, and the court has wide discretion to make orders, taking into account expenses incurred and benefits received. The Act makes vast improvements over the previous common law position and facilitates a more equitable settlement of rights and remedies in the event of frustration.

10.38 As with many areas of contract law, the application of the doctrine of frustration is subject to the parties' freedom of contract. Contracting parties may come to an agreement as to how they wish to deal with supervening events. By and large, such wishes receive the endorsement of the courts.

CHAPTER 11 Mistake

PARAGRAPHS

Introduction and Legal Consequences of a Mistake

11.1 Introduction
11.2 Is There a Doctrine of Mistake to Begin With?
11.3 Categories of Mistake
Legal Consequences of Mistake
11.4 (1) Where Contract is Void under Common Law
11.5 (2) Where Contract is Voidable in Equity
11.6 (3) Importance of Distinction Between Voidness and Voidability

Common Mistake

11.7–11.9 Introduction
Common Mistake at Common Law
11.10 (1) Introduction—*Bell v Lever Brothers, Ltd*
11.11–11.14 (2) Modern Law—The *Associated Japanese Bank* case
11.15–11.16 (3) Local Position
Common Mistake in Equity
11.17–11.19 (1) English Position
11.20–11.21 (2) Local Position
11.22–11.25 Relationship Between Common Mistake at Common Law and Common Mistake in Equity—Proposed Reform: Merger of the Two Doctrines
11.26–11.27 Rectification

11.28–11.30 **Mutual Mistake**

Unilateral Mistake

11.31–11.32 Introduction
11.33–11.37 'Rule in Smith v Hughes'
Mistaken Identity
11.38 (1) Introduction
(2) Face-to-Face or *Inter Praesentes* Cases
11.39–11.41 (a) Introduction and General Principles
11.42 (b) The 'Infamous' Trilogy of Cases (1)—*Phillips v Brooks, Ltd*

PARAGRAPHS

Unilateral Mistake (continued)

11.43–11.44 (c) The 'Infamous' Trilogy of Cases (2)—*Ingram v Little*

11.45 (d) The 'Infamous' Trilogy of Cases (3)—*Lewis v Averay*

11.46 (e) Taking Stock—Confusion and Complexity

11.47 (f) Latest Development—*Shogun Finance Ltd v Hudson*

11.48–11.52 (3) Non-Face-to-Face or Non-*Inter Praesentes* Cases

11.53–11.56 ***Non Est Factum***

11.57 **Future Directions**

Introduction and the Legal Consequences of a Mistake

Introduction

11.1 There would be little doubt that many would, adopting a layperson's perspective, be of the view that a mistake should allow the party who is negatively affected to avoid the contract concerned. However, that would raise, from a *legal* point of view, the issue as to *how* one would be able to ascertain whether or not the mistake was sufficiently serious to merit the court allowing the party adversely affected to avoid the contract. After all, the court would also have to take into account the rights of the other party as well. In fact, as we shall see, the issue of mistake often arises in situations where *neither* party is to blame. For example, the parties may be the victims of a rogue who cheats one party of his or her property and then sells it on to the other party. In such a situation, which of the two innocent parties ought to bear the burden of what essentially is a wrong committed by a third party (here, the rogue)? There are, it is suggested, no easy answers.

Is There a Doctrine of Mistake to Begin With?

11.2 Added to the basic difficulty briefly laid down in the preceding paragraph, there is the additional difficulty of a potentially devastating critique of the entire law of mistake itself. To elaborate briefly, it has been argued by some writers that there is no independent doctrine of mistake and that it all depends, in the final analysis, upon the construction of the terms of the contract itself (see, eg Slade, 'The Myth of Mistake in the English Law of Contract' (1954) 70 *Law Quarterly Review* 385; PS Atiyah, '*Couturier v Hastie* and The Sale of Non-Existent Goods' (1957) 73 *Law Quarterly Review* 340; as well as PS Atiyah and FAR Bennion, 'Mistake in the Construction of Contracts' (1961) 24 *Modern Law Review* 421, amongst other pieces; and see, further, the much cited Australian High Court decision of *McRae v Commonwealth Disposals Commission* (1951) as well as paragraph 11.10, below). In a related (and, in some ways more specific) vein, it has been argued, for example, that alternative substantive doctrines (such as offer and acceptance) are the actual basis for the court's decision (rather than a doctrine of mistake as such).

Notwithstanding the doubts expressed above, the doctrine of mistake in contract law nevertheless continues to be alive and well and this is confirmed by the relatively large number of cases that have been handed down recently.

Categories of Mistake

11.3 It would be useful if we note from the outset the various categories of mistake which we will briefly cover in the present chapter. They are as follows:

(1) *Common Mistake*—this occurs where both parties are of one mind but are mistaken as to the underlying contractual subject-matter (see

generally below, paragraph 11.7 ff). There are, in fact, two further sub-categories of common mistake at common law and common mistake in equity.

(2) *Mutual Mistake*—this occurs where both parties are completely mistaken as to what is being offered and what is being accepted (see paragraph 11.28 ff, below).

(3) *Unilateral Mistake*—this occurs where only one party is mistaken and the other party knows about it. However, the precise criteria to establish this particular category of mistake are not altogether clear. There are also a number of established categories, which include the so-called 'Rule in *Smith v Hughes*' (discussed in paragraphs 11.33 ff, below) as well as rules relating to mistaken identity (discussed in paragraphs 11.38 ff, below).

(4) *Non Est Factum*—this particular category of mistake is rather more specific and pertains to documents mistakenly signed (see, generally, paragraphs 11.53 ff, below).

It should be added that as the focus is on mistake under the law of contract, we will not be considering other areas of the law relating to mistake which, whilst relevant, are not at the centre of the area we are currently interested in. It should, however, be noted that the Singapore courts have since followed the landmark House of Lords decision in *Kleinwort Benson Ltd v Lincoln City Council* (1998) which allows recovery for money paid under a mistake of *law* (as opposed to that paid under a mistake of fact); see the Singapore High Court decision of *Management Corporation Strata Title No 473 v De Beers Jewellery Pte Ltd* (2001), which was recently affirmed by the Singapore Court of Appeal in *Management Corporation Strata Title No 473 v De Beers Jewellery Pte Ltd* (2002).

Legal Consequences of Mistake

(1) *Where Contract is Void under Common Law*

11.4 It is also vitally important to note at the outset what the *consequences* of a mistake are *vis-à-vis* the contract concerned.

An operative mistake at *common law* renders the contract completely *void*. In other words, the contract ceases to have effect in the most complete and absolute sense: in traditional legal parlance, it is void *ab initio* (right from the outset). The result, in other words, is as if the contract never existed. This is particularly important in relation to third party rights. This is the situation by way of a simple diagrammatic representation:

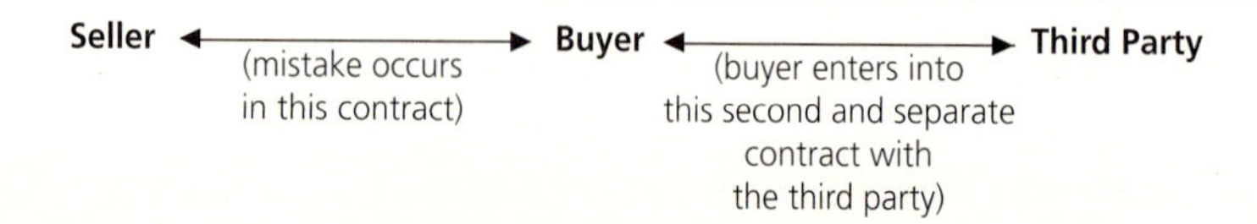

Related Issues: (1) What rights does the third party have under the second contract?
(2) Can the seller claim back the contractual subject-matter from the third party?

There are two contracts in the above diagram. The operative mistake occurs in the first—between the seller and the buyer (this could fall under any of the categories of mistake briefly outlined in the preceding paragraph). One assumes, further, that it is the seller who is negatively impacted by the mistake and, hence, wishes to recover the contractual subject-matter which he or she had sold to the buyer in the first instance. The third party is an actual contracting party, but only with regard to the second contract. The issue is whether or not, despite the mistake, the third party can retain his rights to the contractual subject-matter by virtue of the (second) contract he or she has entered into.

Where a contract is void, no rights or obligations can pass under it at all. This means that if the party has then transferred the contractual subject-matter on to a third party, that third party can receive no rights under this second contract because no rights had passed to the party concerned in the first instance (ie the buyer). The corollary of this is that the party who was the original owner of the contractual subject-matter under the first contract (ie the seller) can recover the contractual subject-matter even though the third party may have purchased it in complete ignorance of the circumstances under which the mistake arose in the first place. At this juncture, it should be noted that both the original owner of the contractual subject-matter and the third party are innocent, and so the really difficult issue is this: as between two equally innocent parties, who is to suffer?

The consequences are quite different under the same factual scenario where the contract is only *voidable* in *equity*.

(2) *Where Contract is Voidable in Equity*

11.5 Where, however, the contract is not void, but only *voidable*, in *equity* (*all operative mistakes at common law* render the contract *void*), the consequences are (as already mentioned) quite different. We assume the same factual scenario which was diagrammatically represented above (in paragraph 11.4).

Where the contract is only voidable (as opposed to being void), the contract can indeed be avoided or rescinded by the seller. *However, the contract (in which the operative mistake occurs) continues in force and subsists until such time that the seller indicates his or her intention to rescind the said contract*. This is extremely significant insofar as the third party's rights are concerned. The result is that if the contractual subject-matter has *already* been sold to the third party (here, by the buyer), it is *too late* for the seller to recover the contractual subject-matter. Since, as just mentioned, the contract continues in force until the seller rescinds, there are still rights that could be passed from the buyer to the third party under the second (and later) contract. This being the case, the attempt by the seller to rescind the original contract between both him or her and the buyer comes *too late, because rights to the contractual subject-matter have already passed to the third party under the (second) contract between the buyer and the third party*.

(3) *Importance of the Distinction Between Voidness and Voidability*

11.6 From both practical as well as theoretical perspectives, therefore, the distinction between void and voidable contracts may well be crucial. This would be the case, for instance, where the buyer turns out to be a rogue and absconds with the third party's money. At this juncture, there is no legal redress available for the seller if the contract is only voidable: the third party, if he or she has paid the buyer for the contractual subject-matter in good faith and without any notice (actual or constructive) of the buyer's fraud in the original contract (between seller and buyer), is legally entitled to the contractual subject-matter. The seller can succeed in recovering the contractual subject-matter *only if he or she can prove that the contract is void* (and *not* merely voidable). If the contract is void, it is treated as never having existed and, therefore, no property rights in the contractual subject-matter could have passed to the third party. The seller is hence at liberty to claim back the contractual subject-matter. Therefore, it may be quite crucial (depending on the *specific fact situation*) whether a contract is void at common law or is only voidable in equity.

Where, however, *no* third party rights have intervened, one could assume (in the ordinary run of events) that it would make *no difference* whether the contract concerned is void at common law or merely voidable in equity. In *both* situations, the plaintiff (in our fact situation above, the seller) can recover the contractual subject-matter back from the defendant (in our fact situation above, the buyer). Reference may also be made to paragraph 11.12, below.

Let us now turn to the various categories of mistake proper.

Common Mistake

Introduction

11.7 A common mistake occurs when, although both offer and acceptance are otherwise properly effected, both the contracting parties are, however, mistaken as to the basis upon which they contracted. In other words, although both parties thought that they were contracting with respect to a certain specific contractual subject-matter, it turns out that, in point of fact, the actual contractual subject-matter is radically different. However, whilst the general concept is easily stated, the criteria for establishing a common mistake and (more importantly) application of those criteria may (as we shall see) be quite a difficult task indeed.

11.8 A preliminary note on *terminology* may also be in order. The terminology is, unfortunately, very variable. On occasion, the term '*mutual* mistake' has been used instead. However, because the traditional terminology would include (as we do in the present chapter) a quite different category which is *also* termed 'mutual mistake', it is proposed that the term 'common mistake' be used throughout instead—if nothing else, then to avoid any possible confusion with the quite separate category just mentioned.

11.9 As already mentioned (see paragraph 11.3, above), the category of common mistake can, in turn, be classified into two further categories, viz common mistake at common law and common mistake in equity. We will now proceed to discuss each of these further categories in turn.

Common Mistake at Common Law

(1) *Introduction—Bell v Lever Brothers, Ltd*

11.10 In this comparatively rare instance, the briefest of historical excursus would not be amiss. Up till relatively recently, it was thought, in some quarters at least, that the doctrine of common mistake was non-existent in the first place. The vast ambiguity was perpetuated in no small measure by the vagueness in the then leading House of Lords decision of *Bell v Lever Brothers, Ltd* (1932). The entire report of the case is lengthy, to say the least (spanning some 78 pages of the Law Reports). More importantly, a close perusal of the case itself would reveal that the issue of common mistake was not raised as a major issue as such. Hence, the fact that a significant proportion of the various judgments is concerned, rather, with points of pleading and not with the substantive law of mistake as such. And of the remainder of the respective judgments, one cannot be sure whether or not a doctrine of common mistake at common law is being propounded in the first instance.

A close perusal of the material parts of the judgment in *Bell v Lever Brothers, Ltd* will, however, reveal that there are concrete theoretical formulations of a *broader* doctrine of common mistake at common law in at least two of the judgments (viz those of Lord Atkin and Lord Thankerton). It is a little unfortunate, though, that most of the illustrations utilised (see pp 217, 218 and 236) as well as authorities cited in these two judgments concern, in fact, *narrower* categories of mistake.

There is, insofar as the narrow categories of mistake are concerned, first, the doctrine of *res extincta* (where the contractual subject-matter had already been destroyed or extinguished: see the oft-cited English case of *Couturier v Hastie* (1856); *contra* the Australian High Court decision of *McRae v Commonwealth Disposals Commission* (1951), also referred to in paragraph 11.2, above, which held that *Couturier v Hastie* turned on the issue of construction of the contract and was not a case on common mistake as such).

A second established narrower category is that of *res sua* (where the property purchased already belonged to the purchaser, even though he or she was unaware of this).

There is little doubt that these narrower and more specific categories are established. If, however, an operative common mistake at common law is confined merely to these two narrower categories, the real thrust of the doctrine would have (in practice, if not in theory) been taken away simply because, as the present writer has ventured to suggest elsewhere, 'the real advantage of the doctrine is to be found precisely in those fact situations which do not fall within these narrower categories' (see A Phang, 'Common Mistake in English Law: The Proposed Merger of

Common Law and Equity' (1989) 9 *Legal Studies* 291, p 293). Given all these various difficulties, it is no surprise, therefore, that there was great uncertainty as to whether or not there was indeed a broader doctrine of common mistake at common law in the first instance. *However*, all this has changed with the very important decision by Steyn J (as he then was) in the English decision of *Associated Japanese Bank (International) Ltd v Crédit du Nord SA* (1989); its significance is even more remarkable, given that it was a judgment at first instance. Its clarificatory effect has, however, been enormous and the case will therefore be dealt with in some detail.

(2) *Modern Law—The Associated Japanese Bank Case*

11.11 In the *Associated Japanese Bank* case, one Bennett, whose fraud was responsible for the present action, concluded a sale and leaseback transaction of four micro-textile compression packaging machines with the plaintiffs, the Associated Japanese Bank (International) Ltd (hereafter referred to as 'AJB'). The transaction (comprising two contracts, viz the sale of the machines by Bennett to AJB and the leaseback of the same by AJB to Bennett) would not have come to pass if Bennett had not succeeded in persuading the defendants, Crédit du Nord (hereafter 'CDN') to guarantee his (Bennett's) obligations under the leaseback. CDN, in so effecting this guarantee, entered into a third contract (a contract of guarantee) with AJB. Unknown to *both* AJB and CDN, however, the machines in question never existed. AJB had, in the meantime, paid out a sum in excess of £1 million to Bennett. Bennett, in turn, who had paid only the first quarterly rental, was subsequently arrested and (not surprisingly) duly defaulted on the rest of the payments under the lease. Bennett was (again, not surprisingly) soon adjudged bankrupt. AJB turned to CDN for recovery, basing their claim upon the contract of guarantee between them. Although there was also a tracing claim against CDN, this was settled prior to trial, thus leaving the court with the central issue as to whether or not CDN were liable to AJB on the said contract of guarantee.

11.12 Steyn J held in favour of the defendants (CDN) on several alternative grounds.

First, he held (on the issue of *construction*) that there was either an express or an implied condition precedent in the guarantee that the machines concerned existed and, as the machines did not in fact exist, the plaintiff's (AJB's) claim should fail. This does indeed support the argument briefly canvassed above to the effect that there is no real doctrine of mistake as such and that it all depends, in the final analysis, upon the construction or interpretation of the terms of the contract itself. However, as we shall see in a moment, Steyn J did not adopt such an 'all-or-nothing' approach: he was prepared to utilise both construction *and* the doctrine of mistake as *alternative doctrines* (which, on the facts of the present case, enabled the court to arrive at the *same result*). This is an intriguing compromise which should give much food for thought to the reader. However, another related point is this: because of this particular holding, it would appear that the rest of the holdings in the case are, strictly speaking, *obiter dicta*; see also per Steyn J himself, where the learned judge observed (at p 264):

> 'Notwithstanding these conclusions, which are *determinative* of the case, I will now consider the arguments as to common or mutual mistake which played such a large part at the hearing of this case' (emphasis added).

Secondly, Steyn J held that there had been a *common mistake at common law* which rendered the contract of guarantee void in any event. Interestingly, the learned judge endorsed and applied the principles laid down in *Bell v Lever Brothers, Ltd*. This is highly significant in the light of the many difficulties associated with *Bell v Lever Brothers, Ltd*, which have been briefly recounted above (see paragraph 11.10, above).

Thirdly, Steyn J held (albeit without much discussion as such) that even if the doctrine of common mistake at common law were inapplicable, the doctrine of *common mistake in equity* would apply—with the *same result*. It is important to revert, at this particular juncture, to a more general point made earlier: that where *no* third party rights are involved (as was the case here), then it makes no difference, in effect, whether the doctrine of common mistake at common law or the doctrine of common mistake in equity is applied (and see paragraph 11.6, above). Indeed, as we shall see (in paragraph 11.24, below), there is, in any event, very little difference (in substance) between these two doctrines.

Finally, Steyn J went quickly over a number of miscellaneous issues which are not germane to the present chapter and will therefore not be discussed here.

11.13 Turning specifically to the doctrine of common mistake at common law, Steyn J 'reinstated' *Bell v Lever Brothers, Ltd* as an authority dealing with common mistake at common law. There is, in other words, no more controversy as to whether or not a *broader* doctrine of common mistake at common law exists (see also the subsequent English Court of Appeal decision of *William Sindall Plc v Cambridgeshire County Council* (1994)). As Steyn J very pertinently pointed out, there was substantial discussion of the doctrine of common mistake in the judgments of Lord Atkin and Lord Thankerton (see also paragraph 11.10, above), from which the learned judge in fact extracted the basic test (see Proposition 4 set out in paragraph 11.14, below).

Steyn J also rebutted an argument in a leading textbook to the effect that the *actual result* in *Bell v Lever Brothers, Ltd* rendered the broader doctrine of common mistake at common law nugatory (see the then current edition of MP Furmston, *Cheshire, Fifoot and Furmston's Law of Contract* (11th ed, 1986), pp 225–226). Indeed, the learned judge summarised the position taken in that textbook very well, as follows (see p 267):

> 'In substance the argument was that the actual decision in *Bell v Lever Bros Ltd* contradicts the language of the speeches. If the test was not satisfied there, so the argument runs, it is difficult to see how it could ever be satisfied …'

Steyn J then proceeded to explain why such an interpretation of *Bell v Lever Brothers, Ltd* was unpersuasive on a closer examination of the merits of that case itself, as follows (see p 267):

> 'But there are indications in the speeches that the so-called "merits" were not all in favour of Lever Bros. The company was most anxious, because of a corporate merger, to terminate the two service agreements. There was apparently a doubt whether the voidability of the service agreements if revealed to the company *at the time of the severance contract* would have affected the company's decision. Lord Thankerton said ... :
>
> > " ... I do not find sufficient material to compel the inference that the appellants, at the time of the contract, regarded the indefeasibility of the service agreements as an essential and integral element in the subject-matter of the bargain."
>
> ... It is noteworthy that Lord Atkin commented on the scarcity of evidence as to the subsidiaries from the boards of which the two employees resigned ... Lord Blanesburgh emphasised that Lever Bros secured the *future* co-operation of the two employees for the carrying through of the amalgamation. ... And the burden, of course, rested squarely on Lever Brothers. With the deference to the distinguished authors who have argued that the actual decision in *Bell v Lever Bros Ltd* contradicts the principle enunciated in the speeches it seems to me that their analysis is altogether too simplistic, and that the actual decision was rooted in the particular facts of the case' (emphasis added).

The learned judge's re-interpretation of *Bell v Lever Brothers, Ltd* above may, it is respectfully submitted, be somewhat too wide insofar as it considers *each and every merit* in a particular given fact situation. But one thing is sure—after the *Associated Japanese Bank* case, the doctrine of common mistake at common law has clearly received a new lease of life.

11.14 We shift now to consider the *specific principles* laid down in the *Associated Japanese Bank* case. From a practical perspective, the following *summary of the law* by Steyn J is of first importance (see pp 268–269; the writer's comments follow after each proposition):

> *Proposition 1*
>
> 'The first imperative must be that the law ought to uphold rather than destroy apparent contracts.'

This first proposition is straightforward and reflects the courts' generally strict approach inasmuch as they would be extremely reluctant to unravel contracts save in exceptional circumstances. The emphasis is also on certainty and predictability, although (as we shall see) there are possible avenues where justice can be achieved in the special circumstances of the case at hand. One such avenue is of course by the successful pleading of the doctrine of common mistake at common law, although this route is much more onerous than pleading common mistake in equity (as to which see, generally, paragraphs 11.17–11.19, below).

Proposition 2

'Secondly, the common law rules as to a mistake regarding the quality of the subject matter, *like the common law rules regarding commercial frustration*, are designed to cope with the impact of *unexpected and wholly exceptional circumstances* on apparent contracts' (emphasis added).

Comments with regard to Proposition 4, below, would apply to this particular proposition as well.

Proposition 3

'Thirdly, such a mistake in order to attract legal consequences must *substantially* be shared by *both* parties and must relate to facts as they existed *at the time the contract was made*' (emphasis added).

This proposition is straightforward. For instance, it is clear that the mistake must 'substantially be shared by both parties' in order for there to be an issue as to *common* mistake in the first place.

Equally straightforward is the point made in this particular proposition to the effect that the material time at which there would be an operative mistake would be with respect to 'facts as they existed at the time the contract was made'. This is because the doctrine of mistake must necessarily relate to the *formation* of the contract concerned. As we shall see in a moment, however, Steyn J does draw a *parallel* between common mistake at common law and the doctrine of discharge by *frustration* (for the doctrine of frustration, see generally Chapter 10, above). *However*, despite the fact that the tests with regard to both doctrines are very similar, there remains a difference insofar as the *timing* of the material event (that leads to a mistake or frustration, respectively) is concerned: the doctrine of mistake (as we have just seen) relates to the time *at or before* the contract was *formed*; in *contrast*, the doctrine of frustration only applies *after* the contract has been *formed*, dealing (as it does) with the *discharge* of the contract (in this instance, by operation of law).

Proposition 4

'Fourthly, and this is the point established by *Bell v Lever Bros Ltd* ..., the mistake must render the subject matter of the contract *essentially and radically different from the subject matter which the parties believed to exist*' (emphasis added).

This proposition concerns the main test for ascertaining whether or not the doctrine of common mistake at common law should operate. We have just seen the close parallel this particular test has (the issue of timing apart) with that for the doctrine of frustration. This is in fact reiterated in Proposition 2 above.

There is also a considerable linkage to Proposition 1 above inasmuch as the assumption is that the courts will be as strict in finding an operative common mistake at common law as they are with respect to finding the particular contract discharged by frustration.

Proposition 5

'Fifthly, there is a requirement which was *not specifically discussed* in *Bell v Lever Bros Ltd* ... In my judgment a party cannot be allowed to rely on a common mistake where the mistake consists of a belief which is entertained by him *without any reasonable grounds* for such [a] belief ... That is not because principles such as estoppel or negligence require it, but simply because *policy and good sense* dictate that the positive rules regarding common mistake should be so qualified. Curiously enough this qualification is similar to the civilian concept where the doctrine of error *in substantia* is tempered by the principles governing *culpa in contrahendo. More importantly*, a recognition of this qualification is *consistent with* the general approach in *equity* where fault on the part of the party adversely affected will generally preclude the granting of equitable relief ...' (emphasis added).

The present writer has in fact ventured to suggest elsewhere that this particular proposition has a historical antecedent in the Australian High Court decision of *McRae v Commonwealth Disposals Commission* (1951) (especially p 408), although there could be some controversy as to this particular point (see A Phang, 'Common Mistake in English Law: The Proposed Merger of Common Law and Equity' (1989) 9 *Legal Studies* 291 at pp 296–297).

There is, as we shall see, also *an analogue* of this proposition in the context of common mistake in *equity* (see paragraph 11.17, below).

(3) *Local Position*

11.15 Although it is open to the Singapore courts to decide whether or not it ought even to adopt the doctrine of common mistake at common law, it is suggested that there is no reason in principle why the present English position (as embodied in the *Associated Japanese Bank* case) ought not to be followed. It does allow the courts to do justice in exceptional circumstances. Further, as we shall see below, the doctrine of common mistake in *equity* clearly exists under *Singapore* law in any event (see paragraphs 11.20–11.21, below; though cf paragraph 11.19 and cf (in turn) paragraph 11.21, below).

11.16 However, a slight possible anomaly may be present in the local context and centres around section 6 of the UK Sale of Goods Act 1979 (which is part of Singapore law (see Cap 393, 1999 Rev Ed) by virtue of the Application of English Law Act (Cap 7A, 1994 Rev Ed)), which was originally enacted to embody what was perceived to be the traditional view of *Courturier v Hastie* (and see paragraph 11.10, above). Section 6 itself reads as follows:

> 'Where there is a contract for the sale of specific goods [defined in section 61(1) of the Act] and the goods without the knowledge of the seller have perished at the time when the contract is made, the contract is void.'

The Singapore decision of *Chop Ngoh Seng v Esmail and Ahmad Bros* (1948) raises interesting issues with regard to the provision just quoted that (unfortunately) have not yet been resolved. These centre around the viability of the doctrine of *res extincta* (see paragraph 11.10, above) and its relationship to section 6 itself. The *Chop Ngoh Seng* case appears to accept the doctrine of *res extincta*, although the pronouncements therein on the relationship between that doctrine and the Sale of Goods Act are ambiguous. The present writer has in fact suggested elsewhere that for 'any future problem in this context, ... this case should be utilized as a point of departure for further analysis' (see A Phang, *The Development of Singapore Law—Historical and Socio-Legal Perspectives* (1990), p 84).

Common Mistake in Equity

(1) *English Position*

11.17 Unlike its common law counterpart, the doctrine of common mistake in *equity* appears to be established, and has often been said to be embodied within the following statement of principles by Denning LJ (as he then was) in the English Court of Appeal decision of *Solle v Butcher* (1950) (at pp 692–693):

> 'The court, it was said, had power to set aside the contract whenever it was of opinion that it was unconscientious for the other party to avail himself of the legal advantage which he had obtained ... It is now clear that a contract will be set aside if the mistake of the one party has been induced by a material misrepresentation of the other, even though it was not fraudulent or fundamental; or if one party, knowing that the other is mistaken about the terms of an offer, or the identity of the person by whom it is made, lets him remain under his delusion and conclude a contract on the mistaken terms instead of pointing out the mistake ... A contract is also liable to be set aside if the parties were under *a common misapprehension* either as to facts or as to their respective rights, *provided that the misapprehension was fundamental and that the party seeking to set it aside was not himself at fault*' (emphasis added).

It should be noted, though, that Lord Denning has consistently denied that there is a doctrine of common mistake at common law, although it is submitted that this approach must now be suspect in view of the very clear pronouncements to the contrary by Steyn J in the *Associated Japanese Bank* case (as to which see, generally, paragraphs 11.11–11.14, above). Further, it is submitted that so long as the doctrine of common mistake at common law is not applied too liberally in order to unravel contracts too frequently, it is an excellent legal instrument which courts could utilise in order to ensure that justice is achieved in situations where third party rights are involved without always having to find in favour of the third party if *only* the doctrine of common mistake in equity were available (and see, generally, paragraphs 11.4–11.6, above, with regard to the consequences of a finding of operative mistake in the context of voidness and voidability).

11.18 It appears, from the case law, that it is relatively easier to obtain a remedy in common mistake in equity compared to the invocation of the doctrine of common mistake at common law (see, eg the oft-cited English precedents of *Grist v Bailey* (1967); *Magee v Pennine Insurance Co Ltd* (1969); *Laurence v Lexcourt Holdings Ltd* (1978) and the *Associated Japanese Bank* case itself; though cf the Singapore Court of Appeal decision of *Projection Pte Ltd v The Tai Ping Insurance Co Ltd* (2001)).

It should also be noted, from the perspective of *remedies*, that as *Solle v Butcher* itself demonstrates, there is much more flexibility: the court can, when exercising its jurisdiction in equity upon the finding of an operative common mistake, set aside the contract *on terms*. In this regard, the following observation by Steyn J in the *Associated Japanese Bank* case should also be noted (see p 270): 'Equity will give relief against common mistake in cases where the common law will not, and it provides more flexible remedies, including the power to set aside the contract on terms.'

11.19 *However*, the English Court of Appeal delivered a recent judgment so startling and radical that it has to be dealt with here in more than a cursory fashion. Indeed, in *Great Peace Shipping Limited v Tsavliris (International) Limited* (2002), the court held that its previous decision in *Solle v Butcher* (see paragraph 11.17, above) was inconsistent with the House of Lords decision in *Bell v Lever Brothers Ltd* (see paragraph 11.10, above), and ought therefore not to be followed. There is, as a result, no longer any doctrine of common mistake in *equity*—at least for the present moment. There are, however, many unanswered questions from the perspectives of technical detail as well as wider considerations of fairness, justice and flexibility. The *Great Peace Shipping* case could well be appealed to the House of Lords and, if so, it is hoped that the House would restore the necessary flexibility by reinstating the equitable doctrine first enunciated in *Solle v Butcher*. The present writer has dealt with this particular case in more detail in a forthcoming piece entitled 'Controversy in Common Mistake' (forthcoming in [2003] *The Conveyancer and Property Lawyer*).

(2) *Local Position*

11.20 The system of case law is not particularly conducive to ascertaining what the present law is, particularly when (as is the case with Singapore) the local law is very heavily dependent upon English law (see, generally, Chapter 1). The present situation is an extremely good illustration of the more general point just made.

The Singapore decision of *Alsagoff v Robin* (1965) considered the doctrine of common mistake in equity and in fact cited the leading English decisions of *Solle v Butcher* (see paragraph 11.17, above) and *Cooper v Phibbs* (1867). Had the court in that case proceeded no further, the existing local law would have been completely in tandem with the then English position above (see, generally, paragraphs 11.17–11.18, above). Somewhat unfortunately, however, the court then proceeded to cite the *Australian* decision of *Svanasio v McNamara* (1956), which tends to *narrow* the ambit of the operation of the doctrine of common mistake in equity quite considerably, not least because the operative element in that (Australian) case centred on total failure of consideration (cf also, in this regard, the Malaysian decision of *Hong Leong Leasing Sdn Bhd v Tan Kim Cheong* (1994), pp 187–188). When *Alsagoff v Robin* went on *appeal*, the (then) Federal Court of Singapore adopted a very similar approach (see *Robin v Goh Boon Choo* (1965)). In summary, a literal adherence to the existing case law would, in effect, necessitate having recourse to the *older Australian* case law, rather than the existing (and *broader*) position as embodied in the *Associated Japanese Bank* case (which, in fact, does not depart from the position laid down in the much earlier decision of *Solle v Butcher*).

11.21 It is submitted, however, that the *broader* position as laid down, *inter alia*, in the *Associated Japanese Bank* case ought to be followed for at least two reasons.

First, the *present Australian* position is *quite different* from the previous position embodied in *Svanasio v McNamara* (see paragraph 11.20, above). Indeed, the present position is clearly expounded by the Australian High Court in *Taylor v Johnson* (1983), which adopts a *much more liberal* position. Hence, to allow the local law to be confined to the *older* Australian position would, it is submitted, be to take (in effect) a step *backwards* and should thus be avoided.

Secondly, and as a closely related point (albeit on a more general level), there appears to be no reason in principle why the Singapore courts should feel constrained by the existing case law which dates back to nearly four decades ago. Indeed, *Alsagoff v Robin* is, in fact, an appropriate example for the application of the general approach just mentioned. *That* decision adopted the *then current* Australian position. In other words, what is most important is to adopt *the most cogent position available at any given point in time*. Indeed, Singapore, being an independent nation state, is *not* bound by any particular position and Singapore courts are free to choose what is the most persuasive position that will enable them to do justice in the case at hand (and see paragraphs 1.46–1.51, above). Looked at in this light, it is submitted that, having regard to the more limited scope embodied within the older Australian precedent of *Svanosio v McNamara*, that position should now be abandoned in favour of the broader English position (principally that embodied in *Solle v Butcher* (see paragraph 11.17, above)). However, this is not to argue for a slavish adherence to English precedent. However, where the (here, English) law is suitable to local circumstances, there is no reason in principle why it should not be followed (see also, with regard to the doctrine of fundamental breach in the context of exception clauses, paragraphs 6.27–6.28, above).

The approach just suggested has in fact been confirmed by the decision of Judith Prakash J in the Singapore High Court decision of *Ho Seng Lee Construction Pte Ltd v Nian Chuan Construction Pte Ltd* (2001), which raises a great number of interesting issues and where the principles in the *Associated Japanese Bank* case were applied. Indeed, the learned judge provided valuable guidance as well as commentary on some of the five principles set out by Steyn J (as he then was) in that case and which we considered in paragraph 11.14, above. For further details and commentary, see A Phang, 'Contract Law' (2001) *Singapore Academy of Law Annual Review of Singapore Cases* 118 at pp 136–138.

However, the English Court of Appeal, as we have seen, has rejected the doctrine of common mistake in equity (as embodied in *Solle v Butcher*) altogether (see the *Great Peace Shipping* case, considered at paragraph 11.19, above). As has been briefly argued, however, such an approach is undesirable and it is hoped that the status quo would be restored.

Relationship Between Common Mistake at Common Law and Common Mistake in Equity—Proposed Reform: Merger of the Two Doctrines

11.22 It appears that as between the doctrines of common mistake at common law and common mistake in equity, the former should be pleaded first (and see eg the approach of Steyn J (as he then was) in the *Associated Japanese Bank* case (discussed in paragraphs 11.11–11.14, above)).

11.23 The approach mentioned in the preceding paragraph is logical as it has been well-established in the case law that that the doctrine of common mistake at common law is *much stricter* than the corresponding doctrine in equity insofar as the *consequences* are concerned (see, generally, paragraphs 11.4–11.6, above). To briefly recapitulate, common mistake at *common law* renders the contract *void*, whereas common mistake in *equity* only renders the contract *voidable*. As we have seen, this difference has profound consequences with regard to the rights of innocent third parties who benefit from the contract concerned that has been held voidable, rather than void (see, generally, paragraphs 11.4–11.6, above). It is suggested in fact that this is the reason why the common law doctrine is so much stricter and, hence, the probability of successfully pleading the doctrine is so much lower compared to the situation where the doctrine of common mistake in equity is being pleaded. In other words, the consequences of a successful finding of common mistake at common law are so devastating with respect to third party rights that the courts are generally much less likely to make such a finding.

It should, however, be noted that where *no* third party rights are involved, it really does not matter which doctrine is pleaded. However, because the case law has established a much stricter legal regime with regard to common mistake at common law, the chances of success are therefore much higher when pleading the doctrine of common mistake in equity instead.

11.24 The writer of the present chapter has in fact ventured to suggest elsewhere that a comparison of the linguistic formulations for both doctrines (as to which see above, paragraphs 11.14 and 11.17, respectively) are, in effect, so similar as to be identical (see generally A Phang, 'Common Mistake in English Law: The Proposed Merger of Common Law and Equity' (1989) 9 *Legal Studies* 291). Any difference, therefore, between the two doctrines really hinges on the difference in *result or consequences* as we have seen in the preceding paragraph and for the reason stated therein. It was therefore suggested that both doctrines ought to be *merged* in order both to prevent artificiality as well as to systematically simplify the law (see Phang, ibid, especially pp 301–306). This proposal is not without objections, the chief of which is that the common law and the equitable rules are different in substance (see Phang, ibid, pp 302–306). However, these objections are by no means insuperable (particularly if one has regard to the *substance* of the two doctrines and their respective formulations) and the proposal itself has been at least referred to or seriously considered in some leading textbooks (see eg GH Trietel, *The Law of Contract* (10th ed, 1999), p 286, note 11; S Wheeler and J Shaw, *Contract Law—Cases, Materials and Commentary* (1994), pp 699–700; JE Martin, *Hanbury & Martin—Modern Equity* (16th ed, 2001), p 845, note 12; and C Boyle and DR Percy (eds), *Contracts: Cases and Commentaries* (5th ed, 1994), p 542). Notwithstanding the deeply embedded distinction between the common law on the one hand and equity on the other, to persist in such artificial demarcation does, with respect, no credit to the development of the law in this particular area.

If, however, such a merger were to be effected, a decision would have to be arrived at as to the *consequences* that would follow from such a merged doctrine. It would appear that the most practical way forward would be for the contract concerned to be rendered *voidable*. However, such an approach would appear to have swung the pendulum clearly in favour of third party rights. It is suggested that one solution to achieve a more equitable balance would be to legislatively delegate powers for adjustment of third party rights to the courts.

11.25 It should, however, be noted that there are certain observations by Evans LJ in the English Court of Appeal decision of *William Sindall Plc v Cambridgeshire County Council* (1994) which appear to militate against the merger proposed above. Whilst not expressing a concluded view as such, Evans LJ nevertheless suggested that the test for common mistake at common law was a stricter one compared to that for common mistake in equity. However, this proposition does not, with respect, take into account the other arguments made (in Phang, above, at paragraph 11.24).

It should also be noted that recent case law holds that there is *no longer* any doctrine of common mistake in equity (see paragraph 11.19, above). However, it has been suggested that this is too radical an approach to adopt and it is hoped that the situation will revert back to the status quo (see paragraph 11.19, above).

Rectification

11.26 This doctrine encompasses a more specific situation in which written agreements do not truly reflect the intention of the parties themselves. The court has, in such a situation, a discretion (in equity) to *rectify* the document concerned in order that it truly reflect the parties' intention.

11.27 It should be noted that the prior agreement need not itself be legally enforceable, so long as there is a *common* intention between the parties themselves which is both clear and unambiguous (see eg the oft-cited English decision of *Joscelyne v Nissen* (1970)). In addition, '[t]here must be a prior common *and continuing* intention right up to the time of the written agreement' (emphasis added) (see per Ajaib Singh J in the Malaysian decision of *Yuson Bien v Bankers Trust Co Ltd* (1980), p 32).

Mutual Mistake

11.28 This is in fact probably the least problematic branch of the law relating to mistake in contract law. The only tangible difficulty is really a conceptual one: put shortly, it has been argued that this particular category of mistake ought not really to be classified as a mistake in the first instance because in such a situation, the alleged mistake arises as a result of a *total lack of coincidence between offer and acceptance*. For instance, S offers to sell a brand new car but B accepts the offer, thinking that S is offering to sell, instead, a second-hand car. Critics of this particular branch of mistake argue (and quite persuasively at that) that such a situation is really one that falls more appropriately under the rubric of offer and acceptance instead.

11.29 It should be noted that there is not all that much by way of case law authority. Indeed, the decision most often cited, *Raffles v Wichelhaus* (1864), does not appear to be particularly well-reported to admit (unambiguously, at least) any substantive propositions of law as such.

11.30 Returning to the problems from classification very briefly canvassed in paragraph 11.28 above, it is at least arguable that no great damage is wrought to principle by classifying the situation presently considered as falling under a separate category of mistake, notwithstanding the fact that the underlying rationale is premised upon the principles relating to offer and acceptance. However, it is admitted that of all the various arguments proffered *against* having a doctrine of mistake, this is perhaps the most persuasive.

Unilateral Mistake

Introduction

11.31 As the title of this category suggests, the focus is on a situation where one party is mistaken but the other party is (or ought to be) aware of the first party's mistake. Situations of unilateral mistake are traditionally sub-classified into two further categories, viz the 'Rule in *Smith v Hughes*' and *mistaken identity*, respectively. The latter sub-category (viz mistaken identity) can be further sub-divided into two more categories—situations where the parties are face-to-face ('*inter praesentes*' cases) and those where the parties are contracting at a distance ('non-*inter praesentes*' cases), respectively.

11.32 As these various sub-categories of unilateral mistake are based on the *common law*, the contract concerned will become *void* (instead of voidable).

The issue as to whether or not there is indeed a doctrine of unilateral mistake in *equity* appears to be still an open one, notwithstanding the allusion to such a doctrine in the Australian High Court decision of *Taylor v Johnson* (1983). However, in the more recent English decision of *Clarion Ltd v National Provident Institution* (2000), the doctrine of unilateral mistake in an equitable context was in fact raised (although it should be noted that no third party rights were involved, so it did not matter whether the case was premised at common law or in equity). In this case, the learned judge, in holding that there had not been an operative mistake, drew a distinction between a mistake that went to the terms of the contract and one that went merely to the commercial effect—an approach similar to that adopted in *Smith v Hughes* (see especially paragraphs 11.35–11.36, below), which was itself also cited in the case itself. For further commentary on the *Clarion* case, see A Phang, 'Commercial Certainty, Mistake, Unconscionability and Implied Terms' (2002) 1 *Journal of Obligations and Remedies* 21.

'Rule in Smith v Hughes'

11.33 It should be noted at the outset that although this particular category of unilateral mistake clearly applies to the situation of a sale of goods, it is not as clear whether it would apply to more *general* situations as well. The present writer would tentatively put forward the proposition to the effect that an at least moderately persuasive case could be made out in favour of a more generalised application.

11.34 In *Smith v Hughes* (1871) itself, a new trial was ordered, with judgment in favour of the defendant purchaser being overturned in the process. The statements of principle contained therein, however, are instructive. The tenor of the judgments suggests that the doctrine of mistake in this particular context will not be applied liberally. This is consistent with the parsimonious attitude of the courts with regard to common mistake at common law simply because the effect of a successful finding of mistake is to render the contract *void*, thus impairing *third party* rights as well (and see paragraphs 11.22–11.23).

11.35 Turning to the substantive principles proper, it would appear, however, that the principles themselves are not, with respect, particularly clear and hence require some careful elaboration. *Smith v Hughes* was a case involving the *passive acquiescence* of the contracting party who knew (unilaterally, of course) of the mistake of the other party. The seller knew that the defendant purchaser had committed a mistake—in this instance, a kind of self-deception. The purchaser had in fact intended to buy old (as opposed to new) oats but, instead, bought what were in point of fact new oats (but thinking that they were old oats). Insofar as the 'Rule in *Smith v Hughes*' is concerned, such a mistake would *not* constitute an operative unilateral mistake, *notwithstanding* the knowledge by (here) the seller of the purchaser's mistake. As Cockburn CJ observed (at p 603):

> 'I take the true rule to be that, where a specific article is offered for sale, without express warranty, or without circumstances from which the law will imply a warranty—as where, for instance, an article is ordered for a specific purpose—and the buyer has full opportunity of inspecting and forming his own judgment, if he chooses to act on his own judgment, the rule *caveat emptor* applies. If he gets the article he contracted to buy, and that article corresponds with what it was sold as, he gets all he is entitled to, and is bound by the contract.'

There *would*, however, have been an operative unilateral mistake if the purchaser had been under the mistaken belief (of course *known* to the seller, as was the case in *Smith v Hughes* as well and which therefore gives rise to a scenario of possible unilateral mistake in the first place) that the seller was *contracting or warranting* that the oats were in fact old oats. In other words, in order for there to be an operative unilateral mistake, that particular mistake *must* relate to a *contractual* promise. The mere knowledge of one of the contracting parties that the other contracting party had made a mistake alone is therefore a necessary, but not sufficient, condition for the finding by the court of an operative unilateral mistake. The mistake must—at the expense of repetition—*also* relate to a *contractual* promise. If the mistake related merely to the quality of the subject matter (as was the case in *Smith v Hughes*), it would be insufficient to found an operative unilateral mistake, notwithstanding the knowledge of the mistake by the other contracting party not under the influence of the said mistake. Indeed, in *Smith v Hughes* itself, Blackburn J (commenting on the direction by the trial judge to the jury which he held to be inadequate) observed thus (at p 608):

> 'But I doubt whether [the direction by the trial judge] would bring to the minds of the jury the *distinction* between agreeing to take the oats under the belief that they were old, and agreeing to take the oats under the belief that the plaintiff *contracted* that they were old' (emphasis added).

Indeed, it is only with respect to the latter situation that an operative unilateral mistake could arise. The point was also succinctly put by Hannen J, as follows (at p 611):

> 'In order to relieve the defendant it was necessary that the jury should find not merely that the plaintiff believed the defendant to believe that he was buying old oats, but that he believed the defendant to believe that he, the plaintiff, was *contracting* to sell old oats' (emphasis added).

11.36 In the light of the discussion in the preceding paragraph, the reader might quite justifiably ask whether the distinction or line drawn between knowledge of a mistake relating to the mere belief in the quality of the contractual subject matter on the one hand and knowledge of a mistake relating to the belief that the other party (ie the party *not* in mistake) was *contracting or promising* that the contractual subject matter was of a particular quality on the other is a rather fine one. In theory at least, the line may indeed (on occasion at least) be a rather fine one. This might conceivably explain why there has been a relative dearth of cases where this particular category of mistake has been canvassed. On the other hand, where the relevant evidence is in fact forthcoming, there appears to be no reason in principle why the distinction ought not to be workable in practice (though cf A Phang, 'Commercial Certainty, Mistake, Unconscionability and Implied Terms' (2002) 1 *Journal of Obligations and Remedies* 21, especially at p 22).

11.37 An important (and related) issue that arises from the 'Rule in *Smith v Hughes*' is this: assuming that the criteria just considered are present, what ought to be the criterion with regard to the process of ascertaining whether or not the contracting party who is alleged to have known of the mistake did actually know (ie possess knowledge of) the mistake in the first instance. In this regard, given the actual nature of the doctrine of unilateral mistake itself as well as the actual elements of the Rule itself, the *subjective knowledge* of the party concerned is required. In other words, did the contracting party *actually and personally know* that the other contracting party was labouring under a mistake? How, then, is this test to be reconciled with the objective test in contract law? A possible response is that, practically speaking, no court will be able to actually 'read the mind' of the contracting party in question and that, therefore, the objective test is still necessary as well as useful in the following way: whether or not the contracting party concerned actually (or *subjectively*) knew of the other contracting party's mistake is *objectively ascertained*.

The leading English decision of *Hartog v Colin & Shields* (1939) illustrates the point just made very well. In that case, the reference to verbal as well as written negotiations prior to the sale concerned and the expert evidence with respect to the prevalent trade practice (in this case, with regard to the pricing unit, around which the central dispute in fact lay) tilted the court's decision in favour of the defendant sellers who, Singleton J held, had obviously made a mistake which was equally and obviously clear to the plaintiff buyer—having regard to the *objective facts and evidence* just referred to. In the words of the learned judge (at p 568):

> '[T]here was an accident. The offer [by the defendant sellers] was wrongly expressed, and the defendants *by their evidence, and by their correspondence*, have satisfied me that the plaintiff *could not reasonably* have supposed that that offer contained the offeror's *real intention*' (emphasis added).

Reference, in this regard, may also be made to the Australian High Court decision of *Taylor v Johnson* (1983), where it was held that there would be a possible situation of unilateral mistake where a contracting party either *actually* knows *or, as a reasonable person, ought to have* known of the other contracting party's mistake. As has already been sought to be shown above, the line between these two particular categories of knowledge is a fine one and is, in fact, often blurred inasmuch as even the first (viz *actual* knowledge) must (in virtually all cases) be premised on some *objective* evidence in the first instance. Reference may also be made to the recent Singapore High Court decision of *Ho Seng Lee Construction Pte Ltd v Nian Chuan Construction Pte Ltd* (2001) especially at pp 426–427.

Mistaken Identity

(1) *Introduction*

11.38 As already mentioned above, this particular category of unilateral mistake is sub-divided further into two more categories—situations where the parties are face-to-face ('*inter praesentes*' cases) and those where the parties are contracting at a distance ('non-*inter praesentes*' cases), respectively (and see above, paragraph 11.31). We will now briefly examine each sub-category in turn.

(2) *Face-to-Face or* Inter Praesentes *Cases*

(a) Introduction and General Principles

11.39 There is an 'infamous' trilogy of three leading English decisions, with one further (and extremely interesting) decision having been handed down by the English Court of Appeal only very recently. The *facts* of each case are important and, indeed, an analysis of the facts of these cases in relation to the general legal principles laid down reveals a huge amount of complexity and confusion. Indeed, one could go so far as to state that the various cases cannot be reconciled, hence generating a rather intractable situation indeed. Given these circumstances, it might be best first to attempt to lay down what appear to be the general legal principles before proceeding to an analysis of the leading cases themselves.

11.40 Most generally, it would appear that an operative mistake under this particular category would not be easily found by the courts at all. One chief factor is that this doctrine operates at common law and thus, any finding of an operative mistake would render the contract concerned *void ab initio*, hence impairing third party rights where they are present (and cf, especially, paragraphs 11.22–11.23, above).

11.41 More specifically, it would appear that there is a rebuttable presumption that the person seeking to set aside the contract for mistaken identity in a face-to-face transaction intended to deal with the *physical person* in front of him or her, and that a valid and binding contract would therefore be deemed to have been concluded in the absence of any rebutting evidence to the contrary.

In order to rebut the abovementioned presumption, it appears that evidence must be adduced to prove that the person seeking to set aside the contract actually intended to deal with *a certain specific person and that person only*, the latter of whose *identity* (as opposed merely to his or her attributes) were thus of *crucial importance*.

There is also a recent general statement of principle (albeit *obiter*) by Sir Nicolas Browne-Wilkinson V-C (as he then was) in the English Court of Appeal decision of *Hector v Lyons* (1988) as follows (at pp 158–159):

> 'In the case of a face to face sale, where the sale is over a counter or between two individuals, the law is well established that the mere fact that the vendor V is under a misapprehension as to the identity of the person in front of him does not operate so as to render the contract void for mistake, it being a mere unilateral mistake as to the quality of the purchaser; only in cases where the *identity of the purchaser is of direct and important materiality* in inducing the vendor to enter into the contract is a mistake of that kind capable of avoiding the contract' (emphasis added).

As we shall see, however, the general principles enunciated here are by no means easy to apply and may themselves give rise to possible difficulties (particularly with regard to the distinction, drawn above, between identity on the one hand and attributes on the other; see the above quotation, as well as below, paragraphs 11.43 and 11.46). This would therefore be an appropriate juncture at which our attention may turn to actual case law itself, as exemplified in the leading cases themselves.

(b) The 'Infamous' Trilogy of Cases (1)—*Phillips v Brooks, Ltd*

11.42 Turning to the *first* decision, that of Horridge J in *Phillips v Brooks, Ltd* (1919), we find that, in that case, a rogue represented himself to the plaintiff jeweller as 'Sir George Bullough of St James's Square'. The plaintiff in fact knew that there was such a person and confirmed the address in the directory. The rogue gave a cheque in exchange for a ring. He then pledged the ring with the defendant pawnbrokers who (in good faith and without notice of the fraud) advanced money to the rogue accordingly. Not surprisingly, the rogue absconded and the cheque was of course dishonoured. The plaintiff then sought the return of the ring or the value of the ring plus damages for detention.

It should be noted at this juncture that *third party rights* (here, that of the defendant pawnbrokers) were involved. And in the nature of things, although the plaintiff could have sought to set aside the contract with the rogue for fraudulent misrepresentation, it was too late insofar as the rogue had already passed the property in the ring to the defendants who acted in good faith and without any notice of the rogue's fraud.

Horridge J held in favour of the defendants, rejecting the plaintiff's argument from mistaken identity. In the learned judge's words, 'although he [ie the plaintiff] believed the person to whom he was handing the ring was Sir George Bullough, he in fact contracted to sell and deliver it to the person who came into his shop' (see p 246). Horridge J added (at pp 248–249): 'I think the seller *intended to contract with the person present*, and there was no error as to the person with whom he contracted, although the plaintiff would not have made the contract if there had not been a fraudulent misrepresentation' (emphasis added). In other words (and having regard to the general principles set out in paragraph 11.41, above), the presumption that (here) the plaintiff intended to contract with the *physical person* in front of him had *not* been rebutted by any countervailing evidence.

(c) The 'Infamous' Trilogy of Cases (2)—*Ingram v Little*

11.43 The *second* decision is that of the English Court of Appeal in *Ingram v Little* (1961). The facts were not totally unlike those in *Phillips v Brooks, Ltd.* In this case, the rogue represented himself to two elderly sisters as 'Mr PGM Hutchinson who lived at Stanstead House, Stanstead Road, Caterham'. The sisters were in fact joint owners of a car and were negotiating with the rogue to sell it to him. One sister went to the nearby post office to verify the name and address given by the rogue in the telephone directory. The sisters then closed the deal for the sale of the car to the rogue, handing him the car in return for his cheque. Not surprisingly, the rogue disposed of the car for cash, selling it to the defendant who purchased the vehicle in good faith and without notice of the fraud. The rogue (again, not surprisingly) absconded. The cheque was of course dishonoured and the two sisters brought an action against the defendant to recover either the car or its value.

It is significant to note that, yet again, *third party rights* were involved, thus necessitating (as was the situation in *Phillips v Brooks, Ltd*) the invocation of the doctrine of mistaken identity in order that the contract between the plaintiffs and the rogue could be rendered *void*, in which case no property in the car could then have been passed from the rogue to the defendant under their contract.

Unlike *Phillips v Brooks, Ltd*, however, the court in the present case held that there *had* been an operative mistake and the plaintiffs thus succeeded in their claim.

Sellers LJ was of the view that the result of the case might have been different had less been said by the rogue and if nothing had been done by the plaintiffs to confirm his (the rogue's) statements. Insofar as *Phillips v Brooks, Ltd* was concerned, the learned judge was of the view that in that case, the plaintiff had intended to deal with the rogue as a *customer only*, and that (see p 51):

> 'It [ie *Phillips v Brooks, Ltd*] is not an authority to establish that where an offer or acceptance is addressed to a person (although under a mistake as to his identity) who is present in person, then it must in all circumstances be treated as if actually addressed to him. I would regard the issue as a question of fact in each case depending on what was said and done and applying the elementary principles of offer and acceptance ...'

Pearce LJ drew a distinction between mere attributes on the one hand (which did not result in an operative mistake) and identity on the other (which did); in the learned judge's words (at p 56; cf also per Nicholas Browne-Wilkinson V-C in *Hector v Lyons*, quoted above, paragraph 11.41 and see below, paragraph 11.46):

> 'The real problem in the present case is whether the plaintiffs were in fact intending to deal with the person physically present and who had fraudulently endowed himself with the attributes of some other identity or whether they were intending only to deal with that other identity.'

Pearce LJ also expressed the view that *Phillips v Brooks, Ltd* was not an easy case to evaluate because the facts were far from clear, the contract having (possibly at least) been concluded *before* the representation by the rogue had been made. The learned judge thought that the case had, in any event, been decided on its own particular facts (see p 60 as well as the quotation from his judgment immediately following; cf also per Sellers LJ, above). Pearce LJ's own view was that (see pp 57 and 61):

> 'Yet clearly, though difficult, it is not impossible to rebut the *prima facie* presumption that the offer can be accepted by the person to whom it is physically addressed.
>
> ...
>
> Each case must be decided on its own facts. The question in such cases is this. Has it been sufficiently shown in the particular circumstances that, contrary to the *prima facie* presumption, a party was not contracting with the physical person to whom he uttered the offer, but with another individual whom (to the other party's knowledge) he believed to be the physical person present. The answer to that question is a finding of fact.'

11.44 Notwithstanding the reasoning of the court in *Ingram v Little*, it is suggested that it is very difficult to draw any meaningful distinction between *Phillips v Brooks, Ltd* on the one hand and *Ingram v Little* on the other in order that the cases (arriving as they did at different results) might possibly be reconciled. One also notes, in this regard, that recourse to the facts, in the final analysis, whilst not inaccurate, is not particularly helpful: not least because there is an at least implicit shift away from the search for *normative* standards. In a similar vein, there are no *other* real guidelines as to when the presumption that one intends to deal with the physical person present should be rebutted.

In addition, one should note a rather powerful dissenting judgment by Devlin LJ (as he then was) in *Ingram v Little* itself. The learned judge was of the view that the presumption mentioned above could *not* in fact be rebutted on the facts. Creditworthiness, although important in this case as well as other cases, was not (in his view) one that went to *identity*—it was 'not a basic fact; it is only a way of expressing the belief that each party normally holds that the other will honour his promise' (see p 69). In other words, creditworthiness was *too general* a quality—in and of itself—to go to identity. It is suggested, however, that the time may have arrived to review not only the distinction between identity and attributes but also the more specific role of creditworthiness itself (and see below, paragraph 11.46).

(d) The 'Infamous' Trilogy of Cases (3)—*Lewis v Averay*

11.45 The final decision in the trilogy of cases is that of (again) the English Court of Appeal in *Lewis v Averay* (1972). The *modus operandi* was, again, quite similar. As was the situation in *Ingram v Little*, the present case also concerned the sale of a car. The plaintiff had placed an advertisement in the newspaper with the intention of selling his car. The rogue responded, test drove the car, and also introduced himself as 'Richard Green' who was then a fairly famous actor. The rogue then wrote a cheque in payment for the car. When asked for proof of his identity, he showed the plaintiff *a special pass of admission to Pinewood Studios which not only bore the rogue's photograph but also had an official stamp*. The plaintiff duly accepted the rogue's cheque which was of course dishonoured. The rogue, in the meantime, took possession of the car and sold it on to the defendant who purchased the vehicle in good faith and without notice of the rogue's fraud.

Once again, we find the intervention of *third party rights* (here, the defendant's). Indeed, the plaintiff, not surprisingly, brought an action against the defendant for conversion of the car since the rogue had absconded and was nowhere to be found. In the circumstances, the plaintiff had no choice but to invoke the doctrine of mistaken identity in order that the title to the vehicle would remain in him, notwithstanding his contract with the rogue.

The court held that there had *not* been an operative mistake. Significantly, Lord Denning MR was of the view that the material facts in *Phillips v Brooks, Ltd* and *Ingram v Little* were 'quite indistinguishable the one from the other' (see p 206). More significantly, the learned Master of the Rolls was of the view that the distinction between a mistake as to the *identity* of a person and a mistake as to that same person's *attributes* was *too fine* a distinction to draw. Lord Denning then went *even further*, expressing the view that any operative mistake would *always* render the contract concerned *voidable*. However, it is submitted, with respect, that retaining the doctrine of mistaken identity at common law would furnish the courts with the necessary flexibility to do justice in egregious cases where third party rights are involved and where it is felt that the original owner's rights should prevail over the third party's rights. The common law doctrine, by rendering the contract concerned *void*, permits such flexibility (and see generally paragraphs 11.4–11.6, above). Lest, however, there be fears that third party rights would be unnecessarily displaced, it should be noted that the courts do apply the common law doctrine *very strictly*.

Phillimore LJ adopted a much more direct approach, simply applying *Phillips v Brooks, Ltd* to the facts of the present case and, of course, arriving at the same result (ie that there had been no operative mistake). In the learned judge's view (at p 208): 'I think this case really is on all fours with *Phillips v Brooks Ltd*, which has been good law for over 50 years.'

The remaining judge, Megaw LJ, found it difficult to understand the basis of the test laid down by the majority of the Court of Appeal in *Ingram v Little*. However, *unlike* Lord Denning (whose views we have briefly canvassed above), Megaw LJ was of the view that there was, in the present case, only a mistake as to the *attributes* of the rogue (viz creditworthiness), which was *insufficient* to constitute an operative mistake which would have rendered the contract void.

(e) Taking Stock—Confusion and Complexity

11.46 Taking brief stock of the 'infamous' trilogy of cases, it can immediately be seen how difficult it would be to attempt to reconcile the cases. Indeed, if one looks closely at all the facts in the three cases, it would appear that the *strongest* case for an operative mistake is the fact situation which existed in *Lewis v Averay* (see paragraph 11.45, above). *However*, as we have seen, the court in that particular case held that there had *not* been an operative mistake.

Matters are, it is suggested, further complicated by the fact that the court, in *Ingram v Little* (see paragraph 11.43, above), held that there *had* been an operative mistake, *notwithstanding* the fact that the material facts in the case itself were in no way stronger than those that existed in *Phillips v Brooks, Ltd* (see paragraph 11.42, above) and (*a fortiori*) *Lewis v Averay* (see paragraph 11.45, above). Indeed, as we have already seen, Lord Denning MR, in *Lewis v Averay*, was of the view that the facts in *Phillips v Brooks, Ltd* and *Ingram v Little* were virtually indistinguishable (and see paragraph 11.45, above).

It would appear, on balance, that the task facing a party seeking to argue that there has been an operative mistake is an extremely daunting one indeed. However, the latest case, *Shogun Finance Ltd v Hudson* (2002), to be discussed briefly in paragraph 11.47, below, throws at least some doubt on this proposition.

However, one issue that does merit a reconsideration centres on the distinction (already fairly firmly established in the case law, as we have seen) between identity and attributes. There is much to be said for Lord Denning's view (see above, paragraph 11.45) that this distinction was too fine. Indeed, a person is usually able to demonstrate his or her identity *by reference to his or her attributes—usually an amalgam of a number of attributes*. Looked at in this light, the distinction between identity and attributes is highly artificial and rather impractical. Professor Treitel does in fact suggest a closely related alternative: the *most important attribute*, having regard to the particular factual matrix concerned, should *go to identity* (see GH Treitel, *The Law of Contract* (10th ed, 1999), pp 277–278). It is true, however, that a certain amount of discretion would still need to be exercised by the courts and that the facts would (as is the case in all other areas of the law) still be very important (cf, though, the discussion in paragraph 11.44, above).

(f) Latest Development—*Shogun Finance Ltd v Hudson*

11.47 The most recent decision (at the time of writing) is that of the English Court of Appeal in *Shogun Finance Ltd v Hudson* (2002). The facts were very similar to those which we encountered in the 'infamous' trilogy of cases. In this case, a rogue obtained a motor vehicle fraudulently by signing a hire-purchase agreement with a forged signature. He then sold on the vehicle to the defendant, who purchased in good faith and without notice of the fraud. The rogue had in fact had his identity 'verified' by producing a genuine driving licence which he had procured unlawfully. The dealer's sales manager at the car showroom telephoned the rogue's details to the plaintiffs' sales support centre before faxing on a copy of both the licence and the draft agreement with the rogue's (forged) signature. The plaintiffs then made a computer search (including ascertaining the relevant credit rating). They also compared the signatures on the faxed documents and found them satisfactory. They then informed the dealer that the proposal had been accepted. After payment of a deposit, the dealer handed over the vehicle to the rogue who (as already mentioned) sold on the vehicle to the defendant. The rogue of course absconded and the plaintiff brought the present action against the defendant.

Constraints of space preclude an extensive discussion. It suffices for our present purposes to note that whilst Dyson LJ held that there had been an operative mistaken identity, Sedley LJ (whilst not differing from Dyson LJ insofar as the basic principles with respect to face-to-face transactions were concerned) was of the view that there had been no operative mistake. The third judge, Brooke LJ, was content to agree with Dyson LJ on the final result (in favour of the plaintiffs), but on another ground and hence did not consider the issue of mistaken identity. The views of Dyson LJ were interesting, not least because there is at least a suggestion that the artificial distinction between identity and attributes (see above, paragraph 11.46) has been undermined. The learned judge also evinced an ostensibly more liberal approach in locating an operative mistake on the facts. For further commentary on this particular decision, see A Phang, 'Mistake in Contract Law—Two Recent Cases' [2002] *Cambridge Law Journal* 272 at pp 273–276.

(3) *Non Face-to-Face or Non-*Inter Praesentes *Cases*

11.48 Compared to face-to-face situations (just discussed above), it appears relatively easier to plead successfully the doctrine of mistaken identity in non-face-to-face situations (ie where the contracting parties are not in physical contact with each other but, instead, contract at a distance).

11.49 Notwithstanding the relative liberality mentioned in the preceding paragraph, there must nevertheless be sufficient factual evidence of a mistake. The English decision of *Boulton v Jones* (1857) illustrates this point. In that case, the court did in fact hold that there had been an operative mistake inasmuch as it was proven to its satisfaction that the defendant had not intended to contract with the plaintiff but, rather, with the latter's *predecessor* (one Brocklehurst). In this regard, the *crucial evidence* consisted in the fact that the defendant had, in fact, a *set-off against Brocklehurst,* thus pointing clearly to the fact that the defendant had *intended to contract with Brocklehurst—and Brocklehurst only.* As Bramwell B observed (at p 566):

> 'If the plaintiff were now at liberty to sue the defendants, they would be deprived of their right of set-off as against Brocklehurst. When a contract is made, in which the personality of the contracting party is or may be of importance, as a contract with a man to write a book, or the like, or where there might be a set-off, no other person can interpose and adopt the contract.'

11.50 The leading decision under this particular category of mistaken identity is that of the House of Lords in *James Cundy & T Bevington v Thomas Lindsay* (1878), the facts of which were as follows.

The plaintiffs, manufacturers of goods, were based in Ireland. The rogue, on the other hand, one Alfred Blenkarn, wrote to the plaintiffs with an order. He gave his address as '37, Wood St, Cheapside' and signed his letters in such an ambiguous manner that they appeared to read as 'Blenkiron & Co'. Perhaps unsurprisingly, the plaintiffs were under the impression that the orders were from a respectable firm bearing the name of 'Blenkiron & Co' which was in fact an actual firm *operating from Wood St* (*albeit at number 123 instead of number 37*). The plaintiffs duly despatched the goods ordered to the rogue who, in turn, sold them on to the defendants who were entirely ignorant of the fraud perpetrated by the rogue. The main issue arose as to whether or not the plaintiffs could succeed on the basis that there had been an operative mistake in its transaction with the rogue, the defendants here being *third parties*. The House, accepting the plaintiff's argument, held in their favour. Lord Cairns LC observed thus (at pp 465–466):

> '[H]ow is it possible to imagine that in that state of things any contract could have arisen between the respondents [here, the plaintiffs] and *Blenkarn*, the dishonest man? Of him they knew nothing, and of him they never thought. With him they never intended to deal. Their minds never, even for an instant of time rested upon him, and as between him and them there was no *consensus* of mind which could lead to any agreement or any contract whatsoever. As between him and them there was merely the one side to a contract, where, in order to produce a contract, two sides would be required.'

The decision of the House can be supported on the special facts of the case itself. There did in point of fact exist a company called 'Blenkiron & Co' and that company did operate from the same street the rogue stated in his letters. Further, the rogue's signature conveyed the impression that the orders were indeed being placed by 'Blenkiron & Co'.

Interestingly, Lord Hatherley would have at least been prepared to have changed his mind had the rogue (Blenkarn) *personally* called at the firm: in which case it would have been a face-to-face situation. The learned Law Lord observed (at p 469) that 'the parting with the goods in that case [in a face-to-face transaction] might possibly—I say no more—have passed the property' (and on the principles relating to face-to-face transactions, see, generally, paragraphs 11.39–11.47, above).

11.51 More importantly, perhaps, the Singapore Court of Appeal decision of *Tribune Investment Trust Inc v Soosan Trading Co Ltd* (2000) may also be noted. In that case, the court, applying the principle in *Cundy v Lindsay* (discussed at paragraph 11.50, above), held that there had been no contract between the plaintiffs and the defendants and that whilst there might have been an intention on the part of the plaintiffs for the defendants to contract with them, in point of fact, the defendant's intention was (at all times) to contract with *yet another party only*. Yong Pung How CJ observed thus (at p 426):

> 'To summarise, the principle espoused in [*Cundy v Lindsay*] is

> simply that a person cannot make another a contracting party with himself, when he knows or ought to know that the other intends to contract not with him but with another. [W]hen an offer meant for A is purportedly accepted by B, any apparent contract formed is void and cannot confer rights on anyone.'

The approach adopted in the present case appears to support the argument (noted above in paragraph 11.2) to the effect that there is no real doctrine of common mistake as such and that everything turns, in the final analysis, on the issue of construction only. However, one might also usefully note (by way of contrast) the recent English Court of Appeal decision of *West Sussex Properties Ltd v Chichester District Council* (unreported judgment dated 28 June 2000) where the leading English Court of Appeal decision of *Solle v Butcher* (considered above at paragraph 11.17) was endorsed as good law, despite academic criticisms to the contrary (although see, more recently, paragraph 11.19, above). However, as already noted above (paragraph 11.2), the doctrine of mistake continues to remain alive and well (see also A Phang, 'Common Mistake in English Law: The Proposed Merger of Common Law and Equity' (1989) 9 *Legal Studies* 291 at pp 293–294 as well as paragraph 11.13, above).

11.52 It should, however, be noted that where a party enters into a contract with a *non-existent entity*, it will generally be held by the courts that that party has contracted with *the writer of the correspondence* and that there would therefore *not* be an operative mistake as such: see the oft-cited English decision of *King's Norton Metal Co (Ltd) v Edridge, Merrett, and Co (Ltd)* (1897).

Non Est Factum

11.53 This specific doctrine of mistake pertains to the situation where the contracting party seeking to set aside the contract pleads that his or her signature on the contractual document concerned is, in fact, not his or her signature inasmuch as his or her mental assent did not accompany the signature actually penned (hence, the Latin equivalent of the doctrine which forms the heading to this particular part).

11.54 The leading decision is that of the House of Lords in *Saunders v Anglia Building Society* (1971), where the House held that there must be 'a *radical difference*' between what the person signed and what he or she thought he or she was signing in order that the doctrine of *non est factum* could be invoked successfully. Indeed, the terms 'fundamental', 'serious' and 'very substantial' were also utilised by the House (see per Lord Reid at p 1017). Lord Hodson thought that the difference must 'be in a particular which goes to the substance of the whole consideration or to the root of the matter' (see p 1019).

Not surprisingly, the actual facts and circumstances of the case are of great importance. It should, however, be noted that the House *rejected* the former distinction drawn between the character of the document on the one hand and its contents on the other. Under the previous case law, it was thought that only a radical difference in the character of the document could result in a successful invocation of the doctrine of *non est factum*. Such an approach could lead to ludicrous results, and there was no logical reason why a radical difference with regard to the contents of the document could not also result in a successful invocation of the doctrine.

11.55 There is, however, a *second* requirement before the doctrine of *non est factum* can succeed. The party seeking to rely upon the doctrine must also prove that he or she *took care, ie was not negligent*. *However*, the negligence referred to here does *not* refer to the concept of negligence in its narrower (and more technical) *legal* sense (viz a duty of care).

11.56 It should be noted that the position in Singapore *vis-à-vis* the doctrine of *non est factum* is based on the *English* position as briefly set out above (and see, generally, A Phang, *Cheshire, Fifoot and Furmston's Law of Contract—Second Singapore and Malaysian Edition* (1998), pp 436–438).

Future Directions

11.57 With the advent of the new economy, various related issues arise for consideration. One interesting issue that arises is whether or not the provisions with respect to electronic as well as digital signatures in the Singapore Electronic Transactions Act (Cap 88, 1999 Rev Ed, and which is discussed generally in Chapter 2 above at paragraphs 2.48–2.53) either reduce or enlarge (or simply do not change) the scope for arguments centring on the doctrine of mistake, particularly that aspect of the doctrine pertaining to mistaken identity. As a tentative observation of sorts, it is suggested that a close perusal of the salient provisions does not (unfortunately) furnish us with a definitive answer and that, hence, more research as well as analysis are required. However, since the doctrine of mistake in all its various aspects operates within a very narrow compass in any event, the Act may not actually make a significant difference to the actual practical *outcomes* that would have obtained even prior to its enactment, although (and here the Act *does* have at least some relevance) many *potential* difficulties could perhaps be avoided by the increased utilisation of trusted third parties (such as certification authorities).

Another interesting issue which arises is whether if a particular contracting party has access to reliable information, it would then be difficult for him or her to argue that there has been an operative mistake entitling him or her to treat the contract concerned as being either void or voidable, as the case may be. More empirical research is necessary, as would also be the case for transactions in cyberspace that are not wholly impersonal but which are not, however, precisely the same as face-to-face transactions as such (these would include video-conferencing and link-ups).

There are also other issues, such as whether or not there ought to be legislative clarification on the issue of ascription of responsibility for actions of computer agents in the formation of electronic contracts and whether the substantive law of mistake should be modified in order to give greater allowance in electronic contracting for one party to either nullify or withdraw from the transaction concerned. See generally for these (as well as the issues briefly alluded to above), A Phang and TM Yeo, 'The Impact of Cyberspace on Contract Law' (presented at the Inaugural Symposium for the Technology Law Development Group of the Singapore Academy of Law on 5 April 2002, and since published in D Seng (ed), *The Impact of the Regulatory Framework on E-Commerce in Singapore* (2002), pp 39–58) at paragraphs 28–33.

CHAPTER 12 Misrepresentation

PARAGRAPHS

12.1–12.4 **Introduction**

Operative Misrepresentation

12.5 Elements of Misrepresentation

Statement of Fact

12.6 (1) Puff

12.7 (2) Opinions

12.8 (3) Intentions

12.9–12.10 (4) Law

Representation by Conduct

12.11 (1) Express Representations

12.12 (2) Conduct

12.13–12.17 (3) Silence

12.18 Ambiguity and Falsity

12.19 Materiality

12.20–12.21 Inducement

12.22–12.25 Addressed to the Other Party

Types of Misrepresentation

12.26 Introduction

12.27–12.29 Fraudulent Misrepresentation

Negligent Misrepresentation

12.30 (1) Negligence at Common Law

12.31 (2) Section 2(1) of the Misrepresentation Act

12.32 (3) Measure of Damages

12.33–12.34 (4) Burden of Proof

12.35 Innocent Misrepresentation

12.36–12.37 **Representation as a Term**

Rescission

12.38–12.40 General

12.41 (1) Restitution Impossible

12.42 (2) Affirmation

12.43 (3) Lapse of Time

12.44 (4) Third Party Rights

PARAGRAPHS

Rescission (continued)

Section 2(2) of the Misrepresentation Act

12.45 (1) General

12.46 (2) Types of Misrepresentation

12.47 (3) Where Right to Rescind is Lost

12.48–12.49 (4) Measure of Damages

12.50–12.54 **Exclusion of Liability**

12.55–12.56 **Conclusion**

Introduction

12.1 The aim of a business is to sell a product or a service and, sometimes, in a bid to secure a sale, much more is said than should have been said. If an untrue statement is part of the contract, the innocent party has his rights for breach of contract. But if the statement is not part of the contract, the innocent party may still have rights under the law of misrepresentation.

12.2 The law of misrepresentation is found in the common law, equity and statute. Originally, at common law, there was liability for misrepresentation only if the misrepresentation was fraudulent or formed part of the contract. Subsequently, after the House of Lords decision in *Hedley Byrne v Heller & Partners* (1964) (referred to at paragraph 12.30, below), there was also, possibly, liability for negligent misrepresentation. Non-contractual statements which were neither fraudulent nor negligent did not give rise to a claim for damages although the representee could seek, in equity, rescission and, possibly, an indemnity.

The UK Misrepresentation Act 1967 was made applicable by the Application of English Law Act (Cap 7A, 1994 Rev Ed). Under this Act, a representee could claim damages for negligent misrepresentation in the same way as he could claim had the representation been fraudulent (see below, paragraph 12.31). Compared to the common law claim under the *Hedley Byrne* case, this species of 'statutory negligence' is easier to mount as a cause of action.

12.3 It should be mentioned that the law of misrepresentation straddles the two broad areas of contract law and tort law. As such, in a situation of misrepresentation, the innocent party may have rights under both contract and tort. The concurrent existence of duties in contract and tort was recently confirmed by the House of Lords in *Henderson v Merrett Syndicates Ltd* (1995).

12.4 As a final introductory remark, it may be observed that misrepresentation sometimes overlaps with breach of contract. Indeed, where a representation is or becomes part of the contract, the innocent party may have remedies in both misrepresentation and breach, and section 1 of the Act makes it clear that a person is not to be deprived of the right to rescind for misrepresentation merely because the representation has become part of the contract.

In general, there are some broad similarities between the liabilities and remedies for misrepresentation and those for breach. For example, in each area, the innocent party generally has remedies of termination and damages. However, as one goes into the details, there are significant differences between these two areas of law.

Operative Misrepresentation

Elements of Misrepresentation

12.5 A misrepresentation is a false statement of fact made by one party to the other party which induced the other party to enter into the contract. The statement must be one of a past or an existing fact, not a commendatory puff, an opinion, a statement of intention, or a statement of law.

It has been said that a statement will be treated as true if it is substantially correct and the difference would not have induced a reasonable person to enter into the contract (per Rix J in the English decision of *Avon Insurance v Swire Fraser* (2000)).

Statement of Fact

(1) *Puffs*

12.6 It is usual for salespersons to use glowing terms to describe their product, such as 'best value money can buy', 'excellent product' or 'very fast car'. In general, such commendatory expressions or puffs are harmless and are regarded as mere sales talk, to which the law attaches no legal liability. However, as the statements get more detailed or precise, they are more likely to be representations, for example, going beyond saying a car is fast to asserting that it has a top speed of 200 kmh.

(2) *Opinions*

12.7 In general, a statement of opinion which turns out to be unfounded does not give rise to liability. But there are exceptions. First, a statement of opinion can be a statement of fact in that the representor impliedly stated that he held the opinion. If he did not hold the opinion or could not, as a reasonable man having his knowledge, honestly have held it, there would be a misrepresentation. The misrepresentation here would be one concerning his state of mind, and it has been said that the state of a person's mind is 'as much a fact as the state of his digestion' (per Bowen LJ in *Edgington v Fitzmaurice* (1885)).

Likewise, a statement of another person's opinion involves an assertion that the latter holds that opinion. Secondly, a statement of opinion may carry with it the implication that the representor had an objectively reasonable basis for his opinion, for example, that he had the handbook which contained the information.

(3) *Intentions*

12.8 A statement of intention is an expression as to the future and does not involve any past or existing fact. However, as with opinions, if the intention was not so held, there would be a false statement of fact. Likewise also, a person who states his intention to do something may be impliedly asserting that he has reasonable grounds for thinking that he has the capacity to do it.

(4) *Law*

12.9 The traditional view is that a statement of law cannot be a misrepresentation. As with opinions and intentions, a statement of law can be a misrepresentation if the representor did not hold that opinion or belief of the law, or if the statement carries an implication of fact which is untrue. Where the statement involves both fact and law, the tendency of the courts is to regard it as a statement of fact.

12.10 Recently, the House of Lords in *Kleinwort Benson v Glasgow City Council (No 2)* (1997) allowed a restitutionary claim for money paid under a mistake of law, jettisoning the traditional distinction between payments made under a mistake of fact and those made under a mistake of law. One can expect that in the near future, the distinction will also be abandoned as regards misrepresentation.

Representation by Conduct

(1) *Express Representations*

12.11 The most obvious form of express representation is the spoken or written word. But expression can also be through a picture, a photograph, a drawing, a chart or any other visual media.

(2) *Conduct*

12.12 Representation can also be through a person's conduct. For example, a person who sits down in a restaurant and orders a meal impliedly represents that he has the ability to pay for the meal. Likewise, a nod of the head may signify agreement, just as a shake of the head may show disapproval. So long as it is intended to induce the other party to believe in a certain state of facts, the gesture or conduct can amount to a representation (see *Walters v Morgan* (1861)).

In the situations just discussed, the conduct is intended to convey a certain message. Sometimes, the conduct may be intended to conceal certain facts. A very simple example is where a fruit seller deliberately sticks the label on the part of the fruit that is damaged. In principle, such conduct would also amount to a representation. In the case of the fruit seller, the implied representation is that the fruit is undamaged.

(3) *Silence*

12.13 The general rule is that silence in itself does not amount to a representation; some active conduct is required. Under general contract law, one party does not have a duty to disclose to the other party material facts which the former knows may influence the latter's decision whether or not to enter into the contract. This rule is subject to several exceptions.

12.14 The first is where the silence makes what has been said a half-truth or an untruth. For example, to say that a pop group currently comprises five named individuals without going on to say that one of them will be leaving, is a misrepresentation (see *Spice Girls v Aprilia World Service*

(2002)). While a contracting party has no duty to make statements, once he begins, he must make full and frank disclosure.

12.15 Secondly, where a statement (which the representor knows is false) is made by the representee or by a third party to the representee while the representor listens in silence, his reticence may amount to tacit confirmation of the truth of the statement (see *Pilmore v Hood* (1838)). By keeping silent, he is impliedly representing that the statement is true.

12.16 The law regards a representation as having a continuing effect until the contract is concluded. For this reason, if a statement which is true when made to the representor's knowledge ceases to be true before the contract is concluded, the representor is required to inform the representee of the change in circumstances. The representor has a duty to ensure that his representation remains true up to the time of the contract (see, eg *With v O'Flanagan* (1936) and *Spice Girls v Aprilia World Service* (2002)).

12.17 Finally, in certain contracts, the law imposes a duty of utmost good faith. The prime example of this is the insurance contract, where the law imposes on the proposed insured the duty to disclose to the insurer all material facts that may influence the insurer's decision whether or not to insure. Such non-disclosure entitles the insurer to avoid the contract of insurance. The rationale for this is that often the special facts and risks are known to the insured but not the insurer.

Ambiguity and Falsity

12.18 Sometimes, a statement may be ambiguous and may bear two (or more) meanings, one of which is true and the other false. Whether such a statement by a contracting party amounts to a misrepresentation depends on two things. First, the representee must prove that he understood the statement in the sense which is in fact false. Secondly, the representor must have intended the statement to be understood in the sense that is false; he is not liable if he honestly intended it in the sense that is true. This is so even if the sense in which the representee understood the statement is the one which, on its true construction, it ought to bear (see *Akerhielm v De Mare* (1959)).

It would appear from the treatment of commentators (see, eg J Cartwright, *Misrepresentation*, Sweet & Maxwell (2002) at paragraph 4.18) that ambiguous statements can amount to fraudulent misrepresentation but not negligent or innocent misrepresentation. The logicality of such dichotomy is not so evident. The representor's intention is relevant for determining the type of misrepresentation: fraudulent, negligent or innocent; whether or not there is falsity (as opposed to culpability) should be an objective matter. Also, from the point of policy, it may not be unjust that the maker of statements be given the major share of responsibility, especially when one bears in mind the general position that there is no need for a contracting party to disclose any material facts.

Materiality

12.19 There is doubt whether the law requires a misrepresentation to be material, in the sense that a reasonable man would have been influenced by it to enter into the contract. Is there misrepresentation if the representee was induced by a misstatement which a reasonable man would have ignored? While there are some judicial statements which support a requirement of materiality, the position is not settled. Certainly, a representee who is induced by an immaterial misrepresentation will have difficulty persuading the court that he was so induced. But it is another matter to deny a representee who was truly induced by the misrepresentation. Commentators are divided on this issue. Treitel, in *The Law of Contract* (10th ed, 1999), pp 311–312, confidently asserts that materiality is a requirement and, in this writer's view, argues his case convincingly. For an alternative viewpoint, see, eg *Chitty on Contracts*, Vol 1 (28th ed, 1999) at paragraph 6-040.

Inducement

12.20 In order for a misrepresentation to be operative, it must induce the representee to enter into the contract. Stated another way, the representee must have relied on the representation. This requirement is an obvious and logical one. There are several scenarios where the representee is not induced by the false statement. The first is where he was not even aware of the representation. Secondly, the representee may have been aware of the representation but knew it was untrue or did not believe it to be true. The third situation is that he simply was not influenced by it, as where he would have entered into the contract even if he had known the true facts. In all these situations, there is no inducement and therefore no operative misrepresentation.

The misrepresentation need not be the sole cause that induced the representee to enter into the contract. It is sufficient that, in deciding whether to enter into the contract, he was materially influenced by the misrepresentation, as where the representee was induced by a misrepresentation as well as by his own mistaken belief (see *Edgington v Fitzmaurice* (1885), followed by the Singapore Court of Appeal in *Panatron v Lee Cheow Lee* (2001)).

12.21 Sometimes, the representee has the opportunity to verify or ascertain the truth for himself. Generally, the fact that a representee had the opportunity to discover the truth but did not use the opportunity does not disentitle him from relief (*Redgrave v Hurd* (1881)). But where it is reasonable to expect the representee to avail himself of the opportunity to discover the truth, the legal position is less clear. In *Panatron v Lee Cheow Lee* (2001), Yong CJ held that once inducement is proved, it is no defence that the representee failed to take the steps which a prudent man would have taken to verify the truth. One should note, however, that the case concerned fraudulent misrepresentation, and one is inclined to agree with Treitel's suggestion (*The Law of Contract* (10th ed, 1999) at p 314) that the representee's failure to take reasonable steps to verify should be a defence for the representor if the misrepresentation is negligent or innocent but not if it is fraudulent. Also, if the representee conducted his own investigations and did not rely on the representor's representation at all, there would be no liability (see, eg *Attwood v Small* (1838)).

Addressed to the Other Party

12.22 Generally speaking, it is the direct addressee or recipient of a representation who may bring an action for misrepresentation. It should be noted that a direct recipient can be a person who is a member of a class of persons to whom the representation is addressed, such as through a media announcement. There are situations, however, where one who is not a direct recipient may have recourse.

12.23 The first is where the representation was made to the representee's authorised agent. Here, there are two possible scenarios. In the first scenario, the recipient, to the representor's knowledge, is only an agent for passing on the representation to his principal. In the second, the representor intends that both the agent and principal will be influenced by the representation, as in the case of partners of a firm. In the first, the principal is the representee, while in the latter, both the principal and the agent are representees.

12.24 The second situation is where, even though there is no agency between the direct recipient and the indirect recipient, the representor intended or reasonably expected the representation to be passed on to the indirect recipient. Thus, where A by a misrepresentation induces B to buy an item and B later induces C by a similar misrepresentation to buy it from B, C could rely on the misrepresentation as against A if A knew that B intended to resell and was likely to repeat the misrepresentation (see *Gross v Lewis Hillman* (1970)).

12.25 It should be noted that an indirect misrepresentation arises either through agency or through the intention or knowledge of the representor. In the past decade and a half, there has been, in the context of guarantees and mortgages by spouses, substantial development on the issue of the extent of a bank's liability for misrepresentation (and other misconduct) of the principal debtor. In essence, the position is that the bank is affected by the principal debtor's misrepresentation to the guarantor if either the principal debtor may be regarded as the bank's agent or the bank had constructive notice of the misrepresentation. For the detailed rules as to when a bank would be put on inquiry and the reasonable steps it would then have to take, see the recent House of Lords decision in *Royal Bank of Scotland v Etridge (No 2)* (2001), as well as (generally) paragraph 13.36 ff, below.

Types of Misrepresentation

Introduction

12.26 As mentioned above, it is now clear that there can be three types of misrepresentation and that they are, on a scale of diminishing culpability, fraudulent misrepresentation, negligent misrepresentation and innocent misrepresentation. Broadly speaking, the remedies of rescission and damages are available for all three. As we shall see, however, there are differences in the respective legal positions insofar as the recovery of damages is concerned.

Fraudulent Misrepresentation

12.27 At common law, fraud is defined quite narrowly, as a charge of fraud 'is such a terrible thing as to bring against a man that it cannot be maintained unless it is shown that he had a wicked mind' (per Lord Esher in *Le Lievre v Gould* (1893) at p 498). In *Derry v Peek* (1889), the House of Lords held that a fraudulent statement is one made knowingly, without belief of its truth, or recklessly—not caring whether it is true or false. A person who deliberately shuts his eyes to the facts or purposely abstains from investing the facts does not have an honest belief in its truth. Where there has been a fraudulent misrepresentation, the representee may recover damages in an action under the tort of deceit. Damages are awarded to compensate the representee for all the losses which can properly be said to have been caused by his reliance on the fraudulent misrepresentation (as contrasted with the contract measure of expectation loss): see the House of Lords decision in *Smith New Court Securities v Scrimgeor Vickers (Asset Management)* (1997). Further, in such an action, contributory negligence is not a defence (see *Standard Chartered Bank v Pakistan National Shipping* (2000)).

12.28 The motive of the representor is irrelevant. It is not necessary that he had a bad motive or intended to cause loss to the representee; it suffices that the false statement was made knowingly with the intention that the representee should act upon it (see *Standard Chartered Bank v Pakistan National Shipping (No 2)* (2000)). It is also immaterial that the representor thought the statement irrelevant or unimportant.

12.29 Where the responsibility for a statement is shared between a principal and an agent, or between two agents, the position is more complex. If an agent knowingly makes a false statement within the scope of his authority, the principal is liable for fraudulent misrepresentation; likewise, if an agent knowingly makes a false statement to another agent intending that agent to pass the statement on to a third party.

If the agent makes a statement which he honestly believes is true but which the principal knows is untrue, then the position depends on the culpability of the principal. If the principal was aware that the statement will be or had been made and did not intervene, the principal is liable for fraudulent misrepresentation. If he was not aware that the statement will be or had been made, he is not liable (see *Armstrong v Strain* (1952)).

Negligent Misrepresentation

(1) *Negligence at Common Law*

12.30 A negligent misrepresentation is one which is made carelessly, or without reasonable grounds for believing it to be true. Prior to and apart from the Misrepresentation Act, a misrepresentation would not be considered negligent unless the representor owed a duty of care to the representee. A 'special relationship' must have existed between the parties before such duty of care can arise (*Hedley Byrne v Heller & Partners* (1964)). The law on negligent misstatements was further developed and qualified by subsequent cases (see, generally, paragraph 19.35 ff, below). So far as negligent misrepresentation is concerned, the importance of these refinements is largely eclipsed by the Misrepresentation Act.

(2) *Section 2(1) of the Misrepresentation Act*

12.31 Section 2(1) of the Misrepresentation Act (Cap 390, 1994 Rev Ed) provides as follows:

> 'Where a person has entered into a contract after a misrepresentation has been made to him by another party thereto and as a result thereof he suffered loss, then, if the person making the misrepresentation would be liable to damages in respect thereof had the misrepresentation been made fraudulently, that person shall be so liable notwithstanding that the misrepresentation was not made fraudulently, unless he proves that he had reasonable ground to believe and did believe up to the time the contract was made that the facts represented were true.'

The uninitiated reader may find the above paragraph at best awkward and at worst incomprehensible. Adopting what has been termed a 'fiction of fraud', the provision first says indirectly that a non-fraudulent misrepresentation has the same liability as a fraudulent misrepresentation. It then gives the qualification that the representee will not be liable if he proves that he had reasonable grounds to believe that his statement was true. In effect, what the section does is to provide that a negligent misrepresentation (that is, one where the representee does not have reasonable grounds to believe his statement is true) attracts the same liability as a fraudulent misrepresentation.

(3) *Measure of Damages*

12.32 There is much debate as to the correct basis for measuring damages for negligent misrepresentation. One view is that the contract measure—to put the representee into the position he would have been had the representation been true—should apply. Another view is that the tort measure is the appropriate one. In tort, the claimant is to be put in a position he would have been if the tort (the misrepresentation) had not been committed. If the tort measure is the correct one, there is a further complication: Should the deceit (fraud) measure or the negligence measure be applied? In cases of fraud, losses may be recoverable even though they were not of a foreseeable kind; this is not the case for negligence. There are no easy answers to this problem. For further discussion of these issues, see A Phang, *Cheshire, Fifoot & Furmston's Law of Contract* (Second Singapore and Malaysian Edition, 1998) at pp 488–489 and *Chitty on Contracts*, Vol 1 (28th ed, 1999) at paragraphs 6-069–6-071.

(4) *Burden of Proof*

12.33 At common law, a representee who alleges fraudulent misrepresentation bears the burden of proving fraud and the onus is a heavy one. Upon reading section 2(1), it is clear that for negligent misrepresentation, the burden is reversed. Once the representee proves that the statement was false, the burden shifts to the representor to prove that he had reasonable grounds to believe that the statement was true. In effect, the representor has to show that his misrepresentation was not negligently made. In this respect, negligent misrepresentation is a more favourable option for the representee than fraudulent misrepresentation.

12.34 Although the use of the words 'reasonable grounds' may give rise to the argument that negligent misrepresentation, like negligent misstatement at common law, requires the representee to establish a duty of care and a special relationship, it is clear from the cases that this is not so (see *Howard Marine & Dredging v Ogden & Sons (Excavations)* (1978); *Ng Buay Hock v Tan Keng Huat* (1997)). On the contrary, it is the representor's responsibility to show that he was not 'negligent'. In similar vein, a representee's claim for damages for negligent misrepresentation in principle would not be reduced by the representor's allegation that the representee was contributorily negligent (see *Chitty on Contracts*, Vol 1 (28th ed, 1999) at paragraph 6-074).

Innocent Misrepresentation

12.35 The least culpable type of misrepresentation is innocent misrepresentation. Here, the false statement is made honestly and with care. The common law provided no remedies for an innocent misrepresentation but, in equity, the representee is entitled to rescission and, possibly, an indemnity. The latter remedy allows the representee to be indemnified against all obligations necessarily created by the contract (see *Whittington v Seal-Hayne* (1900)).

Representation as a Term

12.36 A representation is a statement made before or at the time of the contract and which induced the representee to enter into the contract. It is conceivable, perhaps even likely, that such a statement could be a term of the contract. There are several guidelines for determining whether a pre-contractual statement is a term. For one, the statement is unlikely to be a term if the representor asks the representee to verify its truth (*Ecay* *v Godfrey* (1947)). Another consideration is the relative abilities of the parties: if the representee is in a better position, for instance through special knowledge or experience, to ascertain the truth, the representation is unlikely to be a term (*Oscar Chess Ltd v Williams* (1957)). Finally, the importance of the statement is relevant. If the statement is so important that the representee would not have entered into the contract had the statement not been made, the statement is likely to be a term of the contract (*Bannerman v White* (1861)).

12.37 A representation may, however, be precluded from being a term of contract by the parol evidence rule (see paragraph 5.6 ff, above). The rule basically says that where a contract is in writing, extrinsic (including oral) evidence cannot be used to add to, vary or contradict the terms of the written agreement. An exception to this is the collateral contract. The argument here is that there are two agreements: the main (written) agreement and the collateral oral contract. A representation may amount to a collateral contract upon which the representee may bring an action.

Rescission

General

12.38 An operative misrepresentation makes the contract voidable at the option of the representee. The representee is entitled to rescind the contract, that is, to terminate it *ab initio*—from the beginning, as if the contract never existed. In contrast, where a contract is rescinded for a breach of contract, the contract is terminated as regards the future; while the parties are released from obligations that have not fallen due, they are still liable for obligations which had accrued before the repudiation.

12.39 The right to rescind for a misrepresentation is one which existed prior to the Misrepresentation Act. At common law, a representee had a right to rescind for fraudulent misrepresentation while, in equity, rescission was available for innocent misrepresentation and, presumably, negligent misrepresentation. With section 2(1) of the Act, it is now certain that rescission is available for negligent misrepresentation. However, with regard to negligent and innocent misrepresentation, the right to rescind is subject to the court's discretion to award damages in lieu of rescission under section 2(2) (see paragraph 12.45, below).

12.40 As the effect of rescission can be quite severe for the representor or for third parties, the law puts some bars or restrictions on its availability. These are: where restitution is impossible, where there has been affirmation or lapse of time, where third party rights are affected, and the court's statutory discretion to give damages in lieu of rescission.

(1) *Restitution Impossible*

12.41 Rescission contemplates the representee terminating the contract and returning what he received under the contract. For example, a buyer who wishes to rescind for misrepresentation and recover his purchase money must return the goods to the seller. If such restoration or restitution is not possible, it make sense that rescission should not be permitted. However, what is required is not precise restitution but substantial restitution; equity allows a representee to rescind if he returns the subject matter in its altered state and makes an allowance for any diminution in its value or accounts for any benefit he derived from using it. Equity seeks to make such adjustments as are necessary to do practical justice as between the parties.

Where substantial restitution is not possible, the representee is not barred from rescinding if the diminution is due either to the very defect in the subject matter which it was represented not to have or to external causes, such as damage caused by a third party.

(2) *Affirmation*

12.42 Upon discovery of the misrepresentation, the representor may choose either to affirm or to rescind the contract. Upon affirmation, the right to rescission is lost. Affirmation can be express or implied by conduct. An example of the latter is where the representor uses the goods after knowing of the misrepresentation. Without knowledge of the untruth of the representation, there can be no affirmation.

(3) *Lapse of Time*

12.43 If, subsequent to the discovery of the truth, a reasonable period of time has passed and the representee still does not exercise his right to rescind, his inaction may be evidence of affirmation. Apparently, for innocent and, it would appear, negligent misrepresentation, the lapse of reasonable time may be a bar to rescission even if the representee had not discovered the truth (see *Leaf v International Galleries* (1950)). Such a position is somewhat disconcerting since there can be no affirmation without knowledge of the untruth. So far as fraudulent misrepresentation is concerned, lapse of time without discovery of the truth would not prevent a representee from rescinding.

(4) *Third Party Rights*

12.44 Misrepresentation makes a contract voidable, not void. If before a representee avoids (rescinds) a contract, an innocent third party (that is, one who acts in good faith and gave consideration) has acquired an interest in the subject matter, the right to rescission is lost.

Section 2(2) of the Misrepresentation Act

(1) *General*

12.45 Section 2(2) provides as follows:

> 'Where a person has entered into a contract after a misrepresentation has been made to him otherwise than fraudulently, and he would be entitled, by reason of the misrepresentation, to rescind the contract, then, if it is claimed… that the contract ought to be or has been rescinded, the court… may declare the contract

> subsisting and award damages in lieu of rescission, if of opinion that it would be equitable to do so, having regard to the nature of the misrepresentation and the loss that would be caused by it if the contract were upheld, as well as to the loss that rescission would cause to the other party.'

Essentially, the provision fetters the representor's right to rescission for negligent and innocent misrepresentation. It gives the court the discretion to declare that the contract subsists and to award damages in place of rescission. In deciding the amount of damages, it gives regard to the nature of the contract, the loss that upholding the contract would cause as well as the loss that rescission would cause.

(2) *Types of Misrepresentation*

12.46 The subsection does not apply to fraudulent misrepresentation; the representee's right at common law to rescission and to damages are unaffected. As for negligent misrepresentation, the representee's right to rescission and damages is affected in that the right to rescission is now subject to the court's power to give damages instead. Technically speaking, the representee to a negligent misrepresentation may get two sets of damages: he may claim damages as of right (under section 2(1)) and may also be awarded damages in lieu of rescission (section 2(2)). As for innocent misrepresentation, the representee's rights in equity to rescission and indemnity are now qualified by the court's power to award damages in lieu of rescission.

(3) *Where Right to Rescind is Lost*

12.47 There is substantial controversy as to whether section 2(2) allows a court to award damages in lieu where the representee had lost the right to rescind. For example, he may have affirmed the contract or third party rights may have intervened. A purely linguistic interpretation suggests that the entitlement to rescind must still be available in order for damages to be given in lieu (see *Government of Zanzibar v British Aerospace (Lancaster House)* (2000)).

(4) *Measure of Damages*

12.48 There is uncertainty as to how damages under section 2(2) are to be assessed. Two possibilities are the tortious measure and the contractual measure, respectively. The tortious measure seems inappropriate for innocent misrepresentation since no tort has been committed. For negligent misrepresentation, the further complication is whether the tortious measure, assuming it is to apply, is the fraud measure or the negligence measure (and see paragraph 12.32, above).

12.49 Section 2(3) goes on to provide that damages may be awarded under subsection (2) whether or not the representor is liable to damages under subsection (1), and that any damages awarded under subsection (2) will be taken into account in assessing the damages under subsection (1).

Exclusion of Liability

12.50 Contracting parties sometimes seek to exclude the consequences of misrepresentation by inserting a clause to that effect in the contract. At common law, apart from where the representor is fraudulent, such a clause is valid and is subject to the normal rules of construction applicable to exclusion clauses. This freedom to include exclusion clauses is now circumscribed by statute.

12.51 Section 3 of the Misrepresentation Act, as amended by section 8 of the Unfair Contract Terms Act, reads:

> 'If a contract contains a term which would exclude or restrict (a) any liability to which a party to a contract may be subject by reason of any misrepresentation made by him before the contract was made; or (b) any remedy available to another party to the contract by reason of such a misrepresentation, that term shall be of no effect except in so far as it satisfies the requirement of reasonableness as stated in section 11(1) of the Unfair Contract Terms Act, and it is for those claiming that the term satisfies that requirement to show that it does.'

In essence, the provision invalidates exclusion clauses that exclude or restrict any liability or remedy for misrepresentation unless they are reasonable. It should be noted that the burden of proving that an exclusion clause is reasonable lies with the party seeking to rely on it.

12.52 For exclusion clauses in general, a distinction can be drawn between clauses which exclude liability and those which seek to prevent liability from arising by negativing one or more of the elements of liability; with the former attracting the operation of the UCTA provision but not the latter. As regards misrepresentation, examples of the former would include one which expressly seeks to exclude liability, such as 'All liabilities for and all remedies in respect of any misrepresentations made are excluded' and one which states that the contract is not cancellable or voidable by either party. It should be noted that clauses which seek to limit rather than altogether exclude liability, for example, by limiting liability to a certain sum of money, are viewed less stringently by the courts (*Ailsa Craig Fishing v Malvern Fishing* (1983)). On exclusion clauses generally, see Chapter 6.

12.53 *Overbrooke Estate v Glencombe Properties* (1974) provides a good example of a clause which seeks to prevent misrepresentation liability from arising. In that case, the defendants were successful bidders for a property. A few days before the auction, they made enquiries with the auctioneers and received inaccurate answers. The terms of the sale included a clause which stated that 'neither the auctioneers nor any person in the employment of the auctioneers has any authority to make or give any representation or warranty'. The court held that the provision was not an exclusion clause but a limitation on the apparent authority of the auctioneers.

Other clauses which seek to negative the elements of misrepresentation include clauses stating that no representation has been made or that neither party has relied on any representation. The general approach of the law is that if the clause is genuine, that is, that there really had been no representation, or no reliance, or no authority (as the case may be), then the clause is effective to prevent misrepresentation liability from arising (see, eg *Government of Zanzibar v British Aerospace (Lancaster House)* (2000)). The clause should not avail, for example, where the party seeking to rely on the clause is well aware that representations have in fact been made (see *Cremdean Properties Ltd v Nash* (1977)).

12.54 In deciding whether a clause excluding liability for misrepresentation is reasonable, a relevant factor is the relative knowledge or access to knowledge of the parties (see *South Western General Property v Marton* (1982)). If, for example, the facts on which the representation was based were only within the knowledge of the representor, the clause is likely to be unreasonable. The guidelines set out in Second Schedule of the UCTA, such as the relative bargaining power, are also generally applicable (see, generally, paragraph 6.51 ff).

Conclusion

12.55 The law of misrepresentation performs the important function of providing rights and remedies against false statements in the contractual context, especially if these statements do not find their way into the written agreement. The elements of an operative misrepresentation are clear enough, apart from the nagging doubt regarding materiality. Although misrepresentation provides a drastic remedy in the form of rescission, its availability is moderated by sensible restrictions. This is especially the case for negligent and innocent misrepresentation, where the court has discretion to award remedies in lieu of rescission. The protection which the law of misrepresentation provides is further safeguarded by the legislative requirement that any attempt to exclude or restrict liability for misrepresentation must be reasonable to be valid.

12.56 Fundamental to understanding the law of misrepresentation is an appreciation of the Misrepresentation Act provisions—what they mean to say and how they modify the previous position. The manner by which negligent misrepresentation is established as a recognised concept is unfortunate. Indeed, the indirect approach of using the 'fiction of fraud' results in confusion and several legal issues still remain debatable and speculative. However, taking a holistic view of the subject, one may conclude that the law of misrepresentation does provide a reasonably satisfactory regime for ensuring accountability for the making of pre-contractual statements.

CHAPTER 13

Economic Duress, Undue Influence and Unconscionability

PARAGRAPHS	
13.1–13.3	**Introduction**
	Economic Duress
13.4–13.10	Introduction and Possible Conceptual Difficulties
13.11–13.18	General Principles
13.19–13.20	Position in Singapore
13.21–13.22	Relationship Between Economic Duress and Consideration and the Future of Economic Duress
	Undue Influence
13.23–13.24	Introduction
13.25	Categories of Undue Influence and General Principles Arising Therefrom
13.26	(1) Class 1 Undue Influence
13.27	(2) Class 2 Undue Influence
13.28	(a) Class 2A Undue Influence
13.29	(b) Class 2B Undue Influence
13.30	(3) Independent Advice as a Factor
13.31	(4) Requirement of Manifest Disadvantage
13.32	(5) Requirement of Manifest Disadvantage Abrogated for Class 1 Undue Influence and Its Continued Weakening Under Class 2 Undue Influence
13.33–13.35	(6) Requirement of Manifest Disadvantage—An Historical Error
13.36–13.40	Undue Influence, Creditors and Doctrine of 'Infection'
	Position in Singapore
13.41	(1) Introduction
13.42	(2) Demise of Manifest Disadvantage in the Singapore Context?
	Unconscionability
13.43	Introduction
13.44–13.48	General Principles
13.49–13.50	Position in Singapore

PARAGRAPHS

Linkages Amongst Economic Duress, Undue Influence and Unconscionability—A New Umbrella Doctrine of Unconscionability?

13.51 Introduction

Linkages Amongst the Categories of Undue Influence

13.52 (1) Class 1 and Class 2 Undue Influence

13.53 (2) Class 2A Undue Influence

13.54 Linkage Between Undue Influence and Economic Duress

13.55 Linkage Between Undue Influence and Unconscionability

13.56 Linkage Between Economic Duress and Unconscionability

13.57–13.59 A Broader Umbrella Doctrine of Unconscionability?

Introduction

13.1 'A person's word is his or her bond.' This popular saying is enshrined—in the legal sphere—in the related ideas of freedom as well as sanctity of contract. In other words, the law states that parties who enter into contracts must honour them and that any attempt to play fast and loose with contractual obligations will be sanctioned by the courts—principally by the award of damages against the party in breach (on damages and other remedies, see Chapters 15 and 16).

Indeed, in a business or commercial context, the ideas just mentioned are even more important. Whatever the actual reality (which will differ from situation to situation), the established perception is that *certainty* is imperative to the smooth and efficient conduct of business. In fact, the essence of business centres around risk-taking and if contracting parties were allowed to throw out contracts whenever they were making losses, chaos and uncertainty would result; more importantly, the very essence of transacting (particularly in the business or commercial context) would be wholly undermined.

13.2 Notwithstanding the need for certainty in the business or commercial context, one has to bear in mind a number of other factors as well. Many contracts, for example, are entered into by parties that do not (primarily, at least) seek to make a profit. On the other hand, there are many transactions where one of the contracting parties is of unequal strength compared to the other party. In such situations, the party with the stronger bargaining power might exploit the weaker party. It is at this point that many difficult issues arise, the foremost of which is how the courts are to *balance* the need to allow commercial exploitation on the one hand (in order to maximise profits, which is the *raison d'etre* of doing business) as well as the need to ensure that illegitimate advantage of the weaker party is not taken on the other. This is, in fact, one of the key policy issues in the law relating to economic duress. This more general issue of *line-drawing* is also a central issue with regard to the other two doctrines considered in this chapter, viz undue influence and unconscionability, respectively. Indeed, all three doctrines are, as we shall see, closely related (see generally paragraphs 13.51–13.59, below). Put somewhat simplistically and crudely, there is a *constant tension* between certainty on the one hand and fairness on the other.

13.3 The doctrines considered in the present chapter address precisely those situations where the law deems contracting parties to have 'crossed the line', where, in other words, the exploitation of the other party is no longer viewed as legitimate. However, the very ideas of freedom as well as sanctity of contract mean that such doctrines must be utilised by the courts *sparingly*. To allow an overly liberal application of these doctrines would result in the very unravelling of contracts (with the related consequences of both chaos and uncertainty) that is to be avoided in the first place.

Unfortunately, the line facing the court is a very fine one and the specific facts of the situation concerned become crucial determinants in the overall decision-making process of the court itself. However, it would be highly unsatisfactory if one were to argue that legal rules and principles are really immaterial and that it all depends on the facts of the particular case concerned. This would be the very abandonment of the law itself and signal a descent into arbitrariness that the law is intended to prevent. It is suggested that the difficulty in applying these doctrines occurs precisely because they concern (if successfully invoked) that 'messier' (albeit no less important) sphere of fairness. Indeed, it may be argued that there are in fact competing conceptions of fairness since certainty (the other competing desideratum) is also (as we have seen) a value, particularly in the business or commercial context. On occasion, however, it *is* necessary—even at the expense of unravelling a contract otherwise validly formed—to ensure that a contracting party is not unfairly exploited: hence, the importance of the three doctrines considered in the present chapter.

Economic Duress

Introduction and Possible Conceptual Difficulties

13.4 This part deals with *economic* duress. Not surprisingly, therefore, this particular doctrine is of recent origin. The older law relating to duress was much narrower, being confined (as it was) to duress to the physical person and (to an even more limited extent) that of duress to goods (see, generally, MP Furmston, *Cheshire, Fifoot and Furmston's Law of Contract* (14th ed, 2001) at pp 337–338).

13.5 The doctrine of economic duress proper may be traced to the relatively recent decision of *Occidental Worldwide Investment Corp v Skibs A/S Avainti, Skibs A/S Glarona, Skibs A/S Navalis (The 'Siboen' and the 'Sibotre')* (1976). In that case, Kerr J (as he then was) delivered a seminal formulation of the doctrine, holding that in order for the doctrine of economic duress to be pleaded successfully, there must be coercion of the will that vitiates consent. This has come popularly to be known as the 'overborne will theory'. However, this particular theory has generated considerable controversy.

13.6 The principal critic of the 'overborne will theory' has been Professor Patrick Atiyah, who views this theory as being misleading inasmuch as it suggests that the party who is allegedly the victim of economic duress did not know what he or she was doing, ie was acting as if he or she were under some form of 'automatism' (see PS Atiyah, 'Economic Duress and the "Overborne Will"' (1982) 98 *Law Quarterly Review* 197; see, further, the following exchange: D Tiplady, 'Concepts of Duress' (1983) 99 *Law Quarterly Review* 188 and PS Atiyah, 'Duress and the Overborne Will Again' (1983) 99 *Law Quarterly Review* 353). This criticism is well-made simply because it is true that the party concerned must have known what he or she was doing, although the action concerned was effected under illegitimate pressure by the other party. This, in fact, leads us to the alternative (and competing) rationale for economic duress.

13.7 The competing view is popularly known as the 'illegitimate pressure theory'. As the very terminology suggests, this theory holds that there is economic duress only where the pressure exerted by the stronger party is *illegitimate*. As we shall see, however, this particular theory is also not without difficulties, the principal problem being how one is to distinguish between what is legitimate commercial pressure on the one hand and illegitimate pressure (constituting economic duress) on the other (see paragraph 13.11 ff, below).

13.8 Notwithstanding the specific difficulties with the 'illegitimate pressure theory', it appears to be the view accepted by the courts in at least both England and Australia; see the House of Lords decisions of *Universe Tankships Inc of Monrovia v International Transport Workers Federation* (1983) at pp 384 and 400, and *Dimskal Shipping Co SA v International Transport Workers Federation* (1992), as well as the New South Wales Court of Appeal decision of *Crescendo Management Pty Ltd v Westpac Banking Corp* (1988), respectively. Reference may also be made to the recent New Zealand Privy Council decision of *'R' v Her Majesty's Attorney-General for England and Wales* (2003) (which also raises interesting issues of application).

13.9 However, there might be some complications insofar as the *local* context is concerned. The Hong Kong Privy Council decision of *Pao On v Lau Yiu Long* (1980) endorsed, in fact, the 'overborne will theory' (see paragraphs 13.5–13.6, above). Although appeals to the Privy Council have been abolished in the Singapore context, decisions of the Board—even from other jurisdictions—nevertheless continue to carry great weight. More importantly, the Singapore Court of Appeal decision in *Third World Development v Atang Latief* (1990) referred to the *Pao On* case and appears to have followed the 'overborne will theory'.

13.10 It would appear that the 'illegitimate pressure theory' is to be preferred, the ambiguity generated in the local context notwithstanding. The present writer has, however, ventured to observe elsewhere that both the 'overborne will theory' and the 'illegitimate pressure theory' could possibly *co-exist* as follows (see A Phang, 'Economic Duress—Uncertainty Confirmed' (1992) 5 *Journal of Contract Law* 147 at p 151):

> 'The key is a simple one: that the same concept can have different meanings in different contexts. Words such as "coercion" and phrases such as "vitiation of consent" can, on one view, point to the simplistic and reductionist "automatism" which Professor Atiyah rejects. They can ... *also* refer simply to "coercion" or "vitiation of consent" in the sense of pressure that *so distorts the voluntariness* of the consent that the *law* regards such pressure as *illegitimate*—and what the law regards as illegitimate becomes, from *that* perspective, no consent at all. It is significant to note that the former would fall within the broader compass of the latter' (emphasis in original).

It should also be noted that the practical factors laid down in the *Pao On* case are also helpful (and see generally paragraph 13.12, below; though cf paragraph 13.13, below).

General Principles

13.11 What, then, about the *practical* steps that can be taken by both lawyers and the courts in order to ascertain whether or not economic duress has indeed been exercised? One guideline—already alluded to above—is to distinguish between mere commercial pressure (which is allowable) on the one hand from illegitimate pressure on the other (which would constitute economic duress which is, of course, not allowable). However, as the present writer has sought to argue elsewhere, it is by no means easy at all to make a clear distinction, at least with regard to many fact situations (see, generally, A Phang, 'Whither Economic Duress? Reflections on Two Recent Cases' (1990) 53 *Modern Law Review* 107).

13.12 Although the Hong Kong Privy Council decision of *Pao On v Lau Yiu Long* endorses what appears at present to be the less popular 'overborne will theory' (see paragraph 13.9, above), the judgment of the Board (delivered by Lord Scarman) does lay down some helpful practical factors and guidelines as follows:

> 'In determining whether there was a coercion of will such that there was no true consent, it is material to inquire whether the person alleged to have been coerced did or did not protest; whether, at the time he was allegedly coerced into making the contract, he did or did not have an alternative course open to him such as an adequate legal remedy; whether he was independently advised; and whether after entering the contract he took steps to avoid it.'

It should be noted that the *final* factor mentioned in the above quotation is directly relevant to one of the *bars* to a finding of economic duress, viz affirmation or approbation (see also the English High Court decision of *North Ocean Shipping Co Ltd v Hyundai Construction Co Ltd, The Atlantic Baron* (1979) by way of illustration, as well as paragraph 13.18, below).

13.13 Although the practical factors and guidelines laid down in the preceding paragraph are helpful and are (presumably) intended to aid us in distinguishing mere commercial pressure from illegitimate pressure (see paragraph 13.11, above), once again, however, these guidelines are not easy to apply and may well result in excessive open-endedness and uncertainty (see, generally, A Phang, 'Whither Economic Duress? Reflections on Two Recent Cases' (1990) 53 *Modern Law Review* 107). Indeed, the main (umbrella) factor appears to be that of whether or not the alleged victim had a reasonable alternative course open to him or her. It should, however, be noted that other cases have usefully added another factor: in order for there to be a finding of economic duress, the alleged victim must prove that he or she had acted *reasonably* in taking the other party's threats seriously (see, for example, the (English) decisions of *The Alev* (1989) at pp 142 and 146, as well as *Atlas Express Ltd v Kafco (Importers and Distributors) Ltd* (1989) at p 644).

13.14 Unfortunately, however, later cases have exacerbated what is already a rather ambiguous set of principles. In the English Court of Appeal decision of *CTN Cash and Carry Ltd v Gallaher Ltd* (1994), Steyn LJ (as he then was) observed (at p 719) thus:

> 'We are being asked to extend the categories of duress of which the law will take cognisance. That is not necessarily objectionable, but it seems to me that an extension capable of covering the present case, involving "*lawful* act duress" in a *commercial* context *in pursuit of a bona fide claim*, would be *a radical one with far-reaching implications.* It would *introduce a substantial and undesirable element of uncertainty in the commercial bargaining process. Moreover*, it will often enable *bone fide* settled accounts to be reopened when parties to commercial dealings fall out. ... Outside the field of protected relationships, and in *a purely commercial context*, it might be *a relatively rare case* in which *"lawful act duress"* can be established. And it might be *particularly difficult* to establish duress if the defendant *bona fide* considered that his demand was valid. In this *complex and changing branch of the law I deliberately refrain from saying "never"*. But as the law stands, I am satisfied that the defendants' conduct in this case did not amount to duress' (emphasis added).

The line between mere commercial pressure and illegitimate pressure is, with respect, no clearer. More significantly, perhaps, the present case tends to emaciate the doctrine of economic duress as there is more than a clear implication that, where the situation concerned pertains to *lawful acts involving two commercial parties*, there will *almost always* only be mere commercial pressure and, therefore, *no* economic duress. The reluctance of the court to interfere may be understandable in light of the general reluctance of the courts not to interfere with compromise agreements. The present writer has, nonetheless, argued that 'the need to uphold compromise agreements must always be subsidiary to the broader question of economic duress' for '[t]his is, in part, to avoid a vicious circularity in reasoning where it might be argued that there is no illegitimate pressure by the mere fact of the existence of the compromise agreement itself; such reasoning clearly does not address the more important issue, which is whether the compromise agreement was *itself* the result of illegitimate pressure, which pressure could be the result of factors *other than* the fact of the compromise arrangement itself' (emphasis in original) (see A Phang, 'Economic Duress: Recent Difficulties and Possible Alternatives' [1997] *Restitution Law Review* 53 at pp 59–60). It should be noted that this article just mentioned also contains a comprehensive analysis of the *CTN Cash and Carry* case itself.

13.15 As already argued above, one ought not to argue that only the facts are relevant. However, it is true that the very nature of economic duress suggests that the facts and circumstances of the case are clearly important. This being the case, the appellate court will pay great deference to the trial judge's findings of fact (see, eg the Singapore High Court decision of *Visvasam v Sathasivam* (1980))—a practical point that ought to be noted.

13.16 Insofar as the issue of *causation* is concerned, it used to be thought that so long as the illegitimate pressure was *a* reason for the victim entering into the contract, that would be sufficient in a plea of economic duress (see the Australian Privy Council decision of *Barton v Armstrong* (1976)). However, this proposition of law was *rejected* by Mance J in the English High Court decision of *Huyton SA v Peter Cremer GmbH & Co* (1999); in the words of the learned judge (at p 636):

> 'The minimum basic test of subjective causation in economic duress ought, it appears to me, to be a "but for" test. The illegitimate pressure must have been such as actually caused the making of the agreement, in the sense that it would not otherwise have been made either at all or, at least, in the terms in which it was made. In that sense the pressure must have been decisive or clinching.'

It should be noted that the approach now advocated by Mance J brings the law relating to causation in economic duress in line with that relating to causation in undue influence (as to which see paragraph 13.34, below). It is also suggested that the present approach is also preferable simply because the case of *Barton v Armstrong*—which, as we have seen, was relied upon for the *old* proposition—necessarily adopted a much broader test of causation as the case itself concerned a situation where a threat of serious (even fatal) physical injury to the victim was involved (and see also per Mance J at p 638).

13.17 It is important to note the *legal effect* of a finding of economic duress. The legal effect is to render the contract *voidable* (*not void* (see, eg *Pao On v Lau Yiu Long* (1980), pp 635–636; for the distinction between these two concepts see above, paragraphs 11.4–11.6).

13.18 It should also be noted that even if the court would otherwise have held the contract concerned voidable for economic duress, the victim might be prevented from rescinding the contract if he or she is found to have *affirmed* the contract (and see paragraph 13.12, above).

Position in Singapore

13.19 It can be safely stated that the position in Singapore tracks very closely the situation under English law. It is true that there might be a slight ambiguity insofar as the rationale of the doctrine is concerned (having regard to *Third World Development v Atang Latief*, considered above at paragraph 13.9), but even this is but a minor hiccup since the conflicting theories are reconcilable (see paragraph 13.10, above) and, in any event, the practical guidelines are settled. Indeed, in *Third World Development v Atang Latief* (1990), the Singapore Court of Appeal not only considered the various factors enunciated in the *Pao On* case (see paragraph 13.12, above) but also demonstrated the application of the specific factor of (in this case, the absence of) *protest*. Insofar as the factor of independent advice is concerned, readers might usefully refer to the Singapore High Court decision of *Tan Sim Lay v Lim Kiat Seng* (1996) (at p 778).

13.20 The doctrine of economic duress was the central issue in the recent Singapore High Court decision of *Sharon Global Solutions Pte Ltd v LG International (Singapore) Pte Ltd* (2001) (see also above, paragraph 3.41; the case is noted by D Tan, 'Grounds of Economic Duress—Further Clarification or Further Confusion?' [2001] *Singapore Journal of Legal Studies* 268 and P Koh, 'Economic Duress and a Drop of Fairness—A Singapore Perspective', *Journal of Business Law* (forthcoming)). Because of its relative vintage and its suitability as an illustration to which we can apply the various points in the preceding paragraph, this particular decision will be dealt with in relatively greater detail than would otherwise have been the case in a work of this nature.

In this case, the plaintiff, a small Singapore company, contracted to sell a steel product (Hot Briquette Iron, hereafter referred to as 'HBI') to the defendant, a Singapore-incorporated subsidiary of a large Korean conglomerate (the LG Group). The HBI was intended, in point of fact, for the Pohang Iron and Steel Co Ltd of Korea (POSCO), which happened to have a longstanding and important business relationship with the LG Group (which, it will be recalled, was the parent company of the defendant). Not surprisingly, the supply of the HBI to POSCO was of the utmost importance to the defendant, which importance was conveyed to the plaintiff. To this end, on confirmation by POSCO of its interest in the HBI, the plaintiff purchased the HBI from a Venezuelan steel mill and sold it to the defendant. The defendant would, in turn, enter into a back-to-back agreement to sell the HBI to POSCO. However, as time wore on, the plaintiff's managing director had not secured the necessary vessel for transportation of the HBI, although this was not due to any bad faith: a point accepted by the defendant. Not surprisingly, the defendant began to get anxious and both the plaintiff and the defendant met twice. During the second meeting, the plaintiff told the defendant that unless the defendant agreed to compensate the plaintiff by sharing the increased cost of freight in order to secure the necessary vessel, the plaintiff would refuse to confirm the charter of the said vessel and was, in fact, prepared, therefore, to default on its obligations (here, to secure the required vessel). The defendant acceded to what the plaintiff desired, and an agreement securing these terms was entered into by both parties. The vessel was secured and the HBI duly delivered to POSCO. However, the defendant, whilst making the first 25% of the payment to the plaintiff under the terms of the agreement just mentioned, subsequently refused to pay the remaining 75% and brought, instead, an action to recover the 25% payment already made. The plaintiff then brought the present proceedings for the outstanding 75% of the payment. The defendant pleaded two defences: first, that the agreement it had entered into with the plaintiffs was unenforceable because of economic duress and, secondly, that the agreement was not, in any event, supported by consideration. It is useful, at this juncture, to note what is often a close linkage between the doctrine of consideration on the one hand and that of economic duress on the other (see paragraph 13.21, below).

Turning to the substantive issues proper, the court held that there had indeed been sufficient consideration. Insofar as the argument from economic duress was concerned, Kan Ting Chiu J pertinently pointed out that '[e]conomic duress as a ground for avoiding contractual obligations is in its formative stage of development' (see p 375; see also paragraph 13.5, above). The learned judge also relied heavily on *Chitty on Contracts* (28th ed, 1999), Vol 1 at paragraphs 7-023, 7-024 and 7-029. Interestingly, in the last-cited paragraph, the language utilised by the learned author actually supports the view the present writer has proffered to the effect that there are, *inter alia*, strong linkages between the doctrine of economic duress on the one hand and that of unconscionability on the other (see, generally, paragraph 13.56, below). Returning to the case at hand, Kan J was of the view that '[a] threat to break a contract, eg a refusal to supply goods sold under a contract, may be economic duress' (see p 375). The learned judge also observed, in a more general vein, thus (at p 376):

> 'In my view, it is necessary to consider all the circumstances, including the states of mind of the parties before coming to a conclusion on whether a case for avoidance on the ground of economic duress is made out.'

The proposition just cited may appear, at first blush, to be rather straightforward and commonsensical but is not any less important for all that. As we have already observed (see paragraph 13.15, above), the importance of the facts of the case concerned, particularly in relation to the issue of fairness and justice, cannot be gainsaid.

At this preliminary (and more general) juncture, it should also be noted that Kan J also observed (at p 377) that '[w]hen a defence of economic duress is raised, it is incumbent on the party raising it to show that the duress placed it in a position where it was compelled to accede to the other party's demands'.

Kan J then proceeded to a detailed examination of the facts and circumstances. The learned judge held, first, that 'the spirit of the venture must be taken into account', and the defendant's willingness to contribute to the increased costs of freight 'was another reflection of this' (see p 376). He also held that the plaintiff's demand was due to its inexperience and that it (the plaintiff) was prepared to bear a greater financial burden by bearing its share of the additional freight compared to the loss it would incur by simply defaulting on its obligations (a financial burden that was in fact met by the plaintiff having to borrow the necessary funds from its shareholder or her husband) (see p 376). Kan J thus concluded thus (at pp 376–377):

> 'Against this background it cannot be said that the plaintiff was seeking to exploit the situation to increase its profits when it informed the defendant that it would not charter the vessel unless the defendant agreed to share the additional costs.'

Interestingly the reference in the above quotation to the concept of 'exploitation' is not inconsistent with the broader doctrine of unconscionability very briefly referred to above. Kan J was of the view that the plaintiff was *truthfully* stating that it could not perform without the defendant's promised extra payment and that the key issue, therefore, was whether this constituted an illegitimate threat within the ambit of the doctrine of economic duress itself (see p 377). Two factual matters were, in the learned judge's view, of especial significance in this regard (see p 377):

> 'First, the plaintiff was not seeking to improve its financial position … Second, the plaintiff was not seeking to shift the burden of the additional costs entirely to the defendant, and had agreed to bear a share of it even when it did not have the funds for that purpose.'

However, all this focuses on the *plaintiff's* perspective and it could be persuasively argued that the presence or absence of economic duress depends, instead, on a *holistic* analysis, which takes into account the *defendant's* perspective as well. Not surprisingly, therefore, Kan J also examined the facts and issues from the *defendant's* standpoint. The learned judge was of the view that the consummation of its (the defendant's) contract with POSCO was (as we have also already seen) of vital importance to it and that any failure in this regard would (according to the defendant) have had 'serious commercial consequences' (see p 377) (and this included the defendant's own 'reputation and standing with its parent company [ie, the LG Group] in Korea', although the learned judge expressly observed that the defendant had *not* in fact referred to this in its defence (see p 377)). *However*, Kan J was of the view (see p 377) that '[w]ithout elucidation from the defendant, I do not understand what the serious commercial consequences alluded to [with regard to POSCO] were'. As we have just seen, the learned judge also noted (see ibid) that the defendant had not itself referred to the potentially adverse effect that non-fulfilment of its legal obligations owed to POSCO would have on its reputation and standing with its parent company (the LG Group). Further, the defendant 'did not say that it could not bear the financial repercussions of non-performance, or the nature of the damage non-performance would inflict on the relationship with POSCO' (see p 377). The learned judge also pointed (see ibid) to the fact that the defendant was prepared and was already contemplating to contribute towards the additional freight costs *even prior to* the actual meetings and subsequent entry into the present contract itself. In the event, Kan J held, on the facts and evidence (see, in this regard, especially at p 378) that the eventual agreement was not one procured by the plaintiff's alleged economic duress but, rather, was 'the result of commercial negotiation' (see p 377). The plaintiff, in the learned judge's view, had given 'a *legitimate* notice of its inability to perform rather than an illegitimate threat' (emphasis added) (see p 378). He further added that '[o]n the part of the defendant, [he] did *not* have a clear picture that it [the defendant] *had no alternative but to* accept the plaintiff's terms because it had to fulfill its obligations to POSCO under any circumstances' (emphasis added) (see p 378).

The learned judge's meticulous consideration as well as analysis of the facts of the present case is very persuasive. This case also illustrates, once again, how very difficult it often is to distinguish between mere commercial pressure on the one hand and illegitimate pressure on the other. Further, Kan J did find, as we have seen, what was in effect a lack of sufficient evidence as to precisely what the commercial consequences for the defendant were. However, it is submitted, with respect, that a lingering doubt may nevertheless remain: the plaintiff had been prepared to *break his contract* to that extent the pressure exerted was one that embodied a threat (or at least something approaching a threat) to do an *unlawful or illegal act*. This is quite different from a threat to commit a wholly lawful act; indeed, where this is the case, the court will (at least in the commercial sphere) be extremely reluctant to find economic duress (see, in particular, the discussion of the *CTN Cash and Carry* case at paragraph 13.14, above).

It is, with respect, also rather odd that the court mentioned the factor of a reasonable alternative so late in the case and gave it relatively cursory consideration. As we have seen above, this is an important umbrella factor (see paragraph 13.13, above). To the extent that Kan J considered (and fairly thoroughly at that) the specific facts of the case itself, it could be argued that the learned judge must *necessarily* have been addressing himself, in a *simultaneous* fashion, to a resolution under this broader 'umbrella factor' as well. Looked at in this light, the cursory manner in which the factor of a reasonable alternative was dealt with may be more apparent than real. However, even if this argument is accepted, it is submitted, with respect, that, given the obvious importance of the factor, it ought to have been mentioned and emphasised right at the outset of the judgment itself.

One point of at least possible interest remains. Kan J held (at pp 379–380) that 'as the difficulties the parties encountered arose from the plaintiff's inaptitude in making a proper provision for the freight costs and in securing the vessel, [he] awarded the plaintiff half the costs of the actions'. Admittedly, this is, literally speaking, a wholly different issue but it does, it is suggested, illustrate the flexibility available to the court to balance the interests of the parties so as to achieve a measure of fairness and justice in a balanced fashion *vis-à-vis* the case at hand.

Relationship Between Economic Duress and Consideration and the Future of Economic Duress

13.21 It is not surprising that there is a close relationship between economic duress on the one hand and consideration on the other (on consideration, generally, see Chapter 3). This is because where there occur situations of possible *extortion*, the party attempting to impugn the transaction may argue either that there was insufficient consideration for the transaction or that there had been economic duress. The successful invocation of *either* doctrine would enable this party to extricate himself or herself from the unfortunate bargain.

13.22 Although, as we have seen, the doctrine of economic duress is not without its fair share of problems, in comparison with the doctrine of consideration, it might be persuasively argued that the latter doctrine is in even worse shape. If so, then it might be argued that the doctrine of economic duress ought to *replace* the doctrine of consideration. This presupposes, of course, that any perceived difficulties with economic duress can be successfully solved, or at least accommodated satisfactorily. One advantage that economic duress has over consideration is the fact that its very nature suggests more consistency with present-day commercial needs and circumstances (particularly where *blackmail* and *exploitation* are involved).

It could, of course, also be argued that the doctrine of economic duress should exist side-by-side with that of consideration. Under such circumstances, it might be argued further that consideration would probably take a backseat to economic duress; in the words of Hobhouse J (as he then was) in *The 'Alev'*, for instance (at p 147):

> 'Now that there is a properly developed doctrine ... of economic duress, there is no warrant for the Court to fail to recognize the existence of some consideration even though it may be insignificant and even though there may have been no mutual bargain in any realistic use of that phrase.'

However, if this is so, is there any reason to retain the doctrine of consideration, given its other (and manifold) weaknesses as well as difficulties (as to which, see paragraphs 3.67–3.71, above)? This, at the expense of repetition, assumes that the doctrine of economic duress has been rationalised and put on a stable footing. However, the emaciation of the doctrine in the commercial context (at least insofar as lawful threats are concerned) does not bode well for the doctrine (and see paragraph 13.14, above). We shall also consider, below, the possibility of subsuming both economic duress and undue influence under a broader umbrella doctrine of unconscionability (see generally paragraphs 13.51–13.59, below). This would, in fact, be an appropriate juncture at which to turn to a consideration of the next major—and related—doctrine in this chapter, viz undue influence.

Undue Influence

Introduction

13.23 The doctrine of undue influence is equitable in origin. Compared to the doctrine of economic duress just discussed, it is a doctrine of much greater antiquity. Hence, the various rules and principles are well-settled. However, and as we shall see, there have been extremely recent developments that suggest significant changes to the present rules and principles.

13.24 Although the doctrine is not intended to save persons from their own folly, it is clear that it is intended to *prevent victimisation*.

Categories of Undue Influence and General Principles Arising Therefrom

13.25 The doctrine of undue influence has traditionally been classified into two main categories—*Class 1 (or actual)* undue influence and *Class 2 (or presumed)* undue influence, respectively.

(1) *Class 1 Undue Influence*

13.26 No special relationship between the parties is presumed. The alleged victim bears the burden of proving that the alleged guilty party had exercised undue influence over him or her. In the apt language of Lindley LJ in the leading English Court of Appeal decision of *Allcard v Skinner* (1887) (at p 181):

> 'First, there are the cases in which there has been some unfair and improper conduct, some coercion from outside, some overreaching, some form of cheating, and generally, though not always, some personal advantage obtained by a donee placed in some close and confidential relation to the donor.'

In other words, the defendant has exercised such domination over the plaintiff victim's mind that his or her independence of decision was substantially—or even totally—undermined. As the reader will notice, this is a *very crude and obvious form* of undue influence and is not unlike the doctrine of economic duress considered earlier in this chapter.

(2) *Class 2 Undue Influence*

13.27 Here, there is *no actual* undue influence being exercised by the defendant over the plaintiff (this would, of course, constitute *Class 1 (or actual)* undue influence). This particular category of undue influence concerns, instead, a situation where the *relationship* between the contracting parties is such as to raise the *presumption* that the defendant has exercised undue influence over the plaintiff. *The defendant* then bears the burden of proof of *rebutting this presumption* by proving that the plaintiff had exercised a truly independent will. In other words, there is *a clear shift in the burden of proof*: whereas the plaintiff would normally bear the burden of proving his or her case, it is now the defendant who has to rebut the said presumption, lest the plaintiff succeed instead.

However, *not every* relationship between the parties will raise the presumption of undue influence. This having been said, there are in fact certain categories which have been clearly established in the case law as giving rise to the presumption. These include the following relationships: parent-child; guardian-ward; doctor-patient; lawyer-client; director-company; religious adviser-disciple; and trustee-beneficiary. As the presumption arises automatically by law as a result of the relationship itself, it is known as *Class 2A* undue influence (see paragraph 13.28, below).

There is also case law, however, where it has been held that, for certain specific relationships, *no* presumption of undue influence can arise. The following relationships are examples: employer-employee; agent-principal; husband-wife; and brothers. This having been said, it may equally be said that *the categories of undue influence are not closed.*

Indeed, as we shall see below, the relationship of the parties, *based on the specific facts of the case itself*, might raise a presumption of undue influence. However, the relationship of the parties per se does not—*unlike* Class 2A undue influence (see paragraph 13.28, below)—give rise to such a presumption. To reiterate, the *specific facts* must be looked at and are therefore of crucial importance (see paragraph 13.29, below).

(a) Class 2A Undue Influence

13.28 This sub-category of Class 2 undue influence comprises *established relationships where the presumption of undue influence arises almost automatically by force of law* (discussed in paragraph 13.27, above).

(b) Class 2B Undue Influence

13.29 There is yet *another* sub-category of Class 2 (or presumed) undue influence where a presumption is not raised by virtue of the relationship concerned itself. Under such circumstances, although a presumption would not normally be raised, the court might *still* raise a presumption of undue influence *provided the facts and surrounding circumstances of the case justified it*. Such justification occurs only where it could be proven that, *on the facts*, there had arisen a relationship whereby *trust and confidence* had been reposed by the plaintiff in the defendant. This particular sub-category of undue influence has been termed *Class 2B* undue influence in order to distinguish it from the Class 2A sub-category just discussed.

It might be stated that Class 2A undue influence raises presumptions on *a more general or universal level, where an established category of relationships is said to raise the presumption of undue influence by operation of law without more*. On the other hand, Class 2B undue influence operates at *a much more specific level, in effect, at the level of the facts of the particular case itself and where, on the facts, a specific relationship (of trust and confidence) is found, hence raising the presumption of undue influence.*

(3) *Independent Advice as a Factor*

13.30 An *important factor* that ought to be considered with respect to all categories of undue influence is whether or not the plaintiff had received *independent (in particular, legal) advice*. It should be added, though, that the absence of independent advice will not automatically result in a finding of undue influence.

A leading decision is that of the Privy Council (on appeal from the Court of Appeal of the Straits Settlements) of *Inche Noriah v Shaik Allie bin Omar* (1929). The Board held, first, that independent legal advice, whilst an extremely helpful factor, was *not* the *only* way in which the presumption of undue influence could be rebutted. Secondly, it held that the independent legal advice need not necessarily have had to be taken in order for the presumption to be held to have been rebutted. Thirdly, the Board observed that the legal adviser must give his or her advice 'with a knowledge of all relevant circumstances and must be such as a competent and honest adviser would give if acting solely in the interests of the donor' (see pp 135–136).

Where the legal advice is tendered by a lawyer who is acting for the *defendant*, it *cannot* by any stretch of the imagination be argued that such advice is *independent* (and see, eg *Bank of Montreal v Jane Jacques Stuart* (1911)).

(4) *Requirement of Manifest Disadvantage*

13.31 The House of Lords held, in *National Westminster Bank Plc v Morgan* (1985), that the transaction concerned must have been to the *manifest disadvantage* of the plaintiff. It followed the Indian Privy Council decision of *Poosathurai v Kannappa Chettiar* (1911). Not surprisingly, the House also rejected the attempt by Lord Denning MR in the English Court of Appeal decision of *Lloyds Bank v Bundy* (1975) to introduce the very broad concept of inequality of bargaining power. Indeed, this last-mentioned concept would not have required any manifest disadvantage on the part of the alleged victim; on the contrary, mere inequality of bargaining power between the parties would have allowed the court to set aside the transaction in question.

Although overruled by *CIBC Mortgages Plc v Pitt* (1994) with regard to the endorsement of the requirement of manifest disadvantage for Class 1 undue influence (see paragraph 13.32, below), the English Court of Appeal decision of *Bank of Credit and Commerce International SA v Aboody* (1989) does nevertheless still contain some valuable guidance on the nature and guidelines surrounding the requirement of manifest disadvantage itself. For example, the court held that 'the overall disadvantageous nature of a transaction cannot be said to be manifest, if it only emerges after a fine and close evaluation of its various beneficial and detrimental features. It must be obvious' (see p 780). Further, the material time at which the nature of the transaction is to be judged must be by reference to 'circumstances subsisting at the date of the transaction, though ... subsequent events may conceivably throw light on what could reasonably have been foreseen as at that date' (see p 780).

More importantly, perhaps, and insofar as the actual process of weighing is concerned, the court advocated *a balancing process* which, in the context of a guarantee, 'must [thus] depend on the balance of two factors, namely, (a) the seriousness of the risk of enforcement to the giver [ie here, the surety wife], in practical terms; and (b) the benefits gained by the giver in accepting the risk' (see p 780).

(5) *Requirement of Manifest Disadvantage Abrogated for Class 1 Undue Influence and Its Continued Weakening Under Class 2 Undue Influence*

13.32 The requirement of manifest disadvantage has been subjected to much (in particular, academic) critique. Not surprisingly, perhaps, the House of Lords, in *CIBC Mortgagees Plc v Pitt* (1994), *cut back* on its previous decision in the *Morgan* case (see the preceding paragraph), and held that manifest disadvantage was *no longer a requirement* with regard to *Class 1 (or actual) undue influence*. The underlying rationale for the House's decision was that Class 1 undue influence was actually 'a species of fraud' and that, hence, the innocent party was entitled to have the transaction set aside 'as of right' (see p 808).

The question that arises is whether or not, with the decision of the House in *Pitt*, the days of manifest disadvantage—even in the context of *Class 2* undue influence—are numbered. There is no denial, of course, that the factor of manifest disadvantage may have a powerful *evidential* impact in the case at hand (see, eg the English Court of Appeal decision in *Royal Bank of Scotland v Etridge (No 2)* (1998) at pp 713 and 714). The *latest (English) development* is, in fact, embodied in the relatively recent House of Lords decision in *Royal Bank of Scotland v Etridge (No 2)* (2001), which was a consolidated appeal from not only the preceding decision mentioned but also from seven other decisions as well. The House went further and, as will be seen, limited the role of manifest disadvantage yet further. The decision itself is in fact the subject of a comprehensive article elsewhere (see A Phang and H Tjio, 'The Uncertain Boundaries of Undue Influence' [2002] *Lloyd's Maritime and Commercial Law Quarterly* 231) and therefore only some main points will be canvassed very briefly. The House took pains to emphasise the *evidential* nature of Class 2 (or presumed) undue influence. More specifically, and insofar as the requirement of manifest disadvantage is concerned, it is now clear that, whilst this requirement has been retained for Class 2 undue influence, it merely performs a *sifting* function for this particular category by constituting a catalyst for the invocation of the presumption of undue influence. The role of manifest disadvantage has thus been *greatly reduced* (see, generally, Phang and Tjio, ibid, at pp 234–236; and for a recent summary of the *Etridge* case, see the recent New Zealand Privy Council decision of *'R' v Her Majesty's Attorney-General for England and Wales* (2003)). Indeed, in the following paragraph, we look at *other* reasons why the requirement of manifest disadvantage ought not to have been introduced into the law of undue influence in the first instance.

(6) *Requirement of Manifest Disadvantage—An Historical Error*

13.33 The present writer has in fact argued elsewhere that, insofar as the House of Lords in the *Morgan* case relied upon the Indian Privy Council decision of *Poosathurai* (see paragraph 13.31, above), this was, with respect, misconceived because the *Poosathurai* case was concerned with the interpretation of section 16 of the Indian Contract Act, *where the requirement of manifest disadvantage was statutorily mandated* (see A Phang, 'Undue Influence—Methodology, Sources and Linkages' [1995] *Journal of Business Law* 552 at pp 558–563). Indeed, one might also usefully refer to the later acknowledgment by the English Court of Appeal in *Barclays Bank Plc v Coleman* (2001) to similar effect.

It is also arguable that there was *no* requirement of manifest disadvantage at the point in time when the *Poosathurai* case was decided. Further, even if there was such a requirement, there was no reason in principle why the House in the *Morgan* case ought to have simply accepted the requirement of manifest disadvantage without more—not, at least, without analysing the suitability of the requirement in the light of both reason and principle as well as the present-day commercial context.

It is also interesting (and significant) that the House of Lords, in the *Pitt* case (see paragraph 13.32, above), expressed the view that the requirement of manifest disadvantage might have to be reconsidered in the light of the broader principle of abuse of confidence in the fiduciary context (see p 809 of the case report).

And, as we shall see (see paragraph 13.42, below), the position in *Singapore* might well have moved away from, and (with respect) ahead of, the current English law.

13.34 Insofar as the issue of *causation* is concerned, the English Court of Appeal observed, in *Bank of Credit and Commerce International SA v Aboody* (1989) (which is also considered in paragraph 13.31, above), thus (at p 779):

> 'We think that, at least in ordinary circumstances, it would not be appropriate for the court to exercise this jurisdiction [ie to give relief for undue influence] in a case where the evidence establishes that on balance of probabilities the complainant would have entered into the transaction in any event.'

But cf the very recent (also) English Court of Appeal decision of *UCB Corporate Services Ltd v Williams* (2002), especially at paragraph 91 (however, if the proposition in this case is accepted instead, it would appear—on the court's reasoning—to clearly be persuasive only in situations of *Class 1* (*or actual*) undue influence.)

13.35 The *effect* of undue influence is to render the contract concerned *voidable* (on the distinction between voidness and voidability, see above, paragraphs 11.4–11.6).

The courts will attempt their level best to restore the parties concerned to as close to their original positions as possible, the key guideline here being the achievement of 'practical justice' between them (for an excellent illustration, see the English Court of Appeal decision of *Cheese v Thomas* (1994)).

Undue Influence, Creditors and Doctrine of 'Infection'

13.36 The main issue here is whether or not a creditor—not itself guilty of undue influence (or even misrepresentation, for that matter, as to which see, generally, Chapter 10)—can nevertheless have its rights 'infected' by virtue of having knowledge of the wrongdoing of one of the actual parties (hereafter the 'guilty party', with the wrongdoing constituting, for example, undue influence exercised over the other party (who is the guarantor or surety)). In other words, if the knowledge of the wrongdoing can be 'brought home' to the creditor, then it will not be allowed to enforce its rights under the contract, as those rights would be 'infected' by the guilty party's conduct. The guarantor or surety would, on the contrary, be allowed to set aside the transaction concerned, with the effect that the creditor would be treated *as if* it had actually perpetrated the undue influence (or other wrongdoing) itself.

13.37 The creditor would be 'infected' in one of two main ways. First, it might have entrusted the guilty party as its *agent* with the task of obtaining the execution of the document it is presently suing under. If so, there is 'infection' by way of *agency*.

Secondly, the creditor might have had *constructive notice* of the wrongdoing by the guilty party and, hence, its rights would be 'infected' accordingly. It is this particular concept that has generated a considerable amount of case law.

However, in the House of Lords decision of *Barclays Bank Plc v O'Brien* (1994), Lord Browne-Wilkinson was of the view that situations of agency are likely to be rare (see p 195) and was of the view that the doctrine of constructive notice would constitute the main doctrine in this regard (see pp 194 and 195). In this latter regard, the learned Law Lord was of the view that 'a creditor is put on inquiry when a wife offers to stand surety for her husband's debts by the combination of two factors: (a) the transaction is on its face not to the financial advantage of the wife; and (b) there is a substantial risk in transactions of that kind that, in procuring the wife to act as surety, the husband has committed a legal or equitable wrong that entitles the wife to set aside the transaction' (see p 196). And when the creditor is thus put on inquiry, it has to take reasonable steps to ensure that it is not fixed with constructive notice of the wife's rights. In this regard, Lord Browne-Wilkinson offered the following important guidelines (at pp 196–197):

> 'Normally the reasonable steps necessary ... consist of making inquiry of the person who may have the earlier right (ie the wife) to see whether such right is asserted. It is plainly impossible to require of banks and other financial institutions that they should inquire of one spouse whether he or she has been unduly influenced or misled by the other. But in my judgment the creditor, in order to avoid being fixed with constructive notice, can reasonably be expected to take steps to bring home to the wife the risk she is running by standing as surety and to advise her to take independent advice. As to past transactions, it will depend on the facts of each case whether the steps taken by the creditor satisfy this test. However for the future in my judgment a creditor will have satisfied these requirements if it insists that the wife attend a private meeting (in the absence of the husband) with a representative of the creditor at which she is told of the extent of her liability as surety, warned of the risk she is running and urged to take independent legal advice. ... I should make it clear that I have been considering the ordinary case where the creditor knows only that the wife is to stand surety for her husband's debts. I would not exclude exceptional cases where a creditor has knowledge of further facts which render the presence of undue influence not only possible but probable. In such cases, the creditor to be safe will have to insist that the wife is separately advised.'

13.38 There have been in fact a great many (especially English) decisions since the *O'Brien* case as to whether or not creditors (in particular, banks) had taken reasonable steps to avoid being fixed with constructive notice of the respective wives' rights. The present writer has dealt with many of these decisions elsewhere (see, generally, A Phang, *Cheshire, Fifoot and Furmston's Law of Contract—Second Singapore and Malaysian Edition* (1998) at pp 543–547). It will suffice for our present purposes to note that the courts have adopted a relatively liberal approach which accords, *inter alia*, great weight as well as trust to the judgment of the creditor's solicitor, except in situations where the solicitor concerned clearly did not advise the victim (here, the wife) adequately (including situations where the solicitor concerned has a conflict of interests or duties but nevertheless proceeds to advise the victim anyway; cf, for example, the English High Court decision of *Halifax Mortgage Services Ltd v Stepsky* (1995), with the Court of Appeal managing to avoid the issue by recourse to an express statutory provision: see *Halifax Mortgage Services Ltd v Stepsky* (1996)).

The House of Lords, in *Royal Bank of Scotland v Etridge (No 2)* (2001), has also recently elaborated helpfully on both the nature of constructive notice as well as the role of legal advice and the reader is strongly urged to read the judgments closely. Further analysis may be found in A Phang and H Tjio, 'The Uncertain Boundaries of Undue Influence' [2002] *Lloyd's Maritime and Commercial Law Quarterly* 231 at pp 236–241. In the article just mentioned, the following points (by way of *summary*) were also enunciated and may be usefully quoted here (at pp 244–245):

> '... The nature of constructive notice in this particular situation is, arguably, somewhat idiosyncratic (particularly when compared with traditional conceptions of constructive notice and the application thereof) but nevertheless fulfils an important pragmatic function of striking a balance between the need to protect the surety whilst allowing the wealth that inheres in the matrimonial home to be safely used as collateral.
>
> ...
>
> The House laid down a number of reasonable steps to be followed by banks as well as a "core minimum" (per Lord Nicholls) that had to be contained within the legal advice given to the surety. Insofar as the actual actions by the solicitor are concerned, the central guiding principle is that the solicitor must act for the *surety* in the relevant transaction. Whilst not providing a perfect or even elegant solution, we argue that the individual steps required of the bank and solicitor are not burdensome and should adequately protect the surety in *most* transactions, although difficulties remain where it is specifically pleaded that the bank or solicitor has had something drawn to its attention that arouses suspicion that the surety's will has been overborne (and this is particularly so with regard to interlocutory appeals)' (emphasis in original).

13.39 The House of Lords decision in *Barclays Bank Plc v Boulter* (1999) should also be noted, where it was held that *the onus of proof* is on *the debtor* to plead and prove that it did *not* have constructive notice. This does not, of course, assist the situation insofar as sureties in general and wives in particular are concerned.

13.40 It was also held, in *Barclays Bank Plc v O'Brien* (1994), that there was *no* 'special equity' in favour of wives inasmuch as married women, who had provided security for their respective husbands' debts, did not constitute an automatically protected class where the doctrine of 'infection' could apply, notwithstanding the absence of either agency or constructive notice on the part of the creditor concerned.

It should be noted, however, that the *Australian High Court*, in *Garcia v National Australian Bank Ltd* (1998), has adopted a *completely opposite* approach—endorsing the 'special equity' in favour of married women (see, generally, A Phang and H Tjio, 'From Mythical Equities to Substantive Doctrines—Yerkey in the Shadow of Notice and Unconscionability' (1999) 14 *Journal of Contract Law* 72).

It should be noted further that the Malaysian Court of Appeal, in *Tengku Abdullah ibni Sultan Abu Bakar v Mohd Latiff bin Shah* (1996), *refused to follow* the principles laid down in the *O'Brien case* insofar as *extra-marital relationships* were concerned (for further discussion, see paragraph 14.48, below).

Position in Singapore

(1) *Introduction*

13.41 The position in Singapore generally follows the English law. Hence, the principles hitherto discussed would also apply in the Singapore context (see, generally, A Phang, *Cheshire, Fifoot and Furmston's Law of Contract—Second Singapore and Malaysian Edition* (1998) at p 521 ff). *However*, there are some indications that the requirement of manifest disadvantage may no longer hold in the Singapore context and, if this is the case, the Singapore position would, as shall be argued below, be an improvement over the current English law.

(2) *Demise of Manifest Disadvantage in the Singapore Context?*

13.42 The approach of Lim Teong Qwee JC in the Singapore High Court decision of *Kushvinder Singh Chopra v Mooka Pillai Rajagopal* (1996) suggests that there is *no longer any requirement of manifest disadvantage in the Singapore context*. In particular, the learned judge observed thus (at p 399):

> 'I do not think that *National Westminster Bank Plc v Morgan* [see paragraph 13.31, above] decided that where undue influence is presumed yet the transaction will not be set aside unless it is also shown that it is manifestly disadvantageous to the person challenging it. It seems to me to be contrary to logic that where actual undue influence is proved manifest disadvantage need not be shown but where undue influence is presumed manifest disadvantage has to be shown. In my judgment it is *not necessary* to show that the transaction is manifestly disadvantageous to the person relying on undue influence *whether actual or presumed*' (emphasis added).

Inasmuch as the holding with regard to manifest disadvantage in the *Morgan* case is at least historically flawed (see paragraph 13.33, above), Lim JC's approach is to be welcomed. Indeed, if accepted, the learned judge's approach represents *an advance by Singapore law over the current English law*. On the other hand, however, it is submitted, with respect, that the reasoning, as embodied in the above quotation, may not be wholly persuasive. It is not really contrary to logic for the requirement of manifest disadvantage to be dispensed with with regard to Class 1 (or actual) undue influence (which was in fact the holding in the *Pitt* case; see paragraph 13.32, above) but not with regard to Class 2 (or presumed) undue influence. There are, nevertheless, *other* reasons (briefly considered earlier at paragraph 13.33, above) as to why the requirement of manifest disadvantage ought, in any event, to be done away with.

The learned judge also appeared to suggest that something more than a solicitor-client relationship was required before a presumption of undue influence could arise. However, this is at odds with the received understanding to the effect that such a relationship, in and of itself, generated a presumption of undue influence under the sub-category of Class *2A* undue influence (see paragraphs 13.27 and 13.28, above). Indeed, Lim JC appeared to be suggesting that if a presumption arises at all, it would have to arise based on an examination of the specific facts of the case itself (ie it would be a situation of Class *2B* undue influence instead (see paragraph 13.29, above)). However, one possible (and *alternative*) interpretation is that the learned judge had not altered the established view just referred to but was, rather, simply stating that there had been no solicitor-client relationship *based on the specific facts of the case itself*.

Lim JC's decision was reversed by the Singapore Court of Appeal (see *Mooka Pillai Rajagopal v Kushvinder Singh Chopra* (1996)). However, the court did not need to rule on (especially) the point of manifest disadvantage simply because it held that there *had* been manifest disadvantage on the facts of the case itself. The court also held that, even if no presumption were otherwise operative, there was nevertheless sufficient evidence to establish *Class 1 (or actual)* undue influence in any event. Hence, there has been no clear affirmation of Lim JC's views with regard to the requirement of manifest disadvantage. However, as the present writer has argued earlier, there are extremely persuasive reasons as to why the requirement ought to be done away with (see paragraph 13.33, above) and the requirement in the English context has in fact been further diminished as a result of the latest House of Lords decision in *Royal Bank of Scotland v Etridge (No 2)* (2001) (see paragraph 13.32, above).

Unconscionability

Introduction

13.43 Like undue influence, the doctrine of unconscionability is equitable in origin. However, it has, under English law at least, hitherto been confined to a narrow compass. This is due, in large part, to a fear of the exercise of excessive judicial discretion because, as we shall see, the general criteria underlying the doctrine are rather broad. The doctrine is, nevertheless, rather attractive to those who tend to allocate much weight towards the attainment of a *fair* outcome. We encounter, once again, the perennial tension between the need for (general) certainty on the one hand and (specific) fair outcomes on the other. Whilst it is true that, in most situations, both can be achieved simultaneously, this is not always the case. On occasion at least, in order to achieve a fair result in a particular case, the court might have to ignore or even effectively contradict previously enunciated rules and principles. However, if these rules and principles are generally fair and were therefore operating well, their legitimacy would be undermined for the sake of achieving a fair and just result in just one case, hence, the oft-cited saying that 'hard cases make bad law'. The court's duty, therefore, is to constantly *balance* this tension. It seems clear, however, that the doctrine of unconscionability does tend, as already mentioned, to lean towards the side of fairness as opposed to general certainty: thus, leading to a fear of opening the 'floodgates' of judicial discretion. The present writer will return to this fear at the end of this part and briefly ascertain whether such a fear is in fact justified in the first place.

General Principles

13.44 As already mentioned, the doctrine of unconscionability is confined to a rather narrow compass under *English* law. The principal areas where there was some scope for operation of the doctrine related to transactions involving expectant heirs and improvident transactions, respectively. Let us turn to briefly consider the latter as, by its very nature, the principles considered therein might have—potentially at least—a somewhat broader application.

13.45 In an oft-cited statement of principle, Megarry J (as he then was), in the English High Court decision of *Cresswell v Potter* (1978) (which was curiously decided in 1968, a decade earlier), observed (referring to the judgment of Kay J in *Fry v Lane* (1888)), thus (at p 257):

> 'The judge [ie, Kay J] thus laid down *three requirements. ... first*, whether the plaintiff is *poor and ignorant*; *second*, whether the sale was at *a considerable undervalue*; and *third*, whether the vendor had *independent advice*' (emphasis added).

Megarry J did, however, modify the principles just stated somewhat in order to bring them into sync with modern conditions. The learned judge was of the view that the word 'poor' should be replaced by the phrase 'a member of the lower income group' or similar terminology, whilst the word 'ignorant' should be replaced by the phrase 'less highly educated'. He was also of the view that 'poverty' was not confined to destitution (see, generally, p 257).

13.46 In another oft-cited decision, also from the English High Court, Judge Peter Millett (as he then was) made the following observations in

Alec Lobb (Garages) Ltd v Total Oil Great Britain Ltd (1983) (at pp 94–95) (reference may also be made to the Court of Appeal decision (1985) at pp 312–313):

> '... if the cases are examined, it will be seen that *three elements* have almost invariably been present before the court has interfered. *First*, one party has been *at a serious disadvantage to the other*, whether through *poverty, or ignorance, or lack of advice, or otherwise, so that circumstances existed of which unfair advantage could be taken ... secondly*, this weakness of the one party has been *exploited by the other* in some *morally culpable manner* ... and *thirdly*, the *resulting transaction* has been *not merely hard or improvident, but overreaching and oppressive*. Where there has been a sale at an undervalue, the undervalue has almost always been substantial, so that it calls for an explanation, and is in itself indicative of the presence of some fraud, undue influence, or other such feature. *In short, there must ... be some impropriety, both in the conduct of the stronger party and in the terms of the transaction itself (though the former may often be inferred from the latter in the absence of an innocent explanation) which in the traditional phrase "shocks the conscience of the court", and makes it against equity and good conscience of the stronger party to retain the benefit of a transaction he has unfairly obtained*' (emphasis added).

13.47 The observations in the preceding paragraph suggest a potentially much broader application for the doctrine of unconscionability. However, the general tenor under English law continues to be fairly conservative, although a possible larger role for the doctrine itself was emphasised by (not surprisingly) Millett LJ (now Lord Millett) in the English Court of Appeal decision of *Credit Lyonnais Bank Nederland NV v Burch* (1997) (discussed in more detail in A Phang, 'Vitiating Factors in Contract Law—The Interaction of Theory and Practice' (1998) 10 *Singapore Academy of Law Journal* 1 at pp 49–52). Here, the learned judge was of the view that, on the facts of the case (which were rather egregious), the transaction concerned could be set aside either on the basis of undue influence (discussed in the preceding part of this chapter) or unconscionability (see p 153). Indeed, this last-mentioned point is relevant to the issue of *linkages*, which is considered below (see paragraph 13.51 ff, below). And there has been some indication, in the recent House of Lords decision in *Royal Bank of Scotland v Etridge (No 2)* (2001) (discussed above in paragraph 13.32 with regard to the doctrine of undue influence) that a broader approach (which appears to point towards the doctrine of unconscionability) might be appropriate (see, in particular, the judgments of Lord Nicholls of Birkenhead and Lord Hobhouse, which are elaborated upon in A Phang and H Tjio, 'The Uncertain Boundaries of Undue Influence' [2002] *Lloyd's Maritime and Commercial Law Quarterly* 231 at pp 241–243).

In *Australia*, however, there are clear signs of a broader development. The oft-cited decision in this regard is that of the Australian High Court in *Commercial Bank of Australia Ltd v Amadio* (1983). Deane J, for example, observed thus (at p 423):

> 'The jurisdiction [to relieve against unconscionable dealing] is long established as extending to circumstances in which (i) a party to a transaction was under a special disability in dealing with the other party with the consequence that there was an absence of any reasonable degree of equality between them, and (ii) that disability was sufficiently evident to the stronger party to make it *prima facie* unfair or "unconscientious" that he procure, or accept, the weaker party's assent to the impugned transaction in the circumstances in which he procured or accepted it. Where such circumstances are shown to have existed, an onus is cast upon the stronger party to show that the transaction was fair, just and reasonable ....'

And whether or not the stronger party had the requisite knowledge to support a finding of unconscionabilty is premised on an *objective* test. In the words of Mason J in the same case (at p 417):

> '[I]f A, having *actual* knowledge that B occupies a situation of special disadvantage in relation to an intended transaction, so that B cannot make a judgment as to what is in his own interests, takes unfair advantage of his (A's) superior bargaining power or position by entering into that transaction, his conduct in so doing is unconscionable. And if, instead of having actual knowledge of that situation, *A is aware of the possibility that that situation may exist or is aware of facts that would raise that possibility in the mind of any reasonable person, the result will be the same*' (emphasis added).

Reference may also be made to the (also) Australian High Court decision of *Louth v Diprose* (1992). A useful summary of principles may also be found in the Privy Council decision on appeal from the Court of Appeal of the Eastern Caribbean Supreme Court (Antigua and Barbuda) in *Boustany v Pigott* (1993). Unfortunately, this last mentioned case does reiterate the distinction often drawn between *procedural* fairness on the one hand and *substantive* fairness on the other (though cf per Millett LJ in the *Credit Lyonnais* case, above; reference may also be made, in this regard, to the seminal article by A Leff, 'Unconscionability and the Code —The Emperor's New Clause' (1967) 115 *University of Pennsylvania Law Review* 485. This distinction, as we shall see below, is rather artificial and unsatisfactory (see paragraph 13.59, below)).

13.48 For more information on this important as well as developing area of the law, see, eg Phang at paragraph 13.49, below; M Cope, 'The Review of Unconscionable Bargains in Equity' (1983) 57 *Australian Law Journal* 279; NY Chin, 'Unconscionable Contracts in Anglo-Australian Law' (1985) 16 *Western Australian Law Review* 162; SR Enman, 'Doctrines of Unconscionability in Canadian, English and Commonwealth Contract Law' (1987) 16 *Anglo-American Law Review* 191; D Vaver, 'Unconscionability: Panacea, Analgesic or Loose Can(n)on?' (1988) 14 *Canadian Business Law Journal* 40; AH Angelo and EP Ellinger, 'Unconscionable Contracts: A Comparative Study of the Approaches in England, France, Germany, and the United States' (1992) 14 *Loyola of Los*

Angeles International and Comparative Law Journal 455; and N Bamforth, 'Unconscionability as a Vitiating Factor' [1995] *Lloyd's Maritime and Commercial Law Quarterly* 538.

Position in Singapore

13.49 The Singapore position is not wholly clear. It does appear to track (relatively closely) the English position, but (as we have seen) even the English courts might at least be possibly moving towards a more liberal approach towards the doctrine of unconscionability (see paragraph 13.47, above). The local cases clearly endorse the narrower English position embodied in cases such as *Cresswell v Potter* (as to which see paragraph 13.45, above); see, eg *Lim Geok Hian v Lim Guan Chin* (1994) and *Pek Nam Kee v Peh Lam Kong* (1996). There has in fact been at least one decision where the *Amadio* case (see paragraph 13.47, above) was cited but there was no substantive discussion or development as such; see *United Malayan Banking Corp Bhd v Masagoes* (1994). The more recent Singapore High Court decision of *Fong Whye Koon v Chan Ah Thong* (1996), however, suggests a broader approach towards the doctrine of unconscionability. However, a close perusal of the judgment of Warren LH Khoo J does not (unfortunately) clearly confirm that the broader approach ought to prevail in the local context (for further analysis of this case as well as the local position generally, see A Phang, 'Vitiating Factors in Contract Law —The Interaction of Theory and Practice' (1998) 10 *Singapore Academy of Law Journal* 1 at pp 53–56). And, in the later (also) Singapore High Court decision of *Rajabali Jumabhoy v Ameerali R Jumabhoy* (1997), affirmed by the Court of Appeal (1998), (but without any consideration of this particular issue), Judith Prakash J expressed difficulty with accepting the broader Australian position (see paragraph 13.47, above), which the learned judge thought to be too wide (see p 858). Prakash J did also appear to equate the doctrine of unconscionability with that of inequality of bargaining power. However, it is submitted, with respect, that the doctrine of unconscion ability entails *more* than mere inequality of bargaining power. Indeed, the learned judge did in fact acknowledge that the doctrine of unconscionability would otherwise be 'a useful jurisprudential tool' (see at p 858). See, further, Phang, ibid, at pp 57–58.

13.50 The present writer submits that a broader approach should be adopted towards the doctrine of unconscionability. As we shall see below, the objection from excessive judicial discretion is not a conclusive objection by any means (see paragraph 13.58, below). And, as already pointed out (see paragraph 13.47, above), there are some signs that the English position, which is very influential in Singapore (see generally Chapter 1), may itself be open to such a broader development as well.

Indeed, this would be an appropriate point at which to turn to the linkages amongst all the three doctrines hitherto considered in this chapter and, in the process, respond, *inter alia*, to the objection from excessive judicial discretion as well.

Linkages Amongst Economic Duress, Undue Influence and Unconscionability—A New Umbrella Doctrine of Unconscionability?

Introduction

13.51 There are indeed a number of linkages amongst the different categories of undue influence. There are also linkages between undue influence and economic duress as well as between undue influence and unconscionability, not to mention between economic duress and unconscionabilty. The present writer has dealt with these linkages in more comprehensive detail elsewhere (see A Phang, 'Undue Influence —Methodology, Sources and Linkages' [1995] *Journal of Business Law* 552).

Linkages Amongst the Categories of Undue Influence

(1) *Class 1 and Class 2 Undue Influence*

13.52 Despite the fact that manifest disadvantage is no longer a requirement for the establishment of Class 1 (or actual) undue influence (see paragraph 13.32, above), the present writer has argued that manifest disadvantage is *necessarily* present—by virtue of its egregious nature—in actual undue influence (see A Phang, paragraph 13.51, above). If so, then the line between actual undue influence and Class 2 (or presumed) undue influence remains *blurred*.

In particular, there is, in effect, very little difference between Class 1 undue influence and *Class 2B* undue influence (see Phang, paragraph 13.51, above, especially at pp 563–564). As the present writer has observed ibid at pp 563–564:

> 'Bearing in mind ... the fact that under Class 2B undue influence, the innocent party must prove the existence of a relationship whereby trust and confidence was reposed in the alleged wrongdoer (thus raising the presumption that the wrongdoer has then to rebut), it is, with respect, difficult to see much significant difference, in a *practical* context, between this situation and that involving Class 1 undue influence which also requires proof of actual undue influence being exercised by the alleged wrongdoer' (emphasis in original).

Indeed, the House of Lords, in its relatively recent decision in *Royal Bank of Scotland v Etridge (No 2)* (2001) emphasised the *evidential* nature of Class 2 (or presumed) undue influence and, in effect, sounded the death knell for Class 2B undue influence (see, generally, A Phang and H Tjio, 'The Uncertain Boundaries of Undue Influence' [2002] *Lloyd's Maritime and Commercial Law Quarterly* 231 at pp 232–234 for elaboration and analysis), although, with respect, the House did not articulate the justification for such an approach by explicit reference to the relationship between Class 2B and Class 1 undue influence (which has just, however, been alluded to earlier in this paragraph).

(2) *Class 2A Undue Influence*

13.53 The criteria for ascertaining whether or not a particular fact situation falls within this category of undue influence is unclear. The present writer has in fact ventured to suggest elsewhere that given such uncertainty, it might be preferable to *abolish* this particular category of undue influence altogether (see Phang, paragraph 13.51, above especially at pp 564–565).

Linkage Between Undue Influence and Economic Duress

13.54 Economic duress and Class 1 (or actual) undue influence are also very similar in substance (see Phang, paragraph 13.51, above, especially at pp 565–566). As the present writer has argued ibid at pp 565–566:

> '[C]lass 1 undue influence relates to the *actual* exercise of undue influence which must be of a *dominating* kind. It is suggested that the coercive effect of economic duress, whilst not (theoretically at least) coincident with Class 1 undue influence, is nevertheless very similar' (emphasis in original).

Linkage Between Undue Influence and Unconscionability

13.55 There is a very close relationship between undue influence and unconscionability (see Phang, paragraph 13.51, above, at pp 566–570, for a fuller analysis).

Linkage Between Economic Duress and Unconscionability

13.56 Not surprisingly (especially given the close linkage between (at least Class 1) undue influence and economic duress, as to which see paragraph 13.54, above), there is also a very close relationship between economic duress and unconscionability (see also Phang, paragraph 13.51, above, at p 570, where it is observed that '[a] common thread centres on the element of domination of the will of the innocent party').

A Broader Umbrella Doctrine of Unconscionability?

13.57 Given the numerous linkages mentioned briefly above, the present writer has argued that there was no reason in logic or principle why it was not possible 'to subsume all three doctrines [economic duress, undue influence and unconscionability] under one broad heading of unconscionable conduct' (see Phang, paragraph 13.51, above, at p 570; cf also the recent New Zealand Privy Council decision of *'R' v Her Majesty's Attorney-General for England and Wales* (2003), especially at paragraph 29—at least insofar as the doctrines of undue influence and unconscionability are concerned). One has, however, to bear in mind, at present at least, that the doctrine of unconscionability has not been unambiguously established in the Singapore context (see paragraph 13.49, above).

13.58 The general objection against the proposed umbrella doctrine from excessive judicial discretion meets the response to the effect that judges must necessarily exercise discretion in all but the rarest of instances. There is no reason, therefore, to believe that they would be any less able to exercise discretion with regard to the doctrine of unconscionability, especially since it is expected that general factors and guidance will emerge as has been the case with the common law throughout its illustrious history. Indeed, to adopt an unduly pessimistic approach would be tantamount to expressing a lack of confidence in the entire enterprise of the law itself.

13.59 It should, finally, be noted that writers and courts presently draw a distinction between procedural fairness on the one hand and substantive fairness on the other. It is suggested that this distinction stems from a fear of subjectivity or relativity and the opening up of the floodgates of judicial discretion. As briefly argued in the preceding paragraph, the argument from excessive judicial discretion is unpersuasive. And the distinction between procedure and substance is, in the final analysis, an artificial one. As Professor Atiyah has very persuasively argued, procedural and substantive fairness often impact on, as well as interact with, each other (see PS Atiyah, 'Contract and Fair Exchange' (1985) 35 *University of Toronto Law Journal* 1 (reprinted as Essay 11 in PS Atiyah, *Essays on Contract* (1986))).

CHAPTER 14

Illegality and Public Policy

PARAGRAPHS

14.1–14.6 **Introduction**

Statutory Illegality

14.7–14.11 Introduction
14.12–14.13 Express Prohibition
14.14–14.19 Implied Prohibition
14.20–14.23 Formation vs Performance
14.24–14.27 Situations Where There is Neither Express nor Implied Prohibition

Illegality at Common Law

14.28–14.29 Introduction
14.30–14.32 Contracts Prejudicial to Administration of Justice
14.33 Contracts to Deceive Public Authorities
14.34–14.38 Contracts to Oust Jurisdiction of the Courts
14.39 Contracts to Commit (or Involving) a Crime, Tort or Fraud
14.40–14.41 Contracts Prejudicial to Public Safety
14.42–14.43 Contracts Prejudicial to Status of Marriage—Marriage Brokage Contracts
14.44–14.45 Other Contracts Prejudicial to Status of Marriage
14.46–14.48 Contracts Promoting Sexual Immorality
14.49–14.50 Contracts That are Liable to Corrupt Public Life
14.51 Contracts Restricting Personal Liberty

Consequences or Effects of Illegality

14.52 Introduction
14.53–14.54 Recovery Under Illegal Contract
Recovery of Benefits Conferred Under Illegal Contract (Restitution)
14.55 (1) Introduction
(2) Recovery Where Parties are Not *In Pari Delicto*
14.56 (a) Introduction
14.57 (b) Class Protection Statutes
14.58 (c) Fraud, Duress or Oppression
(3) Recovery Under an Independent Cause of Action
14.59 (a) Introduction
14.60–14.62 (b) Tort
14.63 (c) Collateral Contract

PARAGRAPHS

Consequences or Effects of Illegality (continued)
14.64–14.66 (4) Repentance or Timely Repudiation
14.67 (5) Equitable Exceptions?

Contracts in Restraint of Trade
14.68–14.71 Introduction
14.72–14.77 General Principles
14.78–14.79 Sale of a Business
14.80–14.85 Employment Contracts
14.86–14.88 Exclusive Dealing Arrangements—Focus on Solus Agreements
14.89–14.91 Other Categories

Severance
14.92–14.94 Introduction
14.95–14.96 Severance of Entire Clauses—Illegality of Part of the Consideration Test
14.97–14.99 Severance Within Covenants—'Blue Pencil Test'

14.100 **Proof of Illegality**

14.101–14.102 **Reform**

Introduction

14.1 The topic of illegality and public policy constitutes perhaps the most complex area of the law of contract. This is not surprising because the very concept of public policy is a very nebulous creature indeed. The focus here is not so much on the individual as such but, rather, on society. To this end, the courts are prepared to override the contractual rights of the parties concerned if to do so would give effect to the greater public good. Indeed, in virtually all situations concerning illegality of contract or a contract that is otherwise contrary to public policy, the general rule is that the loss will lie where it falls. In other words, the courts will not aid any of the parties since to do so would be to enforce a contract that has already been decreed to be anathema to the greater public good: inaction would appear to be the order of the day. There are, as we shall see, exceptions to this general rule but one would not go far wrong in proceeding from this premise in the first instance.

14.2 The concept of public policy, as already mentioned, is a rather 'slippery' creature. As Burroughs J put it in his oft-cited observations in *Richardson v Mellish* (1824), public policy is 'a very unruly horse, and when once you get astride it you never know where it will carry you. It may lead you from the sound law' (see p 252). Lord Denning MR, on the other hand, adopted a far more optimistic approach, observing, in *Enderby Town FC Ltd v The Football Association Ltd* (1971) thus: 'With a good man in the saddle, the unruly horse can be kept in control. It can jump over obstacles' (see p 606).

14.3 There is also the thorny issue as to whether or not the heads of public policy can be extended. This is especially important with regard to illegality at *common law* (see, generally, paragraph 14.28 ff, below). The general view, at least under English and (presumably) Singapore law, is that the heads of public policy will not be easily extended at all. This does not, however, mean that public policy is wholly static. On the contrary, the heads of public policy ought to be developed to meet the rapidly changing circumstances over time and, indeed, even existing heads of public policy may, as we shall see, evolve over time as well. However, the *actual practice* has evinced a general reluctance by the courts to extend the heads of public policy, except under very special circumstances. Perhaps, this is due, in part at least, to the fact that the (in particular, English) judiciary prefers to leave the resolution of problematic areas of law to the *legislature* instead as the latter is perceived to be better equipped to consider difficult areas of law which necessarily entail broader societal factors. It may also be the case that the courts perceive no small measure of subjectivity in the very process of developing as well as encompassing within legal structures the societal values necessarily involved. This point is, of course, closely related to the preference by the courts to leave the process of reform to the legislature. But, then again, legislative time is often rare and at a great premium (see paragraph 14.28, below, for some further reflections on this particular issue).

14.4 The law in this area is traditionally divided into two broad areas—*statutory* illegality on the one hand and (with regard to a category already referred to) illegality at *common law* on the other. Indeed, we shall see that, in addition to the difficulties generated by the concept of public policy, the specific area of statutory illegality is subject to much controversy as well (see, generally, paragraph 14.7 ff, below). This is due, in large part, to the lack of a coherent theoretical framework as well as the difficulties to be expected when the court attempts to ascertain the legislative intention of the provision(s) concerned.

14.5 This chapter begins with a discussion of statutory illegality, followed by a brief rendition of the established categories of illegality at common law. The *consequences* of illegality are then discussed.

Contracts *in restraint of trade* are becoming increasingly important and are therefore discussed in a separate part. The present chapter then concludes with a brief look at the important doctrine of *severance*, which might possibly 'save' at least part of the contract concerned from the draconian effects of a finding of illegality, as well as (in the briefest of fashions) the question of the proof of illegality and (finally) the topic of *reform*.

It should be noted that more difficult and (more importantly) *specialised* topics are outside the scope of the present work in general and the present chapter in particular. For example, the reader is referred to a brief discussion of conflict of laws issues in the context of illegality in A Phang, 'Illegality and Public Policy' in MP Furmston (ed), *Butterworths Common Law Series—The Law of Contract* (2nd ed, 2003) at paragraphs 5.235–5.236 (cf also the Singapore Court of Appeal decision of *Peh Teck Quee v Bayerische Landesbank Girozentrale* (2000)).

14.6 In addition to the relevant chapters in the leading contract textbooks, there have been a number of recent works dealing specifically with this rather difficult area of contract law. These include *Illegal Transactions* (1998) by N Enonchong and *Illegality and Public Policy* by RA Buckley (2002). Another work is by the present writer entitled 'Illegality and Public Policy' in MP Furmston (ed), *Butterworths Common Law Series—The Law of Contract* (2nd ed, 2003), Chapter 5, and mentioned in the preceding paragraph. For specific (local) updates, see A Phang, *Developments in Singapore Law Between 1996 and 2000* (Sweet & Maxwell Asia, 2001), pp 299–385 at pp 364–373 and, by the same author, 'Contract Law' (2001) *Singapore Academy of Law Annual Review of Singapore Cases* 118 at pp 149–152.

Statutory Illegality

Introduction

14.7 As already mentioned, the sphere of statutory illegality is by no means an easy topic to expound upon. However, a self-evident point that can be made right at the outset is that in order for any issue of statutory illegality to arise in the context of the law of contract, there must, of course, have been a contravention of the statute in question. Absent such contravention, there is no basic starting-point in the first instance.

14.8 It should also be noted that contravention of *subsidiary legislation* (as opposed to primary acts or legislation) might also result in adverse consequences under the law relating to contractual illegality. This is not surprising in view of the fact that subsidiary legislation also has, of course, the force of law. Where, however, guidelines do *not* have the force of law, there will be no legal consequences in accordance with the general and obvious principle stated in the preceding paragraph (see, for example, the Singapore High Court decision of *Sim Tony v Lim Ah Ghee (t/a Phil Real Estate & Building Services)* (1994) affirmed by the Court of Appeal in *Sim Tony v Lim Ah Ghee (t/a Phil Real Estate & Building Services)* (1995) as well as the Singapore High Court decision of *Shaikh Faisal t/a Gibca v Swan Hunter Singapore Pte Ltd* (1995)).

14.9 Even if there is a contravention, however, there will be no adverse civil consequences if the provision(s) of the statute itself expressly state that no such consequences will follow as a result of such contravention (see also per Augustine Paul J in the Malaysian High Court decision of *Rengamah a/p Rengasamy v Tai Yoke Lai* (1998) at p 269).

14.10 Further, even in the event of a contravention, it does *not necessarily* follow that adverse *civil* consequences *will* follow. There will surely be the relevant *criminal* consequences for contravention (which is virtually always embodied within the statutory provisions themselves). However, whether or not the *contract* itself will be rendered void as a result (in the *civil* sphere) depends very much on the *interpretation* of the provision(s) themselves in order to ascertain whether or not such a drastic consequence was indeed part of the *legislative intention* itself. This is, of course, not at all—in most cases, at least—easy and, indeed, the entire process of statutory interpretation is a major topic in and of itself.

14.11 Contracts, under the general rubric of 'statutory illegality', are traditionally classified under two further categories, viz '*express* prohibition' and '*implied* prohibition', respectively.

Express Prohibition

14.12 This particular category of statutory illegality comprises contracts which are *expressly* declared to be illegal by a particular statute (or, more commonly and accurately, a provision(s) thereof). It follows that the legislative intention is clear on the face of the provision(s) themselves and there is thus no need to invoke the tools of statutory interpretation in order to ascertain the relevant legislative intention.

Where the statutory language is clear, 'it is not open to the court to ascertain the intention of the legislature by considering how the law stood before the enactment of the [statute] and by looking at the objects and reasons set out in the original bill to discover the mischief which was intended to be suppressed' (per Ambrose J in the Singapore decision of *Turquand, Young & Co v Yat Yuen Hong Co Ltd* (1967) at p 292).

14.13 Examples of such statutory provisions are not rare in the Singapore context; they include sections 11 and (especially) 12 of the Professional Engineers Act (Cap 253, 1992 Rev Ed); the Sale of Commercial Properties Act (Cap 281, 1985 Rev Ed); and the Residential Property Act (Cap 274, 1985 Rev Ed).

Perhaps some brief mention might be made of the more specific area of *gaming contracts*. The position appears to be very strict, particularly with the attempt to recover under gaming and waging contracts within the scope of section 5 of the Civil Law Act (Cap 43, 1999 Rev Ed). The reader is referred, by way of some general background, especially to A Phang, *Developments in Singapore Law Between 1996 and 2000* (Sweet & Maxwell Asia, 2001) at pp 366–368 and, by the same author, 'Contract Law' (2001) *Singapore Academy of Law Annual Review of Singapore Cases* 118 at pp 150–152 (and, especially, the local cases cited and analysed in these two pieces). It should, however, be noted that although the law with regard to recovery of sums of money alleged to be won upon a wager may be rather strict (see, in particular, the recent Singapore Court of Appeal decision of *Star City Pty Ltd v Tan Hong Woon* (2002)), it is still well-established law that a *loan* for gaming or wagering, which is *valid* by the law of the place where the loan was made, is recoverable (see the Singapore High Court decision of *Las Vegas Hilton Corp v Khoo Teng Hock Sunny* (1997)).

Implied Prohibition

14.14 By its very nature, this is the more problematic category. As mentioned above (see paragraph 14.10), the ascertainment of the legislative intention where it is not clear on the face of the statute itself (in which case, it would be *express* prohibition) is not always easy. Indeed, it is often difficult and controversial (although previous relevant precedents furnish a helpful—albeit not necessarily conclusive—guide). It might therefore be helpful to state right at the outset of this section that the *key focus* is whether the *object* of the statute (or, more appropriately provision(s) thereof) is *only* to prohibit the *conduct* that is the subject of the statutory penalty *or* is the object *also* to prohibit *the very contract itself. Adverse civil consequences vis-à-vis the contract concerned follow only where the latter question is also answered in the affirmative. The contract, at this point, is impliedly prohibited.*

14.15 The leading exposition, in the present writer's view, is to be found in the judgment of Devlin J (as he then was) in the English High Court decision of *St John Shipping Corporation v Joseph Rank Ltd* (1957). It is perhaps ironic that the leading decision is one only at first instance but, then again, Lord Devlin was considered one of the most brilliant judges of the twentieth century, although he opted for an early retirement.

In the *St John Shipping* case, a ship was overloaded in contravention of the Merchant Shipping (Safety and Load Line Conventions) Act 1932. The master of the ship was prosecuted, convicted and fined. The defendant was the holder of a bill of lading. It had in fact paid most of the freight due to the plaintiff shipowners. However, together with another cargo owner, the defendant withheld a sum equivalent to the freight on the additional cargo by which the ship had been overloaded. The plaintiff sued for the balance of the freight and the defence was raised to the effect that there had been contractual illegality. There was no express prohibition as such. Devlin J held that there had not been any implied prohibition as well. The learned judge also delivered the now-famous warning that the courts ought not to be too quick to strike down a contract due to contractual illegality, particularly when 'so much of commercial life is governed by regulations of some sort or another, which may easily be broken without wicked intent' (see p 288).

When, then, would a contract be impliedly prohibited? Devlin J proffered the following extremely important statement of general principle (at p 287):

> 'The fundamental question is whether the statute means to prohibit the contract. The statute is to be construed in the ordinary way; one must have regard to all relevant considerations and no single consideration, however important, is conclusive.
>
> Two questions are involved. The first ... is: does the statute mean to prohibit contracts at all? But if this be answered in the affirmative, then one must ask: does this contract belong to the class which the statute intends to prohibit?'

14.16 Readers might also like to contrast two further leading decisions emanating from the English Court of Appeal. In *Archbolds (Freightage) Ltd v S Spanglett Ltd* (1961), it was held that the Road and Rail Traffic Act did not intend to prohibit the contract concerned and was intended, instead, 'to provide an orderly and comprehensive service' (see p 386, per Pearce LJ).

In *Anderson, Ltd v Daniel* (1924), on the other hand, the court held that the Fertilisers and Feeding Stuffs Act 1906 *did* intend to prohibit the contract concerned in the event of contravention. In that case, it was held that 'the penalty is imposed wholly for the protection of the public, and the purchaser is entitled to take the objection that as the vendors have failed to give the required invoice the contract of sale is illegal and they cannot sue for the price' (see p 144, per Bankes LJ).

14.17 There are many *local* decisions as well. However, they generally follow the English position, which has been set out briefly above (see, generally, A Phang, *Cheshire, Fifoot and Furmston's Law of Contract—Second Singapore and Malaysian Edition* (1998) at p 589 ff; and, with regard to *express* prohibition, see paragraphs 14.12–14.13, above).

14.18 Unfortunately, however, there appears to be *a quite different approach* towards ascertaining whether or not a particular contract is impliedly prohibited, which was advocated by Kerr LJ in the English Court of Appeal decision of *Phoenix General Insurance Co of Greece SA v Administratia Asiguralor de Stat* (1988), and where the learned judge observed as follows (at p 273):

> '(i) Where a statute prohibits *both* parties from concluding or

performing a contract when both or either of them have no authority to do so, the contract is *impliedly* prohibited: see *Mahmoud and Ispahani's* case ... and its analysis by Pearce LJ in the *Archbold's* case ... with which Devlin LJ agreed.

(ii) But where a statute merely prohibits one party from entering into a contract without authority and/or imposes a penalty on him if he does so (ie, a *unilateral* prohibition) it *does not follow* that the *contract* itself is *impliedly* prohibited so as to render it illegal and void. Whether or not the statute has this effect depends on considerations of public policy in the light of the mischief which the statute is designed to prevent, its language, scope and purpose, the consequences for the innocent party, and any other relevant considerations' (emphasis added).

A perusal of the above observations suggests that a distinction is now to be drawn between *bilateral* prohibitions (see (i), above) and *unilateral* prohibitions (see (ii), above) of the *parties*, whereas the hitherto accepted statement of general principle focuses very simply upon whether or not the provision(s) of the statute concerned intend to prohibit the *contract* (see paragraph 14.15, above). This generates a number of difficulties, which will now be dealt with briefly.

14.19 One difficulty is that Kerr LJ's statement (i), above, seems to be correlated with *express* prohibition. There is, first, the citation of the leading English decision of *Re Mahmoud and Ispahani* (1921), which concerns a situation of express prohibition. Secondly, unlike statement (ii), *no* inquiry into the legislative intention of parliament is required, which is precisely what happens when there is express prohibition (see paragraph 14.12, above). *However*, statement (i) itself talks about *implied* prohibition! But, as we have seen, because of the fact that in a situation of implied prohibition, the legislative intention is unclear, it is imperative that the court concerned attempts to ascertain such intention. *Yet*, a close perusal of statements (i) and (ii) by Kerr LJ in the preceding paragraph demonstrates that the ascertainment of legislative intention is only required in the latter, but not the former. To complicate matters yet further, both statements (i) and (ii) appear to pertain to *different aspects of implied prohibition*.

To summarise, the *traditional approach* requires the ascertainment of legislative intention in *all* situations of *implied* prohibition since it is only in situations of express prohibition that the legislative intention is clear on the face of the statute itself. *However*, Kerr LJ's approach (in the preceding paragraph) suggests that the ascertainment of legislative intention is *not* required in *all* situations of implied prohibition; it is only required where there is a *unilateral* prohibition (see his statement (ii), above), *but not* with regard to *bilateral* prohibition (see his statement (i), above).

The result is rather confusing since—at the expense of repetition—the ascertainment of legislative intention must necessarily be involved whenever it is not expressly stated and *regardless of* whether one or both *parties* is targeted by the provision(s) of the statute concerned (*contra*, however, per Kerr LJ). One *alternative* explanation is to argue that Kerr LJ's category of *bilateral* prohibition (see his statement (i), above) is merely an *alternative way* of describing the more traditional category of *express* prohibition (as to which see paragraph 14.12, above), whereas the learned judge's category of *unilateral* prohibition (see his statement (ii), above) is merely an *alternative way* of describing the (also more traditional) category of *implied* prohibition. *However, this argument is inconsistent with the language utilised by Kerr LJ himself.* As we have seen, *both* statements (i) *and* (ii) above pertain—in the learned judge's view at least—to *implied* prohibition.

There is a yet further difficulty with the alternative explanation just considered: if we consider Kerr LJ as correlating *express* prohibition (of the *contract*) with *bilateral* prohibition (of both *parties*) and as correlating *implied* prohibition (again, of the *contract*) with *unilateral* prohibition (of *only one party*), *difficulties of linkage arise.* To elaborate on the point just made (with regard to *linkage*), this alternative explanation operates on the premise that there is *a necessary linkage* between *the nature of the contractual prohibition* on the one hand and *who are the parties prohibited* on the other. The present writer would argue that there is *no necessary linkage*, for it is entirely possible for a statute to *expressly* prohibit the *contract without* directing the prohibition at *both parties* (ie it is only directed at *one* party, a situation of *unilateral* prohibition). By the same token, it is possible for a statute to *impliedly* prohibit the *contract even though* the prohibition itself *is* directed at *both parties* (ie a situation of *bilateral* prohibition). The focus, insofar as *the nature of* the prohibition is concerned, ought (the present writer would argue) to be on *the intention of the legislature* with regard to *the contract itself*. Whether or not the actual language of the statute is directed at one or both *parties* really relates to *the mechanics and details* of the prohibition itself, which (in turn) *may or may not* impact on *the nature of the prohibition* on the *contract* (ie whether there is an express or implied prohibition of *the contract*). It is admitted that a statutory provision which is directed against *both parties* is *more likely* to be constituted in a manner that is classified as an *express prohibition of the contract*, compared to one which is directed at *only one of the parties*. *However*, the final answer *cannot* be made to depend solely or even mainly on (with respect) a *simplistic one-dimensional* correlation with the mechanics and details of the prohibition of the *parties* themselves.

To summarise, the problem with Kerr LJ's approach (see the preceding paragraph) is that it has focused on the *parties* when it ought (with respect) to have focused, instead, on whether or not the *contract* has been prohibited (whether expressly or impliedly). The latter focus is indeed the focus of the traditional approach which the present writer would therefore argue is clearly to be preferred. In other words, the focus and approach ought, in the final analysis, to be on ascertaining whether or not the prohibition contained in the statute concerned prohibits *the contract*, utilising the general principles laid down by Devlin J in the *St John Shipping* case (see paragraph 14.15, above). The actual details or mechanics of prohibition (in Kerr LJ's terminology, whether one or both *parties* are affected by the prohibition) can only be taken into account as helpful factors *and no more*. Hence, where, for example, the statutory proscription *only affects one of the parties* (ie a situation of *unilateral* prohibition of one party), it must *not* be concluded—without more—that the situation is one of *implied* prohibition of *the contract* if a plain reading of the statutory language suggests that the *contract* is *expressly* prohibited. As already observed above, however, where the statutory proscription is directed against *both of the parties* (ie a situation of *bilateral* prohibition of the *parties*), it is *more likely* to be constituted (and, hence, construed) as an *express* prohibition of *the contract*, although this is, once again, *only a rebuttable presumption* and is *not* a rule written in stone.

Formation vs Performance

14.20 The various textbooks draw a distinction between contracts illegal as *formed* and illegal as *performed* (a distinction which is also equally applicable in the common law context as well, as to which see, generally, paragraph 14.28 ff, below). Contracts which are *expressly* prohibited (see paragraph 14.12, above) are necessarily illegal as *formed* as the provision(s) concerned clearly prohibit the very formation of the contract itself. However, such a result is not invariably the case with regard to contracts which are *impliedly* prohibited (as to which see, generally, paragraph 14.14 ff, above). It appears that this distinction between formation and performance is of real practical importance as a contract illegal as formed would clearly preclude any recovery whatsoever, whereas this draconian consequence need not necessarily follow with regard to contracts illegal as performed.

14.21 However, the present writer has argued elsewhere that this distinction between formation and performance is unhelpful (see A Phang, 'Vitiating Factors in Contract Law—The Interaction of Theory and Practice' (1998) 10 *Singapore Academy of Law Journal* 1 at pp 64–66). One possible pitfall occurs when there is the temptation—in the absence of a direct reference to the contract in the statute concerned and, hence, the need to refer directly to the prohibited *conduct* in the first instance—to equate implied prohibition with contracts which are illegal as performed. However, whilst the concept of 'prohibited *conduct*' refers to conduct that contravenes the statute and is (in all likelihood) subject to *criminal* penalties, the concept of 'illegal *performance*' is a term of art that centres around the issue as to whether or not there are *additional (and adverse) civil consequences beyond the criminal penalty in a situation where the prohibition is not express but, rather, implied*. There are, in other words, *two notions* of the concept of 'illegal performance', both of which are *quite different*. The *first* refers to *literal* (illegal) performance, without which no issue of illegality can arise in the first place; *criminal* penalties may attach but it still remains to be considered whether *additional (adverse) civil consequences* will attach. The *second* refers to illegal performance which is held in law to *entail adverse civil consequences*, having regard to the legislative intention concerned.

Returning to the *latter* concept, in order to ascertain whether the additional civil consequences indeed attach to the contract in question, the central inquiry (as just alluded to above) is whether or not the *legislative intention* was to *prohibit the contract, in addition to the conduct* (see paragraph 14.15, above). It will be seen that the inquiry just stated (in the context of *implied* prohibition) is *identical* to that applied to the category of *express* prohibition. The only difference in practice is that, insofar as the category of *express* prohibition is concerned, the legislative intention is so obvious on the face of the statute (see paragraph 14.12, above) that there is no need for the court to take any further steps in order to ascertain what the legislative intention in fact is. But if this is so, then, logic would demand that if we treat contracts under the category of *express* prohibition as going to *formation* (see paragraph 14.20, above), then the *same* treatment ought to be accorded to contracts under the category of *implied* prohibition *as well*. Indeed, such treatment *is* justifiable on its own terms, for if the legislative intention is to prohibit the contract (even where this is not apparent on the face of the statutory provision(s), ie *implied* prohibition), then the statutory contravention strikes, *in substance*, at *the very root of the contract itself*. This would make the entire situation (of *implied* prohibition), *in effect*, one pertaining to a contract illegal as *formed*. If so, then the distinction drawn between contracts illegal as formed and contracts illegal as performed becomes blurred, even erased.

14.22 The argument proffered in the preceding paragraph to the effect that there is, in the final analysis, little or no difference (in substance) between the contracts illegal as formed and contracts illegal as performed derives more than a modicum of support from Devlin J in the *St John Shipping* case (see paragraph 14.15, above). In that case, the learned judge observed thus (at p 281):

> 'When fully considered it is plain that they [ie the earlier precedents] do not proceed upon the basis that in the course of performing a legal contract an illegality was committed; but on the *narrower basis* that the way in which the contract was performed *turned it into the sort of contract that was prohibited by the statute*' (emphasis added).

In other words, *literal* performance in contravention of the statute is *not*—in and of itself—sufficient to result in adverse *civil* consequences (this is the *first conception* of the concept of 'illegal performance' considered above in paragraph 14.21). What *does* result in adverse *civil* consequences, however, is the fact that the literal (illegal) performance has, *by virtue of the legislative intention, related back* to and (in Devlin J's words just quoted above) '*turned*' the *contract* into one that is *prohibited*—a situation similar in all respects to one where the contract is illegal as *formed*, a point made in the preceding paragraph. Indeed, in the *St John Shipping* case, Devlin J also observed, in a similar vein, thus (at p 284):

> 'But whether it is the terms of the contract or the performance of it that is called in question, the test is *just the same*: is the *contract, as made or as performed*, a contract that is prohibited by the statute?' (emphasis added)

14.23 Given the fact that the distinction between contracts illegal as formed and contracts illegal as performed is not helpful in the least because where the contract is indeed rendered void and unenforceable owing to the legislative intention, then regardless of which category we are dealing with, the contract is—in *both* categories—struck right at *its root, at its very formation*, this distinction ought (it is submitted) to be done away with.

Situations Where There is Neither Express nor Implied Prohibition

14.24 If, in fact, there is neither an express nor implied prohibition of the contract (as to which, see, generally, above in paragraphs 14.12–14.13 and 14.14–14.19, respectively), it would appear, having regard to the discussion above, that the transaction is wholly untainted by illegality, at least insofar as adverse civil consequences are concerned. This is indeed both logical as well as the general rule. *However*, there is a *qualification* which needs to be dealt with here, albeit if only briefly.

14.25 The qualification to the general rule that the contract will be upheld in the civil sphere centres around the *intention of one or both of the contracting parties*. Once again, the following observations by Devlin J in the *St John Shipping* case (discussed above in paragraphs 14.15 and 14.22) are apposite (at p 283):

> '[A] contract which is entered into *with the object of committing an illegal act is unenforceable.* The application of this principle *depends upon proof of the intent, at the time the contract was made, to break the law*; *if* the intent is *mutual* the contract is *not enforceable at all*, and, *if unilateral*, it is *unenforceable at the suit of the party who is proved to have it*' (emphasis added).

14.26 To summarise, where a party enters into a contract *with the intention of contravening the statute*, he or she (as a '*guilty party*') *cannot* enforce his or her rights under the terms of the contract. If, of course, *both* contracting parties enter into the contract with such an intention, then *both* of them would *not* be allowed to enforce their respective rights under the terms of the contract (ie both would be considered, in such a situation, to be '*guilty parties*').

All this is eminently logical and commonsensical. If the courts would otherwise have allowed the contracting party or parties (as the case may be) to enforce the contract, it is *itself a general affront to public policy* to allow either or both to do so *if either or both had the intention of contravening the provision(s) of the statute concerned.*

14.27 It should be noted that in order to become a 'guilty party' (see the preceding paragraph), there has, *in addition to* knowledge of the illegality, some form of *participation* on the part of the party concerned: see the English Court of Appeal decision of *Ashmore, Benson, Pease & Co Ltd v AV Dawson Ltd* (1973), especially at pp 832 and 836, per Lord Denning MR and Scarman LJ (as he then was), respectively. Cf also the Singapore High Court decision of *Dimpex Gems (Singapore) Pte Ltd v Yusoof Diamonds Pte Ltd* (1988).

Illegality at Common Law

Introduction

14.28 We have already seen that the heads of public policy, at least under English and (presumably) Singapore law, will not be extended liberally (see paragraph 14.3, above). It is suggested, however, that such an approach—already strict by its very nature—ought not to be taken too far. What is important is that the courts must bring within its scrutiny general situations that so require its attention, taking into account the fact that circumstances must necessarily change with the times and so, with it, the various facets of public policy itself. The law must, in this regard, continue to keep pace with these inevitable changes in societal values as well as public policy.

14.29 The rather strict approach notwithstanding, there are nevertheless not a few established situations of illegality at common law. Before proceeding to describe and analyse them, it is important to note that the very *fact* that there are such established situations buttresses the view just proffered to the effect that the strict approach against public policy ought not to be taken too far. After all, if this (strict) approach were to be applied rigidly, there would have been extremely few—if any—heads of public policy today: the main issue raised, in this particular regard, being how the so-called existing heads of public policy arose in the first place.

Contracts Prejudicial to Administration of Justice

14.30 These include, for example, *contracts to stifle a prosecution*. However, there is no taint of illegality where the alleged offence is not one of public concern (see the leading English decision of *Keir v Leeman* (1844)).

14.31 Another category relates to *contracts savouring of maintenance or champerty*. 'Maintenance' involves the stirring up of litigation by furnishing aid to a party to either commence or defend a claim without just cause. 'Champerty' occurs when there is the *additional* agreement that the person furnishing such aid will receive a share of what is recovered in the action. There have been a great many developments in both the statutory as well as common law sphere in England in recent years, with greater liberality now being provided by both statute as well as accompanying subsidiary legislation (for further details, see, generally, A Phang, 'Illegality and Public Policy' MP Furmston (ed), *Butterworths Common Law Series—The Law of Contract* (2nd ed, 2003) at paragraphs 5.67–5.72). The law in Singapore would appear to be more settled, albeit (it is submitted) rather strict, although the general trend now (including, as just mentioned, that in England) is towards greater liberality.

14.32 For an interesting case relating to an action by a registered police informer against a police inspector and his chief constable for breach of contract, see the English Court of Appeal decision of *Carnduff v Rock* (2001). Here, the action was to recover payment for information and assistance rendered to the police as well as damages for consequential loss and damage caused by the defendants' alleged breach of contract and arising from the plaintiff's role as a police informer being uncovered as a result of the present action. The court held in favour of the defendants, observing, *inter alia*, that the various matters in issue 'cannot be litigated consistently with the public interest' (see p 1795, per Laws J; see also, for further details, A Phang, 'Illegality and Public Policy' in MP Furmston (ed), *Butterworths Common Law Series—The Law of Contract* (2nd ed, 2003) at paragraph 5.74).

Contracts to Deceive Public Authorities

14.33 One oft-cited specific instance of this particular category of contracts concerns a contract to defraud the revenue (the English decision most oft-cited under this particular category is *Alexander v Rayson* (1936)). Indeed, this category of contracts is also well-established in the local case law (see A Phang, *Cheshire, Fifoot and Furmston's Law of Contract—Second Singapore and Malaysian Edition* (1998) at pp 645–646; and for further discussion (including discussion of other instances), see A Phang, 'Illegality and Public Policy' in MP Furmston (ed), *Butterworths Common Law Series—The Law of Contract* (2nd ed, 2003) at paragraphs 5.75–5.77).

Contracts to Oust Jurisdiction of the Courts

14.34 This category of contracts is closely connected to the preceding category just discussed. Not surprisingly, such contracts are against public policy and, hence, void and unenforceable. However, more leeway has been given where alternative dispute resolution (in particular, arbitration) is involved. In the leading House of Lords decision of *Scott v Avery* (1856), it was held that a condition precedent to the effect that no legal proceedings could be instituted until the award of an arbitrator on a question of law was handed down was not unlawful. However, the agreement would be unlawful if there had been a blanket prohibition against ever instituting legal proceedings in a court of law.

14.35 What is the position with respect to an arbitration agreement if the underlying contract is illegal? In order for the arbitrator(s) to have jurisdiction over the matter, the arbitration agreement must of course be enforceable. Colman J, in the English High Court decision of *Westacre Investments Inc v Jugoimport-SPDR Ltd* (1998) expressed the view (at p 794) that this depended:

> 'upon whether the nature of the illegality is such that, in the case of statutory illegality the statute has the effect of impeaching that [arbitration] agreement as well as the underlying contract and, in the case of illegality at common law, public policy requires that disputes about the underlying contract should not be referred to arbitration.'

There is the related issue with regard to the *enforcement* of the arbitration award. Here, there appears to be some difference of opinion in the English context, and the reader is referred to A Phang, 'Illegality and Public Policy' in MP Furmston (ed), *Butterworths Common Law Series—The Law of Contract* (2nd ed, 2003) at paragraph 5.93 (see, in particular, now, the English Court of Appeal decision in *Westacre Investments Inc v Jugoimport-SPDR* (2000), which affirmed the decision of Colman J referred to above and the majority approach of which tends towards upholding the enforcement of arbitration awards).

14.36 Insofar as internal rules embodied within the contract with regard to domestic remedies are concerned, regard may be had to the following statement of general principles by Goff J in the English decision of *Leigh v National Union of Railwaymen* (1970) as follows (at p 334):

> 'The first [principle] is that even where there is an express provision in the rules that the plaintiff must first exhaust his domestic remedies, the court is not absolutely bound by that because its jurisdiction cannot be ousted, but the plaintiff will have to show cause why it should interfere with the contractual position. This is consonant with the rule in the case of a submission to arbitration where the court always has a discretion whether to stay an action but cause must be shown why it should not. The second proposition is largely the converse of the first, namely, that in the absence of such a provision the court can readily, or at all events more readily, grant relief without prior recourse to the domestic remedies, but may require the plaintiff to resort first to those remedies.'

14.37 It should also be noted that agreements by wives not to apply to the court for maintenance are *prima facie* contrary to the public interest as this would undermine the sanctity of marriage and throw the financial burden on public funds instead (see, for example, the English decisions of *Hyman v Hyman* (1929) and *Sutton v Sutton* (1984)). The United Kingdom (only) has since enacted legislation to modify the situation and allow the wife recourse to the agreement, provided it is in writing (see section 34 of the UK Matrimonial Causes Act 1973).

14.38 Even more generally, any attempt by a contracting party to exclude the operation of *mandatory* rules of law will generally be held to be invalid. Much will, of course, depend on the precise language as well as policy of the statute concerned (see also, for example, the English House of Lords decision of *Johnson v Moreton* (1980)).

Contracts to Commit (or Involving) a Crime, Tort or Fraud

14.39 This is also a straightforward category and it is easy to see why the courts would prohibit such contracts as being contrary to public policy. There may also be a possible linkage to statutory illegality inasmuch as a contract to contravene a statutory provision—even if not otherwise prohibited by such a contravention—is nevertheless still illegal inasmuch as it is a contract to commit a crime at common law (see, further, A Phang, 'Illegality and Public Policy' in MP Furmston (ed), *Butterworths Common Law Series—The Law of Contract* (2nd ed, 2003) at paragraph 5.83).

Contracts Prejudicial to Public Safety

14.40 The paradigm example under this particular category of contracts are contracts which involve *trading with the enemy*. The location of the parties and the elements of the contract are the most important considerations, rather than the mere nationalities of the parties themselves (see, for example, the English decisions of *Porter v Freudenberg* (1915) and *Sovracht (V/O) v Van Udens Scheepvart en Agentuur Maatschappij (NV Gebr)* (1943); see also A Phang, 'Illegality and Public Policy' in MP Furmston (ed), *Butterworths Common Law Series—The Law of Contract* (2nd ed, 2003) at paragraph 5.79).

14.41 A contract that will harm the welfare of a foreign and friendly country is also prohibited, being a breach of international comity (see, for example, the leading House of Lords decision of *Regazzoni v KC Sethia (1944) Ltd* (1958); and for further elaboration, see, generally, A Phang, 'Illegality and Public Policy' in MP Furmston (ed), *Butterworths Common Law Series—The Law of Contract* (2nd ed, 2003) at paragraphs 5.80–5.82).

Contracts Prejudicial to Status of Marriage—Marriage Brokage Contracts

14.42 Where, in return for a reward, there is a contract between the parties whereby one party agrees to procure a marriage for the other party, this is contrary to public policy under English law as constituting a marriage brokage contract (the leading decision being that of *Hermann v Charlesworth* (1905)).

Nevertheless, there is some indication, even under English law, that marriage brokage contracts were not frowned upon as much by the courts. This takes the form of the courts permitting the recovery of money already paid (pursuant to the procurement of a marriage) on a broad equitable ground.

14.43 In the *local* context, the position is less clear, with cases going either way (see, generally, A Phang, *Cheshire, Fifoot and Furmston's Law of Contract—Second Singapore and Malaysian Edition* (1998) at pp 691–692). It is suggested that perhaps the best approach is to examine the *underlying rationale* behind the English rule prohibiting such contracts. The public interest is, not surprisingly, cited in *Hermann v Charlesworth* (1905). More specifically, the payment of a monetary consideration, the abuse of power by parents and guardians, and the prevention of reckless and inappropriate marriages are reasons that are given for the above-mentioned prohibition. But are these reasons applicable in the *local* context? Are there local customs or practices to the contrary? But what about the influence of modernisation and industrialisation? What *exactly is* the position in Singapore at the present time? Clearly, more *empirical research* would be very helpful. However, even without such further research, it should be noted that, in the *Singapore* context at least, the case *against* marriage brokage contracts has taken on an added dimension. Changed social conditions, particularly with regard to increasing numbers of unmarried graduate women, have necessitated the setting up of government-sponsored marriage-facilitating institutions such as the Social Development Unit (or SDU) and the Social Development Section (or SDS). There have been private institutions set up as well that conduct a variety of activities and also have match-making facilities. It could perhaps be argued that no monetary consideration has passed, although membership fees may be a problem and it is believed that—for the private organisations at least—the fees paid might in fact be rather high. Then, of course, there are the other factors—mentioned briefly above—which constituted part of the original rationale behind the proscription of marriage brokage contracts. It could well be the case, however, that, in the *Singapore* context at least, times have changed and that the rule prohibiting marriage brokage contracts ought to be *abolished*. Certainly, it would appear to the present writer that despite this rule being part of the Singapore legal landscape, it is *ignored in practice* in any event.

For further reading, see R Powell, 'Marriage Brokage Agreements' [1953] *Current Legal Problems* 254 and V Sinnadurai, 'Contracts Relating to Marriage' (1979) 6 *Journal of Malaysian and Comparative Law* 303 (Part I); (1980) 7 *Journal of Malaysian and Comparative Law* 1 (Part II).

Other Contracts Prejudicial to Status of Marriage

14.44 What about agreements by married persons to marry? This would appear contrary to public policy, although the House of Lords decision in *Fender v St John Mildmay* (1938) held that, where such a promise was made by a married person *after* he or she had obtained a decree *nisi* of divorce (but before the decree was made final), such a promise would not be contrary to public policy (*contra* if divorce was merely contemplated and, *a fortiori*, where no divorce proceedings were contemplated at all). Although breach of promise to marry was abolished as a cause of action in England, this is not the case in Singapore.

14.45 What about agreements between spouses for *future* separation? Such agreements are *prima facie* invalid as being contrary to public policy (see, for example, *Brodie v Brodie* (1917)). However, there are a couple of exceptions. First, the prohibition will not apply when the spouses are already separated (see, for example, *Wilson v Wilson* (1848)). Secondly, if such an agreement is made during a reconciliation of estranged spouses, the agreement is valid on the basis that public policy is enhanced rather than undermined since, in the absence of such an agreement, such reconciliation would have been less likely to occur (see, for example, *Harrison v Harrison* (1910)).

Contracts Promoting Sexual Immorality

14.46 The oft-cited decision under this particular category is the English decision in *Pearce v Brooks* (1866), where the defendant prostitute hired an ornamental brougham (a type of horse-drawn coach) 'for the purpose of display, that is, for the purpose of enabling the defendant to pursue her calling' (see p 220). The plaintiffs were coach-builders, who sued for the hire owed. The court held that there could be no recovery as the entire transaction was tainted by illegality.

It should be noted, however, that Pollock CB drew a distinction between things supplied which are both necessary and useful for ordinary purposes (although they could also be used for immoral purposes) and things supplied which could *probably only* be used for immoral purposes (see p 221). It is suggested that this is a very commonsensical distinction to draw.

14.47 The decision in *Pearce v Brooks* (1866) has, in fact, been applied in the *local* context. It was not, however, referred to in the Singapore High Court decision of *Berenger v Rozario (mw)* (1953), although this case is also a good illustration of a contract under this particular category. There was here a claim, *inter alia*, for the return of a car. The plaintiff and defendant —hitherto cohabitees—had fallen out with each other. The court held that there could be no action on the contract as such, although it did hold that there could be a claim for the return of the car based on *an independent cause of action*. The rationale for, as well as a brief analysis of, this latter cause of action will be undertaken later (see paragraph 14.59 ff, below).

14.48 As with the case of marriage brokage contracts (see paragraph 14.43, above), the issue arises as to whether or not, in an *extra-legal context*, the rather strict approach of the courts under this particular category of contracts ought to be continued. More specifically, the question arises as to what *precisely* are *the culture and social mores of the local population*. In England, at least, there appears to be a more liberal approach adopted by the courts, having regard to the fact that many couples simply cohabit together (see, for example, the English Court of Appeal decision of *Heglibiston Establishment v Heyman* (1978) especially at p 571, per Browne LJ; and for an even stronger example, see the Queensland Supreme Court decision of *Andrews v Parker* (1973)). There are certainly some indications in the *local* context that (in particular) youths are becoming more liberal in terms of their relationships. This does not, of course, mean that the courts ought to follow slavishly changes in social values. On the contrary, it is suggested that the overriding public policy in Singapore is to frown upon sexual immorality and that the courts would therefore still incline towards a stricter approach. Certainly, the views of the government as well as the various mainstream religions would tend to support the stricter view. More *empirical research* is obviously desirable. In the meantime, however, the views expressed by Gopal Sri Ram JCA in the Malaysian Court of Appeal decision of *Tengku Abdullah Sultan Abu Bakar v Mohd Latiff bin Shah* (1996) may be usefully noted. In that decision, the learned judge was responding to the observations of Lord Browne-Wilkinson in the House of Lords decision of *Barclays Bank Plc v O'Brien* (1994) (discussed above, at paragraph 13.37 ff), where the learned Law Lord had observed thus (at p 198): 'Now that unmarried cohabitation, whether heterosexual or homosexual, is widespread in our society, the law should recognise this.' Gopal Sri Ram JCA responded as follows (see pp 309–310):

> 'The views expressed in *O'Brien's* case merely reflect the law's attempt to keep in tandem with the moral standards of the society in which an *English* court functions. Our society, on the other hand, has *an entirely different set of moral standards.* It would *therefore be quite wrong to blindly follow all foreign decisions if the result would facilitate moral decadence within our social structure.*
>
> Accordingly, on grounds of *public policy*, this court will *not* extend the doctrine to those *non-marital relationships* alluded to by Lord Browne-Wilkinson ... Our refusal to act in such cases is based upon the *policy consideration* that refusing to accede to such an extension *may deter a fall in the moral standards of our society'* (emphasis added).

It is suggested that, as alluded to above, a similar position would probably be adopted in the *Singapore* context.

Contracts That are Liable to Corrupt Public Life

14.49 What would be the legal position if a member of a political party entered into an agreement with his or her political party that he or she would contribute a substantial proportion of his or her monthly allowance as Member of Parliament if, indeed, he or she were in fact elected into Parliament? What if that person further agreed that if he or she did any act that was perceived to be against the interest of the political party, he or she would forfeit his or her seat in Parliament? This was precisely what happened in the Malaysian Federal Court decision of *Datuk Ong Kee Hui v Sinyium Anak Mutit* (1983). Not surprisingly, it was held that these arrangements were illegal: the monthly allowance was intended to respond to the temptation to abuse one's political position for gain, whilst the agreement to forfeit the Parliamentary seat interfered with the Member's duty to exercise his or her independent judgment on behalf of the people who had voted him or her into Parliament.

14.50 The buying and selling of public offices and titles would also come within the present proscription, as would other agreements that would compromise the proper effecting of public duties, an instance of which was noted in the preceding paragraph. It is important, however, to emphasise that contracts falling under this particular category must pertain to the *public* administration.

Contracts Restricting Personal Liberty

14.51 There are, not surprisingly, not many such cases. It appears that there must be a very severe restriction of a contracting party's liberty before illegality 'bites'. The difficulty, again, not surprisingly, is to know where precisely the line is to be drawn (contrast, for example, the English decisions of *Horwood v Millar's Timber and Trading Co* (1917) and *Denny v Denny* (1919)).

Consequences or Effects of Illegality

Introduction

14.52 For the layperson, at least, this is arguably the most important part of the law relating to contractual illegality simply because he or she would clearly like to know what the *consequences* or *effects* of illegality are on the contract itself.

To this end, the consequences of illegality under the law of contract have been traditionally classified into two main categories. The *first* pertains to recovery under the illegal contract itself. The *second* pertains to recovery of benefits that have hitherto passed under the contract (which itself constitutes a form of *restitution*, rather than recovery under the contract itself). By definition, recovery under this latter category is more restricted because the recovery of *full* contractual loss is obviously not on the cards at all.

Recovery Under Illegal Contract

14.53 This has already been alluded to during our discussion of statutory illegality above. The principle is fairly straightforward: *no recovery whatsoever is permitted with respect to a contract that has either been expressly or impliedly prohibited by statute*. This is a draconian and prophylactic rule inasmuch as the intentions or culpability of the contracting parties is immaterial.

Insofar as the *common law* is concerned, the situation should, by its very nature, depend on whether or not either or both of the contracting parties were 'guilty parties', where their intention is of course crucial and where the basic principles concerned were in fact canvassed earlier with regard to statutory illegality (see paragraphs 14.25–14.27).

14.54 It does not follow, however, that no recovery whatsoever is possible. As already alluded to above, there might be some recovery by way of restitution.

Recovery of Benefits Conferred Under Illegal Contract (Restitution)

(1) *Introduction*

14.55 Recovery of benefits conferred under an illegal contract by way of restitution (as opposed to recovery of full contractual damages) may possibly be obtained through a number of avenues.

However, it used to be thought, under what was popularly termed the '*public conscience* test', that even if recovery were otherwise permitted under one or more of the legal avenues just referred to, the court could still exercise its discretion to *refuse* recovery if to allow recovery would shock the conscience of the court. It should be noted that the 'public conscience test' has been firmly *rejected* by the House of Lords in *Tinsley v Milligan* (1994). Despite some potential difficulties, the *Singapore* position ought, the present writer has argued elsewhere, to be the same as that in England and that such an approach would not represent a slavish adherence to English law but would be justified on principle (see also A Phang, 'Trends in the Core Areas of Singapore Law Between 1990 and 1995—Contract' in *Review of Judicial and Legal Reforms in Singapore Between 1990 and 1995* (1996), pp 250–317, especially at pp 292–294).

(2) *Recovery Where Parties are Not* In Pari Delicto

(a) Introduction

14.56 The underlying theme or strand here is that where one of the parties is deemed, in law, *not to be equally at fault*, that party will be allowed to recover benefits conferred under the illegal contract. Using the oft-cited Latin phrase, the parties are, in such a situation, not *in pari delicto*.

Such a situation can arise in one of at least two ways, which we will now briefly consider.

(b) Class Protection Statutes

14.57 The rationale underlying this particular approach is very straightforward: if, either expressly or on a true construction of the statute (or, rather, relevant provision(s) thereof), the legislative intention is to protect a class of persons to whom one of the contracting parties belongs, then that particular contracting party will be allowed to recover benefits conferred under the illegal contract (see, for example, the oft-cited Privy Council decision of *Kiriri Cotton Co Ltd v Ranchhoddas Keshavji Dewani* (1960) and, for an illustrative case closer to home, the Malaysian decision of *Beca (Malaysia) Sdn Bhd v Tan Choong Kuang* (1986); for possible conceptual as well as practical difficulties, see A Phang, *Cheshire, Fifoot and Furmston's Law of Contract—Second Singapore and Malaysian Edition* (1998) at p 673). It will be seen that, under such a category, the contracting parties are *not equally at fault* at least insofar as that particular statute is concerned.

(c) Fraud, Duress or Oppression

14.58 This is, again, a straightforward category as the presence of fraud, duress or oppression would clearly render the contracting parties *not equally at fault* and that, therefore, one of the parties would *not* be *in pari delicto* (for an illustration of fraudulent misrepresentation, see the English Court of Appeal decision of *Shelley v Paddock* (1980) (for fraudulent misrepresentation generally, see paragraph 12.27 ff, above) and for an illustration of oppression, see the judgment of Fry LJ in the (also) English Court of Appeal decision of *Kearley v Thomson* (1890), the latter decision of which is also discussed with regard to repentance or timely repudiation, which was in fact the main focus of that particular case).

(3) *Recovery Under an Independent Cause of Action*

(a) Introduction

14.59 The rationale for this particular set of categories of recovery in restitution is also relatively straightforward. Where the party who has conferred the benefit under the illegal contract premises his or her *legal right to recovery* on *an independent cause of action and not on the illegal contract as such*, there is no reason in principle why his or her right to recovery should be denied by the court. To put it another way, recovery is permitted because the plaintiff relies upon a cause of action *independent of (and, therefore, independent of the taint of) the illegality in question.*

There are at least two main categories of recovery under this particular approach—in tort and under a collateral contract.

(b) Tort

14.60 It should be noted at the outset that the law of torts covers a variety of topics and substantive causes of action, only some of which are germane to the present section.

One possible and popular action is for the tort of *conversion*, where the plaintiff can recover what was transferred on the basis that the defendant has unlawfully converted it to his or her use, provided that the plaintiff still has title to the property concerned (see, in this regard, the leading English Court of Appeal decision of *Bowmakers, Ltd v Barnet Instruments, Ltd* (1945); reference may also be made to the leading Malaysian Privy Council decision of *Sajan Singh v Sardara Ali* (1960) (which, however, dealt with the closely related action of detinue, now abolished in England but still, presumably, the law in Singapore)). The *Bowmakers* case itself is not, however, without controversy; see, for example, B Coote, 'Another Look at *Bowmakers v Barnet Instruments*' (1972) 35 *Modern Law Review* 38. Another illustrative situation is an action for *fraudulent misrepresentation* (see, for example, *Shelley v Paddock* (1980), referred to at paragraph 14.58, above; however, it would appear that for the plaintiff to succeed, he or she must prove ignorance of the illegality *and* that the defendant's conduct has been such that the defendant has been primarily responsible for the mistake of law).

The principle in the *Bowmakers* case has in fact been recently applied in the context of resulting trusts in the leading House of Lords decision of *Tinsley v Milligan* (1994). In this case, a successful action was permitted in favour of the defendant on her counterclaim, the counterclaim being based on a resulting trust held by the plaintiff in her (the defendant's) favour. There has, however, been some criticism of *Tinsley v Milligan* and, indeed, the Australian High Court, in *Nelson v Nelson* (1995), refused to follow *Tinsley v Milligan* (on the technical distinction drawn between the presumption of a resulting trust on the one hand and the presumption of advancement on the other, with the rebutting of the latter presumption requiring reliance on the illegal transaction). The controversy is outside the purview of the present work and the interested reader is referred to literature elsewhere (see, for example, A Phang, 'Of Illegality and Presumptions—Australian Departures and Possible Solutions' (1996) 11 *Journal of Contract Law* 53).

14.61 The present writer has in fact ventured to suggest that reliance on the illegal contract is in fact inevitable and that it might well be preferable—and less artificial—to develop an independent and substantive doctrine of restitution instead: an approach that would not in fact entail (at least critical) reliance on the illegal contract as such (see Phang, paragraph 14.60, above for a full development of this argument as well as responses to possible difficulties as well as objections).

14.62 Towards the end of the *Bowmakers* case (see, also, paragraph 14.60, above), du Parcq LJ observed thus (see p 72):

> 'It must not be supposed that the general rule which we have stated [allowing for recovery under an independent cause of action: see paragraph 14.60, above] is subject to no exception. Indeed, there is one obvious exception, namely, that class of case in which the goods claimed are of such a kind that it is unlawful to deal in them at all, as for example, obscene books. *No doubt, there are others, but it is unnecessary, and would we think be unwise, to seek to name them all or to forecast the decisions which would be given in a variety of circumstances which may hereafter arise*' (emphasis added).

Despite the apparently broad tenor of the above observation, recent (English) case law suggests that it must be confined to a somewhat narrower compass (see, for example, the English Court of Appeal decisions of *Costello v Chief Constable of Derbyshire Constabulary* (2001) and *Webb v Chief Constable of Merseyside Police* (2000) (the latter decision concerned an action by the plaintiffs for the return of money lawfully seized by the police on the suspicion that it constituted the proceeds of drug trafficking and it was held that du Parcq LJ's exception did *not* apply as 'money is not something which it is unlawful to deal in at all' (see p 444, per May LJ)) and see, generally, A Phang, 'Illegality and Public Policy' in MP Furmston (ed), *Butterworths Common Law Series—The Law of Contract* (2nd ed, 2003) at paragraph 5.215.

(c) Collateral Contract

14.63 Although we are presently considering recovery in restitution, this particular avenue of recovery threatens to go much further and, as a result, sits rather uneasily in this particular section. The possible (even probable) contradiction consists in the fact that if recovery is permitted by way of a collateral contract, there is every possibility that the plaintiff would be allowed to recover what could not otherwise be recovered under the illegal contract which (as we have seen in paragraph 14.53, above) precludes all recovery whatsoever. What results, in other words, is a possible 'backdoor' opening for the plaintiff to recover what he or she could not otherwise have recovered via the 'frontdoor'. It is perhaps because of the very real possibility of contradiction that we have had such few precedents on this particular point. Indeed, the one true decision of any real significance is a fairly dated one: the English Court of Appeal case of *Strongman (1945) Ltd v Sincock* (1955).

In *Strongman*, the defendant architects had employed the plaintiff builders to convert certain buildings. The defendants undertook to obtain the necessary building licences. Licences were obtained. Unfortunately, the licences were for work valued at far below the value of the actual work that was ultimately done. The plaintiffs were under the impression that the licences (to the requisite value) had been obtained; they continued with the work. The plaintiffs later sued the defendants for the remaining sum owed. As there had been a contravention of the licensing requirement, the contract was tainted by illegality. However, the court held in favour of the plaintiffs. It held that the assurance with regard to the licences given by the defendants and accepted by the plaintiffs constituted *a collateral contract*. However, as already pointed out above, possible anomalies and contradictions can result from the finding of a collateral contract. Hence, there is a need to *limit* the use of the device of a collateral contract (and see Birkett LJ's acknowledgment that '[t]he number of cases of this nature which will arise will not be many' (see p 95)). Professor Treitel has also pointed to the fact that the work in this particular case had already been completed and, hence, the granting of the remedy to the plaintiffs by way of a collateral contract did not provide the plaintiffs with any incentive to commit the illegal act (see GH Treitel, *The Law of Contract* (10th ed, 1999) at p 450). And Denning LJ (as he then was) indicated that in order for plaintiffs to succeed, they must not themselves be guilty of any culpable negligence. These various considerations are, it is suggested, to limit the otherwise potentially broad scope of such a device.

(4) *Repentance or Timely Repudiation*

14.64 Where a party to an illegal contract 'repents' in time (before the illegal purpose is effected), it might be possible for that party to recover benefits conferred on the other party under the illegal contract. The Latin phrase often used in this regard is '*locus poenitentiae*' (a place for repentance). In other words, the party concerned is afforded an opportunity to change his or her mind and help 'undo' the illegality before it comes to fruition, so to speak. The rationale for this doctrine is straightforward: it is to encourage contracting parties to back out of illegal contracts.

14.65 The leading (English) decision is that of *Kearley v Thomson* (1890). In this case, the defendants were solicitors. They promised the plaintiff that, in return for payment of their (the defendants') costs, they would not appear at the public examination of a bankrupt who was the plaintiff's friend. In addition, the defendants promised the plaintiff that they would not oppose the bankrupt's discharge. It should be noted that the defendants entered into such a contractual arrangement as the bankrupt's estate, from which their costs were to be paid, lacked the requisite funds. The defendants did not appear at the public examination, which the bankrupt passed. The plaintiff then sued for the return of money already paid to the defendants. The court held in favour of the defendants as it was *too late* for the plaintiff to 'repent'. It held that although the bankrupt had not yet applied for an order of discharge, a substantial part of the agreement had nevertheless already been performed as the defendants had fulfilled the first part of the agreement—which was not to appear at the public examination of the bankrupt. The court held that it was too late for repudiation of the illegal contract as there had been 'a partial carrying into effect of an illegal purpose in a substantial manner' (see p 747, per Fry LJ).

14.66 It should also be noted that in order for 'repentance' to be successful, it must be both *genuine and voluntary* so that, where the contracting party concerned had no choice but to repent because the fulfilment of the illegal purpose was no longer possible owing to external circumstances beyond the control of the parties, the doctrine will not apply (see the leading English decision of *Bigos v Boustead* (1951)). *However*, in the more recent English Court of Appeal decision of *Tribe v Tribe* (1995), only voluntariness, as opposed to the genuineness, of repentance was emphasised.

(5) *Equitable Exceptions?*

14.67 As already alluded to above, there is the possibility of recovery on broad equitable grounds insofar as *marriage brokage* contracts are concerned (see paragraph 14.42). However, there does not appear to be a similar approach adopted with regard to other categories of contracts. There is also the possible danger that such a jurisdiction may, in the absence of more concrete criteria, generate too vague and *ad hoc* results.

Contracts in Restraint of Trade

Introduction

14.68 Covenants in restraint of trade are extremely common today—especially in employment contracts. It is not surprising, therefore, that a fairly substantive body of case law has been developed over the years.

14.69 Covenants in restraint of trade inhibit or restrict *freedom of trade*. *However*, there is a *countervailing* policy that is based on the idea of *freedom of contract*. In the present context, this means that if a contracting party voluntarily enters into an agreement restricting or limiting his or her freedom to trade, then this should be given effect to by the courts.

14.70 Courts initially came down firmly on the side of *freedom of trade*, holding that *all* covenants in restraint of trade were *absolutely void*. Such an approach was not, however, found to be commercially practical. For example, a person desiring to sell his or her business would find it extremely difficult to do so and, if he or she did, the purchaser would find himself or herself at the mercy of the seller or vendor.

To take another common example: if an employee were not subject to any covenants in restraint of trade, he or she could, after ceasing employment with the employer, proceed to exploit the former employer's trade secrets and/or entice away the former employer's customers. Also, potential employers would be reluctant to employ and train apprentices as well.

14.71 In order to achieve a more equitable balance, the courts began to adopt a more relaxed approach towards covenants or clauses in restraint of trade. The courts distinguished between general and partial restraints of trade, holding the former to be totally void whilst holding the latter (which were confined to a particular area) valid if reasonable. However, this distinction was based on the criterion of area—a criterion that soon became meaningless in the light of rapid improvements in the communications network across the world. Not surprisingly, it, too, was rejected.

General Principles

14.72 The law hence developed further and the general principles as we know them today were laid down by Lord Macnaghten in the seminal House of Lords decision in *Nordenfelt v Maxim Nordenfelt Guns and Ammunition Co* (1894) as follows (at p 565):

> 'All interference with individual liberty of action in trading, and all restraints of trade of themselves, if there is nothing more, are contrary to public policy, and therefore void. This is the general rule. But there are exceptions: restraints of trade ... may be justified by the special circumstances of the particular case. *It is a sufficient justification, and indeed it is the only justification, if the restriction is reasonable—reasonable, that is, in reference to the interests of the parties concerned and reasonable in reference to the interests of the public*, so framed and so guarded as to afford adequate protection to the party in whose favour it is imposed, while at the same time it is in no way injurious to the public' (emphasis added).

In summary, there is no longer a distinction between general and partial restraints of trade. The general rule—as laid down above—is that *all covenants in restraint of trade are* prima facie *void, but may in fact be proven to be valid if reasonable both in the interests of the parties and in the interests of the public*. The controlling concept, as it were, is that of *reasonableness*, which is to be analysed from two (cumulative) perspectives: from the perspective of *the parties and* from the perspective of *the public*.

14.73 Given the general principles and test enunciated in the preceding paragraph, it is clear that the precise facts and circumstances of each case are very important. It should also be noted that the burden of proof is on the party seeking to rely upon the covenant in restraint of trade. Further, the material time for ascertaining whether or not the covenant in question is reasonable is the time at which the contract was made (see, generally, for this, as well as the proposition immediately preceding it, A Phang, *Cheshire, Fifoot and Furmston's Law of Contract—Second Singapore and Malaysian Edition* (1998) at pp 703 and 702, respectively).

14.74 Two factors are of especial importance in aiding the courts in ascertaining whether or not a covenant in restraint of trade is reasonable: *area and time*, respectively. However, neither is necessarily conclusive (indeed, as we have seen, the sole reliance on area was rejected quite early on; see paragraph 14.71, above). For example, a covenant which fetters indefinitely could still be held to be reasonable, depending on the specific facts of the case itself (see, for example, the House of Lords decision of

Fitch v Dewes (1921), discussed in paragraph 14.84, below).

It might be interesting, in this regard, to consider whether, given *the very small land area of Singapore*, this might impact—in certain instances at least—on the validity of restraint of trade clauses. Interestingly, in the Singapore High Court decision of *Heller Factoring (Singapore) Ltd v Ng Tong Yang* (1998), GP Selvam J observed thus (at pp 307–308):

> '[A]s to the geographical limit, the area must be no more than adequate for the protection of the plaintiffs. This in effect means the area where the plaintiffs' customers are situate. In the case of Singapore, a small country, a prohibition applicable for the whole country would be necessary in the context of the factoring industry. Customers would be spread all over the island and it would be well nigh impossible to specify pockets to which the clause should be restricted. Further, a competitor of the plaintiffs could be situate anywhere in Singapore. For these reasons the space limit is also eminently reasonable.'

14.75 However, there has been a tendency—under *English law*—to *merge* the two aspects of reasonableness embodied in Lord Macnaghten's statement of principle in the *Nordenfelt* case (as to which see paragraph 14.72, above). More specifically, the focus appeared to be on reasonableness as between *the parties* (cf the oft-cited English decision of *Wyatt v Kreglinger and Fernau* (1933); though cf per Lord Birkenhead (*obiter*) in the House of Lords decision in *McEllistrim v Ballymacelligott Co-operative Agricultural and Dairy Society* (1919) (see p 583)), with reasonableness in the interests of *the public* being largely neglected.

A slight difference in approach is discernible from the leading House of Lords decision of *Esso Petroleum Co Ltd v Harper's Garage (Stourport) Ltd* (1968) (also considered in paragraphs 14.87, 14.88 and 14.89, below), where Lord Pearce, for example, observed as follows (at p 324).

> 'There is not, as some cases seem to suggest, a separation between what is reasonable on grounds of public policy and what is reasonable as between the parties. There is *one broad question*: is it in the interests of the community that this restraint should, as between the parties, be held to be reasonable and enforceable?' (emphasis added)

Both aspects of reasonableness have thus been telescoped, as it were, into one broad question.

14.76 The *Singapore* approach towards both the abovementioned aspects of reasonableness has *diverged* from the position under English law. This is a rarity of sorts and should—for this reason, if nothing else—be noted especially. The Singapore High Court decision of *Thomas Cowan & Co Ltd v Orme* (1961) embodies this quite different approach.

In this case, the plaintiff employer brought an action against the defendant employee for the alleged breach of a covenant in restraint of trade. The plaintiff was in the fumigation business. The covenant concerned read as follows: that the employee '[o]n leaving the services of the employer for any reason whatsoever either pursuant to this

Agreement or on any breach of this Agreement shall not carry on the business of White Ant Exterminator or Fumigator anywhere in the island of Singapore either by himself or in partnership with others nor shall he take employment with any person, firm or corporation carrying on the business of White Ant Exterminators or Fumigators or any such similar business until the period of three years has expired from the date of the employee leaving the services of the employer'.

Chua J first adopted the general principles embodied in Lord Macnaghten's statement quoted above (see paragraph 14.72, above; see also, to like effect, the recent Singapore High Court decision of *Asia Polyurethane Mfg Pte Ltd v Woon Sow Liong* (1990)). This is relatively straightforward thus far. The learned judge then proceeded to find that the covenant was reasonable as between the *parties*. Again, this is straightforward. *However*, Chua J then proceeded to consider, *separately*, the *public interest*, and held that the covenant failed on this particular count. Recall that such an approach is *very different* from that which obtains in the English context (as to which see paragraph 14.75, above). Indeed, on the facts of this particular case, Chua J was of the view that the evidence demonstrated that since the defendant's firm had commenced business in competition with the plaintiff, the charges for fumigation had in fact dropped, with there being no evidence that the standard of fumigation for ships had deteriorated. It is suggested, in fact, that Chua J's approach in this decision is preferable and ought to be adopted. It is also faithful to the two separate aspects of reasonableness laid down by Lord Macnaghten in the *Nordenfelt* case (as to which see paragraph 14.72, above). Indeed, it should be noted that there is not inconsiderable Commonwealth authority that supports this approach as well (see, generally, A Phang, 'Illegality and Public Policy' of MP Furmston (ed), *Butterworths Common Law Series—The Law of Contract* (2nd ed, 2003) in paragraph 5.109).

The present writer would also venture to suggest that any objection to the effect that the courts are ill-equipped to deal with the larger issue of the public interest is inconsistent with the general practice of the courts which is not to act like 'mini-legislatures' but which is also not to avoid issues relating to the public interest where it is necessary to do so. Besides, the reference to the public interest was originally formulated by *a judge* in the first place (Lord Macnaghten in the *Nordenfelt* case at paragraph 14.72, above)! Finally, it should be noted that parliamentary time is, more often than not, at a premium in any event.

14.77 Whilst still on the topic of general principles, it has also been clearly established that the courts will not countenance a bare and blatant restriction of freedom to trade embodied in what is popularly termed as a 'covenant in gross'. *There must be a legitimate proprietary interest which the covenant is intended to protect* (see the leading Canadian Privy Council decision of *Vancouver Malt and Sake Brewing Co Ltd v Vancouver Breweries Ltd* (1934)).

What constitutes a legitimate proprietary interest depends on both the broad category under which the contract in question falls (the main categories will be considered below) as well as the specific facts and circumstances of the case itself. And the covenant concerned can go no further than is necessary to protect that legitimate proprietary interest.

Sale of a Business

14.78 Insofar as this specific category is concerned, the courts are more liberal towards restraint of trade clauses. Unlike employment contracts, such contracts concern purchasers who are purchasing something tangible (including the very important factor of goodwill), which would be eroded without the protection of a covenant in restraint of trade. In contrast, an employer will not be deprived of what he or she has paid for when the employment contract is terminated; on the contrary, the employer would have received what he or she has in fact paid for, ie the employee's services. There is also more likely to be equality of bargaining power in a sale of business context as opposed to an employment context.

14.79 There is the need for a legitimate proprietary interest (see paragraph 14.77, above). This would include, as already mentioned, the important element of goodwill. The covenant must of course go no further than is necessary to protect the legitimate proprietary interest.

Employment Contracts

14.80 As mentioned above, the courts adopt a stricter attitude compared to covenants in restraint of trade contained in contracts for the sale of businesses. It should also be noted that, in the leading House of Lords decision of *Herbert Morris Ltd v Saxelby* (1916); also briefly discussed below in paragraph 14.83), Lord Atkinson observed that every person had to be at liberty to work for himself or herself, and that he or she ought not (in principle) to deprive himself or herself, or the state, of his or her labour, skill, or talent.

14.81 Notwithstanding the stricter approach adopted by the courts towards covenants in restraint of trade, the courts do attempt to achieve a fair balance. Therefore, although it is acknowledged that when the employee leaves his or her employment, the employer would have received what he or she had paid for (viz the employee's services), there are at least two areas of interest where the employer might still require the protection of a reasonable covenant in restraint of trade. Indeed, the two interests represented are so important that the courts will ensure that no abuse results even where there has been no express covenant.

The *first* interest pertains to *trade secrets*. In this regard, the following observations in the English Court of Appeal decision of *Faccenda Chicken Ltd v Fowler* (1986) which, whilst not dealing with an express covenant as such, are nevertheless very instructive insofar as the factors or guidelines aiding the court in ascertaining whether something constitutes a trade secret or its equivalent (at pp 626–627, per Neill LJ, delivering the judgment of the court):

(1) *Nature of the employment*: where confidential information is habitually

handled, a higher obligation of confidentiality may be imposed.
(2) *Nature of the information itself*: the information concerned must be a trade secret *or* material which, whilst not properly described as a trade secret as such, is (having regard to all the circumstances) of such a highly confidential nature as to require the same protection as a trade secret.
(3) *Whether the employer impressed on the employee the confidentiality of the information.*
(4) *Whether the relevant information can be easily isolated from other information which the employee is free to use or disclose*: although this factor (as the court pointed out) is by no means a conclusive one.

It should be noted that the abovementioned principles were followed in the Singapore High Court decision of *Medivac International Management Pte Ltd v John Walter Moore* (1988) and the Singapore Court of Appeal decision of *Tang Siew Choy v Certact Pte Ltd* (1993).

14.82 Whilst a legitimate proprietary interest of the employer will be protected by law, the courts will not enforce a covenant in restraint of trade in order to prevent the employee from exercising his or her own natural talent and skill. The latter would involve, in effect, a 'covenant in gross' (as to which see paragraph 14.77, above).

In the leading House of Lords decision of *Mason v Provident Clothing and Supply Co Ltd* (1913), for example, it was held, *inter alia*, that the success of the defendant employee was due primarily to the employee's natural gifts and only secondarily to the training provided by the employer.

14.83 Another useful case illustration is another House of Lords decision, that of *Herbert Morris Ltd v Saxelby* (1916), where the fact that the plaintiff employer's charts and drawings had always had to be returned by their employees and the fact that it was impossible for any single employee to memorise the enormous amount of complex detail contained therein meant that the information concerned could not be considered a trade secret. It should also be noted, however, that there was an admission by the managing director of the plaintiff that the real object of the covenant concerned was to preclude competition by the defendant employee, a draftsman, who, in point of fact, was merely using his general knowledge and skill. It might, however, well be the case that, with increased access to instruments of reproduction, the situation, if it occurred today, might well be different, depending on whether or not the employee concerned had been able to smuggle out copies from the workplace.

14.84 The *second* interest the courts will protect in the employment context is that of *trade custom or trade connection*. There must, in this respect, be *personal knowledge of as well as influence over the customers of the employer*. In this regard, a somewhat extreme illustration may be found in the House of Lords decision of *Fitch v Dewes* (1921). In this case, a solicitor's managing clerk covenanted that he would not be engaged in solicitors' work within seven miles of the town hall of the town where the plaintiff (a solicitor and his (the defendant managing clerk's) employer) was practising. The House upheld the validity of the covenant, even though it was *unlimited in point of time*. This was because of the other special facts present—in particular, that the area concerned was *extremely limited*.

14.85 A useful summary of the various general principles may be found in the following observations of Judith Prakash J in the Singapore High Court decision of *Buckman Laboratories (Asia) Pte Ltd v Lee Wei Hoong* (1999), as follows (at p 341):

> 'It is well-known that an employer who wishes to enforce a restraint of trade provision in a contract with an ex-employee must show that it was intended to protect the employer's legitimate interests and that it was reasonable in all the circumstances. In ascertaining the validity of such a clause, the first step is to determine what those interests are and the second is to consider whether the clause as drafted is no wider than is necessary to protect such interests. The court will not give effect to a clause if its main function is to inhibit competition in business.
>
> To determine the interest intended to be protected by a restraint of trade covenant, the court must first of all construe the contractual wording to determine whether it indicates what that interest is. Where the wording of a restriction does not specifically state the interest of the employer which it is intended to protect, the court is entitled to look both at the wording and the surrounding circumstances for the purpose of ascertaining that interest by reference to what appear to have been the intentions of the parties. But if the employer states specifically what interest the covenant is intended to protect, the employer cannot thereafter seek to justify it by reference to a separate interest which has not been specified.'

Exclusive Dealing Arrangements—Focus on Solus Agreements

14.86 A solus agreement is one that is entered into between an oil company and a garage proprietor (a proprietor of a petrol station, in more traditional parlance). The typical solus agreement will contain three covenants. There is, first, a tying covenant where the garage proprietor agrees to purchase all petrol and related products from the oil company. Secondly, there is typically a compulsory trading covenant where the garage proprietor covenants to keep the garage or station open at all reasonable times. Thirdly, there is a continuity covenant under which the garage proprietor undertakes to extract similar undertakings from any potential buyer during the period of the solus agreement. The *benefit* to the garage proprietor is that he or she obtains rebates on the products sold and also often obtains advances of money or loans in order to aid in the purchase and/or development of the premises. On the other hand, the abovementioned covenants benefit the oil company as it is enabled to systematically plan as well as organise its business over a considerable period of time (see, generally, GH Treitel, *The Law of Contract* (10th ed, 1999) at p 431).

14.87 It used to be thought that in order for the restraint of trade doctrine to operate in a solus agreement, the covenantor (here, the garage proprietor) had to give up some freedom or right he or she would have had prior to the entry into the solus agreement itself. The paradigm example where the doctrine will be held applicable is where the petrol station or garage premises are owned by the covenantor (see, for example, the leading House of Lords decision of *Esso Petroleum Co Ltd v Harper's Garage (Stourport) Ltd* (1968)). Anomalous and artificial results may, however, occur and this proposition has been critiqued powerfully by Professor Heydon (see JD Heydon, 'The Frontiers of the Restraint of Trade Doctrine' (1969) 85 *Law Quarterly Review* 229; see also, by the same author, *The Restraint of Trade Doctrine* (2nd ed, 1999) at p 52). Professor Heydon gives the example where all the landowners in Yorkshire agree not to trade on their land; in such a situation, the restraint of trade doctrine would apply because these landowners would give up some freedom they would otherwise have had. If, on the other hand, an individual purchases all the land in Yorkshire, covenanting with each vendor not to trade on the land purchased, the restraint of trade doctrine would *not* apply and all the covenants would be enforceable. These two illustrations differ only in form and yet lead to such diametrically opposed results, clearly demonstrating the anomaly and artificiality just referred to.

It should, however, be noted that the above rule could still be adhered to with anomalies and artificiality being kept to a minimum if the focus is on the substance rather than the form. This is well-illustrated by the English Court of Appeal decision of *Alec Lobb (Garages) Ltd v Total Oil (Great Britain) Ltd* (1985), where the plaintiff company (a family company) leased their service station to the defendant oil company. The defendant then granted a leaseback to Mr Lobb and his mother, rather than to the plaintiff. The solus agreement was in fact contained in the leaseback. The defendant argued that the restraint of trade doctrine was precluded because Mr Lobb and his mother had no previous right to give up as the previous occupier was the plaintiff company. Note, once again, that the plaintiff company was a family company, of which *Mr Lobb and his mother were the proprietors*. Not surprisingly, this argument was rejected. Dillon LJ put it well when he observed that the granting of the leaseback by the defendant was 'a palpable device in an endeavour to evade the doctrine of restraint of trade' (see p 178).

Somewhat more radically, perhaps, a relatively recent Singapore High Court decision attempted to free the law from this rule by casting doubt on the distinction contained therein: see *Shell Eastern Petroleum (Pte) Ltd v Chuan Hong Auto (Pte) Ltd* (1995) at p 288 (this decision was affirmed, but without consideration of this particular issue; see *Chuan Hong Auto (Pte) Ltd v Shell Eastern Petroleum (Pte) Ltd* (1996)). Lim Teong Qwee JC preferred, instead, yet another approach of another Law Lord in the *Esso Petroleum* case: Lord Wilberforce, who adopted a much broader approach based on trade practice, with the relevant agreements becoming 'accepted as part of the structure of a trading society' (see p 335). The situation has been fairly well-canvassed in the Australian context although the overall situation still appears relatively open (see A Phang, 'Illegality and Public Policy' in MP Furmston (ed), *Butterworths Common Law Series—The Law of Contract* (2nd ed, 2003) at paragraph 5.125).

14.88 As to actual application, there are, unfortunately, no definitive guidelines. This is perhaps only to be expected in the nature of things. In the *Esso Petroleum Co Ltd v Harper's Garage (Stourport) Ltd* (1968), there were two agreements: one for four years five months, the other for 21 years. The House held that the former agreement was valid whereas the latter was not. Yet, mere quantum of time is not, in and of itself, conclusive. In the *Alec Lobb* case, for example (see paragraph 14.87, above), the leaseback was for 21 years but the agreement was nevertheless held to be valid. There were other factors: there was a provision for termination of the leaseback (and, hence, the solus agreement) after either seven or 14 years; the court also emphasised the broader policy reason to the effect that there ought to be encouragement to rescue firms that were (like the one in the present case) on the verge of bankruptcy.

Other Categories

14.89 The categories of restraint of trade are by no means closed: see per Lord Wilberforce in *Esso Petroleum Co Ltd v Harper's Garage (Stourport) Ltd* (1968) at p 337. And the same sentiment was enunciated in the local context by Chao Hick Tin JA, delivering the judgment of the court in the recent Singapore Court of Appeal decision of *National Aerated Water Co Pte Ltd v Monarch Co, Inc* (2000) at p 33. There are therefore other categories, of which two will be mentioned here.

14.90 There is a fairly broad and open category where there is extreme inequality between the parties. The case most often cited in this regard is that of the House of Lords in *A Schroeder Music Publishing Co Ltd v Macaulay* (1974). In this case, the plaintiff (then an unknown song writer) entered into a standard form contract with the defendants, who were music publishers. The agreement was extremely unfair and unfavourable to the plaintiff. The House held that the agreement was contrary to public policy and void.

An interesting and possible linkage relates to the fledgling doctrine of unconscionability that was considered in Chapter 13 (see, generally, paragraph 13.43 ff). The judgment of Parker LJ in the English High Court decision of *Panayiotou v Sony Music Entertainment (UK) Limited* (1994) may also usefully be noted for although the learned judge does distinguish between the doctrines of restraint of trade and unconscionability, respectively, the possible linkages are also illustrated as well.

14.91 There are also what the present writer would term 'hybrid situations', of which the Hong Kong Privy Council decision of *Deacons v Bridge* (1984) is an excellent illustration. In this case, the plaintiff firm of solicitors, which was large and well-established, was divided into several specialist departments. The defendant was a senior partner who was in charge of the firm's intellectual property and trademarks department. He also received a 5% share in the partnership business and assets (including its goodwill). The partnership agreement contained a covenant in restraint of trade which stipulated that after a person had ceased to be a partner in the firm, he was not to act as a solicitor in Hong Kong for a period of five years for any client of the firm or any person who had been a client of the firm in the three years preceding his departure from the firm. The defendant resigned and soon set up his own practice, acting for former clients of the plaintiffs. Not surprisingly, the plaintiffs brought an action against the defendant for an injunction to enforce the restrictive covenant. The Board held that the covenant was reasonable and therefore enforceable by the plaintiffs.

The point of interest, in the present writer's view, is the fact that the Board found that the partnership agreement did not fall squarely within either the sale of business or employment categories (as to which, see paragraphs 14.78–14.79 and 14.80–14.85, respectively), although it bore some resemblance to *both*. The Board then proceeded to apply the general principles enunciated earlier in this chapter and held that the plaintiffs had a legitimate proprietary interest meriting protection inasmuch as although there were many separate departments, there was, in substance, *one* single practice in which each of the partners had an interest. In addition, the different nature of the work in the plaintiff firm meant varying degrees of client contact. It was therefore *not* feasible—as the defendant had argued—to have had a covenant only restricting the retiring partner from acting for clients for whom he or she had *personally* acted or for whose work he or she was generally responsible. In the circumstances, the covenant concerned was reasonable, although it applied across the board. More specifically, the Board also held that the scope as well as duration of the covenant were reasonable, having regard to the intermittent nature of a solicitor's employment and the fact that the partnership agreement itself had been carefully drafted by legally trained persons. The Board also considered *the public interest*, which it held would be served by the covenant, observing thus (at p 25, per Lord Fraser of Tullybelton, delivering the judgment of the Board):

> '[T]here is a clear public interest in facilitating the assumption by established solicitors' firms of younger men as partners. It benefits clients by tending to secure continuity in practice. It also tends to encourage the entry of younger men into the profession. … the continuing partners in the plaintiff firm would only feel able to take on new capital partners if they knew that in doing so they would not run the risk that the new partners would acquire a connection with clients of the firm and then depart with that part of the firm's goodwill. Conversely, the new capital partners in the plaintiff firm are required to purchase their share of its goodwill, but they could not reasonably be expected to do that if a retiring partner could freely remove part of the goodwill.'

It might also be interesting to note that the Board in effect adopted the 'two-stage' approach advocated above—considering *both* whether the covenant in restraint of trade was reasonable as between the parties *and* whether it was also in the interest of the public (see paragraph 14.76, above).

Severance

Introduction

14.92 This is an extremely important doctrine. The basic idea is to attempt to save a contract, which would otherwise be illegal or contrary to public policy, by excising or cutting away the illegal portion. This could take the form of excising whole terms or clauses; alternatively, portions within clauses could be excised, if appropriate.

Practically speaking, lawyers would do well to draft contracts in such a fashion that severance would be facilitated, if necessary.

14.93 Although the point is not entirely clear from the various textbooks, it would appear that the doctrine of severance is not uniformly applicable to all categories of illegal contracts. It would appear that the doctrine would not apply to contracts involving the more extreme forms of illegality. Indeed, the vast majority of cases dealing with the doctrine of severance involve the restraint of trade doctrine, which doctrine ranks rather low on the scale of illegality. On the other hand, it is suggested that the doctrine of severance would probably not apply to contracts that are either expressly or impliedly prohibited by *statute*. The situation is probably less clear with regard to contracts that are illegal under *the common law*. It is suggested that the doctrine of severance ought to be more likely to be applicable in categories where the original rationale for holding the contract as illegal under the common law is now questionable (owing, for example, to a change in social circumstances and policy). A more comprehensive discussion of the various issues (and others) canvassed in the present paragraph can in fact be found in A Phang, 'Illegality and Public Policy' in MP Furmston (ed), *Butterworths Common Law Series—The Law of Contract* (2nd ed, 2003) at paragraphs 5.223–5.224.

14.94 There are in fact traditionally two broad categories of severance—severance of whole or entire clauses and severance within the otherwise tainted covenant itself. We shall deal with each category briefly.

Severance of Entire Clauses—Illegality of Part of the Consideration Test

14.95 As already mentioned, this form of severance results in the excision of *whole or entire covenant(s)* which allegedly constitute the illegal consideration. The general criterion or test is whether the illegal promise(s) embodied in the said covenant(s) constitute the whole or main consideration for the promise sought to be enforced. The doctrine of severance will *not* apply if the illegal promise(s) do in fact so constitute the whole or main consideration for the promise sought to be enforced. Conversely, if this is not the case, the doctrine of severance will apply.

Two oft-cited English decisions (with contrasting results) are *Goodinson v Goodinson* (1954) and *Bennett v Bennett* (1952), respectively. A more recent illustration is to be found in the Privy Council decision of *Phillip William Carney v John Edward Herbert* (1985). In that case, it was held that the illegal mortgages intended as security for the main transaction (which comprised the sale of shares) were merely ancillary to the main transaction. The doctrine of severance could therefore operate and the personal guarantee given by the defendant (which was *also* intended as security for the main transaction) could therefore be enforced.

14.96 It would appear, however, that if the policy and object of a given statute would be best served by applying the doctrine of severance (in a situation of statutory illegality), then the doctrine will indeed be applied even if the test laid down in the preceding paragraph would have otherwise prevented the application of the doctrine (see the English decision of *Ailion v Spikermann* (1976)).

Severance Within *Covenants—'Blue Pencil Test'*

14.97 As mentioned above, this *second* form of severance results in the excision of promises *within* a covenant that would suffice to enable that particular covenant to be saved since the promises excised are the portions rendering the covenant illegal or contrary to public policy in the first place.

The general guideline is that such excision is permissible so long as the 'blue pencil' running through and excising the offending words in the covenant(s) concerned does not alter the meaning of the covenant(s) *and* does not 'mutilate' the covenant(s) to the point where they do not make any sense (grammatically or otherwise). The reason that this test is popularly known as the 'blue pencil test' is also now clearer.

14.98 Two contrasting and oft-cited English decisions are *Goldsoll v Goldman* (1915) and *Attwood v Lamont* (1920), respectively. It has been suggested that one way of reconciling these two decisions is to argue that the former case related to a sale of business whilst the latter case related to the employment context (and, hence, disallowing the application of the doctrine of severance): see MP Furmston, *Cheshire, Fifoot and Furmston's Law of Contract* (14th ed, 2001), especially at p 475. In the more recent English Court of Appeal decision of *T Lucas & Co Ltd v Mitchell* (1974), however, severance was allowed even though the case itself was one relating to the employment context.

More generally, for a recent local illustration of this form of severance, see the Singapore Court of Appeal decision of *National Aerated Water Co Pte Ltd v Monarch Co, Inc* (2000) (at pp 36–37); the case is also referred to at paragraph 14.89, above.

14.99 Although the courts will attempt their level best to adhere to the 'blue pencil test' (see paragraph 14.97, above), it should nevertheless be noted that the line between re-writing the covenant (which is not permitted) and merely excising portions which will not alter the meaning of the covenant (which is permitted) can often be a very fine one. Indeed, it might be argued persuasively that whenever the 'blue pencil' is utilised to excise material, there must *necessarily* be *at least some* re-writing of the contract *in most instances*—quite apart from the literal changes made. This having been said, the distinction between re-drafting and mere severance is nevertheless an established one, although the courts occasionally come very close to the line indeed. A good illustrative case is that of the English Court of Appeal in *Littlewoods Organisation Ltd v Harris* (1977), where it is suggested that the dissenting judgment by Browne LJ was more persuasive as the learned judge's approach did not result in unduly straining the language of the covenant in question.

Proof of Illegality

14.100 The basic principles with regard to the issue of the proof of illegality have been clearly summarised by Devlin J (as he then was) in the English decision of *Edler v Auerbach* (1950), as follows (at p 371):

> '[F]irst, that, where a contract is *ex facie* illegal, the court will not enforce it, whether the illegality is pleaded or not; secondly, that, where ... the contract is not *ex facie* illegal, evidence of extraneous circumstances tending to show that it has an illegal object should not be admitted unless the circumstances relied on are pleaded; thirdly, that, where unpleaded facts, which taken by themselves show an illegal object, have been revealed in evidence (because, perhaps, no objection was raised or because they were adduced for some other purpose), the court should not act on them unless it is satisfied that the whole of the relevant circumstances are before it; but, fourthly, that, where the court is satisfied that all the relevant facts are before it and can see clearly from them that the contract had an illegal object, it may not enforce the contract, whether the facts were pleaded or not.'

Reform

14.101 The area of contractual illegality is, as we have seen, an astonishingly complex one. It has been the almost unanimous view across the Commonwealth that the law is in need of reform. However, to date, only the *New Zealand* Illegal Contracts Act 1970 represents some tangible reform. More recently, the *UK Law Commission* published a consultation paper entitled *Illegal Transactions: The Effect of Illegality on Contracts and Trusts* (Law Commission Consultation Paper No 154 (1999), and available online (at the time of writing) at the UK Law Commission's website at http://www.lawcom.gov.uk).

14.102 The present writer has in fact dealt with the issue of reform in some detail elsewhere and the reader is referred to the discussion as well as the literature cited therein (see A Phang, 'Illegality and Public Policy' in MP Furmston (ed), *Butterworths Common Law Series—The Law of Contract* (2nd ed, 2003) at paragraphs 5.237–5.244). It will suffice for the moment to observe that the most feasible area for reform is in the sphere of *remedies* (ie the *possible relief* that could be obtained) and that the most appropriate vehicle by which such reform may be effected is probably *legislative* in nature (rather than having resort to the common law). Most importantly, perhaps, it should be noted that the Law Reform Committee of the Singapore Academy of Law recently published a report entitled *Relief from Unenforceability of Illegal Contracts and Trusts* (dated 5 July 2002 and published online at http://www.lawnet.com.sg) which also contains a draft Act that attempts to integrate, in the main, what is perceived to be the best in the New Zealand Illegal Contracts Act 1970, the proposals in the UK Law Commission Consultation Paper and the draft British Columbia Contract Law Reform Act.

CHAPTER 15

Remedies for Breach of Contract I: Damages

PARAGRAPHS

15.1	**Introduction**
15.2	Types of Court-Ordered Remedies
15.3–15.4	Common Law and Equitable Remedies
15.5	Final and Interlocutory Remedies
15.6–15.8	Interest
15.9	Other Remedies
15.10–15.12	Losing One's Judicial Remedies
	Damages
15.13	General
15.14	(1) Types of Damages
	(2) Purpose for Awarding Damages
15.15–15.16	(a) Compensation Versus Punishment
15.17–15.21	(b) Looking Forwards Versus Looking Back
15.22–15.23	(c) Absolute Versus Relative Obligations
15.24–15.25	(3) Time of Quantification
15.26	Causation
	Types of Loss
15.27–15.35	(1) Expectation, Reliance, Incidental and Indemnity Losses
15.36	(2) Differences in Terminology
15.37–15.46	(3) Other Types of Losses
	Quantification of Unliquidated Damages
15.47	(1) Difficulty of Assessment No Bar to Recovery
15.48–15.52	(2) Assessment of Reliance and Indemnity Losses
15.53–15.59	(3) Assessment of Expectation Losses: Diminution in Value or Cost of Cure?
15.60–15.67	(4) Non-Pecuniary Losses
	Restrictions on Assessment of Unliquidated Damages
15.68–15.75	(1) Remoteness
15.76–15.83	(2) Mitigation
15.84–15.87	(3) Compensating Advantages
15.88	(4) Intervening Cause Breaking Chain of Causation
15.89–15.90	(5) Contributory Negligence

PARAGRAPHS

Damages (continued)
15.91 Contractually Agreed Damages and Other Techniques to Recover Losses or Discourage Breach
15.92–15.94 (1) Liquidated Damages Clauses and Penalty Clauses
15.95 (2) Simulating Penalty Clauses
15.96 (a) 'Accelerated Payment' Clauses
15.97–15.98 (b) 'Earnest Money' and 'Forfeiture' Clauses
15.99 (c) Guarantees
15.100 (d) 'Discount' Clauses
15.101 (e) 'Alternative Performance' Clauses
15.102–15.106 (f) 'Withholding' Clauses
15.107 No Damages in Equity?

Introduction

15.1 In the previous chapters, we have considered:

- how a contractual relationship can arise between parties;
- what rights and obligations are owed by the parties to the contract to each other; and
- how such rights and obligations can be infringed or breached.

Assuming we can prove that there has been a breach of contract (and no vitiating factors apply), how can the party injured by such breaches obtain a remedy for his losses?

Types of Court-Ordered Remedies

15.2 In this chapter and the next, we will be focussing on some of the most common 'court-ordered' remedies:

- The *common law* remedy of *damages*: generally speaking, every party who is injured by a breach of contract is entitled to monetary compensation *as of right* for the loss suffered thereof;
- Specific remedies, which may be subdivided into the following types:
  (1) The *common law action for a fixed sum*: where the obligation which is breached is the obligation to pay a fixed sum (for example, the price for goods sold or for services rendered), the injured party is entitled as of right to have the court order the payment of the sum in question;
  (2) The *equitable* remedy of *specific performance*: where the obligation which is breached (or is threatened to be breached) is something other than an obligation to pay a fixed sum, the injured party may ask the court to exercise its discretion to order the party in actual (or anticipatory) breach to perform the contractual promise; and
  (3) The *equitable* remedy of *injunction*: where the obligation in question is a negative one (that is, *not* to do something), the injured party may ask the court to exercise its discretion to issue an injunction which orders the party in breach to cease and desist from acting in a manner that is contrary to its contractual promise;
- The *common law* remedy of *restitution*: where the injured party has paid money, or has tendered goods or services to the party in breach and, due to the breach, has not obtained that which he bargained for, the injured party may recover the money paid, or the money value of those goods or services. Exceptionally, he may recover a 'restitutionary' award that is based not on the value transferred to the party in breach, but based on any gains made by the party in breach. It should be noted that these restitutionary remedies are based on a separate branch of the law (the law of unjust enrichment) outside of the law of contract and the interaction between these two areas is still undergoing intense academic debate. In addition, given that these remedies are a response to events of '*unjust enrichment*', it may be that such remedies are available to parties who are

themselves in breach of contract, but who have nonetheless, provided benefits in money or in kind.

Damages will be discussed in this chapter while the specific remedies and restitution will be left to Chapter 16.

Common Law and Equitable Remedies

15.3 The distinction between common law remedies (which are available as of right) and equitable remedies (which are granted at the court's discretion) is significant, as a plaintiff cannot be sure that a court will exercise its discretion in his favour. If he is entitled to a remedy as of right, he is assured that he will recover something (even albeit nominal).

15.4 In any event, the plaintiff is free to choose whether to frame his claim to recover damages or to ask the court to order specific performance—he may seek an order for specific performance, whether exclusively or as an alternative to damages. However, if he proceeds with his suit in the alternative, at the trial he must elect to pursue either specific performance or damages for breach, but not both (save for the availability of court-ordered damages in lieu of specific performance, sometimes termed 'equitable damages', discussed in the next chapter).

Final and Interlocutory Remedies

15.5 Usually, the court will only order remedies at the end of a trial between disputing contracting parties and this chapter will focus on these 'final remedies'. However, in certain circumstances, 'interlocutory relief' may be granted by the court in the form of 'interim orders' for specific performance or injunctions, as the case requires, even though the case has not been finally resolved. Monetary awards may also be made in the form of 'interim damages', even before the trial is ultimately completed.

Interest

15.6 Following a breach of contract, if the court orders a monetary payment (whether by way of damages, debt or restitution) to remedy the breach, it may also order interest to be paid on it.

15.7 All 'courts of record' in Singapore (this includes the High Court, the District Court and the Magistrates' Court) are given a discretionary power to award interest on damages or debts from the time the cause of action accrues to the plaintiff, up to the time of judgment (sometimes called *pre-judgment* interest). See section 12 of the Civil Law Act (Cap 43, 1999 Rev Ed).

15.8 In the case of interest on the judgment sum (or *post-judgment* interest), section 18(2) read with paragraph 6 of the First Schedule to the Supreme Court of Judicature Act (Cap 322, 1999 Rev Ed) and sections 31(1) and 52 of the Subordinate Courts Act (Cap 321, 1999 Rev Ed) empower the

High Court, the District Court and the Magistrates' Court, respectively, to award post-judgment interest.

Other Remedies

15.9 Although this chapter will focus on contractual remedies, it must be borne in mind that contract law does not operate in a vacuum. Thus, court-ordered remedies for breach of contract are not the only ones available. Some remedies do not require the intervention of a court order, and hence may be termed *self-help* remedies. These include termination of the contract for breach of a condition or an innominate term (the breach of which deprives the innocent party of substantially the whole of the benefit of the contract). Depending on the terms within a contract, other types of self-help remedies may also be available (for example, a 'forfeiture of deposits' clause—this type of clause is discussed at paragraphs 15.97–15.98 below).

Outside of contract law, fact situations involving contracts may also interact with aspects of tort law (such as in the case of misrepresentation and the tort of negligence where advice is negligently given), and even with the law of unjust enrichment (such as where the parties were labouring under a common mistake that they were bound by a legally enforceable contract). Therefore, apart from the court-ordered contractual remedies discussed in this chapter, one should keep an open mind that other types of remedies beyond the law of contract may be applicable to the dispute in question.

Losing One's Judicial Remedies

15.10 Judicial remedies may be lost if the plaintiff is barred from bringing his cause of action to court due to a lapse of time. This can arise through the operation of the Limitation Act (Cap 163, 1996 Rev Ed); as amended by the Singapore Limitation (Amendment) Act (No 22 of 1992) and Arbitration Act 2001 (No 37 of 2001), or through the equitable doctrine of *laches*.

15.11 So far as the Limitation Act is concerned, generally speaking, a plaintiff must commence his legal action within six years from the time his cause of action 'accrues' (see section 6). Usually, for a suit based on breach of contract, this starts from the time the contract was breached. For torts, a similar period is imposed: 'accrual' of the cause of action will ordinarily commence at the time the tort is committed (keeping in mind that usually, there is no tort until damage has occurred).

Some provisions are made to delay the commencement of the limitation period, for example, where the plaintiff was ignorant of the breach of contract or the commission of the tort. The Limitation Act, however, does not apply to any legal action rooted purely in unjust enrichment (see the decision of the Singapore Court of Appeal in *Management Corporation Strata Title No 473 v De Beers Jewellery Pte Ltd* (2002) at p 13).

15.12 Apart from the statutory limitation periods, section 32 of the Limitation Act has preserved the operation of the equitable doctrine of *laches* which operates to bar plaintiffs who have been dilatory in prosecution of their claims. It applies equally to contract, tort or unjust enrichment claims and will bar access to equitable remedies when the plaintiff is seen by the court to have been tardy in bringing his case to court. Two important factors to be considered will be the length of delay (from the time the plaintiff knew he could have brought the case to court), and whether the defendant acquiesced in the delay.

Damages

General

15.13 One leading commentator in this area defines an award of damages to be:

> '... the sum of money payable as compensation for an injury resulting from a tort or breach of contract' (AI Ogus, *The Law of Damages* (1973) at p 1).

Further discussion of damages for tort can be found in Chapters 19 and 20. For the purposes of this chapter however, all references to 'damages' shall only refer to damages for breach of contract unless otherwise specified.

(1) *Types of Damages*

15.14 Often, damages may be referred to as being one of the following types:

- Unliquidated damages: these are damages that are not numerically ascertainable prior to the court making a determination of the appropriate compensatory sum.
- Liquidated damages: these are damages that have been agreed upon between the parties, prior to any litigation.
- Substantial and nominal damages: when the court finds that there has been a breach of contract by the defendant, the general rule is that the plaintiff is entitled as of right to some monetary compensation, or damages. However, the plaintiff has the burden of proof to establish that he has suffered significant losses which the defendant should be responsible for, in which case, substantial damages will be awarded. However, sometimes, the plaintiff is unable to do this. If so, the court will award the plaintiff only nominal damages (which sometimes may be as little as $2).

(2) *Purpose for Awarding Damages*

(a) Compensation Versus Punishment

15.15 As was pointed out in the House of Lords case of *Addis v Gramophone Company, Ltd* (1909), the common law does not traditionally award punitive damages in cases of breach of contract. This may be contrasted with damages that may be awarded in tort; it is accepted that exemplary and punitive damages may be awarded by the courts against a wrongdoer who has committed a particularly serious tort.

15.16 There are, however, some indications that this may no longer be universally true. For example, the decision of the House of Lords in the case of *Attorney General v Blake* (2001) where the profits from the sale of a book of memoirs authored by Blake, a former spy, in breach of his contractual duty to maintain confidentiality, were ordered to be paid over to the British Government, does, in some respects, reflect some punitive element in response to Blake's breach of contract. In that case, the information revealed in Blake's memoir had in fact become public knowledge, and it was therefore difficult to establish any substantial loss on the part of the British Government.

An even more obvious case of punitive damages in the context of a contractual breach can be found in the Canadian Supreme Court case of *Whiten v Pilot Insurance Co* (2002). Mrs Whiten had a contract of insurance with the Pilot Insurance Co ('Pilot'), insuring her home against the risk of fire. Unfortunately, Mrs Whiten's home was razed in a fire and as a result, Mrs Whiten claimed on her insurance policy. Pilot contested the claim, alleging arson on the part of Mrs Whiten or members of her family, even though there was absolutely no evidence in support of such an allegation. This appeared to be a cynical ploy on Pilot's part to force Mrs Whiten to settle her claim for a lower sum than she was otherwise entitled to.

Unsurprisingly, given the lack of any evidence to support their claim of arson, Pilot's defence against Mrs Whiten's suit failed and they were ordered to pay her a sum of around C$300,000 based on the terms of their insurance policy with Mrs Whiten. However, Pilot was also found to have contested her claim in bad faith, thereby breaching their duty of good faith and fair dealing under the contract of insurance. At the end of the trial, the jury also awarded C$1 million to Mrs Whiten as punitive damages in denunciation of Pilot's exceptionally reprehensible behaviour.

An appeal was brought before the Canadian Supreme Court and one of the grounds of appeal was whether punitive damages could be awarded for a contractual breach. Six out of seven of the Canadian Supreme Court judges held that punitive damages for a breach of contract could indeed be awarded if the party-in-breach (Pilot, in this case) had committed an 'actionable wrong' over and above the breach sued upon (that is to say, the non-payment of the approximately C$300,000 claimed under the insurance policy). The majority held that such an actionable wrong could take a number of forms, for example, a tort, a breach of a fiduciary duty, or as in this case, a breach of a contractual duty to act in good faith. Although it remains unclear just precisely when a breach of contract can amount to an 'actionable wrong', the Canadian Supreme Court has opened the door to awards of punitive damages in denunciation of exceptionally shocking breaches of contractual duties which depart markedly from ordinary standards of decent behaviour.

It remains to be seen, however, whether these English and Canadian developments will be adopted in Singapore's courts.

(b) Looking Forwards Versus Looking Back

15.17 When awarding damages for breach of contract, a court will seek to award an amount which would place the plaintiff in the position as though the contract had been completely performed. As observed by Parke B in *Robinson v Harman* (1848) (at p 855):

> 'The rule of the common law is, that where a party sustains a loss by reason of a breach of contract, he is, so far as money can do it, to be placed in the same situation, with respect to damages, as if the contract had been performed.'

15.18 On the other hand, when awarding damages in tort, a court will seek to award an amount that would place the plaintiff in a position as though the tort had never occurred. Hence, in *Livingstone v Rawyards Coal Co* (1880) (at p 39), Lord Blackburn stated that:

> '… where any injury is to be compensated by damages, in setting the sum of money to be given for reparation of damages you should as nearly as possible get at that sum of money which will put the party who has been injured, or who has suffered, in the same position as he would have been in if he had not sustained the wrong [that is, the tort] for which he is now getting his compensation or reparation.'

15.19 Sometimes, the difference between the two kinds of damages may influence a plaintiff who has concurrent causes of action in contract and tort to press forward with an action for breach of contract. Since, in the first instance, contract damages seek to place the plaintiff in the position as though the contract was performed (and are therefore 'forward-looking'), they often incorporate an element of profit.

15.20 This may be contrasted with the purpose of damages in tort, which would essentially enable the plaintiff to recover only his costs and expenses resulting from the tortious act in question. However, this is just a starting point. With the rise of tortious liability in negligent advice and the availability of recovery for economic losses in tort, it may well be that even in tort, 'forward-looking' damages are also recoverable (see, for example, the English Court of Appeal case of *East v Maurer* (1991)).

15.21 Conversely, it has long been recognised that the court may also make an order for damages which merely places the plaintiff in the position as though the contract had never been made (see, for example, the Australian case of *McRae v Commonwealth Disposals Commission* (1951)). Such types of damages in contract seek to protect the plaintiff's *reliance interest* and may be described as being 'backward-looking' in nature. Generally, however, in cases where the plaintiff is clearly able to prove that he would have made a profit of some sort and increased his overall wealth, if not for the defendant's breach of contract, the plaintiff would be better served by trying to frame his claim in a way which also protects his *expectation interest* (as in the example discussed below from paragraph 15.27 onwards).

(c) Absolute Versus Relative Obligations

15.22 Since contract damages are supposed to put the plaintiff in a position, so far as money can do so, as though the contract had been performed, we must first consider what precisely was promised by the defendant under the contract, and then, in what way he has breached such obligations.

15.23 Generally speaking, contract obligations may be divided into two categories:

- 'Absolute' or 'strict' obligations: where the defendant has bound himself absolutely to deliver a certain result (for example, the obligation to deliver the stated quantity of goods at the specified time and place in a contract for sale of goods); and/or
- 'Relative' obligations: where the defendant has bound himself only to take reasonable care in the performance of his contractual duties (for example, the contractual obligation to carry out a survey of the plaintiff's land with reasonable care).

In relation to the first type of obligation, in order to place the plaintiff in the position as though the contract had been fully performed, the defendant ought to provide damages which would enable the plaintiff (if he so chooses) to obtain a replacement for the result that had been promised but which was not delivered.

On the other hand, in relation to the second type of obligation, since the defendant does not promise a particular result, but merely promises that he would take reasonable care, the plaintiff's damages should only be so much as would put the plaintiff in the position as though the defendant's defective performance of his contractual duties had never happened.

(3) *Time of Quantification*

15.24 At which point in time should damages be quantified? Damages could be ascertained at the time of the breach, at the time the proceedings are first brought, at the time the court makes its award, or any point in between. This is an important issue, since awards of damages are often quantified by taking the difference between market prices and the contractually stipulated price for a service or good to be provided under the contract. Given that market prices can fluctuate wildly even in the course of a few days (and in the case of publicly traded corporate securities such as shares and bonds, in the course of a few minutes), the time at which damages should be ascertained can sometimes be critical.

The current position in Singapore appears to be a flexible one: the court is given a wide discretion to determine which point in time would best serve the justice of the case, given the particular facts of the case and keeping in mind the need for the plaintiff to mitigate his losses (see, for example, the Singapore Court of Appeal decision of *Tay Joo Sing v Ku Yu Sang* (1994) which concurred with the House of Lords decision of *Johnson v Agnew* (1980) in holding that where appropriate, damages could be assessed at a point in time *other* than the date of breach). In the

Singapore High Court case of *Min Hong Auto Supply Pte Ltd v Loh Chun Seng & Anor* (1993), involving a contractual option to purchase a shop unit, the damages payable by the defendant vendors (as a result of refusing to honour the terms of the option when it was exercised) were assessed at a later point in time when the shop unit was subsequently auctioned by the defendant vendor's mortgagee bank, instead of the time of breach.

Such flexibility may, Professor Treitel suggests (at pp 893–898 of *The Law of Contract* (10th ed, 1999)), be guided by the following:

- As a starting point, one should ascertain the damage suffered by the plaintiff *as at the time of the breach*. This assumes that the plaintiff knows of the breach once it has been committed, and is able to take steps to mitigate his losses.
- If it was not possible for the plaintiff to have known of the breach, or have discovered it with reasonable diligence at the time it occurred, then the court is likely to assess damages at the time when the plaintiff would have discovered the breach with reasonable diligence.
- However, if at the time of reasonable discovery, it was not possible to act on that knowledge to cut his losses (or to 'mitigate' them), then the court may delay assessment until the point in time when it is possible for the plaintiff to do so.
- Given reasonable discovery and possibility of mitigation, if the plaintiff can nonetheless demonstrate that he failed to act to mitigate at that point in time because there was a reasonable probability that the defendant would make good his default, then the court may defer the time of assessment until the time when it was no longer probable that this would be the case.
- In cases of late performance (as opposed to non-performance), it appears that the time of assessment will be the time of the late performance, and not the time when it ought to have been performed.
- Lastly, in cases of an anticipatory breach which has been accepted, as a starting point, the court will also assess damages as at the time when the defendant ought to have performed his part of the bargain, and not the point in time when the anticipatory breach was accepted. This is, of course, a starting point only, and the considerations discussed above may apply so as to persuade a court to adopt an alternative point in time for assessment of damages.

15.25 Having established the point in time at which damages should be assessed, the following sections will deal with the following areas:

- Causation;
- Types of losses which can be remedied by contractual damages;
- Quantification of such losses; and
- Restrictions on recovery for such losses.

Causation

15.26 Common sense dictates that the plaintiff can only recover compensation from the defendant if he can prove that his loss was *caused* by the defendant's breach of contract. This is also the position in *law*. However, there is little guidance as to what level of causation is required. Ultimately, this seems to be an evidential and factual enquiry, and it is hence difficult to establish any general rule.

This, however, does not mean that causation is unimportant, as illustrated by the House of Lords decision in *South Australia Asset Management Corporation v York Montague Ltd* (1997) (sometimes referred to as the *Banque Bruxelles Lamberts SA v Eagle Star Insurance Co* or the *SAAMCO* (1997) case).

SAAMCO (1997) was a consolidated appeal from three different cases. All were concerned with the damages which ought to be recovered by lenders who had been advised carelessly by valuers of certain assets which were provided as security for loans made by the lenders. In breach of their contractual obligation to carry out such valuation with reasonable care, the valuers over-valued the security. The lenders alleged that this caused them to make loans which they would never have made otherwise. After the loans were made, the general market for the assets in question fell tremendously, and the lenders claimed that the entire loss suffered by them following from defaults in the loans should be recovered from the valuers.

The answer, according to the House of Lords in *SAAMCO* (1997), was that the valuer's duty of care (whether in contract or even in the tort of negligence) did not cause all the loss claimed by the plaintiffs. Even if the valuers had done their job properly, the general fall in the market value would still have occurred and would still have caused loss to the vendors. The only damage which the valuers 'caused' then, was the extent of the over-valuation of the assets in question, at the time of the original valuation. The cause of any further losses was really the fall in the market. Since the valuers were only obliged to provide one piece of information which the lenders would take into consideration in formulating their decision whether or not to proceed with the transaction, it was not correct to make the valuers responsible for all subsequent market fluctuations. To do so would amount to making the valuers insurers for the viability of the transactions.

Types of Loss

(1) *Expectation, Reliance, Incidental and Indemnity Losses*

15.27 In order to better understand the various types of losses which may be incurred by a plaintiff due to a defendant's breach of his contractual obligations, it may be useful to consider the following example:

- Peter has inherited a run-down warehouse and sets up a wholesale food and beverage business in Singapore. He starts his business with cash-in-hand of $100,000 as capital.

- On 1 January, he enters into a contract (governed by Singapore law) to buy 500 bottles of French wine originating from one particular vineyard from David, a wine importer based in Singapore and the exclusive distributor for that vineyard. Peter pays the total contract price of $30,000 in advance, with delivery on 1 February.
- While awaiting delivery, Peter contracts to resell the wine to Tim, (who runs a number of French restaurants) for $50,000, with payment upon delivery on 15 February. This resale contract provides that damages for non-delivery of the wine are agreed in the liquidated sum of $60,000 (as Tim's usual profit margin for wine sold at his restaurants hover around the 20% mark).
- The warehouse is in suitable condition to store most types of goods. However, as wine needs to be stored at a cool temperature, certain insulation works have to be carried out to ensure that the wine is kept cool. Peter therefore contracts with Richard to install the insulation for the warehouse for $6,000 so it can be used to store the wine when it is delivered on 1 February, before delivery to Tim on 15 February. If not for the contract with David, Peter would not have made any renovations at all. Again, Peter pays Richard in full, and Richard immediately starts work (and completes it on 14 January).
- On 1 February, David delivers the *wrong* type of wine—instead of the promised French wine, David delivers 500 bottles of Italian wine of completely different description to Peter, telling Peter that he has found a buyer who is willing to pay a much higher price for the French wine, and he is therefore supplying the Italian wine in substitution.
- Peter refuses to accept the substitution and instead discharges the contract due to David's actual repudiatory breach. This releases him from having to pay David anything, since delivery was a pre-condition to payment. In turn, he regretfully informs Tim that he will be unable to deliver the French wine as contracted, since there is no distributor for the wine other than David.
- Tim accepts David's anticipatory repudiatory breach and discharges their contract, but insists on compliance with the liquidated damages clause—so Peter pays Tim $60,000 as liquidated damages.
- Peter also incurs $3,000 in transport costs in sending the Italian wine back to David when David unreasonably refuses to take back the defective shipment of wine.
- Peter is now left with $31,000 of capital (and no wine). In principle, what can Peter recover in damages from David?

15.28 The first type of loss that Peter can try to recover from David is his *(net) expectation loss*. This is the *net profit* which Peter *expects* to make on the basis that his contract with David is performed, that is, the difference between the resale price of $50,000 and the cost price of $30,000, less any further expenses which Peter must incur in order to earn that profit (this would be the $6,000 paid to Richard for the renovation). Thus, Peter can recover his *net expectation loss* of $14,000.

15.29 Peter has also suffered an expectation loss in relation to the value of the performance which David was expected to have provided in exchange for the payment of the $30,000, ie the value of the 500 bottles of French wine. Since these were not delivered, Peter has suffered a second form of expectation loss based on the value of this wine, which in most cases, will be taken to be their contractually agreed price: $30,000.

15.30 The $6,000 paid to Richard can, however, be recovered by Peter as his *reliance loss*. In *reliance* on David performing his side of the contract, Peter *actually* incurred $6,000 in renovation costs.

15.31 In most cases of breach of contract, the primary focus of attention will be the expectation and/or reliance losses suffered by the plaintiff. In many instances, there will be no issue of indemnity or consequential losses simply because they have not arisen on the facts.

15.32 However, on the facts of our example above, Peter has suffered losses over and above what can be classified as 'expectation' or 'reliance' loss: Peter has also suffered a loss of $60,000 which he paid as liquidated damages to Tim. This is sometimes referred to as Peter's *'indemnity loss'*. Lastly, the $3,000 worth of transport costs in sending the wine back to David incurred by Peter *after* David's breach had come to his attention may also be recoverable as what is sometimes referred to as *'incidental loss'*.

15.33 *In principle*, without considering any of the many restrictions on recovery (which will be discussed in the sections commencing from paragraph 15.68), Peter will be able to recover the following losses from David:

- net expectation loss ($14,000);
- expectation loss for value of goods not delivered ($30,000);
- reliance loss ($6,000);
- incidental loss ($3,000); and
- indemnity loss ($60,000).

15.34 Peter should therefore recover damages totalling $113,000 (being his expectation losses, reliance loss, incidental loss and indemnity loss). Taken together with the $1,000 of capital that Peter had left, assuming David complies with the court order in full, Peter's capital will now total $114,000.

This reflects the fundamental compensatory principle underlying recovery in contract: that the plaintiff is to be put in the position as though the contract was fully performed.

If the contract had been fully performed, Peter, who started out with cash-in-hand of $100,000 in capital, would have made a net profit of $14,000 (being the difference between the $50,000 in revenue he would have earned from the resale contract and the 'necessary expenses' of the $30,000 cost price for the wine and the $6,000 renovation expenses required to 'earn' that profit), bringing his total cash-in-hand up to $114,000. However, as a result of David's breach of contract, Peter ends up with only $1,000 (being $100,000–less $30,000 paid to David, less $6,000 paid to Richard, less $60,000 paid to Tim, less $3,000 incurred for transporting the Italian wine back to David). The shortfall between the position Peter should have been in, had the contract been performed fully by David, and Peter's position now, as a result of David's breach, is $113,000. Therefore, in order to place Peter in the position as though the contract had been fully performed, Peter should be awarded an amount totalling $113,000—which in fact is the sum total of the various components as outlined in paragraph 15.33 above.

15.35 At this juncture, there are some points to note. Firstly, there is no 'punitive' element in any of the sums recovered. It may also be observed that these losses are 'pecuniary' in nature, that is, they are capable of being completely compensated for in terms of money and are an attempt to compensate the plaintiff for his loss of wealth. This may be contrasted with 'non-pecuniary' losses such as loss of reputation, inconvenience, or more generally, mental distress over the breach which will be discussed further below (see text from paragraph 15.60 onwards).

Secondly, the figures in paragraph 15.33 have been quantified using the 'loss of bargain' or 'expectation loss' basis of assessment. However, damages can also be assessed in the alternative using the 'reliance loss' basis (which will be discussed in paragraph 15.36, below).

(2) *Differences in Terminology*

15.36 At this point, we should consider some difficulties relating with terminology. To begin with, the courts have traditionally concerned themselves primarily with two types of losses in contractual disputes: *expectation* as opposed to *reliance losses*. In many cases, the courts have used the term expectation loss to refer to *gross expectation losses* or *gross profit*, which would incorporate, some or all of the costs which would have been incurred by the plaintiff, in order to 'earn' the expected gross profit. In our example above, these costs would include the $6,000 paid to Richard.

It might thus be said that Peter's gross expectation loss or gross profit would be $20,000 (being the difference between the cost of the wine and his expected resale price). This global figure amalgamates the net expectation loss (as set out in paragraph 15.33, above), as well as the $6,000 reliance loss in the form of the renovation costs paid to Tim (as set out in paragraph 15.33, above). Apart from this, Peter will still recover his indemnity loss of $60,000 as well as the incidental loss of $3,000.

Arithmetically, there is no difference in the result (Peter still recovers a total of $113,000), but the difference in terminology must be noted, because where the plaintiff uses a *gross* basis to determine expectation loss, it is obvious that the plaintiff cannot then *also* recover any form of reliance loss which is already incorporated therein, since this would result in double-recovery which would put the plaintiff in a position *better* than if the contract had been performed in full.

Secondly, the term 'reliance loss' itself should also be used with care, since the kinds of payments which might be said to constitute 'reliance loss' may change, depending on whether the damages are assessed on the 'expectation loss' basis or the 'reliance loss' basis. On one analysis, it could be said that the $30,000 price paid to David *also* represents part of Peter's *reliance loss*. Hitherto, we have assessed Peter's losses on the 'expectation loss' basis. As will be discussed at greater length below (at paragraphs 15.48–15.52), subject to certain limits, a plaintiff may choose to assess his losses on the 'reliance loss' basis instead. By assessing his damages in this manner (often because of insuperable difficulties in proving the magnitude of his expectation loss), the plaintiff is choosing to forego recovery of the potential profits *and* the value of the contractual performance under the contract, had the contract been performed in full. Assessed on the reliance loss basis, Peter's damages would be the total of *all* sums paid by him in reliance on the contract being performed. This would *include* the $30,000 price for David's French wine (which was paid in fulfilment of Peter's obligations under their sale contract), as well as the reliance loss of $6,000 for renovations (which was *not* an obligation owed to anyone under that sale contract). In this context, 'reliance loss' is used as an *alternative* to expectation loss: Peter's damages on the *reliance loss* basis completely excludes any net expectation loss. In contrast, 'reliance loss' may be used to *complement* net expectation loss if damages are assessed on the expectation loss basis as was the case at paragraph 15.33 (although 'reliance loss' should be disregarded if expectation loss is reckoned on the 'gross' basis discussed in the immediately preceding paragraphs).

Lastly, it could be said that there was a 'total failure of consideration' on David's part for Peter's advance payment. In effect, Peter obtained nothing of which he bargained for and the $30,000 that was paid to David may be recovered as a refund, pursuant to the law of *unjust enrichment* (assuming none of the restrictions on such recovery are applicable). There are a number of cases where such recovery has been said to constitute part of the damages awarded to the innocent party. However, true recovery in unjust enrichment due to total failure of consideration has nothing to do with damages since they are aimed at the reversal and restoration of benefits conferred instead of compensation for loss. The better view, therefore, is that they are wholly distinct from a claim for damages for breach of contract. Further examination of recovery on the restitutionary basis of total failure of consideration will be carried out in the next chapter (see, in particular, the discussion from paragraphs 16.55–16.73).

(3) *Other Types of Losses*

15.37 We should note that in the above example, Peter entered into the contract with David with the aim of recovering the cost price of the goods through subsequent resale. In other words, the purpose of the contract was one of resale for profit. An analogous type of expectation may be found in contracts to purchase machinery or components where the purchaser expects to use the machinery or parts to produce goods of his own for the purpose of resale; in which case, the purchaser's aim is also to recover the cost price of the machinery or components through profitable resale of the goods manufactured.

15.38 Many contracts, however, do not encompass any such expectation. In most consumer contracts, for example, the aim of the contract is simply for one party to consume and enjoy the contractual performance of the other party, with no thought of economic profit or gain in mind. In such circumstances, the usefulness of labels such as 'expectation loss', 'reliance loss' or 'indemnity loss' will be very much reduced.

15.39 Consider the following example:

- Paula wants to buy a wide-screen television for her living room. She has her eye on a particular model because it is the only model on the market that comes in a pastel green casing (instead of the usual boring black).
- Paula visits her neighbourhood electrical goods shop, a sole-proprietorship owned by a distant cousin, Doreen. Paula spots the model she has in mind on sale for a very attractive price of $800.
- Doreen tells Paula that she does not have any stock at the moment, but will deliver it in two weeks' time. Paula does not mind the delay and buys the television anyway, paying Doreen in full.
- Two days later, Doreen abruptly ceases business and goes into hiding in Genting Highlands in Malaysia as she owes various loan sharks large amounts of money. Since she is a distant relative, Doreen e-mails Paula to tell her that she is sorry about how things have turned out, but she is now not in a position to fulfil her part of the bargain. Nor is she in a position to give Paula a refund.
- Ultimately, Paula buys her television from another retailer for $1,500.
- Now, instead of being out of pocket by $800, Paula has spent a further $1,500 in order to get the television set she expected to have under the original contract with Doreen. She then finds that Doreen has returned to Singapore, having managed to pay off the loan sharks using winnings from her visits to the casinos in Genting Highlands. What can Paula do?

15.40 In relation to this type of contract, Paula should recover $1,500 in contractual damages from Doreen for her breach of their contract. If Doreen had performed without renouncing the contract, Paula would not have been out of pocket by this additional amount.

15.41 This type of loss, of having to incur additional expense in order to obtain a replacement for what was originally promised (but was not delivered), might crudely be described as a form of 'expectation loss', since what Paula expected was that she would have the benefit of the pastel green wide-screen television and only be out of pocket by $800. Instead, due to Doreen's breach, she is out of pocket by $2,300.

15.42 The theoretical possibility remains, of course, that Paula might try to recover the $800 alone as compensation for her 'reliance loss' (on the reliance loss basis). Where there is a 'bad bargain' such that the defendant can show that the plaintiff would not have recovered her costs of the transaction and would have made a loss anyway (regardless of any breach by the defendant), the plaintiff does not have the option to choose between framing her loss in terms of her expectation interest or her reliance interest (see the section commencing from paragraph 15.50, below). This limitation does not appear to apply to Paula, but she is unlikely to exercise her option to frame her claim on the basis of her reliance loss since such action would be contrary to her pecuniary interest. She would recover more by framing her claim based on her expectation loss.

15.43 What is clear, though, is that Paula cannot recover both the $800 *as well as* the $1,500, since had the contract been performed properly by Doreen, Paula would still have been out of pocket by $800. To recover both would clearly put Paula in a better position than if the contract had in fact been performed.

15.44 Admittedly, there is yet a further possibility. Given the above discussion, it could be argued that Paula has suffered a *total failure of consideration*, and as a result, she ought to be entitled to restitution of the $800 paid to Doreen. However, as discussed in the next chapter (see, in particular, the discussion at paragraphs 16.58–16.69), such recovery on top of recovery for damages for Paula's expectation or reliance loss would result in double-recovery, and is therefore not permissible.

15.45 Recent case-law developments have further indicated that the English courts are increasingly amenable to considering other non-traditional types of losses. These include:

- *restitutionary* losses beyond the types discussed above, for example, in the case of *Attorney General v Blake* (2001), which dealt with the recovery of the profits made by a defendant from his breach of contract with the plaintiff (these are further discussed in the next chapter at paragraphs 16.91–16.92);
- *performance* losses wherein the plaintiff is awarded damages purely to compensate him for the failure of the defendant to perform his part of the contract.
  (1) For example, in the case of *Ruxley Electronics and Construction Ltd v Forsyth* (1996), where the plaintiff was awarded damages for 'loss of amenity' when the defendant builder built the plaintiff a swimming pool which was six inches shallower than the contractually specified depth, but was not otherwise of less value than what was contractually specified. By 'loss of amenity', the court had in mind Mr Forsyth's *subjective* loss in terms of disappointment that his *personal preference* for the contractually specified depth of pool had not been realised.
  (2) Similarly, in the case of *Farley v Skinner* (2002), the House of Lords allowed a claim for damages relating to the use and enjoyment of a house which was afflicted by aircraft noise. In that case, the purchaser specifically asked his surveyor to advise on whether the house would be affected by aircraft noise prior to purchase. The surveyor conducted the survey negligently and informed the purchaser that there was no such problem. The purchaser proceeded to buy the house only to discover that the surveyor was wrong. The purchaser was permitted to recover damages

for the surveyor's failure to provide the performance that he had specifically agreed to provide. On one view, this reflects an acceptance that damage done to the interest of a contracting party in the full and precise performance of the contract itself, is amenable to compensation, that is to say, that the *performance interest* of the victim of a breach of contract may be compensated for by damages.

This is not without controversy, and an alternative analysis exists, based on a long-accepted exception to the rules of recovery in damages for *non-pecuniary* losses relating to mental distress from a breach of contract. This alternative analysis is explored at paragraphs 15.60–15.61 below.

(3) The development of damages to compensate for damage to the performance interest has not received complete and unanimous support in the UK. This can be most clearly seen in the divergent strands of reasoning relied upon by the minority in the House of Lords case of *Alfred McAlpine Construction Ltd v Panatown Ltd* (2001) wherein Lords Goff and Millett argued strenuously in favour of recognition of and compensation for the damage done to the performance interest of a contracting party resulting from negligent construction works by a builder on land owned by a third party, but who sustained no pecuniary loss. In contrast, the majority judgments led by Lord Browne-Wilkinson steadfastly refused to recognise such a loss and concentrated on the rule that in such a case, the 'loss' was in reality the financial loss of the third party, and accordingly, only nominal damages would be awarded (unless a narrow exception to this rule was available). This case and its implications are explored more thoroughly in Chapter 8 (see paragraph 8.23);

- *consequential* losses which are recoverable simply because they are consequent upon a breach of contract. Although often used loosely to refer to any kind of loss as a consequence of a breach of contract (in particular a loss of profits, or perhaps reliance losses), Professor Treitel's *Law of Contract* (10th ed, 1999) defines them (at p 879) as: '... further harm, such as personal injury or damage to property, suffered as a result of breach: for example, where a cow is sold under a warranty of soundness but is diseased and infects other cattle of the buyer, which die. The seller is prima facie liable for the loss of the other animals, even though, when the buyer put the cow with them, the possibility of disease, or the risk of its spreading, was not present to his [presumably the seller's] mind at all.'

It may well be that in the appropriate case, a Singapore court will allow recovery for these types of losses.

15.46 To summarise, an award for damages may be made in order to make good the plaintiff's:

- (Net) Expectation loss;
- Reliance loss;

- Incidental loss;
- Indemnity loss;
- Restitutionary loss (under the law of unjust enrichment);
- Performance loss; and/or
- Consequential loss.

Quantification of Unliquidated Damages

(1) *Difficulty of Assessment No Bar to Recovery*

15.47 The difficulty of assessment of damages is no bar to an attempt being made (subject to the limits of remoteness, mitigation and so forth discussed in the sections to follow). One example of this can be found in the case of *Chaplin v Hicks* (1911).

The defendant in this case was a well-known theatrical agent and manager who made a unilateral offer in a newspaper to engage 12 ladies for his agency as actresses. The offer took the form of a contest, wherein ladies were invited to send in their photographs together with an application form to the newspaper. The plaintiff successfully passed the initial rounds of screening and was among the final 50 'contestants', and in fact emerged as the top choice among the section of the public who had seen her picture in their district. Unfortunately, when the defendant mailed her an invitation for a final meeting where he would select the 'winning' 12 ladies, the plaintiff failed to receive it until after the date of the meeting had passed. The winning 12 were selected from the other 49 ladies who had received their invitations. When the plaintiff finally received notice of the meeting, she tried to make another, but this was refused by the defendant (although no mention was made in the original offer that there would only be one meeting). Consequently, the plaintiff sued the defendant for causing her to lose the chance of being selected and therefore losing the chance of 'winning' the prize. At the end of the trial, the jury awarded the plaintiff £100 as damages. The defendant's appeal was then unanimously dismissed by the English Court of Appeal. Farwell LJ held (at pp 798–799) that:

> '... the defendant has committed a breach of his contract, the damages claimed are a reasonable and probable consequence of that breach, and loss has accrued to the plaintiff at the time of action. ... [I]n the present competition we find chance upon chance, two of which the plaintiff had succeeded in passing; from being one of six thousand she had become a member of a class of fifty, and, as I understand it, was first in her particular division by the votes of readers of the paper; out of those fifty there were to be selected twelve prize-winners; it is obvious that her chances were then far greater and more easily assessable than when she was only one of the original six thousand. ... In my opinion the existence of a contingency, which is dependent on the volition of a third person, is not enough to justify us in saying that the damages are incapable of assessment.'

(2) *Assessment of Reliance and Indemnity Losses*

15.48 The assessment of pecuniary losses such as indemnity loss and reliance loss is generally straightforward. In both cases, the plaintiff merely has to identify the amount of money that has been spent to indemnify third parties as compensation for the defendant's breach of contract, or the amount of money which has been spent in reliance.

15.49 Sometimes, due to the excessively speculative nature of the expectation losses in a particular case, reliance and/or indemnity losses may be the *only* types (or heads) of loss that are recoverable by a plaintiff. A good example of this is the case of *Anglia Television Ltd v Reed* (1972):

Oliver Reed entered into a contract with Anglia Television to act in a film to be produced by them. Reed then changed his mind and informed Anglia Television that he no longer wished to act in the film. Prior to the actual signing of the contract and following on from the signing, Anglia Television had expended a significant amount of money in preparation for the production of the film. Anglia Television sued Reed for breach of contract. However, given the speculative nature of the likely profitability of films, Anglia Television sought to recover its reliance losses instead of its expectation losses from Reed. The English Court of Appeal agreed that it was impossible to establish what profits would have been made and held that Anglia Television could indeed recover damages on the reliance basis. However, when it came to quantifying the amount of such reliance, Anglia Television was permitted to recover both the expenses incurred following from the time the contract was signed and (more controversially), the expenses incurred *prior* to its formation, subject to satisfaction of the tests of remoteness.

Therefore, it appears that expenditure made by the plaintiff *before* the contract was entered into can also be recovered as reliance loss, assuming they are not too remote (which is one of the factors which can limit recovery of damages, and is discussed below).

15.50 Recovery for reliance loss in such a context is in substitution for a claim for expectation loss. A necessary assumption to this type of claim, then, is that the contract represented a 'good bargain' for the plaintiff, in that had it been performed, it would have enabled the plaintiff to obtain, at the very least, sufficient revenue to cover his costs and expenses in performing his part of the bargain.

15.51 If the *defendant* is able to demonstrate to the court that the bargain was a *bad bargain* in that the plaintiff would never have recovered the whole of his costs in any event, even if the contract had been performed in full, then such a claim for reliance loss would be capped by reference to what would have been recovered by the plaintiff had the contract been performed; see, for example, the cases of *C & P Haulage v Middleton* (1983) and *CCC Films (London) Ltd v Impact Quadrant Films Ltd* (1985). The facts of *CCC Films (London)* are particularly interesting.

CCC contracted to pay Impact US$12,000 for a licence allowing them to exploit, distribute and exhibit in various countries three motion pictures. A deposit of 25% was paid by CCC in advance, with the remaining 75% to be paid when Impact were in a position to deliver the taped recordings of the films. Having paid the 75%, CCC requested that the tapes be sent by Impact to Munich via recorded delivery, together with the appropriate insurance. In fact, Impact sent the tapes uninsured by ordinary post. The tapes never arrived at their destination. Nor were replacement tapes provided by Impact. Ultimately, CCC brought an action against Impact for breach of contract. Since CCC could produce no evidence of loss of profits from their inability to exhibit or otherwise exploit the films, they pursued an alternative claim for the US$12,000 spent in acquiring the licence. On the other hand, no evidence was adduced by Impact to show that CCC would have failed to recoup their expenditure had there been no breach at all.

Faced with a situation where neither party provided any evidence as to whether CCC would have made a profit on the transaction, Hutchison J held that a plaintiff's choice whether to claim loss of profits or wasted expenditure can only be limited if the *defendant* is able to prove that the plaintiff would never have recovered his expenditure in reliance on the contract, even if the contract had been properly performed. This is a reversal of the usual burden of proof—usually, the plaintiff has to establish every element of his claim. However, since it was the defendant's breach which had caused this situation to arise, the usual burden of proof would be reversed.

15.52 Apart from the above, one other area of complexity is in relation to any possible issues of double-compensation between expectation, reliance and indemnity losses and care should be taken to minimise this.

(3) *Assessment of Expectation Losses: Diminution in Value or Cost of Cure?*

15.53 Expectation losses may be assessed from two viewpoints or measures:

- the 'diminution in value' measure; or
- the 'cost of cure' measure.

15.54 An award based on diminution of value aims to give the plaintiff the financial benefit that he would otherwise have obtained if the contract had been performed. This may take two forms: either the difference between the market or resale value of the contractual performance and the value as stated in the contract; or, where the contractual performance entails the production of something which the plaintiff intends to use in order to generate a profit, the loss of user profit which ought to have been earned had the defendant performed his obligations.

15.55 On the other hand, an award based on cost of cure aims to give the plaintiff a sum of money to repair any defects due to the defendant's breach of contract. As a result, he is put in as good a position as if the defendant had performed his part of the contract, that is, it aims to award the plaintiff the sum which he has paid or would have to pay for substitute performance equivalent to that which the defendant ought to have provided under the contract.

15.56 We have already encountered the *diminution in value* measure in the example involving Peter and David set out above in paragraph 15.27

above. In determining Peter's gross expectation loss to be $20,000, we were in effect measuring the difference in value between what Peter expected to obtain as a result of David's performance (the resale price of $50,000 from Tim) and the amount he had paid David in order to 'earn' that amount (the cost price of $30,000 for the wine).

15.57 The difference between 'diminution in value' and 'cost of cure' may also be illustrated by considering the following example:

- Henry has bought a new house for $750,000 and would like to have it renovated; in particular, he would like to replace the roof. He receives the keys to his new house on 15 January and enters into a contract with Connie to supply materials and labour for the replacement works for a total fee of $15,000.
- Connie's staff finish the re-roofing works on schedule. However, the works are defective and there are leaks all over the house. In addition, due to the poor quality of the tiles supplied, all of the tiles have become discoloured.
- Henry gets a quotation from a rival contractor to perform rectification works to replace the entire roof, and is quoted $20,000. Henry also gets a valuation from a valuer as to the market value of his property in its current defective state, and is told that it is now only valued at $720,000 due to the hideous state of the roof. How much should Henry recover in damages: $30,000 (diminution in value of the house due to Connie's defective work), or $20,000 (cost of cure)?

15.58 In the above example, Henry cannot recover both the diminution in value as well as the cost of cure. He has to elect to recover one or the other. Since they are alternatives, there is no linkage between the two. This is strikingly demonstrated by the case of *Radford v De Froberville* (1977) which stands for the proposition that cost of cure can be recovered *even if there is no diminution in value*. In that case, it was agreed that the defendant would erect a permanent wall (specified to be seven feet high, with bricks of a specific type or alternatively, subject to the plaintiff's approval) to screen off the plaintiff's property from a new property development. In breach of contract, the defendant failed to build the wall. This did not cause any change in the market value of the plaintiff's property, but it could not be denied that the plaintiff had not been supplied with what he had contracted for. In such circumstances, Oliver J observed (at p 1270) that:

> 'If he [the plaintiff] contracts for the supply of that which he thinks serves his interests—be they commercial, aesthetic or merely eccentric—then if that which is contracted for is not supplied by the other contracting party I do not see why, in principle, he should not be compensated by being provided with the cost of supplying it through someone else or in a different way, subject to the proviso, of course, that he is seeking compensation for a genuine loss and not merely using a technical breach to secure an uncovenanted profit.'

The plaintiff's damages were assessed as the full cost of erecting the wall in accordance with the very detailed specifications contained in the agreement. The court declined to award a smaller sum sufficient merely to build a lower cost pre-fabricated boundary fence (as was suggested by the defendants), even though this would arguably provide the plaintiff with an equivalent degree of security against encroaching weeds and trespassers.

15.59 Are there any clear principles, then, that limit the plaintiff's choices as to how he is to quantify his expectation loss? The cases are not completely consistent with one another, but in Professor Burrows' *Remedies for Torts and Breach of Contract* (2nd ed, 1994), it has been suggested (at p 141) that the following factors may influence the court:

- Where the plaintiff has sought to mitigate his losses, he will recover the cost of cure where he has, or ought to have, incurred that cost in reasonably seeking to minimise his losses;
- Where the plaintiff has cured or intends to cure the defective performance by the defendant, the court is more likely to allow the award of damages based on the cost of cure;
- Lastly, the plaintiff's intentions or aims in entering into the contract and desiring the defendant's performance may be important; so if the plaintiff wanted performance in order to profit from it, in the sense of making an economic gain, difference in value would more likely than not be adequate compensation; if the plaintiff wanted performance for other purposes, perhaps for his own use and enjoyment, difference in value would not, or not as fully, compensate him.

These three factors provide some guidance to determine when recovery on a cost of cure measure would be reasonable. In particular, the last issue can be seen to have been critical in the court's assessment of reasonableness in cases such as *Tito v Waddell (No 2)* (1977), *Ruxley Electronics and Construction Ltd v Forsyth* (1996), *Radford v De Froberville* (1977) and *Dean v Ainley* (1987). In the first two cases, the courts were not satisfied that recovery on the cost of cure basis would be reasonable since it was not clear that the plaintiff intended to use such damages (if awarded) to make good the defective performance of the defendant. Accordingly, the courts refused to order damages based on the cost of cure measure. In contrast, in the third and fourth cases, the plaintiff was able to satisfy the court that he intended to use the damages to rectify the defendant's defective performance—cost of cure damages were therefore viewed as being reasonable, and were ordered accordingly.

These factors, though, are really just indications as to whether it would be reasonable to award cost of cure damages. As observed by Lord Jauncey in *Ruxley Electronics and Construction Ltd v Forsyth* (1996) (at p 359):

> '[I]n the normal case the court has no concern with the use to which a plaintiff puts an award of damages for a loss which has been established. Thus irreparable damage to an article as a result of a breach of contract will entitle the owner to recover the value of the article irrespective of whether he intends to replace it with a similar one or to spend the money on something else. Intention,

or lack of it, to reinstate can have relevance only to reasonableness and hence to the extent of the loss which has been sustained.'

Consequently, it is not the case that the plaintiff must demonstrate that he intends to use the damages (if awarded) to 'cure' the breach, before the court is willing to allow them. Instead, it is all a question of reasonableness of such an award and a number of other factors may come into play. For example, Lord Jauncey in *Ruxley Electronics and Construction Ltd v Forsyth* (1996) (at p 358) appears to have also been influenced by the fact that contractual objectives for the construction of the swimming pool had been 'achieved to a substantial extent'. Lord Mustill in the same case was influenced (at p 361) by the perception that the cost of cure measure would result in damages which were 'disproportionate to the non-monetary loss suffered by the employer [Forsyth]'. Therefore, it may well be that even if there had been a finding of fact by the court of first instance that Forsyth had formed the intention to rebuild the pool, or had given an undertaking to the court that he would do so, the House of Lords would still have refused to allow recovery on the cost of cure measure, since Forsyth could not be allowed, '... to create a loss, which does not exist, in order to punish the defendants for their breach of contract. ...' (per Lord Lloyd in *Ruxley Electronics and Construction Ltd v Forsyth* (1996) at p 373).

Interestingly, it appears that Lords Jauncey and Lloyd were both applying an *objective* test as to what was *reasonable* or *proportionate* in the circumstances so as to limit the employer's ability to recover his loss in the context of *quantification*. To put it baldly, Mr Forsyth was not allowed to recover damages based on the cost of digging up the imperfectly built (though perfectly safe and adequate) swimming pool and re-constructing it to the contractual dimensions because, in the *court's opinion*, such actions were *unreasonable*. This may be distinguished from the more-or-less *subjective* tests used in relation to establishing *remoteness of damage* (which will be discussed at length at paragraphs 15.68–15.75, below), wherein the courts are concerned with establishing the kinds of losses which are irrecoverable because they are too remote from the contemplation of the contracting parties, given the state of their knowledge as to each others' affairs and the general conduct of contractual obligations at the time of the contract.

(4) *Non-Pecuniary Losses*

15.60 The kinds of loss that we have discussed above may be referred to as pecuniary losses—roughly speaking, they are losses of wealth. However, they are not the only types of loss that result from a breach of contract—loss may be incurred apart from a loss of wealth. These are termed 'non-pecuniary losses'. Examples of these would include losses in terms of emotional distress, embarrassment, hurt feelings, and so forth. For convenience, damages for these types of non-pecuniary loss will be generally termed as 'mental distress damages' from this point on.

Generally speaking, recovery of mental distress damages for non-pecuniary losses as a result of a breach of contract is not as straightforward as recovery for pecuniary losses. Although every breach of a contract will probably result in some inconvenience and disappointment to the injured party, generally speaking, these are not recoverable 'losses'. Bingham LJ pointed out in the case of *Watts v Morrow* (1991) (at p 1445) that:

> '[a] contract-breaker is not in general liable for any distress, frustration, anxiety, displeasure, vexation, tension or aggravation which his breach of contract may cause to the innocent party. This rule is not, I think, founded on the assumption that such reactions are not foreseeable, which they surely are or may be, but on considerations of policy.'

Any loss of reputation or embarrassment suffered by the injured party because of the breach of contract is also not recoverable (see *Addis v Gramophone Company, Ltd* (1909)). This reluctance to allow recovery for such losses can also be found in local cases, for example, the decision of GP Selvam J in the High Court decision of *Arul Chandran v Gartshore* (2000).

15.61 The strict position against allowing recovery of mental distress damages, however, is not a complete bar. Even in *Addis v Gramophone Company, Ltd* (1909), Lord Atkinson accepted (at p 495) that three exceptions were well-known (as at 1909):

> '...[1] actions against a banker for refusing to pay a customer's cheque when he has in his hands funds of the customer's to meet it, [2] actions for breach of promise of marriage, and [3] actions ... where the vendor of real estate, without any fault on his part, fails to make title. I know of none other.'

15.62 As Professor Phang has observed (in 'The Crumbling Edifice?—The Award of Contractual Damages for Mental Distress' [2003] *Journal of Business Law* 341 at p 347; hereinafter referred to as 'Crumbling Edifice'), there does not appear to be any underlying coherence to these three exceptions. This lack of coherence is further exacerbated by the fact that Lord Atkinson's three 'well-known' exceptions do not appear to be exhaustive and clearly do not represent the current state of the law. Apart from the three mentioned above, the courts have also been willing to allow recovery for mental distress damages in the following situations:

- Where there is substantial physical inconvenience or discomfort as a result of the breach of contract (*Hobbs v The London and South Western Railway Company* (1875); *Bailey v Bullock* (1950)).
- Where distress is directly consequent upon physical loss caused by the breach of contract (*Perry v Sidney Phillips & Son* (1982): anxiety and distress of living in a house in poor condition which had been bought in reliance on negligence in breach of contract in a surveyor's report; *Calebar Properties Ltd v Stitcher* (1984): unpleasantness of living in deteriorating premises until they became uninhabitable because of landlord's delay in repairs).
- Where loss of reputation caused by grossly defective performance of an employer's obligations results in financial loss to the employee (*Malik v Bank of Credit & Commerce International SA* (1998): here, the court was willing to imply a term of implied trust and confidence

between employer and employee wherein the employer was obliged not to conduct its affairs in such a corrupt and dishonest way as would tarnish the reputation of its employees).

- Where the very object or purpose of the contract is to provide enjoyment or to prevent distress (*Jarvis v Swans Tours Ltd* (1973); *Heywood v Wellers (a firm)* (1976); *Diesen v Sampson* (1971); *Reed v Madon* (1989); *Farley v Skinner* (2002)).

15.63 *Farley v Skinner* (2002) in particular, points to a possibly more expansive view in a number of these categories. In relation to the category of physical discomfort, Lord Scott observed (at p 768) as follows:

> 'In my opinion, the critical distinction to be drawn is not a distinction between the different types of inconvenience or discomfort of which complaint may be made but a distinction based on the cause of the inconvenience or discomfort. If the cause is no more than disappointment that the contractual obligation has been broken, damages are not recoverable even if the disappointment has led to a complete mental breakdown. But, if the cause of the inconvenience or discomfort is a sensory (sight, touch, hearing, smell, etc) experience, damages can, subject to the remoteness rules, be recovered.'

Farley v Skinner (2002) also points to a potentially more relaxed approach where non-pecuniary losses by *consumers* are concerned. Lord Steyn observed (at p 748):

> '... I am satisfied that in the real life of our lower courts non-pecuniary damages are regularly awarded on the basis that the defendant's breach of contract deprived the plaintiff of the very object of the contract, *viz* pleasure, relaxation, and peace of mind. The cases arise in diverse contractual contexts, *eg* the supply of a wedding dress or double glazing, hire purchase transactions, landlord and tenant, building contracts, and engagements of estate agents and solicitors. The awards in such cases seem modest. For my part what happens on the ground casts no doubt on the utility of the developments since the 1970s in regard to the award of non-pecuniary damages in the exceptional categories. ...'

In other words, it appears that the courts will be prepared to take a rough and ready approach to do justice in light of the facts of each individual case.

15.64 Such 'rough justice', dependent on the court's readiness to imply contractual terms, or to draw up categories of cases where it is prepared to allow mental distress damages, is unsatisfactory, but is there a way forward?

One possibility has been suggested by Professor Phang in 'Crumbling Edifice' (ibid). Professor Phang suggests, that the difficulties in these cases could be simply resolved using the limitation on liability set by the rules on remoteness of damages (to be discussed below, starting from paragraph 15.68).

To begin with, if one steps back and looks at the cases where mental distress damages were *not* allowed (for example, the cases of *Addis v Gramophone Company, Ltd* (1909), and more recently, the House of Lords case of *Johnson v Gore Wood & Co (a firm)* (2001)), these were cases far removed from the 'consumer' cases noted by Lord Steyn in *Farley v Skinner* (2002). Could it not be said that in a 'commercial' contract, as opposed to a 'consumer' one, the recovery of mental distress damages will *generally* be 'too remote' (that is to say, 'too far from the reasonable contemplation of the parties at the time the contract is formed'), and are therefore *irrecoverable*?

Of course, this begs the question: when is a contract 'commercial'? It is unlikely that any legal rule can be devised to determine whether a contract is one or the other since this is essentially a factual enquiry, dependent in large part on the intentions of the parties at the time of contract; in particular, whether there was a 'view to profit'.

15.65 This factor has been highlighted by some English judges as being particularly important in determining whether mental distress damages are available or not. See, for example, the decision of Lord Millett in the House of Lords case of *Johnson v Unisys Ltd* (2001) where Lord Millett accepted that the rule in *Addis*, 'is not limited to contracts of employment but is of general application in the law of contract,' (at p 1098) and was a 'sound one, *at least in relation to ordinary commercial contracts* entered into by both parties *with a view to profit*' (emphasis added) (at p 1099). He then went on to say:

> 'In [cases with a view to profit] non-pecuniary loss such as mental suffering consequent on breach is not within the contemplation of the parties and is accordingly too remote. The ordinary feelings of anxiety, frustration and disappointment caused by any breach of contract are also excluded, but seemingly for the opposite reason: they are so commonly a consequence of a breach of contract that the parties must be regarded not only as having foreseen it but as having agreed to take the risk of its occurrence ... Contracts which are not purely commercial but which have as their object the provision of enjoyment, comfort, peace of mind or other non-pecuniary personal or family benefits (as in *Jarvis v Swans Tours Ltd* ... and similar cases) are usually treated as exceptions to the general rule, though in truth they would seem to fall outside its rationale. Such injury is not only within the contemplation of the parties but is the direct result of the breach itself and not the manner of the breach. Indeed the avoidance of just such non-pecuniary injury can be said to be a principal object of the contract.'

15.66 As proposed by Professor Phang in 'Crumbling Edifice' (ibid), these observations may be synthesised in the form of a *rebuttable presumption* that unless otherwise demonstrated with adequate evidence, a contract 'with a view to profit' is one where damages for mental distress will be *too remote* and hence will be irrecoverable.

15.67 Even with this suggested approach, however, many other difficulties remain. To begin with, should the purposes of a contract be determined from an objective standpoint, or perhaps, from the subjective perspective of the party suffering the non-pecuniary loss as a result of the breach? If we have determined that there are in fact *mixed* purposes, should the presence of some profit motive bar mental distress damages altogether? Or should mental distress damages be available so long as the profit-motive is *not* the *primary* purpose? If the latter, more relaxed position is adopted, should primacy of the purpose of the contract be measured in terms of *specificity of the injured party's worries and concerns at the time of the contract*, or in terms of the *objective importance* of the contractual obligation which was ultimately breached? No easy answers exist for these and many other issues in the area of mental distress damages, and some of the positions suggested in the cases conflict. Given the introductory nature of this work, a more thorough discussion beyond the foregoing would be excessive. Reference, however, may be made to Professor Phang's work on this area in 'Crumbling Edifice' (ibid) for a more thorough discussion.

Restrictions on Assessment of Unliquidated Damages

(1) *Remoteness*

15.68 Even where the plaintiff has demonstrated that his losses are factually caused by the defendant's breach of contract, and has also shown that his loss (pecuniary or otherwise) is a type which can be compensated for by damages, he still has to contend with the possibility that the loss is too 'remote'.

The law does not compel the defendant to take responsibility for all the loss suffered by the plaintiff due to the breach. The primary rule as to remoteness of damages was set out by Alderson B in the case of *Hadley v Baxendale* (1854) (at pp 354–355) as follows:

> '... Where two parties have made a contract which one of them has broken, the damages which the other party ought to receive in respect of such breach of contract should be such as may fairly and reasonably be considered either arising naturally, ie according to the usual course of things, from such breach of contract itself, or such as may reasonably be supposed to have been in the contemplation of both parties, at the time they made the contract, as the probable result of the breach of it. Now, if the special circumstances under which the contract was actually made were communicated by the plaintiffs to the defendants, and thus known to both parties, the damages resulting from the breach of such a contract, which they would reasonably contemplate, would be the amount of injury which would ordinarily follow from a breach of contract under these special circumstances so known and communicated. But ... if these special circumstances were wholly unknown to the party breaking the contract, he, at the most, could only be supposed to have had in his contemplation the amount of injury which

> would arise generally, and in the great multitude of cases not affected by any special circumstances, from such a breach of contract. For, had the special circumstances been known, the parties might have specially provided for the breach of contract by special terms as to the damages in that case; and of this advantage it would be very unjust to deprive them ....'

This quotation sets out the two traditional limbs relating to remoteness of damages in contract. The first limb relates to loss that flows 'naturally' from the breach. On the other hand, the second limb relates to 'unusual' or 'special' loss which does not flow naturally from the breach, and which is due to special circumstances.

15.69 Under both limbs, the knowledge of the defendant as to the likelihood and nature of the losses that could be suffered by the plaintiff in the event of a breach of contract is critical. This point was highlighted in the judgment of Asquith LJ in *Victoria Laundry (Windsor) Ld v Newman Industries Ld* (1949). Here, two types of knowledge were distinguished:

- Imputed knowledge—knowledge which everyone, as reasonable persons, must be taken to know; and
- Actual knowledge—knowledge which one actually has.

As noted by Asquith LJ (at p 539) in his judgment,

> '... In cases of breach of contract the aggrieved party is only entitled to recover such part of the loss actually resulting as was at the time of the contract *reasonably foreseeable* as *liable* to result from the breach. ... What was at that time reasonably so foreseeable depends on the knowledge then possessed by the parties or, at all events, by the party who later commits the breach. ... *For this purpose, knowledge "possessed" is of two kinds; one imputed, the other actual*. Everyone, as a reasonable person, is taken to know the "ordinary course of things" and consequently what loss is liable to result from a breach of contract in that ordinary course. This is the subject matter of the "first rule" in *Hadley v Baxendale*. ... But to this knowledge, which a contract-breaker is assumed to possess whether he actually possesses it or not, there may have to be added in a particular case knowledge which he actually possesses, of special circumstances outside the "ordinary course of things", of such a kind that a breach in those special circumstances would be liable to cause more loss. Such a case attracts the operation of the "second rule" so as to make additional loss also recoverable' (emphasis added).

Therefore, where the plaintiff is trying to recover ordinary losses which flow naturally from the defendant's breach, there is no need to prove that the defendant had any actual knowledge that this might be the result of his breach—such knowledge will be imputed to him by the court and he is taken to know that such damage would ordinarily result from his breach.

On the other hand, if the plaintiff is trying to recover special losses that would not ordinarily be expected to flow from a breach, he can only recover if he can prove that the defendant had actual knowledge of the special circumstances that gave rise to these special losses.

15.70 How does a plaintiff satisfactorily prove that the defendant had actual knowledge of such special circumstances? It appears that an objective test will be imposed, as was observed by Robert Goff J in his judgment in *Satef-Huttenes Albertus SpA v Paloma Tercera Shipping Co SA (The Pegase)* (1981) (at p 183):

> '… have the facts in question come to the defendant's knowledge in such circumstances that a reasonable person in the shoes of the defendant would, if he had considered the matter at the time of making the contract, have contemplated that, in the event of a breach by him, such facts were to be take into account when considering his responsibility for loss suffered by the plaintiff as a result of such breach.'

Hence, the remoteness rules are not wholly subjective.

15.71 The complexity of the law on remoteness entails one last matter: the information or knowledge must be within the actual or imputed knowledge of the defendant, but what must the defendant know? In order for the plaintiff's loss to be sufficiently proximate, the defendant must actually, or by way of imputation, reasonably contemplate that the damage in question is *liable to result* from the breach. In other words, given the knowledge which the defendant actually or imputedly possesses, a reasonable man would have foreseen that there was an appreciable degree of likelihood that damage would result from the defendant's breach.

The exact degree of perceived probability as to whether the damage will occur as a result of the breach is still a matter of some dispute. In *Victoria Laundry (Windsor) Ld v Newman Industries Ld* (1949), Asquith LJ described (at p 540) the requisite degree of probability as being 'on the cards'. This colloquial phraseology was roundly criticised by the House of Lords in the case of *Koufos v C Czarnikow Ltd, The Heron II* (1969),where Lord Reid suggested that the degree of probability required was that the occurrence of the damage following the breach must have been 'not unlikely'; Lord Morris of Borth-y-Gest preferred the term 'liable to result or at least … not unlikely to result'; Lord Hodson also put forward the term 'liable to result' (while rejecting the phrase 'likelihood'); and lastly, both Lord Pearce and Lord Upjohn were in favour of the terms 'serious possibility' and 'real danger'. There is also some authority to say that their Lordships accepted that the degree of probability required to demonstrate that contract damages are not too remote is higher than that in tort. (The analogous test in tort only requires 'reasonable foreseeability'—see *Overseas Tankship (UK) Ltd v Morts Dock & Engineering Co Ltd (The Wagon Mound No 1)* (1961) (in relation to the tort of negligence) and *Overseas Tankship (UK) Ltd v The Miller Steamship Co Pty* (1967) (in relation to other torts)—both cases were decided by the Privy Council, on appeal from the Supreme Court of New South Wales.)

The confusion as to the precise level of probability required, post-*Heron II*, has been noted by Lord Denning MR in the difficult case of *H Parsons (Livestock) Ltd v Uttley Ingham & Co Ltd* (1978). In that case, the defendants supplied the plaintiff a defective container for pig feed which caused the nuts stored inside to become mouldy. When these mouldy nuts were fed to the plaintiff's pigs, they contracted a rare intestinal disease and subsequently died. On appeal, the English Court of Appeal held that the damage suffered by the plaintiff in the loss of his pigs was not too remote. Lord Denning MR, after making reference to the impossibility of dealing with the 'sea of semantic exercises' posed by the judgments of the House of Lords in the *Heron II*, went on to propose (at pp 802–803) an unconventional approach involving two tests for remoteness depending on the type of damage or loss involved: where the loss was physical, a more relaxed test of 'reasonable foreseeability' of the type of damage as a bare possibility (similar to that applied in tort cases) should be applied; on the other hand, in cases involving economic losses (for example, loss of profit) in contract, the stricter approach of 'reasonable contemplation' was more appropriate. Lord Denning MR characterised the damage suffered by the plaintiff before him as falling within the first category and applied a test of 'reasonable foreseeability'. Since it was reasonably foreseeable that the defective hopper would cause the nuts stored within it to become mouldy, and there was a foreseeable possibility that pigs fed such nuts would fall ill, the damage suffered by the plaintiff was not too remote.

15.72 Lord Denning's approach in *H Parsons (Livestock) Ltd v Uttley Ingham & Co Ltd* (1978) is difficult, as it requires the court to characterise the damage suffered into 'physical' and 'economic' categories. This may not be as simple as it looks. On the facts of *H Parsons (Livestock) Ltd v Uttley Ingham & Co Ltd* (1978) itself, it cannot be denied that the plaintiff, ultimately, was interested in recovering the profits that he would have made, had his pigs survived and made it to market, as opposed to the pigs themselves. Perhaps the difficulty of characterisation prompted the majority of the English Court of Appeal in *H Parsons (Livestock) Ltd v Uttley Ingham & Co Ltd* (1978) to put forward another approach, which distinguished between the *type* and the *extent* of the damage.

In *H Parsons (Livestock) Ltd v Uttley Ingham & Co Ltd* (1978), Scarman LJ proposed (at p 813) as follows:

> '... it would be absurd to regulate damages in such cases upon the necessity of supposing the parties had a prophetic foresight as to the exact nature of the injury that does in fact arise. It is enough if upon the hypothesis predicated physical injury must have been a serious possibility. ... It does not matter ... if they [the defendants] thought that the chance of physical injury, loss of profit, loss of market, or other loss as the case may be, was slight, or that the odds were against it, provided they contemplated as a serious possibility the *type* of consequence, *not necessarily* the *specific* consequence, that ensued upon breach' (emphasis added).

Orr LJ agreed with Scarman LJ's reasoning. On the majority view, the plaintiff's damage (that the pigs would fall ill because of mouldy nuts caused by the defendant's breach of contract by the supply of a defective hopper) was reasonably within the contemplation of the defendant as liable to occur. This constituted a *type* of damage that could be reasonably contemplated as liable to occur. The eventual death of the pigs because they had contracted a rare intestinal disease would not have been within reasonable contemplation. However, this was irrelevant because the outcome (death) was merely reflective of the *extent* of the damage.

15.73 The approach of the majority in *H Parsons* is not completely ideal either, since it is also difficult to characterise whether particular damage suffered and claimed by the plaintiff constitutes a distinct type or merely goes towards extent. It should be apparent that the two concepts are not distinct sets, but represent points along a continuum.

One could consider the facts of the case in *Victoria Laundry (Windsor) Ld v Newman Industries Ld* (1949) itself. The facts of the case were as follows:

Victoria Laundry entered into a contract to purchase a boiler from the defendants in order to expand their business. The defendants contracted to deliver a certain boiler of the specified capacity on 5 June. This boiler, however, was damaged prior to actual delivery, and was not actually delivered until 8 November. The defendants were aware of Victoria Laundry's business and had been informed many times before the contract was concluded that Victoria Laundry were 'most anxious' to put the boiler to use in the 'shortest possible space of time'. In light of the delay, Victoria Laundry sued to recover damages from the defendants in respect of the following losses from their inability to take on:

- large numbers of new customers in the course of their laundry business (which was held by the English Court of Appeal to be recoverable as being part of the usual loss that would follow as a matter of course and of which everyone has imputed knowledge); and
- a number of highly lucrative dyeing contracts for the Ministry of Supply (which was ultimately held to be irrecoverable since it was an unusual loss of which the defendants had no prior actual knowledge).

Could it not be said that the exceptional loss of profit from the potential Ministry of Supply contracts represented merely the extent of the plaintiff's loss; and that such losses should be recoverable as they were of a type (loss of profit from contracts which would have been entered into if not for the defendant's breach) which was reasonably within the contemplation of the defendants in that case?

15.74 To date, Lord Denning's approach has not been followed. On the other hand, despite its difficulties, the approach put forward by Scarman LJ and Orr LJ has been applied in a series of cases, and quite recently, in *Brown v KMR Services Ltd* (1995). Brown was a 'Lloyd's name', meaning he was a member of a number of Lloyds' syndicates which operate as insurers and re-insurers. In particular, he was a member of a large number of high risk 'disaster' insurance syndicates. Unfortunately for Brown, a succession of huge claims was made on members of the Lloyd's syndicates from 1987 to 1990, causing Brown to suffer substantial losses.

Brown sued KMR Services for breach of their contractual obligation to advise him adequately as to the level of risk he was assuming. The court of first instance found that there was indeed a breach of contract by KMR Services and found that they should be responsible for all such losses, rejecting the argument that such losses were too remote. On appeal to the English Court of Appeal, Hobhouse LJ made the following observations (at p 556):

> 'Reduced to its essentials [the argument from KMR Services] amounts to the following. The reasonable person in the position of the contracting parties would not have predicted that in the years 1988, 1989 and 1990 there would have been such a concatenation of major catastrophes as in fact occurred. The expectation and prediction of the reasonable man would have been that only one or two catastrophes would occur in any of those years. It follows that the reasonable man would not have foreseen losses on anything like the scale which was subsequently suffered. It is therefore said that the recoverable damages should be limited to such losses as would reasonably have been foreseen.
>
> ... In the present case the potential direct consequence of the defendants' breach was, and must always have been foreseen to be, that the plaintiff [Mr Brown] would be a member of an excessive number of high risk syndicates with excessive allocations of premium to those syndicates. Accordingly, the direct and wholly foreseeable consequence would be that the plaintiff [Mr Brown] would be liable for the losses made by those syndicates to an excessive extent, whatever those losses might turn out to be. Having identified that the natural, direct and foreseeable consequence of inadequate or improper advice was that the plaintiff [Mr Brown] would incur a liability as a member of high risk syndicates, the plaintiff [Mr Brown] has established what he needs to show—that the damages he is seeking to recover are not too remote.'

These developments focussing on 'type' and 'extent' of damages suggest that the apparently simple division put forward in *Hadley v Baxendale* (1854) and *Victoria Laundry (Windsor) Ld v Newman Industries Ld* (1949) between losses of ordinary profits and losses of exceptional profits may no longer be so clear. As has been observed by Professor Andrew Phang in his contribution to the *International Encyclopaedia of Laws (Contract): Singapore* (2000) at p 421, the approach taken by the majority in *H Parsons (Livestock) Ltd v Uttley Ingham & Co Ltd* (1978) threatens to blur the division between the two limbs. The unusual profit that would have been earned from a successful tender for a Ministry of Supply contract which was classified as special damage under the second limb of *Hadley v Baxendale* (1854) could be reclassified, following the majority in *H Parsons (Livestock) Ltd*, as merely going to the *extent* of the damage. If so, such loss could constitute a *type* of loss which might conceivably fall within the first limb instead.

15.75 Leaving such difficulties aside, in summary, damage suffered by a plaintiff may be recoverable as not being too remote if he can demonstrate that:

- the defendant can be taken to have known or actually knew of the circumstances surrounding the plaintiff which resulted in the plaintiff's loss; and
- it would have been obvious to a reasonable man in the defendant's shoes that if he breached the contract, there was a significant likelihood or serious possibility that such a breach would result in loss of the type which the plaintiff suffered.

(2) *Mitigation*

15.76 The plaintiff seeking to recover damages for a defendant's breach of contract is often said to have a 'duty' to mitigate his loss. As stated by Viscount Haldane LC in the case of *British Westinghouse Electric and Manufacturing Co Ltd v Underground Electric Railways Company of London Ltd* (1912) (at p 689):

> 'I think that there are certain broad principles which are quite well settled. The first is that, as far as possible, he who has proved a breach of a bargain to supply what he contracted to get is to be placed, as far as money can do it, in as good a situation as if the contract had been performed.
>
> The fundamental basis is thus compensation for pecuniary loss naturally flowing from the breach; but this first principle is qualified by a second, which imposes on a plaintiff the duty of taking all reasonable steps to mitigate the loss consequent on the breach, and debars him from claiming any part of the damage which is due to his neglect to take such steps.
>
> ... [T]his second principle does not impose on the plaintiff an obligation to take any step which a reasonable and prudent man would not ordinarily take in the course of his business'.

15.77 On the other hand, where the plaintiff does take steps to try and mitigate, but incurs additional losses (which might not have occurred had the plaintiff done nothing), such additional losses can still be recovered. As was said by Lord Macmillan in *Banco de Portugal v Waterlow & Sons Ltd* (1932) (at p 508):

> 'The law is satisfied if the party placed in a difficult situation by reason of the breach of a duty owed to him has acted reasonably in the adoption of remedial measures, and he will not be held disentitled to recover the cost of such measures merely because the party in breach can suggest that other measures less burdensome to him might have been taken.'

15.78 These observations have been approved and followed in Singapore, in cases such as the Singapore High Court decision of *Tan Soo Leng David v Lim Thian Chai Charles* (1998):

> 'The rule of mitigation of damages does not require the innocent party to do more than is reasonably required to stem the loss. As it is the party in default who has brought about a situation

> which calls for measures to mitigate loss, he is in no position to be astute in criticising the adequacy of the mitigating steps taken by the innocent party' (per Warren LH Khoo J at p 931).

15.79 Ultimately, as noted by Bankes LJ in *Payzu, Limited v Saunders* (1919) (at p 588), everything turns on the reasonableness of the plaintiff's actions to try and minimise his loss and:

> '[i]t is plain that the question [of] what is reasonable for a person to do in mitigation of his damages cannot be a question of law but must be one of fact in the circumstances of each particular case.'

15.80 As to what facts might suggest that the actions taken by the plaintiff were reasonable, some consideration might be made as to the following:

- 'In certain cases of personal service it may be unreasonable to expect a plaintiff to consider an offer from the other party who has grossly injured him; but in commercial contracts it is generally reasonable to accept an offer [of alternative performance] from the party in default' (per Scrutton LJ in *Payzu, Limited v Saunders* (1919) at p 589);
- the plaintiff is not usually required to take steps in mitigation of its loss which it is financially unable to afford;
- the plaintiff is not required to take steps in mitigation of its loss, which would place its commercial reputation or good public relations at risk;
- the plaintiff is not required to take steps in mitigation of its loss that would involve complex litigation.

15.81 Since the 1980s, there has been a view that casting mitigation as a 'duty' of the plaintiff is misleading. Hence, in the case of *Sotiros Shipping Inc and Aeco Maritime SA v Sameiet Solholt (The Solholt)* (1983), Sir John Donaldson MR observed (at p 608) that:

> '[a] plaintiff is under *no duty* to mitigate his loss, *despite* the habitual use by the lawyers of the phrase "duty to mitigate". He is completely free to act as he judges to be in his best interests. On the other hand, a defendant is not liable for all loss suffered by the plaintiff in consequence of his so acting. A defendant is only liable for such part of the plaintiff's loss as is properly to be regarded as caused by the defendant's breach of duty' (emphasis added).

This recasting of the language of mitigation highlights the similarity between mitigation and the issue of causation. One might then wonder, what would happen if a mitigation attempt goes seriously wrong: does this break the chain of causation?

Some guidance, may be found in the judgment of Lord Hoffmann in the *SAAMCO* (1997) case (discussed earlier at paragraph 15.26 above) wherein the answer appears to be 'no'. Lord Hoffmann quoted with approval the New Zealand case of *McElroy Milne v Commercial Electronics Ltd* (1993). In *McElroy*, a lawyer was engaged by a property developer to prepare certain documentation relating to a lease. The lawyer negligently failed to ensure that the lease contained a guarantee from the lessee's parent company. As a result, instead of being able to sell the property together with the benefit of the lease soon after completion, the developer found himself in dispute with the parent company. The dispute dragged on for more than two years, during which time the market fell.

The New Zealand Court of Appeal in *McElroy* held that the developer was entitled to the difference between what the property would have fetched if sold soon after its completion with a guaranteed lease and what it eventually fetched two years later. The lawyer had a duty to take reasonable care to ensure that his client got a properly guaranteed lease. He was therefore responsible for the consequences of his error, which was producing a situation in which the client had a lease which was not guaranteed. All the reasonably foreseeable consequences of that situation were therefore within the scope of the duty of care. The only remaining issue, then, was whether the developer's delay in selling the property negatived the causal connection between that situation and the ultimate loss. The New Zealand Court of Appeal decided this question by asking whether the client had reacted reasonably to his predicament.

Therefore, it seems that so long as the attempt at mitigation is reasonable, there is little to suggest that a court will find that it has broken the chain of causation, even if the mitigation has worsened the loss.

15.82 Even if the language of 'duty' is cast aside, the burden of proof remains on the defendant to show that the plaintiff has not taken steps towards mitigation of his loss: on a balance of probability, he has not mitigated his loss. This is unlikely to be easy, since the courts appear to be willing to find in favour of the plaintiff even in doubtful cases (see *Strutt v Whitnell* (1975)).

15.83 Before leaving mitigation, a few words on where mitigation has *no* application are apposite. Firstly, the need to mitigate only arises *after the contract has been discharged*, following the breach of contract. As discussed previously in Chapter 9 (at paragraphs 9.63–9.65), the victim of a breach of contract has the option whether or not to accept a breach of contract so as to discharge the contract and mitigation has no part to play in limiting his freedom to exercise this choice.

Secondly, mitigation has no relevance in relation to the manner in which the victim of the breach seeks to have his damages quantified. As decided by Oliver J in the case of *Radford v de Froberville* (1977), a plaintiff can be awarded damages to enable him to have performed for him, what the defendant failed to provide under their agreement, *even if more cost-effective ways of enabling him to achieve that performance can be found*. Among others, Oliver J reasoned (at p 1284) that:

> '... [i]t [a pre-fabricated brick wall] was not what the plaintiff stipulated for and what, in effect, he paid for when he sold the plot. I know of no principle of damages which would dictate that a plaintiff who has stipulated for an article of a certain quality should be fobbed off with an inferior substitute merely because it is cheaper for a defendant who has broken his contract to supply it.'

(3) *Compensating Advantages*

15.84 It is conceivable that sometimes, a plaintiff may end up in a better position because of the breach, than if the contractual breach had never happened at all.

Where such 'compensating advantages' arise from the plaintiff's act(s) of mitigation, it appears that such benefits *will* be taken into account to *discount* the damages that the plaintiff may recover from the defendant. The leading case illustrating this principle is the case of *British Westinghouse Electric and Manufacturing Co Ltd v Underground Electric Railways Company of London Ltd* (1912). In this case, the plaintiffs were supplied with defective turbines by the defendants. The plaintiffs attempted to mitigate their loss by obtaining replacement turbines supplied by another company. These turbines turned out to be extremely efficient, and gave rise to significant savings in operational cost that amounted to more than the losses caused by the defendant's defective performance. The House of Lords held that since their losses had been more than completely mitigated by the replacement turbines, the plaintiffs could only recover nominal damages.

15.85 In contrast, 'indirect' compensating advantages that arise apart from any acts of mitigation will be *ignored*. This can be seen in the case of *Lavarack v Woods of Colchester* (1967). In this case, the plaintiff was bound in his contract of employment not to engage in or be interested in any other business, whilst he was employed by the defendants. The defendants wrongfully terminated the plaintiff's employment. This breach of contract by the defendants had the effect of freeing the plaintiff from all outstanding obligations. Following his dismissal, the plaintiff found a job in a company called Martindale at a lower salary. However, he acquired half the shares in Martindale and also bought shares in another company called Ventilation, both of which subsequently rose in value. When the plaintiff sued the defendants in damages for his wrongful termination, the English Court of Appeal held that although the plaintiff's salary and shares in Martindale had to be taken into consideration to discount the damages payable by the defendants, his profits from the rise in the price of Ventilation shares was not. They were too 'indirect' to be taken into account.

15.86 What remains, then, is the difficulty in deciding what constitutes a benefit which is 'too indirect'. In Lord Denning's words in *Lavarack v Woods of Colchester* (1967) (at p 290):

> '... the benefit from that investment [in Ventilation shares] was not a direct result of his dismissal. It was an entirely collateral benefit, for which he need not account to his employers.'

This does not really advance our understanding of the principles involved very much, but it has been suggested by Professor Burrows in *Remedies for Torts and Breach of Contract* (2nd ed, 1994) at p 121 that this requirement of 'directness' operates in an analogous fashion to 'remoteness' and perhaps to 'causation' of damages, only in a reverse manner. Just as when considering remoteness and causation, we are concerned with the outer limits of what can fairly be ascribed to the defendant in terms of the obligation he has agreed to expose himself to, similarly, there should be an outer limit to what the defendant can expect the plaintiff to 'save' as a result of his own breach.

15.87 Lastly, it must be borne in mind that the above discussion relates to compensating advantages that accrue to the plaintiff as a direct result of the breach by the defendant. In cases where a benefit is accrued to the plaintiff *regardless* of the defendant's breach, such a benefit cannot be taken into consideration at all. An example of this is the case of *Thompson (WL) Ld v Robinson (Gunmakers) Ld* (1955).

In this case, the defendant ordered a new motor-car from the plaintiffs. Prior to delivery, the defendant changed his mind and cancelled the order, thereby breaching the contract of sale. The defendants subsequently managed to sell the motor-car to another buyer at the same price as in their contract with the defendant.

At first blush, this might be a suggestion that the plaintiff had fully mitigated his loss, and therefore, like the case of *British Westinghouse Electric and Manufacturing Co Ltd v Underground Electric Railways Company of London Ltd* (1912), any damages awarded would only have been nominal. However, what was extremely significant in this case was that there was an over-supply of motor-cars in the market. In other words, since there was a glut of motor-cars on the market, the effect of the defendant's breach was that the plaintiff made one fewer sale than they would have, had the defendant paid and accepted delivery. To the extent, then, that the plaintiff would have made the subsequent sale of the car to another buyer *in any event regardless of the plaintiff's breach*, the profit made from this subsequent sale had to be disregarded.

The position would, of course, be very different if demand had outstripped supply.

(4) *Intervening Cause Breaking Chain of Causation*

15.88 As noted above, the test for causation of damage in contract is relatively simple and factual. However, even though it may be said that the actions by a defendant in breach may constitute a factual cause for the subsequent damage by the plaintiff, it is possible that the causal link may be broken by an intervening cause (a '*novus actus interveniens*'). Examples of such an intervening event could include:

- the plaintiff's own unreasonable acts. For example, in the case of *Quinn v Burch Bros (Builders) Ltd* (1966), the defendants breached their contractual obligation to supply a ladder to the plaintiff. The plaintiff made use of a trestle instead. He fell and injured himself. The court held that in this case, the plaintiff had acted unreasonably in using the trestle instead of obtaining a more secure form of support, and his own unreasonableness had broken the chain of causation. Accordingly, the plaintiff failed to recover damages for his injuries.

- acts of a third party. In the case of *Stansbie v Troman* (1948), Stansbie was hired by Troman to carry out some decorative work on his house. At some point in the afternoon, Stansbie was left alone in the house to carry out his work. Unfortunately, Stansbie found that he needed to obtain some wallpaper and left the house to go to a neighbouring shop, but he failed to lock the empty house. When he returned, he found the front door was open, and afterwards learnt that a quantity of articles had been stolen. Ultimately, Troman sought to claim the value of the stolen articles from Stansbie. The English Court of Appeal found that on these facts, as Stansbie had a responsibility as to the state of the premises should it be left empty, and he had breached it by leaving the premises unlocked when he left, Stansbie was the cause of the loss. It could not be said that the action of the unknown thief was an intervening cause. In cases of intervention by a third party, then, the court will probably focus on whether the plaintiff was owed a contractual duty of care by the defendant, to prevent such third party intervention. Locally, see *Salcon Ltd v United Cement Pte Ltd* [2004] 4 SLR 353.
- other external factors. Generally, in relation to other external factors such as natural events, it would be a rare case where such events can amount to an intervening cause unless it can be said that the plaintiff was owed some duty of care to prevent the occurrence or influence of such an event. For example, in the case of *Galoo v Bright Grahame Murray* (1994), an auditor was in breach of contract in negligently auditing the client's accounts. Subsequently, the client made trading losses and became insolvent. The court found that the auditor's breach was not the effective cause of the losses. In other words, market forces (and the company's own decisions) acted as intervening causes, breaking the causal link between the auditor's breach, and the subsequent loss, and it could not be said that the auditor owed any duty of care in relation to the operation of the market in these circumstances. The House of Lords came to a similar conclusion in the *SAAMCO* (1997) case (discussed at paragraph 15.26, above).

(5) *Contributory Negligence*

15.89 Issues of mitigation as well as *novus actus interveniens* and causation will often also lead us to consider the possibility of raising contributory negligence as a defence to reduce the monetary damages that may be payable by the defendant.

This defence is found in section 3 of the Contributory Negligence and Personal Injuries Act (Cap 54, 2002 Rev Ed). Section 3(1), in particular, empowers the court of first instance to reduce the damages payable in a just and equitable fashion, in accordance with the plaintiff/claimant's degree of responsibility or fault. In turn, 'fault' is defined in section 2 of the Act to mean:

> '... negligence, breach of statutory duty or other act or omission which gives rise to a liability in tort or would, apart from this Act, give rise to the defence of contributory negligence.'

15.90 The question then, is whether these provisions apply where there is a breach of contract. These provisions were modelled on the English Law Reform (Contributory Negligence) Act 1945 and the analogous provisions (section 1(1) of the 1945 Act) were analysed by Hobhouse J in his decision in *Forsikringsaktieselskapet Vesta v Butcher* (1986), and his analysis was subsequently approved by a majority in the English Court of Appeal in *Forsikringsaktieselskapet Vesta v Butcher* (1988). This position has been expressly adopted and approved by the Singapore Court of Appeal in the case of *Fong Maun Yee v Yoong Weng Ho Robert (practising under the name and style of Yoong & Co)* (1997) (at pp 316–317):

> '... it has been held by the English Court of Appeal in *Forsikringsaktieselskapet Vesta v Butcher* ... that where a defendant's liability in contract is concurrent with an identical duty in tort, the defence of contributory negligence is available to the defendant. In our respectful opinion the English Court of Appeal's decision makes much sense and we have no hesitation in adopting it and following it in this appeal.'

Contractually Agreed Damages and Other Techniques to Recover Losses or Discourage Breach

15.91 Given the many complexities pertaining to the quantification of unliquidated damages and the restrictions on their recovery in the form of the rules on remoteness, mitigation, and so forth, it should not be surprising that parties to a contract (and their lawyers) have adopted various techniques to avoid these uncertainties. In this section, we will have a look at some of them.

(1) *Liquidated Damages Clauses and Penalty Clauses*

15.92 Just as parties are free to set out their mutual rights and obligations which would constitute proper performance of the contract, they can also come to an agreement as to the quantum of damages which will be payable in compensation for any losses suffered in consequence of breach. Such an agreement will often take the form of a provision for 'liquidated damages' based upon a genuine pre-estimate of the loss which may be suffered as a result of a breach of contract.

15.93 If a contract containing a liquidated damages clause has been breached, the party-in-breach will then have to pay the innocent party the amount stipulated in the liquidated damages clause without anything more. There is no need for the innocent party to prove that in actual fact, any loss was suffered.

Contractually agreed clauses stipulating an amount of money payable by the party-in-breach to the innocent party are thus enforceable so long as they are intended to compensate for the losses suffered by an innocent party and are not a 'penalty' aimed at punishing the party-in-breach for his failure to perform. Penalties, which are not genuine pre-estimates of loss, will be struck down. If, however, the sum specified to be a 'penalty' is a lower figure than the actual loss suffered by the innocent party, there does not appear to be any impediment in allowing the innocent party to recover the larger sum in damages, as was the case in *Public Works Commissioner v Hills* (1906).

15.94 The principles setting out the distinctions between a liquidated damages clause and a penalty clause were summarised in the House of Lords case of *Dunlop Pneumatic Tyre Co Ltd v New Garage & Motor Co Ltd* (1915) by Lord Dunedin (at pp 86–88) as follows:

> '... I shall content myself with stating succinctly the various propositions which I think are deducible from the decisions which rank as authoritative:—
>
> 1. Though the parties to a contract who use the words "penalty" or "liquidated damages" may prima facie be supposed to mean what they say, yet the expression used is not conclusive. The Court must find out whether the payment stipulated is in truth a penalty or liquidated damages. This doctrine may be said to be found passim in nearly every case.
> 2. The essence of a penalty is a payment of money stipulated as *in terrorem* of the offending party; the essence of liquidated damages is a genuine covenanted pre-estimate of damage ...
> 3. The question whether a sum stipulated is penalty or liquidated damages is a question of construction to be decided upon the terms and inherent circumstances of each particular contract, *judged of as at the time of the making of the contract*, not as at the time of the breach ...
> 4. To assist this task of construction various tests have been suggested, which if applicable to the case under consideration may prove helpful, or even conclusive. Such are:
>   (a) It will be held to be penalty if the sum stipulated for is extravagant and unconscionable in amount in comparison with the greatest loss that could conceivably be proved to have followed from the breach. ...
>   (b) It will be held to be a penalty if the breach consists only in not paying a sum of money, and the sum stipulated is a sum greater than the sum which ought to have been paid. ...
>   (c) There is a presumption (but no more) that it is penalty when "a single lump sum is made payable by way of compensation, on the occurrence of one or more or all of several events, some of which may occasion serious and others but trifling damage" ...
>
> On the other hand:
>
> (d) It is no obstacle to the sum stipulated being a genuine pre-estimate of damage, that the consequences of the breach are such as to make precise pre-estimation almost an impossibility. On the contrary, that is just the situation when it is probable that pre-estimated damage was the true bargain between the parties. ...'

(2) *Simulating Penalty Clauses*

15.95 Just as it is said that there are many ways to skin a cat, there are many ways in which a breach of contract can be discouraged without resorting to a penalty clause. Examples of clauses which could have a similar effect in practice include:

- 'accelerated payment' clauses;
- 'earnest money' and 'forfeiture' clauses;
- guarantees;
- 'discount' clauses;
- 'alternative performance' clauses; and
- 'withholding' clauses.

The effectiveness of these clauses will depend on whether they can avoid being characterised as a penalty and they are discussed in greater detail below.

(a) 'Accelerated Payment' Clauses

15.96 In contracts which provide for payment in instalments, the contracts will very often incorporate a clause which makes the entire sum outstanding immediately due and outstanding upon a breach of the contract by the debtor. Such a clause, if effective, will therefore 'accelerate' the payment of the sum outstanding upon breach of the contract, commonly, because of late payment of an instalment. Such clauses are commonplace in hire-purchase contracts.

On a simplistic view, it might appear that such clauses can never amount to a penalty since they do not impose any additional burden on the debtor; he merely pays what he was supposed to pay all along, only earlier. However, this ignores the time value of money: just as a bird in the hand is worth two in the bush, payment received early is worth more than payment received late. Therefore, it is usually expected that some 'discount' should be given to reflect this. If some discount is given, it is more unlikely that the acceleration clause will be viewed as being intended to terrorise the debtor. It is therefore more likely to be upheld and might not be treated as a penalty.

(b) 'Earnest Money' and 'Forfeiture' Clauses

15.97 In some contracts, an advance payment is requested to demonstrate that the payer is serious about honouring his contractual obligations; in other words, the payer is guaranteeing that he will perform in accordance with the contract. Such an advance payment is called 'earnest money' and it may be intended that if the contract is fully performed, the earnest money will be taken into account as part of the price payable for the performance of the contract. If the contract is terminated due to breach by the payer, such earnest money is not recoverable. The payee is entitled to forfeit the earnest money.

However, most advance payments are not intended to take the form of earnest money. Instead, they are merely intended to constitute early payment of the total price, that is, a 'deposit'. In general, deposits paid on a contract which is subsequently terminated due to a breach by the payer may be refundable (most probably, because the basis for the advance payment had failed; see the discussion on recovery based on total failure of consideration by a contract-breaker in the next chapter). Hence, in the case of *Dies v British and International Mining and Finance Corp Ltd* (1939), Stable J observed (at pp 744–745) that:

> '... there would be a manifest defect in the law if, where a buyer had paid for the goods but was unable to accept delivery, the vendor could retain the goods and the money quite irrespective of whether the money so retained bore any relation to the amount of the damage, if any, sustained as a result of the breach. The seller is already amply protected, since he can recover such damage as he has sustained and can, it seems, set off his claim for damages against the claim for the return of the purchase price.'

Such deposits, then, may have to be refunded to the payer because the basis for their payment (the benefits that would have resulted if the contract had been performed) has failed. To prevent this, then, the payee may provide in the contract a 'forfeiture' clause. Such a clause might provide that deposits paid by the payer would be forfeited in the event the payer breached the contract, for example, by renouncing the contract and refusing to allow the payee to perform his part of the contract. Such clauses, then, would allow the payee to keep the deposit, as if it was 'earnest money'.

15.98 It is clear that the controls relating to penalties do not apply to either type of forfeiture. However, that is not to say that there is no possibility of relief. Recognising that forfeiture of earnest-monies or deposits could be overly harsh, the courts of equity developed the doctrine of 'equitable relief from forfeiture'. Usually, this will take the form of an order to the parties to allow the payer additional time (the length of which is fixed by the court) to fulfil his part of the bargain. Thus, the Singapore Court of Appeal in the case of *Pacific Rim Investments Pte Ltd v Lam Seng Tiong* (1995) observed (at p 23) that:

> 'In our opinion, the grant of the relief against forfeiture is a prelude to an order of specific performance. The court, in essence, is asked to disregard the rescission or termination of the contract by the vendor as a form of relief prior to the grant of specific performance. The fundamental principle upon which equity acts is that a party having a legal right shall not be permitted to exercise it in such a way that the exercise amounts to unconscionable conduct ... Needless to say, such jurisdiction would only be exercised in exceptional circumstances since the courts would not ordinarily countenance a departure from contractual rights and obligations. Hence, in order to invoke successfully the courts' jurisdiction, the circumstances of the case must reveal elements of unconscionability and injustice.'

(c) Guarantees

15.99 Some contracts provide for more than one party to be responsible for the performance of the contract. For example, in many loan contracts, the lender will frequently require a third party to *guarantee* that the borrower will repay the loan. This is achieved by entering into an agreement with the third party to indemnify the lender in the event the principal obligor (the borrower) fails to fulfil his obligation to repay. Where the borrower is a company, say, and the third party is a director of that company, it is easy to see that the third party will exert pressure on the borrower company to perform its obligations under the loan contract so as to ensure that he does not himself become personally liable on the indemnity. Similarly, it is common practice to require a parent company or principal shareholder of a borrower company to provide this type of guarantee as part of the consideration for the loan itself. Further, to avoid any difficulties with the enforceability of such an agreement due to lack of consideration from the guarantor, often, such guarantees will be made under seal.

Limited restrictions on the efficacy of this type of clause may be found in section 4 of the Unfair Contract Terms Act (Cap 396, 1994 Rev Ed) which provides that such guarantees or indemnities, if given by a person 'dealing as a consumer' may be invalid if they do not satisfy the requirement of reasonableness set out in that Act. This provision, however, is of very limited use in most situations since it is difficult to see that the guarantor/indemnifier is a 'consumer' as defined in section 12 of the Act.

On the other hand, the common law vitiating factors (in particular *duress* and *undue influence*) have often been found to be present where guarantees have been given for the benefit of third parties. Where the guarantor was coerced or was unduly influenced into entering into the guarantee, and if the creditor having the benefit of the guarantee had *notice* of such inequitable activity, the guarantee may be set aside. This is further discussed in Chapter 13.

(d) 'Discount' Clauses

15.100 In some contracts for sale of goods, there may be a clause providing for different prices to be paid, depending on when payment is made (lower if early, higher if later), or for a 'discount' to be given upon 'early payment'. If a higher price is ultimately paid due to payment on a later date, it does not take much imagination to see that this has practically the same effect as a penalty clause imposed in response to a late payment.

(e) 'Alternative Performance' Clauses

15.101 A clause which provides for payment of a certain sum of money upon the occurrence of an event *other than breach* should not be viewed as a penalty clause. Otherwise, in a contract for the sale of goods, one might be forced to view the payment of the price of the goods in exchange for the delivery of those goods to be a penalty!

On the other hand, some contracts may provide that a sum of money is to be payable by one party, upon the exercise of a contractual right of termination of the contract by the other party. This might not appear to be controversial if the right of termination arises out of an event which has nothing to do with any potential breach of contract. Confusion, however, arises if the event which entitles one party to exercise its contractual right of termination is actually a breach of contract in itself, which would also have created a liability in damages for the breach. Let us consider the following example:

- David enters into a sole-distribution agency agreement with Peter who is a manufacturer of high-end audiophile hi-fi components. Under this agreement, Peter agrees to develop a market and distribute David's hi-fi components in Singapore on a commission basis. The contract provides that David is obliged for the next ten years to supply the goods to Peter and will not enable any other person to sell the same goods within Singapore.
- The contract also provides that once sales figures reach 5,000 components a year, either David or Peter may bring the distribution agreement to an end. If David exercises this power, however, David must also pay Peter $750,000 in lieu of further performance of his own obligations under the contract.
- Peter is very successful in building up a market for David. Within six months, Peter's efforts have managed to shift 5,200 components for David, generating revenues of $650,000 from sale of the components. David is now confident that he can take over the sales from Peter as his brand is sufficiently established. This also triggers David's alternate performance to pay Peter $750,000.

Given the facts above, the wording of the contract suggests that David and Peter intended the payment of the $750,000 to be an alternate mode of performance. However, it is not otherwise clear why this should not be treated as a penalty: on a purely objective view, there is little to differentiate the effect of such a clause from that of a penalty clause. What seems to be clear, though, is that the intentions of David and Peter in drafting the payment in this manner will probably be critical in inclining courts to take the former view rather than the latter.

(f) 'Withholding' Clauses

15.102 Where the contract provides that payments for the performance by one party is to be made in stages (depending on the progress made), or only upon completion of all of the obligations, it is not uncommon to find that the scheduled payments may be delayed or withheld if there is any defect in the performance. This may take the form of delays in progress, or perhaps, in defects in the performance itself, for example, defective quality or short quantity of goods, defects in services provided, and so forth. So long as the defect is not made good, the corresponding payment is withheld. Since the payment is still outstanding, merely delayed, it should not be viewed as a penalty.

15.103 The problem lies with more draconian clauses which seek to *permanently* withhold such sums, with the ultimate effect that the payor pays a smaller amount in total. It is not difficult to see that this can have the effect of a 'penalty' in the form of the goods or performance which are not paid for.

In cases such as *Gilbert-Ash (Northern) Ltd v Modern Engineering*

(Bristol) Ltd (1974), the House of Lords had to consider a contractual clause which permitted a main contractor to suspend or withhold payment of any moneys due or becoming due to his sub-contractor, however large, if the sub-contractor breached any of the terms of the contract between them, regardless of the severity of the breach. In the words of Viscount Dilhorne (at p 711): 'Read literally this [clause] provides for the imposition of a penalty which may be wholly disproportionate to the damage suffered by the contractor.'

15.104 On the other hand, if the withholding is effected simply by making full payment due only upon the *strict, full and complete performance* of the contract, so long as there is no such performance, the sum will never become due and in effect, the withholding will have become permanent. An example of this type of clause was considered and upheld by the English Court of Appeal in *Eshelby v Federated European Bank* (1932).

15.105 Withholding clauses may also be re-worded to apply to withholding or withdrawal of performance of an obligation other than payment of money. Thus, it is common in hire contracts that the owner of a chattel hired to the hirer can withdraw his permission for the hirer to use that chattel, if the hirer is late in payment of the hire fees. Again, such acts to withhold performance do not appear to contravene the rules against penalties and are regularly upheld.

15.106 Of course, in appropriate circumstances, it could be argued that such permanent withholdings or deductions are really forfeitures, in which case *equitable relief against forfeiture* should arguably be available (discussed above at paragraph 15.98). However, where sums are withheld because they are not due as the payee has not fully performed his obligations under the contract (as suggested above), it seems that the courts will be reluctant to exercise their jurisdiction to grant equitable relief (see, for example, the English decision of Rattee J in *Nutting v Baldwin* (1995)).

In *Nutting*, certain members of an insurance syndicate breached their contractual obligation to contribute sums of money for the purpose of funding any litigation which the syndicate might mount. As a result of this breach, the defaulting members were disentitled under the contract from participating in any 'profits' made by the syndicate. Since no sums were due, nothing was payable to the defaulting members and such withholding could not be viewed as a penalty. Rattee J accepted that the defaulting members had proprietary rights in the profits, and that this withholding had the effect of a forfeiture. When asked, however, to order equitable relief against forfeiture, Rattee J refused, primarily because the members' contributions to the fund were the very essence of the contract itself. By contributing, the members would share in the risks of the endeavour as well as the benefits from it. To order relief would completely negate this. Accordingly, no relief was granted against forfeiture.

No Damages in Equity?

15.107 Unlike the courts at common law, the courts of equity did not originally have the power to award monetary damages in compensation for losses caused by breach of contract (although it did award equitable compensation for breaches of fiduciary duties). The primary remedies of the courts of equity in response to a simple breach of contract were the equitable remedies of specific performance and injunction (which will be discussed in the next chapter). As a general rule, therefore, no damages may be awarded in equity for breach of contract.

This is not a particularly difficult problem nowadays, since our courts are empowered to exercise both equitable and common law jurisdiction and may award either or both types of remedies where appropriate. In some unusual situations, however, it may well be that the court is faced with a problem where no common law damages can be awarded, and yet the equitable remedies are also not available. In such a situation, the court does have a residual power to award damages *in lieu* of an order for specific performance or an injunction. This is discussed further in the next chapter (see paragraphs 16.45–16.47).

CHAPTER 16

Remedies for Breach of Contract II: Specific Performance and Injunctions

PARAGRAPHS

16.1–16.2 **Specific Remedies**

Common Law Action for Fixed Sum

16.3 (1) Where the Plaintiff is Blameless

16.4 (2) Action for Fixed Sum Distinct from Claim for Damages

16.5–16.6 (3) No Election Between Action for Fixed Sum and Claim for Damages

(4) Exceptions Permitting Damages for Breach of Obligation to Pay Money

16.7 (a) Contractual Provision for Interest

16.8 (b) Knowledge That Breach Would Cause Losses

16.9–16.10 (c) Damages Arising Apart from Non-Payment

16.11 (5) Timing of Claim

16.12–16.14 (6) Where Plaintiff is in Breach of Contract

16.15–16.19 Equitable Remedies

(1) Specific Performance

16.20–16.21 (a) Common Law Remedies Inadequate

16.22–16.23 (b) Exercise of Court's Discretion Would Be Just and Equitable

16.24–16.25 (c) Contract Was Discharged Due to Breach

16.26–16.27 (d) Contracts for Personal Service

16.28–16.29 (e) Constant Supervision/Uncertainty in Definition of Obligation

16.30 (2) Injunction

16.31–16.42 (a) Prohibitory Injunctions

16.43–16.44 (b) Mandatory Injunctions

16.45–16.46 (3) Damages in Lieu of or in Addition to Specific Performance or Injunction

16.47 (4) Effect of Non-Compliance

16.48–16.53 **Restitutionary Awards**

16.54 Unjust Enrichment where Plaintiff is Blameless

PARAGRAPHS

Restitutionary Awards (continued)

16.55 (1) Benefits in Money: Total Failure of Consideration
16.56–16.57 (a) Terminology
16.58–16.60 (b) Overlap with Breach of Contract
16.61–16.64 (c) Where Loss Suffered is Equal or Less Than Sum Paid
16.65–16.69 (d) Where Loss Suffered is Greater Than Sum Paid
16.70–16.73 (e) Requirement of 'Total' Failure
16.74–16.75 (2) Benefits in Kind: *Quantum Meruit* and *Quantum Valebant*
16.76–16.84 (a) Where Plaintiff has Completed Some Obligations
16.85–16.87 (b) Where Plaintiff has Completed All Obligations
(3) Restitutionary Damages for Breach of Contract
16.88–16.90 (a) General Position: Breach of Contract *Simpliciter*
16.91–16.92 (b) More Than Just Breach of Contract
16.93–16.94 Unjust Enrichment Where Plaintiff is in Breach of Contract
16.95–16.97 (1) Benefits in Money: Total Failure of Consideration?
16.98–16.101 (2) Benefits in Kind: *Quantum Meruit*?
16.102–16.104 Where Contract is Discharged for Reasons Other than Breach
16.105–16.106 (1) Contracts Discharged by Agreement
16.107–16.109 (2) Contracts Discharged by Frustration
16.110–16.111 (3) Contracts Vitiated by Illegality
16.112–16.119 Restrictions on Recovery for Unjust Enrichment

Specific Remedies

16.1 Apart from awarding damages for breach of contract, more direct means of enforcement are available from the courts, for example, the 'specific remedies'. Instead of compensation, the plaintiff sometimes just wants what is due or owed to him (whether in money or in kind) from the defendant.

16.2 As mentioned at the beginning of the previous chapter, specific remedies which give the innocent party what is due to him stem from two different legal traditions and may be divided into the following categories:

- the *common law* action for a fixed sum (sometimes, this is referred to as an action for an agreed sum, or an action for repayment of a debt);
- the *equitable* remedy of specific performance; and
- the *equitable* remedy of injunction.

Common Law Action for Fixed Sum

(1) *Where Plaintiff is Blameless*

16.3 This type of claim is most common in situations where the defendant's breach of contract simply consists of his failure to pay a contractually stipulated sum of money to the plaintiff. For example, if the plaintiff has performed all of his obligations and yet does not receive payment of the agreed price for that performance, he is entitled to sue the defendant for that price. This would be a liquidated claim for a precise sum which is owed to the plaintiff.

(2) *Action for Fixed Sum Distinct from Claim for Damages*

16.4 In an action for a fixed sum, concepts such as remoteness of damages and mitigation of damages are *irrelevant*. These issues are only relevant in claims for damages for breach of a contractual term (whether liquidated or unliquidated). This should be obvious once we appreciate that the action for a fixed sum or debt has nothing to do with compensation. Such a claim simply allows the innocent party to recover what was promised to him, and is not a 'money-substitute' for it. As observed by GP Selvam J in the Singapore High Court case of *MP-Bilt Pte Ltd v Oey Widarto* (1999) (at p 602):

> 'Common sense and authorities affirm the principle that there is no duty to mitigate where a debt is claimed. A creditor is entitled to recover a debt and it is independent of his duty to mitigate damages if and when he accepts a breach by the other party.
> ... By definition a debt is a sum of money fixed by the contract for the completed performance of a given obligation while the contract is alive. ... It follows that once a debt has crystallized there is nothing for the creditor to mitigate. Once a debt always a debt. There being no claim for damages no duty to mitigate can arise. ...'

(3) *No Election Between Action for Fixed Sum and Claim for Damages*

16.5 Where the breach of contract solely relates to an obligation to pay money, the general rule is that no damages can be recovered for such a breach. Instead, the only possible remedy is an action for a fixed sum. As observed by GP Selvam J in *MP-Bilt Pte Ltd v Oey Widarto* (1999) (at p 602), '[a]fter a debt has fallen due the debtor cannot decide to dishonour it and convert it into damages'. This position was set out in the old House of Lords case of the *London, Chatham and Dover Railway Company v The South Eastern Railway Company* (1893) where Lord Herschell made the following observations (at p 437):

> '[T]he appellants contended that … interest might be given by way of damages in respect of the wrongful detention of their debt. I confess that I have considered this part of the case with every inclination to come to a conclusion in favour of the appellants, to the extent at all events, if it were possible, of giving them interest from the date of the action … But I have come to the conclusion, upon a consideration of the authorities, agreeing with the Court below, that it is not possible to do so …'

The above position was reviewed by the House of Lords in the case of *President of India v La Pintada Compania Navigacion SA* (1985) but although it was unanimous that the rule was undesirable, they refused to overrule *London, Chatham and Dover Railway* (1893). In coming to this decision, the House of Lords was heavily influenced by Parliament's apparent satisfaction with the status quo when it did not accept a proposal in 1982 by the UK Law Commission for that case to be legislatively overruled.

16.6 The view taken in these cases, however, fails to consider the commercial reality of the time cost of money. In the commercial context, it does not take much imagination to realise that late payment costs money, either because the payor is unable to benefit from interest upon that sum, or because he has to incur interest because he is not able to reduce any outstanding loans which he may have with the proceeds from the late payment. The law has therefore left open some exceptions to this general rule.

(4) *Exceptions Permitting Damages for Breach of Obligation to Pay Money*

(a) Contractual Provision for Interest

16.7 Parties are permitted to contractually provide for the payment of interest in the event of late payment. Ideally, this should be expressly provided for, but on the appropriate facts, the courts may be willing to imply such a provision, for example, in the English Court of Appeal case of *F G Minter v Welsh Health Technical Services Organisation* (1980).

(b) Knowledge That Breach Would Cause Losses

16.8 In the case of *Wadsworth v Lydall* (1981), the English Court of Appeal had to consider whether a plaintiff could recover interest and costs incurred from having to undertake additional financing arrangements due to cover a shortfall in his finances because of the defendant's failure to fully honour a money debt. The facts were as follows:

The defendant and the plaintiff were informal partners holding a tenancy of a farm on which the plaintiff lived. When the partnership was dissolved, it was agreed that the plaintiff would give up possession of the farm by a specified date when he would receive £10,000 from the defendant. Relying on this agreement, the plaintiff agreed to purchase another property from a third party. This required him to pay the £10,000, which by then he should have received, to the third party. Unfortunately, the defendant only paid £7,600 and as a result, the plaintiff had to take out a mortgage from the third party for the balance. Ultimately, the plaintiff sued the defendant and tried to recover the interest incurred on the mortgage and the transaction costs involved as *special damages*.

On appeal to the English Court of Appeal, Brightman LJ said (at p 603):

> '... If a plaintiff pleads and can prove that he has suffered special damage as a result of the defendant's failure to perform his obligation under a contract, and such damage is not too remote on the principle of *Hadley v Baxendale*..., I can see no logical reason why such special damage should be irrecoverable merely because an obligation on which the defendant defaulted was an obligation to pay money and not some other type of obligation.'

This case was subsequently approved by the House of Lords in *President of India v La Pintada Compania Navigacion SA* (1985). A fuller discussion as to the principles of *Hadley v Baxendale* (1854) is set out at paragraphs 15.68–15.75 in Chapter 15. As for the reference to *special* damages used by Brightman LJ, it should be noted that this has been clarified to refer to the second limb of *Hadley v Baxendale* (1854) (not least by Lord Brandon in the *La Pintada* case) relating to unusual losses which do not flow naturally from the breach. As clarified by subsequent judges, Brightman LJ was not referring to special damages in the context of legal pleadings (where special damages refer to claims which must be specifically pleaded or itemised in a plaintiff's statement of claim).

(c) Damages Arising Apart from Non-Payment

16.9 In many cases, loss may be incurred as a result of matters other than the non-payment of money. Although damages are not available to compensate for losses incurred from the late or non-payment of money *per se,* if it is possible to characterise the loss as arising from matters which are distinct from the failure to pay, the bar is lifted. In such a case, the plaintiff could possibly recover both in an action for a fixed sum, as well as damages.

16.10 *Overstone Ltd v Shipway* (1962) is an example of such a case. The facts of the case were as follows:

Shipway entered into a hire-purchase contract with Overstone Ltd for the hire-purchase of a car. The contract provided that Shipway, as hirer, should pay the sums specified in the agreement punctually and interest on any late payments. The contract also provided that any default in punctual payment or any breach of the conditions would entitle Overstone Ltd to terminate the hiring and retake possession of the vehicle. Shipway paid the deposit and took delivery of the car but paid none of the monthly instalments. In consequence, Overstone Ltd terminated the contract and re-possessed the car. On 22 January 1960, Overstone Ltd sued and recovered the four monthly instalments then due from Shipway in an action for debt. Meanwhile, they sold the car for £265 and subsequently brought a second action claiming £48 15s 4d in damages, being the balance of the price they would have recovered under the agreement if it had not been terminated, less the total of the following items: the initial deposit (£73), the four monthly instalments recovered earlier in the action for debt (totalling £43 3s 8d), the proceeds from the sale of the car (£265), and a rebate of interest charges (£23 14s).

A majority of the judges sitting in the English Court of Appeal held that this claim for damages was not precluded by the earlier action for debt. The majority of the English Court of Appeal accepted that, here, Overstone Ltd rightfully accepted Shipway's repudiatory breach in failing to make any payments at all and terminated the contract as a result of such breach, instead of relying on its contractual right of termination. Following from this, Overstone was entitled to make a claim for damages arising from that breach. Holroyd Pearce LJ, one of the majority judges, observed (at p 123) as follows:

> 'There is clear authority which establishes that a plaintiff may not bring separate actions for different heads of damage arising from the same cause of action. But here the first cause of action was based on a different cause of action from the second. The first was a claim for money due under the contract, namely, instalments which fell to be paid before the hiring was terminated. ... The second action claimed damages for breach of the contract resulting in the termination of the hiring. In my judgment it is impossible to hold that a claim for sums due [as a debt] under the hiring is the same cause of action as a claim for damages for breach.'

(5) *Timing of Claim*

16.11 A claim in debt can only be successful if the debt is due—that is to say, when the contractual obligation to pay the innocent party has arisen. Thus, in the case of *White and Carter (Councils) Ltd v McGregor* (1962) (discussed in Chapter 9 at paragraphs 9.63–9.64), the plaintiffs only pressed their suit for payment of the contract price for their services after they had finished performance of the contractually stipulated obligations on their part. Once they had done so, according to the terms of their contract with the defendants, the defendants were obliged to pay, and when the defendants refused, the plaintiffs were perfectly entitled to sue them to recover the sum owed in an action for debt (subject, of course, to the possible limitation of *legitimate interest* raised in *White and Carter (Councils) Ltd v McGregor* (1962)).

(6) *Where Plaintiff is in Breach of Contract*

16.12 Thus far, we have assumed that the plaintiff has not breached any of his contractual obligations to the defendant. What happens when the plaintiff is himself in breach of contract? What if, for example, in a contract of sale of goods between the plaintiff (vendor) and the defendant (purchaser), the plaintiff failed to perform his part of the bargain precisely by delivering goods which did not conform to the contract description? Clearly, the plaintiff would be liable to pay damages to the defendant in compensation for any losses resulting from the breach. However, would such a breach prevent the plaintiff from making a claim for the sums which would have been owed to him under the contract?

16.13 These issues have already been discussed in Chapter 9 on Discharge by Performance, Breach and Agreement. In summary:

- Where the plaintiff is himself in breach, it may be that he can still successfully make a claim for some, if not all of the price if the term which is breached is not a condition nor an innominate term which goes to the root of the contract.
- Firstly, if the plaintiff's breach is *de minimis*, that is, so inconsequential in all the circumstances it can be regarded as being trifling, it will be ignored and the full price is payable.
- Secondly, even if the plaintiff's breach cannot be said to be *de minimis*, if he has substantially performed his part of the bargain, he may still be entitled to recover the full price. If the defective performance has caused the defendant loss, however, the defendant may recover damages to compensate him for such loss from the plaintiff. Therefore, where the plaintiff attempts to sue the defendant for the price of his substantial but defective performance, he will most probably have to set off as against the price any damages which the defendant may claim to compensate him for his losses.
- Thirdly, if the contract (expressly or impliedly) provides that payment is to be in proportion to the amount of work done, then upon the ascertainment of the amount of work done, the proportionate price becomes due and may be claimed by the plaintiff as a debt. This is sometimes referred to as a claim for *quantum meruit* under contract.
- Fourthly, if the contract is severable, and it can be said that the plaintiff has completely performed his obligations under each severable component, then the price payable for each completed component can be recovered as a separate debt. Of course, in relation to any severable parts of the contract which have been defectively performed, the associated payment cannot be claimed, unless arguments like those in the three preceding paragraphs can be made for those parts, in which case partial payment for those portions completed may be possible.

16.14 In the discussion on discharge of contract by performance in Chapter 9, we also discussed the possibility of making a *quantum meruit* claim under the *law of unjust enrichment*. Such a claim is not a claim for debt. Instead, it falls more aptly under a claim for a restitutionary award and will be dealt with in that section (see below from paragraph 16.48 onwards).

Equitable Remedies

16.15 Damages are the usual remedy when a contract is breached. In most cases, this would be adequate to compensate the aggrieved plaintiff. However, in some situations, damages for breach are not adequate or appropriate. For example, when a vendor who has agreed to sell his land to a purchaser breaches that obligation, an award of damages to the purchaser is unlikely to be adequate compensation since no two pieces of land are alike: even if damages are awarded, it is not possible for the plaintiff to obtain a substitute piece of land to replace what he ought to have had under the contract.

16.16 In response, the courts of equity developed equitable remedies to compel 'specific performance' of such contractual obligations. In effect, such orders *compel the performance of the contract, according to its terms,* as far as is equitable in the circumstances. Failure to obey such an order would amount to a contempt of court, and would attract penal sanctions such as a fine, or even imprisonment. Given that non-compliance results in such draconian penalties, equitable remedies are not granted as a matter of course.

16.17 Unlike the position with respect to awards of damages or actions for a fixed sum, however, it is not clear if *all* courts of record in Singapore have the power and/or jurisdiction to grant these equitable remedies. So far as the High Court and District Courts are concerned, the position appears to be clear, based on the wording of section 18(2) read with paragraph 14 of First Schedule to the Supreme Court of Judicature Act (Cap 322, 1999 Rev Ed), and sections 31(1) and 31(2) of the Subordinate Courts Act (Cap 321, 1999 Rev Ed), respectively. The position in relation to Magistrates' Courts, though, is obscure as it appears that only section 31(1) is applicable to the Magistrates' Court (by virtue of the wording of section 52 of the Subordinate Courts Act), but not section 31(2). To circumvent any possible difficulty, in practice, parties have tended to avoid bringing their case before a Magistrates' Court if they are seeking specific performance or an injunction.

16.18 The equitable remedy of injunction may also be sought in situations where the primary obligations of a contract have been discharged, but where breach of an ancillary obligation is threatened, for example, where following the discharge of a contract, one of the parties acts in breach of a restraint of trade clause. If such a clause is reasonable and is not illegal and void, often, the only way in which an appropriate remedy can be fashioned is to grant an injunction. Other types of ancillary obligations like choice of law, jurisdiction or arbitration clauses, which determine how and where the parties may legitimately bring their legal disputes for hearing may similarly most appropriately be remedied via an injunction.

16.19 Injunctions may also be sought to remedy breaches of duties owed in other areas of the law. The discussion below, however, will first focus on the availability of specific performance, followed by an examination of injunctions in the context of contract law.

(1) *Specific Performance*

(a) Common Law Remedies Inadequate

16.20 Specific performance of a contractual obligation is an equitable remedy which was developed to supplement (and not supplant) the remedies which had already been developed by the common law (chief of which is the common law remedy of damages). Hence, it has been said that:

> 'The court gives specific performance instead of damages, only when it can by that means do more perfect and complete justice' (per Lord Selbourne LC in *Wilson v Northampton and Banbury Junction Railway Company* (1874) at p 284).

16.21 Examples of such situations where the equitable remedy does better justice would include contracts for the sale of unique goods (such as land, rare antiquities and so forth) and also cases where damages would not reflect the true extent of the loss suffered. A good example of a situation where damages would have been inadequate is the case of *Beswick v Beswick* (1968). The facts of the case were as follows:

Peter Beswick was a coal merchant who sold his business to John, his nephew. In consideration for the sale, John agreed that (1) so long as Peter continued to live, John would pay him £6 10s a week and (2) following Peter's death, John would pay Peter's wife an annuity of £5 a week, so long as she survived Peter. John paid Peter in accordance with the agreement until Peter passed away about 21 months later. He made one £5 payment to Peter's widow, but made no other payments thereafter. Peter's widow sued John, first, in her personal capacity, and secondly, in her capacity as the administratrix of Peter's estate.

In relation to her claim as administratrix, the House of Lords held that this was an appropriate case to order specific performance of John's contractual obligation to pay Peter's widow £5 a week as promised. It was clear that, as administratrix for Peter's estate, only nominal damages could have been awarded since Peter's estate suffered no loss as a result of this breach. However, had Peter been alive and the annuity been payable within his lifetime instead of only after his death, it could not be denied that he would have been able to obtain an order of specific performance. Naturally, his administratrix (who in a sense, merely steps into the shoes of the deceased) was equally entitled to seek such a remedy. Even if damages were available, on these facts:

> '... specific performance [was] more convenient than an action for arrears of payment followed by separate actions as each sum [fell] due. Moreover, damages for breach would be a less appropriate remedy since the parties to the agreement were intending an annuity for a widow; and a lump sum of damages [would] not accord with this' (per Lord Pearce at p 88).

(b) Exercise of Court's Discretion Would Be Just and Equitable

16.22 Unlike the common law actions for the recovery of damages or debt (which are available *as of right*), an order for specific performance is *discretionary*. Lord Parker observed (at p 419) in the House of Lords case of *Stickney v Keeble* (1915) that 'the dominant principle has always been that equity will only grant specific performance if, under all the circumstances, it is just and equitable so to do'.

Similarly, Karthigesu JA observed in the Singapore Court of Appeal case of *Tay Ah Poon v Chionh Hai Guan* (1997) (at p 370) that '[t]he right [to seek specific performance of a contract] exists in equity independently of any contractual provision that stipulates for its preservation. After all whether the right will be granted or not is in the discretion of the court'.

16.23 Obviously, the court will not exercise its discretion in an arbitrary manner. The court will consider the actions of both the plaintiff and the defendant, the severity of the impact of an order for specific performance on the defendant as opposed to the benefits to be obtained by the plaintiff, as well as all the surrounding circumstances. For example, in the case of *Co-operative Insurance Society Ltd v Argyll Stores (Holdings) Ltd* (1998), the House of Lords declined to make an order of specific performance to compel Argyll Stores to continue operating their business as a supermarket (which was closed because it was loss-making) for the period they had undertaken to run it for in premises they had leased from the Co-operative Insurance Society. Therefore, the court will have to balance the justice of the case before deciding whether or not to grant an order of specific performance. The presence of the following, for example, may well disincline it from granting such orders:

- where the party making the application (the 'applicant') does not come to court with 'clean hands', for example, where he has tried to exploit an obvious mistake by the other party (the respondent);
- where the order would impose an excessively burdensome and perhaps futile (or even impossible) obligation on the respondent;
- where the order would adversely affect the rights of third parties to the contract between the applicant and the respondent;
- where the order would not achieve any significant practical benefit to any of the parties to the contract; and/or
- where there is a want of 'mutuality' between the two parties.

'Mutuality' in this context, refers to whether the court would have been able to make an order of specific performance had the tables been turned: had it been the applicant who had been in breach of contract, could the court have also been able to make an order of specific performance against him?

Some degree of uncertainty persists as to when and how this factor operates. However, following the English Court of Appeal case of *Price v Strange* (1978), it seems that the following may be discerned:

- mutuality is ascertained at the time the contract is formed (per Goff LJ at p 357 and Buckley LJ at p 367); and
- although mutuality is *a* matter to be taken into account by the court in deciding whether to exercise its discretion in favour of granting

specific performance or refusing it, its *absence* does *not* mean the court is unable to grant such an order if the circumstances otherwise merit it (per Buckley J at p 370).

(c) *Contract Was Discharged Due to Breach*

16.24 Given that specific performance is meant to be a remedy for breach of contract, without such a breach, it is not open for the court to order a contract to be specifically performed. Although this seems to be an obvious point, there may be confusion when a contract is brought to an end not because of breach, but due to some other mechanism. In such a case, there may be confusion as to whether specific performance is available or not.

16.25 A case which neatly illustrates this problem can be found in the local case of *Tay Ah Poon v Chionh Hai Guan* (1997). The facts were as follows:

Mr and Mrs Chionh contracted to sell their flat to Mr and Mrs Tay for $228,000, accepting a deposit of $5,000 when the contract was signed. The contract of sale was to be completed on 15 September 1995 and provided in 'Clause 5' that:

> 'In the event the purchaser(s) ... fails to complete the purchase, the vendor(s) shall forfeit the deposit and the purchaser(s) shall further pay a sum equivalent to ten percent (10%) of the sale price as compensation to the vendor(s) immediately. Similarly, in the event the vendor(s) ... fails to complete the sale, the vendor(s) shall refund to the purchasers all monies paid herein and shall further pay a sum equivalent to ten percent (10%) of the sale price as compensation to the purchaser(s) immediately. Thereafter neither party shall have any claim against the other.'

On 22 August 1995, the government announced that certain blocks of flats were to be compulsorily acquired for demolition and redevelopment. In exchange, owners of acquired flats would be given a compensation package. The Chionhs' flat fell within this scheme and as the compensation package was extremely attractive, the Chionhs decided not to complete the sale. In compliance with Clause 5, the Chionhs sent the Tays a cheque of $27,800 (comprising the $5,000 deposit and the 10% of the sale price as mentioned in that clause). Mr and Mrs Tay refused to accept the cheque and sued Mr and Mrs Chionh for breach of contract. To remedy this breach, Mr and Mrs Tay sought specific performance of the contract and complete the sale.

At first instance, the registrar hearing this matter decided that the government's compulsory acquisition of the Chionhs' flat had not frustrated the contract of sale. This finding was not appealed against. The registrar also dismissed the Tays' application for an order of specific performance against the Chionhs to complete the sale. The Tays appealed against this part of the registrar's decision and the matter was eventually brought before the Singapore Court of Appeal. The Chionhs argued that no order for specific performance for the completion of the sale could be granted because Clause 5 was a clause which defined their obligations under the contract, and in fact, permitted the Chionhs to perform one of two alternative sets of obligations: they had the option of either (a) completing the sale; or (b) paying the Tays the amounts specified in Clause 5. An order to specifically perform option (a) would thus be inappropriate since the contract had provided that the Chionhs were to have a choice; they were not under any absolute obligation to perform option (a).

The Tays argued otherwise. In their view, Clause 5 was just a liquidated damages clause which operated as a reasonable pre-estimate of the losses that might be suffered by them if the Chionhs breached the contract. Nonetheless, since there was a breach of contract, it was open for them to seek specific performance instead of damages. Given further that this was a contract for sale of real property, monetary damages would be inadequate and instead, specific performance was more appropriate.

The decision of the court hinged on the interpretation of Clause 5. Karthigesu JA observed (at p 369) that:

> '... The court must always construe the contractual provision in question to determine whether it is intended by the parties to provide the vendor with a choice of an alternative method of performance, or whether it is intended by the parties to be a true liquidated damages clause that sets out the question of damages in the event of the vendor's non-performance of the contract. In the former case, the equitable remedy of specific performance is not available to the purchaser, while in the latter case, the purchaser may elect to seek specific performance of the contract or claim liquidated damages.'

Falling to the task of interpreting Clause 5, the court went on to say (at p 369) that:

> 'On their plain reading these words do not have the effect of conferring on the vendors [the Chionhs] the right to choose between two different methods of performing the agreement. All that the clause seeks to do, in our judgment, is to fix the amount of damages payable by the defaulting party to the innocent party should the defaulting party bring an action for damages.'

Having accepted the Tays' arguments, the Singapore Court of Appeal allowed their application and ordered the Chionhs to complete the sale.

(d) Contracts for Personal Service

16.26 It is a well-settled rule that the courts will not order specific performance of a contract for personal service. The best example of such a contract is the contract between an employer and employee.

16.27 There are a number of reasons for the courts' reluctance to order specific performance of this type of contract. However, the most obvious reason would be that an order for specific performance of a contract of personal service could result in involuntary servitude, converting 'contracts of service into contracts of slavery' (per Fry LJ in the case of *De Francesco v Barnum* (1890) at p 438).

Further, contracts of personal service invariably require a relationship of mutual trust, confidence and respect in order to operate satisfactorily. If that has broken down, an order of specific performance cannot restore it. Indeed, it may worsen the breakdown in the relationship between the parties and lead to additional disputes.

Lastly, the adequacy of performance of such contracts is usually also a discretionary matter; the issue as to whether a particular employee is working reasonably hard, or is slacking off, is a matter of fine judgment. If an order of specific performance was ordered against such an employee, it would be difficult to determine with any certainty (save in the most extreme cases), whether it had been breached—one cannot discount the possibility that the employer may have excessively unreasonable expectations of his employees. This brings us neatly to the next factor limiting the courts' discretion to order specific performance.

(e) Constant Supervision/Uncertainty in Definition of Obligation

16.28 In *Ryan v Mutual Tontine Westminster Chambers Association* (1893), the English Court of Appeal was asked to order specific performance of a lessor's obligation to his tenants to appoint a resident porter who would be 'constantly in attendance' to carry out certain services for the tenants, or, if called away, would appoint in his place a trustworthy assistant. The porter who was actually appointed was absent every weekday for a few hours as he was also employed as a cook in a neighbouring club, and he would just appoint boys or charwomen to take his place, leading one of the tenants to bring an application for specific performance before the English Court of Appeal. The application failed, although the basis of the court's decision is unclear. However, Lopes LJ noted (at p 125) that:

> '... [w]hat was contracted for was not the mere appointment of a porter who might be useless, but the employment of a competent porter who should perform the specified duties. I think that it is an entire contract. If that be so, it is clear that it is such a contract that, *in order to give effect to it by an order for specific performance, the Court would have to watch over and supervise its execution*. But it is a recognised rule that the Court cannot enforce a contract by compelling specific performance, where the execution of the contract requires such watching over and supervision by the Court. ...' (emphasis added).

This case has thus been said to support the proposition that specific performance will not be ordered if doing so will require constant supervision by the court.

16.29 Following the more recent House of Lords decision of *Co-operative Insurance Society Ltd v Argyll Stores (Holdings) Ltd* (1998) though, the bias against specific performance due to 'difficulties in supervision' may appear to be weaker than was previously thought. In that case, Lord Hoffmann observed (at p 12) that:

> '... [t]he judges who have said that the need for constant supervision was an objection to such orders were no doubt well

aware that supervision would in practice take the form of rulings by the court, on applications made by the parties, as to whether there had been a breach of the order. It is the possibility of the court having to give an indefinite series of such rulings in order to ensure the execution of the order which has been regarded as undesirable.

Why should this be so? A principal reason is that … the only means available to the court to enforce its order is the quasi-criminal procedure of punishment for contempt. This is a powerful weapon; so powerful, in fact, as often to be unsuitable as an instrument for adjudicating upon the disputes which may arise over whether a business is being run in accordance with the terms of the court's order. …'

Lord Hoffmann then went on to distinguish (at p 13) between:

'… orders which require a defendant to carry on an activity, such as running a business over or more or less extended period of time, and orders which require him to achieve a result. The possibility of repeated applications for rulings on compliance with the order which arises in the former case does not exist to anything like the same extent in the latter. Even if the achievement of the result is a complicated matter which will take some time, the court, if called upon to rule, only has to examine the finished work and say whether it complies with the order.'

Thus, in cases of the latter type where the defendant is required 'to achieve a result', the requirement to 'supervise' is much less, and accordingly, the court should be less disinclined to refuse making an order of specific performance. However, this is not the end of the enquiry: even if the court is asked to consider a contract of this type, other limits may apply. In Lord Hoffman's words (at pp 13–14):

'If the terms of the court's order, reflecting the terms of the obligation, cannot be precisely drawn, the possibility of wasteful litigation over compliance is increased. So is the oppression caused by the defendant having to do things under threat of proceedings for contempt. The less precise the order, the fewer the signposts to the forensic minefield which he has to traverse. The fact that the terms of a contractual obligation are sufficiently definite to escape being void for uncertainty, or to found a claim for damages, or to permit compliance to be made a condition of relief against forfeiture, does not necessarily mean that they will be sufficiently precise to be capable of being specifically enforced.'

(2) *Injunction*

16.30 Specific performance is just one of two remedies available to a court of equity to enforce a contract. The second is the equitable remedy of injunction which can take either *prohibitory* or *mandatory* forms. These will usually only be ordered at the conclusion of the hearing of the dispute as a *final* order. However, given that the litigation process takes time, the courts are sometimes amenable to grant *interim* orders of injunction, pending the final outcome of the hearing if there are extenuating circumstances (the intricacies of which are beyond the scope of this textbook). We will, however, proceed to examine some of the more general principles governing the grant of injunctions.

(a) Prohibitory Injunctions

16.31 Where a contractual obligation is negative in nature (taking the form of an express or implied promise *not* to do something), its breach may best be remedied by the issue of a prohibitory injunction. Essentially, this is an order from the court for the defendant to cease his infringing activity. As a result, the defendant is restrained from committing any further breaches *in the future* on pain of committing contempt of court.

16.32 Generally speaking, although still discretionary, the likelihood that a court will grant a prohibitory injunction is higher as compared with an application for specific performance or a mandatory injunction (discussed in the next section). Although in theory, it ought only to be granted after consideration as to whether damages would be an adequate remedy, this bar has been overcome in the past with little difficulty.

16.33 This, however, may no longer be completely accurate. As observed by the English Court of Appeal in *Warren v Mendy* (1989) (at p 868):

> 'In most of the decided cases it is assumed that damages will not be an adequate alternative remedy to the grant of an injunction and the point is not much discussed. Thus in *Lumley v Wagner* itself it was assumed that the mere chance of any damages which a jury might give was not worth very much. Now that these damages are invariably assessed by a judge or master we do not think that it can be assumed that they will always be an inadequate remedy.'

In Singapore's court system, all damages are assessed by judges or other judicial officers and not by jury. Further, with the development of contractual damages which go *beyond* compensation for pecuniary losses (discussed in the previous chapter at paragraph 15.45, as well as paragraphs 16.91–16.92, below), it may be the case that our courts today will no longer be as ready to accept that damages are indeed inadequate in the circumstances.

16.34 Apart from the requirement that damages must be an inadequate remedy, there are three main grounds on which the court may refuse to issue this type of injunction. They are:

- where the applicant has acted in an inequitable manner;
- where the applicant has acquiesced (or broadly speaking 'consented') to the breach of contract by the respondent; and/or
- where the prohibitory injunction would amount to indirect specific performance of a contractual obligation for which specific performance would not have been ordered.

The first two grounds are sufficiently clear, and in practice, are rarely brought up in court. Much of the discussion, however, centres on the last ground, in particular, with the prohibition against ordering specific performance of contracts of personal service.

16.35 A good case illustrating the problem can be found in *Page One Records Ltd v Britton* (1968):

Britton and three others were members of a 1960's pop group, 'The Troggs'. In February 1966, the Troggs entered into a written agreement with Page One Records Ltd. Under this agreement, Page One Records were appointed to manage affairs relating to the professional careers of the Troggs on a worldwide basis for five years. The Troggs also agreed that during the period of the agreement, they would *not* 'engage any other person, firm or corporation to act as managers or agents for' the Troggs. In April 1966, the Troggs appointed another company as their personal representative, agent and manager in breach of their February agreement. Page One Records then applied to court for a prohibitory injunction to stop the Troggs from acting in breach of their agreement.

This order was refused by Stamp J as he took the view this would amount to an order of indirect specific performance of a contract of personal service. Such contracts, as we have seen above, are not susceptible to specific performance. As a 'practical matter', preventing the Troggs from employing another manager would compel them to carry on with Page One Records.

16.36 Before going on to discuss the many inconsistencies in the cases dealing with this area of the law, we should keep in mind the following points:

Firstly, where there is *only* a positive obligation by one party to provide services to another, *unaccompanied* by any express (or implied) negative obligation *not* to provide those services to any third parties (that is, a negative obligation), no injunction can be granted to prevent the breach of the positive obligation.

Secondly, where the parties to a contract have expressly (or perhaps impliedly) provided for such negative obligations which are to operate so long as the contract is not otherwise discharged, such clauses should be distinguished from restraint of trade clauses which operate to restrict one's freedom of employment or trade *after* one's primary obligations under the contract have been discharged.

The kinds of clauses under consideration operate during the currency of the contract between the parties, *prior* to its discharge. Such clauses could, of course, be viewed as an illegal restraint of trade clause which may then be vitiated (and hence void) if found to be unreasonable (as was discussed in Chapter 14). In practice, however, it appears that such clauses are unlikely to be viewed as being so unreasonable as to be void. Therefore, although the doctrine of illegal restraint of trade may be applicable to a contractual obligation of exclusivity during the currency of the contract, it will probably only be in the worst cases of abuse that such a clause will be found to be illegal and void. Such a finding, however, is rare (see, for example, the cases of *Warner Brothers Pictures, Incorporated v Nelson* (1937), and more recently, the decision of the English Court of Appeal in *Symbian Ltd v Christensen* (2001)).

Thirdly, the remedy of injunction is discretionary. It is for the first-instance judge to consider whether all of the facts of the case are such that he can be moved to grant it. Given that it is an exercise of his *discretion*, even if the parties disagree and appeal against his decision, it is unlikely to be overturned unless the appellate courts can be convinced that the discretion was not exercised at all or was exercised in a way which was *plainly wrong*.

Fourthly, and perhaps most significantly, given the discretionary nature of the remedy, its 'grant or refusal, ..., depends on the infinitely variable facts of the individual case. Although statements of the principles on which the discretion ought to be exercised in some particular area are often authoritative, they are principles of practice rather than of law, whose application may be rendered inappropriate by the finest of factual variations between one case and another' (per Nourse LJ of the English Court of Appeal case of *Warren v Mendy* (1989) at p 860).

16.37 Keeping the above distinctions in mind, a survey of the many cases dealing with the exercise of the court's discretion to order an injunction reveals, not unsurprisingly, a litter of inconsistencies.

16.38 For example, in the early case of *Lumley v Wagner* (1852):

Miss Wagner entered into a contract to perform at Lumley's theatre for three months. The contract provided that she would not, during this period, perform at any other theatre without Lumley's written consent. In breach of this term, Wagner contracted to perform at another theatre for a higher fee, without obtaining the necessary consent.

Based on these facts, Lord St Leonards LC affirmed the decision of the first instance judge to grant an injunction to restrain Wagner from performing at any theatre other than Mr Lumley's.

16.39 Even more problematically, there is the decision of Branson J in English High Court case of *Warner Brothers Pictures, Incorporated v Nelson* (1937), concerning a contractual dispute between Mrs Nelson, an actress (more popularly known by her stage name, Bette Davis) and the Warner Brothers movie studio.

In 1931, Mrs Nelson contracted to 'render her exclusive services as a motion picture and/or legitimate stage actress' to Warner Brothers for 52 weeks. The contract could be extended at the discretion of Warner Brothers. She also agreed that during the term of the contract, she would not 'render any services for or in any other phonographic, stage or motion picture production or productions or business of any other person ... or engage in any other occupation without the written consent of the producer being first had and obtained.'

In 1937, after repeated extensions of her contract at increasing levels of salary, there was a dispute over whether Mrs Nelson should be paid even more. Mrs Nelson then contracted with a third party to perform as an actress and Warner Brothers sought to restrain her from breaching her negative obligations under her contract.

Branson J held that the arrangements within Mrs Nelson's

employment contract were not void as an illegal restraint of trade. He went on to hold that it was appropriate for the court to exercise its discretion to prevent Mrs Nelson from breaching her negative obligation *vis-à-vis* Warner Brothers:

> '... [I]t would, of course, be impossible to grant an injunction covering all the negative covenants in the contract. That would, indeed, force the defendant to perform her contract or remain idle; but this objection is removed by the restricted form in which the injunction is sought. It is confined to forbidding the defendant, without the consent of the plaintiffs, to render any services for or in any motion picture or stage production for any one other than the plaintiffs.
>
> It was also urged that the difference between what the defendant can earn as a film artiste and what she might expect to earn by any other form of activity is so great that she will in effect be driven to perform her contract. *That is not the criterion adopted in any of the decided cases*. The defendant is stated to be a person of intelligence, capacity and means, and *no evidence was adduced to show that, if enjoined from doing the specified acts otherwise than for the plaintiffs, she will not be able to employ herself both usefully and remuneratively in other spheres of activity, though not as remuneratively as in her special line*' (per Branson LJ at pp 219–220).

16.40 This shockingly harsh decision has been heavily criticised. Fortunately, times have changed since then. Nourse LJ, delivering the judgment of the English Court of Appeal in *Warren v Mendy* (1989), quoted (at pp 864–865) the following observations of Oliver J with approval:

> '... It simply does not, with respect, seem to me to be realistic to say that nothing short of idleness and starvation is compulsive, and therefore no injunction which involves anything less than that can be said to infringe the principle that the court will not specifically enforce a contract of personal services. The injunction in *Warner Brothers Pictures Inc v Nelson* did not in practice leave the defendant in that case much freedom of choice if she wanted to pursue her chosen profession. *No doubt it might have been quite otherwise if, as in the other previous cases in which similar injunctions had been granted, the contract had been a very short-term one*' (emphasis added) (per Oliver J in *Nichols Advanced Vehicle Systems Inc v De Angelis* (1979)).

Following up on this observation, the English Court of Appeal agreed that although the decided cases could be explained on their own facts, it could not be denied that:

> 'the most significant feature of each of those [cases] in which an injunction was granted before *Warner Brothers Pictures Inc v Nelson* was that the term of the engagement was short, in none of them exceeding 20 weeks. ...' (per Nourse LJ in *Warren v Mendy* (1989) at p 865).

16.41 If we focus on the length of time for which the injunction would be operational, most of the cases in this area of the law can be reconciled with one another. For example, since the three-month engagement in *Lumley v Wagner* (1852) was 'short-term', the impact of an injunction would be less devastating than, say, the five-year engagement in *Page One Records Ltd v Britton* (1968). In the latter case, an injunction would have had severe effects on the careers of the Troggs and was therefore not appropriate or equitable.

Warner Brothers Pictures, Incorporated v Nelson (1937), however, cannot be rationalised on this basis. Possibly, Branson J's uniquely unsympathetic stance in the *Warner Brothers* case can only be understood on the special facts of that case, in particular, the lack of evidence from Mrs Nelson to explain her actions since she refused to testify in court. As observed by the English Court of Appeal in *Warren v Mendy* (1989) (at p 865), '[i]n the absence of evidence from her [Mrs Nelson], the judge no doubt thought that it was not for the court to assume that she could not or would not employ herself both, usefully and remuneratively in other spheres of activity'.

16.42 Locally, Lim Teong Qwee JC has also highlighted the significance of the time frame of any prohibition imposed by an injunction in deciding whether or not it would amount to indirect specific performance. In the Singapore High Court case of *Pub 1997 Pte Ltd v Scorpion* (1994), Lim JC was faced with an application for an injunction by the managers of a 'Canto-pop' band (the Scorpions) who wished to have a change of management and to perform at other venues besides that of Pub 1997. Lim JC noted (at p 187) that:

> '... [t]he career of a "Canto pop" musician is uncertain and by no means likely to be long. ... [The defendants] need to perform as a "Canto pop" band and they need to do so publicly and professionally. They have to interact with the patrons of the night club and its management. ... An injunction may well terminate their careers unless they succumb to the compulsion to perform for the plaintiff. ... I am satisfied that enforcement of the negative obligation not to render any public performance or to be engaged by any other pub by the grant of injunctions in the terms of this application would effectively compel the defendants to perform a positive obligation under the contract. It would amount to a decree of specific performance of the positive obligation to perform for the plaintiff exclusively.'

(b) Mandatory Injunctions

16.43 Sometimes, matters may have reached the point where it is not enough that the defendant merely cease his infringing activity. In some circumstances, it may be necessary to order the defendant to take certain positive steps to reverse a breach of contract that has occurred *in the past*. If so, a 'mandatory injunction' is necessary to restore the plaintiff to the position he would have been in had there been no breach of contract by the defendant. As a result, a defendant may be compelled to tear down buildings or remove roads constructed in contravention of contractual requirements, and so forth.

16.44 Failure to comply with a mandatory injunction also amounts to a contempt of court and attracts penalties such as court fines or imprisonment in the most flagrant cases. Given its drastic nature, the courts are reluctant to grant mandatory injunctions unless they are confident that doing so would be fair and just in all the circumstances. Both the needs of the plaintiff as well as the detriment that the defendant will probably suffer must be considered and balanced against one another and many of the factors considered above in relation to specific performance and prohibitory injunctions will be just as relevant.

(3) *Damages in Lieu of or in Addition to Specific Performance or Injunction*

16.45 What happens if the court takes the view that an order of specific performance or injunction cannot be made? If this occurs where only nominal damages could have been recovered by the plaintiff, the plaintiff may be left without any effective remedy. In response to this, the English courts of equity have long been given (via statute) the power to award damages in lieu of or in addition to an order for specific performance or injunction.

16.46 The courts in Singapore are similarly empowered under the Supreme Court of Judicature Act (Cap 322, 1999 Rev Ed) wherein paragraph 14 of the First Schedule (read with section 18(2)) provides that the High Court has:

> '[p]ower to grant all reliefs and remedies at law and in equity, including damages in addition to, or in substitution for, an injunction or specific performance.'

One example where the High Court exercised this power may be found in the case of *Ho Kian Siang v Ong Cheng Hoo* (2000). This case also highlights the fact that damages in lieu of or in addition to specific performance or injunction are also discretionary, and hence are distinct from damages for breach of contract (which are available as of right). Although both are compensatory, there is no direct analogy in terms of the *time of assessment*. Hence, in *Ho Kian Seng* (at p 388), Lee Seiu Kin JC followed the English position on the matter (as set out in paragraph 960 of Volume 44(1) of *Halsbury's Laws of England* (4th ed, 1984)):

> 'Where damages are awarded in lieu of specific performance, the principle that damages should be assessed as at the date of the breach of contract (which is the usual rule in relation to commercial contracts) does not normally apply. The selection of the appropriate date is a matter for the court's discretion, but *the date usually chosen is the date at which the remedy of specific performance ceases to be available*' (emphasis added).

These powers are also extended to District Courts and Magistrates' Courts via section 31(1) and section 52 of the Subordinate Courts Act (Cap 321, 1999 Rev Ed), respectively.

(4) *Effect of Non-Compliance*

16.47 One final issue remains: what happens if a defendant should fail to comply with a court order for specific performance or an injunction?

In the first place, such failure could amount to contempt of court and could expose the offending party to penal sanctions such as a fine or even imprisonment. These draconian measures, would of course, only be used as a final resort in the face of inexcusable and repeated disregard for the orders of the court. However, a party who has elected and obtained the remedy of specific performance or injunction does not irrevocably shut the door on common law damages for breach of contract. As observed by Lord Wilberforce in the House of Lords decision of *Johnson v Agnew* (1980) (at p 398), a litigant 'who seeks (and gets) specific performance is merely electing for a course which may or may not lead to implementation of the contract—what he elects for is not eternal and unconditional affirmation, but a continuance of the contract under the control of the court which control involves the power, in certain events, to terminate it'. Should such an application be made, upon discharge of the contract, the litigant would then be entitled 'on grounds of normal and accepted principle, to damages appropriate for a breach of contract... [although the] court would not make an order dissolving the decree of specific performance and terminating the contract (with recovery of damages) if to do so would be unjust, in the circumstances then existing, to the other party' (at p 399).

Restitutionary Awards

16.48 'Restitution' is not, strictly speaking, a response to breach of contract. Unlike damages which seek to provide monetary compensation for loss suffered by a plaintiff due to a defendant's breach of contract, restitution seeks to reverse any '*unjust enrichment*' gained by the defendant at the expense of the plaintiff. Some academic commentators (and indeed judges) place the remedy of restitution within an entirely different legal regime, that of the law of unjust enrichment.

16.49 The law of unjust enrichment forms a different area of the law and confers a distinct 'cause of action' with its own rules and principles (just as the law of tort is distinct from the law of contract). It is a rapidly developing area and much of its boundaries remain undefined. Even the name of this area of the law is the subject of academic debate: whether it should be called the law of 'unjust enrichment,' 'restitution' or more archaically, 'quasi-contract'.

16.50 What is common ground amongst most Commonwealth academics in this area is that the plaintiff can establish liability for unjust enrichment so long as he can show that:

- the defendant was *enriched*;
- at the *expense* of the plaintiff;
- in circumstances such that the enrichment was '*unjust*', which is to say that there is some reason (an 'unjust factor' or on some views, the lack of any justificatory factor) within the law which would make it unfair for the defendant to keep that enrichment; and
- there is *no defence* available to the defendant to resist the justice of disgorgement of his unjust enrichment in favour of the plaintiff.

16.51 It is also commonly accepted that the law of unjust enrichment is 'subservient' to the law of contract. That is to say, where a contract is binding between parties, unjust enrichment issues will not arise—any dispute between the parties will be resolved in accordance with contract law. It is only when there is no contract at all, or perhaps, after a contract has been terminated or vitiated that the law of unjust enrichment may be applied to determine the rights and liabilities between parties. See, for example, the reasoning of the Singapore High Court in *Info-communications Development Authority of Singapore v Singapore Telecommunications Ltd (No 2)* (2002) wherein Lai Kew Chai J observed that, '... before restitution comes into play, and in order to avoid contradicting a valid contractual obligation to render the benefit, the plaintiff almost always has to establish, according to contractual rules, the invalidity of the contract' (at p 517).

16.52 There are still, however, large areas of academic dispute and judicial uncertainty. Apart from the list of 'unjust factors' and defences (both of which are still the subject of debate), firstly, it is not yet settled whether restitution as a remedy is solely a response to unjust enrichment, or whether it is also a possible response to various 'wrongs'.

The widest possible view of the ambit of unjust enrichment suggests that the commission of a wrongful act 'at the expense of the plaintiff' falls within unjust enrichment. Other commentators have taken a more restrictive view of 'at the expense of the plaintiff' to only mean '*subtractive* from the wealth of the plaintiff'. These academics therefore accept that restitution may be ordered outside the law of unjust enrichment, for example, where there have been breaches of fiduciary duties. This is not at all unusual, since similar types of remedies may be ordered for different causes of action. Take damages, for example, which can be ordered for breaches of contract, or for breaches of duties owed in tort.

16.53 Secondly, there is also some dispute as to whether these principles apply regardless of whether the plaintiff seeking restitution is himself 'at fault' for breaching contractual obligations with the defendant or not. For the purposes of our discussion in the following sections, we will first focus on cases where the plaintiff is not at fault and is not himself a party-in-breach or 'contract-breaker' as the position for these cases is relatively settled. We will then consider the position of a contract-breaker towards the end of this chapter.

Unjust Enrichment Where Plaintiff is Blameless

16.54 Coming back to the topic at hand, we will now examine three areas where restitutionary remedies often intersect with breaches of contract:

- total failure of consideration;
- *quantum meruit* and *quantum valebant;*
- restitutionary damages for breach of contract.

(1) *Benefits in Money: Total Failure of Consideration*

16.55 The common law courts have long recognised that money which has been paid to a defendant on the basis that he will perform his obligations under a contract may be recovered if he fails to perform those obligations in such a way that it can be said that the basis of the money payment has failed. This is known as the doctrine of 'total failure of consideration' and is a clear example of the law of unjust enrichment in action.

(a) Terminology

16.56 The terminology is deceptive and likely to cause confusion with the concept of consideration in relation to the formation of a contract. The two were clearly demonstrated to be distinct by Viscount Simon LC in the House of Lords case, *Fibrosa Spolka Akcyjna v Fairbairn Lawson Combe Barbour Ltd* (1943) ('*Fibrosa* (1943)'). Viscount Simon LC observed (at p 48) as follows:

> '... In English law, an enforceable contract may be formed by an exchange of a promise for a promise, or by the exchange of a promise for an act ... and thus, in the law relating to the formation of contract, the promise to do a thing may often be the consideration, but when one is considering the law of failure of consideration and of the quasi-contractual right to recover money on that ground, it is, generally speaking, not the promise which is referred to as the consideration, but the performance of the promise. The money was paid to secure performance and, if performance fails the inducement which brought about the payment is not fulfilled.'

16.57 Therefore, 'consideration' in the context of a claim in unjust enrichment does not necessarily refer to the same consideration which is furnished by either party at the time the contract is formed. As observed by some commentators, it would probably be more accurate to describe the doctrine as 'total failure of basis'. That is to say, when the basis for a payment has completely failed, then that payment ought to be returned to the payor. In the case of a contract for sale of goods, if there has been a payment of money on the basis that the contract goods will be delivered in good order and condition at the date and time specified, and such goods are in fact never delivered at all, the basis for the initial payment will have failed. Or, in other words, there has been a 'total failure of consideration'. 'Consideration' here, therefore, refers to the actual performance and completion of any executory consideration (if any), and not to the presence or absence of any executory consideration at the time the contract was formed.

(b) Overlap with Breach of Contract

16.58 Failure of consideration (or basis) can occur in many different contexts, some contractual, some not (for example, in relation to failed gifts). However, in the business context, the most common reason for failure of consideration is the termination or vitiation of an otherwise valid contractual relationship. Some academic commentators have therefore analysed the effect of frustration and the vitiating factors on a contract as examples of unjust enrichment. Such analysis is beyond the scope of this textbook. However, the courts routinely apply total failure of consideration reasoning where a contractual obligation has been breached to the extent that defendant has completely failed to provide the performance of the obligation contracted for.

16.59 The overlap with breach of contract arises because severe breaches of contract, such as where the defendant completely fails to perform any part of his bargain, necessarily mean that the plaintiff gets nothing of what he paid for. The two causes of action may overlap and the plaintiff has to choose whether to allege *total failure of consideration* (to secure a refund or restoration of money paid over to the defendant in anticipation of the benefits which the defendant promised to provide) *or* a claim for *damages for breach of contract* (to compensate the plaintiff for all expenses incurred in reliance on the performance of the contract).

16.60 The two types of recovery can, however, be distinguished in the following ways:

- Contractual damages (whether on the expectation loss or reliance loss bases) are aimed at compensating the plaintiff for his losses, which naturally raises concerns that he should minimise (or mitigate) them. However, restitution involves restoration of benefits that would otherwise give the defendant an unjust enrichment—it is not concerned with compensation. Hence there is no concept of mitigation in restitution.
- Contractual damages are related to the concept of bargain and therefore, they are limited to losses which are not so far from the parties' initial understanding of their obligations under the contract (and the risks undertaken) to be too 'remote'. Restitution, however, is not centred on bargain and 'remoteness' is an irrelevant issue.
- Contractual damages assessed on a reliance loss basis, however, will closely overlap with restitution of benefits given to the defendant. The difference is that reliance damages encompass recovery of *all* expenses reasonably incurred in reliance on the performance of the contract by the party-in-breach, whether paid to the party-in-breach or not, and may even include reasonable expenses incurred prior to the time the contract was entered into (see *Anglia Television Ltd v Reed* (1972), the facts of which are discussed at paragraph 15.49). Restitution, however, only requires the return of sums paid to the party-in-breach, if the retention of such benefit would be unjust.

The questions then arise: when would the plaintiff choose one over the other, and does the plaintiff have a free choice? To answer the latter question first, it appears that the courts do not restrict the plaintiff's freedom to choose between these two different causes of action. The plaintiff is free to choose whichever cause of action would afford him a more complete remedy allowing for greater recovery. However, it sometimes appears that the plaintiff is not allowed to recover in both total failure of consideration *as well as* damages for breach of contract.

(c) Where Loss Suffered is Equal or Less Than Sum Paid

16.61 Consider the following scenario:

- Philip works freelance from home as a graphics designer. As his old colour laser printer is nearing the end of its life-cycle, Philip contracts to buy a replacement from Derek for $2,500 and makes a down-payment of $750.
- However, Derek's stocks have run out, and it is agreed that delivery will be made two weeks later, when his stock is replenished after he places a new order with the Singapore sole-distributor the following day.
- The following day, Derek discovers that the sole-distributor has jacked up the price of this particular model of laser printer by 150% because it has received highly favourable reviews in a well-respected computing trade journal. Derek orders it anyway since there are no alternative sources of supply.
- Derek calls Philip to inform him that as the sole-distributor has raised the price by 150% and thus, he is no longer able to supply the printer to him at the original price of $2,500. However, he is willing to absorb some of the price increase and will only charge Philip $5,200 for it.
- Philip is naturally outraged and calls Derek a cheat, refusing to pay anything more than what was contractually agreed. Derek, in turn, is incensed by Philip's outburst and tells him: 'Sue me if you like, but you can kiss your down-payment goodbye!'
- Philip hunts around for a replacement and finds that what Derek said was true. No one in the market is retailing this particular model for anything less than $5,200. As the nature of his work requires very accurate colour-matching with those used by commercial printers, and this particular model provides the closest match, Philip cannot use any other model.
- In the meantime, Philip's old laser printer has given up the ghost. As Philip is in the middle of a very important project, he needs a replacement urgently in order to meet the deadline. Fortunately for him, he mentions his dilemma to one of his relatives who is an employee of the sole-distributor. Philip's relative manages to get one for him at a hugely discounted 'employee's' price of $1,500. This colour laser printer is identical to the one ordered from Derek.

16.62 It is clear once promises between Philip and Derek are exchanged, an enforceable and binding contract is formed. Philip has furnished executed consideration in the form of the down-payment and executory consideration in the form of his own promise to make eventual full payment in support of Derek's promise of delivery. Conversely, Derek has furnished executory consideration in the form of his own promise to deliver the printer two weeks later to support Philip's promise to make full payment at a later date. There are no issues on these facts relating to privity, intention to create legal relations, or any vitiating factors.

16.63 When Derek unjustifiably refuses to perform his end of the bargain,

Philip is entitled to sue Derek for breach of contract. However, due to Philip's successful attempt to mitigate his losses by obtaining a replacement printer, it appears that Philip has been put in a position which is *better* than it would have been had Derek performed. Given that the two printers are comparable, had Derek performed his end of the bargain, Philip would have been out of pocket by $2,500. Now, however, Philip is out of pocket by $2,250 (being the sum of his down-payment to Derek and the amount paid to his relative for the replacement printer). Accordingly, only nominal damages may be awarded to Philip.

16.64 This result seems to be perverse since it seems to reward Derek for his breach of contract as a result of Philip's efforts to mitigate. Fortunately, the common law has developed the doctrine of 'total failure of consideration' to address this problem.

Applying this doctrine to the problem set out above, it must be obvious that the basis for the down-payment of $750 has failed. Notwithstanding the fact that there was valid executory consideration at the time the contract was made, the basis for the payment was the eventual performance of Derek's promise to deliver the laser printer to Philip. Since Derek *never performed* his promise, the basis for Philip's down-payment has failed. Not only that, on these facts, it has *completely* failed—Philip has obtained nothing of what he bargained for. Accordingly, the common law doctrine of total failure of consideration can be applied in Philip's favour, and he is entitled to recover the down-payment from Derek and is not restricted to nominal damages only.

(d) Where Loss Suffered is Greater Than Sum Paid

16.65 The question then arises: what if Philip's attempts at mitigation had been less successful? Is it possible for Philip to recover both the down-payment and damages? In most cases, the answer would be 'no'.

16.66 Assuming that Philip's relative had not enabled Philip to obtain a replacement at below-market prices, Philip could have sued and recovered substantial damages from Derek. From the facts of the problem, since the market price from other suppliers is at least $5,200, Philip would have mitigated his losses by acquiring a replacement printer at this price. His total outlay at this point in time would then be $5,200 plus $750, which totals $5,950. If the contract had been performed without any breach, Philip's total outlay would have been $2,500. Therefore, in order to put him in the position as if the contract had been performed, the court should order damages of $3,450 (being the difference between what he has had to pay as a result of the breach, and what he ought to have paid had there been no breach).

16.67 The above calculation incorporates the $750 down-payment as part of Philip's damages. At the conclusion of the contract, Philip expected that he would have the benefit of the laser printer and only be out of pocket by a further $1,750 (having already paid $750 as a down-payment). Instead, on the facts as modified in paragraph 16.66, he has had to pay $5,200 to another supplier for the printer. The $3,450 difference between these two figures ($1,750 and $5,200) can crudely be said to represent Philip's expectation loss. Such recovery in damages, however, is subject to the usual limitations on recovery (notably, mitigation and remoteness, limitation of liability clauses, and so forth).

16.68 Although he could do so, it is unlikely that Philip would give up his claim for damages of $3,450 and opt for a *refund* of the $750 down-payment on the basis of total failure of consideration. Doing so would obviously be contrary to his pecuniary interest. It is also clear that he cannot claim for a refund of the $750 down-payment *in addition* to the damages assessed at $3,450 as this would place Philip in a position *better* than he would have been, had Derek performed the contract in full. Furthermore, it could be said that concurrent claims for contractual damages and restitution are logically contradictory: the former seek to place the innocent party in the position as if the contract had been performed, whereas the latter seek to restore parties to a position as if the contract had never existed.

16.69 Despite the attractiveness of the logic, it should nonetheless be recognised that the courts have sometimes awarded a combination of refunds of advance payments for total failure of consideration, damages for wasted expenditure and/or lost profits—see, for example, the decision of Branson J in *Millar's Machinery Co Ltd v David Way & Son* (1935) which was subsequently upheld on appeal by the English Court of Appeal. Commenting on these and other cases, Professor Treitel takes the view at p 878 in his treatise *The Law of Contract* (10th ed, 1999) that, '[t]he true principle is not that there is any logical objection to combining the various types of claim, but that the claimant cannot combine them so as to recover more than once for the same loss.' Applying this view to the modified facts in paragraph 16.66, if the courts are willing to let Philip assess his damages in a somewhat different fashion, for example, by letting him assert that he has suffered damages of only $2,700 (being the difference between the $2,500 he *expected to pay in total* for the printer, and the $5,200 he *actually had to pay* as a result of Derek's breach: $5,200), he will have side-stepped the problem of double-recovery, and may well be entitled to raise a concurrent claim for restitution of the $750 down-payment paid to Derek (although this would necessarily rule out any possibility of recovering the $750 down-payment as 'reliance loss').

(e) Requirement of 'Total' Failure

16.70 The language of 'total failure' suggests that success of such a claim depends on being able to establish that plaintiff got no part of the promised benefit. Unfortunately, the decided cases demonstrate the determination of exactly what was promised and what constitutes 'benefit' for this purpose is by no means clear cut.

16.71 For example, in the case of *Rowland v Divall* (1923), the English Court of Appeal had to decide whether there had been total failure of consideration by a vendor of a car, when it turned out that the vendor, through no fault of his own, had no title to it (he had been sold the car by a fraudster who had stolen the car from the true owner). The plaintiff purchaser of the stolen car had to return it to the true owner, after having driven it for only two months or so, and sought a refund of its purchase price from the defendant vendor. The English Court of Appeal held that as the plaintiff had not been given good title to the car, there was indeed a total failure of consideration and ordered the defendant to refund the purchase price to him.

16.72 Even more strikingly, in *Fibrosa* (1943), the plaintiffs paid the defendants to manufacture and deliver certain machinery. Advance payment of £1,000 was made but before the machinery could be completed and delivered, the contract was frustrated by the outbreak of World War II. This case was decided before the enactment of the English Law Reform (Frustrated Contracts) Act 1943 and the House of Lords held that here, there was indeed a total failure of consideration, despite the fact that the defendants had expended significant sums in the manufacture of the contract machinery.

16.73 Further evidence of the importance of characterising what the plaintiff was supposed to receive as benefit from the contract can be seen in the decision of the English Court of Appeal in *Rover International Ltd v Cannon Film Sales Ltd* (1989). This case involved multiple suits by a number of different parties against Cannon Film. One such party was Rover International who had agreed to dub and distribute films owned by Cannon Film in Italy. The agreement provided that Rover International would make large advance payments to Cannon Film, and would then reimburse themselves out of ticket sales over the duration of the contract. In addition, at the end of the agreement, Cannon Film would reimburse Rover International if there remained any difference between the total of the advance payments and the net ticket receipts. After making the advance payments and putting considerable efforts into dubbing and distribution of Cannon Film's products, it was discovered that the agreement was void as it had been entered into prior to Rover International's incorporation as a corporate entity. Among other things, Rover International sought a refund of the advance payments on the basis of total failure of consideration. Kerr LJ held that their claim was well founded even though Rover International had received and screened some films from Cannon Film. He observed (at p 923) that:

> '... [t]he question whether there has been a total failure of consideration is not answered by considering whether there was any consideration sufficient to support a contract or purported contract. The test is whether or not the party claiming total failure of consideration has in fact received any part of the benefit bargained for under the contract or purported contract.'

Applying this test to the facts, Kerr LJ held that the bargain was for Rover International to at least break even from the transaction, or even make some profits. Due to the invalidity of the agreement, this had not been achieved and hence, Rover International 'got nothing of what they had bargained for, and there was clearly a total failure of consideration' (per Kerr LJ at p 925).

None of the above, however, precludes the possibility of partial restitution of payments made in exchange for a consideration which is *severable*. See, for example, p 531 of the Singapore High Court case of *Info-communications Development Authority of Singapore v Singapore Telecommunications Ltd (No 2)* (2002) wherein Lai Kew Chai J quoted with approval the observations by Gleeson CJ, Gaudron J and Hayne J in the Australian High Court decision of *Roxburgh v Rothmans of Pall Mall Australia* (2001) (at paragraph 14) that: '... where the consideration is severable, complete failure of part may form a ground for recovering a proportionate part of the money paid for it ...'

(2) *Benefits in Kind: Quantum Meruit and Quantum Valebant*

16.74 When the basis for the payment of money has completely failed, the common law looks to the law of total failure of consideration. What about situations where the basis for a benefit *in kind* has completely failed? Is there a doctrine that provides for restitution of non-monetary benefits (such as goods and/or services) that mirrors total failure of consideration?

16.75 Extension of the doctrine of total failure of consideration to a situation where goods or services are supplied on a particular basis which has failed is not completely straightforward. Practically speaking, there may be difficulties with returning goods, and services once rendered cannot be readily returned. So very often, what we are thinking about when we consider the possibility of a 'refund' of goods or services is their money's worth.

Two scenarios will be considered in the following sections.

(a) Where Plaintiff has Completed Some Obligations

16.76 We have already mentioned at paragraph 16.13 above, the sequence of arguments which may be made by a plaintiff who has performed his contractual obligations imperfectly. Most of these fall squarely within the law of contract. However, it is possible to also raise a parallel argument within the law of unjust enrichment based on the *quantum meruit* (which relates to services) and *quantum valebant* (which relates to goods). For the sake of convenience, '*quantum meruit*' will be used hereafter to describe this type of claim in unjust enrichment, regardless of whether the subject matter relates to goods or services.

16.77 Consider the following scenario where:

- the basis for which the provision of goods or services has failed (very often, because the payment for those goods or services is not forthcoming from the defendant, the plaintiff is entitled to terminate the contract for the defendant's breach);
- the plaintiff has given the defendant some benefit in the form of partial or imperfect delivery of those goods or provision of those services (which does not amount to a breach of a condition or an innominate term going to the root of the contract); and
- it can be demonstrated that such partial or imperfect performance nonetheless still represents a benefit to the defendant.

Given the above, what should the court order? If the defendant still has the goods in hand, should the court order him to return those goods (assuming there has been no significant deterioration)? Or should it order payment of their money's worth to the plaintiff? If the goods have deteriorated such that they cannot be restored to the plaintiff in something approximating their original condition, then only the latter option, or *quantum meruit*, is available. However, if both choices are available, then it appears that the plaintiff has a free choice as to which to opt for.

16.78 There are numerous cases based on a reasonable valuation of benefits provided by a plaintiff and although none expressly provides that they are merely manifestations of the doctrine of total failure of consideration, extended to include non-monetary 'refunds', the reasoning seems obvious enough and an award for *quantum meruit* appears to be unobjectionable so long as such an award would be less than any possible award for damages for breach of contract.

16.79 We have noted above that in principle, there does not seem to be any bar to prevent a refund of moneys paid upon a total failure of consideration, even if it can be shown that the breach of contract which caused the total failure, caused no loss to the plaintiff. In the example of Philip and Derek (at paragraph 16.61 above), this arose because of the operation of mitigation. But any of the other limitation factors may have the same effect. So, for example, if the defendant can show that the plaintiff had made a bad bargain and would never have made any profit in the first place, although the plaintiff will not be allowed to recover damages assessed on the reliance loss basis, this is no reason why he should not be allowed to recover the price paid to the defendant on the basis of a total failure of consideration.

16.80 The next question then, is whether the same approach can be applied to non-money 'payments', that is, whether *quantum meruit* may be successfully pleaded by a plaintiff who has provided non-money benefits to the defendant, where the value of such *quantum meruit* would exceed the contractually agreed price, had such price been payable. There appears to be no local or English case on this point as yet, but the famous Californian case of *Boomer v Muir* (1933) suggests that it can.

In *Boomer v Muir* (1933), the plaintiffs contracted to build a dam for the defendants for a certain sum (to be paid in instalments). Prior to payment of the last instalment of $20,000, the defendants prevented the plaintiffs from finishing the construction works. As a result, the plaintiffs could not claim to be entitled to payment of the last instalment, since the project was incomplete. Therefore, the plaintiffs sued the defendants on a *quantum meruit* to recover a reasonable value for the work actually done. The court of first instance found in favour of the plaintiffs and assessed the reasonable value of the plaintiff's works as amounting to $257,000 (the reason for this was because construction costs had risen astronomically from the time when the contract was first entered into). The defendants then appealed, arguing that this amounted to a windfall for the plaintiffs: if the contract had not been breached, the plaintiffs would only have been paid another $20,000. Relying on Californian case and statutory authority, the appellate court found no difficulty dismissing the appeal. In the words of Justice *pro tem* Dooling (at p 577):

> 'To hold that payments under the contract may limit recovery where the contract is afterwards rescinded through the defendant's fault seems to us to involve a confusion of thought. A rescinded contract ceases to exist for all purposes. How then can it be looked to for one purpose, the purpose of fixing the amount of recovery?'

16.81 Within the Commonwealth, there is the authority of *Lodder v Slowey* (1904), a decision of the Privy Council on appeal from the New Zealand Court of Appeal. In that case, Slowey was contracted to carry out certain construction works by Lodder. In breach of the agreement, Lodder prevented Slowey from completing his work. Without considering at all what Slowey could have recovered from Lodder under the terms of the contract had he been allowed to complete his work, Lord Davey, delivering the opinion of the Privy Council, agreed with the decision of the New Zealand Court of Appeal and allowed Slowey to recover on the basis of *quantum meruit* for the value of the work he had completed up to the time when the contract was breached, and therefore brought to an end by Lodder.

16.82 These two cases suggest that recovery on the basis of *quantum meruit* need not be related to the contractually agreed price for the plaintiff's work. This does not, however, mean that the contract price is *completely irrelevant*.

16.83 Firstly, what is apparent from the two cases of *Boomer v Muir* (1933) and *Lodder v Slowey* (1904), is that the defendants in both cases were taken to have benefited from the part-performance of their respective plaintiffs. However, it should not be assumed that every case of partial performance of an obligation amounts to a benefit to a defendant since 'benefit', in this context, is determined *subjectively*. In other words, the defendant is sometimes entitled to '*subjectively devalue*' the plaintiff's partial performance by arguing that he does not *subjectively* find the partial performance to be of any benefit at all. Such an argument is extremely difficult where the benefit is *incontrovertible*, as in the case where the benefit takes the form of money: receipt of a sum of money is invariably valuable and beneficial, even if it is only a partial payment. However, the position is less clear in relation to benefits in kind. In some of these cases, the plaintiff may be able to show that his partial provision of goods and services has relieved the defendant from expenses which he would inevitably have had to incur. If so, the defendant's benefit of having saved *inevitable and necessary expenses* should be treated as an incontrovertible benefit and *cannot* be subjectively devalued. One clear example of this might take the form of partial completion of refurbishment works to a car which has been resold by the defendant prior to trial, and which would have been completely unmarketable or which would have fetched a *lower* price had no refurbishment works been carried out at all. In such cases of *incontrovertible benefit*, the pro rata contract price should rightfully be ignored. As observed by Professor Burrows (at p 346) in the *Law of Restitution* (2nd ed, 2002):

> '... if one regards the defendant as having been incontrovertibly benefitted by "necessary expense saved" there should be no restriction to the pro rata contract price, for this would be contradictory: if the expense saved were really necessary the defendant would have been prepared to pay at the market price rather than merely at the particular contract price.'

Secondly, as incontrovertibly beneficial partial performance is likely to be the exception rather than the rule, most plaintiffs will have to demonstrate benefit by other means. As observed by Professor Burrows (at p 23) in *The Law of Restitution*, since full performance must have been regarded by the defendant to be beneficial to him (why else would he enter into it?) and non-payment of the price would amount to a saved expense (which he would otherwise have been willing to incur), '[b]y similar reasoning, even if the defendant receives only part of what it bargained for, it can be rebuttably presumed that [the defendant] has been saved part of the expense that it would otherwise have incurred'. Professor Burrows goes on to suggest (at p 24) that it is a '... factual truth that in general—but clearly not always—a defendant who has bargained for a performance considers itself to be benefited by each part of that performance even if it has only agreed to pay on completion'. *Subjective devaluation* is therefore still available to the defendant to show that the plaintiff's partial performance was not a benefit at all in his particular case, thereby rebutting the presumption that the defendant has received a *'bargained-for'* benefit. One obvious example of such a 'bargained-for' benefit being subjectively devalued would be where 'the cost of completing performance would now be as much as the whole of the original bargain price for full performance' (see *The Law of Restitution* at p 24). Professor Burrows then suggests (at p 346) that 'bargained-for' benefit is necessarily subject to a valuation ceiling, based on the pro rata contract price, '... for to allow the claimant the objective market price in excess of this would be to re-encounter subjective devaluation in that the defendant can validly argue that it was only willing to pay at the contractual rate'. This analysis therefore suggests that the position taken by the courts in *Boomer* and *Lodder* to disregard the contract price as a limit to the value of the partially performed contractual obligations may not be of universal application—one first has to note whether the benefit to the defendant is *incontrovertible* or is derived from the *'bargained-for'* presumption.

16.84 Still, interesting as these views are, it remains to be seen if a court will adopt them in Singapore.

(b) Where Plaintiff has Completed All Obligations

16.85 In this case, where the goods or services to be provided by the plaintiff have in fact been provided in full, if the defendant refuses to pay the money sum that is due, the plaintiff can simply sue the defendant to recover the price in an action for a fixed sum (as discussed above from paragraph 16.3 onwards). Note also paragraph 16.5, pointing out that the remedy of damages is not usually available for a breach of an obligation merely to pay money.

16.86 If the failure to pay the price amounts to a breach that is sufficiently serious to terminate the contract, in theory, the unpaid plaintiff might pursue a claim based on *quantum meruit* as discussed above, instead of a claim in price. This is unusual, since the time of payment of the price is most commonly viewed only as a warranty (or at best, an innominate term) unless the contract specifically provides that it is a condition. If the contract has been terminated for breach, though, due to the uncertainties in proving what would amount to a reasonable valuation of the plaintiff's work, it is unlikely that this type of claim will be pursued in preference to a simple claim for the price.

16.87 Factors which might tip the plaintiff towards pursuing such a claim, notwithstanding the vagaries of proof of reasonableness, might include issues as to limitation, or perhaps, where due to changes in the market, the amount recoverable in *quantum meruit* would be greater than the contractually agreed price, as was the case in *Boomer v Muir* (1933).

(3) *Restitutionary Damages for Breach of Contract*

(a) General Position: Breach of Contract *Simpliciter*

16.88 As previously mentioned, the traditional view is that restitution is not awarded for a breach of contract. As a result, a defendant cannot be made to *disgorge* gains made as a result of his breach of contract. Neither can the plaintiff insist that the defendant account for any expenses which he *saves* as a result of the breach. This view can be clearly observed in the holding of Sir Robert Megarry VC in *Tito v Waddell (No 2)* (1977).

In that case, the defendants were contractually obliged to restore the vegetation to an island in the Pacific Ocean after denuding it in order to carry out mining operations. This was not done, and the island remained uninhabitable. The islanders sought to recover from the defendants the expenses it had saved by not performing its obligation to replant the trees on the island, but failed. In the words of Sir Robert Megarry VC (at p 332):

> '… [I]t is fundamental to all questions of damages that they are to compensate the plaintiff for his loss or injury by putting him as nearly as possible in the same position as he would have been in had he not suffered the wrong. The question is not one of making the defendant disgorge what he has saved by committing the wrong, but one of compensating the plaintiff.'

16.89 Similarly, in the case of *Surrey County Council v Bredero Homes Ltd* (1993), the English Court of Appeal refused to award damages based on the excess profit earned by the defendants as a result of their breach of contract. The defendants had bought land from the plaintiffs on the basis that only a certain number of houses were to be built on it. In breach of that agreement, the defendants built more than they were contractually permitted to and therefore made a greater profit. Unfortunately, as the plaintiffs could not prove any loss on the basis of any change in market value, they were only awarded nominal damages.

16.90 Where the breach of contract involves nothing more, then, as these two cases demonstrate, it appears that restitution of expenses saved or profits earned by a defendant as a result of his breach will not be ordered by the courts.

(b) More Than Just Breach of Contract

16.91 In situations where proprietary rights have been infringed, the courts have traditionally been open to awarding restitution. A good example is the English case of *Wrotham Park Estate Co Ltd v Parkside Homes Ltd* (1974). Here, the plaintiffs were the beneficiaries of a restrictive covenant which 'ran' with the defendant's land: the land had been sold to the defendants on the basis that it would comply with a particular plan of development. When the defendants deviated from that plan, Brightman J held that the defendants could be made to disgorge the profits it had made from the deviation to the plaintiffs because the deviation had, in a sense, violated the plaintiff's *proprietary* rights.

16.92 The highly restrictive approach to awards of damages on a restitutionary basis may, however, be open to change. This is typified in the approach of the House of Lords in the case of *Attorney General v Blake* (2001). The facts of the case were as follows:

Blake was a spy for the British government and signed an undertaking as part of his employment contract not to divulge any official information gained as a result of his employment. However, Blake was really spying for and disclosed valuable secret information to the Soviet Union. He was apprehended and convicted of spying. After serving five years of his sentence, he managed to escape to Moscow where he continued to remain until 1989. In 1989 he wrote an autobiography, substantial parts of which were based on information he had acquired in the course of his employment as a spy—none of this information, however, was 'secret' anymore as they had become public knowledge. In breach of his undertaking of confidentiality, Blake entered into a publishing contract with a publisher under which he was to receive an advance of £50,000, a further £50,000 on delivery of the final manuscript and £50,000 on publication. No approval or permission was obtained from the British government to do any of this. On behalf of the British government, the Attorney General sought to restrain the publishers from making any further payments to Blake, and to force Blake to disgorge any profits he had made from his breach of the undertaking to maintain confidentiality.

The House of Lords held that in an 'exceptional' case where the normal remedies of damages, specific performance and injunction were inadequate, the court could, if justice demanded it, grant the discretionary remedy of requiring the defendant to account to the plaintiff for the benefits received from the breach of contract. It drew an analogy between Blake's confidentiality undertaking with the obligations of a 'fiduciary'; where a fiduciary breaches his obligations of confidentiality, an account of profits is a standard remedy in response. Also, in order to ensure that there were no financial incentives for other members of the intelligence service to breach their undertakings and that the morale and trust between members of the service when engaged in secret and dangerous operations was not undermined, the Crown had a legitimate interest in preventing the defendant profiting from the serious and damaging breach of his undertaking. For all these reasons, although the information disclosed was no longer confidential (and hence no loss was suffered by the British government) and orders of specific performance and injunction would be ineffective (since the book had been released globally), it was appropriate to order Blake to account for his profits from breaching his obligation to maintain confidentiality.

Unjust Enrichment Where Plaintiff is in Breach of Contract

16.93 As mentioned earlier, where the plaintiff is blameless in causing the contract to come to an end, the courts are fairly open to the award of restitutionary remedies to order the repayment of money paid to a defendant (or *quantum meruit* for non-money benefits) where there is a total failure of consideration. In the exceptional case of *Attorney General v Blake* (2001), we also observed how in extreme cases of breach of contract, where ordinary contractual damages are not adequate and the equitable remedies of specific performance or injunction are not available, restitutionary damages might be ordered if the plaintiff had some special interest in ensuring performance by the defendant of his contractual obligations, and also some interest in deterring future breaches by others who might have been tempted to breach their obligations in a similar fashion.

16.94 On the other hand, when the plaintiff who is trying to persuade the court to grant him a restitutionary remedy is himself the party 'at fault' for causing the contract to come to an end, the position is very different depending on whether the benefit given to the defendant is in money or in kind. In the former case, there is some authority to suggest that it is possible. In the latter case of benefits in kind, however, the position is not as clear.

(1) *Benefits in Money: Total Failure of Consideration?*

16.95 Two cases are regularly referred to in the academic literature to support the argument that there should be no restriction on an action for unjust enrichment where the benefit provided is in the form of money, depending on whether the plaintiff is a contract-breaker or not (see, for example, Professor Burrows' *The Law of Restitution* (2nd ed, 2002), pp 350–354). The first of these cases is *Dies v British and International Mining and Finance Corporation, Ltd* (1935). The facts of the case were as follows:

The plaintiff in this case contracted to buy guns and ammunition from the defendant. An advance payment of £100,000 was made to the defendants. However, the plaintiff breached the contract because it was not able to take delivery of the guns and ammunition—presumably, this breach was accepted by the defendants and the contract was then discharged. Ultimately, the defendants were sued for the return of the advance payment. This claim was brought before Stable J who allowed the claim.

The facts and the outcome of the case suggest that restitution was ordered, even though the plaintiff was 'at fault'. Unfortunately, in coming to his decision, Stable J held as follows (at p 744):

> 'In my judgment, the real foundation of the right which I hold exists in the present case is not a total failure of consideration but the right of the purchaser, derived from the terms of the contract and the principle of law applicable, to recover back his money.'

This could be explained on the basis that in 1935 (when *Dies* was decided), Stable J did not yet have the benefit of the explanation in *Fibrosa* (1943) by the House of Lords as to the meaning of 'consideration' in the doctrine of total failure of consideration. If so, Stable J's decision is not inconsistent with the proposition that there is no restriction on restitution of benefits in money in these circumstances.

16.96 The second case which is often cited in support from the proposition that it does not matter whether or not the plaintiff is a contract-breaker is the case of *Rover International Ltd v Cannon Film Sales Ltd* (1989).

The facts and holding of this case in relation to one of the suits of in this case (between Rover International and Cannon Film) have already been discussed at paragraph 16.73 above. For our present purposes, we are interested in the other suit within this case, the one between Proper Film Ltd and Cannon Film. The facts of this suit were as follows:

Proper Film contracted with Cannon Film for the right to screen certain films on Italian television for a total of £1,000,000 (or three instalments of US$900,000 each). The first two instalments were paid without incident. However, there was a dispute over the payment of the third instalment because Cannon Film was in breach of the contractual arrangement: they were unable to supply one of the films to Proper Film. Nonetheless, the contract between Proper Film and Cannon Film continued to bind the two parties as Proper Film maintained that they did not wish to discharge the contract, despite Cannon Film's breach of this term. Due to the dispute over whether or not Cannon Film had breached the contract, Proper Film did not pay Cannon Film the final instalment and offered to pay it into a special account, pending the outcome of the litigation over this matter. However, their contract expressly provided that time of payment of the instalments was of the essence. Accordingly, failure to pay the third payment on time constituted a breach of condition entitling Cannon Film to discharge the contract, which Cannon Film did. Cannon Film then sued Proper Film for the final instalment of US$900,000 as a debt owed to them.

The issue before the court was whether Cannon was entitled to recover the final instalment even though they had discharged the contract due to Proper Film's breach of condition of timely payment. Proper Film argued that if they had paid this instalment before discharge of the contract for breach, then it would now be recoverable by them on the basis of total failure of consideration (since they had not been given any films to exhibit at all). Consequently, and *a fortiori*, since there was now no contract at all, they could not be held liable to pay it. The English Court of Appeal agreed with Proper Film's arguments and dismissed Cannon Film's claims for the last instalment to be payable to them as a debt, although it recognised that Cannon Film could still recover damages for Proper Film's breach.

This part of the case is said to support the position that a contract-breaker claimant can still have restitution because of certain observations by the two judges who delivered the reasons for their decision (the third agreed with both of them). Most obviously, Kerr LJ observed (at p 932) that:

> 'In the present case it is entirely clear, in my view, that this instalment was payable in advance of any consideration for the payment which fell to be provided from the side of Thorn EMI/ Cannon. Indeed, when Proper declined to pay it, it was rightly pointed out on behalf of Cannon that nothing in the way of performance was as yet due from their side. This instalment would accordingly have been recoverable by Proper if it had been paid, and it is therefore irrecoverable by Cannon for the same reason. The only claim open to them would have been a claim for damages if they had shown that they had suffered any as the result of the termination of the contract.'

The basis for dismissing Cannon Film's claim for the final instalment was therefore total failure of consideration: if Proper Film had paid the final instalment, since there was a total failure of consideration and Proper Film had obtained nothing of the benefit bargained for under the contract, Proper Film would have been entitled to a repayment. Consequently, it made no sense to allow Cannon Film to recover the last instalment as a debt, only to have to return it to Proper Film. Given this line of reasoning, it would have followed that Proper Film could also have recovered the first two instalments which were actually paid to Cannon Film—however, strangely, Proper Film did not pursue a claim to recover those amounts.

At p 931, Kerr LJ also quoted the following portion of the judgment of Stable J in *Dies v British and International Mining and Finance Corporation, Ltd* (1935) with approval:

> 'Where there is a contract for the sale of goods, and a part payment for the goods is made, but no goods are delivered or tendered by reason of the default of the buyer, the seller's only remedy is to recover damages for the default, while the buyer, notwithstanding that it is by reason of his default that the contract has not been performed, is entitled to recover the purchase price that he has paid, subject possibly to the right of the seller to set

off against that claim the damages to which he can establish his title' (per Stable J at pp 736–737).

16.97 Reviewing these two cases, we must conclude that there is some support for the view that it is irrelevant whether the plaintiff is himself a contract-breaker. However, keeping in mind that although it appears that the defendant to a claim by a contract-breaker plaintiff for restitution of advance payments must make restitution of those payments, it may ultimately be a pyrrhic victory for the plaintiff—the plaintiff himself, being a contract-breaker, is still liable to the defendant for breach of contract. If the defendant sues the plaintiff to recover damages, and those damages exceed the pre-paid amount, then the defendant will only recover the amount in excess. In such a case, if the defendant is made to return the pre-payment (due to a successful claim in unjust enrichment by the plaintiff, following the reasoning in *Dies v British and International Mining and Finance Corporation, Ltd* (1935) or *Rover International Ltd v Cannon Film Sales Ltd* (1989)), he will then be allowed to recover the *full* amount of damages assessed. Perhaps this is why such cases have only rarely appeared before the courts.

(2) *Benefits in Kind: Quantum Meruit?*

16.98 In contrast with the position of a contract-breaker who has provided benefits in the form of money, where the contract-breaker has provided benefits in *kind* to the defendant in the form of goods or services, the courts have tended to shy away from allowing restitution of the benefits in the form of their money's worth, that is, *quantum meruit*. Two of the leading cases in this area are *Sumpter v Hedges* (1898) and *Bolton v Mahadeva* (1972). The facts of *Sumpter v Hedges* (1898) were as follows:

Sumpter was contracted by Hedges to build two houses and a stable on Hedges' land. It was agreed that Hedges would pay Sumpter a total of £565 upon completion of the works. In breach of the contract, Sumpter abandoned the contract after completing some of the work (which was valued at £333). Hedges then finished the construction work on his own account.

One of Sumpter's claims was to recover for his work done before abandoning the contract (on a *quantum meruit* basis). Using the language of unjust enrichment, it would appear that Hedges had been unjustly enriched since he had the benefit of Sumpter's work—even though incomplete, Hedges was saved the expense for the work completed up to that stage. However, the English Court of Appal rejected Sumpter's claim.

16.99 In *Bolton v Mahadeva* (1972), the issue was whether Bolton could recover in *quantum meruit* for the work he had done in installation of a heating system for Mahadeva's house. It was clear that Bolton was in breach of contract because the system installed did not provide sufficient heat and also gave out fumes. When asked to remedy these problems, Bolton refused to do so and Mahadeva engaged a third party to carry out rectification work. On these facts, the English Court of Appeal also rejected Bolton's claim for *quantum meruit*.

16.100 Both of these judgments were decided on the basis that the obligations on the part of the plaintiffs to complete the works were 'entire'. Therefore, unless and until the plaintiffs completed performance of their parts of the bargain (in the case of *Sumpter v Hedges* (1898), completion of all three buildings, and in the case of *Bolton v Mahadeva* (1972), installation of a heating system which functioned in a reasonably adequate manner), the defendants had obtained none of the benefit that had been bargained for. Accordingly, there was no basis for them to pay. In a sense, therefore, these cases reflect the idea brought out in *Rover International Ltd v Cannon Film Sales Ltd* (1989): if the payments had been made, they would have had to be restored to the payors, as the basis for their payment had failed.

16.101 If the obligations in *Sumpter v Hedges* (1898) and *Bolton v Mahadeva* (1972) had not been 'entire', though, there is some support for the argument that *quantum meruit* should also be available to a contract-breaker. This can be inferred from the decision in the House of Lords case of *Hain Steamship Company Ltd v Tate & Lyle Ltd* (1936). In *obiter dicta*, Lord Wright considered the following example (at p 612):

> '... Let me put a quite possible case: A steamer carrying a cargo of frozen meat from Australia to England deviates by calling at a port outside the usual or permitted route [and deviation from the route is invariably a condition of contracts for carriage of goods by sea]: it is only the matter of a few hours extra steaming: no trouble ensues except the trifling delay. The cargo is duly delivered in England at the agreed port. The goods owner has had for all practical purposes the benefit of all that his contract required; he has had the advantages of the use of a valuable ship, her crew, fuel, refrigeration and appliances, canal dues, port charges, stevedoring. ... [I cannot] help feeling that the court would not be slow to infer an obligation when the goods are received at destination to pay, not indeed the contract freight, but a reasonable remuneration....'

Admittedly, this *dictum* does not make it clear whether Lord Wright was considering *quantum meruit* in the context of an implied term or as a species of unjust enrichment, but it is not inconsistent with the latter.

Locally, however, the Singapore Court of Appeal decision of *Lee Siong Kee v Beng Tiong Trading, Import and Export (1988) Pte Ltd* (2000) (discussed below at paragraphs 16.105–16.106) raises the hint of a suggestion that *quantum meruit* is not available to a contract-breaker. Even so, this problem was not specifically in issue before the court and the true position has yet to be clearly and authoritatively formulated. It is hoped that the courts may be able to clarify the position further in an appropriate case.

Where Contract is Discharged for Reasons Other Than Breach

16.102 Since this is a chapter on remedies for breach of contract, in this section we have concentrated on the restitutionary remedies where a prior contractual relationship between plaintiff and defendant has come to an end due to breach of a term which entitles the plaintiff to discharge the contract.

16.103 A contract, however, may come to an end in various other ways. In addition to discharge by way of breach, it may be discharged by way of agreement, performance, as well as frustration. A contract may also come to an end when it is vitiated, that is to say, when it is found to be *void*, or where it has been rescinded and hence *avoided*. In either case, the contract is unwound and is treated as though it never came into existence. In some of these instances, it may be possible that the law of unjust enrichment may also play a part.

16.104 In any case where a contract is discharged or vitiated, if the plaintiff can show that the defendant has obtained some benefit from the plaintiff, it may be the case that a cause of action in unjust enrichment is also available to the plaintiff. For example, where a contract is found to be void for mistake, if the plaintiff had provided benefits to the defendant on the (wrong) assumption that there was a contract between them, those benefits ought to be subject to restitution. Arguing from first principles, it would appear to be that so long as the requirements for a restitutionary claim are fulfilled, restoration of benefits given in the form of money or *quantum meruit* for benefits given in kind should be available in any circumstance where there is a failure of basis, regardless of the reason for that failure (subject to the further considerations discussed in the following sections).

Three of these categories of failure of basis merit additional consideration.

(1) *Contracts Discharged by Agreement*

16.105 Logically, the manner in which a pre-existing contractual relationship is discharged (whether such discharge is effected by agreement, performance, frustration or breach) should not affect the availability of *quantum meruit* as a remedy. However, certain comments made by the Singapore Court of Appeal in the case of *Lee Siong Kee v Beng Tiong Trading, Import and Export (1988) Pte Ltd* (2000) (hereafter, '*Lee Siong Kee* (2000)') have cast some doubts on the proposition just mentioned. The facts of the case itself were as follows:

Beng Tiong Trading, Import and Export (1988) Pte Ltd ('Beng Tiong') were interested in purchasing certain properties owned by the estate of Shaik Ahmad (deceased) (the 'estate'). To facilitate the acquisition, Beng Tiong appointed Lee Siong Kee ('Lee') to act as their agent under an agency agreement. Beng Tiong then advanced $250,000 to Lee when the agency agreement was signed and agreed to make further advances of up to $150,000 between 1 November 1993 and 15 July 1994 (the 'further advances'). Lee promised under this agreement to have the sale agreement of the properties to Beng Tiong for a consideration of $8.25 million executed by 15 July 1994, failing which the agency agreement would become null and void, and Lee would refund all moneys advanced to him by Beng Tiong. In turn, Beng Tiong promised that they would leave all contact and communications with the beneficiaries of the estate to Lee. The 15 July 1994 deadline was subsequently varied and extended to 31 December 1994 (the 'extended deadline'). Due to various reasons, the sale of the property was not completed by the extended deadline, despite Lee's efforts. Lee also discovered in November 1993 that in breach of their agreement, Beng Tiong had in fact directly approached some of the beneficiaries of the estate. In addition, after having received $110,000 out of the $150,000 'further advances', he requested an advance of the balance $40,000 in early 1994, but this request was denied by Beng Tiong. Nonetheless, Lee continued with his efforts to negotiate with the beneficiaries of the estate in order to try and arrange for the sale to be completed by 31 December 1994. Unfortunately, he was not able to do so. Lee then sued Beng Tiong. Among other things, Lee sued Beng Tiong and claimed for a *quantum meruit* award.

After holding that Beng Tiong's breaches of the agency agreement did not have the effect of discharging the contract as it was clear that Lee had affirmed the contract, the Singapore Court of Appeal held that Lee's claim in *quantum meruit* was unsustainable. As noted earlier in Chapter 9, a *quantum meruit* claim can be raised pursuant to an express or implied term within the contract itself, or it could be based on the law of unjust enrichment (on a pure 'restitutionary basis'). Insofar as the claim was based on an express or implied term, it failed because there was no such term, nor could it be implied since the contract had specifically provided for the return of the moneys claimed upon the expiration of the advances if the sale of the properties was not completed by 31 December 1994. What interests us most, though, are the observations by LP Thean JA (delivering the judgment of the Singapore Court of Appeal) on the validity of Lee's claim in *quantum meruit* based on the law of unjust enrichment. LP Thean JA commented (at p 573) that:

> '[t]he crux of such a claim against a party for a *quantum meruit* on a restitutionary basis is the premise that the contract was terminated prematurely *as a result of a breach of that party. That principle has no application here.* The agency agreement was not terminated prematurely by reason of the breaches on the part of Beng Tiong. The agreement ... came to an end on the expiry of the extended deadline by which Lee was to secure (which he did not) the execution ... of the sale and purchase agreement for the sale of the properties to Beng Tiong' (emphasis added).

Accordingly, since the contract had not been terminated by Beng Tiong's breach, but had instead been terminated pursuant to the terms of the contract itself (that is, by agreement), *quantum meruit* on a restitutionary basis was not available to Lee and his claim on this ground was dismissed.

16.106 Following this decision, what seems clear is that in a case where there has been a breach of contract resulting in the discharge of the contract, the innocent party is entitled to recover in *quantum meruit* on a restitutionary basis. Where the contract is discharged by *agreement, Lee*

Siong Kee (2000) suggests that it is not. While this position may be justified where the agreement to discharge the contract clearly provides that no restitutionary remedies are to be made available, there is nothing in the judgment of the Singapore Court of Appeal to suggest that the width of their ruling is so limited. It is therefore unclear if the limitation of *quantum meruit* in unjust enrichment to cases of discharge of contract by breach is merely a rule of interpretation (in which case, it could be displaced given adequate demonstration that the parties intended otherwise), or if it is a rule of law (in which case, it applies regardless of the intentions of the parties). Also outstanding is the question as to whether this limitation applies also to a restitutionary claim based on total failure of consideration. Lastly, the passage from the judgment quoted above, read closely, also raises the inference that *quantum meruit* is only available to an innocent part *against* a party whose breach has discharged the contract. These points were not fully considered by the Singapore Court of Appeal in *Lee Siong Kee* (2000). It is therefore to be hoped that these issues will be revisited and perhaps clarified in a future decision of the court.

(2) *Contracts Discharged by Frustration*

16.107 In England, prior to the enactment of the Law Reform (Frustrated Contracts) Act 1943, all situations where the defendant's non- or defective performance resulted in a total failure of consideration would have been analysed using the doctrine of total failure of consideration. Following 1943 then, cases such as *Fibrosa* (1943) would no longer be decided the same way.

16.108 In Singapore, an Ordinance was passed in 1959 with largely similar provisions as the Law Reform (Frustrated Contracts) Act 1943. This has been updated and the local analogue to the position set out in the Law Reform (Frustrated Contracts) Act 1943 can now be found in the Frustrated Contracts Act (Cap 115, 1997 Rev Ed). Other than numbering, the provisions are *in pari materia*. (For a discussion on the operation of this Act, please refer to Chapter 10.)

16.109 Accordingly, the likelihood of overlap between the doctrine of total failure of consideration and the law of frustration (so far as English and Singaporean courts are concerned), is now very minimal. In other words, *quantum meruit* now has no part to play where the Frustrated Contracts Act is applicable. However, *quantum meruit* may still be relevant for the categories of contracts which are excluded (see section 3(5) of the Act).

(3) *Contracts Vitiated by Illegality*

16.110 As discussed in Chapter 14, special considerations operate to modify and preclude the availability of restitution following the rescission of a contract found to be void for illegality. In brief, sums of money which are paid under a contract which is subsequently found to be void for illegality are *not* to be restored to the payor, even though the basis for that payment (that is, the purported contract) has completely failed. The maxim 'the loss falls where it lies' overrides the usual position mandating restitution and it does not appear to matter that the payee may have been 'unjustly enriched'. Nonetheless, in some circumstances, restitution of benefits provided pursuant to an illegal contract may be possible. Details of such circumstances are discussed within Chapter 14 (see generally, paragraphs 14.55–14.58 in Chapter 14).

16.111 It should also be noted that there is also some academic debate as to the status of 'illegality' within the law of contract and the law of unjust enrichment. It should be apparent that there is significant (if not complete) overlap between the concepts of a contract void for illegality, and the concept of total failure of basis. In some analyses (for example, Professor Birks' *An Introduction to the Law of Restitution* (Rev ed, 1989), and Professor Burrows' *The Law of Restitution* (2nd ed, 2002)), illegality has been viewed as a possible defence to a claim in unjust enrichment for restitution following a total failure of basis (as well as constituting an 'unjust factor' which triggers restitution in its own right). The various exceptions to the rule of 'the loss falling where it lies' would then merely be instances where the defence of illegality to an unjust enrichment claim following a total failure of basis is *not* allowed to succeed.

Restrictions on Recovery for Unjust Enrichment

16.112 In the section on damages, we discussed how quantification of such damages is restricted by doctrines such as mitigation, remoteness, and so forth. Is restitution for unjust enrichment subject to any restrictions?

16.113 Even in its present nascent form, the law of unjust enrichment recognises that having established a cause of action, certain defences may nonetheless apply to restrict recovery.

A number of defences have been posited in different jurisdictions and by different academics. However, apart from the defence of 'change of position', (which will be expanded upon in the next few paragraphs), the extent to which a number of other 'restitutionary' defences will be applied in the courts of Singapore is doubtful, following the decision of the Singapore Court of Appeal in the case of *Management Corporation Strata Title No 473 v De Beers Jewellery Pte Ltd* (2002) ('De Beers (2002)') (see pp 17–19 of the judgment). In particular, the Court of Appeal in *De Beers* (2002) rejected the applicability of *estoppel* as a defence to a claim under unjust enrichment, since the requirements for estoppel (discussed above in Chapter 3 at paragraphs 3.48–3.59) overlap greatly with those for 'change of position' and yet would be overly broad, since it would prevent any recovery at all, and not just that portion of the benefit which had been dissipated by the defendant's change of position. It did, however, suggest in *obiter dicta* that a number of other defences were possible, for example, a defence of 'payment under a settled view of the law'. Since this chapter is focussed on remedies for breach of contract, it is probably inappropriate to provide a detailed discussion of the various viewpoints and approaches. Therefore, we will just provide a brief outline of the defence of 'change of position' which has clearly been approved and applied locally.

16.114 The defence of change of position was recognised in England by the House of Lords in the case of *Lipkin Gorman (a firm) v Karpnale Ltd* (1991). Locally, the Singapore Court of Appeal in *Seagate Technology Pte Ltd v Goh Han Kim* (1995) has recognised that it is applicable in Singapore.

16.115 This defence has most recently been considered in Singapore in the Singapore High Court case of *Info-communications Development Authority of Singapore v Singapore Telecommunications Ltd (No 2)* (2002) wherein Lai Kew Chai J identified four constituent elements. To wit, a defendant recipient of a benefit from the plaintiff will be able to resist or minimise restitution if:

- the payee has changed his position;
- the change is *bona fide;*
- it would be inequitable to require him to make restitution or to make restitution in full; and
- there is a causal link between receipt of the benefit and the recipient's change of position.

16.116 An example as to the application of the defence might take the following form. Following receipt of a benefit in money from the plaintiff, the defendant spends the increase in his wealth on an expensive luxury holiday which he would not have gone on if not for the benefit received. Since he would not have decreased his overall wealth by expenditure on such a holiday but for the benefit from the plaintiff, it would be inequitable now to require him to disgorge that benefit. In the words of Professor Birks and Dr Mitchell in their contribution to the second volume of *English Private Law* (2000) (at p 610):

> '... if, by the happening of an event which would not have happened but for the enrichment, the defendant's wealth is reduced, his obligation to make restitution is to that extent extinguished. In short the defence of change of position seems usually to be a defence of disenrichment.'

16.117 The payee's disenrichment would not be *bona fide* if he had acted dishonestly or in bad faith. The disenrichment would also not be *bona fide* if he had accepted the benefit knowing of facts which would entitle the plaintiff to restitution. However, care must be taken not to assume that every *bona fide* disenrichment would result in a change of position. As observed by Lord Goff in *Lipkin Gorman (a firm) v Karpnale Ltd* (1991) (at p 580):

> '... the mere fact that the defendant has spent the money, in whole or in part, does not of itself render it inequitable that he should be called upon to repay, because the expenditure might in any event have been incurred by him in the ordinary course of things.'

16.118 As for causality— '[i]t is clear that ... the change of position must occur after the receipt of the payment ...' (per Lai Kew Chai J at p 530 of *Info-communications Development Authority of Singapore v Singapore Telecommunications Ltd (No 2)* (2002)).

16.119 The requirement of inequity, however, awaits further elucidation in our courts.

PART III

The Law of Agency

CHAPTER 17 Agency

PARAGRAPHS

17.1–17.3	**Introduction**
17.4	True Agency Against Commercial Agency
17.5	**How Agency Arises**
17.6–17.7	By Agreement
17.8	(1) Express Authority
17.9–17.11	(2) Implied Authority
17.12	Without Agreement
17.13–17.17	(1) Apparent Authority
17.18–17.19	(2) Agency of Necessity
17.20–17.21	Ratification
17.22–17.25	(1) The Requirements
17.26–17.29	(2) The Effects
17.30	**Effect of Agency**
17.31	Principal–Third Party Relationship
17.32–17.33	(1) Disclosed Agency
17.34–17.35	(2) Undisclosed Agency
17.36	Principal–Agent Relationship
17.37–17.38	(1) Duties of Agent
17.39	(a) Duty to Avoid a Conflict of Interests
17.40	(b) Duty Not to Make a Secret Profit
17.41–17.42	(c) Duty Not to Delegate
17.43–17.45	(2) Rights of Agent
17.46–17.48	Agent–Third Party Relationship
17.49–17.52	**Termination of Agency**

Introduction

17.1 The law of agency is an important part of commercial law. This is because agents are integral to the conduct of modern business. An agent, at the most rudimentary level, is one who acts on someone else's behalf, and a significant part of the law of agency deals with the ability of the agent to affect the legal position of that someone else. It has often been observed that commercial activity would be severely curtailed if all business transactions had to be conducted personally. Indeed, personal attention to all aspects of a business would not only be inconvenient but also be impracticable where time, knowledge or expertise is lacking, and certain business structures, like the partnership and the company, would not be able to operate at all.

17.2 The term 'agent' is bandied about very frequently in the marketplace, especially when referring to middlemen, or persons who represent others. Thus it is common to find persons described as employment agents, sales agents, estate agents, insurance agents and sole agents. This led to Lord Herschell's observation in *Kennedy v De Trafford* (1897) (at p 188) that '[n]o word is more commonly and constantly abused than the word "agent"'. It needs to be pointed out however, that the law of agency may not necessarily apply in all of these situations. Thus, in the words of Lord Herschell again, 'a person may be spoken of as an "agent" and no doubt in the popular sense of the word may properly be said to be an "agent", although when it is attempted to suggest that he is an "agent" under such circumstances as create the legal obligations attaching to agency that use of the word is only misleading'.

17.3 What exactly then, is agency? A leading textbook on the subject defines it as 'a branch of law under which one person, the agent, may directly affect the legal relations of another person, the principal, as regards yet other persons, called third parties, by acts which the agent is said to have the principal's authority to perform on his behalf and which when done are in some respects treated as the principal's acts' (see FMB Reynolds, *Bowstead & Reynolds on Agency* (17th ed, 2001), paragraph 1-003). Gummow J, in the High Court of Australia, observed in *Scott v Davis* (2000) (at p 1451) that 'the term "agency" is best used ... to connote an authority or capacity in one person to create legal relations between a person occupying the position of principal and third parties ... Usually the legal relations so created will be contractual in nature ... The resultant contract is formed directly between the principal and the third party and there is no contract between the agent and the third party which is attributed to the principal'.

The agency relationship is sometimes represented as being triangular as it involves three parties: the agent, the principal on whose behalf the agent acts and the third party, with whom the principal ultimately contracts. The agency relationship may also be analysed in terms of an internal aspect, which is the relationship between the agent and his principal, and an external aspect, which affects the legal position of the principal *vis-à-vis* the third party. In any case, what is crucial in the relationship is the power of the agent to alter his principal's legal position, and the complementary liability of the principal on the altered position (see Dowrick, 'The Relationship of Principal and Agent' (1954) 17 *Modern Law Review* 24 at p 36). Whilst the agent might have been responsible for negotiating, concluding and perhaps even executing (but in the name or on behalf of the principal) the contract, he is himself typically not personally bound by the concluded contract between his principal and the third party. It is therefore often said that, provided he acts within his authority, the agent 'drops out of the picture' as soon as the contract is concluded. Any recourse that the third party has under the contract will therefore be against the principal and not the agent.

True Agency Against Commercial Agency

17.4 Many commonly called agents are really not, in the legal sense, genuine agents because they are themselves in fact acting as principals. A distributor of goods for the manufacturer, for example, may refer to itself as the 'sole agent' or 'exclusive agent' for these goods. In legal reality, the distributor probably *buys* the products, and then *resells* these to consumers. The sale contracts with ultimate consumers are not made by the distributor on behalf of the manufacturer; rather, any contract of sale entered into by the distributor will be on its own behalf as principal.

The distributor may undertake, under the contract of supply, to furnish the necessary advertising and promotion, in return for exclusive distributorship rights. In such contracts, the manufacturer could be in breach of contract if it sells the goods itself. Thus, in the case of *WT Lamb & Sons v Goring Brick Co* (1932), a manufacturer of bricks and other building materials, who appointed the plaintiffs as 'sole selling agents of all bricks and other materials manufactured at their works' for a certain period was held to be in breach of contract when it decided to sell all bricks manufactured by it without the intervention of an agent before the expiration of this period. Clearly, if the relationship had been one of agency, the manufacturer would (as principals) have been free to sell as well. The Court of Appeal found, however, on a proper construction of the agreement, that it was one of vendor and purchaser and not one of agency, and the manufacturer was thus precluded contractually from so selling.

How Agency Arises

17.5 An agency relationship may arise as a result of an *agreement* between the principal and agent, but may also arise in the *absence* of such an agreement by the doctrine of ostensible or apparent authority, and where the law imposes an agency of necessity. An agency relationship might even arise *retrospectively* by operation of the doctrine of ratification. The significance of establishing that there is an agency relationship is that it confers on the agent the power to bind his principal.

By Agreement

17.6 Typically, an agency relationship arises when there is an *agreement* between the principal and the agent that the latter should act for former. The essence of such an agency is *consent*. It is, however, not necessary for the agreement to amount to a *contract*. In *Yasuda Fire and Marine Insurance Co of Europe Ltd v Orion Marine Insurance Underwriting Agency Ltd* (1995), Colman J observed (at p 57) that:

> 'Although in modern commercial transactions agencies are almost invariably founded upon a contract between principal and agent, there is no necessity for such a contract to exist. It is sufficient if there is consent by the principal to the exercise by the agent of authority and consent by the agent to his exercising such authority on behalf of the principal.'

This consent is objectively ascertained because whether an agency relationship exists or not is a question of law. As Lord Pearson explained in *Garnac Grain Co Inc v HMF Faure & Fairclough Ltd* (1968) (at p 1137), the principal and the agent 'will be held to have consented if they have agreed to what amounts in law to such a relationship, even if they do not recognise it themselves and even if they have professed to disclaim it ... But the consent must have been given by each of them, either expressly or by implication from their words and conduct.' This test was applied by Judith Prakash J in the Singapore decision of *Win Line (UK) Ltd v Masterpart (Singapore) Pte Ltd* (2000).

17.7 In agencies that are premised on agreements, it is important to determine the scope of the agent's authority, because the principal is only bound by the agent's acts when the agent has acted *within* his authority. In such cases, the agent is said to be conferred *actual*, or real, authority, which may be either expressly or impliedly conferred.

(1) *Express Authority*

17.8 Express authority is, as the description implies, conferred by express appointment and the agent would be specifically told what he is authorised to do. There is no formality required in the appointment of an agent and an oral appointment is equally effective to confer express authority. The scope and extent of the agent's authority will primarily be determined on a true construction of the words of the appointment itself.

Where the appointment is contained in a written agreement, the extent of the agent's authority will depend generally on an examination of the agreement, applying the ordinary principles for the construction of contracts. Where the agreement is oral, this will be a matter of evidence. In *Ashford Shire Council v Dependable Motors Pty Ltd* (1961), Lord Reid observed that 'the extent of an agent's authority, if in doubt, must be determined by inference from the whole circumstances' (at p 349).

(2) *Implied Authority*

17.9 Authority may arise by implication or inference from the conduct or the relationship of the parties. Sometimes, a person is made an agent by his appointment to a particular post or designation. He would then have the implied authority to do all those things that would normally be necessary for the proper execution of his duties in that particular post or designation. As Lord Denning MR explained in *Hely-Hutchinson v Brayhead Ltd* (1968) (at p 583):

> '[actual authority] is implied when it is inferred from the conduct of the parties and the circumstances of the case, such as when the board of directors appoint one of their number to be managing director. They thereby impliedly authorise him to do all such things as fall within the usual scope of that office.'

17.10 Additionally, an agent, who is conferred express authority, will have the implied authority to do all such things that are incidental to and necessary for the execution of that express authority.

17.11 Finally, an agent appointed in a particular trade, business or profession, will be impliedly authorised to do those things that are normally or ordinarily done in that trade, business or profession.

Without Agreement

17.12 An agency relationship may arise even without the parties' agreement.

(1) *Apparent Authority*

17.13 Sometimes, a person, by his conduct or representation, creates an *impression* that another, the 'agent', has the requisite authority to act on his behalf. If the third party had relied on the impression so created and altered his legal position, then the person creating that impression is not allowed to deny the purported agent's authority, and would therefore be bound by that agent's acts. Apparent, or ostensible, authority, therefore, is the authority which an agent *appears* to have but in fact does not.

17.14 What are the essential elements of apparent authority? In *Rama Corporation v Proved Tin and General Investments Ltd* (1952), Slade J said (at pp 149–150):

> 'Ostensible or apparent authority ... is merely a form of estoppel, indeed, it has been termed agency by estoppel, and you cannot call in aid an estoppel unless you have three ingredients: (i) a representation, (ii) a reliance on the representation, and (iii) an alteration of your position resulting from such reliance.'

17.15 The basis of apparent authority is therefore the principal's 'holding out', or *representation*, to the third party that the 'agent' is authorised to act as his agent. This representation of authority is often implied from the conduct of the principal in appointing the agent to a particular position, which might usually carry with it the authority to conclude contracts of the type in question, or from a previous course of dealings between the principal and the third party.

Thus, a representation of authority could be made when the supposed principal *allowed* the alleged agent, who had *not* in fact been properly appointed as agent, *to appear* as if he was the principal's agent. This occurred in *Freeman & Lockyer v Buckhurst Park Properties (Mangal) Ltd* (1964) (see also paragraph 18.30, below). The articles of association of the company authorised the board of directors to appoint a managing director, but none was in fact appointed. The board, however, allowed one director to act as managing director, and he contracted with a third party to do some work for the company. The company claimed that it was not bound by the contract because the director had no authority. It was held that although the director had no *actual* authority to so contract, the company had, through its board of directors, created an impression of authority by acquiescing in the director's conduct. The company was therefore bound by any act within the ambit of that apparent authority. Diplock LJ explained (at p 503) the basis of apparent authority:

> 'An "apparent" or "ostensible" authority ... is a legal relationship between the principal and the contractor (third party) created by a representation, made by the principal to the contractor, intended to be and in fact acted upon by the contractor, that the agent has authority to enter on behalf of the principal into a contract of a kind within the scope of the "apparent" authority, so as to render the principal liable to perform any obligations imposed upon him by such a contract. To the relationship so created the agent is a stranger. He need not be (although he generally is) aware of the existence of the representation but he must not purport to make the agreement as principal himself. The representation, when acted upon by the contractor by entering into a contract with the agent, operates as an estoppel, preventing the principal from asserting that he is not bound by the contract. It is irrelevant whether the agent had actual authority to enter into the contract.'

Perhaps more commonly, the impression of authority is generated when the principal either revokes or limits the authority his agent actually possessed, but fails to inform those third parties with whom the agent had dealings. In this situation, the agent would appear to continue to possess authority, when in fact his actual authority has either been revoked or curtailed. The previous course of dealings therefore constitutes the principal's representation. Lord Denning gave an example of this in *Hely-Hutchinson v Brayhead Ltd* (1968) (at p 583):

> '[W]hen the board appoint one of their number to be managing director, they invest him not only with implied authority, but also with ostensible authority to do all such things as fall within the usual scope of that office. Other people who see him acting as managing director are entitled to assume that he has the usual authority of a managing director. But sometimes ostensible authority exceeds actual authority. For instance, when the board appoint the managing director, they may expressly limit his authority by saying he is not to order goods worth more than £500 without the sanction of the board. In that case his actual authority is subject to the £500 limitation, but his *ostensible*

authority includes all the usual authority of a managing director. The company is bound by his ostensible authority in his dealings with those who do not know of the limitation' (emphasis in original).

It should be noted that the representation must come from the principal, or someone actually authorised by the principal, in order for the estoppel to arise against him. It is insufficient for the representation to have come from the agent himself. In *United Bank of Kuwait v Hammond* (1988), Lord Donaldson MR observed (at p 1066) that 'it is trite law that an agent cannot ordinarily confer ostensible authority on himself. He cannot pull himself up by his own shoe laces'.

17.16 The second element that is necessary to establish the estoppel against the principal is that the third party must have *relied* on the representation. There can be no reliance if the third party did not deal with the 'agent' as agent. Equally, where the third party knows, ought to know or suspects that the agent is in fact without authority, he will not then be allowed to rely on the doctrine of apparent authority to bind the principal.

17.17 Finally, there must be an alteration of the third party's position as a result of the reliance. The third party's entering into the contract is sometimes considered sufficient alteration (see, eg *Arctic Shipping Co Ltd v Mobilia AB, The Tatra* (1990) at p 59) although other cases appear to require that the third party suffer a detriment (*Norfolk County Council v Secretary of State for the Environment* (1973)).

(2) *Agency of Necessity*

17.18 In certain limited circumstances, the law confers authority on a person to act for, and bind, another because he is confronted with a situation that requires him to act expeditiously in order to protect the property or interests of that other person. The origin of this doctrine lies in mercantile law, particularly in shipping cases, where the shipmaster was given authority to act as the ship owner's agent in emergencies so as to preserve the ship and its cargo.

The doctrine applies, in cases of *pre-existing* agencies, to confer on an authorised agent a further or more extensive authority, and also to confer authority by necessity on a person who was hitherto *not* in any agency relationship with the principal. In both situations, there are policy concerns with over-extending the applicability of the doctrine. In the first, the concern is over condoning, in the name of necessity, all that an agent does such that the agent becomes in effect the principal. In the second, the law is disinclined to confer authority on the 'officious intermeddler' (see I Brown, 'Authority and Necessity in the Law of Agency' (1992) 55 *Modern Law Review* 414 at p 418) so as to subject the principal to obligations without his consent. The doctrine is therefore kept within narrow boundaries.

17.19 The doctrine of necessity has specific requirements. First, the agent must have been unable to obtain, or it must have been practically impossible to obtain, instructions from the principal on time. Second, the agent must have acted, reasonably and in good faith, in the interests of the principal and, third, there must have been a necessity or emergency that compelled the agent to act as he did.

Ratification

17.20 An agent, who has neither actual nor ostensible authority, cannot bind the so-called principal to third parties by his acts. However, the principal may choose to adopt, or *ratify*, the agent's acts subsequently. When this occurs, an agency relationship arises *retrospectively* and the principal thereby assumes full contractual obligations and rights with respect to the agent's earlier acts. Lord Sterndale MR in *Koenigsblatt v Sweet* (1923) explained (at p 325) the concept in the following terms:

> '[Ratification] is equivalent to an antecedent authority ... and when there has been ratification the act that is done is put in the same position as if it had been antecedently authorised.'

17.21 Ratification may be express or implied from the principal's conduct, although in the latter case, the principal's conduct must unequivocally indicate an affirmation of the agent's acts.

(1) *The Requirements*

17.22 There are a number of requirements for ratification to be effective.

17.23 With regard to *who* may ratify, *Bowstead and Reynolds on Agency* (17th ed, 2001) states (at paragraph 2-060) as follows:

> 'The only person who has power to ratify an act is the person in whose name or on whose behalf the act purported to be done, and it is necessary that he should have been in existence at the time when the act was done, and competent at that time and at the time of ratification to be the principal of the person doing the act; but it is not necessary that at the time the act was done he was known, either personally or by name, to the third party.'

Thus, if a person purports to act on his own, and not on the principal's behalf, or who intended to act on the principal's behalf but fails to disclose this fact to the third party, the principal cannot ratify. The facts of *Keighley, Maxted & Co v Durant* (1901) illustrate this point. An agent was authorised to purchase, at a certain price, wheat on a joint account for himself and the defendants. Acting in excess of authority, he purchased wheat at a higher price from the plaintiffs but in his own name and without disclosing that he was also buying on behalf of the defendants. The defendants ratified the purchase the next day but failed subsequently to take delivery of the wheat. The House of Lords held that the action for breach of contract must fail. The purported ratification was ineffective as the agent had contracted in his own name. The defendants were therefore under no contractual obligation to the plaintiffs.

The requirement as to the existence and competence of the principal at the time the transaction was completed presented difficulties in the context of *pre-incorporation* contracts entered into by the incorporators (or promoters) of a company that is yet to be incorporated. At common law, a company was not bound by contracts made prior to its incorporation and it could not ratify the contract either. The position has been legislatively changed by section 41 of the Companies Act (Cap 50, 1994 Rev Ed) which provides as follows:

> 'Any contract or other transaction purporting to be entered into by a company prior to its formation or by any person on behalf of a company prior to its formation may be ratified by the company after its formation and thereupon the company shall become bound by and entitled to the benefit thereof as if it had been in existence at the date of the contract or other transaction and had been a party thereto.'

Where the company does *not* ratify, or where the company fails to get incorporated, section 41(2) provides for the *promoter*, in the absence of any express agreement otherwise, to be personally liable on the pre-incorporation contract (reference may also be made to paragraph 7.34, above).

17.24 With regard to *what* transactions may be ratified, the general rule is that anything that can be done through an agent, including even unlawful acts, may be ratified by the person on whose behalf that act was done. However, a transaction that is void at its inception cannot be ratified, neither can acts that are prohibited by statute.

17.25 Finally, the ratification must be in time. If there is a time fixed for the performance of the contract, ratification must clearly be within this particular period of time. If there is no fixed time, then the ratification should occur within a reasonable time of the principal acquiring knowledge of the unauthorised transaction.

(2) *The Effects*

17.26 Ratification has a *retroactive* effect, which means that the parties involved, viz the principal, the third party and the agent, will be placed in the position they would respectively have been in if the agent's acts had been authorised all along. In *Bolton Partners v Lambert* (1889), Cotton LJ said (at p 306):

> 'The rule as to ratification by a principal of acts done by an assumed agent is that the ratification is thrown back to the date of the act done, and that the agent is put in the same position as if he had had authority to do the act at the time the act was done by him.'

Thus, the principal acquires rights and obligations under the contract with the third party, and the agent drops out of the picture.

17.27 This rule, known as the doctrine of *relation-back*, does at first glance appear to favour the principal unfairly over the third party. Whilst the principal may or may not decide to ratify, the third party does not have the same choice.

Under the rules of offer and acceptance (see Chapter 2), we know that an offer may be revoked anytime prior to it being accepted. But in this agency context, if the principal *does* later ratify, the effect of ratification is retrospective, and relates back to the time the agent purportedly contracted on behalf of the principal. Thus, although the principal is not bound by the contract until he ratifies, the third party would appear to be effectively bound from the date of the contract. The facts of *Bolton Partners v Lambert* illustrate the point.

Scratchley, a director of the plaintiff company, was unauthorised to bind the plaintiff but nevertheless accepted an offer made by the defendant. Prior to the plaintiff's ratification, the defendant purported to withdraw his offer. The plaintiff subsequently ratified. The court held that the defendant was bound to the contract. In the words of Cotton LJ (at pp 307–308):

> 'I think the proper view is that the acceptance by Scratchley did constitute a contract, subject to its being shewn that Scratchley had authority to bind the company. If that were not shewn there would be no contract on the part of the company, but when and as soon as authority was given to Scratchley to bind the company the authority was thrown back to the time when the act was done by Scratchley, and prevented the Defendant withdrawing his offer because it was then no longer an offer, but a binding contract.'

17.28 This perceived inequity of the doctrine of relation-back should not, however, be over-stated. The real 'hardship' or inconvenience suffered by the third party is the uncertainty as to whether and when the principal will ratify the transaction. In this regard, it has already been pointed out that ratification must be effected within a reasonable time. As to what amounts to a 'reasonable time', Bowen LJ said in *Re Portuguese Consolidated Copper Mines Limited* (1890) (at p 35) that:

> 'there is no hard-and-fast line in any case: the measure of the reasonableness of the time depends entirely upon the circumstances of the case. You cannot take a hypothetical case and say that if this had been an instance of an offer made and nothing done, with all the parties silent and the silence continuing for two or three months, then the [ratification] would have come too late ... It must be a question of fact in each case what the reasonable limit is. Mere time is nothing except with reference to the circumstances.'

On the facts of *Re Portuguese Consolidated Copper Mines Limited*, the English Court of Appeal placed considerable emphasis on the fact that the third party did not 'repudiate' or intimate that he would like to withdraw the offer on the ground of the agent's lack of authority in concluding that a ratification that came after two to three months was effected within a reasonable time. It would therefore be open to the third party to require the principal to ratify quickly or not at all.

17.29 The doctrine of relation-back has no application when the agent contracts subject to the principal's approval or ratification and the third party may therefore withdraw his offer anytime prior to ratification. As Maugham J explained in *Watson v Davies* (1931) (at pp 468–469):

> 'In a case where the agent for one party to a negotiation informs the other party that he cannot enter into a contract binding his principal except subject to his approval, there is in truth no contract or contractual relation until the approval has been obtained. The agent has incurred no responsibility ... An acceptance by an agent subject in express terms to ratification by his principal is legally a nullity until ratification, and is no more binding on the other party than an unaccepted offer which can, of course, be withdrawn before acceptance.'

Effect of Agency

17.30 When an agency is created or imposed by law, this has effects on all three sides of the triangular relationship that results from the agency. The most important characteristic of agency is the agent's power to affect the legal position of the principal *vis-à-vis* third parties. As such, we will begin this section with a consideration of this aspect, and proceed thereafter to consider the effects of agency on the principal-agent relationship and the agent-third party relationship.

Principal–Third Party Relationship

17.31 In the normal agency situation, the third party when dealing with the agent would know that the agent is in fact acting on behalf of someone else (the principal). The third party therefore deals with the agent *as an agent*. The principal in these cases is known as a *disclosed* principal. Where the third party is aware of the *existence* of the principal, it does not appear relevant that the principal is *unnamed*. An unnamed principal is still a disclosed principal.

There are also situations in which the third party deals with the agent in the latter's capacity as *principal*, and who is therefore *unaware* of the existence of the agent's own principal, and that the agent was in fact acting on behalf of his principal. In these situations, the principal is said to be *undisclosed*. The undisclosed principal, notwithstanding the third party's ignorance of his existence, has a right to enforce the contract against the third party if the agent has acted within his authority. The rules to determine the principal's rights against the third party depend partly on the distinction between disclosed and undisclosed principals. As such, each category will be dealt with separately in the ensuing paragraphs.

(1) *Disclosed Agency*

17.32 Generally, where an agent acts within the scope of his actual authority, whether express or implied, a disclosed principal is bound by and becomes liable for the acts of his agent. Direct contractual relations would therefore be established between the principal and the third party. The main concern in such cases is to determine the *scope* of the agent's authority. If the agent's acts fall *within* the scope of his authority, his principal is not only imposed with obligations to the third party, but also acquires rights against the third party. Even where the agent has acted *outside* the scope of his authority, the disclosed principal may ratify the contract. When this occurs, the principal may sue and be sued on the contract with the third party. The agent drops out the picture, and accordingly, neither the third party nor the principal can, as a general rule, discharge their respective liability to each other by settling with the agent.

Thus, in *Butwick v Grant* (1924), payment for goods by a third party purchaser to the agent of the seller did not discharge the third party's liability to the principal-seller. The court held that authority to an agent to *sell* goods does not necessarily imply authority to *receive* payment for the goods.

In *Irvine & Co v Watson & Sons* (1880), the *principal's* payment to his own agent, of the purchase price for the oil that the latter had contracted for on the principal's behalf, did not discharge his liability to the third party. Bramwell LJ said (at p 416):

> 'I think it is impossible to say that it discharged them, unless they were misled by some conduct of the plaintiffs into the belief that the broker had already settled with the plaintiffs, and made such payment in consequence of such belief.'

17.33 The situation is slightly different when the agent acts without authority and the principal does not ratify. If the agent had acted within an authority he appeared to possess, ie his apparent or ostensible authority, the principal will undoubtedly be liable to the third party. However, it is unlikely that the principal will be able to initiate an action against the third party on contracts purportedly made by these 'apparent agents'.

(2) *Undisclosed Agency*

17.34 An undisclosed principal, as alluded to before, may be able to enforce a contract entered into by his agent with a third party, and this is so even though the third party was under the impression that he was dealing only with the agent in the latter's own capacity. As such, this rule is generally thought of as anomalous because it goes against the fundamental principles of privity of contract, which is logically only established between the third party and the *agent*. The rule is, however, justified on grounds of commercial convenience (per Lord Lloyd in *Siu Yin Kwan v Eastern Insurance Co Ltd* (1994) at p 207). Lord Lindley explained the justification in *Keighley, Maxsted & Co v Durant* (1901) (at p 260) in the following manner:

> 'As a contract is constituted by the concurrence of two or more persons and by their agreement to the same terms, there is an anomaly in holding one person bound to another of whom he did not, in fact, intend to contract. But middlemen, through whom contracts are made, are common and useful in business transactions, and in the great mass of contracts it is a matter of indifference to either party whether there is an undisclosed principal or not. If he exists it is, to say the least, extremely

> convenient that he should be able to sue and be sued as a principal, and he is only allowed to do so upon terms which exclude injustice.'

17.35 The rules that apply to an undisclosed agency was summarised by Lord Lloyd of Berwick in *Siu Yin Kwan v Eastern Insurance Co Ltd* (1994) (at p 207) as follows:

> '(1) An undisclosed principal may sue and be sued on a contract made by an agent on his behalf, acting within the scope of his actual authority. (2) In entering into the contract, the agent must intend to act on the principal's behalf. (3) The agent of an undisclosed principal may also sue and be sued on the contract. (4) Any defence which the third party may have against the agent is available against his principal. (5) The terms of the contract may, expressly or by implication, exclude the principal's right to sue, and his liability to be sued. The contract itself, or the circumstances surrounding the contract, may show that the agent is the true and only principal.'

In order for the undisclosed principal to intervene in the contract made by his agent, it is of great importance that the agent acted within his *actual* authority, and that he *intended* to act on his principal's behalf. The undisclosed principal's right of intervention is 'subject to any defences or equities which without notice may exist against the agent' (per Sir Montague Smith in *Browning v Provincial Insurance Co of Canada* (1873) at p 272). Thus, the third party may utilise any right of set-off against the agent which may have accrued in his favour before he had notice of the principal's existence. In a similar manner, if the third party had settled on the contract with the agent prior to his discovery of the principal's existence, this would provide a complete defence to any action brought by the principal. The position here is clearly different from that of the *disclosed* principal (discussed in paragraph 17.32, above), because the undisclosed principal had allowed the agent to act as though *he* (ie the agent) were the principal.

As long as the principal remains undisclosed, the agent, who has contracted with the third party in his own name, will be able to sue and be sued on the contract. However, once the principal decides to intervene in the contract, the agent loses his right to sue.

Once the *third party* becomes aware of the existence of the principal, the law confers on the former the right to elect (or choose) whether to sue the principal or the agent on the contract. In the words of Earl Cairns LC in *Kendall v Hamilton* (1879) (at p 514):

> '... where an agent contracts in his own name for an undisclosed principal, the person with whom he contracts may sue the agent, or he may sue the principal, but if he sues the agent and recovers judgment, he cannot afterwards sue the principal, even although the judgment does not result in satisfaction of the debt.'

Point (5) in the quotation above is necessary in order to prevent any injustice that an unqualified right to intervene by the principal may cause to the third party because of the third party's ignorance of the principal's existence. Thus, the undisclosed principal will not be permitted to intervene if this would contradict the express or implied terms of the contract.

Principal–Agent Relationship

17.36 The rights and duties of the principal and the agent derive from the terms of the contract, if any, between the parties. Additionally, and independently of contract, certain duties arise from the very agency relationship itself.

(1) *Duties of Agent*

17.37 Where the agent is appointed under a contract, he is clearly bound to perform in accordance with the terms of the contract and with the instructions stipulated therein. The obligation to perform with reasonable care and diligence will, if not expressly stipulated, be an implied term of the contract (see Chapter 5). If he acts in a manner that is not authorised, he will be in breach of the contract. Even an agent who is not appointed pursuant to a contract is required to act with due care and skill, although it is not unlikely that a higher standard might be expected of a *paid*, as opposed to a *gratuitous*, agent.

17.38 In addition, agents are *fiduciaries*. A fiduciary is a person who stands in a position of trust and confidence *vis-à-vis* another, and who is conferred discretion to act for the benefit of that other (ie the beneficiary). A fiduciary possesses the mandate to exercise individual discretion, and is able (like the agent) to affect the legal position of the beneficiary. However, the very power held by the fiduciary that allows him to benefit the other, also allows him to 'indulge his own interest and to injure' that other (see DA DeMott, 'Beyond Metaphor: An Analysis of Fiduciary Obligation' [1988] *Duke Law Journal* 879 at p 914). Thus, as McCardie J explained in *Armstrong v Jackson* (1917) (at p 826):

> 'The position of principal and agent gives rise to particular and onerous duties on the part of the agent, and the high standard of conduct required from him springs from the fiduciary relationship between his employer and himself. His position is confidential. It readily lends itself to abuse. A strict and salutary rule is required to meet the special situation.'

A number of fiduciary duties are therefore imposed on agents. A breach of the agent's fiduciary obligations will render the agent liable to surrender his ill-gotten gains to his principal. The main fiduciary obligations are discussed below.

(a) Duty to Avoid a Conflict of Interests

17.39 An agent is under an obligation not to put himself in a position where his duties as agent conflict with his personal interests unless the conflict has been fully disclosed to the principal and the latter's consent obtained. This rule is necessary because of the agent's power to affect his principal's legal position. Its premise is prophylactic because 'human infirmity' (per

Eldon LC in *Ex Parte Bennett* (1805) at p 897) renders it difficult to resist the temptation to favour oneself over one's principal. This temptation is particularly acute if the agent, employed to buy, were allowed to purchase his own goods on behalf of his principal or if the agent, employed to sell, were allowed to himself buy the principal's property.

(b) Duty Not to Make a Secret Profit

17.40 In a similar vein, the agent is not allowed to use his position (including property or confidential information acquired in his position as agent), without the knowledge and assent of the principal, to make personal profits or for a personal advantage. Neither is he allowed to accept bribes or secret commissions from the third parties with whom he is dealing on behalf of his principal. Slade J defined, in *Industries and General Mortgage Co Ltd v Lewis* (1949) (at p 575), a 'bribe' as follows:

> 'A bribe means a payment of a secret commission, which only means (i) that the person making the payment makes it to the agent of the other person with whom he is dealing; (ii) that he makes it to that person knowing that that person is acting as the agent of the other person with whom he is dealing; and (iii) that he fails to disclose to the other person with whom he is dealing that he has made that payment to the person whom he knows to be the other person's agent.'

Both the agent who receives the bribe and the third party who pays it may be criminally liable under the Prevention of Corruption Act (Cap 241, 1993 Rev Ed). In addition, the bribe received by the agent may be confiscated or forfeited under the Corruption, Drug Trafficking and Other Serious Crimes (Confiscation of Benefits) Act (Cap 65A, 2000 Rev Ed).

(c) Duty Not to Delegate

17.41 The general rule is that an agent cannot appoint and delegate his authority to a sub-agent except with the express or implied authority of the principal, and where confidence in the person of the agent is the root of the agency relationship, the authority to delegate cannot be implied as an ordinary incident in the contract (per Thesiger LJ in *De Bussche v Alt* (1878) at p 310).

However, it is recognised that the exigencies of business do sometimes require that a sub-agent be appointed. The authority to delegate may (in such situations) be implied, as Thesiger LJ explained (at p 310):

> '... where, from the conduct of the parties to the original contract of agency, the usage of trade, or the nature of the particular business which is the subject of the agency, it may reasonably be presumed that the parties to the contract of agency originally intended that such authority should exist, or where, in the course of the employment, unforeseen emergencies arise which impose upon the agent the necessity of employing a substitute.'

17.42 However, even where such authority to delegate exists, there appears to be no general principle of law that *privity* of contract then arises as between the principal and the sub-agent so that the sub-agent, and not the agent, becomes directly responsible to the principal in connection with the performance of the original mandate. Wright J stated, in *Calico Printers' Association Ltd v Barclays Bank* (1930) (at p 109) as follows:

> '... English law ... has in general applied the rule that even where the sub-agent is properly employed there is still no privity between him and the principal. The latter is entitled to hold the agent liable for breach of the mandate which he has accepted, and cannot in general claim against the sub-agent for negligence or breach of duty. I know of no English case in which a principal has recovered against a sub-agent for negligence. The agent does not as a rule escape liability to the principal merely because employment of the sub-agent is contemplated. To create privity it must be established not only that the principal contemplated that a sub-agent would perform part of the contract, but also that the principal authorised the agent to create privity of contract between the principal and the sub-agent, which is a very different matter requiring precise proof. In general, where a principal employs an agent to carry out a particular employment, the agent undertakes responsibility for the whole transaction and is responsible for any negligence in carrying it out, even if the negligence be that of the sub-agent properly or necessarily engaged to perform some part, because there is no privity between the principal and the sub-agent.'

(2) *Rights of Agent*

17.43 The agent has a number of rights against his principal. Very importantly, the agent has a right to being remunerated for carrying out his mandate, but this is a right that depends on the agreement between the parties. Where the agent is appointed pursuant to a contract, the terms of the contract will govern his right to remuneration.

17.44 The agent is also entitled to be reimbursed for expenses incurred and indemnified by the principal against all liabilities which he has reasonably incurred in the execution of his mandate. However, the agent is not entitled to reimbursement or to an indemnity in respect of expenses incurred outside of his authority unless the principal ratifies the agent's acts. This rule applies equally to expenses that result from illegal acts or from the agent's own breach of duty.

17.45 Finally, an agent is entitled to a lien over his principal's property in respect of all claims against the principal that arise out of the agency. A lien is essentially a security interest that allows the agent to retain possession of his principal's property until the principal satisfies all of the agent's claims.

Agent–Third Party Relationship

17.46 The general rule is that the agent who contracts on behalf of his principal owes no liability to, nor does he have any rights against, the third party.

17.47 There are, however, exceptions.

An agent may have agreed or undertaken to be personally liable. This is a matter of proper construction of the contract concluded with the third party. Or it may be usual in the particular trade or business for the agent to be personally liable and entitled, or this could be the usual course of business between the specific parties. The agent may also be liable, as we saw above, where the principal is an undisclosed principal.

Statute may also render an agent personally liable. Section 26 of the Bills of Exchange Act (Cap 23, 1999 Rev Ed), for example, provides that 'where a person signs a bill as drawer, indorser, or acceptor, and adds words to his signature, indicating that he signs for or on behalf of a principal, or in a representative character, he is not personally liable thereon; but the mere addition to his signature of words describing him as an agent, or as filling a representative character, does not exempt him from personal liability'. In a similar manner, section 41 of the Companies Act (see paragraph 17.23) renders the agent (ie the promoter of the company) personally liable on pre-incorporation contracts if these are not subsequently ratified by the company after it is incorporated.

17.48 An agent who contracted in excess of authority, and whose principal does not adopt the agent's acts through the process of ratification, may be liable to the third party for breach of the agent's implied warranty of authority. In the words of Willes J in *Collen v Wright* (1857) (at p 657):

> '... a person who induces another to contract with him as the agent of a third party by an unqualified assertion of his being authorised to act as such agent, is answerable to the person who so contracts for any damages which he may sustain by reason of the assertion of authority being untrue ... The fact that the professed agent honestly thinks that he has the authority affects the moral character of his act; but his moral innocence, so far as the person whom he has induced to contract is concerned, in no way aids such person or alleviates the inconvenience and damage which he sustains.'

It should be obvious that if the third party knows or must be taken to know of the agent's lack of authority, the agent cannot be made liable on this ground. Also, where the principal ratifies the agent's unauthorised acts, the agent will also not be liable for a breach of warranty of authority.

Termination of Agency

17.49 Agency may be terminated by the acts of the parties themselves or by operation of law. Certain classes of agency are, however, deemed by law to be irrevocable.

17.50 Where the agency is created by an agreement that amounts to a *contract*, it may, as a general rule, be determined in a similar manner as a contract. Thus the contract of agency may be discharged by performance and breach or frustration (see Chapters 9 and 10 respectively). As agency is mostly a consensual relationship based on agreement between the parties, its termination too may be effected by agreement. Either party may also give notice of his intention to withdraw from the agency, subject to liability in damages if the agency is derived from a contract. Whilst these acts terminate the relationship of principal and agent, they do not necessarily terminate the agent's apparent or ostensible authority, unless the third party had notice of this. *Vis-à-vis* the *third party*, therefore, the principal may remain liable for the acts of his former agent.

17.51 Even where the parties do not themselves act to terminate the agency, certain events do so by operation of law. Death of either party determines the agency, whether the surviving party had notice of the death or not. But where it is the *principal* who has died, the agent may be liable to the third party for breach of warranty of authority. In a similar manner, the supervening insanity of either the principal or the agent determines the agency.

Whilst the bankruptcy of the principal (which amounts to legal incapacity) will automatically terminate the agency relationship, the bankruptcy of the agent will determine the relationship only if the agent is thereby made unfit to perform his duties.

17.52 The authority of an agent may become irrevocable in certain situations. Specifically, an authority, given to an agent by contract or deed for the purpose of protecting a pre-existing interest of the agent, cannot be revoked by the principal without the agent's consent. In this sense, the authority is irrevocable.

The facts of *Gaussen v Morton* (1830) illustrate the operation of the doctrine. A principal owed money to another, and therefore conferred authority on the latter to sell certain property and to use the proceeds to discharge the debt. The purpose of the creation of the agency was therefore to secure a benefit to the agent (ie the repayment of the debt). It was therefore held that the agent's authority could not be revoked without the agent's consent.

PART IV

Business Organisations

CHAPTER **18**

Business Organisations

PARAGRAPHS

Introduction

18.1–18.3 Overview
18.4–18.6 Registering a Business

Companies

18.7 Overview
18.8 Reform
18.9–18.13 Categories and Classification
18.14–18.17 Company Formation
Persona Ficta
18.18–18.20 (1) Legal Personality
18.21–18.23 (2) Looking Behind the Veil of Incorporation
How Companies Operate
18.24–18.26 (1) Rules of Attribution
18.27–18.28 (2) Division of Powers
18.29–18.32 (3) Corporate Contracting
Directors
18.33–18.35 (1) General
18.36–18.38 (2) Directors' Obligations and Duties
18.39–18.41 (a) Equitable and Fiduciary Duties
18.42 (b) The Duty of Skill, Care and Diligence
18.43–18.44 (3) Enforcement of Directors' Duties
Relationship Between Shareholders
18.45–18.46 (1) Statutory Contract
18.47–18.49 (2) Majority Rule and Protection of the Minority

Non-Corporate Business Organisations

18.50 Sole Proprietorships
Partnerships
18.51–18.52 (1) General Partnership
18.53 (a) Dealings with Third Parties
18.54 (b) Unlimited Personal Liability of Partners
18.55 (c) Dissolution
18.56–18.57 (2) Limited Partnership
18.58–15.59 (3) Limited Liability Partnerships

Introduction

Overview

18.1 A person contemplating starting a business has a number of options as to how to structure his business. The major basic structures are, traditionally, the sole proprietorship, the partnership and the company, and these will be considered in this chapter. In addition, recent reform proposals recommend the introduction of the limited partnership and the limited liability partnership with a view to widening the options available for businesses and investments in Singapore (see the Report of the Company Legislation and Regulatory Framework Committee, October 2002). The limited partnership is really a variant of the ordinary partnership as the general principles of partnership law still apply. The limited liability partnership attempts to combine the favourable attributes of the ordinary partnership and the company. We will revisit these forms later in the chapter.

In addition, there are organisational structures such as societies, co-operative societies and trusts. These are generally utilised for purposes *other* than that of business and profit-making.

18.2 There are also methods of *association* that may be used for business purposes. The joint venture is one such common example. Other examples include the syndicate and the consortium. These are effectively facilitative arrangements between two or more parties (who may themselves be individuals, partnerships or companies) who come together to cooperate commercially for a particular purpose. The actual legal form through which these associations pursue their shared undertaking is usually either the partnership or the company.

18.3 The law does not, as a general rule, dictate which structure a business must adopt. However, if the proposed association is formed for the purposes of gain and which consists of more than 20 persons, then section 17(3) of the Companies Act (Cap 50, 1994 Rev Ed) mandates that it be incorporated as a company. Otherwise, the particular business form chosen is very much a private decision. The final decision as to which form to adopt will depend, first of all, on whether the businessman goes at it alone or with others, and secondly, on a careful evaluation and weighing of a number of factors including the nature of the business contemplated, the potential for liability, the management process, the present and future capital requirements of the business and tax incentives.

Registering a Business

18.4 There is one other matter that needs to be at least briefly mentioned before we look in more detail at the basic business forms, and this is the requirement for the registration of businesses. The Business Registration Act (Cap 32, 2001 Rev Ed) (hereinafter the 'BRA') makes it compulsory for every person who intends to carry on a business in Singapore to make an application to the Registrar of Businesses (which in Singapore is also the Registrar of Companies) in the prescribed manner for the registration of the business under the BRA. This application must be made *before* the commencement of business (section 5). Section 4 exempts from registration certain small businesses (as listed in the First Schedule including that carried on by licensed hawkers, taxi drivers, trishaw riders and, subject to certain conditions, craftsmen and farmers) and businesses that are carried on by bodies already regulated under other laws (accountants and lawyers would fall within this exemption). Although companies are regulated under the Companies Act (Cap 50, 1994 Rev Ed) and registration under the BRA is therefore generally not necessary, registration is nevertheless required if the company carries on a business under a name that is not its corporate name (section 4(2)).

The requirement for registration serves to provide the public with a repository of information on persons who do business in Singapore, and in so doing, protects the public against being misled as to the real identity of such persons. To ensure that the registered information is kept updated, the BRA imposes the further obligation to notify the Registrar of any changes to particulars already registered (section 12).

18.5 There are both civil and criminal consequences on a failure to register. Section 17 provides that a person who defaults on the registration requirements in respect of a business (including the requirement to update registered particulars) shall not be able to enforce his rights under any contract which relates to that particular business. The section does not prejudice the rights of the *other* party to the affected contract; the intention is clearly to penalise only the defaulting party. It should be obvious, however, that if the disability were to be a strict and absolute one, the section might stand to be abused by the other contracting party as a means to *avoid* his contractual obligations and injustice would thereby be suffered by the defaulter. The disability therefore is *not* absolute and the court is given 'the widest possible powers of granting relief to persons in default' (per Christopher Lau JC in *Federal Lands Commissioner v Benfort Enterprises & Anor* (1998) at p 859) where it is satisfied that the default was 'accidental or due to inadvertence or some other sufficient cause, or that on other grounds it is just and equitable to grant relief' (section 17(2)). The justification for this is explained by Lush J (with whom Christopher Lau JC expressly agreed) in *Weller v Denton* (1921) as follows (at p 109):

> 'The reason why this wide power of granting relief should be given to the court can well be understood. Where the defendant has not been misled, and knew the members of the firm or other persons with whom he was dealing, it might be most unjust and inequitable to hold that the plaintiff's action should not be maintained merely because he did not know that he ought to have been registered under the Act.'

Whilst this might give the impression that relief is readily granted on request as long as the defaulter 'did not know that he ought to have been registered', this is not the case. In *Watson v Park Royal (Caterers) Ltd*

(1961), Edmund Davies J made it clear that however broadly the English equivalent of section 17 is to be construed, it is still a requirement that the court be satisfied of the matters set out therein as grounds for relief. In his Honour's words, 'to hold that [relief] is automatically granted on request would simply be to put a pencil through the provisions of an Act of Parliament which obviously had security and stability in business dealings as its object' (at p 736).

18.6 Section 23 imposes criminal sanctions for non-compliance with the BRA. This does not, however, render the contract entered into by a defaulter one that is void on the ground of illegality (*Lim Feng Chieh (formerly trading as Intra-Smit Agencies) v GS Auto Supply Pte Ltd* (1993)). On the BRA generally, see HM Zafrullah, 'The Law of Business Registration in Singapore' [1985] 2 *Malayan Law Journal* ccxvii.

Companies

Overview

18.7 The word 'company' is used in this chapter to denote a corporation that is formed through the process of registration or incorporation laid down in the Companies Act (Cap 50, 1994 Rev Ed) (hereinafter the 'CA'). Indeed, this is the definition the CA ascribes to the word. The effect of complying with the requirements of registration is to bring into being 'a body corporate by the name contained in the memorandum capable forthwith of exercising all the functions of an incorporated company and of suing and being sued and having perpetual succession and a common seal with power to hold land' (section 19(5)).

Companies are therefore really a sub-category of associations known as 'bodies corporate' or 'corporations', all of which share in common the possession of corporate *status*. This means that the law conceptualises the corporation as an entity possessing artificial personality. The effect of this will be discussed in the ensuing paragraphs.

Corporations include those that are created directly by an Act of Parliament. The Civil Aviation Authority of Singapore, for example, is a body corporate created directly by the Civil Aviation Authority of Singapore Act (Cap 41, 1985 Rev Ed). These statutory corporations do not fall within the definition of 'corporations' that are subject to the provisions of the CA (section 4).

Reform

18.8 Singapore's company law is currently undergoing major reform. The Final Report of the Company Legislation and Regulatory Framework Committee (hereinafter the 'CLRFC') was published in October 2002 (hereinafter the 'Report') and the Singapore government has accepted all its recommendations. In the years following the publication of the Report, we will be seeing amendments to the CA. Indeed, some of the more procedural and technical changes have already been the subject of amendment bills released in 2003. References to the more substantive proposals will be made in this chapter where appropriate.

Categories and Classification

18.9 The CA provides for three types of companies classified according to the method by which the liability of the members to contribute to the assets of the company is determined. In the unlimited company, there is no limit placed on the liability of its members who may therefore be personally liable for the whole of the company's liabilities to its creditors. In the limited company, this liability is restricted to an amount fixed by reference to the terms by which shares are held or by the company's constitutional documents.

18.10 The CA recognises two types of limited company, and these are the company limited by shares and the company limited by guarantee.

18.11 A company limited by shares has a share capital. Most of the companies registered under the CA are companies limited by shares as this provides perhaps the most appropriate form for commercial purposes. A share represents the holder's financial undertaking in the company and provides the basis on which he is conferred member rights, such as the right to vote and the entitlement to participate, in the form of dividends, in the profits of the company. The terms 'shareholder' and 'member' are generally used interchangeably, although technically, a shareholder becomes a 'member' only when his name is entered into the company's register of members (section 19(6) of the CA).

The liability of a member or shareholder of a company limited by shares is limited to the amount that remains unpaid on his shares. For example, if a company allots to X a share at the price of $1, and X pays $0.50 to the company on the issue of that share, X's maximum potential liability to meet the company's debts is then limited to the outstanding balance of $0.50. The company may require X to contribute the outstanding amount by making a *call* on the unpaid balance even when the company is not being wound up. An unpaid call amounts to a *debt* owing to the company.

18.12 In a company limited by guarantee, a member (note that there cannot be 'shareholders' in such companies as there is no share capital) is only liable to contribute to the assets of the company in the event of its winding up, and then only at the (usually nominal) amount fixed by the memorandum. Such companies are used mainly for non-profit making purposes such as charities or recreational clubs. The Singapore Management University, for example, is a company limited by guarantee. This chapter deals only with the company limited by shares.

18.13 The CA also classifies companies as private or public. Under the CA, only companies having a share capital may be incorporated as private companies. A private company must, in its memorandum or articles of association, restrict the right to transfer its shares and limit the number of its members to 50 (section 18(1)). Although there is currently a requirement that there must also be, in the constitution, a prohibition against the raising of funds from the public, the CLRFC is recommending that this requirement be removed. Once this proposal is put into effect, private companies will be allowed to raise funds by offering its shares or debentures for investment as long as this is undertaken through private, as opposed to public, means. It is proposed that a comprehensive list of what would amount to private offerings be provided.

Within this class of private companies, there is a further division into companies that are conferred *exempt* status and those that are not. An exempt private company is defined in the CA as 'a private company in the shares of which no beneficial interest is held directly or indirectly by any corporation and which has not more than 20 members' or any private company wholly held by the Government and which is declared, in the national interest, as an exempt private company (section 4). These companies are exempted from certain accounting requirements under the CA.

A public company is any company that is not a private company (section 4). Public companies, because of their generally unrestricted ability to raise funds from the public, are subject to a correspondingly higher degree of regulation by the law. Additionally, the shares of a public company are usually listed on a stock exchange which provides a ready market for the company's shares. The stock exchange will have its own listing and on-going requirements that will have to be complied with by listed companies. Listed companies are regulated separately by the Securities and Futures Act (Cap 289, 2002 Rev Ed).

Company Formation

18.14 The CA prescribes the process of incorporation. It requires the drawing up of the company's constitution, which is to be 'subscribed' to by (currently) two subscribers, and the lodging of this with the Registrar of Companies, together with certain prescribed forms and the prescribed fee (section 19). If all is in order, the Registrar will issue a certificate of incorporation whereupon 'the subscribers to the memorandum together with such other persons as may from time to time become members of the company shall be a body corporate' (section 19(5)).

Currently, the CA requires companies to have a minimum of two shareholders and two directors. The CLRFC is of the view that there is no continuing policy reason for this and is therefore proposing that private companies be allowed to be incorporated with the minimum of one shareholder and one director, who can be the same person. This will reduce incorporation and maintenance costs.

18.15 Currently, the company's constitution comprises two documents, the memorandum of association and the articles of association. Section 22 of the CA prescribes the minimum information that must be contained in the memorandum, including the *objects* of the company. This statement of the company's objects formed the basis for the development of the difficult '*ultra vires*' doctrine.

The doctrine is a rule of company law that is concerned with the *capacity* of the company. By the doctrine, a company could not do anything that was not within the scope of its objects clause as it would be without the capacity to. In the eyes of the law, an *ultra vires* transaction would be null and void, and would not be capable of being authorised or ratified (retrospectively approved), not even by a unanimous decision of the shareholders. Operating together with the doctrine of constructive notice, which deems all who deal with the company to have notice of the contents of the company's constitution and other lodged documents, the doctrine of *ultra vires* was the cause of significant injustice to outsiders who may have supplied goods or services to the company for a purpose not contained in the memorandum.

Section 25 of the CA reformed the doctrine of *ultra vires*. The section provides that, with respect to outsiders, 'no act or purported act of a company… shall be invalid by reason only of the fact that the company was without capacity or power to do such act…', but as a matter of internal administration, the fact of corporate incapacity may be relied upon by a member who wants to restrain the company from doing an *ultra vires* act. Unlike the position at common law where the *ultra vires* transaction is automatically void, restraint or the setting aside of the *ultra vires* transaction under section 25(3) will only be ordered if the court considers that it would be just and equitable to do so. The company's lack of capacity may also be relied upon in any action by the company or by any member against the company's officers for breach of duty.

The CLRFC is thinking of going further by recommending that the doctrine of *ultra vires* be totally abolished and the company be statutorily conferred with all the powers of a natural person. However, where the constitution of the company places limits on its capacity and powers, the CLRFC has recommended that the doctrine remains available as a basis for internal redress by members against the directors.

18.16 The articles of association of the company regulate the internal administration of the company. The Fourth Schedule of the CA contains Table A, a default set of articles which may be adopted by companies who do not have articles specially drafted for them.

18.17 The CLRFC is recommending that the requirement for separate memorandum and articles of association be eliminated and replaced by a single model constitution (Report, Recommendation 1.10).

Persona Ficta

(1) *Legal Personality*

18.18 According to Lord Hoffman in *Meridian Global Funds Management Asia Ltd v Securities Commission* (1995), a company 'exists because there is a rule (usually in a statute) which says that a *persona ficta* shall be deemed to exist and to have certain of the powers, rights and duties of a natural person' (at p 506). Legal personality is the capacity to enjoy legal rights and owe legal obligations. It is possessed, not only by 'natural persons', ie human beings, but also by 'artificial persons' created by the law through the process of incorporation. The company is one such artificial person.

18.19 A consequence of being a *persona ficta* is that the company is considered separate and distinct from the humans who caused the company to be incorporated. This means that the company may, on its own account, hold property, make contracts and carry on business irrespective of its current shareholders. The corollary to this is that, individually, the shareholders do not own the company's assets or property, and any rights or obligations that arise out of the company's contracts do not belong to the shareholders.

The well-known case of *Saloman v Saloman & Co Ltd* (1897) illustrates the effect of this principle. Mr Saloman ran a successful boot and shoe manufacturing business as a sole proprietor. He incorporated a limited liability company to take over the business. He with his wife and five grown-up children were the subscribers to the memorandum (ie the initial shareholders). His business was transferred to the company, which gave Mr Saloman in consideration therefor, £1,000 in cash, £10,000 in debentures (which represented the company's indebtedness to Mr Saloman repayable at a later time) and 20,000 shares of £1 each. The company unfortunately fell on difficult times and had to be wound up. While the company's assets were sufficient to pay off the debentures, there would in that event be nothing left to pay the trade creditors. It was therefore alleged on behalf of the trade creditors that the debentures were invalid as Mr Saloman and the company were one and the same, and he therefore could not lend money to himself. The House of Lords held that 'the company is at law a different person altogether from the subscribers to the memorandum; and though it may be that after incorporation the business is precisely the same as it was before, and the same persons are managers, and the same hands receive the profits, the company is not in law the agent of the subscribers or trustee for them. Nor are the subscribers as members liable in any shape or form ...' (per Lord MacNaughten at p 51). The debentures were therefore valid and Mr Saloman was entitled to repayment.

18.20 The other consequence of incorporation is that the company has perpetual succession. This means that, once incorporated, the company continues to exist notwithstanding changes in its shareholders until it is properly wound up through the legal process of liquidation. This is one of the advantages that the corporate form has over non-incorporated business forms like the general partnership, which generally dissolve should there be a change in its constitution, whether through death, discharge or bankruptcy.

(2) *Looking Behind the Veil of Incorporation*

18.21 The conferment of a separate legal status on the company upon incorporation is often likened to a 'veil of incorporation' that descends to separate the human incorporators from the company. Because this veil shields the shareholders from being liable on the company's debts, there is potential for the corporate form to be abused by persons seeking to avoid their legal obligations and liabilities. Where this is the case, the courts will 'lift the veil' and ignore the separate personality of the company, affixing liability on the wrongdoing shareholders.

18.22 In *Trade Facilities Pte Ltd v Public Prosecutor* (1995), the company was implicated in the sale of adulterated Hennessy XO in genuine Hennessy XO bottles, and was later prosecuted for selling and importing goods to which a trade mark had been falsely applied. Looi owned all but one share in the company and was its sole directing mind and will. On the question whether Looi or the company did the prohibited act, the High Court of Singapore held that as the evidence showed that the company was nothing more than a vehicle that Looi employed as and when it suited him, it was the alter ego of Looi. It would therefore be appropriate to lift the corporate veil and impose liability on Looi. However, the fact that the corporate veil had been lifted did not absolve the company of all liability. As it had allowed itself to be used as a vehicle of Looi's, it was also liable.

18.23 The corporate veil, particularly that which exists between a parent company and its subsidiaries within the same group, is, however, not to be cast aside merely because it would appear just to do so. As the English Court of Appeal explained in *Adams v Cape Industries plc* (1990) (at p 536):

> '... save in cases which turn on the wording of particular statutes or contracts, the court is not free to disregard the principle of *Saloman v A Saloman and Co Ltd* merely because it considers that justice so requires. Our law, for better or worse, recognises the creation of subsidiary companies, which though in one sense the creatures of their parent companies, will nevertheless under the general law fall to be treated as separate legal entities with all the rights and liabilities which would normally attach to separate legal entities.'

How Companies Operate

(1) *Rules of Attribution*

18.24 Although a company has legal existence, its existence is really only a legal fiction. In practical terms, it cannot operate except through human individuals. It is therefore a necessary part of corporate personality that there be 'rules of attribution' to help us ascertain what acts should count as acts of the company. This is necessary for deciding not only what rights a company is entitled to, but also what liabilities it is subject to. There are 'primary' as well as 'general' rules of attribution.

18.25 The primary rules of attribution, as Lord Hoffman explained in *Meridian Global Funds Management Asia Ltd v Securities Commission* (1995), attributes decisions taken by the company's *organs* to the company. The shareholders in general meeting and the board of directors are the two organs of the company, and decisions of each organ (known as *resolutions*) are usually made at *meetings*. The meeting, and its *collective* nature, is therefore the bedrock of corporate decision-making. The constitution of the company, typically the articles of association, lays down the framework by which the company is run internally, including details as to the proper conduct of shareholder as well as directors' meetings. As long as the proper procedure for decision-making by these organs is followed, the company's organs are 'identified' with the company. Decisions made at a general meeting of the shareholders, or at a meeting of the board of directors are then considered decisions of the company.

Decisions are taken by shareholders in general meeting through a process of voting and by a majority of votes. In most cases, a simple majority (ie more than half of the shareholders present and voting) is sufficient to carry the decision, but a higher percentage of majority may be required for certain decisions. A decision to wind up the company, for example, requires a majority of at least 75%. Resolutions that are carried by a simple majority are known as *ordinary* resolutions, whilst resolutions requiring a minimum majority of 75%, passed at a meeting of which not less than 21 days' notice had been given, are known as *special* resolutions (section 184 of the CA). It should be pointed out that it is also possible for a decision of the shareholders to be made *without* a formal meeting, and this occurs when all the shareholders (who are entitled to attend and vote at general meetings) *unanimously* assent to a particular course of action (*Jimat bin Awang v Lai Wee Ngen* (1995) at p 776).

The directors are appointed by the shareholders in general meeting, and together they comprise the board. The board's powers to act as the company is a collective one, ie through a board resolution. Individual directors therefore do not, unless specifically authorised, have the power to bind the company. Directors are generally left to regulate their meetings as they think fit (article 79, Table A of the CA).

18.26 However, it should be obvious that a company does not act *only* through board or shareholder resolutions which, because of the formal requirements for the holding of valid meetings, can be significantly slower and more cumbersome to obtain. It is therefore usual for the company to appoint *agents* to act on its behalf. The *general* rules of attribution, which are the principles of agency, attribute the acts of the agents to the company. These rules, which are also applicable to natural persons, were considered in the preceding chapter. To recapitulate, an individual (the agent), who is actually or apparently authorised to act on behalf of another (the principal), will be able to bind that other if the agent had acted within this actual or apparent authority.

In a similar manner, the company will be bound by the acts of its agents if these agents have been either actually or apparently authorised. However, unlike the comparatively straightforward case of a human individual appointing an agent, an additional question needs to be addressed in the case of the company: whether the company has, by the rules of attribution, taken the decision to *appoint* an agent. The answer is determined both by application of the primary rules of attribution and, somewhat circuitously, also by the general rules of attribution. It is not unusual for the articles of association to provide that the power to make commercial decisions is vested in the board, and further for the board to have the power to *delegate* its functions to one or more of its number. When the power to delegate is exercised by the board, this would be a decision of the company by the *primary* rule of attribution. The director to whom certain functions of the board is delegated is then an authorised agent and when *he* acts to appoint yet other agents, his act will bind the company by the general rules of attribution.

The agency principles, when applied to companies, are additionally affected by the operation of two other company law doctrines, the indoor management rule and the rule of constructive notice. These concepts will be explained in later paragraphs.

(2) *Division of Powers*

18.27 How the company is managed depends on its constitution. Where the articles delegate general managerial powers to the board, the courts have consistently maintained that it is not open to the shareholders in general meeting to intervene in or dictate the exercise of those powers. Thus, although the shareholders are the owners of the company, they cannot countermand what their appointed directors have done which are within the latter's powers, even if they are unhappy with the directors' actions.

In the oft-quoted words of Greer LJ in *John Shaw & Sons (Salford) Ltd v Shaw* (1935), 'if powers of management are vested in the directors, they and they alone can exercise these powers. The only way in which the general body of the shareholders can control the exercise of powers vested by the articles in the directors is by altering their articles, or if opportunity arises under the articles, by refusing to re-elect the directors of whose actions they disapprove. They cannot themselves usurp the powers which by the articles are vested in the directors any more than the directors can usurp the powers vested by the articles in the general body of shareholders ...' (at p 134).

18.28 It is possible for the constitution to specifically reserve the right to manage the company in the shareholders. The question is ultimately one of construction of the particular constitutional provision. In *Credit Development Pte Ltd v IMO Pte Ltd* (1993), the Singapore High Court had to interpret an article which provided as follows:

> 'The business of the company shall be managed by the directors, who may exercise all such powers of the company as are not, by the statutes or by these articles, required to be exercised by the company in general meeting, subject nevertheless ... to such regulations, being not inconsistent with the said provisions and articles, as may be prescribed by the company in general meeting; but no regulation made by the company in general meeting shall invalidate any prior act of the directors which would have been valid if that regulation had not been made.'

Lim Teong Qwee JC held that, on its true construction, the article provided that, in the management of the business of the company, the directors must also comply with such regulations as are prescribed by the shareholders in general meeting, as long as these are not inconsistent with the other articles in the constitution and with legislation.

(3) *Corporate Contracting*

18.29 Two issues inevitably arise when considering the enforceability of contracts purportedly entered into by companies. The first relates to the capacity of the company, as determined by the doctrine of *ultra vires*. This doctrine, as we saw earlier, is no longer as significant as it used to be. The second but more relevant issue relates to the *authority* of the company's *agents* to bind the company.

18.30 As we saw in the preceding discourse, the constitution of a company will usually specify that management of the company is to be in the hands of the board of directors. The board may, and indeed often will, in turn delegate certain decision-making powers to a particular director. The constitution may also specify a particular office—the office of the *managing director* for example—which is authorised to act for the company, and any limitation that is placed on the scope of that officer's authority.

A company's agent may therefore be appointed through a board resolution which delegated board functions to him, or by appointment to a particular office. The actual authority of these agents will depend on the relevant provisions of the constitution, as well as the terms of any board resolution that appointed them. In addition, these agents may *themselves* appoint or employ yet other agents, and the scope of authority of these agents will then depend on their respective contracts of employment.

We saw in the preceding chapter that apparent or ostensible authority is the authority that an agent *appears* to have. Certainly a managing director, by virtue of his appointment to that position, may appear to have more authority than he *actually* has. The doctrine of ostensible authority is premised on principles of estoppel, ie where there is a representation of authority by the principal, which induced a person to alter his position (usually by contracting with the principal through the agent), the principal is estopped from denying that the agent had the requisite authority. It appears that only representations that are made by agents who have *actual* (as opposed to *apparent*) authority from the company will be capable of founding the estoppel against the company.

In the corporate context, the representation by the company may be made by either of the company's organs or by an agent who has been authorised to make representations on the company's behalf. It should be noted that the making of such a representation is *itself* an act of management of the company's business (per Diplock LJ in *Freeman & Lockyer v Buckhurst Park Properties (Mangal) Ltd* (1964) (at p 505)).

The representation may take the form of an appointment to a particular position within the company's hierarchy or the acceptance of or acquiescence to a particular factual state. The facts of *Freeman & Lockyer v Buckhurst Park Properties (Mangal) Ltd* (1964) illustrate this.

The company was a property development company incorporated to buy and resell a large piece of land, the shares of which were held equally by K and H. The board of directors comprised K and H and a nominee of each. Although the company's constitution provided for the appointment of a managing director, none was appointed. H travelled frequently and left the day-to-day management of the company to K. K employed a firm of architects for the purposes of applying for planning permission for the development of the land. When this fell through, the company refused to pay the firm's fees on the grounds that K did not have the authority to appoint it. The court found that the board of directors was aware throughout that K was effectively running the company's affairs on a day-to-day basis. As such, although K did not have the actual authority to appoint the architect as he was never appointed to the office of managing director, he nevertheless had the apparent authority to do so. As Diplock LJ explained (at p 505):

> 'The commonest form of representation by a principal creating an "apparent" authority of an agent is by conduct, namely, by permitting the agent to act in the management or conduct of the principal's business. Thus, if in the case of a company the board of directors who have "actual" authority under the memorandum and articles of association to manage the company's business permit the agent to act in the management or conduct of the company's business, they thereby represent to all persons dealing with such agent that he has authority to enter on behalf of the corporation into contracts of a kind which an agent authorised to do acts of the kind which he is in fact permitted to do usually enters into in the ordinary course of such business.'

18.31 We also saw in the preceding chapter that where the other contracting party is aware of the agent's lack of authority, he will not be able to raise the estoppel against the principal. In the corporate context, the company's constitution may place limitations on the agent's scope of authority. If so, the contracting party seeking to rely on the agent's apparent authority to bind the company will be affected by the doctrine of constructive notice. By this doctrine, third parties are deemed to know the contents of a company's lodged documents even if they had not read the documents. The presumption of notice applies also to *special* resolutions which are, by section 186 of the CA, required to be lodged with the Registrar of Companies within a month after they are passed.

A failure on the part of the third party to check a company's lodged documents before contracting with it might therefore result in the contract being subsequently set aside if those documents contain some limitation on the power of the board or on the authority of the company's representative. The problem is, as Professor Sealy observed, that 'it was not at all a necessary step to reason that, because the law gave everyone the *opportunity* to find out about a company's registered documents, there was a corresponding *duty* to do so ... Businessmen need to make decisions promptly and for them the documents held by the registrar are accessible only at too great a cost in time and trouble' (emphasis in original) (L Sealy, *Cases & Materials in Company Law* (7th ed, 2001) at pp 215–216).

The doctrine is therefore potentially capable of causing significant injustice. Whilst the doctrine has, for this reason, been abolished in the UK (section 711A of the UK Companies Act 1985) and partially abolished in Australia (section 130 of the Corporations Act 2001), it remains very much a part of Singapore's company law.

18.32 However, there is another rule which was developed and operates to ameliorate the injustice that could be caused by the doctrine of constructive notice. This is the rule in *Turquand's* case, also known as the 'indoor management rule'. This rule provides that third parties, who deal with the company in good faith and with no notice of any irregularity, are entitled to assume that matters relating to the internal administration and regulation of the company have been duly complied with. The facts of *Turquand's* case (*Royal British Bank v Turquand* (1856)) itself illustrate this rule. The company had given a bond for £2,000, under the seal of the company and signed by two directors and the secretary, to the plaintiff bank. However, the company, by its constitution, could issue bonds of only such sums as was authorised by the company in general meeting, and it was alleged that no specific resolution had been passed. The court held that a third party, like the plaintiff bank, on reading the company's constitution, 'would find, not a prohibition from borrowing, but a permission to do so on certain conditions. Finding that the authority might be made complete by a resolution, he would have a right to infer the fact of a resolution authorising that which on the face of the document appeared to be legitimately done' (at p 332). Thus, as all that was required to authorise the borrowing was an *ordinary* resolution, which unlike a special resolution does not have to be lodged with the Registry, the doctrine of constructive notice would not apply and the third party was entitled to assume that the resolution had been properly obtained.

Directors

(1) *General*

18.33 Every company (except the proposed single-member company) must have at least two directors, one of whom is ordinarily resident in Singapore (section 145 of the CA). The first directors are to be named in the company's constitution, and later directors are usually elected by the shareholders in general meeting, which will also fix their remuneration (articles 66 and 70, Table A). The general meeting is also conferred the power to remove any director by an ordinary resolution (article 69, Table A).

18.34 We have already been introduced to the managing director, who would be an *executive* director. Executive directors are the working directors of the company, and they are frequently appointed pursuant to service contracts. They are, in addition to holding the *office* of director, in effect *employees* of the company. A removal of a director prior to the end of his contractual term, even if done in accordance with the provisions of the constitution, could amount to a breach of the service contract (*Southern Foundries (1926) Ltd v Shirlaw* (1940)).

18.35 Non-executive (or outside) directors are directors without more and thus do not hold a managing or executive position in the company. They are therefore not involved in the day-to-day running of the company's affairs. Non-executive directors play an important role in corporate governance as independent monitors of management decisions in *public* companies.

(2) *Directors' Obligations and Duties*

18.36 Directors owe a number of duties to the company. These duties are found, not only in the rules of common law and equity, but also in the terms of any extrinsic contract with the company, and in the provisions of the CA. In addition, the CA, as well as the regulations promulgated under it, contain many requirements and rules with which the directors have to comply.

18.37 The law does not draw any distinction between the executive and the non-executive director for the purposes of imposing duties on them, although the standard of skill, care and diligence expected of an executive director is likely to be higher than that expected of a non-executive director.

18.38 The area of directors' duties is not an easy area of company law, not least of all because of the overlapping common law, equitable and statutory rules. In fact, there are many unresolved issues beyond the scope of this chapter but which will become patent on reading the specialist texts on company law. It is with the stated objective of clarifying this area of the law, and making the principles more accessible to the ordinary director, that UK's Company Law Review Steering Group, tasked with looking into the reform of UK's company law, proposed the enactment of an all-inclusive statement of directors' duties. The CLRFC is recommending that Singapore adopt UK's draft restatement, subject to such adaptation as are necessary (Recommendation 3.6). In the words of the CLRFC, 'the enactment of these general principles, bolstered by statutory remedies to enforce directors' duties, will form the bedrock of directors' duties, which would continue to be amenable to evolution through case law'. The ensuing paragraphs introduce the directors' duties as they *currently* stand. The proposed restatement is meant to *codify* the existing duties, and as such, does not alter the *substance* of these obligations and duties.

(a) Equitable and Fiduciary Duties

18.39 Directors have wide management powers conferred on them, and as such, stand not only in a position of trust and responsibility *vis-à-vis* the company, but also in a position of considerable power and control. The law therefore obliges the directors, as a collegiate body, to exercise the powers conferred on them in good faith and in the company's interests. In addition, the law treats the director as being in a *fiduciary* relationship with the company. Being a fiduciary obliges the director, as an individual, to always place the company's interests *ahead* of his own.

18.40 The basic equitable duty owed by the directors is to act *bona fide* in what they believe (and not what a court may consider) to be in the interests of the company. But with whom should the 'company' be identified for the purposes of ascertaining its interests in this context? Other than most obviously the shareholders, present and future, there are other stakeholders in the company whose interests might be of relevance and should be considered. The claims of the company's employees, for example, are recognised legislatively (section 159 of the CA). The proposed restatement requires the director to 'act in the way he decides, in good faith, would be most likely to promote the success of the company for the benefit of its members as a whole' but allows the director to 'take into account in good faith of all the material factors that it is practicable in the circumstances for him to identify', including matters such as the company's need to foster its business relationships and its need to maintain a reputation for high standards of business conduct.

A corresponding duty requires the directors to exercise the powers conferred on them for proper and not collateral purposes.

A breach of the director's equitable duties will entitle the company to equitable compensation.

18.41 As a fiduciary, the director owes a strict duty of loyalty to the company. There are two aspects to this duty. First, he must not allow his personal interest to come into conflict with the company's interest, and secondly, he must not make a profit out of his position unless the informed consent of the company has been obtained.

A conflict of interests is present if, in any transaction to which the company is party, the director has an interest *adverse* to, or different from, that of the company. In the absence of disclosure, the company may avoid the transaction. Thus, a director cannot, without full disclosure, enter into a contract with the company, or cause the company to enter into a transaction if he has an interest in that contract. This rule is supplemented statutorily by an obligation to disclose on pain of criminal penalties (section 156 of the CA). The articles will usually also require the interested director to abstain from voting on the transaction (article 81, Table A).

Interestingly, and somewhat inconsistently, directors are permitted, as a general rule, to serve on the boards of more than one company at a time, and even to compete with the company on their own account (*London & Mashonaland Explorations Co Ltd v New Mashonaland Exploration Co Ltd* (1891)). Whilst this position was assumed correct by Lord Blanesburgh in *Bell v Lever Bros Ltd* (1932) (at p 195), many company law commentators (see, eg PL Davies, *Gower's Company Law* (6th ed, 1997), p 622) have expressed doubt over its correctness. In the recent UK Court of Appeal decision of *Plus Group Ltd and Others v Pyke* (2002), Sedley LJ opined that 'if one bears in mind the high standard of probity which equity demands of fiduciaries, and the reliance which shareholders and creditors are entitled to place upon it, the *Mashonaland* principle is a very limited one' (at paragraph 84). Clearly, there is nothing objectionable about competing with the company (whether as a director on the board of a competing company or on the director's own account) if the director concerned had disclosed and obtained the company's consent. The question is whether consent is *likely* to be given. For further reading on this topic, see M Christie, 'The Director's Fiduciary Duty Not to Compete' (1992) 55 *Modern Law Review* 506.

The no-profit rule prohibits the director from making a secret profit out of his office, and he cannot divert corporate contracts or business opportunities meant for the company to himself. This rule is strictly applied, even if the director had acted in good faith and for the benefit of the company because 'liability arises from the mere fact of a profit having, in the circumstances, been made' (per Lord Russell in *Regal (Hastings) Ltd v Gulliver* (1942) at p 386).

The company is entitled to ask for an account of the profits made by the director in breach of his fiduciary duties.

(b) The Duty of Skill, Care and Diligence

18.42 Directors are expected to exercise, when performing their functions as directors, at least that level of skill, care and diligence that might reasonably be expected of any director occupying a similar position. The standards may be further elevated if the director in question possessed specific qualifications or expertise.

(3) *Enforcement of Directors' Duties*

18.43 Directors owe their duties to the company and not to individual shareholders (*Percival v Wright* (1902)). Breach of a common law or equitable duty owed to the company is therefore a civil wrong against the company, and enforceable only by the company. The power to commence and conduct litigation in the name of the company is generally considered a management power and therefore vested in the board of directors. However, where the board as a whole has committed a wrong against the company, the power to call the directors to account must rightly revert to the company in general meeting, where the decision rests with the majority.

18.44 There is an alternative procedure for the redress of a corporate wrong, including a breach of directors' duties, which may be commenced by an *individual* shareholder. This is the statutory derivative action under section 216A of the CA.

Section 216A lays down a *procedure* by which a shareholder, or other 'proper person', may apply to court for leave to commence an action in the name of the company. To convince the court, the applicant bears the burden of showing not only that he is acting in good faith, but also that it is *prima facie* in the interests of the company that the action be brought. In recognition of the fact that the course of action is a corporate one, the applicant must have first given notice to the company's board of directors of his intention to bring the action. This gives the board, acting as the company, the opportunity to take over the action itself.

It should be pointed out that the section 216A procedure is available only in respect of *unlisted* companies.

Relationship Between Shareholders

(1) *Statutory Contract*

18.45 The relationship between the shareholders of a company is governed by the constitution. Pursuant to section 39 of the CA, the constitution takes effect as a *contract* which binds the company and the shareholders as if it had been 'signed and sealed by each member and contained covenants on the part of each member to observe all the provisions' of the constitution.

18.46 This 'contract' is however unlike the normal contract that is dealt with in the other chapters of this book. First, it is alterable by special resolution, which as we saw earlier, requires only a three-fourths majority, not unanimity, so that the alteration takes effect even if there are members who do not agree. Second, the cases have held that this statutory contract binds members *qua members* only. What this means is that the 'contract' can only be relied upon to enforce what are properly *members'* rights, and not other non-member or outsider rights. In *Beattie v E & F Beattie Ltd* (1938), for example, a director was sued for the return of certain sums that had allegedly been improperly paid to him. As he was also a member of the company, he sought, relying on a clause contained in the articles of association, to refer the dispute to arbitration. The court, however, held that as the dispute had arisen in his capacity as a director and not in his capacity as a member, he could not rely on the 'contract' comprised in the articles.

(2) *Majority Rule and Protection of the Minority*

18.47 We saw earlier that decisions are made for the company by either of its two organs on the basis of the majority vote. Whilst the director's vote is controlled by strict fiduciary duties, there are no such constraints on the shareholder's vote. As Dixon J of the High Court of Australia explained, 'shareholders are not trustees for one another, and, unlike directors, they occupy no fiduciary position and are under no fiduciary duties. They vote in respect of their shares, which are property, and the right to vote is attached to the share itself as an incident of property to be enjoyed and exercised for the owner's personal advantage' (see *Peter's American Delicacy Co Ltd v Heath* (1939) at p 504).

The shareholders who control the majority of the votes in a company therefore wield substantial power in the company which is likely to be run in accordance with their wishes. Indeed, this must naturally be so as the majority's control is a result of the correspondingly higher investment that it has made in the company. The greater say therefore comes at a higher price. The shareholders who fall in the minority must generally accept this as a fact of commercial life.

Acknowledging this, however, does not mean that the minority has to accept unfair or wrongful acts that result from abuses of the majority power, opportunity for which clearly exists. Attempts have been made, both legislatively and judicially, to achieve some balance between the opposing interests of the majority and the minority. In this chapter, we consider in brief the duty imposed on the majority, in seeking to alter the company's constitution, to vote *bona fide* for the benefit of the company as a whole, and the oppression action under section 216 of the CA.

18.48 The relationship between the members and their rights *inter se* are usually governed by the company's constitution. But, as we saw earlier, it is possible for the provisions of the constitution to be altered with a three-fourths majority. The opportunity thus exists for such a majority to alter the constitution to improve their position at the expense of the minority. The courts have therefore laid down the rule that the power to alter the constitution must be exercised *bona fide* for the benefit of the company as a whole (*Allen v Gold Reefs of West Africa Ltd* (1900)).

In *Allen v Gold Reefs of West Africa Ltd*, the company's articles gave it a lien (which is a security interest) for all debts and liabilities of any member 'upon all shares (not being fully paid) held by such member'. Z owed the company money and was the only holder of fully- paid shares. An alteration was made to the articles to give the company a lien over fully-paid shares as well. The court held that the alteration was valid. Although Z was at the time of the alteration the only holder of paid-up shares, the alteration applied to *all* holders of fully-paid shares and did not distinguish amongst them. Since the alteration would allow the company to recover moneys owing to it, it was made *bona fide* for the benefit of the company.

There are, however, difficulties with the application of the test, and these were pointed out by the Australian High Court in *Peter's American Delicacy Co Ltd v Heath* (1939). Dixon J explained (at p 512):

> 'If the challenged alteration relates to an article which does or may affect an individual, as, for instance, a director appointed for life or a shareholder whom it is desired to expropriate or to an article affecting the mutual rights and liabilities *inter se* of shareholders or different classes or descriptions of shareholders, the very subject matter involves a conflict of interests and advantages. To say that the shareholders forming the majority must consider the advantage of the company as a whole in relation to such a question seems inappropriate, if not meaningless...'

In view of these application difficulties, the CLRFC is recommending that the common law position be restated legislatively.

18.49 Legislatively, section 216 of the CA gives any member the right to petition to court if the affairs of the company are being conducted in a manner that is oppressive or in disregard of his interests, or some act of the company has been done or is being threatened that unfairly discriminates against him, or is otherwise prejudicial to him. In the Privy Council decision (on appeal from the Federal Court of Malaysia) of *Re Kong Thai Sawmill (Miri) Sdn Bhd* (1978), Lord Wilberforce made the following comments (at p 229):

> '[T]he mere fact that one or more of those managing the company possess a majority of the voting power and, in reliance on that power, make policy or executive decisions, with which the complainant does not agree, is not enough. Those who take interests in companies limited by shares have to accept majority rule. It is only when majority rule passes over into rule oppressive of the minority, or in disregard of their interests, that the section can be invoked ... [T]here must be a visible departure from the standards of fair dealing and a violation of the conditions of fair play which a shareholder is entitled to expect before a case of oppression can be made ... And similarly "disregard" involves something more than a failure to take account of the minority's interest: there must be awareness of that interest and an evident decision to override it or brush it aside or to set at naught the proper company procedure ....'

His Lordships' comments have been adopted and followed in *Re Gee Hoe Chan Trading Co Pte Ltd* (1991) and *Low Peng Boon v Low Janie* (1999).

In *Low Peng Boon v Low Janie*, the Singapore Court of Appeal observed that the court's discretionary power to make an appropriate order is unfettered and that each case has to be considered on its own merits.

Non-Corporate Business Organisations

Sole Proprietorships

18.50 The sole proprietorship is essentially a business that is owned and managed by one person, the proprietor. Apart from the requirement for the registration of the business name under the Business Registration Act (Cap 32, 2001 Rev Ed), there are no other formalities that need to be complied with in the creation of a sole proprietorship. The debts of the business are really the debts of the person, for which the sole proprietor is personally liable, without limit. There is also no legal process for the business to carry on following the sole proprietor's incapacity or death.

The main advantage of the sole proprietorship as a form of business structure is the flexibility that accompanies its operation. This results not only from the relative lack of formal requirements, but also from the fact that the sole proprietor is the only person in control. The necessary corollary to this latter point, however, is that he has to rely primarily on himself to finance his business.

Partnerships

(1) *General Partnership*

18.51 Partnership is the associative relationship that subsists between two or more persons carrying on a business in common with a view to profit (section 1 of the Partnership Act (Cap 391, 1994 Rev Ed)). It is essentially a *contractual* relationship, as it involves an agreement between and amongst the partners. The contract of partnership may be created by an express agreement, or it may be inferred from the parties' course of dealings. The partners have considerable freedom in deciding how to regulate their relationship with each other. Whilst the Partnership Act contains rules as to the interests of partners in the partnership property and their rights and duties in relation to the partnership, these rules are mostly subject to the agreement between the partners.

18.52 The law does not recognise the partnership firm as having any collective legal personality. Consequently, 'partners carry on business both as principals and as agents for each other within the scope of the partnership business' (per Farwell LJ in *Sadler v Whiteman* (1910) at p 889).

(a) Dealings with Third Parties

18.53 Section 5 of the Partnership Act provides that every partner is an agent of the other partners and of the partnership. Thus, such acts of his as are 'for the carrying on in the usual way business of the kind carried on by the firm' will bind the firm and all the partners. Where the partners have agreed to restrict the authority of individual partners, the restriction does not affect the partners' liability to outside parties unless the restriction was made known to the outside parties (section 8 of the Partnership Act).

(b) Unlimited Personal Liability of Partners

18.54 Whilst the partners may agree amongst themselves that the liability of one or more of them shall be limited, this remains an agreement between the partners only and does not affect outsiders. By section 9 of the Partnership Act, the partners remain jointly liable for all debts and obligations of the firm.

(c) Dissolution

18.55 The partnership, like the sole proprietorship, does not enjoy perpetual succession, as it has no legal existence of its own. The partnership is dissolved automatically if a partner dies, leaves or retires.

(2) *Limited Partnership*

18.56 Unlike a general partnership, there are two classes of partners in a limited partnership: general partners and limited partners. General partners are, like the partners in a general partnership, liable for all debts and obligations of the firm whilst limited partners, who contribute to the partnership's capital and share in its profits, are not liable beyond the amount contributed. Limited partners have no right to participate in the management of the firm and cannot bind the firm.

18.57 The CLRFC is recommending that the limited partnership be introduced in Singapore to widen the menu of business vehicles available. It is recommended that the Singapore Limited Partnership Act be modelled after the UK Limited Partnerships Act 1907.

(3) *Limited Liability Partnerships*

18.58 The limited liability partnership ('LLP') is a hybrid creature. Its partners enjoy limited liability and the LLP is conferred separate legal status. It is, however, treated as a partnership for tax purposes and the internal relations between the partners are governed by agreement. There is also no requirement for the public filing of financial statements.

18.59 Although the UK has recently enacted the Limited Liability Partnerships Act 2000, the CLRFC's recommendation is that Singapore adopts, subject to appropriate adaptations, the US Delaware Revised Uniform Partnership Act as the base model.

PART V

The Law of Tort

CHAPTER 19 Negligence

PARAGRAPHS

19.1–19.3 **Introduction**

19.4 **Elements of Negligence: Introduction**

Elements of Negligence (1): The Duty of Care

19.5 Introduction

19.6–19.10 The Beginning: The 'Neighbour Principle'

Liability for Pure Economic Loss: Development, Complexity and a Suggested Resolution

19.11–19.13 (1) Public Policy Test

19.14 (2) The Test of 'Foreseeability Including Policy'

19.15–19.16 (3) The 'Two-Stage Test'

19.17 (4) The 'Two-Stage Test' and Liability for Nervous Shock or Psychiatric Harm

19.18 (5) Coherence of the 'Two-Stage Test'

19.19 (6) Decline of the 'Two-Stage Test'

19.20 (7) The 'Three-Part Test'

19.21 (8) An Unwarranted Critique of the 'Two-Stage Test'

19.22–19.24 (9) The Elusiveness of 'Proximity'

19.25–19.26 (10) What Does 'Fair, Just and Reasonable' Mean?

19.27 19.32 (11) Position in Singapore

19.33–19.34 (12) Summing-Up

19.35–19.40 (13) Liability for Negligent Misstatements Under the Rule in Hedley Byrne

19.41 (14) Recovery of Economic Loss Consequential Upon Physical Injury or Damage

19.42–19.45 **Elements of Negligence (2): Breach of the Duty of Care**

Elements of Negligence (3): Causation, Remoteness and Mitigation

19.46–19.48 Causation

19.49–19.50 Remoteness of Damage

PARAGRAPHS

Elements of Negligence (3): Causation, Remoteness and Mitigation (continued)

19.51 Mitigation of Damage
19.52–19.53 Proof of Negligence and the Doctrine of *Res Ipsa Loquitur*
19.54 'Thin Skull Rule'

Defences

19.55–19.56 Illegality
19.57–19.58 Voluntary Assumption of Risk
19.59 Contributory Negligence

Negligence and Cyberspace

19.60–19.61 Introduction
Computer Viruses and Negligence
19.62–19.67 (1) Establishing a Duty of Care
19.68 (2) Establishing the Requisite Standard of Care
19.69 (3) Potential Problems of Causation
19.70 (4) Potential Problems of Remoteness of Damage
19.71 (5) When is the Defence of Contributory Negligence Available?
19.72 (6) When is the Defence of Assumption of Risk Available?
Negligent Misstatements in Cyberspace
19.73 (1) Application of General Principles
19.74 (2) Negligent Misstatements and Hyperlinking

19.75 **Conclusion**

Introduction

19.1 Many legal difficulties and liability arise principally in that general area of law known as the law of contract. The law of contract, however, relates to legal relations arising from *a valid agreement* between the parties to the contract concerned. On the other hand, many potential legal difficulties arise between persons who are *not* in a contractual relationship with each other. This can arise, for example, where the defendant manufactures a defective product which is later sold by the retailer to the plaintiff consumer. The plaintiff suffers damage as a result of the defective product. The consumer has no contractual relationship with the defendant manufacturer, although it would have one with the retailer. The plaintiff might decide to sue the manufacturer. It cannot do so in contract. Does the law offer it an alternative cause of action? Another common instance is when the defendant casts negative aspersions on its plaintiff rival's products. Such aspersions are wholly unfounded and the plaintiff suffers a loss of business as a result. The two—being rivals —do not (unsurprisingly) have a contractual relationship with each other. Does the plaintiff have a cause of action outside the law of contract?

The law ought, and does, give legal redress in appropriate circumstances in the situations just mentioned. The principal avenue through which the law gives such redress is through the law of *tort*. A tort is, basically put, *a civil wrong*. A breach of contract is also a civil wrong but necessarily involves a valid legal contract, whereas the law of tort does not contain such a requirement. The most important tort is, not surprisingly, that of *negligence*. In the first situation mentioned above, there could be possible liability if the defective product was the result of negligence on the part of the manufacturer. Liability in negligence can—as we shall see—also extend to *words* as well, in the context of negligent *misstatements*. However, as we shall also see, problems of potential 'floodgates' of liability also arise, particularly in relation to pure economic loss.

There are also *other* torts that are relevant to the business context. For example, the second situation mentioned above may result in possible legal liability in *malicious falsehood* (which is considered in Chapter 20). The present chapter considers the tort of negligence, whilst other relevant business torts are dealt with in the next chapter.

19.2 It should also be noted that there may be a possible *overlap* between tortious and contractual liability. There might, for example, be the breach of a *contractual* duty to take care which might simultaneously constitute the breach of a duty to take care in *tortious* negligence. It has been clearly established, however, that where there is *concurrent* liability in contract and tort, the plaintiff ought generally to avail itself of its contractual cause of action in the first instance (see, for example, the leading House of Lords decision of *Henderson v Merrett Syndicates Ltd* (1995)).

On the other hand, there could be the mounting of both contractual *and* tortious causes of action *simultaneously*. For example, the plaintiff could mount an action in tort for deceit or negligent misstatement (as the case may be; and see paragraphs 12.27–12.29 and 12.30–12.34 as well as paragraphs 19.35–19.40, respectively) *as well as* for breach of a misrepresentation that has *become a term of the contract* (and see above, paragraph 12.4). Logically and commonsensically, of course, there can be no double-recovery as such.

19.3 An extremely brief word about *vicarious liability* may also be appropriate at this juncture. Under this particular doctrine, an employer will be held *vicariously* responsible or liable for torts (including, for example, negligence) committed by its employee in the course of its (the employee's) employment. Hence, for example, a company will be vicariously liable for the negligence of its employee which is committed during the course of his or her employment. Where, however, the tortfeasor (the person responsible for the tort) is not an employee but an independent contractor, obviously no vicarious liability will result. On a practical level, the issue of vicarious liability is an important one as it will—more often than not—be the employer who will have 'deeper pockets' and who will therefore be a more 'attractive' defendant compared to the employee who actually committed the tort that gave rise to the cause of action in the first place. And, of course, the doctrine of vicarious liability would—by its very (general) nature—also be relevant to *all* torts and is not confined to negligence only.

It is by no means easy to ascertain whether the tortfeasor is an employee or an independent contractor. The usual rubric is to distinguish between a contract *of* service (in which case the tortfeasor would be considered an employee) and a contract *for* services (in which case the tortfeasor would be considered an independent contractor). However, on a practical level, there are many factors that need to be taken into account. One oft-cited factor is that of the degree of control by the employer, although it is by no means conclusive. In the English decision of *Market Investigations Ltd v Minister of Social Security* (1969), for example, Cooke J observed (at pp 184–185) thus:

> 'No exhaustive list has been compiled and perhaps no exhaustive list can be compiled of the considerations which are relevant ..., nor can strict rules be laid down as to the relative weight which the various considerations should carry in particular cases. The most that can be said is that control will no doubt always have to be considered, although it can no longer be regarded as the sole determining factor; and that factors which may be of importance are such matters as whether the man performing the services provides his own equipment, whether he hires his own helpers, what degree of financial risk he takes, what degree of responsibility for investment and management he has, and whether and how far he has an opportunity of profiting from sound management in the performance of his task.
>
> The application of the general test may be easier in a case where the person who engages himself to perform the services does so in the course of an already established business of his own; but this factor is not decisive, and a person who engages

himself to perform services for another may well be an independent contractor even though he has not entered into any contract in the course of an existing business carried on by him.'

However, no failsafe, universal test exists and much would depend on the facts of the case concerned; see *Clerk & Lindsell on Torts* (18th ed, 2000) at paragraph 5-11. See also, for general accounts, *Clerk & Lindsell on Torts*, ibid, at Chapter 5 as well as M Brazier and J Murphy, *Street on Torts* (10th ed, 1999) at Chapter 25.

The reader is also referred to section 5 of the Government Proceedings Act (Cap 121, 1985 Rev Ed) insofar as the liability of the government in tort is concerned.

Elements of Negligence: Introduction

19.4 There are, traditionally, three elements that, taken together, constitute the tort of negligence. In order to establish the defendant's liability in negligence, the plaintiff has, *first*, to demonstrate that the defendant owed a *duty of care* to the plaintiff.

Secondly, the plaintiff must prove that the defendant had *breached* that duty of care.

Thirdly, the plaintiff must prove that he had suffered *damage or loss* as a result of the breach of the duty of care. It should, however, be noted that there are constraints on the scope of recovery. As in the parallel situation in the law of contract, for example (see above, paragraph 15.68 ff), damages recoverable under the tort of negligence are also subject to rules of *remoteness of damage* (although the precise rules themselves would, of course, differ; see, generally, paragraphs 19.49–19.50, below). There are also issues with respect to *causation* as well as *mitigation of damage* (as to which see, generally, below, paragraphs 19.46–19.48 and 19.51, respectively).

We turn now to consider these various elements in turn.

Elements of Negligence (1): The Duty of Care

Introduction

19.5 This is the logical starting-point, for without the existence of a duty of care in the first place, there can be no breach of that duty which gives rise to tortious liability upon the proof of tangible damage to the plaintiff. However, as we shall see, although the initial contours of the concept of the duty of care were fairly clear and straightforward, the present law is more than moderately complex. This is due, in no small part, to the fact that as plaintiffs began to sue for recovery for alleged negligence in the context of *pure economic loss*, it became increasingly difficult (and some would even say, impossible) to draw clear and intelligible lines that would enable the court concerned to either impose or not impose legal liability. As we shall see, this is due, in large part, to the fact that, *unlike* a situation involving *physical* damage, the potential scope for liability insofar as pure economic loss is concerned is far too broad.

As we briefly trace the history as well as principles with regard to the duty of care, it would be appropriate at this juncture to pay tribute to the excellent overview by Professor KF Tan in his article entitled 'The Three-Part Test: Yet Another Test of Duty in Negligence' (1989) 31 *Malaya Law Review* 223. It is true that, owing to its vintage, some updating is required. However, this article does lay down a very clear and perceptive foundation and what follows owes much to the insightful analysis contained therein—although the present writer's views (particularly with regard to the *underlying reasons for the complexity of the present law*) will also be evident throughout.

The Beginning: The 'Neighbour Principle'

19.6 The modern law of negligence, whilst having a rather chequered history to date, is not, in fact, of very ancient vintage by any means. It took a lengthy period of time before the famous *'neighbour principle'*, first formulated by Lord Atkin in the seminal House of Lords decision of *Donoghue v Stevenson* in 1932, emerged—a development that literally revolutionised the law in England by establishing what was, in essence, a completely new (and potentially wide-ranging) tort. Lord Atkin himself observed (at p 580) as follows:

> 'The rule that you are to love your neighbour becomes in law, you must not injure your neighbour; and the lawyer's question, Who is my neighbour? receives a restricted reply. You must take reasonable care to avoid acts or omissions which you can reasonably foresee would be likely to injure your neighbour. Who, then, in law is my neighbour? The answer seems to be – persons who are so closely and directly affected by my act that I ought reasonably to have them in contemplation as being so affected when I am directing my mind to the acts or omissions which are called in question.'

It is of interest to note that the actual decision in *Donoghue v Stevenson* was decided by a 3-2 majority, which is perhaps not surprising in view of the seminal nature of the case itself. Nevertheless, one ought also to note Lord Macmillan's observation (at p 619) that '[t]he categories of negligence are never closed'. Indeed, as we shall see, this particular decision marked only the beginning of some very interesting, albeit complex and even confusing, developments ahead.

19.7 Professor Tan classifies Lord Atkin's 'neighbour principle' as embodying a '*pure foreseeability* test' (see, generally, above, paragraph 19.5 at pp 224–226), although, as we shall see, it is arguable that it might be narrower in scope (see paragraph 19.21, below, and see the critique of an overly broad reading as well as application of *Donoghue v Stevenson* (1932) in JC Smith and P Burns, 'Donoghue v. Stevenson—The Not So Golden Anniversary' (1983) 46 *Modern Law Review* 147). As the learned author argues, such a test is of course entirely appropriate insofar as *physical* damage is concerned (and cf per GP Selvam JC (as he then was) in the Singapore High Court decision of *Swiss Singapore Overseas Enterprise Pte Ltd v Horng*

Chang Enterprise Pte Ltd (1993) at p 486, where the learned judge observed that '*Donoghue v Stevenson* was concerned with biological injury and not economic loss for which the law does not afford a comprehensive remedy in tort'). In other words, there is little, or no, danger of opening the 'floodgates' of legal liability in such a situation. The very *nature* of physical damage itself necessarily limits the scope of liability: persons/ plaintiffs who could be foreseen to have been adversely impacted by the breach of a duty of care on the part of the defendant would, of course, naturally be limited to those who had actually suffered the physical harm or damage. There would, in other words (and in the famous words of that great American judge, Cardozo CJ, in *Ultramares Corporation v Touche* (1931)) not be the danger of 'liability in an indeterminate amount for an indeterminate time to an indeterminate class' (see p 444) (although cf the observation of Lord Buckmaster, *dissenting* in the seminal decision of *Donoghue v Stevenson* (1932), observing, *inter alia* (at p 577): 'If one step, why not fifty?'). In the House of Lords decision *Hedley Byrne & Co Ltd v Heller & Partners Ltd* (1964), Lord Pearce observed (at p 534) that '[d]amage by negligent acts to persons or property ... is more visible and obvious; its limits are more easily defined, and it is with this damage that the earlier cases were more concerned' (reference may also be made to p 536). And, in the House of Lords decision of *Murphy v Brentwood District Council* (1991), Lord Oliver of Aylmerton observed (at pp 486-487) thus (and reference may also be made to the learned Law Lord's observations in *Caparo Industries Plc v Dickman* (1990) at p 632):

> 'In the *straightforward case* of the direct infliction of *physical injury* by the act of the plaintiff there is, indeed, *no need to look beyond the foreseeability of the defendant* of the result in order to establish that he is in a "proximate" relationship with the plaintiff' (emphasis added).

In summary, the 'neighbour principle' enunciated by Lord Atkin in the preceding paragraph and which, in effect, mandates a test of foreseeability would be eminently suitable in a situation where *physical* damage or harm was concerned (though cf the argument that this 'neighbour principle' actually focuses on the concept of *proximity* instead; see paragraph 19.21, below).

19.8 *However*, the House of Lords decision in *Marc Rich & Co AG v Bishop Rock Marine Co Ltd* (1996) suggests that even in a situation involving physical injury or damage, mere foreseeability is insufficient to establish liability in negligence (at least where the physical injury or damage is *indirect*), and that the concept of proximity as well as the requirement that liability be 'fair, just and reasonable' are also relevant (this is in fact the application of the 'three-part test' considered at paragraph 19.20, below). Indeed, in this case, the court held—in the context of an action against a classification society in the shipping context—that it would, the presence of physical damage notwithstanding, not be fair, just and reasonable to impose a duty of care on the defendant, having regard to the broader context (but see the powerful dissent by Lord Lloyd of Berwick (who was of the view (at p 230) that '[a]ll that is required [was] a straightforward application of *Donoghue v Stevenson*') as well as the equally powerful critique by KF Tan (see 'Of Duty' (1996) 112 *Law Quarterly Review* 209), where alternative approaches are also canvassed; and cf the English Court of Appeal decision of *Perrett v Collins* (1998), where the *Marc Rich* case was sought to be distinguished).

19.9 The 'pure foreseeability test' does *not*, however, work as well in a situation where *non*-physical damage or harm is involved. In particular, where *pure economic loss* is concerned, *the potential spread of liability is enormous and, to all intents and purposes in some situations at least, virtually unlimited.* In other words, the danger referred to by Cardozo CJ at paragraph 19.7, above, would have been realised—in spades.

A vivid illustration of the enormity of the problem may be seen in the facts of an oft-cited decision which occurred relatively earlier on in the development of the principles relating to pure economic loss, that of the English Court of Appeal in *Spartan Steel & Alloys Ltd v Martin & Co (Contractors) Ltd* (1973), where the facts were as follows. The defendants' employees, whilst digging up a road, negligently damaged an electric cable which resulted in the cut-off of electricity supply to the plaintiffs' factory. Although the court allowed the plaintiffs to recover damages for the loss of profit resulting from physical damage to the plaintiffs' product, it did *not* allow recovery for pure economic loss (comprising the further profit that could have been made but for the cut-off of the electricity supply but which was economic loss independent of the physical damage). Interestingly, Edmund Davies LJ (as he then was) dissented, preferring to utilise the much broader test of pure foreseeability instead, which is clearly too wide as we shall see in the very next paragraph.

19.10 It can be readily seen, therefore, how the application of the 'pure foreseeability test' could result in an almost geometric increase in the defendant's potential liability in the situation of *pure economic loss* (as opposed to physical damage). It could, of course, be argued that there is nothing wrong in this inasmuch as if the defendant could have reasonably foreseen that its actions could have caused damage to others, then it ought, in principle, to be liable to every such person. However, it could also be argued that the concept of reasonable foreseeability takes liability 'too far afield' and that it is unfair for the defendant to be held legally liable simply because it ought—on an objective test or basis—to have foreseen that the plaintiffs concerned could have been adversely impacted by its actions and that this is all the more so where pure economic loss—as opposed to physical damage or harm—is concerned. Simply put, the net cast is simply too wide to be fair insofar as the defendant is concerned. The ideal approach, of course, is to strike a *balance*. But, herein lies the nub of the problem or dilemma. *How and where is one to draw the line?* The present writer suggests that if the reader constantly bears in mind this question, then he or she would have far fewer difficulties deciphering what is, with respect, the somewhat convoluted actions of the courts in the paragraphs that follow. *Put simply,* *what the courts have sought to achieve is a balance between justice or fairness to the plaintiff on the one hand and justice or fairness to the defendant on the other. However, in attempting to strike this balance, the courts have, unfortunately, generated more confusion than clarity. It is submitted that if we bear this central thesis of sorts constantly in mind, we would be able to understand better why the law is so complex. In a nutshell, it is so complex simply because the courts have not yet been able to locate an ideal approach that comes even close to achieving the balance just referred to.*

With these caveats in mind, we can now proceed to consider briefly the development of the concept of the duty of care insofar as pure economic loss—as opposed to physical damage or harm—is concerned. It should, however, be mentioned at this juncture that the reader who wants an overview of what the position in Singapore is and what the writer's own views are with regard to this extremely complex area of the law can bypass the discussion of the various stages, concepts and difficulties that follows and go straight to paragraphs 19.27–19.30 and 19.33–19.34, respectively. Indeed, two summary charts of both the general position as well as the position in Singapore are also to be located at paragraph 19.34, below.

Liability for Pure Economic Loss: Development, Complexity and a Suggested Resolution

(1) *Public Policy Test*

19.11 We have, in fact, already briefly considered the *Spartan Steel* case (1973) (see paragraph 19.9, above). Lord Denning MR adopted the view that liability in negligence for pure economic loss is simply a question of *public policy* (and see Professor Tan's article at paragraph 19.5 at pp 226-229). The learned Master of the Rolls observed thus (at p 37; and cf per Lawton LJ at p 49):

> 'The more I think about these cases, the more difficult I find it to put each into its proper pigeon-hole. Sometimes I say: "There was no duty." In others I say: "The damage was too remote." So much so that I think the time has come to discard those tests which have proved so elusive. It seems to me better to consider the particular relationship in hand, and see whether or not, *as a matter of policy*, economic loss should be recoverable, or not.'

It is not in the least surprising that this approach of public policy has not found favour with the English (and, presumably, Singapore) courts. At this point, it is important to emphasise the fact that both English and Singapore courts basically share the same legal culture (and see, generally, Chapter 1), which is, in fact, one that emphasises the importance of *rules*. It is far more *formal* in nature, the underlying idea being that any recourse to the more nebulous creature of public policy would result, necessarily, in the conferment of excessive discretion on judges and the courts—with such discretion leading, presumably, to arbitrariness and the undermining of the very idea of the rule of law itself. However, whilst one ought indeed to guard against the conferment of excessive judicial discretion, one ought also to be careful about not swinging it too far, as it were, in the opposite direction. The exercise of judicial discretion is an inevitable and integral part of the legal landscape. More importantly, one cannot satisfactorily resolve legal issues without, on most occasions at least, recourse to the *extra*-legal factors that are an integral part of public policy. To put it another way, recourse to legal rules—*and legal rules alone*—will never enable courts to arrive at substantively fair outcomes. This is due, in no small part, to the fact that the very concept of substantive fairness or justice—so much, it should be added, a part of the purpose of the law in general and the purpose of the law of negligence in particular—entails a consideration of the *values underlying the legal rules themselves*.

19.12 It is true, however, that one popular conception is that legal principles lie more appropriately within the province of the *courts*, whereas policy lies more appropriately within the province of the *legislature* (see, for example, Professor Ronald Dworkin's views in 'Hard Cases', *Taking Rights Seriously* (Rev ed, 1978) Chapter 4; and see the contrasting views embodied by some judges in the House of Lords decision of *McLoughlin v O'Brian* (1983), with Lord Scarman apparently adopting the view closest to Dworkin's (see p 430)). However, it should be noted that, *even in theory*, the line between principle on the one hand and policy on the other is often very blurred indeed. It could well be said that 'one person's principle is another's policy' and vice versa. This is not in the least surprising because, as has already been argued, the consideration of policy cannot be avoided when applying rules and principles. However, this does not, unfortunately, resolve even most of the difficulties present. This is due to the fact that the mere consideration of factors relating to public policy does not readily allow the judges and courts to know *where precisely* the line is to be drawn. Nevertheless, it is clear that *notwithstanding* their reluctance to countenance an *explicit* recognition of public policy as the, or at least a, major criterion, the courts have in fact incorporated at least an element of public policy into the *present* criteria with respect to the duty of care in the context of pure economic loss during the second stage of the 'two-stage test' (see paragraph 19.15, below) and the '*fair, just and reasonable*' element of the 'three-part test', which is discussed in more detail below (see below, paragraphs 19.25–19.26).

19.13 We have hitherto been referring to the concept of 'public policy'. It must also be noted, however, that Lord Millett has recently distinguished, in the House of Lords decision of *McFarlane v Tayside Health Board* (2000), between '*legal*' policy on the one hand and '*public*' policy on the other (see p 108; and see also, generally, *Clerk & Lindsell on Torts* (18th ed, 2000) at paragraphs 17.17–17.18). Might it therefore be argued that the courts are correct in rejecting the concept of *public* policy? Once again, however, the question arises as to whether or not there is, with respect, any *meaningful* distinction between 'legal' policy and 'public' policy. More importantly and specifically, perhaps, if '*legal*' policy refers, in effect, to the concept of *legal rules and principles*, then we are really back to where we had begun. At this point, we have, therefore, returned to the argument just made above to the effect that one cannot realistically (and, even theoretically) divorce the legal context from the extra-legal one. If, on the other hand, *'legal'* policy refers to factors residing and to be considered in the *extra*-legal context, then another question arises: what, then, is the difference between 'legal' policy on the one hand and 'public' policy on the other since *both* would, *ex hypothesi*, involve *extra*-legal factors? It might be argued that *'legal'* policy (*compared to 'public'* policy) concerns factors in the extra-legal context that enable the courts to strike a better balance between the plaintiff and the defendant in the context of the law of negligence, particularly insofar as attempted recovery for pure economic loss is concerned. It is submitted, with respect, however, that such an argument is mere assertion: the nub of the inquiry is whether or not, given the presence of *extra*-legal factors, it is *possible, in the first instance, to formulate workable criteria that would enable the courts to strike the balance just referred to.* It is therefore submitted that there is no effective distinction between 'legal' policy and 'public' policy and that the courts are, in the final analysis, still left with the basic dilemma as to what criteria precisely they are to utilise in order to strike a balance between the interests of the plaintiff on the one hand and the interests of the defendant on the other. *And this is the reason why we cannot—despite acknowledging the necessary role of public policy in the entire process—adopt, without more, the criterion of public policy advocated by Lord Denning MR in the Spartan Steel case as the sole determinant of the duty of care in the context of pure economic loss.*

(2) *The Test of 'Foreseeability Including Policy'*

19.14 Professor Tan then points—in the development of the law itself—to yet *another test*: the *'foreseeability including policy* test' or the so-called *'composite* test' (see, generally, above, paragraph 19.5 at pp 229–230). Under this particular test, the duty of care is perceived as being based on the concept or element of foreseeability (which, taken alone, it will be recalled, constitutes the *first* test we looked at at paragraphs 19.7–19.9, above) that *includes and encompasses policy* factors. The present writer submits that this particular test does not aid the court in any substantive fashion. Although an improvement over the pure 'public policy test' (as to which see generally paragraphs 19.11–19.13), a close analysis of this particular test will reveal that, by *relying heavily upon the 'public policy test' itself*, it would be subject to *the same weaknesses* already identified which afflict that particular test. Indeed, under the present *composite* nature of the present test, it is, both practically as well as conceptually, difficult to distinguish, in *substance*, between this test and the 'public policy test'. This is because *the element of public policy, being an integral part of the test itself, would, it is submitted, infuse the test so much that, in the final analysis, the entire test would be 'overwhelmed' by the public policy element and therefore be subsumed within it.* At this juncture, the earlier reference to a 'heavy reliance' upon the 'public policy test' insofar as the present test is concerned becomes, in effect, a gross understatement indeed.

(3) *The 'Two-Stage Test'*

19.15 The next major development—and which, as we shall see, is clearly a *landmark test*—is what Professor Tan characterises as the '*two-stage* test', which is embodied in the following (oft-cited) passage in the judgment of Lord Wilberforce in the House of Lords decision of *Anns v Merton London Borough Council* (1978) (at pp 751–752):

> '[I]n order to establish that a duty of care arises in a particular situation, it is not necessary to bring the facts of that situation within those of previous situations in which a duty of care has been held to exist. Rather the question has to be approached in *two stages*. First one has to ask whether, as between the alleged wrongdoer and the person who has suffered damage there is *a sufficient relationship of proximity or neighbourhood* such that, in the reasonable contemplation of the former, carelessness on his part may be likely to cause damage to the latter—in which case a *prima facie duty of care* arises. Secondly, if the first question is answered affirmatively, it is necessary to consider whether there are any considerations which ought to *negative, or to reduce or limit the scope of* the duty *or* the class of persons to whom it is owed or the damages to which breach of it may give rise' (emphasis added).

The present writer submits that the key virtue of this particular test is that whilst acknowledging the importance of the element of public policy, this element is nevertheless *kept separate and distinct from the overall test*. It is, as Lord Wilberforce clearly put it, *a constraining or limiting factor* insofar as the *first* element of what is, in effect, *foreseeability* is concerned (hence, the label '*two-stage* test', the first of which, therefore, concerns whether or not the conduct complained of is *foreseeable* and the second of which then asks whether there are any *public policy* factors that ought to limit the reach of liability established by the test of foreseeability). It should, however, be noted that Lord Wilberforce may in fact have been referring not to foreseeability *per se* but, rather, the *narrower* concept of '*proximity*', a point to which we will return in more detail later (see paragraph 19.21, below).

However, assuming that Lord Wilberforce was referring to the concept of foreseeability in its widest and most literal sense, we have seen that that concept (or even the narrower concept of 'proximity' for that matter) is potentially too broad when it is applied to a context other than physical damage or harm (see paragraph 19.9, above). Hence, wider considerations of public policy operate, in appropriate situations, to limit an overextension, as it were, of liability by cutting down on the scope of the duty of care: in Lord Wilberforce's own words, 'it is necessary to consider whether there are any considerations which ought to negative, or to reduce or limit the scope of the duty or the class of persons to whom it is owed or the damages to which breach of it may give rise'. It should be noted that the learned Law Lord does not explicitly utilise the rubric of 'public policy'. However, it is clear, from both the context as well as tenor of the language of his judgment, that the limiting factors or considerations must necessarily fall within the concept of 'public policy'. This does not, of course, resolve the problem of how the court is to draw the line when faced with the application of *extra*-legal factors and considerations. What this test *does avoid*, however, is the danger of making this very difficult task of applying public policy factors and considerations *even more intractable by making it a central part of the test itself*. Indeed, this particular (*two-stage*) test is, in this respect, to be contrasted with the 'composite test' (as to which, see paragraph 19.14, above).

19.16 In the *Anns* case itself (see paragraph 19.15, above), Lord Wilberforce's 'two-stage test' was applied in the following fashion. The plaintiffs, who were long lessees, brought an action against the defendant local authority for loss caused by the inadequate foundations in their building. Although the loss was foreseeable (stage *one*), the House of Lords nevertheless proceeded to hold that the scope of the duty of care was too wide if based on foreseeability alone. The House held that the fact that the defendant was a statutory body was a relevant factor that went towards narrowing the scope of the duty of care (stage *two*).

(4) *The 'Two-Stage Test' and Liability for Nervous Shock or Psychiatric Harm*

19.17 The 'two-stage test' advocated by Lord Wilberforce in the *Anns* case was subsequently applied by the House of Lords in the context of *nervous shock or psychiatric harm* in *McLoughlin v O'Brian* (1983) with regard (it should be noted) to *secondary* victims (viz those who suffer psychiatric illness that results from the fear for the safety of a related person). In this decision, the House was of the view that the qualifying public policy factors (stage *two*) did *not* exclude recovery for *nervous shock or psychiatric harm*. However, the House then proceeded to enunciate some *further* factors that would *narrow* the scope of the application of the test of 'pure foreseeability'—centring on three elements, viz the class of persons who should succeed (relational), the proximity of the plaintiffs concerned to the accident (spatial) and the means by which the shock is caused (perceptional, and which is not restricted to sight or hearing of the event only, but includes its 'immediate aftermath' as well). Note, once again, the *underlying rationale* of preventing the 'floodgates of liability' opening. We need not spend too much time on the context of nervous shock as pure instances in the specifically *business* context are quite rare. However, it will suffice for our present purposes to note that the context of nervous shock is a rather special one and that the factors mentioned above (viz relational, spatial and perceptional in nature) are specially 'tailored' to that particular context. More importantly, it is suggested, with respect, that the factors just mentioned *do*—contrary to the views of the House—pertain to *public policy*, albeit in relation to the more specific context of nervous shock. One other possibility is to classify these factors as going to the concept of '*proximity*' instead (on the concept of 'proximity', see paragraph 19.22 ff, below). However, the classification of these factors under the heading of 'proximity' only serves to generate more confusion, both terminological and otherwise. Indeed, it is (as we shall see) precisely because of such conceptual and terminological confusion that the law is in the unsatisfactory state it is today (and see, generally, paragraph 19.22 ff, below). *Significantly*, though, it was *Lord Wilberforce* who laid down these three factors. *If, therefore*, the three elements mentioned above indeed go towards the concept of 'proximity', *then it would appear that Lord Wilberforce had not in fact endorsed the concept of 'foreseeability' and had not neglected the concept of 'proximity' after all (for this criticism, see paragraph 19.19, below)—this argument is in fact buttressed by the discussion in paragraph 19.21, below*. Support for the argument that the three elements above go towards the ascertainment of *proximity* may be found in the judgment of Lord Oliver of Aylmerton in *Alcock v Chief Constable of South Yorkshire Police* (1992) (especially at p 411). Further, in the Singapore High Court decision of *Pang Koi Fa v Lim Djoe Phing* (1993), Amarjeet JC referred to Lord Wilberforce's three elements as the 'three *proximities*' (emphasis added) (see p 324; see, further, pp 326–344), although the learned judge also thought that Lord Wilberforce had expressed them 'as policy considerations in the second stage of the *Anns* two-stage test' (see p 324). This last-mentioned proposition in fact supports the argument, made above, to the effect that these three elements pertain to *public policy*. However, Amarjeet JC did also then refer to the 'three-part test' in the *Caparo* case (considered at paragraph 19.20, below) and expressed the view that that particular test had 'redefined' the basic test for the duty of care, characterising the concept of 'proximity' as one that pertained to 'a legal threshold' which was thus *separate and distinct from* that of policy (see, generally, pp 325–326). Interestingly, the learned judge equated policy considerations with the requirement of what was 'fair, just and reasonable' (see also below, paragraphs 19.25–19.26).

The decision in *McLoughlin v O'Brian* was in fact followed by the subsequent House of Lords decision of *Alcock v Chief Constable of South Yorkshire Police* (1992) as well as by the Singapore High Court in *Pang Koi Fa v Lim Djoe Phing* (1993). It bears repeating that both these decisions actually concerned harm caused to *related secondary* victims. Insofar as *non*-relative *secondary* victims are concerned, in the House of Lords decision of *White v Chief Constable of South Yorkshire Police* (1998), it was held (by a majority) that the plaintiff could recover only if he or she was within the area of physical danger and could therefore recover on the basis of being an endangered *primary* victim.

What, then, about *primary* victims (viz those who suffer nervous shock or psychiatric illness as a result of the *direct* fear of physical injury to himself or herself)? Primary victims are in fact treated even more favourably under the existing law. In the House of Lords decision of *Page v Smith* (1996), it was held that where the plaintiff was the *primary* victim, he or she was entitled to recovery *even when* the *psychiatric* illness suffered was *not reasonably foreseeable—provided that* the *physical injury which was apprehended* (which *need not* actually *have occurred*, as was the actual situation in this case) *and which gave rise to the psychiatric illness was foreseeable*. In this regard, Lord Lloyd of Berwick observed thus (at pp 188–189):

> 'Liability for physical injury [to a primary victim] depends on what was reasonably foreseeable by the defendant before the event. It could not be right that a negligent defendant should escape liability for psychiatric injury just because, though serious physical injury was foreseeable, it did not in fact transpire. Such a result in the case of a primary victim is neither necessary, logical nor just.'

The learned Law Lord also delivered a useful summary (at p 197), which merits quotation in full, as follows:

> 'In conclusion, the following propositions can be supported. 1. In cases involving nervous shock, it is essential to distinguish between the primary victim and secondary victims. 2. In claims by secondary victims the law insists on certain control mechanisms, in order as a matter of policy to limit the number of potential claimants. Thus, the defendant will not be liable unless psychiatric injury is foreseeable in a person of normal fortitude. These control mechanisms have no place where the plaintiff is the primary victim. 3. In claims by secondary victims, it may be legitimate to use hindsight in order to be able to apply the test of reasonable foreseeability at all. Hindsight, however, has no part to play where the plaintiff is the primary victim. 4. Subject to the above qualifications, the approach in all cases should be the same, namely, whether the defendant can reasonably foresee that his conduct will expose the plaintiff to the risk of personal injury, whether physical or psychiatric. If the answer is yes, then the duty of care is established, even though physical injury does not, in fact, occur. There is no justification for regarding physical and psychiatric injury as different "kinds of damage". 5. A defendant who is under a duty of care to the plaintiff, whether as primary or secondary victim, is not liable for damages for nervous shock unless the shock results in some recognised psychiatric illness. It is no answer that the plaintiff was predisposed to psychiatric illness. Nor is it relevant that the illness takes a rare form or is of unusual severity. The defendant must take his victim as he finds him.'

It should be noted, however, that the decision in *Page v Smith* was arrived at by a bare majority of 3–2, and has been subject to a perceptive and rather persuasive critique; see KF Tan, 'Nervous Shock to Primary Victims' [1995] *Singapore Journal of Legal Studies* 649.

The present law relating to liability for nervous shock is both complex and confusing and is in fact in need of urgent reform. For both a background of the law as well as proposals for reform, see KF Tan, *Discussion Paper on Liability for Negligently Inflicted Psychiatric Illness* (prepared for the Law Reform Committee of the Singapore Academy of Law, August 2000; available online at http://www.lawnet.com.sg). Also of interest and assistance is the UK Law Commission's Report entitled *Liability for Psychiatric Illness* (Law Com No 249, 1998).

(5) *Coherence of the 'Two-Stage Test'*

19.18 *Returning to* our discussion of the 'two-stage test' by Lord Wilberforce in the *Anns* case (see, in particular, paragraph 19.15, above), the present writer submits that it is both cogent and coherent (see also KF Tan at paragraph 19.5, above). *Foreseeability* (*or*, perhaps, *proximity*)—always an essential element—is considered at the *first* stage, with *qualifying policies* coming into play (where present and applicable) at the *second*. At the expense of repetition, it is important to emphasise, once again, that this does not mean that the problems of application that will inevitably arise when public policy factors are considered will thereby be resolved. However, as we have seen (see paragraph 19.11, above), it is difficult to conceive of a situation where public policy factors can be dispensed with, whilst still limiting the otherwise broad reach of—or even the opening of the 'floodgates' by—foreseeabilty, especially in unusual situations. *The main strategy, it is submitted, is to minimise the opportunities for public policy factors to 'run wild', so to speak. Looked at in this light, the 'two-stage test' is probably the best approach available in the case law.*

Unfortunately, however, the 'two-stage test' enunciated by Lord Wilberforce in the *Anns* case has, more recently, been *frowned upon and, ultimately, rejected*. We have, in its place, a '*three-part test*' instead (for yet another variation in the interim, see Professor Tan's article, cited at paragraph 19.5, above, at pp 236–243, where the '*two-part* test' of 'foreseeability and proximity' was mooted). Before proceeding to consider this latest test, however, it might be appropriate to consider, briefly, the gradual shift *against* the 'two-stage test' in the *Anns* case, which, at one stage, was thought (on the contrary) to be in the ascendancy (see, in particular, the House of Lords decision of *Junior Books Ltd v Veitchi Co Ltd* (1983)).

(6) *Decline of the 'Two-Stage Test'*

19.19 In the Hong Kong Privy Council decision of *Yuen Kun Yeu v Attorney-General of Hong Kong* (1988), Lord Keith of Kinkel, delivering the judgment of the Board, observed (at p 191) that '[t]heir Lordships venture to think that the two stage test formulated by Lord Wilberforce for determining the existence of a duty of care in negligence has been elevated to a degree of importance greater than it merits, and greater perhaps than its author intended'. And, in a similar vein, Lord Brandon of Oakbrook observed, in the House of Lords decision of *Leigh and Sillavan Ltd v Aliakmon Shipping Co Ltd* (1986) that Lord Wilberforce's observations in the *Anns* case do 'not provide, and cannot … have been intended by Lord Wilberforce to provide, a universally applicable test of the existence and scope of a duty of care in the law of negligence'. Less than encouraging signs continued to issue from the House of Lords itself (see, for example, *Governors of the Peabody Donation Fund v Sir Lindsay Parkinson & Co Ltd* (1985) and *D & F Estates Ltd v Church Commissioners for England* (1989)). There are also the following oft-cited observations by Brennan J in the Australian High Court decision of *Sutherland Shire Council v Heyman* (1985) (at p 481):

> 'It is preferable, in my view, that the law should develop novel categories of negligence incrementally and by analogy with established categories, rather than by a massive extension of a *prima facie* duty of care restrained only by indefinable considerations which ought to negative, or to reduce or limit the scope of the duty or the class of person to whom it is owed.'

The 'campaign against' *Anns*—in England at least—culminated in the House of Lords decision of *Murphy v Brentwood District Council* (1991), where the House disallowed attempted recovery by the plaintiff for alleged negligence for pure economic loss against the defendant council as a result of it (the defendant) having passed building plans that were based on the negligent advice of the consulting engineers (who were independent contractors). Even more significantly, the House *clearly departed from* the *Anns* case; Lord Keith of Kinkel observed (at p 471):

> 'In my opinion it is clear that *Anns* did not proceed upon any basis of established principle, but introduced a new species of liability governed by a principle indeterminate in character but having the potentiality of covering a wide range of situations, involving chattels as well as real property, in which it had never hitherto been thought that the law of negligence had any proper place.'

(7) *The 'Three-Part Test'*

19.20 We turn now to the *'three-part* test' enunciated most notably in the House of Lords decision of *Caparo Industries Plc v Dickman* (1990). In this case, the plaintiffs, a public limited company, brought an action against the defendants who were directors and auditors, respectively, of a company which had in fact been the subject of a take-over by the plaintiffs themselves. The plaintiffs had initially purchased shares in the said company. They alleged that, as a result of the report announcing the accounts of the company, they had purchased *further* shares, ultimately taking over the company itself. The plaintiffs now claimed that they had acted upon accounts that were inaccurate and misleading. The House held in favour of the defendants, holding that no duty of care existed *vis-à-vis* the plaintiffs. In the words of Lord Oliver of Aylmerton (at p 654):

> 'In my judgment … the purpose for which the auditors' certificate is made and published is that of providing those entitled to receive the report with information to enable them to exercise in conjunction those powers which their respective proprietary interests confer on them and not for the purposes of individual speculation with a view to profit.'

In a similar vein, Lord Jauncey of Tullichettle observed (at p 662) thus:

> 'I … conclude that the purpose of annual accounts, so far as members are concerned, is to enable them to question the past management of the company, to exercise their voting rights, if so advised, and to influence future policy and management. Advice to individual shareholders in relation to present or future

investment in the company is no part of the statutory purpose of the preparation and distribution of accounts.'

The House also acknowledged that Lord Wilberforce's statement of principle in the *Anns* case (see paragraph 9.15, above) had been criticised. Lord Bridge of Harwich then proceeded to observe (at pp 617–618) thus:

> 'What emerges is that, *in addition to the foreseeability of damage, necessary* ingredients in any situation giving rise to a duty of care are that there should exist between the party owing the duty and the party to whom it is owed *a relationship characterised by the law as one of "proximity" or "neighbourhood" and* that the situation should be one in which the court considers it *fair, just and reasonable* that the law should impose a duty of a given scope upon the one party for the benefit of the other' (emphasis added).

This is, in fact, the latest *tripartite 'three-part test'*, comprising foreseeability, proximity and the need that imposition of the duty of care be 'fair, just and reasonable', respectively. The House also endorsed the *incremental* approach advocated by Brennan J in the *Sutherland Shire Council* case (see paragraph 19.19, above). Lord Bridge of Harwich observed (at p 618) that '[w]hilst recognising, of course, the importance of the underlying general principles common to the whole field of negligence, I think the law has now moved in the direction of attaching greater significance to the more traditional categorisation of distinct and recognisable situations as guides to the existence, the scope and the limits of the varied duties of care which the law imposes'.

(8) *An Unwarranted Critique of the 'Two-Stage Test'*

19.21 The nub of the critique of Lord Wilberforce's 'two-stage test' in the *Anns* case centres around the fact that the learned Law Lord had, in the first stage of his test, utilised the concept of foreseeability in its most literal and widest sense. This presupposes, however, that the Atkinian 'neighbour principle' (see paragraph 19.6, above) relied upon by Lord Wilberforce in fact embraced such a very broad concept. This is not necessarily the case.

One possibility is to argue that the 'neighbour principle' enunciated by Lord Atkin in *Donoghue v Stevenson* was actually a reference to the narrower principle of 'proximity' (narrower, because it is encompassed within the much broader concept of 'foreseeability' in its most literal and widest sense). This is a view that has found favour with a relatively large number of courts and judges (see, for example, per Lord Keith of Kinkel in *Governors of the Peabody Donation Fund v Sir Lindsay Parkinson & Co Ltd* (1985) at p 240 as well as, by the same Law Lord, delivering the judgment of the Privy Council in *Yuen Kun Yeu v Attorney-General of Hong Kong* (1988) (at p 191); per Lord Jauncey of Tullichettle in *Murphy v Brentwood District Council* (1991) (at p 492); and per Lord Ackner in *Alcock v Chief Constable of South Yorkshire Police* (1992) (at p 402); cf also per Lord Devlin in *Hedley Byrne & Co Ltd v Heller & Partners Ltd* (1964) (at pp 514–515, 524–525 and 530–531), although it is arguable that the learned Law Lord, whilst using the rubric of 'proximity', was, in substance, actually referring to the broader concept of 'foreseeability' (see, especially, at p 525); cf, further, the Malaysian High Court decision of *Uniphone Sdn Bhd v Chin Boon Lit* (1998) at p 446, per Kamalanathan Ratnam JC).

However, it is arguable, *on the other hand*, that the 'neighbour principle' really embodied *only* the *broader* concept of *'foreseeability'*—not least because this principle was merely (and literally) in its infancy at the time it was expounded. And in *Murphy v Brentwood District Council* (1991), Lord Oliver of Aylmerton was of the view that Lord Atkin was focusing on 'the infliction of direct physical injury' and, in that context, 'clearly equated "proximity" with the reasonable foresight of damage' (see p 486; cf also per the same Law Lord in *Caparo Industries Plc v Dickman* (1990) at p 632). In the *Anns* case itself, Lord Wilberforce does refer to 'a sufficient relationship of proximity or neighbourhood' (see paragraph 19.15, above), but Deane J, in the Australian High Court decision of *Sutherland Shire Council v Heyman* (1985) thought that the learned Law Lord was, notwithstanding his reference to the concept of 'proximity', referring, in substance, to the concept of 'foreseeability' instead (see pp 506–507). A close reading of *McLoughlin v O'Brian* (1983), however, tends to suggest, with respect, that Deane J might not be wholly correct; in this case, Lord Wilberforce himself referred to a part of Lord Atkin's judgment with respect to the 'neighbour principle' ('persons who are so closely and directly affected by my act that I ought reasonably to have them in contemplation as being so affected': see paragraph 19.6, above) and expressed the view (at p 420) that '[t]his is saying that *foreseeability must* be *accompanied by the law's judgment* as to persons who ought, according to its standards of value or justice, to have been in contemplation' (emphasis added). This suggests that Lord Wilberforce thought (at least in *McLoughlin v O'Brian*) that the 'neighbour principle' embraced *both* foreseeability *and* proximity (with the latter being the narrower *legal* conception of whether or not a duty of care should be imposed in the situation concerned). However, it should be noted that the learned Law Lord then proceeded to speak of 'foreseeability' not only as involving an objective test but also as a 'limiting' concept with regard to persons to whom a duty of care would be declared by the courts was owing (see ibid). This appears, with respect, rather odd, although this particular view does *still include* the narrower concept of *'proximity'*. To complicate matters further, the learned Law Lord then reiterated his views expressed in the *Anns* case (see paragraph 19.15, above) to the effect that the concept of foreseeability alone did not automatically lead to a duty of care, but that *policy* factors had to be taken into account as well (see ibid).

However, given the preceding discussion, Lord Wilberforce's use of the term 'foreseeability' must *not* be taken *literally*, ie as a *factual* concept, which he was at pains to disavow explicitly. As already seen, his conception of 'foreseeability' was indeed a *legal* one which, the present writer suggests, is the counterpart of the concept of *'proximity'*. *In other words, Lord Wilberforce in both the* Anns *case and (now)* McLoughlin v O'Brian *was actually utilising both 'foreseeability' and 'proximity' interchangeably as well as in a narrower (legal) sense—which concept would then be limited (in appropriate circumstances) by policy factors (which may well be the counterpart of the third element of 'fair, just and reasonable' in the 'three-part test': see above, paragraph 19.20)*. Looked at in this light, Lord Wilberforce had not, in fact, radically changed the law. *Indeed, it may be argued that the 'three-part test' has in fact introduced a vacuous concept of (literal) foreseeability, which must always necessarily be present in any event before proximity can be established*. Looked at in this light, there was no need for Lord Wilberforce to set out (literal) foreseeability as an additional element (although the 'three-part test' does). *What matters, even in Lord Wilberforce's view, is that, in the eyes of the law, there is a kind or type of 'foreseeability', which is (it is submitted) the equivalent of the so-called 'new' concept of 'proximity'*. In this regard, the reader is also referred to the discussion in paragraph 19.15, above as well as the supporting observations by Lord Nicholls of Birkenhead in *Stovin v Wise* (1996) (at p 932). *If the arguments made thus far are accepted, then it is clear that there is no difference, in substance, between Lord Wilberforce's 'two-stage test' and the Caparo 'three-part test'*—a point to which we shall return below (see paragraph 19.34).

(9) *The Elusiveness of 'Proximity'*

19.22 However, we are still left with what is arguably the most important question: what precisely is '*proximity*', assuming that it is a concept that is narrower than 'foreseeability'? Various answers have been proffered by the courts, not all of which have been particularly helpful. In the *Caparo* case (1990) itself, Lord Bridge of Harwich expressed the view (at p 618) that 'the concepts of proximity and fairness ... are *not susceptible of any such precise definition as would be necessary to give them utility as practical tests, but* amount in effect to *little more than convenient labels to attach to the features of different specific situations which, on a detailed examination of all the circumstances, the law recognises pragmatically as giving rise to a duty of care of a given scope*' (emphasis added). And in the same case, Lord Roskill observed, in a similar vein, thus (at p 628):

> 'Phrases such as "foreseeabilty", "proximity", "neighbourhood", "just and reasonable", "fairness", "voluntary acceptance of risk", or "voluntary assumption of responsibility" will be found used from time to time in the different cases. But, as your Lordships have said, such phrases are *not precise* definitions. *At best they are but labels or phrases descriptive of the very different factual situations which can exist in particular cases and which must be carefully examined in each case before it can be pragmatically determined whether a duty of care exists and, if so, what is the scope and extent of that duty*' (emphasis added).

19.23 Lord Oliver of Aylmerton also observed, in *Alcock v Chief Constable of South Yorkshire Police* (1992), that 'in the end, it has to be accepted that the concept of "proximity" is an *artificial* one which depends more upon the court's perception of what is the reasonable area for the imposition of liability than upon any logical process of analogical deduction' (emphasis added) (see p 411; see also, by the same Law Lord in *Caparo Industries Plc v Dickman* (1990) at p 633).

There have, nevertheless, been other attempts at making the concept of 'proximity' more concrete. For example, in the Hong Kong Privy Council decision of *Yuen Kun Yeu v Attorney-General of Hong Kong* (1988), Lord Keith of Kinkel, who delivered the judgment of the Board, referred (at p 194) to the concept of 'close and direct relations' (see also at p 192; cf also per Deane J in the Australian High Court decision of *Sutherland Shire Council v Heyman* (1985) at p 496, referring to the actual language utilised in Lord Atkin's judgment, with the learned judge also referring (at pp 497–498) to the concepts of physical, circumstantial as well as causal proximity).

Perhaps the best balanced summary is encompassed within the following observations by Lord Nicholls of Birkenhead (dissenting, but not on this particular point) in the House of Lords decision of *Stovin v Wise* (1996) (at p 932):

> 'The *Caparo* tripartite test elevates proximity to the dignity of a separate heading. This formulation tends to suggest that proximity is a separate ingredient, distinct from fairness and reasonableness, and capable of being identified by some other criteria. This is not so. Proximity is a slippery word. Proximity is not legal shorthand for a concept with its own, objectively identifiable characteristics. Proximity is convenient shorthand for a relationship between two parties which makes it fair and reasonable one should owe the other a duty of care. This is only another way of saying that when assessing the requirements of fairness and reasonableness regard must be had to the relationship of the parties.'

The learned Law Lord also proceeded to observe thus (see ibid):

> '[T]he pithy, tripartite formulation has advantages. The relationship between the parties is an important ingredient in the overall assessment. The tripartite test is useful in focusing attention specifically on this feature and also in clearly separating this feature from foreseeability of damage.'

19.24 The Supreme Court of *Canada* decision in *Cooper v Hobart* (2001) (noted by SGA Pitel, 'Negligence: Canada Remakes the *Anns* Test' [2002] *Cambridge Law Journal* 252) should also be usefully considered. In this case, Major J, who delivered the judgment of the court, observed thus (at paragraphs 31, 32, 34 and 35):

> 'Two things may be said [about the concept of "proximity"]. The first is that "proximity" is generally used in the authorities to characterize the type of relationship in which a duty of care may arise. The second is that sufficiently proximate relationships are identified through the use of categories. The categories are not closed and new categories of negligence may be introduced. But generally, proximity is established by reference to these categories. This provides certainty to the law of negligence, while still permitting it to evolve to meet the needs of new circumstances.
>
> On the first point, it seems clear that the word "proximity"

> in connection with negligence has from the outset and throughout its history been used to describe the type of relationship in which a duty of care to guard against foreseeable negligence may be imposed. "Proximity" is the term used to describe the "close and direct" relationship that Lord Atkin described as necessary to grounding a duty of care in [*Donoghue v Stevenson*; see paragraph 9.6, above]. … Defining the relationship may involve looking at expectations, representations, reliance, and the property or other interests involved. Essentially, these are factors that allow us to evaluate the closeness of the relationship between the plaintiff and the defendant and to determine whether it is just and fair having regard to that relationship to impose a duty of care in law upon the defendant.
>
> The factors which may satisfy the requirement of proximity are diverse and depend on the circumstances of the case. One searches in vain for a single unifying characteristic.'

(10) *What Does 'Fair, Just and Reasonable' Mean?*

19.25 There is also, under the 'three-part test' the important issue as to what the *third* part ('fair, just and reasonable') means and what its relationship is to the other two parts, viz foreseeability and proximity. Indeed, in the English Court of Appeal decision of *James McNaughton Paper Group Ltd v Hicks Anderson & Co* (1991), Neill LJ stated (at pp 123–124) that this particular concept (which he referred to as one of 'fairness') 'is elusive and may indeed be no more than one of the criteria by which proximity is to be judged'. In a similar vein, Lord Nicholls of Birkenhead, in *Stovin v Wise* (1996), observed—perhaps a little more optimistically (at p 933)—thus:

> 'The basic test of fair and reasonable is itself open to criticism for vagueness. Indeed, it is an uncomfortably loose test for the existence of a legal duty. But no better or more precise formulation has emerged so far, and a body of case law is beginning to give the necessary further guidance as courts identify the factors indicative of the presence or absence of a duty.'

19.26 It is in fact suggested that the third criterion of 'fair, just and reasonable' might be best viewed as a facet of *public policy*—although it could be argued that the idea of fairness underlying the concept of 'fair, just and reasonable' may pertain more to the *specific* situation of fairness between the parties themselves rather than broader considerations of public policy (cf per Lord Morris of Borth-y-Gest in *Home Office v Dorset Yacht Co Ltd* (1970) at p 1039). There is in fact some apparent support for the equation of this third criterion with that of policy in the Singapore High Court decision of *Pang Koi Fa v Lim Djoe Phing* (1993), especially at p 336 (see also paragraph 19.17, above; cf also the Malaysian High Court decisions of *Pilba Trading & Agency v South East Asia Insurance Bhd* (1998) at pp 61–62 and *Uniphone Sdn Bhd v Chin Boon Lit* (1998) at pp 446–447). However, it could be argued that even if this criterion be equated with the concept of 'policy', there could be different conceptions of this concept—viz the narrower concept of 'legal' policy and the much broader concept of 'public' policy (as to which see generally the discussion at paragraph 19.13 as well as *Clerk & Lindsell on Torts* (18th ed, 2000) at paragraph 7-15 ff).

(11) *Position in Singapore*

19.27 What, then, is the position in *Singapore*? As we shall see, the position is none too clear: although there has been *a clear departure from the existing English law* as embodied in *Murphy v Brentwood District Council* (1991) (see paragraph 19.19, above).

The seminal decision in this regard is that of the Singapore Court of Appeal in *RSP Architects Planners and Engineers v Ocean Front Pte Ltd* (1996). In this case, the plaintiff management corporation of a condominium brought an action against the defendant developers, alleging faulty construction of common property, resulting in concrete spalling in the ceilings of certain basement car parks as well as water ponding of certain common areas and corridors around the lift lobbies. The developers then joined the architects as third parties. The situation was obviously one pertaining only to pure economic loss. If the *Murphy* case were followed, there could be no duty of care imposed on the defendants. However, the court held *otherwise*; it held that the defendants owed a duty to the plaintiffs to exercise reasonable care to avoid the damage that had been sustained. Significantly, however, the court declined to follow Lord Wilberforce's 'two-stage test' in *Anns* case (see paragraph 19.15, above), observing (at p 126) that the learned Law Lord's pronouncements were in fact 'purely obiter' (and see paragraph 1.66 ff, above, on the distinction between *obiter dicta* and *ratio decidendi*). Indeed, the court proceeded to survey the then existing English law in an extremely comprehensive fashion. It *also* surveyed the *contrasting* case law in *other Commonwealth jurisdictions as well*. It considered the Australian High Court decision of *Bryan v Maloney* (1995), for example, where the court expressly declined to follow the *Murphy* case. It also pointed to similar departures in the New Zealand context (which has since been confirmed by the Privy Council in *Invercargill City Council v Hamlin* (1996)) as well as in the Canadian context (where the Supreme Court of Canada decision in *Winnipeg Condominium Corp No 36 v Bird Construction Co* (1995) was referred to).

LP Thean JA, who delivered the judgment of the court, concluded (at p 138) that 'there is no single rule or set of rules for determining, first, whether a duty of care arises in a particular circumstance and, second, the scope of that duty'. The learned judge further observed thus (see ibid):

> 'In determining the existence of a duty of care and scope of such duty in different categories of cases, different judges have used different expressions: some say they are doing so as a matter of policy; some justify their approach by common sense, pragmatism, justice and reasonableness.'

Indeed Thean JA then proceeded to cite Lord Roskill's, Lord Bridge of Harwich's and Lord Oliver of Aylmerton's observations in the *Caparo* case (1990), already referred to, in varying degrees of detail, earlier (see paragraph 19.22, above). The learned judge then observed (at p 139) thus:

> 'But the approach of the court has been to examine a particular circumstance to determine whether there exists that degree of *proximity* between the plaintiff and the defendant as would give rise to a duty of care by the latter to the former with respect to the damage sustained by the former. Such proximity is the "determinant" of the duty of care and also the scope of such duty' (emphasis added).

Thean JA held that such proximity was indeed present on the facts of the present case. Indeed, the learned judge observed (at p 140) that:

> '[T]he management corporation at the time of its creation was, in fact, *the developers themselves who alone constitute the management corporation. At that stage, the management corporation was the developers' alter ego.* It is only at a later stage as and when the developers completed the sales of the various lots to purchasers that the constitution of the management corporation changed and subsidiary proprietors other than the developers then constituted the management corporation. Even at that stage, the subsidiary proprietors who formed the management corporation were parties with each of whom the developers had a contractual relationship. [T]he management corporation was *in fact the creation of the developers. Historically there existed a very close proximity in the relationship between the developers and the management corporation. It was therefore clearly foreseeable by the developers that if in the construction of the common property they failed to exercise reasonable care and skill, the burden of making good any defects arising from their failure would inevitably redound on their successor, the management corporation*' (emphasis added).

The learned judge then proceeded (at pp 141–142) to delve more specifically into 'the following facts of crucial importance in determining that there is sufficient proximity between the developers and the management corporation which gives rise to the duty of care: (i) the management corporation was an entity conceived and created by the developers; (ii) the developers were the party who built and developed the condominium including the common property and undertook the obligations to construct it in a good and workmanlike manner and were alone responsible for such construction; (iii) after completion of the condominium the developers were the party solely responsible for the maintenance and upkeep of the common property; (iv) the management corporation as the successor of the developers took over the control, management and administration of the common property and has the obligations of upkeeping and maintaining the common property; (v) the performance of these obligations is very much dependent on the developers having exercised reasonable care in the construction of the common property; (vi) the developers obviously knew or ought to have known that if they were negligent in their construction of the common property the resulting defects would have to be made good by the management corporation. The relationship between the developers and management corporation is as close as it could be short of actual privity of contract. In our judgment, there is a duty on the part of the developers in the construction of the common property a duty to take reasonable care to avoid the kind of damage sustained by the management corporation.'

What is as significant, perhaps, is the fact that the court then proceeded 'to consider whether there is *any policy consideration in negativing such duty of care*' (emphasis added) (see p 142). It found that there was *not* inasmuch as '[t]he amount recoverable is the cost of repair and making good the defects in the common property and in no way can it be said to be indeterminate. The class of persons is finite and definable. As for the duration, the time span is also not indeterminate, as the maximum period of time in which the developers can possibly be exposed to liability is limited by the Limitation Act [Cap 163, 1996 Rev Ed]' (see ibid). As to the argument that 'recovery for economic loss would result in an indefinitely transmissible warranty', the court held that '[t]he common property has been and will continue to remain in the control and under the management of the management corporation' and that there was therefore 'no question of any transmissible warranty to any other party' (see ibid).

It would appear that the *Ocean Front* case, whilst not expressly endorsing the approach of Lord Wilberforce in the *Anns* case, has, *in substance*, adopted it. It has adopted an approach that actually *departs from* that adopted in the *Murphy* case. More importantly, it has—again *in substance*—adopted a *two-stage* approach inasmuch as the court examined, first, the relationship between the parties before proceeding next to consider whether or not there were any policy factors that militated against the finding of a duty of care. It is of course true that the court did not adopt—at the first stage—a test of foreseeability in its most literal sense. It did examine, as we have seen, the relationship between the parties very closely indeed, although the issue of what the concept of 'proximity' precisely is continues to be a problem (and see paragraph 19.22, above). However, as we have seen, Lord Wilberforce may *not*, at least arguably, have been referring to a test of foreseeability in its most literal sense in the first stage of his 'two-stage test' in any event (see paragraph 19.21). Indeed, the present decision supports the proposition —made above at paragraph 19.21 and below at paragraph 19.34—to the effect that there may, in the final analysis, be very little difference in substance between the *Anns* 'two-stage test' and the *Caparo* 'three-part test'.

19.28 A *second* Singapore decision, however, ought also to be noted. It also emanated from the Court of Appeal: see *RSP Architects Planners & Engineers (Raglan Squire & Partners FE) v Management Corporation Strata Title Plan No 1075* (1999). This case also concerned alleged defective construction in a condominium. However, this time around, whilst the plaintiffs were (once again) the management corporation, the defendants were the architects, who (in turn) joined as third parties the main contractor for the development. The plaintiffs alleged negligence on the part of the architects with regard to the design and supervision of the construction of the condominium (bricks and brick tiles forming part of a gable end wall of one block having fallen off and causing damage to the roof and contents of a unit in another block). Although there was, in this respect, physical damage, the main expenses incurred by the plaintiffs was the rectification of the wall claddings which had not yet fallen, in order to avoid future injury to persons and/or damage to property. In this respect, therefore, the claim was for pure economic loss. What is of significance in the present decision was the fact that, unlike the *Ocean Front* case, the court in the present case *expressly rejected* Lord Wilberforce's 'two-stage test' in the *Anns* case. LP Thean JA, who delivered the judgment of the court, observed thus (at pp 456–457):

> 'It seems to us that what is objectionable in that passage [containing Lord Wilbeforce's test in the *Anns* case] is firstly his Lordship's sweeping proposition of a single general rule or principle which can be applied in every situation to determine whether a duty of care arises and secondly the fact that the test propounded by his Lordship in the first stage was based on foreseeability of damage alone.'

It should be noted that Thean JA also delivered the judgment of the court in the *Ocean Front* case. Indeed, the learned judge proceeded, after reviewing the decision in the *Ocean Front* case itself, to observe thus (at p 465):

> 'It is abundantly clear that in *Ocean Front* this court did *not* follow the broad proposition laid down by Lord Wilberforce in *Anns*. True, the court reached its conclusion by *a two-stage process. In principle, there is no objection to such approach*. It depends on what is involved and considered in each stage. The court certainly did not apply the first test in *Anns*. The court's finding that there was sufficient degree of proximity giving rise to a duty on the part of the developers to avoid the loss sustained by the management corporation was not premised on foreseeability of damage alone, but on the consideration of other relevant facts. Nor did the court accept Lord Wilberforce's proposition that in any given situation, a single general rule or principle can be applied to determine whether a duty of care arises.
>
> It does not follow from the mere fact that the court in the course of their determination examined the facts by the *two-stage process* that the court in effect followed *Anns*' (emphasis added).

Thean JA also observed as follows (at p 466):

> 'Stripped of the verbiage, the crux of such approach [ie the 'two-stage process'] is no more than this: the court first examines and considers the facts and factors to determine whether there is *sufficient degree of proximity* in the relationship between the party who has sustained the loss and the party who is said to have caused the loss which would give rise to a duty of care on the

part of the latter to avoid the kind of loss sustained by the former. … *Next*, having found such degree of proximity, the court next considers whether there is *any material factor or policy which precludes such duty from arising*' (emphasis added).

Applying the law to the facts of the present case, it was held that a duty of care was owed by the defendants to the plaintiffs: the defendant architects had assumed the responsibility of professional competence with regard to the developers who (in turn) had relied on the defendants to exercise reasonable care and skill. 'The management corporation which later came into existence was merely a statutory creation and was a successor to the developers with respect to the common property' and 'the architects knew that the management corporation would be in charge and would be managing the common property and would depend on their care and skill in the design and supervision of the construction of the common property' (see p 469). The court thus concluded that 'there was sufficient degree of proximity in the relationship between the management corporation and the architects as would give rise to a duty on the part of the architects to avoid the loss as sustained by [the plaintiffs] in this case' (see ibid).

Insofar as *broader policy factors* were concerned, the court referred to two factors which were considered in the Australian High Court decision of *Bryan v Maloney* (1995) as follows (see p 470):

> 'Firstly, the investment in real property is likely to represent a significant, if not the most significant, investment in an individual's lifetime (as opposed to the purchase of a mere chattel). The scale of the investment in money terms is far greater than what is involved in the acquisition of a chattel. Secondly, the permanence of the structure may give rise to a greater expectation than a chattel. We think those arguments *apply a fortiori in Singapore, where land is not only scarce but expensive*. We think that to treat houses and consumer goods alike would be to ignore simple realities, realities which, to our mind, are instrumental in dictating the expectations and degree of reliance placed upon the persons developing, building or designing the structure which stands upon it' (emphasis added).

Another argument, which is perhaps more specific, was in fact also referred to in *Bryan v Maloney* (1995) itself; in a joint judgment, Mason CJ, Deane and Gaudron JJ observed thus (at p 628):

> 'It is difficult to see why, as a matter of principle, policy or common sense, a negligent builder should be liable for ordinary physical injury caused to any person or to other property by reason of the collapse of a building by reason of the inadequacy of the foundations but be not liable to the owner of the building for the cost of remedial work necessary to remedy the inadequacy and to avert such damage.'

Such broader arguments are, it is suggested, of not inconsiderable significance. In the Supreme Court of Canada decision of *Winnipeg Condominium Corporation No 36 v Bird Construction Co Ltd* (1995), for example, it was observed by La Forest J, delivering the judgment of the court (at paragraph 37) that there was 'also a strong underlying policy justification for imposing liability' in such cases inasmuch as such an approach 'serves to encourage, rather than discourage, reckless and hazardous behaviour' (although it should be noted that the court here confined its holding to the cost of repair of *dangerous* defects). Indeed, it must surely be the case that the court concerned is free to develop the law in a manner that is best suited to the conditions of the country concerned (and see the New Zealand Privy Council decision of *Invercargill City Council v Hamlin* (1996), especially at pp 640 and 642; see also paragraphs 1.5, 1.46–1.51 and 1.198, above).

19.29 It is submitted that notwithstanding its express rejection of Lord Wilberforce's 'two-stage test' in the *Anns* case, the present decision nevertheless continues—like the *Ocean Front* case—to apply that *same* test: at least *in substance*. However, the approach is now characterised as a *'two-stage process'* rather than a *'two-stage test'*. It is submitted, with respect, that this is a distinction without a real difference. It is admitted that only insofar as Lord Wilberforce in the *Anns* case was adopting a test of foreseeability in its most literal sense can the approach in the present decision be considered to be different in substance. However, as already mentioned, Lord Wilberforce may, in fact, have adopted a narrower test which is entirely consistent with the argument from *proximity* advocated in the present case (see paragraph 19.21, above). Further, as we have seen, the very concept of 'proximity' itself may well be problematic (see paragraph 19.22). It should also be noted that the court continued to endorse the *departure* from the English position and reiterated the fact that this was the position in other Commonwealth jurisdictions as well (see p 471). In this regard, it is significant that in many instances—particularly in the Canadian and New Zealand contexts—the approach adopted in the *Anns* case had in fact been *endorsed*.

19.30 In the (also) Singapore Court of Appeal decision of *Ikumene Singapore Pte Ltd v Leong Chee Leng* (1993), the court in fact endorsed the *Caparo* 'three-part test' (see paragraph 19.20, above), holding that there was no duty of care on the part of the auditor to a guarantor of the company. There are also other Singapore cases where the *Caparo* 'three-part test' has been endorsed (see, for example, *Swiss Singapore Overseas Enterprise Pte Ltd v Horng Chang Enterprise Pte Ltd* (1993); *Standard Chartered Bank v Coopers & Lybrand* (1993); and *Mohd bin Sapri v Soil-Build (Pte) Ltd* (1996)). *However*, if the argument just made is correct, then it *does not matter* whether the *Anns* 'two-stage test' *or* the *Caparo* 'three-stage test' is applied since both are—*in substance*—the *same*.

19.31 It might be interesting to note, however, that insofar as the *Canadian* context is concerned, the Supreme Court of Canada recently 'revisited' the 'two-stage test' enunciated by Lord Wilberforce in the *Anns* case in *Cooper v Hobart* (2001) (which has already been briefly considered at paragraph 19.24, above). The issue in this case was neatly put by the court (at paragraph 20), as follows: 'Does a statutory regulator owe a private law duty of care to members of the investing public for (alleged) negligence in failing to properly oversee the conduct of an investment company licensed by the regulator?' The court held that no such duty was owed. It is interesting that, whilst endorsing the 'two-stage test' by Lord Wilberforce in *Anns* case, the court did in fact emphasise (at paragraph 22) that 'foreseeability alone was not enough; there must also be a close and direct relationship of proximity or neighbourhood'. More importantly, perhaps, it observed that '[t]he importance of *Anns* lies in *its recognition* that *policy considerations* play *an important role* in *determining proximity in new situations*' (emphasis added) (see paragraph 25). Even more importantly, Major J, who delivered the judgment of the court, observed thus (at paragraph 28):

> 'We continue in the view, repeatedly expressed by this Court, that the *Anns* two-stage test, properly understood, does not involve duplication because different types of policy considerations are involved at the two stages. In our view, *Anns* continues to provide a useful framework in which to approach the question of whether a duty of care should be imposed in a new situation.'

Most importantly, in the present writer's view, is the following statement of principle which merits quotation in full (see paragraph 30):

> 'In brief compass, we suggest that at this stage in the evolution of the law, both in Canada and abroad, the *Anns* analysis is best understood as follows. At the first stage of the *Anns* test, two questions arise: (1) was the harm that occurred the reasonably foreseeable consequence of the defendant's act? and (2) are there reasons, notwithstanding the proximity between the parties established in the first part of this test, that tort liability should not be recognized here? The proximity analysis involved at the first stage of the *Anns* test focuses on factors arising from the *relationship* between the plaintiff and the defendant. These factors include questions of policy in the broad sense of that word. If foreseeability and proximity are established at the first stage, a *prima facie* duty of care arises. At the second stage of the *Anns* test, the question still remains whether there are residual policy considerations outside the relationship of the parties that may negative the imposition of a duty of care. It may be, as the Privy Council suggests in [*Yuen Kun Yeu v Attorney-General of Hong Kong* (1988)], that such considerations will not often prevail. However, we think it useful expressly to ask, before imposing a new duty of care, whether despite foreseeability and proximity of relationship, there are other policy reasons why the duty should not be imposed' (emphasis in original).

Elaboration in this particular case of the first part of the *Anns* test insofar as the concept of 'proximity' is concerned has already been touched on above (see paragraph 19.24). Insofar as the *second* stage of the *Anns* test is concerned, 'residual policy considerations fall to be considered here. These are not concerned with the relationship between the parties, but with the effect of recognizing a duty of care on other legal obligations, the legal system and society more generally' (see paragraph 37). Major J then proceeded to elaborate thus (see paragraphs 37 and 39):

> 'Does the law already provide a remedy? Would recognition of the duty of care create the spectre of unlimited liability to an unlimited class? Are there other reasons of broad policy that suggest that the duty of care should not be recognised? ... The second step of *Anns* generally arises only in cases where the duty of care asserted does not fall within a recognized category of recovery. Where it does, we may be satisfied that there are no overriding policy considerations that would negative the duty of care. ... However, where a duty of care in a novel situation is alleged, ... we believe it necessary to consider both steps of the *Anns* test ... This ensures that before a duty of care is imposed in a new situation, not only are foreseeability and relational proximity present, but there are no broader considerations that would make imposition of a duty of care unwise.'

19.32 Returning to general principles, on a *practical* level, the following advice by Neill LJ (at p 123) in *James McNaughton Paper Group Ltd v Hicks Anderson & Co* (1991), although still quite general, is nevertheless pragmatic: 'It therefore becomes necessary, in the absence of some general principle, to examine each individual case in the light of the concepts of foreseeability, proximity and fairness'. This is, admittedly, still rather vague and general. However, given the confused as well as confusing manner in which the law in this area has developed, any attempt to state what the basic principles are would appear to be foolhardy. Still, in a work of this nature, it would be undesirable to simply leave everything 'up in the air'. Hence, an *extremely qualified* attempt follows in the very next section.

(12) *Summing-Up*

19.33 What seems clear is that mere foreseeability in its most *literal, factual* sense is *insufficient* to establish a *legal* duty of care. It would appear that the better view is that the 'neighbour principle' represented the *latter* (ie *legal* foreseeability or proximity) and not the former (ie *literal* foreseeability; and see, generally, paragraph 19.21, above). It is suggested —obviously with great tentativeness—that this latter concept (viz a *legal* conception of the concept of 'foreseeability') is what the courts (particularly during more recent times) term the concept of 'proximity'. Although it appears that this interpretation is probably the most coherent and persuasive, it *does* generate difficulties, not least because the 'three-part test' (see, generally, paragraph 19.20, above), which appears to represent the present law (see also paragraph 19.30, above), would literally be thrown out of kilter. Indeed, acceptance of the present argument would 'collapse' the first two parts of this test into one. One way of avoiding such an 'embarrassment' is to argue that the concept of 'foreseeability' in the first part of the 'three-part test' actually refers to foreseeability in its most *literal, factual* sense. *However*, such an approach would, it is suggested, be unsatisfactory for at least two reasons. First, as we have already seen, such a concept of foreseeability is unhelpful at best and may contribute to confusion at worst. Secondly, and in a related vein, such a concept is also *redundant* inasmuch as in order to establish proximity (or, on the assumption proceeded upon here, a *legal* conception of the concept of 'foreseeability'), there *must* obviously have been literal and factual foreseeability in the first instance. In other words, literal and factual foreseeability does not necessarily lead to a finding of 'legal' foreseeability (or *proximity*), although a finding of such 'legal' foreseeability must *necessarily* include a finding of literal and factual foreseeability in the first place. Looked at in this light, there is some merit to the use of the term 'proximity' in *this* (*legal*) sense (in order to avoid the confusion that might otherwise arise from the use of the term 'foreseeability' in more than one (here, at least two) senses).

What seems *equally* clear is that, notwithstanding the criticisms (in England) of Lord Wilberforce's 'two-stage test' in the *Anns* case, *that element in* the learned Law Lord's *second* stage (viz that of a 'constraining' *public policy*) is *still very much alive and well today*. Indeed, the concept of public policy has been, either explicitly or implicitly, the main factor in many decisions for the courts finding that there is, in the final analysis, no legal duty of care (see, for example, the House of Lords decisions of *Hill v Chief Constable of West Yorkshire* (1989) and *Stovin v Wise* (1996); and cf the (also) House of Lords decisions of *Home Office v Dorset Yacht Co Ltd* (1970); *X (Minors) v Bedfordshire County Council* (1995); *Barrett v Enfield London Borough Council* (1999); and *Phelps v Hillingdon London Borough Council* (2000)). It would also appear that where a *statutory power* is involved, the consideration of the *statutory policy* is both inevitable as well as necessary (see, for example, *Stovin v Wise* (1996); presumably, since a statute is involved, no problems arise with regard to the distinction hitherto drawn between principle and policy (as to which see paragraph 19.13, above)). Finally, it should also be noted that the nature of public policy *might differ from country to country*. An excellent illustration of this in the local context is the Singapore Court of Appeal decision of *Chong Yeo & Partners v Guan Ming Hardware & Engineering Pte Ltd* (1997), where the court held that the then immunity recognised by the House of Lords in *Rondel v Worsley* (1967) with regard to lawyers did *not* apply in the Singapore context. Yong Pung How CJ, who delivered the judgment of the court, observed (at p 744) that 'the *Rondel v Worsley* immunity does not apply in Singapore. A claim in negligence against an advocate and solicitor is not barred save where that claim is against the conduct of a criminal case'. Indeed, the entire judgment repays careful analysis and illustrates the more general proposition that English law, whilst the foundation of the Singapore legal system, will not be slavishly adhered to. Significantly, the English law itself has since been changed: see the House of Lords decision of *Arthur JS Hall & Co (a firm) v Simons* (2002).

On a related note, recent (English) decisions have also considered the 'policy/operational' dichotomy laid down by Lord Wilberforce in the *Anns* case (1978) at p 754, where it was held that, whilst in essence 'probably a distinction of degree', there was 'an operational area'—as distinct from a 'policy area' with regard to the decisions of public authorities—that the courts would not interfere with. This distinction was recently accepted and restated by Lord Browne-Wilkinson in the House of Lords decision of *X (Minors) v Bedfordshire County Council* (1995) at p 738 as follows:

> 'Where Parliament has conferred a statutory discretion on a public authority, it is for that authority, not for the courts, to exercise the discretion: nothing which the authority does within the ambit of the discretion can be actionable at common law. If the decision complained of falls outside the statutory discretion, it *can* (but not necessarily will) give rise to common law liability. However, if the factors relevant to the exercise of the discretion include matters of policy, the court cannot adjudicate on such policy matters and therefore cannot reach the conclusion that the decision was outside the ambit of the statutory discretion. Therefore a common law duty of care in relation to the taking of decisions involving policy matters cannot exist' (emphasis in original).

Once again, we find the distinction between policy and principle being favoured by the courts (see also paragraph 19.13, above). *However*, it should also be noted that the distinction did *not* find favour with Lord Hoffmann in the (also) House of Lords decision of *Stovin v Wise* (1996) (see pp 951-953; and cf per Lord Slynn of Hadley in the House of Lords decision of *Barrett v Enfield London Borough Council* (1999) at p 96). Of interest, too, are the following observations of Major J, delivering the judgment of the court in the Supreme Court of Canada decision of *Cooper v Hobart* (2001) (see paragraph 38; also considered above at paragraphs 19.24 and 19.31, respectively):

> 'In our view, the exclusion of liability for policy decisions is properly regarded *as an application of the second stage* of the *Anns* test. The exclusion does not relate to the relationship between the parties. Apart from the legal characterization of the government duty as a matter of policy, plaintiffs can and do recover' (emphasis added).

19.34 If, however, the arguments above are persuasive, it would appear that there is, *in substance, very little difference* between the *Anns* 'two-stage test' and the *Caparo* 'three-part test' (see also paragraph 19.21, above; cf also KF Tan, 'Of Duty' (1996) 112 *Law Quarterly Review* 209, especially at pp 213–214, as well as, by the same author, paragraph 19.5, above, at p 247). Indeed, in *Stovin v Wise* (1996), Lord Nicholls of Birkenhead was of the view (at p 931) that '[t]he difference is perhaps more a difference of presentation and emphasis than substance'. In the same case, Lord Hoffmann thought that both tests were different ways of approaching the same issue: the *Anns* 'two-stage test' 'involves starting with a prima facie assumption that a duty of care exists if it is reasonably foreseeable that carelessness may cause damage and then asking whether there are any considerations which ought to "negative, or to reduce or limit the scope of the duty or the class of person to whom it is owed or the damages to which a breach of it may arise"', whereas the *Caparo* 'three-part test' approaches 'the question the other way around, starting with situations in which a duty has been held to exist and then asking whether there are considerations of analogy, policy, fairness and justice for extending it to cover a new situation … *It can be said that, provided that the considerations of policy etc. are properly analysed, it should not matter whether one starts from one end or the other*' (emphasis added) (see p 949).

Establishing a Duty of Care:
The *General* Position

***Physical* Damage** (Simpler)

- Covered by the Atkinian 'neighbour principle' in *Donoghue v Stevenson* [**19.6**]
  - *Literal* or *Factual* Foreseeability (wider)
    - Sufficient to establish liability in *virtually all* cases—*But* see the possible qualifications even in this context in the *Marc Rich* case, which appears to adopt a narrower approach, at least in certain circumstances. [**19.8**]
  - *Legal* Foreseeability (or *Proximity*) (narrower)

Pure *Economic* Loss (Complex)

(A) Tests

'Interim' Tests (1):
(1) The *Public Policy* Test [**19.11–19.13**]
(2) The Test of '*Foreseeability Including Policy*'/The '*Composite* Test' [**19.14**]

* ***Anns* '*Two-Stage* Test'** [**19.15–19.19**] → *Elements:*
(1) '[A] sufficient relationship of proximity or neighbourhood'.
(2) Constraining *policy* factors that 'ought to negative, or to reduce or limit the scope of the duty or the class of persons to whom it is owed or the damages to which breach of it may give rise'.

'*Interim*' Test (2): The Test of '*Foreseeability and Proximity*'/The '*Two-Part* Test' [**19.18**]

[Attack on, and Decline of, the '*Two-Stage* Test' [**19.19**]

* ***Caparo* '*Three-Part* Test'** [**19.20**] → *Elements:*
(1) *Foreseeability*
(2) *Proximity*
(3) *Fair, Just and Reasonable* to impose liability (cf [**19.12–19.13**]).

(B) Specific Situations
(1) Liability for *Negligent Misstatements* under the Rule in *Hedley Byrne* [**19.35–19.40**]
(2) Liability for *Nervous Shock or Psychiatric Illness* (*Quaere* whether the *Anns* test is also still relevant) [**19.14**]

Tests ***different*** if: Take and compare the elements in each test *literally—ie 3 does not fit into 2.*

Tests the ***same*** if:
(1) '[A] sufficient relationship of proximity or neighbourhood' (Element (1) in the *Anns* test, though often characterised in later cases as *Literal or Factual* Foreseeability) = *Legal* Foreseeability or *Proximity* (Element (2) in the *Caparo* test) ([**19.21**], cf [**19.22–19.24**] with regard to 'Proximity')
(2) Constraining *policy* factors (Element (2) in the *Anns* test) = The element of 'fair, just and Reasonable' (Element (3) in the *Caparo* test) [**19.25–19.26**]
(3) The element of 'Foreseeability' (Element (1) in the *Caparo* test). *But*, in such a situation, the concept of 'foreseeability' is *redundant*, because *Legal* Foreseeability or *Proximity* ***presupposes*** *Literal or Factual* Foreseeability in the first instance. [**19.33**] = *Literal or Factual* Foreseeability

** **CONCLUSION**
This interpretation is to be preferred: see generally [**19.33–19.34**]

Establishing a Duty of Care for *Pure Economic Loss*: The Position in *Singapore*

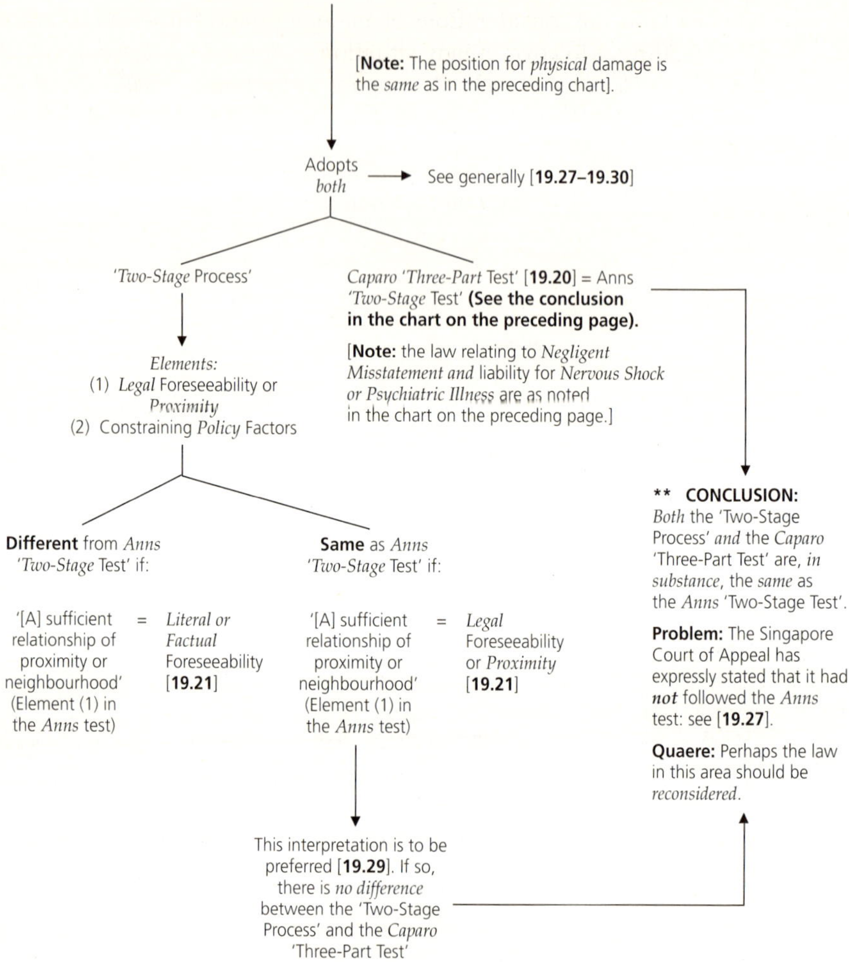

(13) *Liability for Negligent Misstatements Under the Rule in Hedley Byrne*

19.35 What *has* been clearly established—in the context of *pure economic loss*—is that there can indeed be legal liability for *negligent misstatements* under *certain circumstances*, where a '*special relationship*' exists (for possible liability for *nervous shock*, see, generally, above, paragraph 19.17). The seminal decision in this regard is that of the House of Lords in *Hedley Byrne & Co Ltd v Heller & Partners Ltd* (1964). In this case, the plaintiffs (a firm of advertising agents) sought advice on the financial position of a company (Easipower Ltd) from the defendants, who were Easipower Ltd's bankers. Although the defendants furnished favourable references, these were stipulated to be 'without responsibility'. The plaintiffs acted on these references and placed substantial orders for advertising time at various venues on behalf of Easipower Ltd, but incurred losses when Easipower Ltd itself went into liquidation. The House held that there was a duty of care owed by the defendants to the plaintiffs. *However,* such a duty of care was *negated* by the *disclaimer* by the defendants themselves.

19.36 However, subsequent elaboration of the circumstances under which a negligent misstatement will found legal liability has resulted in some possible controversy, although the basic structure of the inquiry (viz the '*three-part* test' enunciated in *Caparo Industries Plc v Dickman* (1990), itself a case involving alleged liability for negligent misstatement and discussed above at paragraph 19.20; see also the Singapore decisions of *Ikumene Singapore Pte Ltd v Leong Chee Leng*, *Swiss Singapore Overseas Enterprise Pte Ltd v Horng Chang Enterprise Pte Ltd*, and *Standard Chartered Bank v Coopers & Lybrand*, all of which are referred to at paragraph 19.30, above) continues to apply. Simply put, there is a difference of opinion as to whether or not the basis of legal liability for a negligent misstatement is the *reasonable reliance by the plaintiff* on the misstatement concerned *or* the *voluntary assumption of responsibility by the defendant* who made the said misstatement. There is authority for both the former (see, for example, per Lord Reid, Lord Morris of Borth-y-Gest and Lord Hodson in the *Hedley Byrne* case (1964) at pp 483, 496 and 514, respectively; per Lord Templeman in *Smith v Eric S Bush* (1990) at p 848 and per Lord Slynn of Hadley in *Spring v Guardian Assurance Plc* (1995) at p 332; and cf per Lord Browne-Wilkinson in *White v Jones* (1995) at p 272, as well as (especially) pp 272–273, where there was, instead, more of a focus on assumption of responsibility) as well as the latter (see, for example, per Lord Morris of Borth-y-Gest and Lord Devlin in the *Hedley Byrne* case (1964) at pp 494–495, 497, 502–504 as well as 528–530, respectively; per Lord Keith of Kinkel, delivering the judgment of the Privy Council in *Yuen Kun Yeu v Attorney-General of Hong Kong* (1988) at p 192; per Lord Templeman and Lord Jauncey of Tullichettle in *Smith v Eric S Bush* (1990) at pp 847 and 870, respectively; per Lord Goff of Chieveley and Lord Browne-Wilkinson in *Henderson v Merrett Syndicates Ltd* (1995) at pp 181 and 205, respectively; *White v Jones* (1995), especially per Lord Goff of Chieveley at p 268 (see also per Lord Browne-Wilkinson at pp 272–273); and per Lord Goff of Chieveley in *Spring v Guardian Assurance Plc* (1995) at p 316; *contra* per Lord Griffiths in *Smith v Eric S Bush* (1990) at p 862 and per Lord Roskill in the *Caparo* case (1990) at p 628).

What *is* clear, however, is that *both* bases are to be ascertained on an *objective* basis. This is why reliance has to be reasonable and, insofar as assumption of responsibility is concerned, Lord Goff, in *Henderson v Merrett Syndicates Ltd* (1995) observed (at p 181) that the entire process of inquiry was the subject of 'an objective test'. Interestingly, the learned Law Lord also observed (ibid) that where the principle in the *Hedley Byrne* case applied, 'there should be no need to embark upon any further enquiry whether it is "fair, just and reasonable" to impose liability for economic loss' (which is the third part of the 'three-part test' discussed above (see above, paragraph 19.20); though cf per Lord Woolf in *Spring v Guardian Assurance Plc* (1995) at p 342). And, in *White v Jones* (1995), Lord Browne-Wilkinson observed—insofar as the voluntary assumption of responsibility was concerned—that 'the assumption of responsibility referred to is the defendants' assumption of responsibility for *the task not* the assumption of *legal liability*' (emphasis added) (see p 273).

In point of fact, it is submitted that authority for the bases of *both* reasonable reliance *and* voluntary assumption of responsibility can be found in the *Hedley Byrne* case itself. More importantly, it is further submitted that there is, at bottom, no real conflict between both bases. Indeed, it is suggested that one ought to view the basis or rationale of reasonable reliance as centring on the *plaintiff's* perspective and the basis or rationale of voluntary assumption of responsibility as centring on the *defendant's (or maker of the statement's)* perspective. *In other words, both perspectives just mentioned are merely two sides of the same coin and ought therefore to be viewed in a holistic and integrated fashion*. Indeed, it comes, therefore, as no surprise that courts and judges frequently refer to *both* bases in the same case or judgment, respectively (see, for example, per Lord Morris of Borth-y-Gest in the *Hedley Byrne* case (1964), especially at pp 502–503; per Lord Templeman in *Smith v Eric S Bush* (1990) at pp 847–848; per Lord Goff of Chieveley in *Spring v Guardian Assurance Plc* (1995) at pp 318 and 319 (this last-mentioned reference is significant as Lord Goff has consistently focused on the concept of voluntary assumption of liability (as we have seen above); reference may also be made (albeit in a slightly different context) to the Australian High Court decision of *Bryan v Maloney* (1995)). And in the recent House of Lords decision of *Williams v Natural Life Health Foods Ltd* (1998), Lord Steyn observed (at p 836) that '[i]f reliance is not proved, it is not established that the assumption of personal responsibility had causative effect'; indeed, the learned Law Lord appeared to suggest (at p 837) that it was precisely because the element of reliance was present that the criticism of the concept of the voluntary assumption of liability from the perspective of fiction or artificiality was misplaced.

19.37 There also used to be some controversy as to whether or not, in order for a special relationship within the principle in the *Hedley Byrne* case to arise, the defendant had to be in the business of giving that particular type of (here, negligent) advice or that there was some profession that it (the defendant) possessed the requisite skill and competence to render such advice. This was in fact what the majority of the Board held in the Australian Privy Council decision of *Mutual Life and Citizens' Assurance Co Ltd v Evatt* (1971). *However*, it is now generally accepted that the *minority* position (adopted by Lord Reid and Lord Morris of Borth-y-Gest) ought to represent the law instead (see, for example, *Clerk & Lindsell on Torts* (18th ed, 2000) at paragraph 7-114, and the authorities cited therein). As the minority put it (at p 811), '[i]t may be going too far to say that a duty to take care can only arise where advice is sought and given in a business or professional context, for there might be unusual cases requiring a wider application of this principle'. It also observed (at p 812) thus:

> 'In our judgment when an inquirer consults a business man in the course of his business and makes it plain to him that he is seeking considered advice and intends to act on it in a particular

> way, any reasonable business man would realise that, if he chooses to give advice without any warning or qualification, he is putting himself under a moral obligation to take some care. It appears to us well within the principles established by the *Hedley Byrne* case to regard his action in giving such advice as creating a special relationship between him and the inquirer and to translate his moral obligation into a legal obligation to take such care as is reasonable in the whole circumstances.'

19.38 On a more practical level, Neill LJ, in *James McNaughton Paper Group Ltd v Hicks Anderson & Co* (1991) set out various matters 'which are likely to be of importance in most cases in reaching a decision as to whether or not a duty [of care] exists' (see p 125). These include: the purpose for which the statement was made, the purpose for which the statement was communicated; the relationship between the adviser, the advisee and any relevant third party, the size of any class to which the advisee belongs, the state of knowledge of the adviser, and reliance by the advisee (see generally pp 125–127).

19.39 It should also be noted that although a *disclaimer* of liability can—as was the case in the *Hedley Byrne* case itself—negate the existence of a duty of care, the later House of Lords decision in *Smith v Eric S Bush* (1990) establishes that such a disclaimer must nevertheless pass muster under the UK Unfair Contract Terms Act 1977, which is also—in very slightly modified form—applicable in the Singapore context as well (and see generally paragraph 6.35, above).

19.40 Finally, it should be further noted that liability for negligent misstatement under the principles first enunciated in the *Hedley Byrne* case is also relevant to, and indeed is, on appropriate occasions, an integral part of, the law relating to *misrepresentation* (as to which see generally Chapter 12, above).

(14) *Recovery of Economic Loss Consequential Upon Physical Injury or Damage*

19.41 It should be mentioned that it is possible to argue that economic loss is recoverable if it is consequential upon physical injury to the plaintiff's property or person (as distinguished from pure economic loss; and see the Singapore Court of Appeal decision of *RSP Architects Planners and Engineers v Ocean Front Pte Ltd* (1996) at p 124). However, the line between pure economic loss on the one hand and economic loss consequential upon such physical injury is not always clear.

Elements of Negligence (2): Breach of the Duty of Care

19.42 In an oft-cited passage, Alderson B, in *Blythe v Birmingham Waterworks Co* (1856) observed (at p 784) that 'negligence is the omission to do something which a reasonable man, guided upon those considerations which ordinarily regulate human affairs, would do, or doing something which a prudent and reasonable man would not do'.

More specifically, and in the context of *professionals*, the following observations by McNair J in *Bolam v Friern Hospital Management Committee* (1957) have also often been cited as well (see p 586):

> 'The test is the standard of the ordinary skilled man exercising and professing to have that special skill. A man need not possess the highest expert skill; it is well established now that it is sufficient if he exercised the ordinary skill of an ordinary competent man exercising that particular art.'

And, as Lord Fraser of Tullybelton put it in the more recent House of Lords decision of *Whitehouse v Jordan* (1981) (at p 263):

> 'Merely to describe something as an error of judgment tells us nothing about whether it is negligent or not. The true position is that an error of judgment may, or may not, be negligent; it depends on the nature of the error. If it is one that would not have been made by a reasonably competent professional man professing to have the standard and type of skill that the defendant held himself out as having, and acting with ordinary care, then it is negligent. If, on the other hand, it is an error that such a man, acting with ordinary care, might have made, then it is not negligent.'

19.43 However, the test in the *Bolam* case (above), whilst rational and commonsensical, has nevertheless often been criticised, particularly as being unfair to plaintiffs. As one textbook puts it: 'A major criticism of *Bolam* was that it supported medical paternalism, particularly when applied in consent to treatment cases' (see V Harpwood, 'Negligence: Breach of Duty' in Chapter 13 of A Grubb (Gen ed), *Butterworths Common Law Series—The Law of Tort* (2002) at paragraph 13.30). However, closer scrutiny of the testimony of expert witnesses has been advocated in the House of Lords decision of *Bolitho v City and Hackney Health Authority* (1997), which has in fact modified the test in the *Bolam* case by requiring that 'the court has to be satisfied that the exponents of the body of opinion relied on can demonstrate that such opinion has a logical basis' (see per Lord Browne-Wilkinson at p 778; and see Harpwood, ibid, at paragraph 13.31). Although both the *Bolam* and *Bolitho* cases (and, indeed, *Whitehouse v Jordan* as well) involved cases in the medical context, '[i]t has become clear that the *Bolam* test as modified by *Bolitho* does apply outside the healthcare context' (see Harpwood, ibid, at paragraph 13.40; cf *Dr Khoo James & Anor v Gunapathy d/o Muniandy* (2002) at p 435).

Both the *Bolam* and *Bolitho* cases have been applied in the Singapore context, most recently, in the Singapore Court of Appeal decision of *Dr Khoo James & Anor v Gunapathy d/o Muniandy*, just referred to above, which also provides a very comprehensive overview of the existing law.

19.44 On a *theoretical* level, the concept of the duty of care (considered in the preceding part) and the standard of care (presently considered) have often been confused and/or conflated. They are, however, conceptually distinct. And, as a leading textbook put it (see M Brazier and J Murphy, *Street on Torts* (10th ed, 1999) at p 231):

> 'Although it is not uncommon for the standard of care to be treated as part of the "duty", it seems preferable to confine "duty"

to the question of whether the defendant is under an obligation to the plaintiff and to treat separately the question of the extent of the duty owed.'

And, in a similar vein, another leading textbook put it thus (see D Howarth, 'Duty of Care—Incorporating Misrepresentation and Deceit' in Chapter 12 of A Grubb (Gen ed), *Butterworths Common Law Series—The Law of Tort* (2002) at p 505):

'The difference between breach issues and duty issues is that breach issues are about whether, taking both the risks and benefits of the defendant's conduct into account, the defendant acted reasonably; duty issues are about whether defendants should be held to be not liable even though they might have acted unreasonably, that is whether the rule of requiring conduct to be reasonable should apply in the first place.'

19.45 On a *practical* level, what factors would guide the courts in ascertaining —on an objective, reasonable person, basis—the appropriate standard of care in a given situation? A leading textbook has set out a number of relevant factors as follows: the likelihood of harm; the seriousness of the risk and the risk of serious injury; the utility of the act of the defendant; and the cost of avoiding the harm (see generally M Brazier and J Murphy, *Street on Torts* (10th ed, 1999) at pp 233–235).

Elements of Negligence (3): Causation, Remoteness and Mitigation

Causation

19.46 The breach of the duty of care must, of course, have been the *operative cause* of the plaintiff's damage (see, generally, *Clerk & Lindsell on Torts* (18th ed, 2000) at Chapter 2, entitled 'Causation in Tort: General Principles'). Generally, the courts apply the 'but for' test, which asks whether the damage to the plaintiff would have occurred 'but for' the defendant's breach of his or her duty of care owed to the plaintiff. However, as been aptly observed (see *Clerk & Lindsell on Torts*, ibid, at paragraph 2-06):

'It is worth bearing in mind that the "but for" test functions as an exclusionary test, *i.e.* its purpose is to exclude from consideration irrelevant causes. The fact that the defendant's conduct is found to be *a* cause, applying the "but for" test, is not conclusive as to whether he should be held responsible in law since the function of the causal enquiry in law is to determine which causes have significance for the purpose of attributing legal responsibility. It is sometimes said that the law seeks the *causa causans* (effective factor) rather than the *cause sine qua non* (factor(s) without which damage could not have occurred)' (emphasis in original).

The text just quoted proceeds to note an equally important and related principle which should also be noted (see ibid at paragraph 2-15):

> 'The claimant does not have to prove that the defendant's breach of duty was the sole, or even main, cause of his damage provided he can demonstrate that it made a *material contribution* to the damage' (emphasis added).

A very recent and interesting House of Lords decision might also be noted very briefly. In *Fairchild v Glenhaven Funeral Services Ltd* (2002), it was held that, where the plaintiff had brought an action against more than one defendant, all of whom were former employers *and* (more importantly) who were guilty of negligence, but where the plaintiff could not—based on current medical knowledge—establish (in accordance with the 'but for' test above) which particular defendant was responsible for his existing medical condition, then the court ought to adopt a *modified and less strict* approach towards the proof of causation. The House therefore held that *each* defendant's wrongdoing had materially increased the risk of the plaintiff contracting his disease and that the causal requirements for liability of the defendants had therefore been established. The concern to achieve a fair result was undoubtedly an extremely important and influential factor.

19.47 It is possible, though, for an intervening act (termed, in Latin, a '*novus actus interveniens*') to *break the chain of causation* and hence relieve the defendant from further liability (and see generally *Clerk & Lindsell on Torts* (18th ed, 2000) at paragraphs 2-36–2-59). The entire process, though, is one which is heavily dependent on the particular facts of the case at hand and (see ibid at paragraph 2-36) 'may take three forms: (i) some natural event independent of any human agency; (ii) an act (or omission) by a third party; (iii) the conduct of the claimant himself'.

19.48 Insofar as *concurrent causes* are concerned, it has been observed thus (see M Brazier and J Murphy, *Street on Torts* (10th ed, 1999) at p 273):

> 'If the defendant commits a tort (or an act which will become a tort if non-remote damage ensues) and, before his act spends its force, some later tortious act combines with it to produce a particular result which would not have been produced without the operation of the second act, then the defendant will be liable if, and only if, it is found … that his act caused the damage.'

Remoteness of Damage

19.49 It is also clear that even if there is a duty of care and that duty has been breached, with the damage clearly being caused by the defendant, the defendant might still escape legal liability if the damage is *too remote* (and see generally *Clerk & Lindsell on Torts* (18th ed, 2000) at paragraphs 2-60–2-66; and for an analogous limitation under the law of *contract*, see paragraph 15.68 ff, above); the *policy* reason underlying such a limitation or constraint on liability should be noted (see ibid at paragraph 2-60):

> 'The possible consequences of any human conduct are endless. The defendant's wrongdoing may trigger a series of events which "but for" his fault would never have occurred. The law does not, however, impose indefinite liability. A line must be drawn

to confine the responsibility of the defendant to those consequences of his fault which it is proper for him to shoulder. Damage must not be too remote. Remoteness of damage is concerned not so much with causation as setting the outer limits of the defendant's responsibility.'

Insofar as the law relating to negligence is concerned, it has been clearly established, since the seminal Privy Council decision in *Overseas Tankship (UK) Ltd v Morts Dock & Engineering Co, The Wagon Mound (No 1)* (1961), that the test of remoteness of damage is one of *reasonable foreseeability*; in other words, the defendant would only be liable for damage that is reasonably foreseeable (contrast this with the special situation with regard to fraudulent misrepresentation or deceit where the scope and range of liability is very much broader; see the chapter on 'Misrepresentation' at paragraph 12.27, above). It should be noted, however, that so long as the *type* of damage caused is reasonably foreseeable, the damage is deemed not to be too remote, although it might well be the case that the *extent* of the damage itself is not reasonably foreseeable (see also paragraph 19.54, below).

19.50 What, then, about the relationship between the concept of remoteness of damage on the one hand and the concept of the duty of care on the other: particularly since both involve (albeit in different ways) the idea of reasonable foreseeability? A leading textbook perceptively puts it this way (see *Clerk & Lindsell on Torts* (18th ed, 2000) at paragraph 2-66):

> 'In the tort of negligence there is clearly a relationship between the remoteness of damage and the nature and scope of the defendant's duty of care. Since remoteness is concerned with setting the outer limits of the defendant's responsibility in circumstances where the damage has occurred in unusual or unanticipated ways, it makes no sense to attempt to identify those limits without also addressing the question of what consequences the duty of care imposed upon the defendant was designed to avoid.'

Mitigation of Damage

19.51 A plaintiff will not be allowed to either unreasonably increase his or her loss and/or fail to take reasonable steps to decrease such loss. The key test here is that of *reasonableness* and hence depends very much on the facts of the case (and see generally *Clerk & Lindsell on Torts* (18th ed, 2000) at paragraphs 29-08–29-09).

Proof of Negligence and the Doctrine of Res Ipsa Loquitur

19.52 The onus or burden of proof generally lies on the *plaintiff* to prove his or her case on a balance of probabilities.

19.53 On occasion, however, the doctrine of *res ipsa loquitur* (the Latin phrase meaning 'the situation speaks for itself') may in fact operate in order to raise the inference that the defendant has been negligent. The basic elements of the doctrine are to be found in the following oft-cited statement of principle by Erle CJ in the seminal English decision in this area of *Scott v London and St Katherine Docks Co* (1865) (at p 601):

> 'There must be reasonable evidence of negligence. But where the thing is shewn to be under the management of the defendant or his servants, and the accident is such as in the ordinary course of things does not happen if those who have the management use proper care, it affords reasonable evidence, in the absence of explanation by the defendants, that the accident arose from want of care.'

In summary, the doctrine of *res ipsa loquitur* can be applied if the event concerned would not normally have happened in the absence of negligence; the thing causing the damage to the plaintiff was under the sole management and control of the defendant or his servants; and the cause of the event itself was unknown to the plaintiff (and see, generally, *Clerk & Lindsell on Torts* (18th ed, 2000) at paragraphs 7-192–7.196 as well as F Trindade and KF Tan, '*Res Ipsa Loquitur*: Some Recent Cases in Singapore and Its Future' [2000] *Singapore Journal of Legal Studies* 186).

In the Singapore High Court decision of *Ooi Han Sun v Bee Hua Meng* (1991) (also discussed below at paragraph 19.56), Yong Pung How CJ, after having cited the statement of principle by Erle CJ just quoted above, applied the general principles to the facts at hand (which involved a road accident) as follows (see p 827):

> 'In the present case, the pick-up was at all times under the control and management of the defendant, and the accident which resulted in the pick-up overturning in the middle of the road could not have happened in the ordinary course of things without negligence on the defendant's part. A burden is therefore cast upon the defendant, and he must show how the accident actually occurred, and how this was consistent with due care on his part. In other words, he must rebut the inference of negligence raised against him ...'

'Thin Skull Rule'

19.54 It is established law that the defendant must 'take the plaintiff as he or she finds him or her'. This is the essence of the 'eggshell skull rule' (sometimes also known as the 'thin skull rule'). Professor Michael Jones described this rule well, in his learned work, *Textbook on Torts* (8th ed, 2002), as follows (at pp 272–273):

> 'The [rule] is ... used to describe the notion that where the claimant is suffering from a latent physical or psychological predisposition to a particular injury or illness which the harm inflicted by the defendant triggers off, the defendant is responsible for the additional, unforeseeable damage that his negligence has produced. This is commonly called the 'thin-skull' or the 'eggshell-skull' rule. The rule can apply to almost any type of weakness or predisposition, such as a fragile skull. ...

> The eggshell-skull rule overlaps, but is not coextensive, with the general principle that the extent of the harm need not be foreseeable. Where the claimant's predisposition simply exacerbates the otherwise foreseeable type of harm, then it is little more than the mechanism by which the principle comes into effect. And clearly, the general principle can apply in the absence of any predisposition in the plaintiff ... The eggshell-skull rule arguably goes beyond this, however, by allowing recovery for harm of a different type from that which is foreseeable.'

An oft-cited illustration is the English decision of *Smith v Leech Brain & Co Ltd* (1962). In this case, the plaintiff's husband was burnt on the lower lip by a piece of molten metal at his workplace. It was found that he had received inadequate protection and that this was due to the negligence of the defendant employer. Unfortunately, the burn triggered a cancer, which the plaintiff's husband died from some three years later (the cancer developed from the tissues in his lip which were already in a pre-malignant condition). The court held that defendant was liable for the plaintiff's husband's death. As Lord Parker CJ put it (at p 414), '[i]t has always been the law of this country that a tortfeasor takes his victim as he finds him'; and he observed, later in his judgment, thus (at p 415):

> 'The test is not whether these employers could reasonably have foreseen that a burn would cause cancer and that he would die. The question is whether these employers could reasonably foresee the type of injury he suffered, namely, the burn. What, in the particular case, is the amount of damage which he suffers as a result of that burn, depends upon the characteristics and constitution of the victim.'

Defences

Illegality

19.55 The defence of *illegality* is not easily available. The mere occurrence of an illegal act will not, *per se*, result in the successful invocation of the defence. There must be a sufficient linkage, an example of which occurred in the English Court of Appeal decision of *Pitts v Hunt* (1991). In this case, the plaintiff was a pillion passenger on a motor cycle which was involved in an accident. The personal representative of the (deceased) rider of the motor cycle was the first defendant and the other vehicle involved in the accident was driven by the second defendant. Both the plaintiff and the rider had been drinking prior to the accident. The plaintiff also knew that the rider did not hold a driving licence and was uninsured and yet encouraged him (the rider) to drive in a reckless and dangerous manner such that if someone else had been killed as a result, it would have amounted to manslaughter by the commission of a dangerous act. The court held that the plaintiff was precluded, on grounds of public policy, from recovering any compensation for the injuries that he had sustained. Balcombe LJ also held that the plaintiff and the rider had been involved in a 'joint illegal enterprise' which was 'such as to disable the court from determining the standard of care to be observed' (see p 50).

19.56 The following passage from *Halsbury's Laws of Singapore—Tort* (2000) at pp 46–47 is also instructive:

> 'The maxim *ex turpi causa non oritur actio* has only a very limited application in tort. In general, the fact that the plaintiff is involved in some wrongdoing does not of itself provide the defendant with a good defence. However, if the injury arises from an act done in the direct execution of the illegal common purpose, the plaintiff may be debarred from recovering on the principle that an action which arises from an immoral cause cannot be sustained.'

Indeed, in the Singapore High Court decision of *Ooi Han Sun v Bee Hua Meng* (1991) (also considered above with regard to the doctrine of *res ipsa loquitur* at paragraph 19.53, above), Yong Pung How CJ observed thus (at pp 830–831):

> 'A a rule of public policy, the maxim *ex turpi causa non oritur actio* (no cause of action arises out of a base cause) will apply in the law of contract to prevent a plaintiff founding a claim on an illegal act or agreement [and see generally Chapter 14 of the present work, above]. It is clear, however, that the maxim has only very limited application in tort and, in general, the fact that the plaintiff is involved in some wrongdoing does not of itself provide the defendant with a good defence ... The only exceptions would appear to be the limited range of cases in which, on the facts of the case, an injury can be held to have been directly incurred in the course of the commission of a crime [citing, *inter alia*, *Pitts v Hunt*, discussed above in this paragraph]. These decisions would also be in line with the public policy in Singapore which is reflected in the Contributory Negligence and Personal Injuries Act [Cap 54, 1989 Rev Ed] ... under which a claim will not be defeated by reason of the fault of the person suffering the damage [and see the discussion at paragraph 19.59, below]; and in the Workmen's Compensation Act [Cap 354, 1998 Rev Ed] ... which provides that a workman will not be prevented from suing for recovery of compensation even under an illegal contract.'

In this case, the defendant had in fact argued that one of the plaintiff passengers (a Malaysian who had been injured) did not possess a valid work permit at the time the accident occurred. The court held that this particular plaintiff could not thereby be precluded from claiming against the defendant. However, it should be noted that there was nevertheless an effect on the *quantum of damages awarded*. Yong CJ observed (at p 833) as follows:

> 'In my judgment, the assessment of the first plaintiff's loss of earnings should be based on an estimate, however, difficult and imprecise this might be, of what he would have earned in

> Malaysia had there been no accident to him. The immigration laws and regulations which require work permits to be obtained by foreign workers before they can work in Singapore were not designed merely to raise a little extra revenue, but to implement a basic public policy. To compensate the first plaintiff on the basis of what he might have earned by working illegally in Singapore without a valid work permit would be against public policy and wholly improper.'

Voluntary Assumption of Risk

19.57 Another defence is that embodied in the Latin maxim *'volenti non fit injuria'*, which centres around the concept of consent or the voluntary assumption of risk. In order for this particular defence to succeed, the plaintiff must not only have fully known as well as appreciated the extent of the risk but must also have both consented as well as voluntarily accepted the said risk as well (and see generally M Brazier and J Murphy, *Street on Torts* (10th ed, 1999) at pp 292–300).

19.58 However, this particular defence must be distinguished from the next (viz contributory negligence, considered at paragraph 19.59, below). As was aptly observed in *Halsbury's Laws of Singapore—Tort* (2000) at p 234:

> 'This defence is to be distinguished from the plea of contributory negligence, for a plaintiff may have voluntarily exposed himself to the risk of being injured while himself exercising the utmost care for his own safety and conversely, while knowledge of the risk may show contributory negligence it does not prove voluntary assumption of risk.'

It should also be noted that 'contributory negligence operates to reduce damages according to the degree of fault, *volenti* is a total defence' (see *Clerk & Lindsell on Torts* (18th ed, 2000) at paragraph 3-99).

Contributory Negligence

19.59 The present law is embodied within the Contributory Negligence and Personal Injuries Act (Cap 54, 1989 Rev Ed) which is, in turn, based upon the UK Law Reform (Contributory Negligence) Act 1945 (and see generally D Howarth, 'General Defences' in Chapter 5 of A Grubb (Gen ed), *Butterworths Common Law Series—The Law of Tort* (2002) at paragraphs 5.2–5.40).

The main provision is to be found in *section 3* of the Act, which reads as follows:

> '(1) Where any person suffers damage as the result partly of his own fault and partly of the fault of any other person or persons, a claim in respect of that damage shall not be defeated by reason of the fault of the person suffering the damage, but the damages recoverable in respect thereof shall be reduced to such extent as the court thinks just and equitable having regard to the claimant's share in the responsibility for the damage.

Provided that —
(2) Subsection (1) shall not operate to defeat any defence arising under a contract.
(3) Where any contract or written law providing for the limitation of liability is applicable to the claim, the amount of damages recoverable by the claimant under subsection (1) shall not exceed the maximum limit so applicable.
(4) Where damages are recoverable by any person under subsection (1) subject to such reduction as is therein mentioned, the court shall find and record the total damages which would have been recoverable if the claimant had not been at fault.
(5) Where any person dies as the result partly of his own fault and partly of the fault of any other person or persons, and accordingly if an action were brought for the benefit of the estate under section 10 of the Civil Law Act (Cap 43), the damages recoverable would be reduced under subsection (1), any damages recoverable in an action brought for the benefit of —
(a) the dependants of that person under section 20 of the Civil Law Act; or
(b) any person under section 21 of the Civil Law Act,
shall be reduced to a proportionate extent.
(6) Where, in any case to which subsection (1) applies, one of the persons at fault avoids liability to any other such person or his personal representative by pleading the Limitation Act or any other written law limiting the time within which proceedings may be taken, he shall not be entitled to recover any damages or contributions from that other person or personal representative by virtue of that subsection.'

And 'fault' is defined in *section 2* of the Act as meaning 'negligence, breach of statutory duty or other act or omission which gives rise to a liability in tort or would, apart from this Act, give rise to the defence of contributory negligence'.

The defence of contributory negligence does not necessitate a duty of care being owed by the plaintiff to the defendant as such.

The apportionment of damages under the Act 'will generally be reached on a commonsense basis'; see M Brazier and J Murphy, *Street on Torts* (10th ed, 1999) (at p 291).

Negligence and Cyberspace

Introduction

19.60 There are many intriguing issues that are raised as a result of the interface between the law of negligence on the one hand and cyberspace on the other. However, no definitive conclusions can, in the main, be drawn. This not surprising in view of the fact that lawyers and judges are only just beginning to delve into the many fascinating issues that have arisen as a result of the introduction of cyberspace—itself a relatively new development. It should also be mentioned that the many difficulties that hinder resolution of the various issues are due, in the main, to the fact that we have, for the time being at least, only more traditional concepts which were originally formulated during quite different times and in an obviously quite different environment. However, it is the present writer's view that most of the existing legal concepts do not need to be altered radically although the courts will need great wisdom as well as intellectual dexterity to apply existing concepts to the many new scenarios that have arisen as a result of the introduction of cyberspace.

It should nevertheless also be noted that the *potential* liability is, by the very nature of cyberspace, much greater: if nothing else, because information over the Internet is much more widely as well as efficiently circulated.

19.61 Only a few issues can be dealt with, albeit cursorily, in this chapter, not least because, as already mentioned, they are very new and have (for the most part) not been dealt with in any conclusive manner by the courts themselves.

Computer Viruses and Negligence

(1) *Establishing a Duty of Care*

19.62 One important issue which arises is also a very practical and important one: what is the tortious liability insofar as the spread of *computer viruses* are concerned? As already alluded to above, there is no easy answer to this particular issue. Although the originators of such viruses are subject to criminal penalties under the Computer Misuse Act (Cap 50A, 1998 Rev Ed), we are concerned here with *civil* (in particular, *tortious*) liability. It should also be noted that even where criminal liability is concerned, the originator of such viruses is usually beyond the criminal jurisdiction of the local courts in any event—all the more so since such viruses travel literally round the globe.

As already mentioned, existing tortious doctrines may not fit easily with possible legal liability in the context of cyberspace. Various doctrines have been mentioned by writers as possible ways of imposing legal liability for the spread of computer viruses. These include the tort of trespass to goods, strict liability under the rule in *Rylands v Fletcher* (1868), as well as negligence (see generally GJH Smith, *Internet Law and Regulation* (3rd ed, 2002) at paragraphs 5-012–5-020). Although it is true that the present chapter focuses, in any event, on the law of negligence, it is equally true that the possible application of the former two doctrines just mentioned is probably less potentially effective compared to the application of the general principles of the law of negligence itself (and see generally Smith, ibid at paragraphs 5-020 and 5-016–5-019, respectively; reference may also be made, insofar as possible liability under the rule in *Rylands v Fletcher* is concerned, to C Gringras, *The Laws of the Internet* (2nd ed, 2003) at p 113). For example, the rule in *Rylands v Fletcher* requires, *inter alia*, that the defendant accumulate dangerous material (here, in his or her personal computer); this is of course highly improbable (save, perhaps, insofar as the originator of the computer virus is concerned), for 'most people do not set out to maintain collections of computer viruses' and that '[t]heir systems become infected by accident and they pass on the viruses by accident or neglect' (see Smith, ibid at paragraph 5-017). Indeed, even insofar as the originator of the computer virus is concerned, it would, more often than not, be extremely difficult, to say the least, to mount a successful cause of action against him or her for a number of reasons (including the fact that he or she would probably have operated from another country altogether). And insofar as the tort of *trespass* is concerned, it is arguable 'that virus damage to the data on a computer disk would constitute damage to goods for the purposes of trespass' (see Smith, ibid at paragraph 5-019).

19.63 Turning to what is suggested is a more substantive possible claim in *negligence*, it might be argued that even if the defendant had not been the originator of the computer virus, he or she might nevertheless be liable in negligence for not having taken reasonable care—this breach of the duty of care having resulted in the transmission of the virus to the personal computer(s) of the plaintiff(s) concerned. However, it might be argued that to impose a duty of care under such circumstances would be to open the floodgates since computer viruses can spread extremely far and wide, causing different varieties as well as large amounts of damage. The problem is, of course, particularly acute when the damage consists of *pure economic loss* (and see, generally, paragraphs 19.11–19.41, above). It could of course be argued that there ought to be no difficulties insofar as *physical* damage to the personal computer and (at least possibly) its software is concerned (cf C Gringras, *The Laws of the Internet* (2nd ed, 2003) at pp 95 and 97). Could it then be argued that any economic loss which flows thereafter is consequential upon the physical damage and/or only goes to the extent (and not the type) of damage?

It is envisaged that the basic principles discussed earlier in this chapter would apply. It may well be argued that to find a duty of care under such circumstances would not be 'fair, just and reasonable' under the third part of the 'three-part test' enunciated in the *Caparo* case (1990), which apparently represents the present law (although the reader should also note the critique of the 'three-part test' by the present writer as well; cf also C Gringras, *The Laws of the Internet* (2nd ed, 2003) at pp 91–92, on the application of the element of 'fair, just and reasonable'). On the other hand, could it be argued that it is 'fair, just and reasonable' that if a particular computer virus is particularly notorious, reasonable individuals and corporations ought then to take the necessary precautions or else face the legal consequences accordingly? But, leaving aside this broader element, could it be argued that there would be insufficient 'proximity' between the plaintiff and the defendant? It is suggested that this really depends, in the final analysis, upon the precise facts of the case concerned. This is, admittedly, not a particularly satisfactory answer. However, the myriad possibilities of factual permutations, especially in the context of cyberspace, must be borne in mind. Ought, for example, the defendant be liable to a plaintiff who happens to be in his or her e-mail address book without more? Would it make a difference if the defendant and plaintiff had had a close business association in the past? If, of course, the defendant *knew* that the e-mail sent was infected, a duty of care would obviously arise (and see, in this regard, C Gringras, *The Laws of the Internet* (2nd ed, 2003) at p 89). Such reasoning would of course apply, *a fortiori*, to institutions and corporations; indeed, as one writer puts it (see C Gringras, *The Laws of the Internet* (2nd ed, 2003) at p 90):

> 'In the workplace, many people other than the system operator send emails. If an internal network is infected, the system operator should block all emails from leaving the system until the suspected malicious code is treated. If it is technically difficult to block emails leaving, the system operator has a duty to external recipients to inform the employees not to send potentially infected material. … [V]iruses are often spread because system operators do not act quickly enough to prevent other users of the system from infecting others.'

19.64 There is also the potential liability (in negligence) of Internet Service Providers (ISPs) as well. The additional complication is often that of *control* (or, rather the *lack* thereof). It should, however, be noted that, in addition to the attempted invocation of contractual disclaimers or exception clauses (briefly touched on below), a 'network service provider' is afforded some protection against civil or criminal liability under *section 10 of the Electronic Transactions Act* (Cap 88, 1999 Rev Ed). Section 10 is, in effect, a '*statutory* defence', and for other possible defences at common law, the reader is referred to the discussion below (see below, paragraphs 19.71–19.72). The material provisions of the section itself read as follows:

> '(1) A *network service provider* shall not be subject to any civil or criminal liability under any rule of law in respect of third-party material in the form of electronic records to which he *merely provides access* if such liability is founded on —
> (a) the making, publication, dissemination or distribution of such materials or any statement made in such material; or
> (b) the infringement of any rights subsisting in or in relation to such material.
> (2) Nothing in this section shall affect —
> (a) any obligation founded on contract;
> (b) the obligation of a network service provider as such under a licensing or other regulatory regime established under any written law; or
> (c) any obligation imposed under any written law or by a court to remove, block or deny access to any material.
> (3) For the purposes of this section —
> "provides access", in relation to third-party material, means the provision of the necessary technical means by which third-party material may be accessed and includes the automatic and temporary storage of the third-party material for the purpose of providing access;

"third-party", in relation to a network service provider, means a person over whom the provider *has no effective control*' (emphasis added).

It should be noted that the emphasised phrases above do indicate not only the key elements of the provision but also highlight potential areas of ambiguity in the context of interpretation and application (for example, the fact that the term 'network service provider' has not been defined in the Act itself).

However, in order to avoid legal liability (particularly where, for some reason or other, the statutory protection mentioned above does *not* apply), it might be prudent to take the necessary precautions (these would apply equally to website hosts and other controllers as well). In the words of one writer (see C Gringras, *The Laws of the Internet* (2nd ed, 2003) at p 90):

> 'Technical solutions obviously include ensuring that no files can be uploaded before passing through the site's anti-viral program first. This will probably be sufficient to extinguish the controller's liability to his visitors, although it would be legally safer if a contractual disclaimer is also provided [as to which see paragraph 19.66, below]. Additionally it may be evidentially useful for the controller to maintain a log of which person leaves which file. If a claim is brought against the controller, it may be crucial that the claimant can add, as co-defendant, the person who deposited the virus initially.'

19.65 Where, of course, the virus is transmitted via a *website*, the argument of the lack or absence of control becomes much weaker since the owner of the website has direct control over the content as well as processes of his or her website (and see C Gringras, *The Laws of the Internet* (2nd ed, 2003) at p 91). Indeed, for this very reason, the website owner would do well to put into place the precautions mentioned in the preceding paragraph.

19.66 Liability could of course be sought to be avoided by way of *contractual disclaimers*. Generally speaking, the law relating to exception clauses (discussed in Chapter 6) would apply and the reader is referred to the discussion in that particular chapter.

19.67 It would seem clear, however, that it would be prudent for any individual to *take the proper practical precautions* which, it is submitted, would enable him or her to safeguard himself or herself against any possible legal liability in negligence (insofar as Internet Service Providers are concerned, see paragraph 19.64, above). For example, the individual concerned could *scan any e-mail containing an attachment first before* sending it to other users (viz the potential plaintiffs). It should be noted, however, that computer viruses often replicate themselves *without any knowledge or intent on the part of the defendant*.

The individual concerned could also *ensure that there is a clear and adequate warning in his or her e-mail*, so that if any other individual should suffer damage or loss as a result of the deleterious effects of a computer virus, the former could probably successfully invoke the defence of *volenti non fit injuria* (or voluntary assumption of risk, as to which see, generally, paragraphs 19.57–19.58, above, as well as paragraph 19.72, below).

(2) *Establishing the Requisite Standard of Care*

19.68 The appropriate *standard of care* also poses some possible difficulties. Would *industry practice* be the best guide (a point that also arises when we discuss the possible defence of contributory negligence and which is potentially problematic, particularly since there are so very many different kinds of individuals with different levels of competence in information technology; see below, paragraph 19.71 as well as GJH Smith, *Internet Law and Regulation* (3rd ed, 2002) at paragraph 5-015 and C Gringras, *The Laws of the Internet* (2nd ed, 2003), especially at p 93)? It is arguable that the more dangerous the computer virus, the greater the obligation to take adequate precautions to prevent its spread—a point that is wholly consistent with the general principles in the area (and see Gringras, ibid at p 94). And insofar at least as the larger institutions and organisations are concerned, the standard of care might include installing the latest anti-viral software as well (see Gringras, ibid).

(3) *Potential Problems of Causation*

19.69 There are also potentially complex issues of *causation*. For example, can the defendant argue that the plaintiff's personal computer had *already* been infected by an *unrelated* website? What if the argument is that the damage to the plaintiff's personal computer had been caused by a *different* computer virus altogether? There would also undoubtedly be situations where it is unclear whether the computer virus concerned had actually caused the damage in question. At this juncture, an effective response would arguably not lie in the sphere of the law as such but, rather, in the spheres of both technology as well as the experts in technology, although the basic principles of causation briefly mentioned above (see paragraphs 19.46–19.48) would continue to apply. It should be noted that these—and other—issues are dealt with generally in C Gringras, *The Laws of the Internet* (2nd ed, 2003) at pp 98–101.

(4) *Potential Problems of Remoteness of Damage*

19.70 There are possible arguments from *remoteness of damage* as well. This particular issue is an especially acute one in the context of cyberspace where the boundaries of liability can be virtually limitless. Where, then, is the court to draw the line and can the line drawn be justified by legal principle? Undoubtedly, the basic principles (see paragraph 19.49, above) would also continue to apply but their *application* would be rather more complex because of the change in context.

(5) *When is the Defence of Contributory Negligence Available?*

19.71 Another issue which arises, in the context of a possible *defence*, is whether or not if the plaintiff does not install anti-virus software (or, perhaps, even the latest anti-virus software), he or she is guilty of *contributory negligence* (as to which see, generally, paragraph 19.59, above, as well as C Gringras, *The Laws of the Internet* (2nd ed, 2003) at pp 106–107). There is no easy answer to this particular issue. One argument might be that the current practice is to install such software and that, hence, the plaintiff ought to have done so. On the other hand, it could be argued that this may not be the case—or at least may not be the case in certain countries; this, in turn, depends on the level of competence insofar as information technology is concerned in that particular country. But it is suggested that, even within a particular country, ascertaining what the prevailing practice is may not be at all easy since levels of competence will vary from group to group as well as from individual to individual. Where, however, large corporations are concerned, it is probably difficult for such organisations to argue that the absence of adequate protective measures (such as firewalls) is not indicative of at least some contributory negligence on their part.

Could it also be argued that the plaintiff ought *not* to have *opened* the e-mail attachment containing the virus *without scanning it with anti-virus software* in the *first instance*? Would such conduct itself amount to contributory negligence? *Or* ought it to depend upon the *type* of computer virus in question and whether or not the plaintiff knew—or ought, as a reasonable person, to have known—of the existence of the virus concerned and the dangers it posed?

And where software and/or data has been damaged or lost, could it be argued that the plaintiff ought to have had a *backup or replacement copy* in the first instance (cf Gringras, ibid at pp 107–08)?

(6) *When is the Defence of Assumption of Risk Available?*

19.72 The defence of *volenti non fit injuria* or the voluntary assumption of risk may well arise especially in the context of plaintiffs whose personal computers have been infected by a computer virus originating from the defendant's website as it is arguable that the plaintiff had at least impliedly consented to the risk of such infection by accessing the defendant's website (cf C Gringras, *The Laws of the Internet* (2nd ed, 2003) at p 108). Where, of course, the defendant clearly placed a warning in the requisite language on his or her website, this would clearly strengthen the chances of such a defence succeeding.

Where an infected e-mail is concerned, we have already seen that this defence might also be available where a clear and adequate warning has been placed by the defendant in the text of his or her e-mail to the plaintiff (and see paragraph 19.67, above; see also C Gringras, *The Laws of the Internet* (2nd ed, 2003) at p 90).

Negligent Misstatements in Cyberspace

(1) *Application of General Principles*

19.73 Yet another important issue concerns one already examined above, but in the context of *cyberspace*. What are the legal principles which govern legal liability for *negligent misstatements in cyberspace*? It is submitted that the basic principles already considered above would continue to apply (and see, generally, paragraphs 19.35–19.40, above). However, the *new* *context* does result in various difficult issues of *application*. How, for instance, does the court treat information contained in websites (assuming that we could, in the main at least, treat situations involving correspondence via electronic mail as analogous to those in the traditional sense)? This is an important issue simply because there are thousands upon thousands of websites on the Internet. This might suggest that there should be a presumption against finding a duty of care. This is certainly a persuasive argument insofar as *general* information contained in the website is concerned. *However*, where *specific* information is given in response to a *specific* request, the situation might conceivably be quite different (and see, generally, GJH Smith, *Internet Law and Regulation* (3rd ed, 2002) at paragraph 5-008); indeed, such a scenario would support the establishment of the requisite degree of *proximity* required in order for a duty of care to arise in law (whether the rationale is reasonable reliance or voluntary assumption of responsibility, although an *integrated* approach has been proposed earlier: see paragraph 19.36). More specifically, assuming that reasonable reliance is an element relating to liability in this particular context (and see paragraph 19.36, above), is it, as a point of general principle, reasonable to rely on information from the Internet in the first instance? It would appear that the distinction just drawn between very general information on the one hand and specialised information (particularly when furnished at the plaintiff's request) on the other may be helpful. Where, for instance, the response is a casual one, there is less likelihood of a duty of care arising compared to one where the response is a considered one (see also C Gringras, *The Laws of the Internet* (2nd ed, 2003) at p 116). Here, the precise *nature* of the website itself would be of great importance (see also Gringras, ibid, at pp 116–117).

In situations involving specificity of relationship, there might of course be a *contractual* relationship as well—upon which legal liability (if applicable) can of course be more conveniently based (and see Smith, ibid at paragraph 5-010). Finally, the following (related) observations are also of some interest (see Smith, ibid at paragraph 5-008):

> 'One sure prediction, however, is that at least some of today's personal, custom-tailored, individually provided professional advice services will be tomorrow's branded, mass-provided interactive information services. That trend can only increase the pressure to widen the scope of liability for economic loss caused by incorrect information. The courts are currently set against this. But only a few years before *Donoghue v Stevenson* imposed product liability on manufacturers, judges were insistent that such liability should not be contemplated.'

However, could it be argued that the vastness of the Internet might well cut the other way, so to speak. In other words, could it be argued that inasmuch as the plaintiff would have access to other alternative sources of information on the Internet, he or she might not have relied on the defendant's alleged negligent misstatement in the first instance, or that he or she ought not, as a reasonable person, to have relied on such an alleged misstatement? Could it also possibly be argued that the plaintiff ought, in the light of alternative sources of information, to have been disabused of any errors in the defendant's alleged negligent misstatement? However, the assumption here is that the plaintiff ought —as a reasonable person—to have effected checks for such alternative sources of information. Once again, whether or not such an assumption is itself reasonable has not, to the best of the present writer's knowledge, been canvassed in any Commonwealth jurisdiction yet.

There are also possibly preliminary issues as well, for example, identifying who made the statement concerned in the first instance (see, generally, C Gringras, *The Laws of the Internet* (2nd ed, 2003) at pp 114–115).

(2) *Negligent Misstatements and Hyperlinking*

19.74 Finally, what about situations of *hyperlinking* to other websites? Much, it is submitted, would depend on the precise facts as well as context. However, one possible way of avoiding any legal liability for content outside one's own website is to have a notice stating that no liability is assumed for such content. One writer observes, in this regard, as follows (see C Gringras, *The Laws of the Internet* (2nd ed, 2003) at p 120):

> 'There are two situations where such a notice is used: first, where the linked site is a "subsidiary" of the main site, second, where the linked site is not associated with the first. Clearly, for the first situation, if the site is within the overall control of the website owner, say where a set of websites are collected together under the same domain, the controller will have some responsibility to viewers of the other sites. In the second situation, however, it is difficult to see how a duty would arise from providing a link to another's site.'

The same writer also observes (at p 121) that '[a] cleaner approach is merely to use a heading for the linked sites, "Other sites of interest". This simple statement distances the website owner from the other content and should be general enough not to form considered advice.'

Conclusion

19.75 It is clear that a great many issues in the context of cyberspace remain unresolved. Indeed, an even close to comprehensive analysis as well as a canvassing of their probable solutions would require a separate work of its own. However, it is hoped that, within the more modest compass of this part of this chapter, the reader would have obtained a 'flavour' of the main issues as well as the possible ways forward.

CHAPTER 20 Economic Torts

PARAGRAPHS

20.1 **Introduction**

Interference with Trade and Economic Interest

20.2–20.5 General Framework
20.6 Inducing Breach of Contract
20.7–20.9 (1) Knowledge and Intention
(2) Procurement
20.10 (a) Direct Procurement
20.11–20.12 (b) Direct Intervention
20.13–20.14 (c) Indirect Intervention
20.15 (d) Inconsistent Dealings
20.16–20.17 (3) Breach
20.18–20.20 (4) Damage
20.21–20.23 (5) Justification
20.24 Inducing Breach of Other Obligations
20.25 Intimidation
20.26 (1) Threat
20.27 (2) Unlawful Conduct
20.28 (3) Damage
20.29–20.30 (4) Two- and Three-Party Liability
20.31 Conspiracy
(1) Conspiracy to Injure
20.32 (a) Combination
20.33 (b) Predominant Purpose to Injure
20.34 (c) Damage
20.35 (2) Conspiracy by Unlawful Means
20.36 (a) Intention
20.37–20.38 (b) Unlawful Means
20.39–20.40 Unlawful Interference with Trade
20.41–20.42 (1) Intention
20.43 (2) Unlawful Means
20.44 (a) Tort
20.45–20.46 (b) Breach of Contract
20.47 (c) Crime and Breach of Statutory Duty
20.48 (i) The Construction Test
20.49 (ii) A General Approach?

PARAGRAPHS

Interference with Trade and Economic Interest (continued)

20.50 (3) Unlawful Interference as a Genus Tort

Malicious Falsehood

20.51 Introduction
Elements of Tort
20.52 (1) Falsehood
20.53 (2) Malice
20.54 (3) Special Damage
20.55 Malicious Falsehood Distinguished from Defamation

Defamation

20.56–20.58 Introduction
Elements of the Tort
(1) Defamatory Statements
20.59–20.60 (a) What Constitutes a Defamatory Statement
20.61 (b) Form
20.62–20.67 (c) Interpretation
20.68–20.69 (2) Reference to the Plaintiff
20.70–20.72 (3) Publication
Defences
20.73 (1) Justification
20.74 (2) Fair Comment
20.75–20.76 (a) Comment
20.77 (b) Comment is Based on True Facts
20.78 (c) Comment is Fair
20.79 (d) Public Interest
20.80 (e) Effect of Malice
20.81 (3) Absolute Privilege
20.82 (a) Parliamentary Proceedings
20.83 (b) Judicial Proceedings
20.84 (c) Executive Matters
(4) Qualified Privilege
20.85 (a) Malice
20.86–20.87 (b) Communications Between Persons with Corresponding Interests and Duties
20.88 (c) Statements Made to Protect Self-Interests
20.89 (d) Reports of Proceedings
20.90 (5) Innocent Dissemination
20.91 (6) Offer of Amends
20.92–20.93 Remedies
20.94–20.99 Defamation on the Internet

Introduction

20.1 In this chapter, we turn to a category of torts which serves to protect trade or economic interests but which are distinguished from the tort of negligence in that they are usually committed intentionally. For present purposes, this broad category of torts may be divided into two sub-categories, the first of which encompasses acts which amount to an interference with trade or economic interests, with the second relating to torts committed by way of false representations, such as defamation and malicious falsehood.

Interference with Trade and Economic Interests

General Framework

20.2 It should be noted at the outset that this is a sphere of tort law that has developed in a haphazard fashion and is therefore not given to neat classification or simple rationalisation. One reason for the significant uncertainties that surround these torts is that, at its crux, the law is grappling with a complex policy question: where should the line be drawn between lawful and unlawful interference with another's economic interests? Inherent in the notion of free competition—the basic tenet of our economy—is the acceptance that one should be permitted to advance one's own interests even if it is to the disadvantage of others. Yet, notwithstanding the virtues and importance of competition, it is also indisputable that such competition must be based on a fair premise. It is therefore necessary for the law to define the boundaries beyond which one's competitive conduct becomes unfair or unlawful. Cases involving economic torts continually seek to strike a proper *balance* between these two divergent aims.

Although the law in this regard is still evolving to meet the needs of the modern economy, the broad framework may be stated with a reasonable degree of confidence.

20.3 In resolving the tension between free and fair competition, the law gives primacy to the former by acknowledging the general liberty to engage in competitive practices. Competition, together with its resultant injurious effects on one's competitors, do not, without more, amount to a tort. In *Mogul Steamship Co Ltd v McGregor Gow & Co* (1892), several shipowners formed an association with the objective of monopolising a particular trade by offering extremely favourable terms to customers and agents who dealt exclusively with them. As a result, the plaintiff shipowners, not being part of the association, were forced to carry on the trade at a loss. Even though the plaintiffs had clearly been harmed economically by the defendants' cooperation, it was held that the defendants had committed no tort; they were aggressively enlarging their market share through the elimination of competition but had not, in so doing, committed any unlawful act.

20.4 The appropriate indicators of unfair or unlawful competition must therefore be found in considerations other than the injury sustained by the plaintiff. For this purpose, three concepts are commonly employed. Firstly, economic torts have generally been confined to intentional conduct, so that one who incidentally injures another in the course of advancing his own interests would generally not be guilty of having committed a tort. A second restriction is to require that the means utilised by the tortfeasor be of an unlawful nature. (The tort of conspiracy to injure, though, is a notable exception in this regard, see paragraph 20.33, below.) Finally, in the absence of any independently unlawful conduct, one's competitive acts may be tortious if they in fact result in the interference of another's pre-existing legal rights.

20.5 One further preliminary point should be noted. It will be apparent, from the discussion which follows, that a great number of cases in this subject concern the legitimacy of trade union actions in the UK. Although trade union activism is not characteristic of the industrial scene in Singapore, the principles laid down in the leading cases have nonetheless been substantially endorsed by the local judiciary for general application to instances of abuse of economic power.

Inducing Breach of Contract

20.6 Where A, knowing that a contractual relationship exists between B and C, and by word or conduct, procures or induces C to break his contract with B without any reasonable justification or excuse and as a result of which B sustains damage, then A commits a tort as against B. In *Lumley v Gye* (1853), the plaintiff had contracted with Johanna Wagner, an opera singer, to perform exclusively at his theatre for a specified period of time. Subsequently, however, Wagner refused to honour her contractual obligation with the plaintiff but instead performed at the defendant's theatre for a higher fee. The defendant was found to be liable to the plaintiff in tort as he had knowingly induced or procured Wagner to break her contractual obligation with the plaintiff.

(1) *Knowledge and Intention*

20.7 There are two distinct aspects to the mental ingredient of this tort. First, the defendant must be shown to have knowledge of the existence of the contract. The test for determining the existence of such knowledge is an objective one. It is thus not necessary to show that the defendant had actual knowledge of the contract. Instead, the defendant is deemed to possess such knowledge if the existence of the contract is obvious or may reasonably be inferred from the surrounding circumstances. Further, it is unnecessary to show that the defendant has knowledge of the precise terms of the contract. The requirement is also satisfied if a defendant does not in fact know of the existence of the contract at the time of the breach but subsequently learns of it whilst the breach is continuing.

20.8 The second aspect of the mental ingredient requires that defendant must have intended the breach of the contract (see *Tribune Investment Trust Inc v Soosan Trading Co Ltd* (2000)). This does not, however, mean that the defendant must have acted maliciously, in the sense of ill-will or spite, as the defendant's motive is largely irrelevant.

20.9 A question which is as yet unresolved relates to whether the requirement for intention is satisfied when a person does not specifically intend to injure the plaintiff, but commits an act which would inevitably result in such injury. In *Millar v Bassey* (1994), Shirley Bassey was a renowned singer who had contracted her recording services to Dreampace, a recording company. Dreampace wished to produce an album of Bassey's songs and engaged Millar, a record producer, for that purpose. After various arrangements were made for the booking of the recording studios as well as the attendance of the accompanying musicians, Bassey refused to turn up for the rehearsals and eventually withdrew from the project. Millar sued Bassey for procuring the breach by Dreampace of its contractual obligation to Millar. The trial judge found that Bassey's refusal to perform was motivated mainly by considerations of her own career advancement and was not therefore aimed at disabling Dreampace from fulfilling its contractual obligation to Bassey. As such, the trial judge concluded that Bassey did not have the requisite intention to commit the tort and Millar's action was accordingly struck out as disclosing no cause of action. The decision was, however, reversed on appeal. In the English Court of Appeal, Beldam LJ took the view that the intention requirement of the tort could be satisfied if Bassey knew that her refusal to perform would render it impossible for Dreampace to fulfil its contractual obligation with Millar, even if she did not, by doing so, specifically intend to affect Dreampace's contract with Millar. The main difficulty with this view is that it substantially extends the scope of the tort and renders a person accountable to a class of persons whose legal rights he or she had no intention of affecting. It has been observed in the local decision of *Tribune Investment Trust Inc v Soosan Trading Co Ltd* (2000) that the procurer must have intended to interfere with the plaintiff's contract and that it is 'not sufficient that the resulting breach of contract was a mere natural consequence of the defendant's conduct' (per Yong Pung How CJ at p 413). It is therefore submitted that Beldam LJ's view in *Millar v Bassey* is unlikely to find favour in the courts of Singapore.

(2) *Procurement*

(a) Direct Procurement

20.10 Direct persuasion is the most common and straightforward means of procurement. Such persuasion is applied directly on one of the contracting parties and may take the form of peaceful dialogue, or it may be accompanied by bribes, bounties or threats. Generally, the communication of information would not amount to procurement. It is also said that mere advice does not constitute persuasion. However, this distinction is not always helpful as it is sometimes difficult to distinguish between advice and persuasion. Ultimately, the issue is one of causation, in that the defendant's words or conduct must be shown to have been a direct and effective cause of the contracting party's decision to default on his contractual obligation.

(b) Direct Intervention

20.11 A person may also be guilty of inducing a breach of contract if he intervenes to prevent another from performing his contractual obligations by, for instance, kidnapping the contracting party or removing the only available tools needed for performance. In *GWK Ltd v Dunlop Rubber Co Ltd* (1926), a motor car manufacturer had contracted with the plaintiffs to exhibit, at a forthcoming motor show, cars which were fitted with the plaintiffs' tyres. Subsequently, however, the defendants unlawfully removed and substituted the plaintiffs' tyres with their own. The defendants were found liable for inducing the car manufacturer's contractual breach.

20.12 It was observed in *DC Thomson & Co Ltd v Deakin* (1952) that the intervening act must be of an unlawful nature in order for liability to arise. If so, then it would appear that cases involving direct intervention should more appropriately be classified as a species of unlawful interference with trade (see paragraphs 20.39–20.50, below; see, however, criticisms of this requirement by R Bagshaw, 'Inducing Breach of Contract' in J Horder (ed), *Oxford Essays in Jurisprudence* (2000)).

(c) Indirect Intervention

20.13 Indirect intervention occurs where A procures B to commit a wrongful act against C with the intention of disabling C from fulfilling its contractual obligations with D. The intervention is indirect in such a case as the defendant, A, does not directly approach the contracting party, C. In *J T Stratford & Sons Ltd v Lindley* (1965), the defendant trade union embargoed its members against handling goods on barges owned by the plaintiffs. This caused the plaintiffs' customers (who hired the barges for the carriage of cargo) to breach their contractual obligation with the plaintiffs as they were unable to discharge the cargo and return the barges to the plaintiffs in time. The House of Lords held that the defendants could be liable for procuring these breaches of contracts between the plaintiffs and their customers on these facts, even though their interference was carried out indirectly through the instrumentality of their members.

20.14 Where the intervention is indirect, liability will only arise if *unlawful* means are used. In *J T Stratford & Sons Ltd v Lindley*, this requirement was satisfied as the members who obeyed the embargo were in fact acting in breach of their employment contracts by refusing to handle the plaintiffs' barges. By contrast, this element was absent in *DC Thomson & Co Ltd v Deakin* (1952), where the employees of Bowaters (a supplier of paper), who refused to deliver paper to the plaintiffs in response to a boycott organised by the defendant trade union, were found not to be in breach of their employment contracts since Bowaters did not actually require them to make the deliveries to the plaintiffs. As a result, the trade unions were not liable for procuring the breach of Bowaters' contract with the plaintiffs. As we shall see in paragraph 20.50 below, it has been argued that cases of indirect intervention are, by reason of the additional requirement for unlawful means, in fact, a species of the genus tort of interferences with trade by unlawful means. Hence, the true objection to this type of interference is not that the defendant has interfered with a contractual or pre-existing legal obligation as such, but, rather, that the defendant was guilty of utilising unlawful means.

(d) *Inconsistent Dealings*

20.15 It has been said that the tort may also be committed by a person who knows of a contract between the contract breaker and another, and yet deals with the contract breaker in a way which is inconsistent with that contract. In *British Motor Trade Association v Salvadori* (1949), the plaintiff association required all purchasers of new motor cars to undertake not to resell the cars except in the manner permitted by their contracts. The defendants then purchased motor cars from third parties in circumstances which they knew would violate the undertakings which the third parties had given to the plaintiffs. The defendants were found to be liable for procuring the said violation. There is, however, some concern as to whether this would mean that a person who has done no more than merely agreeing to a transaction which he or she knows to be inconsistent with the offeror's other obligations thereby commits the tort. One commentator has strenuously argued that such minimal degree of interference should not amount to a tort, since in such a case it was really the contract breaker's own conduct, and not any inducement on the part of the defendant, which caused the breach. If, however, this version of the tort did in fact require some active conduct on the part of the defendant, then it might be asked if this were not merely an instance of direct procurement discussed under paragraph 20.10 above (see H Carty, *An Analysis of the Economic Torts* (2001) at pp 56–61).

(3) *Breach*

20.16 By definition, the tort only arises where the defendant's inducement results in the *breach* of a contractual obligation, which may be either a primary or a secondary obligation (such as an obligation to pay damages arising from the breach of a primary obligation). It logically follows that there can be no tort where the contract may be terminated by the induced party at pleasure, or where the contract is void, for instance, on the ground of illegality or incapacity, or where it is voidable (at least insofar as the person induced is the party who has the right to rescind). The element does not, however, require that the contract breaker (who acted in response to the defendant's inducement) be actually liable to the plaintiff. In *Torquay Hotel Co Ltd v Cousins* (1969), the defendant trade union was found liable for causing Esso's breach of its contractual obligation to deliver fuel to the plaintiff's hotel, even though Esso was in fact exempted from liability by virtue of a *force majeure* clause in the contract.

20.17 An issue which has arisen in some cases is whether the tort could be constituted by *bare interference* not resulting in the breach of a contract. In *Torquay Hotel Co Ltd v Cousins*, Lord Denning (at p 138) attempted to extend the scope of the tort in this manner by holding that:

> '…there must be interference in the execution of the contract. The interference is not confined to the procurement of a breach of the contract. It extends to a case where a third person prevents or hinders one party from performing his contract, even though it be not a breach.'

This approach was in fact approved by the House of Lords in *Merkur Island Corporation v Laughton* (1983). However, this development has been severely criticised as it has the effect of casting the net of the tort too widely, thereby placing in jeopardy competitive conduct which is otherwise generally regarded as legitimate in a commercial context. It would thus appear that the better view is that breach remains an essential ingredient of the tort. The majority of the judges did in fact find a contractual breach on the facts of *Torquay Hotel v Cousins* (see paragraph 20.16, above) and the House of Lords' decision in *Merkur Island Corporation v Laughton* (1983) may be more appropriately understood as an instance of interference with trade by unlawful means which, as we shall see in paragraph 20.39 below, is a different genus of torts which does not require the proof of any breach of obligation. (See *Clerk & Lindsell on Torts* (18th ed, 2000) at paragraphs 24-31–24-34; H Carty, *An Analysis of the Economic Torts* (2001) at pp 54–55; and T Weir, *A Casebook on Tort* (9th ed, 2000) at p 608.)

(4) *Damage*

20.18 Finally, the plaintiff must prove that he or she has suffered *damage* as a result of the breach of contract. In *Jones Bros (Hunstanton) Ltd v Stevens* (1955), the defendant had employed the plaintiffs' servant and continued to do so even after learning of the earlier employment. It was, however, held that no action in tort could be sustained as the servant would not in any event have returned to the plaintiffs' service and, hence, the plaintiffs had not sustained any damage as a result of the defendant's inducement.

20.19 The damages which are recoverable for this tort include all intended damage, as well as damages which are not too remote at the time of breach. Further, it is not necessary to prove particular damage; damage may be *inferred* from the circumstances if the breach were of such nature as would in the ordinary course of events inflict injury on the innocent party.

20.20 Where the tort is established, the court may, upon the request of the plaintiff and subject to the satisfaction of the relevant conditions (see paragraphs 16.30–16.44, above), grant injunctions to restrain the defendant from future interferences.

(5) *Justification*

20.21 Exceptionally, the defendant who has interfered with the plaintiff's contract may be able to raise the *defence* of justification. This is a little-known defence not given to any precise definition, but it is generally accepted that in considering its availability, 'regard might be had to the nature of the contract broken; the position of the parties to the contract; the grounds for the breach; the means employed to procure the breach; the relation of the person procuring the breach to the person who breaks the contract; and I think also to the object of the person in procuring the breach' (per Romer LJ in *Glamorgan Coal Co v South Wales Miners' Federation* (1903) at p 574).

20.22 It has been said that the defence must relate to the fulfilment of a *moral duty* of the interferer, and not merely the protection of his personal interests. It is therefore not sufficient to show that the defendant has acted honestly, nor that a trade union or an association is acting in the interests of its members. In *Brimelow v Casson* (1924), the defendants induced theatre proprietors to breach their contracts with the plaintiffs, a theatrical manager, so as to compel the plaintiffs to increase the wages of chorus girls, who were otherwise resorting to prostitution to supplement their meager earnings. The defendants' conduct was justified as they had a duty to safeguard the moral standards of the theatrical profession.

20.23 Another instance in which justification may arise is where the defendant has a legal right to protect which is *equal or superior* to that of the plaintiff. In *Edwin Hill & Partners v First National Finance Corporation* (1989), the defendant bankers had extended a loan, secured by a charge on freehold property, to a developer who was neither able to proceed with the development nor raise further finance for that purpose. Although the defendants were entitled to call on the loan and exercise their right of sale as mortgagee, they chose not to do so but agreed, instead, to extend further loans to the developer on the condition that the developer dismissed the plaintiffs and appoint in their place a more prestigious firm of architects. The plaintiffs sued the defendants for procuring a breach of their contract with the developer. The plaintiffs' action failed as the defendants' rights as mortgagee to be repaid under the loan agreement was superior to the plaintiffs' contractual rights; the plaintiffs would have been no better off if the defendants had exercised their right of sale under the mortgage. In the same way, a defendant's rights under a pre-existing contract with the contract breaker would be equal or superior to that of the plaintiff under a subsequent inconsistent agreement. However, this defence will not succeed if the defendant's contractual rights arose under an antecedent but independent contract with the plaintiff.

Inducing Breach of Other Obligations

20.24 Since *Lumley v Gye* (1853), the tort of inducing breach of contract has been extended to other types of enforceable obligations. Thus, a person commits a tort if he knowingly and intentionally induces a breach of a statutory duty or an enforceable equitable obligation. However, it is *not* necessary, as is the case for inducing breach of contracts, to show that the defendant has employed unlawful means in procuring the breach of these other obligations.

Intimidation

20.25 If A threatens to use unlawful means to cause B to do or refrain from doing some act which he is entitled to do, resulting in harm to B or a third party C, A commits the tort of intimidation. In the leading case of *Rookes v Barnard* (1964), the defendants, executive members of a trade union AESD, threatened British Overseas Airways Corporation (BOAC) with a labour strike unless it ceased to employ the plaintiff (Rookes) as its draughtsman. The defendants' motive was to sanction Rookes for terminating his union membership. Fearing the adverse impact of a labour withdrawal, BOAC terminated the plaintiff's employment by giving due notice in accordance with the employment terms. That being the case, the contract was terminated lawfully and the plaintiff did not have an action against the defendants for procuring breach of contract. However, the defendants' threat of strike, if carried out, would in fact have been a breach of the workers' employment terms. The House of Lords held the defendants liable for intimidation: their threat to BOAC involved the use of an unlawful means (ie breach of contract) which resulted in loss to the plaintiff. This was in fact a significant extension of the law as prior thereto, the tort of intimidation had generally arisen only in connection with threats of violence and other tortious acts. The House of Lords was however unwilling to so confine the tort as '[threatening] a breach of contract may be a far more coercive weapon than threatening a tort, particularly when the threat is directed against a company or corporation' (per Lord Reid at p 1169).

(1) *Threat*

20.26 To establish the tort, the plaintiff must prove that the defendant has made a threat that is *coercive* in nature, ie it has the effect of compelling another to comply with the defendant's wishes so as to avoid adverse consequences which the defendant may otherwise bring about. Thus it is not sufficient if the defendant merely inflicted 'idle abuses'. Threats must also be distinguished from warnings or advice intended mainly to inform the recipient and therefore generally lack coercive force. In practice, however, this distinction is not always easy to draw.

(2) *Unlawful Conduct*

20.27 The threat must relate to unlawful conduct or means. As Lord Reid explained in *Rookes v Barnard* (see paragraph 20.25, above):

> 'So long as the defendant only threatens to do what he has a legal right to do he is on safe ground. .... But I agree with Lord Herschell that there is a chasm between doing what you have a

> legal right to do and doing what you have no legal right to do, and there seems to me to be the same chasm between threatening to do what you have a legal right to do and threatening to do what you have no legal right to do' (at p 1168).

This element of unlawfulness lies at the heart of the tort. The wrongfulness of the tort lies not in the making of a threat, nor the bad motive which underlies the threat, but the threatened use of unlawful means. For this reason, the tort of intimidation is generally seen to be the paradigm of the broader genus tort of interference by unlawful means (see paragraphs 20.39–20.50, below). Since the commonality of these torts lies in the use of unlawful means, logic dictates that the same concept of 'unlawfulness' should apply to all torts falling within this genus (see *Clerk & Lindsell on Torts* (18th ed, 2000) at paragraph 24-94). It would also follow that the scope and content of this element of unlawfulness are more appropriately examined within the broader framework of unlawful interference (see paragraphs 20.43–20.49, below). It should, however, be noted that there is as yet no judicial support for such a general approach (see, further, paragraph 20.50, below).

(3) *Damage*

20.28 The plaintiff must have sustained damage as a result of the defendant's threat. Such damage would include all intended losses as well as those that are not too remote.

(4) *Two- and Three-Party Liability*

20.29 In *Rookes v Barnard* (see paragraph 20.25, above), the tort of intimidation arose in a three-party situation where the injured plaintiff was distinct from the victim of the threat. The tort may, however, also arise in a two-party situation. Thus, if A threatens to inflict physical harm on B so as to coerce B to cease a particular trade, there is, in principle, no reason why B should not, after succumbing to A's threat, seek damages against A on the ground of intimidation. However, difficult issues arise as regards the interrelation of tort and contract where the threatened act is one of a breach of contract.

20.30 As noted in paragraph 20.25 above, the House of Lords extended the concept of 'unlawful act' to include a breach of contract in *Rookes v Barnard*. In a two-party setting, however, this will mean that A commits the tort of intimidation or unlawful interference if he threatens to breach his contract with B, thereby causing B loss. It will also follow that B will be entitled to choose between alternative remedies in tort (for intimidation) and in contractual (for anticipatory breach or, where he has yielded to the threat, economic duress, on which see generally, Chapter 13, above). The conflation of tort and contractual principles in such a situation has given rise to the suggestion that a threatened breach of contract should only constitute an unlawful act in a three-party but not a two-party situation (see H Carty, *An Analysis of the Economic Torts* (2001) at pp 94–97). We shall return to examine these difficulties in paragraphs 20.45–20.46, below.

Conspiracy

20.31 The tort of conspiracy arises where two or more persons agree on a course of conduct to cause damage to another. A conspiracy to commit an illegal act or to do a legal act by illegal means is also a criminal offence under section 120A of the Penal Code (Cap 224, 1985 Rev Ed) but the discussion in this section shall be confined to the *civil* sphere. The tort of conspiracy may take either one of two forms: conspiracy to injure *or* conspiracy by unlawful means. Two features distinguish these two forms of the tort: first, the former does not involve the use of unlawful means but the latter does, and secondly, the former requires the conspirators to have acted with the predominant purpose of injuring the victim but the latter does not. Thus, in the case of a conspiracy to injure (or simple conspiracy), the wrongfulness of the tort lies solely in the concerted action of the conspirators to harm the plaintiff, even though the same conduct would not have been unlawful had it been effected, instead, by one person acting independently. For this reason, this form of conspiracy is often said to be anomalous as it renders an otherwise lawful act unlawful merely by reason of the 'magic of plurality'. The unsatisfactory basis of this form of conspiracy is borne out by Lord Diplock's observations in *Lonrho Ltd v Shell Petroleum Co Ltd (No 2)* (1982) that 'to suggest today that acts done by one street-corner grocer acting in concert with a second are more oppressive and dangerous to a competitor than the same acts done by a string of supermarkets under a single ownership … is to shut one's eyes to what has been happening in the business and the industrial world since the turn of the century' (at p 189). That said, his Lordship nevertheless felt constrained by precedent to accept that this tort is 'too well-established to be discarded' (at p 189).

(1) *Conspiracy to Injure*

(a) Combination

20.32 There must be a combination or some concerted action between two or more persons. The agreement between the conspirators need not be express but may be of a tacit nature. The conspirators need not join in at the same time and may indeed have different aims, as the essential question in each case is whether they are aware of the plan and took part in its execution. Directors may conspire with their company since the latter is a separate legal entity. An employer is not unusually regarded as being involved in a conspiracy with its employee where the latter merely goes about his or her business, though the employer could be vicariously liable for the conspiracy of his employees committed in the course of their employment. If one does an action which may facilitate another in causing harm to the plaintiff, such facilitation does not by itself amount to a combination if the former does not have control over or interest in the latter's acts (see *CBS Songs Ltd v Amstrad* (1988), which concerns the issue of liability as joint tortfeasors, but the same principles appear to apply to the issue of complicity in the tort of conspiracy). Further, the requirement of combination is not satisfied by evidence of mere agreement between the defendants. It must be established that each of the alleged conspirators has acted or taken some step to further the common design of the parties.

(b) Predominant Purpose to Injure

20.33 The essence of the tort of simple conspiracy lies in the defendants' intention to inflict damage on the victim. Such intention must be the predominant purpose of the defendants' engagement in the conspiracy. Thus, where it is established that the defendants have been acting in pursuit of a legitimate interest, the fact that damage to the plaintiff is an inevitable or foreseeable result of the defendants' conduct is not sufficient. In *Crofter Hand Woven Harris Tweed Co Ltd v Veitch* (1942), the defendant trade union officials were informed by mill-owners (whose workers were members of the union) that they were unable to raise the wages of their workers due to competition from the plaintiffs, who operated at lower cost by importing their yarn supplies. Consequently, the defendants acted in combination with the mill-owners to prevent the plaintiffs from obtaining their yarn supplies. Such action did not, however, involve the use of any unlawful means. The House of Lords held that the combination was legitimate as the predominant purpose of the defendants was to protect the industry on which the wages of the workers depended. It follows from this decision that the pursuit of self-interest is generally regarded as legitimate for the purposes of this tort. However, once it is established that the defendants' predominant motive is to injure the plaintiff, it is of no assistance to plead that their conduct also serves the subsidiary purpose of protecting their own interests. In practice, this requirement for predominant purpose severely restricts the scope of the tort as it is often not difficult to show that the defendants' conduct is actuated principally by the desire to protect self-interests.

(c) Damage

20.34 The tort is only actionable on proof of damage. For this purpose, the plaintiff has to show that he has suffered some pecuniary loss. However, the assessment of such damages is not subject to the proof of particular losses but may be inferred from the circumstances. In *Lonrho v Fayed (No 5)* (1993), it was held that the plaintiff could not claim damages for injury to reputation and feelings in an action for conspiracy as such damages are more appropriately dealt with under the rules relating to defamation (see paragraphs 20.56–20.99, below).

(2) *Conspiracy by Unlawful Means*

20.35 This form of conspiracy shares the features of combination and damage respectively discussed in paragraphs 20.32 and 20.34 above. As noted, however, it differs from simple conspiracy in that it involves the use of unlawful means but does not require the presence of a predominant purpose to harm the victim. The discussion which follows will focus on these two points of distinction.

(a) Intention

20.36 In *Lonrho v Fayed* (1992), the House of Lords held that it is *not* essential, in an action concerning unlawful conspiracy, to prove that the conspirators acted with the predominant purpose to harm the plaintiff. In that case, the plaintiff's plans to acquire a controlling stake in the holding company of Harrods, the renowned departmental store in London, had been suspended whilst awaiting the endorsement of the Monopolies and Mergers Commission ('MMC'). However, the defendants made a rival bid for and acquired control of the company just before the MMC released its report (which was favourable to the plaintiff). The plaintiff sued the defendants alleging, amongst others, that they had unlawfully conspired to injure the plaintiff by misleading the Secretary of State, through various fraudulent misrepresentations, into abstaining from referring their bid to the MMC with the result that they could proceed with their bid ahead of the plaintiff's. It was, however, found that the defendants had not acted with the predominant motive of injuring the plaintiff. Nonetheless, the defendants' attempt to strike out the plaintiff's action on this ground failed as the tort of conspiracy by unlawful means did not require the proof of a predominant purpose to injure. Thus where unlawful means are used, it is sufficient that the conspirators intend to injure the plaintiff, even if such intention is not their predominant motive. In Singapore, this aspect of *Lonrho v Fayed* (1992) has been affirmed and applied by the Court of Appeal in *Quah Kay Tee v Ong & Co Pte Ltd* (1997) and *Chew Kong Huat v Ricwil (Singapore) Pte Ltd* (2001).

(b) Unlawful Means

20.37 The clarification of the law in *Lonrho v Fayed* (1992) was necessary and important because the House of Lords had, in the earlier decision of *Lonrho v Shell Petroleum (No 2)* (1982), appeared to suggest the contrary. By this clarification, *Lonrho v Fayed* (1992) underscored the distinctive rationales of the two forms of the tort. As explained in paragraph 20.31 above, the objection to simple conspiracies is founded on the collective will of a group of people to harm another. Where unlawful means are used, however, it is the use of such means which renders the combination tortious.

20.38 Generally, the commission of another tort would suffice as unlawful means. Since intimidation and procuring breach of contract are torts, it would also follow that a combination to intimidate by threatening a breach of contract, or to procure a breach of contract, would amount to unlawful means. While it is as yet unclear whether the definition of 'unlawful means' in the context of conspiracy is or should be identical to that in the context of unlawful interference, it would appear that the many uncertainties surrounding that concept in the latter context are also true of the tort of unlawful conspiracy (see paragraphs 20.43–20.49, below).

Unlawful Interference with Trade

20.39 It is now recognised that there is a tort of unlawful interference with trade or business, the ingredients of which are: (1) the interference by one with another's trade or business (2) using unlawful means (3) with the intention to injure that other and which (4) in fact results in damage to that other person. In one respect, this tort has a wider ambit than torts which interfere with pre-existing legal obligations (examined in paragraphs 20.6–20.24, above) in that it does not require the breach of a subsisting obligation, be it contractual, statutory or otherwise. Thus, in *J T Stratford v Lindley* (1965) (discussed in paragraph 20.13, above), two of the Law Lords were prepared to find the defendant trade union liable for unlawfully interfering with the plaintiff's business as the embargo against the handling of the plaintiffs' barges did not only result in the breach of the plaintiffs' existing contracts, but also prevented them from doing any new business as a result of the non-availability of the barges.

20.40 Notwithstanding the undisputed reception of this tort in case law, much uncertainty remains as regards its scope and reach. The difficulties centre around the meaning of two essential elements of the tort—intention and unlawful means, respectively.

(1) *Intention*

20.41 Although the point is not entirely settled, the preponderance of judicial and academic view appear to favour a narrower definition of intention, ie that the defendant must have intended to injure the plaintiff by *targeting or directing his conduct at the plaintiff*. Where the defendant's act is not specifically aimed at the plaintiff, it will generally not suffice to show that the plaintiff's damage is an inevitable, probable or even foreseeable result of the defendant's conduct. Thus, in one case, the defendant union called on their members, who were employed by the Meat and Livestock Commission ('MLC') and were responsible for certifying both livestock and deadstock for export, to go on one-day 'lightning strikes' in a bid to coerce the MLC to agree to improve pay structures. The plaintiffs, who were abattoir owners and others involved in the meat trade, unsuccessfully sought to restrain the defendants from proceeding with the strikes on the ground that such conduct would amount to unlawful interference with their business. One of the reasons given for the rejection of this claim was that the defendant's action was in fact targeted at MLC and not the plaintiffs. The defendant could not be said to have intended to injure the plaintiffs, even though the disruption to the plaintiffs' business was an inevitable consequence of the strikes; see *Baretts & Baird (Wholesale) Ltd v Institute of Professional Civil Servants* (1987). It should, however, be noted that the actual decision was in fact rationalised on the ground that it was not the defendants' predominant purpose to injure the plaintiffs, but the correctness of this approach must now be doubted in the light of the English Court of Appeal's decision in *Lonrho v Fayed* (1990).

20.42 The requirement for some form of targeted or specific intent must not be confused with the issue of the defendant's *motive*. In *Lonrho v Fayed* (1990), the English Court of Appeal rejected the proposition that the tort of unlawful interference with trade required the proof of a predominant purpose to injure (this aspect of the decision was not the subject of the appeal before the House of Lords; see paragraph 20.36, above). Thus the requisite mental element is satisfied even if the primary motive of the defendant's conduct, which is targeted at the plaintiff, is that of advancing his own interests rather than damaging the interests of the plaintiff. This is in line with the general principle laid down in the seminal case of *Allen v Flood* (1898), which renders irrelevant the defendant's motive for purposes of economic torts since a lawful act does not become unlawful by reason only of the malevolence with which it is committed (but see the exceptional position as regards the tort of conspiracy to injure, discussed in paragraph 20.33, above).

(2) *Unlawful Means*

20.43 The use of unlawful means is the essence of the tort. It is arguably also the most problematic aspect of the tort because it is not every unlawful act or means which would give rise to an action for unlawful interference. Moreover, a simple and exhaustive definition of the concept is not readily discernible from the relevant case law. These difficulties will become apparent as we examine the various categories of unlawful means or conduct.

(a) Tort

20.44 All torts, including other economic torts, suffice as unlawful means. What remains unsettled is whether the torts constituting the unlawful means must be independently actionable by the third party at whom the tort is directed. The better view appears to dispense with such a requirement. In *Lonrho v Fayed* (1990) (the facts of which have been stated in paragraph 20.36, above), the defendants contended that the deceit which they had allegedly practiced on the Secretary of State could not constitute the requisite unlawful means (for the purposes of the plaintiffs' suit for unlawful interference) as the Secretary of State, not having suffered any financial damage on account of the deceit, did not have a complete cause of action against the defendants. The Court of Appeal rejected this argument as it took the view that the tort (in this case, that of deceit) did not cease to be unlawful only because it might not have been actionable by the third party on whom it was inflicted. It has been said that this approach is 'in line with the "magic" of the tort'—the focus of the tort is on the use of unlawful means and the attribute of unlawfulness is satisfied once it is shown that the conduct in question falls within the ambit of tort law (see H Carty, *An Analysis of the Economic Torts* (2001) at pp 110–101). The fact that the third party has not been damaged as a result does not affect the unlawful nature of the conduct.

(b) Breach of Contract

20.45 We have seen in paragraph 20.25 above that *Rookes v Barnard* (1964) established that it is unlawful to threaten a breach of contract so as to cause damage to another. We have also seen that the inference that necessarily arose from the decision is that a deliberate breach of contract could by itself suffice as an unlawful means in the law of tort (see paragraphs 20.29–20.30, above). For, as Lord Reid observed in that case, 'it would be absurd to make [a defendant] liable for threatening to do [an act] but not for doing it' (at p 1168). But the acceptance of a breach of contract as an unlawful act entails some rather startling consequences which were perhaps not intended by the House of Lords. In a two-party scenario, the effect of accepting a deliberate breach of contract as an unlawful act is to 'tortify' the contractual breach in that it could (in theory, at least) transform every deliberate breach of contract into a tort—such a proposition would eradicate the tort-contract divide and is therefore widely rejected as heretical. It may therefore be necessary, as suggested in paragraph 20.30 above, to confine the principle in *Rookes v Barnard* to a three-party situation. While that may serve as a practical solution to the conundrum, it does not, however, resolve the conceptual inconsistency of attributing an unlawful character to the same breach in a three-party situation but not in a two-party situation.

20.46 The decision in *Rookes v Barnard* presents yet another difficulty in the three-party situation in that it appears to offend the doctrine of privity of contract (and see, generally, Chapter 8, above) by according to a person a right of action on the basis of a contract to which he is not a party. In *Rookes v Barnard* itself, Lord Reid dismissed this objection on the ground that the plaintiff's action 'does not sound in contract' (at p 1168) but in tort. As one commentator explained, '[with] intimidation, the plaintiff's claim is not based on breach of contract, though that is the heart of the threat. Rather, it is an action brought against a defendant who has used unlawful means as a deliberate weapon against the plaintiff' (see H Carty, *An Analysis of the Economic Torts* (2001) at p 94). However, while the argument just cited may clarify the rationale of the tort, it does not deny its incursory effect on the privity doctrine. It is not difficult to see that, by extending 'unlawful means' to include a breach of contract, the tort does in fact place the plaintiff in the same position as if the contract between the defendant and the threatened intermediary had been performed. Thus, the crux of the issue may in fact be one of *policy*, ie whether contractual principles should be subordinated to those of tort law so as to curb the use of economic power (as embodied in contractual rights) as a means of inflicting damage on another (see KW Wedderburn, 'Intimidation and the Right to Strike' (1964) 27 *Modern Law Review* 257).

(c) Crime and Breach of Statutory Duty

20.47 At first sight, it must seem evident that crimes, commonly assumed to be the exemplification of reprehensible conduct, should as a matter of course constitute unlawful means. Indeed such an assumption may be confidently made in respect of crimes which include elements of dishonest intent or the use of physical force. The position as regards statutory offences is, however, much less straightforward.

(i) The Construction Test

20.48 In *Lonrho v Shell Petroleum (No 2)* (1982), the House of Lords held, consistently with its earlier decision in *Gouriet v Union of Post Office Workers* (1978), that whether civil liability could be founded on the breach of a penal statute depends on the proper *construction* of the statute. The general rule is that a statutory duty which is expressed to be enforceable by criminal prosecution only may not be enforced in any other manner. To this general rule, there are two exceptions: firstly, where the statutory provision is imposed, on its true construction, for the benefit of a particular class of individuals and the plaintiff is a member of that class, and secondly, where the statute creates a public right and the plaintiff suffers special damage over and above that which is suffered by the public at large. In *Lonrho v Shell Petroleum (No 2)* (1982), the UK government enacted criminal sanctions against the supply by UK-incorporated companies of petroleum to Southern Rhodesia after the latter unilaterally declared independence. The plaintiffs (Lonrho) alleged that the defendants (Shell and BP) had continued to supply petroleum products in contravention of the statutory prohibitions, thereby prolonging the illegal regime and causing loss to the plaintiffs who were prevented (by the same legislation) from operating a pipeline to transport petroleum to Southern Rhodesia for the duration of that regime. The House of Lords held that the statutory contraventions did not give rise to any civil liability. The relevant legislation, on its true construction, was intended neither for the benefit of a particular class (ie those who engage in the trade of supplying petroleum products to Southern Rhodesia) nor for the protection of the public at large. On the contrary, the legislation was designed to withdraw the citizens' pre-existing rights to trade in petroleum products with Southern Rhodesia. The approach set out in *Lonrho v Shell Petroleum (No 2)* was endorsed by the High Court of Singapore in *Management Corp Strata Title No 586 v Menezes* (1992).

(ii) A General Approach?

20.49 Prior to *Lonrho v Shell Petroleum (No 2)* (1982), a line of authorities appeared to advocate a more general approach. Notably, Lord Denning MR observed in *Ex p Island Records Ltd* (1978) that '[a] man who is carrying on a lawful trade or calling has a right to be protected from any unlawful interference with it' (at p 136) and that such unlawfulness may take the form of a tort, a crime or *any* breach of a statute, even one that is punishable only as a criminal offence. Under this broader approach, it would be unnecessary to ascertain the underlying intent of the statutory provision since any breach would suffice as an unlawful means. This was, however, categorically rejected by Lord Diplock in *Lohrho v Shell Petroleum (No 2)*, who, as explained in paragraph 20.48 above, reasserted the construction test as the correct approach. It should, nonetheless, be noted that there appears to have been a resurgence of the more general approach in a number of decisions subsequent to *Lonrho v Shell Petroleum (No 2)*. For example, the English Court of Appeal was prepared to accept, in *Associated British Ports v Transport and General Workers' Union* (1989), that a breach by employees of their statutory duty to work for a reasonable period of time was not actionable by the employer as a tort, but such breach could suffice as 'unlawful means' for the purposes of determining whether the trade union was liable for unlawfully interfering with the employers' business by inciting the employees to go on strike.

With the state of authorities as it is, it is not possible to conclude with absolute confidence that *Lonrho v Shell Petroleum (No 2)* has indeed conclusively spelt the demise of the general approach propounded by Lord Denning in *Ex p Island Records Ltd.* Ultimately, the issue at hand is whether there are cogent policy reasons for expanding the scope of this particular tort.

(3) *Unlawful Interference as a Genus Tort*

20.50 In *Merkur Island Corporation v Laughton* (1983), Lord Diplock regarded unlawful interference with trade as a 'genus tort' which embraces other economic torts such as inducing breach of contract. The rationale of the tort rests on the desire to protect one's business and economic interests against the intentional interference of another by unlawful means. Undoubtedly, the introduction of such a unifying principle is a positive development likely to import order and coherence into an area of law plagued by uncertainties and inconsistencies. In particular, it must logically follow that all torts falling within the ambit of this wider tort must share the common concepts of intention and unlawful means. That said, however, there is as yet no general consensus on which torts come within the ambit of the wider tort. As mentioned, it seems uncontroversial that the tort of intimidation and procuring breach of contract by indirect intervention could be placed on the same foundation as the wider tort. Beyond that, however, views differ. A leading authority in this subject suggests that all economic torts involving the use of unlawful means would fall within this wider genus, including unlawful interferences with contract, indirect procurement of breach of contract, intimidation and unlawful conspiracies (see *Clerk & Lindsell on Torts* (18th ed, 2000) at paragraphs 24-88–24-90 and 24-94). Direct inducement of breach of contract may (more controversially) be included if one regards the contractual breach itself as an unlawful means. However, another view contends that the tort of direct inducement of breach of contract and unlawful conspiracies are better viewed as torts which create secondary liability based on the primary wrong (the breach of contract or the unlawful means employed). Analogising with the principles underlying the doctrine of joint tortfeasance, the defendant's liability in such cases arises from his or her complicity in the commission of the primary wrong (see H Carty, *An Analysis of the Economic Torts* (2001) at pp 271–273). Thus the current position is that while the existence of the genus tort of unlawful interference is indisputable, its precise ambit is ill-defined. Until and unless the boundaries of the tort are clearly demarcated by definitive rulings as regards which torts fall within its ambit, one will have to continue to wade through the muddied waters of the relevant precedents to understand the scope and meaning of each tort.

Malicious Falsehood

Introduction

20.51 The common law has long recognised that one's trade and business interests may be harmed not just by conduct but also by words and representations. Thus we saw in Chapter 12 above that the tort of deceit safeguards a person against any injury which directly results from relying on another's fraudulent statements. In this section, we consider the tort of malicious falsehood, which arises in situations where false representations are made maliciously in order to injure the plaintiff's goodwill or economic reputation.

Elements of the Tort

(1) *Falsehood*

20.52 The plaintiff bears the burden of proving that that the defendant had practised some form of falsehood. Such falsehood may take the form of oral or written statements or even misleading conduct. Although the tort was originally conceived to protect interests relating to land, it has since been extended to apply to economic interests generally. Thus the loss of business resulting from the defendant's false publication in the latter's newspaper that the plaintiff had ceased business is actionable (*Radcliffe v Evans* (1892)). Obviously, the false representation must bear some relation to the plaintiff, his property or trade. It must also have been published to third persons other than the plaintiff himself, since a publication to the plaintiff alone is unlikely to result in any actual financial damage.

(2) *Malice*

20.53 The concept of malice here is similar to that which we will discuss in the context of qualified privilege (see paragraph 20.85, below). A defendant acts maliciously if he makes a statement knowing that it is untrue or is reckless as regards its truth, ie not caring whether it is true or false. However, mere negligence alone is not malice. Evidence of personal ill-will and spite, or an intention to injure would suffice in proving malice.

(3) *Special Damage*

20.54 At common law, a plaintiff has to prove that he has suffered special damage as a result of the falsehood practiced by the defendant. Such damage could include, for instance, diminution in asset values and general decline in sales and customs. This requirement for special damage has, however, been modified by legislation. Under section 6 of the Defamation Act (Cap 75, 1985 Rev Ed), it is not necessary to prove special damage in an action for malicious falsehood if the words or statements complained of are published in writing or permanent form, or where the words used are calculated to cause pecuniary damage to the plaintiff in respect of any office, profession, calling, trade or business held or carried on by him at the time of publication.

Malicious Falsehood Distinguished from Defamation

20.55 As the tort of malicious falsehood is essentially concerned with protecting trade reputation, there is an obvious resemblance between this tort and the tort of defamation, which we shall examine in the following part. Indeed, these two torts may often overlap and in such situations, the plaintiff will have a choice of which action to pursue. Nonetheless, it must be remembered that the elements of the two torts are distinctly different. For malicious falsehood, the operative statements must be false, but they need neither relate to the plaintiff's reputation or character, nor impute a defamatory meaning. Further, malicious falsehood is actionable upon proof of malice, but malice is not generally a requirement of defamation. Finally, malicious falsehood is essentially founded on the proof of special damage resulting from the defendant's false representations but substantial damages may generally (other than instances of slander which require proof of particular damage) be claimed in a defamation suit without proof of particular damage.

Defamation

Introduction

20.56 The law of defamation protects a person's reputation and good name. It is therefore unlike the torts discussed in the preceding sections in that it is not immediately concerned with the safeguarding of economic interests. Nonetheless, the relationship between a good name and economic interests is far from distant. Where individuals are concerned, a disparaging remark could, at worst, destroy a person's livelihood. For businesses, repute and goodwill are now commonly regarded as one of the most significant assets and thus any damage to it would in all likelihood translate directly into significant financial losses. The discussion of the tort of defamation in this chapter is therefore both necessary and fitting.

20.57 Although no more than an introductory account of the law will be attempted here, the reader will do well to note that this is in fact a complex subject as it strives to balance the competing demands of two very important concepts of liberty: the right to free speech and the right to protect one's reputation. In recent years, the difficulties surrounding this delicate balancing exercise have been compounded by the revolutionary impact of the Internet, elevating the problems to a transnational level. It is perhaps fair to say that the legal developments which we have seen to date are but the tip of the iceberg as the full thrust of these technological changes has yet to be seen and understood. One can therefore justifiably expect significant developments of this aspect of the law in time to come.

20.58 Several preliminary comments are in order. First, the law of defamation is essentially constituted by and developed through case law. The Defamation Act (Cap 75, 1985 Rev Ed) does not supplant the common law but merely modifies it in a limited number of ways. Secondly, the making of a defamatory statement may in some circumstance also constitute a criminal offence under section 499 of the Penal Code (Cap 224, 1985 Rev Ed). The elements of (and defences to) the criminal offence do, however, differ from the civil tort in material ways. For instance, it is an element of the criminal offence that the accused must have made the publication with the *intention* to harm the reputation of the defamed party, or knows or has reason to believe that such injury would result (see section 499(1) of the Penal Code (Cap 224, 1985 Rev Ed)). By contrast, the defendant's subjective state of mind is not an element of the civil wrong. The discussion which follows will, in keeping with the theme of this work, focus on the civil tort alone. Finally, a defamatory publication may take either of two forms: where the publication is made in a permanent form, it is published as a *libel*; and where the mode of publication is temporal or transient, the tort is actionable as a *slander*. It is important to distinguish between these two forms because damages are presumed to result from a libel and hence it is actionable without the proof of *special damage*, ie actual and material loss capable of being measured in monetary terms. By contrast, an action for slander would require the proof of special damage unless it falls within certain common law and statutory exceptions (see, eg sections 4 and 5 of the Defamation Act (Cap 75, 1985 Rev Ed)).

Elements of the Tort

(1) *Defamatory Statements*

(a) What Constitutes a Defamatory Statement

20.59 There is no single exhaustive test for determining whether a statement is of a defamatory nature, but it is often said that a defamatory statement is one which exposes the plaintiff to 'hatred, contempt or ridicule' (per Parke B in *Parmiter v Coupland* (1840) at p 108), or which '[lowers] the plaintiff in the estimation of right-thinking members of society' (per Lord Atkin in *Sim v Stretch* (1936) at p 1240) or which causes him to be shunned or avoided. A statement is defamatory if it has the *tendency* to excite adverse opinion against the plaintiff, though it is not necessary to prove that such adverse opinion has in fact arisen. The question whether a statement is defamatory must not be confused with the question of its truth. A statement is not defamatory by reason only that it is untrue, though its truth may avail the defendant of the defence of justification (see paragraph 20.73, below).

20.60 The standard of opinion to be applied is the views of 'right-thinking members' of society. This is an *objective* standard and hence the subjective intention of the maker of the statement is irrelevant. Thus a statement is not defamatory merely because the maker of the statement intends to injure the plaintiff. The views of the community must be considered as a whole and not just that of a limited class. A statement is therefore not defamatory if it is only regarded as disparaging by a group whose views are so radical as not to be fairly representative of that of the community. Strong language, vulgarities and words spoken in the heat of the moment are not defamatory if a reasonable person would understand them to be no more than mere abuses or insults the literal meaning of which is not intended.

(b) Form

20.61 Other than spoken or written words, defamatory assertions may also take the form of cartoons, caricatures, visual images, statues, signs and gestures. In all cases, however, the test for determining whether a defamatory imputation arises remains the same.

(c) Interpretation

20.62 To decide if a statement is defamatory, the court first construes or interprets the statement to ascertain its *natural and ordinary meaning*, ie the meaning which would be conveyed to 'ordinary persons using their general knowledge and common sense' (per LP Thean J in *Lee Kuan Yew v Davies* (1989) at p 1080). For this purpose, the court has to (somewhat artificially) ignore the fact that words may mean different things to different people and seek to ascertain its *one and only* meaning. The words complained of must be considered, not in isolation, but in the light of the publication as a whole. In some cases, a statement is defamatory because its natural and ordinary meaning bears a clearly adverse imputation, for example, A is a liar or a murderer. In other cases, the disparagement does not arise directly but may be reasonably inferred by ordinary persons not guided by any special knowledge.

20.63 A defamatory imputation may also arise by way of an *innuendo*. This occurs where the words or expressions used are *prima facie* innocuous, but could in fact convey a disparaging meaning when made to persons who have knowledge of special facts which are not otherwise generally known. Such innuendos are commonly referred to as 'true' or 'legal' innuendos. In one case, the defendant newspaper published the picture of Mr C with Ms X together with an announcement that Mr C and Ms X were to be engaged. Although both the picture and the words were not objectionable in themselves, they were found to be defamatory of the plaintiff (Mrs C, the lawful wife of Mr C) as they suggested to those who knew that the plaintiff lived with Mr C as his wife that she was doing so out of wedlock and was therefore an immoral woman (see *Cassidy v Daily Mirror Newspapers Ltd* (1929)). The adverse imputation did not therefore arise directly from the published materials but as an extended meaning thereof established by reference to the special facts known to those to whom the publication was made.

20.64 Legal or true innuendos must be distinguished from 'false' innuendos. The latter refers to inferences which may reasonably be drawn from the plain wording of the statements without any reference to external facts or evidence (and is therefore unlike true or legal innuendos in that respect). As explained in paragraph 20.62 above, false innuendos are really part and parcel of the natural and ordinary meaning ascribed to statements. In practice, it is not always easy to distinguish between a legal and a false innuendo; however, a useful clue lies in whether the facts relied upon to support the innuendo are indeed known only to a select group of people or generally known to the public. In the latter case, the inference would be in the nature of a false innuendo. In *Chiam See Tong v Ling How Doong* (1997), the internal strife amongst the members of the Singapore Democratic Party ('SDP') culminated in the issue of a statement by the defendants (members of the SDP's executive committee) calling for the cessation of the plaintiff's party membership. The plaintiff alleged that the statement gave rise to various defamatory innuendos including, *inter alia*, that he was a puppet, stooge or lackey of the People's Action Party and that he was not a man of principle and honour as he had betrayed the interests of his own party. It was held, however, that the plaintiff could not rely on the events leading to the issue of the statement as 'special facts' supporting the alleged legal innuendos since these facts were well-known to the public at large. Thus the proper approach was to examine the statement and ask if the natural and ordinary meaning of the words would, having regard to the state of knowledge of the general public, give rise to the imputations alleged by the plaintiff.

20.65 It is important to distinguish between the different ways in which defamatory imputations arise because the evidentiary and pleading rules differ according to the type of imputation alleged. Thus, where it is alleged that words are defamatory on their natural and ordinary meaning, the plaintiff need only plead the words themselves. In fact, no evidence as regards the sense in which the words are understood is admissible as such meaning should be apparent from the words themselves.

20.66 In the case of false innuendos, the plaintiff will have to plead the meaning he ascribes to the words since such meaning will not be apparent from the bare words themselves.

20.67 As regards legal innuendos, the plaintiff will have to plead the special facts giving rise to the innuendo and adduce evidence that such facts were in fact known to one or more persons to whom the statement was published. It is possible that a particular publication may be defamatory both on its natural and ordinary meaning as well as on the basis of legal innuendos arising therefrom but such a pleading would in fact give rise to two separate causes of action.

(2) *Reference to the Plaintiff*

20.68 An action in defamation can only be made out if the plaintiff can prove that the defamatory matter has been published *of and concerning him*. It is not necessary that the plaintiff be expressly identified, though obviously if he were, the requirement would be satisfied. It is sufficient if ordinary and sensible people who are acquainted with the plaintiff or who have knowledge of the special facts might reasonably understand the words to be referring to the plaintiff. Where the plaintiff is clearly identified, the plaintiff may sue for defamation even if the statement was intended to refer to some other person with the same name or identification (see *Hulton v Jones* (1910)). Generally, the subjective intention of the maker of the statement is irrelevant in determining whether the statement is made with reference to the plaintiff, though such intention may, as we shall see in paragraphs 20.80, 20.85 and 20.92 below, affect the defences and damages available.

20.69 If a castigating statement is made in respect of a class, such a statement is actionable neither by the class nor a member of that class. Thus a remark to the effect that all lawyers are liars is not actionable unless it could be proved to be referring to a particular individual. Where, exceptionally, an allegedly defamatory statement could, as a matter of construction, be reasonably understood to refer to *each and every* member of a *determinate* class, such a statement may be actionable (see *DHKW Marketing v Nature's Farm Pte Ltd* (1999)).

(3) *Publication*

20.70 To maintain an action for defamation, it must be proven that the allegedly defamatory matter has been published, ie that the defamatory matter has been made known to a third person other than the plaintiff. Thus a person cannot complain of being defamed if the defamatory matter was communicated to him alone. The rationale is that a person's reputation is the esteem with which others regard him and not his self-estimation. The requirement is only satisfied where the defamatory meaning of the words have been conveyed. Thus there is no publication if the person to whom the matter was communicated did not understand the language in which it was expressed.

20.71 It is not necessary to prove in every case that the defamatory matter has in fact been shown or communicated to a third person. It is sufficient if the plaintiff could show that the statement or material would, in the ordinary course of events, be reasonably expected to come to the attention of third parties. Thus, if a libel is written on the back of a postcard and sent by post, it may reasonably be assumed that its content thereof has been read by third parties in the course of delivery. Similarly, it could be reasonably foreseen that a defamatory letter sent to a woman in a sealed envelope may be opened and read by her husband. Conversely, the originator of the statement is not liable if it is not reasonable to anticipate that a statement would be communicated to a third party. Thus A is not liable if he sends a defamatory letter addressed to B but the letter is in fact opened by C, who is not authorised to do so.

20.72 Liability for defamation is not restricted to the original author alone. Once the fact of publication is established, every person who publishes, or procures or takes part in a publication is liable as a publisher. Where a defamatory statement has been *reproduced*, liability generally lies with the party responsible for the reproduction and not the original maker thereof. Hence, the journalist, newspaper and printer of a libellous article are liable for repeating libellous remarks even where they have attributed such remarks to their original sources (though such attribution may be a relevant mitigating factor for purposes of assessing damages). Where, however, the originator of the statement has intended or authorised the third parties to whom the statements were made to publish them, then he will be liable for their subsequent publication together with the third parties.

Defences

(1) *Justification*

20.73 As we have noted (see paragraph 20.59, above), it is not part of the plaintiff's case to prove that the defamatory statement is untrue. The defendant may, however, raise the defence of justification by proving that the defamatory statement is true in substance and in fact. The onus is on the defendant to demonstrate that the substance or gist of the charge is true, but he is not required to substantiate every detail or comment that does not materially add to the main charge (see further, section 8 of the Defamation Act (Cap 75, 1985 Rev Ed)). Obviously, the justification proferred must relate to the precise words that are the subject of the plaintiff's complaint and not a version which is materially different from that asserted by the plaintiff. It must also relate to the full breadth of the offending statement. Thus the defence would fail in relation to an allegation that the plaintiff is a 'libellous journalist' if it were merely proven that he had once incurred liability for libel because a single incident would not justify the imputation that the plaintiff is habitually libellous (see *Wakley v Cooke* (1849)). Where an innuendo is pleaded, both the basic facts of the offending statement and the inuendo will have to be justified. If a defamatory statement comprises a comment, the defendant must establish that both the truth of the facts on which the comment was based and that the comment itself are warranted on those facts (but see paragraph 20.76, below, on the distinction between this defence and that of fair comment). Generally, where justification is established, it acts as a *complete* defence against the plaintiff's claims. Significantly, however, it has been observed, *obiter*, in the unreported decision of *Arul Chandran v Chew Chin Aik* (2000) that exceptionally, *public policy* may intervene to defeat the defence of justification where the defendant has engaged in malicious muck-raking by resurrecting events of buried past with the *sole* intention of inflicting injury on the plaintiff.

(2) *Fair Comment*

20.74 This defence seeks to protect honest and fair criticisms on matters of public interest. The defence succeeds where it can be established that (1) the words complained of are in the nature of a comment, (2) the comment is based on true facts, (3) the comment or opinion expressed is fair and (4) it relates to a matter of public interest.

(a) Comment

20.75 The defence only applies to statements which are in the nature of a comment or opinion, as opposed to assertions of facts. The question whether a statement is one of fact or opinion is determined *objectively*, ie 'whether an ordinary reasonable reader on reading the whole article would understand the words as a comment or a statement of fact' (per LP Thean J in *Lee Kuan Yew v Davies* (1989) at p 1087). This distinction is not always easy to draw, as the same words may be factual in one context and yet constitute a comment in another. This was illustrated by LP Thean J, who observed that 'if it is said of a member of the Bar that he is unfit to be a member of the Bar, that statement by itself is one of fact. On the other hand, if the same statement was prefaced by a statement that the member of the Bar has been convicted of cheating, then the statement becomes a comment' (at p 1087). Ultimately, the answer would depend on the nature of the imputation made, as well as the context and circumstances in which the words were published.

20.76 The restriction of the fair comment defence to expressions of opinion serves as an important distinction between the defences of fair comment and justification, since the latter applies to *both* facts and opinions. Further, a defendant pleading fair comment is not required to prove the truth of the comment, but only that it is fair and honestly held. If justification is sought in respect of an opinion, the defendant will have to satisfy the more onerous burden of proving that the opinion expressed is correct.

(b) Comment is Based on True Facts

20.77 A fair comment must be based on true facts. It is not necessary to prove that all facts pleaded in support of the comment are true, but only those facts that are material and sufficient to form the basis of the comment (see further, section 9 of the Defamation Act (Cap 75, 1985 Rev Ed)). A defendant may not rely on facts which only arose subsequent to the publication to substantiate his comments. It seems, however, that reliance may be placed on facts which are publicly known at the time of the publication even if they are not specifically set out in the publication containing the offending comment.

(c) Comment is Fair

20.78 A comment is fair if it is an opinion which could be honestly held by a fair-minded person and 'every allowance or latitude is to be given for any prejudice and exaggeration entertained by such a fair-minded man' (per LP Thean J in *Lee Kuan Yew v Davies* (1989) at p 1092) in making the assessment. This requirement does not therefore mandate a balanced or impartial view and may even admit comments that are biased, exaggerated or wrong. Ultimately, the honesty (or lack thereof) with which the opinion is held is the most critical factor in each case.

(d) Public Interest

20.79 A matter is of public interest if it is 'such as to affect people at large, so that they may be legitimately interested in, or concerned at, what is going on; or what may happen to them or others' (per Lord Denning in *London Artists Ltd v Littler Grade Organisation Ltd* (1969) at p 391). This requirement elucidates the rationale underlying the defence: that honest criticism is essential to the proper and efficient management of public institutions and offices. Examples of matters of public interests include matters relating to politics, religion, the public acts of public figures, the workings of public institutions, publications, performances and any other works intended for public consumption.

(e) Effect of Malice

20.80 The defence of fair comment will be defeated if the plaintiff succeeds in adducing evidence that the defendant's comments are in fact motivated by malice. The presumption is that a comment that is coloured or distorted by malice cannot be fair. So long as the element of malice is established, the defence cannot stand even if the same comment could have been made by some other person honestly and without malice (see *Thomas v Bradbury, Agnew & Co Ltd* (1906)).

(3) *Absolute Privilege*

20.81 The defence of absolute privilege is borne out of the law's recognition that there are occasions on which one must be assured complete liberty to express oneself without the fear of incurring liability for defamation. Once a communication or publication falls within the recognised categories of protected occasions, no civil action may be commenced by anyone in respect thereof. The privilege accorded is *absolute* because it may not (unlike matters protected by qualified privilege as to which see paragraph 20.85, below) be defeated even by evidence that the privileged publication has been actuated by malice. The various occasions on which absolute privilege arises may broadly be categorised as follows:

(a) Parliamentary Proceedings

20.82 Absolute privilege is accorded to all parliamentary proceedings pursuant to the provisions of the Parliament (Privileges, Immunities and Powers) Act (Cap 217, 2000 Rev Ed). Members of Parliament are therefore immune from both civil and criminal law suits for any potentially slanderous remarks made in the course of parliamentary proceedings. The immunity is extended to all reports, papers and journals relating to such proceedings the publication of which is directly authorised by Parliament. The reproduction of extracts from such materials are, however, only accorded qualified privilege (see sections 7 and 8 of the Parliament (Privileges, Immunities and Powers) Act (Cap 217, 2000 Rev Ed)).

(b) Judicial Proceedings

20.83 The privilege attached to judicial proceedings is founded primarily on the common law. No action may therefore be brought against any person taking part in a legal suit including judges, counsels, witnesses and parties. The protection is not, however, limited to statements made during trial but extends to all stages of judicial proceedings. The same privilege also attaches to statements made in the course of proceedings conducted in tribunals or bodies recognised by law and acting judicially. Under section 11 of the Defamation Act (Cap 75, 1985 Rev Ed), a fair, accurate and contemporaneous report of judicial proceedings which are publicly heard is absolutely privileged. A similar privilege is attached to any comment on such report if the comment is 'fair and *bona fide*'.

(c) Executive Matters

20.84 Some cases have held that certain communications made by ministers and civil servants concerning the affairs of the state are absolutely privileged. Thus the advice given by a minister to the government and official communications made between officers of state in the course of their duty would fall within the province of this defence. It should be noted that the exact ambit of this head of absolute privilege has yet to be defined, though the general view is that it does not purport to afford a blanket protection of all communications made within the civil service (see W Rogers, *Winfield & Jolowicz on Tort* (16th ed, 2002) at p 447).

(4) *Qualified Privilege*

(a) Malice

20.85 Qualified privilege differs from absolute privilege in that the former does not afford the defendant complete immunity regardless of his motives. Thus, where it is shown that the offending communication is made by a defendant maliciously, the plea of qualified privilege cannot be maintained. Malice is the use of a privileged occasion for an indirect or wrong purpose, ie a purpose other than that for which the law confers protection. Thus, a defendant acts maliciously if he makes a statement with the main object of causing injury to the plaintiff, since such a purpose would clearly not be condoned by the law. The strongest evidence of malice is the defendant's unbelief in the truth of his statement, but mere carelessness in ascertaining its truth is not sufficient. Malice may also be inferred from the publication itself, as where the words used are greatly exaggerated or bear little or no relation to the facts, or where the publication is disseminated to a much wider group of people than is in fact warranted. Evidence of the parties' relations before and after the publication, as well as the defendant's conduct in the course of the proceedings, will also be relevant to the question of malice.

(b) Communications Between Persons with Corresponding Interests and Duties

20.86 If A has an interest or duty (whether legal, social or moral) to communicate information regarding B to C, and C has a corresponding interest or duty to receive that information, then such communication is protected by qualified privilege even if it is in fact defamatory of B. Since the privilege is founded on the respective interests and duties of the communicating parties, it logically follows that it will only extend to communication which is relevant to such duty and interests; extraneous and unconnected statements are therefore not protected. Character references given by employers in respect of former employees (*Kelly v Partington* (1833)), communication between a trade association and its member on the credit standing of a trader (*London Association for Protection of Trade v Greenlands Ltd* (1916)) and communications made by solicitors in furtherance of clients' interests (*Wee Richard v Wong Meng Meng & Partners* (1995)) are some examples of privileged communications.

20.87 The reciprocity of duty or interest between the speaker and the recipient is an essential feature of this defence but that does not require the respective interests or duties of the two parties to be identical. Thus, in *Watt v Longsdon* (1930), the defendant, a director of the Scottish Petroleum Company ('SPC'), received a letter from one B (a manager of SPC's operations in Morocco) accusing the plaintiff (the managing director of same operations) of immorality, drunkenness and dishonesty. The defendant replied to B stating his own suspicions of the same conduct and showed it to S, the chairman of SPC, as well as the defendant's wife. All the allegations against the plaintiff were unfounded. It was held that the publication of the reply to B and S was clearly privileged. The defendant and B, being employees of the same company, had a common interest in the affairs of the company. The defendant also owed a moral duty to inform S, whose interest in the matter arose from the fact of the plaintiff's employment by the company and the fact that he might be required to provide testimonials to the plaintiff's future employers. The publication to the plaintiff's wife was, however, not privileged. Whilst the wife undoubtedly had an interest in any information relating to her husband's conduct, the defendant had no interest or duty to communicate the information to her particularly in view of the doubtful source from which the information was derived.

(c) Statements Made to Protect Self-Interests

20.88 Qualified privilege is also conferred on statements made with a view to defend the defendant's own interests. If, for instance, a defendant has been accused of cheating, he may legitimately respond by denying the accusation and accuse the plaintiff of lying. Even though such counter-accusation may, upon publication to a third party, be defamatory in nature, it may nonetheless not be actionable by the plaintiff by virtue of the fact that it is privileged. Again, it should be noted that such privilege would only be as extensive as is necessary for the purposes of the protection of the defendant's interests and would not attach to excessive or extraneous remarks (*Adam v Ward* (1917)).

(d) Reports of Proceedings

20.89 At common law, reports of parliamentary and judicial proceedings which are *fair and accurate* are the subject of qualified privilege. As we have seen in paragraphs 20.82–20.83 above, however, substantial legislative inroads have been made in this regard, conferring absolute privilege on reports of both parliamentary and judicial proceedings. Nonetheless, the privilege conferred at common law remains relevant as it affects a much broader class of reports. Significantly, section 12 of the Defamation Act (Cap 75, 1985 Rev Ed) expressly preserves the availability of qualified privilege for newspaper reports of parliamentary and judiciary proceedings and extends the privilege to similar reports of proceedings in the Commonwealth.

(5) *Innocent Dissemination*

20.90 A person who, not being the author, first or main publisher and printer of a defamatory statement, participated in the distribution of such a statement may be exonerated from liability on account of innocent dissemination, if he can prove that he did not know that the printed material contained a libel, that there was nothing in the circumstances or the work that could have alerted him to its libellous content and that such ignorance was not due to any negligence on his part (*Vizetelly v Mudie's Select Library Ltd* (1900)). This defence generally protects innocent intermediaries such as retail vendors, libraries and delivery agents.

(6) *Offer of Amends*

20.91 It has been noted (see paragraph 20.68, above) that one may be liable for defaming someone without the slightest intention to do so. This occurs, for instance, where more than one person answers to the description of the subject referred to in a defamatory publication. Strict enforcement of such liability does, however, often appear unduly harsh. A procedure for ameliorating the rigour of the law in such a situation is provided for under section 7 of the Defamation Act (Cap 75, 1985 Rev Ed), which essentially allows a person who has innocently defamed another to acquire a defence against liability by making an 'offer of amends'. Such an offer must include the offer to publish a public apology to the aggrieved party and to take such steps that may be reasonably practical to inform those to whom copies of the original publication have been distributed that the content of the publication is alleged to be defamatory of the aggrieved party. If the offer of amends is accepted by the aggrieved party and is duly performed, then the aggrieved party may not bring any action in respect thereof, or, in the event where such action has already been commenced, to discontinue such proceedings. If, however, the aggrieved party does not accept the offer of amends, then such an offer shall constitute a defence against any libel or slander suit instituted by the aggrieved party against the publisher.

Remedies

20.92 Where a plaintiff succeeds in a defamation suit, damages would generally be awarded to compensate him for the loss of his reputation. Except for cases of slander which require proof of special damage (see paragraph 20.58, above), damages for defamation are said to be 'at large', ie although 'damages cannot be precisely quantified in money terms but the plaintiff is entitled to a substantial award for the wrong against him' (see W Rogers, *Winfield & Jolowicz on Tort* (16th ed, 2002) at p 750). The award of damages may be aggravated by factors such as the defendant's malicious motives, the standing and prominence of both the plaintiff and the defendant, the gravity of the libel, the manner and extent of the publication as well as the defendant's conduct from the time of publication to the closure of proceedings. Conversely, the award may be mitigated by evidence of an honest belief in the truth of the publication, the publication of or an offer to publish an apology (see section 10 of the Defamation Act (Cap 75, 1985 Rev Ed)), any misconduct of the plaintiff at a material time and evidence of his general bad reputation. Exemplary or punitive damages are not generally available in a libel suit except where the compensatory award is insufficient to 'punish' the defendant for his outrageous conduct and even then, only in the limited circumstances enunciated by the House of Lords in *Cassell v Broome* (1972). Special damages may be recoverable in respect of both slander and libel provided that the usual conditions of causation and remoteness are satisfied.

20.93 A successful plaintiff in a defamation suit may also seek an injunction to prevent the future publication of any defamatory matter where such further publication is reasonably apprehended. More rarely, an interlocutory injunction may be awarded to forestall the publication of an allegedly defamatory matter but the courts are understandably more guarded in dispensing such orders so as not to impose any undue restraint on the right to free speech. Thus a court will generally not grant any such order unless the plaintiff is able to prove, at the interlocutory proceedings, that defendant is not likely to succeed in establishing any defence at the eventual trial (see *Bonnard v Perryman* (1891)).

Defamation on the Internet

20.94 For many of us, the transformation brought about by the Internet is now very much a way of life. A whole host of information is accessible at the mere click of a mouse in the privacy of our home or place of work. International communications are near-instantaneous but cost only a trifle. Not surprisingly, such exponential growth in global communications has given rise to much anxiety over the possibility of increased liability connected therewith and the correspondingly more extensive damage which a potential plaintiff may suffer. Indeed, in the realm of defamation law, such anxiety is more than justified. The risk of making a libellous publication on the Internet is many times magnified by the culture of unrestrained expression amongst the pioneering net-users and the ease with which such publication is conveyed to a large number of readers regardless of geographical boundaries. Moreover, while the basic elements required to prove the tort remain unchanged, difficult and novel issues haves arisen from attempts to apply these established concepts in the virtual realm. Owing to constraints of space, we will illustrate these difficulties by focusing on two particular sets of problems which have of late been the subject of spirited debate and discussion. (For a comprehensive analysis of this interesting subject, see M Collins, *The Law of Defamation and the Internet* (2001)).

20.95 The first relates to the role and responsibility of intermediaries such as Internet Service Providers ('ISP'). Publication on the Internet is not usually made by a single party but through the assistance of a third party, commonly the ISP. As we have noted in paragraph 20.72 above, all persons who participated in the publication of a defamatory statement could be liable as a publisher thereof and that would obviously include an ISP in the virtual context. From the perspective of the defamed party, bringing a suit against the ISP is no doubt an attractive option, given the occasional difficulties of identifying the original authors of the offending statements, as well as the fact that ISPs are usually commercial entities which are better able to meet substantial financial awards. It seems, however, intuitively unjust and undesirable to burden ISPs with the general responsibility for any defamatory content, since, in most instances, the ISPs have no hand in crafting such content and could not reasonably be expected to sift through the colossal number of materials passing through its network daily in order to avoid such liability. In Singapore, the legislature has responded to this problem by enacting section 10 of the Electronic Transactions Act (Cap 88, 1999 Rev Ed; hereafter the 'ETA'), the main text of which has been set out in paragraph 19.64, above. In essence, this provision protects an ISP from any liability arising from the 'making, publication, dissemination or distribution' (section 10(1)(a) of the ETA) of third-party materials if the ISP has done no more than *merely providing access* to such materials. The intent of the legislature, as evidenced by records of the relevant parliamentary debates, is to create a statutory defence akin to the common law defence of innocent dissemination (see paragraph 20.90, above). The precise ambit and effect of this defence is, however, not as clear as it may initially appear.

20.96 In the English decision of *Godfrey v Demon Internet Ltd* (2000), the plaintiff, an academic, brought an action against the defendant ISP in respect of a 'squalid, obscene and defamatory' posting by an unknown person in the US on the pretence that it was posted by the plaintiff. The posting was subsequently disseminated through the defendant's newsgroup. On discovering the posting, the plaintiff informed the defendants of the forgery and requested that the posting be removed. The defendants, however, did not do so until some 10 days later. The court held that the defendants could not rely on the relevant English statutory defence of innocent dissemination (see section 1 of the Defamation Act 1996) because their conduct in failing to remove the offending materials after receipt of the plaintiff's notification could not fairly be described as 'innocent', an important ingredient of the defence. Following this decision, it could reasonably be anticipated that a prudent ISP would err on the side of caution by expeditiously removing all materials in respect of which complaints have been received. Although section 10 of the ETA is drafted more broadly than its English counterpart in that it does not expressly require the defendant to show that he has no reason to believe that he has caused or contributed to the publication of a defamatory statement, nonetheless it is arguable that an ISP who refuses to remove allegedly defamatory materials would not be 'merely providing access' within the meaning of the provision, but may in effect be adopting or condoning such content.

20.97 Another difficulty arising from section 10 of the ETA is that it appears, paradoxically, to punish the prudent while protecting the reckless. By restricting the defence to ISPs who *merely provides access* for third-party materials, the inference which arises is that if an ISP adopts the prudent practice of editing such material with a view to censoring any undesirable or libellous content, it is more likely to lose the immunity provided by section 10 of the ETA since it will not then be merely providing access to such materials. To the extent that this defence may encourage ISPs to adopt a 'bury your head in the sand' strategy, public interest in the transmission of truthful information is not well served. Undoubtedly, intermediaries such as ISPs have a useful role to play in safeguarding the free transmission of truthful information but such a role must be balanced against their commercial interests (see L Edwards, 'Defamation and the Internet' in L Edwards and C Waelde (eds), *Law and the Internet —A Framework for Electronic Commerce* (2nd ed, 2000) at pp 261–264 and C Gringras, *The Laws of the Internet* (2nd ed, 2003) at pp 132–139). Admittedly, the relevant laws are still very much at a stage of infancy and thus one can only hope that the balance would be adjusted and improved over time.

20.98 The second and equally intractable set of problems relate to the determinations of the appropriate forum to sue as well as the law which should govern such an action. It is not difficult to see why this is a particularly prickly problem in the setting of cyberspace. Existing laws as regards jurisdictional and choice of law issues are developed with reference to geographical boundaries. The Internet, however, knows of no similar constraints. The resultant incongruity is thus patent. If A makes a defamatory posting of B in the US which is then transmitted to a newsgroup in the UK but finally downloaded and read by C in Singapore, in which jurisdiction should B be permitted to commence his action against A? What national law should the court apply to resolve the dispute? The answers are far from obvious. These issues were most recently considered by the Australian High Court in *Dow Jones & Company v Gutnick* (2002), where the plaintiff (Gutnick) brought an action in Victoria (Australia) against the defendants in respect of a defamatory article published in both the online as well as a printed version of the latter's newspaper. The online version of the article was uploaded in New Jersey in the US, where the defendants maintained their servers. The trial judge found that the plaintiff had decided to litigate in Victoria so as to vindicate his reputation in the place where he resided and where much of his business and social life was conducted. Before the High Court, the defendants strenuously argued that the action should be governed by the law and heard in a place where the publishers maintained their servers, ie New Jersey; such a rule would enable online publishers to identify in advance the relevant set of laws to comply with prior to publication. To hold otherwise, they contended, would place the publishers in the near-impossible position of having to comply with the laws of almost every country on earth. The High Court judges unanimously rejected these arguments. The Victorian court's jurisdiction to hear the case was founded on the relevant rules of court, which permitted the service of proceedings on a defendant residing outside Australia if the tort was committed in Victoria; or, if the plaintiff sustained damage in Victoria (the local equivalent of these rules can be found in the Singapore Rules of Court, Order 11, rule 1(f)(i) and (ii)). The latter requirement was satisfied as the plaintiff clearly had a reputation in Victoria which could have been injured when the defamatory article was accessed by the defendants' subscribers in Victoria. The former condition was also satisfied because the tort was committed in the place in which damage was sustained, ie Victoria. It was further held that Victorian law, being the law of the place in which the tort was committed, was the appropriate governing law.

20.99 At its crux, the law of defamation seeks to balance the individual's interests in protecting his good name against the publisher's conflicting liberty to express. In this instance, the former clearly outweighed the latter because the court considered it fundamental that a person should be entitled to defend his name in the place where it was most vulnerable. In comparison, to require publishers intending to publish a potentially libellous matter to take cognizance of the defamation laws of the places in which the subject has a reputation does not seem an excessive burden. The High Court's resistance to the defendants' proposition (to adopt the law of the place where the servers were maintained) underscored yet another material consideration. The evidence before the court was that, currently, the vast majority of web servers reside in the US. An endorsement of the defendants' argument would therefore be tantamount to importing US laws in the preponderance of Internet defamation suits. But such a result would be unacceptable having regard to the distinct legal culture which has moulded US defamation laws, which provides extremely strong protection to the right of free speech under the First Amendment of the US Constitution—a culture which is not necessarily shared by other legal jurisdictions. While it remains to be seen whether Singapore courts would adopt the reasoning of this case, there is no doubt that this decision has at the very least apprised us of the complex national and transnational issues likely to arise in Internet defamation suits.

PART VI

Law of Intellectual Property

CHAPTER 21

Law of Intellectual Property

PARAGRAPHS

21.1 **Introduction to Intellectual Property Law**
21.2 Property Rights
21.3 Characteristics of Intellectual Property Rights
21.4 Justification for Intellectual Property Protection

Law of Copyright
21.5 What is Copyright?
21.6 General Principles of Copyright Law
Copyright Protection Under Copyright Act 1987
21.7 (1) In What Subject Matter Can You Claim Copyright?
21.8 (2) Connecting Factor: Are You a Protected Person?
21.9 (3) Requirement of Originality
21.10 (4) Reduction into Material Form
21.11 Duration of Copyright
21.12–21.13 Ownership of Copyright/Assignments and Licences
21.14 Exclusive Rights of Copyright Owner
21.15–21.17 Primary Infringement of Copyright in Authors' Works
21.18–21.19 Infringing Authorisation (Authorising Primary Infringement)
21.20 Secondary Infringement of Copyright
21.21 Groundless Threats of Legal Proceedings
21.22 Civil Remedies
21.23 Border Enforcement Measures
21.24–21.26 Defences to Infringement
21.27 Rights in Performances (Performers' Rights)
21.28–21.29 Moral Rights
21.30 Rights Management Information
21.31–21.34 Liability of Network/Internet Service Providers
21.35 Browsing (User Caching)
21.36–21.39 Hyper-linking and Meta-tagging

21.40–21.46 **Industrial Designs**

Law of Patents
21.47 General Introduction
21.48–21.50 Meaning of 'Invention' and Elements of Patentability

PARAGRAPHS

Law of Patents (continued)
21.51–21.53 (1) Novelty
21.54–21.55 (2) Inventive Step (Non-Obviousness)
21.56–21.57 (3) Industrial Application
21.58–21.60 Patent Infringement
21.61 Defences to Patent Infringement
21.62 Remedies for Patent Infringement
21.63 Groundless Threats of Infringement Proceedings
21.64 Assignments and Licences

21.65–21.70 **Trade Secrets and the Law of Confidence**

Law of Trade Marks
21.71 General Introduction
21.72–21.73 What is a Trade Mark?
21.74–21.75 Absolute or Relative Grounds for Refusal of Registration
21.76–21.77 Applying for a Trade Mark in Singapore and Duration of Trade Mark Protection
21.78 Exclusive Rights of Registered Proprietor
21.79 Trade Mark Infringement
Defences to Trade Mark Infringement
21.80 (1) Comparative Advertising
21.81 (2) Other Acts Not Amounting to Infringement
21.82 (3) Prior Use
21.83 (4) Exhaustion of Rights and Parallel Imports
21.84 Remedies for Trade Mark Infringement
21.85 Border Enforcement Measures
21.86 Remedy for Groundless Threats of Infringement Proceedings
21.87 Assignments and Licences
21.88 Madrid Protocol

21.89–21.90 **Law of Passing Off and Cybersquatting**
21.91 Goodwill
21.92 Misrepresentation
21.93–21.96 Cybersquatting

21.97–21.99 **Geographical Indications Act 1998**

21.100 **Concluding Thoughts**

Introduction to Intellectual Property Law

21.1 It is fair to say that few branches of the law have, in recent times, developed as swiftly and explosively across jurisdictions as the law of intellectual property and its associated laws of information technology, electronic commerce and biotechnology. One simple reason for this phenomenon is that many countries, including developing countries, have come to realise the intrinsic worth and value of intellectual property and have taken steps to ensure that such intangible assets are given due protection in today's knowledge-based economy.

The law of intellectual property is basically a system of law which aims to protect the fruits of intellectual effort and labour from piracy and unfair competition. Traditionally though, a number of intellectual property rights (including patents, trade marks and designs) were known collectively as industrial property. With the development of the law of copyright, the term intellectual property was later used to describe the entirety of rights and it has since become standard terminology.

One notable characteristic of intellectual property law is that it plays a pivotal role in many aspects of everyday life, for example, in industry (inventions in the form of new products and processes), science (research in biotechnology and in new software applications), arts and craft (paintings, plays, music and film) and in business (trading reputation, trade secrets and other forms of confidential information). Owing to the breadth of the subject, this chapter will only attempt to introduce to the reader the basic principles governing this area of the law. Many of the detailed rules and complexities have therefore been omitted.

Property Rights

21.2 Intellectual property is a form of personal property (unlike land which is known as real property) and is intangible in nature (as opposed to tangible forms of personal property like chattels or goods). As with any other property, intellectual property can be owned and exploited. For example, such property rights can be assigned or transferred for a price or otherwise licensed in return for royalties. Intellectual property can also be used as security for loans, such as by way of a mortgage or charge.

Characteristics of Intellectual Property Rights

21.3 In order to protect the different varieties of creations emanating from the human intellect, it is not surprising that intellectual property law does not just comprise one set of legal rules. Rather, the phrase intellectual property is really a 'handy shorthand for a whole slew of disparate rights ... which share the feature that they protect some products of the human mind, for varying periods of time, against use by others of those products in various ways' (D Vaver, 'Intellectual Property: The State of the Art' (2000) 116 *Law Quarterly Review* 621 at p 621). The different branches of intellectual property law, which we shall soon be examining in greater detail, therefore deal with different aspects of intellectual property.

Some intellectual property rights are secured by way of formal registration, that is, upon the successful completion of a formal application and registration procedure. These would include trade marks, patents and registered designs. Other rights like copyright and performance rights can be acquired automatically without the need for registration.

It is also important to note that intellectual property rights are largely territorial in nature. Owners of intellectual property do not, by acquiring intellectual property rights in Singapore, enjoy protection on a 'world-wide' basis and those who wish to obtain protection overseas will generally be required to comply with all the formalities and other substantive requirements imposed by each overseas country in which protection is sought. Intellectual property protection therefore does not extend beyond the territorial confines of each jurisdiction. However, in order to facilitate trade and commerce between nations, there has been for some time a concerted drive towards greater harmonisation of national laws in the field of intellectual property.

In view of its intrinsic value as a marketable commodity, intellectual property is often linked to international trade issues and to trade relations between countries. Many years ago, developed countries including the United States began to exert pressure on developing nations to increase the level of intellectual property protection in their domestic laws (in an effort to clamp down on global piracy, amongst other things) and this eventually led to the inclusion of intellectual property protection issues in the agenda for the Uruguay Round of multilateral trade talks under the auspices of GATT (General Agreement on Tariffs and Trade). In turn, the World Trade Organisation ('WTO'), the successor to GATT, was established and one of its major responsibilities was to administer a highly significant instrument known as the Agreement on Trade Related Aspects of Intellectual Property Rights ('TRIPS Agreement'). The TRIPS Agreement, which came into force on 1 January 1995, laid down minimum standards of protection and enforcement for each facet of intellectual property law and all WTO member countries had to ensure (for fear of the imposition of trade sanctions) that their domestic laws complied with these minimum standards within specified time frames.

The TRIPS Agreement is arguably the most important international initiative in the field of intellectual property in recent times in that it provides an effective enforcement mechanism through the linking of trade rights with the need for adequate protection of intellectual property rights. It promotes two long-established objectives: firstly, the principle of national treatment that there should be non-discriminatory treatment of foreign nationals within each WTO member country (ie each member country must afford to nationals of other member countries the same protection as it affords to its own nationals) and secondly, the movement towards greater harmonisation of national intellectual property laws through the adoption of minimum standards of protection.

Singapore's intellectual property laws are largely in compliance with TRIPS. The word 'largely' is used here (and elsewhere in this chapter) because commentators have argued that some aspects of Singapore's intellectual property laws still require 'fine-tuning'. For example, in the realm of copyright law, certain defences and exceptions spelt out in the Copyright Act 1987 (eg sections 38, 106 and 114) may need to be re-examined in the light of article 13 of TRIPS, which states that 'Members shall confine limitations or exceptions to exclusive rights to certain special cases which do not conflict with a normal exploitation of the work and do not unreasonably prejudice the legitimate interests of the right holder'. This issue is raised and discussed by Professor George Wei in his book, *The Law of Copyright in Singapore* (2nd ed, 2000) at paragraphs 9.20, 9.60–9.62 and 9.181.

Justification for Intellectual Property Protection

21.4 Why should intellectual property rights be protected in the first place? Although there are several rationales and justifications for such protection, only two of these will be briefly mentioned in this chapter.

The conventional wisdom has been that authors, inventors and entrepreneurs ought to receive legal protection for their works and inventions because they should be compensated and rewarded for their time, energy and expense in creating end-products which invariably benefit society, whether scientifically, technologically or culturally. Some *economic* arguments that have been raised include the need to encourage and reward innovation, to promote investment, to provide economic incentives for further innovation so as to lead to the creation of new knowledge and technology, and to generate income and employment. Such arguments are particularly cogent for products and inventions which generate good revenue and remain commercially viable in the long term.

Quite apart from monetary returns however, there is the additional and distinct justification of *moral rights* over a work. As Professor Wei explains, '[t]he moral rights theory supports not just the creation of economic rights, but also rights which protect other legitimate expectations of authorship' (G Wei, *The Law of Copyright in Singapore* (2nd ed, 2000) at p 22). For example, the person who creates a work should have the right to be identified as the author of the work (viz the moral right of paternity). He should also have the right to control the use and exploitation of it (viz the moral right of integrity), not simply for economic reasons but also to prevent unauthorised distortion, mutilation or modification to the work where this is prejudicial to the integrity of the work or to the 'honour' or 'reputation' of the author. This latter example is premised on the idea that because the work in question is a product of the author's intellectual effort, it thereby becomes part of the author's own personality.

Law of Copyright

What is Copyright?

21.5 As its name suggests, copyright confers on the owner of the copyright subsisting in a work (or some other authorised third party) the right to do certain acts in relation to the work, such as to make copies of (or to reproduce) the work. The unauthorised reproduction of copyright material by persons who have not obtained permission from the copyright owner may therefore amount to an infringement of copyright, for which the copyright owner can seek redress in a court of law. In Singapore, copyright is governed by the Copyright Act 1987 (Cap 63, 1999 Rev Ed).

Unless otherwise stated, all statutory references in this section on the law of copyright are to the Copyright Act 1987 (Cap 63, 1999 Rev Ed)

General Principles of Copyright Law

21.6 Copyright is often viewed as a 'partial', 'weak' or 'quasi' monopoly right. The reason for this is that in order to sue for copyright infringement, the copyright owner must prove the element of 'copying', that the alleged infringer has actually copied his work (we shall discuss the topic of copyright infringement in greater detail below). Weaker monopolies like copyright, however, tend to be compensated with longer protection periods, for example, for the life of the author plus 50 years after death (as in the case of authors' works in Singapore). This term of protection for copyright works is the minimum set out in the Berne Convention for the Protection of Literary and Artistic Works. Many countries however (including the UK and the US) have increased the period of protection to life of the author plus 70 years after death, and Singapore will soon follow suit (in view of the recently-concluded US-Singapore Free Trade Agreement). The US Supreme Court, for example, recently confirmed that the Sonny Bono Copyright Term Extension Act 1998 was constitutional and upheld the extension (by the US Congress) of the term of protection for copyright works in the US from the life of the author plus 50 years after death to plus 70 years after death (see *Eldred v Ashcroft* (2003)).

Known as the idea-expression dichotomy, this fundamental principle states that copyright only protects ideas which have been expressed/ fixed in some material or tangible form and will not protect the underlying ideas themselves (which must be free for all to take, unless protected by the law of confidence). Take, for example, a book written by your friend on his life as a university undergraduate. Although the idea *per se* (of writing a book on life as a university undergraduate) does not attract copyright protection, the form of expression is, however, protected by copyright (the book actually written by your friend, whether published or otherwise). This distinction between 'idea' and 'expression', although easy to state in theory, can be difficult to apply in practice.

Unlike patents and trade marks (which are registrable rights), copyright in most countries (including Singapore) subsists automatically without the need for registration nor compliance with other formalities.

Copyright Protection Under Copyright Act 1987

(1) *In What Subject Matter Can You Claim Copyright?*

21.7 Copyright can subsist in two broad categories of subject matter, namely authors' works and subject matter other than works (which, for our purposes, we shall label 'neighbouring rights').

Authors' works include:

(a) literary works, eg expressions in print/writing like articles and books, tables/compilations of data, computer programs, or basically works which afford 'either information and instruction, or pleasure in the form of literary enjoyment' to the reader (see section 7A and *Exxon Corporation v Exxon Insurance Consultants International Ltd* (1982));

(b) musical works;

(c) artistic works, viz paintings, sculptures, drawings, engravings, photographs, buildings or models of buildings, all of which are capable of protection irrespective of 'artistic quality', or works of artistic craftsmanship (see the definition of an 'artistic work' in section 7(1));

(d) dramatic works, eg a choreographic show if described in writing in the form in which the show is to be presented, or a script/scenario for a cinematograph film (see the definition of a 'dramatic work' in section 7(1)).

The rights subsisting in 'subject matter other than works' are sometimes known as neighbouring or entrepreneurial rights because these rights typically owe their existence to persons (typically entrepreneurs) who are not the authors of the original work but who nevertheless undertake the risk of exploiting new technology and of promoting and investing in the works of authors. Sound recordings, cinematograph films, television and sound broadcasts, cable programmes and published editions of authors' works all fall within the rubric of neighbouring rights.

It should be noted that different copyrights can co-exist in one particular product and that they can belong to different parties. Take, for example, a CD recording of songs: the lyrics or words to the songs are protected by literary copyright, the music itself has musical copyright whilst sound recording rights reside in the CD recording.

(2) *Connecting Factor: Are You a Protected Person?*

21.8 In view of the territorial nature of intellectual property rights, copyright protection is only available if the owner of the copyright or the copyright material itself is in some way connected to Singapore. In the case of unpublished authors' works, the author must be a 'qualified person' at the time when the work was made (section 27(1)) and the phrase 'qualified person' has been defined to mean a citizen of Singapore or a person resident in Singapore (section 27(4)). As for authors' works which have been published (please refer to section 24 for more information on the concept of 'publication'), copyright will subsist only if the author was a 'qualified person' at the time when the work was first published or if the work was first published in Singapore (section 27(2)). Turning to neighbouring rights (to sound recordings and cinematograph films in particular), the general position is that the maker has to be a 'qualified person' at the time when the recording or film was made, or that the recording or film was made or first published in Singapore (sections 87 and 88; see also sections 89–91).

Thus far, our discussion has been on local copyright material. Can foreign works and neighbouring rights also secure copyright protection in Singapore? As mentioned above, the principle of national treatment (an important objective in the 'internationalisation' of intellectual property law) necessitates that Singapore should extend to foreigners the same level of copyright protection enjoyed by locals. For this purpose, citizens/nationals or residents of a WTO member country or a country which is party to the Berne Convention for the Protection of Literary and Artistic Works can generally avail themselves of the provisions of the Singapore Copyright Act (section 184 read with the Copyright (International Protection) Regulations).

(3) *Requirement of Originality*

21.9 One of the cardinal principles of copyright law is that the work for which protection is sought must be original (note that the requirement of originality only applies to authors' works and not to neighbouring rights; see section 27). This basically means that the work must have originated from the author; it must have been independently created and not copied from some other source. Whilst there is no statutory definition for originality, case law has made it clear that simplicity of the work *per se* is not a bar to copyright protection, meaning that merit and quality are generally irrelevant considerations (*Kenrick v Lawrence* (1890); *British Northrop v Texteam* (1974)). Instead, a work will be treated as original for copyright purposes if sufficient effort, skill, labour and judgment has been expended in creating the work (*Macmillan & Co Ltd v K & J Cooper* (1923); *Re AUVI Trademark* (1992)). It is therefore possible, though unlikely, for two persons to independently produce identical pieces of work such that each person will be considered to be the author of his own work for copyright purposes.

(4) *Reduction into Material Form*

21.10 Another prerequisite for copyright protection is that the work in question must have been reduced to material (or tangible) form, as for example, when the work is first reduced to writing or when it is stored in a computer (sections 16 and 17). This requirement follows logically from the fact that copyright law does not protect ideas *per se* but only the expression of such ideas.

Duration of Copyright

21.11 The rules for determining the duration of copyright protection depend on the type of work in question and they can generally be summarised as follows:

(1) For authors' works (except photographs), copyright subsists for the lifetime of the author plus another 50 years after his death (section 28(2); see also the qualification in section 28(3) for works which remain unpublished at the time of death of the author);

(2) For photographs, copyright subsists for 50 years from first publication (section 28(6));

(3) For neighbouring rights, copyright generally subsists for 50 years from first publication or production (sections 92–95);

(4) For published editions of works, copyright (to be claimed by the publishers) subsists for 25 years from first publication (section 96).

Ownership of Copyright/Assignments and Licences

21.12 As a general rule, the author of a literary, dramatic, musical or artistic work is the first owner of the copyright in the work (section 30(2)). Similarly, the maker of a sound recording or cinematograph film is entitled to claim ownership of the copyright subsisting in the recording or film (sections 97(2) and 98(2)). There are also works of joint authorship which have been produced by the collaboration of two or more authors and in which the contribution of each author is not separate from the contribution of the other author or the contributions of other authors (see the definition of a 'work of joint authorship' in section 7(1)).

There are however some exceptions to this basic rule and they apply mainly to works produced by employed journalists (section 30(4)) and to certain commissioned works (sections 30(5), 97(3) and 98(3)). In addition, if an author produces a piece of work in the course of his employment (the author must be employed under a contract of service or apprenticeship), then it is his employer who will be entitled to the copyright in the work (section 30(6)). Note however that these exceptions can be excluded or modified by mutual agreement between the parties (section 30(3); see also sections 97(3) and 98(3)).

21.13 Like other forms of personal property, copyright may be assigned or licensed. For an assignment of copyright (whether total or partial) to be effective at law, it must be in writing and signed by or on behalf of the assignor (section 194(3)). Whilst an assignment of copyright results in a transfer of ownership, a licence (which, except for an exclusive licence, does not need to comply with any formalities like writing) merely authorises the licensee to do certain acts which fall within the scope of exclusive rights of the copyright owner (see next paragraph).

Exclusive Rights of Copyright Owner

21.14 How can the copyright owner, who has acquired copyright protection for his work under the Copyright Act 1987, now exploit his work and deal with the copyright therein? What is the scope of rights exclusive to the copyright owner? We turn to section 26 for the answer—but do note that section 26 only deals with exclusive rights in relation to authors' works (the reader is referred to sections 82–86 for the corresponding provisions on neighbouring rights).

For authors' works in general, the copyright owner has the exclusive right to do any of the following acts:

(1) to reproduce the work in a material form (see section 15 generally);
(2) to publish the work, if the work is unpublished;
(3) to broadcast the work;
(4) to include the work in a cable programme.

Further, for literary, dramatic and musical works only, the copyright owner has the exclusive right to do any of the following additional acts:

(5) to perform the work in public;
(6) to make an adaptation of the work (see the definition of 'adaptation' in section 7(1));
(7) to do any of the six acts specified above in relation to the adaptation.

There is also a special category of rights known as rental rights which the owners of copyright in computer programs and sound recordings can now exploit. These copyright owners have been conferred the right (via commercial rental arrangements) to authorise or prohibit the commercial rental to the public of originals or copies of computer programs and sound recordings (sections 26(1)(c), 82(1)(b) and 25A).

Primary Infringement of Copyright in Authors' Works

21.15 The reader is advised that infringement of copyright (both primary and secondary) in relation to neighbouring rights will not be discussed here (please refer to sections 103–105 for further information).

If a person (the 'defendant') does any act in Singapore which falls within the scope of rights exclusive to the copyright owner (the 'plaintiff') without the permission or licence of the plaintiff, then he is said to have infringed the plaintiff's copyright in the work in question (section 31). This is known as primary copyright infringement, for example, where the defendant makes a photocopy of the plaintiff's book without first seeking his permission.

21.16 Before an action can be brought against the defendant for copyright infringement, the plaintiff must first satisfy two elements: (1) a causal connection between the plaintiff's work and the defendant's copy, and (2) a substantial taking by the defendant of the plaintiff's work.

The first element of causal connection simply requires the plaintiff to show that the defendant has copied his work, for example, that there is sufficient objective similarity between the two works in question and that the defendant has had prior access (or an opportunity to gain access) to the plaintiff's work (*LB (Plastics) Ltd v Swish Products Ltd* (1979)). This therefore means that there can be no copyright infringement if the defendant has created his work, albeit identical in all respects to the plaintiff's, independently of the plaintiff's work.

The second element of substantial taking makes it clear that copyright may be infringed even if the defendant has not copied the plaintiff's work in its entirety, so long as the defendant has taken a substantial part of the plaintiff's work (section 10(1)). The question of substantiality (which is largely a matter of fact and degree) has been interpreted by the courts as referring to the quality of what has been taken rather than its quantity in relation to the whole (*Ladbroke v William Hill* (1964)). On this basis, copying a small portion of a work can infringe copyright if the portion copied is important in relation to the whole work. Further, in view of the idea-expression dichotomy, it is necessary for the plaintiff to show, in an action for copyright infringement, that the defendant has copied the form of expression and not merely the underlying idea in his work.

21.17 It should be noted that the copyright in an artistic work which is in two-dimensional form (eg a drawing of a toy car) may be infringed by the defendant's production of a three-dimensional model (toy car) based on the artistic work (see section 15(3)). However, no infringement is made out in such a case if, to a non-expert (possibly a lay person of reasonable intelligence), the three-dimensional model created by the defendant does not appear to be a reproduction of the two-dimensional artistic work (see section 69). The reader should also be aware that there are complex provisions dealing with the use of copyright to protect industrial designs and also with the relationship between copyright and registered design protection (see sections 70, 73 and 74). The position of industrial designs is outlined later in this chapter.

Infringing Authorisation (Authorising Primary Infringement)

21.18 Sometimes, it may not be in the interest of the plaintiff to target the primary infringer (ie the party guilty of primary copyright infringement), who may be elusive and hence difficult to trace or who would probably not come to court with deep pockets. Instead, the plaintiff may wish to commence an action against the defendant who has authorised the act of primary copyright infringement.

> Section 31(1) reads: '… the copyright in a … work is infringed by a person who, not being the owner of the copyright, and without the licence of the owner of the copyright, … *authorises* the doing in Singapore of any act comprised in the copyright' (emphasis added).

Section 103(1) is the parallel provision for neighbouring rights.

Take, for example, a shop which provides self-service photocopying facilities. It is not unreasonable to assume that some of its customers/users would have, at some point in time, infringed copyright by photocopying books and other reading material in their entirety (without the permission of the relevant copyright owners). Instead of targeting these customers/users (who could very well be students), copyright owners may be better off suing the vendor for having authorised (or, at the very least, for having acquiesced in) such acts of primary copyright infringement. For our purposes, we shall use the term 'infringing authorisation' to denote this cause of action.

21.19 To succeed in an action for infringing authorisation, the plaintiff must (at the least) prove that the defendant had under his control the means by which an infringement of copyright may be committed (eg a photocopying machine) and that the defendant had in some way, expressly or impliedly, approved or authorised the act of infringement (for example, the defendant knew or had reasonable grounds to suspect that primary copyright infringement would be committed but failed to take reasonable steps to prevent it; see *Moorhouse v University of New South Wales* (1976)). It should be noted, however, that with the House of Lords' decision in *CBS Songs v Amstrad* (1988) and the Singapore Court of Appeal's decision in *Ong Seow Pheng v Lotus Development* (1997), the element of authorisation is now more strictly construed: to authorise now means to 'grant or purport to grant' to a third party the right to do the infringing act in question. This means that merely conferring on the third party the power to copy or even facilitating the third party's act of copying is insufficient to amount to an act of authorisation.

Secondary Infringement of Copyright

21.20 Secondary infringement of copyright occurs when infringing copies of copyright material (eg copies of pirated software) are exploited commercially (eg offered for sale to the public). The distinction therefore between primary infringement and secondary infringement of copyright is that the former involves the actual making of the infringing copies whilst the latter involves the commercial exploitation of these infringing copies.

It should be noted that secondary infringement of copyright attracts both civil and criminal liability. The copyright owner can bring a civil suit against the defendant who, without the licence/consent of the copyright owner, imports into Singapore for purposes of sale or distribution or who actually sells in Singapore infringing copies of copyright material. The copyright owner in this case would, however, have to show that the secondary infringer (the defendant) actually knew or ought reasonably to have known (ie having knowledge of facts which would put an honest and reasonable person on enquiry) that the copies imported or sold were infringing copies. This, of course, is merely a simplified reading of sections 32 and 33 (for a fuller understanding of the intricacies surrounding secondary infringement and the issue of parallel imports, the reader is advised to read sections 32 and 33 (and the parallel provisions for neighbouring rights, sections 104 and 105) and sections 25(3) and 25(4) in detail as well as the local case of *PP v Teo Ai Nee* (1995)).

As mentioned above, such acts of infringement also amount to criminal offences, for which the penalty is a fine or term of imprisonment or both (section 136).

Groundless Threats of Legal Proceedings

21.21 For many innocent traders, the threat of a copyright infringement action may be worrisome. This is particularly so where the threat is serious and has an adverse effect on a trader's business (eg where customers or potential customers are driven away by the threat of action). Fortunately, those who are aggrieved by such threats can now deal with them by way of a statutory cause of action.

Section 200(1) provides that a person who, by circulars, advertisements or otherwise, threatens to institute legal proceedings against another person for copyright infringement may himself be faced with a civil action for having made such threats (to which the only defence is proof of actual infringement). The aggrieved party may claim the following relief: an injunction (against the continuance of the threats), damages (in respect of any loss which the aggrieved party may have sustained as a result of the threats) and a declaration (to the effect that the threats are unjustifiable). Note, however, that a mere notification of the existence of copyright does not in itself constitute a threat.

Civil Remedies

21.22 The remedies for copyright infringement are set out in Part V of the Copyright Act 1987 (see, in particular, sections 119, 120 and 120A). According to section 119(2), the copyright owner (the plaintiff) can ask the court for an injunction (basically a stop-order to prevent further acts of infringement) and either damages (monetary compensation) or an account of profits. However, as against a defendant who was not aware or who had no reasonable grounds for suspecting that what he had done amounted to an infringement of copyright, the plaintiff is only entitled to an account of profits and not to damages (section 119(3)). Further, in appropriate circumstances, the court may award the plaintiff additional damages after having taken into account, amongst other factors, the flagrancy of the infringement and the benefit which has accrued to the defendant by reason of the infringement (section 119(4)). Finally, the court may, upon application by the plaintiff, order the defendant to deliver up infringing copies of copyright material to the plaintiff and may also make an order for the disposal/destruction of these copies.

Border Enforcement Measures

21.23 Division 6 of Part V of the Copyright Act 1987, together with the Copyright (Border Enforcement Measures) Regulations 1998, provide for border enforcement measures to prevent the importation of infringing copies of copyright material into Singapore. Basically, the owner of the copyright in copyright material (including the exclusive licensee) may give written notice to the Director-General of Customs and Excise, stating that infringing copies of copyright material (not being copies of copyright material which are goods in transit) are expected to be imported at a certain time and place specified in the notice and that he objects to such importation (section 140B(1)). If such infringing copies are indeed imported into Singapore for the purpose of sale, hire, distribution or trade generally, the customs officer is empowered to seize the infringing copies (section 140B(7)). Senior customs officers also have the power to search vessels, aircraft and vehicles for such infringing copies of copyright material (section 140M(1)).

Defences to Infringement

21.24 Whilst the law of copyright seeks to protect original works and neighbouring rights from the unauthorised acts of third parties, it too recognises that not all dealings with such works should amount to an infringement of copyright. Society at large must be allowed to benefit in some way from the intellectual output of authors and the fair dealing defences (amongst other defences and exceptions) in the Copyright Act 1987 go some way towards achieving this purpose. The general difficulty here, of course, lies in delineating the precise extent of allowable defences and exceptions under copyright law and in finding the right balance (if at all possible) between the rights and interests of the creators of intellectual property on the one hand, and users and the general public on the other. It should be remembered though that the various qualifications and exceptions to intellectual property rights ought to be consistent with the principles set out in article 13 of TRIPS. This chapter will only examine the fair dealing defences.

21.25 A fair dealing with a work for the purpose of research or private study, or for the purpose of criticism or review, or for the purpose of reporting current events shall not constitute an infringement of the copyright in the work (see, generally, sections 35–37 for authors' works and sections 109–111 for neighbouring rights). In determining whether a dealing with a work (by way of making a copy of the whole work or a part of the work) constitutes fair dealing for the purpose of *research or private study*, section 35(2) sets out certain guidelines for consideration:

(1) the purpose and character of the dealing, including whether such dealing is of a commercial nature or is for non-profit educational purposes;
(2) the nature of the work;
(3) the amount and substantiality of the part copied taken in relation to the whole work; and
(4) the effect of the dealing upon the potential market for, or value of, the work.

Notwithstanding section 35(2), certain dealings with a work for the purpose of *research or private study* are deemed to be fair dealings under section 35(3):

(1) if the work is an article in a periodical publication (eg *Newsweek*), copying the whole or a part of that article (note, however, that according to section 35(4), the defence of fair dealing does not apply to the copying of the whole or a part of an article if another article in the same issue/publication, being an article dealing with a different

subject-matter, is also copied);

(2) in all other cases (eg published books/works), copying not more than a 'reasonable portion' of the work (eg not more than 10% of the total number of pages in a book of at least 10 pages (or not more than 10% of the total number of bytes of the work as stored on any medium by electronic means) *or* not more than one chapter of the book/work, whichever is more). Do note, however, that this is a simplified reading of sections 7(2) and 7(2A), which set out, non-exhaustively, the meaning of the expression 'reasonable portion'. For completeness, these provisions are reproduced in full below:

Section 7(2) Without limiting the meaning of the expression 'reasonable portion' in this Act, where a literary, dramatic or musical work is contained in a published edition of that work, being an edition of not less than 10 pages, a copy of part of that work, as it appears in that edition, shall be taken to contain only a reasonable portion of that work if the pages that are copied in the edition—

(a) do not exceed, in the aggregate, 10% of the number of pages in that edition; or

(b) in a case where the work is divided into chapters—exceed, in the aggregate, 10% of the number of pages in that edition but contain only the whole or part of a single chapter of the work.

Section 7(2A) Without limiting the meaning of the expression 'reasonable portion' in this Act, where a literary, dramatic or musical work is contained in a published edition of that work, being an edition which is stored on any medium by electronic means and is not divided into pages, a copy of part of that work, as it appears in that edition, shall be taken to contain only a reasonable portion of that work if the part that is copied in the edition—

(a) does not exceed, in the aggregate, 10% of the total number of bytes in that edition; or

(b) in a case where the work is divided into chapters, exceeds, in the aggregate, 10% of the total number of bytes in that edition but contains only the whole or part of a single chapter of the work.

21.26 A fair dealing with a literary, dramatic, musical or artistic work shall not constitute copyright infringement if it is for the purpose of *criticism or review* or *the reporting of current events* (eg in a newspaper or magazine), so long as a sufficient acknowledgment of the work is made (viz an acknowledgment identifying the work by its title and identifying the author; see the definition of 'sufficient acknowledgement' in section 7(1)). Note, however, that there is no need for an acknowledgment where the reporting of current events is by means of broadcasting or a cable programme service or in a cinematograph film.

Although there are no statutory guidelines for 'fair dealing' here, it is not unreasonable to suggest that they should be similar to those for research or private study (see section 35(2)). Indeed, there is support for this view in the case authorities, of which the following are instructive: *Hubbard v Vosper* (1972); *Pro Sieben Media AG v Carlton UK Television Ltd* (1999); *Hyde Park Residence Ltd v Yelland* (2000).

Rights in Performances (Performers' Rights)

21.27 Part XII of the Copyright Act 1987, titled 'Performers' Protection', extends to artistes and performers certain rights which prohibit the bootlegging of *live* performances given by them (see section 246 *et seq*). Basically, during the protection period of the performance (which is 50 years from the time of performance), a third party cannot, amongst other things, make an unauthorised direct sound recording of the 'live' performance (nor make copies of such unauthorised recordings) nor broadcast 'live' the performance without the permission of the performer.

To avail himself of such protection, however, the performer must be a 'qualified person' (ie a citizen of Singapore or a person resident in Singapore) or that the 'live' performance must have been given in Singapore, whether in the presence of an audience or otherwise. Therefore, if a Singapore citizen or a person resident in Singapore gives a 'live' performance in England, that performance will be protected in Singapore. Likewise, if any foreign national or resident gives a 'live' performance in Singapore, that performance will also be protected because it had taken place in Singapore.

It should also be noted that pursuant to section 256, regulations have been made by the Minister to apply the provisions in Part XII of the Copyright Act on performers' rights to foreign countries. The reader's attention is therefore also drawn to regulation 3(8) of the Copyright (International Protection) Regulations.

Moral Rights

21.28 Moral rights, which exist independently of economic rights, are personal to the author of a work—generally speaking, they cannot be assigned. The purpose of moral rights is to grant the author the respect he deserves for his intellectual output. This is because '[m]oral rights are based on the idea that a work being a product of the author's intellectual effort, becomes part of the author's personality' (G Wei, *The Law of Copyright in Singapore* (2nd ed, 2000) at p 22). As one commentator puts it, moral rights 'recognise the creator's contribution, a way of giving legal effect to the fact that the act of producing a work is an act of creation and that the creator has a link or bond with the work which should be preserved regardless of hard economic considerations' (D Bainbridge, *Intellectual Property* (5th ed, 2002) at p 28).

Moral rights are most closely associated with countries in Continental Europe (countries which adopt the civil law system), whereas common law countries in general prefer to place greater emphasis on protecting the economic interests of authors.

Many European civil law countries recognise four main moral rights: the right to claim authorship (moral right of paternity), the right to protect the integrity of the work (moral right of integrity), the right of publication and the right of recall. Article 6*bis* of the Berne Convention for the Protection of Literary and Artistic Works requires member countries to specifically protect the moral right of paternity and the moral right of integrity. It should be noted however that article 9(1) of the TRIPS Agreement had expressly excluded the need for WTO member countries (like Singapore) to comply with article 6*bis* of the Berne Convention. Yet, by virtue of the fact that Singapore acceded to the Berne Convention on 21 September 1998 and that the Convention came into effect in Singapore on 21 December 1998, Singapore is obliged, in due course, to comply with article 6*bis* of Berne.

21.29 There are provisions in the Copyright Act 1987 which protect the moral rights of authors in certain respects. For example, Part IX of the Act (specifically section 188) imposes on third parties a statutory duty not to attribute falsely the authorship of a copyright work (there is, however, no specific provision in the Act as yet which gives a positive right to the author to claim authorship). Simply put, no one should be allowed to insert/affix another person's name on a piece of work originating from the author, in such a way as to imply that the other person is the author of the work. Given that Singapore has also joined the Berne Convention, the Copyright Act 1987 ought, in due course, to be amended to introduce specific provisions relating to the protection of the moral rights of paternity and integrity (as is required by article 6*bis* of the Berne Convention).

Rights Management Information

21.30 Part XIII of the Copyright Act 1987, which deals with 'Rights Management Information' (or 'RMI'), is basically concerned with protecting the integrity of information provided on or in association with works (and other copyright subject-matter) so as to enable the copyright owner to better administer the rights that he enjoys. As Professor Wei explains, '[t]his is perhaps especially important in the digital environment or cyberspace on account of the ease by which works and other copyright subject-matter may be reproduced and exploited through the use of information technology. If the copyright owner is able to fix rights management information onto licensed copies, he may be in a better position to track the reproduction and so forth of that copy in the digital environment' (G Wei, *The Law of Copyright in Singapore* (2nd ed, 2000) at p 1372).

RMI, in relation to a copy of a work (for simplicity, discussion of RMI in a recording of a performance is omitted), is defined in section 260(4) to mean:

(1) information which identifies the work;
(2) information which identifies the author of the work or the owner of copyright in the work;

(3) information about the terms and conditions of use of the copy of the work;
(4) any numbers or codes that represent the information in (1) to (3) above.

RMI, however, excludes any information which relates to a user of a copy of the work, such as the name, account, address or other contact information of the user.

RMI is thus protected in the following way: a person who provides the RMI (in an *electronic form* and attached to a copy of the work in question *or* where RMI in an *electronic form* appears in connection with materials made available on a network) can bring an action against a third party who, without his consent and knowingly and with intent to *mislead* or to *induce or facilitate an infringement* of the copyright in the work, *removes or alters* the RMI (see sections 260(1), 260(2) and 260(3)). The court may grant the plaintiff in such a case an injunction or damages or both, and may also make an order for the delivery-up or destruction of the offending article (section 261).

Liability of Network/Internet Service Providers

21.31 Another important development in the law of copyright concerns the liability of Network Service Providers in respect of copyright infringement committed over the Internet and other computer networks. Examples of Network Service Providers include Internet Service Providers ('ISPs') and operators of a local area network ('LAN'). For simplicity, however, we shall adopt the term 'ISP' here. As the primary role of ISPs is to facilitate access to material on the Internet, ISPs often run the risk of being held liable for the material hosted by them on behalf of their subscribers on the Internet. It would therefore appear that where infringing material has been made available on a network which is operated and controlled solely by an ISP (eg when the ISP hosts such material for its subscribers on its network file server), the ISP may potentially be liable for infringing authorisation if it fails to inform its subscribers of the implications of copyright law and of the importance of not infringing copyright and, additionally, fails to monitor the material made available through its service. Whether the ISP is ultimately liable for infringing authorisation or indeed primary infringement will of course depend very much on the actual facts and circumstances. Suffice it to say that the facts may well be complex and the legal issues tricky and ever evolving.

21.32 Fortunately, ISPs may be able to absolve themselves from liability in respect of such infringing material by relying on sections 193B and 193C(1) (a similar though more widely worded provision is to be found in section 10 of the Electronic Transactions Act 1998 (Cap 88, 1999 Rev Ed)). Basically, the owner of copyright material cannot sue the ISP for performing any act in relation to an electronic copy of that material made available on a network (such electronic copies of material can be stored in a network file server or uploaded and stored onto a bulletin board) if

(1) the ISP has merely acted as a data conduit by providing the necessary technical means to enable users of the network to access the electronic copy (eg enabling network users to view the electronic copy on their computer monitors), or (2) the infringing act (performed in the course of storing, transmitting, routing or providing connections to the electronic copy on the network) is done at the express/implied direction of a user of the network and the ISP does not deliberately modify the contents of the electronic copy.

21.33 Note, however, that according to section 193C(2), the ISP is precluded from relying on the special immunity granted under section 193C(1) if:

(1) the electronic copy of the copyright material was made available on a network operated and controlled solely by the ISP (eg where the ISP operates and controls the network servers and any relevant network operating system);
(2) the owner of the copyright material has furnished the ISP with a statutory declaration setting out, in good faith, the details of the alleged infringement; and
(3) the ISP fails within a reasonable time to take reasonable steps to remove the infringing copy from the network or to disable access to the material on the network.

21.34 Should the ISP, on the other hand, proceed to remove the infringing copy from its network or disable access to it pursuant to its receipt of a statutory declaration, the ISP will be exempt from any civil/criminal liability which may otherwise arise as a result of such removal or disabling, even if it is ultimately determined that copyright in the material has not been infringed (section 193D). This basically means that the user of the network (or the 'mastermind' behind the infringing copy) cannot later turn around and sue the ISP for removing the infringing copy. The ISP is therefore shielded from liability and its interests are thereby protected.

Browsing (User Caching)

21.35 Does an Internet user, for example, infringe copyright by browsing/surfing the website of Amazon.com on his own computer? It may be argued that by browsing the website of Amazon.com, the user would have created/reproduced a transient electronic copy of Amazon's web page in his computer's random access memory ('RAM') and probably in the cache of his browser software. Section 193E however provides that the mere browsing of a website will not amount to an infringement of copyright so long as 'the making of a transient or incidental electronic copy' of material found on a network is 'required for the viewing, listening or utilisation of the material' by the user. Further, it can be argued that by the very act of displaying copyright material on the World Wide Web, the copyright owner is effectively granting an implied licence to Internet users to visit his website.

Hyper-linking and Meta-tagging

21.36 An example of the many challenges in applying traditional intellectual property regimes in cyberspace involves the extension of copyright and trade mark principles to deal with questions of legal liability arising from common Internet practices like hyper-linking (allowing the web-user to link from one website to another) and meta-tagging (involving the use of certain words and phrases in a website's HTML coding to attract Internet traffic to the site through 'hits' generated by search engines).

21.37 For the convenience of web-users, hypertext links are often incorporated in the overall layout and design of Internet web pages. Some of these links may contain marked-up text or graphic images (icons) or even the name or logo of a particular company or business entity. In most cases though, this would not be of any real concern to the company or business entity concerned (known in our context as the owner of the linked website). Disputes may, however, arise when, instead of linking to the home page of the linked website, the link in question (on the linking website) directs web-users to one of the 'inner' pages of the linked website. This Internet routing process (also known as 'deep-linking') is objectionable because the home page of the linked website, which usually carries web advertisements which are themselves a significant source of revenue for the owner of the linked website, is inevitably bypassed. Accordingly, the owner of the linked website may seek to combat 'deep-linking' by basing his legal claim on, *inter alia*, copyright infringement (would, for example, the use of an icon or marked-up text as a hyperlink infringe the artistic or literary copyright of the owner of the linked website?) and/or trade mark infringement (assuming, in the first instance, that the offending link takes the form of a registered trade mark belonging to the plaintiff).

21.38 Insofar as meta-tagging is concerned, the issue here is whether the use of meta-tags incorporating the famous trade marks of third parties will be disallowed on the basis of trade mark infringement (the law of trade marks is discussed in greater detail below). The problem arises in the following way. Information (in the form of key words and phrases) that is found in these meta-tags is often 'picked up' by search engines (such as *Yahoo* and *AltaVista*) whilst they generate their databases and direct web-users to the relevant 'hit' sites. The intrinsic value of meta-tags becomes immediately apparent and businessmen (especially those who trade over the Internet) are savvy enough to incorporate famous trade marks belonging to third parties as part of the key information of their own meta-tags, so as to generate more search 'hits' and, in turn, Internet traffic to their own websites. The argument will go that the defendant's use of the plaintiff's trade mark in its meta-tags to lure customers and other web-users to its website is likely to mislead and confuse them as regards the relationship between the disputing parties. It therefore comes as no surprise that the owners of famous trade marks are anxious to stop such unscrupulous conduct by seeking, on the premise of trade mark infringement, a complete removal of all offending words and phrases from the meta-tags concerned.

21.39 A proper discussion of these issues is, unfortunately, beyond the scope of this chapter. The reader may therefore wish to refer to other specialist texts in the area (eg L Edwards and C Waelde (eds), *Law and the Internet —A Framework for Electronic Commerce* (2nd ed, 2000), Chapter 8 generally; C Reed, *Internet Law: Text and Materials* (2000), Chapter 3, pp 67–76) and to KFK Low and KCF Loi, 'Links, Frames and Meta-tags: More Challenges from the Wild Wild Web' (2000) 12 *Singapore Academy of Law Journal* 51 for a flavour of the various controversies.

Industrial Designs

21.40 Industrial designs are often recorded as two-dimensional drawings (eg engineering drawings) of objects that would later be industrially applied / produced in three-dimensional form. Take, as a simple example, a design drawing of a container for a drink. It is possible, at least in theory, to protect this design drawing under copyright law (as an artistic work), registered designs law and even trade mark law (which now allows for the registration of shape marks). This part of the chapter however concentrates on registered designs law and only brief mention will be made of copyright protection.

Such designs (in their two-dimensional form) used to be protected under the law of copyright for a limited 15-year period as artistic works if (1) the designs were of a functional nature and hence excluded from design registration (designs which generally lacked eye / aesthetic appeal and which usually led to the production of objects having an intrinsic utilitarian function, such as spare part components), and (2) the designs had been industrially applied anywhere in the world (eg there had been more than 50 reproductions of the drawings as three-dimensional objects for the purposes of sale). This short-term protection for unregistrable but industrially applied designs under copyright law was, however, removed with the amendment to section 70(1) of the Copyright Act 1987, due in part to feedback from industry that there was no longer a need to protect such designs (section 70(1) of the Copyright Act 1987 was amended by section 76(1)(a) of the Registered Designs Act 2000 (Act 25 of 2000); see also the speech made by Associate Professor Ho Peng Kee, Minister of State for Law, during the second reading of the Registered Designs Bill on 25 August 2000).

21.41 Industrial designs are generally protected under registered designs law. Singapore now operates its own design registration system; the Registered Designs Act 2000 (Cap 266, 2001 Rev Ed) ('RDA') was passed by Parliament in August 2000. In the past, however, design owners in Singapore had to first register their designs in the United Kingdom (under the UK Registered Designs Act 1949) before they could acquire design protection in Singapore. This 'piggy-back' system was operational under the now repealed United Kingdom Designs (Protection) Act (Cap

339, 1985 Rev Ed). Since 13 November 2000, design owners have been able to file their design applications directly with the Registry of Designs of the Intellectual Property Office of Singapore ('IPOS'). Whilst design protection in the UK (as extended to Singapore in the past) was for a 25-year period, design owners now only get a maximum protection period of 15 years in Singapore (see sections 21(1) and 21(2) of the RDA).

21.42 An interesting issue arises as to the meaning and scope of a 'design'. What constitutes a 'design'? A 'design' has been defined in section 2(1) of the RDA to mean features of shape, configuration, pattern or ornament applied to an article by any industrial process, but it does not include the following:

(1) a method or principle of construction;
(2) features of shape or configuration of an article which—
 (a) are dictated solely by the function which the article has to perform;
 (b) are dependent upon the appearance of another article of which the article is intended by the designer to form an integral part ('must-match' exception or 'integral part' exception); or
 (c) enable the article to be connected to, or placed in, around or against, another article so that either article may perform its function.

Note that the design in question must not be dictated purely by the function which the article is to perform (point 2a, above). The issue here is whether the shape of the article is actually attributable to or prompted by its function. If the answer is in the positive, then such a design will be excluded from registration. As for the 'must-match' or 'integral part' exception, the RDA provides that the design in question must not be dependent on the appearance of another article of which the article in question is intended by the designer to form an integral part. This necessarily excludes the registration of designs for many vehicle spare parts, such as design drawings for the door panels and bonnet tops of a car. Clearly, the design of a door panel is dependent on and must integrate with the appearance of the car as a whole.

21.43 The RDA further provides that a design is not registrable if its publication or use would be contrary to public order or morality (see section 6). It should be noted that computer programs and layout-designs of integrated circuits are also unregistrable under the RDA (see section 7); the former can generally be protected under copyright and patent law whilst protection for the latter is now governed by the Layout-Designs of Integrated Circuits Act 1999 (Cap 159A, 2000 Rev Ed).

21.44 Section 5 of the RDA sets out clearly the registrability criteria for designs. Only designs which are *new* qualify for design registration in Singapore. Novelty in a design is preserved so long as it is not identical with or materially similar to a design which had been previously registered or one which had been published in Singapore *or elsewhere* prior to the date of the instant application.

Such designs must also be registered in respect of some specified article.

In Singapore, a self-assessment mechanism is adopted for design registration (as well as for patent registration). This means that the Registrars at IPOS will only conduct a formalities examination for each design application to determine that the application satisfies all the formal requirements. The Registrars are not obliged to consider or have regard to the registrability of the design in determining whether to accept the application for registration (see section 19 of the RDA).

21.45 Once a design has been successfully registered, the owner of the registered design has the right to prevent third parties from making in Singapore or importing into Singapore for commercial purposes (eg sale/hire), or from commercially exploiting (eg selling/hiring) in Singapore articles to which the registered design (or a design not substantially different from it) has been applied (see section 30 of the RDA). Accordingly, the right in a registered design is infringed if a third party does any of these acts without the consent of the owner of the registered design. There are of course other provisions on design infringement which will not be discussed here. For this, the reader is referred to section 30 of the RDA as well as to Division 3 of Part III of the RDA generally for the remedies available to the owner of the registered design.

There are certain defences to design infringement set out in sections 30(5) and 30(6) of the RDA. The right in a registered design is not infringed by (1) the doing of any act for a private, non-commercial purpose, or (2) the doing of any act for the purpose of evaluation, analysis, research or teaching. Further, the right in a registered design is not infringed by the reproduction of a feature of the design which, by virtue of paragraph (2) of the definition of 'design' in section 2(1) of the RDA (see paragraph 21.42, above), was left out when the registrability of the design was being determined (eg the reproduction of that part of the design which, in itself, is dictated solely by the function which the article, as a whole, has to perform).

21.46 It has been mentioned above that industrial designs are essentially two-dimensional drawings of three-dimensional articles. Whilst we recognise the fact that registrable designs may be afforded protection under registered designs law, it should be remembered that such designs (in the form of drawings) are, in their own right, artistic works (which have traditionally been protected under the law of copyright). However, this does not mean that a registered design is entitled to dual protection, both under the law of registered designs as well as the law of copyright. The Copyright Act 1987 contemplates two possible scenarios:

(1) With regard to a design which is registrable and which has in fact been registered under the RDA and in which artistic copyright subsists, section 74(1) of the Copyright Act 1987 provides that during the period when the registered design monopoly is in subsistence, it is not an infringement of the copyright in the two-dimensional design (artistic work) to do any act which is an infringement of the registered design right. In other words, if the infringing act in question is prohibited under the RDA, the plaintiff should proceed with an action against the defendant under the RDA since he cannot

sustain an action for copyright infringement against the defendant. Once the registered design protection comes to an end, the denial of copyright protection becomes even wider. The plaintiff now has no legal right whatsoever under the Copyright Act nor the RDA to stop third parties from doing acts that fall within the scope of the registered design monopoly (eg making in Singapore three-dimensional articles from the two-dimensional design for the purpose of sale), as extended to all associated designs and articles (see section 73(2)(b) of the Copyright Act 1987). Basically, the scope of the registered design monopoly is now extended to cover every possible design that is a modification or variation of the registered design (such modification or variation must, however, not alter the character of the registered design nor substantially affect its identity) for all articles for which registration could have been obtained. In either case, however, the plaintiff only has a residual action in copyright if the infringing act in question does not fall within the scope of the registered design monopoly (as, for example, where the defendant makes a two-dimensional reproduction or photocopy of the plaintiff's design drawing).

(2) With regard to a design which is registrable but has *not* been registered under the RDA and in which artistic copyright subsists, sections 74(2), 74(3) and 74(4), when read together, provide that during a period of 15 years from the time the articles to which the design had been applied industrially were first sold or let for hire, it shall not be an infringement of the copyright in the design (artistic work) to do any act which would have fallen within the scope of the registered design monopoly, if the design had in fact been registered. In other words, if the infringing act in question were to be prohibited under the RDA, the plaintiff would have no recourse at all against the defendant: no registered design rights (since the design had not been registered) and no action for copyright infringement. After the expiry of this 15-year period, the denial of copyright protection is similarly broadened: the plaintiff has no legal right whatsoever under the Copyright Act nor the RDA to stop third parties from doing acts which would have fallen within the scope of the registered design monopoly, as extended to all associated designs and articles. In either case, however, the plaintiff only retains a residual action in copyright which is similar to that mentioned in (1) above.

From the tenor of these provisions, it is clear that design owners ought to register their industrial designs under the RDA, especially if such designs qualify for design registration. Failure to do so may, as we have seen, leave these design owners with very little intellectual property protection, if any, over their designs.

Law of Patents

General Introduction

21.47 The patent system rewards inventors with the grant of a strong monopoly right over their individual inventions for a limited period of time. In Singapore, the law of patents is governed by the Patents Act 1994 (Cap 221, 2002 Rev Ed), as amended by the Patents (Amendment) Act 1995, the Intellectual Property Office of Singapore Act 2001 (Cap 140, 2002 Rev Ed) and the Patents (Amendment) Act 2001 (which introduced a new Part XIX to regulate the patent agent profession in Singapore).

Inventions can either be product-based (eg a machine or drug) or process-based (eg a process or sequence leading to the production of a semi-conductor chip). Unlike copyright, patent rights do not arise automatically—an application for a patent must be filed and a patent must be granted. It is advisable for inventors to file their patent applications promptly as Singapore has, in this regard, adopted the first-to-file system (unlike the United States which has adopted the first-to-invent system). This means that the inventor who files a patent application for the invention first will be entitled to the patent for that invention, even though some other party may have been the first to invent.

Patent rights, like any other intellectual property right, are territorial in nature and hence are effective only in the country in which the grant has been obtained. They are also strong monopoly rights because, unlike copyright, there is no requirement for proof of copying in an action for patent infringement. In any event, since an application for a patent eventually results in the publication of the patent specification (which, according to section 25(4) of the Patents Act 1994, must disclose the invention in a manner that is clear and complete for the invention to be performed by a person skilled in the art), it is only fair that the patentee, in return for making such information available to the public, obtains powerful rights over the use and exploitation of the invention in question.

On the international front, Singapore is a signatory to the Paris Convention for the Protection of Industrial Property, the Patent Co-operation Treaty and the Budapest Treaty on the International Recognition of the Deposit of Micro-organisms for the Purposes of Patent Procedure. A Singapore patent may therefore be obtained by the filing of either a national application with the Registry of Patents of IPOS or an international application designating Singapore under the Patent Co-operation Treaty ('PCT') at one of the international PCT offices (including our local Registry of Patents).

Unless otherwise stated, all statutory references in this section on the law of patents are to the Patents Act 1994 (Cap 221, 2002 Rev Ed).

Meaning of 'Invention' and Elements of Patentability

21.48 A patent for an invention is valid only if the invention in question is a patentable invention. Failure to satisfy this condition may result in the revocation of the patent (section 80(1)(a)). Section 13(1) states clearly that a patentable invention is one that satisfies three criteria: (1) the invention must be new, (2) it must involve an inventive step and (3) it must be capable of industrial application. These are the three elements of patentability which we shall explore in greater detail below. Section

13(2) further provides that if the publication or exploitation of an invention is expected to encourage offensive, immoral or anti-social behaviour, then such an invention is not a patentable invention.

21.49 More fundamentally, it is to be observed that the Patents Act 1994 does not contain a definition of what an 'invention' is. What is certain is that inventions can either be product inventions or process inventions (see section 66(1)). It may be argued that logically, one should first determine if the invention in issue can properly be described as an invention before considering whether it satisfies the prescribed conditions for patentability. The lack of a statutory definition was explained by Lord Hoffmann in *Biogen v Medeva* (1997) in the following terms (at p 41):

> 'Article 52 [of the European Patent Convention ('EPC')] also has no definition of an invention. It seems that the parties to the EPC were unable to agree upon one … But the reason why the parties were content to do without a definition was that they recognised that the question would almost invariably be academic.'

Lord Hoffmann, however, went on to recognise (at p 41) that the prescribed conditions for patentability 'probably also contain every element of the concept of an invention in ordinary speech' (in other words, the basic requirements of novelty, inventive step and industrial application, as defined by statute and as interpreted by the courts, would in most cases produce an effective and practical explanation of the word 'invention' for the purposes of the law of patents) and he therefore conveniently suggested that '[t]here may one day be a case in which it is necessary to decide whether something which satisfies the conditions can be called an invention, but that question can wait until it arises' (at p 42).

21.50 Another interesting development is that before section 13(2) was repealed by the Patents (Amendment) Act 1995 (which came into force on 1 January 1996), it categorically stated that the following were *not* inventions for the purposes of the Patents Act:

(1) a discovery, scientific theory or mathematical method;
(2) a literary, dramatic, musical or artistic work or any other aesthetic creation whatsoever;
(3) a scheme, rule or method for performing a mental act, playing a game or doing business, or a program for a computer;
(4) the presentation of information.

These exceptions, however, were confined only to claims over the respective subject matter 'as such', meaning that inventions which solely comprised such subject matter *per se* were excluded from patent registration. To qualify for patent registration, such subject matter (eg computer programs and methods for doing business) had to exhibit some practical/technical effect or make some technical contribution.

Now that section 13(2) has been deleted from the statute, it is arguable, at least on one view, that there should no longer be any bars to patentability in respect of inventions which incorporate such subject matter *per se*. Nevertheless, it would appear that a discovery *per se*, even with the repeal of section 13(2), is very unlikely to be regarded as an invention and that difficult questions still remain (especially of policy and ethics) as to the future of business method patents and patents over gene sequences. Indeed, with the repeal of section 13(2), the general question of what an invention is for patent law has become even more important.

(1) *Novelty*

21.51 The first requirement of patentability is that the invention in question must be new. According to section 14(1), this means that the invention must not form part of the state of the art, which is taken to comprise all matter which has been made available to the public (in Singapore or elsewhere) at any time before the priority date of the invention (section 14(2)). In other words, the novelty of an invention is preserved so long as the invention has not been anticipated by any publicly available material found anywhere in the world before the priority date of the invention.

The *priority date* of an invention is generally the date of filing of the patent application. If, however, the applicant had previously filed a patent application in a Paris Convention country within a period of 12 months immediately preceding the filing date of the later application, the priority date of the later application shall be the date of filing of the earlier application, so long as the invention in the later application is supported by matter disclosed in the earlier application. The reader is referred to section 17 of the Patents Act and other related provisions for further details.

21.52 The question of novelty is largely a question of fact and it entails a comparison between the state of the art (or the prior art as it is sometimes known) and the invention in issue to determine if the invention has been anticipated by the prior art. Only if the prior art leads directly, clearly and unmistakably to the invention in issue will novelty in the latter be defeated. As the English Court of Appeal in *General Tire v Firestone Tyre* (1972) observed (at p 486):

> 'A signpost, however clear, upon the road to the patentee's invention will not suffice. The prior inventor must be clearly shown to have planted his flag at the precise destination before the patentee.' (These remarks were endorsed by the Singapore Court of Appeal in *Merck v Pharmaforte* (2000) and again in *Genelabs Diagnostics v Institut Pasteur* (2001).)

21.53 It should be noted, however, that some exceptions in the form of non-prejudicial disclosures are provided for in section 14(4). Basically, matters, which would otherwise form part of the state of the art, may be disregarded when determining novelty if the disclosure of such matters had occurred within a period of 12 months before the date of filing of the patent application and was broadly due to one of the following circumstances:

(1) the information disclosed had been obtained unlawfully or obtained in breach of confidence;
(2) the information had been disclosed in breach of confidence;
(3) the disclosure was made at a display of the invention at an international exhibition (see section 2(1) for the definition of an 'international exhibition');
(4) the disclosure was made by the inventor describing the invention in a paper read by him (or by another person with his consent or on his behalf) before any learned society or published with his consent in the transactions of any learned society (see section 14(5) for the definition of a 'learned society').

(2) *Inventive Step (Non-Obviousness)*

21.54 The second requirement of patentability is that the invention must involve an inventive step, ie the invention must not appear to be obvious to a person skilled in the art (or otherwise known as the hypothetical skilled addressee) (section 15). The question of inventiveness or non-obviousness, which is largely a question of fact, is to be determined against the same background of knowledge and state of the art as that for the requirement of novelty discussed above. This view is supported by a plain reading of section 15.

The hypothetical skilled addressee refers to an averagely skilled person who is generally well-acquainted with his field and who possesses common general knowledge (ie information that is generally known and accepted in the field) but who does not have inventive capacity.

21.55 One way of approaching this issue is to ask whether the invention is obvious to the hypothetical skilled addressee, having regard to all matter made available to the public anywhere in the world before the priority date of the invention, in such a way that the invention is well worth trying out to solve a recognised problem at hand (*Johns-Manville Corporation's Patent* (1967); *Beecham Group Limited's (Amoxycillin) Application* (1980)). In other words, would the hypothetical skilled addressee, in using his common general knowledge, immediately recognise that the adoption of the invention in issue would be a technically or practically obvious way of overcoming the particular problem at hand? If the answer is in the affirmative, then the invention in issue necessarily lacks inventive step.

On occasion, certain other factors are also taken into account in determining the question of non-obviousness, for example, the commercial success of the invention in issue and whether or not the invention satisfies a long-felt want of the public/consumers. The reader is also referred to the four-step approach used by Oliver LJ in *Windsurfing International v Tabur Marine* (1985) (at p 73) to determine if an invention involved an inventive step.

(3) *Industrial Application*

21.56 The third and final requirement of patentability is that the invention in issue must be capable of industrial application. This requirement is easily established by showing that the invention can be made or used in any kind of industry, including agriculture (section 16(1)). It should be noted, however, that an invention will fail for lack of industrial application if it relates to a *method* of treatment of the human or animal body by surgery or therapy or a diagnostic method practised on the human or animal body (section 16(2)). Section 16(3) qualifies this exception by providing that a product consisting of a *substance* or *composition* will not be treated as being incapable of industrial application merely because it has been invented for use in any such method of treatment or diagnosis. This essentially means that whilst the medical process itself is not patentable, the tools or drugs used in surgery or therapy potentially are.

21.57 It should be noted that Singapore adopts a self-assessment mechanism for patent registration, meaning that the patent application may still proceed to grant even if, for example, the three elements of patentability have not been satisfied. The onus is therefore on the applicant to ensure that his invention complies with the substantive requirements of patentability, failing which he may run the risk of having his patent revoked at a later date (section 80(1)(a)). A patent, once granted, shall be effective for a maximum period of 20 years from the date of filing of the patent application, subject to the timely payment of renewal fees (section 36).

Section 34 imposes certain national security restrictions on the filing of overseas patent applications by Singapore residents. It is a criminal offence for any person residing in Singapore to file a patent application overseas without first obtaining written permission from the Registrar of Patents. Note, however, that no written permission is required if the overseas application for the *same* invention was filed two months after the filing of the application in Singapore and if the Registrar had not made any directions prohibiting or restricting the publication of information contained in the local patent application (such information being prejudicial to the defence of Singapore or to the safety of the public) (see section 33).

Patent Infringement

21.58 In examining the issue of patent infringement, it is important to determine at the outset the patentee's scope of monopoly claimed in the invention. According to section 113(1), an invention shall be taken to be that specified in a *claim* of the specification of the application as interpreted by the description and any drawings contained in that specification. The extent of the protection conferred by the patent is to be determined accordingly. It therefore follows that since a patent is granted on the basis of the claims in the specification, it is to the patent claims that a court must initially refer in order to determine whether the patent has been infringed.

21.59 Textual infringement (or exact literal infringement) is said to occur when the alleged infringer (the defendant) duplicates every single feature of the claimed invention. However, where the alleged infringement is not a direct copy but a variant (eg where some feature of the claimed invention has been changed), difficulties may arise in determining whether the variant has indeed infringed the patent. The court will have to construe the patent specification and claims to find out if the grant extends to the variant. In this regard, the general position is that the patent will be infringed so long as the defendant has taken the 'pith and marrow' (or the essential features) of the claimed invention and that a purposive approach (as opposed to a purely literal approach) should now be adopted by the court in the construction of the patent specification.

In the leading House of Lords decision of *Catnic Components Ltd v Hill & Smith Ltd* (1982), the plaintiff owned a patent for load-bearing steel lintels, which had a rear support member that was described in the relevant patent claim as 'extending vertically'. The rear support member of the defendant's modified lintel was, however, inclined at six degrees to the vertical. The plaintiff sued for infringement and the House of Lords held that the plaintiff's patent had been infringed. Lord Diplock was of the view that even though the words 'extending vertically' were used in the patent claim, they were not intended (by the patentee) to take on a strict, literal meaning and were certainly broad enough to encompass a slant of six degrees to the vertical.

Lord Diplock then identified the question in each case as being whether practical persons who are skilled in the art would understand from the language of the patent claim that strict compliance with a particular descriptive word or phrase in the claim was intended by the patentee to be an essential requirement of the invention. If so, any variant that did not comply would fall outside the patent claim, even though it would have had no material effect on the way the invention worked. Obviously, if the variant did have a material effect on the way the invention worked, there would be no infringement. This approach adopted by Lord Diplock was later reformulated into a three-part test by Hoffmann J in *Improver Corp v Remington* (1990).

What is therefore clear from the above account is that the inventor must be cautious in drafting his claims to ensure that they are not framed too narrowly, such that some slight and insignificant variation may be effected without infringing the patent.

21.60 Having looked at how the courts interpret patent claims in general, we turn now to consider the various types of infringing acts which are prohibited by statute. Section 66(1) provides that an infringement is made out if the defendant does any of the following acts *in Singapore* in relation to the invention without the consent of the patent owner:

(1) *vis-à-vis* a product invention—to make, dispose of (eg sell), offer to dispose of, use or import an infringing product, or to keep it for disposal or otherwise (section 66(1)(a));
(2) *vis-à-vis* a process invention—(a) to use an infringing process in Singapore, or to offer an infringing process for use in Singapore, when the defendant knows, or when it is obvious to a reasonable

person in the circumstances, that such use without the consent of the patent owner would have been an infringement of the patent (section 66(1)(b)); or (b) to dispose of, offer to dispose of, use or import any product obtained directly by means of an infringing process, or to keep any such product for disposal or otherwise (section 66(1)(c)).

Defences to Patent Infringement

21.61 Section 66(2) sets out a list of statutory defences to an action for patent infringement.

(1) Section 66(2)(a): The *private user* defence allows a third party to perform an infringing act privately and for purposes which are not commercial;
(2) Section 66(2)(b): The *experimentation* defence allows the infringing act to be performed for experimental purposes relating to the subject matter of the invention;
(3) Section 66(2)(g) allows the *import*, use, disposal or offer to dispose of any patented product, or any product obtained by means of a patented process or to which a patented process has been applied, which is produced by or with the consent (conditional or otherwise) of the patent owner or his licensee. This provision is seen as countenancing, amongst other things, the parallel importation of genuine products into Singapore, ie products which have been made by or with the consent of the patent owner.

Another available defence is the *prior user* defence in section 71(1). Essentially, a third party who, at any time before the priority date of the invention in issue, has in good faith been doing in Singapore any act which would have amounted to an infringement of a patent (if it were in force) may continue to do that act even after the grant of the patent. This defence extends to a third party who, at any time before the priority date of the invention in issue, has in good faith been making in Singapore effective and serious preparations to do any such act. Note, however, that the right conferred on the prior user under section 71(1) to continue to do the infringing act is a mere personal right. The prior user cannot subsequently grant a licence to another party to perform the infringing act, unless the infringing act was initially done (or preparations were made) in the course of a business (in which case, the prior user may license the prior user right to any of his business partners) (see sections 71(2) and 71(3)).

According to section 82(1)(a), the validity of a patent may also be challenged by way of a defence to an action for patent infringement. The defendant may therefore ask the court to revoke the plaintiff's patent on the basis that it has been anticipated by certain prior art or that it is obvious to a person skilled in the art.

Remedies for Patent Infringement

21.62 Before discussing the issue of remedies, there is an important question which must first be answered. When can the patent owner bring infringement proceedings against the third party infringer? It is clear from section 76(3) that infringement proceedings can only be brought after the patent in question has been granted. This may appear somewhat unfair to the patent owner as it is conceivable that acts of infringement may occur between the time the patent application is filed and the time the patent is actually granted (this could take as long as 54 months; see section 30(1) and rule 47(1) of the Patents Rules 1995). Section 76(1) therefore confers on the patent owner certain 'retrospective rights', such that when the patent owner is later entitled to bring infringement proceedings against the third party infringer (after the patent has been granted), his right to sue for patent infringement would accrue from the time the patent application is *published*. In other words, the patent owner has effective protection over his invention from the date of publication of the patent application.

The remedies which are generally available to the patent owner in an action for patent infringement include an injunction (or restraining order), an order for delivery-up or destruction of the infringing product or of any article in which the infringing product is inextricably comprised, a declaration of patent validity, and either damages or an account of profits (sections 67(1) and 67(2)). Note, however, that the court will not make an order for damages nor an order for an account of profits against an 'innocent' infringer, who can prove that, at the time of the infringement, he was not aware, and had no reasonable grounds for supposing, that the patent existed (section 69(1)).

Groundless Threats of Infringement Proceedings

21.63 Section 77 provides that where a patent owner (for example) threatens by way of circulars, advertisements or otherwise to sue another person for patent infringement, the person aggrieved by such threats may institute legal proceedings against the patent owner for making such groundless threats and claim the following relief: an injunction (against the continuance of the threats), damages (in respect of any loss which the aggrieved party may have sustained as a result of the threats) and a declaration (to the effect that the threats are unjustifiable). In defence of an action brought by the aggrieved party, the patent owner can prove that an actual infringement has taken place (the patent owner should, however, ensure that his patent is not invalid for any reason). It should be noted that a mere notification by the patent owner of the existence of a patent does not in itself constitute a threat. Further, the aggrieved party cannot institute legal proceedings against the patent owner under section 77 if the threats made by the patent owner are in relation to the following infringing acts, viz making or importing a product for disposal, or using a process.

Assignments and Licences

21.64 Patent rights, like other intellectual property rights, can be dealt with as personal property; they can be assigned, mortgaged or licensed (section

41). An assignment or a mortgage of a patent is considered void in law unless it is in writing and is signed by or on behalf of the parties to the transaction. A licence, on the other hand, does not need to comply with such formalities. A person who has acquired the property in a patent by virtue of an assignment, a mortgage, licence or any other transaction (known for our purposes as an 'earlier transaction') is well advised to register the transaction with the Registry of Patents at IPOS for two reasons. Firstly, a third party who claims to have acquired the property in the patent by virtue of a *later* transaction will take priority and be entitled to the property in the patent if the earlier transaction had not been so registered and if this third party (who is claiming under the *later* transaction) did not know of the earlier transaction (section 43(1)). Secondly, where such a person becomes the proprietor (assignee) or an exclusive licensee of the patent by virtue of the earlier transaction and the patent is subsequently infringed, the court or the Registrar will not award him damages or an account of profits in respect of the infringement (note, in this respect, that an assignment of a patent and an exclusive licence granted under any patent may confer on the assignee or licensee, as the case may be, the right to bring proceedings for a previous infringement; see section 41(7)) unless (a) the earlier transaction had been registered within six months, or (b) the court or the Registrar is satisfied that it was not practicable to register the said transaction within the six-month period and that the transaction was registered as soon as practicable thereafter (see section 75).

Trade Secrets and the Law of Confidence

21.65 What, if at all, is the relationship between the law of confidence and the law of patents? Take, for example, the research work being carried out on a new product (which we assume to be patentable) by personnel from the R&D department of a company. The company obviously has plans to file, in due course, a patent application for this invention. Notwithstanding the fact that the invention is *prima facie* patentable, should the secrets or workings behind the invention be disclosed or leaked out by these R&D personnel to some third party or to the public at large prior to the company's filing of the patent application, the invention will no longer be considered novel and hence will not be patentable under the Patents Act. It is therefore necessary to bind these R&D personnel to such information (usually of a confidential nature) and to other trade secrets in their contracts of employment via *confidentiality clauses* or, in the absence of an employer-employee relationship, via *non-disclosure agreements*.

Seen in this light, we can better appreciate why the law of confidence affords good protection when the subject matter or invention in question is still in an embryonic state (eg cutting-edge ideas yet to be concretised into workable inventions). The law of confidence therefore complements the patent system by protecting such inventions from unwarranted disclosure until the actual filing of the patent application.

This, however, does not mean that just because a patentable invention is made that it should be patented as a matter of course. It may be better in some cases to rely on bars of confidence. For example, if the invention in question is easy to reverse engineer, it is advisable for the inventor to file for a patent (since, upon publication of the patent document, the invention becomes public knowledge). Conversely, if the invention in question is not easily reverse engineered, then the inventor, in the right circumstances, may be better off protecting the information leading to the making of the invention as a trade secret under the law of confidence.

21.66 The action for breach of confidence is premised on the equitable notion of good faith. Essentially, a person who has received information in confidence is bound in good faith to keep that information confidential. The leading case of *Coco v Clark* (1969) sets out the three elements of the action:

(1) The information must have the necessary quality of confidence about it, ie the information must generally be of a confidential nature—such information must not be common/public knowledge or information in the public domain (a secret therefore remains a secret until it enters the public domain) and should not be mere 'trivial tittle-tattle' (mere trivia). It follows that the publication of a patent specification would generally destroy the confidentiality of the invention as the information or teachings leading to the manufacture of the invention would have entered the public domain upon such publication.

(2) The information must have been communicated in circumstances importing an obligation of confidence on the part of the defendant. The question to ask here is whether a reasonable man in the shoes of the recipient of the information would have realised upon reasonable grounds that the information was given to him in confidence. The recipient of the information is normally taken to be a direct or an intended recipient, ie someone to whom the plaintiff/confider has directly disclosed confidential information. However, it appears that a third party who indirectly receives confidential information (eg through disclosure of such information by the direct recipient in breach of confidence) may also be subject to the obligation of confidence where he knows or ought to have known that the information was disclosed in breach of confidence. A third party who, on the other hand, receives confidential information innocently and with no notice of the breach of confidence will not have the obligation of confidence imposed on him until he acquires the necessary knowledge of the breach.

Thus far, our discussion of the law of confidence has centred on third party *recipients* of information. Interesting issues (concerning, *inter alia*, an individual's right of privacy) also arise with regard to third party *takers* of information, as for example, where a third party obtains the confidential information surreptitiously or in circumstances involving industrial espionage. A discussion of this area of law is unfortunately beyond the scope of this chapter and the reader is therefore referred to other textbooks on the law of intellectual property (eg D Bainbridge, *Intellectual Property* (5th ed, 2002), Chapter 11, generally).

(3) There must be unauthorised use or disclosure of the information by the defendant, ie use by the defendant of the plaintiff's information without his consent (possibly resulting in a detriment to the plaintiff).

21.67 The remedies which are available to a plaintiff in an action for breach of confidence include an injunction and either damages or an account of profits. It has been suggested that where the information disclosed is of a personal nature (eg some personal secret), the injunction may be the more appropriate remedy. On the other hand, where the information disclosed is largely of a commercial character, the court may make an order for an account of profits, although damages remain the primary remedy. Further, the court may, as part of its inherent equitable jurisdiction, make an order for the delivery-up and destruction of articles which have been made by using the confidential information.

21.68 A defence of public interest is generally available in an action for breach of confidence. The plaintiff will not be entitled to relief where the disclosure of confidential information is justified in the public interest (eg where it concerns the administration of justice). However, whether or not the public interest defence applies would depend on the scope and nature of the disclosure. Public interest can be served by the disclosure of information to a limited section of the public or, on other occasions, to the public at large, depending on the circumstances of each case. What is clear, however, is that the defendant must have disclosed the information to persons who have a proper interest to receive such information (*Initial Services Ltd v Putterill* (1968)). Further, it is also important to distinguish between information which the public would generally find interesting (eg mere gossip or other private information of no real concern to the public) and information which the public would generally have a right to know (eg matters which are of real public concern); see *Lion Laboratories Ltd v Evans* (1984).

21.69 An obligation of confidence is commonly established and delineated by a formal contract between the parties. The employer-employee relationship is often used as an illustrative example as it shows how the law in this respect seeks to strike a fair balance between protecting the interests of the employer and those of the employee, who must be allowed, at some stage, to freely utilise all the skills and knowledge which he had acquired on the job (especially when seeking other employment).

During the subsistence of the contract of employment, an employee is usually bound by a duty of confidence to his employer under the express terms of the employment contract. In the absence of express confidentiality clauses, the court is inclined to imply into the contract a duty of fidelity (or a duty of good faith) on the part of the employee. The employee is expected to respect the confidentiality of the information which he acquires during his employment and to act in the best interests of his employer (eg by not engaging in activities which are in direct competition with his employer's interests and which expose his employer's interests to risk).

After the expiration of the contract of employment, the employer may attempt to impose a continuing duty of confidence on the employee by enforcing certain restrictive terms found in the employment contract (usually referred to as covenants in restraint of trade). Such covenants are often expressed in terms of preventing the employee from working for a competitor or from setting up a competing business within a given geographical area and for a given period of time. Covenants in restraint of trade are *prima facie* void, unless they can be shown to be reasonable in the interest of the parties and in the interest of the public. Apart from such restrictive clauses, there is also an implied term imposing an obligation of confidence on the employee after the termination of his employment. The implied obligation of confidence imposed on the employee here is, however, more restricted in scope as compared to the employee's implied duty of fidelity (discussed above). The employee is only expected to keep confidential his employer's trade secrets and such other information which is of a sufficiently high degree of confidentiality as to amount to a trade secret. The following factors are relevant in determining whether or not the information in question possesses the required degree of confidentiality as to merit the protection of the law:

(1) the nature of the employment (ie in what capacity is the employee employed?);
(2) the nature of the information itself;
(3) whether the employer had impressed upon the employee the confidentiality of the information;
(4) whether the relevant information can be easily isolated from other information which the employee is free to use or disclose.

(See also paragraphs 14.80 ff.)

Essentially, the law does not prevent a former employee from making use of the body of skill, knowledge and experience acquired in the course of his previous career to earn a new living elsewhere. The former employee is merely prohibited from using or disclosing identifiable trade secrets (or their equivalent) belonging to his former employer (see *Faccenda Chicken v Fowler* (1986); *Tang Siew Choy v Certact* (1993)).

21.70 At present, there are no data protection laws in Singapore which specifically protect an individual's right to privacy (cf the UK Data Protection Act 1998). Disparate torts are, however, available to deal, at least indirectly, with invasions of privacy, eg nuisance, trespass, defamation and the law of confidence (in this regard, it is noteworthy that the English courts have begun to recognise the possibility that an action for breach of confidence may give rise to a separate right of privacy—a development which, arguably, is supported by the UK Human Rights Act 1998. See, in particular, the speeches of Sedley LJ and Keene LJ in the English Court of Appeal decision of *Douglas v Hello! Ltd* (2001)). Although harassment is generally not an established tort in Singapore, Judicial Commissioner Lee Seiu Kin (as he then was) in the local decision of *Malcomson Nicholas Hugh Bertram & Anor v Naresh Kumar*

Mehta (2001) was of the opinion that the time has come in Singapore to recognise a tort of harassment (at pp 473–474).

There is also the Computer Misuse Act 1993 (Cap 50A, 1998 Rev Ed) which basically deals with computer crimes like computer hacking. As its long title suggests, one of the aims of the Computer Misuse Act ('CMA') is to prevent the unauthorised access to or modification of computer material and the unauthorised use or interception of a computer to obtain computer services. It is therefore an offence for any person to knowingly cause a computer to perform any function for the purpose of securing unauthorised access to any program or data held in the computer (see section 3 of the CMA). Similarly, it is also an offence for any person to do any act which he knows will cause an unauthorised modification of the contents of any computer (see section 5 of the CMA).

Law of Trade Marks

General Introduction

21.71 Trade marks are, arguably, the best known and most commonly encountered form of intellectual property. They are usually the first contact that the public has with a particular business or company, as trade marks are often advertised on the front door of a shop or above the shop's front entrance, or even in the media. For this reason, trade marks have long been used by manufacturers and traders to identify their goods and, more importantly, to distinguish them from those made or sold by their competitors. With time, trade marks develop into valuable forms of intellectual property as they become associated with quality and consumer expectations in a particular brand of product. Certain products have today become almost synonymous with their trade names, for example *Coca-Cola*, *Milo*, *Nescafé*, *Tupperware*, *Rollerblade* and *Walkman*. Given the high potential value of trade marks as an effective marketing tool for businesses, it is not surprising that proprietors of trade marks would want to vigorously assert and defend their rights and to safeguard their business reputation and goodwill.

The most effective way of protecting trade marks in Singapore is to register them under the Trade Marks Act 1998 (Cap 332, 1999 Rev Ed). Registration of trade marks is, however, not compulsory and unregistered marks may be protected under the common law action of passing off (discussed below). Unless otherwise stated, all statutory references in this section on the law of trade marks are to the Trade Marks Act 1998 (Cap 332, 1999 Rev Ed).

What is a Trade Mark?

21.72 A 'trade mark', as defined in section 2(1), is 'any visually perceptible *sign* capable of being represented graphically and which is capable of distinguishing goods or services dealt with or provided in the course of trade by a person from goods or services so dealt with or provided by any other person'. A 'sign' is, in turn, defined to include 'any letter, word, name, signature, numeral, device, brand, heading, label, ticket, shape, colour, aspect of packaging or any combination thereof'.

Some pertinent observations arise from these two definitions. First of all, the scope of registrable subject matter appears to be fairly wide. Apart from trade names, logos and slogans, it is now possible to register as a trade mark a particular colour, shape or aspect of packaging (eg the shape of the *Coca-Cola* bottle). Unlike in the UK, however, sounds (eg musical jingles) and smells (eg perfumes) are not registrable in Singapore as trade marks (although the law in this area is likely to change in view of the recently-concluded US-Singapore Free Trade Agreement). Secondly, marks are registrable in relation to the provision, in the course of trade, of both goods (trade marks) and services (service marks). Section 2(2) further provides that a trade mark is registrable in relation to services whether or not such services are provided for money or money's worth. Accordingly, retail services may be protected in Singapore under a registered trade mark. Thirdly, the 'sign' in question must be capable of distinguishing the goods or services of one trader from those of another. In other words, the trade mark must serve as a guarantee of trade origin—there must be a connection (in the minds of the public) between a particular trader and the goods or services in question.

21.73 Brief mention will be made here of the protection of well-known trade marks. A trade mark which is entitled to protection under the Paris Convention or the TRIPS Agreement as a well-known trade mark is also protected under the Trade Marks Act 1998 (the 'Act'). Such well-known trade marks are accorded protection whether or not they are registered as trade marks under the Act. Essentially, the Act prohibits the unauthorised registration (sections 8(1) and 8(2); note that the phrase 'earlier trade mark' found in section 8 is defined in section 2(1) to include a trade mark which is entitled to protection under the Paris Convention or the TRIPS Agreement as a well-known trade mark) and the unauthorised use (section 55) of a mark which is identical with or similar to a well-known trade mark for goods or services which are identical with or similar to those for which the well-known trade mark is protected, where there exists a likelihood of confusion. Note, however, that where the registration is for a mark which is *identical* with the well-known trade mark for *identical* goods or services (as in section 8(1)), the likelihood of confusion is presumed.

In the section 55 scenario, it is important to highlight that the entitlement to protection is not conditional upon there being actual use of the well-known trade mark in Singapore, so long as the well-known trade mark is also well-known in Singapore (section 55(1)). The question of whether or not a mark is well-known is essentially one of fact. Section 2(7) states that in deciding whether a trade mark is well-known in Singapore, 'one shall take into account the extent to which the trade mark is known within the relevant sector of the public, whether as a result of the promotion of the trade mark or any other reason'.

Section 8(3) further protects well-known trade marks which are also well-known in Singapore against the registration of identical or similar marks in relation to *dissimilar* goods or services, where:

(1) the use of the conflicting mark (in relation to goods or services which are *not similar* to those for which the well-known trade mark is protected) would indicate a connection between those goods or services and the proprietor of the well-known trade mark;

(2) there exists a likelihood of confusion on the part of the public because of such use; and

(3) the interests of the proprietor of the well-known trade mark are likely to be damaged by such use.

Section 8 is discussed in greater detail below.

Absolute or Relative Grounds for Refusal of Registration

21.74 A trade mark application may only be refused either on absolute (section 7) or relative (section 8) grounds. Section 7(1) states that the following shall not be registered:

(1) signs which do not satisfy the definition of a trade mark in section 2(1);

(2) trade marks which are *devoid of any distinctive character;*

(3) trade marks which consist exclusively of signs or indications which may serve, in trade, to designate the kind, quality, quantity, intended purpose, value, geographical origin, the time of production of goods or of rendering of services, or other characteristics of goods or services;

(4) trade marks which consist exclusively of signs or indications which have become customary in the current language or in the *bona fide* and established practices of the trade.

Some examples of trade marks which have been held to be devoid of any distinctive character include the mark 'P.R.E.P.A.R.E.' (because it so closely resembled the word 'PREPARE'; see *P.R.E.P.A.R.E. Trade Mark* (1997)) and the mark 'FROOT LOOPS' (because it was the phonetic equivalent of 'FRUIT LOOPS'; see *FROOT LOOPS Trade Mark* (1998)). Clearly, marks such as 'SOAP' (for soap) and 'PERFECT' (for a particular kind of product) are also unregistrable, as they comprise common, everyday words or words found in the English language (in any event, these words are also descriptive of the goods or are laudatory in nature). Not only is it unfair for a particular trader to acquire a monopoly over common vocabulary (especially words which describe the character or quality of the goods or services to which they are to be applied), the important question to ask here is whether or not such words can in fact perform the task of distinguishing the goods or services of one trader from those of other traders in the field. Notwithstanding this argument, a descriptive or laudatory mark may be capable of registration if, before the date of the trade mark application, the mark has *in fact* acquired a distinctive character as a result of the *use* made of it (ie such a mark has become factually distinctive by reason of *prior use*) (see section 7(2)). Compelling evidence of extensive use of the mark is, however, required to establish factual distinctiveness in the case of common laudatory/

descriptive words, as such words are naturally capable of application to the goods or services of any trader.

According to section 7(3), a sign shall not be registered as a trade mark if it consists exclusively of (a) the shape which results from the nature of the goods themselves (eg the shape of an American football for American footballs or the shape of a lemon for lemons), (b) the shape of goods which is necessary to obtain a technical result (ie where the shape purely serves a functional purpose, for example the shape of a three-headed rotary shaver), or (c) the shape which gives substantial value to the goods (eg where the shape, with eye-appeal, serves a purely decorative or aesthetic purpose). Further, a trade mark shall not be registered if:

(1) it is contrary to public policy or to morality, or if it is of such a nature as to deceive the public (for instance as to the nature, quality or geographical origin of the goods or services) (section 7(4));
(2) its use is prohibited in Singapore by any written law or rule of law (section 7(5));
(3) the application is made in bad faith (section 7(6)).

21.75 We now consider the relative grounds for refusal of registration. Sections 8(1) and 8(2) essentially state that a trade mark will not be registrable if it is identical with or similar to an 'earlier trade mark' and if it is used upon goods or services which are identical with or similar to those for which the 'earlier trade mark' is protected. Section 8(3), on the other hand, prohibits the registration of a trade mark which is in conflict with an 'earlier trade mark' (which itself is well-known in Singapore) and which is used on goods or services which are *not similar* to those for which the 'earlier trade mark' is protected. An 'earlier trade mark' is defined in section 2(1) as, in effect, an earlier registered trade mark or an earlier pending trade mark application (as mentioned above, the section 2(1) definition of an 'earlier trade mark' also includes a trade mark which is entitled to protection under the Paris Convention or the TRIPS Agreement as a well-known trade mark).

This prohibition in section 8 generally exists because of the likelihood of confusion which may arise on the part of the public. In determining whether a trade mark is similar to or in conflict with an 'earlier trade mark', the Registrar will usually consider the following factors: (1) the look of the two marks, (2) the sound of the two marks, (3) the goods or services to which the marks are to be applied, (4) the nature and kind of customer who would be likely to buy those goods or use those services and (5) all the surrounding circumstances (per Parker J in *Pianotist Co's Application* (1906) at p 777). It should also be noted that despite the citation(s) raised by the Registrar pursuant to any of the provisions in section 8, a trade mark may still be accepted for registration if (1) the proprietor of the 'earlier trade mark' consents to the registration (section 8(6)), or (2) there is evidence of honest concurrent use of the trade mark in the course of trade in Singapore by the applicant (unless the proprietor of the 'earlier trade mark' objects to such registration in opposition proceedings) (section 9(1)).

Applying for a Trade Mark in Singapore and Duration of Trade Mark Protection

21.76 A trade mark may be obtained in Singapore by the filing of a trade mark application with the Registry of Trade Marks at IPOS. As Singapore is a signatory to the Paris Convention, an applicant who has lodged a corresponding trade mark application in any of the member countries within the last six months may make a priority claim based on the corresponding application (section 10(1)). The local application must also state that the trade mark is being used by the applicant (or with his consent) in the course of trade or that there is a *bona fide* intention to so use the mark (section 5(2)). Further, registration must be sought in respect of the specific classes of goods and/or services for which the mark is used or is to be used (section 6). The reader is referred to the Third Schedule of the Trade Marks Rules 1998 for the specific classification of goods and services.

21.77 A trade mark, once registered, is valid for a period of ten years from the date of registration (this is usually the filing/priority date of the trade mark application) and may be subsequently renewed for further periods of ten years upon payment of the prescribed renewal fee. So long as there is timely payment of renewal fees, a trade mark may effectively receive perpetual protection (sections 18 and 19; see also sections 15(2) and 15(3)). Note, however, that a registered trade mark may be revoked if, within a period of five years from the date of completion of the registration procedure, it has not been put to genuine use by the proprietor (or with his consent) in the course of trade in Singapore and if there are no proper reasons for non-use (section 22(1)(a); see, generally, section 22 for the grounds of revocation of a registered trade mark). Further, a registered trade mark may be declared invalid either by the Registrar or by the court on the ground of fraud in the registration or that the registration was obtained by misrepresentation (section 23(4); see, generally, section 23 for the grounds for invalidity of a trade mark registration).

Exclusive Rights of Registered Proprietor

21.78 The proprietor of a registered trade mark has the exclusive rights to *use* the trade mark and to *authorise* other persons to use the trade mark (eg through licensing) in relation to the goods or services for which the trade mark is registered (section 26(1)). The word 'use' is defined in section 2(4) to include use 'otherwise than by means of a graphic representation' and would cover the following acts: (1) to apply the mark to the proprietor's goods or to their packaging, (2) to offer or expose the goods bearing the mark for sale, (3) to import or export goods bearing the mark, (4) to use the mark on an invoice, wine list, catalogue, business letter, business paper, price list or other commercial document, and (5) to use the mark in advertising (section 27(4)).

Trade Mark Infringement

21.79 The acts amounting to infringement of a registered trade mark are set out in section 27. Infringement is generally made out if the defendant, without the consent of the plaintiff (ie the proprietor of the trade mark), *uses* in the course of trade a sign which is identical with or similar to the registered trade mark in relation to goods or services which are identical with or similar to those for which the trade mark is registered (sections 27(1) and 27(2)). The meaning of the word 'use' has already been discussed in the preceding paragraph. Section 27(3), on the other hand, deals with the infringement of a registered trade mark which is well-known in Singapore.

It will be noticed that the section 8 (relative) grounds for refusal of registration (discussed above) have a close parallel in terms of the ways in which registered trade marks can be infringed. It is therefore not surprising that the action for infringement is similarly premised on the need to protect the public against a likelihood of confusion, which may arise as a result of the similarity of the conflicting marks. The factors which are relevant here in assessing the likelihood of confusion should also be similar to those spelt out by Parker J in *Pianotist Co's Application* (discussed above).

According to section 27(5), a person who applies a sign to any material used or intended to be used for labelling or packaging goods, or who uses it on any document described in section 27(4)(d) or in advertising, is deemed *not* to have used the sign if, at the time of such application or use, he *does not know nor has reason to believe* that the proprietor or a licensee of the registered trade mark did not consent to such application or use of the sign. This provision can be seen as defining the limits to an action for contributory infringement, whereby a person (such as a printer or packager) who applies a trade mark in the aforesaid manner shall be treated as a party to any infringing use of the trade mark only if, when he applied the mark, he knew or had reason to believe that the application of the mark was not authorised by the registered proprietor (or his licensee).

Defences to Trade Mark Infringement

(1) *Comparative Advertising*

21.80 It is not an infringement to use a registered trade mark for the purpose of identifying goods or services as those of the proprietor or a licensee, so long as such use is in accordance with *honest practices* in industrial or commercial matters. If it is not, then such use will infringe if, without due cause, it takes *unfair advantage* of, or is *detrimental* to, the distinctive character or repute of the trade mark (section 27(6)). The primary objective of this provision is that it allows for comparative advertising, with the proviso that the use of a competitor's trade mark must be honest and fair. There should therefore be a prohibition where, for example, misleading statements have been made either about particular qualities of the products (eg that they are the same when they are not, or that they differ in some respect when they do not) or about such factors as price or after-sale services.

(2) *Other Acts Not Amounting to Infringement*

21.81 Essentially, section 28(1) states that a person does not infringe a registered trade mark when:

(1) he uses his own name or the name of his place of business;
(2) he uses a sign to indicate the kind, quality, quantity, intended purpose, value, geographical origin or other characteristic of goods or services, or to indicate the time of production of goods or of the rendering of services; or
(3) he uses the trade mark to indicate the intended purpose of goods (in particular as accessories or spare parts) or services,

so long as such use is in accordance with *honest practices* in industrial or commercial matters.

(3) *Prior Use*

21.82 It is not an infringement for a person to use an unregistered mark that is identical with or similar to a registered trade mark in relation to goods or services which are identical with or similar to those for which the trade mark is registered if this person had *continuously used* the unregistered mark in the course of trade in relation to those goods or services.

More specifically, he should have continuously used the unregistered mark from a time *prior* to (1) the date of registration of the registered trade mark, or (2) the date the proprietor of the registered trade mark first used the trade mark, whichever is the earlier (section 28(2)). In simple terms, this means that if the defendant had, arguably in good faith, used the trade mark prior to the plaintiff's registration of it, then the defendant cannot be said to have infringed the plaintiff's registered trade mark.

(4) *Exhaustion of Rights and Parallel Imports*

21.83 According to section 29(1), a registered trade mark is not infringed by the use of the trade mark in relation to goods which have been put on the market, whether in Singapore or outside Singapore, under that trade mark by the proprietor of the registered trade mark or with his express or implied consent (conditional or otherwise). The defence in section 29(1), however, does not apply where the condition of the goods has been changed or impaired after they have been put on the market, and the use of the registered trade mark in relation to those goods is detrimental to the distinctive character or repute of the registered trade mark (section 29(2)).

Section 29(1) expressly sanctions the parallel importation of genuine goods. Note, however, that the proviso in section 29(2) kicks in if 'the condition of the goods has been changed or impaired', as, for example, when the parallel importer imports goods manufactured by the registered proprietor but then changes or adapts (maybe even adulterates) them to suit Singapore's climate before selling them off to consumers under the registered trade mark.

Remedies for Trade Mark Infringement

21.84 The court may grant the following relief in an action for infringement:

(1) an injunction (section 31(2)(a));
(2) either damages or an account of profits (section 31(2)(b));
(3) an order for the erasure/removal/obliteration of the offending sign from the infringing goods, or, if this is not reasonably practicable, an order for the destruction of the infringing goods in question (section 32(1));
(4) an order for delivery-up and disposal (destruction/forfeiture) of the infringing goods (sections 33(1) and 34(1)).

Apart from being the subject of a civil action, infringement of a registered trade mark may also amount to a criminal offence (see, generally, Part VI of the Trade Marks Act 1998). For example, counterfeiting a registered trade mark attracts the penalty of a fine not exceeding $100,000 or imprisonment for a term not exceeding five years or both (section 46(1)). Section 46(2) states that a person who makes a sign identical to or so nearly resembling a registered trade mark as to be calculated to deceive, or who falsifies a genuine registered trade mark (whether by alteration, addition, effacement, partial removal or otherwise), without the consent of the proprietor of the registered trade mark, shall be deemed to counterfeit a registered trade mark. It is also an offence for a person to falsely apply a registered trade mark to goods or services (see section 47 generally).

Border Enforcement Measures

21.85 Part X of the Trade Marks Act 1998, together with the Trade Marks (Border Enforcement Measures) Rules 1999, provide for border enforcement measures to prevent the importation of infringing goods into Singapore. In line with international trends, the Act has designated the Customs and Excise Department to handle border enforcement issues in Singapore.

The proprietor of a registered trade mark or a licensee may give written notice to the Director-General of Customs and Excise stating that infringing goods are expected to be imported for the purpose of trade at a certain time and place specified in the notice and that he objects to such importation (section 82(1)). If such goods (not being 'goods in transit', as defined in section 81) are indeed imported into Singapore and if, in the opinion of the customs officer, these goods (or their packaging) bear a sign that is identical with or similar to the proprietor's registered trade mark, the officer is empowered to seize the goods (section 82(4)). Senior customs officers also have the power to search vessels, aircraft and vehicles for goods liable to be seized under section 82 (section 94(1)).

Remedy for Groundless Threats of Infringement Proceedings

21.86 This remedy, found in section 35, is available to 'any aggrieved person' who has been threatened with proceedings for infringement of a registered trade mark (except where the threat relates to (1) the application of the mark to goods or to material used or intended to be used for labelling or packaging goods, or (2) the importation of goods to which, or to the packaging of which, the mark has been applied, or (3) the supply of services under the mark). The aggrieved person may apply for any of the following relief:

(a) a declaration that the threats are unjustifiable;
(b) an injunction against the continuance of the threats;
(c) damages in respect of any loss he has sustained by the threats.

Note, however, that the aggrieved person (the plaintiff) will not be entitled to such relief if the defendant (who may be the proprietor of the registered trade mark) shows that the acts, in respect of which proceedings were threatened, constitute an infringement of the registered trade mark in question, unless the former can show that the registration of the trade mark is invalid or ought to be revoked in a relevant respect. Further, it should be noted that the mere notification that a trade mark is registered, or that an application for registration has been made, does not in itself constitute a threat of infringement proceedings.

Assignments and Licences

21.87 A registered trade mark is personal property (section 36). It is therefore assignable and transmissible in the same way as other personal or movable property and either in connection with the goodwill of a business or independently (section 38(1)). An assignment of a registered trade mark may be partial (ie limited so as to apply in relation to some but not all of the goods or services for which the trade mark is registered). However, for assignments in general to be legally effective, they must be in writing and signed by or on behalf of the assignor (sections 38(2) and 38(3)).

According to section 42(1), a licence to use a registered trade mark may also be general or limited (ie limited so as to apply in relation to some but not all of the goods or services for which the trade mark is registered). Like an assignment, a licence to use a registered trade mark is not legally effective unless it is in writing and signed by or on behalf of the grantor (section 42(3)).

Both an assignment and the grant of a licence are considered 'registrable transactions' under the Trade Marks Act 1998 (section 39(2)). Either the assignor/licensor or the assignee/licensee may apply to the Registrar to have the prescribed particulars of such transactions registered (section 39(1)). The reader is referred to rule 54 of the Trade Marks Rules 1998 for the list of prescribed particulars pertaining to an assignment and the grant of a licence. If the prescribed particulars of a registrable transaction are not registered, the transaction is *ineffective* as against a person acquiring a conflicting interest in or under the registered trade mark in *ignorance* of it (section 39(3)(a)). Failure to register the prescribed particulars of the grant of a licence will also cause the licensee to lose the rights which would otherwise have been conferred on him by section 44 or 45 (section 39(3)(b)), for example, the right to commence infringement proceedings in his own name. Section 39(4) further provides that a person who becomes the proprietor or a licensee of a registered trade mark by virtue of a registrable transaction will not be entitled to damages or an account of profits in respect of any infringement of the registered trade mark occurring *after* the date of the transaction and *before* the date of application for registration of the prescribed particulars of the transaction. The message is therefore clear: it will be in the interest of the parties to the transaction to have these prescribed particulars registered.

Madrid Protocol

21.88 Singapore acceded to the Madrid Protocol on 31 July 2000 and the Protocol came into operation here on 31 October 2000. Before 31 October 2000, trade mark applications in various jurisdictions around the world had to be filed separately in each respective jurisdiction. With Singapore's accession to the Madrid Protocol, local trade mark applicants or proprietors of registered trade marks who wish to have the same mark registered overseas need only file their application through IPOS, which, in turn, will help them disseminate their request to foreign intellectual property offices. Similarly, an overseas applicant of a member country to the Protocol can also designate Singapore as one of the countries in which trade mark protection is sought. For more information on the Madrid Protocol, the reader is referred to CL Saw, 'Singapore's Accession to the Madrid Protocol: The Dawn of a New Era for the International Registration of Marks' (2001) 31 *Asia Business Law Review* 61.

Law of Passing Off and Cybersquatting

21.89 The tort of passing off, which is often described as the common law form of trade mark law, is largely used to protect owners of unregistered trade marks. It is also available to owners of registered trade marks and is often pleaded as an alternative cause of action in infringement proceedings (see section 4(2) of the Trade Marks Act 1998). Passing off, in relation to goods, occurs when the defendant uses on his own goods a trade mark or get-up that belongs to the plaintiff (or one that is very similar to the plaintiff's), with the effect of misrepresenting to the public that his goods are those of the plaintiff (ie that the defendant's goods have the same trade origin as or at least some business connection/association with the plaintiff's goods). In the process, the defendant takes an unfair advantage of the goodwill/reputation of the plaintiff's business, and this is likely to cause confusion amongst the public as to the true origin and nature of the defendant's goods (since there may be an unjustifiable imputation of quality to the defendant's goods which is widely and normally recognised in connection with the goods of the more established plaintiff trader). The point should, however, be made that passing off can arise even where the defendant's misrepresentation was innocent and not at all deliberate.

21.90 To succeed in an action for passing off, the plaintiff must establish the following three elements (see *Reckitt & Colman Products Ltd v Borden Inc* (1990)):

(1) There is sufficient goodwill associated with the plaintiff's business/trade which has been acquired through the mark or get-up used by the plaintiff on his goods or services;
(2) There is a misrepresentation by the defendant that his goods or services are those of the plaintiff, thereby leading to confusion or deception on the part of the public; and
(3) The plaintiff has suffered or is likely to suffer damage as a result of the defendant's misrepresentation (eg where there has been an actual reduction in the volume of sales in the plaintiff's business or, in the latter scenario, where the defendant's goods or services directly compete with the plaintiff's goods or services in the same market).

Goodwill

21.91 It must be emphasised at the outset that the law of passing off does not directly protect a trader's name, mark or get-up *per se*. Rather, it is in connection with the goodwill of the plaintiff's business as a whole that the law of passing off is concerned. 'Goodwill' should also not be confused with the word 'reputation', although the two are often used interchangeably. Unlike reputation *per se*, goodwill does not exist on its own; it must be attached to a business within the jurisdiction. To establish goodwill, the plaintiff usually needs to show that he has a business/trading presence and consequently, a pool of customers in Singapore. Whether or not sufficient goodwill has been established by the plaintiff is purely a factual determination, depending on factors such as volume of sales and volume of advertising.

Note, however, that a Singapore Court of Appeal decision (*CDL Hotels International Ltd v Pontiac Marina Pte Ltd* (1998)) has clarified that, in some instances, pre-trading activity in the form of pre-launch publicity may suffice in generating the requisite goodwill. Whether this is so is a question of fact and depends on the nature and intensity of the activity in question. For example, was there large-scale advertising and media coverage or any other form of pre-launch publicity? In the *CDL Hotels* case, LP Thean JA, on behalf of the court, held that the extensive advertising campaigns undertaken by the plaintiffs (viz Pontiac Marina Pte Ltd) to promote their business and services in Singapore had generated sufficient goodwill for their trade name, despite the fact that the plaintiffs had not officially commenced business in Singapore at the relevant time. The learned judge cautioned, however, that merely taking steps to register a trade mark in Singapore does not in itself suffice in generating the requisite goodwill.

In light of this decision and of the factual nature of a passing off action, it is advisable for traders to keep proper records of all invoices of actual sales (showing annual turnover), all invoices of advertising expenditure and copies of all advertisements published (eg in the local newspapers, magazines, brochures/pamphlets, or over the Internet).

In addition, it would generally be difficult for the plaintiff to show that he has acquired sufficient goodwill in his business if the mark or get-up used is not distinctive of the plaintiff's goods or services (or, in other words, is unable to identify the plaintiff to the exclusion of all other traders). As such, names which are *descriptive* in nature (eg 'Coffeemix' and other laudatory/non-invented words which are common in the English language, such as 'Perfect') are generally not distinctive of the plaintiff's goods or services, unless the plaintiff can show that the descriptive name in question has acquired a *secondary meaning* (ie the name must have somehow become distinctive of the plaintiff's business through, for example, evidence of long usage), *or* that the descriptive name in question is a mere *fancy name* (ie one that has no obvious relevance to the character or quality of the plaintiff's goods or services). See, in particular, the Singapore Court of Appeal decision in *Lifestyle 1.99 Pte Ltd v S$1.99 Pte Ltd (t/a ONE.99 SHOP)* (2000) and the Singapore High Court decision in *Nippon Paint (Singapore) Co Pte Ltd v ICI Paint (Singapore) Pte Ltd* (2001).

Misrepresentation

21.92 For the defendant to have misrepresented that his goods or services are those of the plaintiff trader, the defendant need not have used an exact copy of the plaintiff's mark or get-up on his own goods or services. Similarity between the two identifying get-up (be it visual or aural) sufficient to cause confusion amongst the public will suffice, although it should be noted that confusion *alone* does not necessarily amount to a material misrepresentation. However, it has been suggested that evidence of actual confusion is always relevant and may be decisive in judging whether or not passing off has occurred. Confusion or deception on the part of the public is generally established by survey evidence (although the courts are often wary of this) and such surveys are usually conducted by professional survey companies.

The paramount test here, therefore, is whether, on an objective analysis, the defendant's misrepresentation would have misled or deceived a significant number of purchasers or consumers into believing either that the goods or services of the defendant were those of the plaintiff or that there was a connection/association between the plaintiff and the defendant in relation to the goods or services provided by them (eg in terms of quality).

Further, where two traders adopt descriptive words or words in common use as part of their trade names or get-up (eg 'ONE.99 shop' vs 'Lifestyle 1.99'), it is inevitable that some risk of public confusion would arise. In such cases, the court would normally accept comparatively small differences between the competing get-up (eg slight differences in name, colour or design of the logo) as sufficient to avert such confusion (see, in particular, the House of Lords decision in *Office Cleaning Services Ltd v Westminster Window & General Cleaners Ltd* (1946)).

Cybersquatting

21.93 An interesting development in the law of passing off concerns disputes over Internet domain names. The sudden popularity of domain names across the globe is due in no small part to the fact that many businesses have now come to realise the true commercial potential of the Internet. Just as trade marks serve as business identifiers in the terrestrial world, domain names take on the same function in the virtual world as they give individual businesses a unique 'global' presence. Domain names (comprising gTLDs or ccTLDs, which denote generic top-level domains (eg .com domain names) and country-code top-level domains (eg .sg domain names) respectively) are generally registered on a first-come, first-served basis and this registration procedure has, rather unfortunately, resulted in the proliferation of cybersquatting cases. Cybersquatting is essentially an unfair trade practice where a third party (eg a business competitor) deliberately registers as domain names certain trade marks or well-known names belonging to other business entities, hoping to later sell them for a profit to those rightfully entitled or to use them to redirect Internet traffic to his own, often unrelated website.

21.94 Depending on the circumstances of each particular case, disputes involving the cybersquatting of gTLD domain names may be resolved through the Uniform Domain Name Dispute Resolution Policy ('UDRP') (where parties submit to a 'mandatory administrative proceeding') or through litigation (in the United States, the aggrieved party may have recourse to the Anticybersquatting Consumer Protection Act 1999 (S1255)). The UDRP was adopted by the Internet Corporation for Assigned Names and Numbers ('ICANN') in October 1999. When a gTLD domain name is registered with a Registrar accredited by ICANN, the UDRP is incorporated by reference into the Registration Agreement. Under paragraph 4(a) of the UDRP, the registrant of a gTLD domain name is required to submit to a mandatory administrative proceeding when a complainant asserts that:

(1) the registrant's domain name is identical or confusingly similar to a trade mark or service mark in which the complainant has rights;
(2) the registrant has no rights or legitimate interests in respect of the domain name; and
(3) the registrant's domain name has been registered and is being used in bad faith.

Further, paragraph 4(b) of the UDRP deems certain circumstances as evidence of the registration and use of a domain name in bad faith, whilst paragraph 4(c) of the UDRP deems certain circumstances as demonstrating the registrant's rights to or legitimate interests in the domain name in question.

21.95 Disputes involving the cybersquatting of ccTLD (eg .sg) domain names may be resolved through non-adversarial or alternative methods of dispute resolution (eg negotiation, mediation or arbitration) or through the court process. The aggrieved party in a .sg domain name dispute can also rely on Singapore's version of the UDRP for the resolution of the domain name dispute. The Singapore Domain Name Dispute Resolution Policy ('SDRP'), which is modelled after the UDRP, was launched by the ccTLD administrator in Singapore, the Singapore Network Information Centre (SGNIC), on 15 November 2001. The first case that was decided pursuant to a mandatory administrative proceeding under the SDRP involved a dispute over the domain name 'mtv.com.sg'; see *Viacom International Inc v Elitist Technologies Co Ltd* (Case No SDRP-2002/0001(F)). For a fuller understanding of the domain name system and how domain name disputes are resolved generally, as well as for a detailed analysis of the *Viacom* decision, the reader is referred to HC Phang, 'Resolving Domain Name Disputes—A Singapore Perspective' (2002) 14 *Singapore Academy of Law Journal* 85.

21.96 Should the aggrieved party decide to commence legal proceedings in court (especially in a Singapore court), there is an instructive case emanating from England which can serve as a useful precedent. It was held by the English Court of Appeal in *British Telecommunications Plc v One In A Million Ltd* (1998) that the defendants' registration of well-known trade names (eg marksandspencer.com) as Internet domain names amounted, *inter alia*, to a case of passing off (the defendants, who were dealers in Internet domain names, had previously registered a string of domain names which comprised well-known names and trade marks such as 'bt.org' and 'sainsbury.com'). The defendants had, through such registration, made a false representation to the public that they were associated or connected with the well-known British chain (Marks & Spencer), and had equipped themselves with or intended to equip others with instruments of fraud (names which would, by reason of their similarity to the names of other well-known business entities, inherently give rise to actions in passing off were likely to be instruments of fraud). In such cases, the court opined that injunctive relief was appropriate.

Geographical Indications Act 1998

21.97 The aim of the Geographical Indications Act 1998 (Cap 117B, 1999 Rev Ed) ('GIA') is, according to its long title, 'to provide for the protection of geographical indications in relation to goods' in Singapore. Singapore did not have specific legislation governing the use of geographical indications prior to the enactment of the GIA (which was in compliance with our obligations under the TRIPS Agreement). In the past, therefore, geographical indications were protected either by registering them as certification trade marks (see section 61 and the Second Schedule of the Trade Marks Act 1998), or, if they failed to satisfy the registrability requirements under the Trade Marks Act 1998, by the common law tort of passing off.

A 'geographical indication' is defined in section 2 of the GIA to mean any indication used in trade to identify goods (ie any natural or agricultural product or any product of handicraft or industry) as originating from a place (country or territory), provided that—

(1) the place (country or territory) is a member of the World Trade Organisation, or is a party to the Paris Convention, or is designated by the Minister as a qualifying country; and
(2) a given quality, reputation or other characteristic of the goods is essentially attributable to that place.

Some well-known examples of geographical indications include 'Champagne', 'Bordeaux', 'Sherry' and 'Parma Ham'.

21.98 In line with the TRIPS Agreement, there is no requirement under the GIA for the registration of a protectable geographical indication. Unlike the protection of trade marks under the Trade Marks Act 1998, protection of geographical indications is not contingent upon registration and the rights conferred are therefore not limited to any period of time. Instead, the GIA allows a producer or trader of goods identified by a geographical indication to institute legal proceedings against a person who commits a prohibited act (section 3(1)). The following acts are prohibited under the GIA (section 3(2)):

(1) use of a geographical indication in relation to goods which did not originate in the place indicated by the geographical indication, in a manner which misleads the public as to the geographical origin of the goods;
(2) use of a geographical indication which constitutes an act of unfair competition within the meaning of article 10*bis* of the Paris Convention (ie any act of competition which is contrary to honest practices in industrial or commercial matters, including, but not limited to, acts of such a nature as to cause confusion);
(3) use of a geographical indication (being a geographical indication which identifies a wine/spirit, eg 'Champagne') in relation to a wine/spirit which did not originate from the place indicated by the geographical indication, whether or not—
    (a) the true geographical origin of the wine/spirit (eg Singapore) is used together with the geographical indication (as in 'Singapore Champagne');
    (b) the geographical indication is used in translation; or
    (c) the geographical indication is accompanied by expressions such as 'kind', 'type', 'style', 'imitation' or the like (eg 'Champagne-type').

This last-mentioned provision (viz sections 3(2)(c) and 3(2)(d) of the GIA) prohibits the *use* of a geographical indication (being a geographical indication which identifies a wine/spirit) in relation to a wine/spirit which did not originate from the place indicated by the geographical indication. The reader should note that similar provisions exist in the Trade Marks Act 1998 (viz sections 7(7)–7(10)) which prohibit the *registration of a trade mark* which consists of a geographical indication in respect of a wine/spirit and which is used or intended to be used in relation to a wine/spirit not originating from the place indicated in the geographical indication.

21.99 There are, however, certain exceptions to the protection of geographical indications. No relief or protection may be sought, for example, where the geographical indication is contrary to public policy or morality, or where the geographical indication has ceased to be protected in its country or territory of origin or has fallen into disuse (see, generally, sections 6–9 of the GIA). The remedies which are available to a plaintiff who successfully brings an action against a person under the GIA for carrying out a prohibited act include an injunction (to restrain the further carrying out of the act) and/or damages or an account of profits (see section 4).

Concluding Thoughts

21.100 It is appropriate to conclude this chapter by citing, where relevant, excerpts from an article by Professor David Vaver (see D Vaver, 'Intellectual Property: The State of the Art' (2000) 116 *Law Quarterly Review* 621).

Whilst it is true that all of Singapore's intellectual property legislation are largely in compliance with the minimum standards of protection laid down by the TRIPS Agreement, there is still a need to subject them, and indeed to subject the whole body of intellectual property law, to constant and detailed review.

> 'If intellectual property were seen as a form of subsidy—a willingness by society at large to provide economic benefits to one sector in return for the prospect of larger benefits to all—then few would question the need to keep intellectual property under constant review to ensure the scheme was working well. It would not be enough to say that intellectual property *as a whole* was returning social benefits that outweighed its costs *as a whole*. As with any other subsidy, each element within the scheme would need to be examined to see if it passes its own A level—and with distinction. A strong case for such systematic reviews must surely exist' (at p 636) (emphasis in original).

It is perhaps not surprising that there will continue to be demands for greater intellectual property protection from the owners of such rights all over the world. However, it is equally important to guard against an over-indulgence in one's pursuit of such protection as it may ultimately result in the suppression of other values (such as freedom of expression and the right to compete). The difficulty here, of course, lies in the way intellectual property should be reconciled with these other values. How can we achieve the right balance between having a monopoly over the marketplace of ideas and having a free flow of information which is so central to the vitality of the Internet and the vibrancy of democracy? The starting premise must then be that owners of intellectual property should not always insist on reaping all that they have sowed.

Finally, there is a sombre message underlying this area of the law.

For the intellectual property system to survive and to continue to serve its useful purpose, 'it must gain and keep public respect'. As Professor Vaver argues (at p 637):

> 'To be respected, it must be known. To be known, it must be understood. To be understood, it must be coherent and persuasive. There are now calls that the public should become better educated about intellectual property. Such calls are, naturally, music to the ears of any educator. But one must be prepared for the consequence that an educated public is entitled to demand greater coherence and persuasiveness from the intellectual property system than that system presently exhibits. If those calls are not met and answered, then greater knowledge will not produce greater public respect, but instead cynicism, disregard and avoidance. Perhaps that is the first lesson which those who would educate the public may wish to teach themselves.'

The law of intellectual property is, in many ways, a demanding and complex subject and is an area of the law that will continue to evolve in the years to come. It is hoped that this introductory chapter has given the reader a feel for the subject and has laid the foundation for a more detailed study at a later time.

For the intellectual property system to survive and to continue to serve its useful purposes, it must gain and keep public respect. As Professor Vaver suggested:

> "To be respected, it must be known. To be known, it must be understood. To be understood, it must be coherent and [illegible]"

PART VII

Law and International Business

CHAPTER 22

Law and International Business

PARAGRAPHS

22.1 **Introduction: Globalisation, Law and International Business**

22.2 **Public International Law**
22.3 Sources of Public International Law
22.4 Status of International Law in a Country
22.5 Jurisdiction in Public International Law
22.6 Nationality

22.7 **Conflict of Laws**

22.8 **WTO and International Trade**
22.9 Dumping
22.10 Subsidies

22.11 **International Sales**

22.12 **Trade Terms: INCOTERMS**

Forms of Doing Business Overseas
22.13 Introduction
22.14 Agents and Distributors
22.15 Branches
22.16 Management and Technical Assistance Arrangements
22.17 Companies
22.18 Project Finance/SPVs and BOTs
22.19 Representative Offices
22.20 Franchises
22.21 Contract Manufacturing

Foreign Direct Investment
22.22 Introduction
22.23 Expropriation and Nationalisation
22.24 Bilateral Investment Treaties

PARAGRAPHS

Foreign Direct Investment (continued)

22.25 US–Singapore Free Trade Agreement
22.26 WTO and FDI
22.27 Resolution of FDI Disputes

Dispute Settlement

22.28 Introduction
22.29 Model Law and New York Convention
22.30 The Model Law
22.31 Limited Role of Court
22.32 Conduct of Proceedings
22.33 Making of the Award
22.34 Enforcement of Arbitral Award

22.35 **Preventive Tools: Due Diligence and Opinions of Counsel**

22.36 **Conclusion**

Introduction: Globalisation, Law and International Business

22.1 The term 'globalisation' means different things to different people. For our present purposes we can consider the term to describe the increased movement across boundaries of persons such as IT professionals and guest-workers, money in forms such as loans and investment, goods, and services such as insurance and accountancy and the sale and purchase of various products and services either in cyberspace or in the real world. Such movements and trade flows, with the exception of cyberspace transactions, have gone on for centuries but, in the recent past, it is the speed and impact of such flows that have increased, and governmental restrictions on these trade flows that have decreased.

Transactions across national boundaries have features that are not present in purely domestic transactions. The parties to cross-border transactions live in different countries, speak different languages, use different currencies, and live under different political systems with different levels of economic development. Often, these transactions require supplementary transactions with banks, insurance companies, and transportation companies. Despite features that contain the potential for many things to go wrong in such interactions, hundreds of millions of dollars worth of transactions are conducted every day without any problems. At the same time, some transactions do fail and the disaffected party may decide to seek remedies under the law.

To determine how the law becomes relevant and applicable in cross-border commercial relationships, it is useful to perceive the legal structure relating to international business transactions as a pyramid that contains three interlocking tiers as follows:

The first segment comprising the top tier of the pyramid consists of the conduct of parties that gives rise to legal consequences. Usually, such conduct consists of agreements between parties that they regard as legally binding. However, of late, there are more non-consensual events that give rise to legal consequences. These are usually legal wrongs or torts. For example, if a product manufactured in America is used in Indonesia and injures a French national, employed by a Singapore company, working on an offshore oil-rig off the island of Java, the injured employee may seek relief against various potential defendants in several countries.

The second segment, comprising the middle tier of the pyramid, consists of national laws that provide the legal context for, and attaches legal consequences to, the conduct of parties that makes up the first tier of the pyramid. Persons may agree on many matters but unless the relevant law says that such agreements are contracts, the agreements have no legal force. Some countries may require particular types of contract to be in writing or to be notarised, and, of course, common law countries require that there be consideration for a contract to be valid. In the area of tort, some countries impose strict product liability while other countries may require proof of negligence, which is a fault-based concept.

The third segment, the bottom tier of the pyramid, consists of rules of public international law that regulate relationships among sovereign countries, specify a country's rights and obligations, and also accord force and recognition to the laws and regulations of individual countries. This body of law will lay down the limits of a country's jurisdiction to make laws so that country X will not be able to pass a law that the citizens of country Y must behave in a certain way when they are in country Y. Of late, the rules of public international law have become more important because most of the trade and commerce that takes place is subject to international law rules supervised by the World Trade Organization. There also have been treaties, or agreements between countries, such as the Free Trade Agreements between Singapore and the US, Japan, the European Union and Australia which provide for increased trade flows in goods and services among countries, the protection of intellectual property rights, and how the foreign direct investment of nationals from one country will be respected and treated in the other country.

Public International Law

22.2 Public international law, as a subject, embraces a vast array of topics ranging from the peaceful uses of outer space to the treatment of prisoners of war. Even in the narrower area of international business, public international law contains rules relating to such diverse topics as the immunity of states in commercial transactions and the obligations of states to enact laws prohibiting commercial bribery abroad. In this section, we will only discuss, at a basic level, four issues as they pertain to law and international business. First, the ways in which public international law is made. Second, the status of public international law in the legal system of a particular country. Third, the rules of prescriptive jurisdiction whereby countries are allowed to make and enforce their laws. Finally, the rule of nationality which links a country to a person or an asset and permits that country to assert an interest with respect to the way that person or asset is treated.

Sources of Public International Law

22.3 One of the institutions established after World War II was the International Court of Justice ('ICJ'), and scholars regard article 38(1) of the charter establishing the ICJ as enumerating four sources of international law. These are treaties and conventions, customary international law, general principles of law accepted by civilised nations and (as a subsidiary source) judicial precedent of both the ICJ as well as decisions of national courts and the writings of international law scholars.

Treaties are agreements between two or more countries. Much of international business is affected by the contents of treaties that address such issues as the protection of investments, the customs duties that could be levied upon imports, the avoidance of double taxation of profits, and preventing bribery in commercial transactions. Treaties relating to the law of the sea specify how maritime resources can be exploited and the rights and obligations of countries relating to the use of the oceans.

Another treaty, known as the Vienna Convention on the Law of Treaties (1969) contains rules that govern how treaties are made, interpreted and terminated and how in the case of multilateral treaties, a state may not submit to some of the obligations contained in such multilateral treaty by means of 'reservations'. This Convention can be perceived as the 'law of contract' that governs written contracts among countries.

The next source of law concerns rules of public international law derived from custom described as a 'constant and uniform usage, accepted as law': see the *Asylum (Columbia v Peru)* (1950). For a customary rule of international law to exist, two conditions must be satisfied: (1) a widespread and clear practice followed by states. Complete uniformity is not required so long as substantial uniformity is present and no precise length of time is required: see the *North Sea Continental Shelf* case (1969); and (2) a showing that such widespread and clear practice is followed by states because they believe that they are obligated to do so as a matter of legal duty rather than as a courtesy: see *Lotus* case (*France v Turkey*) (1927). Many of the older rules of public international law, before they were codified by treaty provisions on the subject, were customary rules of international law. Thus, the immunity of ambassadors, the right of ships to sail on the high seas and rules of prescriptive jurisdiction had their origins in rules of customary international law. Customary international law is still important as evidenced by the US–Singapore Free Trade Agreement ('FTA') which establishes standards of conduct that are based on customary international law.

The third source comprises those general principles of law that are common to civilised nations. For example, most legal systems recognise the principle that once a case is tried and finally decided, it cannot be retried again. The principle of estoppel was invoked in *Temple of Preah Vihear (Cambodia v Thailand)* (1962) where a map showing the disputed temple located in Cambodia was accepted without protest by the Government of Thailand. In *Corfu Channel Case (United Kingdom v Albania)* (1949), the use of circumstantial evidence to prove matters was allowed by the tribunal.

Finally, article 38(1) of the ICJ statute authorises resort to past judgments of various tribunals including that of the ICJ, its predecessor, the Permanent Court of International Justice, national courts, and arbitral tribunals. Often, these decisions contain influential statements of international law and sometimes provide useful general principles that could be applied to specific problems. For example, a dispute between two states in a federal state such as the United States or Australia about the use of a common river by those states may provide guidance for a court that has to decide the problem when the dispute about the rivers is between two countries. However, these decisions, although highly influential, are not binding but merely give guidance on how a matter could be decided.

Status of International Law in a Country

22.4 Are rules of international law part of the law of a country? Different countries, depending on their respective constitutions, have different answers to this question.

In most common law countries including Singapore, international law becomes a part of the local law when the legislature incorporates a treaty either by passing a law that gives effect to the substance of the treaty or by stating that the treaty will become a part of the law. The courts, too, give effect to international law principles provided that these do not conflict or are inconsistent with local law. In *Trendtex Trading Corpn v Central Bank of Nigeria* (1977), Lord Denning MR was of the view that rules of customary international law are incorporated into English law automatically and are considered to be part of English law unless they are in conflict with an Act of Parliament. The constitutions of some civil law European countries make international law the supreme law of the land. In the United States, article II, section 2 of the American Constitution accords the force of law to treaties that have received the advice and consent of the US Senate. American constitutional law also recognises another species of agreement known as executive agreements. Some of these executive agreements, especially trade agreements, have been made under prior authorisation by the US Congress while others have been made on the sole constitutional authority of the President. Both types of executive agreements have survived constitutional challenges in American courts.

Jurisdiction in Public International Law

22.5 International law recognises the rights of countries to make laws that would bind persons in certain circumstances. This is known as 'prescriptive jurisdiction'. Although countries claim that they can enact laws that govern conduct in a variety of circumstances, international law recognises only a few categories as follows.

Territorial Jurisdiction refers to the power that any country has to regulate the conduct of people, whether they are its own citizens or others, within its borders. Thus, country X may pass laws that regulate how people, whether they be citizens of country X or foreigners, must behave in country X. Often, some part of the prohibited conduct is conducted or completed in a particular country. The decision in the *Lotus* case validates the exercise of jurisdiction where the prohibited action is completed in the country asserting jurisdiction. The position is less clear when the consequences complained of are economic. The US has asserted jurisdiction over conduct abroad that has anti-competitive effects within the US while other countries have strongly resisted the extraterritorial reach of American anti-trust laws by passing retaliatory claw-back legislation: see *United States v Aluminum Co of America* (1945).

Nationality Jurisdiction refers to the jurisdiction of a country to regulate the conduct of its citizens or nationals wherever they may be. Usually, the exercise of nationality jurisdiction coincides with the exercise of territorial jurisdiction as for example when a country passes a law requiring its male citizens to perform national service. But a country can even legislate on what its nationals may or may not do while they are abroad. The United States and some other countries prohibit their companies from engaging in commercial bribery even when they are abroad. A country can punish acts of treason committed by its nationals when abroad: see, eg *Joyce v DPP* (1946). Singapore prohibits her citizens from ingesting prohibited substances even when they are outside Singapore under section 8A of the Misuse of Drugs Act (Cap 185, 2001 Rev Ed).

Jurisdiction based on the protective principle allows a country to proscribe conduct abroad that is designed to affect the peace and security of the country making the laws. For instance, a country can prohibit the counterfeiting of its currency wherever this may occur. Drug trafficking and terrorism are crimes that afflict many countries in the world. The planning of terrorism may take place outside the affected country's borders but international law recognises the jurisdiction of a country to punish such overseas conduct: see *United States v Yousef* (2000). Closely aligned with the protective principle is the passive nationality principle of jurisdiction that allows a country to prohibit conduct designed to injure its nationals and undertaken because the victims are nationals of that country.

Universal Jurisdiction refers to a type of jurisdiction where any country has jurisdiction regardless of where the act in question was committed. Piracy at sea has for a long time been regarded as an offence over which any country had jurisdiction. Recently, other offences such as genocide, torture and terrorism have been added to that list so that any country has the right to pass laws that allow its courts to try offenders for these crimes: *R v Bow Street Metropolitan Stipendiary Magistrate, Ex Parte Pinochet Ugurte (No 2)* (2000).

Nationality

22.6 Nationality refers to the link between a person or asset and a country. In *Nottebohm (Liechtenstein v Guatemala)* (1955), the court recognised that it is for every sovereign state to settle by its own legislation the rules relating to the acquisition of its nationality. The laws of each country will determine the circumstances under which that country will confer nationality on a natural person. Constitutional provisions of some countries, such as the Fourteenth Amendment to the US Constitution, provide that any person born within the borders of that country becomes a citizen. Yet, other countries require some link such as one parent being a citizen of that country.

The issue of nationality is not confined to human beings. Companies may have a nationality and the general rule is that a company has the nationality of the country in which it is incorporated; see, eg *Barcelona Traction, Light and Power Company, Limited (Belgium v Spain)* (1970). However, most bilateral investment treaties now treat foreign direct investment companies in which the shareholders are foreign as non-local companies in those circumstances where there has been a dispute over nationalisation or expropriation of the assets or shares of such companies. Applicable treaties provide that ships and aircraft have the nationality of the countries in which they are registered.

Nationality is relevant in the area of international business law because the relevant country has a right of protection when the company or the asset in question is taken over or harassed by a government in a foreign country. Many bilateral treaties, including the US–Singapore FTA and bilateral investment treaties, provide that the countries that are parties to the treaties would give certain protection and benefits to the nationals of the countries to the agreement. Thus, it is necessary to ascertain whether certain natural persons or assets qualify as nationals under these agreements.

Conflict of Laws

22.7 The subject of conflict of laws, or private international law as it is sometimes called, deals with the set of rules that the courts use to determine how to handle a case that has a legally significant foreign element. For instance, a legally significant foreign element would be present if the contract in question was performed overseas, the plaintiff was injured overseas, or the land that is the subject of the dispute is situated in a different country. Unlike public international law, conflict of laws rules are rules made in each country either by the legislature or the courts for dealing with disputes where there is a foreign element that is both present and material.

In international business, a contract may be between parties who are nationals of two different countries and may envisage performance in a third country. The case may be brought in a fourth country because the courts of that country have a high reputation. Multinationals have operations in many countries and some of these operations may cause death or injury to both employees as well as third parties as in the case of the Union Carbide plant in Bhopal, India: In *Re Union Carbide Corp* (1986). Employees of a mining company who were injured in the course of their work may decide to sue the parent company in the courts of the foreign country in which the parent company is located: see *Lubbe v Cape Plc* (2000). Products may be manufactured in France and although used in French Caledonia causing injury to an Australian plaintiff there, the plaintiff may decide to sue in Australia: see *Renault v Zhang* (2002).

Conflict of laws principles address three issues where the transaction involves a significant foreign element: First, what law must the court apply? Second, may the court hear the case despite the presence of the foreign element? Finally, under what circumstances will the court enforce a judgment that is given by a foreign court?

The rules of conflict of laws provide a strategic advantage to parties and must be considered both when planning a transaction as well as selecting a forum once a dispute has arisen. In agreeing to a cross-border contract, the parties would want to consider what law they would choose to be the governing law of the contract. The contract law of some countries is highly detailed, sophisticated and predictable and will thus enable the parties to estimate their respective risks and plan accordingly. The contract law of yet other countries may be vague and unsatisfactory and contracts with such governing laws may require highly detailed drafting to cover eventualities because the application of the contract law to these would be uncertain. The general rule in the common law courts of the Commonwealth is that the parties to a contract may expressly choose the law to govern their contract provided that the choice was made in good faith and was legal and that there was no reason for avoiding the choice on the ground of public policy: see, eg *Vita Food Products Inc v Unus Shipping Co Ltd* (1939). Other rules of conflict of laws will determine whether the parties to the contract had the capacity to contract and ancillary issues.

Another important matter to be considered is whether a court will hear a case in which a foreigner is a defendant. For instance, a court in Singapore will be reluctant to compel a defendant who lives in Japan to appear before a Singapore court and defend an action. In most Commonwealth countries, the circumstances in which a court will allow a plaintiff to sue a foreign defendant are specified in a set of rules known as Order 11 rules. Some of these circumstances involve the defendant submitting to the jurisdiction of the forum specified in the contract or where the contract is to be performed in the country in which the court is located.

In international litigation, for several years, there has been a practice known as 'forum shopping' where a party seeks to have the dispute tried in the courts of one country as opposed to another because of the advantages perceived in the former. A hoary rule of conflict of laws is that the laws of the forum govern procedural matters and the procedural law of the forum may affect issues such as the quantum of damages and the pre-trial discovery rights of the parties. It is thus not uncommon to see litigants conflict over where to try the case so that this outcome can affect an out-of-court settlement favourable to the party that can litigate in a forum perceived as beneficial to that party. This practice has given rise to abuses and common law courts have shaped two main tools to deal with the problem. The first relates to the doctrine of *forum non conveniens* where a court that is authorised to hear a case decides not to hear the action because another court is better suited to hear the case. The second relates to an antisuit injunction.

The doctrine of *forum non conveniens* becomes relevant when a court that can hear a case is asked by the defendant not to hear that case because another court, usually a foreign court, is better positioned to hear the case. In *Spiliada Maritime Corp v Cansulex Ltd* (1987), the highest court in England (the House of Lords) held that an English court will stay an action if the foreign court proposed by the defendant is clearly more appropriate than the English court and that it would be in the interests of justice to not hear the case in England. Usually, a foreign court would be regarded as clearly more appropriate if that foreign court is the 'natural forum', by which is meant that most of the important factors such as the critical events which took place and important witnesses are found in the country of that foreign court. If the court agrees that there is another court in a foreign country that is clearly more appropriate to try the case, it will stay the action in favour of the foreign court unless the plaintiff can show that he will not be able to get justice in that foreign court. When a plaintiff seeks to serve a writ under Order 11 on a foreign defendant, it is the plaintiff who must satisfy the court under *The Spiliada* principles that the court, and not some foreign court, is appropriate to hear the case. The Singapore High Court has adopted the test set forth in *The Spiliada* case to determine a plea by the defendant that a Singapore court, while it could hear a case, should not hear the case because there is a foreign court able to hear the case that is clearly more appropriate than the Singapore court: see *Brinkerhoff Maritime Drilling Corp v PT Airfast Services Indonesia* (1992).

An antisuit injunction is an order given by a court to someone within its jurisdiction not to start or proceed with an action in a foreign court. The order is given to the actual or potential plaintiff and it is not given to a foreign court itself because one court will not order a foreign court to not hear the case. In *Societe Nationale Industrielle Aerospatiale v Lee Kui Jak* (1987), the Privy Council held that the plaintiff, a widow whose husband perished in a helicopter accident in Brunei, could not sue the manufacturer in the state of Texas. Antisuit injunctions are not easily obtained because their effect is to prevent a foreign court from hearing the case. The person seeking an antisuit injunction must demonstrate that the action that is threatened or is continuing in the foreign forum will be vexatious and oppressive. The House of Lords in subsequent decisions such as *Airbus Industrie GIE v Patel* (1999) and *Turner v Grovit* (2002) has elucidated further the principles that govern the issuance of an antisuit injunction. Singapore courts follow the principles relating to the granting of antisuit injunctions set forth by the Privy Council in the *Lee Kui Jak* case: see *Djoni Widjaja v Bank of America* (1993).

The Reciprocal Enforcement of Commonwealth Judgments Act (Cap 264, 1997 Rev Ed) and the Reciprocal Enforcement of Foreign Judgments Act (Cap 264, 1997 Rev Ed) specify the circumstances in which judgments rendered in a Commonwealth or non-Commonwealth foreign court, respectively, may be enforced in Singapore. Foreign judgments that satisfy the criteria of these Acts will be entitled to enforcement in Singapore as if they were issued by a Singapore court. The familiar exceptions such as lack of jurisdiction of the foreign court, fraud and public policy are found in this legislation which denies enforcement to judgments that are so tainted.

WTO and International Trade

22.8 For thousands of years, people have traded goods and services across national boundaries. After World War II, many important trading countries attempted to establish a trade organisation known as the International Trade Organization. This attempt failed and for several decades trade was conducted under an agreement known as the General Agreement on Tariffs and Trade ('GATT') the purpose of which was to liberalise trade by bringing down barriers to trade and cutting tariffs. The GATT provided the framework for several trade negotiating 'rounds' designed to lower tariffs and other trade barriers. The World Trade Organization, hereafter the 'WTO', now oversees the implementation of scores of trade liberalisation agreements negotiated among countries: see the *Marrakesh Agreement Establishing the World Trade Organization, Final Act Embodying the Results of the Uruguay Round of Multilateral Trade Negotiations, April 15, 1994*. Some of these agreements such as the Agreement on Trade Related Aspects of Intellectual Property Rights ('TRIPS' discussed in Chapter 21) reflect features of a modern economy that recognises wealth not only in the form of tangible goods but also in the intangible form of intellectual property.

In the early part of the 19th century, the English economist, David Ricardo, using a simple example of England and Portugal producing wheat and wine, showed that although one country, Portugal, may have an absolute advantage in producing both commodities, it would be beneficial for both countries to specialise. England would have the comparative advantage of producing wheat while Portugal would have the comparative advantage of producing wine. While the theory of comparative advantage demonstrated the benefits of free trade to countries, in practice, governments have used protectionist devices to keep out imports and yet other devices to promote exports.

Traditionally, countries have attempted to regulate the import of goods by way of two categories of barriers, viz tariff and non-tariff barriers, respectively. Tariffs are duties or taxes that are levied by the importing country and are usually based on a percentage of the value of the product. Non-tariff barriers are hosts of measures, some legitimate and some illegitimate, that have the effect of making importation of goods difficult, if not impossible. One type of non-tariff barrier is a quota whereby a country allows only a certain number of products to be imported. Other types of non-tariff barriers are those that concern labeling, health and safety inspections, as well as those based on national security.

Under the various GATT rounds and the negotiations conducted during the various WTO meetings, tariffs have been progressively reduced. Membership of the WTO brings with it most favoured-nation status in respect of tariffs. This means that a country X that has, for example, a tariff of 2% on a particular item must allow imports of that particular item from all other WTO member countries at 2% and it is no argument that this low tariff is meant to reward country Y. Once goods enter a country that is a WTO member, that country must extend *national* treatment to these goods, by which is meant that there should be no discrimination against these goods, and their sale and distribution must be regulated in the same way that goods produced locally are regulated.

A WTO member cannot demand most favoured-nation status from another WTO member in respect of trade benefits when these are part of a package confined to a customs union such as the European Union or a free trade arrangement such as the US–Singapore Free Trade Agreement or the North American Free Trade Agreement ('NAFTA').

The WTO supervises and administers a wide variety of agreements devoted to various trade issues. The WTO agreement also contains three principal instruments relating to trade defence and two of these address issues that have been prominent sources of trade friction among countries, viz the issues of dumping and subsidies. These are supposed to be instances of unfair competition and the country affected is authorised, where it follows the rules, to take actions that neutralise the trade distorting impact of these practices. Singapore's legislation conforming to WTO agreements on dumping and subsidies is contained in the Countervailing and Anti-Dumping Duties Act 1966 (Cap 65B, 1997 Rev Ed).

Dumping

22.9 When a company exports its products to another country at a price that is less than the price in its home market, and the exported products cause or threaten to cause material injury to the domestic industry in that importing country, then that importing country may levy an additional tax, the anti-dumping duty, that is meant to offset the unfair advantage of the dumped product.

Many industrialised countries have had anti-dumping legislation for several decades and exporters have charged that these laws have been misused to protect inefficient domestic industry. The WTO Anti-Dumping Agreement, unlike its predecessor under GATT, binds all WTO members and provides for more detailed rules for calculating the amount of dumping and more detailed procedures for investigation. The main focus of this agreement is on the reaction of the importing country so that anti-dumping retaliation can take place only in carefully circumscribed circumstances. The Agreement lays down substantive standards to ascertain if there is really dumping, procedural safeguards that are meant to ensure that the investigation is conducted properly and a dispute settlement mechanism whereby the failure by the importing country to respect either the substantive or procedural requirements can be taken to the WTO dispute settlement body.

The important substantive requirements are that (1) there must be dumping. This means that the exporter's product must cost less in its domestic market or, if there is no domestic market for that product, the exporter's price in a third country or the cost arrived at by taking into account production and associated costs. Section 2 of the Countervailing and Anti-Dumping Duties Act 1966 (Cap 65B, 1997 Rev Ed) defines dumping margin as 'the amount by which the normal value of the subject goods exceeds the export price'; (2) the dumping must be in respect of 'like goods' which section 2 of the Singapore legislation states are 'any goods which the Minister determines are identical in all respect to the subject goods or, in the absence of such goods, any other goods which the Minister determines has characteristics closely resembling those of the subject goods' (for example, would a computer printer be considered a like good with regard to an electric typewriter or a scanner?); and (3) there must be injury to the domestic industry.

The procedural requirements are meant to thwart a rush to judgment. The relevant records must be examined and the exporting company must be given an opportunity to defend itself.

If the procedural and substantive requirements are satisfied, the government of the importing country is allowed to levy anti-dumping duties or tariffs to offset the effects of the dumping but these duties may be levied only for a limited time; see the Countervailing and Anti-Dumping Duties Act 1966 (Cap 65B, 1997 Rev Ed), Part III.

Subsidies

22.10 While dumping is carried on by exporting companies, subsidies are given by governments and are regarded as having a trade distorting effect because they give an unfair advantage to companies that receive the subsidy. Sometimes a government can subsidise exports to a country such that the exports of a third country to the importing country are adversely affected. The WTO Agreement on Subsidies and Countervailing Measures addresses two separate topics: (1) multilateral disciplines regulating the provisions of subsidies. These are rules to determine whether or not a member country is providing a subsidy and these can be directly enforced by an affected member country through the use of the WTO dispute settlement mechanism; and (2) the circumstances under which the government of the importing country can use countervailing measures to offset injury caused by subsidised imports. Here, the government is acting unilaterally and can impose the duty after determining that the criteria set forth in the agreement are satisfied. In both instances, the subsidy provided must be 'specific'. This Agreement conspicuously does not address the issue of agricultural subsidies.

For a subsidy to exist, three elements must be present: (1) there must be a financial contribution; (2) by a government or any public body; and (3) the contribution must confer a benefit. A financial contribution can be made in many ways such as loan guarantees, the purchase of goods or the provision of goods and services. Sometimes the requirement of benefit can be easily proven and at other times this is a complex issue requiring comparison with the market-place.

Since only specific subsidies are the subject of the Agreement, subsidies that benefit the entire economy are not regarded as distorting the economy. These four types of specific subsidies are: (1) enterprise-specific subsidies; (2) industry-specific subsidies; (3) subsidies granted to a specific geographical region; and (4) prohibited subsidies.

The Agreement also divides subsidies into two basic categories: (1) prohibited subsidies; and (2) actionable subsidies.

Subsidies that fall into the category of 'prohibited subsidies' are 'export subsidies', where the receipt of the subsidy is contingent upon export performance, and 'local content subsidies' where the subsidy is contingent upon the use of domestic over imported goods. These subsidies are prohibited because they are considered aggressive and designed to impact trade to the detriment of other member countries.

'Actionable subsidies', while not prohibited, are subject to challenge either directly before the WTO or through countervailing duties imposed by the government of the importing country if they cause adverse effects to the interests of another country. Adverse effects exist when the subsidy causes injury to the domestic industry of the importing country, or serious prejudice as when the market of the subsidising member or that of a third country becomes less attractive for exports of the complaining country, or there is nullification or impairment of benefits such that the improved market access presumed to flow from tariff reductions are undercut by the subsidies.

In some recent high profile rulings, the WTO has ruled that the US business organisation known as the 'Foreign Sales Corporation' and the support given by Canada to its aircraft manufacturer, Bombardier Inc, constitute subsidies given by the respective governments.

A member country may not impose countervailing duties unless it can be shown that there is a causal link between the subsidy and the domestic industry. In Singapore, section 3 of the Countervailing and Anti-Dumping Duties Act 1966 (Cap 65B, 1997 Rev Ed) requires the Minister to find that a countervailable subsidy is being provided as well as that a specific type of injury exists.

International Sales

22.11 Sales of goods across national borders have features absent in purely domestic sales. Distance and time play an important part with the result that the seller will be anxious because she fears that she will not be paid and the buyer will be concerned that the seller, who has already been paid, will either not ship the goods at all or ship inferior goods. Also, intermediaries, such as banks (buyer's and seller's), insurance companies and transportation companies, play crucial facilitative roles in international sales transactions with the resulting complexity in legal exposure. Finally, a majority of international sales contracts are 'string contracts' meaning that the buyer in one transaction is usually a seller to another buyer who in turn is a seller to another (and so on) with respect to the same goods.

The law that regulates the relationship between the seller and the buyer in a country can either be a domestic sale of goods Act (in Singapore, the Sale of Goods Act (Cap 393, 1999 Rev Ed)) or, in the context of international sales, the United Nations Convention on the International Sale of Goods ('CISG') if that country has become a party to this convention. The CISG attempts to provide a common framework for international sale of goods transactions. The CISG has been adopted and made part of the local law by most trading countries, including Singapore (see the Sale of Goods (United Nations Convention) Act (Cap 283A, 1996 Rev Ed)) and the US, but not by the UK.

The CISG attempts to blend common law and civil law concepts relating to the sale of goods and its primary objective is to give as much autonomy to the buyer and seller to arrange the specifics of the transaction. In order to be 'user friendly', the CISG uses plain, non-technical language.

Article 1(1)(a) of the CISG makes it applicable where the buyer and the seller are from different countries that are parties to the Convention. This fact, that the seller and the buyer are from different countries, must have been evident in the contract or must have been known to the parties at or before the time the sales contract was made. The CISG will apply by default in these circumstances but the parties are free to exclude its application and specify another law either expressly or by implication. Usually, if the CISG is not applicable, the Singapore Sale of Goods Act referred to above will be applicable if the governing law of the contract is Singapore law.

An important principle underlying the CISG is the principle of good faith in international trade.

The CISG applies only to transactions involving the sale of goods. Transactions excluded from the scope of the CISG are those involving goods purchased for family or household use, electricity sales, sales of shares and sales of ships and aircraft (article 2). It also does not apply to sales where the purchaser supplies much of the materials necessary for the finished product (article 3). The CISG does not address liability issues arising from death or injury (article 5). Many topics such as the validity of the contract as affected by mistake and misrepresentation, as well as the passing of property, are also not addressed in the CISG and these issues are to be resolved by applying the relevant domestic law.

Part II of the CISG deals with rules governing the formation of contracts. Like all contracts, a contract under the CISG is formed when there is a valid offer that is matched by a valid acceptance. There is a valid offer when a proposal for making a contract is addressed to a specific person indicating, clearly, (1) the intention of the offeror to be bound in case of acceptance and (2) the goods, their quantity and price. Although the offer becomes effective when it reaches the offeree, the offeror may withdraw the offer by sending a notice of withdrawal that reaches the offeree either before or at the same time the offer reaches the offeree. Under article 16(1), the offeror can revoke the offer before an acceptance is dispatched. But article 16(2) states that an offeror may not revoke her offer if the original offer provided for a fixed time for acceptance or otherwise indicated that it is irrevocable or where the offeree has acted in reliance on the offer. Article 18(2) states that there is a valid acceptance 'at the moment the indication of assent reaches the offeror'. A counter-offer destroys the original offer but an acceptance that contains additional terms that do not materially alter the terms of the offer constitutes an acceptance, unless the offeror objects to these without undue delay (article 19(2)). But an acceptance with additional terms that relate to price, payment, quality and quantity of goods would constitute a counter-offer as such terms would be considered material terms (article 19(3)).

Part III of the CISG covers the obligations of the seller and the buyer, the passing of risk, the remedies for breach. The fundamental principle enshrined in Part III is the primacy of the contract so that parties are free to choose the terms of their bargain and displace contrary rules in the CISG. Article 25 declares a breach to be 'fundamental' if it results in such detriment to the other party as substantially to deprive him of what he is entitled to expect under the contact. If the other party did not foresee, and a reasonable person could not have foreseen that result, the breach is not fundamental.

Chapter II is entitled 'Obligations of the Seller' and article 30 states the basic obligation of the seller which are to deliver the goods, hand over any documents relating to them and transfer the property in the goods. The articles following, articles 31 to 44, specify the manner in which the seller must fulfil his obligations. These include the obligations to deliver conforming goods (article 35) and to deliver goods free from any right or claim of a third party (article 41).

Chapter III is entitled 'Obligations of the Buyer' and article 53 states the basic obligation which is to 'pay the price for the goods and take delivery of them as required by the contract' and the CISG. The parties' agreement takes precedence over the CISG provisions, such as the determination of the price (article 54), place of payment (article 57) and time for payment (article 58). These provisions will apply if the parties have not addressed these key items or if what they have agreed upon is obscure.

Articles 66 to 70 deal with the passing of risk. For instance, if the risk of loss has passed to the buyer, he cannot refuse to pay on the ground that he has not received the goods. The general rule is that the risk passes from the seller to the buyer at the moment of delivery. The CISG provisions on the passing of risk attempt to place the risk of loss on the party who is better able to seek remedies against third parties such as the insurer or the carrier.

Chapter V, entitled 'Provisions Common to the Obligations of the Seller and the Buyer', deals with topics such as anticipatory breaches, the right to avoid the contract and damages. Article 71 authorises a party to suspend performance of his obligations if it becomes apparent that the other party will not perform a substantial part of his obligations as a result of a serious deficiency in his ability to perform, or in his creditworthiness, or in his conduct in preparing to perform or in performing the contract. The suspending party is required to give notice to the other and must continue performance if the other party provides adequate assurance of his performance.

Article 72 allows a party to declare the contract avoided if it becomes clear that the other party will commit a fundamental breach of contract. Under article 82, avoidance releases both parties from their obligations under the contract, subject to any damages which may be due. Article 74 states the general rule as to damages which is that the sum is 'equal to the loss, including the loss of profit, suffered by the other party as a consequence of the breach'. Such damages must not exceed the loss that the party in breach foresaw or ought to have foreseen at the time of the contract, taking into account matters that the breaching party was aware of or should have known.

Trade Terms: INCOTERMS

22.12 Sales transactions can be completed quickly because business has developed a vocabulary of trade terms that denote the rights and obligations of buyers and the sellers. These well-recognised abbreviations identify what the seller has to do in terms of arranging transport and insurance, the buyer's obligations to make payment and the place and the time of the risk of transfer. Trade terms not only enable the buyer and seller to quickly exchange information on price, delivery and other significant terms because of their common vocabulary regardless of the actual languages spoken or understood by the parties but is also a shorthand for fixing liability in ways that reputable commercial courts in the world will understand and honour.

'Incoterms' are trade terms published by the International Chamber of Commerce ('ICC'). The most recent version is known as 'Incoterms 2000' issued by the ICC as ICC Pub No 560. Incoterms can be grouped into four main categories. The 'E' terms are to be used when the seller will make available the goods to the buyer at the seller's premises. The 'F' terms are used when the seller must deliver the goods to a carrier appointed by the buyer. The 'C' terms are used when the seller will be required to make shipping arrangements but will not assume the risk of loss or damage to the goods, or of additional costs that may occur after shipment or dispatch. The 'D' terms require the seller to bear all costs and risks needed to bring the goods to the place of destination. The most well known terms are 'CIF', 'C&F', and 'FOB'. These terms are also used in the domestic law in the UK and the US and may have different meanings from that assigned to them in Incoterms 2000. Accordingly, when these terms are used to denote rights and obligations under Incoterms, it is advisable to specify that the Incoterms 2000 definitions will be applicable.

Forms of Doing Business Overseas

Introduction

22.13 A rudimentary form of doing business across borders consists in buying and selling goods. However, business interaction in a complex global economy requires a range of modes of doing business. In response to particular needs, businesspersons together with their professional advisors have developed many ways of conducting business across borders some of which are quite recent. A foreign business intending to do business in a host country will consider a series of factors that would include considerations of tax, political risk, start up costs and the risks flowing from an inadequate intellectual property regime in the host country. Many countries have a tax concept called the 'permanent establishment' which means that a foreign company having a permanent establishment will have all of its host country-derived income taxed at the same rate at which a resident of that host country is taxed. Effective tax planning and the judicious use of tax havens can sometimes provide the decisive competitive advantage to a company that locates a part of its operations overseas.

Of late, the protection of intellectual property has become a pressing concern to foreign companies that are concerned with the protection of their intellectual property and are averse to doing business in countries where intellectual property piracy is widespread.

Agents and Distributors

22.14 A foreign manufacturer will find it necessary to appoint a local agent or distributor in the host country. An agent can accept orders, make sales and promote the interests of the principal. As a practical necessity, anyone seriously wishing to do business in a foreign country must consider an agent who will advertise the principal's products or services, keep customers satisfied especially in the area of consumer products where product warranties are common and alert the principal to new opportunities as well as intellectual property violations in respect of the principal's products or services.

Because the agent will invest funds in establishing and developing the agency, a host country may by law prevent parallel importing of products so that the agent's margin is not undercut in the gray market. Likewise, many host country laws protect the agent from early termination by the principal even for cause. For example, Decree No 295 of the Ministry of Trade and Industry of Indonesia requires exclusive agencies for a minimum term and is implemented in such a way that a dissatisfied principal must pay a large amount of compensation even to an under-performing agent whose agency it wishes to terminate. Consequently, great care must be taken in selecting an agent since the principal must select not only a host country national that possess the requisite influence but also one who will not use that influence against the principal in case of a dispute with the principal.

Branches

22.15 In most countries, branches of foreign businesses are not allowed. The exception to this rule is banks that rarely incorporate in the host country but instead carry on their business through branches. A consequence of operating as a branch is that the company in question is liable for all the obligations of the branch and cannot hide behind the veil of a corporation as a parent company could in the case of a subsidiary.

Management and Technical Assistance Arrangements

22.16 In many fields, the owner of a prospective investment may lack the management, marketing and financial skills that are required to make the investment successful. The hotel industry is full of examples where well-known hotel chains manage hotel properties owned by host country nationals. Less familiar examples are management contracts with respect to airlines and consultancy firms. The central feature of management contracts is the sale of specialised know-how usually bundled with the licensing of a trademark.

Companies

22.17 A standard mode of doing business is to incorporate under the laws of the host countries. The result is that the foreign investor is the sole or majority shareholder of a local company that is subject to local laws. Not infrequently, a foreign investor incorporating a company will form a corporate joint venture with a local shareholder either because it is required by local law or because of strategic reasons. The host country's company law, including laws designed to improve corporate governance and related legislation, such as employment, tax and environmental laws, will apply to the company so formed. With many countries amending their company law to provide rights to minority shareholders and prevent shareholder oppression, a foreign majority shareholder might find that it cannot direct the local company to do whatever it wants should the local shareholders object.

Project Finance/SPVs and BOTs

22.18 In many parts of the world, infrastructure in the form of power plants and airports need to be built, resources such as natural gas fields can be exploited and other large scale projects, such as building an oil pipeline, require the involvement of companies with specialist skills and experience in completing large projects. A feature of these projects is that once completed they are expected to generate stable revenue flows either because an institutional intermediary guarantees purchase through an off-take agreement or a take-or-pay undertaking.

Financing these projects usually takes place through project finance where the necessary funds are not provided through share capital but through loans from banks and bondholders who look primarily to the revenue stream from the completed project for repayment and interest. Project financing involves a complex series of arrangements and in order to undertake the project, the sponsor will normally incorporate a single purpose company, known as a 'special purpose vehicle' ('SPV'). For more than a decade, a variant of project finance arrangements has been the build-operate-and-transfer ('BOT') arrangement where a sponsor builds a capital intensive plant, such as a power plant, operates the plant for a specified period during which the sponsor derives revenues from selling the power usually through an off-take agreement with a government utility, and at the end of the period, transfers the plant. Many Asian countries have enacted BOT legislation to streamline the procurement process and minimise the risk of commercial corruption. See, for example, the Philippine Build-Operate-Transfer Law [Republic Act No 7718].

Because the revenue from the project due to its sponsor is denominated in hard currency, such as US dollars, and the price charged to the eventual consumer is in local currency, there have been catastrophic shortfalls in revenue in some projects, especially those involving independent power producers ('IPPs'), after the recent financial crisis that saw steep devaluations of the local currencies against the US dollars. Several projects have thus been shelved and the IPPs have sued host governments.

Representative Offices

22.19 A representative office is not allowed to buy and sell but can serve as a listening post as well as a trade promotion bureau for the foreign business concerned. Aircraft manufacturers, large equipment manufacturers and construction companies intending to build on infrastructure projects will typically have representative offices. Usually, a representative office will be deemed to be a permanent establishment in the host country for tax purposes.

Franchises

22.20 The ubiquitous golden arches testify to the pervasive reach of franchises around the world. In a franchise, the franchisor will own specialised know-how and intellectual property, such as brand names and trademarks, the use of which will be licensed to the franchisee on condition that the latter work the licensed property subject to the instructions of the franchisor. To prevent unfair conditions being imposed on franchisees who quite often lack a good bargaining position, many states in the US have franchising laws that protect the franchisee from the over-reaching by the franchisor. In most countries of Asia, such protective legislation is missing and as a consequence, the franchisee must carefully scrutinise its potential exposure under the franchise agreement.

The International Institute for the Unification of Private Law ('Unidroit') has produced 'A Guide to International Master Franchise Arrangements' that was cast into a model law and released in 2002. Unidroit has refrained from proposing 'relationship legislation' between the franchisor and the franchisee. Instead, article 6 of the document lists the range of information, including contract details for existing franchisees and the conditions governing the renewal of the franchise, that franchisors must disclose to prospective franchisees.

Contract Manufacturing

22.21 Sellers of popular consumer items, such as branded clothing and athletic wear, have long supply chains and their operations are rarely vertically integrated. These companies contract out the manufacturing of these consumer items to businesses in the developing world. For several years, many brand name owners have been accused of condoning sweat shops and child labour abuses by these contract manufacturers who, it is alleged, pay less than subsistence wages, expose workers to hazardous chemicals and sexually abuse female workers. Responding to these complaints, many owners of popular brand names have undertaken to impose ethical procurement codes. One auditing tool that is used is Social Accountability 8000 which comprises a set of standards meant to eliminate child labour and harassment, provide decent working conditions and a minimum wage.

Foreign Direct Investment

Introduction

22.22 Foreign Direct Investment ('FDI') may be contrasted with foreign portfolio investment. In FDI, the investor purchases an asset in a foreign country or runs a business such as manufacturing, mining or services, usually through a company incorporated in the foreign country. In foreign portfolio investment, on the other hand, the investor's stake is in the form of shares purchased solely for investment purposes. Such shares can be bought and sold on the basis of returns and growth expectations on the local stock exchange. The main difference, therefore, is that in FDI, the foreign investor has a large degree of managerial control. The country in which the foreign investor makes the investment is known as the 'host country' while the country from which the investor originates is known as the 'home country'.

Businesses engage in foreign direct investment for a variety of reasons. Often, it is cheaper to manufacture and sell in a large market than try to export the product to such a market where it will attract high tariffs. Many Asian countries attract FDI because businesses find it cheaper to manufacture in these countries and export the products back to their markets than to try to manufacture in their home countries. Finally, in certain sectors such as telecommunications, there is a huge domestic market that is waiting to be tapped.

Expropriation and Nationalisation

22.23 The treatment of FDI by host governments has generated much controversy in the history of international law. The term 'expropriation' refers to the transfer of title to the foreigner's property whether directly by means of a compelled transfer of title to the property in question or indirectly where the practical effect is the transfer of title even though there is no outright seizure or formal transfer of title. 'Nationalisation' is a subset of expropriation and describes acts of expropriation undertaken on a wide scale and impersonally. Host country governments have asserted a right to expropriate the investments of foreigners with little or no compensation for such takings. Nationalistic governments have argued that the foreign investor takes away precious foreign exchange from the country, or that the investment was made in unfavourable circumstances when the host country was a colony of the home country or that it is undesirable that foreigners should control a local strategic industry. Home country governments, usually capital exporting, have challenged these assertions arguing that an expropriation can be justified only if it is done for a public purpose on a non-discriminatory basis and if the dispossessed foreign investor is entitled to adequate compensation in hard currency. To promote foreign direct investment, donor institutions, such as the World Bank have issued guidelines for foreign investment. The World Bank has also set up the Multilateral Investment Guarantee Agency ('MIGA') (1985), which insures the investment of foreign investors from member countries against the risk of nationalisation in the host countries that are also members of MIGA.

Bilateral Investment Treaties

22.24 For more than three decades, capital exporting countries (the industrialised countries) and capital importing countries (the developing countries) have made FDI the subject of treaties known as bilateral investment treaties. These treaties usually address topics such as the types of foreign investment that would be entitled to protection, the obligation on the country receiving the FDI not to discriminate against the foreign investor and the obligation to allow the foreign investor the right to send out profits in the form of foreign exchange.

US–Singapore Free Trade Agreement

22.25 Singapore has concluded free trade agreements with the European Union, Japan, Australia and China and also recently, a comprehensive agreement, with the US which becomes effective on January 2004. Chapter XV of the recently concluded US–Singapore Free Trade Agreement ('FTA') deals with the subject of foreign investment and significantly expands the rights and privileges of foreign investors found in traditional bilateral investment agreements. For example, article 15.4.1 gives the investor from the home country the same rights as that of the host country national in establishing and operating an enterprise in the host country. Thus, a Singapore national has the same rights as an American national to establish and operate a business in the US and vice versa: the national treatment obligation. In addition, if the host country grants a benefit to an investor of a third country, then the investor from the home country will automatically be entitled to that benefit: the most-favoured nation obligation. The FTA requires the host government to allow the foreign investor to repatriate profits and capital without any capital controls. The host government may nationalise the foreign investment only for a public purpose and in a non-discriminatory manner but compensation will always be payable to the foreign investor. The foreign investor who has a dispute with the host government is given the right to seek final resolution of the dispute in an arbitration.

WTO and FDI

22.26 Two instruments resulting from the Uruguay Round of negotiations that led to the establishment of the WTO are the Agreement on Trade Related Investment Measures ('TRIMS') and the General Agreement on Trade in Services ('GATS'). The purpose of the TRIMS Agreement is to eliminate performance requirements on a foreign investor while GATS will open up a host country's market for foreign businesses providing services such as banking and insurance.

Resolution of FDI Disputes

22.27 One of the major sources of tension between capital importing and exporting countries has been the scope of protection that the home country government has asserted that it has the right to extend on behalf of its aggrieved investor. On the other hand, foreign investors have distrusted the courts of the host country to provide them with the expected standard of fair treatment. To resolve this tension, the World Bank established the International Centre for the Settlement of Investment Disputes ('ICSID') which on the one hand guarantees to the foreign investor the right to seek arbitration against a host country in respect of an investment dispute but at the same time makes this the exclusive remedy for the foreign investor who foregoes what host governments regard as the heavy-handed protection of the home government.

The basis of ICSID jurisdiction is consent to its jurisdiction from both the host government and the foreign investor. This consent to ICSID jurisdiction could be contained in the investment agreement between the host government and the foreign investor, in a bilateral investment treaty, a free trade agreement, such as the FTA (between Singapore and the US) or in the foreign investment law of the host country.

An award made by ICSID is final and subject to review and appeal within the ICSID framework. This means that a national court may not review the correctness of the award. Most capital exporting and capital importing countries are members of the ICSID Convention. As a result, the ICSID award may be enforced in any member country. For example, if X, Y and Z are member countries of ICSID, then if a foreign investor from X wins an award against Y, she can enforce that award in Z against the government of Y.

Singapore has enacted the Arbitration (International Investment Disputes) Act (Cap 11, 1985 Rev Ed) to implement the ICSID Convention.

Dispute Settlement

Introduction

22.28 Cross-border transactions, like domestic transactions, will generate their own share of disputes. However, while disputing parties who are nationals of one state may willingly go to their national courts to have their disputes settled, disputing parties who are not nationals of the same country may lack confidence in the judiciary of each other's country or be advised that litigation in one country affords one party an unfair advantage. Moreover, litigating in national courts means that the parties would have to accommodate their schedules to the court's calendar and this would raise costs since witnesses including expert witnesses would have to be ready at times not of their own choosing and the parties may have to spend much time attending court when they would prefer to be attending to their business.

In recognition of this reality and with a need to promote international trade and commerce, those who have done business across borders have, for hundred of years, agreed that they would bypass the court system and submit their disputes for settlement by means other than the court system. These methods are referred to collectively as alternative dispute resolution. Disputing parties may ask a third party to act as a mediator in a process known as mediation. They may ask for a third party to act as a conciliator in the process known as conciliation. Finally, they may submit a dispute for settlement by arbitration. The arbitration may be conducted by a single arbitrator or by several.

In none of these methods of alternative dispute resolution must the third party be a judge or even a lawyer. This is an advantage sometimes when the nature of the dispute, eg construction disputes, is such that a person from the discipline involved, eg engineer or architect, would be better suited to hear and settle the dispute.

Despite the fact that arbitration is a private proceeding, it cannot succeed unless there is a backup by the courts. The *lex arbitri* or the law of the country where the arbitration is conducted will apply to the procedures adopted by the arbitral tribunal in conducting the arbitration even though that tribunal may apply a substantive law other than the country in question. For example, in a dispute governed by New York law that is arbitrated in Singapore, the tribunal will apply New York law as the *lex causae* but Singapore law will govern how the proceedings are conducted. Often, the party who loses in an arbitration may choose not to comply with the award against him. Sometimes, a party who has agreed to go to arbitration may disregard this agreement and go to court instead. In yet other instances, a party may claim that the arbitrator is biased or corrupt and should be disqualified or that there is some defect in the award that it should not therefore be enforced. In these and other circumstances, courts are required to intervene and support the arbitration process by enforcing the award, restraining parties from ignoring their arbitration agreement or supporting the orders of the arbitral tribunal.

Model Law and New York Convention

22.29 Parties will be more likely to assume the risks of doing business across national borders if they are able to plan for and quantify the risks of the transaction. Being able to settle disputes fairly and with a minimum of costs and expense are factors that will promote international business. Many countries, both industrialised and developing, have adopted two instruments relating to arbitration that allow parties to choose meaningful alternate dispute resolution when planning business transactions. The first of these instruments, the New York Convention of the Recognition and Enforcement of Foreign Arbitral Awards ('New York Convention'), was opened for signature in 1958 and most of the important commercial countries are now parties to this convention. The thrust of this convention is that it obligates the courts of the member countries to recognise and enforce arbitral awards rendered in other member countries except in limited circumstances. The other instrument is the Model Law on International Commercial Arbitration ('Model Law') issued by the United Nations Commission on International Trade Law ('UNCITRAL'). The Model Law must be distinguished from the UNCITRAL arbitration rules which provide in detail how an arbitration will be conducted. As more countries adopt the Model Law, planners of business transactions can anticipate how a country that has adopted the Model Law will respond to the various issues and problems that arise during an arbitration. Moreover, as we shall see, since courts that apply article V of the New York Convention may refuse to enforce an award that has been set aside by the courts of the country in which the arbitration was held, it is important to know the circumstances in which the courts of such countries will set aside the award in order to minimise the risk of non-enforcement of the award. The Model Law states the law on how the arbitration will progress and the role of the courts in the country that has adopted the Model Law but does not state the law that would be applied to the substance of the dispute. For example, a Thai national and a Malaysian national may enter into a business contract governed by New York law with disputes to be settled by arbitration in Singapore. Since Singapore has adopted the Model Law (International Arbitration Act (Cap 143A, 2002 Rev Ed)) the parties to this contract will know how the Singapore courts will relate to the arbitration. However, the arbitral tribunal will apply New York law to the dispute and even if it makes a technical mistake when applying New York law, the parties will know that, because of the Model Law, the Singapore courts will not intervene and correct the legal mistake made by the arbitral tribunal.

The Model Law

22.30 The Model Law applies only to arbitrations that are both international and commercial. Satisfaction of both these criteria will be easy in most cases because the terms 'international' and 'commercial' are defined in broad language. The 'international' requirement is satisfied if the parties to the agreement have their business in different countries or where the place of arbitration or the place where substantial part of the contract is to be performed is in a country that is outside their place of business. The parties may also agree that the subject matter of the arbitration relates to more than one country and this will satisfy the 'international' requirement (article 1(3) of the Model Law). The Model Law requires the term 'commercial' to be given a wide interpretation 'so as to cover matters arising from all relationships of a commercial nature, whether contractual or not' (article 1(1) of the Model Law).

The Model Law applies only to arbitration agreements that are in writing. The agreement to arbitrate may be a part of a larger contract or in a separate agreement. The writing requirement may be satisfied in a variety of ways including telex, telegrams and arguably by email.

Limited Role of the Court

22.31 Arbitral tribunals, unlike courts, are private institutions that have no power to make orders that are enforceable by the state. Courts, on the other hand, while possessing the powers of compulsion can damage the workings of an arbitral tribunal if they interfere and obstruct the work of the tribunal. The Model Law identifies the circumstances in which a court could intervene in the arbitration. Apart from these specific instances, the Model Law does not permit a court to interfere in the arbitration (article 5 of the Model Law). These instances, some of which are given below, are immediately seen to be necessary so that the arbitration can not only progress but also that it satisfies the basic concepts of fairness and justice that are embedded in judicial systems.

The court must stay proceedings brought before it by one party when the other party alleges that both parties had agreed that the subject of the dispute would be referred to arbitration (article 8 of the Model Law). In such an instance, the court will in effect ask the plaintiff to abide by her agreement to settle disputes only through arbitration and ask her to settle the dispute through the agreed arbitration procedure.

The court is allowed to grant an interim order of protection. It takes time before an arbitral tribunal can be set up and one party may, in the meantime, sell the disputed asset or destroy evidence (article 9 of the Model Law). By making an interim order, the court can ensure that one party does not abuse the delays caused by an arbitration procedure to defeat the rights of the other.

The Model Law also provides a role for the court in the appointment and termination of appointment of an arbitrator in order to safeguard the arbitration process. The arbitration agreement may require each party to appoint an arbitrator and the two arbitrators so appointed choose a third arbitrator. If one party fails to appoint an arbitrator or if the arbitrators cannot agree on a third arbitrator, the court is allowed to make the appointment. The arbitration agreement may require that the persons to be appointed have certain qualifications, for example, an engineering qualification, and one party may appoint as an arbitrator someone whom the other party does not think satisfies the engineering qualification requirement. The court can rule on this challenge. The court is also authorised to remove an incapacitated arbitrator, eg when an arbitrator falls seriously ill and cannot do his job.

Unlike a court, an arbitral tribunal cannot compel third parties to give evidence. The Model Law allows a court to assist a tribunal by giving assistance in the taking of evidence.

Conduct of Proceedings

22.32 The Model Law requires the arbitral tribunal to conduct its proceedings in accordance with the basic concepts of justice and fair treatment. Parties must be given equal treatment and must be allowed to submit evidence and be otherwise heard (article 18 of the Model Law). A certain amount of flexibility is allowed in that the tribunal can meet at a venue that is appropriate so that convenience is achieved. The language of the tribunal is that specified in the arbitral agreement but failing such designation, the tribunal can choose the language in which proceedings will be conducted (article 22 of the Model Law).

Making of the Award

22.33 In the introduction, the intimate relationship between national legal systems and the conduct of the parties was noted. Parties to a transaction arrange the components of that transaction according to the rights and obligations provided by the governing law of the transaction. The Model Law requires the arbitral tribunal to respect the choice of law chosen by the parties (article 28 of the Model Law). Thus, if a Malaysian and an Indonesian party chose New York law to govern the transaction, the arbitral tribunal cannot disregard the choice and state that Singapore law would have been be a better choice of law. However, the Model Law does allow the tribunal to take into account the usages of the trade applicable to the transaction to supplement the terms of the contract. Unlike a court which has to make its decision strictly according to law, an arbitral tribunal may make an award that is based on justice and fairness even if this is in variance with the strict letter of the law but only if the parties have empowered the tribunal to make an award based on this standard, known as *ex aequo et bono* (article 28(3) of the Model Law).

Sometimes, during the course of a proceeding, the parties may decide to settle their dispute. If this happens, then the terms of the settlement could be submitted to the arbitral tribunal which would then make the settlement as a part of its award (article 30 of the Model Law). The effect of this is to prevent one party from subsequently repudiating the settlement.

Enforcement of Arbitral Award

22.34 The most significant element of international commercial arbitration is that an award once rendered can be enforced in all but limited circumstances in the many countries that are parties to the 1958 New York Convention on the Recognition and Enforcement of Foreign Arbitral Awards (International Arbitration Act, Second Schedule (Cap 143A, 2002 Rev Ed)). This is in contrast with judicial decisions where the degree of recognition awarded to a foreign court decision will vary from country to country. For instance, in Singapore, decisions of some foreign courts will be recognised and enforced as if they were Singapore court decisions while decisions of other foreign courts will be denied such recognition. The Reciprocal Enforcement of Commonwealth Judgments Act (Cap 264, 1985 Rev Ed) and the Reciprocal Enforcement of Foreign Judgments Act (Cap 265, 2001 Rev Ed) are referred to in paragraph 22.7.

The New York Convention states that as a general rule a court from a country that is a party to the New York Convention must recognise and enforce a foreign arbitral award that relates to a commercial matter except in very limited circumstances. The Model Law mirrors these principles to a large extent. Two sets of circumstances provide the basis for denying enforcement of a foreign arbitral award. In the first set of circumstances, the party resisting enforcement satisfies the court that there was a flaw that fatally undermined the very arbitration process itself. None of these objections go to the correctness of the decision. In the second set of circumstances, the court finds that public policy reasons dictate that enforcement should be denied. Since article V states that the court before which enforcement is sought *may*, instead of *shall*, decline enforcement, in the circumstances specified in article V, some American decisions hold that a court has the discretion to enforce the award despite the fact that a condition for non-enforcement listed in article V has been satisfied; see *Chromalloy Aeroservices v Arab Republic of Egypt* (1996). The corresponding French text of article V would not appear to support such an interpretation giving the enforcing court the discretion to enforce an award regardless of the satisfaction of a criterion for non-enforcement of such award specified in article V.

A party resisting the enforcement of the award is allowed to show that the arbitration agreement upon which the whole arbitration was based was itself not valid. Since the arbitration springs from a freely negotiated agreement to arbitrate, a showing that the agreement was invalid destroys the validity of the arbitration that followed. If the party resisting arbitration can show that she was not served notice of arbitration or was not able to present her case to the arbitral tribunal, then there would be a showing of such basic unfairness that would authorise a court to refuse to enforce the award. An arbitral award that goes beyond the scope of the dispute subject to arbitration will not be enforced because the entire basis of arbitration is that it is consensual and the jurisdiction of the arbitral tribunal is restricted to the four corners of the arbitrable dispute. To guard against a court holding that the award exceeds the scope of the arbitration mandate, it is usual for an arbitration agreement to use language such as 'arising out of or in connection with' the subject matter of the contract. The enforcing court may also decline to enforce an arbitral award where the composition of the tribunal or the arbitral procedure was not in accordance with the arbitration agreement. This ground is an illustration of the larger principle that the very basis of arbitration is the agreement among the parties, and if the arbitral tribunal which, for example, is supposed to be composed of engineers is instead composed of architects who are not engineers, that consensus is destroyed and the tribunal lacks authority to make a binding award. Likewise, if a procedure has been agreed upon and the tribunal follows another procedure, either party should be entitled to complain and resist enforcement of the award. Finally, where the award has been suspended or set aside by a court of the country where the award was made or the court of the country the law of which was the governing law of the contract, the court before which enforcement is sought can refuse to enforce that award. The policy behind this exception is that where a court that was intimately connected with the proceeding or the governing law has set aside or suspended the award, it is unsafe for the enforcing court to disregard these factors and enforce the award; see article V(1) of the New York Convention.

The above are circumstances where the party resisting enforcement should justifiably be aggrieved by the award. The Model Law and the New York Convention also authorise the enforcing court to decline enforcement where enforcing an award would be in conflict with important interests of the country in question; see article V(2) of the New York Convention. Accordingly, if the subject matter of the dispute is not capable of settlement by arbitration under the law of the state in which enforcement is sought, the court can refuse enforcement. For example, a country may have a policy that claims for breach of contract caused by sexual harassment should be only litigated in the courts. However, if standard form contracts in a particular industry, eg the securities industry, provide that all disputes shall be resolved by arbitration and this also includes sexual harassment claims, a country that has a strong policy of deterring sexual harassment might want exclusive judicial supervision of this policy and would not tolerate such issues being decided by an arbitral tribunal. A court is also allowed to refuse enforcement where recognition or enforcement of the award would be contrary to the public policy of the country in which enforcement is sought. In the US, it is not uncommon for large amounts of punitive damages to be awarded for a breach of contract and an arbitral tribunal may award punitive damages; see *Mastrobuono v Sherson Lehman Hutton* (1995). On the other hand, a Commonwealth court that takes a conservative view of the proper scope of the damages remedy would find the award of punitive damages for the breach of contract to be a violation of a fundamental tenet of its contract law which is that damages must be compensatory and not punitive, or such court may take the view that only courts and not arbitral panels must be allowed to award punitive damages (and cf above, paragraphs 15.15–15.16). Accordingly, such a court asked to enforce an award of punitive damages rendered in the US would probably refuse to enforce the award on the ground that it violates the public policy of that enforcing court.

Preventive Tools: Due Diligence and Opinions of Counsel

22.35 The interaction of the agreement of the parties with different national laws and applicable rules of public international law on issues such as double taxation, money laundering, intellectual property rights and commercial bribery requires the input of professionals such as accountants, lawyers and bankers from different countries while structuring the transaction. Often, international contracts list a set of requirements known as 'conditions precedent' which must be satisfied before the contract becomes operational. Reflecting the complexity of international business transactions that cut across several legal systems, two well-known conditions precedent are the satisfactory completion of a due diligence process as well as opinions of foreign and local counsel.

The due diligence process involves a detailed checklist relating to various matters including obtaining the necessary governmental approvals and permits for the venture, the establishment of a company, sometimes known as a 'Special Purpose Vehicle' or 'SPV' through which the project will be performed and the approval of loans and other types of funding for the project. To ensure that the proposed transaction complies with all applicable laws, opinions of counsel from major international law firms as well as domestic law firms confirming that the proposed transaction complies with the applicable laws will be necessary before the transaction can become operative.

Conclusion

22.36 In the foregoing sections, an attempt was made to identify some of the areas of international business that are of importance to Asia and to consider how legal rules have shaped and have been shaped by the policies and values of interested participants in these areas. A focus on these areas should, however, not ignore the larger context of globalisation that includes supply chains that run halfway across the globe and the concerns about sweat-shop labour alleged to constitute some of the links in the chain, the reshaping of societies and their cultures through the Internet, mass media and entertainment products, the threats to the environment including global warming caused by polluting industry, the steady destruction of rainforests and animal habitats, and massive rural migration to cities and the ease with which deadly viruses with pandemic potential, such as AIDS and SARS, cross national boundaries. In all of these critical areas, law can only play a limited facilitative role and many areas that require urgent legal regulation will continue to be ignored, for even in an obviously interdependent world, the scope of legal regulation will necessarily be limited until most of the powerful that shape law and policy send not to ask for whom the bell tolls.

Index

A

- Acceptance
  - bilateral contract *2.20*
  - Convention on the International Sale of Goods (CISG), under *22.11*
  - definition *2.20*
  - 'no-fault' rule *2.23*
  - offer, of *2.2*
    - communication of *2.5, 2.22–2.23*
    - conduct, by *2.22, 2.29*
    - electronic mail, by, *see* electronic mail *2.23, 2.28., 2.49*
    - final and unqualified *2.4, 2.21*
    - ignorance, and *2.32–2.34*
    - instantaneous *2.23, 2.51*
    - mistake *11.28, 11.42*
    - performance, through *2.5, 2.14*
    - postal acceptance rule *2-24–2.28, 2.51*
    - silence, by *2.29–2.31*
  - unilateral contract *2.20*
- Accord and satisfaction
  - definition *9.86*
  - discharge of contract *9.69, 9.87*
- Advertisement
  - offer, whether an, *see* offer
- Agency
  - contract *17.3*
  - creation of *17.5*
    - consent required *17.6*
    - contract not required *17.6*
  - definition *17.3*
  - distributorship, distinguished *17.4*
  - estoppel, by *17.14*
  - frustration of contract, and *10.11*
  - indirect misrepresentation *12.25*
  - irrevocable, that is *17.52*
  - legal effects *17.30*
  - nature of *17.2, 17.3*
  - necessity, of *17.18*
    - requirements *17.19*
    - pre-existing agency *17.18*
  - privity of contract, *see* privity of contract
  - relationship *17.3*
  - rules of attribution *18.26*
  - termination *17.49*
    - bankruptcy *17.51*
    - contract, by *17.50*
    - death *17.51*
    - insanity *17.51*
    - statute *17.51*
  - undue influence, *see* undue influence
- Agent
  - actual authority *9.63, 17.7, 17.15, 18.30*
    - express *17.8*
    - implied *17.9*
  - apparent authority *17.5, 17.13, 17.15, 17.33, 18.30*
    - conduct, created by *17.09, 17.13, 18.30*
    - elements *17.14–17.17*
    - principal's representations *17.13–17.16*
  - appointment, *see also* director *17.8, 17.9*
  - authority to act on behalf of company *18.26*
  - bribery *17.40*
  - commission *17.40*
  - company, acting as *18.19*
  - definition *17.1*
  - director as *17.9, 18.26, 18.29*
    - appointment *18.30*
    - ostensible authority *17.13, 18.30*
    - powers *18.30*
  - duties *17.37*
    - act within authority, to *17.3, 17.37, 17.48*
    - conflict of interests *17.39*
    - delegation *17.41*
    - due care and skill *17.37*
    - fiduciary duty *17.38*
    - reasonable care and diligence *17.37*
    - secret profit-making *17.40*
  - international trade, in *22.14*
  - liability *17.3, 17.44*
    - sub-agent's acts *17.42*
    - undisclosed principal *17.35*
  - misrepresentation to *12.23, 12.25, 12.29*
  - necessary authority, *see* agency
  - ostensible authority *9.63, 17.5, 17.13, 17.33*
  - partner, as *18.53*
  - principal
    - agent, relationship with *17.3, 17.36*
    - disclosed *17.31, 17.32*
    - liability for agent's acts *17.7, 17.13, 17.15, 17.20, 17.32, 17.33*
    - rights *17.32, 17.34, 17.35*
    - sub-agent, relationship with *17.42*
    - third party, relationship with *17.3, 17.13, 17.15, 17.31*
    - undisclosed *17.31, 17.34*
  - promoter as *17.23, 17.47*
  - ratification *17.20*
    - legal effects *17.26*
    - pre-incorporation contracts *7.34, 17.23, 17.47*
    - reasonable time, within *17.25, 17.28*

relation-back doctrine *17.26, 17.27*
requirements *17.22 ff*
representations *18.30*
rights
indemnity *17.3, 17.44*
lien *17.45*
reimbursement *17.44*
remuneration *17.43*
sub-agent *17.41*
privity of contract *17.42*
third party
agent's liability *17.35, 17.46*
bills of exchange *17.47*
exception to rule *17.34, 17.47*
principal's liability *17.32–17.35*
rights *17.35*
Agreement
bargain, distinguished *3.69*
contract, distinguished *2.37*
discharge of contract by *9.68*
accord and satisfaction *9.69, 9.87*
existing contract *9.69, 9.70*
mutual release *9.69, 9.73, 9.78, 9.83*
subsequent agreement *9.69, 9.72, 9.78, 9.88*
unilateral release (release under seal) *9.69, 9.72*
variation *9.78*
waiver *9.58, 9.66*
non-disclosure *21.65*
solus *14.86*
Alternative dispute resolution *1.155, 21.95*
advantages *1.178–1.180*
arbitration *1.157, 1.170, 1.183, 22.28*
Contract (Rights of Third Parties) Act 2001 *8.33*
illegal contract *14.34, 14.35*
New York Convention on the Recognition and Enforcement of Foreign Arbitral Awards 1958 *1.158, 1.188, 22.29, 22.34*
Singapore International Arbitration Centre *1.159, 1.184, 1.185–1.189*
UNCITRAL Model Law on International Commercial Arbitration *1.158, 1.186, 22.29, 22.30, 22.31, 22.34*
award *22.33*
court intervention *22.31*
proceedings *22.32*
US–Singapore Free Trade Agreement *22.25*
Committee on Alternative Dispute resolution *1.160*
conciliation *22.28*
foreign arbitral awards
when not enforced *22.34*
International Centre for the Settlement of Investment Disputes *22.27*
jurisdiction *22.27*
international contracts
lex arbitri 22.28
mediation *1.160–1.163, 1.168–1.169, 1.181–1.182, 22.28*
Singapore Mediation Centre *1.159, 1.179, 1.184, 1.190–1.196*
mediation-arbitration *1.171, 1.174–1.175*
mini-trial *1.171, 1.172–1.173*
negotiation *1.165–1.167*
Arbitration, *see* alternative dispute resolution
Articles of association, *see also* company
alteration *18.46, 18.48*
powers of director *18.26, 18.27, 18.28*
relationship between shareholders *18.45, 18.46*
Assessment of damages, *see also* damages, expectation loss *and* reliance loss
bad bargain *15.51*
consequential loss *15.45*
defamation *20.92*
expectation interest *15.21*
expectation loss *15.27, 15.28, 15.33, 15.36, 15.41, 15.50, 15.53*
cost of cure *15.55, 15.59*
diminution of value *15.54*
incidental loss *15.27, 15.32*
indemnity loss *15.27, 15.32, 15.48*
limitations to recovery *15.68 ff*
loss of amenity *15.45*
loss of profits *15.28, 15.36, 15.51, 15.73*
non-pecuniary loss *15.35, 15.60*
commercial vs consumer contracts *15.64 ff*
definition *15.60*
limitations to recovery *15.60*
when recovery allowed *15.62*
pecuniary loss *15.35, 20.34, 20.54*
performance loss *15.45*
reliance interest *15.21*
reliance loss *9.15, 15.27, 15.30, 15.36, 15.42, 15.48, 16.59, 16.69*
restitutionary loss *15.45*
time at which damages are quantified *15.24*
unliquidated damages *15.47*

B

Bailment
privity of contract, and, *see* privity of contract
Bank
branches in foreign entity *22.15*
misrepresentation to guarantor *12.25*
Bilateral contract *2.5, 2.20*
unilateral contract, distinguished *2.5*
Bill of exchange
liability
agent-third party *17.47*
privity of contract *2.31*
Bill of lading
privity of contract *8.16*

Bodies corporate, *see also* companies and incorporate entities *18.7*
Breach
- confidence, of, *see also* confidence, law of *21.66*
- contract, of, *see* breach of contract
- duty of care, in contract, *see* duty of care
- duty of care, in negligence, *see* negligence

Breach of contract *2.6, 2.11, 9.1, 9.7, 9.25, 13.1*
- actual *9.26, 9.41*
  - affirmation *9.42, 9.61*
- anticipatory *9.27, 9.44, 15.24, 20.30*
  - affirmation *9.47, 9.62*
- condition, breach of *5.4, 5.10, 5.22, 9.7, 9.12, 9.25, 9.29, 9.41, 15.9, 16.13*
  - promissory *9.28*
- Convention on the International Sale of Goods, under *22.11*
- damages, *see* damages and assessment of damages
- *de minimis* rule *9.3–9.5, 9.23, 16.13*
- election to affirm or discharge contract, *see also* repudiation *9.48, 9.49*
- innominate term, breach of *5.4 5.19, 5.22, 9.6, 9.7, 9.12, 9.25, 9.29, 9.36, 15.9, 16.13*
- interdependent obligations *9.30–9.31*
- legal effects *9.49*
- methods *9.25*
- misrepresentation *12.4*
- privity of contract, *see* privity of contract
- remedy, *see* remedies
- repudiation
  - anticipatory breach *9.27, 9.44, 15.24*
  - conduct, by *9.35, 9.40*
  - omission, by *9.37*
  - oral or written *9.33–9.34*
- restitutionary remedies *16.54 ff*
- warranty, breach of *5.4, 5.19, 5.22, 9.6, 9.12, 9.29*

Business name, *see* company name

C

Carriage of goods
- privity of contract *8.31*

Causation
- breach of duty of care in negligence
  - 'but for' test *19.46*
- damages, in breach of contract *15.26*
  - *novus actus interveniens* *15.88*
- damages, in negligence, *see also* negligence *15.26*
  - computer viruses, spread of *19.69*
  - *novus actus interveniens* *19.47*
- economic duress, *see* economic duress
- tort, in inducing breach of contract *20.10*
- undue influence, *see* undue influence

Circularity of actions *8.17*
Civil law *1.83 ff*
Civil law (legal tradition) *1.78*
- balance of probabilities *1.86*
- common law, distinguished *1.80*
- criminal law, distinguished *1.83–1.86*

Collateral contract *2.8, 2.9, 2.38*
- exception clause *6.29*
- parol evidence rule *5.9, 6.30*
- privity of contract, *see* privity of contract
- recovery independent of illegal contract *14.63*
- representation *5.9, 12.37*

Common law
- equity, and *1.75*
- legislation, and *1.77*

Common law (legal tradition)
- civil law, distinguished *1.80*
- development of *1.58*

Company, *see also* corporations and incorporate businesses
- agent, *see* agent
- articles of association, *see also* articles of association *7.35, 18.15, 18.16, 18.25*
- categories *18.9*
- classification *18.13*
- constructive notice, doctrine of *18.15*
  - agency *18.31*
  - *Turquand's* case (indoor management rule) *18.32*
- corporate veil, *see* corporate veil
- debentures, *see* debentures
- definition *18.7*
- directors, *see* directors
- incorporation, *see* incorporation
- limited, *see also* limited company *18.9*
  - by guarantee *18.10, 18.12*
  - by shares *18.10, 18.11*
- management *18.24 ff*
- managing director, *see* managing director
- meetings, *see* meetings of company
- members, *see* members of company
- memorandum of association *7.35, 18.15*
- name *18.4*
- nationality *22.6*
- partnership, *see* partnership
- *persona ficta* *18.18 ff*
  - corporate veil, lifting of *18.21*
  - legal personality *18.18*
- private *18.13*
- public *18.13, 18.35*
- registration *18.4*
- rules of attribution *18.24*
  - general *18.26*
  - primary *18.25, 18.26*
- shareholders, *see* shareholders and members of company
- structures *18.1, 18.2*
- subsidiaries *18.23*
- trade mark infringement *18.22*
- trade secrets *14.81, 21.69*
- *ultra vires* doctrine *18.15*
  - member's right to restrain *18.15*
- unlimited *18.9*
- winding up *18.2, 18.20*
  - percentage of votes required *18.25*

Company name *18.4*
Company officer, *see also* director, managing director, agent
  breach of duty *18.15, 19.20*
Condition of contract
  breach, *see* breach of contract
  consideration, distinguished *3.7*
  secondary usage of term *5.20*
  warranty, distinguished, *see* terms of contract
Confidence, law of *21.65 ff*
  breach of confidence *21.66*
    defences *21.68*
    remedy *21.67*
  duty of fidelity *21.69*
  employment contract *21.69*
  restraint of trade *21.69*
Consideration
  adequate *3.20*
  agent *8.9*
  condition, distinguished *3.7*
  definition *3.1, 3.3, 3.4*
  economic duress, and *3.21, 3.42, 3.43, 13.20, 13.21–13.22*
  executed *3.10, 3.11, 3.12, 3.16*
  executory *3.4, 3.11, 16.61, 16.62*
  intention to create legal relations *3.43, 3.68, 4.15*
  joint promisee doctrine *3.18, 8.36*
  mutual release from contract *9.69, 9.73*
  nature *3.6, 3.14*
  past *3.9, 3.13–3.14, 3.24*
    executed consideration, distinguished *3.10, 3.12*
  privity of contract, *see* privity of contract
  promisee, move from *3.17*
  promisor, requested by *3.6*
  promissory estoppel, *see also* promissory estoppel *3.47 ff*
  promissory note *3.25*
  release under seal *3.2, 9.72*
  severance of illegal contract *14.95*
  sufficient *3.20 ff*
    compromise *3.28*
    conduct exceeding existing legal/contractual duty *3.31, 3.32, 3.35*
    existing contractual duty owed to promisor *3.34 ff*
    existing contractual duty owed to third party *3.33*
    existing public/legal duty *3.30 ff*
    forbearance *3.28, 3.29*
    intangibles *3.23*
    moral obligation *3.24 ff*
    partial payment of debt *3.44 ff*
    practical/factual benefit, enjoyed *3.27, 3.36 ff, 3.46, 3.70, 4.15, 9.80*
  total failure of *16.54–16.73*
  value, must be of *3.6, 3.8, 3.22*
  variation of contract *9.79*
  waiver *9.83*
Consortium *18.2*
Constitution, *see* articles of association *and* memorandum of association
Contract
  acceptance, *see* acceptance
  agency, *see* agency
  agreement, distinguished *2.37*
  bilateral *2.5*
  breach of, *see also* breach of contract *2.6 2.11, 13.1*
  certain and complete terms, *see* terms of contract
  collateral , *see* collateral contract
  consideration, *see* consideration
  corporations, *see* corporations
  discharge, *see* discharge of contract
  drunkard, *see* drunkard
  Electronic Transactions Act, under *2.48–2.53*
  exclusion clause, *see* exception clauses
  formation of
    United Nations Convention on the International Sale of Goods *22.11*
  freedom of *6.2, 14.69*
  gaming and wagering, *see* illegal contract
  good faith, negotiate in *2.38*
  illegal, *see* illegal contract
  intention, *see* intention to create legal relations
  mental patient, *see* mental patient
  minor, *see* minor
  misrepresentation, *see* misrepresentation
  mistake, *see* mistake
  multilateral, *see* multilateral contract
  offer, *see* offer
  oral *5.6, 5.9, 5.16*
  pre-contractual statements *5.10, 5.11, 12.36*
  pre-incorporation *7.34, 7.47, 16.73, 17.23*
  privity of, *see* privity of contract
  quasi-, *see also* unjust enrichment, law of *and* restitution *9.20*
  'shrinkwrap' licence *2.41*
  standard form *6.3, 6.19, 22.34*
  terms, *see* terms of contract
  ultra vires *7.35*
  unilateral *2.5, 2.18, 2.20, 2.33*
  vitiation of
    economic duress, *see* economic duress
    incapacity, *see* incapacity
    mistake, *see* mistake
    unconscionability, *see* unconscionability
    undue influence, *see* undue influence
Constitution, *see* articles of association *and* memorandum of association
Contributory negligence *15.89, 19.59, 19.72*
Co-operative societies *18.1*
Copyright *21.1, 21.3, 21.5*

assignment *21.13*
authors' works *21.7*
caching *21.35*
Copyright Act 1987 *21.3 ff*
definition *21.5*
exclusive rights *21.14*
entrepreneurial rights *21.7*
fair dealing *21.25*
criticism or review *21.26*
'reasonable portion' *21.25*
reporting of current events *21.26*
research or private study *21.25*
hyperlinks *21.36, 21.37*
infringement *21.15*
border enforcement measures *21.23*
defences *21.24*
primary *21.15, 21.18*
remedy, civil *21.22*
secondary *21.20*
test *21.16, 21.19*
licence *21.13*
material form, reduced to *21.10*
moral rights *21.28*
neighbouring rights *21.7, 21.14, 21.18, 21.20*
network service providers *21.31*
originality *21.9*
ownership *21.12*
employment, in the course of *21.12*
performers' rights *21.27*
principles *21.6*
protection
Berne Convention *21.6, 21.8, 21.28*
duration *21.6, 21.11*
prerequisites *21.7 ff*
qualified person *21.8*
rental rights *21.14*
rights management information *21.30*
subject matter other than works *21.7*
Corporate veil
hiding behind *18.21 ff, 22.15*
lifting of *18.23*
Corporations, *see also* company
articles of association, *see also* articles of association *and* company *7.35*
capacity to contract *7.33*
Companies Act, section 41, under *7.34, 17.23*
objects clause, outside *7.35*
pre-incorporation *7.34*
representative, by *7.34, 7.37, 7.38*
contract, enforcement of
ultra vires 7.35, 7.37
law *1.152*
memorandum of association *7.35*
name *18.4*
objects clause *7.35–7.36*
voidable contract
ratification *7.34*
Counter-offer *2.15, 2.16, 2.21*
Convention on the International Sale of Goods, under *22.11*
request for information, distinguished *2.16*
standard forms *2.43–2.47*
Criminal law
beyond reasonable doubt *1.86*
civil law, distinguished *1.83–1.86*
Customary international law *22.3, 22.4*

D

Damages, *see also* assessment of damages, mitigation of damage, remedies *and* reliance loss
accelerated payment clause *15.96*
alternative performance *15.101*
breach of contract *5.4, 9.5, 9.7, 9.41, 9.45, 9.46, 15.17*
in tort, distinguished *15.18, 15.19, 15.20*
causation *15.26*
duty of care, advisors *15.26, 15.81*
novus actus interveniens 15.88
common law action for fixed sum, distinguished *16.4*
compensatory advantage *15.84*
indirect *15.85*
contract vs tort *15.17*
contributory negligence *15.89*
copyright infringement *21.22*
definition *15.13*
director's breach of duty *18.40, 18.41*
discounts *15.100*
earnest money *15.97*
deposit, distinguished *15.97*
expectation loss, *see* assessment of damages *and* expectation loss
forfeiture *15.97*
'equitable relief from forfeiture doctrine' *15.98, 15.106*
geographical indications
infringement *21.99*
guarantee *15.99*
illegal contract *14.52*
interest on *15.6*
liquidated *15.14, 15.27, 15.92, 16.25*
penalty, distinguished *15.94*
mental distress, *see* assessment of damages, non-pecuniary loss
misrepresentation *12.2, 12.32, 12.45*
mitigation *9.63, 9.65, 15.24, 15.76, 16.60, 20.72*
causation, and *15.81*
principles *15.76*
reasonable actions towards *15.80*
when not applicable *15.83*
nominal *15.14, 16.89*
privity of contract, *see* privity of contract
obligations, breach of
absolute *15.23*
relative *15.23*
strict *15.23*

patent infringement *21.67*
penalty *15.93*
pre-contractual loss *15.49*
privity of contract, *see* privity of contract
punitive *15.15, 15.16, 20.93, 22.34*
reliance loss, *see* assessment of damages *and* reliance loss
remoteness, in contract *15.68, 16.60*
actual knowledge *15.69, 15.70, 15.71*
damages due to special circumstances *15.68–15.70, 16.8*
damages flowing naturally from breach *15.68*
Hadley v Baxendale rule *15.68*
imputed knowledge *15.69, 15.71*
probability of occurrence *15.71*
ordinary course of things *15.69*
remoteness, in tort
probability of occurrence *15.71*
special *16.8*
substantial *15.14*
tort, in *15.9, 15.18*
trade mark infringement *21.84*
types *15.14*
unliquidated *15.14*
assessment of *15.47 ff*
withholding clause *15.102*
penalty, and *15.103*

Death
termination of agency *17.51*
termination of offer *2.19*

Debentures *18.19*

Deeds *3.2*

Defences
copyright infringement *21.24*
defamation *20.73 ff*
justification, in tort *20.21*
negligence *19.55 ff*
patent infringement *21.61*
registered design infringement *21.45*
trade mark infringement *21.79, 21.80 ff*

De minimis rule *9.3–9.5, 9.23, 9.63*

Design, *see* industrial design

Director
agent, as, *see also* agent *18.26, 18.29*
construction notice, doctrine of, *see* company
appointment *18.25, 18.33*
delegation of functions *18.26*
duties *18.36 ff*
breach of *18.40, 18.41, 18.43*
disclose, to *18.41*
enforcement of *18.43*
equitable (act *bona fide*) *18.40*
use power for proper purpose *18.40*
fiduciary *18.39, 18.41*
conflict of interest *18.41*
no-profit rule *18.41*
skill, care and diligence *18.37, 18.42*
executive *18.34*
managing, *see* managing director
non-executive *18.35*
powers *18.25, 18.40, 18.43*
resolutions, *see* meetings of company
service contract *18.34*
serving on board of more than one company *18.41*

Discharge of contract
agreement, by, *see also* agreement *9.1, 9.68 ff*
quantum meruit, claim for *16.105–16.106*
breach, due to, *see* breach of contract
frustration, *see also* frustration *9.1, 9.38, 10.1, 17.50*
quantum meruit, claim for *16.109*
limitation to right of discharge
affirmation of contract *9.57–9.65*
estoppel *9.66*
exclusion of right in contract *9.55–9.56*
waiver *9.58, 9.66, 9.83*
performance, *see also* performance of contract *9.1, 9.2, 9.67, 17.50*
repudiation *9.33, 9.40*
conduct, by *9.35*
express *9.33*
omission, by *9.37*

Disclosure of facts
misrepresentation *12.16, 12.17*

Dissolution
partnership, *see* partnership
sole proprietorship, *see* sole proprietorship

Drunkard
contract, enforcement of *7.30–7.32*
valid contract
'necessary goods' *7.32*
voidable contract *7.30*
ratification *7.31*

Duress, *see* economic duress

Duty
care, of, *see* duty of care
director, *see* director
equitable (act *bona fide*)
director *18.40*
fidelity, of *21.69*
fiduciary
director *18.39, 18.41*
majority shareholders *18.47*

Duty of care
agent *17.37*
breach, *see* breach
contract, in *15.23, 15.26, 15.90, 18.42, 19.2*
negligence, in *19.2, 19.4 ff*
breach, *see* negligence
composite test *19.14, 19.15*
computer viruses, spread of, *see also* negligence *19.62, 19.63*
'fair, just and reasonable' *19.8, 19.12, 19.17, 19.25, 19.35, 19.63*

foreseeability *19.7, 19.8, 19.9, 19.15, 19.18, 19.21*
proximity, interchangeable with *19.21, 19.33*
negligent misstatement, *see* negligent misstatement
neighbour principle *19.6, 19.21, 19.33*
nervous shock *19.17*
non-related secondary victim *19.17*
primary victim *19.17*
psychiatric harm, resulting in *19.17*
related secondary victim *19.17*
proximity *19.7, 19.8, 19.15, 19.21, 19.22, 19.27, 19.63, 19.73*
confusion over *19.23*
public policy *19.11 ff, 19.18, 19.21, 19.26, 19.33*
legal policy, cf *19.13, 19.26*
principle, and *19.13, 19.33*
pure foreseeability test *19.9, 19.10*
relational, spatial, perceptional elements *19.17*
standard of care, distinguished *19.44*
three-part test *19.8, 19.12, 19.18, 19.20, 19.23, 19.30, 19.35*
two-stage test, relationship with *19.21, 19.27, 19.30, 19.33, 19.34*
two-stage process *19.28, 19.29*
two-stage test *19.12, 19.15–19.19, 19.27, 19.30, 19.31*
criticism of *19.19*
two-stage process, distinguished *19.28*
negligence in bailment *8.20*
negligent misrepresentation *12.30, 12.34*
negligent misstatement *12.34*

E

Economic duress *13.4 ff, 13.54, 13.56, 20.30*
causation *13.16*
consideration, and *3.21, 3.42, 13.20, 13.21–13.22*
illegitimate pressure theory *13.7–13.8, 13.10*
legal effect *13.17, 14.58*
'overborne will theory' *13.5–13.6, 13.9, 13.12*
pressure, commercial vs illegitimate *13,11, 13.14, 13.20*
principles *13.11 ff*
unconscionablility, and *13.20, 13.25*
Economic loss
physical injury or damage recoverability *19.41*
Electronic mail
acceptance by *2.23, 2.28, 2.49*
Employment contract
confidentiality clause *21.65, 21.69*
breach of *16.92*
frustration *10.11*
implied terms in *5.27*
privity of contract *8.31*
restraint of trade *14.80*
Enforcement
contract, of
consideration *3.1, 3.2*
corporations, *see* corporations
director as agent *18.26, 18.29 ff*
drunkard, *see* drunkard
intentions to create legal relations chapter 4
mental patient, *see* mental patient
minor, *see* minor
non-registration of business *18.5*
third parties, by, *see* privity of contract
foreign arbitral award *22.34*
letter of comfort, of *4.12 ff*
Equitable (*bona fide*) duty
director *18.40*
Equity
common law, and *1.75*
development of *1.74*
remedies under *1.76*
Estoppel
agency by *17.14*
agent's ostensible duty *18.30*
promissory, *see also* promissory estoppel *3.47 ff*
unjust enrichment, law of *16.113*
Exception clauses
business transactions *6.3, 6.19*
collateral contract *6.29*
construction *6.21*
contra preferentum rule *6.21, 6.22–6.23, 6.24*
fundamental breach, exclusion of *6.27*
inconsistent terms *6.29*
negligence, liability in contract *6.24–6.26, 6.40*
negligence, liability in tort *6.33, 6.34, 6.40*
consumer protection, and *6.61*
consumer transactions *6.3, 6.8, 6.19, 6.38, 6.47*
'dealing as consumer' *6.38, 6.47, 6.49*
definition *6.1*
discharge of contract *9.56*
electronic contracts *6.16, 6.56, 6.57*
incorporation in contract *6.8ff*
methods of incorporation *6.9*
notice, by *6.12*
sufficient *6.13*
time of notice *6.14, 6.15*
previous dealings between parties, by *6.17*
signature, by *6.10*
exception to rule *6.11*
trade custom, by *6.18*

whether document is binding *6.9*
indemnity clause *6.1*
limitation of liability clause *6.1*
distinguished *6.5, 12.52, 12.53*
misrepresentation *6.11, 12.50*
negligence
computer viruses, spread of *19.64, 19.66*
offer and acceptance *2.39*
performance of contract *6.44, 6.45*
privity of contract, *see* privity of contract
reasonableness test *6.11, 6.32, 6.35*
requirement to be legally effective *6.7*
sale of goods *6.36, 6.39, 6.47*
standard form contracts *6.3, 6.11, 6.19, 6.44*
unsigned document, and *6.20*
Unfair Contract Terms Act 1994 *6.6, 6.31 ff, 8.32, 12.51*
reasonableness test, under *6.43, 6.46, 6.47, 6.48, 6.51 ff*
when applicable *6.36*
when not applicable *6.37*
Expectation loss, *see also* assessment of damages *15.27 ff*
reliance loss, distinguished *15.36*
Express terms, *see* terms of contract

F

Fiduciary duty
agent *17.38*
breach of
restitution *16.52, 16.92*
director *18.39, 18.41*
shareholder *18.47*
Forebearance *3.28*
Foreign judgment
enforcement of *22.3, 22.7*
Foreseeability
frustration, *see* frustration
Fraudulent misrepresentation *11.42, 11.43, 12.2, 12.18, 12.21, 12.27, 14.60*
agent *12.29*
burden of proof *12.33*
damages *12.27, 19.49*
definition *12.27*
recovery independent of illegal contract *14.60*
rescission *12.39, 12.43*
Frustration
agency contract *10.11*
building contracts *10.10*
classification
illegality *10.15*
impossibility *10.10*
radical change *10.16*
consideration, and *10.29*
death *10.11*
definition *10.4*
delay in performance *10.17*
destruction of subject matter *10.10*
discharge of contract *11.14*
elements
foreseeability *10.8, 10.28*
foresight *10.8, 10.28*
parties not at fault *10.6*
radically different performance *10.5*
time of frustration *10.7, 10.17*
employment contract *10.11*
failure of source of goods *10.13*
force majeure 9.67, 10.24, 20.16
impracticability *10.18*
lease of land *10.19*
legal effect *10.2, 10.29*
mistake, distinguished *10.1, 11.14*
negligence, and *10.21*
partial *10.23*
performance impossible, method of *10.14*
performance of some contracts *10.22*
personal incapacity *10.11*
purpose of contract, failure of *10.16*
'radically different', principle *10.4, 10.5, 10.14, 10.16*
remedy *10.30*
Frustrated Contracts Act 1985 *10.30*
restitution *16.107*
sale of goods *10.10*
sale of land *10.19*
self-induced *10.6, 10.20*
supervening event *10.5, 10.22*
supervening illegality *10.15, 10.24*
unavailability of subject matter *10.12*

G

Geographical indications
definition *21.97*
Geographical Indications Act 1998 *21.97*
infringement
remedy *21.99*
test *21.98*
protection
duration *21.98*
registration *21.98*
trade marks, and *21.98*
Goods
minor, supplied to, *see* minor
Guarantee
company limited by *18.12*
consideration, as *15.99*
damages, as *15.99*
misrepresentation *12.25*
mistake, *see* mistake
undue influence *13.31, 15.99*

I

Illegal contract
common law, at *14.3, 14.4, 14.28 ff, 14.93*
contract to commit crime, tort or fraud *14.39*
contract corrupting public life *14.49*
contract to deceive public authority *14.33*

contract ousting jurisdiction of court *14.34*
contract prejudicial to administration of justice *14.30*
contract prejudicial to public safety *14.40*
contract promoting sexual immorality *14.46*
contract restricting personal liberty *14.51*
marriage brokerage contract *14.42, 14.67*
frustration *10.15*
legal consequences *14.52*
recovery *14.53*
repentance/repudiation *16.64*
restitution *14.55, 16.110*
non-registration of business *18.6*
proof of illegality
principles *14.100*
remedy *14.102, 16.110, 16.111*
restraint of trade *14.68*
during vs after operation *16.36*
employment *14.80, 14.91, 14.97, 16.36, 21.69*
exclusive dealings (solus agreement) *14.86*
principles *14.72, 14,77*
sale of a business *14.78, 14.97*
severance *14.92*
covenant, of part of *14.97*
covenant, of whole *14.95*
statutory illegality *14.4, 14.7, 14.93*
bilateral prohibition *14.18, 14.19*
express prohibition *14.12, 14.19, 14.20, 14.23*
formation vs performance of contract *14.20 ff*
gaming and wagering contract *14.13*
implied prohibition *14.14, 14.19, 14.20, 14.23*
principle *14.15*
legislative intention *14.10, 14.12, 14.19*
principle *14.7*
subsidiary legislation, contravention of *14.8*
unilateral prohibition *14.18, 14.19*
Implied terms, *see* Terms of contract
Incapacity
contract, to
corporations, *see* corporations
drunkard, *see* drunkard
mental patient, *see* mental patient
minor, *see* minor
ultra vires acts *7.35, 7.37, 18.15*
Incorporation
guideline *18.3*
legal effect *18.18 ff*
process *18.14*
Incoterms *22.12*
Indemnity
misrepresentation *12.2, 12.35*
Indirect misrepresentation *12.24, 12.25*
Indoor management
rule *18.32*
Inducement
promissory estoppel *3.55*
letter of comfort *4.14*
misrepresentation *12.20*
Industrial design *21.1, 21.3*
copyright, and *21.7, 21.40, 21.46*
definition *21.42*
infringement
defences *21.45*
proprietor's rights *21.45*
protection
duration *21.41*
registrable *21.41*
criteria *21.44*
Injunction *1.76*
breach of contract *15.2, 16.2, 16.18, 16.30 ff*
copyright infringement *21.22*
damages, in lieu of *16.45 ff*
geographical indications
infringement *21.99*
mandatory *16.30, 16.43, 16.44*
patent infringement *21.62*
prohibitory *16.30, 16.31*
contract of personal service *16.34 ff*
specific performance, and *16.34*
when awarded *16.34, 16.36*
tort *2.93, 20.20, 20.93*
trade mark fringement *21.84*
Innocent misrepresentation *12.18, 12.21, 12.35*
damages *12.46*
indemnity *12.35*
rescission *12.35, 12.39, 12.43*
Insurance
privity of contract, *see* privity of contract
Intellectual property
characteristics *21.2, 21.3*
copyright, *see* copyright
designs, *see* industrial design
geographical indications, *see* geographical indications
moral rights *21.4*
patents, *see* patents
performance rights *21.3*
protection
Agreement on Trade Related Aspects of Intellectual Property Rights *21.3, 22.8*
international *22.1*
reasons for *21.4*
trade mark, *see* trade mark
trade secrets, *see* trade secrets
Intention to create legal relations
actual reliance on agreement *4.7, 4.14*
business agreements *4.9*
certainty of terms *4.7, 4.11, 4.14*

commercial agreements *4.9*
honour clause *4.11*
letter of comfort *4.12*
consideration, and *3.43, 3.68, 4.15*
domestic agreements *4.4, 4.15*
offer *2.3, 2.4, 2.5, 2.6*
social agreements *4.4*
websites *2.7*

Interest
common law action for fixed sum *16.5, 16.6, 16.7–16.8*
damages, on *15.6 ff*

International contracts
condition precedent *22.35*
due diligence *22.35*
opinions of counsel *22.35*
conflict of laws *22.7*
dispute resolution, *see* alternative dispute resolution
exception clause, applicability *6.39*
governing laws, application of *2.1, 22.7*
Inconterms *22.12*
jurisdiction of courts
anti-trust injunction *22.7*
forum non conveniens *22.7*
Order 11 rules *22.7*
sale of goods *22.11*
Convention on the International Sale of Goods *22.11*

International law
customary, *see* customary international law
enforcement *22.4, 22.7*
executive agreements *22.4*
private, *see* private international law
public, *see* public international law
treaties and conventions, *see* treaties and conventions

International trade
agents *22.14*
alternative dispute resolution, *see* alternative dispute resolution
branches *22.15*
build-operate-and-transfer *22.18*
comparative advantage theory *22.8, 22.10*
contract manufacturing *22.21*
dispute resolution, *see* alternative dispute resolution
distributors *22.14*
dumping, *see also* World Trade Organization *22.9*
foreign direct investment
bilateral investment treaties *22.24*
dispute resolution *22.27*
expropriation *22.23*
foreign portfolio investment, distinguished *22.22*
nationalisation *22.23, 22.25*
nationality of company *22.6*
US–Singapore Free Trade Agreement *22.25*
World Trade Organization *22.26*
franchise *22.20*
incorporation in foreign entity *22.17*
International Institute for the Unification of Private Law *22.20*
management contracts *22.16*
permanent establishment *22.13, 22.19*
project finance *22.18*
protectionist measures *22.8*
representative office *22.19*
special purpose vehicle *22.18, 22.35*
subsidies, *see also* World Trade Organization *22.10*
taxation *22.13*
treaties and conventions, *see* treaties and conventions

Internet Corporations for Assigned Names and Numbers *21.95*

Invalid contract
ultra vires doctrine *18.15*

J

Joint ventures *18.2, 22.17*

Judiciary
court hierarchy and structure *1.109–1.133*
information technology, use of *1.141–1.146*
International Court of Justice *22.3*
judgments
law-making *1.59*
obiter dictum *1.67, 1.68*
precedents, *see also stare decisis* *1.61, 1.62 ff, 1.68, 1.107*
exceptions to doctrine *1.72*
foreign jurisdictions, from *1.137*
ratio decidendi *1.66, 1.68, 1.69*
judicial commissioners *1.47, 1.111*
jurisdiction, meaning of *1.108*
Privy Council *1.45, 1.48, 1.50, 1.110, 1.136*
role of *1.106–1.107*
statutory interpretation *1.138-1.140*
general approaches *1.138*
technical rules *1.140*
Subordinate Courts *1.106, 1.112–1.124*
District Courts *1.112, 1.114, 1.119, 1.121, 1.129, 1.130*
appeals from *1.129–1.130*
equitable remedies, jurisdiction to grant *16.17*
judges *1.121*
Magistrates' Courts *1.108, 1.114, 1.118, 1.129, 1.130*
appeals from *1.129–1.130*
jurisdiction *1.119–1.120, 16.17*
Small Claims Tribunal *1.108, 1.112, 1.114, 5.18*
appeals from *1.117*
mediation *1.159, 1.182*
jurisdiction *1.115–1.116*
Supreme Court *1.18, 1.35, 1.106, 1.109, 1.125*

Court of Appeal *1.48, 1.50, 1.110, 1.131*
jurisdiction *1.131–1.133*
stare decisis *1.136*
Constitutional Tribunal *1.51, 1.109*
High Court *1.45, 1.108, 1.117, 1.123, 1.126*
appeals from *1.133*
jurisdiction *1.126–1.130, 1.132, 16.17*
judges *1.111, 1.125*
Technology Court *1.143*
Jurisdiction of courts, *see also* judiciary
equitable remedies, award of *16.17, 16.22, 16.46*

L

Land
law
privity of contract, *see* privity of contract
privity of estate *8.15*
Lease
frustration of contract *10.19*
Legal profession
admission to the bar *1.148*
advocate and solicitor *1.147*
non-practising *1.149, 1.151*
practising *1.148–1.150*
law corporation *1.152*
Law Society of Singapore *1.153*
partnership *1.152*
practice, setting up of *1.152*
qualified person *1.148*
Roll of the Supreme Court *1.148*
striking off *1.150, 1.151*
Singapore Academy of Law *1.154*
sole proprietorship *1.152*
training *1.148*
Legal system
alternative dispute resolution, *see* alternative dispute resolution
common law, *see* common law
Constitution *1.28, 1.29, 1.38, 1.43, 1.47, 1.51, 1.88*
history and development *1.4–1.56*
Council of Presidential Advisers *1.101*
equity, *see* equity
Executive *1.88, 1.100 ff*
Attorney-General *1.103-1.104*
Attorney-General's Chambers *1.104*
powers *1.103*
Cabinet *1.100, 1.101, 1.102*
accountability to Parliament *1.102*
composition *1.102*
President *1.97*
powers *1.101, 1.51, 1.56*
Prime Minister *1.102, 1.103*
Solicitor-General
powers *1.105*
Judiciary, *see also* judiciary *1.46, 1.88, 1.106 ff*
law, meaning of *1.1*
law-making process *1.96*
legal profession, *see* legal profession
legislation, *see* legislation
Legislature *1.59, 1.60, 1.88, 1.90, 19.12*
Committee of the Whole House *1.97*
Members of Parliament *1.53–1.55*
Parliament *1.43, 1.44, 1.90*
Committee *1.93–1.95*
composition *1.90–1.92*
President *1.51, 1.56*
Presidential Council for Minority Rights *1.44-1.97*
Select Committees *1.94, 1.97*
separation of powers *1.89*
UK influence *1.4, 1.7 ff*
common law, application of *1.23, 1.57*
Legislation
enactment process *1.96–1.99*
interpretation *1.138–1.140*
primary *1.98*
privity of contract, *see* privity of contract
subsidiary *1.98–1.99*
Letter of comfort *2.38, 4.12*
acceptance *2.31*
Liability
agent, *see* agent
exclusion of, *see* exception clause
principal, *see* agent
Limitation clause,
privity of contract, *see* privity of contract
Limited company
guarantee, limited by *18.10, 18.12*
liability *18.9*
shares, limited by *18.10, 18.11*
Litigation process
dispute resolution, compared *1.176–1.180*
Rules of Court *1.156, 1.177*

M

Managing director *18.30, 18.34*
agent, as *17.9, 17.15*
Meetings of company *18.25*
resolutions *18.25*
legal effect *18.25*
ordinary (simple majority) *18.25, 18.32, 18.33*
special (75% majority) *18.25, 18.31, 18.46*
unanimous *18.25*
voting *18.25*
Members of company, *see also* shareholder
liability
company limited by guarantee *18.12*
company limited by shares
unpaid call *18.11*
relationship with company
statutory contract *18.45*
rights
enforcement *18.46*
participation *18.11*

voting *18.11*
shareholder, distinguished *18.11*
liability *18.11*
Memorandum of Association *7.35, 18.15*
Mental patient
contract, enforcement of *7.26–7.29*
valid contract
'necessary goods' *7.29*
voidable contract *7.27*
sale of land *2.28*
Minor
age of majority *7.4*
contract, enforcement of *7.8*
definition *7.4–7.7*
goods supplied/to be supplied *7.17*
invalid contract *7.11*
restitution, liability in *7.18, 7.22–7.25*
fraud *7.23*
Minors' Contracts Act, under *7.25*
quasi-contract *7.23*
sale of goods *7.16*
tort, liability in *7.20*
valid contract *7.9*
'necessary goods' *7.9*
services *7.10*
void contract
loan *7.17*
Infants Relief Act 1874 (UK), under *7.17, 71.18, 71.19*
voidable contract *7.12*
age of majority, on reaching *7.13, 7.15*
consideration, lack of *7.14*
lease *7.12*
liability *7.14, 7.15*
marriage, settlement of *7.12*
partnership *7.12*
ratification *7.15*
recovery *7.14*
sale/purchase of land *7.12*
Minority protection, *see* shareholders
Misrepresentation *5.3, 5.11, 12.1 ff, 19.40*
ambiguous *12.18*
common law, at *12.2, 12.30*
conduct, by *12.12*
damages *12.2, 12.32, 12.45, 15.9*
definition *12.5*
disclosure of facts *12.16, 12.17*
elements *12.5*
exception clause *6.11, 12.50*
express *12.11*
fraudulent *12.2, 12.18, 12.21, 12.26, 14.60*
indemnity *12.2*
indirect *12.24, 12.25*
inducement *12.20*
innocent *12.18, 12.21, 12.35*
intentions *12.5, 12.8*
material *12.19, 12.20*
Misrepresentation Act, under *5.18*
negligent *12.21, 12.30 ff*
non-contractual statements *12.2, 12.16*
opinion *12.5, 12.7*
passing off *21.89, 21.90, 21.92*
policy *12.18*
puff *12.5, 12.6*
representee's obligation *12.21*
rescission *5.17, 12.2, 12.4, 12.47*
affirmation *12.42*
lapse of time *12.43*
restitution impossible *12.41*
third party rights *12.44*
silence *12.13*
statement of law *12.5, 12.9*
statutory *12.2*
who can bring action *12.22*
Mistake
common *11.3, 11.7–11.27, 11.51*
Associated Japanese Bank case *11.11–11.14, 11.20, 11.21*
common law, at *11.3, 11.10 ff, 11.22*
doctrine *11.7*
equity, in *11.3, 11.12, 11.17 ff, 11.22*
rectification of contract *11.26*
res extincta *11.10, 11.16*
res sua *11.10*
test *11.14, 11.25*
doctrine *11.2*
electronic signature *11.57*
fact, of *11.3*
frustration, distinguished *10.1, 11.14*
guarantee *11.11–11.12*
law, of *11.13*
mutual *11.3, 11.8, 11.28–11.30*
non est factum *11.53–11.56*
rectification of contract *5.7, 11.26*
res extincta *11.10, 11.16*
res sua *11.10*
sale of goods *11.16*
unilateral *11.3, 11.32–11.53*
common law, at *11.32*
contractual promise *11.35*
equity, in *11.32*
mistaken identity *11.3, 11.31, 11.38 ff*
inter praesentes cases *11.39 ff*
non-*inter praesentes* cases *11.48 ff*
Smith v Hughes rule *11.3, 11.31, 11.32, 11.33*
test *11.37*
void contract under common law
legal effect *11.4*
voidable contract in equity
legal effect *11.5*
Mitigation of damage, *see* also damages *9.63, 9.65, 15.24, 15.76*
fixed sum, in action for *16.4*
negligence *19.51*
Mortgage
misrepresentation *12.25*
Multilateral contract
privity of contract, *see* privity of contract
Mutual release from contract *9.69, 9.73*
variation of contract, distinguished *9.78*
waiver, distinguished *9.83*

N

Negligence, *see also* pure economic loss
  breach of duty of care *19.4, 19.42 ff*
    burden of proof *19.52*
    causation *19.46*
    professionals, test for *19.42*
    reasonably foreseeable test *19.54*
    res ipsa loquitur *19.53*
  computer viruses, spread of *19.60*
    damage suffered
      causation *19.69*
      contributory negligence *19.70*
      remoteness *19.70*
    defences *19.64*
    duty of care *19.62*
    standard of care *19.68*
  damage suffered *19.4*
    'but for' test *19.46*
    causation *19.46, 19.69*
    eggshell skull rule *19.54*
    mitigation *19.4, 19.51*
    reasonable foreseeability *19.49*
    remoteness *19.4, 19.49, 19.70*
      duty of care, relationship with *19.50*
  defences
    contributory negligence *15.89, 19.59, 19.71*
    ex turpi causa non oritur actio *19.56*
    illegality *19.55*
    voluntary assumption of risk *19.57, 19.72*
      contributory negligence, distinguished *19.58*
  duty of care, *see also* duty of care, in negligence *19.4 ff*
    bailment, in *8.20*
    breach of *19.4, 19.42 ff*
    computer viruses, spread of 19.62, 19.63
    'fair, just and reasonable' *19.8, 19.25*
    foreseeability *19.7, 19.8, 19.9, 19.15, 19.21*
    neighbour principle *19.6, 19.21, 19.31*
    proximity *19.7, 19.8, 19.21, 19.22, 19.27*
    public policy *19.11, 19.21, 19.26*
    pure foreseeability test *19.9, 19.20*
  exception clause to exclude liability
    contract, in *6.24, 6.41*
    tort, in *6.33, 6.34, 6.42*
  frustration of contract, and *10.21*
  internet service providers
    duty of care *19.64*
  misrepresentation, *see* negligent misrepresentation
  misstatement, *see* negligent misstatement
  nervous shock, *see also* duty of care
    two-stage test *19.17*
  pure economic loss, *see* pure economic loss
  three-part test, *see* duty of care in negligence
  two-stage process, *see* duty of care in negligence
  two-stage test, *see* duty of care in negligence
Negligent misrepresentation *12.2, 12.18, 12.21 ff, 12.30, 19.2*
  assessment of damages *12.48*
  burden of proof *12.33*
  common law, at *12.30*
  damages *12.32, 12.46*
  'fiction of fraud' principle *12.31*
  liability *12.31*
  rescission *12.39, 12.43*
Negligent misstatement *12.30, 15.9, 19.2, 19.35*
  burden of proof *12.34*
  duty of care
    assumption of responsibility *19.36, 19.73*
    disclaimer *19.39*
    Hedley Byrne v Heller *19.35*
    reliance on advice *19.36, 19.73*
    special relationship *19.35, 19.37*
      elements of *19.38*
      requisite skill and competence *19.37*
  internet, on the *19.73*
    hyperlink *19.74*
    specific information given *19.73*
  pure economic loss *19.35*
Non-disclosure agreement
  patent *21.65*
Non-incorporated businesses
  business partnership, *see* partnership
  legal effect *18.20*
  sole proprietorship, *see* sole proprietorship

O

Offer
  acceptance, and, *see also* acceptance *11.2*
    principles *2.2, 2.3*
    unqualified response *2.6*
  advertisement to the whole world *2.5, 2.9*
  auctions *2.9*
  bilateral contract *2.5*
  communication of *2.4*
  consideration, and, *see* consideration
  counter-offer *2.15, 2.21*
    request for information, distinguished *2.16*
  cross-offers *2.35*
  definition *2.4*
  intention to be bound by *2.4, 2.6, 2.7*
  intention to create legal relations *2.3, 2.4, 2.5, 2.6, 2.7, 4.1 ff*
  invention to treat, distinguished *2.6*
    goods on display *2.7*
    principle, arguments against *2.7*
    software *2.7*

puff, distinguished *2.5*
quotations, distinguished *2.10*
tender, and *2.8*
termination of
counter-offer *2.15–2.16*
death *2.19*
failure of condition *2.18*
lapse of time *2.5, 2.17*
rejection *2.15*
revocation *2.11, 17.27*
unilateral contract *2.5, 2.18, 2.20, 2.33*
United Nations Convention on the International Sale of Goods, under *22.11*
whole world, to *2.5*
website, and *2.7*

P

Parol evidence rule *5.3, 5.6, 5.10*
collateral contract *5.9*
exceptions to rule
common law *5.7, 5.16*
statute *5.8*
rule *5.6, 6.30*
Singapore Evidence Act, and *5.6, 5.7, 5.8*
Partnership *18.1, 18.51*
agent, partner as *18.53*
characteristics *18.51, 18.52*
definition *18.51*
dissolution *18.55*
general *18.51*
limited *18.1, 18.56*
general partners *18.56*
liability *18.56*
limited partners *18.56*
limited liability *18.1, 18.57*
unlimited liability *18.54*
Passing off *21.71, 21.89*
definition *21.89*
goodwill *21.91*
Internet domain names (cybersquatting), and *21.93*
misrepresentation
test *21.90, 21.92*
trade mark, unregistered *21.71*
Patents *21.1, 21.3*
application process *21.47*
assignment and licence *21.64*
Budapest Treaty *21.47*
characteristics *21.47*
confidence, and law of *21.65*
breach and remedy *21.66, 21.67*
defences against breach *21.68*
European Patent Convention *21.49*
infringement *21.58*
defences *21.61*
remedy *21.62*
statutory *21.60*
test *21.60*
international application
restrictions *21.57*
invention
definition *21.49*
inventor's rights *21.47*
Paris Convention *21.47*
Patent Co-operation Treaty *21.47*
patentable inventions *21.48, 21.50*
industrial application *21.56*
inventive step *21.54*
novelty *21.51*
process-based *21.47, 21.49, 21.60*
product-based *21.47, 21.49, 21.60*
protection
duration *21.57*
retrospective rights *21.62*
Performance of contract *10.2*
ancillary obligations *9.43*
condition precedent *9.7, 9.11*
de minimis rule *9.3–9.5, 9.23, 9.63*
discharge of contract *9.1, 9.2*
divisible covenants and obligations, performance of *9.21, 9.34, 16.13*
exception clause *6.44 ff*
frustration, *see* frustration
non-/partial performance due to *10.1 ff*
partial *9.9, 9.11, 16.76*
quantum meruit, restitution by *16.76, 16.98*
precise *9.2, 16.85*
quantum meruit, restitution by *16.86*
specific, *see also* specific performance *15.2, 15.3, 16.2, 16.16*
substantial *9.11*
Persona ficta, *see* company
Principal
agent, and, *see* agent
third party, liability to, *see* agent
Private company *18.13*
exempt status *18.13*
share capital *18.13*
Private international law *22.7*
conflict of laws *22.7*
public international law, distinguished *22.7*
Privity of contract
benefit to third party *8.2, 8.5, 8.16, 8.18, 8.23, 8.24, 8.25*
breach of contract *8.21, 8.23*
consideration *3.18, 8.9, 8.10, 8.16, 8.24, 8.35, 8.36*
'joint promisees' doctrine *8.36*
Contracts (Rights of Third Parties) Act 2001 *8.24 ff*
exception to rule
agency *8.8–8.11, 8.16, 17.34*
bailment *8.20*
benefit to third party *8.6, 8.7, 8.16, 8.18, 8.23, 8.24, 8.25*
collateral contract *8.12*
damages *8.21, 8.23*

drafting *8.17*
exception clause *8.16, 8.17, 8.32*
'Himalaya clause' *8.16*
insurance, in *8.19*
land law *8.15*
limitation clause *8.18, 8.31*
multilateral contract *8.12*
negligence in bailment *8.20*
shipping *8.16*
specific performance *8.21, 8.22*
statute *8.24, 8.32*
trust *8.14*
unilateral contract *8.16*
mistake, and *11.4, 11.5*
rule *8.1*
sub-agent and principal, between *17.42*
third-party liability in tort, conflict with *20.46*
Prohibition
bilateral, *see* illegal contract
express, *see* illegal contract
implied, *see* illegal contract
unilateral, *see* illegal contract
Promissory estoppel, *see also* consideration
breach of contract, and *3.58, 9.66*
cause of action, as a *3.56, 3.65*
clear and unequivocal promise *3.48*
consideration, and *3.47 ff, 3.63 ff*
defence, only used as *3.56*
discharge of contract *9.66, 9.74*
implied promise *3.49*
inequitable to go back on promise *3.54*
legal effects *3.60 ff*
principle *3.47*
reliance on promise *3.50, 3.54, 3.65, 9.74, 9.84*
revocation of offer *2.14*
silent promise *3.49*
suspension of obligation *3.60 ff*
waiver, and *9.84*
Promissory note
consideration, and *3.25*
privity of contract *8.31*
Promoter
liability for pre-incorporation contract *17.23, 17.47*
Property
intellectual, *see* intellectual property
shares as *18.47*
Public international law *22.1, 22.2 ff*
enforcement *22.4*
jurisdiction *22.5*
territorial *22.5*
universal *22.5*
nationality *22.6*
sources *22.3*
Public company
share capital *18.13*
Public policy
contract against *14.1 ff, 14.19, 14.32, 14.33, 14.34, 14.46, 14.90*
Puff *2.5, 4.10, 5.10, 12.5, 12.6*
representation, distinguished *12.6*
Pure economic loss, *see also* negligence *and* duty of care in negligence
composite test 15.71, 19.14, 19.15,
computer viruses, spread of 19.63
negligence, due to 15.9, 15.20, 19.5
negligent misstatement 19.35
physical loss, distinguished 15.71, 19.7, 19.10
public policy test 19.11
pure foreseeability test 19.9
recoverability 15.72, 19.11 ff
three-part test, *see* duty of care in negligence
two-stage process, *see* duty of care in negligence
two-stage test, *see* duty of care in negligence

Q

Quantum meruit
contract, by *9.16*
discharge of contract by
agreement, on *16.105–16.106*
frustration, on *10.5, 16.107-16.109*
recovery by *2.36, 16.13, 16.74 ff*
implied at common law
officious bystander test *9.18*
partial performance of contract *9.8, 9.13–9.14, 16.13*
restitution by *9.20, 16.54, 16.74 ff*
revocation of offer *2.14*
sale of goods, payment for *9.17*
unjust enrichment, law of , and *9.8, 9.20, 16.14, 16.74 ff*
benefits in kind, valuation of *16.74, 16.98*

R

Ratification
agent, acts of *17.20*
legal effects *17.26*
pre-incorporation contract *7.34, 17.23*
reasonable time, within *17.25, 17.28*
relation-back doctrine *17.26, 17.27*
requirements *17.22*
void contract *17.24*
voidable contract
corporations, *see* corporations
drunkard, *see* drunkard
minor, *see* minor
Real property law
privitiy of contract *8.15*
Registrar of businesses *18.4*
Registrar of companies *18.4*
memorandum of association *18.14*
special resolutions, lodgement of *18.31*
Registration
company *18.4, 18.14*

exceptions *18.4*
failure to register *18.5, 18.6*
geographical indications *21.98*
industrial design *21.41*
patent *21.48*
trade mark *21.71*
Reliance loss, *see also* assessment of damages *9.15, 15.27, 15.30, 15.42, 16.59*
expectation loss, distinguished *15.36*
Remedies, *see also* damages
common law action for fixed sum *15.3, 16.2, 16.3 ff*
damages, distinguished *16.4*
exceptions to rule *16.7*
quantum meruit, vs *16.85*
copyright infringement, *see* copyright
damages vs restitution
total failure of consideration, under *16.60, 16.68*
defamation *20.92 ff*
equitable *15.3, 15.107, 16.15–16.47*
jurisdiction of courts *16.17*
forfeiture *15.9, 15.97–15.98*
frustration *10.30*
geographical indications
illegal contract, under, *see* illegal contract
infringement *21.99*
injunction, *see also* injunction *15.2, 16.2, 16.30, 20.20*
interim orders *15.5, 16.30*
interlocutory *15.5*
limitation of actions
laches *15.10, 15.12*
lapse of time *15.10, 15.11*
patent
infringement, *see* patent
payment of fixed sum *15.2, 16.1–16.14*
restitution, *see* restitution
self-help *15.9*
specific performance, *see also* specific performance *15.2, 15.3, 16.15–16.29*
trade mark
infringement, *see* trade mark
Remoteness
damage due to negligence *19.49*
computer viruses, spread of *19.70*
damages for breach of contract, *see* damages
Representations
agent, by, *see* agent
collateral contract *12.37*
conduct *12.12*
express *12.11*
implied *12.12*
misrepresentation, *see* misrepresentation
parol evidence rule *5.6, 5.10, 12.37*
pre-contractual statement *5.10, 5.11, 12.36*
silence *12.13*
term of contract, as a *12.36*
distinguished *5.3, 5.10*
importance of statement *5.14*
oral statements *5.16*
request to verify *5.13*
special skill and knowledge *5.17*
timing of statement *5.15*
written contract *5.16*
Repudiation
contract, of, *see also* breach of contract *9.33–9.37, 9.41-9.48, 15.27*
discharge of contract, *see* discharge
election to affirm or discharge contract *9.48, 9.49, 9.57, 15.83*
communication of election *9.50, 9.60*
limitation of right to elect *9.63*
legal effects *9.52*
loss of right to discharge *9.54*
illegal contract *14.64*
rescission *ab initio*, distinguished *9.52*
Rescission
mistake *11.5*
misrepresentation *5.17, 12.2, 12.4, 12.35, 12.38 ff, 12.47*
repudiation *ab initio*, distinguished *9.52*
Res ipsa loquitur 19.53
Restitution *9.20, 15.2, 16.48*
contract discharged
agreement, by *16.105*
breach of contract, by *16.48 ff*
frustration, by *16.107*
contract vitiated by
illegality *14.42, 14.53, 14.55, 16.110*
illegal contract, *see* illegal contract
minor's liability in *7.22 ff*
misrepresentation *12.41*
mitigation under *16.60*
quantum meruit, by *9.20, 16.54, 16.76, 16.105*
quantum valebant, by *16.54, 16.76*
quasi-contract *9.20*
remoteness under *16.60*
restitutionary damages for breach of contract *16.88*
total failure of consideration *7.14, 15.44, 15.97, 16.54, 16.55, 16.95*
breach of contract, and *16.58, 16.64, 16.68*
consideration in formation of contract, distinguished from *16.56*
definition *16.57, 16.70*
illegal contract, and *16.111*
Restraint of trade
legality of contract *14.68*
employment contract, *see* illegal contract
exclusive dealings (solus agreement), *see* illegal contract
sale of a business, *see* illegal contract
party interest/benefit *14.72, 14.76, 14.86, 14.91*
public interest *14.72, 14.76, 14.91*
reasonableness *14.72, 14.73, 14.75, 14.76,*

14.91
duration of contract *14.74, 14.85, 14.91*
geographical area *14.74*
severance of contract, *see* illegal contract
unconscionability, and *14.90*
Revocation
offer, of
implied *2.13, 2.14*
'two-offer approach' *2.14*
unilateral contract, in *2.14*

S

Sale of goods
damages *16.2, 22.11*
exception clause *6.36, 6.39, 6.47*
mental patient, to, *see* mental patient
minor, to, *see* minor
mistake, *see* mistake
payment
quantum meruit *9.17*
risk, passing of *10.10, 22.11*
Sale of Goods (United Nations Convention) Act *5.29, 22.11*
Sale of land
frustration of contract *10.19*
Severance
illegal part of contract *14.92*
Shareholder, *see also* member of company
director, appointment of *18.25*
foreign majority *22.17*
individual
legal action against board of directors *7.38, 18.44*
liability
company limited by shares *18.11, 18.21, 18.22, 18.24*
majority *18.47*
member, distinguished *18.11*
minority protection *18.47*
discrimination, legal action against *18.49*
oppressive act, legal action against *18.49, 22.17*
ownership of company assets *18.19, 18.24*
powers of director, and *18.27, 18.28*
resolutions, *see* meetings of company
Shares
company limited by *18.10, 18.11*
definition *18.11*
dividend *18.11*
property, as *18.47*
share capital *18.11*
Silence
acceptance by *2.29–2.31*
misrepresentation *12.14*
promissory estoppel *3.49*
rule *12.14*
exceptions *12.14, 12.15*
Shipping
exception clause
privity of contract, *see* privity of contract
Signature
electronic *2.52*
mistake, *see* mistake, *non est factum*
Singapore Academy of Law
Law Reform Committee *1.154*
illegal contracts, reform of *14.102*
Singapore Domain Name Dispute Resolution Policy *21.95*
Societies *18.1*
Sole proprietorship *18.1, 18.19, 18.50*
advantages and disadvantages *18.50*
business name *18.50*
definition *18.50*
dissolution *18.50*
unlimited liability *18.50*
Specific performance *1.76, 8.22, 15.2, 15.3, 16.2, 16.16, 16.18, 16.20–16.29*
damages in lieu of or in addition to *16.45*
mutuality test *16.23*
personal service, contract for *16.26, 16.35*
privity of contract, *see* privity of contract
when awarded *16.20, 16.23, 16.24, 16.26*
Standard form contracts *6.3, 6.19, 22.34*
Stare decisis *1.63, 1.64, 1.71, 1.72, 1.73*
horizontal *1.70, 1.134, 1.135–1.137*
vertical *1.70, 1.134*
Subsidiaries *18.23*
Syndicate *18.2*

T

Tender
offer, distinguished *2.8*
exceptions to rule *2.8*
Termination
acceptance *2.27*
breach of contract *5.4, 15.9*
offer, *see* offer
Terms of contract
breach of *9.28–9.32*
certain and complete *2.36, 3.48, 4.7, 5.1, 5.6, 5.7, 13.1, 13.43*
'lock-in' agreement *2.38*
charterparty *5.22*
classification *5.19*
Sale of Goods Act 1979 (UK) *5.22*
condition *5.4, 5.5, 5.19*
contingent *5.20, 9.28*
promissory *5.20, 9.28*
warranty, distinguished *5.21*
exception clause, *see* exception clauses
express *5.2*
implied *2.36, 5.2, 5.20, 5.23, 10.3, 17.37*
business efficacy *5.24, 5.25, 9.18*
custom of trade *5.7, 5.30*
employment contract *5.23, 5.27*
in fact *5.2, 5.23, 5.24*
in law *5.2, 5.23, 5.26*
default terms *5.23, 5.26*
statute *5.23, 5.29*
specialist contract *5.23*

when implied *5.25*
indemnity clause *6.1*
innominate *5.4, 5.5, 5.19*
Hong Kong Fir approach *5.21, 5.22*
limitation of liability clause *6.1*
oral *5.6, 5.16*
parol evidence rule, *see also* parol evidence rule *5.3, 5.6, 6.30*
pre-contractual statements *5.10, 5.11, 12.36, 12.37*
puff *2.5, 4.10, 5.10, 12.5, 12.6*
reasonableness, ascertained through *2.36, 5.28*
representations, *see* representations
warranty *5.4, 5.5, 5.19, 5.20*
condition, distinguished *5.21*

Third party
agent's liability to, *see* agent
principal's liability to, *see* agent
privity of contract, *see* privity of contract
rescission of contract *12.44*
rights
agency, under *17.35, 17.47*
void contract, under *11.4, 11.23*
voidable contract, under *11.5, 11.23, 12.44*

Tort
competition, and *20.2*
when tortious *20.4*
conspiracy by unlawful means *20.35, 20.37*
intention *20.36*
conspiracy to injure *20.32*
conspiracy by unlawful means, distinguished *20.31*
damage, proof of *20.34*
predominant intention to injure *20.33*
contractual liability, overlap *19.2*
conversion *2.29, 14.60*
damages, *see* damages
deceit *12.27*
defamation *19.1, 20.34, 20.55, 20.56 ff*
civil vs criminal *20.58*
defamatory statement *20.59*
defence
absolute privilege *20.81*
fair comment *20.74*
innocent dissemination *20.90, 20.96*
justification *20.73, 20.76*
offer of amends *20.91*
qualified privilege *20.82, 20.85*
form of statement *20.61*
elements *20.59 ff*
innuendo *20.63*
false *20.64, 20.66*
legal *20.63, 20.64, 20.67*
Internet, on the *20.94 ff*
Internet Service Provider liability *20.95, 20.97*
jurisdiction of trial *20.98*
interpretation of statement *20.62*
natural and ordinary meaning *20.62, 20.65, 20.67*
libel *20.58*
publication *20.70*
refers to party injured *20.68*
remedy *20.92*
slander *20.58*
statement must be published *20.70*
test *20.60*
definition *19.1*
fraudulent misrepresentation, *see* fraudulent misrepresentation
inducing breach of contract *20.6, 20.50*
breach, requirement of *20.16*
damage *20.18*
defence of justification *20.21*
knowledge and intention *20.7*
procurement
bare interference not resulting in breach *20.17*
direct intervention *20.11, 20.50*
direct procurement *2.10*
inconsistent dealings *20.15*
indirect intervention *20.13*
statutory duty, breach of *20.24*
intimidation *20.25, 20.50*
damage *20.28*
threat *20.26*
three-party liability, applies only in *20.30, 20.45, 20.46*
unlawful conduct *20.27*
malicious falsehood *20.51 ff*
damage *20.54*
defamation, distinguished *20.55*
misrepresentation, *see* misrepresentation
negligence, *see* negligence
negligent misrepresentation, *see* negligent misrepresentation
negligent misstatement, *see* negligent misstatement
passing off *21.89*
privity of contract, conflict with *20.46*
recovery independent of illegal contract *14.60*
Rylands v Fletcher liability *19.62*
tortfeasor *19.3*
employee vs independent contractor *19.3*
trespass to goods *19.62*
unlawful interference with trade *20.12, 20.14, 20.39*
contract, breach of *20.45*
crime *20.47*
inducing breach of contract, distinguished *20.39*
intention to injure *20.41*
statutory duty, breach of *20.48*
vicarious liability *19.3*

Trade mark *21.1, 21.3*
- application *21.76*
- assignment *21.87*
- confusion between *21.75, 21.92*
- definition *21.72*
- descriptive/laudatory mark *21.74, 21.91*
- identical/similar and dissimilar goods/services, for *21.73, 21.75*
- infringement *21.79*
  - border enforcement measures *21.85*
  - defence *21.79, 21.80*
  - remedy *21.84*
- invalidity *21.77, 21.87*
- licensing *21.78, 21.87*
- Madrid Protocol *21.88*
- meta-tagging *21.38*
- passing off, *see* passing off
- proprietary rights *21.78*
- protection *21.73*
  - duration *21.77*
  - Paris Convention *21.73*
  - passing off *21.71*
- registration *21.71*
  - rejection *21.74, 21.75*
- revocation *21.77, 21.86*
- scope *21.72, 21.74*
- service marks *21.72*
- Trade Marks Act 1998 *21.71 ff, 21.97, 21.98*
- TRIPS Agreement *21.73*
- 'well-known' *21.73*

Trade secrets *21.65 ff*
- confidentiality clause *21.65, 21.69*
- data protection *21.70*
- non-disclosure agreement *21.65*
- patent *21.65*

Treaties and conventions, *see also* Table of Treaties and Conventions *22.3*
- Agreement on Trade Related Investment Measures (TRIMS) *22.26*
- UNCITRAL
  - Model Law on Electronic Commerce *2.48, 2.49, 2.51*
  - Model Law on International Commercial Arbitration *1.158, 1.186*
- United Nations Convention on the International Sale of Goods *22.11*
  - application *22.11*
  - provisions *22.11*
- US–Singapore Free Trade Agreement 2003 *2.1, 21.6, 21.72, 22.3, 22.6, 22.8, 22.25*
- Vienna Convention on the Law of Treaties 1969 *22.3*

Trust *18.1*
- privity of contract, *see* privity of contract

Trustee
- company as *18.19*

U

UK law
- application in Singapore *1.19, 1.49, 7.6, 7.7, 7.9, 7.17, 8.4, 11.16, 12.2, 13.19, 18.39*
  - Application of English Law Act 1993 *1.22, 1.49, 2.9, 5.11, 5.22, 5.29, 6.6, 6.48, 11.16, 12.2*

UK Law Commission
- illegal contract, reform of *14.101*
- minors, on *7.19*

Ultra vires acts *7.35, 7.37, 18.15*
- Member's right to restrain *18.15*

UNCITRAL
- Model Law on Electronic Commerce *2.48, 2.49, 2.51*
- Model Law on International Commercial Arbitration *1.158, 1.186*

Unconscionability *13.43 ff, 13.55, 13.56, 15.57*
- inequality of bargaining power, and *13.49*
- principles *13.44*
- promissory estoppel, and *3.64, 3.66*
- restraint of trade, and *14.90*
- test *13.47*
- umbrella doctrine, as *13.57 ff*

Undue influence *13.23 ff, 13.55*
- bargaining power, and *13.31*
- causation *13.34*
- Class 1 (actual) *13.26, 13.52, 13.54*
- Class 2 (presumed) *13.27, 13.52*
  - Class 2A *13.27, 13.28, 13.42, 13.53*
  - Class 2B *13.27, 13.29–13.30, 13.42*
- economic duress, and *13.54*
- infection, doctrine of *13.36*
  - agency *13.37, 13.40*
  - constructive notice *13.37 ff*
- manifest disadvantage *13.31, 13.32, 13.41 ff, 13.52*
- principles *13.25 ff*

Uniform Domain Name Dispute Resolution Policy *21.94*

Unilateral contract *2.5, 2.20, 2.33, 2.18*
- bilateral contract, distinguished *2.5*
- privity of contract, *see* privity of contract

Unilateral release from contract *9.69, 9.72*

Unincorporation, *see* Non-incorporated businesses

Unjust enrichment, law of, *see also* restitution *15.2, 15.9, 15.11, 16.48*
- limitation on recovery under *16.112*
  - estoppel *16.113*
  - 'change of position' *16.113, 16.114*
- *quantum meruit*, and *9.8, 9.20, 16.14, 16.105*
- test *16.50*
- void contract, and *16.103*

Unlimited company
- liability *18.9*

US law
- UK law, distinguished *8.4*

V

Valid contract
- drunkard, *see* drunkard
- mental patient, *see* mental patient
- minor, *see* minor

Variation of contract
- consideration *9.79*
  - counter-promise for payment of money *9.80, 9.81*
- definition *9.78, 9.79*
- mutual release from contract, distinguished *9.78*

Vitiation of contract
- economic duress, *see* economic duress
- illegality, *see* illegal contract
- misrepresentation, *see* misrepresentation
- mistake, *see* mistake
- unconscionability, *see* unconscionability
- undue influence, *see* undue influence

Void contract, *see also* illegal contract
- *ab initio* *10.15, 11.4, 11.40*
- minor, *see* minor
- non-registration of business *18.6*
- third-party rights *11.4, 11.23*
- *ultra vires* doctrine *18.15*
- unjust enrichment, law of *16.103*
- voidable contract, distinguished *11.6*

Voidable contract
- drunkard, *see* drunkard
- economic duress *13.17–13.18*
- mental patient, *see* mental patient
- minor, *see* minor
- misrepresentation *12.38*
- third-party rights *11.5, 11.23*

W

Waiver
- affirmation of contract *9.85*
- consideration *9.83*
- definition *9.83*
- discharge of contract by *9.58, 9.66, 9.74*
- mutual release from contract, distinguished *9.83*
- promissory estoppel, and *9.84*
- total waiver, distinguished *9.58*

Warranty
- breach, *see* breach of contract
- condition, distinguished, *see* terms of contract
- secondary usage of term *5.20*

Winding up
- company limited by guarantee, of member's liability to assets *18.12*
- Minister of Finance, by *7.38*

World Bank *22.23, 22.27*

World Trade Organization *22.1, 22.8*
- dumping *22.9*
  - Agreement on Anti-dumping *22.9*
  - proof of *22.9*
- most-favoured nation status *22.8*
- subsidies *22.10*
  - actionable *22.10*
  - Agreement on Subsidies and Counterveiling Measures *22.10*
  - prohibited *22.10*
  - proof of *22.10*